MAJOR AMERICAN WRITERS
Third Edition

VOLUME TWO

MAJOR AMERICAN WRITERS

THIRD EDITION

Edited by HOWARD MUMFORD JONES

Harvard University

ERNEST E. LEISY

Southern Methodist University

RICHARD M. LUDWIG

Princeton University

VOLUME TWO

HARCOURT, BRACE AND COMPANY   *NEW YORK*

LIST OF COPYRIGHTS AND ACKNOWLEDGMENTS

The authors record their thanks for the use of the selections reprinted in this book by permission of the following publishers and copyright holders:

APPLETON-CENTURY-CROFTS, INC., for *The Red Badge of Courage,* by Stephen Crane, copyright 1895.

DOUBLEDAY, DORAN AND COMPANY, INC., for selections from *Leaves of Grass* by Walt Whitman, reprinted by permission of Doubleday, Doran and Company, Inc., authorized publishers; from *The Sheltered Life* by Ellen Glasgow, copyright 1932 by Doubleday, Doran and Company.

DUELL, SLOAN & PEARCE, INC., for *The Irresponsibles* by Archibald MacLeish, reprinted by permission of the publishers.

FABER & FABER, for selections from *Collected Poems of T. S. Eliot,* copyright 1936; and from *Selected Essays of T. S. Eliot,* copyright 1932, 1936, 1950.

HARCOURT, BRACE AND COMPANY, INC., for selections from *A Certain Measure* by Ellen Glasgow, copyright 1938, 1943; from *Smoke and Steel* by Carl Sandburg, copyright 1920; from *Slabs of the Sunburnt West* by Carl Sandburg, copyright 1922; from *Good Morning, America* by Carl Sandburg, copyright 1928; from *The People, Yes* by Carl Sandburg, copyright 1936; from *Babbitt* by Sinclair Lewis, copyright 1922; from *Collected Poems of T. S. Eliot,* copyright 1936; and from *Selected Essays of T. S. Eliot,* copyright 1932, 1936, 1950.

HARPER AND BROTHERS, for selections from *The Gilded Age* and *Life on the Mississippi* by Mark Twain, and for *The Mysterious Stranger* by Mark Twain, copyright 1916 by Harper and Brothers, copyright 1944 by Clara Clemens Gabrilowitsch; for four poems from *Bolts of Melody: New Poems by Emily Dickinson,* edited by Mabel Loomis Todd and Millicent Todd Bingham, published by Harper and Brothers, copyright 1945 by Millicent Todd Bingham.

HENRY HOLT AND COMPANY, INC., for selections from *Collected Poems, A Further Range,* and *A Witness Tree* by Robert Frost; from *Chicago Poems* and *Cornhuskers* by Carl Sandburg.

HOUGHTON MIFFLIN COMPANY, for selections from *Mont St. Michel and Chartres* by Henry Adams; from *The Education of Henry Adams;* from *Poems, 1924-1933* by Archibald MacLeish; all used by arrangement with and permission of the publishers.

MISS MILDRED HOWELLS and JOHN MEAD HOWELLS, for selections from *Criticism and Fiction* by William Dean Howells, copyright 1891 by Harper and Brothers, copyright 1918 by W. D. Howells; from *A Traveler from Altruria* by William Dean Howells, copyright 1894 by Harper and Brothers, copyright 1921 by Mildred Howells and John Mead Howells; from *A Modern Instance* by William Dean Howells, copyright by Mildred Howells and John Mead Howells.

ALFRED A. KNOPF, INC., for the selection reprinted from *A Book of Prefaces* by H. L. Mencken, by permission of Alfred A. Knopf, Inc. Copyright 1917, 1944 by Alfred A. Knopf, Inc.

LITTLE, BROWN, AND COMPANY, for selections from *The Poems of Emily Dickinson,* edited by Martha Dickinson Bianchi and Alfred Leete Hampson, reprinted by permission of Little, Brown & Company.

LONGMANS, GREEN AND COMPANY, for "The Will to Believe" and a selection from *Pragmatism* by William James.

MACMILLAN COMPANY, for selections from *Partial Portraits* by Henry James; from *Collected Poems* and *Tristram* by Edwin Arlington Robinson. By permission of The Macmillan Company, Publishers.

NEW DIRECTIONS, for the selection from *The Crack-Up* by F. Scott Fitzgerald, published by New Directions, 333 Sixth Avenue, New York City 14; copyright 1945 by New Directions.

RANDOM HOUSE, INC., for "The Bear" from *Go Down, Moses* by William Faulkner, copyright 1942 by William Faulkner.

CHARLES SCRIBNER'S SONS, for selections from Sidney Lanier; from *History of the United States* by Henry Adams; from *Children of the Night* and *Town Down the River* by Edwin Arlington Robinson; from *The Fifth Column and the First Forty-nine Stories* by Ernest Hemingway, copyright, 1938, by Ernest Hemingway, published by Charles Scribner's Sons; from *All the Sad Young Men* by F. Scott Fitzgerald; copyright 1926 by Charles Scribner's Sons; used by permission of the publishers.

PREFACE

T HE PURPOSE of the editors of this anthology in this, its third revision, is
to supply for introductory college courses in American literature a
body of selections from the chief writers of the eighteenth and nineteenth centuries, and of representative writers of the seventeenth and twentieth
centuries. The alteration from the original concentration of the book upon
the eighteenth and nineteenth centuries seems to be made necessary by changes
in the introductory course.

Nevertheless, it is still the conviction of the editors that the introductory
course in American literature has suffered from trying to include too much,
with the result that the student leaves the subject in a confused state of mind
because he has tried to study too many authors in too short a time. In making
this revision the authors hope that they have clung to the original purpose of
the collection.

The editors trust that the selections are representative of various important
phases of the authors chosen. The authors representing the eighteenth and
nineteenth centuries are, they hope, major American writers in the sense that
they constitute the core of the national letters. The authors representing the
seventeenth and twentieth centuries are, they trust, representative, even though
the question of greatness and genius in their cases is under perpetual debate.

Great care has been taken to establish reputable texts. Without prejudice to
the labors of others, it has seemed to the editors that in no field is the need of
establishing reputable texts more necessary than in the field of American
literature. The editors have, however, been catholic in their choices, sometimes
printing first editions, sometimes the latest versions to appear in an author's
lifetime, sometimes a posthumous version appearing close to the date of the
author's demise. They have also preserved the punctuation and spelling of the
originals. To many, this will seem pedantry; but the flavor and cadence of
literature are often changed for the worse when an editor "improves" or mod-
ernizes the punctuation or spelling of the original. Fortunately for the beginning student, American literature is still too young not to be readily grasped
in its verbal meanings, even when the spelling is not twentieth-century spelling
and the punctuation is that older, rhetorical punctuation we have abandoned
under the impact of the newspaper and the linotype machine.

The texts have been heavily annotated where they need it. Years of experience in teaching have shown the editors that little general information can be
expected of all members of any class, and the editors have therefore preferred
to err on the side of generosity. If a footnote seems obvious, let the reader
pleasantly remember that it may not be obvious to those less well informed
than he is.

There is, of course, a school which holds that it is the business of the student
to look up references. Doubtless there is something to be said for this Spartan

practice, but there is not very much to be said for it. In the first place, references are not always easy to look up—as the editors have discovered to their sorrow; in the second place, students do not always look them up; and in the third place, no adult expects to run constantly to a dictionary or an encyclopaedia when he is trying to get pleasure from a masterpiece. Why should the student, to whom the teacher is trying to make reading attractive, be subjected to "busy work" that the adult does not perform? The editors believe that literature will be attractive in proportion as its meaning is made clear. To that end they have given the meanings of all obscure words and phrases where they have understood them, as well as the meanings of all words, the sense of which has been altered with the passage of time. They have also explained all the allusions they could, and they have tried to fix the sources of the quotations with which good writers abound. If an allusion or a reference goes unexplained, it is because the editors could not, after reasonable search, pin it down with accuracy.

In planning the contents of this collection the editors have chosen selections which should leave the student free to read such novels as *The Scarlet Letter, Typee, Moby Dick, Huckleberry Finn, The Rise of Silas Lapham,* or *The Portrait of a Lady,* which cannot be adequately represented in an anthology.

It is a pleasure to record the generous spirit of co-operation shown by the trustees and officials of the Henry E. Huntington Library in permitting the editors to print for the first time an accurate transcript of that portion of Franklin's *Autobiography* included in this book; and to acknowledge also their help in the matter of Poe. Equally cordial thanks should be given the officials of the University of Michigan Library, particularly Miss Ella M. Hymans and her assistant, Miss Pauline G. Waite, who, in the Reserved Book Room of that institution, have charge of a remarkable collection of American first editions. The unfailing patience and courtesy of Miss Hilda M. Rankin, Miss Mary E. Mixer, and their colleagues in the Reference Library have helped to make scholarly research a pleasure. The co-operation of the library officials of Southern Methodist University is also gratefully acknowledged.

CONTENTS

FOR VOLUME TWO

HERMAN MELVILLE

1819-1891

I. "THE MAN WHO LIVED AMONG THE CANNIBALS" (1819–1844)

1819   August 1, born in New York City, second son and third child of Allan and Maria Gansevoort Melville.

1824   Attended elementary schools in New York. Visits to the Gansevoort family in Albany during the summers.

1830   His business failing, Allan Melville removed with his family to Albany. Melville entered the Albany Academy.

1832   Death of the father left the family in straitened circumstances.

1834   Melville became a clerk in the New York State Bank, Albany; and also in his brother's store.

1836   Visited his uncle's home in Pittsfield, Massachusetts. Taught school.

1837–1841   Years of obscurity. Among other activities Melville taught school at Greenbush (East Albany), New York.

1839   Melville's first published articles, two "Fragments from a Writing Desk" in the *Democratic Press and Lansingburgh Advertiser,* May 4 and 18. Sailed for Liverpool on June 5 aboard the *St. Lawrence.* Discharged on return of ship.

1841   January 3, shipped on the *Acushnet* whaling vessel from Fairhaven, Massachusetts, bound for the Pacific.

1842   July 9(?), deserted in the Marquesas Islands; and with Richard Tobias Greene ("Toby") went to live among the Typees (cannibals). "Rescued" and went aboard the *Lucy Ann* whaler. In September, with other members of the crew, under technical arrest in Tahiti, which he left with a companion to work as a laborer on a neighboring island. Taken on the *Leviathan* whaler, and voyaged with her to Japan(?) and the Hawaiian Islands.

1843   August 17, enlisted at Honolulu as a common sailor on the U.S.S. *United States.* During the voyage to Boston, Melville narrowly avoided having to endure an unjust flogging; and just escaped death by drowning.

1844   October 14, discharged at Boston.

II. "FROM MY TWENTY-FIFTH YEAR I DATE MY LIFE" (1844–1853)

1844   Living at Lansingburg (near Albany) with his mother and family, and writing *Typee.*

1845   *Typee* completed; published by John Murray in London (New York ed., 1846; "expurgated" edition, 1849).

1847   January, *Omoo* published. August 4, married Elizabeth Shaw of Boston. Removed to New York City later in the year.

1849   February 16, Malcolm Melville born. *Mardi* published, April; *Redburn,*

August. At work on *Whitejacket*. Sailed to London October 11 to arrange for publication of two last named, returning February 2, 1850.

1850   Melville and the family went to Pittsfield for the summer, and in October bought Arrowhead farm near Pittsfield, Hawthorne being a near neighbor (at Lenox) until November, 1851. At work on *Moby Dick*.

1851   *Moby Dick* published. At work on *Pierre*.

1852   *Pierre* published. Denounced by critics.

1853   Plates of Melville's novels destroyed by fire at the publisher's.

III. DEEPENING SHADOWS (1853–1891)

1853   Sought consular appointment in vain. Contributed to *Putnam's Monthly Magazine* and *Harper's Magazine* (to 1856).

1855   *Israel Potter* published, after appearing serially in *Putnam's*.

1856   *Piazza Tales* published. Trip to London, the Mediterranean, and Palestine laid the foundation for *Clarel*.

1857   *The Confidence Man* published. Tried lecturing, which he continued for three years. Commenced composition of verse.

1860   Trip to San Francisco with his brother, returning by Panama.

1863   October, removed to New York City with the family.

1866   *Battle-Pieces* (first book of verse) published. December 5, Melville appointed customs inspector, holding the post to January, 1886, when an inheritance received by his wife enabled him to resign.

1876   *Clarel* (second book of verse) published.

1888   *John Marr and Other Poems* published.

1891   *Timoleon* published. *Billy Budd* completed. September 28, Melville died in New York City.

1924   *Billy Budd* published.

BIOGRAPHIES: R. M. Weaver, *Herman Melville, Mariner and Mystic,* Doran, 1921; John Freeman, *Herman Melville,* Macmillan, 1926; Lewis Mumford, *Herman Melville,* Harcourt, Brace, 1929; W. E. Sedgwick, *Herman Melville: The Tragedy of Mind,* Harvard University Press, 1944. Eleanor M. Metcalfe, ed., *Journal of a Visit to London and the Continent, by Herman Melville, 1848-1850,* Harvard University Press, 1948.

BIBLIOGRAPHY AND EDITIONS: There is no separate bibliography, but see *Literary History of the United States,* Vol. III, pp. 647-54. The standard edition is *Works of Herman Melville,* Wells, 1922-24, 16 vols., but another edition is in progress, having been passed from publisher to publisher. Of this edition there have appeared *Collected Poems,* ed. Howard P. Vincent, Packard, 1945, 1947; *Piazza Tales,* ed. E. S. Oliver, Hendricks House, 1948; *Pierre,* ed. Henry S. Murray, Hendricks House, 1949. See also *The Shorter Novels of Herman Melville,* ed. Raymond Weaver, Liveright, 1928; *Moby Dick,* ed. Willard Thorp, Oxford, 1947; and *Melville's Billy Budd,* ed. F. B. Freeman, Harvard University Press, 1948.

CRITICISM: The flood of critical articles on Melville should be followed in the usual bibliographical guides. For useful critical books see Charles R. Anderson, *Melville in the South Seas,* Columbia University Press, 1939, and William Braswell, *Melville's Religious Thought,* Duke University Press, 1943. Excellent both for bibliographical guidance and for interpretation is Willard Thorp, ed., *Representative Selections from Herman Melville,* American Book Co., 1938.

The two most remarkable facts about the literary fame of Herman Melville are the almost complete neglect into which he fell in the latter part of the nineteenth century, and the lyrical enthusiasm of the rediscovery of him in the twentieth. To the nineteenth century he was largely the teller of sea tales—an American rival of Captain Marryat; to the twentieth, he has become the epitome of the bitter fate of the artist under the industrial régime. Pursuing this interpretation, critics have read into his novels symbolical meanings which are perhaps not always intended; and, fortified by large draughts of Freudian psychology, have developed what amounts to a Melville legend. As in other such cases, the pointer is likely to stabilize itself somewhere between these two extremes. The nineteenth century certainly overlooked the larger philosophical implications of works like *Moby Dick* and *Mardi,* and the twentieth has tended to overlook, minimize, or excuse the grave artistic blemishes (especially in point of style) of Melville's novels.

Like Borrow, whom he in many points resembles, Melville spun the stuff of autobiography into books that are neither fiction nor fact but a middle term between the two. His romances are a vast confession, but a confession veiled in both deliberate and unconscious obscurities. These obscurities arise from a number of causes, among which a certain wilfulness must be counted; but they arise also from a certain confusion in Melville himself. In his writing there is a perpetual tension between romantic and realistic elements, between a thirst for epic largeness and a vivid sense of the actual. Thus in "Benito Cereno" Melville bases his tale upon a highly factual record in a forgotten travel book, but certain portions of the narrative are embroidered with much romantic and macabre detail; and not content to let his story speak for itself, he insists at the end on driving home its philosophic implications. Similar threads of artistic method are woven into the huge tapestry which is *Moby Dick.* Touched by the transcendental atmosphere of his creative period, Melville was yet compelled to base what he wrote upon the actual, upon what he had himself seen and experienced and felt; and these "realistic" elements, under the spell of his dilating imagination, frequently swell to abnormal proportions. Hence arise both the greatness and the failure of his method, and hence it is that the riddle of his personality and the enigma of his purposes have so fascinated the contemporary literary world.

BENITO CERENO

"Benito Cereno" was first published serially in *Putnam's Monthly Magazine* for October, November, and December, 1855; and then collected into the *Piazza Tales* (1856). The text of the *Piazza Tales,* here reprinted, was revised, and differs both in minor matters of substance and in punctuation from the magazine version. The most important changes in substance are indicated in the notes. Melville founded his story on Chapter XVIII of *A Narrative of Voyages and Travels, in the Northern and Southern Hemispheres: Comprising Three Voyages Round the World; together with a Voyage of Survey and Discovery, in the Pacific Ocean and Oriental Islands* by Amasa Delano (Boston, 1817). This chapter has been conveniently reprinted in the *Publications of the Modern Language Association,* Vol. XLIII, No. 2 (June, 1928, pp. 502-32), in an article by Harold H. Scudder entitled "Melville's *Benito Cereno* and Captain Delano's Voyages." Melville used his original much as Shakespeare used Holinshed's *Chronicles;* generally speaking, he took over the substance of the narrative, and found most of his characters in Delano's book. He added the atmospheric effects, the macabre details, the detailed description of the Spanish ship, the oakumpickers and the hatchet-polishers, and various details of the plot. He also changed the names of the ships and the time of the action.

The island of Santa Maria, where the action takes place, is just off the coast of north-central Chile, not very far from the city of Concepción. A study of the map of the Pacific will make clear most of the geographical details.

Where the text of the *Putnam's Monthly Magazine* version differs importantly from that of the version in the *Piazza Tales,* this is indicated in the footnotes by (P).

I N THE year 1799, Captain Amasa Delano, of Duxbury, in Massachusetts, commanding a large sealer and general trader, lay at anchor with a valuable cargo, in the harbor of St. Maria—a small, desert, uninhabited island towards the southern extremity of the long coast of Chili. There he had touched
5   for water.

On the second day, not long after dawn, while lying in his berth, his mate came below, informing him that a strange sail was coming into the bay. Ships were then not so plenty in those waters as now. He rose, dressed, and went on deck.
10   The morning was one peculiar to that coast. Everything was mute and calm; everything gray. The sea, though undulated into long roods of swells, seemed fixed, and was sleeked at the surface like waved lead that has cooled and set in the smelter's mould. The sky seemed a gray surtout. Flights of troubled gray fowl, kith and kin with flights of troubled gray vapors among which they
15   were mixed, skimmed low and fitfully over the waters, as swallows over meadows before storms. Shadows present, foreshadowing deeper shadows to come.

To Captain Delano's surprise, the stranger, viewed through the glass, showed no colors; though to do so upon entering a haven, however unhabited in its shores, where but a single other ship might be lying, was the custom among
20   peaceful seamen of all nations. Considering the lawlessness and loneliness of the spot, and the sort of stories, at that day, associated with those seas, Captain Delano's surprise might have deepened into some uneasiness had he not been a person of a singularly undistrustful good nature, not liable, except on extraordinary and repeated incentives, and hardly then, to indulge in personal
25   alarms, any way involving the imputation of malign evil in man. Whether, in view of what humanity is capable, such a trait implies, along with a benevolent heart, more than ordinary quickness and accuracy of intellectual perception, may be left to the wise to determine.

But whatever misgivings might have obtruded on first seeing the stranger,
30   would almost, in any seaman's mind, have been dissipated by observing that, the ship, in navigating into the harbor, was drawing too near the land; a sunken reef making out off her bow. This seemed to prove her a stranger, indeed, not only to the sealer, but the island; consequently, she could be no wonted freebooter on that ocean. With no small interest, Captain Delano con-
35   tinued to watch her—a proceeding not much facilitated by the vapors partly mantling the hull, through which the far matin light from her cabin streamed equivocally enough; much like the sun—by this time hemisphered on the rim of the horizon, and, apparently, in company with the strange ship, enter-

---

4. **southern extremity**—It is not clear why Melville has shifted the position of the island southward. 11. **roods**—A rood is a linear measure of about 7 or 8 yards. 13. **surtout**—"mantle" (P). 17. **glass**—telescope. 24. **incentives**—"excitement" (P). 31-32. **land; a sunken reef**—"land, for her own safety's sake, owing to a sunken reef" (P). 37. **hemisphered**—"crescented" (P).

ing the harbor—which, wimpled by the same low, creeping clouds, showed not unlike a Lima intriguante's one sinister eye peering across the Plaza from the Indian loop-hole of her dusk *saya-y-manta*.

It might have been but a deception of the vapors, but, the longer the stranger was watched the more singular appeared her manoeuvres. Ere long it seemed   5 hard to decide whether she meant to come in or no—what she wanted, or what she was about. The wind, which had breezed up a little during the night, was now extremely light and baffling, which the more increased the apparent uncertainty of her movements.

Surmising, at last, that it might be a ship in distress, Captain Delano or-   10 dered his whale-boat to be dropped, and, much to the wary opposition of his mate, prepared to board her, and, at the least, pilot her in. On the night previous, a fishing-party of the seamen had gone a long distance to some detached rocks out of sight from the sealer, and, an hour or two before daybreak, had returned, having met with no small success. Presuming that the   15 stranger might have been long off soundings, the good captain put several baskets of the fish, for presents, into his boat, and so pulled away. From her continuing too near the sunken reef, deeming her in danger, calling to his men, he made all haste to apprise those on board of their situation. But, some time ere the boat came up, the wind, light though it was, having shifted, had   20 headed the vessel off, as well as partly broken the vapors from about her.

Upon gaining a less remote view, the ship, when made signally visible on the verge of the leaden-hued swells, with the shreds of fog here and there raggedly furring her, appeared like a white-washed monastery after a thunderstorm, seen perched upon some dun cliff among the Pyrenees. But it was no   25 purely fanciful resemblance which now, for a moment, almost led Captain Delano to think that nothing less than a ship-load of monks was before him. Peering over the bulwarks were what really seemed, in the hazy distance, throngs of dark cowls; while, fitfully revealed through the open port-holes, other dark moving figures were dimly descried, as of Black Friars pacing the   30 cloisters.

Upon a still nigher approach, this appearance was modified, and the true character of the vessel was plain—a Spanish merchantman of the first class, carrying negro slaves, amongst other valuable freight, from one colonial port to another. A very large, and, in its time, a very fine vessel, such as in those   35 days were at intervals encountered along that main; sometimes superseded Acapulco treasure-ships, or retired frigates of the Spanish king's navy, which, like superannuated Italian palaces, still, under a decline of masters, preserved signs of former state.

As the whale-boat drew more and more nigh, the cause of the peculiar pipe-   40 clayed aspect of the stranger was seen in the slovenly neglect pervading her. The spars, ropes, and great part of the bulwarks, looked woolly, from long unacquaintance with the scraper, tar, and the brush. Her keel seemed laid, her ribs put together, and she launched, from Ezekiel's Valley of Dry Bones.

2. intriguante—flirtatious woman. **3. saya-y-manta**—skirt-and-shawl. **16. soundings**—shallower water near the shore. **36. main**—ocean, that is, main ocean. **37. Acapulco treasure-ships**—In the eighteenth century Spanish ships regularly carried gold from this port in Mexico to Spain. **44. Ezekiel's Valley**—*Cf.* Ezek. 37: 1-10.

In the present business in which she was engaged, the ship's general model and rig appeared to have undergone no material change from their original warlike and Froissart pattern. However, no guns were seen.

5 The tops were large, and were railed about with what had once been octagonal net-work, all now in sad disrepair. These tops hung overhead like three ruinous aviaries, in one of which was seen perched on a ratlin, a white noddy, a strange fowl, so called from its lethargic somnambulistic character, being frequently caught by hand at sea. Battered and mouldy, the castellated forecastle seemed some ancient turret, long ago taken by assault, and then left to decay.

10 Toward the stern, two high-raised quarter galleries—the balustrades here and there covered with dry, tindery sea-moss—opening out from the unoccupied state-cabin, whose dead-lights, for all the mild weather, were hermetically closed and calked—these tenantless balconies hung over the sea as if it were the grand Venetian canal. But the principal relic of faded grandeur was the

15 ample oval of the shield-like stern-piece, intricately carved with the arms of Castile and Leon, medallioned about by groups of mythological or symbolical devices; uppermost and central of which was a dark satyr in a mask, holding his foot on the prostrate neck of a writhing figure, likewise masked.

Whether the ship had a figure-head, or only a plain beak, was not quite

20 certain, owing to canvas wrapped about that part, either to protect it while undergoing a re-furbishing, or else decently to hide its decay. Rudely painted or chalked, as in a sailor freak, along the forward side of a sort of pedestal below the canvas, was the sentence, *"Seguid vuestro jefe"* (follow your leader); while upon the tarnished head-boards, near by, appeared, in stately capitals,

25 once gilt, the ship's name "SAN DOMINICK," each letter streakingly corroded with tricklings of copper-spike rust; while, like mourning weeds, dark festoons of sea-grass slimily swept to and fro over the name, with every hearse-like roll of the hull.

As, at last, the boat was hooked from the bow along toward the gangway

30 amidship, its keel, while yet some inches separated from the hull, harshly grated as on a sunken coral reef. It proved a huge bunch of conglobated barnacles adhering below the water to the side like a wen—a token of baffling airs and long calms passed somewhere in those seas.

Climbing the side, the visitor was at once surrounded by a clamorous throng

35 of whites and blacks, but the latter outnumbering the former more than could have been expected, negro transportation-ship as the stranger in port was. But, in one language, and as with one voice, all poured out a common tale of suffering; in which the negresses, of whom there were not a few, exceeded the others in their dolorous vehemence. The scurvy, together with a fever, had

3. **Froissart pattern**—This phrase is apparently peculiar to Melville. He seems to have in mind the early Tudor sailing vessels. 4. **tops**—A top is a platform surrounding the head of the lower mast, serving, among other uses, as a standing-place for the sailors. 6. **ratlin**—a transverse rope attached to the shrouds of a vessel; the ratlins serve as ladders. 10. **quarter galleries**—platforms on the after parts of the vessel's sides. 12. **dead-lights**—shutters fitted over the port, or cabin, windows of the ship, to keep out the water. 16. **Castile and Leon**—The kingdom of Spain was formed by the union of the kingdoms of Castile and Leon. 25. **San Dominick**—The proper form would be San Domingo. In reality the Spanish ship was called the *Tryal*. 29. **was hooked**—that is, was held off from the vessel's side with a boat hook, and then hooked along to the gangway.

swept off a great part of their number, more especially the Spaniards. Off
Cape Horn, they had narrowly escaped shipwreck; then, for days together,
they had lain tranced without wind; their provisions were low; their water
next to none; their lips that moment were baked.

While Captain Delano was thus made the mark of all eager tongues, his one   5
eager glance took in all the faces, with every other object about him.

Always upon first boarding a large and populous ship at sea, especially a
foreign one, with a nondescript crew such as Lascars or Manilla men, the impression varies in a peculiar way from that produced by first entering a strange
house with strange inmates in a strange land. Both house and ship—the one by   10
its walls and blinds, the other by its high bulwarks like ramparts—hoard from
view their interiors till the last moment; but in the case of the ship there is
this addition; that the living spectacle it contains, upon its sudden and complete disclosure, has, in contrast with the blank ocean which zones it, something of the effect of enchantment. The ship seems unreal; these strange cos-   15
tumes, gestures, and faces, but a shadowy tableau just emerged from the deep,
which directly must receive back what it gave.

Perhaps it was some such influence, as above is attempted to be described,
which, in Captain Delano's mind, heightened whatever, upon a staid scrutiny,
might have seemed unusual; especially the conspicuous figures of four elderly   20
grizzled negroes, their heads like black, doddered willow tops, who, in venerable contrast to the tumult below them, were couched sphynx-like, one on the
starboard cat-head, another on the larboard, and the remaining pair face to
face on the opposite bulwarks above the main-chains. They each had bits of
unstranded old junk in their hands, and, with a sort of stoical self-content,   25
were picking the junk into oakum, a small heap of which lay by their sides.
They accompanied the task with a continuous, low, monotonous chant; dron-
ing and druling away like so many gray-headed bag-pipers playing a funeral
march.

The quarter-deck rose into an ample elevated poop, upon the forward verge   30
of which, lifted, like the oakum-pickers, some eight feet above the general
throng, sat along in a row, separated by regular spaces, the cross-legged figures
of six other blacks; each with a rusty hatchet in his hand, which, with a bit
of brick and a rag, he was engaged like a scullion in scouring; while between
each two was a small stack of hatchets, their rusted edges turned forward   35
awaiting a like operation. Though occasionally the four oakum-pickers would
briefly address some person or persons in the crowd below, yet the six hatchet-
polishers neither spoke to others, nor breathed a whisper among themselves,
but sat intent upon their task, except at intervals, when, with the peculiar love
in negroes of uniting industry with pastime, two-and-two they sideways clashed   40
their hatchets together, like cymbals, with a barbarous din. All six, unlike the
generality, had the raw aspect of unsophisticated Africans.

2. **Cape Horn**—the southernmost point of South America, dreaded for its storms. 8. **Lascars**
—East Indian sailors employed on European vessels. 8. **Manilla**—The Philippine Islands then belonged to Spain. 21. **doddered**—deprived of branches through age. 23. **cat-head**—a projecting
timber near the bow of the ship, to which the anchor is hoisted. 24. **main-chains**—chains having
to do with the mainmast. 25. **junk**—pieces of old cordage. 26. **oakum**—loose fiber picked from
old ropes, and used to calk seams. 30. **quarter-deck**—that part of the upper deck abaft of the
mainmast, reserved for the officers and passengers.

But that first comprehensive glance which took in those ten figures, with scores less conspicuous, rested but an instant upon them, as, impatient of the hubbub of voices, the visitor turned in quest of whomsoever it might be that commanded the ship.

5   But as if not unwilling to let nature make known her own case among his suffering charge, or else in despair of restraining it for the time, the Spanish captain, a gentlemanly, reserved-looking, and rather young man to a stranger's eye, dressed with singular richness, but bearing plain traces of recent sleepless cares and disquietudes, stood passively by, leaning against the main-mast,

10 at one moment casting a dreary, spiritless look upon his excited people, at the next an unhappy glance toward his visitor. By his side stood a black of small stature, in whose rude face, as occasionally, like a shepherd's dog, he mutely turned it up into the Spaniard's, sorrow and affection were equally blended.

15 Struggling through the throng, the American advanced to the Spaniard, as-suring him of his sympathies, and offering to render whatever assistance might be in his power. To which the Spaniard returned, for the present but grave and ceremonious acknowledgments, his national formality dusked by the saturnine mood of ill-health.

20 But losing no time in mere compliments, Captain Delano, returning to the gangway, had his basket of fish brought up; and as the wind still continued light, so that some hours at least must elapse ere the ship could be brought to the anchorage, he bade his men return to the sealer, and fetch back as much water as the whale-boat could carry, with whatever soft bread the steward

25 might have, all the remaining pumpkins on board, with a box of sugar, and a dozen of his private bottles of cider.

Not many minutes after the boat's pushing off, to the vexation of all, the wind entirely died away, and the tide turning, began drifting back the ship helplessly seaward. But trusting this would not long last, Captain Delano

30 sought, with good hopes, to cheer up the strangers, feeling no small satisfac-tion that, with persons in their condition he could—thanks to his frequent voyages along the Spanish main—converse with some freedom in their native tongue.

While left alone with them, he was not long in observing some things tend-

35 ing to heighten his first impressions; but surprise was lost in pity, both for the Spaniards and blacks, alike evidently reduced from scarcity of water and provisions; while long-continued suffering seemed to have brought out the less good-natured qualities of the negroes, besides, at the same time, impairing the Spaniard's authority over them. But, under the circumstances, precisely this

40 condition of things was to have been anticipated. In armies, navies, cities, or families, in nature herself, nothing more relaxes good order than misery. Still, Captain Delano was not without the idea, that had Benito Cereno been a man of greater energy, misrule would hardly have come to the present pass. But the debility, constitutional or induced by the hardships, bodily and mental, of

45 the Spanish captain, was too obvious to be overlooked. A prey to settled de-jection, as if long mocked with hope he would not now indulge it, even when it had ceased to be a mock, the prospect of that day or evening at furthest,

lying at anchor, with plenty of water for his people, and a brother captain to
counsel and befriend, seemed in no perceptible degree to encourage him. His
mind appeared unstrung, if not still more seriously affected. Shut up in these
oaken walls, chained to one dull round of command, whose unconditionality
cloyed him, like some hypochondriac abbot he moved slowly about, at times   5
suddenly pausing, starting, or staring, biting his lip, biting his finger-nail, flushing, paling, twitching his beard, with other symptoms of an absent or moody
mind. This distempered spirit was lodged, as before hinted, in as distempered
a frame. He was rather tall, but seemed never to have been robust, and now
with nervous suffering was almost worn to a skeleton. A tendency to some pul- 10
monary complaint appeared to have been lately confirmed. His voice was like
that of one with lungs half gone—hoarsely suppressed, a husky whisper. No
wonder that, as in this state he tottered about, his private servant apprehen-
sively followed him. Sometimes the negro gave his master his arm, or took
his handkerchief out of his pocket for him; performing these and similar of- 15
fices with that affectionate zeal which transmutes into something filial or fraternal acts in themselves but menial; and which has gained for the negro the
repute of making the most pleasing body-servant in the world; one, too, whom
a master need be on no stiffly superior terms with, but may treat with familiar
trust; less a servant than a devoted companion.   20

Marking the noisy indocility of the blacks in general, as well as what seemed
the sullen inefficiency of the whites, it was not without humane satisfaction
that Captain Delano witnessed the steady good conduct of Babo.

But the good conduct of Babo, hardly more than the ill-behavior of others,
seemed to withdraw the half-lunatic Don Benito from his cloudy languor. Not 25
that such precisely was the impression made by the Spaniard on the mind of his
visitor. The Spaniard's individual unrest was, for the present, but noted as a
conspicuous feature in the ship's general affliction. Still, Captain Delano was
not a little concerned at what he could not help taking for the time to be Don
Benito's unfriendly indifference toward himself. The Spaniard's manner, too, 30
conveyed a sort of sour and gloomy disdain, which he seemed at no pains to
disguise. But this the American in charity ascribed to the harassing effects of
sickness, since, in former instances, he had noted that there are peculiar natures
on whom prolonged physical suffering seems to cancel every social instinct of
kindness; as if forced to black bread themselves, they deemed it but equity 35
that each person coming nigh them should, indirectly, by some slight or affront,
be made to partake of their fare.

But ere long Captain Delano bethought him that, indulgent as he was at the
first, in judging the Spaniard, he might not, after all, have exercised charity
enough. At bottom it was Don Benito's reserve which displeased him; but the 40
same reserve was shown toward all but his personal attendant. Even the formal
reports which, according to sea-usage, were at stated times made to him by
some petty underling, either a white, mulatto or black, he hardly had patience
enough to listen to, without betraying contemptuous aversion. His manner
upon such occasions was, in its degree, not unlike that which might be sup- 45

23. **Babo**—In the original narrative the confidential servant is Muri; but Melville apparently
preferred the suggestive name of Babo.

posed to have been his imperial countryman's, Charles V., just previous to the anchoritish retirement of that monarch from the throne.

This splenetic disrelish of his place was evinced in almost every function pertaining to it. Proud as he was moody, he condescended to no personal man-
5 date. Whatever special orders were necessary, their delivery was delegated to his body-servant, who in turn transferred them to their ultimate destination, through runners, alert Spanish boys or slave boys, like pages or pilot-fish within easy call continually hovering round Don Benito. So that to have beheld this undemonstrative invalid gliding about, apathetic and mute, no landsman could
10 have dreamed that in him was lodged a dictatorship beyond which, while at sea, there was no earthly appeal.

Thus, the Spaniard, regarded in his reserve, seemed as the involuntary victim of mental disorder. But, in fact, his reserve might, in some degree, have pro-ceeded from design. If so, then here was evinced the unhealthy climax of that
15 icy though conscientious policy, more or less adopted by all commanders of large ships, which, except in signal emergencies, obliterates alike the mani-festation of sway with every trace of sociality; transforming the man into a block, or rather into a loaded cannon, which, until there is call for thunder, has nothing to say.
20 Viewing him in this light, it seemed but a natural token of the perverse habit induced by a long course of such hard self-restraint, that, notwithstanding the present condition of his ship, the Spaniard should still persist in a demeanor, which, however harmless, or it may be, appropriate, in a well-appointed vessel, such as the San Dominick might have been at the outset of the voyage, was any-
25 thing but judicious now. But the Spaniard, perhaps, thought that it was with captains as with gods: reserve, under all events, must still be their cue. But probably this appearance of slumbering dominion might have been but an attempted disguise to conscious imbecility—not deep policy, but shallow device. But be all this as it might, whether Don Benito's manner was designed or not,
30 the more Captain Delano noted its pervading reserve, the less he felt uneasiness at any particular manifestation of that reserve towards himself.

Neither were his thoughts taken up by the captain alone. Wonted to the quiet orderliness of the sealer's comfortable family of a crew, the noisy con-fusion of the San Dominick's suffering host repeatedly challenged his eye.
35 Some prominent breaches, not only of discipline but of decency, were observed. These Captain Delano could not but ascribe, in the main, to the absence of those subordinate deck-officers to whom, along with higher duties, is entrusted what may be styled the police department of a populous ship. True, the old oakum-pickers appeared at times to act the part of monitorial constables to
40 their countrymen, the blacks; but though occasionally succeeding in allaying trifling outbreaks now and then between man and man, they could do little or nothing toward establishing general quiet. The San Dominick was in the condition of a transatlantic emigrant ship, among whose multitude of living freight are some individuals, doubtless, as little troublesome as crates and bales;

1. **Charles V.**—Charles V (1500-1558), the most powerful European monarch of his age, retired to a monastery before his death. 7. **pilot-fish**—a species of fish which accompany sharks. 14. **here**—"in Don Benito" (P).

but the friendly remonstrances of such with their ruder companions are of not so much avail as the unfriendly arm of the mate. What the San Dominick wanted was, what the emigrant ship has, stern superior officers. But on these decks not so much as a fourth-mate was to be seen.

The visitor's curiosity was roused to learn the particulars of those mishaps 5 which had brought about such absenteeism, with its consequences; because, though deriving some inkling of the voyage from the wails which at the first moment had greeted him, yet of the details no clear understanding had been had. The best account would, doubtless, be given by the captain. Yet at first the visitor was loth to ask it, unwilling to provoke some distant rebuff. But pluck- 10 ing up courage, he at last accosted Don Benito, renewing the expression of his benevolent interest, adding, that did he (Captain Delano) but know the particulars of the ship's misfortunes, he would, perhaps, be better able in the end to relieve them. Would Don Benito favor him with the whole story.

Don Benito faltered; then, like some somnambulist suddenly interfered with, 15 vacantly stared at his visitor, and ended by looking down on the deck. He maintained this posture so long, that Captain Delano, almost equally disconcerted, and involuntarily almost as rude, turned suddenly from him, walking forward to accost one of the Spanish seamen for the desired information. But he had hardly gone five paces when, with a sort of eagerness Don Benito invited him 20 back, regretting his momentary absence of mind, and professing readiness to gratify him.

While most part of the story was being given, the two captains stood on the after part of the main-deck, a privileged spot, no one being near but the servant.   25

"It is now a hundred and ninety days," began the Spaniard, in his husky whisper, "that this ship, well officered and well manned, with several cabin passengers—some fifty Spaniards in all—sailed from Buenos Ayres bound to Lima, with a general cargo, Paraguay tea and the like—and," pointing forward, "that parcel of negroes, now not more than a hundred and fifty, as you 30 see, but then numbering over three hundred souls. Off Cape Horn we had heavy gales. In one moment, by night, three of my best officers, with fifteen sailors, were lost, with the main-yard; the spar snapping under them in the slings, as they sought, with heavers, to beat down the icy sail. To lighten the hull, the heavier sacks of mata were thrown into the sea, with most of the 35 water-pipes lashed on deck at the time. And this last necessity it was, combined with the prolonged detentions afterwards experienced, which eventually brought about our chief causes of suffering. When—"

Here there was a sudden fainting attack of his cough, brought on, no doubt, by his mental distress. His servant sustained him, and drawing a cordial from 40 his pocket placed it to his lips. He a little revived. But unwilling to leave him unsupported while yet imperfectly restored, the black with one arm still encircled his master, at the same time keeping his eye fixed on his face, as if to watch for the first sign of complete restoration, or relapse, as the event might prove.   45

34. slings—ropes to support a yard. 34. heavers—bars. 35. mata—Apparently Melville has a South American plant in mind. 36. water-pipes—water casks.

The Spaniard proceeded, but brokenly and obscurely, as one in a dream.

—"Oh, my God! rather than pass through what I have, with joy I would have hailed the most terrible gales; but—"

His cough returned and with increased violence; this subsiding, with red-
5 dened lips and closed eyes he fell heavily against his supporter.

"His mind wanders. He was thinking of the plague that followed the gales," plaintively sighed the servant; "my poor, poor master!" wringing one hand, and with the other wiping the mouth. "But be patient, Señor," again turning to Captain Delano, "these fits do not last long; master will soon be himself."

10 Don Benito reviving, went on; but as this portion of the story was very brokenly delivered, the substance only will here be set down.

It appeared that after the ship had been many days tossed in storms off the Cape, the scurvy broke out, carrying off numbers of the whites and blacks. When at last they had worked round into the Pacific, their spars and sails
15 were so damaged, and so inadequately handled by the surviving mariners, most of whom were become invalids, that, unable to lay her northerly course by the wind, which was powerful, the unmanageable ship, for successive days and nights, was blown northwestward, where the breeze suddenly deserted her, in unknown waters, to sultry calms. The absence of the water-pipes now proved
20 as fatal to life as before their presence had menaced it. Induced, or at least aggravated, by the more than scanty allowance of water, a malignant fever followed the scurvy; with the excessive heat of the lengthened calm, making such short work of it as to sweep away, as by billows, whole families of the Africans, and a yet larger number, proportionably, of the Spaniards, including,
25 by a luckless fatality, every remaining officer on board. Consequently, in the smart west winds eventually following the calm, the already rent sails, having to be simply dropped, not furled, at need, had been gradually reduced to the beggar's rags they were now. To procure substitutes for his lost sailors, as well as supplies of water and sails, the captain, at the earliest opportunity, had
30 made for Baldivia, the southernmost civilized port of Chili and South America; but upon nearing the coast the thick weather had prevented him from so much as sighting that harbor. Since which period, almost without a crew, and almost without canvas and almost without water, and, at intervals, giving its added dead to the sea, the San Dominick had been battle-dored about by
35 contrary winds, inveigled by currents, or grown weedy in calms. Like a man lost in woods, more than once she had doubled upon her own track.

"But throughout these calamities," huskily continued Don Benito, painfully turning in the half embrace of his servant, "I have to thank those negroes you see, who, though to your inexperienced eyes appearing unruly, have, indeed,
40 conducted themselves with less of restlessness than even their owner could have thought possible under such circumstances."

Here he again fell faintly back. Again his mind wandered; but he rallied, and less obscurely proceeded.

"Yes, their owner was quite right in assuring me that no fetters would be
45 needed with his blacks; so that while, as is wont in this transportation, those

13. scurvy—a disease due to the lack of fresh fruit and vegetables.

negroes have always remained upon deck—not thrust below, as in the Guinea-men—they have, also, from the beginning, been freely permitted to range within given bounds at their pleasure."

Once more the faintness returned—his mind roved—but, recovering, he resumed: 5

"But it is Babo here to whom, under God, I owe not only my own preservation, but likewise to him, chiefly, the merit is due, of pacifying his more ignorant brethren, when at intervals tempted to murmurings."

"Ah, master," sighed the black, bowing his face, "don't speak of me; Babo is nothing; what Babo has done was but duty."   10

"Faithful fellow!" cried Captain Delano. "Don Benito, I envy you such a friend; slave I cannot call him."

As master and man stood before him, the black upholding the white, Captain Delano could not but bethink him of the beauty of that relationship which could present such a spectacle of fidelity on the one hand and confidence on   15
the other. The scene was heightened by the contrast in dress, denoting their relative positions. The Spaniard wore a loose Chili jacket of dark velvet; white small-clothes and stockings, with silver buckles at the knee and instep; a high-crowned sombrero, of fine grass; a slender sword, silver mounted, hung from a knot in his sash—the last being an almost invariable adjunct, more for   20
utility than ornament, of a South American gentleman's dress to this hour. Excepting when his occasional nervous contortions brought about disarray, there was a certain precision in his attire, curiously at variance with the unsightly disorder around: especially in the belittered Ghetto, forward of the main-mast, wholly occupied by the blacks.   25

The servant wore nothing but wide trowsers, apparently, from their coarseness and patches, made out of some old topsail; they were clean, and confined at the waist by a bit of unstranded rope, which, with his composed, deprecatory air at times, made him look something like a begging friar of St. Francis.

However unsuitable for the time and place, at least in the blunt-thinking   30
American's eyes, and however strangely surviving in the midst of all his afflictions, the toilette of Don Benito might not, in fashion at least, have gone beyond the style of the day among South Americans of his class. Though on the present voyage sailing from Buenos Ayres, he had avowed himself a native and resident of Chili, whose inhabitants had not so generally adopted the plain 35
coat and once plebeian pantaloons; but, with a becoming modification, adhered to their provincial costume, picturesque as any in the world. Still, relatively to the pale history of the voyage, and his own pale face, there seemed something so incongruous in the Spaniard's apparel, as almost to suggest the image of an invalid courtier tottering about London streets in the time of the plague.   40

The portion of the narrative which, perhaps, most excited interest, as well as some surprise, considering the latitudes in question, was the long calms spoken of, and more particularly the ship's so long drifting about. Without communicating the opinion, of course, the American could not but impute at least part of the detentions both to clumsy seamanship and faulty navigation.   45

1-2. **Guinea-men**—slave ships bringing Negroes from the African coast to the New World.

Eyeing Don Benito's small, yellow hands, he easily inferred that the young captain had not got into command at the hawse-hole but the cabin-window; and if so, why wonder at incompetence, in youth, sickness, and gentility united?

But drowning criticism in compassion, after a fresh repetition of his sympa-
5 thies, Captain Delano, having heard out his story, not only engaged, as in the first place, to see Don Benito and his people supplied in their immediate bodily needs, but, also, now further promised to assist him in procuring a large permanent supply of water, as well as some sails and rigging; and, though it would involve no small embarrassment to himself, yet he would spare three of his
10 best seamen for temporary deck officers; so that without delay the ship might proceed to Conception, there fully to refit for Lima, her destined port.

Such generosity was not without its effect, even upon the invalid. His face lighted up; eager and hectic, he met the honest glance of his visitor. With gratitude he seemed overcome.

15 "This excitement is bad for master," whispered the servant, taking his arm, and with soothing words gently drawing him aside.

When Don Benito returned, the American was pained to observe that his hopefulness, like the sudden kindling in his cheek, was but febrile and transient.

20 Ere long, with a joyless mien, looking up towards the poop, the host invited his guest to accompany him there, for the benefit of what little breath of wind might be stirring.

As, during the telling of the story, Captain Delano had once or twice started at the occasional cymballing of the hatchet-polishers, wondering why such an
25 interruption should be allowed, especially in that part of the ship, and in the ears of an invalid; and moreover, as the hatchets had anything but an attractive look, and the handlers of them still less so, it was, therefore, to tell the truth, not without some lurking reluctance, or even shrinking, it may be, that Captain Delano, with apparent complaisance, acquiesced in his host's invitation. The
30 more so, since, with an untimely caprice of punctilio, rendered distressing by his cadaverous aspect, Don Benito, with Castilian bows, solemnly insisted upon his guest's preceding him up the ladder leading to the elevation; where, one on each side of the last step, sat for armorial supporters and sentries two of the ominous file. Gingerly enough stepped good Captain Delano between them,
35 and in the instant of leaving them behind, like one running the gauntlet, he felt an apprehensive twitch in the calves of his legs.

But when, facing about, he saw the whole file, like so many organ-grinders, still stupidly intent on their work, unmindful of everything beside, he could not but smile at his late fidgety panic.

40 Presently, while standing with his host, looking forward upon the decks below, he was struck by one of those instances of insubordination previously alluded to. Three black boys, with two Spanish boys, were sitting together on the hatchets, scraping a rude wooden platter, in which some scanty mess had

2. hawse-hole—one of the holes in a ship's bow, through which a cable passes. That is, the captain had not had practical experience as a seaman. 3. gentility—"aristocracy" (P). 3. united? —"Such was his democratic conclusion" is added in (P). 39. fidgety—"fidgeting" (P). 40. his host—"Don Benito" (P).

recently been cooked. Suddenly, one of the black boys, enraged at a word dropped by one of his white companions, seized a knife, and, though called to forbear by one of the oakum-pickers, struck the lad over the head, inflicting a gash from which blood flowed.

In amazement, Captain Delano inquired what this meant. To which the pale 5 Don Benito dully muttered, that it was merely the sport of the lad.

"Pretty serious sport, truly," rejoined Captain Delano. "Had such a thing happened on board the Bachelor's Delight, instant punishment would have followed."

At these words the Spaniard turned upon the American one of his sudden, 10 staring, half-lunatic looks; then, relapsing into his torpor, answered, "Doubtless, doubtless, Señor."

Is it, thought Captain Delano, that this helpless man is one of those paper captains I've known, who by policy wink at what by power they cannot put down? I know no sadder sight than a commander who has little of command 15 but the name.

"I should think, Don Benito," he now said, glancing towards the oakum-picker who had sought to interfere with the boys, "that you would find it advantageous to keep all your blacks employed, especially the younger ones, no matter at what useless task, and no matter what happens to the ship. Why, 20 even with my little band, I find such a course indispensable. I once kept a crew on my quarter-deck thrumming mats for my cabin, when, for three days, I had given up my ship—mats, men, and all—for a speedy loss, owing to the violence of a gale, in which we could do nothing but helplessly drive before it." 25

"Doubtless, doubtless," muttered Don Benito.

"But," continued Captain Delano, again glancing upon the oakum-pickers and then at the hatchet-polishers, near by, "I see you keep some, at least, of your host employed."

"Yes," was again the vacant response. 30

"Those old men there, shaking their pows from their pulpits," continued Captain Delano, pointing to the oakum-pickers, "seem to act the part of old dominies to the rest, little heeded as their admonitions are at times. Is this voluntary on their part, Don Benito, or have you appointed them shepherds to your flock of black sheep?" 35

"What posts they fill, I appointed them," rejoined the Spaniard in an acrid tone, as if resenting some supposed satiric reflection.

"And these others, these Ashantee conjurors here," continued Captain Delano, rather uneasily eying the brandished steel of the hatchet-polishers, where, in spots, it had been brought to a shine, "this seems a curious business they are at, 40 Don Benito?"

"In the gales we met," answered the Spaniard, "what of our general cargo was not thrown overboard was much damaged by the brine. Since coming into

22. thrumming—To thrum is to insert short pieces of rope yarn or spun yarn in a piece of canvas to make a rough surface suitable for wrapping about rigging to prevent chafing. 31. pows —heads. 33. dominies—masters (usually used of ministers). 38. Ashantee—a district on the west coast of Africa whence slaves were sold.

calm weather, I have had several cases of knives and hatchets daily brought up for overhauling and cleaning."

"A prudent idea, Don Benito. You are part owner of ship and cargo, I presume; but not of the slaves, perhaps?"

5   "I am owner of all you see," impatiently returned Don Benito, "except the main company of blacks, who belonged to my late friend Alexandro Aranda."

As he mentioned this name, his air was heart-broken; his knees shook; his servant supported him.

Thinking he divined the cause of such unusual emotion, to confirm his sur-
10 mise, Captain Delano, after a pause, said: "And may I ask, Don Benito, whether —since awhile ago you spoke of some cabin passengers—the friend, whose loss so afflicts you, at the outset of the voyage accompanied his blacks?"

"Yes."

"But died of the fever?"

15   "Died of the fever.—Oh, could I but—"

Again quivering, the Spaniard paused.

"Pardon me," said Captain Delano, lowly, "but I think that, by a sympathetic experience, I conjecture, Don Benito, what it is that gives the keener edge to your grief. It was once my hard fortune to lose at sea, a dear friend, my own
20 brother, then supercargo. Assured of the welfare of his spirit, its departure I could have borne like a man; but that honest eye, that honest hand—both of which had so often met mine—and that warm heart; all, all—like scraps to the dogs—to throw all to the sharks! It was then I vowed never to have for fellow-voyager a man I loved, unless, unbeknown to him, I had provided every req-
25 uisite, in case of a fatality, for embalming his mortal part for interment on shore. Were your friend's remains now on board this ship, Don Benito, not thus strangely would the mention of his name affect you."

"On board this ship?" echoed the Spaniard. Then, with horrified gestures, as directed against some spectre, he unconsciously fell into the ready arms of his
30 attendant, who, with a silent appeal toward Captain Delano, seemed beseeching him not again to broach a theme so unspeakably distressing to his master.

This poor fellow now, thought the pained American, is the victim of that sad superstition which associates goblins with the deserted body of man, as ghosts with an abandoned house. How unlike are we made! What to me, in
35 like case, would have been a solemn satisfaction, the bare suggestion, even, terrifies the Spaniard into this trance. Poor Alexandro Aranda! what would you say could you here see your friend—who, on former voyages, when you, for months, were left behind, has, I dare say, often longed, and longed, for one peep at you—now transported with terror at the least thought of having you
40 anyway nigh him.

At this moment, with a dreary grave-yard toll, betokening a flaw, the ship's forecastle bell, smote by one of the grizzled oakum-pickers, proclaimed ten o'clock, through the leaden calm; when Captain Delano's attention was caught by the moving figure of a gigantic black, emerging from the general crowd be-
45 low, and slowly advancing towards the elevated poop. An iron collar was about his neck, from which depended a chain, thrice wound round his body; the terminating links padlocked together at a broad band of iron, his girdle.

"How like a mute Atufal moves," mumured the servant.

The black mounted the steps of the poop, and, like a brave prisoner, brought up to receive sentence, stood in unquailing muteness before Don Benito, now recovered from his attack.

At the first glimpse of his approach, Don Benito had started, a resentful 5
shadow swept over his face; and as with the sudden memory of bootless rage, his white lips glued together.

This is some mulish mutineer, thought Captain Delano, surveying, not without a mixture of admiration, the colossal form of the negro.

"See, he waits your question, master," said the servant.   10

Thus reminded, Don Benito, nervously averting his glance, as if shunning, by anticipation, some rebellious response, in a disconcerted voice, thus spoke:—

"Atufal, will you ask my pardon now?"

The black was silent.

"Again, master," murmured the servant, with bitter upbraiding eyeing his 15
countryman, "again, master; he will bend to master yet."

"Answer," said Don Benito, still averting his glance, "say but the one word, *pardon,* and your chains shall be off."

Upon this, the black, slowly raising both arms, let them lifelessly fall, his links clanking, his head bowed; as much as to say, "No, I am content."   20

"Go," said Don Benito, with inkept and unknown emotion.

Deliberately as he had come, the black obeyed.

"Excuse me, Don Benito," said Captain Delano, "but this scene surprises me; what means it, pray?"

"It means that that negro alone, of all the band, has given me peculiar 25
cause of offence. I have put him in chains; I——"

Here he paused; his hand to his head, as if there were a swimming there, or a sudden bewilderment of memory had come over him; but meeting his servant's kindly glance seemed reassured, and proceeded:—

"I could not scourge such a form. But I told him he must ask my pardon. 30
As yet he has not. At my command, every two hours he stands before me."

"And how long has this been?"

"Some sixty days."

"And obedient in all else? And respectful?"

"Yes."   35

"Upon my conscience, then," exclaimed Captain Delano, impulsively, "he has a royal spirit in him, this fellow."

"He may have some right to it," bitterly returned Don Benito; "he says he was king in his own land."

"Yes," said the servant, entering a word, "those slits in Atufal's ears once 40
held wedges of gold; but poor Babo here, in his own land, was only a poor slave; a black man's slave was Babo, who now is the white's."

Somewhat annoyed by these conversational familiarities, Captain Delano turned curiously upon the attendant, then glanced inquiringly at his master; but, as if long wonted to these little informalities, neither master nor man 45
seemed to understand him.

"What, pray, was Atufal's offence, Don Benito?" asked Captain Delano; "if it was not something very serious, take a fool's advice, and, in view of his general docility, as well as in some natural respect for his spirit, remit his penalty."

"No, no, master never will do that," here murmured the servant to himself,
5 "proud Atufal must first ask master's pardon. The slave there carries the padlock, but master here carries the key."

His attention thus directed, Captain Delano now noticed for the first time, that, suspended by a slender silken cord, from Don Benito's neck, hung a key. At once, from the servant's muttered syllables, divining the key's purpose, he
10 smiled and said:—"So, Don Benito—padlock and key—significant symbols, truly."

Biting his lip, Don Benito faltered.

Though the remark of Captain Delano, a man of such native simplicity as to be incapable of satire or irony, had been dropped in playful allusion to the
15 Spaniard's singularly evidenced lordship over the black; yet the hypochondriac seemed in some way to have taken it as a malicious reflection upon his confessed inability thus far to break down, at least, on a verbal summons, the entrenched will of the slave. Deploring this supposed misconception, yet despairing of correcting it, Captain Delano shifted the subject; but finding his com-
20 panion more than ever withdrawn, as if still slowly digesting the lees of the presumed affront above-mentioned, by-and-by Captain Delano likewise became less talkative, oppressed, against his own will, by what seemed the secret vindictiveness of the morbidly sensitive Spaniard. But the good sailor, himself of a quite contrary disposition, refrained, on his part, alike from the appearance as
25 from the feeling of resentment, and if silent, was only so from contagion.

Presently the Spaniard, assisted by his servant somewhat discourteously crossed over from his guest; a procedure which, sensibly enough, might have been allowed to pass for idle caprice of ill-humor, had not master and man, lingering round the corner of the elevated skylight, began whispering together
30 in low voices. This was unpleasing. And more: the moody air of the Spaniard, which at times had not been without a sort of valetudinarian stateliness, now seemed anything but dignified; while the menial familiarity of the servant lost its original charm of simple-hearted attachment.

In his embarrassment, the visitor turned his face to the other side of the ship.
35 By so doing, his glance accidentally fell on a young Spanish sailor, a coil of rope in his hand, just stepped from the deck to the first round of the mizzen-rigging. Perhaps the man would not have been particularly noticed, were it not that, during his ascent to one of the yards, he, with a sort of covert intentness, kept his eye fixed on Captain Delano, from whom, presently, it passed, as if by
40 a natural sequence, to the two whisperers.

His own attention thus redirected to that quarter, Captain Delano gave a slight start. From something in Don Benito's manner just then, it seemed as if the visitor had, at least partly, been the subject of the withdrawn consultation going on—a conjecture as little agreeable to the guest as it was little flattering
45 to the host.

27. **his guest**—"Captain Delano" (P).

The singular alternations of courtesy and ill-breeding in the Spanish captain were unaccountable, except on one of two suppositions—innocent lunacy, or wicked imposture.

But the first idea, though it might naturally have occurred to an indifferent observer, and, in some respects, had not hitherto been wholly a stranger to Captain Delano's mind, yet, now that, in an incipient way, he began to regard the stranger's conduct something in the light of an intentional affront, of course the idea of lunacy was virtually vacated. But if not a lunatic, what then? Under the circumstances, would a gentleman, nay, any honest boor, act the part now acted by his host? The man was an impostor. Some low-born adventurer, masquerading as an oceanic grandee; yet so ignorant of the first requisites of mere gentlemanhood as to be betrayed into the present remarkable indecorum. That strange ceremoniousness, too, at other times evinced, seemed not uncharacteristic of one playing a part above his real level. Benito Cereno— Don Benito Cereno—a sounding name. One, too, at that period, not unknown, in the surname, to supercargoes and sea captains trading along the Spanish Main, as belonging to one of the most enterprising and extensive mercantile families in all those provinces; several members of it having titles; a sort of Castilian Rothschild, with a noble brother, or cousin, in every great trading town of South America. The alleged Don Benito was in early manhood, about twenty-nine or thirty. To assume a sort of roving cadetship in the maritime affairs of such a house, what more likely scheme for a young knave of talent and spirit? But the Spaniard was a pale invalid. Never mind. For even to the degree of simulating mortal disease, the craft of some tricksters had been known to attain. To think that, under the aspect of infantile weakness, the most savage energies might be couched—those velvets of the Spaniard but the velvet paw to his fangs.

From no train of thought did these fancies come; not from within, but from without; suddenly, too, and in one throng, like hoar frost; yet as soon to vanish as the mild sun of Captain Delano's good-nature regained its meridian.

Glancing over once again towards his host—whose side-face, revealed above the skylight, was now turned toward him—he was struck by the profile, whose clearness of cut was refined by the thinness incident to ill-health, as well as ennobled about the chin by the beard. Away with suspicion. He was a true off-shoot of a true hidalgo Cereno.

Relieved by these and other better thoughts, the visitor, lightly humming a tune, now began indifferently pacing the poop, so as not to betray to Don Benito that he had at all mistrusted incivility, much less duplicity; for such mistrust would yet be proved illusory, and by the event; though, for the present, the circumstance which had provoked that distrust remained unexplained. But when that little mystery should have been cleared up, Captain Delano thought he might extremely regret it, did he allow Don Benito to become aware that he

16. **supercargoes**—A supercargo is the officer in charge of the commercial concerns of a voyage. 16-17. **Spanish Main**—See note 39, p. 605. 19. **Rothschild**—the Rothschild family, famous in the banking annals of England, but with branches in other European countries. 21. **cadetship**—Cadet refers here to a young brother or son of a particular family, earning his spurs, in this case in business. 31. **his host**—"Don Benito" (P). 32. **he**—"Captain Delano" (P). 35. **hidalgo**—here about equivalent to blue-blood.

had indulged in ungenerous surmises. In short, to the Spaniard's black-letter text, it was best, for a while, to leave open margin.

Presently, his pale face twitching and overcast, the Spaniard, still supported by his attendant, moved over towards his guest, when, with even more than his
5 usual embarrassment, and a strange sort of intriguing intonation in his husky whisper, the following conversation began:—

"Señor, may I ask how long you have lain at this isle?"

"Oh, but a day or two, Don Benito."

"And from what port are you last?"
10 "Canton."

"And there, Señor, you exchanged your seal-skins for teas and silks, I think you said?"

"Yes. Silks, mostly."

"And the balance you took in specie, perhaps?"
15 Captain Delano, fidgeting a little, answered—

"Yes; some silver; not a very great deal, though."

"Ah—well. May I ask how many men have you, Señor?"

Captain Delano slightly started, but answered—

"About five-and-twenty, all told."
20 "And at present, Señor, all on board, I suppose?"

"All on board, Don Benito," replied the Captain, now with satisfaction.

"And will be to-night, Señor?"

At this last question, following so many pertinacious ones, for the soul of him Captain Delano could not but look very earnestly at the questioner, who, in-
25 stead of meeting the glance, with every token of craven discomposure dropped his eyes to the deck; presenting an unworthy contrast to his servant, who, just then, was kneeling at his feet, adjusting a loose shoe-buckle; his disengaged face meantime, with humble curiosity, turned openly up into his master's downcast one.
30 The Spaniard, still with a guilty shuffle, repeated his question:

"And—and will be to-night, Señor?"

"Yes, for aught I know," returned Captain Delano—"but nay," rallying himself into fearless truth, "some of them talked of going off on another fishing party about midnight."
35 "Your ships generally go—go more or less armed, I believe, Señor?"

"Oh, a six-pounder or two, in case of emergency," was the intrepidly indifferent reply, "with a small stock of muskets, sealing-spears, and cutlasses, you know."

As he thus responded, Captain Delano again glanced at Don Benito, but the
40 latter's eyes were averted; while abruptly and awkwardly shifting the subject, he made some peevish allusion to the calm, and then, without apology, once more, with his attendant, withdrew to the opposite bulwarks, where the whispering was resumed.

At this moment, and ere Captain Delano could cast a cool thought upon

1-2. black-letter text—Early printed books were in black letter, imitative of manuscript letters, and, to modern eyes, difficult to read.

what had just passed, the young Spanish sailor, before mentioned, was seen
descending from the rigging. In act of stooping over to spring inboard to the
deck, his voluminous, unconfined frock, or shirt, of coarse woolen, much spotted
with tar, opened out far down the chest, revealing a soiled under garment of
what seemed the finest linen, edged, about the neck, with a narrow blue ribbon, 5
sadly faded and worn. At this moment the young sailor's eye was again fixed
on the whisperers, and Captain Delano thought he observed a lurking significance in it, as if silent signs, of some Freemason sort, had that instant been
interchanged.

This once more impelled his own glance in the direction of Don Benito, and, 10
as before, he could not but infer that himself formed the subject of the conference. He paused. The sound of the hatchet-polishing fell on his ears. He
cast another swift side-look at the two. They had the air of conspirators. In
connection with the late questionings, and the incident of the young sailor,
these things now begat such return of involuntary suspicion, that the singular 15
guilelessness of the American could not endure it. Plucking up a gay and
humorous expression, he crossed over to the two rapidly, saying:—"Ha, Don
Benito, your black here seems high in your trust; a sort of privy-counsellor, in
fact."

Upon this, the servant looked up with a good-natured grin, but the master 20
started as from a venomous bite. It was a moment or two before the Spaniard
sufficiently recovered himself to reply; which he did, at last, with cold constraint:—"Yes, Señor, I have trust in Babo."

Here Babo, changing his previous grin of mere animal humor into an intelligent smile, not ungratefully eyed his master.   25

Finding that the Spaniard now stood silent and reserved, as if involuntarily,
or purposely giving hint that his guest's proximity was inconvenient just then,
Captain Delano, unwilling to appear uncivil even to incivility itself, made some
trivial remark and moved off; again and again turning over in his mind the
mysterious demeanor of Don Benito Cereno.   30

He had descended from the poop, and, wrapped in thought, was passing near
a dark hatchway, leading down into the steerage, when, perceiving motion
there, he looked to see what moved. The same instant there was a sparkle in the
shadowy hatchway, and he saw one of the Spanish sailors, prowling there, hurriedly placing his hand in the bosom of his frock, as if hiding something. Before 35
the man could have been certain who it was that was passing, he slunk below
out of sight. But enough was seen of him to make it sure that he was the
same young sailor before noticed in the rigging.

What was that which so sparkled? thought Captain Delano. It was no lamp
—no match—no live coal. Could it have been a jewel? But how come sailors 40
with jewels?—or with silk-trimmed under-shirts either? Has he been robbing
the trunks of the dead cabin-passengers? But if so, he would hardly wear one
of the stolen articles on board ship here. Ah, ah—if, now, that was, indeed, a
secret sign I saw passing between this suspicious fellow and his captain awhile
since; if I could only be certain that, in my uneasiness, my senses did not de- 45
ceive me, then——

Here, passing from one suspicious thing to another, his mind revolved the strange questions put to him concerning his ship.

By a curious coincidence, as each point was recalled, the black wizards of Ashantee would strike up with their hatchets, as in ominous comment on the
5 white stranger's thoughts. Pressed by such enigmas and portents, it would have been almost against nature, had not, even into the least distrustful heart, some ugly misgivings obtruded.

Observing the ship now helplessly fallen into a current, with enchanted sails, drifting with increased rapidity seaward; and noting that, from a lately
10 intercepted projection of the land, the sealer was hidden, the stout mariner began to quake at thoughts which he barely durst confess to himself. Above all, he began to feel a ghostly dread of Don Benito. And yet when he roused himself, dilated his chest, felt himself strong on his legs, and coolly considered it—what did all these phantoms amount to?

15 Had the Spaniard any sinister scheme, it must have reference not so much to him (Captain Delano) as to his ship (the Bachelor's Delight). Hence the present drifting away of the one ship from the other, instead of favoring any such possible scheme, was, for the time at least, opposed to it. Clearly any suspicion, combining such contradictions, must need be delusive. Beside, was it not
20 absurd to think of a vessel in distress—a vessel by sickness almost dismanned of her crew—a vessel whose inmates were parched for water—was it not a thousand times absurd that such a craft should, at present, be of a piratical character; or her commander, either for himself or those under him, cherish any desire but for speedy relief and refreshment? But then, might not general distress,
25 and thirst in particular, be affected? And might not that same undiminished Spanish crew, alleged to have perished off to a remnant, be at that very moment lurking in the hold? On heart-broken pretence of entreating a cup of cold water, fiends in human form had got into lonely dwellings, nor retired until a dark deed had been done. And among the Malay pirates, it was no unusual
30 thing to lure ships after them into their treacherous harbors, or entice boarders from a declared enemy at sea, by the spectacle of thinly manned or vacant decks, beneath which prowled a hundred spears with yellow arms ready to upthrust them through the mats. Not that Captain Delano had entirely credited such things. He had heard of them—and now, as stories, they recurred.
35 The present destination of the ship was the anchorage. There she would be near his own vessel. Upon gaining that vicinity, might not the San Dominick, like a slumbering volcano, suddenly let loose energies now hid?

He recalled the Spaniard's manner while telling his story. There was a gloomy hesitancy and subterfuge about it. It was just the manner of one mak-
40 ing up his tale for evil purposes, as he goes. But if that story was not true, what was the truth? That the ship had unlawfully come into the Spaniard's possession? But in many of its details, especially in reference to the more calamitous parts, such as the fatalities among the seamen, the consequent prolonged beating about, the past sufferings from obstinate calms, and still con-
45 tinued suffering from thirst; in all these points, as well as others, Don Benito's

---

1-2. revolved the strange questions—"revolved the point of the strange questions" (P).

story had corroborated not only the wailing ejaculations of the indiscriminate multitude, white and black, but likewise—what seemed impossible to counterfeit—by the very expression and play of every human feature, which Captain Delano saw. If Don Benito's story was, throughout, an invention, then every soul on board, down to the youngest negress, was his carefully drilled recruit 5 in the plot: an incredible inference. And yet, if there was ground for mistrusting his veracity, that inference was a legitimate one.

But those questions of the Spaniard. There, indeed, one might pause. Did they not seem put with much the same object with which the burglar or assassin, by day-time, reconnoitres the walls of a house? But, with ill purposes, to 10 solicit such information openly of the chief person endangered, and so, in effect, setting him on his guard; how unlikely a procedure was that? Absurd, then, to suppose that those questions had been prompted by evil designs. Thus, the same conduct, which, in this instance, had raised the alarm, served to dispel it. In short, scarce any suspicion or uneasiness, however apparently rea- 15 sonable at the time, which was not now, with equal apparent reason, dismissed.

At last, he began to laugh at his former forebodings; and laugh at the strange ship for, in its aspect someway siding with them, as it were; and laugh, too, at the odd-looking blacks, particularly those old scissors-grinders, the Ashantees; and those bed-ridden old knitting women, the oakum-pickers; and almost at 20 the dark Spaniard himself, the central hobgoblin of all.

For the rest, whatever in a serious way seemed enigmatical, was now good-naturedly explained away by the thought that, for the most part the poor invalid scarcely knew what he was about; either sulking in black vapors, or putting idle questions without sense or object. Evidently, for the present, the 25 man was not fit to be intrusted with the ship. On some benevolent plea withdrawing the command from him, Captain Delano would yet have to send her to Conception in charge of his second mate, a worthy person and good navigator—a plan not more convenient for the San Dominick than for Don Benito; for, relieved from all anxiety, keeping wholly to his cabin, the sick man, under 30 the good nursing of his servant, would probably, by the end of the passage, be in a measure restored to health, and with that he should also be restored to authority.

Such were the American's thoughts. They were tranquilizing. There was a difference between the idea of Don Benito's darkly pre-ordaining Captain 35 Delano's fate, and Captain Delano's lightly arranging Don Benito's. Nevertheless, it was not without something of relief that the good seaman presently perceived his whale-boat in the distance. Its absence had been prolonged by unexpected detention at the sealer's side, as well as its returning trip lengthened by the continual recession of the goal. 40

The advancing speck was observed by the blacks. Their shouts attracted the

---

7. his—"the Spanish captain's" (P). 8-15. But those . . . dispel it—Omitted in (P). 15. In short—(P) here begins a new paragraph, which continues to line 21, the first sentence of which reads "In short, scarce an uneasiness entered the honest sailor's mind but, by a subsequent spontaneous act of good sense, it was ejected." 17. his former—"these" (P). 20-21. and almost at the dark Spaniard—"and, in a human way, he almost began to laugh at the dark Spaniard" (P). 25. idle—"random" (P). 29. a plan not more convenient—"a plan which would prove no wiser" (P).

attention of Don Benito, who, with a return of courtesy, approaching Captain Delano, expressed satisfaction at the coming of some supplies, slight and temporary as they must necessarily prove.

Captain Delano responded; but while doing so, his attention was drawn to
5 something passing on the deck below: among the crowd climbing the landward bulwarks, anxiously watching the coming boat, two blacks, to all appearances accidentally incommoded by one of the sailors, violently pushed him aside, which the sailor someway resenting, they dashed him to the deck, despite the earnest cries of the oakum-pickers.

10 "Don Benito," said Captain Delano quickly, "do you see what is going on there? Look!"

But, seized by his cough, the Spaniard staggered, with both hands to his face, on the point of falling. Captain Delano would have supported him, but the servant was more alert, who, with one hand sustaining his master, with
15 the other applied the cordial. Don Benito restored, the black withdrew his support, slipping aside a little, but dutifully remaining within call of a whisper. Such discretion was here evinced as quite wiped away, in the visitor's eyes, any blemish of impropriety which might have attached to the attendant, from the indecorous conferences before mentioned; showing, too, that if the servant
20 were to blame, it might be more the master's fault than his own, since, when left to himself, he could conduct thus well.

His glance called away from the spectacle of disorder to the more pleasing one before him, Captain Delano could not avoid again congratulating his host upon possessing such a servant, who, though perhaps a little too forward now
25 and then, must upon the whole be invaluable to one in the invalid's situation.

"Tell me, Don Benito," he added, with a smile—"I should like to have your man here, myself—what will you take for him? Would fifty doubloons be any object?"

"Master wouldn't part with Babo for a thousand doubloons," murmured the
30 black, overhearing the offer, and taking it in earnest, and, with the strange vanity of a faithful slave, appreciated by his master, scorning to hear so paltry a valuation put upon him by a stranger. But Don Benito, apparently hardly yet completely restored, and again interrupted by his cough, made but some broken reply.

35 Soon his physical distress became so great, affecting his mind, too, apparently, that, as if to screen the sad spectacle, the servant gently conducted his master below.

Left to himself, the American, to while away the time till his boat should arrive, would have pleasantly accosted some one of the few Spanish seamen
40 he saw; but recalling something that Don Benito had said touching their ill conduct, he refrained; as a ship-master indisposed to countenance cowardice or unfaithfulness in seamen.

While, with these thoughts, standing with eye directed forward towards

7-8. one of the sailors, . . . which—"one of the sailors, flew out against him with horrible curses, which" (P). 8. they—"the two blacks" (P). 8. deck, despite—"deck, and jumped upon him, despite" (P). 22. glance called—"glance thus called" (P). 23. his host—"Don Benito" (P).

that handful of sailors, suddenly he thought that one or two of them returned the glance and with a sort of meaning. He rubbed his eyes, and looked again; but again seemed to see the same thing. Under a new form, but more obscure than any previous one, the old suspicions recurred, but, in the absence of Don Benito, with less of panic than before. Despite the bad account given of the sailors, Captain Delano resolved forthwith to accost one of them. Descending the poop, he made his way through the blacks, his movement drawing a queer cry from the oakum-pickers, prompted by whom, the negroes, twitching each other aside, divided before him; but, as if curious to see what was the object of this deliberate visit to their Ghetto, closing in behind, in tolerable order, followed the white stranger up. His progress thus proclaimed as by mounted kings-at-arms, and escorted as by a Caffre guard of honor, Captain Delano, assuming a good-humored, off-hand air, continued to advance; now and then saying a blithe word to the negroes, and his eye curiously surveying the white faces, here and there sparsely mixed in with the blacks, like stray white pawns venturously involved in the ranks of the chess-men opposed.

While thinking which of them to select for his purpose, he chanced to observe a sailor seated on the deck engaged in tarring the strap of a large block, a circle of blacks squatted round him inquisitively eyeing the process.

The mean employment of the man was in contrast with something superior in his figure. His hand, black with continually thrusting it into the tar-pot held for him by a negro, seemed not naturally allied to his face, a face which would have been a very fine one but for its haggardness. Whether this haggardness had aught to do with criminality, could not be determined; since, as intense heat and cold, though unlike, produce like sensations, so innocence and guilt, when, through casual association with mental pain, stamping any visible impress, use one seal—a hacked one.

Not again that this reflection occurred to Captain Delano at the time, charitable man as he was. Rather another idea. Because observing so singular a haggardness to be combined with a dark eye, averted as in trouble and shame, and then, again recalling Don Benito's confessed ill opinion of his crew, insensibly he was operated upon by certain general notions which, while disconnecting pain and abashment from virtue, as invariably link them with vice.

If, indeed, there be any wickedness on board this ship, thought Captain Delano, be sure that man there has fouled his hand in it, even as now he fouls it in the pitch. I don't like to accost him. I will speak to this other, this old Jack here on the windlass.

He advanced to an old Barcelona tar, in ragged red breeches and dirty nightcap, cheeks trenched and bronzed, whiskers dense as thorn hedges. Seated between two sleepy-looking Africans, this mariner, like his younger shipmate, was employed upon some rigging—splicing a cable—the sleepy-looking blacks

1. one or two of them—"some of them" (P). 12. kings-at-arms—literally, chief heraldic officers. 12. Caffre—the Caffre or Kafir tribe of Negroes in South Africa. 18-19. block, a circle —"block, with a circle" (P). 31-32. and then . . . operated upon—"and then, however illogically, uniting in his mind his own private suspicions of the crew with the confessed ill-opinion on the part of their captain, he was insensibly operated upon" (P). 39. Barcelona tar—Barcelona, a seaport in northeastern Spain, was notable for its sailors.

performing the inferior function of holding the outer parts of the ropes for
him.

Upon Captain Delano's approach, the man at once hung his head below its
previous level; the one necessary for business. It appeared as if he desired to
be thought absorbed, with more than common fidelity, in his task. Being addressed, he glanced up, but with what seemed a furtive, diffident air, which
sat strangely enough on his weather-beaten visage, much as if a grizzly bear,
instead of growling and biting, should simper and cast sheep's eyes. He was
asked several questions concerning the voyage—questions purposely referring
to several particulars in Don Benito's narrative, not previously corroborated
by those impulsive cries greeting the visitor on first coming on board. The
questions were briefly answered, confirming all that remained to be confirmed
of the story. The negroes about the windlass joined in with the old sailor;
but, as they became talkative, he by degrees became mute, and at length quite
glum, seemed morosely unwilling to answer more questions, and yet, all the
while, this ursine air was somehow mixed with his sheepish one.

Despairing of getting into unembarrassed talk with such a centaur, Captain
Delano, after glancing round for more promising countenance, but seeing none,
spoke pleasantly to the blacks to make way for him; and so, amid various
grins and grimaces, returned to the poop, feeling a little strange at first, he
could hardly tell why, but upon the whole with regained confidence in Benito
Cereno.

How plainly, thought he, did that old whiskerando yonder betray a consciousness of ill desert. No doubt, when he saw me coming, he dreaded lest I,
apprised by his Captain of the crew's general misbehavior, came with sharp
words for him, and so down with his head. And yet—and yet, now that I think
of it, that very old fellow, if I err not, was one of those who seemed so earnestly
eying me here awhile since. Ah, these currents spin one's head round almost
as much as they do the ship. Ha, there now's a pleasant sort of sunny sight;
quite sociable, too.

His attention had been drawn to a slumbering negress, partly disclosed
through the lace-work of some rigging, lying, with youthful limbs carelessly
disposed, under the lee of the bulwarks, like a doe in the shade of a woodland
rock. Sprawling at her lapped breasts, was her wide-awake fawn, stark naked,
its black little body half lifted from the deck, crosswise with its dam's; its
hands, like two paws, clambering upon her; its mouth and nose ineffectually
rooting to get at the mark; and meantime giving a vexatious half-grunt, blending with the composed snore of the negress.

The uncommon vigor of the child at length roused the mother. She started
up, at a distance facing Captain Delano. But as if not at all concerned at the
attitude in which she had been caught, delightedly she caught the child up,
with maternal transports, covering it with kisses.

There's naked nature, now; pure tenderness and love, thought Captain
Delano, well pleased.

This incident prompted him to remark the other negresses more particularly than before. He was gratified with their manners; like most uncivilized
women, they seemed at once tender of heart and tough of constitution; equally

ready to die for their infants or fight for them. Unsophisticated as leopardesses; loving as doves. Ah! thought Captain Delano, these, perhaps, are some of the very women whom Ledyard saw in Africa, and gave such a noble account of.

These natural sights somehow insensibly deepened his confidence and ease. At last he looked to see how his boat was getting on; but it was still pretty 5 remote. He turned to see if Don Benito had returned; but he had not.

To change the scene, as well as to please himself with a leisurely observation of the coming boat, stepping over into the mizzen-chains, he clambered his way into the starboard quarter-gallery—one of those abandoned Venetian-looking water-balconies previously mentioned—retreats cut off from the deck. 10 As his foot pressed the half-damp, half-dry sea-mosses matting the place, and a chance phantom cats-paw—an islet of breeze, unheralded, unfollowed—as this ghostly cats-paw came fanning his cheek; as his glance fell upon the row of small, round dead-lights—all closed like coppered eyes of the coffined—and the state-cabin door, once connecting with the gallery, even as the dead-lights 15 had once looked out upon it, but now calked fast like a sarcophagus lid; and to a purple-black, tarred-over panel, threshold, and post; and he bethought him of the time, when that state-cabin and this state-balcony had heard the voices of the Spanish king's officers, and the forms of the Lima viceroy's daughters had perhaps leaned where he stood—as these and other images flitted 20 through his mind, as the cats-paw through the calm, gradually he felt rising a dreamy inquietude, like that of one who alone on the prairie feels unrest from the repose of the noon.

He leaned against the carved balustrade, again looking off toward his boat; but found his eye falling upon the ribbon grass, trailing along the ship's water- 25 line, straight as a border of green box; and parterres of sea-weed, broad ovals and crescents, floating nigh and far, with what seemed long formal alleys between, crossing the terraces of swells, and sweeping round as if leading to the grottoes below. And overhanging all was the balustrade by his arm, which, partly stained with pitch and partly embossed with moss, seemed the charred 30 ruin of some summer-house in a grand garden long running to waste.

Trying to break one charm, he was but becharmed anew. Though upon the wide sea, he seemed in some far inland country; prisoner in some deserted chateau, left to stare at empty grounds, and peer out at vague roads, where never wagon or wayfarer passed. 35

But these enchantments were a little disenchanted as his eye fall on the corroded main-chains. Of an ancient style, massy and rusty in link, shackle and bolt, they seemed even more fit for the ship's present business than the one for which she had been built.

Presently he thought something moved nigh the chains. He rubbed his eyes, 40

3. **Ledyard**—"Mungo Park" (P). Why Melville changed the name of the traveler is not evident. John Ledyard (1751-1788) published his *Life and Travels* in 1828, but seems not to have been especially interested in Africa. Mungo Park (1771-1805) is remembered especially for his *Travels in the Internal Districts of Africa* (1799). 8. **mizzen-chains**—chains having to do with the mizzenmast. 19. **Lima viceroy's**—Lima was formerly the seat of the Spanish viceroy, the nominal ruler of the Spanish possessions in South America. 26. **parterres**—A parterre is strictly an ornamental arrangement of flower plots or grass plots. 39. **which she had been**—"which probably she had been" (P).

and looked hard. Groves of rigging were about the chains; and there, peering from behind a great stay, like an Indian from behind a hemlock, a Spanish sailor, a marlingspike in his hand, was seen, who made what seemed an imperfect gesture towards the balcony, but immediately, as if alarmed by some
5 advancing step along the deck within, vanished into the recesses of the hempen forest, like a poacher.

What meant this? Something the man had sought to communicate, unbeknown to any one, even to his captain. Did the secret involve aught unfavourable to his captain? Were those previous misgivings of Captain Delano's about
10 to be verified? Or, in his haunted mood at the moment, had some random, unintentional motion of the man, while busy with the stay, as if repairing it, been mistaken for a significant beckoning?

Not unbewildered, again he gazed off for his boat. But it was temporarily hidden by a rocky spur of the isle. As with some eagerness he bent forward,
15 watching for the first shooting view of its beak, the balustrade gave way before him like charcoal. Had he not clutched an outreaching rope he would have fallen into the sea. The crash, though feeble, and the fall, though hollow, of the rotten fragments, must have been overheard. He glanced up. With sober curiosity peering down upon him was one of the old oakum-pickers,
20 slipped from his perch to an outside boom; while below the old negro, and, invisible to him, reconnoitering from a port-hole like a fox from the mouth of its den, crouched the Spanish sailor again. From something suddenly suggested by the man's air, the mad idea now darted into Captain Delano's mind, that Don Benito's plea of indisposition, in withdrawing below, was but a pre-
25 tense: that he was engaged there maturing some plot, of which the sailor, by some means gaining an inkling, had a mind to warn the stranger against; incited, it may be, by gratitude for a kind word on first boarding the ship. Was it from foreseeing some possible interference like this, that Don Benito had, beforehand, given such a bad character of his sailors, while praising the
30 negroes; though, indeed, the former seemed as docile as the latter the contrary? The whites, too, by nature, were the shrewder race. A man with some evil design, would he not be likely to speak well of that stupidity which was blind to his depravity, and malign that intelligence from which it might not be hidden? Not unlikely, perhaps. But if the whites had dark secrets con-
35 cerning Don Benito, could then Don Benito be any way in complicity with the blacks? But they were too stupid. Besides, who ever heard of a white so far a renegade as to apostatize from his very species almost, by leaguing in against it with negroes? These difficulties recalled former ones. Lost in their mazes, Captain Delano, who had now regained the deck, was uneasily advancing
40 along it, when he observed a new face; an aged sailor seated cross-legged near the main hatchway. His skin was shrunk up with wrinkles like a pelican's empty pouch; his hair frosted; his countenance grave and composed. His hands were full of ropes, which he was working into a large knot. Some blacks were about him obligingly dipping the strands for him, here and there, as the
45 exigencies of the operation demanded.

3. marlingspike—a pointed tool used by sailors in splicing rope; usually, marlinspike.

Captain Delano crossed over to him, and stood in silence surveying the knot;
his mind, by a not uncongenial transition, passing from its own entanglements
to those of the hemp. For intricacy such a knot he had never seen in an American ship, or indeed any other. The old man looked like an Egyptian priest,
making Gordian knots for the temple of Ammon. The knot seemed a com-   5
bination of double-bowline-knot, treble-crown-knot, back-handed-well-knot,
knot-in-and-out-knot, and jamming-knot.

At last, puzzled to comprehend the meaning of such a knot, Captain Delano addressed the knotter:—

"What are you knotting there, my man?"   10
"The knot," was the brief reply, without looking up.
"So it seems; but what is it for?"
"For some one else to undo," muttered back the old man, plying his fingers
harder than ever, the knot being now nearly completed.

While Captain Delano stood watching him, suddenly the old man threw   15
the knot towards him, saying in broken English,—the first heard in the ship,—
something to this effect: "Undo it, cut it, quick." It was said lowly, but with
such condensation of rapidity, that the long, slow words in Spanish, which
had preceded and followed, almost operated as covers to the brief English
between.   20

For a moment, knot in hand, and knot in head, Captain Delano stood mute;
while, without further heeding him, the old man was now intent upon other
ropes. Presently there was a slight stir behind Captain Delano. Turning, he
saw the chained negro, Atufal, standing quietly there. The next moment the
old sailor rose, muttering, and, followed by his subordinate negroes, removed   25
to the forward part of the ship, where in the crowd he disappeared.

An elderly negro, in a clout like an infant's, and with a pepper and salt
head, and a kind of attorney air, now approached Captain Delano. In tolerable Spanish, and with a good-natured, knowing wink, he informed him that
the old knotter was simple-witted, but harmless; often playing his old tricks.   30
The negro concluded by begging the knot, for of course the stranger would
not care to be troubled with it. Unconsciously, it was handed to him. With a
sort of congé, the negro received it, and, turning his back, ferreted into it like
a detective custom-house officer after smuggled laces. Soon, with some African
word, equivalent to pshaw, he tossed the knot overboard.   35

All this is very queer now, thought Captain Delano, with a qualmish sort
of emotion; but, as one feeling incipient sea-sickness, he strove, by ignoring the
symptoms, to get rid of the malady. Once more he looked off for his boat. To
his delight, it was now again in view, leaving the rocky spur astern.

The sensation here experienced, after at first relieving his uneasiness, with   40
unforeseen efficacy soon began to remove it. The less distant sight of that well-
known boat—showing it, not as before, half blended with the haze, but with
outline defined, so that its individuality, like a man's, was manifest; that boat,
Rover by name, which, though now in strange seas, had often pressed the
beach of Captain Delano's home, and, brought to its threshold for repairs,   45

5. **Gordian . . . Ammon**—See note 14, p. 999. 16. **saying**—"and said" (P). 33. **congé**—
farewell. 41. **efficacy**—"efficiency" (P).

had familiarly lain there, as a Newfoundland dog; the sight of that household
boat evoked a thousand trustful associations, which, contrasted with previous
suspicions, filled him not only with lightsome confidence, but somehow with
half humorous self-reproaches at his former lack of it.

5   "What, I, Amasa Delano—Jack of the Beach, as they called me when a lad—
I, Amasa; the same that, duck-satchel in hand, used to paddle along the water-
side to the school-house made from the old hulk—I, little Jack of the Beach,
that used to go berrying with cousin Nat and the rest; I to be murdered here
at the ends of the earth, on board a haunted pirate-ship by a horrible Spaniard?
10 Too nonsensical to think of! Who would murder Amasa Delano? His conscience is clean. There is some one above. Fie, fie, Jack of the Beach! you are
a child indeed; a child of the second childhood, old boy; you are beginning to
dote and drule, I'm afraid."

    Light of heart and foot, he stepped aft, and there was met by Don Benito's
15 servant, who, with a pleasing expression, responsive to his own present feelings, informed him that his master had recovered from the effects of his
coughing fit, and had just ordered him to go present his compliments to his
good guest, Don Amasa, and say that he (Don Benito) would soon have the
happiness to rejoin him.

20   There now, do you mark that? again thought Captain Delano, walking the
poop. What a donkey I was. This kind gentleman who here sends me his
kind compliments, he, but ten minutes ago, dark-lantern in hand, was dodging
round some old grind-stone in the hold, sharpening a hatchet for me, I thought.
Well, well; these long calms have a morbid effect on the mind, I've often
25 heard, though I never believed it before. Ha! glancing towards the boat;
there's Rover; good dog; a white bone in her mouth. A pretty big bone
though, seems to me.—What? Yes, she has fallen afoul of the bubbling tide-
rip there. It sets her the other way, too, for the time. Patience.

    It was now about noon, though, from the grayness of everything, it seemed
30 to be getting towards dusk.

    The calm was confirmed. In the far distance, away from the influence of
land, the leaden ocean seemed laid out and leaded up, its course finished, soul
gone, defunct. But the current from landward, where the ship was, increased;
silently sweeping her further and further towards the tranced waters beyond.

35   Still, from his knowledge of those latitudes, cherishing hopes of a breeze,
and a fair and fresh one, at any moment, Captain Delano, despite present
prospects, buoyantly counted upon bringing the San Dominick safely to anchor
ere night. The distance swept over was nothing; since, with a good wind,
ten minutes' sailing would retrace more than sixty minutes', drifting. Mean-
40 time, one moment turning to mark "Rover" fighting the tide-rip, and the next
to see Don Benito approaching, he continued walking the poop.

    Gradually he felt a vexation arising from the delay of his boat; this soon
merged into uneasiness; and at last—his eye falling continually, as from a
stage-box into the pit, upon the strange crowd before and below him, and,
45 by-and-by, recognizing there the face—now composed to indifference—of the

6. **duck-satchel**—satchel made of duck or cotton.

Spanish sailor who had seemed to beckon from the main-chains—something of his old trepidations returned.

Ah, thought he—gravely enough—this is like the ague: because it went off, it follows not that it won't come back.

Though ashamed of the relapse, he could not altogether subdue it; and so, 5 exerting his good-nature to the utmost, insensibly he came to a compromise.

Yes, this is a strange craft; a strange history, too, and strange folks on board. But—nothing more.

By way of keeping his mind out of mischief till the boat should arrive, he tried to occupy it with turning over and over, in a purely speculative sort of 10 way, some lesser peculiarities of the captain and crew. Among others, four curious points recurred:

First, the affair of the Spanish lad assailed with a knife by the slave boy; an act winked at by Don Benito. Second, the tyranny in Don Benito's treatment of Atufal, the black; as if a child should lead a bull of the Nile by the 15 ring in his nose. Third, the trampling of the sailor by the two negroes; a piece of insolence passed over without so much as a reprimand. Fourth, the cringing submission to their master of all the ships' underlings, mostly blacks; as if by the least inadvertence they feared to draw down his despotic displeasure.

Coupling these points, they seemed somewhat contradictory. But what then, 20 thought Captain Delano, glancing towards his now nearing boat—what then? Why, Don Benito is a very capricious commander. But he is not the first of the sort I have seen; though it's true he rather exceeds any other. But as a nation—continued he in his reveries—these Spaniards are all an odd set; the very word Spaniard has a curious, conspirator, Guy-Fawkish twang to it. And 25 yet, I dare say, Spaniards in the main are as good folks as any in Duxbury, Massachusetts. Ah, good! At last "Rover" has come.

As, with its welcome freight, the boat touched the side, the oakum-pickers, with venerable gestures, sought to restrain the blacks, who, at the sight of three gurried water-casks in its bottom, and a pile of wilted pumpkins in its 30 bow, hung over the bulwarks in disorderly raptures.

Don Benito, with his servant, now appeared; his coming, perhaps, hastened by hearing the noise. Of him Captain Delano sought permission to serve out the water, so that all might share alike, and none injure themselves by unfair excess. But sensible, and, on Don Benito's account, kind as this offer was, it 35 was received with what seemed impatience; as if aware that he lacked energy as a commander, Don Benito, with the true jealousy of weakness, resented as an affront any interference. So, at least, Captain Delano inferred.

In another moment the casks were being hoisted in, when some of the eager negroes accidentally jostled Captain Delano, where he stood by the gangway; 40 so that, unmindful of Don Benito, yielding to the impulse of the moment, with good-natured authority he bade the blacks stand back; to enforce his words making use of a half-mirthful, half-menacing gesture. Instantly the blacks paused, just where they were, each negro and negress suspended in his

or her posture, exactly as the word had found them—for a few seconds continuing so—while, as between the responsive posts of a telegraph, an unknown syllable ran from man to man among the perched oakum-pickers. While the visitor's attention was fixed by this scene, suddenly the hatchet-polishers half
5 rose, and a rapid cry came from Don Benito.

Thinking that at the signal of the Spaniard he was about to be massacred, Captain Delano would have sprung for his boat, but paused, as the oakum-pickers, dropping down into the crowd with earnest exclamations, forced every white and every negro back, at the same moment, with gestures friendly and
10 familiar, almost jocose, bidding him, in substance, not be a fool. Simultaneously the hatchet-polishers resumed their seats, quietly as so many tailors, and at once, as if nothing had happened, the work of hoisting in the casks was resumed, whites and blacks singing at the tackle.

Captain Delano glanced toward Don Benito. As he saw his meagre form
15 in the act of recovering itself from reclining in the servant's arms, into which the agitated invalid had fallen, he could not but marvel at the panic by which himself had been surprised on the darting supposition that such a commander, who, upon a legitimate occasion, so trivial, too, as it now appeared, could lose all self-command, was, with energetic iniquity, going to bring about his
20 murder.

The casks being on deck, Captain Delano was handed a number of jars and cups by one of the steward's aids, who, in the name of his captain, entreated him to do as he had proposed—dole out the water. He complied, with republican impartiality as to this republican element, which always seeks one level,
25 serving the oldest white no better than the youngest black; excepting, indeed, poor Don Benito, whose condition, if not rank, demanded an extra allowance. To him, in the first place, Captain Delano presented a fair pitcher of the fluid; but, thirsting as he was for fresh water, the Spaniard quaffed not a drop until after several grave bows and salutes. A reciprocation of courtesies which the
30 sight-loving Africans hailed with clapping of hands.

Two of the less wilted pumpkins being reserved for the cabin table, the residue were minced up on the spot for the general regalement. But the soft bread, sugar, and bottled cider, Captain Delano would have given the whites alone, and in chief Don Benito; but the latter objected; which disinterestedness
35 not a little pleased the American; and so mouthfuls all around were given alike to whites and blacks; excepting one bottle of cider, which Babo insisted upon setting aside for his master.

Here it may be observed that as, on the first visit of the boat, the American had not permitted his men to board the ship, neither did he now; being un-
40 willing to add to the confusion of the decks.

Not uninfluenced by the peculiar good-humor at present prevailing, and for the time oblivious of any but benevolent thoughts, Captain Delano, who, from recent indications, counted upon a breeze within an hour or two at furthest,

---

3-4. the visitor's—"Captain Delano's" (P). 22. his captain—"Don Benito" (P). 28. the Spaniard—"Don Benito" (P). 29. salutes. A reciprocation—"salutes: a reciprocation" (P). 33. whites—"Spaniards" (P). 34-35. disinterestedness not a little—"disinterestedness, on his part, not a little" (P).

dispatched the boat back to the sealer, with orders for all the hands that could
be spared immediately to set about rafting casks to the watering-place and
filling them. Likewise he bade word be carried to his chief officer, that if,
against present expectation, the ship was not brought to anchor by sunset, he
need be under no concern; for as there was to be a full moon that night, he   5
(Captain Delano) would remain on board ready to play the pilot, come the
wind soon or late.

As the two captains stood together, observing the departing boat—the servant, as it happened, having just spied a spot on his master's velvet sleeve, and
silently engaged rubbing it out—the American expressed his regrets that the   10
San Dominick had no boats; none, at least, but the unseaworthy old hulk of
the long-boat, which, warped as a camel's skeleton in the desert, and almost
as bleached, lay pot-wise inverted amidships, one side a little tipped, furnishing a subterraneous sort of den for family groups of the blacks, mostly women
and small children; who, squatting on old mats below, or perched above in   15
the dark dome, on the elevated seats, were descried, some distance within, like
a social circle of bats, sheltering in some friendly cave; at intervals, ebon flights
of naked boys and girls, three or four years old, darting in and out of the
den's mouth.

"Had you three or four boats now, Don Benito," said Captain Delano, "I   20
think that, by tugging at the oars, your negroes here might help along matters
some. Did you sail from port without boats, Don Benito?"

"They were stove in the gales, Señor."

"That was bad. Many men, too, you lost then. Boats and men. Those must
have been hard gales, Don Benito."   25

"Past all speech," cringed the Spaniard.

"Tell me, Don Benito," continued his companion with increased interest,
"tell me, were these gales immediately off the pitch of Cape Horn?"

"Cape Horn?—who spoke of Cape Horn?"

"Yourself did, when giving me an account of your voyage," answered Cap-   30
tain Delano, with almost equal astonishment at this eating of his own words,
even as he ever seemed eating his own heart, on the part of the Spaniard.
"You yourself, Don Benito, spoke of Cape Horn," he emphatically repeated.

The Spaniard turned, in a sort of stooping posture, pausing an instant, as
one about to make a plunging exchange of elements, as from air to water.   35

At this moment a messenger-boy, a white, hurried by, in the regular performance of his function carrying the last expired half-hour forward to the
forecastle, from the cabin time-piece, to have it struck at the ship's large bell.

"Master," said the servant, discontinuing his work on the coat sleeve, and
addressing the rapt Spaniard with a sort of timid apprehensiveness, as one   40
charged with a duty, the discharge of which, it was foreseen, would prove irksome to the very person who had imposed it, and for whose benefit it was
intended, "master told me never mind where he was, or how engaged, always
to remind him, to a minute, when shaving-time comes. Miguel has gone to
strike the half-hour afternoon. It is *now,* master. Will master go into the   45
cuddy?"

6-7. come the wind—"should the wind come" (P). **46. cuddy**—small cabin.

"Ah—yes," answered the Spaniard, starting, as from dreams into realities; then turning upon Captain Delano, he said that ere long he would resume the conversation.

"Then if master means to talk more to Don Amasa," said the servant, "why
5 not let Don Amasa sit by master in the cuddy, and master can talk, and Don Amasa can listen, while Babo here lathers and strops."

"Yes," said Captain Delano, not unpleased with this sociable plan, "yes, Don Benito, unless you had rather not, I will go with you."

"Be it so, Señor."

10 As the three passed aft, the American could not but think it another strange instance of his host's capriciousness, this being shaved with such uncommon punctuality in the middle of the day. But he deemed it more than likely that the servant's anxious fidelity had something to do with the matter; inasmuch as the timely interruption served to rally his master from the mood which had
15 evidently been coming upon him.

The place called the cuddy was a light deck-cabin formed by the poop, a sort of attic to the large cabin below. Part of it had formerly been the quarters of the officers; but since their death all the partitionings had been thrown down, and the whole interior converted into one spacious and airy marine hall;
20 for absence of fine furniture and picturesque disarray of odd appurtenances, somewhat answering to the wide, cluttered hall of some eccentric bachelor-squire in the country, who hangs his shooting-jacket and tobacco-pouch on deer antlers, and keeps his fishing-rod, tongs, and walking-stick in the same corner.

25 The similitude was heightened, if not originally suggested, by glimpses of the surrounding sea; since, in one aspect, the country and the ocean seem cousins-german.

The floor of the cuddy was matted. Overhead, four or five old muskets were stuck into horizontal holes along the beams. On one side was a claw-footed old
30 table lashed to the deck; a thumbed missal on it, and over it a small, meagre crucifix attached to the bulk-head. Under the table lay a dented cutlass or two, with a hacked harpoon, among some melancholy old rigging, like a heap of poor friars' girdles. There were also two long, sharp-ribbed settees of Malacca cane, black with age, and uncomfortable to look at as inquisitors' racks, with a
35 large, misshapen arm-chair, which, furnished with a rude barber's crotch at the back, working with a screw, seemed some grotesque engine of torment. A flag locker was in one corner, exposing various colored bunting, some rolled up, others half unrolled, still others tumbled. Opposite was a cumbrous wash-stand, of black mahogany, all of one block, with a pedestal, like a font, and
40 over it a railed shelf, containing combs, brushes, and other implements of the toilet. A torn hammock of stained grass swung near; the sheets tossed, and the pillow wrinkled up like a brow, as if whoever slept here slept but illy, with alternate visitations of sad thoughts and bad dreams.

The further extremity of the cuddy, overhanging the ship's stern, was pierced
45 with three openings, windows or port-holes, according as men or cannon might

· **36. grotesque engine**—"grotesque middle age engine" (P).

peer, socially or unsocially, out of them. At present neither men nor cannon were seen, though huge ring-bolts and other rusty iron fixtures of the wood-work hinted of twenty-four-pounders.

Glancing towards the hammock as he entered, Captain Delano said, "You sleep here, Don Benito?"   5

"Yes, Señor, since we got into mild weather."

"This seems a sort of dormitory, sitting-room, sail-loft, chapel, armory, and private closet together, Don Benito," added Captain Delano, looking round.

"Yes, Señor; events have not been favorable to much order in my arrange-ments."   10

Here the servant, napkin on arm, made a motion as if waiting his master's good pleasure. Don Benito signified his readiness, when, seating him in the Malacca arm-chair, and for the guest's convenience drawing opposite one of the settees, the servant commenced operations by throwing back his master's collar and loosening his cravat.   15

There is something in the negro which, in a peculiar way, fits him for avo-cations about one's person. Most negroes are natural valets and hair-dressers; taking to the comb and brush congenially as to the castinets, and flourishing them apparently with almost equal satisfaction. There is, too, a smooth tact about them in this employment, with a marvelous, noiseless, gliding briskness,   20 not ungraceful in its way, singularly pleasing to behold, and still more so to be the manipulated subject of. And above all is the great gift of good-humor. Not the mere grin or laugh is here meant. Those were unsuitable. But a cer-tain easy cheerfulness, harmonious in every glance and gesture; as though God had set the whole negro to some pleasant tune.   25

When to all this is added the docility arising from the unaspiring content-ment of a limited mind, and that susceptibility of blind attachment sometimes inhering in indisputable inferiors, one readily perceives why those hypochon-driacs, Johnson and Byron—it may be something like the hypochondriac, Benito Cereno—took to their hearts, almost to the exclusion of the entire white race,   30 their serving men, the negroes, Barber and Fletcher. But if there be that in the negro which exempts him from the inflicted sourness of the morbid or cyn-ical mind, how, in his most prepossessing aspects, must he appear to a benevo-lent one? When at ease with respect to exterior things, Captain Delano's na-ture was not only benign, but familiarly and humorously so. At home, he had 35 often taken rare satisfaction in sitting in his door, watching some free man of color at his work or play. If on a voyage he chanced to have a black sailor, in-variably he was on chatty, and half-gamesome terms with him. In fact, like most men of a good, blithe heart, Captain Delano took to negroes, not philan-thropically, but genially, just as other men to Newfoundland dogs.   40

Hitherto the circumstances in which he found the San Dominick had re-pressed the tendency. But in the cuddy, relieved from his former uneasiness, and, for various reasons, more sociably inclined than at any previous period of the day, and seeing the colored servant, napkin on arm, so debonair about

---

31. **Barber and Fletcher**—For Francis Barber, the devoted Negro servant of Dr. Samuel Johnson, consult the index to a good edition of Boswell's *Life of Johnson*. There seems to be no record that William Fletcher, the body servant of Lord Byron, was a Negro.

his master, in a business so familiar as that of shaving, too, all his old weakness for negroes returned.

Among other things, he was amused with an odd instance of the African love of bright colors and fine shows, in the black's informally taking from the flag-locker a great piece of bunting of all hues, and lavishly tucking it under his master's chin for an apron.

The mode of shaving among the Spaniards is a little different from what it is with other nations. They have a basin, specially called a barber's basin, which on one side is scooped out, so as accurately to receive the chin, against which it is closely held in lathering; which is done, not with a brush, but with soap dipped in the water of the basin and rubbed on the face.

In the present instance salt-water was used for lack of better; and the parts lathered were only the upper lip, and low down under the throat, all the rest being cultivated beard.

These preliminaries being somewhat novel to Captain Delano he sat curiously eying them, so that no conversation took place, nor, for the present, did Don Benito appear disposed to renew any.

Setting down his basin, the negro searched among the razors, as for the sharpest, and having found it, gave it an additional edge by expertly stropping it on the firm, smooth, oily skin of his open palm; he then made a gesture as if to begin, but midway stood suspended for an instant, one hand elevating the razor, the other professionally dabbling among the bubbling suds on the Spaniard's lank neck. Not unaffected by the close sight of the gleaming steel, Don Benito nervously shuddered; his usual ghastliness was heightened by the lather, which lather, again, was intensified in its hue by the contrasting sootiness of the negro's body. Altogether the scene was somewhat peculiar, at least to Captain Delano, nor, as he saw the two thus postured, could he resist the vagary, that in the black he saw a headsman, and in the white a man at the block. But this was one of those antic conceits, appearing and vanishing in a breath, from which, perhaps, the best regulated mind is not free.

Meantime the agitation of the Spaniard had a little loosened the bunting from around him, so that one broad fold swept curtain-like over the chair-arm to the floor, revealing, amid a profusion of armorial bars and ground-colors—black, blue and yellow—a closed castle in a blood-red field diagonal with a lion rampant in a white.

"The castle and the lion," exclaimed Captain Delano—"why, Don Benito, this is the flag of Spain you use here. It's well it's only I, and not the King, that sees this," he added with a smile, "but"—turning towards the black,—"it's all one, I suppose, so the colors be gay;" which playful remark did not fail somewhat to tickle the negro.

"Now, master," he said, readjusting the flag, and pressing the head gently further back into the crotch of the chair; "now, master," and the steel glanced nigh the throat.

Again Don Benito faintly shuddered.

"You must not shake so, master. See, Don Amasa, master always shakes

34. **closed castle . . . field diagonal**—heraldic terms.

when I shave him. And yet master knows I never yet have drawn blood, though it's true, if master will shake so, I may some of these times. Now, master," he continued. "And now, Don Amasa, please go on with your talk about the gale, and all that; master can hear, and between times, master can answer."   5

"Ah yes, these gales," said Captain Delano; "but the more I think of your voyage, Don Benito, the more I wonder, not at the gales, terrible as they must have been, but at the disastrous interval following them. For here, by your account, have you been these two months and more getting from Cape Horn to St. Maria, a distance which I myself, with a good wind, have sailed in a few   10 days. True, you had calms, and long ones, but to be becalmed for two months, that is, at least, unusual. Why, Don Benito, had almost any other gentleman told me such a story, I should have been half disposed to a little incredulity."

Here an involuntary expression came over the Spaniard, similar to that just before on the deck, and whether it was the start he gave, or a sudden gawky   15 roll of the hull in the calm, or a momentary unsteadiness of the servant's hand, however it was, just then the razor drew blood, spots of which stained the creamy lather under the throat; immediately the black barber drew back his steel, and remaining in his professional attitude, back to Captain Delano, and face to Don Benito, held up the trickling razor, saying, with a sort of half   20 humorous sorrow, "See, master—you shook so—here's Babo's first blood."

No sword drawn before James the First of England, no assassination in that timid King's presence, could have produced a more terrified aspect than was now presented by Don Benito.

Poor fellow, thought Captain Delano, so nervous he can't even bear the   25 sight of barber's blood; and this unstrung, sick man, is it credible that I should have imagined he meant to spill all my blood, who can't endure the sight of one little drop of his own? Surely, Amasa Delano, you have been beside yourself this day. Tell it not when you get home, sappy Amasa. Well, well, he looks like a murderer, doesn't he? More like as if himself were to be done   30 for. Well, well, this day's experience shall be a good lesson.

Meantime, while these things were running through the honest seaman's mind, the servant had taken the napkin from his arm, and to Don Benito had said—"But answer Don Amasa, please, master, while I wipe this ugly stuff off the razor, and strop it again."   35

As he said the words, his face was turned half round, so as to be alike visible to the Spaniard and the American, and seemed, by its expression, to hint, that he was desirous, by getting his master to go on with the conversation, considerately to withdraw his attention from the recent annoying accident. As if glad to snatch the offered relief, Don Benito resumed, rehearsing to Captain Delano,   40 that not only were the calms of unusual duration, but the ship had fallen in with obstinate currents; and other things he added, some of which were but repetitions of former statements, to explain how it came to pass that the passage from Cape Horn to St. Maria had been so exceedingly long; now and then mingling with his words, incidental praises, less qualified than before, to   45

22. James the First—Fearful of assassination, James I of England (1566-1625) wore padded clothing, and forbade the drawing of swords in his presence.

the blacks, for their general good conduct. These particulars were not given consecutively, the servant, at convenient times, using his razor, and so, between the intervals of shaving, the story and panegyric went on with more than usual huskiness.

5　To Captain Delano's imagination, now again not wholly at rest, there was something so hollow in the Spaniard's manner, with apparently some reciprocal hollowness in the servant's dusky comment of silence, that the idea flashed across him, that possibly master and man, for some unknown purpose, were acting out, both in word and deed, nay, to the very tremor of Don Benito's

10　limbs, some juggling play before him. Neither did the suspicion of collusion lack apparent support, from the fact of those whispered conferences before mentioned. But then, what could be the object of enacting this play of the barber before him? At last, regarding the notion as a whimsy, insensibly suggested, perhaps, by the theatrical aspect of Don Benito in his harlequin ensign,

15　Captain Delano speedily banished it.

The shaving over, the servant bestirred himself with a small bottle of scented waters, pouring a few drops on the head, and then diligently rubbing; the vehemence of the exercise causing the muscles of his face to twitch rather strangely.

20　His next operation was with comb, scissors and brush; going round and round, smoothing a curl here, clipping an unruly whisker-hair there, giving a graceful sweep to the temple-lock, with other impromptu touches evincing the hand of a master; while, like any resigned gentleman in barber's hands, Don Benito bore all, much less uneasily, at least, than he had done the razoring;

25　indeed, he sat so pale and rigid now, that the negro seemed a Nubian sculptor finishing off a white statue-head.

All being over at last, the standard of Spain removed, tumbled up, and tossed back into the flag-locker, the negro's warm breath blowing away any stray hair which might have lodged down his master's neck; collar and cravat

30　readjusted; a speck of lint whisked off the velvet lapel; all this being done; backing off a little space, and pausing with an expression of subdued self-complacency, the servant for a moment surveyed his master, as, in toilet at least, the creature of his own tasteful hands.

Captain Delano playfully complimented him upon his achievement; at the

35　same time congratulating Don Benito.

But neither sweet waters, nor shampooing, nor fidelity, nor sociality, delighted the Spaniard. Seeing him relapsing into forbidding gloom, and still remaining seated, Captain Delano, thinking that his presence was undesired just then, withdrew, on pretense of seeing whether, as he had prophesied, any

40　signs of a breeze were visible.

Walking forward to the mainmast, he stood awhile thinking over the scene, and not without some undefined misgivings, when he heard a noise near the cuddy, and turning, saw the negro, his hand to his cheek. Advancing, Captain Delano perceived that the cheek was bleeding. He was about to ask the cause,

45　when the negro's wailing soliloquy enlightened him.

---

2. at convenient times—"now and then" (P). **37. forbidding**—"forbidden" (P).

"Ah, when will master get better from his sickness; only the sour heart that sour sickness breeds made him serve Babo so; cutting Babo with the razor, because, only by accident, Babo had given master one little scratch; and for the first time in so many a day, too. Ah, ah, ah," holding his hand to his face.

Is it possible, thought Captain Delano; was it to wreak in private his Span-   5
ish spite against this poor friend of his, that Don Benito, by his sullen manner, impelled me to withdraw? Ah, this slavery breeds ugly passions in man.—Poor fellow!

He was about to speak in sympathy to the negro, but with a timid reluctance he now re-entered the cuddy.   10

Presently master and man came forth; Don Benito leaning on his servant as if nothing had happened.

But a sort of love-quarrel, after all, thought Captain Delano.

He accosted Don Benito, and they slowly walked together. They had gone but a few paces, when the steward—a tall, rajah-looking mulatto, orientally   15
set off with a pagoda turban formed by three or four Madras handkerchiefs wound about his head, tier on tier—approaching with a salaam, announced lunch in the cabin.

On their way thither, the two captains were preceded by the mulatto, who, turning round as he advanced, with continual smiles and bows, ushered them   20
in, a display of elegance which quite completed the insignificance of the small bare-headed Babo, who, as if not unconscious of inferiority, eyed askance the graceful steward. But in part, Captain Delano imputed his jealous watchfulness to that peculiar feeling which the full-blooded African entertains for the adulterated one. As for the steward, his manner, if not bespeaking much dig-   25
nity of self-respect, yet evidenced his extreme desire to please; which is doubly meritorious, as at once Christian and Chesterfieldian.

Captain Delano observed with interest that while the complexion of the mulatto was hybrid, his physiognomy was European—classically so.

"Don Benito," whispered he, "I am glad to see this usher-of-the-golden-rod   30
of yours; the sight refutes an ugly remark once made to me by a Barbados planter; that when a mulatto has a regular European face, look out for him; he is a devil. But see, your steward here has features more regular than King George's of England; and yet there he nods, and bows, and smiles; a king, indeed—the king of kind hearts and polite fellows. What a pleasant voice he   35
has, too?"

"He has, Señor."

"But, tell me, has he not, so far as you have known him, always proved a good, worthy fellow?" said Captain Delano, pausing, while with a final genuflexion the steward disappeared into the cabin; "come, for the reason just men-   40
tioned, I am curious to know."

"Francesco is a good man," rather sluggishly responded Don Benito, like a phlegmatic appreciator, who would neither find fault nor flatter.

"Ah, I thought so. For it were strange, indeed, and not very creditable to

<hr />

27. **Chesterfieldian**—The reference is to the famous *Letters* of the Earl of Chesterfield (1694-1773), intended to teach polite and worldly conduct. 30. **usher-of-the-golden-rod**—An usher bearing a black rod is an official of the English Parliament.

us white-skins, if a little of our blood mixed with the African's, should, far from improving the latter's quality, have the sad effect of pouring vitriolic acid into black broth; improving the hue, perhaps, but not the wholesomeness."

"Doubtless, doubtless, Señor, but"—glancing at Babo—"not to speak of ne-
5 groes, your planter's remark I have heard applied to the Spanish and Indian intermixtures in our provinces. But I know nothing about the matter," he list-lessly added.

And here they entered the cabin.

The lunch was a frugal one. Some of Captain Delano's fresh fish and pump-
10 kins, biscuit and salt beef, the reserved bottle of cider, and the San Dominick's last bottle of Canary.

As they entered, Francesco, with two or three colored aids, was hovering over the table giving the last adjustments. Upon perceiving their master they withdrew, Francesco making a smiling congé, and the Spaniard, without
15 condescending to notice it, fastidiously remarking to his companion that he relished not superfluous attendance.

Without companions, host and guest sat down, like a childless married couple, at opposite ends of the table, Don Benito waving Captain Delano to his place, and, weak as he was, insisting upon that gentleman being seated
20 before himself.

The negro placed a rug under Don Benito's feet, and a cushion behind his back, and then stood behind, not his master's chair, but Captain Delano's. At first, this a little surprised the latter. But it was soon evident that, in taking his position, the black was still true to his master; since by facing him he
25 could the more readily anticipate his slightest want.

"This is an uncommonly intelligent fellow of yours, Don Benito," whispered Captain Delano across the table.

"You say true, Señor."

During the repast, the guest again reverted to parts of Don Benito's story,
30 begging further particulars here and there. He inquired how it was that the scurvy and fever should have committed such wholesale havoc upon the whites, while destroying less than half of the blacks. As if this question repro-duced the whole scene of plague before the Spaniard's eyes, miserably remind-ing him of his solitude in a cabin where before he had had so many friends
35 and officers round him, his hand shook, his face became hueless, broken words escaped; but directly the sane memory of the past seemed replaced by insane terrors of the present. With starting eyes he stared before him at vacancy. For nothing was to be seen but the hand of his servant pushing the Canary over towards him. At length a few sips served partially to restore him. He made
40 random reference to the different constitutions of races, enabling one to offer more resistance to certain maladies than another. The thought was new to his companion.

Presently Captain Delano, intending to say something to his host concerning the pecuniary part of the business he had undertaken for him, especially—
45 since he was strictly accountable to his owners—with reference to the new suit of sails, and other things of that sort; and naturally preferring to conduct such affairs in private, was desirous that the servant should withdraw; imag-

ining that Don Benito for a few minutes could dispense with his attendance.
He, however, waited awhile; thinking that, as the conversation proceeded, Don
Benito, without being prompted, would perceive the propriety of the step.

But it was otherwise. At last catching his host's eye, Captain Delano, with
a slight backward gesture of this thumb, whispered, "Don Benito, pardon me, 5
but there is an interference with the full expression of what I have to say to
you."

Upon this the Spaniard changed countenance; which was imputed to his
resenting the hint, as in some way a reflection upon his servant. After a moment's pause, he assured his guest that the black's remaining with them could 10
be of no disservice; because since losing his officers he had made Babo (whose
original office, it now appeared, had been captain of the slaves) not only his
constant attendant and companion, but in all things his confidant.

After this, nothing more could be said; though, indeed, Captain Delano
could hardly avoid some little tinge of irritation upon being left ungratified 15
in so inconsiderable a wish, by one, too, for whom he intended such solid
services. But it is only his querulousness, thought he; and so filling his glass
he proceeded to business.

The price of the sails and other matters was fixed upon. But while this was
being done, the American observed that, though his original offer of assistance 20
had been hailed with hectic animation, yet now when it was reduced to a
business transaction, indifference and apathy were betrayed. Don Benito, in
fact, appeared to submit to hearing the details more out of regard to common
propriety, than from any impression that weighty benefit to himself and his
voyage was involved.   25

Soon, this manner became still more reserved. The effort was vain to seek
to draw him into social talk. Gnawed by his splenetic mood, he sat twitching
his beard, while to little purpose the hand of his servant, mute as that on the
wall, slowly pushed over the Canary.

Lunch being over, they sat down on the cushioned transom; the servant 30
placing a pillow behind his master. The long continuance of the calm had now
affected the atmosphere. Don Benito sighed heavily, as if for breath.

"Why not adjourn to the cuddy," said Captain Delano; "there is more air
there." But the host sat silent and motionless.

Meantime his servant knelt before him with a large fan of feathers. And 35
Francesco coming in on tiptoes, handed the negro a little cup of aromatic
waters, with which at intervals he chafed his master's brow; smoothing the
hair along the temples as a nurse does a child's. He spoke no word. He only
rested his eye on his master's, as if, amid all Don Benito's distress, a little to
refresh his spirit by the silent sight of fidelity.   40

Presently the ship's bell sounded two o'clock; and through the cabin-windows
a slight rippling of the sea was discerned; and from the desired direction.

"There," exclaimed Captain Delano, "I told you so, Don Benito, look!"

He had risen to his feet, speaking in a very animated tone, with a view the
more to rouse his companion. But though the crimson curtain of the stern- 45
window near him that moment fluttered against his pale cheek, Don Benito
seemed to have even less welcome for the breeze than the calm.

Poor fellow, thought Captain Delano, bitter experience has taught him that one ripple does not make a wind, any more than one swallow a summer. But he is mistaken for once. I will get his ship in for him, and prove it.

Briefly alluding to his weak condition, he urged his host to remain quietly
5 where he was, since he (Captain Delano) would with pleasure take upon him-self the responsibility of making the best use of the wind.

Upon gaining the deck, Captain Delano started at the unexpected figure of Atufal, monumentally fixed at the threshold, like one of those sculptured porters of black marble guarding the porches of Egyptian tombs.
10 But this time the start was, perhaps, purely physical. Atufal's presence, sin-gularly attesting docility even in sullenness, was contrasted with that of the hatchet-polishers, who in patience evinced their industry; while both spectacles showed, that lax as Don Benito's general authority might be, still, whenever he chose to exert it, no man so savage or colossal but must, more or less, bow.
15 Snatching a trumpet which hung from the bulwarks, with a free step Captain Delano advanced to the forward edge of the poop, issuing his orders in his best Spanish. The few sailors and many negroes, all equally pleased, obediently set about heading the ship toward the harbour.

While giving some directions about setting a lower stu'n'-sail, suddenly
20 Captain Delano heard a voice faithfully repeating his orders. Turning, he saw Babo, now for the time acting, under the pilot, his original part of captain of the slaves. This assistance proved valuable. Tattered sails and warped yards were soon brought into some trim. And no brace or halyard was pulled but to the blithe songs of the inspirited negroes.
25 Good fellows, thought Captain Delano, a little training would make fine sailors of them. Why see, the very women pull and sing, too. These must be some of those Ashantee negresses that make such capital soldiers, I've heard. But who's at the helm? I must have a good hand there.

He went to see.
30 The San Dominick steered with a cumbrous tiller, with large horizontal pullies attached. At each pulley-end stood a subordinate black, and between them, at the tiller-head, the responsible post, a Spanish seaman, whose counte-nance evinced his due share in the general hopefulness and confidence at the coming of the breeze.
35 He proved the same man who had behaved with so shame-faced an air on the windlass.

"Ah,—it is you, my man," exclaimed Captain Delano—"well, no more sheep's-eyes now;—look straight forward and keep the ship so. Good hand, I trust? And want to get into the harbor, don't you?"
40 The man assented with an inward chuckle, grasping the tiller-head firmly. Upon this, unperceived by the American, the two blacks eyed the sailor in-tently.

Finding all right at the helm, the pilot went forward to the forecastle, to see how matters stood there.
45 The ship now had way enough to breast the current. With the approach of evening the breeze would be sure to freshen.

40. **The man assented**—" 'Si, Señor,' assented the man" (P). **41. intently**—"askance" (P).

Having done all that was needed for the present, Captain Delano, giving his last orders to the sailors, turned aft to report affairs to Don Benito in the cabin; perhaps additionally incited to rejoin him by the hope of snatching a moment's private chat while his servant was engaged upon deck.

From opposite sides, there were, beneath the poop, two approaches to the 5 cabin; one further forward than the other, and consequently communicating with a longer passage. Marking the servant still above, Captain Delano, taking the highest entrance—the one last named, and at whose porch Atufal still stood—hurried on his way, till, arrived at the cabin threshold, he paused an instant, a little to recover from his eagerness. Then, with the words of his in- 10 tended business upon his lips, he entered. As he advanced toward the seated Spaniard, he heard another footstep, keeping time with his. From the opposite door, a salver in hand, the servant was likewise advancing.

"Confound the faithful fellow," thought Captain Delano; "what a vexatious coincidence." 15

Possibly, the vexation might have been something different, were it not for the brisk confidence inspired by the breeze. But even as it was, he felt a slight twinge, from a sudden indefinite association in his mind of Babo with Atufal.

"Don Benito," said he, "I give you joy; the breeze will hold, and will increase. By the way, your tall man and time-piece, Atufal, stands without. By 20 your order, of course?"

Don Benito recoiled, as if at some bland satirical touch, delivered with such adroit garnish of apparent good breeding as to present no handle for retort.

He is like one flayed alive, thought Captain Delano; where may one touch him without causing a shrink? 25

The servant moved before his master, adjusting a cushion; recalled to civility, the Spaniard stiffly replied: "you are right. The slave appears where you saw him, according to my command; which is, that if at the given hour I am below, he must take his stand and abide my coming."

"Ah now, pardon me, but that is treating the poor fellow like an ex-king 30 indeed. Ah, Don Benito," smiling, "for all the license you permit in some things, I fear lest, at bottom, you are a bitter hard master."

Again Don Benito shrank; and this time, as the good sailor thought, from a genuine twinge of his conscience.

Conversation now became constrained. In vain Captain Delano called atten- 35 tion to the now perceptible motion of the keel gently cleaving the sea; with lack-lustre eye, Don Benito returned words few and reserved.

By-and-by, the wind having steadily risen, and still blowing right into the harbor, bore the San Dominick swiftly on. Rounding a point of land, the sealer at distance came into open view. 40

Meantime Captain Delano had again repaired to the deck, remaining there some time. Having at last altered the ship's course, so as to give the reef a wide berth, he returned for a few moments below.

I will cheer up my poor friend, this time, thought he.

"Better and better, Don Benito,["] he cried as he blithely re-entered: "there 45

11-12. **the seated Spaniard, he**—"the Spaniard, on the transom, he" (P). **17. brisk—** "buoyant" (P). **18. indefinite—**"involuntary" (P). **31. indeed—**"denied" (P).

will soon be an end to your cares, at least for awhile. For when, after a long, sad voyage, you know, the anchor drops into the haven, all its vast weight seems lifted from the captain's heart. We are getting on famously, Don Benito. My ship is in sight. Look through this side-light here; there she is; all a-taunt-o!
5 The Bachelor's Delight, my good friend. Ah, how this wind braces one up. Come, you must take a cup of coffee with me this evening. My old steward will give you as fine a cup as ever any sultan tasted. What say you, Don Benito, will you?"

At first, the Spaniard glanced feverishly up, casting a longing look towards
10 the sealer, while with mute concern his servant gazed into his face. Suddenly the old ague of coldness returned, and dropping back to his cushions he was silent.

"You do not answer. Come, all day you have been my host; would you have hospitality all on one side?"
15 "I cannot go," was the response.

"What? It will not fatigue you. The ships will lie together as near as they can, without swinging foul. It will be little more than stepping from deck to deck; which is but as from room to room. Come, come, you must not refuse me."
20 "I cannot go," decisively and repulsively repeated Don Benito.

Renouncing all but the last appearance of courtesy, with a sort of cadaverous sullenness, and biting his thin nails to the quick, he glanced, almost glared, at his guest, as if impatient that a stranger's presence should interfere with the full indulgence of his morbid hour. Meantime the sound of the parted waters
25 came more and more gurglingly and merrily in at the windows; as reproaching him for his dark spleen; as telling him that, sulk as he might, and go mad with it, nature cared not a jot; since, whose fault was it, pray?

But the foul mood was now at its depth, as the fair wind at its height.

There was something in the man so far beyond any mere unsociality or
30 sourness previously evinced, that even the forbearing good-nature of his guest could no longer endure it. Wholly at a loss to account for such demeanor, and deeming sickness with eccentricity, however extreme, no adequate excuse, well satisfied, too, that nothing in his own conduct could justify it, Captain Delano's pride began to be roused. Himself became reserved. But all seemed
35 one to the Spaniard. Quitting him, therefore, Captain Delano once more went to the deck.

The ship was now within less than two miles of the sealer. The whale-boat was seen darting over the interval.

To be brief, the two vessels, thanks to the pilot's skill, ere long in neighborly
40 style lay anchored together.

Before returning to his own vessel, Captain Delano had intended communicating to Don Benito the smaller details of the proposed services to be rendered. But, as it was, unwilling anew to subject himself to rebuffs, he resolved, now that he had seen the San Dominick safely moored, immediately to quit her,
45 without further allusion to hospitality or business. Indefinitely postponing his

42. smaller—"practical" (P).

ulterior plans, he would regulate his future actions according to future circumstances. His boat was ready to receive him; but his host still tarried below.
Well, thought Captain Delano, if he has little breeding, the more need to
show mine. He descended to the cabin to bid a ceremonious, and, it may be,
tacitly rebukeful adieu. But to his great satisfaction, Don Benito, as if he began   5
to feel the weight of that treatment with which his slighted guest had, not
indecorously, retaliated upon him, now supported by his servant, rose to
his feet, and grasping Captain Delano's hand, stood tremulous; too much
agitated to speak. But the good augury hence drawn was suddenly dashed,
by his resuming all his previous reserve, with augmented gloom, as, with   10
half-averted eyes, he silently reseated himself on his cushions. With a corresponding return of his own chilled feelings, Captain Delano bowed and
withdrew.

He was hardly midway in the narrow corridor, dim as a tunnel, leading
from the cabin to the stairs, when a sound, as of the tolling for execution   15
in some jail-yard, fell on his ears. It was the echo of the ship's flawed bell,
striking the hour, drearily reverberated in this subterranean vault. Instantly, by
a fatality not to be withstood, his mind, responsive to the portent, swarmed
with superstitious suspicions. He paused. In images far swifter than these
sentences, the minutest details of all his former distrusts swept through   20
him.

Hitherto, credulous good-nature had been too ready to furnish excuses for
reasonable fears. Why was the Spaniard, so superfluously punctilious at times,
now heedless of common propriety in not accompanying to the side his
departing guest? Did indisposition forbid? Indisposition had not forbidden   25
more irksome exertion that day. His last equivocal demeanor recurred. He
had risen to his feet, grasped his guest's hand, motioned toward his hat; then,
in an instant, all was eclipsed in sinister muteness and gloom. Did this imply
one brief, repentant relenting at the final moment, from some iniquitous plot,
followed by remorseless return to it? His last glance seemed to express a   30
calamitous, yet acquiescent farewell to Captain Delano forever. Why decline
the invitation to visit the sealer that evening? Or was the Spaniard less
hardened than the Jew, who refrained not from supping at the board of him
whom the same night he meant to betray? What imported all those day-
long enigmas and contradictions, except they were intended to mystify, pre-   35
liminary to some stealthy blow? Atufal, the pretended rebel, but punctual
shadow, that moment lurked by the threshold without. He seemed a sentry,
and more. Who, by his own confession, had stationed him there? Was the
negro now lying in wait?

The Spaniard behind—his creature before: to rush from darkness to light   40
was the involuntary choice.

The next moment, with clenched jaw and hand, he passed Atufal, and
stood unharmed in the light. As he saw his trim ship lying peacefully at her
anchor, and almost within ordinary call; as he saw his household boat, with
familiar faces in it, patiently rising and falling on the short waves by the   45

33. **Jew**—*Cf.* Matt. 26: 25.

San Dominick's side; and then, glancing about the decks where he stood, saw the oakum-pickers still gravely plying their fingers; and heard the low, buzzing whistle and industrious hum of the hatchet-polishers, still bestirring themselves over their endless occupation; and more than all, as he saw the
5   benign aspect of nature, taking her innocent repose in the evening; the screened sun in the quiet camp of the west shining out like the mild light from Abraham's tent; as his charmed eye and ear took in all these, with the chained figure of the black, the clenched jaw and hand relaxed. Once again he smiled at the phantoms which had mocked him, and felt something like
10 a tinge of remorse, that, by indulging them even for a moment, he should, by implication, have betrayed an almost atheist doubt of the ever-watchful Providence above.

There was a few minutes' delay, while, in obedience to his orders, the boat was being hooked along to the gangway. During this interval, a sort of
15 saddened satisfaction stole over Captain Delano, at thinking of the kindly offices he had that day discharged for a stranger. Ah, thought he, after good actions one's conscience is never ungrateful, however much so the benefited party may be.

Presently, his foot, in the first act of descent into the boat, pressed the
20 first round of the side-ladder, his face presented inward upon the deck. In the same moment, he heard his name courteously sounded; and, to his pleased surprise, saw Don Benito advancing—an unwonted energy in his air, as if, at the last moment, intent upon making amends for his recent discourtesy. With instinctive good feeling, Captain Delano, withdrawing his foot, turned and
25 reciprocally advanced. As he did so, the Spaniard's nervous eagerness increased, but his vital energy failed; so that, the better to support him, the servant, placing his master's hand on his naked shoulder, and gently holding it there, formed himself into a sort of crutch.

When the two captains met, the Spaniard again fervently took the hand of
30 the American, at the same time casting an earnest glance into his eyes, but, as before, too much overcome to speak.

I have done him wrong, self-reproachfully thought Captain Delano; his apparent coldness has deceived me; in no instance has he meant to offend.

Meantime, as if fearful that the continuance of the scene might too much
35 unstring his master, the servant seemed anxious to terminate it. And so, still presenting himself as a crutch, and walking between the two captains, he advanced with them towards the gangway; while still, as if full of kindly contrition, Don Benito would not let go the hand of Captain Delano, but retained it in his, across the black's body.

40 Soon they were standing by the side, looking over into the boat, whose crew turned up their curious eyes. Waiting a moment for the Spaniard to relinquish his hold, the now embarrassed Captain Delano lifted his foot, to overstep the threshold of the open gangway; but still Don Benito would not let go his hand. And yet, with an agitated tone, he said, "I can go no further;
45 here I must bid you adieu. Adieu, my dear, dear Don Amasa. Go—go!"

6-7. **light . . . tent**—The reference is apparently to Abraham's entertaining three strangers; see Gen. 18: 1 ff. **24. withdrawing**—"revoking" (P).

suddenly tearing his hand loose, "go, and God guard you better than me, my best friend."

Not unaffected, Captain Delano would now have lingered; but catching the meekly admonitory eye of the servant, with a hasty farewell he descended into his boat, followed by the continual adieus of Don Benito, standing rooted 5 in the gangway.

Seating himself in the stern, Captain Delano, making a last salute, ordered the boat shoved off. The crew had their oars on end. The bowsmen pushed the boat a sufficient distance for the oars to be lengthwise dropped. The instant that was done, Don Benito sprang over the bulwarks, falling at the 10 feet of Captain Delano; at the same time, calling towards his ship, but in tones so frenzied, that none in the boat could understand him. But, as if not equally obtuse, three sailors, from three different and distant parts of the ship, splashed into the sea, swimming after their captain, as if intent upon his rescue. 15

The dismayed officer of the boat eagerly asked what this meant. To which, Captain Delano, turning a disdainful smile upon the unaccountable Spaniard, answered that, for his part, he neither knew nor cared; but it seemed as if Don Benito had taken it into his head to produce the impression among his people that the boat wanted to kidnap him. "Or else—give way for your 20 lives," he wildly added, starting at a clattering hubbub in the ship, above which rang the tocsin of the hatchet-polishers; and seizing Don Benito by the throat he added, "this plotting pirate means murder!" Here, in apparent verification of the words, the servant, a dagger in his hand, was seen on the rail overhead, poised, in the act of leaping, as if with desperate fidelity to 25 befriend his master to the last; while, seemingly to aid the black, the three Spanish sailors were trying to clamber into the hampered bow. Meantime, the whole host of negroes, as if inflamed at the sight of their jeopardized captain, impended in one sooty avalanche over the bulwarks.

All this, with what preceded, and what followed, occurred with such in- 30 volutions of rapidity, that past, present, and future seemed one.

Seeing the negro coming, Captain Delano had flung the Spaniard aside, almost in the very act of clutching him and, by the unconscious recoil, shifting his place, with arms thrown up, so promptly grappled the servant in his descent, that with dagger presented at Captain Delano's heart, the black 35 seemed of purpose to have leaped there as to his mark. But the weapon was wrenched away, and the assailant dashed down into the bottom of the boat, which now, with disentangled oars, began to speed through the sea.

At this juncture, the left hand of Captain Delano, on one side, again clutched the half-reclined Don Benito, heedless that he was in a speechless 40 faint, while his right foot, on the other side, ground the prostrate negro; and his right arm pressed for added speed on the after oar, his eye bent forward, encouraging his men to their utmost.

But here, the officer of the boat, who had at last succeeded in beating off the towing sailors, and was now, with face turned aft, assisting the bowsman at 45

8. bowsmen—"bowsman" (P). 13. three sailors—"three Spanish sailors" (P). 17. Spaniard —"Benito Cereno" (P). 19. Don Benito—"the Spaniard" (P). 44-45. the towing sailors— "the towing Spanish sailors" (P).

his oar, suddenly called to Captain Delano, to see what the black was about;
while a Portuguese oarsman shouted to him to give heed to what the Spaniard
was saying.

Glancing down at his feet, Captain Delano saw the freed hand of the
5 servant aiming with a second dagger—a small one, before concealed in his
wool—with this he was snakishly writhing up from the boat's bottom, at
the heart of his master, his countenance lividly vindictive, expressing the
centred purpose of his soul; while the Spaniard, half-choked, was vainly
shrinking away, with husky words, incoherent to all but the Portuguese.

10 That moment, across the long-benighted mind of Captain Delano, a flash
of revelation swept, illuminating in unanticipated clearness his host's whole
mysterious demeanor, with every enigmatic event of the day, as well as the
entire past voyage of the San Dominick. He smote Babo's hand down, but
his own heart smote him harder. With infinite pity he withdrew his
15 hold from Don Benito. Not Captain Delano, but Don Benito, the black, in
leaping into the boat, had intended to stab.

Both the black's hands were held, as, glancing up towards the San Dominick, Captain Delano, now with the scales dropped from his eyes, saw the
negroes, not in misrule, not in tumult, not as if frantically concerned for
20 Don Benito, but with mask torn away, flourishing hatchets and knives, in
ferocious piratical revolt. Like delirious black dervishes, the six Ashantees
danced on the poop. Prevented by their foes from springing into the water,
the Spanish boys were hurrying up to the topmost spars, while such of the
few Spanish sailors, not already in the sea, less alert, were descried, helplessly
25 mixed in, on deck, with the blacks.

Meantime Captain Delano hailed his own vessel, ordering the ports up,
and the guns run out. But by this time the cable of the San Dominick had
been cut; and the fag-end, in lashing out, whipped away the canvas shroud
about the beak, suddenly revealing, as the bleached hull swung round towards
30 the open ocean, death for the figurehead, in a human skeleton; chalky comment on the chalked words below, *Follow your leader.*

At the sight, Don Benito, covering his face, wailed out: " 'Tis he, Aranda!
my murdered, unburied friend!"

Upon reaching the sealer, calling for ropes, Captain Delano bound the
35 negro, who made no resistance, and had him hoisted to the deck. He would
then have assisted the now almost helpless Don Benito up the side; but Don
Benito, wan as he was, refused to move, or be moved, until the negro should
have been first put below out of view. When, presently assured that it was
done, he no more shrank from the ascent.

40 The boat was immediately dispatched back to pick up the three swimming
sailors. Meantime, the guns were in readiness, though, owing to the San
Dominick having glided somewhat astern of the sealer, only the aftermost
one could be brought to bear. With this, they fired six times; thinking to
cripple the fugitive ship by bringing down her spars. But only a few in-
45 considerable ropes were shot away. Soon the ship was beyond the gun's range,

11. **his host's**—"Benito Cereno's" (P).

steering broad out of the bay; the blacks thickly clustering round the bow-sprit, one moment with taunting cries towards the whites, the next with upthrown gestures hailing the now dusky moors of ocean—cawing crows escaped from the hand of the fowler.

The first impulse was to slip the cables and give chase. But, upon second thoughts, to pursue with whale-boat and yawl seemed more promising.

Upon inquiring of Don Benito what firearms they had on board the San Dominick, Captain Delano was answered that they had none that could be used; because, in the earlier stages of the mutiny, a cabin-passenger, since dead, had secretly put out of order the locks of what few muskets there were. But with all his remaining strength, Don Benito entreated the American not to give chase, either with ship or boat; for the negroes had already proved them-selves such desperadoes, that, in case of a present assault, nothing but a total massacre of the whites could be looked for. But, regarding this warning as coming from one whose spirit had been crushed by misery, the American did not give up his design.

The boats were got ready and armed. Captain Delano ordered twenty-five men into them. He was going himself when Don Benito grasped his arm.

"What! have you saved my life, Señor, and are you now going to throw away your own?"

The officers also, for reasons connected with their interests and those of the voyage, and a duty owing to the owners, strongly objected against their com-mander's going. Weighing their remonstrances a moment, Captain Delano felt bound to remain; appointing his chief mate—an athletic and resolute man, who had been a privateer's-man—to head the party. The more to encourage the sailors, they were told, that the Spanish captain considered his ship as good as lost; that she and her cargo, including some gold and silver, were worth more than a thousand doubloons. Take her, and no small part should be theirs. The sailors replied with a shout.

The fugitives had now almost gained an offing. It was nearly night; but the moon was rising. After hard, prolonged pulling, the boats came up on the ship's quarters, at a suitable distance laying upon their oars to discharge their muskets. Having no bullets to return, the negroes sent their yells. But, upon the second volley, Indian-like, they hurtled their hatchets. One took off a sailor's fingers. Another struck the whale-boat's bow, cutting off the rope there, and remaining stuck in the gunwale like a woodman's axe. Snatching it, quivering from its lodgment, the mate hurled it back. The returned gaunt-let now stuck in the ship's broken quarter-gallery, and so remained.

The negroes giving too hot a reception, the whites kept a more respectful distance. Hovering now just out of reach of the hurtling hatchets, they, with a view to the close encounter which must soon come, sought to decoy the blacks into entirely disarming themselves of their most murderous weapons in a hand-to-hand fight, by foolishly flinging them, as missiles, short of the mark, into the sea. But ere long, perceiving the stratagem, the negroes desisted,

25. privateer's-man—to head—"privateer's-man, and, as his enemies whispered, a pirate—to head" (P). 28. worth more than a thousand—"worth upwards of ten thousand" (P).

though not before many of them had to replace their lost hatchets with hand-spikes; an exchange which, as counted upon, proved, in the end, favorable to the assailants.

Meantime, with a strong wind, the ship still clove the water; the boats
5   alternately falling behind, and pulling up, to discharge fresh volleys.

The fire was mostly directed towards the stern, since there, chiefly, the negroes, at present, were clustering. But to kill or maim the negroes was not the object. To take them, with the ship, was the object. To do it, the ship must be boarded; which could not be done by boats while she was sailing
10 so fast.

A thought now struck the mate. Observing the Spanish boys still aloft, high as they could get, he called to them to descend to the yards, and cut adrift the sails. It was done. About this time, owing to causes hereafter to be shown, two Spaniards, in the dress of sailors, and conspicuously showing
15 themselves, were killed; not by volleys, but by deliberate marksman's shots; while, as it afterwards appeared, during one of the general discharges, Atufal, the black, and the Spaniard at the helm likewise were killed. What now, with the loss of the sails, and loss of leaders, the ship became unmanageable to the negroes.
20 With creaking masts, she came heavily round to the wind; the prow slowly swinging into view of the boats, its skeleton gleaming in the horizontal moonlight, and casting a gigantic ribbed shadow upon the water. One extended arm of the ghost seemed beckoning the whites to avenge it.

"Follow your leader!" cried the mate; and, one on each bow, the boats
25 boarded. Sealing-spears and cutlasses crossed hatches and handspikes. Huddled upon the long-boat amidships, the negresses raised a wailing chant, whose chorus was the clash of the steel.

For a time, the attack wavered; the negroes wedging themselves to beat it back; the half-repelled sailors, as yet unable to gain a footing, fighting as
30 troopers in the saddle, one leg sideways flung over the bulwarks, and one without, plying their cutlasses like carters' whips. But in vain. They were almost overborne, when rallying themselves into a squad as one man, with a huzza, they sprang inboard, where, entangled, they involuntarily separated again. For a few breaths' space there was a vague, muffled, inner sound, as of
35 submerged sword-fish rushing hither and thither through shoals of black-fish. Soon, in a reunited band, and joined by the Spanish seamen, the whites came to the surface, irresistibly driving the negroes toward the stern. But a barricade of casks and sacks, from side to side, had been thrown up by the mainmast. Here the negroes faced about, and though scorning peace or truce, yet
40 fain would have had a respite. But, without pause, overleaping the barrier, the unflagging sailors again closed. Exhausted, the blacks now fought in despair. Their red tongues lolled, wolf-like, from their black mouths. But the pale sailors' teeth were set; not a word spoken; and, in five minutes more, the ship was won.
45 Nearly a score of the negroes were killed. Exclusive of those by the balls,

25. **Sealing-spears**—"Scaling-spears" (P).

many were mangled; their wounds—mostly inflicted by the long-edged sealing-spears—resembling those shaven ones of the English at Preston Pans, made by the poled scythes of the Highlanders. On the other side, none were killed, though several were wounded; some severely, including the mate. The surviving negroes were temporarily secured, and the ship, towed back 5 into the harbor at midnight, once more lay anchored.

Omitting the incidents and arrangements ensuing, suffice it that, after two days spent in refitting, the two ships sailed in company for Conception in Chili, and thence for Lima in Peru; where, before the vice-regal courts, the whole affair, from the beginning, underwent investigation. 10

Though, midway on the passage, the ill-fated Spaniard, relaxed from constraint, showed some signs of regaining health with free-will; yet, agreeably to his own foreboding, shortly before arriving at Lima, he relapsed, finally becoming so reduced as to be carried ashore in arms. Hearing of his story and plight, one of the many religious institutions of the City of Kings opened 15 an hospitable refuge to him, where both physician and priest were his nurses, and a member of the order volunteered to be his one special guardian and consoler, by night and by day.

The following extracts, translated from one of the official Spanish documents, will, it is hoped, shed light on the preceding narrative, as well as, in 20 the first place, reveal the true port of departure and true history of the San Dominick's voyage, down to the time of her touching at the island of St. Maria.

But, ere the extracts come, it may be well to preface them with a remark.

The document selected, from among many others, for partial translation, 25 contains the deposition of Benito Cereno; the first taken in the case. Some disclosures therein were, at the time, held dubious for both learned and natural reasons. The tribunal inclined to the opinion that the deponent, not undisturbed in his mind by recent events, raved of some things which could never have happened. But subsequent depositions of the surviving sailors, bearing 30 out the revelations of their captain in several of the strangest particulars, gave credence to the rest. So that the tribunal, in its final decision, rested its capital sentences upon statements which, had they lacked confirmation, it would have deemed it but duty to reject.

I, DON JOSE DE ABOS AND PADILLA, His Majesty's Notary for the Royal 35 Revenue, and Register of this Province, and Notary Public of the Holy Crusade of this Bishopric, etc.

Do certify and declare, as much as is requisite in law, that, in the criminal cause commenced the twenty-fourth of the month of September, in the year seventeen hundred and ninety-nine, against the Senegal negroes of the ship 40 San Dominick, the following declaration before me was made:

Declaration of the first witness, DON BENITO CERENO.

The same day, and month, and year, His Honor, Doctor Juan Martinez de Rozas,

---

1-2. sealing-spears—"scaling-spears" (P). 2. Preston Pans—At the battle of Prestonpans (1745), the Scotch Highlanders, fighting for the cause of the Stuart Pretender, charged the English army as indicated.

Councilor of the Royal Audience of this Kingdom, and learned in the law of this Intendency, ordered the captain of the ship San Dominick, Don Benito Cereno, to appear; which he did in his litter, attended by the monk Infelez; of whom he received the oath, which he took by God, our Lord, and a sign of the Cross; under
5 which he promised to tell the truth of whatever he should know and should be asked;—and being interrogated agreeably to the tenor of the act commencing the process, he said, that on the twentieth of May last, he set sail with his ship from the port of Valparaiso, bound to that of Callao; loaded with the produce of the country beside thirty cases of hardware and one hundred and sixty blacks, of both
10 sexes, mostly belonging to Don Alexandro Aranda, gentleman, of the city of Mendoza; that the crew of the ship consisted of thirty-six men, beside the persons who went as passengers; that the negroes were in part as follows: . . .

[Here, in the original, follows a list of some fifty names, descriptions, and ages, compiled from certain recovered documents of Aranda's, and also from
15 *recollections of the deponent, from which portions only are extracted.]*

—One, from about eighteen to nineteen years, named José, and this was the man that waited upon his master, Don Alexandro, and who speaks well the Spanish, having served him four or five years; . . . A mulatto, named Francesco, the cabin steward, of a good person and voice, having sung in the Valparaiso churches, native
20 of the province of Buenos Ayres, aged about thirty-five years. A smart negro, named Dago, who had been for many years a grave-digger among the Spaniards, aged forty-six years. . . . Four old negroes, born in Africa, from sixty to seventy, but sound, caulkers by trade, whose names are as follows:—the first was named Muri, and he was killed (as was also his son named Diamelo); the second, Nacta;
25 the third, Yola, likewise killed; the fourth, Ghofan; and six full-grown negroes, aged from thirty to forty-five, all raw, and born among the Ashantees—Matiluqui, Yan, Lecbe, Mapenda, Yambaio, Akim; four of whom were killed; . . . a powerful negro named Atufal, who being supposed to have been a chief in Africa, his owner set great store by him. . . . And a small negro of Senegal, but some years among
30 the Spaniards, aged about thirty, which Negro's name was Babo; . . . that he does not remember the names of the others, but that still expecting the residue of Don Alexandro's papers will be found, will then take due account of them all, and remit to the court; . . . and thirty-nine women and children of all ages.

[The catalogue over, the deposition goes on:]

35   . . . That all the negroes slept upon deck, as is customary in this navigation, and none wore fetters, because the owner, his friend Aranda, told him that they were all tractable; . . . that on the seventh day after leaving port, at three o'clock in the morning, all the Spaniards being asleep except the two officers on the watch, who were the boatswain, Juan Robles, and the carpenter, Juan Bautista Gayete, and the
40 helmsman and his boy, the negroes revolted suddenly, wounded dangerously the boatswain and the carpenter, and successively killed eighteen men of those who were sleeping upon deck, some with hand-spikes and hatchets, and others by throwing them alive overboard, after tying them; that of the Spaniards upon deck, they left about seven, as he thinks, alive and tied, to manoeuvre the ship, and

---

1. **Audience**—The Spanish colonial possessions in the New World were divided into political units known as *audiencias* (judicial districts). 4. **received**—After "received," (P) inserts "before Don José de Abos and Padilla, Notary Public of the Holy Crusade,". 9. **beside thirty cases of hardware**—Omitted in (P). 34. **The catalogue**—In (P), this line reads *"After the catalogue, the deposition goes on as follows:"*

three or four more who hid themselves, remained also alive. Although in the act
of revolt the negroes made themselves masters of the hatchway, six or seven wounded
went through it to the cockpit, without any hindrance on their part; that in the act
of revolt, the mate and another person, whose name he does not recollect, attempted
to come up through the hatchway, but being quickly wounded, were obliged to   5
return to the cabin; that the deponent resolved at break of day to come up the
companion-way, where the negro Babo was, being the ringleader, and Atufal, who
assisted him, and having spoken to them, exhorted them to cease committing such
atrocities, asking them, at the same time, what they wanted and intended to do,
offering, himself, to obey their commands; that, notwithstanding this, they threw,   10
in his presence, three men, alive and tied, overboard; that they told the deponent
to come up, and that they would not kill him; which having done, the negro Babo
asked him whether there were in those seas any negro countries where they might
be carried, and he answered them, No; that the negro Babo afterwards told him to
carry them to Senegal, or to the neighbouring islands of St. Nicholas; and he   15
answered, that this was impossible, on account of the great distance, the necessity
involved of rounding Cape Horn, the bad condition of the vessel, the want of
provisions, sails, and water; but that the negro Babo replied to him he must carry
them in any way; that they would do and conform themselves to everything the
deponent should require as to eating and drinking; that after a long conference,   20
being absolutely compelled to please them, for they threatened him to kill all the
whites if they were not, at all events, carried to Senegal, he told them that what
was most wanting for the voyage was water; that they would go near the coast
to take it, and thence they would proceed on their course; that the negro Babo
agreed to it; and the deponent steered towards the intermediate ports, hoping to   25
meet some Spanish or foreign vessel that would save them; that within ten or
eleven days they saw the land, and continued by it in the vicinity of Nasca; that
the deponent observed that the negroes were not restless and mutinous, because
he did not effect the taking in of water, the negro Babo having required, with
threats, that it should be done, without fail, the following day; he told him he   30
saw plainly that the coast was steep, and the rivers designated in the maps were
not to be found, with other reasons suitable to the circumstances; that the best way
would be to go to the island of Santa Maria, where they might water easily, it
being a solitary island, as the foreigners did; that the deponent did not go to
Pisco, that was near, nor make any other port of the coast, because the negro Babo   35
had intimated to him several times, that he would kill all the whites the very
moment he should perceive any city, town, or settlement of any kind on the shores
to which they should be carried: that having determined to go to the island of
Santa Maria, as the deponent had planned, for the purpose of trying whether, on
the passage or near the island itself, they could find any vessel that should favor   40
them, or whether he could escape from it in a boat to the neighbouring coast of
Arruco, to adopt the necessary means he immediately changed his course, steering
for the island; that the negroes Babo and Atufal held daily conferences, in which
they discussed what was necessary for their design of returning to Senegal, whether
they were to kill all the Spaniards, and particularly the deponent; that eight days   45
after parting from the coast of Nasca, the deponent being on the watch a little after
day-break, and soon after the negroes had their meeting, the negro Babo came to
the place where the deponent was, and told him that he had determined to kill his
master, Don Alexandro Aranda, both because he and his companions could not

5. **but being quickly wounded, were**—"but having been wounded, at the onset, they
were" (P). **15. Senegal**—on the west coast of Africa. **27. Nasca**—city in Chile. **33. water
easily**—"water and victual easily" (P). **34. solitary**—"desert" (P).

otherwise be sure of their liberty, and that to keep the seamen in subjection, he wanted to prepare a warning of what road they should be made to take did they or any of them oppose him; and that, by means of the death of Don Alexandro, that warning would best be given; but, that what this last meant, the deponent did not at
5 the time comprehend, nor could not, further than that the death of Don Alexandro was intended; and moreover the negro Babo proposed to the deponent to call the mate Raneds, who was sleeping in the cabin, before the thing was done, for fear, as the deponent understood it, that the mate, who was a good navigator, should be killed with Don Alexandro and the rest; that the deponent, who was the friend,
10 from youth of Don Alexandro, prayed and conjured, but all was useless; for the negro Babo answered him that the thing could not be prevented, and that all the Spaniards risked their death if they should attempt to frustrate his will in this matter, or any other; that, in this conflict, the deponent called the mate, Raneds, who was forced to go apart, and immediately the negro Babo commanded the
15 Ashantee Martinqui and the Ashantee Lecbe to go and commit the murder; that those two went down with hatchets to the berth of Don Alexandro; that, yet half alive and mangled, they dragged him on deck; that they were going to throw him overboard in that state, but the negro Babo stopped them, bidding the murder be completed on the deck before him, which was done, when, by his orders, the body
20 was carried below, forward; that nothing more was seen of it by the deponent for three days; . . . that Don Alonzo Sidonia, an old man, long resident at Valparaiso, and lately appointed to a civil office in Peru, whither he had taken passage, was at the time sleeping in the berth opposite Don Alexandro's; that awakening at his cries, surprised by them, and at the sight of the negroes with their bloody hatchets in their
25 hands, he threw himself into the sea through a window which was near him and was drowned, without it being in the power of the deponent to assist or take him up; . . . that, a short time after killing Aranda, they brought upon deck his german-cousin, of middle-age, Don Francisco Masa, of Mendoza, and the young Don Joaquin, Marques de Aramboalaza, then lately from Spain, with his Spanish
30 servant Ponce, and the three young clerks of Aranda, José Mozairi, Lorenzo Bargas, and Hermenegildo Gandix, all of Cadiz; that Don Joaquin and Hermenegildo Gandix, the negro Babo, for purposes hereafter to appear, preserved alive; but Don Francisco Masa, José Mozairi, and Lorenzo Bargas, with Ponce the servant, beside the boatswain, Juan Robles, the boatswain's mates, Manuel Viscaya and Roderigo
35 Hurta, and four of the sailors, the negro Babo ordered to be thrown alive into the sea, although they made no resistance, nor begged for anything else but mercy; that the boatswain, Juan Robles, who knew how to swim, kept the longest above water, making acts of contrition, and, in the last words he uttered, charged this deponent to cause mass to be said for his soul to our Lady of Succor: . . . that, during
40 the three days which followed, the deponent, uncertain what fate had befallen the remains of Don Alexandro, frequently asked the negro Babo where they were, and, if still on board, whether they were to be preserved for interment ashore, entreating him so to order it; that the negro Babo answered nothing till the fourth day, when at sunrise, the deponent coming on deck, the negro Babo showed him a
45 skeleton, which had been substituted for the ship's proper figurehead—the image of Christopher Colon, the discoverer of the New World; that the negro Babo asked him whose skeleton that was, and whether, from its whiteness, he should not think it a white's; that, upon discovering his face, the negro Babo, coming close, said words to this effect: "Keep faith with the blacks from here to Senegal, or you
50 shall in spirit, as now in body, follow your leader," pointing to the prow; . . .

15. **Martinqui**—This name first appears as Matiluqui, but Melville apparently became confused. 48. **discovering**—"his covering" (P).

that the same morning the negro Babo took by succession each Spaniard forward, and asked him whose skeleton that was, and whether, from its whiteness, he should not think it a white's; that each Spaniard covered his face; that then to each the negro Babo repeated the words in the first place said to the deponent; . . . that they (the Spaniards), being then assembled aft, the negro Babo harangued them, saying that he had now done all; that the deponent (as navigator for the negroes) might pursue his course, warning him and all of them that they should, soul and body, go the way of Don Alexandro, if he saw them (the Spaniards) speak or plot anything against them (the negroes)—a threat which was repeated every day; that, before the events last mentioned, they had tied the cook to throw him overboard, for it is not known what thing they heard him speak, but finally the negro Babo spared his life, at the request of the deponent; that a few days after, the deponent, endeavoring not to omit any means to preserve the lives of the remaining whites, spoke to the negroes peace and tranquillity, and agreed to draw up a paper, signed by the deponent and the sailors who could write, as also by the negro Babo, for himself and all the blacks, in which the deponent obliged himself to carry them to Senegal, and they not to kill any more, and he formally to make over to them the ship, with the cargo, with which they were for that time satisfied and quieted. . . . But the next day, the more surely to guard against the sailors' escape, the negro Babo commanded all the boats to be destroyed but the long-boat, which was un- seaworthy, and another, a cutter in good condition, which knowing it would yet be wanted for towing the water casks, he had it lowered down into the hold.

*   *   *   *   *   *   *   *

[Various particulars of the prolonged and perplexed navigation ensuing here follow, with incidents of a calamitous calm, from which portion one passage is extracted, to wit:]

—That on the fifth day of the calm, all on board suffering much from the heat, and want of water, and five having died in fits, and mad, the negroes became irritable, and for a chance gesture, which they deemed suspicious—though it was harmless—made by the mate, Raneds, to the deponent in the act of handing a quadrant, they killed him; but that for this they were afterwards sorry, the mate being the only remaining navigator on board, except the deponent.

*   *   *   *   *   *   *   *

—That omitting other events, which daily happened, and which can only serve uselessly to recall past misfortunes and conflicts, after seventy-three days' navigation, reckoned from the time they sailed from Nasca, during which they navigated under a scanty allowance of water, and were afflicted with the calms before mentioned, they at last arrived at the island of Santa Maria, on the seventeenth of the month of August, at about six o'clock in the afternoon, at which hour they cast anchor very near the American ship, Bachelor's Delight, which lay in the same bay, com- manded by the generous Captain Amasa Delano; but at six o'clock in the morning, they had already descried the port, and the negroes became uneasy, as soon as at distance they saw the ship, not having expected to see one there; that the negro Babo pacified them, assuring them that no fear need be had; that straightway he ordered the figure on the bow to be covered with canvas, as for repairs, and had the decks a little set in order; that for a time the negro Babo and the negro Atufal conferred; that the negro Atufal was for sailing away, but the negro Babo would not, and, by himself, cast about what to do; that at last he came to the deponent, pro-

22. towing—"lowering" (P).

posing to him to say and do all that the deponent declares to have said and done to
the American captain; . . . that the negro Babo warned him that if he varied in the
least, or uttered any word, or gave any look that should give the least intimation
of the past events or present state, he would instantly kill him, with all his com-
5 panions, showing a dagger, which he carried hid, saying something which, as he
understood it, meant that that dagger would be alert as his eye; that the negro Babo
then announced the plan to all his companions, which pleased them; that he then,
the better to disguise the truth, devised many expedients, in some of them uniting
deceit and defense; that of this sort was the device of the six Ashantees before
10 named, who were his bravoes; that them he stationed on the break of the poop,
as if to clean certain hatchets (in cases, which were part of the cargo), but in
reality to use them, and distribute them at need, and at a given word he told them;
that, among other devices, was the device of presenting Atufal, his right hand man,
as chained, though in a moment the chains could be dropped; that in every par-
15 ticular he informed the deponent what part he was expected to enact in every device,
and what story he was to tell on every occasion, always threatening him with
instant death if he varied in the least: that, conscious that many of the negroes would
be turbulent, the negro Babo appointed the four aged negroes, who were calkers,
to keep what domestic order they could on the decks; that again and again he
20 harangued the Spaniards and his companions, informing them of his intent, and of
his devices, and of the invented story that this deponent was to tell; charging them
lest any of them varied from that story; that these arrangements were made and
matured during the interval of two or three hours, between their first sighting the
ship and the arrival on board of Captain Amasa Delano; that this happened at
25 about half-past seven o'clock in the morning, Captain Amasa Delano coming in his
boat, and all glady receiving him; that the deponent, as well as he could force
himself, acting then the part of principal owner, and a free captain of the ship, told
Captain Amasa Delano, when called upon, that he came from Buenos Ayres, bound
to Lima, with three hundred negroes; that off Cape Horn, and in a subsequent
30 fever, many negroes had died; that also, by similar casualties, all the sea officers
and the greatest part of the crew had died.

.   .   .   .

[*And so the deposition goes on, circumstantially recounting the fictitious
story dictated to the deponent by Babo, and through the deponent imposed
upon Captain Delano; and also recounting the friendly offers of Captain*
35 *Delano, with other things, but all of which is here omitted. After the fictitious
story, etc., the deposition proceeds:*]

—that the generous Captain Amasa Delano remained on board all the day, till he left
the ship anchored at six o'clock in the evening, deponent speaking to him always
of his pretended misfortunes, under the forementioned principles, without having
40 had it in his power to tell a single word, or give him the least hint, that he might
know the truth and state of things; because the negro Babo, performing the office
of an officious servant with all the appearance of submission of the humble slave,
did not leave the deponent one moment; that this was in order to observe the
deponent's actions and words, for the negro Babo understands well the Spanish;
45 and besides, there were thereabout some others who were constantly on the watch,
and likewise understood the Spanish; . . . that upon one occasion, while deponent
was standing on the deck conversing with Amasa Delano, by a secret sign the
negro Babo drew him (the deponent) aside, the act appearing as if originating with
the deponent; that then, he being drawn aside, the negro Babo proposed to him to

gain from Amasa Delano full particulars about his ship, and crew, and arms; that
the deponent asked "For what?" that the negro Babo answered he might conceive;
that, grieved at the prospect of what might overtake the generous Captain Amasa
Delano, the deponent at first refused to ask the desired questions, and used every
argument to induce the negro Babo to give up this new design; that the negro   5
Babo showed the point of his dagger; that, after the information had been obtained
the negro Babo again drew him aside, telling him that that very night he (the
deponent) would be captain of two ships instead of one, for that, great part of the
American's ship's crew being to be absent fishing, the six Ashantees, without any one
else, would easily take it; that at this time he said other things to the same purpose;   10
that no entreaties availed; that before Amasa Delano's coming on board, no hint
had been given touching the capture of the American ship: that to prevent this
project the deponent was powerless; . . . —that in some things his memory is
confused, he cannot distinctly recall every event; . . . —that as soon as they had
cast anchor at six of the clock in the evening, as has before been stated, the American   15
Captain took leave, to return to his vessel; that upon a sudden impulse, which the
deponent believes to have come from God and his angels, he, after the farewell had
been said, followed the generous Captain Amasa Delano as far as the gunwale, where
he stayed, under the pretense of taking leave, until Amasa Delano should have been
seated in his boat; that on shoving off, the deponent sprang from the gunwale into   20
the boat, and fell into it, he knows not how, God guarding him; that—

.   .   .   .

*[Here, in the original, follows the account of what further happened at the
escape, and how the San Dominick was retaken, and of the passage to the
coast; including in the recital many expressions of "eternal gratitude" to the
"generous Captain Amasa Delano." The deposition then proceeds with   25
recapitulatory remarks, and a partial renumeration of the negroes, making
record of their individual part in the past events, with a view to furnishing,
according to command of the court, the data whereon to found the criminal
sentences to be pronounced. From this portion is the following:]*

—That he believes that all the negroes, though not in the first place knowing to   30
the design of revolt, when it was accomplished, approved it. . . . That the negro,
José, eighteen years old, and in the personal service of Don Alexandro, was the
one who communicated the information to the negro Babo, about the state of
things in the cabin, before the revolt; that this is known, because, in the preceding
midnight, he used to come from his berth, which was under his master's, in the   35
cabin, to the deck where the ringleader and his associates were, and had secret
conversations with the negro Babo, in which he was several times seen by the mate;
that, one night, the mate drove him away twice; . . . that this same negro José was
the one who, without being commanded to do so by the negro Babo, as Lecbe and
Martinqui were, stabbed his master, Don Alexandro, after he had been dragged   40
half-lifeless to the deck; . . . that the mulatto steward, Francesco, was of the first
band of revolters, that he was, in all things, the creature and tool of the negro Babo;
that, to make his court, he, just before a repast in the cabin, proposed, to the negro
Babo, poisoning a dish for the generous Captain Amasa Delano; this is known
and believed, because the negroes have said it; but that the negro Babo, having   45
another design, forbade Francesco; . . . that the Ashantee Lecbe was one of the
worst of them; for that, on the day the ship was retaken, he assisted in the defense

26. **renumeration**—reënumeration.

of her, with a hatchet in each hand, with one of which he wounded, in the breast, the chief mate of Amasa Delano, in the first act of boarding; this all knew; that, in sight of the deponent, Lecbe struck, with a hatchet, Don Francisco Masa when, by the negro Babo's orders, he was carrying him to throw him overboard, alive;
5 beside participating in the murder, before mentioned, of Don Alexandro Aranda, and others of the cabin-passengers; that, owing to the fury with which the Ashantees fought in the engagement with the boats, but this Lecbe and Yan survived; that Yan was bad as Lecbe; that Yan was the man who, by Babo's command, willingly prepared the skeleton of Don Alexandro, in a way the negroes afterwards told the
10 deponent, but which he, so long as reason is left him, can never divulge; that Yan and Lecbe were the two who, in a calm by night, riveted the skeleton to the bow; this also the negroes told him; that the negro Babo was he who traced the inscription below it; that the negro Babo was the plotter from first to last; he ordered every murder, and was the helm and keel of the revolt; that Atufal was his lieutenant
15 in all; but Atufal, with his own hand, committed no murder; nor did the negro Babo; . . . that Atufal was shot, being killed in the fight with boats, ere boarding; . . . that the negresses, of age, were knowing to the revolt, and testified themselves satisfied at the death of their master, Don Alexandro; that, had the negroes not restrained them, they would have tortured to death, instead of simply killing, the
20 Spaniards slain by command of the negro Babo; that the negresses used their utmost influence to have the deponent made away with; that, in the various acts of murder, they sang songs and danced—not gaily, but solemnly; and before the engagement with the boats, as well as during the action, they sang melancholy songs to the negroes, and that this melancholy tone was more inflaming than a different one
25 would have been, and was so intended; that all this is believed because the negroes have said it.
—that of the thirty-six men of the crew, exclusive of the passengers (all of whom are now dead), which the deponent had knowledge of, six only remained alive, with four cabin-boys and ship-boys, not included with the crew; . . . —that the
30 negroes broke an arm of one of the cabin-boys and gave him strokes with hatchets.

[*Then follow various random disclosures referring to various periods of time. The following are extracted:*]

—That during the presence of Captain Amasa Delano on board, some attempts
35 were made by the sailors, and one by Hermenegildo Gandix, to convey hints to him of the true state of affairs; but that these attempts were ineffectual, owing to fear of incurring death, and, furthermore, owing to the devices which offered contradictions to the true state of affairs, as well as owing to the generosity and piety of Amasa Delano, incapable of sounding such wickedness; . . . that Luys Galgo, a
40 sailor about sixty years of age, and formerly of the king's navy, was one of those who sought to convey tokens to Captain Amasa Delano; but his intent, though undiscovered, being suspected, he was, on a pretense, made to retire out of sight, and at last into the hold, and there was made away with. This the negroes have since said; . . . that one of the ship-boys feeling, from Captain Amasa Delano's presence,
45 some hopes of release, and not having enough prudence, dropped some chance-word respecting his expectations, which being overheard and understood by a slave-boy with whom he was eating at the time, the latter struck him on the head with a knife, inflicting a bad wound, but of which the boy is now healing; that likewise, not long before the ship was brought to anchor, one of the seamen, steering

at the time, endangered himself by letting the blacks remark some expression in his countenance, arising from some cause similar to the above; but this sailor, by his heedful after conduct, escaped; . . . that these statements are made to show the court that from the beginning to the end of the revolt, it was impossible for the deponent and his men to act otherwise than they did; . . . —that the third clerk, Her- 5 menegildo Gandix, who before had been forced to live among the seamen, wearing a seaman's habit, and in all respects appearing to be one for the time; he, Gandix, was killed by a musket ball fired through mistake from the boats before boarding; having in his fright run up the mizzen-rigging, calling to the boats—"don't board," lest upon their boarding the negroes should kill him; that this inducing the Ameri- 10 cans to believe he some way favored the cause of the negroes, they fired two balls at him, so that he fell wounded from the rigging, and was drowned in the sea; . . . —that the young Don Joaquin, Marques de Aramboalaza, like Hermenegildo Gandix, the third clerk, was degraded to the office and appearance of a common sea- man; that upon one occasion, when Don Joaquin shrank, the negro Babo com- 15 manded the Ashantee Lecbe to take tar and heat it, and pour it upon Don Joaquin's hands; . . . —that Don Joaquin was killed owing to another mistake of the Americans, but one impossible to be avoided, as upon the approach of the boats, Don Joaquin, with a hatchet tied edge out and upright to his hand, was made by the negroes to appear on the bulwarks; whereupon, seen with arms in his hands and in 20 a questionable attitude, he was shot for a renegade seaman; . . . —that on the person of Don Joaquin was found secreted a jewel, which, by papers that were discovered, proved to have been meant for the shrine of our Lady of Mercy in Lima; a votive offering, beforehand prepared and guarded, to attest his gratitude, when he should have landed in Peru, his last destination, for the safe conclusion of his entire 25 voyage from Spain; . . . —that the jewel, with the other effects of the late Don Joaquin, is in the custody of the brethren of the Hospital de Sacerdotes, awaiting the disposition of the honorable court; . . . —that, owing to the condition of the deponent, as well as the haste in which the boats departed for the attack, the Americans were not forewarned that there were, among the apparent crew, a 30 passenger and one of the clerks, disguised by the negro Babo; . . . —that, beside the negroes killed in the action, some were killed after the capture and re-anchoring at night, when shackled to the ring-bolts on deck; that these deaths were committed by the sailors, ere they could be prevented. That so soon as informed of it, Captain Amasa Delano used all his authority, and, in particular with his own hand, struck 35 down Martinez Gola, who, having found a razor in the pocket of an old jacket of his, which one of the shackled negroes had on, was aiming it at the negro's throat; that the noble Captain Amasa Delano also wrenched from the hand of Bartholomew Barlo, a dagger secreted at the time of the massacre of the whites, with which he was in the act of stabbing a shackled negro, who, the same day, with another negro, 40 had thrown him down and jumped upon him; . . . —that, for all the events, be- falling through so long a time, during which the ship was in the hands of the negro Babo, he cannot here give account; but that, what he has said is the most substantial of what occurs to him at present, and is the truth under the oath which he has taken; which declaration he affirmed and ratified, after hearing it read to 45 him.

He said that he is twenty-nine years of age, and broken in body and mind; that when finally dismissed by the court, he shall not return home to Chili, but betake himself to the monastery on Mount Agonia without; and signed with his honor,

---

1. **some expression**—"a certain unconscious hopeful expression" (P). **8. from the boats**— "from the American boats" (P). **28. disposition**—"decision" (P).

and crossed himself, and, for the time, departed as he came, in his litter, with the
monk Infelez, to the Hospital de Sacerdotes.

BENITO CERENO

DOCTOR ROZAS.

5   If the deposition have served as the key to fit into the lock of the complications which precede it, then, as a vault whose door has been flung back, the
San Dominick's hull lies open to-day.

Hitherto the nature of this narrative, besides rendering the intricacies in
the beginning unavoidable, has more or less required that many things, in-
10   stead of being set down in the order of occurrence, should be retrospectively,
or irregularly given; this last is the case with the following passages, which
will conclude the account:

During the long, mild voyage to Lima, there was, as before hinted, a period
during which the sufferer a little recovered his health, or, at least in some
15   degree, his tranquillity. Ere the decided relapse which came, the two captains
had many cordial conversations—their fraternal unreserve in singular contrast
with former withdrawments.

Again and again, it was repeated, how hard it had been to enact the part
forced on the Spaniard by Babo.

20   "Ah, my dear friend," Don Benito once said, "at those very times when you
thought me so morose and ungrateful, nay when, as you now admit, you
half thought me plotting your murder, at those very times my heart was
frozen; I could not look at you, thinking of what, both on board this ship
and your own, hung, from other hands, over my kind benefactor. And as God
25   lives, Don Amasa, I know not whether desire for my own safety alone could
have nerved me to that leap into your boat, had it not been for the thought
that, did you, unenlightened, return to your ship, you, my best friend, with
all who might be with you, stolen upon, that night, in your hammocks, would
never in this world have wakened again. Do but think how you walked this
30   deck, how you sat in this cabin, every inch of ground mined into honey-
combs under you. Had I dropped the least hint, made the least advance
towards an understanding between us, death, explosive death—yours as mine—
would have ended the scene."

"True, true," cried Captain Delano, starting, "you saved my life, Don
35   Benito, more than I yours; saved it, too, against my knowledge and will."

"Nay, my friend," rejoined the Spaniard, courteous even to the point of
religion, "God charmed your life, but you saved mine. To think of some
things you did—those smilings and chattings, rash pointings and gesturings.
For less than these, they slew my mate, Raneds; but you had the Prince of
40   Heaven's safe conduct through all ambuscades."

"Yes, all is owing to Providence, I know; but the temper of my mind that
morning was more than commonly pleasant, while the sight of so much
suffering, more apparent than real, added to my good-nature, compassion,
and charity, happily interweaving the three. Had it been otherwise, doubtless,

5. have served—"of Benito Cereno has served" (P). 14. the sufferer—"Don Benito" (P).
20. friend—"Don Amasa" (P).

as you hint, some of my interferences might have ended unhappily enough. Besides, those feelings I spoke of enabled me to get the better of momentary distrust, at times when acuteness might have cost me my life, without saving another's. Only at the end did my suspicions get the better of me, and you know how wide of the mark they then proved."

"Wide indeed," said Don Benito, sadly; "you were with me all day; stood with me, sat with me, talked with me, looked at me, ate with me, drank with me; and yet, your last act was to clutch for a monster, not only an innocent man, but the most pitiable of all men. To such degree many malign machinations and deceptions impose. So far may even the best men err, in judging the conduct of one with the recesses of whose condition he is not acquainted. But you were forced to it; and you were in time undeceived. Would that, in both respects, it was so ever, and with all men."

"You generalize, Don Benito; and mournfully enough. But the past is passed; why moralize upon it? Forget it. See, yon bright sun has forgotten it all, and the blue sea, and the blue sky; these have turned over new leaves."

"Because they have no memory," he dejectedly replied; "because they are not human."

"But these mild trades that now fan your cheek, Don Benito, do they not come with a human-like healing to you? Warm friends, steadfast friends are the trades."

"With their steadfastness they but waft me to my tomb, Señor," was the foreboding response.

"You are saved," cried Captain Delano, more and more astonished and pained; "you are saved: what has cast such a shadow upon you?"

"The negro."

There was silence, while the moody man sat, slowly and unconsciously gathering his mantle about him, as if it were a pall.

There was no more conversation that day.

But if the Spaniard's melancholy sometimes ended in muteness upon topics like the above, there were others upon which he never spoke at all; on which, indeed, all his old reserves were piled. Pass over the worst and, only to elucidate, let an item or two of these be cited. The dress so precise and costly, worn by him on the day whose events have been narrated, had not willingly been put on. And that silver-mounted sword, apparent symbol of despotic command, was not, indeed, a sword, but the ghost of one. The scabbard, artificially stiffened, was empty.

As for the black—whose brain, not body, had schemed and led the revolt, with the plot—his slight frame, inadequate to that which it held, had at once yielded to the superior muscular strength of his captor, in the boat. Seeing all was over, he uttered no sound, and could not be forced to. His aspect seemed to say, since I cannot do deeds, I will not speak words. Put in irons in the hold, with the rest, he was carried to Lima. During the passage, Don Benito did not visit him. Nor then, nor at any time after, would he look at him.

1. **might have**—"with the blacks might have" (P). 2. **Besides**—"Besides that," (P). 8. **monster**—"villain" (P). 14. **You generalize**—"I think I understand you. You" (P). 24. **saved,**—"saved, Don Benito," (P)

Before the tribunal he refused. When pressed by the judges he fainted. On the testimony of the sailors alone rested the legal identity of Babo.

Some months after, dragged to the gibbet at the tail of a mule, the black met his voiceless end. The body was burned to ashes; but for many days, the
5 head, that hive of subtlety, fixed on a pole in the Plaza, met, unabashed, the gaze of the whites; and across the Plaza looked towards St. Bartholomew's church, in whose vaults slept then, as now, the recovered bones of Aranda: and across the Rimac bridge looked toward the monastery, on Mount Agonia without; where, three months after being dismissed by the court, Benito
10 Cereno, borne on the bier, did, indeed, follow his leader.

    2. Babo.—(P) here inserts "And yet the Spaniard would, upon occasion, verbally refer to the negro, as has been shown; but look on him he would not, or could not."

WALT WHITMAN

1819-1892

I. "A DREAMY IMPRACTICABLE YOUTH" (1819–1855)

1819 Born May 31, on a farm at West Hills, Long Island, the second child of Walter and Louise Van Velsor Whitman, of English, Welsh, and Dutch ancestry, and in the Quaker tradition.

1823 (May?) Family removed to Brooklyn. Whitman later entered the public schools.

1832 Left school. In 1831-32 his first newspaper work done for the *Long Island Patriot*. Employed in a law office, a doctor's office, and a printing-office.

1833–1836 Journeyman printer in New York City; growing interest in the life of the city, and in theater and opera.

1836–1841 Teacher in seven Long Island country schools; much miscellaneous newspaper work.

1839–1841 Contributed to the *Long Island Democrat* immature essays and conventional poems.

1841–1848 Lived a Bohemian existence in New York City and Brooklyn, writing for various papers. Participated in reform movements of the forties.

1842 Published *Franklin Evans; or, The Inebriate: A Tale of the Times* (didactic novel) in the *New World*.

1846–1848 Editor, *Brooklyn Eagle* (March, 1846-January, 1848); forced to resign because of his support of the Free Soil party.

1848 February 11-June 15, traveled South and to the Mississippi Valley with his brother Jeff. Wrote for the *Crescent,* a New Orleans newspaper (March-May). Probable time of a mysterious liaison in New Orleans.

1848–1849 Editor, the *Freeman,* an antislavery paper in Brooklyn.

1850 March, published first poem in free verse, "Blood-Money," in the New York *Evening Post*. "Resurgemus," first poem to be retained in *Leaves of Grass,* published June 21, in the New York *Daily Tribune*.

1850–1854 Supported himself by newspaper work, carpentering, selling houses, and so forth. Member of a literary and newspaper group meeting at Pfaff's Bohemian Restaurant in New York City.

II. LEAVES OF GRASS AND THE WOUNDS OF WAR (1855–1873)

1855 First edition of *Leaves of Grass* (second, 1856; third, 1860-61; fourth, 1867; fifth, 1871; sixth, 1876 ("Centennial" edition); seventh (London), 1881; "suppressed" edition, 1881-82; "Author's" edition, 1882; other editions that same year).

1857–1859 Editor, Brooklyn *Daily Times*.

1862 December, brother George wounded; Whitman went to the army on the Rappahannock to nurse him. Remained in Washington as a nurse and helper of the wounded, living mainly at the home of W. D. O'Connor. Correspondent for the New York *Times* and other papers. His circle of friends included John Burroughs, E. C. Stedman, Trowbridge, C. W. Eldridge; also Peter Doyle, an illiterate Confederate prisoner on parole, to whom the letters in *Calamus* were written.

1864 Breakdown in health from overwork. Temporary recovery.

1865 February, appointed clerk in the Indian Bureau; dismissed June 30 by James Harlan, Secretary of the Department of the Interior, for having written an immoral book. Appointed almost immediately to a clerkship in the Attorney-General's Department.

1866 (Dated September 2, 1865), W. D. O'Connor published *The Good Gray Poet,* a flaming denunciation of Harlan and vindication of Whitman. *Walt Whitman's Drum Taps* published (1865).

1867 John Burroughs published *Notes on Walt Whitman as Poet and Person,* partly written by Whitman. Whitman's reputation in England steadily increasing.

1868 Rossetti published selections from Whitman in England.

1869–1870 Beginning of the "passionate friendship" of Mrs. Anne Gilchrist for Whitman.

1871 Published *Democratic Vistas;* recited "After All Not to Create Only" at the American Institute, New York City (published as a pamphlet); published *Passage to India.*

1872 Delivered "As a Strong Bird on Pinions Free" at the Dartmouth College commencement (published as a pamphlet); and "Song of the Universal" at Tufts College. Traveled in New England and New York State.

III. "THE LONG AFTERNOON" (1873–1892)

1873 February 22, first paralytic stroke suffered in Washington. Whitman went to Camden, New Jersey, where his mother died in the spring.

1875 Published *Memoranda during the War.*

1876 Partial recovery. Published Centennial edition (*Leaves of Grass* and *Two Rivulets*). In the next few years, traveled in the East, to the West (1879), and to Canada (1880).

1881 Published *Poetry of the Future* (from *North American Review,* February, 1881).

1882 Published *Specimen Days and Collect.*

1883 Richard M. Bucke published *Walt Whitman* (biography).

1884 Bought house in Mickle Street, Camden, Mrs. Davis being his housekeeper. Financial straits.

1887 Published *Specimen Days in America.*

1888 Published *November Boughs.* Fresh paralytic attack confined him to a wheeled-chair. Published *Complete Poems and Prose.*

1889 Added *A Backward Glance o'er Travel'd Roads* to *Leaves of Grass.*

1891 Published *Good-bye My Fancy.* Camden had become a mecca for admirers.

1892 Died at Camden March 26.

1893 Traubel, Bucke, and Harned published *In Re Walt Whitman.*

1897 *Calamus* published.

1898 *The Wound-Dresser* published.

BIOGRAPHIES: Besides those noted above, Bliss Perry, *Walt Whitman,* Houghton Mifflin, 1906; Horace Traubel, *With Walt Whitman in Camden,* Doubleday, Page, 1906-14, 3 vols.; Emory Holloway, *Whitman: An Interpretation in Narrative,* Knopf, 1926; Newton Arvin, *Whitman,* Macmillan, 1938; Mrs. Esther Shephard, *Whitman's Pose,* Harcourt, Brace, 1938; Henry S. Canby, *Walt Whitman: An American,* Houghton Mifflin, 1943.

BIBLIOGRAPHY AND EDITIONS: Carolyn Wells and A. F. Goldsmith, *A Concise Bibliography of the Works of Walt Whitman,* Houghton Mifflin, 1922; *Literary History of the United States,* Vol. III, pp. 759-68.

The Complete Writings of Walt Whitman, Booklovers' Camden edition, Putnam, 1902, 10 vols.; *Complete Poetry and Selected Prose,* ed. Emory Holloway, London, Nonesuch Press, 1938; *Leaves of Grass,* Inclusive edition, ed. by Emory Holloway, Doubleday, Page, 1924; *The Uncollected Poetry and Prose of Walt Whitman,* ed. by Emory Holloway, Doubleday, Page, 2 vols., 1921; *Gathering of the Forces,* ed. by Cleveland Rodgers and John Black, Putnam, 1920, 2 vols.; *The Half-Breed and Other Stories,* ed. by T. O. Mabbott, Columbia University Press, 1927; *Walt Whitman's Workshop,* ed. by C. J. Furness, Harvard University Press, 1928; *Franklin Evans; or, The Inebriate,* ed. by Emory Holloway, Random House, 1929; *I Sit and Look Out,* ed. by Emory Holloway, Columbia University Press, 1932; *Walt Whitman's Backward Glances,* ed. by Sculley Bradley and J. A. Stevenson, University of Pennsylvania, 1947. *Leaves of Grass (1850-1881),* with an introduction by S. P. Sherman, Scribner, 1922, and Floyd Stovall, ed., *Walt Whitman: Representative Selections,* American Book Co., 1939 (rev. ed.) are satisfactory.

Until his middle thirties Walt Whitman showed little indication of developing into the poet who in 1855 presented to the world a revolutionary volume of verse. Study of the great mass of writing which he did in the first part of his life reveals, it is true, many ideas in embryo among the editorials and articles of the journalist which later reached fuller expression in *Leaves of Grass* and the subsequent prose. Journalism, in part at least, also accounts for Whitman's genius for striking titles, the uncertainty of his diction, his habit of making catalogues, and his avid eye for vivid detail. Deeper than these details is the fact that his aimless early years, because they threw him into contact with all sorts and conditions of men, strengthened his mystic sense of human brotherhood. When one adds his irregular but eager reading, his love for drama and opera, and his dislike of a merely disciplined existence, one accounts for much that is in him.

Democracy has shown little interest in the singer of democracy. Whitman appeals rather to intellectual and social radicals than to the audience which admires Mr. Edgar Guest. There are a number of explanations for the repudiation by the plain people of the singer of "powerful uneducated persons"; one reason is, of course, the form of his verse and the repetitiousness of his prose. But it is also true, despite a certain element of charlatanism, that Whitman is difficult reading. The intellectual substance of his writing is tough. A mystic is always hard going; but Whitman is especially hard to understand because of the interweaving of scientific, philosophical, and political speculation in his later work. The reader finds much that is simple and immediate; but he finds also philosophical or pseudo-philosophical passages that depend for meaning upon theories which Whitman picked up, and which he restates with his usual generous looseness of meaning.

Perhaps the very lack in him of verbal precision helps to explain why the communist and the capitalist, the Christian and the atheist, the socialist and the individualist, are each likely to discover in Whitman comfortable support for particular views of human life. Whitman, more than any other great American writer, is all of a piece; his verse and his prose are simply aspects of the vast flowing stuff that is Whitman, so that the influence of his form and his emotional mysticism upon subsequent American literature has been immense and continuous, and is still profound.

PREFACE TO LEAVES OF GRASS

The preface to the original (1855) edition of *Leaves of Grass* is a longer, more rhapsodic, and more eccentrically punctuated document than is the essay here reprinted. The original preface was withdrawn after the edition of 1855, nor did it again appear in conjunction with the poems. Sections of it were worked into poems in the 1856 edition of the *Leaves;* larger and more important sections finally came to rest, much revised, in "By Blue Ontario's Shore" (1870), "To a Foil'd European Revolutionaire" (1870) and "Song of Prudence" (1881). The rest of the original preface, much revised, was then reprinted in the "Collect" section of the *Complete Poems and Prose* of 1882 (1882-83). Meanwhile, the original unrevised preface was reprinted as a pamphlet in London in 1881. The present reprint follows the text of the Camden edition of the *Writings*. Except in minor inaccuracies of capitalization and spelling, the Camden text is, with a few trifling exceptions, an accurate reprint of the 1882 version.

For the "Centennial" edition of his works (1876) Whitman wrote a second, and inferior, preface to *Leaves of Grass,* capitalizing the interest of the centennial year, and laying stress upon the relation of his poetry to politics and science. In addition to this preface, traces of various other prefaces have been discovered; these fragments may be consulted in Furness, *Walt Whitman's Workshop,* pp. 117-74.

A MERICA does not repel the past or what it has produced under its forms or amid other politics or the idea of castes or the old religions— accepts the lesson with calmness—is not impatient because the slough still sticks to opinions and manners in literature while the life which served
5 its requirements has passed into the new life of the new forms—perceives that the corpse is slowly borne from the eating and sleeping rooms of the house—perceives that it waits a little while in the door—that it was fittest for its days—that its action has descended to the stalwart and well-shaped heir who approaches—and that he shall be fittest for his days.
10   The Americans of all nations at any time upon the earth have probably the fullest poetical nature. The United States themselves are essentially the greatest poem. In the history of the earth hitherto, the largest and most stirring appear tame and orderly to their ampler largeness and stir. Here at last is something in the doings of man that corresponds with the broadcast
15 doings of the day and night. Here is action untied from strings, necessarily blind to particulars and details, magnificently moving in masses. Here is the hospitality which forever indicates heroes. Here the performance, disdaining the trivial, unapproach'd in the tremendous audacity of its crowds and groupings, and the push of its perspective, spreads with crampless and flowing
20 breadth, and showers its prolific and splendid extravagance. One sees it must indeed own the riches of the summer and winter, and need never be bank-

rupt while corn grows from the ground, or the orchards drop apples, or the
bays contain fish, or men beget children upon women.

Other states indicate themselves in their deputies—but the genius of the
United States is not best or most in its executives or legislatures, nor in its
ambassadors or authors, or colleges or churches or parlors, nor even in its   5
newspapers or inventors—but always most in the common people, South,
North, West, East, in all its States, through all its mighty amplitude. The largeness of the nation, however, were monstrous without a corresponding largeness
and generosity of the spirit of the citizen. Not swarming states, nor streets and
steamships, nor prosperous business, nor farms, nor capital, nor learning, may   10
suffice for the ideal of man—nor suffice the poet. No reminiscences may
suffice either. A live nation can always cut a deep mark, and can have the
best authority the cheapest—namely, from its own soul. This is the sum of
the profitable uses of individuals or states, and of present action and grandeur,
and of the subjects of poets. (As if it were necessary to trot back generation   15
after generation to the Eastern records! As if the beauty and sacredness of
the demonstrable must fall behind that of the mythical! As if men do not
make their mark out of any times! As if the opening of the Western Continent
by discovery, and what has transpired in North and South America, were
less than the small theatre of the antique, or the aimless sleep-walking of the   20
Middle Ages!) The pride of the United States leaves the wealth and finesse
of the cities, and all returns of commerce and agriculture, and all the magnitude of geography or shows of exterior victory, to enjoy the sight and realization of full-sized men or one full-sized man unconquerable and simple.

The American poets are to enclose old and new, for America is the race of   25
races. The expression of the American poet is to be transcendent and new.
It is to be indirect, and not direct or descriptive or epic. Its quality goes through
these to much more. Let the age and wars of other nations be chanted, and
their eras and characters be illustrated, and that finish the verse. Not so the
great psalm of the republic. Here the theme is creative and has vista. What-   30
ever stagnates in the flat of custom or obedience or legislation, the great poet
never stagnates. Obedience does not master him, he masters it. High up out
of reach he stands turning a concentrated light—he turns the pivot with his
finger—he baffles the swiftest runners as he stands, and easily overtakes and
envelopes them. The time straying toward infidelity and confections and   35
persiflage he withholds by steady faith. Faith is the antiseptic of the soul—it
pervades the common people and preserves them—they never give up believing and expecting and trusting. There is that indescribable freshness and
unconsciousness about an illiterate person, that humbles and mocks the power
of the noblest expressive genius. The poet sees for a certainty how one not a   40
great artist may be just as sacred as the greatest artist.

The power to destroy or remould is freely used by the greatest poet, but
seldom the power of attack. What is past is past. If he does not expose superior

16. **Eastern records**—Whitman has in mind the movement of civilization out of the East
into America by way of Greece and Rome. 19. **transpired**—happened (colloquial meaning).
21. **finesse**—probably about equivalent to "sophistication" as that word is now current. 35. **confections**—loosely equivalent to trivial artificialities.

models, and prove himself by every step he takes, he is not what is wanted.
The presence of the great poet conquers—not parleying, or struggling, or
any prepared attempts. Now he has passed that way—see after him! There is
not left any vestige of despair, or misanthropy, or cunning, or exclusiveness, or
5 the ignominy of a nativity or color, or delusion of hell or the necessity of hell—
and no man thenceforward shall be degraded for ignorance or weakness or
sin. The greatest poet hardly knows pettiness or triviality. If he breathes into
anything that was before thought small, it dilates with the grandeur and life
of the universe. He is a seer—he is individual—he is complete in himself—the
10 others are as good as he, only he sees it and they do not. He is not one of
the chorus—he does not stop for any regulation—he is the president of regulation. What the eyesight does to the rest, he does to the rest. Who knows the
curious mystery of the eyesight? The other senses corroborate themselves, but
this is removed from any proof but its own, and foreruns the identities of the
15 spiritual world. A single glance of it mocks all the investigations of man,
and all the instruments and books of the earth, and all reasoning. What is
marvellous? what is unlikely? what is impossible or baseless or vague?—
after you have once just open'd the space of a peach-pit, and given audience to
far and near, and to the sunset, and had all things enter with electric swiftness,
20 softly and duly, without confusion or jostling or jam?
     The land and sea, the animals, fishes, and birds, the sky of heaven and the
orbs, the forests, mountains and rivers, are not small themes—but folks expect
of the poet to indicate more than the beauty and dignity which always attach
to dumb real objects—they expect him to indicate the path between reality
25 and their souls. Men and women perceive the beauty well enough—probably
as well as he. The passionate tenacity of hunters, woodmen, early risers, culti-
vators of gardens and orchards and fields, the love of healthy women for the
manly form, sea-faring persons, drivers of horses, the passion for light and
the open air, all is an old varied sign of the unfailing perception of beauty,
30 and of a residence of the poetic in outdoor people. They can never be assisted
by poets to perceive—some may, but they never can. The poetic quality is not
marshal'd in rhyme or uniformity, or abstract addresses to things, nor in
melancholy complaints or good precepts, but is the life of these and much else,
and is in the soul. The profit of rhyme is that it drops seeds of a sweeter and
35 more luxuriant rhyme, and of uniformity that it conveys itself into its own
roots in the ground out of sight. The rhyme and uniformity of perfect poems
show the free growth of metrical laws, and bud from them as unerringly and
loosely as lilacs and roses on a bush, and take shapes as compact as the shapes
of chestnuts and oranges, and melons and pears, and shed the perfume im-
40 palpable to form. The fluency and ornaments of the finest poems or music
or orations or recitations are not independent but dependent. All beauty comes
from beautiful blood and a beautiful brain. If the greatnesses are in conjunction

----

     5. ignominy of a nativity—ignominy attaching to birth in a particular social class. **11.
president**—a favorite word of Whitman's for master, controller. **22. orbs**—stars. Whitman
elsewhere uses the word to mean respectively planet, sun, the earth, eye. **31. some**—that is, some
others. **34. rhyme**—Whitman may mean literally rhyme, but it is at least possible he is using the
word as loosely meaning rhythm, poetical discourse.

in a man or woman, it is enough—the fact will prevail through the universe; but the gaggery and gilt of a million years will not prevail. Who troubles himself about his ornaments or fluency is lost. This is what you shall do: Love the earth and sun and the animals, despise riches, give alms to every one that asks, stand up for the stupid and crazy, devote your income and labor to others,   5 hate tyrants, argue not concerning God, have patience and indulgence toward the people, take off your hat to nothing known or unknown, or to any man or number of men—go freely with powerful uneducated persons, and with the young, and with the mothers of families—re-examine all you have been told in school or church or in any book, and dismiss whatever insults your own soul;   10 and your very flesh shall be a great poem and have the richest fluency, not only in its words, but in the silent lines of its lips and face, and between the lashes of your eyes, and in every motion and joint of your body. The poet shall not spend his time in unneeded work. He shall know that the ground is always ready plough'd and manured; others may not know it, but he shall.   15 He shall go directly to the creation. His trust shall master the trust of everything he touches—and shall master all attachment.

The known universe has one complete lover, and that is the greatest poet. He consumes an eternal passion, and is indifferent which chance happens, and which possible contingency of fortune or misfortune, and persuades daily and   20 hourly his delicious pay. What balks or breaks others is fuel for his burning progress to contact and amorous joy. Other proportions of the reception of pleasure dwindle to nothing to his proportions. All expected from heaven or from the highest, he is rapport with in the sight of the daybreak, or the scenes of the winter woods, or the presence of children playing, or with his arm   25 round the neck of a man or woman. His love above all love has leisure and expanse—he leaves room ahead of himself. He is no irresolute or suspicious lover—he is sure—he scorns intervals. His experience and the showers and thrills are not for nothing. Nothing can jar him—suffering and darkness cannot—death and fear cannot. To him complaint and jealousy and envy are   30 corpses buried and rotten in the earth—he saw them buried. The sea is not surer of the shore, or the shore of the sea, than he is of the fruition of his love, and of all perfection and beauty.

The fruition of beauty is no chance of miss or hit—it is as inevitable as life— it is exact and plumb as gravitation. From the eyesight proceeds another eye-   35 sight, and from the hearing proceeds another hearing, and from the voice proceeds another voice, eternally curious of the harmony of things with man. These understand the law of perfection in masses and floods—that it is profuse and impartial—that there is not a minute of the light or dark, nor an acre of the earth or sea, without it—nor any direction of the sky, nor any trade or em-   40 ployment, nor any turn of events. This is the reason that about the proper expression of beauty there is precision and balance. One part does not need to be

<hr>

2. **gaggery**—probably an independent coinage of Whitman's, though gaggery in the sense of hoaxing is a rare word appearing in early nineteenth-century British periodicals. 17. **master . . . attachment**—that is, the poet sings of the timeless, the absolute, and so surpasses or transcends temporal events. 19. **consumes**—that is, is consumed by. 24. **rapport**—another favorite Whitman word; note the construction he forces upon it. 42. **precision and balance**— in the sense of organic unity rather than "classical" precision and balance.

thrust above another. The best singer is not the one who has the most lithe and powerful organ. The pleasure of poems is not in them that take the handsomest measure and sound.

Without effort and without exposing in the least how it is done, the greatest
5 poet brings the spirit of any or all events and passions and scenes and persons, some more and some less, to bear on your individual character as you hear or read. To do this well is to compete with the laws that pursue and follow Time. What is the purpose must surely be there—and the clue of it must be there—and the faintest indication is the indication of the best, and then becomes the
10 clearest indication. Past and present and future are not disjoin'd but join'd. The greatest poet forms the consistence of what is to be, from what has been and is. He drags the dead out of their coffins and stands them again on their feet. He says to the past, Rise and walk before me that I may realize you. He learns the lesson—he places himself where the future becomes present. The
15 greatest poet does not only dazzle his rays over character and scenes and passions—he finally ascends and finishes all—he exhibits the pinnacles that no man can tell what they are for, or what is beyond—he glows a moment on the extremest verge. He is most wonderful in his last half-hidden smile or frown; by that flash of the moment of parting the one that sees it shall be encouraged
20 or terrified afterwards for many years. The greatest poet does not moralize or make applications of morals—he knows the soul. The soul has that measureless pride which consists in never acknowledging any lessons or deductions but its own. But it has sympathy as measureless as its pride, and the one balances the other, and neither can stretch too far while it stretches in company
25 with the other. The inmost secrets of art sleep with the twain. The greatest poet has lain close betwixt both, and they are vital in his style and thoughts.

The art of art, the glory of expression and the sunshine of the light of letters, is simplicity. Nothing is better than simplicity—nothing can make up for excess, or for the lack of definiteness. To carry on the heave of impulse and pierce
30 intellectual depths and give all subjects their articulations, are powers neither common nor very uncommon. But to speak in literature with the perfect rectitude and insouciance of the movements of animals, and the unimpeachableness of the sentiment of trees in the woods and grass by the roadside, is the flawless triumph of art. If you have look'd on him who has achiev'd it you have
35 look'd on one of the masters of the artists of all nations and times. You shall not contemplate the flight of the gray gull over the bay, or the mettlesome action of the blood horse, or the tall leaning of sunflowers on their stalk, or the appearance of the sun journeying through heaven, or the appearance of the moon afterward, with any more satisfaction than you shall contemplate
40 him. The great poet has less a mark'd style, and is more the channel of thoughts and things without increase or diminution, and is the free channel of himself. He swears to his art, I will not be meddlesome, I will not have in my writing any elegance, or effect, or originality, to hang in the way between me and the rest like curtains. I will have nothing hang in the way, not the

---

15. **dazzle**—does not content himself with dazzling characters, scenes, and passions. 16-17.
pinnacles . . . beyond—The construction is ungrammatical but the sense is clear: pinnacles, the purpose of which no man knows.

richest curtains. What I tell I tell for precisely what it is. Let who may exalt
or startle or fascinate or soothe, I will have purposes as health or heat or snow
has, and be as regardless of observation. What I experience or portray shall go
from my composition without a shred of my composition. You shall stand by
my side and look in the mirror with me.   5

The old red blood and stainless gentility of great poets will be proved by
their unconstraint. A heroic person walks at his ease through and out of that
custom or precedent or authority that suits him not. Of the traits of the brotherhood of first-class writers, savans, musicians, inventors and artists, nothing is
finer than silent defiance advancing from new free forms. In the need of   10
poems, philosophy, politics, mechanism, science, behavior, the craft of art, an
appropriate native grand opera, shipcraft, or any craft, he is greatest for ever
and ever who contributes the greatest original practical example. The cleanest
expression is that which finds no sphere worthy of itself, and makes one.

The messages of great poets to each man and woman are, Come to us on   15
equal terms, only then can you understand us, we are no better than you, what
we inclose you inclose, what we enjoy you may enjoy. Did you suppose there
could be only one Supreme? We affirm there can be unnumber'd Supremes,
and that one does not countervail another any more than one eyesight counter-
vails another—and that men can be good or grand only of the consciousness of   20
their supremacy within them. What do you think is the grandeur of storms
and dismemberments, and the deadliest battles and wrecks, and the wildest
fury of the elements, and the power of the sea, and the motion of Nature, and
the throes of human desires, and dignity and hate and love? It is that something in the soul which says, Rage on, whirl on, I tread master here and every-   25
where—Master of the spasms of the sky and of the shatter of the sea, Master
of nature and passion and death, and of all terror and all pain.

The American bards shall be mark'd for generosity and affection, and for
encouraging competitors. They shall be kosmos, without monopoly or secrecy,
glad to pass anything to any one—hungry for equals night and day. They shall   30
not be careful of riches and privilege—they shall be riches and privilege—
they shall perceive who the most affluent man is. The most affluent man is he
that confronts all the shows he sees by equivalents out of the stronger wealth
of himself. The American bard shall delineate no class of persons, nor one
or two out of the strata of interests, nor love most nor truth most, nor the soul   35
most nor the body most—and not be for the Eastern States more than the
Western, or the Northern States more than the Southern.

Exact science and its practical movements are no checks on the greatest poet,
but always his encouragement and support. The outset and remembrance are
there—there are the arms that lifted him first, and braced him best—there he   40

---

9. savans—more commonly, *savants;* literally, "learned persons," but Whitman uses the word
with his customary generosity of meaning. 12. native grand opera—Listening to grand opera
in New York City was a favorite pastime of Whitman in his earlier years; and it has been suspected that the rhythms of Italian musical arias, as well as their floridity, have had their influence
on Whitman's style. 15. The messages—Note the transcendental quality of this paragraph, and
the following. 29. kosmos—usually, cosmos, but Whitman wishes to call attention to his special
meaning. Cosmos means literally the ordered universe, but Whitman tends to use it as meaning
the sum total of experience. 36-37. Eastern . . . Southern—In 1855 sectionalism was fervid.

returns after all his goings and comings. The sailor and traveler—the anatomist, chemist, astronomer, geologist, phrenologist, spiritualist, mathematician, historian and lexicographer, are not poets, but they are the lawgivers of poets, and their construction underlies the structure of every perfect poem. No matter

5　what rises or is utter'd they sent the seed of the conception of it—of them and by them stand the visible proofs of souls. If there shall be love and content between the father and the son, and if the greatness of the son is the exuding of the greatness of the father, there shall be love between the poet and the man of demonstrable science. In the beauty of poems are henceforth the tuft and

10　final applause of science.

Great is the faith of the flush of knowledge, and of the investigation of the depths of qualities and things. Cleaving and circling here swells the soul of the poet, yet is president of itself always. The depths are fathomless, and therefore calm. The innocence and nakedness are resumed—they are neither modest nor

15　immodest. The whole theory of the supernatural, and all that was twined with it or educed out of it, departs as a dream. What has ever happen'd—what happens, and whatever may or shall happen, the vital laws inclose all. They are sufficient for any case and for all cases—none to be hurried or retarded— any special miracle of affairs or persons inadmissible in the vast clear scheme

20　where every motion and every spear of grass, and the frames and spirits of men and women and all that concerns them, are unspeakably perfect miracles, all referring to all, and each distinct and in its place. It is also not consistent with the reality of the soul to admit that there is anything in the known universe more divine than men and women.

25　Men and women, and the earth and all upon it, are simply to be taken as they are, and the investigation of their past and present and future shall be unintermitted, and shall be done with perfect candor. Upon this basis philosophy speculates, ever looking towards the poet, ever regarding the eternal tendencies of all toward happiness, never inconsistent with what is clear to the

30　senses and to the soul. For the eternal tendencies of all toward happiness make the only point of sane philosophy. Whatever comprehends less than that— whatever is less than the laws of light and of astronomical motion—or less than the laws that follow the thief, the liar, the glutton and the drunkard, through this life and doubtless afterward,—or less than vast stretches of time,

35　or the slow formation of density, or the patient upheaving of strata,—is of no account. Whatever would put God in a poem or system of philosophy as contending against some being or influence, is also of no account. Sanity and ensemble characterise the great master—spoilt in one principle, all is spoilt. The great master has nothing to do with miracles. He sees health for himself

40　in being one of the mass—he sees the hiatus in singular eminence. To the

2. **phrenologist**—In 1855 the phrenologist was still regarded by many (including Whitman) as a reputable scientist. 2. **spiritualist**—The vogue of spiritualism began with the table-rappings of the Fox sisters in Hydesville, New York, in 1848, and the publication of *Principles of Nature* (1847) by Andrew Jackson Davis, the "Poughkeepsie Seer," (see note 16, p. 781) which ran through innumerable editions. In 1855 the critical examination of alleged spiritualistic phenomena had not begun, and the movement was of formidable proportions. 9. **demonstrable science**— laboratory science. 25. **Men and women . . .** —*Cf.* with this paragraph such an essay of Emerson's as that on "Spiritual Laws."

perfect shape comes common ground. To be under the general law is great, for that is to correspond with it. The master knows that he is unspeakably great, and that all are unspeakably great—that nothing, for instance, is greater than to conceive children, and bring them up well—that to *be* is just as great as to perceive or tell.   5

In the make of the great masters the idea of political liberty is indispensable. Liberty takes the adherence of heroes wherever men and women exist—but never takes any adherence or welcome from the rest more than from poets. They are the voice and exposition of liberty. They out of ages are worthy the grand idea—to them it is confided and they must sustain it. Nothing has prece-   10 dence of it and nothing can warp or degrade it. . . .

As the attributes of the poets of the kosmos concentre in the real body, and in the pleasure of things, they possess the superiority of genuineness over all fiction and romance. As they emit themselves, facts are shower'd over with light—the daylight is lit with more volatile light—the deep between the setting   15 and rising sun goes deeper many fold. Each precise object or condition or combination or process exhibits a beauty—the multiplication table its—old age its— the carpenter's trade its—the grand-opera its—the huge-hulled clean-shap'd New York clipper at sea under steam or full sail gleams with unmatch'd beauty—the American circles and large harmonies of government gleam with   20 theirs—and the commonest definite intentions and actions with theirs. The poets of the kosmos advance through all interpositions and coverings and turmoils and stratagems to first principles. They are of use—they dissolve poverty from its need, and riches from its conceit. You large proprietor, they say, shall not realize or perceive more than any one else. The owner of the library is not   25 he who holds a legal title to it, having bought and paid for it. Any one and every one is owner of the library (indeed he or she alone is owner) who can read the same through all the varieties of tongues and subjects and styles, and in whom they enter with ease, and make supple and powerful and rich and large.   30

These American States, strong and healthy and accomplish'd, shall receive no pleasure from violations of natural models, and must not permit them. In paintings or mouldings or carvings in mineral or wood, or in the illustrations of books or newspapers, or in the patterns of woven stuffs, or anything to beautify rooms or furniture or costumes, or to put upon cornices or monu-   35 ments, or on the prows or sterns of ships, or to put anywhere before the human eye indoors or out, that which distorts honest shapes, or which creates unearthly beings or places or contingencies, is a nuisance and revolt. Of the human form especially, it is so great it must never be made ridiculous. Of ornaments to a work nothing outré can be allow'd—but those ornaments can be   40 allow'd that conform to the perfect facts of the open air, and that flow out of the nature of the work, and come irrepressibly from it, and are necessary to the completion of the work. Most works are most beautiful without orna-

---

11. degrade it—Here follows in the original form of the preface a long, rhapsodic passage describing the poet as the guardian of liberty and humanity. 19. steam—When the preface was originally written, steamships still commonly used sails as an aid. 33. mouldings—in the sense of casts. 33. mineral—Stone is technically mineral substance, though there seems to be no good reason for Whitman's insistence upon the fact.

ment. Exaggerations will be revenged in human physiology. Clean and vigorous children are jetted and conceiv'd only in those communities where the models of natural forms are public every day. Great genius and the people of these States must never be demean'd to romances. As soon as histories are
5 properly told, no more need of romances.

The great poets are also to be known by the absence in them of tricks, and by the justification of perfect personal candor. All faults may be forgiven of him who has perfect candor. Henceforth let no man of us lie, for we have seen that openness wins the inner and outer world, and that there is no single
10 exception, and that never since our earth gather'd itself in a mass have deceit or subterfuge or prevarication attracted its smallest particle or the faintest tinge of a shade—and that through the enveloping wealth and rank of a state, or the whole republic of States, a sneak or sly person shall be discover'd and despised—and that the soul has never been once fool'd and never can be fool'd—
15 and thrift without the loving nod of the soul is only a foetid puff—and there never grew up in any of the continents of the globe, nor upon any planet or satellite, nor in that condition which precedes the birth of babes, nor in any time during the changes of life, nor in any stretch of abeyance or action of vitality, nor in any process of formation or reformation anywhere, a being whose instinct
20 hated the truth.

Extreme caution or prudence, the soundest organic health, large hope and comparison and fondness for women and children, large alimentiveness and destructiveness and causality, with a perfect sense of the oneness of nature, and the propriety of the same spirit applied to human affairs, are called up of
25 the float of the brain of the world to be parts of the greatest poet from his birth out of his mother's womb, and from her birth out of her mother's. Caution seldom goes far enough. It has been thought that the prudent citizen was the citizen who applied himself to solid gains, and did well for himself and his family, and completed a lawful life without debt or crime. The greatest
30 poet sees and admits these economies as he sees the economies of food and sleep, but has higher notions of prudence than to think he gives much when he gives a few slight attentions at the latch of the gate. The premises of the prudence of life are not the hospitality of it, or the ripeness and harvest of it. Beyond the independence of a little sum laid aside for burial-money, and of
35 a few clapboards around and shingles overhead on a lot of American soil own'd, and the easy dollars that supply the year's plain clothing and meals, the melancholy prudence of the abandonment of such a great being as a man is to the toss and pallor of years of money-making with all their scorching days and icy nights, and all their stifling deceits and underhanded dodgings, or
40 infinitesimals of parlors, or shameless stuffing while others starve, and all the loss of the bloom and odor of the earth, and of the flowers and atmosphere, and of the sea, and of the true taste of the women and men you pass or have to do with in youth or middle age, and the issuing sickness and desperate revolt at the close of a life without elevation or naïveté, (even if you have

---

22. alimentiveness—Alimentiveness, like the following **destructiveness**, is part of the jargon of phrenology. **26. Caution . . .** —*Cf.* with the following passage Emerson's essay "Prudence."

achiev'd a secure 10,000 a year, or election to Congress or the Governorship,) and the ghastly chatter of a death without serenity or majesty, is the great fraud upon modern civilization and forethought, blotching the surface and system which civilization undeniably drafts, and moistening with tears the immense features it spreads and spreads with such velocity before the reach'd 5 kisses of the soul.

Ever the right explanation remains to be made about prudence. The prudence of the mere wealth and respectability of the most esteem'd life appears too faint for the eye to observe at all, when little and large alike drop quietly aside at the thought of the prudence suitable for immortality. What is the 10 wisdom that fills the thinness of a year, or seventy or eighty years—to the wisdom spaced out by ages, and coming back at a certain time with strong reinforcements and rich presents, and the clear faces of wedding-guests as far as you can look in every direction running gaily toward you? Only the soul is of itself—all else has reference to what ensues. All that a person does or thinks 15 is of consequence. Nor can the push of charity or personal force ever be anything else than the profoundest reason, whether it brings arguments to hand or no. No specification is necessary—to add or subtract or divide is in vain. Little or big, learn'd or unlearn'd, white or black, legal or illegal, sick or well, from the first inspiration down the windpipe to the last expiration out of it, 20 all that a male or female does that is vigorous and benevolent and clean is so much sure profit to him or her in the unshakable order of the universe, and through the whole scope of it forever. The prudence of the greatest poet answers at last the craving and glut of the soul, puts off nothing, permits no let-up for its own case or any case, has no particular sabbath or judgment day, 25 divides not the living from the dead or the righteous from the unrighteous, is satisfied with the present, matches every thought or act by its correlative, and knows no possible forgiveness or deputed atonement.

The direct trial of him who would be the greatest poet is to-day. If he does not flood himself with the immediate age as with vast oceanic tides—if he be 30 not himself the age transfigur'd, and if to him is not open'd the eternity which gives similitude to all periods and locations and processes, and animate and inanimate forms, and which is the bond of time, and rises up from its inconceivable vagueness and infiniteness in the swimming shapes of to-day, and is held by the ductile anchors of life, and makes the present spot the passage from 35 what was to what shall be, and commits itself to the representation of this wave of an hour, and this one of the sixty beautiful children of the wave—let him merge in the general run and wait his development.

Still the final test of poems, or any character or work, remains. The prescient poet projects himself centuries ahead, and judges performer or performance 40 after the changes of time. Does it live through them? Does it still hold on untired? Will the same style, and the direction of genius to similar points, be satisfactory now? Have the marches of tens and hundreds and thousands of years made willing détours to the right hand and the left hand for his sake?

20. **inspiration down the windpipe**—medical practice with newborn babies, to get them to breathe; but Whitman may mean simply, drawing one's first breath. 24. **glut**—desire(?); that is, wish to be glutted.

Is he beloved long and long after he is buried? Does the young man think often of him? and the young woman think often of him? and do the middle-aged and the old think of him?

5 A great poem is for ages and ages in common, and for all degrees and complexions, and all departments and sects, and for a woman as much as a man, and a man as much as a woman. A great poem is no finish to a man or woman, but rather a beginning. Has any one fancied he could sit at last under some due authority, and rest satisfied with explanations, and realize and be content and full? To no such terminus does the greatest poet bring—he brings neither 10 cessation nor shelter'd fatness and ease. The touch of him, like Nature, tells in action. Whom he takes with firm sure grasp into live regions previously un-attain'd—thenceforward is no rest—they see the space and ineffable sheen that turn the old spots and lights into dead vacuums. Now there shall be a man cohered out of tumult and chaos—the elder encourages the younger and shows 15 him how—they two shall launch off fearlessly together till the new world fits an orbit for itself and looks unabash'd on the lesser orbits of the stars, and sweeps through the ceaseless rings, and shall never be quiet again.

There will soon be no more priests. Their work is done. A new order shall arise, and they shall be the priests of man, and every man shall be his own 20 priest. They shall find their inspiration in real objects to-day, symptoms of the past and future. They shall not deign to defend immortality or God, or the perfection of things, or liberty, or the exquisite beauty and reality of the soul. They shall arise in America, and be responded to from the remainder of the earth.

25 The English language befriends the grand American expression—it is brawny enough, and limber and full enough. On the tough stock of a race who through all change of circumstances was never without the idea of political liberty, which is the animus of all liberty, it has attracted the terms of daintier and gayer and subtler and more elegant tongues. It is the powerful language of 30 resistance—it is the dialect of common sense. It is the speech of the proud and melancholy races, and of all who aspire. It is the chosen tongue to express growth, faith, self-esteem, freedom, justice, equality, friendliness, amplitude, prudence, decision, and courage. It is the medium that shall well-nigh express the inexpressible.

35 No great literature, nor any like style of behavior or oratory, or social intercourse or household arrangements, or public institutions, or the treatment by bosses of employ'd people, nor executive detail, or detail of the army or navy, nor spirit of legislation or courts, or police or tuition or architecture, or songs or amusements, can long elude the jealous and passionate instinct of American 40 standards. Whether or no the sign appears from the mouths of the people, it throbs a live interrogation in every freeman's and freewoman's heart, after that which passes by, or this built to remain. Is it uniform with my country? Are its disposals without ignominious distinctions? Is it for the ever-growing communes of brothers and lovers, large, well-united, proud, beyond the old models, 45 generous beyond all models? Is it something grown fresh out of the fields, or drawn from the sea for use to me to-day here? I know that what answers for

---

14. cohered—made to cohere. 26. who—which. 28. terms—words.

me, an American, in Texas, Ohio, Canada, must answer for any individual or nation that serves for a part of my materials. Does this answer? Is it for the nursing of the young of the republic? Does it solve readily with the sweet milk of the nipples of the breasts of the Mother of Many Children?

America prepares with composure and good-will for the visitors that have 5
sent word. It is not intellect that is to be their warrant and welcome. The talented, the artist, the ingenious, the editor, the statesman, the erudite, are not unappreciated—they fall in their place and do their work. The soul of the nation also does its work. It rejects none, it permits all. Only toward the like of itself will it advance half-way. An individual is as superb as a nation when 10
he has the qualities which make a superb nation. The soul of the largest and wealthiest and proudest nation may well go half-way to meet that of its poets.

ONE'S-SELF I SING

The growth of *Leaves of Grass* from a pamphlet containing a rhapsodic prose preface and a poem of a little more than eighty pages, loosely divided into twelve sections, to the final form of the work, which, in the Camden edition, occupies two volumes and a part of the third (655 pages in all), is among the prodigies of American poetry. As is evident, Whitman was perpetually revising, adding, canceling, turning prose into poetry, lifting passages out of one poem and putting them into another, shifting titles, and the like, so that a genetic study of *Leaves of Grass* is a highly complicated problem. Part of the confusion arises from the changing significance of the title in Whitman's mind. It was originally the name of a book, but the phrase meant at various times to him the title of a book, the name of a long poem, a name for a particular species of long poems, and a symbolic title for all his poetic output. The present selections follow the order of the Camden edition, with which the text has been collated. This edition has been chosen not because the text is entirely satisfactory, but because it at least represents a norm generally agreed upon.

"One's-Self I Sing" first appeared in the 1867 edition of *Leaves of Grass* as "Inscription," the first poem in a section entitled "Inscriptions." The present form of the text dates from 1871, and the poem is kept consistently as the opening poem of *Leaves of Grass* thereafter.

One's-self I sing, a simple separate person,
Yet utter the word Democratic, the word En-Masse.

Of physiology from top to toe I sing,
Not physiognomy alone nor brain alone is worthy for the Muse, I say the Form
   complete is worthier far,
The Female equally with the Male I sing.   5

Of Life immense in passion, pulse, and power,
Cheerful, for freest action form'd under the laws divine,
The Modern Man I sing.

4. **Many Children**—A short passage, omitted by Whitman in his revision, contains the significant sentence: "The poems distilled from other poems will probably pass away." **12. poets** —In the original form of the preface the last sentence reads: "The proof of a poet is that his country absorbs him as affectionately as he has absorbed it," but Whitman did not allow the sentence to stand.

ME IMPERTURBE

This poem was originally number 18 of the "Chants Democratic" section of the 1860 *Leaves*. In 1867 it became independent of any section. In 1871 it formed one of the various groups entitled "Leaves of Grass," and so remained in 1876. In 1881 it was transferred to the "Inscriptions" section. "Imperturbe" is, of course, a coinage from imperturbable.

Me imperturbe, standing at ease in Nature,
Master of all, or mistress of all, aplomb in the midst of irrational things,
Imbued as they, passive, receptive, silent as they,
Finding my occupation, poverty, notoriety, foibles, crimes, less important than I
    thought,
Me toward the Mexican sea, or in the Mannahatta or the Tennessee, or far north or
    inland,   5
A river man, or a man of the woods or of any farm-life of these States, or of the
    coast, or the lakes, or Kanada,
Me wherever my life is lived, O to be self-balanced for contingencies,
O to confront night, storms, hunger, ridicule, accidents, rebuffs, as the trees and
    animals do.

I HEAR AMERICA SINGING

This poem first appears as number 20 of the "Chants Democratic" section of the 1860 edition of *Leaves of Grass*. The first line then read: "American mouth-songs!" Its present form dates from 1867. In 1881 it was made part of the "Inscriptions" section.

I hear America singing, the varied carols I hear,
Those of mechanics, each one singing his as it should be blithe and strong,
The carpenter singing his as he measures his plank or beam,
The mason singing his as he makes ready for work, or leaves off work,
The boatman singing what belongs to him in his boat, the deck-hand singing on the
    steamboat deck,   5
The shoemaker singing as he sits on his bench, the hatter singing as he stands,
The wood-cutter's song, the ploughboy's on his way in the morning, or at noon
    intermission or at sundown,
The delicious singing of the mother, or of the young wife at work, or of the girl
    sewing or washing,
Each singing what belongs to him or her and to none else,
The day what belongs to the day—at night the party of young fellows, robust,
    friendly,   10
Singing with open mouths their strong melodious songs.

    5. **Mexican sea**—the Gulf of Mexico. 5. **Tennessee**—the Tennessee River.

SONG OF MYSELF

This poem may be regarded as the central poem of *Leaves of Grass,* in so far as any poem deserves that place. It forms the introductory section of the 1855 edition, without title and without section divisions. In 1856 it became "Poem of Walt Whitman, an American." In 1860 it became "Walt Whitman," and the verse paragraphs were numbered consecutively. In 1867 it retained this title and the numbering of the verse paragraphs, but it was also divided into numbered sections. In 1881 this became "Song of Myself," the verse paragraph numbers were dropped, and the section numbers were retained. There are, of course, innumerable textual variations.

1

I celebrate myself, and sing myself,
And what I assume you shall assume,
For every atom belonging to me as good belongs to you.

I loafe and invite my soul,
I lean and loafe at my ease observing a spear of summer grass.   5

My tongue, every atom of my blood, form'd from this soil, this air,
Born here of parents born here from parents the same, and their parents the same,
I, now thirty-seven years old in perfect health begin,
Hoping to cease not till death.

Creeds and schools in abeyance,   10
Retiring back a while sufficed at what they are, but never forgotten,
I harbor for good or bad, I permit to speak at every hazard,
Nature without check with original energy. . . .

[Sections 2-5 dwell upon the interpenetration of Whitman's soul with the phenomena of the universe; his refusal to be swallowed up in the flood of merely temporal things; and the deep peace which comes to him as he realizes the fundamental significance of the relation between his deeper self and the universe.]

6

A child said *What is the grass?* fetching it to me with full hands;
How could I answer the child? I do not know what it is any more than he.   15

I guess it must be the flag of my disposition, out of hopeful green stuff woven.

Or I guess it is the handkerchief of the Lord,
A scented gift and remembrancer designedly dropt,
Bearing the owner's name someway in the corners, that we may see and remark, and
    say *Whose?*

Or I guess the grass is itself a child, the produced babe of the vegetation.   20

Or I guess it is a uniform hieroglyphic,
And it means, Sprouting alike in broad zones and narrow zones,

10-11. **Creeds . . . forgotten**—The looseness of Whitman's syntax is sometimes annoying. The general sense seems to be: Creeds and schools, which no longer suffice me, were yet at one time sufficient, considering what they are. To get the meaning, insert line 13 after "I permit."
18. **remembrancer**—souvenir.

Growing among black folks as among white,
Kanuck, Tuckahoe, Congressman, Cuff, I give them the same, I receive them the
    same.

And now it seems to me the beautiful uncut hair of graves.   25

Tenderly will I use you curling grass,
It may be you transpire from the breasts of young men,
It may be if I had known them I would have loved them,
It may be you are from old people, or from offspring taken soon out of their mothers'
    laps,
And here you are the mothers' laps.   30

This grass is very dark to be from the white heads of old mothers,
Darker than the colorless beards of old men,
Dark to come from under the faint red roofs of mouths.

O I perceive after all so many uttering tongues,
And I perceive they do not come from the roofs of mouths for nothing.   35

I wish I could translate the hints about the dead young men and women,
And the hints about old men and mothers, and the offspring taken soon out of their
    laps.

What do you think has become of the young and old men?
And what do you think has become of the women and children?

They are alive and well somewhere,
The smallest sprout shows there is really no death,   40
And if ever there was it led forward life, and does not wait at the end to arrest it,
And ceas'd the moment life appear'd.

All goes onward and outward, nothing collapses,
And to die is different from what any one supposed, and luckier. . . .   45

[Sections 7-16 dwell upon the poet's mystical union with all things, Sections 8-16 in particular being a long catalogue of varieties of human and animal life which Whitman, in this
sense, interpenetrates.]

17

These are really the thoughts of all men in all ages and lands, they are not original
    with me,
If they are not yours as much as mine they are nothing, or next to nothing,
If they are not the riddle and the untying of the riddle they are nothing,
If they are not just as close as they are distant they are nothing.

This is the grass that grows wherever the land is and the water is,
This the common air that bathes the globe.   50

24. **Kanuck**—colloquial term for French Canadian. 24. **Tuckahoe**—colloquial term for a
Virginian living east of the mountains; a tidewater Virginian. 24. **Cuff**—Cuffey, colloquial term
for Negro. 27. **transpire**—in the literal Latin sense of piercing through (and upward). 46.
These—The general link between this section and the preceding is the thought that, like the grass
in widest commonalty spread, so the soul of the poet is everywhere at one with nature and men.

18

With music strong I come, with my cornets and my drums,
I play not marches for accepted victors only, I play marches for conquer'd and slain
    persons.

Have you heard that it was good to gain the day?
I also say it is good to fall, battles are lost in the same spirit in which they are
    won.   55

I beat and pound for the dead,
I blow through my embouchures my loudest and gayest for them.

Vivas to those who have fail'd!
And to those whose war-vessels sank in the sea!
And to those themselves who sank in the sea!   60
And to all generals that lost engagements, and all overcome heroes!
And the numberless unknown heroes equal to the greatest heroes known! . . .

[Section 19 is a mystical invitation to all persons to share the poet's sense of union.]

20

Who goes there? hankering, gross, mystical nude;
How is it I extract strength from the beef I eat?

What is a man anyhow? what am I? what are you?   65

All I mark as my own you shall offset it with your own,
Else it were time lost listening to me.

I do not snivel that snivel the world over,
The months are vacuums and the ground but wallow and filth.

Whimpering and truckling fold with powders for invalids, conformity goes to the
    fourth remov'd,   70
I wear my hat as I please indoors or out.

Why should I pray? why should I venerate and be ceremonious?

Having pried through the strata, analyzed to a hair, counsel'd with doctors and
    calculated close,
I find no sweeter fat than sticks to my own bones.

In all people I see myself, none more and not one a barley-corn less,   75
And the good or bad I say of myself I say of them.

I know I am solid and sound,
To me the converging objects of the universe perpetually flow,
All are written to me, and I must get what the writing means.

57. embouchures—The embouchure is that part of a musical instrument applied to the
mouth.

I know I am deathless,   80
I know this orbit of mine cannot be swept by a carpenter's compass,
I know I shall not pass like a child's carlacue cut with a burnt stick at night.

I know I am august,
I do not trouble my spirit to vindicate itself or be understood,
I see that the elementary laws never apologize,   85
(I reckon I behave no prouder than the level I plant my house by, after all.)

I exist as I am, that is enough,
If no other in the world be aware I sit content,
And if each and all be aware I sit content.

One world is aware and by far the largest to me, and that is myself,   90
And whether I come to my own to-day or in ten thousand or ten million years,
I can cheerfully take it now, or with equal cheerfulness I can wait.

My foothold is tenon'd and mortis'd in granite,
I laugh at what you call dissolution,
And I know the amplitude of time.   95

21

I am the poet of the Body and I am the poet of the Soul,
The pleasures of heaven are with me and the pains of hell are with me,
The first I graft and increase upon myself, the latter I translate into a new
    tongue.

I am the poet of the woman the same as the man,
And I say it is as great to be a woman as to be a man,   100
And I say there is nothing greater than the mother of men.

I chant the chant of dilation or pride,
We have had ducking and deprecating about enough,
I show that size is only development.

Have you outstript the rest? are you the President?   105
It is a trifle, they will more than arrive there every one, and still pass on.

I am he that walks with the tender and growing night,
I call to the earth and sea half-held by the night.

Press close bare-bosom'd night—press close magnetic nourishing night!
Night of south winds—night of the large few stars!   110
Still nodding night—mad naked summer night.

Smile O voluptuous cool-breath'd earth!
Earth of the slumbering and liquid trees!
Earth of departed sunset—earth of the mountains misty-topt!
Earth of the vitreous pour of the full moon just tinged with blue!   115

82. carlacue—more commonly, curleycue. 86. level—carpenter's spirit level. 115. vitreous
—glassy, glasslike.

Earth of shine and dark mottling the tide of the river!
Earth of the limpid gray of clouds brighter and clearer for my sake!
Far-swooping elbow'd earth—rich apple-blossom'd earth!
Smile, for your lover comes.

Prodigal, you have given me love—therefore I to you give love!   120
O unspeakable passionate love. . . .

[Sections 22-29 are a symphonic development of the mood and thought of the preceding
sections, urging faith in the universe and its goodness, declaring that positive science is but a
form of this faith, and that all parts of the body, all forms of life, are equally significant to the
true spiritual democrat. Section 26 interprets all song as part of a universal song; Sections 27-29
interpret the union of the poet with people and things under various physical symbols.]

30

All truths wait in all things,
They neither hasten their own delivery nor resist it,
They do not need the obstetric forceps of the surgeon,
The insignificant is as big to me as any,   125
(What is less or more than a touch?)

Logic and sermons never convince,
The damp of the night drives deeper into my soul.

(Only what proves itself to every man and woman is so,
Only what nobody denies is so.)   130

A minute and a drop of me settle my brain,
I believe the soggy clods shall become lovers and lamps,
And a compend of compends is the meat of a man or woman,
And a summit and flower there is the feeling they have for each other,
And they are to branch boundlessly out of that lesson until it becomes omnific,   135
And until one and all shall delight us, and we them.

31

I believe a leaf of grass is no less than the journey-work of the stars,
And the pismire is equally perfect, and a grain of sand and the egg of the wren,
And the tree-toad is a chef d'œuvre for the highest,
And the running blackberry would adorn the parlors of heaven,   140
And the narrowest hinge in my hand puts to scorn all machinery,
And the cow crunching with depress'd head surpasses any statue,
And a mouse is miracle enough to stagger sextillions of infidels.

I find I incorporate gneiss, coal, long-threaded moss, fruits, grains, esculent roots,
And am stucco'd with quadrupeds and birds all over,   145
And have distanced what is behind me for good reasons,
But call any thing back again when I desire it.

In vain the speeding or shyness,
In vain the plutonic rocks send their old heat against my approach,

133. **compend**—Whitmanesque for compendium. 137. **journey-work**—daily work, as of
a journeyman worker. 139. **chef d'œuvre**—French phrase for masterpiece. 140. **running
blackberry**—The blackberry sends out runners in the ground. 144. **gneiss**—a metamorphic
rock. 144. **esculent**—edible. 149. **plutonic rocks**—igneous rocks. In the first half of the century geologists tended to divide into the Neptunists, or those who accounted for geologic change by
water, and the Plutonists, or those who attributed change to fire.

In vain the mastodon retreats beneath his own powder'd bones,   150
In vain objects stand leagues off and assume manifold shapes,
In vain the ocean settling in hollows and the great monsters lying low,
In vain the buzzard houses herself with the sky,
In vain the snake slides through the creepers and logs,
In vain the elk takes to the inner passes of the woods,   155
In vain the razor-bill'd auk sails far north to Labrador,
I follow quickly, I ascend to the nest in the fissure of the cliff.

32

I think I could turn and live with animals, they're so placid and self-contain'd,
I stand and look at them long and long.

They do not sweat and whine about their condition,   160
They do not lie awake in the dark and weep for their sins,
They do not make me sick discussing their duty to God,
Not one is dissatisfied, not one is demented with the mania of owning things,
Not one kneels to another, nor to his kind that lived thousands of years ago,
Not one is respectable or unhappy over the whole earth.   165

So they show their relations to me and I accept them,
They bring me tokens of myself, they evince them plainly in their possession.

I wonder where they get those tokens,
Did I pass that way huge times ago and negligently drop them?

Myself moving forward then and now and forever,   170
Gathering and showing more always and with velocity,
Infinite and omnigenous, and the like of these among them,
Not too exclusive toward the reachers of my remembrancers,
Picking out here one that I love, and now go with him on brotherly terms.

A gigantic beauty of a stallion, fresh and responsive to my caresses,   175
Head high in the forehead, wide between the ears,
Limbs glossy and supple, tail dusting the ground,
Eyes full of sparkling wickedness, ears finely cut, flexibly moving.

His nostrils dilate as my heels embrace him,
His well-built limbs tremble with pleasure as we race around and return.   180
I but use you a minute, then I resign you, stallion,
Why do I need your paces when I myself out-gallop them?
Even as I stand or sit passing faster than you. . . .

[Sections 33-43 are mainly a huge catalogue of past and present things and events with
which the poet in turn identifies himself. Section 43 in particular presents Whitman's faith as
embracing all religious faiths. Section 44 (given in the text) is a kind of summing up of the
material developed in Sections 21-43.]

156. razor-bill'd auk—one of the three varieties of auk. The report of Kane's expedition
to the Arctic was published in 1856; Whitman may have picked up this information about the
auk from reports in the newspapers. **172. omnigenous**—Literally, of all kinds; that is, the poet
is mystically part of all the genera and species of animals. **173. remembrancers**—here seems
to refer to the animals themselves as causing the poet to remember.

44

It is time to explain myself—let us stand up.

What is known I strip away, 185
I launch all men and women forward with me into the Unknown.

The clock indicates the moment—but what does eternity indicate?

We have thus far exhausted trillions of winters and summers,
There are trillions ahead, and trillions ahead of them.

Births have brought us richness and variety, 190
And other births will bring us richness and variety.

I do not call one greater and one smaller,
That which fills its period and place is equal to any.

Were mankind murderous or jealous upon you, my brother, my sister?
I am sorry for you, they are not murderous or jealous upon me, 195
All has been gentle with me, I keep no account with lamentation,
(What have I to do with lamentation?)

(I am an acme of things accomplish'd, and I an encloser of things to be.)

My feet strike an apex of the apices of the stairs,
On every step bunches of ages, and larger bunches between the steps, 200
All below duly travel'd, and still I mount and mount.

Rise after rise bow the phantoms behind me,
Afar down I see the huge first Nothing, I know I was even there,
I waited unseen and always, and slept through the lethargic mist,
And took my time, and took no hurt from the fetid carbon. 205

Long I was hugg'd close—long and long.

Immense have been the preparations for me,
Faithful and friendly the arms that have help'd me.

Cycles ferried my cradle, rowing and rowing like cheerful boatmen,
For room to me stars kept aside in their own rings, 210
They sent influences to look after what was to hold me.

Before I was born out of my mother generations guided me,
My embryo has never been torpid, nothing could overlay it.

For it the nebula cohered to an orb,
The long slow strata piled to rest it on, 215
Vast vegetables gave it sustenance,
Monstrous sauroids transported it in their mouths and deposited it with care.

205. fetid carbon—reference to the theory that the earth was originally shrouded in carbonic gas (the **lethargic mist** of line 204). **217. sauroids**—Whitman has huge, prehistoric lizards in mind.

All forces have been steadily employ'd to complete and delight me,
Now on this spot I stand with my robust soul. . . .

[The omitted Section 45 is mainly a restatement of the poet's identity with the evolving universe, the first line of this section being a summation of its thought.]

46

I know I have the best of time and space, and was never measured and never will be
    measured.   220

I tramp a perpetual journey, (come listen all!)
My signs are a rain-proof coat, good shoes, and a staff cut from the woods,
No friend of mine takes his ease in my chair,
I have no chair, no church, no philosophy,
I lead no man to a dinner-table, library, exchange,   225
But each man and each woman of you I lead upon a knoll,
My left hand hooking you round the waist,
My right hand pointing to landscapes of continents and the public road.

Not I, not any one else can travel that road for you,
You must travel it for yourself.   230

It is not far, it is within reach,
Perhaps you have been on it since you were born and did not know
Perhaps it is everywhere on water and on land.

Shoulder your duds dear son, and I will mine, and let us hasten forth,
Wonderful cities and free nations we shall fetch as we go.   235

If you tire, give me both burdens, and rest the chuff of your hand on my hip,
And in due time you shall repay the same service to me,
For after we start we never lie by again.

This day before dawn I ascended a hill and look'd at the crowded heaven,
And I said to my spirit *When we become the enfolders of those orbs, and the*
    pleasure and knowledge of every thing in them, shall we be fill'd and satisfied
    then?   240
And my spirit said *No, we but level that lift to pass and continue beyond.*

You are also asking me questions and I hear you,
I answer that I cannot answer, you must find out for yourself.

Sit a while dear son,
Here are biscuits to eat and here is milk to drink,   245
But as soon as you sleep and renew yourself in sweet clothes, I kiss you with a good-
    by kiss and open the gate for your egress hence.

Long enough have you dream'd contemptible dreams,
Now I wash the gum from your eyes,
You must habit yourself to the dazzle of the light and of every moment of your life.

234. **duds**—one's "belongings"; it is characteristic of Whitman's rhetorical punctuation to omit the comma after duds. 236. **chuff**—Whitman apparently refers to the plump part of the hand underneath the thumb. 241. **lift**—in the sense of height.

Long have you timidly waded holding a plank by the shore,   250
Now I will you to be a bold swimmer,
To jump off in the midst of the sea, rise again, not to me, shout, and laughingly
    dash with your hair. . . .

[Section 47 states the poet's companionship with athletic and outdoor persons.]

48

I have said that the soul is not more than the body,
And I have said that the body is not more than the soul,
And nothing, not God, is greater to one than one's self is,   255
And whoever walks a furlong without sympathy walks to his own funeral drest in
    his shroud,
And I or you pocketless of a dime may purchase the pick of the earth,
And to glance with an eye or show a bean in its pod confounds the learning of all
    times,
And there is no trade or employment but the young man following it may become
    a hero,
And there is no object so soft but it makes a hub for the wheel'd universe,   260
And I say to any man or woman, Let your soul stand cool and composed before a
    million universes.

And I say to mankind, Be not curious about God,
For I who am curious about each am not curious about God,
(No array of terms can say how much I am at peace about God and about death.)

I hear and behold God in every object, yet understand God not in the least.   265
Nor do I understand who there can be more wonderful than myself.

Why should I wish to see God better than this day?
I see something of God each hour of the twenty-four, and each moment then,
In the faces of men and women I see God, and in my own face in the glass,
I find letters from God dropt in the street, and every one is sign'd by God's name, 270
And I leave them where they are, for I know that wheresoe'er I go,
Others will punctually come for ever and ever. . . .

[Section 50 is a brief section, in which the eternity of the universe is found to be happiness.]

51

The past and present wilt—I have fill'd them, emptied them,
And proceed to fill my next fold of the future.

Listener up there! what have you to confide to me?   275
Look in my face while I snuff the sidle of evening,
(Talk honestly, no one else hears you, and I stay only a minute longer.)

Do I contradict myself?
Very well then I contradict myself,
(I am large, I contain multitudes.)   280

I concentrate toward them that are nigh, I wait on the door-slab.

276. sidle—Whitman's image is of the slow, secret drift of evening into night.

Who has done his day's work? who will soonest be through with his supper?
Who wishes to walk with me?

Will you speak before I am gone? will you prove already too late?

52

The spotted hawk swoops by and accuses me, he complains of my gab and my
    loitering.   285

I too am not a bit tamed, I too am untranslatable,
I sound my barbaric yawp over the roofs of the world.

The last scud of day holds back for me,
It flings my likeness after the rest and true as any on the shadow'd wilds,
It coaxes me to the vapor and the dusk.   290

I depart as air, I shake my white locks at the runaway sun,
I effuse my flesh in eddies, and drift it in lacy jags.

I bequeath myself to the dirt to grow from the grass I love,
If you want me again look for me under your boot-soles.

You will hardly know who I am or what I mean,   295
But I shall be good health to you nevertheless,
And filter and fibre your blood.

Failing to fetch me at first keep encouraged,
Missing me one place search another,
I stop somewhere waiting for you.   300

OUT OF THE ROLLING OCEAN THE CROWD

This poem was originally part of the *Drum-Taps* pamphlet, and as such was
united to the 1867 *Leaves.* In 1871 it was made part of "Children of Adam," where
it consistently remained. At one time it was divided into two numbered sections.

Out of the rolling ocean the crowd came a drop gently to me,
Whispering, *I love you, before long I die,*
I have travel'd a long way, merely to look on you to touch you,
For I could not die till I once look'd on you,
For I fear'd I might afterward lose you.   5

Now we have met, we have look'd, we are safe,
Return in peace to the ocean my love,
I too am part of that great ocean, my love, we are not so much separated,
Behold the great rondure, the cohesion of all, how perfect!
But as for me, for you, the irresistible sea is to separate us,   10
As for an hour, carrying us diverse, yet cannot carry us diverse forever;
Be not impatient—a little space—know you I salute the air, the ocean and the land,
Every day at sundown for your dear sake my love.

288. scud—Scud refers literally to a hurried movement, as of clouds.

NATIVE MOMENTS

This poem was originally number eight of the "Enfans d'Adam" section in 1860. In 1867 this section became "Children of Adam," and the poem remained consistently in this group ever after.

Native moments—when you come upon me—ah you are here now,
Give me now libidinous joys only,
Give me the drench of my passions, give me life coarse and rank,
To-day I go consort with Nature's darlings, to-night too,
I am for those who believe in loose delights, I share the midnight orgies of young
    men,   5
I dance with the dancers, and drink with the drinkers,
The echoes ring with our indecent calls, I pick out some low person for my dearest
    friend,
He shall be lawless, rude, illiterate, he shall be one condemn'd by others for deeds
    done,
I will play a part no longer, why should I exile myself from my companions?
O you shunn'd persons, I at least do not shun you,   10
I come forthwith in your midst, I will be your poet,
I will be more to you than to any of the rest.

THE BASE OF ALL METAPHYSICS

This poem was first included in 1871 in the "Calamus" section of the *Leaves,* when it was divided into numbered verse paragraphs. Its present form dates from 1881.

And now, gentlemen,
A word I give to remain in your memories and minds,
As base, and finalè too for all metaphysics.

(So to the students the old professor,
At the close of the crowded course.)   5

Having studied the new and antique, the Greek and Germanic systems,
Kant having studied and stated, Fichte and Schelling and Hegel,
Stated the lore of Plato, and Socrates, greater than Plato,
And greater than Socrates sought and stated, Christ divine having studied long,
I see reminiscent to-day those Greek and Germanic systems,   10
See the philosophies all, Christian churches and tenets see
Yet underneath Socrates clearly see, and underneath Christ the divine I see,

6. **Germanic**—When this poem was first printed, Germany was regarded as peculiarly the home of metaphysical thinking. 7. **Kant**—Immanuel Kant (1724-1804), the founder of the transcendental metaphysical theory. 7. **Fichte, Schelling and Hegel**—Johann Gottlieb Fichte (1762-1814) and Friedrich Wilhelm Joseph von Schelling (1775-1854) taught systems of transcendental philosophy derived from Kant; Georg Wilhelm Friedrich Hegel (1770-1831), usually regarded as more "realistic," taught a system partly derived from Kant and partly opposed to him.

The dear love of man for his comrades, the attraction of friend to friend,
Of the well-married husband and wife, of children and parents,
Of city for city, and land for land.   **15**

I SAW IN LOUISIANA A LIVE-OAK GROWING

This poem was originally number 20 of the "Calamus" section in 1860. In 1867 it was given its present title. It remained consistently in the "Calamus" section of the *Leaves*.

I saw in Louisiana a live-oak growing,
All alone stood it and the moss hung down from the branches,
Without any companion it grew there, uttering joyous leaves of dark green,
And its look, rude, unbending, lusty, made me think of myself,
But I wonder'd how it could utter joyous leaves, standing alone there, without its
    friend, for I knew I could not,   5
And I broke off a twig with a certain number of leaves upon it, and twined around
    it a little moss,
And brought it away, and I have placed it in sight in my room,
It is not needed to remind me as of my own dear friends,
(For I believe lately I think of little else than of them,)
Yet it remains to me a curious token, it makes me think of manly love;   10
For all that, and though the live-oak glistens there in Louisiana solitary in a wide
    flat space,
Uttering joyous leaves all its life, without a friend a lover near,
I know very well I could not.

I HEAR IT WAS CHARGED AGAINST ME

This poem first appears as number 24 of the "Calamus" section of the 1860 edition, when it was without title. The present title and text appear first in 1867.

I hear it was charged against me that I sought to destroy institutions,
But really I am neither for nor against institutions,
(What indeed have I in common with them? or what with the destruction of them?)
Only I will establish in the Mannahatta and in every city of these States inland and
    seaboard,
And in the fields and woods, and above every keel little or large that dents the
    water,   5
Without edifices or rules or trustees or any argument,
The institution of the dear love of comrades.

SONG OF THE OPEN ROAD

As "Poem of the Road" this poem was number 12 of the 1856 *Leaves of Grass*, where it was printed without section numbers. In the 1860 edition the verse para-

    3. uttering—putting forth.

graphs were numbered. In 1867 it took its present title, and was divided into numbered sections. In 1881 the verse paragraph numbers were dropped, but the section divisions were retained, and the present text was achieved. There are, of course, many textual variations among the different versions.

1

Afoot and light-hearted I take to the open road,
Healthy, free, the world before me,
The long brown path before me leading wherever I choose.

Henceforth I ask not good-fortune, I myself am good-fortune,
Henceforth I whimper no more, postpone no more, need nothing,   5
Done with indoor complaints, libraries, querulous criticisms,
Strong and content I travel the open road.

The earth, that is sufficient,
I do not want the constellations any nearer,
I know they are very well where they are,   10
I know they suffice for those who belong to them.

(Still here I carry my old delicious burdens,
I carry them, men and women, I carry them with me wherever I go,
I swear it is impossible for me to get rid of them,
I am fill'd with them, and I will fill them in return.)   15

2

You road I enter upon and look around, I believe you are not all that is here,
I believe that much unseen is also here.

Here the profound lesson of reception, nor preference nor denial,
The black with his woolly head, the felon, the diseas'd, the illiterate person, are not denied;
The birth, the hasting after the physician, the beggar's tramp, the drunkard's stagger, the laughing party of mechanics,   20
The escaped youth, the rich person's carriage, the fop, the eloping couple,
The early market-man, the hearse, the moving of furniture into the town, the return back from the town,
They pass, I also pass, anything passes, none can be interdicted,
None but are accepted, none but shall be dear to me.

3

You air that serves me with breath to speak!   25
You objects that call from diffusion my meanings and give them shape!
You light that wraps me and all things in delicate equable showers!
You paths worn in the irregular hollows by the roadsides!
I believe you are latent with unseen existences, you are so dear to me.

26. call . . . shape—The poet's general interpenetration of the universe of life is given concrete meanings as he sympathizes with particular objects in the universe.

You flagg'd walks of the cities! you strong curbs at the edges!   30
You ferries! you planks and posts of wharves! you timber-lined sides! you distant
    ships!
You rows of houses! you window-pierc'd façades! you roofs!
You porches and entrances! you copings and iron guards!
You windows whose transparent shells might expose so much!
You doors and ascending steps! you arches!   35
You gray stones of interminable pavements! you trodden crossings!
From all that has touch'd you I believe you have imparted to yourselves, and now
    would impart the same secretly to me,
From the living and the dead you have peopled your impassive surfaces, and the
    spirits thereof would be evident and amicable with me.

                                    4

The earth expanding right hand and left hand,
The picture alive, every part in its best light,   40
The music falling in where it is wanted, and stopping where it is not wanted,
The cheerful voice of the public road, the gay fresh sentiment of the road.

O highway I travel, do you say to me *Do not leave me?*
Do you say *Venture not—if you leave me you are lost?*   44
Do you say *I am already prepared, I am well-beaten and undenied, adhere to me?*

O public road, I say back I am not afraid to leave you, yet I love you,
You express me better than I can express myself,
You shall be more to me than my poem.

I think heroic deeds were all conceiv'd in the open air, and all free poems also,
I think I could stop here myself and do miracles,   50
I think whatever I shall meet on the road I shall like, and whoever beholds me shall
    like me,
I think whoever I see must be happy.

                                    5

From this hour I ordain myself loos'd of limits and imaginary lines,
Going where I list, my own master total and absolute,
Listening to others, considering well what they say,   55
Pausing, searching, receiving, contemplating,
Gently, but with undeniable will, divesting myself of the holds that would hold me.

I inhale great draughts of space,
The east and the west are mine, and the north and the south are mine.

I am larger, better than I thought,   60
I did not know I held so much goodness.

All seems beautiful to me,
I can repeat over to men and women You have done such good to me I would do
    the same to you,

   30. flagg'd walks—Before the invention of the cement sidewalk, walks were made of flag-
stones.

I will recruit for myself and you as I go,
I will scatter myself among men and women as I go,   65
I will toss a new gladness and roughness among them,
Whoever denies me it shall not trouble me,
Whoever accepts me he or she shall be blessed and shall bless me.

6

Now if a thousand perfect men were to appear it would not amaze me,
Now if a thousand beautiful forms of women appear'd it would not astonish me.   70

Now I see the secret of the making of the best persons,
It is to grow in the open air and to eat and sleep with the earth.

Here a great personal deed has room,
(Such a deed seizes upon the hearts of the whole race of men,
Its effusion of strength and will overwhelms law and mocks all authority and all
    argument against it.)   75

Here is the test of wisdom,
Wisdom is not finally tested in schools,
Wisdom cannot be pass'd from one having it to another not having it,
Wisdom is of the soul, is not susceptible of proof, is its own proof,
Applies to all stages and objects and qualities and is content,   80
Is the certainty of the reality and immortality of things, and the excellence of things;
Something there is in the float of the sight of things that provokes it out of the soul.

Now I re-examine philosophies and religions,
They may prove well in lecture-rooms, yet not prove at all under the spacious clouds
    and along the landscape and flowing currents.

Here is realization,   85
Here is a man tallied—he realizes here what he has in him,
The past, the future, majesty, love—if they are vacant of you, you are vacant of
    them.

Only the kernel of every object nourishes;
Where is he who tears off the husks for you and me?
Where is he that undoes stratagems and envelopes for you and me?   90

Here is adhesiveness, it is not previously fashion'd, it is apropos;
Do you know what it is as you pass to be loved by strangers?
Do you know the talk of those turning eye-balls?

7

Here is the efflux of the soul,
The efflux of the soul comes from within through embower'd gates, ever provoking
    questions,   95
These yearnings why are they? these thoughts in the darkness why are they?
Why are there men and women that while they are nigh me the sunlight expands
    my blood?

91. adhesiveness—friendship. This term, like efflux, line 94, Whitman drew from the
jargon of phrenology.

Why when they leave me do my pennants of joy sink flat and lank?
Why are there trees I never walk under but large and melodious thoughts descend
    upon me?
(I think they hang there winter and summer on those trees and always drop fruit
    as I pass;)   100
What is it I interchange so suddenly with strangers?
What with some driver as I ride on the seat by his side?
What with some fisherman drawing his seine by the shore as I walk by and pause?
What gives me to be free to a woman's and man's good-will? what gives them to
    be free to mine?

8

The efflux of the soul is happiness, here is happiness,   105
I think it pervades the open air, waiting at all times,
Now it flows unto us, we are rightly charged.

Here rises the fluid and attaching character,
The fluid and attaching character is the freshness and sweetness of man and woman,
(The herbs of the morning sprout no fresher and sweeter every day out of the roots
    of themselves, than it sprouts fresh and sweet continually out of itself.)   110
Toward the fluid and attaching character exudes the sweat of the love of young and
    old,
From it falls distill'd the charm that mocks beauty and attainments,
Toward it heaves the shuddering longing ache of contact.

9

Allons! whoever you are come travel with me!
Traveling with me you find what never tires.   115

The earth never tires,
The earth is rude, silent, incomprehensible at first, Nature is rude and incomprehen-
    sible at first,
Be not discouraged, keep on, there are divine things well envelop'd,
I swear to you there are divine things more beautiful than words can tell.

Allons! we must not stop here,   120
However sweet these laid-up stores, however convenient this dwelling we cannot
    remain here,
However shelter'd this port and however calm these waters we must not anchor here,
However welcome the hospitality that surrounds us we are permitted to receive it
    but a little while.

10

Allons! the inducements shall be greater,
We will sail pathless and wild seas,   125
We will go where winds blow, waves dash, and the Yankee clipper speeds by under
    full sail.

Allons! with power, liberty, the earth, the elements,
Health, defiance, gayety, self-esteem, curiosity;

101. **What . . .** —that is, why do I seem to interchange personalities with strangers? **114.**
Allons!—"Let us go on!"; one of Whitman's importations from the French.

Allons! from all formules!
From your formules, O bat-eyed and materialistic priests.   130

The stale cadaver blocks up the passage—the burial waits no longer.

Allons! yet take warning!
He traveling with me needs the best blood, thews, endurance,
None may come to the trial till he or she bring courage and health,
Come not here if you have already spent the best of yourself,   135
Only those may come who come in sweet and determin'd bodies,
No diseas'd person, no rum-drinker or venereal taint is permitted here.

(I and mine do not convince by arguments, similes, rhymes,
We convince by our presence.)

11

Listen! I will be honest with you,   140
I do not offer the old smooth prizes, but offer rough new prizes,
These are the days that must happen to you:
You shall not heap up what is call'd riches,
You shall scatter with lavish hand all that you earn or achieve,
You but arrive at the city to which you were destin'd, you hardly settle yourself to
    satisfaction before you are call'd by an irresistible call to depart,   145
You shall be treated to the ironical smiles and mockings of those who remain behind
    you,
What beckonings of love you receive you shall only answer with passionate kisses of
    parting,
You shall not allow the hold of those who spread their reach'd hands toward you.

12

Allons! after the great Companions, and to belong to them!
They too are on the road—they are the swift and majestic men—they are the great-
    est women,   150
Enjoyers of calms of seas and storms of seas,
Sailors of many a ship, walkers of many a mile of land,
Habituès of many distant countries, habituès of far-distant dwellings,
Trusters of men and women, observers of cities, solitary toilers,
Pausers and contemplators of tufts, blossoms, shells of the shore,   155
Dancers at wedding-dances, kissers of brides, tender helpers of children, bearers of
    children,
Soldiers of revolts, standers by gaping graves, lowerers-down of coffins,
Journeyers over consecutive seasons, over the years, the curious years each emerging
    from that which preceded it,
Journeyers as with companions, namely their own diverse phases,
Forth-steppers from the latent unrealized baby-days,   160
Journeyers gayly with their own youth, journeyers with their bearded and well-
    grain'd manhood,
Journeyers with their womanhood, ample, unsurpass'd, content,
Journeyers with their own sublime old age of manhood or womanhood,
Old age, calm, expanded, broad with the haughty breadth of the universe,
Old age, flowing free with the delicious near-by freedom of death.   165

129. formules—formulas. In an earlier version Whitman uses the orthodox form of the word.

13

Allons! to that which is endless as it was beginningless,
To undergo much, tramps of days, rests of nights,
To merge all in the travel they tend to, and the days and nights they tend to,
Again to merge them in the start of superior journeys,
To see nothing anywhere but what you may reach it and pass it,)   170
To conceive no time, however distant, but what you may reach it and pass it,
To look up or down no road but it stretches and waits for you, however long but it
    stretches and waits for you,
To see no being, not God's or any, but you also go thither,
To see no possession but you may possess it, enjoying all without labor or purchase,
    abstracting the feast yet not abstracting one particle of it,
To take the best of the farmer's farm and the rich man's elegant villa, and the
    chaste blessings of the well-married couple, and the fruits of orchards and
    flowers of gardens,   175
To take to your use out of the compact cities as you pass through,
To carry buildings and streets with you afterward wherever you go,
To gather the minds of men out of their brains as you encounter them, to gather
    the love out of their hearts,
To take your lovers on the road with you, for all that you leave them behind you,
To know the universe itself as a road, as many roads, as roads for traveling souls.

All parts away for the progress of souls,   181
All religion, all solid things, arts, governments—all that was or is apparent upon
    this globe or any globe, falls into niches and corners before the procession of
    souls along the grand roads of the universe.

Of the progress of the souls of men and women along the grand roads of the uni-
    verse, all other progress is the needed emblem and sustenance.

Forever alive, forever forward,
Stately, solemn, sad, withdrawn, baffled, mad, turbulent, feeble, dissatisfied,   185
Desperate, proud, fond, sick, accepted by men, rejected by men,
They go! they go! I know that they go, but I know not where they go,
But I know that they go toward the best—toward something great.

Whoever you are, come forth! or man or woman come forth!
You must not stay sleeping and dallying there in the house, though you built it,
    or though it has been built for you.   190

Out of the dark confinement! out from behind the screen!
It is useless to protest, I know all and expose it.

Behold through you as bad as the rest,
Through the laughter, dancing, dining, supping, of people,
Inside of dresses and ornaments, inside of those wash'd and trimm'd faces,   195
Behold a secret silent loathing and despair.

No husband, no wife, no friend, trusted to hear the confession,
Another self, a duplicate of every one, skulking and hiding it goes,

   181. parts—departs, gets out of the way.

Formless and wordless through the streets of the cities, polite and bland in the
    parlors,
In the cars of railroads, in steamboats, in the public assembly,   200
Home to the houses of men and women, at the table, in the bedroom, everywhere,
Smartly attired, countenance smiling, form upright, death under the breast-bones,
    hell under the skull-bones,
Under the broadcloth and gloves, under the ribbons and artificial flowers,
Keeping fair with the customs, speaking not a syllable of itself,
Speaking of any thing else but never of itself.   205

14

Allons! through struggles and wars!
The goal that was named cannot be countermanded.

Have the past struggles succeeded?
What has succeeded? yourself? your nation? Nature?
Now understand me well—it is provided in the essence of things that from any
    fruition of success, no matter what, shall come forth something to make a
    greater struggle necessary.   210

My call is the call of battle, I nourish active rebellion,
He going with me must go well arm'd,
He going with me goes often with spare diet, poverty, angry enemies, desertions.

15

Allons! the road is before us!
It is safe—I have tried it—my own feet have tried it well—be not detain'd!   215
Let the paper remain on the desk unwritten, and the book on the shelf unopen'd!
Let the tools remain in the workshop! let the money remain unearn'd!
Let the school stand! mind not the cry of the teacher!
Let the preacher preach in his pulpit! let the lawyer plead in the court, and the
    judge expound the law.

Camerado, I give you my hand!   220
I give you my love more precious than money,
I give you myself before preaching or law;
Will you give me yourself? will you come travel with me?
Shall we stick by each other as long as we live?

CROSSING BROOKLYN FERRY

    In the 1856 volume this was the eleventh poem, under the title "Sun-Down
Poem." The present title appeared in 1860, when the verse paragraphs were numbered. In 1871 the section numbers were added. In 1881 the verse and section numbers were dropped. There are various textual variations.

1

Flood-tide below me! I see you face to face!
Clouds of the west—sun there half an hour high—I see you also face to face.

  220. Camerado—another coinage: comrade.

Crowds of men and women attired in the usual costumes, how curious you are to
me!
On the ferry-boats the hundreds and hundreds that cross, returning home, are more
curious to me than you suppose,
And you that shall cross from shore to shore years hence are more to me, and more
in my meditations, than you might suppose.   5

2

The impalpable sustenance of me from all things at all hours of the day,
The simple, compact, well-join'd scheme, myself disintegrated, every one disinte-
grated yet part of the scheme,
The similitudes of the past and those of the future,
The glories strung like beads on my smallest sights and hearings, on the walk in
the street and the passage over the river,
The current rushing so swiftly and swimming with me far away,   10
The others that are to follow me, the ties between me and them,
The certainty of others, the life, love, sight, hearing of others.

Others will enter the gates of the ferry and cross from shore to shore,
Others will watch the run of the flood-tide,
Others will see the shipping of Manhattan north and west, and the heights of
Brooklyn to the south and east,   15
Others will see the islands large and small;
Fifty years hence, others will see them as they cross, the sun half an hour high,
A hundred years hence, or ever so many hundred years hence, others will see them,
Will enjoy the sunset, the pouring-in of the flood-tide, the falling-back to the sea
of the ebb-tide.

3

It avails not, time nor place—distance avails not,   20
I am with you, you men and women of a generation, or ever so many generations
hence,
Just as you feel when you look on the river and sky, so I felt,
Just as any of you is one of a living crowd, I was one of a crowd,
Just as you are refresh'd by the gladness of the river and the bright flow, I was
refresh'd,
Just as you stand and lean on the rail, yet hurry with the swift current, I stood yet
was hurried,   25
Just as you look on the numberless masts of ships and the thick-stemm'd pipes of
steamboats, I look'd.

I too many and many a time cross'd the river of old,
Watched the Twelfth-month sea-gulls, saw them high in the air floating with mo-
tionless wings, oscillating their bodies,
Saw how the glistening yellow lit up parts of their bodies and left the rest in strong
shadow,
Saw the slow-wheeling circles and the gradual edging toward the south,   30
Saw the reflection of the summer sky in the water,

7. disintegrated—The meaning is obscure, but seems to be that everyone who participates
sympathetically in the scene overflows the boundaries of his own personality, and is therefore more
than himself; that is, not merely and only himself. **28. Twelfth-month**—In 1860 Whitman
dropped the conventional names of the months for the Quaker usage.

Had my eyes dazzled by the shimmering track of beams,
Look'd at the fine centrifugal spokes of light round the shape of my head in the
    sunlit water,
Look'd on the haze on the hills southward and south-westward,
Look'd on the vapor as it flew in fleeces tinged with violet,   35
Look'd toward the lower bay to notice the vessels arriving,
Saw their approach, saw aboard those that were near me,
Saw the white sails of schooners and sloops, saw the ships at anchor,
The sailors at work in the rigging or out astride the spars,
The round masts, the swinging motion of the hulls, the slender serpentine pennants,
The large and small steamers in motion, the pilots in their pilot-houses,   41
The white wake left by the passage, the quick tremulous whirl of the wheels,
The flags of all nations, the falling of them at sunset,
The scallop-edged waves in the twilight, the ladled cups, the frolicsome crests and
    glistening,
The stretch afar growing dimmer and dimmer, the gray walls of the granite store-
    houses by the docks,   45
On the river the shadowy group, the big steam-tug closely flank'd on each side by
    the barges, the hay-boat, the belated lighter,
On the neighboring shore the fires from the foundry chimneys burning high and
    glaringly into the night,
Casting their flicker of black contrasted with wild red and yellow light over the tops
    of houses, and down into the clefts of streets.

4

These and all else were to me the same as they are to you,
I loved well those cities, loved well the stately and rapid river,
The men and women I saw were all near to me,   50
Others the same—others who look back on me because I look'd forward to them,
(The time will come, though I stop here to-day and to-night.)

5

What is it then between us?
What is the count of the scores or hundreds of years between us?   55

Whatever it is, it avails not—distance avails not, and place avails not,
I too lived, Brooklyn of ample hills was mine,
I too walk'd the streets of Manhattan island, and bathed in the waters around it,
I too felt the curious abrupt questionings stir within me,
In the day among crowds of people sometimes they came upon me,   60
In my walks home late at night or as I lay in my bed they came upon me,
I too had been struck from the float forever held in solution,
I too had receiv'd identity by my body,
That I was I knew was of my body, and what I should be I knew I should be of my
    body.

6

It is not upon you alone the dark patches fall,   65
The dark threw its patches down upon me also,

---

46. **lighter**—barge. 62. **float**—stuff that differentiates into the particular. 64. **That**—That
which.

The best I had done seem'd to me blank and suspicious,
My great thoughts as I supposed them, were they not in reality meagre?
Nor is it you alone who know what it is to be evil,
I am he who knew what it was to be evil,   70
I too knitted the old knot of contrariety,
Blabb'd, blush'd, resented, lied, stole, grudg'd,
Had guile, anger, lust, hot wishes I dared not speak,
Was wayward, vain, greedy, shallow, sly, cowardly, malignant,
The wolf, the snake, the hog, not wanting in me,   75
The cheating look, the frivolous word, the adulterous wish, not wanting,
Refusals, hates, postponements, meanness, laziness, none of these wanting,
Was one with the rest, the days and haps of the rest,
Was call'd by my nighest name by clear loud voices of young men as they saw me
       approaching or passing,
Felt their arms on my neck as I stood, or the negligent leaning of their flesh against
       me as I sat,   80
Saw many I loved in the street or ferry-boat or public assembly, yet never told them
       a word,
Lived the same life with the rest, the same old laughing, gnawing, sleeping,
Play'd the part that still looks back on the actor or actress,
The same old role, the role that is what we make it, as great as we like,
Or as small as we like, or both great and small.   85

                                    7

Closer yet I approach you,
What thought you have of me now, I had as much of you—I laid in my stores in
       advance,
I consider'd long and seriously of you before you were born.

Who was to know what should come home to me?
Who knows but I am enjoying this?   90
Who knows, for all the distance, but I am as good as looking at you now, for all
       you cannot see me?

                                    8

Ah, what can ever be more stately and admirable to me than mast-hemm'd Man-
       hattan?
River and sunset and scallop-edg'd waves of flood-tide?
The sea-gulls oscillating their bodies, the hay-boat in the twilight, and the belated
       lighter?

What gods can exceed these that clasp me by the hand, and with voices I love call
       me promptly and loudly by my nighest name as I approach?   95

What is more subtle than this which ties me to the woman or man that looks in my
       face?
Which fuses me into you now, and pours my meaning into you?

We understand then do we not?
What I promis'd without mentioning it, have you not accepted?
What the study could not teach—what the preaching could not accomplish is accom-
       plish'd, is it not?   100

9

Flow on, river! flow with the flood-tide, and ebb with the ebb-tide!
Frolic on, crested and scallop-edg'd waves!
Gorgeous clouds of the sunset! drench with your splendor me, or the men and
    women generations after me!
Cross from shore to shore, countless crowds of passengers!
Stand up, tall masts of Mannahatta! stand up, beautiful hills of Brooklyn!   105
Throb, baffled and curious brain! throw out questions and answers!
Suspend here and everywhere, eternal float of solution!
Gaze, loving and thirsting eyes, in the house or street or public assembly!
Sound out, voices of young men! loudly and musically call me by my nighest name!
Live, old life! play the part that looks back on the actor or actress!   110
Play the old role, the role that is great or small according as one makes it!
Consider, you who peruse me, whether I may not in unknown ways be looking
    upon you;
Be firm, rail over the river, to support those who lean idly, yet haste with the
    hasting current;
Fly on, sea-birds! fly sideways, or wheel in large circles high in the air;
Receive the summer sky, you water, and faithfully hold it till all downcast eyes
    have time to take it from you!   115
Diverge, fine spokes of light, from the shape of my head, or any one's head, in the
    sunlit water!
Come on, ships from the lower bay! pass up or down, white-sail'd schooners, sloops,
    lighters!
Flaunt away, flags of all nations! be duly lower'd at sunset!
Burn high your fires, foundry chimneys! cast black shadows at nightfall! cast red
    and yellow light over the tops of the houses!
Appearances, now or henceforth, indicate what you are,   120
You necessary film, continue to envelop the soul,
About my body for me, and your body for you, be hung our divinest aromas,
Thrive, cities—bring your freight, bring your shows, ample and sufficient rivers,
Expand, being than which none else is perhaps more spiritual,
Keep your places, objects than which none else is more lasting.   125

You have waited, you always wait, you dumb, beautiful ministers,
We receive you with free sense at last, and are insatiate henceforward,
Not you any more shall be able to foil us, or withhold yourselves from us,
We use you, and do not cast you aside—we plant you permanently within us,
We fathom you not—we love you—there is perfection in you also,   130
You furnish your parts toward eternity,
Great or small, you furnish your parts toward the soul.

PIONEERS! O PIONEERS!

This poem was originally included in *Drum Taps* (1865), when the stanzas were
numbered. By 1871 it was lifted out of the "Drum Taps" section of *Leaves of
Grass* and included under "Marches Now the War Is Over." In 1881 it was trans-

---

107. **float of solution**—temporal phenomena conceived of as floating on the universe and
dissolving into it. *Cf.* line 62. 127. **free sense**—senses freed from merely temporal activity.

ferred to the "Birds of Passage" section, where it remained. The verse numberings were dropped with this transfer. There are very few changes in the text during these wanderings.

Come my tan-faced children,
Follow well in order, get your weapons ready,
Have you your pistols? have you your sharp-edged axes?
          Pioneers! O pioneers!

For we cannot tarry here,   5
We must march my darlings, we must bear the brunt of danger,
We the youthful sinewy races, all the rest on us depend,
          Pioneers! O pioneers!

O you youths, Western youths,
So impatient, full of action, full of manly pride and friendship,   10
Plain I see you Western youths, see you tramping with the foremost,
          Pioneers! O pioneers!

Have the elder races halted?
Do they droop and end their lesson, wearied over there beyond the seas?
We take up the task eternal, and the burden and the lesson,   15
          Pioneers! O pioneers!

All the past we leave behind,
We debouch upon a newer mightier world, varied world,
Fresh and strong the world we seize, world of labor and the march,
          Pioneers! O pioneers!   20

We detachments steady throwing,
Down the edges, through the passes, up the mountains steep,
Conquering, holding, daring, venturing as we go the unknown ways,
          Pioneers! O pioneers!

We primeval forests felling,   25
We the rivers stemming, vexing we and piercing deep the mines within,
We the surface broad surveying, we the virgin soil upheaving,
          Pioneers! O pioneers!

Colorado men are we,
From the peaks gigantic, from the great sierras and the high plateaus,   30
From the mine and from the gully, from the hunting trail we come,
          Pioneers! O pioneers!

From Nebraska, from Arkansas,
Central inland race are we, from Missouri, with the continental blood intervein'd,
All the hands of comrades clasping, all the Southern, all the Northern,   35
          Pioneers! O pioneers!

O resistless restless race!
O beloved race in all! O my breast aches with tender love for all!
O I mourn and yet exult, I am rapt with love for all,
          Pioneers! O pioneers!   40

Raise the mighty mother mistress,
Waving high the delicate mistress, over all the starry mistress, (bend your heads all,)
Raise the fang'd and warlike mistress, stern, impassive, weapon'd mistress,
               Pioneers! O pioneers!

      See my children, resolute children,   45
By those swarms upon our rear we must never yield or falter,
Ages back in ghostly millions frowning there behind us urging,
               Pioneers! O pioneers!

      On and on the compact ranks,
With accessions ever waiting, with the places of the dead quickly fill'd,   50
Through the battle, through defeat, moving yet and never stopping,
               Pioneers! O pioneers!

      O to die advancing on!
Are there some of us to droop and die? has the hour come?
Then upon the march we fittest die, soon and sure the gap is fill'd,   55
               Pioneers! O pioneers!

      All the pulses of the world,
Falling in they beat for us, with the Western movement beat,
Holding single or together, steady moving to the front, all for us,
               Pioneers! O pioneers!   60

      Life's involv'd and varied pageants,
All the forms and shows, all the workmen at their work,
All the seamen and the landsmen, all the masters with their slaves,
               Pioneers! O pioneers!

      All the hapless silent lovers,   65
All the prisoners in the prisons, all the righteous and the wicked,
All the joyous, all the sorrowing, all the living, all the dying,
               Pioneers! O pioneers!

      I too with my soul and body,
We, a curious trio, picking, wandering on our way,   70
Through these shores amid the shadows, with the apparitions pressing,
               Pioneers! O pioneers!

      Lo, the darting bowling orb!
Lo, the brother orbs around, all the clustering suns and planets,
All the dazzling days, all the mystic nights with dreams,   75
               Pioneers! O pioneers!

      These are of us, they are with us,
All for primal needed work, while the followers there in embryo wait behind,
We to-day's procession heading, we the route for travel clearing,
               Pioneers! O pioneers!   80

   73. darting bowling orb—either the earth as it "bowls along," or the sun. Whitman is consistently vague in his use of "orb."

O you daughters of the West!
O you young and elder daughters! O you mothers and you wives!
Never must you be divided, in our ranks you move united,
        Pioneers! O pioneers!

        Minstrels latent on the prairies!   85
(Shrouded bards of other lands, you may rest, you have done your work),
Soon I hear you coming warbling, soon you rise and tramp amid us,
        Pioneers! O pioneers!

        Not for delectations sweet,
Not the cushion and the slipper, not the peaceful and the studious,   90
Not the riches safe and palling, not for us the tame enjoyment,
        Pioneers! O pioneers!

        Do the feasters gluttonous feast?
Do the corpulent sleepers sleep? Have they lock'd and bolted doors?
Still be ours the diet hard, and the blanket on the ground,   95
        Pioneers! O pioneers!

        Has the night descended?
Was the road of late so toilsome? did we stop discouraged nodding on our way?
Yet a passing hour I yield you in your tracks to pause oblivious,
        Pioneers! O pioneers!   100

        Till with sound of trumpet,
Far, far off the daybreak call—hark! how loud and clear I hear it wind,
Swift! to the head of the army!—swift! spring to your places,
        Pioneers! O pioneers!

OUT OF THE CRADLE ENDLESSLY ROCKING

   After periodical publication, as "A Child's Reminiscence," this poem first appeared in the 1860 edition as "A Word out of the Sea," and the second, and greater, portion of it is split off from the first and entitled "Reminiscences." In 1867 the poem had its present length, the verse paragraphs were numbered, and the poem was split into numbered sections. In 1871 it was transferred to "Passage to India" as part of the section of "Sea-Shore Memories." It does not appear in the 1876 *Leaves,* but does appear in the *Two Rivulets* volume of that year ("Passage to India"). In 1881 it became the leading poem in the section entitled "Sea-Drift," and the numberings were dropped. There are many textual variations.

Out of the cradle endlessly rocking,
Out of the mocking-bird's throat, the musical shuttle,
Out of the Ninth-month midnight,
Over the sterile sands and the fields beyond, where the child leaving his bed wander'd alone, bareheaded, barefoot,
Down from the shower'd halo,   5
Up from the mystic play of shadows twining and twisting as if they were alive,
Out from the patches of briers and blackberries,

From the memories of the bird that chanted to me,
From your memories sad brother, from the fitful risings and fallings I heard,
From under that yellow half-moon late-risen and swollen as if with tears,   10
From those beginning notes of yearning and love there in the mist,
From the thousand responses of my heart never to cease,
From the myriad thence-arous'd words,
From the word stronger and more delicious than any,
From such as now they start the scene revisiting,   15
As a flock, twittering, rising, or overhead passing,
Borne hither, ere all eludes me, hurriedly,
A man, yet by these tears a little boy again,
Throwing myself on the sand, confronting the waves,
I, chanter of pains and joys, uniter of here and hereafter,   20
Taking all hints to use them, but swiftly leaping beyond them,
(A reminiscence sing.)

Once Paumanok,
When the lilac-scent was in the air and Fifth-month grass was growing,
Up this seashore in some briers,   25
Two feather'd guests from Alabama, two together,
And their nest, and four light-green eggs spotted with brown,
And every day the he-bird to and fro near at hand,
And every day the she-bird crouch'd on her nest, silent, with bright eyes,
And every day I, a curious boy, never too close, never disturbing them,   30
Cautiously peering, absorbing, translating.

Shine! shine! shine!
Pour down your warmth, great sun!
While we bask, we two together.

Two together!   35
Winds blow south, or winds blow north,
Day come white, or day come black,
Home, or rivers and mountains from home,
Singing all time, minding no time,
While we two keep together.   40

Till of a sudden,
May-be kill'd, unknown to her mate,
One forenoon that she-bird crouch'd not on the nest,
Nor return'd that afternoon, nor the next,
Nor ever appear'd again.   45

And thenceforward all summer in the sound of the sea,
And at night under the full of the moon in calmer weather,
Over the hoarse surging of the sea,
Or flitting from brier to brier by day,
I saw, I heard at intervals the remaining one, the he-bird,   50
The solitary guest from Alabama.

23. Paumanok—Long Island. **37. Day come**—This line usually appears as "Day come white, or night come black," but the reading in the text is that of the Camden edition.

Blow! blow! blow!
Blow up sea-winds along Paumanok's shore;
I wait and I wait till you blow my mate to me.

Yes, when the stars glisten'd,   55
All night long on the prong of a moss-scallop'd stake,
Down almost amid the slapping waves,
Sat the lone singer wonderful causing tears.

He call'd on his mate,
He pour'd forth the meanings which I of all men know.   60

Yes my brother I know,
The rest might not, but I have treasur'd every note,
For more than once dimly down to the beach gliding,
Silent, avoiding the moonbeams, blending myself with the shadows,
Recalling now the obscure shapes, the echoes, the sounds and sights after their sorts,
The white arms out in the breakers tirelessly tossing,   66
I, with bare feet, a child, the wind wafting my hair,
Listen'd long and long.

Listen'd to keep, to sing, now translating the notes,
Following you my brother.   70

Soothe! soothe! soothe!
Close on its wave soothes the wave behind,
And again another behind embracing and lapping, every one close,
But my love soothes not me, not me.

Low hangs the moon, it rose late,   75
It is lagging—O I think it is heavy with love, with love.

O madly the sea pushes upon the land,
With love, with love.

O night! do I not see my love fluttering out among the breakers?
What is that little black thing I see there in the white?   80

Loud! loud! loud!
Loud I call to you, my love!

High and clear I shoot my voice over the waves,
Surely you must know who is here, is here,
You must know who I am, my love.   85

Low-hanging moon!
What is that dusky spot in your brown yellow?
O it is the shape, the shape of my mate!
O moon do not keep her from me any longer.

Land! land! O land!   90
Whichever way I turn, O I think you could give me my mate back again if you
*   only would,*
For I am almost sure I see her dimly whichever way I look.

O rising stars!
Perhaps the one I want so much will rise, will rise with one of you.

O throat! O trembling throat!   95
Sound clearer through the atmosphere!
Pierce the woods, the earth,
Somewhere listening to catch you must be the one I want.

Shake out carols!
Solitary here, the night's carols!   100
Carols of lonesome love! death's carols!
Carols under that lagging, yellow, waning moon!
O under that moon where she droops almost down into the sea!
O reckless despairing carols.

But soft! sink low!   105
Soft! let me just murmur,
And do you wait a moment you husky-nois'd sea,
For somewhere I believe I heard my mate responding to me,
So faint, I must be still, be still to listen,
But not altogether still, for then she might not come immediately to me.   110

Hither my love!
Here I am! here!
With this just-sustain'd note I announce myself to you,
This gentle call is for you my love, for you.

Do not be decoy'd elsewhere,   115
That is the whistle of the wind, it is not my voice,
That is the fluttering, the fluttering of the spray,
Those are the shadows of leaves.

O darkness! O in vain!
O I am very sick and sorrowful.   120

O brown halo in the sky near the moon, drooping upon the sea!
O troubled reflection in the sea!
O throat! O throbbing heart!
And I singing uselessly, uselessly all the night.

O past! O happy life! O songs of joy!   125
In the air, in the woods, over fields,
Loved! loved! loved! loved! loved!
But my mate no more, no more with me!
We two together no more.

The aria sinking,   130
All else continuing, the stars shining,
The winds blowing, the notes of the bird continuous echoing,
With angry moans the fierce old mother incessantly moaning,
On the sands of Paumanok's shore gray and rustling,
The yellow half-moon enlarged, sagging down, drooping, the face of the sea almost
     touching,   135

The boy ecstatic, with his bare feet the waves, with his hair the atmosphere dallying,
The love in the heart long pent, now loose, now at last tumultuously bursting,
The aria's meaning, the ears, the soul, swiftly depositing,
The strange tears down the cheeks coursing,
The colloquy there, the trio, each uttering,   140
The undertone, the savage old mother incessantly crying,
To the boy's soul's questions sullenly timing, some drown'd secret hissing,
To the outsetting bard.

Demon or bird! (said the boy's soul,)
Is it indeed toward your mate you sing? or is it really to me?   145
For I, that was a child, my tongue's use sleeping, now I have heard you,
Now in a moment I know what I am for, I awake,
And already a thousand singers, a thousand songs, clearer, louder and more sorrowful
    than yours,
A thousand warbling echoes have started to life within me, never to die.

O you singer solitary, singing by yourself, projecting me,   150
O solitary me listening, never more shall I cease perpetuating you,
Never more shall I escape, never more the reverberations,
Never more the cries of unsatisfied love be absent from me,
Never again leave me to be the peaceful child I was before what there in the night,
By the sea under the yellow and sagging moon,   155
The messenger there arous'd, the fire, the sweet hell within,
The unknown want, the destiny of me.

O give me the clew! (it lurks in the night here somewhere,)
O if I am to have so much, let me have more!

A word then, (for I will conquer it,)   160
The word final, superior to all,
Subtle, sent up—what is it?—I listen;
Are you whispering it, and have been all the time, you sea-waves?
Is that it from your liquid rims and wet sands?

Whereto answering, the sea,   165
Delaying not, hurrying not,
Whisper'd me through the night, and very plainly before daybreak,
Lisp'd to me the low and delicious word death,
And again death, death, death, death,
Hissing melodious, neither like the bird nor like my arous'd child's heart, 170
But edging near as privately for me rustling at my feet,
Creeping thence steadily up to my ears and laving me softly all over,
Death, death, death, death, death.

Which I do not forget,
But fuse the song of my dusky demon and brother,   175
That he sang to me in the moonlight on Paumanok's gray beach,
With the thousand responsive songs at random,
My own songs awaked from that hour,

144. **Demon**—in the sense of *daimon*, or spirit.

And with them the key, the word up from the waves,
The word of the sweetest song and all songs,   180
That strong and delicious word which, creeping to my feet,
(Or like some old crone rocking the cradle, swathed in sweet garments, bending
    aside,)
The sea whisper'd me.

ON THE BEACH AT NIGHT ALONE

In the 1856 *Leaves* this poem appears as number 15 ("Clef Poem"); in the
1860 edition, it becomes the twelfth of "Leaves of Grass," and is divided into eight
numbered verse paragraphs. In 1867 the title was dropped, the poem was radically reworked, and the structure was reduced to two verse paragraphs. In the
Passage to India pamphlet the poem appears as part of the "Sea-Shore Memories" section under its present title. It was retained as part of the "Passage
to India" "annex" to the 1871 *Leaves;* and in the section of *Two Rivulets* under
that title. In 1881 it took its position in the "Sea-Drift" section of *Leaves,* where it
has its present form.

On the beach at night alone,
As the old mother sways her to and fro singing her husky song,
As I watch the bright stars shining, I think a thought of the clef of the universes
    and of the future.

A vast similitude interlocks all,
All spheres, grown, ungrown, small, large, suns, moons, planets,   5
All distances of place however wide,
All distances of time, all inanimate forms,
All souls, all living bodies though they be ever so different, or in different worlds,
All gaseous, watery, vegetable, mineral processes, the fishes, the brutes,
All nations, colors, barbarisms, civilizations, languages,   10
All identities that have existed or may exist on this globe, or any globe,
All lives and deaths, all of the past, present, future,
This vast similitude spans them, and always has spann'd,
And shall forever span them and compactly hold and enclose them.

WHEN I HEARD THE LEARN'D ASTRONOMER

This poem first appeared in *Drum-Taps;* remained in the "Drum-Taps" section of
the 1867 *Leaves;* was transferred to "Songs of Parting" in the 1871 *Leaves;* and
came to rest in "By the Roadside" in 1881.

When I heard the learn'd astronomer,
When the proofs, the figures, were ranged in columns before me,
When I was shown the charts and diagrams, to add, divide, and measure them,
When I sitting heard the astronomer where he lectured with much applause in the
    lecture-room,

3. **clef**—key to the riddle of the universe. 4. **similitude**—in the sense of likeness merely.

How soon unaccountable I became tired and sick, 5
Till rising and gliding out I wander'd off by myself,
In the mystical moist night-air, and from time to time,
Look'd up in perfect silence at the stars.

BEAT! BEAT! DRUMS!

This poem first appeared in *Drum-Taps,* where it was divided into three numbered sections. It remained consistently in the "Drum-Taps" section of *Leaves of
Grass* after 1867. The present form dates from 1881.

Beat! beat! drums!—blow! bugles! blow!
Through the windows—through doors—burst like a ruthless force,
Into the solemn church, and scatter the congregation,
Into the school where the scholar is studying;
Leave not the bridegroom quiet—no happiness must he have now with his bride, 5
Nor the peaceful farmer any peace, plowing his field or gathering his grain,
So fierce you whirr and pound you drums—so shrill you bugles blow.

Beat! beat! drums!—blow! bugles! blow!
Over the traffic of cities—over the rumble of wheels in the streets;
Are beds prepared for sleepers at night in the houses? no sleepers must sleep in those
    beds, 10
No bargainers' bargains by day—no brokers or speculators—would they continue?
Would the talkers be talking? would the singer attempt to sing?
Would the lawyer rise in the court to state his case before the judge?
Then rattle quicker, heavier drums—you bugles wilder blow.

Beat! beat! drums!—blow! bugles! blow! 15
Make no parley—stop for no expostulation,
Mind not the timid—mind not the weeper or prayer,
Mind not the old man beseeching the young man,
Let not the child's voice be heard, nor the mother's entreaties,
Make even the trestles to shake the dead where they lie awaiting the hearses, 20
So strong you thump O terrible drums—so loud you bugles blow.

CAVALRY CROSSING A FORD

The history of this poem is like that of "Beat! Beat! Drums!"

A line in long array where they wind betwixt green islands,
They take a serpentine course, their arms flash in the sun—hark to the musical clank,
Behold the silvery river, in it the splashing horses loitering stop to drink,
Behold the brown-faced men, each group, each person a picture, the negligent rest
    on the saddles,
Some emerge on the opposite bank, others are just entering the ford—while, 5
Scarlet and blue and snowy white,
The guidon flags flutter gayly in the wind.

COME UP FROM THE FIELDS FATHER

This poem was first included in *Drum-Taps,* where the verse paragraphs were numbered. It remained consistently in the "Drum-Taps" section of *Leaves of Grass* after 1867. In 1871 it was divided into numbered sections, but in 1881 took its present form.

Come up from the fields father, here's a letter from our Pete,
And come to the front door mother, here's a letter from thy dear son.

Lo, 'tis autumn,
Lo, where the trees, deeper green, yellower and redder,
Cool and sweeten Ohio's villages with leaves fluttering in the moderate wind, 5
Where apples ripe in the orchards hang and grapes on the trellis'd vines,
(Smell you the smell of the grapes on the vines?
Smell you the buckwheat where the bees were lately buzzing?)
Above all, lo, the sky so calm, so transparent after the rain, and with wondrous clouds,
Below too, all calm, all vital and beautiful, and the farm prospers well. 10

Down in the fields all prospers well,
But now from the fields come father, come at the daughter's call,
And come to the entry mother, to the front door come right away.

Fast as she can she hurries, something ominous, her steps trembling,
She does not tarry to smooth her hair nor adjust her cap. 15

Open the envelope quickly,
O this is not our son's writing, yet his name is sign'd,
O a strange hand writes for our dear son, O stricken mother's soul!
All swims before her eyes, flashes with black, she catches the main words only,
Sentences broken, *gunshot wound in the breast, cavalry skirmish, taken to hospital,*
At present low, but will soon be better. 21

Ah now the single figure to me,
Amid all teeming and wealthy Ohio with all its cities and farms,
Sickly white in the face and dull in the head, very faint,
By the jamb of a door leans. 25

Grieve not so, dear mother, (the just-grown daughter speaks through her sobs,
The little sisters huddle around speechless and dismay'd,)
See, dearest mother, the letter says Pete will soon be better.

Alas poor boy, he will never be better, (nor may be needs to be better, that brave and
    simple soul,)
While they stand at home at the door he is dead already, 30
The only son is dead.

But the mother needs to be better,
She with thin form presently drest in black,

By day her meals untouch'd, then at night fitfully sleeping, often waking,
In the midnight waking, weeping, longing with one deep longing,   35
O that she might withdraw unnoticed, silent from life escape and withdraw,
To follow, to seek, to be with her dear dead son.

GIVE ME THE SPLENDID SILENT SUN

This poem first appeared in *Drum-Taps,* and remained consistently in the "Drum-Taps" section of the *Leaves* after 1867. The present punctuation dates from 1881. It is one of the few poems in which Whitman writes with equal cogency on opposite sides of a situation.

I

Give me the splendid silent sun with all his beams full-dazzling,
Give me juicy autumnal fruit ripe and red from the orchard,
Give me a field where the unmow'd grass grows,
Give me an arbor, give me the trellis'd grape,
Give me fresh corn and wheat, give me serene-moving animals teaching content, 5
Give me nights perfectly quiet as on high plateaus west of the Mississippi, and I
    looking up at the stars,
Give me odorous at sunrise a garden of beautiful flowers where I can walk
    undisturb'd,
Give me for marriage a sweet-breath'd woman of whom I should never tire,
Give me a perfect child, give me away aside from the noise of the world a rural
    domestic life,
Give me to warble spontaneous songs recluse by myself, for my own ears only,   10
Give me solitude, give me Nature, give me again O Nature your primal sanities!

These demanding to have them, (tired with ceaseless excitement, and rack'd by the
    war-strife,)
These to procure incessantly asking, rising in cries from my heart,
While yet incessantly asking still I adhere to my city,
Day upon day and year upon year O city, walking your streets,   15
Where you hold me enchain'd a certain time refusing to give me up,
Yet giving to make me glutted, enrich'd of soul, you give me forever faces;
(O I see what I sought to escape, confronting, reversing my cries,
I see my own soul trampling down what it ask'd for.)

2

Keep your splendid silent sun   20
Keep your woods, O Nature, and the quiet places by the woods,
Keep your fields of clover and timothy, and your corn-fields and orchards,
Keep the blossoming buckwheat fields where the Ninth-month bees hum;
Give me faces and streets—give me these phantoms incessant and endless along the
    trottoirs!
Give me interminable eyes—give me women—give me comrades and lovers by the
    thousand!   25
Let me see new ones every day—let me hold new ones by the hand every day!
Give me such shows—give me the streets of Manhattan!

24. trottoirs—sidewalks.

Give me Broadway, with the soldiers marching—give me the sound of the trumpets
    and drums!
(The soldiers in companies or regiments—some starting away, flush'd and reckless,
Some, their time up, returning with thinn'd ranks, young, yet very old, worn, march-
    ing, noticing nothing;)   30
Give me the shores and wharves heavy-fringed with black ships!
O such for me! O an intense life, full to repletion and varied!
The life of the theatre, bar-room, huge hotel, for me!
The saloon of the steamer! the crowded excursion for me! the torchlight procession!
The dense brigade bound for the war, with high piled military wagons following; 35
People, endless, streaming, with strong voices, passions, pageants,
Manhattan streets with their powerful throbs, with beating drums as now,
The endless and noisy chorus, the rustle and clank of muskets, (even the sight of
    the wounded,)
Manhattan crowds, with their turbulent musical chorus!
Manhattan faces and eyes forever for me.   40

RECONCILIATION

This poem originally appeared in "Sequel to Drum-Taps," bound up with the
Drum-Taps pamphlet in 1865-66. In the 1867 *Leaves* it kept this place. In the 1871
Leaves it was placed under "Drum-Taps," where it consistently remained.

Word over all, beautiful as the sky,
Beautiful that war and all its deeds of carnage must in time be utterly lost,
That the hands of the sisters Death and Night incessantly softly wash again, and
    ever again, this soil'd world;
For my enemy is dead, a man divine as myself is dead,
I look where he lies white-faced and still in the coffin—I draw near,   5
Bend down, and touch lightly with my lips the white face in the coffin.

WHEN LILACS LAST IN THE DOORYARD BLOOM'D

When President Lincoln was assassinated, Whitman had already printed his
pamphlet *Drum-Taps.* He poured out his grief in his memorial poems, printed
them, and bound them up with his previously printed pamphlet as *Sequel to Drum-
Taps,* the extra part being dated 1865-66. In this "When Lilacs Last in the Dooryard
Bloom'd" was included, but the first arrangement of the poem was one of 43 numbered verse paragraphs organized into 21 numbered sections. The text, of course,
differs from the final text. In adding his war poems to the *Leaves* of 1867, he kept
the same arrangement of "Drum-Taps" and "Sequel to Drum-Taps." In 1871 the
four memorial poems were grouped together as a section titled "President Lincoln's
Burial Hymn," and the portion of the poem now printed in italics was printed
in that type face, and headed "Death Carol." In 1876 the same four poems were
printed in *Two Rivulets* as part of the "Passage to India" portion of that volume.
In the 1881 *Leaves* the present poem is part of the "Memories of President Lincoln".
section, and has since remained so. The student should note that Lincoln is not
mentioned by name in "When Lilacs Last in the Dooryard Bloom'd."

1

When lilacs last in the dooryard bloom'd,
And the great star early droop'd in the western sky in the night,
I mourn'd, and yet shall mourn with ever-returning spring.

Ever-returning spring, trinity sure to me you bring,
Lilac blooming perennial and drooping star in the west,   5
And thought of him I love.

2

O powerful western fallen star!
O shades of night—O moody, tearful night!
O great star disappear'd—O the black murk that hides the star!
O cruel hands that hold me powerless—O helpless soul of me!   10
O harsh surrounding cloud that will not free my soul.

3

In the dooryard fronting an old farm-house near the white-wash'd palings,
Stands the lilac-bush tall-growing with heart-shaped leaves of rich green,
With many a pointed blossom rising delicate, with the perfume strong I love,
With every leaf a miracle—and from this bush in the dooryard,   15
With delicate-color'd blossoms and heart-shaped leaves of rich green,
A sprig with its flower I break.

4

In the swamp in secluded recesses,
A shy and hidden bird is warbling a song.

Solitary the thrush,   20
The hermit withdrawn to himself, avoiding the settlements,
Sings by himself a song.

Song of the bleeding throat,
Death's outlet song of life, (for well dear brother I know,
If thou wast not granted to sing thou would'st surely die.)   25

5

Over the breast of the spring, the land, amid cities,
Amid lanes and through old woods, where lately the violets peep'd from the ground,
    spotting the gray debris,
Amid the grass in the fields each side of the lanes, passing the endless grass,
Passing the yellow-spear'd wheat, every grain from its shroud in the dark-brown
    fields uprisen,
Passing the apple-tree blows of white and pink in the orchards,   30
Carrying a corpse to where it shall rest in the grave,
Night and day journeys a coffin.

31. **Carrying**—The reference is to the funeral train which took Lincoln's body from Washington to Springfield, Illinois, for burial. The succeeding portions of the poem are historically
accurate in describing the mourning. Note how the leitmotif of sorrow is sustained by thematic
words like "death," "star," "lilacs," "him I love," and so forth.

6

Coffin that passes through lanes and streets,
Through day and night with the great cloud darkening the land,
With the pomp of the inloop'd flags with the cities draped in black,   35
With the show of the States themselves as of crape-veil'd women standing,
With processions long and winding and the flambeaus of the night,
With the countless torches lit, with the silent sea of faces and the unbared heads,
With the waiting depot, the arriving coffin, and the sombre faces,
With dirges through the night, with the thousand voices rising strong and solemn, 40
With all the mournful voices of the dirges pour'd around the coffin,
The dim-lit churches and the shuddering organs—where amid these you journey,
With the tolling tolling bells' perpetual clang,
Here, coffin that slowly passes,
I give you my sprig of lilac.   45

7

(Nor for you, for one alone,
Blossoms and branches green to coffins all I bring,
For fresh as the morning, thus would I chant a song for you O sane and sacred
    death.

All over bouquets of roses,
O death, I cover you over with roses and early lilies,   50
But mostly and now the lilac that blooms the first,
Copious I break, I break the sprigs from the bushes,
With loaded arms I come, pouring for you,
For you and the coffins all of you O death.)

symbol of his own attitude toward death.

8

O western orb sailing the heaven,   55
Now I know what you must have meant as a month since I walk'd,
As I walk'd in silence the transparent shadowy night,
As I saw you had something to tell as you bent to me night after night,
As you droop'd from the sky low down as if to my side, (while the other stars all
    look'd on,)
As we wander'd together the solemn night, (for something I know not what kept me
    from sleep,)   60
As the night advanced, and I saw on the rim of the west how full you were of woe,
As I stood on the rising ground in the breeze in the cool transparent night,
As I watch'd where you pass'd and was lost in the netherward black of the night,
As my soul in its trouble dissatisfied sank, as where you sad orb,
Concluded, dropt in the night, and was gone.   65

9

Sing on there in the swamp,
O singer bashful and tender, I hear your notes, I hear your call,
I hear, I come presently, I understand you,
But a moment I linger, for the lustrous star has detain'd me,
The star my departing comrade holds and detains me.   70

10

O how shall I warble myself for the dead one there I loved?
And how shall I deck my song for the large sweet soul that has gone?
And what shall my perfume be for the grave of him I love?

Sea-winds blown from east and west,
Blown from the Eastern sea and blown from the Western sea, till there on the
    prairies meeting,   75
These and with these and the breath of my chant,
I'll perfume the grave of him I love.

11

O what shall I hang on the chamber walls?
And what shall the pictures be that I hang on the walls,
To adorn the burial-house of him I love?   80

Pictures of growing spring and farms and homes,
With the Fourth-month eve at sundown, and the gray smoke lucid and bright,
With floods of the yellow gold of the gorgeous, indolent, sinking sun, burning,
    expanding the air,
With the fresh sweet herbage under foot, and the pale green leaves of the trees
    prolific,
In the distance the flowing glaze, the breast of the river, with a wind-dapple here
    and there,   85
With ranging hills on the banks, with many a line against the sky, and shadows,
And the city at hand with dwellings so dense, and stacks of chimneys,
And all the scenes of life and the workshops, and the workmen homeward returning.

12

Lo, body and soul—this land,
My own Manhattan with spires, and the sparkling and hurrying tides, and the
    ships,   90
The varied and ample land, the South and the North in the light, Ohio's shores and
    flashing Missouri,
And ever the far-spreading prairies cover'd with grass and corn.

Lo, the most excellent sun so calm and haughty,
The violet and purple morn with just-felt breezes,
The gentle soft-born measureless light,   95
The miracle spreading bathing all, the fulfill'd noon,
The coming eve delicious, the welcome night and the stars,
Over my cities shining all, enveloping man and land.

13

Sing on, sing on you gray-brown bird,
Sing from the swamps, the recesses, pour your chant from the bushes,   100
Limitless out of the dusk, out of the cedars and pines.

Sing on dearest brother, warble your reedy song,
Loud human song, with voice of uttermost woe.

O liquid and free and tender!
O wild and loose to my soul—O wondrous singer!   105
You only I hear—yet the star holds me, (but will soon depart,)
Yet the lilac with mastering odor holds me.

14

Now while I sat in the day and look'd forth,
In the close of the day with its light and the fields of spring, and the farmers pre-
    paring their crops,
In the large unconscious scenery of my land with its lakes and forests,   110
In the heavenly aerial beauty, (after the perturb'd winds and the storms,)
Under the arching heavens of the afternoon swift passing, and the voices of children
    and women,
The many-moving sea-tides, and I saw the ships how they sail'd,
And the summer approaching with richness, and the fields all busy with labor,
And the infinite separate houses, how they all went on, each with its meals and
    minutia of daily usages,   115
And the streets how their throbbings throbb'd, and the cities pent—lo, then and
    there,
Falling upon them all and among them all, enveloping me with the rest,
Appear'd the cloud, appear'd the long black trail,
And I knew death, its thought, and the sacred knowledge of death.

Then with the knowledge of death as walking one side of me,   120
And the thought of death close-walking the other side of me,
And I in the middle as with companions, and as holding the hands of companions,
I fled forth to the hiding receiving night that talks not,
Down to the shores of the water, the path by the swamp in the dimness,
To the solemn shadowy cedars and ghostly pines so still.   125

And the singer so shy to the rest receiv'd me,
The gray-brown bird I know receiv'd us comrades three,
And he sang the carol of death, and a verse for him I love.

From deep secluded recesses,
From the fragrant cedars and the ghostly pines so still,   130
Came the carol of the bird.

And the charm of the carol rapt me,
As I held as if by their hands my comrades in the night,
And the voice of my spirit tallied the song of the bird.

Come lovely and soothing death,   135
Undulate round the world, serenely arriving, arriving,
In the day, in the night, to all, to each,
Sooner or later delicate death.

Prais'd be the fathomless universe,
For life and joy, and for objects and knowledge curious,   140
And for love, sweet love—but praise! praise! praise!
For the sure-enwinding arms of cool-enfolding death.

(*Dark mother always gliding near with soft feet,*)
Have none chanted for thee a chant of fullest welcome?
Then I chant it for thee, I glorify thee above all,   145
I bring thee a song that when thou must indeed come, come unfalteringly.

Approach strong deliveress,
When it is so, when thou hast taken them I joyously sing the dead,
Lost in the loving floating ocean of thee,
Laved in the flood of thy bliss O death.   150
From me to thee glad serenades,
Dances for thee I propose saluting thee, adornments and feastings for thee,
And the sights of the open landscape and the high-spread sky are fitting,
And life and the fields, and the huge and thoughtful night.

The night in silence under many a star,   155
The ocean shore and the husky whispering wave whose voice I know,
And the soul turning to thee O vast and well-veil'd death,
And the body gratefully nestling close to thee.

Over the tree-tops I float thee a song,
Over the rising and sinking waves, over the myriad fields and the prairies wide, 160
Over the dense-pack'd cities all and the teeming wharves and ways,
I float this carol with joy, with joy to thee O death.

15

To the tally of my soul,
Loud and strong kept up the gray-brown bird,
With pure deliberate notes spreading filling the night.   165
Loud in the pines and cedars dim,
Clear in the freshness moist and the swamp-perfume,
And I with my comrades there in the night.

While my sight that was bound in my eyes unclosed,
As to long panoramas of visions.   170

And I saw askant the armies,
I saw as in noiseless dreams hundreds of battle-flags,
Borne through the smoke of the battles and pierc'd with missiles I saw them,
And carried hither and yon through the smoke, and torn and bloody,
And at last but a few shreds left on the staffs, (and all in silence,)   175
And the staffs all splinter'd and broken.

I saw battle-corpses, myriads of them,
And the white skeletons of young men, I saw them,
I saw the debris and debris of all the slain soldiers of the war,
But I saw they were not as was thought,   180
They themselves were fully at rest, they suffer'd not,
The living remain'd and suffer'd, the mother suffer'd,
And the wife and the child and the musing comrade suffer'd,
And the armies that remain'd suffer'd.

16

Passing the visions, passing the night,   185
Passing, unloosing the hold of my comrades' hands,
Passing the song of the hermit bird and the tallying song of my soul,
Victorious song, death's outlet song, yet varying ever-altering song,
As low and wailing, yet clear the notes, rising and falling, flooding the night,
Sadly sinking and fainting, as warning and warning, and yet again bursting with
      joy,   190
Covering the earth and filling the spread of the heaven,
As that powerful psalm in the night I heard from recesses,
Passing, I leave thee lilac with heart-shaped leaves,
I leave thee there in the dooryard, blooming, returning with spring.

I cease from my song for thee,   195
From my gaze on thee in the west, fronting the west, communing with thee,
O comrade lustrous with silver face in the night.

Yet each to keep and all, retrievements out of the night,
The song, the wondrous chant of the gray-brown bird,
And the tallying chant, the echo arous'd in my soul,   200
With the lustrous and drooping star with the countenance full of woe,
With the holders holding my hand nearing the call of the bird,
Comrades mine and I in the midst, and their memory ever to keep, for the dead I
      loved so well,
For the sweetest, wisest soul of all my days and lands—and this for his dear sake,
Lilac and star and bird twined with the chant of my soul,   205
There in the fragrant pines and the cedars dusk and dim.

O CAPTAIN! MY CAPTAIN!

   The history of this poem is like that of the preceding. In the original form, and
until 1881, the stanzas were numbered. There are minor textual variations in the
several editions.

      O Captain! my Captain! our fearful trip is done,
      The ship has weather'd every rack, the prize we sought is won,
      The port is near, the bells I hear, the people all exulting,
      While follow eyes the steady keel, the vessel grim and daring;
                  But O heart! heart! heart!   5
                  O the bleeding drops of red,
                        Where on the deck my Captain lies,
                        Fallen cold and dead.

      O Captain! my Captain! rise up and hear the bells;
      Rise up—for you the flag is flung—for you the bugle trills,   10
      For you bouquets and ribbon'd wreaths—for you the shores a-crowding,
      For you they call, the swaying mass, their eager faces turning;
                  Here Captain! dear father!
                  This arm beneath your head!
                        It is some dream that on the deck,   15
                        You've fallen cold and dead.

My Captain does not answer, his lips are pale and still,
My father does not feel my arm, he has no pulse nor will,
The ship is anchor'd safe and sound, its voyage closed and done,
From fearful trip the victor ship comes in with object won: 20
       Exult O shores, and ring O bells!
       But I with mournful tread,
       Walk the deck my Captain lies,
       Fallen cold and dead.

THERE WAS A CHILD WENT FORTH

This poem, without title, originally formed part of the 1855 volume, being the
third section from the end. In 1856, under the title "Poem of The Child That Went
Forth, and Always Goes Forth Forever and Forever" it was poem number 25. In
1860 it became number nine of one of the "Leaves of Grass" sections, when it was
divided into numbered verse paragraphs. In 1867 it was the first poem in that section, and was further divided into numbered sections. In 1871 the numbered sections
disappeared. In 1881 it took its place in the "Autumn Rivulets" section, and the
text took its present shape.

There was a child went forth every day,
And the first object he look'd upon, that object he became,
And that object became part of him for the day or a certain part of the day,
Or for many years or stretching cycles of years.

The early lilacs became part of this child,   5
And grass and white and red morning-glories and white and red clover, and the
    song of the phoebe-bird,
And the Third-month lambs and the sow's pink-faint litter, and the mare's foal and
    the cow's calf,
And the noisy brood of the barnyard or by the mire of the pond-side,
And the fish suspending themselves so curiously below there, and the beautiful
    curious liquid,
And the water-plants with their graceful flat heads, all became part of him.   10

The field-sprouts of Fourth-month and Fifth-month became part of him,
Winter-grain sprouts and those of the light-yellow corn, and the esculent roots of
    the garden,
And the apple-trees cover'd with blossoms and the fruit afterward, and wood-
    berries, and the commonest weeds by the road,
And the old drunkard staggering home from the outhouse of the tavern whence
    he had lately risen,
And the schoolmistress that pass'd, and the quarrelsome boys,   15
And the tidy and fresh-cheek'd girls, and the barefoot negro boy and girl,
And all the changes of city and country wherever he went.

His own parents, he that had father'd him, and she that had conceiv'd him in her
    womb, and birth'd him,
They gave this child more of themselves than that,
They gave him afterward every day, they became part of him.   20

6. phoebe-bird—The pewit, or pewee. **12. esculent**—edible.

The mother at home quietly placing the dishes on the supper-table,
The mother with mild words, clean her cap and gown, a wholesome odor falling
    off her person and clothes as she walks by,
The father, strong, self-sufficient, manly, mean, anger'd, unjust,
The blow, the quick loud word, the tight bargain, the crafty lure,
The family usages, the language, the company, the furniture, the yearning and
    swelling heart,   25
Affection that will not be gainsay'd, the sense of what is real, the thought if after
    all it should prove unreal,
The doubts of day-time and the doubts of night-time, the curious whether and how,
Whether that which appears so is so, or is it all flashes and specks?
Men and women crowding fast in the streets, if they are not flashes and specks,
    what are they?
The streets themselves and the façades of houses, and goods in the windows,   30
Vehicles, teams, the heavy-plank'd wharves, the huge crossing at the ferries,
The village on the highland seen from afar at sunset, the river between,
Shadows, aureola and mist, the light falling on roofs and gables of white or brown
    two miles off,
The schooner near by sleepily dropping down the tide, the little boat slack-tow'd
    astern,
The hurrying tumbling waves, quick-broken crests, slapping,   35
The strata of color'd clouds, the long bar of maroon-tint away solitary by itself,
    the spread of purity it lies motionless in,
The horizon's edge, the flying sea-crow, the fragrance of salt marsh and shore mud,
These became part of that child who then went forth every day, and who now goes,
    and will always go forth every day.

THE CITY DEAD-HOUSE

This poem was added to *Leaves of Grass* in 1867. In 1881 it was made part of
the "Autumn Rivulets" section.

By the city dead-house by the gate,
As idly sauntering wending my way from the clangor,
I curious pause, for lo! an outcast form, a poor dead prostitute brought,
Her corpse they deposit unclaim'd, it lies on the damp brick pavement,
The divine woman, her body, I see the body, I look on it alone,   5
That house once full of passion and beauty, all else I notice not,
Nor stillness so cold, nor running water from faucet, nor odors morbific impress me,
But the house alone—that wondrous house—that delicate fair house—that ruin!
That immortal house more than all the rows of dwellings ever built!
Or white-domed capitol with majestic figure surmounted, or all the old high-spired
    cathedrals,   10
That little house alone, more than them all—poor, desperate house;
Fair, fearful wreck—tenement of a soul—itself a soul,
Unclaim'd, avoided house—take one breath from my tremulous lips,

37. sea-crow—Eight or nine varieties of birds are popularly known as sea crows. Whitman
probably has reference to the pewit gull. **4. pavement**—that is, the brick platform on which
corpses were exposed for identification. Cold water (see line 7) was kept running over them for
preservation.

Take one tear, dropt aside as I go, for thought of you,
Dead house of love—house of madness and sin, crumbled, crush'd,   15
House of life, erewhile talking and laughing—but ah, poor house, dead even then,
Months, years, an echoing, garnish'd house—but dead, dead, dead.

PASSAGE TO INDIA

"Passage to India" first appeared in the pamphlet by that title in 1871 (copyright
1870), and was originally divided into 13 sections and 41 verse paragraphs. This
pamphlet was bound in with the 1871 *Leaves* as an "annex" by the same title. In
1876 the whole "Passage to India" section appeared in the *Two Rivulets* volume.
The present form of the poem dates from the 1881 edition.

In 1869 the tracks of the Union Pacific, extending westward from Omaha, were
joined to the tracks of the Central Pacific, extending eastward from San Francisco.
Because of the anxiety over the isolation of the Pacific Coast during the Civil War,
this linking of the continent by the first transcontinental railway system was a
national event of major importance. The reader of the poem will soon discover,
however, that the facilitating of the passage to India becomes for Whitman a symbol
of human progress towards richer and more golden futures.

1

Singing my days,
Singing the great achievements of the present,
Singing the strong light works of engineers,
Our modern wonders, (the antique ponderous Seven outvied,)
In the Old World the east the Suez canal,   5
The New by its mighty railroad spann'd,
The seas inlaid with eloquent gentle wires;
Yet first to sound, and ever sound, the cry with thee O soul,
The Past! the Past! the Past!

The Past—the dark unfathom'd retrospect!   10
The teeming gulf—the sleepers and the shadows!
The past—the infinite greatness of the past!
For what is the present after all but a growth out of the past?
(As a projectile form'd, impell'd, passing a certain line, still keeps on,
So the present, utterly form'd, impell'd by the past.)   15

2

Passage O soul to India!
Eclaircise the myths Asiatic, the primitive fables.

Not you alone proud truths of the world,
Nor you alone ye facts of modern science,
But myths and fables of eld, Asia's, Africa's fables,   20
The far-darting beams of the spirit, the unloos'd dreams,
The deep diving bibles and legends,

4. **Seven**—the Seven Wonders of the World. See any handbook of classical allusions. 5. **Suez canal**—completed in 1869. 7. **seas . . . wires**—The first wholly successful transatlantic cable was laid in 1866. 17. **Eclaircise**—a Whitmanesque coinage from the French: make clear.

The daring plots of the poets, the elder religions;
O you temples fairer than lilies pour'd over by the rising sun!
O you fables spurning the known, eluding the hold of the known, mounting to
    heaven!   25
You lofty and dazzling towers, pinnacled, red as roses, burnish'd with gold!
Towers of fables immortal fashion'd from mortal dreams!
You too I welcome and fully the same as the rest!
You too with joy I sing.

Passage to India!   30
Lo, soul, seest thou not God's purpose from the first?
The earth to be spann'd, connected by network,
The races, neighbors, to marry and be given in marriage,
The oceans to be cross'd, the distant brought near,
The lands to be welded together.   35

A worship new I sing,
You captains, voyagers, explorers, yours,
You engineers, you architects, machinists, yours,
You, not for trade or transportation only,
But in God's name, and for thy sake O soul.   40

3

Passage to India!
Lo soul for thee of tableaus twain,
I see in one the Suez canal initiated, open'd,
I see the procession of steamships, the Empress Eugenie's leading the van,
I mark from on deck the strange landscape, the pure sky, the level sand in the
    distance,   45
I pass swiftly the picturesque groups, the workmen gather'd,
The gigantic dredging machines.

In one again, different, (yet thine, all thine, O soul, the same,)
I see over my own continent the Pacific railroad surmounting every barrier,
I see continual trains of cars winding along the Platte carrying freight and passengers,
I hear the locomotives rushing and roaring, and the shrill steam-whistle,   51
I hear the echoes reverberate through the grandest scenery in the world,
I cross the Laramie plains, I note the rocks in grotesque shapes, the buttes,
I see the plentiful larkspur and wild onions, the barren, colorless sage-deserts,
I see in glimpses afar or towering immediately above me the great mountains, I
    see the Wind river and the Wahsatch mountains,   55

42. tableaus twain—the imaginative pictures of the Suez Canal and of the Pacific railroad,
which make up this section of the poem. 43-44. I see . . . Eugenie—When the Suez Canal
was opened for traffic, Nov. 17-20, 1869, a fleet of 68 vessels streamed through, headed by the
S.S. Aigle, with the Empress Eugénie of France on board. 46. picturesque groups—Construction of the canal had been interrupted by a quarrel over the employment of native laborers, and
the problem was in the public mind. Breaking the original contract (which required the employment of native labor) permitted the use of modern machinery. 49-60. I see . . . meadows—
In imagination Whitman traverses the route of the new railroad to the Pacific, going up the Platte
River (Nebraska), across the plains of eastern Wyoming, through the Wasatch Mountains of Utah,
past the Great Salt Lake, through the Humboldt range in Nevada, past Lake Tahoe (between
Nevada and California), and down the slopes of the Sierra Nevada into the great valley of California.

I see the Monument mountain and the Eagle's Nest, I pass the Promontory, I
    ascend the Nevadas,
I scan the noble Elk mountain and wind around its base,
I see the Humboldt range, I thread the valley and cross the river,
I see the clear waters of lake Tahoe, I see forests of majestic pines,
Or crossing the great desert, the alkaline plains, I behold enchanting mirages of
    waters and meadows,   60
Marking through these and after all, in duplicate slender lines,
Bridging the three or four thousand miles of land travel,
Tying the Eastern to the Western sea,
The road between Europe and Asia.

(Ah Genoese thy dream! thy dream!   65
Centuries after thou art laid in thy grave,
The shore thou foundest verifies thy dream.)

                                       4
Passage to India!
Struggles of many a captain, tales of many a sailor dead,
Over my mood stealing and spreading they come,   70
Like clouds and cloudlets in the unreach'd sky.

Along all history, down the slopes,
As a rivulet running, sinking now, and now again to the surface rising,
A ceaseless thought, a varied train—lo, soul, to thee, thy sight, they rise,
The plans, the voyages again, the expeditions;   75
Again Vasco de Gama sails forth,
Again the knowledge gain'd, the mariner's compass,
Lands found and nations born, thou born America,
For purpose vast, man's long probation fill'd,
Thou rondure of the world at last accomplish'd.   80

                                       5
O vast Rondure, swimming in space,
Cover'd all over with visible power and beauty,
Alternate light and day and the teeming spiritual darkness,
Unspeakable high processions of sun and moon and countless stars above,
Below, the manifold grass and waters, animals, mountains, trees,   85
With inscrutable purpose, some hidden prophetic intention,
Now first it seems my thought begins to span thee.

Down from the gardens of Asia descending radiating,
Adam and Eve appear, then their myriad progeny after them,
Wandering, yearning, curious, with restless explorations,   90
With questionings, baffled, formless, feverish, with never-happy hearts,
With that sad incessant refrain, *Wherefore unsatisfied soul?* and *Whither O*
    mocking life?

----

65. Genoese—Columbus. 76. Vasco de Gama—Vasco da Gama (1469?-1524) in 1497-99
sailed around Africa to India and returned to Portugal. 81. Rondure—the earth. 88. gardens
of Asia—the Garden of Eden.

Ah who shall soothe these feverish children?
Who justify these restless explorations?
Who speak the secret of impassive earth?   95
Who bind it to us? what is this separate Nature so unnatural?
What is this earth to our affections? (unloving earth, without a throb to answer ours,
Cold earth, the place of graves.)

Yet soul be sure the first intent remains, and shall be carried out,
Perhaps even now the time has arrived.   100
After the seas are all cross'd, (as they seem already cross'd,)

After the great captains and engineers have accomplish'd their work,
After the noble inventors, after the scientists, the chemist, the geologist, ethnologist,
Finally shall come the poet worthy that name,
The true son of God shall come singing his songs.   105

Then not your deeds only O voyagers, O scientists and inventors, shall be justified,
All these hearts as of fretted children shall be sooth'd,
All affection shall be fully responded to, the secret shall be told,
All these separations and gaps shall be taken up and hook'd and link'd together,
The whole earth, this cold, impassive, voiceless earth, shall be completely justified,
Trinitas divine shall be gloriously accomplish'd and compacted by the true son of
     God, the poet,   111
(He shall indeed pass the straits and conquer the mountains,
He shall double the cape of Good Hope to some purpose,)
Nature and Man shall be disjoin'd and diffused no more,
The true son of God shall absolutely fuse them.   115

6

Year at whose wide-flung door I sing!
Year of the purpose accomplish'd!
Year of the marriage of continents, climates and oceans!
(No mere doge of Venice now wedding the Adriatic,)
I see O year in you the vast terraqueous globe given and giving all, 120
Europe to Asia, Africa join'd, and they to the New World,
The lands, geographies, dancing before you, holding a festival garland,
As brides and bridegrooms hand in hand.

Passage to India!
Cooling airs from Caucasus far, soothing cradle of man,   125
The river Euphrates flowing, the past lit up again.

Lo, soul, the retrospect brought forward,
The old, most populous, wealthiest of earth's lands,
The streams of the Indus and the Ganges and their many affluents,
(I my shores of America walking to-day behold, resuming all,)   130
The tale of Alexander on his warlike marches suddenly dying,

111. **Trinitas**—Trinity. 119. **doge . . . Adriatic**—While Venice was an independent state, it was the custom for the Doge, in the state barge, annually to throw a gold ring into the Adriatic as a token of the wedding of Venice to the element which had enriched the state. 125. **Caucasus** —Anthropological theory, when this poem was written, held that the Caucasus region was probably the original home of man. 131. **Alexander**—Alexander the Great invaded India, dying 323 B.C. during his return march.

On one side China and on the other side Persia and Arabia,
To the south the great seas and the bay of Bengal,
The flowing literatures, tremendous epics, religions, castes,
Old occult Brahma interminably far back, the tender and junior Buddha,   135
Central and southern empires and all their belongings, possessors,
The wars of Tamerlane, the reign of Aurungzebe,
The traders, rulers, explorers, Moslems, Venetians, Byzantium, the Arabs, Portuguese,
The first travelers famous yet, Marco Polo, Batouta the Moor,
Doubts to be solv'd, the map incognita, blanks to be fill'd,   140
The foot of man unstay'd, the hands never at rest,
Thyself O soul that will not brook a challenge.

The mediaeval navigators rise before me,
The world of 1492, with its awaken'd enterprise,
Something swelling in humanity now like the sap of the earth in spring,   145
The sunset splendor of chivalry declining.

And who art thou sad shade?
Gigantic, visionary, thyself a visionary,
With majestic limbs and pious beaming eyes,
Spreading around with every look of thine a golden world,   150
Enhuing it with gorgeous hues.

As the chief histrion,
Down to the footlights walks in some great scene,
Dominating the rest I see the Admiral himself,
(History's type of courage, action, faith,)   155
Behold him sail from Palos leading his little fleet,
His voyage behold, his return, his great fame,
His misfortunes, calumniators, behold him a prisoner, chain'd,
Behold his dejection, poverty, death.

(Curious in time I stand, noting the efforts of heroes,   160
Is the deferment long? bitter the slander, poverty, death?
Lies the seed unreck'd for centuries in the ground? lo, to God's due occasion,
Uprising in the night, it sprouts, blooms,
And fills the earth with use and beauty.)

7

Passage indeed O soul to primal thought,   165
Not lands and seas alone, thy own clear freshness,
The young maturity of brood and bloom,
To realms of budding bibles.

135. **Brahma . . . Buddha**—The religion associated with Brahma greatly antedates that of Buddha (Gautama), who flourished about 500 B.C. 137. **Tamerlane**—the great Asiatic conqueror Tamerlane (1336-1405). 137. **Aurungzebe**—Aurung-Zebe (1619-1707), the last great emperor of Hindustan. 138. **Moslems . . .** —Whitman's list comprises nations and peoples especially associated with Oriental trade and conquest. 139. **Marco Polo**—(1254-1324) the famous traveler, who visited the Emperor of Cathay. 139. **Batouta**—Muhammed ibn Abd Allah, called Ibn Batutah (1303-1377), whose travels in Asia and Africa were translated into English by Samuel Lee in 1829. 152. **histrion**—actor; in this instance, Columbus, the **Admiral** of line 154. 156. **Palos** —Columbus sailed from the little Spanish seaport in question.

O soul, repressless, I with thee and thou with me,
Thy circumnavigation of the world begin,   170
Of man, the voyage of his mind's return,
To reason's early paradise,
Back, back to wisdom's birth, to innocent intuitions,
Again with fair creation.

8

O we can wait no longer,   175
We too take ship O soul,
Joyous we too launch out on trackless seas,
Fearless for unknown shores on waves of ecstasy to sail,
Amid the wafting winds, (thou pressing me to thee, I thee to me, O soul,)
Caroling free, singing our song of God,   180
Chanting our chant of pleasant exploration.

With laugh and many a kiss,
(Let others deprecate, let others weep for sin, remorse, humiliation,)
O soul thou pleasest me, I thee.

Ah more than any priest O soul we too believe in God,   185
But with the mystery of God we dare not dally.

O soul thou pleasest me, I thee,
Sailing these seas or on the hills, or waking in the night,
Thoughts, silent thoughts, of Time and Space and Death, like waters flowing,
Bear me indeed as through the regions infinite,   190
Whose air I breathe, whose ripples hear, lave me all over,
Bathe me O God in thee, mounting to thee,
I and my soul to range in range of thee.

O Thou transcendent,
Nameless, the fibre and the breath,   195
Light of the light, shedding forth universes, thou centre of them,
Thou mightier centre of the true, the good, the loving,
Thou moral, spiritual fountain—affection's source—thou reservoir,
(O pensive soul of me—O thirst unsatisfied—waitest not there,
Waitest not haply for us somewhere there the Comrade perfect?)   200
Thou pulse—thou motive of the stars, suns, systems,
That, circling, move in order, safe, harmonious,
Athwart the shapeless vastnesses of space,
How should I think, how breathe a single breath, how speak, if, out of myself,
I could not launch, to those, superior universes?   205

Swiftly I shrivel at the thought of God,
At Nature and its wonders, Time and Space and Death,
But that I, turning, call to thee O soul, thou actual Me,
And lo, thou gently masterest the orbs,
Thou matest Time, smilest content at Death,   210
And fillest, swellest full the vastness of Space.

---

200. Waitest—Whitman's punctuation obscures the sense: Thou, the Comrade perfect, waitest haply for us somewhere there.

Greater than stars or suns,
Bounding O soul thou journeyest forth;
What love than thine and ours could wider amplify?
What aspirations, wishes, outvie thine and ours O soul?   215
What dreams of the ideal? what plans of purity, perfection, strength,
What cheerful willingness for others' sake to give up all?
For others' sake to suffer all?

Reckoning ahead O soul, when thou, the time achiev'd,
The seas all cross'd, weather'd the capes, the voyage done,   220
Surrounded, copest, frontest God, yieldest, the aim attain'd,
As filled with friendship, love complete, the Elder Brother found,
The Younger melts in fondness in his arms.

9

Passage to more than India!
Are thy wings plumed indeed for such far flights?   225
O soul, voyagest thou indeed on voyages like those?
Disportest thou on waters such as those?
Soundest below the Sanscrit and the Vedas?
Then have thy bent unleash'd.

Passage to you, your shores, ye aged fierce enigmas!   230
Passage to you, to mastership of you, ye strangling problems!
You, strew'd with the wrecks of skeletons, that, living, never reach'd you.

Passage to more than India!
O secret to the earth and sky!
Of you O waters of the sea! O winding creeks and rivers!   235
Of you O woods and fields! of you strong mountains of my land!
Of you O prairies! of you gray rocks!
O morning red! O clouds! O rains and snows!
O day and night, passage to you!

O sun and moon and all you stars! Sirius and Jupiter!   240
Passage to you!

Passage, immediate passage! the blood burns in my veins!
Away O soul! hoist instantly the anchor!
Cut the hawsers—haul out—shake out every sail!
Have we not stood here like trees in the ground long enough?   245
Have we not grovel'd here long enough, eating and drinking like mere brutes?
Have we not darken'd and dazed ourselves with books long enough?

Sail forth—steer for the deep waters only,
Reckless O soul, exploring, I with thee, and thou with me,
For we are bound where mariner has not yet dared to go,   250
And we will risk the ship, ourselves and all.

228. Sanscrit—the ancient language of the Hindus, in which the Vedas, or holy books, are written.

O my brave soul!
O farther farther sail!
O daring joy, but safe! are they not all the seas of God?
O farther, farther, farther sail!   255

THE LAST INVOCATION

This poem first appears in the *Passage to India* pamphlet, in three numbered sections; was united with the contents of that pamphlet to the 1871 *Leaves;* reappeared in the "Passage to India" part of *Two Rivulets;* and finally came to rest in the "Whispers of Heavenly Death" section of the *Leaves* of 1881.

At the last, tenderly,
From the walls of the powerful fortress'd house,
From the clasp of the knitted locks, from the keep of the well-closed doors,
Let me be wafted.

Let me glide noiselessly forth;   5
With the key of softness unlock the locks—with a whisper,
Set ope the doors O soul.

Tenderly—be not impatient,
(Strong is your hold O mortal flesh,
Strong is your hold O love.)   10

TO A LOCOMOTIVE IN WINTER

This poem first appeared in the "Poems" section of *Two Rivulets* and in 1881 was transferred to "From Noon to Starry Night" in the *Leaves*. The student should look up a picture of the locomotive of the seventies; a picture will explain such phrases as "Thy great protruding head-light."

Thee for my recitative,
Thee in the driving storm even as now, the snow, the winter-day declining,
Thee in thy panoply, thy measur'd dual throbbing and thy beat convulsive,
Thy black cylindric body, golden brass and silvery steel,
Thy ponderous side-bars, parallel and connecting rods, gyrating, shuttling at thy
    sides,   5
Thy metrical, now swelling pant and roar, now tapering in the distance,
Thy great protruding head-light fix'd in front,
Thy long, pale, floating vapor-pennants, tinged with delicate purple,
The dense and murky clouds out-belching from thy smoke-stack,
Thy knitted frame, thy springs and valves, the tremulous twinkle of thy wheels, 10
Thy train of cars behind, obedient, merrily following,
Through gale or calm, now swift, now slack, yet steadily careering:
Type of the modern—emblem of motion and power—pulse of the continent,
For once come serve the Muse and merge in verse, even as here I see thee,
With storm, and buffeting gusts of wind and falling snow,   15
By day thy warning ringing bell to sound its notes,
By night thy silent signal lamps to swing.

Fierce-throated beauty!
Roll through my chant with all thy lawless music, thy swinging lamps at night,
Thy madly-whistled laughter, echoing, rumbling like an earthquake, rousing all, 20
Law of thyself complete, thine own track firmly holding,
(No sweetness debonair of tearful harp or glib piano thine,)
Thy trills of shrieks by rocks and hills return'd,
Launch'd o'er the prairies wide, across the lakes,
To the free skies, unpent and glad and strong.   25

THE MYSTIC TRUMPETER

This poem first appeared in *As a Strong Bird on Pinions Free* in 1872. In 1876 it
appeared in the *Two Rivulets* volume. In 1881 it was made part of "From Noon to
Starry Night" in the *Leaves*.

1

Hark, some wild trumpeter, some strange musician,
Hovering unseen in air, vibrates capricious tunes tonight.

I hear thee trumpeter, listening alert I catch thy notes,
Now pouring, whirling like a tempest round me,
Now low, subdued, now in the distance lost.   5

2

Come nearer bodiless one, haply in thee resounds
Some dead composer, haply thy pensive life
Was fill'd with aspirations high, unform'd ideals,
Waves, oceans musical, chaotically surging,
That now ecstatic ghost, close to me bending, thy cornet echoing, pealing,   10
Gives out to no one's ears but mine, but freely gives to mine,
That I may thee translate.

3

Blow trumpeter free and clear, I follow thee,
While at thy liquid prelude, glad, serene,
The fretting world, the streets, the noisy hours of day withdraw   15
A holy calm descends like dew upon me,
I walk in cool refreshing night the walks of Paradise,
I scent the grass, the moist air and the roses;
Thy song expands my numb'd imbonded spirit, thou freest, launchest me,
Floating and basking upon heaven's lake.   20

4

Blow again trumpeter! and for my sensuous eyes,
Bring the old pageants, show the feudal world.

What charm thy music works! thou makest pass before me,
Ladies and cavaliers long dead, barons are in their castle halls, the troubadours are
　　singing,

Arm'd knights go forth to redress wrongs, some in quest of the holy Graal;   25
I see the tournament, I see the contestants incased in heavy armor seated on stately
    champing horses,
I hear the shouts, the sounds of blows and smiting steel;
I see the Crusaders' tumultuous armies—hark, how the cymbals clang,
Lo, where the monks walk in advance, bearing the cross on high.

5

Blow again trumpeter! and for thy theme,   30
Take now the enclosing theme of all, the solvent and the setting,
Love, that is pulse of all, the sustenance and the pang,
The heart of man and woman all for love,
No other theme but love—knitting, enclosing, all-diffusing love.

O how the immortal phantoms crowd around me!   35
I see the vast alembic ever working, I see and know the flames that heat the world,
The glow, the blush, the beating hearts of lovers,
So blissful happy some, and some so silent, dark, and nigh to death;
Love, that is all the earth to lovers—love, that mocks time and space,
Love, that is day and night—love, that is sun and moon and stars,   40
Love, that is crimson, sumptuous, sick with perfume,
No other words but words of love, no other thought but love.

6

Blow again trumpeter—conjure war's alarums.

Swift to thy spell a shuddering hum like distant thunder rolls,
Lo, where the arm'd men hasten—lo, mid the clouds of dust the glint of bayonets, 45
I see the grime-faced cannoneers, I mark the rosy flash amid the smoke, I hear the
    cracking of the guns;
Nor war alone—thy fearful music-song, wild player, brings every sight of fear,
The deeds of ruthless brigands, rapine, murder—I hear the cries for help!
I see ships foundering at sea, I behold on deck and below deck the terrible tableaus.

7

O trumpeter, methinks I am myself the instrument thou playest,   5c
Thou melt'st my heart, my brain—thou movest, drawest, changest them at will;
And now thy sullen notes send darkness through me,
Thou takest away all cheering light, all hope,
I see the enslaved, the overthrown, the hurt, the opprest of the whole earth,
I feel the measureless shame and humiliation of my race, it becomes all mine,   55
Mine too the revenges of humanity, the wrongs of ages, baffled feuds and hatreds,
Utter defeat upon me weighs—all lost—the foe victorious,
(Yet 'mid the ruins Pride colossal stands unshaken to the last,
Endurance, resolution to the last.)

8

Now trumpeter for thy close,   60
Vouchsafe a higher strain than any yet,
Sing to my soul, renew its languishing faith and hope,

Rouse up my slow belief, give me some vision of the future,
Give me for once its prophecy and joy.

O glad, exulting, culminating song! 65
A vigor more than earth's is in thy notes,
Marches of victory—man disenthrall'd—the conqueror at last,
Hymns to the universal God from universal man—all joy!
A reborn race appears—a perfect world, all joy!
Women and men in wisdom innocence and health—all joy! 70
Riotous laughing bacchanals fill'd with joy!
War, sorrow, suffering gone—the rank earth purged—nothing but joy left!
The ocean fill'd with joy—the atmosphere all joy!
Joy! joy! in freedom, worship, love! joy in the ecstasy of life!
Enough to merely be! enough to breathe!
Joy! joy! all over joy! 75

SPIRIT THAT FORM'D THIS SCENE

Written in Platte Cañon, Colorado

This poem was published in the *Critic,* September 10, 1881, and afterwards included in the "From Noon to Starry Night" section of the 1881 *Leaves.* Whitman visited Colorado in the autumn of 1879.

Spirit that form'd this scene,
These tumbled rock-piles grim and red,
These reckless heaven-ambitious peaks,
These gorges, turbulent-clear streams, this naked freshness,
These formless wild arrays, for reasons of their own, 5
I know thee, savage spirit—we have communed together,
Mine too such wild arrays, for reasons of their own;
Was't charged against my chants they had forgotten art?
To fuse within themselves its rules precise and delicatesse?
The lyrist's measur'd beat, the wrought-out temple's grace—column and polish'd
    arch forgot? 10
But thou that revelest here—spirit that form'd this scene,
They have remember'd thee.

YEARS OF THE MODERN

As "Years of the Unperform'd" this poem originally formed part of *Drum-Taps,*
and was united with that section to the *Leaves* of 1867. In 1871 it became part of
"Songs of Parting" and took its present title. The present text dates from 1881.

Years of the modern! years of the unperform'd!
Your horizon rises, I see it parting away for more august dramas,
I see not America only, not only Liberty's nation but other nations preparing,
I see tremendous entrances and exits, new combinations, the solidarity of races,

9. **delicatesse**—Whitmanesque for "false delicacy."

I see that force advancing with irresistible power on the world's stage,   5
(Have the old forces, the old wars, played their parts? are the acts suitable to them
    closed?)
I see Freedom, completely arm'd and victorious and very haughty, with Law on
    one side and Peace on the other,
A stupendous trio all issuing forth against the idea of caste;
What historic denouements are these we so rapidly approach?
I see men marching and countermarching by swift millions,   10
I see the frontiers and boundaries of the old aristocracies broken,
I see the landmarks of European kings removed,
I see this day the People beginning their landmarks, (all others give way;)
Never were such sharp questions ask'd as this day,
Never was average man, his soul, more energetic, more like a God,   15
Lo, how he urges and urges, leaving the masses no rest!
His daring foot is on land and sea everywhere, he colonizes the Pacific, the archi-
    pelagoes,
With the steamship, the electric telegraph, the newspaper, the wholesale engines of
    war,
With these and the world-spreading factories he interlinks all geography, all lands;
What whispers are these O lands, running ahead of you, passing under the seas? 20
Are all nations communing? is there going to be but one heart to the globe?
Is humanity forming en-masse? for lo, tyrants tremble, crowns grow dim,
The earth, restive, confronts a new era, perhaps a general divine war,
No one knows what will happen next, such portents fill the days and nights;
Years prophetical! the space ahead as I walk, as I vainly try to pierce it, is full of
    phantoms,   25
Unborn deeds, things soon to be, project their shapes around me,
This incredible rush and heat, this strange ecstatic fever of dreams O years!
Your dreams O years, how they penetrate through me! (I know not whether I sleep
    or wake;)
The perform'd America and Europe grow dim, retiring in shadow behind me,
The unperform'd, more gigantic than ever, advance, advance upon me.   30

THE CALMING THOUGHT OF ALL

This poem first appears in the "Sands at Seventy" annex to the *Complete Poems
and Prose* of 1888 (1888-89).

That coursing on, whate'er men's speculations,
Amid the changing schools, theologies, philosophies,
Amid the bawling presentations new and old,
The round earth's silent vital laws, facts, modes continue.

GOOD-BYE, MY FANCY!

From *Good-Bye My Fancy* (1891), which became an "annex" to the *Leaves.*

Good-bye my Fancy!
Farewell dear mate, dear love!

I'm going away, I know not where,
Or to what fortune, or whether I may ever see you again,
So Good-bye my Fancy.   5
Now for my last—let me look back a moment;
The slower fainter ticking of the clock is in me,
Exit, nightfall, and soon the heart-thud stopping.

Long have we lived, joy'd caress'd together;
Delightful!—now separation—Good-bye my Fancy.   10

Yet let me not be too hasty,
Long indeed have we lived, slept, filter'd, become really blended into one;
Then if we die we die together, (yes, we'll remain one,)
If we go anywhere we'll go together to meet what happens,
May-be we'll be better off and blither, and learn something,   15
May-be it is yourself now ushering me to the true songs, (who knows?)
May-be it is you the mortal knob really undoing, turning—so now finally,
Good-bye—and hail! my Fancy.

DEMOCRATIC VISTAS

Democratic Vistas originally appeared in 1871 as a pamphlet of 84 pages entitled
Memoranda. Democratic Vistas. This was printed in Washington. It was collected
into the *Two Rivulets* volume of 1876, and thereafter formed part of the collected
prose, assuming the classificatory title of "Collect." The first paragraph printed in
the text does not appear in 1871; it was added by the time of the appearance of
the essay in *Complete Poetry and Prose* (1888).
  Minor variations of spelling and punctuation between the 1871 text and the final
version are not noted here, but all changes affecting the sense materially are noted
by the symbol (1871). Generally speaking, Whitman spelled the past tense of verbs
ending in "ed" regularly in 1871, and omitted the "e" in later versions. Complete
appreciation of the essay demands that the political corruption of the Grant administrations be kept in mind.

A s THE greatest lessons of Nature through the universe are perhaps the lessons of variety and freedom, the same present the greatest lessons also
in New World politics and progress. If a man were ask'd, for instance, the distinctive points contrasting modern European and American po-
5 litical and other life with the old Asiatic cultus, as lingering-bequeath'd yet in
China and Turkey, he might find the amount of them in John Stuart Mill's
profound essay on Liberty in the future, where he demands two main constitu-
ents, or sub-strata, for a truly grand nationality—1st, a large variety of character—and 2d, full play for human nature to expand itself in numberless and
10 even conflicting directions—(seems to be for general humanity much like the
influences that make up, in their limitless field, that perennial health-action of
the air we call the weather—an infinite number of currents and forces, and
contributions, and temperatures, and cross-purposes, whose ceaseless play of

  5. **cultus**—culture in the broadest sense. **6-7. Mill's . . . Liberty**—John Stuart Mill (1806-
1873) published *On Liberty* in 1859.

counterpart upon counterpart brings constant restoration and vitality). With this thought—and not for itself alone, but all it necessitates, and draws after it—let me begin my speculations.

America, filling the present with greatest deeds and problems, cheerfully accepting the past, including feudalism (as, indeed, the present is but the legitimate birth of the past, including feudalism), counts, as I reckon, for her justification and success (for who, as yet, dare claim success?) almost entirely on the future. Nor is that hope unwarranted. To-day, ahead, though dimly yet, we see, in vistas, a copious, sane, gigantic offspring. For our New World I consider far less important for what it has done, or what it is, than for results to come. Sole among nationalities, these States have assumed the task to put in forms of lasting power and practicality, on areas of amplitude rivaling the operations of the physical kosmos, the moral political speculations of ages, long, long deferr'd, the democratic republican principle, and the theory of development and perfection by voluntary standards, and self-reliance. Who else, indeed, except the United States, in history, so far, have accepted in unwitting faith, and, as we now see, stand, act upon, and go security for, these things?

But preluding no longer, let me strike the key-note of the following strain. First premising that, though the passages of it have been written at widely different times (it is, in fact, a collection of memoranda, perhaps for future designers, comprehenders), and though it may be open to the charge of one part contradicting another—for there are opposite sides to the great question of democracy, as to every great question—I feel the parts harmoniously blended in my own realization and convictions, and present them to be read only in such oneness, each page and each claim and assertion modified and temper'd by the others. Bear in mind, too, that they are not the result of studying up in political economy, but of the ordinary sense, observing, wandering among men, these States, these stirring years of war and peace. I will not gloss over the appaling dangers of universal suffrage in the United States. In fact, it is to admit and face these dangers I am writing. To him or her within whose thought rages the battle, advancing, retreating, between democracy's convictions, aspirations, and the people's crudeness, vice, caprices, I mainly write this essay. I shall use the words America and democracy as convertible terms. Not an ordinary one is the issue. The United States are destined either to surmount the gorgeous history of feudalism, or else prove the most tremendous failure of time. Not the least doubtful am I on any prospects of their material success. The triumphant future of their business, geographic and productive departments, on larger scales and in more varieties than ever, is certain. In those respects the republic must soon (if she does not already) outstrip all examples hitherto afforded, and dominate the world. . . .

[In eleven omitted paragraphs Whitman reiterates his favorite belief that the production of a great literature is the highest problem before the United States, justifying his argument from the

13. **moral political**—"moral and political" (1871). **15. self-reliance**—"self-suppliance" (1871). **18. preluding no longer**—omitted in 1871. **25. and each . . . assertion**—omitted in 1871. **33. I shall use**—New paragraph in 1871. **38. certain**—Whitman here appends a quotation from a speech by Vice President Colfax in 1870, and another quotation from the London *Weekly Times* (June 23, 1882) on the rapid growth in wealth of the United States.

examples of past civilizations, and declaring that the soul of man in America will be satisfied with nothing less. To the problem of spiritual values thus raised "the thinkers of the United States, in general so acute, have either given feeblest attention, or have remain'd, and remain, in a state of somnolence." At this point the text resumes.]

For my part, I would alarm and caution even the political and business reader, and to the utmost extent, against the prevailing delusion that the establishment of free political institutions, and plentiful intellectual smartness, with general good order, physical plenty, industry, &c. (desirable and precious ad-
5 vantages as they all are), do, of themselves, determine and yield to our experiment of democracy the fruitage of success. With such advantages at present fully, or almost fully, possess'd—the Union just issued, victorious, from the struggle with the only foes it need ever fear, (namely, those within itself, the interior ones), and with unprecedented materialistic advancement—society, in
10 these States, is canker'd, crude, superstitious, and rotten. Political, or law-made society is, and private, or voluntary society is also. In any vigor, the element of the moral conscience, the most important, the verteber to State or man, seems to me either entirely lacking, or seriously enfeebled or ungrown.

I say we had best look our times and lands searchingly in the face, like a
15 physician diagnosing some deep disease. Never was there, perhaps, more hollowness at heart than at present, and here in the United States. Genuine belief seems to have left us. The underlying principles of the States are not honestly believ'd in, (for all this hectic glow, and these melo-dramatic screamings), nor is humanity itself believ'd in. What penetrating eye does not everywhere see
20 through the mask? The spectacle is appaling. We live in an atmosphere of hypocrisy throughout. The men believe not in the women, nor the women in the men. A scornful superciliousness rules in literature. The aim of all the *littérateurs* is to find something to make fun of. A lot of churches, sects, &c., the most dismal phantasms I know, usurp the name of religion. Conversation
25 is a mass of badinage. From deceit in the spirit, the mother of all false deeds, the offspring is already incalculable. An acute and candid person, in the revenue department in Washington, who is led by the course of his employment to regularly visit the cities, North, South and West, to investigate frauds, has talk'd much with me about his discoveries. The depravity of the business
30 classes of our country is not less than has been supposed, but infinitely greater. The official services of America, national, state, and municipal, in all their branches and departments, except the judiciary, are saturated in corruption, bribery, falsehood, mal-administration; and the judiciary is tainted. The great cities reek with respectable as much as non-respectable robbery and scoundrel-
35 ism. In fashionable life, flippancy, tepid amours, weak infidelism, small aims, or no aims at all, only to kill time. In business, (this all-devouring modern word, business), the one sole object is, by any means, pecuniary gain. The magician's serpent in the fable ate up all the other serpents; and money-making is our magician's serpent, remaining to-day sole master of the field. The best
40 class we show, is but a mob of fashionably dress'd speculators and vulgarians.

12. verteber—"vertebrae" (1871). 31. The official—"The whole of the official" (1871). 38. magician's serpent—*Cf.* Ex. 7: 9-12.

True, indeed, behind this fantastic farce, enacted on the visible stage of society, solid things and stupendous labors are to be discover'd, existing crudely
and going on in the background, to advance and tell themselves in time. Yet
the truths are none the less terrible. I say that our New World democracy,
however great a success in uplifting the masses out of their sloughs, in ma-   5
terialistic development, products, and in a certain highly-deceptive superficial
popular intellectuality, is, so far, an almost complete failure in its social aspects,
and in really grand religious, moral, literary, and esthetic results. In vain do
we march with unprecedented strides to empire so colossal, outvying the antique, beyond Alexander's, beyond the proudest sway of Rome. In vain have   10
we annex'd Texas, California, Alaska, and reach north for Canada and south
for Cuba. It is as if we were somehow being endow'd with a vast and more
and more thoroughly-appointed body, and then left with little or no soul.

Let me illustrate further, as I write, with current observations, localities, &c.
The subject is important, and will bear repetition. After an absence, I am now   15
again (September, 1870) in New York City and Brooklyn, on a few weeks'
vacation. The splendor, picturesqueness, and oceanic amplitude and rush of
these great cities, the unsurpass'd situation, rivers and bay, sparkling sea-tides,
costly and lofty new buildings, façades of marble and iron, of original grandeur
and elegance of design, with the masses of gay color, the preponderance of   20
white and blue, the flags flying, the endless ships, the tumultuous streets, Broadway, the heavy, low, musical roar, hardly ever intermitted, even at night; the
jobbers' houses, the rich shops, the wharves, the great Central Park, and the
Brooklyn Park of hills, (as I wander among them this beautiful fall weather,
musing, watching, absorbing)—the assemblages of the citizens in their groups,   25
conversations, trades, evening amusements, or along the by-quarters—these, I
say, and the like of these, completely satisfy my senses of power, fulness, motion, &c., and give me, through such senses and appetites, and through my
esthetic conscience, a continued exaltation and absolute fulfilment. Always and
more and more, as I cross the East and North rivers, the ferries, or with the   30
pilots in their pilot-houses, or pass an hour in Wall Street, or the gold exchange,
I realize, (if we must admit such partialisms) that not Nature alone is great
in her fields of freedom and the open air, in her storms, the shows of night
and day, the mountains, forests, seas—but in the artificial, the work of man
too is equally great—in this profusion of teeming humanity—in these in-   35
genuities, streets, goods, houses, ships—these hurrying, feverish, electric crowds
of men, their complicated business genius (not least among the genuises) and
all this mighty, many-threaded wealth and industry concentrated here.

But sternly discarding, shutting our eyes to the glow and grandeur of the
general superficial effect, coming down to what is of the only real importance,   40
Personalities, and examining minutely, we question, we ask, Are there, indeed,
men here worthy the name? Are there athletes? Are there perfect women,
to match the generous material luxuriance? Is there a pervading atmosphere

---

10-11. **have we annex'd**—"do we annex" (1871). 19. **façades**—"the façades" (1871).
26. **trades**—"trade" (1871). 29. **conscience**—consciousness. 36. **hurrying**—"seething, hurrying" (1871). 36. **electric**—omitted in 1871. 40. **superficial**—omitted in 1871.

of beautiful manners? Are there crops of fine youths, and majestic old persons? Are there arts worthy freedom and a rich people? Is there a great moral and religious civilization—the only justification of a great material one? Confess that to severe eyes, using the moral microscope upon humanity, a sort of
5 dry and flat Sahara appears, these cities, crowded with petty grotesques, malformations, phantoms, playing meaningless antics.(Confess that everywhere, in shop, street, church, theatre, bar-room, official chair, are pervading flippancy and vulgarity, low cunning, infidelity—everywhere the youth puny, impudent, foppish, prematurely ripe—everywhere an abnormal libidinousness, unhealthy
10 forms, male, female, painted, padded, dyed, chignon'd, muddy complexions, bad blood, the capacity for good motherhood deceasing or deceas'd, shallow notions of beauty, with a range of manners, or rather lack of manners, (considering the advantages enjoy'd), probably the meanest to be seen in the world.)
    Of all this, and these lamentable conditions, to breathe into them the breath
15 recuperative of sane and heroic life, I say a new founded literature, not merely to copy and reflect existing surfaces, or pander to what is called taste—not only to amuse, pass away time, celebrate the beautiful, the refined, the past, or exhibit technical, rhythmic, or grammatical dexterity—but a literature underlying life, religious, consistent with science, handling the elements and forces
20 with competent power, teaching and training men—and, as perhaps the most precious of its results, achieving the entire redemption of woman out of these incredible holds and webs of silliness, millinery, and every kind of dyspeptic depletion—and thus insuring to the States a strong and sweet Female Race, a race of perfect Mothers—is what is needed.
25   And now, in the full conception of these facts and points, and all that they infer, pro and con—with yet unshaken faith in the elements of the American masses, the composites, of both sexes, and even consider'd as individuals—and ever recognizing in them the broadest bases of the best literary and esthetic appreciation—I proceed with my speculations, Vistas.
30   First, let us see what we can make out of a brief, general, sentimental consideration of political democracy, and whence it has arisen, with regard to some of its current features, as an aggregate, and as the basic structure of our future literature and authorship. We shall, it is true, quickly and continually find the origin-idea of the singleness of man, individualism, asserting itself,
35 and cropping forth, even from the opposite ideas. But the mass, or lump character, for imperative reasons, is to be ever carefully weigh'd, borne in mind,

---

   3-4. Confess—New paragraph in 1871. 4. that—"that rather" (1871). 10. chignon'd—A chignon, fashionable in 1870, was a large mass of hair twisted around a pad and worn at the nape of the neck by the women. 13. world—"Of these rapidly-sketch'd hiatuses the two which seem to me most serious are, for one, the condition, absence, or perhaps the singular abeyance, of moral conscientious fibre all through American society; and, for another, the appaling depletion of women in their powers of sane athletic maternity, their crowning attribute, and ever making the woman, in loftiest spheres, superior to the man.
   "I have sometimes thought, indeed, that the sole avenue and means of a reconstructed sociology depended, primarily, on a new birth, elevation, expansion, invigoration of woman, affording, for races to come, (as the conditions that antedate birth are indispensable), a perfect motherhood. Great, great, indeed, far greater than they know, is the sphere of women. But doubtless the question of such new sociology all goes together, includes many varied and complex influences and premises, and the man as well as the woman, and the woman as well as the man." (Whitman's note) 30. sentimental—elevated(?).

and provided for. Only from it, and from its proper regulation and potency, comes the other, comes the chance of individualism. The two are contradictory, but our task is to reconcile them.

The political history of the past may be summ'd up as having grown out of what underlies the words, order, safety, caste, and especially out of the need of   5
some prompt deciding authority, and of cohesion at all cost. Leaping time, we come to the period within the memory of people now living, when, as from some lair where they had slumber'd long, accumulating wrath, sprang up and are yet active, (1790, and on even to the present, 1870), those noisy eructations, destructive iconoclasms, a fierce sense of wrongs, amid which moves   10
the form, well known in modern history, in the Old World, stain'd with much blood, and mark'd by savage reactionary clamors and demands. These bear, mostly, as on one inclosing point of need.

For after the rest is said—after the many time-honor'd and really true things for subordination, experience, rights of property, &c., have been listen'd to and   15
acquiesced in—after the valuable and well-settled statement of our duties and relations in society is thoroughly conn'd over and exhausted—it remains to bring forward and modify everything else with the idea of that Something a man is (last precious consolation of the drudging poor), standing apart from all else, divine in his own right, and a woman in hers, sole and untouchable   20
by any canons of authority, or any rule derived from precedent, state-safety, the acts of legislatures, or even from what is called religion, modesty, or art. The radiation of this truth is the key of the most significant doings of our immediately preceding three centuries, and has been the political genesis and life of America. Advancing visibly, it still more advances invisibly. Underneath   25
the fluctuations of the expressions of society, as well as the movements of the politics of the leading nations of the world, we see steadily pressing ahead and strengthening itself, even in the midst of immense tendencies toward aggregation, this image of completeness in separatism, of individual personal dignity, of a single person, either male or female, characterized in the main, not from   30
extrinsic acquirements or position, but in the pride of himself or herself alone; and, as an eventual conclusion and summing up (or else the entire scheme of things is aimless, a cheat, a crash), the simple idea that the last, best dependence is to be upon humanity itself, and its own inherent, normal, full-grown qualities, without any superstitious support whatever. This idea of perfect in-   35
dividualism it is indeed that deepest tinges and gives character to the idea of the aggregate. For it is mainly or altogether to serve independent separatism that we favor a strong generalization, consolidation. As it is to give the best vitality and freedom to the rights of the States (every bit as important as the right of nationality, the union), that we insist on the identity of the Union at   40
all hazards.

3. task—"The question hinted here is one which time only can answer. Must not the virtue of modern Individualism, continually enlarging, usurping all, seriously affect, perhaps keep down entirely, in America, the like of the ancient virtue of Patriotism, the fervid and absorbing love of general country? I have no doubt myself that the two will merge, and will mutually profit and brace each other, and that from them a greater product, a third, will arise. But I feel that at present they and their oppositions form a serious problem and paradox in the United States." (Whitman's note) 10. amid—"and amid" (1871). 23. The radiation—New paragraph in 1871.

The purpose of democracy—supplanting old belief in the necessary absoluteness of establish'd dynastic rulership, temporal, ecclesiastical, and scholastic, as
furnishing the only security against chaos, crime, and ignorance—is, through
many transmigrations, and amid endless ridicules, arguments, and ostensible
5 failures, to illustrate, at all hazards, this doctrine or theory that man, properly
train'd in sanest, highest freedom, may and must become a law, and series of
laws, unto himself, surrounding and providing for, not only his own personal
control, but all his relations to other individuals, and to the State; and that,
while other theories, as in the past histories of nations, have proved wise enough,
10 and indispensable perhaps for their conditions, *this,* as matters now stand in
our civilized world, is the only scheme worth working from, as warranting
results like those of Nature's laws, reliable, when once establish'd, to carry on
themselves. . . .

[In 34 succeeding paragraphs, here omitted, Whitman discusses democracy as a political concept,
arguing that the failure of the Civil War to split the country is proof of the strength of democracy,
that the future of democratic government lies in training individuals to rule themselves under fundamental laws, and declaring that a more nearly universal ownership of property is the "gravitation-
hold" of political liberalism. With the din of the crudities of the election of 1868 in his ears, he
yet looks forward confidently to the future success of the democratic experiment, believing that the
growth of the western part of the country will increase the chances of the success of the great experiment. He experiences "the joy of being toss'd in the brave turmoil of these times," and says of the
nation that "we have never deserted, never despair'd, never abandon'd the faith." Here the text
resumes.]

So much contributed, to be conn'd well, to help prepare and brace our edifice,
15 our plann'd Idea—we still proceed to give it in another of its aspects—perhaps
the main, the high façade of all. For to democracy, the leveler, the unyielding
principle of the average, is surely join'd another principle, equally unyielding,
closely tracking the first, indispensable to it, opposite (as the sexes are opposite), and whose existence, confronting and ever modifying the other, often
20 clashing, paradoxical, yet neither of highest avail without the other, plainly
supplies to these grand cosmic politics of ours, and to the launch'd-forth mortal
dangers of republicanism, to-day or any day, the counterpart and offset whereby
Nature restrains the deadly original relentlessness of all her first-class laws.
This second principle is individuality, the pride and centripetal isolation of a
25 human being in himself—identity—personalism. Whatever the name, its acceptance and thorough infusion through the organizations of political commonalty now shooting Aurora-like about the world, are of utmost importance,
as the principle itself is needed for very life's sake. It forms, in a sort, or is to
form, the compensating balance-wheel of the successful working machinery of
30 aggregate America.

And, if we think of it, what does civilization itself rest upon—and what object has it, with its religions, arts, schools, &c., but rich, luxuriant, varied personalism? To that, all bends; and it is because toward such result democracy
alone, on anything like Nature's scale, breaks up the limitless fallows of human-
35 kind, and plants the seed, and gives fair play, that its claims now precede the
rest. The literature, songs, esthetics, &c., of a country are of importance princi-

27. **Aurora-like**—in the sense of dawn-like (not aurora borealis!). 36. **The literature**—
New paragraph in 1871.

pally because they furnish the materials and suggestions of personality for the women and men of that country, and enforce them in a thousand effective ways. As the topmost claim of a strong consolidating of the nationality of these States, is, that only by such powerful compaction can the separate States se- cure that full and free swing within their spheres, which is becoming to them, 5 each after its kind, so will individuality, with unimpeded branchings, flourish best under imperial republican forms.

Assuming Democracy to be at present in its embryo condition, and that the only large and satisfactory justification of it resides in the future, mainly through the copious production of perfect characters among the people, and 10 through the advent of a sane and pervading religiousness, it is with regard to the atmosphere and spaciousness fit for such characters, and of certain nutri- ment and cartoon-draftings proper for them, and indicating them for New- World purposes, that I continue the present statement—an exploration, as of new ground, wherein, like other primitive surveyors, I must do the best I can, 15 leaving it to those who come after me to do much better. (The service, in fact, if any, must be to break a sort of first path or track, no matter how rude and ungeometrical.)

We have frequently printed the word Democracy. Yet I cannot too often repeat that it is a word the real gist of which still sleeps, quite unawaken'd, 20 notwithstanding the resonance and the many angry tempests out of which its syllables have come, from pen or tongue. It is a great word, whose his- tory, I suppose, remains unwritten, because that history has yet to be en- acted. It is, in some sort, younger brother of another great and often-used word, Nature, whose history also waits unwritten. As I perceive, the tenden- 25 cies of our day, in the States, (and I entirely respect them), are toward those vast and sweeping movements, influences, moral and physical, of humanity, now and always current over the planet, on the scale of the impulses of the elements. Then it is also good to reduce the whole matter to the considera- tion of a single self, a man, a woman, on permanent grounds. Even for the 30

3. ways—"After the rest is satiated, all interest culminates in the field of persons, and never flags there. Accordingly in this field have the great poets and literatuses signally toil'd. They too, in all ages, all lands, have been creators, fashioning, making types of men and women, as Adam and Eve are made in the divine fable. Behold, shaped, bred by orientalism, feudalism, through their long growth and culmination, and breeding back in return—(when shall we have an equal series typical of democracy?)—behold, commencing in primal Asia, (apparently formulated, in what beginning we know, in the gods of the mythologies, and coming down thence,) a few sam- ples out of the countless product, bequeath'd to the moderns, bequeath'd to America as studies. For the men, Yudishtura, Rama, Arjuna, Solomon, most of the Old and New Testament characters; Achilles, Ulysses, Theseus, Prometheus, Hercules, Aeneas, Plutarch's heroes; the Merlin of Celtic bards; the Cid, Arthur and his knights, Siegfried and Hagen in the Nibelungen, Roland and Oliver; Roustam in the Shah-Nemah; and so on to Milton's Satan, Cervantes' Don Quixote, Shakspere's Hamlet, Richard II., Lear, Marc Antony, &c., and the modern Faust. These, I say, are models, combined, adjusted to other standards than America's, but of priceless value to her and hers.

"Among women, the goddesses of the Egyptian, Indian and Greek mythologies, certain Bible characters, especially the Holy Mother; Cleopatra, Penelope; the portraits of Brunhelde and Chriemhilde in the Nibelungen; Oriana, Una, &c., the modern Consuelo, Walter Scott's Jeanie and Effie Deans, &c., &c. (Yet woman portray'd or outlin'd at her best, or as perfect human mother, does not hitherto, it seems to me, fully appear in literature.)" (Whitman's note) 3. As the—New paragraph in 1871. 13. cartoon-draftings—preliminary sketches. 15. primitive—in the sense of exploratory. 25. As I—New paragraph in 1871.

treatment of the universal, in politics, metaphysics, or anything, sooner or later we come down to one single, solitary soul.

There is, in sanest hours, a consciousness, a thought that rises, independent, lifted out from all else, calm, like the stars, shining eternal. This is the thought
5 of identity—yours for you, whoever you are, as mine for me. Miracle of miracles, beyond statement, most spiritual and vaguest of earth's dreams, yet hardest basic fact, and only entrance to all facts. In such devout hours, in the midst of the significant wonders of heaven and earth (significant only because of the Me in the centre), creeds, conventions, fall away and become of no account
10 before this simple idea. Under the luminousness of real vision, it alone takes possession, takes value. Like the shadowy dwarf in the fable, once liberated and look'd upon, it expands over the whole earth, and spreads to the roof of heaven. The quality of BEING, in the object's self, according to its own central idea and purpose, and of growing therefrom and thereto—not criticism by other
15 standards, and adjustments thereto—is the lesson of Nature. True, the full man wisely gathers, culls, absorbs; but if, engaged disproportionately in that, he slights or overlays the precious idiocrasy and special nativity and intention that he is, the man's self, the main thing, is a failure, however wide his general cultivation. Thus, in our times, refinement and delicatesse are not only at-
20 tended to sufficiently, but threaten to eat us up, like a cancer. Already, the democratic genius watches, ill-pleased, these tendencies. Provision for a little healthy rudeness, savage virtue, justification of what one has in one's self, whatever it is, is demanded. Negative qualities, even deficiencies, would be a relief. Singleness and normal simplicity and separation, amid this more and
25 more complex, more and more artificialized state of society—how pensively we yearn for them! how we would welcome their return!

In some such direction, then—at any rate enough to preserve the balance— we feel called upon to throw what weight we can, not for absolute reasons, but current ones. To prune, gather, trim, conform, and ever cram and stuff,
30 and be genteel and proper, is the pressure of our days. While aware that much can be said even in behalf of all this, we perceive that we have not now to consider the question of what is demanded to serve a half-starved and barbarous nation, or set of nations, but what is most applicable, most pertinent, for numerous congeries of conventional, over-corpulent societies, already be-
35 coming stifled and rotten with flatulent, infidelistic literature, and polite conformity and art. In addition to establish'd sciences, we suggest a science as it were of healthy average personalism, on original-universal grounds, the object of which should be to raise up and supply through the States a copious race of superb American men and women, cheerful, religious, ahead of any yet
40 known.

America has yet morally and artistically originated nothing. She seems singularly unaware that the models of persons, books, manners, &c., appropriate for former conditions and for European lands, are but exiles and exotics here.

---

11. **dwarf**—vague reference to the conventional episodes in certain stories of the Arabian Nights in which the genie, released from a bottle, is at first small, then swells to gigantic dimensions. 17. **idiocrasy**—idiosyncrasy, quality of being individual. 36. **In addition**—New paragraph in 1871. 41. **America . . . nothing**—"America, leaving out her politics, has yet morally originated nothing." (1871)

No current of her life, as shown on the surfaces of what is authoritatively called her society, accepts or runs into social or esthetic democracy; but all the currents set squarely against it. Never, in the Old World, was thoroughly up-holster'd exterior appearance and show, mental and other, built entirely on the idea of caste, and on the sufficiency of mere outside acquisition—never were 5 glibness, verbal intellect, more the test, the emulation—more loftily elevated as head and sample—than they are on the surface of our republican States this day. The writers of a time hint the mottoes of its gods. The word of the mod-ern, say these voices, is the word Culture.

We find ourselves abruptly in close quarters with the enemy. This word 10 Culture, or what it has come to represent, involves, by contrast, our whole theme, and has been, indeed, the spur, urging us to engagement. Certain ques-tions arise. As now taught, accepted and carried out, are not the processes of culture rapidly creating a class of supercilious infidels, who believe in nothing? Shall a man lose himself in countless masses of adjustments, and be so shaped 15 with reference to this, that, and the other, that the simply good and healthy and brave parts of him are reduced and clipp'd away, like the bordering of box in a garden? You can cultivate corn and roses and orchards—but who shall cultivate the mountain peaks, the ocean, and the tumbling gorgeousness of the clouds? Lastly—is the readily-given reply that culture only seeks to help, 20 systematize, and put in attitude, the elements of fertility and power, a con-clusive reply?

I do not so much object to the name, or word, but I should certainly insist, for the purposes of these States, on a radical change of category, in the distri-bution of precedence. I should demand a programme of culture, drawn out, 25 not for a single class alone, or for the parlors or lecture-rooms, but with an eye to practical life, the West, the working-men, the facts of farms and jack-planes and engineers, and of the broad range of the women also of the middle and working strata, and with reference to the perfect equality of women, and of a grand and powerful motherhood. I should demand of this programme or 30 theory a scope generous enough to include the widest human area. It must have for its spinal meaning the formation of a typical personality of character, eligible to the uses of the high average of men—and *not* restricted by conditions ineligible to the masses. The best culture will always be that of the manly and courageous instincts, and loving perceptions, and of self-respect—aiming to form, 35 over this continent, an idiocrasy of universalism, which, true child of America, will bring joy to its mother, returning to her in her own spirit, recruiting myriads of offspring, able, natural, perceptive, tolerant, devout believers in her, America, and with some definite instinct why and for what she has arisen, most vast, most formidable of historic births, and is, now and here, with wonder- 40 ful step, journeying through Time.

The problem, as it seems to me, presented to the New World, is, under perma-nent law and order, and after preserving cohesion (ensemble-Individuality), at all hazards, to vitalize man's free play of special Personalism, recognizing in

13. **As now**—New paragraph in 1871. 34. **The best**—New paragraph in 1871. 36. **uni-versalism**—in the sense of universality. 38. **offspring**—"men" (1871). 38. **devout . . . her** —"devout, real men, alive and full, believers in her" (1871).

it something that calls ever more to be consider'd, fed, and adopted as the substratum for the best that belongs to us, (government indeed is for it), including the new esthetics of our future.

To formulate beyond this present vagueness—to help line and put before us 5 the species, or a specimen of the species, of the democratic ethnology of the future, is a work toward which the genius of our land, with peculiar encouragement, invites her well-wishers. Already certain limnings, more or less grotesque, more or less fading and watery, have appear'd. We too (repressing doubts and qualms), will try our hand.

10 (Attempting, then, however crudely, a basic model or portrait of personality for general use for the manliness of the States (and doubtless that is most useful which is most simple and comprehensive for all, and toned low enough), we should prepare the canvas well beforehand. Parentage must consider itself in advance. (Will the time hasten when fatherhood and motherhood shall become 15 a science—and the noblest science?) To our model, a clear-blooded, strong-fibred physique, is indispensable; the questions of food, drink, air, exercise, assimilation, digestion, can never be intermitted. Out of these we descry a well-begotten selfhood—in youth, fresh, ardent, emotional, aspiring, full of adventure; at maturity, brave, perceptive, under control, neither too talkative nor 20 too reticent, neither flippant nor sombre; of the bodily figure, the movements easy, the complexion showing the best blood, somewhat flush'd, breast expanded, an erect attitude, a voice whose sound outvies music, eyes of calm and steady gaze, yet capable also of flashing—and a general presence that holds its own in the company of the highest. (For it is native personality, and that alone, 25 that endows a man to stand before presidents or generals, or in any distinguish'd collection, with *aplomb*—and *not* culture, or any knowledge or intellect whatever.)

With regard to the mental-educational part of our model, enlargement of intellect, stores of cephalic knowledge, &c., the concentration thitherward of 30 all the customs of our age, especially in America, is so overweening, and provides so fully for that part, that, important and necessary as it is, it really needs nothing from us here—except, indeed, a phrase of warning and restraint. Manners, costumes, too, though important, we need not dwell upon here. Like beauty, grace of motion, &c., they are results. Causes, original things, being 35 attended to, the right manners unerringly follow. Much is said, among artists, of "the grand style," as if it were a thing by itself. When a man, artist or whoever, has health, pride, acuteness, noble aspirations, he has the motive-elements of the grandest style. The rest is but manipulation (yet that is no small matter).

Leaving still unspecified several sterling parts of any model fit for the future 40 personality of America, I must not fail, again and ever, to pronounce myself on one, probably the least attended to in modern times—a hiatus, indeed, threatening its gloomiest consequences after us. I mean the simple, unsophisticated Conscience, the primary moral element. If I were asked to specify in what quarter lie the grounds of darkest dread, respecting the America of our hopes, 45 I should have to point to this particular. I should demand the invariable appli-

29. **cephalic**—having to do with the head. 33. **Manners**—New paragraph in 1871. 41. **hiatus**—gap.

cation to individuality, this day and any day, of that old, ever-true plumb-rule of persons, eras, nations. Our triumphant modern civilizee, with his all-schooling and his wondrous appliances, will still show himself but an amputa-tion while this deficiency remains. Beyond (assuming a more hopeful tone), the vertebration of the manly and womanly personalism of our Western world, 5 can only be, and is, indeed, to be (I hope) its all penetrating Religiousness.

The ripeness of Religion is doubtless to be looked for in this field of in-dividuality, and is a result that no organization or church can ever achieve. As history is poorly retain'd by what the technists call history, and is not given out from their pages, except the learner has in himself the sense of the well- 10 wrapt, never yet written, perhaps impossible to be written, history—so Religion, although casually arrested, and, after a fashion, preserv'd in the churches and creeds, does not depend at all upon them, but is a part of the identified soul, which, when greatest, knows not bibles in the old way, but in new ways— the identified soul, which can really confront Religion when it extricates itself 15 entirely from the churches, and not before.

Personalism fuses this, and favors it. I should say, indeed, that only in the perfect uncontamination and solitariness of individuality may the spirituality of religion positively come forth at all. Only here, and on such terms, the meditation, the devout ecstasy, the soaring flight. Only here, communion with 20 the mysteries, the eternal problems, whence? whither? Alone, and identity, and the mood—and the soul emerges, and all statements, churches, sermons, melt away like vapors. Alone, and silent thought and awe, and aspiration— and then the interior consciousness, like a hitherto unseen inscription, in magic ink, beams out its wondrous lines to the sense. Bibles may convey, and priests 25 expound, but it is exclusively for the noiseless operation of one's isolated Self, to enter the pure ether of veneration, reach the divine levels, and commune with the unutterable.

To practically enter into politics is an important part of American person-alism. To every young man, North and South, earnestly studying these things, 30 I should here, as an offset to what I have said in former pages, now also say, that may be to views of very largest scope, after all, perhaps the political (per-haps the literary and sociological), America goes best about its development its own way—sometimes, to temporary sight, appaling enough. It is the fashion among dillettants and fops (perhaps I myself am not guiltless) to decry the 35 whole formulation of the active politics of America, as beyond redemption, and to be carefully kept away from. See you that you do not fall into this error. America, it may be, is doing very well upon the whole, notwithstanding these antics of the parties and their leaders, these half-brain'd nominees, the many ignorant ballots, and many elected failures and blatherers. It is the dillettants, 40 and all who shirk their duty, who are not doing well. As for you, I advise you to enter more strongly yet into politics. I advise every young man to do so.

2. civilizee—A coinage, on the model of employee, meaning one who is civilized. Here used derogatively. 4. Beyond—New paragraph in 1871. 6. Religiousness—"The architecture of In-dividuality will ever prove various, with countless different combinations; but here they rise as into common pinnacles, some higher, some less high, only all pointing upward." (Whitman's note, 1871) 7. The ripeness—"Indeed, the ripeness" (1871). 9. technists—specialists. 35. perhaps I— 1871 omits matter in parenthesis. 36. formulation—"formulation and personnel" (1871).

Always inform yourself; always do the best you can; always vote. Disengage yourself from parties. They have been useful, and to some extent remain so; but the floating, uncommitted electors, farmers, clerks, mechanics, the masters of parties—watching aloof, inclining victory this side or that side—such are the
5 ones most needed, present and future. For America, if eligible at all to down-fall and ruin, is eligible within herself, not without; for I see clearly that the combined foreign world could not beat her down. But these savage, wolfish parties alarm me. Owning no law but their own will, more and more combative, less and less tolerant of the idea of ensemble and of equal brotherhood, the
10 perfect equality of the States, the ever-over-arching American ideas, it behooves you to convey yourself implicitly to no party, nor submit blindly to their dictators, but steadily hold yourself judge and master over all of them.

So much, (hastily toss'd together, and leaving far more unsaid), for an ideal, or intimations of an ideal, toward American manhood. But the other sex, in our
15 land, requires at least a basis of suggestion.

I have seen a young American woman, one of a large family of daughters, who, some years since, migrated from her meagre country home to one of the Northern cities, to gain her own support. She soon became an expert seam-stress, but finding the employment too confining for health and comfort,
20 she went boldly to work for others, to housekeep, cook, clean, &c. After trying several places, she fell upon one where she was suited. She has told me that she finds nothing degrading in her position; it is not inconsistent with personal dignity, self-respect, and the respect of others. She confers benefits and receives them. She has good health; her presence itself is healthy and bracing;
25 her character is unstain'd; she has made herself understood, and preserves her independence, and has been able to help her parents, and educate and get places for her sisters; and her course of life is not without opportunities for mental improvement, and of much quiet, uncosting happiness and love.

I have seen another woman who, from taste and necessity conjoin'd, has gone
30 into practical affairs, carries on a mechanical business, partly works at it herself, dashes out more and more into real hardy life, is not abash'd by the coarseness of the contact, knows how to be firm and silent at the same time, holds her own with unvarying coolness and decorum, and will compare, any day, with superior carpenters, farmers, and even boatmen and drivers. For all that, she has not
35 lost the charm of the womanly nature, but preserves and bears it fully, though through such rugged presentation. . . .

[Here follow in the original two additional portraits of admirable womanhood.]

The foregoing portraits, I admit, are frightfully out of line from these imported models of womanly personality—the stock feminine characters of the current novelist, or of the foreign court poems (Ophelias, Enids, princesses, or
40 ladies of one thing or another) which fill the envying dreams of so many poor girls, and are accepted by our men, too, as supreme ideals of feminine excellence to be sought after. But I present mine just for a change.

2. parties—It should be remembered that party lines were much more tightly drawn in the seventies than since. 39. Ophelias, Enids—Ophelia in *Hamlet;* Enid in Tennyson's *The Idylls of the King.*

Then there are mutterings (we will not now stop to heed them here, but they must be heeded) of something more revolutionary. The day is coming when the deep questions of woman's entrance amid the arenas of practical life, politics, the suffrage, &c., will not only be argued all around us, but may be put to decision, and real experiment.   5

Of course, in these States, for both man and woman, we must entirely recast the types of highest personality from what the oriental, feudal, ecclesiastical worlds bequeath us, and which yet possess the imaginative and esthetic fields of the United States, pictorial and melodramatic, not without use as studies, but making sad work, and forming a strange anachronism upon the scenes 10 and exigencies around us. Of course, the old undying elements remain. The task is, to successfully adjust them to new combinations, our own days. Nor is this so incredible. I can conceive a community, to-day and here, in which, on a sufficient scale, the perfect personalities, without noise meet; say in some pleasant Western settlement or town, where a couple of hundred best men and women, of 15 ordinary worldly status, have by luck been drawn together, with nothing extra of genius or wealth, but virtuous, chaste, industrious, cheerful, resolute, friendly and devout. I can conceive such a community organized in running order, powers judiciously delegated—farming, building, trade, courts, mails, schools, elections, all attended to; and then the rest of life, the main thing, 20 freely branching and blossoming in each individual, and bearing golden fruit. I can see there, in every young and old man, after his kind, and in every woman after hers, a true personality, develop'd, exercised proportionately in body, mind, and spirit. I can imagine this case as one not necessarily rare or difficult, but in buoyant accordance with the municipal and general requirements of our times. 25 And I can realize in it the culmination of something better than any stereotyped *éclat* of history or poems. Perhaps, unsung, undramatized, unput in essays or biographies—perhaps even some such community already exists, in Ohio, Illinois, Missouri, or somewhere, practically fulfilling itself, and thus outvying, in cheapest vulgar life, all that has been hitherto shown in best ideal pictures. 30

In short, and to sum up, America, betaking herself to formative action (as it is about time for more solid achievement, and less windy promise), must, for her purposes, cease to recognize a theory of character grown of feudal aristocracies, or form'd by merely literary standards, or from any ultramarine, full-dress formulas of culture, polish, caste, &c., and must sternly promulgate 35 her own new standard, yet old enough, and accepting the old, the perennial elements, and combining them into groups, unities, appropriate to the modern, the democratic, the West, and to the practical occasions and needs of our own cities, and of the agricultural regions. Ever the most precious in the common. Ever the fresh breeze of field, or hill, or lake, is more than any palpitation of 40 fans, though of ivory, and redolent with perfume; and the air is more than the costliest perfumes. . . .

[In three succeeding paragraphs, here omitted, Whitman insists that a truly American culture will sum up past culture, and "move, self-poised, through the ether, and shine like heaven's own suns!"]

8. yet possess—"yet fully possess" (1871). **11. Of course**—New paragraph in 1871. **34. ultramarine**—here, transatlantic

What, however, do we more definitely mean by New World literature?
Are we not doing well enough here already? Are not the United States this
day busily using, working, more printer's type, more presses, than any other?
Do not our publishers fatten quicker and deeper? (helping themselves, under
5 shelter of a delusive and sneaking law, or rather absence of law, to most of
their forage, poetical, pictorial, historical, romantic, even comic, without money
and without price—and fiercely resisting the timidest proposal to pay for it.)
Many will come under this delusion—but my purpose is to dispel it. I say that
a nation may hold and circulate rivers and oceans of very readable print,
10 journals, magazines, novels, library-books, "poetry," &c.—such as the States
to-day possess and circulate—of unquestionable aid and value—hundreds of
new volumes annually composed and brought out here, respectable enough, indeed unsurpass'd in smartness and erudition—with further hundreds, or rather
millions (as by free forage or theft aforemention'd), also thrown into the
15 market—and yet, all the while, the said nation, strictly speaking, may possess
no literature at all.

Repeating our inquiry, what, then do we mean by real literature? especially
the democratic literature of the future? Hard questions to meet. The clues are
inferential, and turn us to the past. At best, we can only offer suggestions,
20 comparisons, circuits. . . .

[In five succeeding paragraphs, here omitted, Whitman pays tribute to the great literature of the
past, but finds the United States possesses no such lofty literature. He denounces the ephemeral literature of the day, of which audiences come to tire.]

Compared with the past, our modern science soars, and our journals serve—
but ideal and even ordinary romantic literature, does not, I think, substantially
advance. Behold the prolific brood of the contemporary novel, magazine-tale,
theatre-play, &c. The same endless thread of tangled and superlative love-story,
25 inherited, apparently from the Amadises and Palmerins of the 13th, 14th, and
15th centuries over there in Europe. The costumes and associations brought
down to date, the seasoning hotter and more varied, the dragons and ogres
left out—but the *thing,* I should say, has not advanced—is just as sensational,
just as strain'd—remains about the same, nor more, nor less.

30 What is the reason our time, our lands, that we see no fresh local courage,
sanity, of our own—the Mississippi, stalwart Western men, real mental and
physical facts, Southerners, &c., in the body of our literature? especially the
poetic part of it. But always, instead, a parcel of dandies and ennuyées, dapper
little gentlemen from abroad, who flood us with their thin sentiment of
35 parlors, parasols, piano-songs, tinkling rhymes, the five-hundredth importation—
or whimpering and crying about something, chasing one aborted conceit after
another, and forever occupied in dyspeptic amours with dyspeptic women.

3. other—"uttering and absorbing more publications than any other?" inserted (1871). 5. law
—The United States had no international copyright law until 1891; the absence of such a statute
permitted the republication of English books without royalty to the author. 8. Many—New paragraph in 1871. 18. democratic—"American" (1871). 25. Amadises and Palmerins—Whitman is probably referring to the *Amadis de Gaul* (1540) by the Frenchman Herberay, a compendium of romantic stories; and to *Palmerin de Inglaterra* (1547) by the Spaniard Luis Hurtado. The
latter was condensed and translated by Robert Southey. 26. associations—"associations are"
(1871).

While, current and novel, the grandest events and revolutions, and stormiest
passions of history, are crossing to-day with unparallel'd rapidity and magnificence over the stages of our own and all the continents, offering new materials,
opening new vistas, with largest needs, inviting the daring launching forth of
conceptions in literature, inspired by them, soaring in highest regions, serving 5
art in its highest (which is only the other name for serving God, and serving
humanity), where is the man of letters, where is the book, with any nobler
aim than to follow in the old track, repeat what has been said before—and, as
its utmost triumph, sell well, and be erudite or elegant?

Mark the roads, the processes, through which these States have arrived, 10
standing easy, henceforth ever-equal, ever-compact, in their range to-day.
European adventures? the most antique? Asiatic or African? old history—
miracles—romances? Rather, our own unquestion'd facts. They hasten, incredible, blazing bright as fire. From the deeds and days of Columbus down
to the present, and including the present—and especially the late secession war 15
—when I con them, I feel, every leaf, like stopping to see if I have not made
a mistake, and fall'n on the splendid figments of some dream. But it is no
dream. We stand, live, move, in the huge flow of our age's materialism—in its
spirituality. We have had founded for us the most positive of lands. The
founders have pass'd to other spheres—but what are these terrible duties they 20
have left us?

Their politics the United States have, in my opinion, with all their faults,
already substantially establish'd, for good, on their own native, sound, long-
vista'd principles, never to be overturned, offering a sure basis for all the rest.
With that, their future religious forms, sociology, literature, teachers, schools, 25
costumes, &c., are of course to make a compact whole, uniform, on tallying principles. For how can we remain, divided, contradicting ourselves, this way?
I say we can only attain harmony and stability by consulting ensemble and the
ethic purports, and faithfullly building upon them. For the New World, indeed, after two grand stages of preparation-strata, I perceive that now a third 30
stage, being ready for (and without which the other two were useless), with
unmistakable signs appears. The First stage was the planning and putting on
record the political foundation rights of immense masses of people—indeed all
people—in the organization of republican National, State, and municipal governments, all constructed with reference to each, and each to all. This is the 35
American programme, not for classes, but for universal man, and is embodied in
the compacts of the Declaration of Independence, and, as it began and has
now grown, with its amendments, the Federal Constitution—and in the State
governments, with all their interiors, and with general suffrage; those having
the sense not only of what is in themselves, but that their certain several things 40

1. **While**—New paragraph in 1871. **17. But it**—New paragraph in 1871. **27. way**—"Note,
to-day, an instructive curious spectacle and conflict. Science, (twin, in its fields, of Democracy in
its)—Science, testing absolutely all thoughts, all works, has already burst well upon the world—a
sun, mounting, most illuminating, most glorious—surely never again to set. But against it, deeply
entrench'd, holding possession, yet remains (not only through the churches and schools, but by
imaginative literature, and unregenerate poetry) the fossil theology of the mythic-materialistic, superstitious, untaught and credulous, fable-loving, primitive ages of humanity." (Whitman's note)
29. For the New—New paragraph in 1871.

started, planted, hundreds of others in the same direction duly arise and follow. The Second stage relates to material prosperity, wealth, produce, labor-saving machines, iron, cotton, local, State and continental railways, inter-communication and trade with all lands, steamships, mining, general employ-
5 ment, organization of great cities, cheap appliances for comfort, numberless technical schools, books, newspapers, a currency for money circulation, &c. The Third stage, rising out of the previous ones, to make them and all illustrious, I, now, for one, promulge, announcing a native expression-spirit, getting into form, adult, and through mentality, for these States, self-contain'd, different
10 from others, more expansive, more rich and free, to be evidenced by original authors and poets to come, by American personalities, plenty of them, male and female, traversing the States, none excepted—and by native superber tableaux and growths of language, songs, operas, orations, lectures, architecture —and by a sublime and serious Religious Democracy sternly taking command,
15 dissolving the old, sloughing off surfaces, and from its own interior and vital principles, reconstructing, democratizing society. . . .

[In five paragraphs, here omitted, Whitman restates with vigor his belief that America needs a new literature; says that good literature is everywhere good, but that there is interwoven in it "the materiality and personality of a land, a race," and finds most current American books "useless and a mockery."]

(Of what is called the drama, or dramatic presentation in the United States, as now put forth at the theatres, I should say it deserves to be treated with the same gravity, and on a par with the questions of ornamental confectionery at
20 public dinners, or the arrangement of curtains and hangings in a ball-room— nor more, nor less.) Of the other, I will not insult the reader's intelligence (once really entering into the atmosphere of these Vistas) by supposing it necessary to show in detail, why the copious dribble, either of our little or well-known rhymesters, does not fulfill, in any respect, the needs and august occasions of
25 this land. America demands a poetry that is bold, modern, and all-surrounding and kosmical, as she is herself. It must in no respect ignore science or the modern, but inspire itself with science and the modern. It must bend its vision toward the future, more than the past. Like America, it must extricate itself from even the greatest models of the past, and, while courteous to them, must
30 have entire faith in itself, and the products of its own democratic spirit only. Like her, it must place in the van, and hold up at all hazards, the banner of the divine pride of man in himself (the radical foundation of the new religion). Long enough have the People been listening to poems in which common humanity, deferential, bends low, humiliated, acknowledging superiors. But
35 America listens to no such poems. Erect, inflated, and fully self-esteeming be the chant; and then America will listen with pleased ears. . . .

[The omitted paragraphs (eight in all) sketch out in some detail the regional possibilities of a future American literature, and call for books expressing a "wholesome extasy."]

In the prophetic literature of these States (the reader of my speculations will miss their principal stress unless he allows well for the point that a new Litera-

8. promulge—"promulgate" (1871). 21. Of the other—New paragraph in 1871. 30. democratic—"original" (1871). 37 ff. the reader . . . Democracy—The material in parentheses does not appear in 1871.

ture, perhaps a new Metaphysics, certainly a new Poetry, are to be, in my
opinion, the only sure and worthy supports and expressions of the American
Democracy), Nature, true Nature, and the true idea of Nature, long absent,
must, above all, become fully restored, enlarged, and must furnish the pervading atmosphere to poems, and the test of all high literary and esthetic com- 5
positions. I do not mean the smooth walks, trimm'd hedges, poseys and nightingales of the English poets, but the whole orb, with its geologic history, the
kosmos, carrying fire and snow, that rolls through the illimitable areas, light as
a feather, though weighing billions of tons. Furthermore, as by what we now
partially call Nature is intended, at most, only what is entertainable by the 10
physical conscience, the sense of matter, and of good animal health—on these
it must be distinctly accumulated, incorporated, that man, comprehending these,
has, in towering superaddition, the moral and spiritual consciences, indicating
his destination beyond the ostensible, the mortal.

To the heights of such estimate of Nature indeed ascending, we proceed to 15
make observations for our Vistas, breathing rarest air. What is I believe called
Idealism seems to me to suggest (guarding against extravagance, and ever
modified even by its opposite) the course of inquiry and desert of favor for our
New World metaphysics, their foundation of and in literature, giving hue to all.

The elevating and etherealizing ideas of the unknown and of unreality must 20
be brought forward with authority, as they are the legitimate heirs of the

    19. all—"The culmination and fruit of literary artistic expression, and its final fields of pleasure
for the human soul, are in metaphysics, including the mysteries of the spiritual world, the soul
itself, and the question of the immortal continuation of our identity. In all ages, the mind of man
has brought up here—and always will. Here, at least, of whatever race or era, we stand on common ground. Applause, too, is unanimous, antique or modern. Those authors who work well in
this field—though their reward, instead of a handsome percentage, or royalty, may be but simply
the laurel-crown of the victors in the great Olympic games—will be dearest to humanity, and their
works, however esthetically defective, will be treasur'd forever. The altitude of literature and
poetry has always been religion—and always will be. The Indian Vedas, the Naçkas of Zoroaster,
the Talmud of the Jews, the Old Testament, the Gospel of Christ and his disciples, Plato's works,
the Koran of Mohammed, the Edda of Snorro, and so on toward our own day, to Swedenborg,
and to the invaluable contributions of Leibnitz, Kant and Hegel—these with such poems only in
which (while singing well of persons and events, of the passions of man, and the shows of the
material universe,) the religious tone, the consciousness of mystery, the recognition of the future,
of the unknown, of Deity over and under all, and of the divine purpose, are never absent, but
indirectly give tone to all—exhibit literature's real heights and elevations, towering up like the
great mountains of the earth. Standing on this ground—the last, the highest, only permanent
ground—and sternly criticising, from it, all works, either of the literary, or any art, we have
peremptorily to dismiss every pretensive production, however fine its esthetic or intellectual points,
which violates or ignores, or even does not celebrate, the central divine idea of All, suffusing universe, of eternal trains of purpose, in the development, by however slow degrees, of the physical,
moral, and spiritual kosmos. I say he has studied, meditated to no profit, whatever may be his
mere erudition, who has not absorb'd this simple consciousness and faith. It is not entirely new—
but it is for Democracy to elaborate it, and look to build upon and expand from it, with uncompromising reliance. Above the doors of teaching the inscription is to appear. Though little or
nothing can be absolutely known, perceiv'd, except from a point of view which is evanescent, yet
we know at least one permanency, that Time and Space, in the will of God, furnish successive
chains, completions of material births and beginnings, solve all discrepancies, fears and doubts, and
eventually fulfil happiness—and that the prophecy of those births, namely spiritual results, throws
the true arch over all teaching, all science. The local considerations of sin, disease, deformity, ignorance, death, &c., and their measurement by the superficial mind, and ordinary legislation and
theology, are to be met by science, boldly accepting, promulging this faith, and planting the seeds
of superber laws—of the explication of the physical universe through the spiritual—and clearing
the way for a religion, sweet and unimpugnable alike to little child or great savan." (Whitman's
note)

known, and of reality, and at least as great as their parents. Fearless of scoffing, and of the ostent, let us take our stand, our ground, and never desert it, to confront the growing excess and arrogance of realism. To the cry, now victorious—the cry of sense, science, flesh, incomes, farms, merchandise, logic, intellect, demonstrations, solid perpetuities, buildings of brick and iron, or even the facts of the shows of trees, earth, rocks, &c., fear not, my brethren, my sisters, to sound out with equally determin'd voice, that conviction brooding within the recesses of every envision'd soul—illusions! apparitions! figments all! True, we must not condemn the show, neither absolutely deny it, for the indispensability of its meanings; but how clearly we see that, migrate in soul to what we can already conceive of superior and spiritual points of view, and, palpable as it seems under present relations, it all and several might, nay certainly would, fall apart and vanish.

(I hail with joy the oceanic, variegated, intense practical energy, the demand for facts, even the business materialism of the current age, our States. But wo to the age or land in which these things, movements, stopping at themselves, do not tend to ideas.) As fuel to flame, and flame to the heavens, so must wealth, science, materialism—even this democracy of which we make so much—unerringly feed the highest mind, the soul. Infinitude the flight: fathomless the mystery. Man, so diminutive, dilates beyond the sensible universe, competes with, outcopes space and time, meditating even one great idea. Thus, and thus only, does a human being, his spirit, ascend above, and justify, objective Nature, which, probably nothing in itself, is incredibly and divinely serviceable, indispensable, real, here. And as the purport of objective Nature is doubtless folded, hidden, somewhere here—as somewhere here is what this globe and its manifold forms, and the light of day, and night's darkness, and life itself, with all its experiences, are for—it is here the great literature, especially verse, must get its inspiration and throbbing blood. Then may we attain to a poetry worthy the immortal soul of man, and which, while absorbing materials, and, in their own sense, the shows of Nature, will, above all, have, both directly and indirectly, a freeing, fluidizing, expanding, religious character, exulting with science, fructifying the moral elements, and stimulating aspirations, and meditations on the unknown.) . . .

[The remaining fourteen paragraphs of the essay are mainly a vigorous rhetorical restatement of the ideas of the preceding portion.]

2. **ostent**—ostentatious (?).

EMILY DICKINSON

1830-1886

I. A NEW ENGLAND GIRLHOOD (1830–1856)

1830 Born December 10 in Amherst, Massachusetts. Her father, Edward Dickinson, was for forty years treasurer of Amherst College. Helen Hunt (Jackson), later author of *Ramona,* was an intimate friend and neighbor, and put her into *Mercy Philbrick's Choice.*

1846 Beginning of lifelong acquaintance with Susan Gilbert, her most sympathetic friend and future sister-in-law.

1847 Attended Mount Holyoke Female Seminary, under Mary Lyon; showed somewhat rebellious spirit toward restrictive regulations.

1848 Resumed work in Amherst Academy. Platonic friendship with Benjamin F. Newton, apprentice in her father's law office, who encouraged her writing of verse. He died in 1853.

1852 "Valentine Extravaganza" printed in Samuel Bowles' *Springfield Republican,* February 26.

1854 On the way to Washington, where her father was a member of Congress, she seems to have fallen in love with the Rev. Charles Wadsworth of Philadelphia, her "dearest earthly friend," in whose image she created the "lover" of her poems. The experience confirmed her Puritan mysticism.

1856 Susan Gilbert married her brother Austin and lived next to the Dickinson homestead. To "Sister Sue" Emily sent poetic epistles.

II. THE LEAF AT LOVE TURNED BACK (1862–1886)

1862 With Wadsworth's removal to San Francisco, Emily withdrew from Amherst society and occupied herself increasingly with poetry. Applied to Thomas Wentworth Higginson for advice and criticism, but, though appreciative, ignored it.

1866 "The Snake" sent to the *Springfield Republican,* published February 14.

1870 Colonel T. W. Higginson visited Emily at Amherst, August 16, and became her "teacher."

1874 Death of her father resulted in Emily's almost complete retirement. Mother paralyzed the next year, dying in 1882.

1878 Publication of the third and last poem during Emily's lifetime, "Success," in Helen Hunt Jackson's *A Masque of Poets.*

1884 Emily suffered a breakdown in health.

1886 Died May 15. Asked that her writings be destroyed, but her devoted sister Lavinia saved them.

III. POSTHUMOUS RECOGNITION (1886–1936)

1890   Posthumous publication of *Poems,* ed. by T. W. Higginson and Mabel L. Todd.

1891   *Poems: Second Series,* ed. by Mabel L. Todd and T. W. Higginson.

1896   *Poems: Third Series,* ed. with an introduction by Mrs. Todd.

1914   *The Single Hound,* ed. by Martha Dickinson Bianchi.

1924   *Complete Poems of Emily Dickinson,* ed. with introduction by Martha Dickinson Bianchi.

1929   *Further Poems,* ed. by Martha Dickinson Bianchi and Arthur L. Hampson.

1936   *Unpublished Poems,* ed. by M. D. Bianchi and A. L. Hampson.

1945   *Bolts of Melody: New Poems,* ed. by Mabel L. Todd and Millicent T. Bingham.

BIOGRAPHIES AND CRITICISM: Mabel Loomis Todd, *Letters of Emily Dickinson,* 2 vols., Harper, 1894; new and enlarged ed., 1931; Martha D. Bianchi, *The Life and Letters of Emily Dickinson,* Houghton Mifflin, 5th printing, 1929; MacGregor Jenkins, *Emily Dickinson, Friend and Neighbor,* Little, Brown, 1930; rev. ed., 1939; Josephine Pollitt, *Emily Dickinson: The Human Background of Her Poetry,* Harper, 1930; Genevieve Taggard, *The Life and Mind of Emily Dickinson,* Knopf, 1930; Martha D. Bianchi, *Emily Dickinson Face to Face,* Houghton Mifflin, 1932; G. F. Whicher, *This Was a Poet: A Critical Biography of Emily Dickinson,* Scribner, 1938; Emilio Cecchi, *Emily Dickinson,* Morcelliana (Brescia), 1939; Millicent T. Bingham, *Ancestor's Brocade,* Harper, 1945. See also T. W. Higginson, *Carlyle's Laugh and Other Surprises,* Houghton Mifflin, 1909, pp. 249-83, and Clement Wood, *Poets of America,* Dutton, 1925, pp. 82-96. For a rich bibliography of critical articles see *Literary History of the United States,* Vol. III, pp. 467-70.

BIBLIOGRAPHIES AND EDITIONS: A. L. Hampson, *Emily Dickinson: A Bibliography,* Northampton, 1930; G. F. Whicher, *Emily Dickinson: A Bibliography,* Jones Library, Amherst, 1930; rev. ed., 1931.

Conrad Aiken, *Selected Poems of Emily Dickinson,* London, Jonathan Cape, 1924, has an excellent critical introduction; the poems are chosen from the Todd-Higginson series. *The Poems of Emily Dickinson,* edd. M. D. Bianchi and A. L. Hampson, Little, Brown, 1937, includes *Further Poems* and *Unpublished Poems.* But a knowledge of the true texts of the poems must await the edition to be prepared by T. H. Johnson from the original manuscripts, now in the Houghton Library at Harvard University.

Emily Dickinson, our major woman poet, wrote during the "Indian summer" of New England, but was not fully appreciated until the rebellious, skeptical nineteen twenties. Her brief, sharply imaged stanzas, when they appeared posthumously, inspired poets like Stephen Crane, Amy Lowell, and the postwar naturalists. Drawing her imagery from flowers, the village world, household doings, Biblical story, and legal phrasings, she quietly rejected the world's values, and expressed her notions about nature, love, and God in her own cryptic way. Some of her poems appear to be communicated in code; a few are fragmentary, or falter to an obscure or inappropriate close. All are touched by mysticism and require an alert imagination for their comprehension. Their elusiveness comes in part from their compression, in part from their whimsical metaphor. They eschew rhyme and assonance, yet have tonal harmony. They are based in part on hymn tunes of her childhood and are the expression of a sensitive soul whose thirst for knowledge of the world about her marks a mind at once daring and naïvely responsive to simple things, beauty, love, justice. They are the product of an impish, sometimes arch, but intensely human spirit, driven to dramatizing itself and finding outlet in a passion for actuality, in a paradoxical swoop of thought, perhaps in an intimation of immortality. The numbering of the poems is not that of *The Complete Poems,* but of this volume. Poems numbered XXXV-XXXVIII are from the new volume, *Bolts of Melody.*

I *

Success is counted sweetest
By those who ne'er succeed.
To comprehend a nectar
Requires sorest need.

Not one of all the purple host   5
Who took the flag to-day
Can tell the definition,
So clear, of victory,

As he, defeated, dying,
On whose forbidden ear   10
The distant strains of triumph
Break, agonized and clear.

II †

If you were coming in the fall,
I'd brush the summer by
With half a smile and half a spurn,
As housewives do a fly.

If I could see you in a year,   5
I'd wind the months in balls,
And put them each in separate drawers,
Until their time befalls.

If only centuries delayed,
I'd count them on my hand,   10
Subtracting till my fingers dropped
Into Van Diemen's land,

If certain, when this life was out,
That yours and mine should be,
I'd toss it yonder like a rind,   15
And taste eternity.

But now, all ignorant of the length
Of time's uncertain wing,
It goads me, like the goblin bee,
That will not state its sting.   20

III

I cannot live with you,
It would be life,
And life is over there
Behind the shelf

The sexton keeps the key to,   5
Putting up
Our life, his porcelain,
Like a cup

* First published in Helen Hunt Jackson, ed., *A Masque of Poets,* 1878. **3. nectar**—a drink of the gods, not to be tasted but "comprehended." **5. purple**—royal; the imagery, based on the dying Civil War soldier, suggests value won through deprivation. † Poems II-XIII are an imaginative reconstruction of the stages of Emily Dickinson's emotional experience with Charles Wadsworth, and perhaps earlier with Ben Newton ("My life closed twice"). They progress from the feeling aroused by Wadsworth's departure for California to the conviction that "A death-blow is a life-blow," and finally to the belief that she will be a heavenly bride. **12. Van Diemen's land**—Tasmania, far beyond California, was being settled at this time.

Discarded of the housewife,
Quaint or broken;   10
A newer Sèvres pleases,
Old ones crack.

I could not die with you,
For one must wait
To shut the other's gaze down,—   15
You could not.

And I, could I stand by
And see you freeze,
Without my right of frost,
Death's privilege?   20

Nor could I rise with you,
Because your face
Would put out Jesus',
That new grace

Glow plain and foreign   25
On my homesick eye,
Except that you, than he
Shone closer by.

They'd judge us—how?
For you served Heaven, you know,   30
Or sought to;
I could not,

Because you saturated sight,
And I had no more eyes
For sordid excellence   35
As Paradise.

And were you lost, I would be,
Though my name
Rang loudest
On the heavenly fame.   40

And were you saved,
And I condemned to be
Where you were not,
That self were hell to me.

So we must keep apart,   45
You there, I here,
With just the door ajar
That oceans are,

And prayer,
And that pale sustenance,   50
Despair!

I V

Not with a club the heart is broken,
   Nor with a stone;
A whip, so small you could not see it,
   I've known

To lash the magic creature   5
   Till it fell,
Yet that whip's name too noble
   Then to tell.

Magnanimous of bird
   By boy descried,   10
To sing unto the stone
   Of which it died.

V

Pain has an element of blank;
It cannot recollect
When it began, or if there were
A day when it was not.

It has no future but itself,   5
Its infinite realms contain
Its past, enlightened to perceive
New periods of pain.

V I

A death-blow * is a life-blow to some
Who, till they died, did not alive become;
Who, had they lived, had died, but when
They died, vitality begun.

V I I

Heart, we will forget him!
   You and I, to-night!

---

11. **Sèvres**—French porcelain. **30. served Heaven**—Wadsworth was a clergyman.
* death-blow—The renunciation of her already married lover seems to be the central fact in her history. The play on words is in the manner of seventeenth-century poets like John Donne.

You may forget the warmth he gave,
  I will forget the light.

When you have done, pray tell me,   5
  That I my thoughts may dim;
Haste! lest while you're lagging,
  I may remember him!

VIII

My life closed twice before its close;
  It yet remains to see
If Immortality unveil
  A third event to me,

So huge, so hopeless to conceive,   5
  As these that twice befell.
Parting is all we know of heaven,
  And all we need of hell.

IX

The soul selects her own society,
Then shuts the door;
On her divine majority *
Obtrude no more.

Unmoved, she notes the chariot's pausing   5
At her low gate;
Unmoved, an emperor is kneeling
Upon her mat.

I've known her from an ample nation
Choose one;   10
Then close the valves of her attention
Like stone.

X

A wife at daybreak I shall be;
Sunrise, hast thou a flag for me?
At midnight I am yet a maid—
How short it takes to make it bride!
Then, Midnight, I have passed from thee   5
Unto the East and Victory.

Midnight, "Good night."
I hear them call.

The angels bustle in the hall,
Softly my Future climbs the stair,   10
I fumble at my childhood's prayer—
So soon to be a child no more!
Eternity, I'm coming, Sir,—
Master, I've seen that face before.

XI

Much madness is divinest sense
To a discerning eye;
Much sense the starkest madness.
'Tis the majority
In this, as all, prevails.   5
Assent, and you are sane;
Demur,—you're straightway dangerous,
And handled with a chain.

XII

Alter? When the hills do.
Falter? When the sun
Question if his glory
Be the perfect one.

Surfeit? When the daffodil   5
Doth of the dew:
Even as herself, O friend!
I will of you!

XIII†

They say that "time assuages,"—
  Time never did assuage;
An actual suffering strengthens,
  As sinews do, with age.

Time is a test of trouble,   5
  But not a remedy.
If such it prove, it prove too
  There was no malady.

XIV

I taste a liquor never brewed,
From tankards scooped in pearl;

---

* **majority**—sanctity. † First published in the *Independent,* May 21, 1896.

Not all the vats upon the Rhine
Yield such an alcohol!

Inebriate of air am I,   5
And debauchee of dew,
Reeling, through endless summer days,
From inns of molten blue.

When landlords turn the drunken bee
Out of the foxglove's door,   10
When butterflies renounce their drams,
I shall but drink the more!

Till seraphs swing their snowy hats,
And saints to windows run,
To see the little tippler   15
Leaning against the sun!

XV

He preached upon "breadth" till it argued
   him narrow,—
The broad are too broad to define;
And of "truth" until it proclaimed him a
   liar,—
The truth never flaunted a sign.

Simplicity fled from his counterfeit presence
As gold the pyrites would shun.   6
What confusion would cover the innocent
   Jesus
To meet so enabled a man!

XVI

I know that he exists
Somewhere, in silence.
He has hid his rare life
From our gross eyes.

'Tis an instant's play,   5
'Tis a fond ambush,
Just to make bliss
Earn her own surprise!

But should the play
Prove piercing earnest,   10

Should the glee glaze
In death's stiff stare,

Would not the fun
Look too expensive?
Would not the jest   15
Have crawled too far?

XVII

It's such a little thing to weep,
   So short a thing to sigh;
And yet by trades the size of these
   We men and women die!

XVIII

I dreaded that first robin so,
But he is mastered now,
And I'm accustomed to him grown,—
He hurts a little, though.

I thought if I could only live   5
Till that first shout got by,
Not all pianos in the woods
Had power to mangle me.

I dared not meet the daffodils,
For fear their yellow gown   10
Would pierce me with a fashion
So foreign to my own.

I wished the grass would hurry,
So when 'twas time to see,
He'd be too tall, the tallest one   15
Could stretch to look at me.

I could not bear the bees should come,
I wished they'd stay away
In those dim countries where they go:
What word had they for me?   20

They're here, though; not a creature failed,
No blossom stayed away
In gentle deference to me,
The Queen of Calvary.

---

3. vats—The Heidelberg tun was one of the celebrated vats of the winegrowing Rhineland.
15. tippler—one who sips. 6. pyrites—fool's gold. 11. glaze—become glassy. 24. Queen of
Calvary—She regards herself as crucified.

Each one salutes me as he goes, 25
And I my childish plumes
Lift, in bereaved acknowledgment
Of their unthinking drums.

XIX

How happy is the little stone
That rambles in the road alone,
And doesn't care about careers,
And exigencies never fears;
Whose coat of elemental brown 5
A passing universe put on;
And independent as the sun,
Associates or glows alone,
Fulfilling absolute decree
In casual simplicity. 10

XX

The bustle in a house
The morning after death
Is solemnest of industries
Enacted upon earth,—

The sweeping up the heart, 5
And putting love away
We shall not want to use again
Until eternity.

XXI

This quiet Dust was Gentlemen and Ladies,
And Lads and Girls;
Was laughter and ability and sighing,
And frocks and curls.
This passive place a Summer's nimble man-
sion, 5
Where Bloom and Bees
Fulfilled their Oriental Circuit,*
Then ceased like these.

XXII

I'm nobody! Who are you?
Are you nobody, too?

Then there's a pair of us—don't tell!
They'd banish us, you know.

How dreary to be somebody! 5
How public, like a frog
To tell your name the livelong day
To an admiring bog!

XXIII

Some keep the Sabbath going to church;
I keep it staying at home,
With a bobolink for a chorister,
And an orchard for a dome.

Some keep the Sabbath in surplice; 5
I just wear my wings,
And instead of tolling the bell for church,
Our little sexton sings.

God preaches,—a noted clergyman,—
And the sermon is never long; 10
So instead of getting to heaven at last,
I'm going all along!

XXIV

The sky is low, the clouds are mean,
A travelling flake of snow
Across a barn or through a rut
Debates if it will go.

A narrow wind complains all day 5
How someone treated him;
Nature, like us, is sometimes caught
Without her diadem.†

XXV

To hear an oriole sing
May be a common thing,
Or only a divine.

It is not of the bird
Who sings the same, unheard, 5
As unto crowd.

* **Oriental Circuit**—bright career. † **diadem**—symbol of royalty.

The fashion of the ear
Attireth that it hear
In dun or fair.

So whether it be rune,   10
Or whether it be none,
Is of within;

The "tune is in the tree,"
The sceptic showeth me;
"No, sir! In thee!"   15

XXVI

To fight aloud is very brave,
But gallanter, I know,
Who charge within the bosom,
The cavalry of woe.

Who win, and nations do not see,   5
Who fall, and none observe,
Whose dying eyes no country
Regards with patriot love.

We trust, in plumed procession,
For such the angels go,   10
Rank after rank, with even feet
And uniforms of snow.

XXVII

What soft, cherubic creatures
  These gentlewomen are!
One would as soon assault a plush
  Or violate a star.

Such dimity * convictions,   5
  A horror so refined
Of freckled human nature,
  Of Deity ashamed,—

It's such a common glory,
  A fisherman's degree!   10
Redemption, brittle lady,
  Be so, ashamed of thee.

XXVIII

He ate and drank the precious words,
His spirit grew robust;
He knew no more that he was poor,
Nor that his frame was dust.
He danced along the dingy days,   5
And this bequest of wings
Was but a book. What liberty
A loosened spirit brings!

XXIX†

A thought went up my mind to-day
That I have had before,
But did not finish,—some way back,
I could not fix the year,

Nor where it went, nor why it came   5
The second time to me,
Nor definitely what it was,
Have I the art to say.

But somewhere in my soul, I know
I've met the thing before;   10
It just reminded me—'twas all—
And came my way no more.

XXX

I had been hungry all the years;
My noon had come, to dine;
I, trembling, drew the table near,
And touched the curious wine.

'Twas this on tables I had seen,   5
When turning, hungry, lone,
I looked in windows, for the wealth
I could not hope to own.

I did not know the ample bread,
'Twas so unlike the crumb   10
The birds and I had often shared
In Nature's dining-room.

10. rune—a mystic song. * dimity—delicate, like thin cotton dressgoods. In this poem Miss Dickinson expresses her contempt for mere respectability. † This poem refers to a mystic experience akin to Wordsworth's "Intimations of Immortality."

The plenty hurt me, 'twas so new,—
Myself felt ill and odd,
As berry of a mountain bush 15
Transplanted to the road.

Nor was I hungry; so I found
That hunger was a way
Of persons outside windows,
The entering takes away. 20

XXXI

After great pain a formal feeling comes—
The nerves sit ceremonious like tombs;
The stiff Heart questions—was it He that
bore?
And yesterday—or centuries before?

The feet mechanical 5
Go round a wooden way
Of ground or air or Ought, regardless
grown,
A quartz contentment like a stone.

This is the hour of lead
Remembered if outlived, 10
As freezing persons recollect the snow—
First chill, then stupor, then the letting go.

XXXII

All overgrown by cunning moss,
All interspersed with weed,
The little cage of "Currer Bell," *
In quiet Haworth laid.

This bird, observing others, 5
When frosts too sharp became,
Retire to other latitudes,
Quietly did the same.

But differed in returning;
Since Yorkshire hills are green, 10
Yet not in all the nests I meet
Can nightingale be seen.

Gathered from any wanderings,
Gethsemane can tell
Through what transporting anguish 15
She reached the asphodel!

Soft falls the sounds of Eden
Upon her puzzled ear;
Oh, what an afternoon for heaven,
When Brontë entered there! 20

XXXIII

These are the days when birds come back,
A very few, a bird or two,
To take a backward look.

These are the days when skies put on
The old, old sophistries of June,— 5
A blue and gold mistake.

Oh, fraud that cannot cheat the bee,
Almost thy plausibility
Induces my belief,

Till ranks of seeds their witness bear, 10
And softly through the altered air
Hurries a timid leaf!

Oh, sacrament of summer days,
Oh, last communion in the haze,
Permit a child to join, 15

Thy sacred emblems to partake,
Thy consecrated bread to break,
Taste thine immortal wine!

XXXIV

To make a prairie it takes a clover and one
bee,—
One clover, and a bee,
And revery.
The revery alone will do
If bees are few. 5

* "Currer Bell"—Charlotte Brontë, to whom this poem is addressed, wrote *Jane Eyre* under this pen name. **14. Gethsemane**—that is, scene of agony. **16. asphodel**—flower of the dead in Greek mythology.

XXXV

Again his voice is at the door,
I feel the old degree,
I hear him ask the servant
For such an one as me;

I take a flower as I go   5
My face to justify,
He never saw me in this life,
I might surprise his eye.

I cross the hall with mingled steps,
I silent pass the door,   10
I look on all this world contains—
Just his face—nothing more!

We talk in venture and in toss,
A kind of plummet strain,
Each sounding shyly just how deep   15
The other's foot had been.

We walk. I leave my dog behind.
A tender thoughtful moon
Goes with us just a little way
And then we are alone.   20

Alone—if angels are alone
First time they try the sky!
Alone—if those veiled faces be
We cannot count on high!

I'd give to live that hour again   25
The purple in my vein;
But he must count the drops himself—
My price for every stain!

XXXVI

We learned the whole of love,
The alphabet, the words,
A chapter, then the mighty book—
Then revelation closed.

But in each other's eyes   5
An ignorance beheld
Diviner than the childhood's,
And each to each a child

Attempted to expound
What neither understood.   10

Alas, that wisdom is so large
And truth so manifold!

XXXVII

Crumbling is not an instant's act,
A fundamental pause;
Dilapidation's processes
Are organized decays.

'Tis first a cobweb on the soul,   5
A cuticle of dust,
A borer in the axis,
An elemental rust.

Ruin is formal, devil's work,
Consecutive and slow—   10
Fail in an instant no man did,
Slipping is crash's law.

XXXVIII

You cannot make remembrance grow
When it has lost its root.
The tightening the soil around
And setting it upright

Deceives perhaps the universe   5
But not retrieves the plant;
Real memory, like cedar feet,
Is shod with adamant.

Nor can you cut remembrance down
When it shall once have grown,   10
Its iron buds will sprout anew
However overthrown.

XXXIX

This is my letter to the world,
    That never wrote to me,—
The simple news that Nature told,
    With tender majesty.

Her message is committed   5
    To hands I cannot see;
For love of her, sweet countrymen,
    Judge tenderly of me!

MARK TWAIN

1835-1910

I. FLUSH TIMES ON THE MISSISSIPPI AND IN THE WEST
(1835–1870)

1835 Samuel Langhorne Clemens born November 30 in Florida, Missouri, son of John Marshall Clemens and Jane Lampton, of Virginia stock.

1839 Removed with his family to Hannibal, Missouri, where he had irregular schooling, but enjoyed free life of this river town.

1847 Death of the father; son apprenticed as a printer the following year. Began contributing to brother's newspaper (1851).

1853–1856 Worked as journeyman printer and wandering journalist in St. Louis, New York, Philadelphia, Keokuk, Cincinnati, contributing letters and humorous sketches to various papers.

1857–1861 Worked as pilot on the Mississippi River where he met a great variety of people.

1861 Set out by stage for Nevada with his brother Orion, who had been made secretary to the territorial governor.

1862–1866 In Nevada and California mining, printing, reporting.

1865 Published "The Celebrated Jumping Frog" in the New York *Saturday Press,* November 18; it was copied widely. Associated in San Francisco with Bret Harte and Artemus Ward, whom he had first met in Nevada.

1866 October 2, delivered his first lecture, in San Francisco, continuing appearances as a lecturer until 1906.

1867 Published *The Celebrated Jumping Frog of Calaveras County, and Other Sketches;* visited Europe, the Mediterranean, and Palestine.

1869 Published *The Innocents Abroad,* based on reports sent to the *Alta California* on his trip.

II. THE GILDED AGE (1870–1890)

1870 Marriage to Olivia Langdon of a conservative family in Elmira, New York; became part owner of the Buffalo *Express* (1869).

1872 Published *Roughing It,* reflecting his experiences in the Far West.

1873–1890 Established home in Hartford, Connecticut.

1873 Published *The Gilded Age* (with Charles Dudley Warner), based on family history.

1875 Published *Sketches, New and Old,* a compilation of previously published work.

1876 Published *The Adventures of Tom Sawyer.*

1880 Published *A Tramp Abroad,* based on walking trip with the Rev. Joseph Twichell in the Black Forest and Switzerland.

1179

1882 Published *The Prince and the Pauper,* a historical novel of the Elizabethan age.

1883 Published *Life on the Mississippi,* enlarged from "Old Times on the Mississippi," which appeared in the *Atlantic Monthly* in 1875.

1884 Published *The Adventures of Huckleberry Finn.*

1888 Received honorary Master of Arts degree from Yale.

1889 Published *A Connecticut Yankee in King Arthur's Court.*

III. THE YEARS OF DISILLUSION (1890–1910)

1891–1900 Extensive travel abroad. Period of close association with William Dean Howells. Unfortunate investments in a typesetting machine and a publishing house.

1892 Published *The American Claimant,* with reintroduction of Colonel Sellers.

1894 Published *Pudd'nhead Wilson* and *Tom Sawyer Abroad.*

1896 Published *Personal Recollections of Joan of Arc* (anonymous); Susan Clemens died August 18.

1897 Published *Following the Equator,* based on his journey around the world.

1898 Wrote *The Mysterious Stranger,* not published until 1916; *What Is Man?* printed in 1906; and "The Man That Corrupted Hadleyburg," 1899.

1900–1908 Lived in New York City. Death of his wife in 1904. Honorary degree of Litt. D. from Oxford University (1907).

1908–1910 Lived at Redding, Connecticut. Death of his daughter Jean, 1909.

1910 Died April 21, at Stormfield, his house at Redding.

1917 Publication of *Mark Twain's Letters.*

1924 Publication of *Autobiography* in two volumes.

BIOGRAPHIES: A. B. Paine, *Mark Twain: A Biography,* Harper, 1912, 3 vols.; *Mark Twain's Letters,* ed. by A. B. Paine, Harper, 1917, 2 vols.; Mary Lawton, *A Lifetime with Mark Twain,* Harcourt, Brace, 1925; Van Wyck Brooks, *The Ordeal of Mark Twain,* Dutton, 1920, rev. ed., 1933; Stephen Leacock, *Mark Twain,* Appleton, 1933; Edward Wagenknecht, *Mark Twain, The Man and His Work,* Yale University Press, 1935; *Mark Twain's Autobiography,* ed. by A. B. Paine, Harper, 1924, 2 vols.; Friedrich Schönemann, *Mark Twain als literarische Persönlichkeit,* Jena, 1925; *Life in Letters of William Dean Howells,* ed. by Mildred Howells, Doubleday, Doran, 1928; Clara Clemens, *My Father, Mark Twain,* Harper, 1931; Bernard DeVoto, *Mark Twain's America,* Little, Brown, 1932; M. M. Brashear, *Mark Twain, Son of Missouri,* University of North Carolina Press, 1934; A. B. Paine, ed., *Mark Twain's Notebook,* Harper, 1935; Ivan Benson, *Mark Twain's Western Years,* Stanford University Press, 1938; *Mark Twain in Eruption: hitherto unpublished pages about men and events,* ed. Bernard DeVoto, Harper, 1940; Bernard DeVoto, *Mark Twain at Work,* Harvard, 1942; De Lancey Ferguson, *Mark Twain: Man and Legend,* Bobbs, Merrill, 1943; Samuel C. Webster, *Mark Twain: Business Man,* 1946.

BIBLIOGRAPHY AND EDITIONS: Merle Johnson, *A Bibliography of the Work of Mark Twain,* rev. ed., Harper, 1935; *Literary History of the United States,* Vol. III, pp. 442-50.

Collected editions offer a variety of puzzles as to text and inclusiveness. The "definitive" edition is Albert B. Paine, ed., *Writings of Mark Twain*, 1922-25, 37 vols. Other collections are the "Author's National" *Writings*, 25 vols., 1907-1918; the "Autograph" *Writings*, 22 vols., 1899-1900; the "Underwood" *Writings*, 1901-1907, 25 vols.; and *Mark Twain's Works*, 23 vols., 1933. These are all published in fact by Harper, though the "Autograph Edition" seems to stem from Hartford, Conn. A variety of books containing uncollected material has appeared outside the collected editions; a list of these can be conveniently found in the bibliography in the *Literary History of the United States*. A scholarly book of extracts is F. L. Pattee, ed., *Mark Twain: Representative Selections*, American Book Co., 1935, but this needs revision.

Keepers of the genteel tradition have been reluctant to admit Mark Twain among the "elect," alleging that he was not "literary." Others aver that since he lived in an age lacking "spiritual exuberance," health was not in him. Still others observe that he was but an improviser, not considering that, as he said, the incongruities he brought together in his purposeless way might be the basis of American art.

Certainly Mark Twain did a great deal to establish an indigenous literature. He had the good fortune to know many parts of his country at first hand; he engaged in various occupations that kept him close to the ordinary idiom and the average point of view. As printer, pilot, miner, reporter, traveler, lecturer, author, publisher, and capitalist he maintained an original attitude toward the issues that confronted the "gilded age." A product of the frontier, he was encumbered by no traditions, no conventional standards of value; rather he was a devout hater of all shams. He made many mistakes, of course—his own promptings led him into hoaxes, burlesques, and fanciful adventures below the level of his best powers. Staking his faith on comfort rather than beauty, he developed in the end a pessimism that was, at bottom, sentimental. But who better than he has given the haunting beauty and picturesque romance of the Mississippi, and the thrill of Western adventure in its hazard of new fortunes?

Out of this material Mark Twain drew an infectious and hilarious humor, as free as the conditions that gave it birth. The frontier experience related him to that tradition of oral anecdote and backwoods fun-making which is characteristic of the American "realistic" attitude. But there is another and a bitterer Mark Twain, equally characteristic of the American people in some moods, the cynical and pessimistic disciple of determinism. Between these two extremes the humorist perpetually swings. Both elements appear in a character like Huckleberry Finn, a world-figure created by a great folk artist. Mark Twain is understood by a democratic people because he is theirs, because he has their morals and their beliefs, their spirit and their speech.

THE GILDED AGE

This satirical novel was written in collaboration with Charles Dudley Warner, and published in 1873. The selections here given comprise Chapters VII and VIII. The fantastic quotations which precede the chapters are here omitted. Earlier chapters relate how the Hawkins family, in response to Colonel Beriah Sellers's eloquent representations of the fortunes to be won, moved from Tennessee to Missouri, and became hopelessly involved. In this chapter Si Hawkins sends his son Washington to his old friend Sellers, for help.

CHAPTER VII

COLONEL SELLERS'S SCHEMES FOR MONEY-MAKING

B EARING Washington Hawkins and his fortunes, the stage-coach tore out of Swansea at a fearful gait, with horn tooting gaily and half the town admiring from doors and windows. But it did not tear any more after it got to the outskirts; it dragged along stupidly enough, then—till it came in sight of the next hamlet; and then the bugle tooted gaily again, and again the vehicle went tearing by the houses. This sort of conduct marked every entry to a station and every exit from it; and so in those days children grew up with the idea that stage-coaches always tore and always tooted; but they also grew up with the idea that pirates went into action in their Sunday clothes, carrying the black flag in one hand and pistoling people with the other, merely because they were so represented in the pictures: but these illusions vanished when later years brought their disenchanting wisdom. They learned then that the stage-coach is but a poor, plodding, vulgar thing in the solitudes of the highway; and that the pirate is only a seedy, unfantastic "rough," when he is out of the pictures.

Toward evening, the stage-coach came thundering into Hawkeye with a perfectly triumphant ostentation—which was natural and proper, for Hawkeye was a pretty large town for interior Missouri. Washington, very stiff and tired and hungry, climbed out, and wondered how he was to proceed now. But his difficulty was quickly solved. Colonel Sellers came down the street on a run and arrived panting for breath. He said:

"Lord bless you—I'm glad to see you, Washington—perfectly delighted to see you, my boy! I got your message. Been on the lookout for you. Heard the stage horn, but had a party I couldn't shake off—man that's got an enormous thing on hand—wants me to put some capital into it—and I tell you, my boy, I could do worse, I could do a deal worse. No, now, let that luggage alone; I'll fix that. Here, Jerry, got anything to do? All right—shoulder this plunder and follow me. Come along, Washington. Lord, I'm glad to see you! Wife and the children are just perishing to look at you. Bless you, they won't know you, you've grown so. Folks all well, I suppose? That's good—glad to hear that. We're always going to run down and see them, but I'm into so many operations, and they're not things a man feels like trusting to other people, and so somehow we keep putting it off. Fortunes in them! Good gracious, it's the country to pile up wealth in! Here we are—here's where the Sellers dynasty hangs out. Dump it on the doorstep, Jerry—the blackest niggro in the state, Washington, but got a good heart—mighty likely boy, is Jerry. And now I suppose you've got to have ten cents, Jerry. That's all right—when a man works for me— when a man—in the other pocket, I reckon—when a man—why, where the mischief *is* that portmonnaie!—when a—well now that's odd—Oh, now I remember, must have left it at the bank; and b' George I've left my check-book, too—Polly says I ought to have a nurse—well, no matter. Let me have a dime, Washington, if you've got—ah, thanks. Now clear out, Jerry, your complexion has brought on the twilight half an hour ahead of time. Pretty fair joke— pretty fair. Here he is, Polly! Washington's come, children!—come now, don't 5 eat him up—finish him in the house. Welcome, my boy, to a mansion that is proud to shelter the son of the best man that walks on the ground. Si Hawkins has been a good friend to me, and I believe I can say that whenever I've had a chance to put him into a good thing I've done it, and done it pretty cheer- fully, too. I put him into that sugar speculation—what a grand thing that was, 10 if we hadn't held on too long!"

True enough; but holding on too long had utterly ruined both of them; and the saddest part of it was, that they never had had so much money to lose before, for Sellers's sale of their mule crop that year in New Orleans had been a great financial success. If he had kept out of sugar and gone back home 15 content to stick to mules it would have been a happy wisdom. As it was, he managed to kill two birds with one stone—that is to say, he killed the sugar speculation by holding for high rates till he had to sell at the bottom figure, and that calamity killed the mule that laid the golden egg—which is but a figurative expression and will be so understood. Sellers had returned home 20 cheerful but empty-handed, and the mule business lapsed into other hands. The sale of the Hawkins property by the sheriff had followed, and the Hawkins hearts been torn to see Uncle Dan'l and his wife pass from the auction-block into the hands of a negro trader and depart for the remote South to be seen no more by the family. It had seemed like seeing their own flesh and blood 25 sold into banishment.

Washington was greatly pleased with the Sellers mansion. It was a two-story- and-a-half brick, and much more stylish than any of its neighbors. He was borne to the family sitting-room in triumph by the swarm of little Sellerses, the parents following with their arms about each other's waists. 30

The whole family were poorly and cheaply dressed; and the clothing, al- though neat and clean, showed many evidences of having seen long service. The Colonel's "stovepipe" hat was napless and shiny with much polishing, but nevertheless it had an almost convincing expression about it of having been just purchased new. The rest of his clothing was napless and shiny, too, but it had 35 the air of being entirely satisfied with itself and blandly sorry for other people's clothes. It was growing rather dark in the house, and the evening air was chilly, too. Sellers said:

"Lay off your overcoat, Washington, and draw up to the stove and make yourself at home—just consider yourself under your own shingles, my boy— 40 I'll have a fire going, in a jiffy. Light the lamp, Polly, dear, and let's have things cheerful—just as glad to see you, Washington, as if you'd been lost a century and we'd found you again!"

By this time the Colonel was conveying a lighted match into a poor little stove. Then he propped the stove-door to its place by leaning the poker against 45 it, for the hinges had retired from business. This door framed a small square of isinglass, which now warmed up with a faint glow. Mrs. Sellers lit a cheap,

showy lamp, which dissipated a good deal of the gloom, and then everybody
gathered into the light and took the stove into close companionship.

The children climbed all over Sellers, fondled him, petted him, and were
lavishly petted in return. Out from this tugging, laughing, chattering disguise
5 of legs and arms and little faces, the Colonel's voice worked its way and his
tireless tongue ran blithely on without interruption; and the purring little wife,
diligent with her knitting, sat near at hand and looked happy and proud and
grateful; and she listened as one who listens to oracles and gospels and whose
grateful soul is being refreshed with the bread of life. By and by the children
10 quieted down to listen; clustered about their father, and resting their elbows
on his legs, they hung upon his words as if he were uttering the music of
the spheres.

A dreary old haircloth sofa against the wall; a few damaged chairs; the
small table the lamp stood on; the crippled stove—these things constituted the
15 furniture of the room. There was no carpet on the floor; on the wall were
occasional square-shaped interruptions of the general tint of the plaster which
betrayed that there used to be pictures in the house—but there were none now.
There were no mantel ornaments, unless one might bring himself to regard as
an ornament a clock which never came within fifteen strokes of striking the
20 right time, and whose hands always hitched together at twenty-two minutes
past anything and traveled in company the rest of the way home.

"Remarkable clock!" said Sellers, and got up and wound it. "I've been offered—well, I wouldn't expect you to believe what I've been offered for that
clock. Old Governor Hager never sees me but he says, 'Come, now, Colonel,
25 name your price—I *must* have that clock!' But my goodness I'd as soon think
of selling my wife. As I was saying to—silence in the court, now, she's begun
to strike! You can't talk against her—you have to just be patient and hold up
till she's said her say. Ah—well, as I was saying, when—she's beginning again!
Nineteen, twenty, twenty-one, twenty-two, twen—ah, that's all. Yes, as I was
30 saying to old Judge—go it, old girl, don't mind me. Now how is that? Isn't
that a good, spirited tone? She can wake the dead! Sleep? Why you might
as well try to sleep in a thunder factory. Now just listen at that. She'll strike
a hundred and fifty, now, without stopping—you'll see. There ain't another
clock like that in Christendom."

35 Washington hoped that this might be true, for the din was distracting—
though the family, one and all, seemed filled with joy; and the more the clock
"buckled down to her work" as the Colonel expressed it, and the more in-
supportable the clatter became, the more enchanted they all appeared to be.
When there was silence, Mrs. Sellers lifted upon Washington a face that
40 beamed with a child-like pride, and said:

"It belonged to his grandmother."

The look and the tone were plain call for admiring surprise, and therefore
Washington said—(it was the only thing that offered itself at the moment):
"Indeed!"

45 "Yes, it did, didn't it, father!" exclaimed one of the twins. "She was my
great-grandmother—and George's too; wasn't she, father! *You* never saw her,
but Sis has seen her, when Sis was a baby—didn't you, Sis! Sis has seen her

most a hundred times. She was awful deef—she's dead, now. Ain't she, father!"

All the children chimed in, now, with one general Babel of information about deceased—nobody offering to read the riot act or seeming to discountenance the insurrection or disapprove of it in any way—but the head twin drowned all the turmoil and held his own against the field:

"It's our clock, now—and it's got wheels inside of it, and a thing that flutters every time she strikes—don't it, father! Great-grandmother died before hardly any of us were born—she was an Old-School Baptist and had warts all over her—you ask father if she didn't. She had an uncle once that was bald-headed and used to have fits; he wasn't *our* uncle, I don't know what he was to us— some kin or another I reckon—father's seen him a thousand times—hain't you, father! We used to have a calf that et apples and just chawed up dishrags like nothing, and if you stay here you'll see lots of funerals—won't he, Sis! Did you ever see a house afire? I have! Once me and Jim Terry—"

But Sellers began to speak now, and the storm ceased. He began to tell about an enormous speculation he was thinking of embarking some capital in—a speculation which some London bankers had been over to consult with him about—and soon he was building glittering pyramids of coin, and Washington was presently growing opulent under the magic of his eloquence. But at the same time Washington was not able to ignore the cold entirely. He was nearly as close to the stove as he could get, and yet he could not persuade himself that he felt the slightest heat, notwithstanding the isinglass door was still gently and serenely glowing. He tried to get a trifle closer to the stove, and the consequence was, he tripped the supporting poker and the stove-door tumbled to the floor. And then there was a revelation—there was nothing in the stove but a lighted tallow candle!

The poor youth blushed and felt as if he must die with shame. But the Colonel was only disconcerted for a moment—he straightway found his voice again:

"A little idea of my own, Washington—one of the greatest things in the world! You must write and tell your father about it—don't forget that, now. I have been reading up some European scientific reports—friend of mine, Count Fugier, sent them to me—sends me all sorts of things from Paris—he thinks the world of me, Fugier does. Well, I saw that the Academy of France had been testing the properties of heat, and they came to the conclusion that it was a non-conductor or something like that, and of course its influence must necessarily be deadly in nervous organizations with excitable temperaments, especially where there is any tendency toward rheumatic affections. Bless you, I saw in a moment what was the matter with us, and says I, out goes your fires!—no more slow torture and certain death for me, sir. What you want is the *appearance* of heat, not the heat itself—that's the idea. Well, how to do it was the next thing. I just put my head to work, pegged away a couple of days, and here you are! Rheumatism? Why a man can't any more start a case of rheumatism in this house than he can shake an opinion out of a mummy! Stove with a candle in it and a transparent door—that's it—it has been the salvation of this family. Don't you fail to write your father about it, Washington. And tell him the idea is mine—I'm no more conceited than most people,

I reckon, but you know it is human nature for a man to want credit for a thing like that."

Washington said with his blue lips that he would, but he said in his secret heart that he would promote no such iniquity. He tried to believe in the health-
5 fulness of the invention, and succeeded tolerably well; but after all he could not feel that good health in a frozen body was any real improvement on the rheumatism.

CHAPTER VIII

COLONEL SELLERS ENTERTAINS WASHINGTON HAWKINS

10 The supper at Colonel Sellers's was not sumptuous, in the beginning, but it improved on acquaintance. That is to say, that what Washington regarded at first sight as mere lowly potatoes, presently became awe-inspiring agricultural productions that had been reared in some ducal garden beyond the sea, under the sacred eye of the duke himself, who had sent them to Sellers; the bread
15 was from corn which could be grown in only one favored locality in the earth and only a favored few could get it; the Rio coffee, which at first seemed exe-crable to the taste, took to itself an improved flavor when Washington was told to drink it slowly and not hurry what should be a lingering luxury in order to be fully appreciated—it was from the private stores of a Brazilian
20 nobleman with an unrememberable name. The Colonel's tongue was a magi-cian's wand that turned dried apples into figs and water into wine as easily as it could change a hovel into a palace and present poverty into imminent future riches.

Washington slept in a cold bed in a carpetless room and woke up in a palace
25 in the morning; at least the palace lingered during the moment that he was rubbing his eyes and getting his bearings—and then it disappeared and he recognized that the Colonel's inspiring talk had been influencing his dreams. Fatigue had made him sleep late; when he entered the sitting-room he noticed that the old haircloth sofa was absent; when he sat down to breakfast the
30 Colonel tossed six or seven dollars in bills on the table, counted them over, said he was a little short and must call upon his banker; then returned the bills to his wallet with the indifferent air of a man who is used to money. The breakfast was not an improvement upon the supper, but the Colonel talked it up and transformed it into an oriental feast. By and by, he said:
35 "I intend to look out for you, Washington, my boy. I hunted up a place for you yesterday, but I am not referring to that, now—that is a mere livelihood— mere bread and butter; but when I say I mean to look out for you I mean something very different. I mean to put things in your way that will make a mere livelihood a trifling thing. I'll put you in a way to make more money
40 than you'll ever know what to do with. You'll be right here where I can put my hand on you when anything turns up. I've got some prodigious operations on foot; but I'm keeping quiet; mum's the word; your old hand don't go around powwowing and letting everybody see his k'yards and find out his little game. But all in good time, Washington, all in good time. You'll see.
45 Now, there's an operation in corn that looks well. Some New York men are

trying to get me to go into it—buy up all the growing crops and just boss the market when they mature—ah, I tell you it's a great thing. And it only costs a trifle; two millions or two and a half will do it. I haven't exactly promised yet—there's no hurry—the more indifferent I seem, you know, the more anxious those fellows will get. And then there is the hog speculation—that's bigger 5 still. We've got quiet men at work," [he was very impressive here,] "mousing around, to get propositions out of all the farmers in the whole West and Northwest for the hog crop, and other agents quietly getting propositions and terms out of all the manufactories—and don't you see, if we can get all the hogs and all the slaughter-houses into our hands on the dead quiet—whew! 10 it would take three ships to carry the money. I've looked into the thing—calculated all the chances for and all the chances against, and though I shake my head and hesitate and keep on thinking, apparently, I've got my mind made up that if the thing can be done on a capital of six millions, that's the horse to put up money on! Why, Washington—but what's the use of talking about it— 15 any man can see that there's whole Atlantic oceans of cash in it, gulfs and bays thrown in. But there's a bigger thing than that, yet—a bigger—"

"Why, Colonel, you can't want anything bigger!" said Washington, his eyes blazing. "Oh, I wish I could go into either of those speculations—I only wish I had money—I wish I wasn't cramped and kept down and fettered with pov- 20 erty, and such prodigious chances lying right here in sight! Oh, it is a fearful thing to be poor. But don't throw away those things—they are so splendid and I can see how sure they are. Don't throw them away for something still better and maybe fail in it! I wouldn't, Colonel. I would stick to these. I wish father were here and were his old self again. Oh, he never in his life had such chances 25 as these are. Colonel, you *can't* improve on these—no man can improve on them!"

A sweet, compassionate smile played about the Colonel's features, and he leaned over the table with the air of a man who is "going to show you" and do it without the least trouble: 30

"Why Washington, my boy, these things are nothing. They *look* large—of course they look large to a novice, but to a man who has been all his life accustomed to large operations—pshaw! They're well enough to while away an idle hour with, or furnish a bit of enjoyment that will give a trifle of idle capital a chance to earn its bread while it is waiting for something to *do,* but— 35 now just listen a moment—just let me give you an idea of what we old veterans of commerce call 'business.' Here's the Rothschilds' proposition—this is between you and me, you understand—"

Washington nodded three or four times impatiently, and his glowing eyes said, "Yes, yes—hurry—I understand—" 40

"—for I wouldn't have it get out for a fortune. They want me to go in with them on the sly—agent was here two weeks ago about it—go in on the sly" [voice down to an impressive whisper, now] "and buy up a hundred and thirteen wildcat banks in Ohio, Indiana, Kentucky, Illinois, and Missouri—notes of these banks are at all sorts of discount now—average discount of the hundred 45 and thirteen is forty-four per cent.—buy them all up, you see, and then all of

37. Rothschilds'—a famous European banking family.

a sudden let the cat out of the bag! Whiz! the stock of every one of those wildcats would spin up to a tremendous premium before you could turn a handspring—profit on the speculation not a dollar less than forty millions!" [An eloquent pause, while the marvelous vision settled into W.'s focus.]

5   "Where's your hogs now! Why, my dear innocent boy, we would just sit down on the front doorsteps and peddle banks like lucifer matches!"

Washington finally got his breath and said:

"Oh, it is perfectly wonderful! Why couldn't these things have happened in father's day? And I—it's of no use—they simply lie before my face and mock

10   me. There is nothing for me but to stand helpless and see other people reap the astonishing harvest."

"Never mind, Washington, don't you worry. I'll fix you. There's plenty of chances. How much money have you got?"

In the presence of so many millions, Washington could not keep from blush-

15   ing when he had to confess that he had eighteen dollars in the world.

"Well, all right—don't despair. Other people have been obliged to begin with less. I have a small idea that may develop into something for us both, all in good time. Keep your money close and add to it. I'll make it breed. I've been experimenting (to pass away the time) on a little preparation for curing sore

20   eyes—a kind of decoction nine-tenths water and the other tenth drugs that don't cost more than a dollar a barrel; I'm still experimenting; there's one ingredient wanted yet to perfect the thing, and somehow I can't just manage to hit upon the thing that's necessary, and I don't dare talk with a chemist, of course. But I'm progressing, and before many weeks I wager the country

25   will ring with the fame of Beriah Sellers's Infallible Imperial Oriental Optic Liniment and Salvation for Sore Eyes—the Medical Wonder of the Age! Small bottles fifty cents, large ones a dollar. Average cost, five and seven cents for the two sizes. The first year sell, say, ten thousand bottles in Missouri, seven thousand in Iowa, three thousand in Arkansas, four thousand in Kentucky,

30   six thousand in Illinois, and say twenty-five thousand in the rest of the country. Total, fifty-five thousand bottles; profit clear of all expenses, twenty thousand dollars at the very lowest calculation. All the capital needed is to manufacture the first two thousand bottles—say a hundred and fifty dollars—then the money would begin to flow in. The second year, sales would reach two

35   hundred thousand bottles—clear profit, say seventy-five thousand dollars—and in the mean time the great factory would be building in St. Louis, to cost, say, one hundred thousand dollars. The third year we could easily sell one million bottles in the United States and—"

"O, splendid!" said Washington. "Let's commence right away—let's—"

40   "—one million bottles in the United States—profit at least three hundred and fifty thousand dollars—and *then* it would begin to be time to turn our attention toward the *real* idea of the business."

"The *real* idea of it! Ain't three hundred and fifty thousand dollars a year a pretty real—"

45   "Stuff! Why, what an infant you are, Washington—what a guileless, short-sighted, easily contented innocent you are, my poor little country-bred know-nothing! Would I go to all that trouble and bother for the poor crumbs a body

might pick up in *this* country? Now do I look like a man who—does my history suggest that I am a man who deals in trifles, contents himself with the narrow horizon that hems in the common herd, sees no further than the end of his nose? Now, *you* know that that is not me—couldn't *be* me. *You* ought to know that if I throw my time and abilities into a patent medicine, 5 it's a patent medicine whose field of operations is the solid earth! its clients the swarming nations that inhabit it! Why what is the republic of America for an eye-water country? Lord bless you, it is nothing but a barren highway that you've got to cross to get *to* the true eye-water market! Why, Washington, in the Oriental countries people swarm like the sands of the desert; every 10 square mile of ground upholds its thousands upon thousands of struggling human creatures—and every separate and individual devil of them's got the ophthalmia! It's as natural to them as noses are—and sin. It's born with them, it stays with them, it's all that some of them have left when they die. Three years of introductory trade in the Orient and what will be the result? Why, 15 our headquarters would be in Constantinople and our hindquarters in Further India! Factories and warehouses in Cairo, Ispahan, Bagdad, Damascus, Jerusalem, Yedo, Peking, Bangkok, Delhi, Bombay, and Calcutta! Annual income —well, God only knows how many millions and millions apiece!"

Washington was so dazed, so bewildered—his heart and his eyes had wan- 20 dered so far away among the strange lands beyond the seas, and such avalanches of coin and currency had fluttered and jingled confusedly down before him, that he was now as one who has been whirling round and round for a time, and, stopping all at once, finds his surroundings still whirling and all objects a dancing chaos. However, little by little the Sellers family cooled down 25 and crystallized into shape, and the poor room lost its glitter and resumed its poverty. Then the youth found his voice and begged Sellers to drop everything and hurry up the eye-water; and he got his eighteen dollars and tried to force it upon the Colonel—pleaded with him to take it—implored him to do it. But the Colonel would not; said he would not need the capital (in his native 30 magnificent way he called that eighteen dollars capital) till the eye-water was an accomplished fact. He made Washington easy in his mind, though, by promising that he would call for it just as soon as the invention was finished, and he added the glad tidings that nobody but just they two should be admitted to a share in the speculation. 35

When Washington left the breakfast-table he could have worshiped that man. Washington was one of that kind of people whose hopes are in the very clouds one day, and in the gutter the next. He walked on air, now. The Colonel was ready to take him around and introduce him to the employment he had found for him, but Washington begged for a few moments in which to 40 write home; with his kind of people, to ride to-day's new interest to death and put off yesterday's till another time, is nature itself. He ran up-stairs and wrote glowingly, enthusiastically, to his mother about the hogs and the corn, the banks and the eye-water—and added a few inconsequential millions to each project. And he said that people little dreamed what a man Colonel Sellers 45 was, and that the world would open its eyes when it found out. And he closed his letter thus:

So make yourself perfectly easy, mother—in a little while you shall have everything you want, and more. I am not likely to stint *you* in anything, I fancy. This
money will not be for me, alone, but for all of us. I want all to share alike; and
there is going to be far more for each than one person can spend. Break it to father
5 cautiously—you understand the need of that—break it to him cautiously, for he has
had such cruel hard fortune, and is so stricken by it that great good news might
prostrate him more surely than even bad, for he is used to the bad but is grown
sadly unaccustomed to the other. Tell Laura—tell all the children. And write to
Clay about it if he is not with you yet. You may tell Clay that whatever I get he
10 can freely share in—freely. He knows that that is true—there will be no need that
I should swear to that to make him believe it. Good-by—and mind what I say:
Rest perfectly easy, one and all of you, for our troubles are nearly at an end.

Poor lad, he could not know that his mother would cry some loving, compassionate tears over his letter and put off the family with a synopsis of its
15 contents which conveyed a deal of love to them but not much idea of his
prospects or projects. And he never dreamed that such a joyful letter could
sadden her and fill her night with sighs, and troubled thoughts, and bodings
of the future, instead of filling it with peace and blessing it with restful sleep.
When the letter was done, Washington and the Colonel sallied forth, and
20 as they walked along Washington learned what he was to be. He was to be a
clerk in a real-estate office. Instantly the fickle youth's dreams forsook the
magic eye-water and flew back to the Tennessee Land. And the gorgeous possibilities of that great domain straightway began to occupy his imagination to
such a degree that he could scarcely manage to keep even enough of his atten-
25 tion upon the Colonel's talk to retain the general run of what he was saying.
He was glad it was a real-estate office—he was a made man now, sure.
The Colonel said that General Boswell was a rich man and had a good and
growing business; and that Washington's work would be light and he would
get forty dollars a month and be boarded and lodged in the General's family—
30 which was as good as ten dollars more; and even better, for he could not live
as well even at the "City Hotel" as he would there, and yet the hotel charged
fifteen dollars a month where a man had a good room.
General Boswell was in his office; a comfortable-looking place, with plenty
of outline maps hanging about the walls and in the windows, and a spec-
35 tacled man was marking out another one on a long table. The office was in
the principal street. The General received Washington with a kindly but reserved politeness. Washington rather liked his looks. He was about fifty years
old, dignified, well preserved, and well dressed. After the Colonel took his
leave, the General talked awhile with Washington—his talk consisting chiefly
40 of instructions about the clerical duties of the place. He seemed satisfied as to
Washington's ability to take care of the books, he was evidently a pretty fair
theoretical bookkeeper, and experience would soon harden theory into practice. By and by dinner-time came, and the two walked to the General's house;
and now Washington noticed an instinct in himself that moved him to keep
45 not in the General's rear, exactly, but yet not at his side—somehow the old
gentleman's dignity and reserve did not inspire familiarity.

LIFE ON THE MISSISSIPPI

Life on the Mississippi was published in 1883. The selections here given (Chapters IV and VII) were published originally in the *Atlantic Monthly* for June and August, 1875. The changes in text were slight.

CHAPTER IV

THE BOYS' AMBITION

WHEN I was a boy, there was but one permanent ambition among my comrades in our village on the west bank of the Mississippi River. That was, to be a steamboatman. We had transient ambitions of 5
other sorts, but they were only transient. When a circus came and went, it left us all burning to become clowns; the first negro minstrel show that ever came to our section left us all suffering to try that kind of life; now and then we had a hope that, if we lived and were good, God would permit us to be pirates. These ambitions faded out, each in its turn; but the ambition to be 10
a steamboatman always remained.

Once a day a cheap, gaudy packet arrived upward from St. Louis, and another downward from Keokuk. Before these events, the day was glorious with expectancy; after them, the day was a dead and empty thing. Not only the boys, but the whole village, felt this. After all these years I can picture that old time 15
to myself now, just as it was then: the white town drowsing in the sunshine of a summer's morning; the streets empty, or pretty nearly so; one or two clerks sitting in front of the Water Street stores, with their splint-bottomed chairs tilted back against the walls, chins on breasts, hats slouched over their faces, asleep—with shingle-shavings enough around to show what broke them 20
down; a sow and a litter of pigs loafing along the sidewalk, doing a good business in watermelon rinds and seeds; two or three lonely little freight piles scattered about the "levee"; a pile of "skids" on the slope of the stone-paved wharf, and the fragrant town drunkard asleep in the shadow of them; two or three wood flats at the head of the wharf, but nobody to listen to the peaceful 25
lapping of the wavelets against them; the great Mississippi, the majestic, the magnificent Mississippi, rolling its mile-wide tide along, shining in the sun; the dense forest away on the other side; the "point" above the town, and the "point" below, bounding the river-glimpse and turning it into a sort of sea, and withal a very still and brilliant and lonely one. Presently a film of dark smoke 30
appears above one of those remote "points"; instantly a negro drayman, famous for his quick eye and prodigious voice, lifts up the cry, "S-t-e-a-m-boat a-comin'!" and the scene changes! The town drunkard stirs, the clerks wake up, a furious clatter of drays follows, every house and store pours out a human contribution, and all in a twinkling the dead town is alive and moving. 35
Drays, carts, men, boys, all go hurrying from many quarters to a common center, the wharf. Assembled there, the people fasten their eyes upon the com-

4. **village**—"Hannibal, Missouri." (Mark Twain's note)

ing boat as upon a wonder they are seeing for the first time. And the boat *is* rather a handsome sight, too. She is long and sharp and trim and pretty; she has two tall, fancy-topped chimneys, with a gilded device of some kind swung between them; a fanciful pilot-house, all glass and "gingerbread," perched on top of the "texas" deck behind them; the paddle-boxes are gorgeous with a picture or with gilded rays above the boat's name; the boiler-deck, the hurricane-deck, and the texas deck are fenced and ornamented with clean white railings; there is a flag gallantly flying from the jack-staff; the furnace doors are open and the fires glaring bravely; the upper decks are black with passengers; the captain stands by the big bell, calm, imposing, the envy of all; great volumes of the blackest smoke are rolling and tumbling out of the chimneys— a husbanded grandeur created with a bit of pitch-pine just before arriving at a town; the crew are grouped on the forecastle; the broad stage is run far out over the port bow, and an envied deck-hand stands picturesquely on the end of it with a coil of rope in his hand; the pent steam is screaming through the gauge-cocks; the captain lifts his hand, a bell rings, the wheels stop; then they turn back, churning the water to foam, and the steamer is at rest. Then such a scramble as there is to get aboard, and to get ashore, and to take in freight and to discharge freight, all at one and the same time; and such a yelling and cursing as the mates facilitate it all with! Ten minutes later the steamer is under way again, with no flag on the jack-staff and no black smoke issuing from the chimneys. After ten more minutes the town is dead again, and the town drunkard asleep by the skids once more.

My father was a justice of the peace, and I supposed he possessed the power of life and death over all men, and could hang anybody that offended him. This was distinction enough for me as a general thing; but the desire to be a steamboatman kept intruding, nevertheless. I first wanted to be a cabin-boy, so that I could come out with a white apron on and shake a table-cloth over the side, where all my old comrades could see me; later I thought I would rather be the deckhand who stood on the end of the stage-plank with the coil of rope in his hand, because he was particularly conspicuous. But these were only daydreams—they were too heavenly to be contemplated as real possibilities. By and by one of our boys went away. He was not heard of for a long time. At last he turned up as apprentice engineer or "striker" on a steamboat. This thing shook the bottom out of all my Sunday-school teachings. That boy had been notoriously worldly, and I just the reverse; yet he was exalted to this eminence, and I left in obscurity and misery. There was nothing generous about this fellow in his greatness. He would always manage to have a rusty bolt to scrub while his boat tarried at our town, and he would sit on the inside guard and scrub it, where we all could see him and envy him and loathe him. And whenever his boat was laid up he would come home and swell around the town in his blackest and greasiest clothes, so that nobody could help remembering that he was a steamboatman; and he used all sorts of steamboat technicalities in his talk, as if he were so used to them that he forgot common people could not understand them. He would speak of the "labboard" side of a horse in an

---

5. **"texas" deck**—a structure on the hurricane deck, containing officers' quarters; the pilot house is directly in front or on top.

easy, natural way that would make one wish he was dead. And he was always talking about "St. Looy" like an old citizen; he would refer casually to
occasions when he was "coming down Fourth Street," or when he was "passing by the Planter's House," or when there was a fire and he took a turn on
the brakes of "the old Big Missouri"; and then he would go on and lie about   5
how many towns the size of ours were burned down there that day. Two or
three of the boys had long been persons of consideration among us because
they had been to St. Louis once and had a vague general knowledge of its
wonders, but the day of their glory was over now. They lapsed into a humble
silence, and learned to disappear when the ruthless "cub"-engineer approached. 10
This fellow had money, too, and hair-oil. Also an ignorant silver watch and a
showy brass watch-chain. He wore a leather belt and used no suspenders. If
ever a youth was cordially admired and hated by his comrades, this one was.
No girl could withstand his charms. He "cut out" every boy in the village.
When his boat blew up at last, it diffused a tranquil contentment among us   15
such as we had not known for months. But when he came home the next
week, alive, renowned, and appeared in church all battered up and bandaged,
a shining hero, stared at and wondered over by everybody, it seemed to us
that the partiality of Providence for an undeserving reptile had reached a point
where it was open to criticism.   20
    This creature's career could produce but one result, and it speedily followed.
Boy after boy managed to get on the river. The minister's son became an engineer. The doctor's and the postmaster's sons became "mud clerks"; the wholesale liquor dealer's son became a barkeeper on a boat; four sons of the chief
merchant, and two sons of the county judge, became pilots. Pilot was the   25
grandest position of all. The pilot, even in those days of trivial wages, had a
princely salary—from a hundred and fifty to two hundred and fifty dollars a
month, and no board to pay. Two months of his wages would pay a preacher's
salary for a year. Now some of us were left disconsolate. We could not get on
the river—at least our parents would not let us.   30
    So, by and by, I ran away. I said I would never come home again till I was
a pilot and could come in glory. But somehow I could not manage it. I went
meekly aboard a few of the boats that lay packed together like sardines at
the long St. Louis wharf, and humbly inquired for the pilots, but got only a
cold shoulder and short words from mates and clerks. I had to make the best 35
of this sort of treatment for the time being, but I had comforting day-dreams
of a future when I should be a great and honored pilot, with plenty of money,
and could kill some of these mates and clerks and pay for them.

CHAPTER VII

A DARING DEED   40

    When I returned to the pilot-house St. Louis was gone, and I was lost. Here
was a piece of river which was all down in my book, but I could make neither
head nor tail of it: you understand, it was turned around. I had seen it when
coming up-stream, but I had never faced about to see how it looked when it

was behind me. My heart broke again, for it was plain that I had got to learn this troublesome river *both ways*.

The pilot-house was full of pilots, going down to "look at the river." What is called the "upper river" (the two hundred miles between St. Louis and
5 Cairo, where the Ohio comes in) was low; and the Mississippi changes its channel so constantly that the pilots used to always find it necessary to run down to Cairo to take a fresh look, when their boats were to lie in port a week; that is, when the water was at a low stage. A deal of this "looking at the river" was done by poor fellows who seldom had a berth, and whose only
10 hope of getting one lay in their being always freshly posted and therefore ready to drop into the shoes of some reputable pilot, for a single trip, on account of such pilot's sudden illness, or some other necessity. And a good many of them constantly ran up and down inspecting the river, not because they ever really hoped to get a berth, but because (they being guests of the boat) it was
15 cheaper to "look at the river" than stay ashore and pay board. In time these fellows grew dainty in their tastes, and only infested boats that had an established reputation for setting good tables. All visiting pilots were useful, for they were always ready and willing, winter or summer, night or day, to go out in the yawl and help buoy the channel or assist the boat's pilots in any way they
20 could. They were likewise welcomed because all pilots are tireless talkers, when gathered together, and as they talk only about the river they are always understood and are always interesting. Your true pilot cares nothing about anything on earth but the river, and his pride in his occupation surpasses the pride of kings.

25 We had a fine company of these river inspectors along this trip. There were eight or ten, and there was abundance of room for them in our great pilot-house. Two or three of them wore polished silk hats, elaborate shirt-fronts, diamond breastpins, kid gloves, and patent-leather boots. They were choice in their English, and bore themselves with a dignity proper to men of solid means
30 and prodigious reputation as pilots. The others were more or less loosely clad, and wore upon their heads tall felt cones that were suggestive of the days of the Commonwealth.

I was a cipher in this august company, and felt subdued, not to say torpid. I was not even of sufficient consequence to assist at the wheel when it was
35 necessary to put the tiller hard down in a hurry; the guest that stood nearest did that when occasion required—and this was pretty much all the time, because of the crookedness of the channel and the scant water. I stood in a corner; and the talk I listened to took the hope all out of me. One visitor said to another:

40 "Jim, how did you run Plum Point, coming up?"

"It was in the night, there, and I ran it the way one of the boys on the *Diana* told me; started out about fifty yards above the wood-pile on the false point, and held on the cabin under Plum Point till I raised the reef—quarter less twain—then straightened up for the middle bar till I got well abreast the
45 old one-limbed cottonwood in the bend, then got my stern on the cottonwood,

32. **Commonwealth**—the Puritan Commonwealth under Oliver Cromwell. 44. **twain**—two fathoms, or twelve feet; but a "quarter less twain" presumably would be ten and one-half feet.

and head on the low place above the point, and came through a-booming—
nine and a half."

"Pretty square crossing, an't it?"

"Yes, but the upper bar's working down fast."

Another pilot spoke up and said: 5

"I had better water than that, and ran it lower down; started out from the
false point—mark twain—raised the second reef abreast the big snag in the
bend, and had quarter less twain."

One of the gorgeous ones remarked:

"I don't want to find fault with your leadsmen, but that's a good deal of   10
water for Plum Point, it seems to me."

There was an approving nod all around as this quiet snub dropped on the
boaster and "settled" him. And so they went on talk-talk-talking. Meantime,
the thing that was running in my mind was, "Now, if my ears hear aright,
I have not only to get the names of all the towns and islands and bends, and   15
so on, by heart, but I must even get up a warm personal acquaintanceship with
every old snag and one-limbed cottonwood and obscure wood-pile that ornaments the banks of this river for twelve hundred miles; and more than that,
I must actually know where these things are in the dark, unless these guests
are gifted with eyes that can pierce through two miles of solid blackness. I   20
wish the piloting business was in Jericho and I had never thought of it."

At dusk Mr. Bixby tapped the big bell three times (the signal to land), and
the captain emerged from his drawing-room in the forward end of the "texas,"
and looked up inquiringly. Mr. Bixby said:

"We will lay up here all night, captain."   25

"Very well, sir."

That was all. The boat came to shore and was tied up for the night. It
seemed to me a fine thing that the pilot could do as he pleased, without asking
so grand a captain's permission. I took my supper and went immediately to
bed, discouraged by my day's observations and experiences. My late voyage's   30
note-booking was but a confusion of meaningless names. It had tangled me
all up in a knot every time I had looked at it in the daytime. I now hoped
for respite in sleep; but no, it reveled all through my head till sunrise again,
a frantic and tireless nightmare.

Next morning I felt pretty rusty and low-spirited. We went booming along,   35
taking a good many chances, for we were anxious to "get out of the river"
(as getting out to Cairo was called) before night should overtake us. But Mr.
Bixby's partner, the other pilot, presently grounded the boat, and we lost so
much time getting her off that it was plain the darkness would overtake us
a good long way above the mouth. This was a great misfortune, especially to   40
certain of our visiting pilots, whose boats would have to wait for their return,
no matter how long that might be. It sobered the pilot-house talk a good deal.
Coming up-stream, pilots did not mind low water or any kind of darkness;
nothing stopped them but fog. But down-stream work was different; a boat
was too nearly helpless, with a stiff current pushing behind her; so it was not   45
customary to run down-stream at night in low water.

There seemed to be one small hope, however: if we could get through the

intricate and dangerous Hat Island crossing before night, we could venture
the rest, for we would have plainer sailing and better water. But it would be
insanity to attempt Hat Island at night. So there was a deal of looking at
watches all the rest of the day, and a constant ciphering upon the speed we
5   were making; Hat Island was the eternal subject; sometimes hope was high
and sometimes we were delayed in a bad crossing, and down it went again.
For hours all hands lay under the burden of this suppressed excitement; it
was even communicated to me, and I got to feeling so solicitous about Hat
Island, and under such an awful pressure of responsibility, that I wished I
10 might have five minutes on shore to draw a good, full, relieving breath, and
start over again. We were standing no regular watches. Each of our pilots ran
such portions of the river as he had run when coming up-stream, because of
his greater familiarity with it; but both remained in the pilot-house constantly.
    An hour before sunset Mr. Bixby took the wheel, and Mr. W. stepped aside.
15 For the next thirty minutes every man held his watch in his hand and was
restless, silent, and uneasy. At last somebody said, with a doomful sigh:
    "Well, yonder's Hat Island—and we can't make it."
    All the watches closed with a snap, everybody sighed and muttered some-
thing about its being "too bad, too bad—ah, if we could *only* have got here
20 half an hour sooner!" and the place was thick with the atmosphere of disappointment. Some started to go out, but loitered, hearing no bell-tap to land.
The sun dipped behind the horizon, the boat went on. Inquiring looks passed
from one guest to another; and one who had his hand on the door-knob and
had turned it, waited, then presently took away his hand and let the knob turn
25 back again. We bore steadily down the bend. More looks were exchanged, and
nods of surprised admiration—but no words. Insensibly the men drew together
behind Mr. Bixby, as the sky darkened and one or two dim stars came out.
The dead silence and sense of waiting became oppressive. Mr. Bixby pulled
the cord, and two deep, mellow notes from the big bell floated off on the night.
30 Then a pause, and one more note was struck. The watchman's voice followed,
from the hurricane-deck:
    "Labboard lead, there! Stabboard lead!"
    The cries of the leadsmen began to rise out of the distance, and were gruffly
repeated by the word-passers on the hurricane-deck.
35   "M-a-r-k three! M-a-r-k three! Quarter-less-three! Half twain! Quarter twain!
M-a-r-k twain! Quarter-less—"
    Mr. Bixby pulled two bell-ropes, and was answered by faint jinglings far
below in the engine-room, and our speed slackened. The steam began to whistle through the gauge-cocks. The cries of the leadsmen went on—and it is a
40 weird sound, always, in the night. Every pilot in the lot was watching now,
with fixed eyes, and talking under his breath. Nobody was calm and easy but
Mr. Bixby. He would put his wheel down and stand on a spoke, and as the
steamer swung into her (to me) utterly invisible marks—for we seemed to be
in the midst of a wide and gloomy sea—he would meet and fasten her there.
45 Out of the murmur of half-audible talk, one caught a coherent sentence now
and then—such as:
    "There; she's over the first reef all right!"

After a pause, another subdued voice:

"Her stern's coming down just *exactly* right, by *George!*"

"Now she's in the marks; over she goes!"

Somebody else muttered:

"Oh, it was done beautiful—*beautiful!*"

Now the engines were stopped altogether, and we drifted with the current. Not that I could see the boat drift, for I could not, the stars being all gone by this time. This drifting was the dismalest work; it held one's heart still. Presently I discovered a blacker gloom than that which surrounded us. It was the head of the island. We were closing right down upon it. We entered its deeper shadow, and so imminent seemed the peril that I was likely to suffocate; and I had the strongest impulse to do *something,* anything, to save the vessel. But still Mr. Bixby stood by his wheel, silent, intent as a cat, and all the pilots stood shoulder to shoulder at his back.

"She'll not make it!" somebody whispered.

The water grew shoaler and shoaler, by the leadsman's cries, till it was down to:

"Eight-and-a-half! E-i-g-h-t feet! E-i-g-h-t feet! Seven-and—"

Mr. Bixby said warningly through his speaking-tube to the engineer:

"Stand by, now!"

"Ay, ay, sir!"

"Seven-and-a-half! Seven feet! *Six*-and—"

We touched bottom! Instantly Mr. Bixby set a lot of bells ringing, shouted through the tube, *"Now,* let her have it—every ounce you've got!" then to his partner, "Put her hard down! snatch her! snatch her!" The boat rasped and ground her way through the sand, hung upon the apex of disaster a single tremendous instant, and then over she went! And such a shout as went up at Mr. Bixby's back never loosened the roof of a pilot-house before!

There was no more trouble after that. Mr. Bixby was a hero that night; and it was some little time, too, before his exploit ceased to be talked about by river-men.

Fully to realize the marvelous precision required in laying the great steamer in her marks in that murky waste of water, one should know that not only must she pick her intricate way through snags and blind reefs, and then shave the head of the island so closely as to brush the overhanging foliage with her stern, but at one place she must pass almost within arm's reach of a sunken and invisible wreck that would snatch the hull timbers from under her if she should strike it, and destroy a quarter of a million dollars' worth of steamboat and cargo in five minutes, and maybe a hundred and fifty human lives into the bargain.

The last remark I heard that night was a compliment to Mr. Bixby, uttered in soliloquy and with unction by one of our guests. He said:

"By the Shadow of Death, but he's a lightning pilot!"

THE MYSTERIOUS STRANGER

A ROMANCE

The Mysterious Stranger was written wholly or in part in 1898, but it was published posthumously in 1916 by Harper and Brothers, with illustrations by N. C.
Wyeth. This edition retained Mark Twain's own punctuation and is therefore here
reprinted. The story later appeared in *The Mysterious Stranger and Other Stories,*
1922, but with unfortunate alterations in the punctuation and a few changes in the
text.

CHAPTER I

I T WAS in 1590—winter. Austria was far away from the world, and asleep;
it was still the Middle Ages in Austria, and promised to remain so forever.
Some even set it away back centuries upon centuries and said that by the
5   mental and spiritual clock it was still the Age of Belief in Austria. But they
meant it as a compliment, not a slur, and it was so taken, and we were all
proud of it. I remember it well, although I was only a boy; and I remember,
too, the pleasure it gave me.

Yes, Austria was far from the world, and asleep, and our village was in the
10   middle of that sleep, being in the middle of Austria. It drowsed in peace in
the deep privacy of a hilly and woodsy solitude where news from the world
hardly ever came to disturb its dreams, and was infinitely content. At its front
flowed the tranquil river, its surface painted with cloud-forms and the reflections of drifting arks and stone-boats; behind it rose the woody steeps to
15   the base of the lofty precipice; from the top of the precipice frowned a vast
castle, its long stretch of towers and bastions mailed in vines; beyond the
river, a league to the left, was a tumbled expanse of forest-clothed hills cloven
by winding gorges where the sun never penetrated; and to the right a precipice overlooked the river, and between it and the hills just spoken of lay
20   a far-reaching plain dotted with little homesteads nested among orchards and
shade trees.

The whole region for leagues around was the hereditary property of a
prince, whose servants kept the castle always in perfect condition for occupancy, but neither he nor his family came there oftener than once in five
25   years. When they came it was as if the lord of the world had arrived,
and had brought all the glories of its kingdoms along; and when they went
they left a calm behind which was like the deep sleep which follows an
orgy.

Eseldorf was a paradise for us boys. We were not overmuch pestered with
30   schooling. Mainly we were trained to be good Christians; to revere the Virgin,
the Church, and the saints above everything. Beyond these matters we were
not required to know much; and, in fact, not allowed to. Knowledge was not
good for the common people, and could make them discontented with the
lot which God had appointed for them, and God would not endure discon-

29. **Eseldorf**—i.e., Donkeytown.

tentment with His plans. We had two priests. One of them, Father Adolf,
was a very zealous and strenuous priest, much considered.

There may have been better priests, in some ways, than Father Adolf, but
there was never one in our commune who was held in more solemn and
awful respect. This was because he had absolutely no fear of the Devil. He   5
was the only Christian I have ever known of whom that could be truly said.
People stood in deep dread of him on that account; for they thought that there
must be something supernatural about him, else he could not be so bold and
so confident. All men speak in bitter disapproval of the Devil but they do it
reverently, not flippantly; but Father Adolf's way was very different; he   10
called him by every name he could lay his tongue to, and it made every one
shudder that heard him; and often he would even speak of him scornfully
and scoffingly; then the people crossed themselves and went quickly out of
his presence, fearing that something fearful might happen.

Father Adolf had actually met Satan face to face more than once, and de-   15
fied him. This was known to be so. Father Adolf said it himself. He never
made any secret of it, but spoke it right out. And that he was speaking true
there was proof in at least one instance, for on that occasion he quarreled
with the enemy, and intrepidly threw his bottle at him; and there, upon the
wall of his study, was the ruddy splotch where it struck and broke.   20

But it was Father Peter, the other priest, that we all loved best and were
sorriest for. Some people charged him with talking around in conversation that
God was all goodness and would find a way to save all his poor human children. It was a horrible thing to say, but there was never any absolute proof
that Father Peter said it; and it was out of character for him to say it, too,   25
for he was always good and gentle and truthful. He wasn't charged with
saying it in the pulpit, where all the congregation could hear and testify, but
only outside, in talk; and it is easy for enemies to manufacture *that*. Father
Peter had an enemy and a very powerful one, the astrologer who lived in a
tumbled old tower up the valley, and put in his nights studying the stars.   30
Every one knew he could foretell wars and famines, though that was not so
hard, for there was always a war and generally a famine somewhere. But
he could also read any man's life through the stars in a big book he had, and
find lost property, and every one in the village except Father Peter stood in
awe of him. Even Father Adolf, who had defied the Devil, had a wholesome   35
respect for the astrologer when he came through our village wearing his tall,
pointed hat and his long, flowing robe with stars on it, carrying his big book
and a staff which was known to have magic power. The bishop himself
sometimes listened to the astrologer, it was said, for, besides studying the
stars and prophesying, the astrologer made a great show of piety, which   40
would impress the bishop, of course.

But Father Peter took no stock in the astrologer. He denounced him openly
as a charlatan—a fraud with no valuable knowledge of any kind, or powers
beyond those of an ordinary and rather inferior human being, which naturally
made the astrologer hate Father Peter and wish to ruin him. It was the as-   45
trologer, as we all believed, who originated the story about Father Peter's
shocking remark and carried it to the bishop. It was said that Father Peter

had made the remark to his niece, Marget, though Marget denied it and implored the bishop to believe her and spare her old uncle from poverty and
disgrace. But the bishop wouldn't listen. He suspended Father Peter indefinitely, though he wouldn't go so far as to excommunicate him on the evi-
5 dence of only one witness; and now Father Peter had been out a couple of
years, and our other priest, Father Adolf, had his flock.

Those had been hard years for the old priest and Marget. They had been
favorites, but of course that changed when they came under the shadow of
the bishop's frown. Many of their friends fell away entirely, and the rest be-
10 came cool and distant. Marget was a lovely girl of eighteen when the trouble
came, and she had the best head in the village, and the most in it. She taught
the harp, and earned all her clothes and pocket money by her own industry.
But her scholars fell off one by one now; she was forgotten when there were
dances and parties among the youth of the village; the young fellows stopped
15 coming to the house, all except Wilhelm Meidling—and he could have been
spared; she and her uncle were sad and forlorn in their neglect and disgrace,
and the sunshine was gone out of their lives. Matters went worse and worse,
all through the two years. Clothes were wearing out, bread was harder and
harder to get. And now, at last, the very end was come. Solomon Isaacs had
20 lent all the money he was willing to put on the house, and gave notice that
to-morrow he would foreclose.

CHAPTER II

Three of us boys were always together, and had been so from the cradle,
being fond of one another from the beginning, and this affection deepened
25 as the years went on—Nikolaus Bauman, son of the principal judge of the
local court; Seppi Wohlmeyer, son of the keeper of the principal inn, the
"Golden Stag," which had a nice garden, with shade trees reaching down
to the riverside, and pleasure boats for hire; and I was the third—Theodor
Fischer, son of the church organist, who was also leader of the village mu-
30 sicians, teacher of the violin, composer, tax-collector of the commune, sexton,
and in other ways a useful citizen, and respected by all. We knew the hills
and the woods as well as the birds knew them; for we were always roaming
them when we had leisure—at least, when we were not swimming or boating
or fishing, or playing on the ice or sliding down hill.

35 And we had the run of the castle park, and very few had that. It was because we were pets of the oldest servingman in the castle——Felix Brandt;
and often we went there, nights, to hear him talk about old times and strange
things, and to smoke with him (he taught us that) and to drink coffee; for
he had served in the wars, and was at the siege of Vienna; and there, when
40 the Turks were defeated and driven away, among the captured things were
bags of coffee, and the Turkish prisoners explained the character of it and
how to make a pleasant drink out of it, and now he always kept coffee by
him, to drink himself and also to astonish the ignorant with. When it stormed

---

30. commune—here, loosely used for "district." 39. siege of Vienna—In 1529 a Turkish
army unsuccessfully besieged Vienna.

he kept us all night; and while it thundered and lightened outside he told us about ghosts and horrors of every kind, and of battles and murders and mutilations, and such things, and made it pleasant and cozy inside; and he told these things from his own experience largely. He had seen many ghosts in his time, and witches and enchanters, and once he was lost in a fierce storm 5 at midnight in the mountains, and by the glare of the lightning had seen the Wild Huntsman rage on the blast with his specter dogs chasing after him through the driving cloud-rack. Also he had seen an incubus once, and several times he had seen the great bat that sucks the blood from the necks of people while they are asleep, fanning them softly with its wings and so keeping 10 them drowsy till they die.

He encouraged us not to fear supernatural things, such as ghosts, and said they did no harm, but only wandered about because they were lonely and distressed and wanted kindly notice and compassion; and in time we learned not to be afraid, and even went down with him in the night to the haunted 15 chamber in the dungeons of the castle. The ghost appeared only once, and it went by very dim to the sight and floated noiseless through the air, and then disappeared; and we scarcely trembled, he had taught us so well. He said it came up sometimes in the night and woke him by passing its clammy hand over his face, but it did him no hurt; it only wanted sympathy and 20 notice. But the strangest thing was that he had seen angels—actual angels out of heaven—and had talked with them. They had no wings, and wore clothes, and talked and looked and acted just like any natural person, and you would never know them for angels except for the wonderful things they did which a mortal could not do, and the way they suddenly disappeared while you were 25 talking with them, which was also a thing which no mortal could do. And he said they were pleasant and cheerful, not gloomy and melancholy, like ghosts.

It was after that kind of a talk one May night that we got up next morning and had a good breakfast with him and then went down and crossed the bridge 30 and went away up into the hills on the left to a woody hill-top which was a favorite place of ours, and there we stretched out on the grass in the shade to rest and smoke and talk over these strange things, for they were in our minds yet, and impressing us. But we couldn't smoke, because we had been heedless and left our flint and steel behind. 35

Soon there came a youth strolling toward us through the trees, and he sat down and began to talk in a friendly way, just as if he knew us. But we did not answer him, for he was a stranger and we were not used to strangers and were shy of them. He had new and good clothes on, and was handsome and had a winning face and a pleasant voice, and was easy and graceful and un- 40 embarrassed, not slouchy and awkward and diffident, like other boys. We wanted to be friendly with him, but didn't know how to begin. Then I thought of the pipe, and wondered if it would be taken as kindly meant if I offered

---

7. Wild Huntsman—According to a widely disseminated legend a spectral huntsman with his dogs frequents certain forests, usually in stormy weather, because, when he was alive, he would not suffer Jesus to drink out of a horse-trough, and he must accordingly ride forever. **8. incubus**—an evil spirit supposed to descend upon sleeping persons, especially upon women. The "great bat" in the next line is the equally legendary vampire bat.

it to him. But I remembered that we had no fire, so I was sorry and disappointed. But he looked up bright and pleased, and said:

"Fire? Oh, that is easy; I will furnish it."

I was so astonished I couldn't speak, for I had not said anything. He took
5 the pipe and blew his breath on it, and the tobacco glowed red, and spirals of blue smoke rose up. We jumped up and were going to run, for that was natural; and we did run a few steps, although he was yearningly pleading for us to stay, and giving us his word that he would not do us any harm, but only wanted to be friends with us and have company. So we stopped and stood,
10 and wanted to go back, being full of curiosity and wonder, but afraid to venture. He went on coaxing, in his soft, persuasive way; and when we saw that the pipe did not blow up and nothing happened, our confidence returned by little and little, and presently our curiosity got to be stronger than our fear, and we ventured back—but slowly, and ready to fly at any alarm.

15 He was bent on putting us at ease, and he had the right art; one could not remain doubtful and timorous where a person was so earnest and simple and gentle, and talked so alluringly as he did; no, he won us over, and it was not long before we were content and comfortable and chatty, and glad we had found this new friend. When the feeling of constraint was all gone we asked
20 him how he had learned to do that strange thing, and he said he hadn't learned it at all; it came natural to him—like other things—other curious things.

"What ones?"

"Oh, a number; I don't know how many."

"Will you let us see you do them?"
25 "Do—please!" the others said.

"You won't run away again?"

"No—indeed we won't. Please do. Won't you?"

"Yes, with pleasure; but you mustn't forget your promise, you know."

We said we wouldn't, and he went to a puddle and came back with water
30 in a cup which he had made out of a leaf, and blew upon it and threw it out, and it was a lump of ice the shape of the cup. We were astonished and charmed, but not afraid any more; we were very glad to be there, and asked him to go on and do some more things. And he did. He said he would give us any kind of fruit we liked, whether it was in season or not. We all spoke at once:
35 "Orange!"

"Apple!"

"Grapes!"

"They are in your pockets," he said, and it was true. And they were of the best, too, and we ate them and wished we had more, though none of us said so.
40 "You will find them where those came from," he said, "and everything else your appetites call for; and you need not name the thing you wish; as long as I am with you, you have only to wish and find."

And he said true. There was never anything so wonderful and so interesting. Bread, cakes, sweets, nuts—whatever one wanted, it was there. He ate nothing
45 himself, but sat and chatted, and did one curious thing after another to amuse us. He made a tiny toy squirrel out of clay, and it ran up a tree and sat on a limb overhead and barked down at us. Then he made a dog that was not much

larger than a mouse, and it treed the squirrel and danced about the tree, excited
and barking, and was as alive as any dog could be. It frightened the squirrel
from tree to tree and followed it up until both were out of sight in the forest.
He made birds out of clay and set them free, and they flew away, singing.

At last I made bold to ask him to tell us who he was.   5

"An angel," he said, quite simply, and set another bird free and clapped his
hands and made it fly away.

A kind of awe fell upon us when we heard him say that, and we were afraid
again; but he said we need not be troubled, there was no occasion for us to be
afraid of an angel, and he liked us, anyway. He went on chatting as simply   10
and unaffectedly as ever; and while he talked he made a crowd of little men
and women the size of your finger, and they went diligently to work and
cleared and leveled off a space a couple of yards square in the grass and began
to build a cunning little castle in it, the women mixing the mortar and carrying
it up the scaffoldings in pails on their heads, just as our work-women have   15
always done, and the men laying the courses of masonry—five hundred of these
toy people swarming briskly about and working diligently and wiping the
sweat off their faces as natural as life. In the absorbing interest of watching
those five hundred little people make the castle grow step by step and course
by course, and take shape and symmetry, that feeling and awe soon passed   20
away and we were quite comfortable and at home again. We asked if we might
make some people, and he said yes, and told Seppi to make some cannon for
the walls, and told Nikolaus to make some halberdiers with breastplates and
greaves and helmets, and I was to make some cavalry, with horses, and in allot-
ting these tasks he called us by our names, but did not say how he knew them. 25
Then Seppi asked him what his own name was, and he said, tranquilly,
"Satan," and held out a chip and caught a little woman on it who was falling
from the scaffolding and put her back where she belonged, and said, "She is
an idiot to step backward like that and not notice what she is about."

It caught us suddenly, that name did, and our work dropped out of our   30
hands and broke to pieces—a cannon, a halberdier, and a horse. Satan laughed,
and asked what was the matter. I said, "Nothing, only it seemed a strange
name for an angel." He asked why.

"Because it's—it's—well, it's his name, you know."

"Yes—he is my uncle."   35

He said it placidly, but it took our breath for a moment and made our hearts
beat. He did not seem to notice that, but mended our halberdiers and things
with a touch, handing them to us finished, and said, "Don't you remember?
—he was an angel himself, once."

"Yes—it's true," said Seppi; "I didn't think of that."   40

"Before the Fall he was blameless."

"Yes," said Nikolaus, "he was without sin."

"It is a good family—ours," said Satan; "there is not a better. He is the only
member of it that has ever sinned."

---

16. **courses**—continuous layers. 23. **halberdiers**—soldiers armed with a halberd or halbert,
a combined spear and battle-axe. 24. **greaves**—armor for the lower half of the legs. 41. **Fall**
—i.e., the fall of Lucifer, not the fall of man. See Isa. 14:12-15.

I should not be able to make any one understand how exciting it all was. You know that kind of quiver that trembles around through you when you are seeing something so strange and enchanting and wonderful that it is just a fearful joy to be alive and look at it; and you know how you gaze, and your
5 lips turn dry and your breath comes short, but you wouldn't be anywhere but there, not for the world. I was bursting to ask one question—I had it on my tongue's end and could hardly hold it back—but I was ashamed to ask it; it might be a rudeness. Satan set an ox down that he had been making and smiled up at me and said:
10 "It wouldn't be a rudeness, and I should forgive it if it was. Have I seen him? Millions of times. From the time that I was a little child a thousand years old I was his second favorite among the nursery angels of our blood and lineage— to use a human phrase—yes, from that time until the Fall, eight thousand years, measured as you count time."
15 "Eight—thousand!"
"Yes." He turned to Seppi, and went on as if answering something that was in Seppi's mind, "Why, naturally I look like a boy, for that is what I am. With us what you call time is a spacious thing; it takes a long stretch of it to grow an angel to full age." There was a question in my mind, and he turned to me
20 and answered it, "I am sixteen thousand years old—counting as you count." Then he turned to Nikolaus and said: "No, the Fall did not affect me nor the rest of the relationship. It was only he that I was named for who ate of the fruit of the tree and then beguiled the man and the woman with it. We others are still ignorant of sin; we are not able to commit it; we are without blemish,
25 and shall abide in that estate always. We—" Two of the little workmen were quarreling, and in buzzing little bumblebee voices they were cursing and swear- ing at each other; now came blows and blood; then they locked themselves together in a life-and-death struggle. Satan reached out his hand and crushed the life out of them with his fingers, threw them away, wiped the red from his
30 fingers on his handkerchief, and went on talking where he had left off: "We cannot do wrong; neither have we any disposition to do it, for we do not know what it is."
It seemed a strange speech, in the circumstances, but we barely noticed that, we were so shocked and grieved at the wanton murder he had committed—for
35 murder it was, that was its true name, and it was without palliation or excuse, for the men had not wronged him in any way. It made us miserable, for we loved him, and had thought him so noble and so beautiful and gracious, and had honestly believed he was an angel; and to have him do this cruel thing— ah, it lowered him so, and we had had such pride in him. He went right on
40 talking, just as if nothing had happened, telling about his travels and the in- teresting things he had seen in the big worlds of our solar system and of other solar systems far away in the remoteness of space, and about the customs of the immortals that inhabit them, somehow fascinating us, enchanting us, charm- ing us in spite of the pitiful scene that was now under our eyes, for the wives of
45 the little dead men had found the crushed and shapeless bodies and were crying over them, and sobbing and lamenting, and a priest was kneeling there with his hands crossed upon his breast, praying; and crowds and crowds of pitying

friends were massed about them, reverently uncovered, with their bare heads
bowed, and many with the tears running down—a scene which Satan paid no
attention to until the small noise of the weeping and praying began to annoy
them, then he reached out and took the heavy board seat out of our swing
and brought it down and mashed all those people into the earth just as if they   5
had been flies, and went on talking just the same.

An angel, and kill a priest! An angel who did not know how to do wrong,
and yet destroys in cold blood hundreds of helpless poor men and women
who had never done him any harm! It made us sick to see that awful deed,
and to think that none of those poor creatures was prepared except the priest,   10
for none of them had ever heard a mass or seen a church. And we were witnesses; we had seen these murders done and it was our duty to tell, and let the
law take its course.

But he went on talking right along, and worked his enchantments upon us
again with that fatal music of his voice. He made us forget everything; we   15
could only listen to him, and love him, and be his slaves, to do with us as he
would. He made us drunk with the joy of being with him, and of looking into
the heaven of his eyes, and of feeling the ecstasy that thrilled along our veins
from the touch of his hand.

CHAPTER III   20

The Stranger had seen everything, he had been everywhere, he knew everything, and he forgot nothing. What another must study, he learned at a glance;
there were no difficulties for him. And he made things live before you when
he told about them. He saw the world made; he saw Adam created; he saw
Samson surge against the pillars and bring the temple down in ruins about   25
him; he saw Cæsar's death; he told of the daily life in heaven; he had seen the
damned writhing in the red waves of hell; and he made us see all these things,
and it was as if we were on the spot and looking at them with our own eyes.
And we felt them, too, but there was no sign that they were anything to him
beyond mere entertainments. Those visions of hell, those poor babes and women   30
and girls and lads and men shrieking and supplicating in anguish—why, we
could hardly bear it, but he was as bland about it as if it had been so many imitation rats in an artificial fire.

And always when he was talking about men and women here on the earth
and their doings—even their grandest and sublimest—we were secretly ashamed,   35
for his manner showed that to him they and their doings were of paltry poor
consequence; often you would think he was talking about flies, if you didn't
know. Once he even said, in so many words, that our people down here were
quite interesting to him, notwithstanding they were so dull and ignorant and
trivial and conceited, and so diseased and rickety and such a shabby, poor,   40
worthless lot all around. He said it in a quite matter-of-course way and without bitterness, just as a person might talk about bricks or manure or any other

---

4. **them**—so the text, but "him" seems to be meant. **24-25. Adam . . . Samson**—*cf.*
Gen. 2:7; Judg. 16:25-31. **26. Cæsar's death**—*cf.* Shakespeare, *Julius Caesar,* Act III, sc. i.
40. rickety—i.e., suffering from rickets (rachitis), a softening and deformation of the bones,
especially of the legs.

thing that was of no consequence and hadn't feelings. I could see he meant no offense, but in my thoughts I set it down as not very good manners.

"Manners!" he said. "Why, it is merely the truth, and truth is good manners; manners are a fiction. The castle is done. Do you like it?"

5   Any one would have been obliged to like it. It was lovely to look at, it was so shapely and fine, and so cunningly perfect in all its particulars, even to the little flags waving from the turrets. Satan said we must put the artillery in place now, and station the halberdiers and display the cavalry. Our men and horses were a spectacle to see, they were so little like what they were intended
10   for; for, of course, we had no art in making such things. Satan said they were the worst he had seen; and when he touched them and made them alive, it was just ridiculous the way they acted, on account of their legs not being of uniform lengths. They reeled and sprawled around as if they were drunk, and endangered everybody's lives around them, and finally fell over and lay
15   helpless and kicking. It made us all laugh, though it was a shameful thing to see. The guns were charged with dirt, to fire a salute, but they were so crooked and so badly made that they all burst when they went off, and killed some of the gunners and crippled the·others. Satan said we would have a storm now, and an earthquake, if we liked, but we must stand off a piece, out of danger.
20   We wanted to call the people away, too, but he said never mind them; they were of no consequence, and we could make more, some time or other, if we needed them.

A small storm-cloud began to settle down black over the castle, and the miniature lightning and thunder began to play, and the ground to quiver,
25   and the wind to pipe and wheeze, and the rain to fall, and all the people flocked into the castle for shelter. The cloud settled down blacker and blacker, and one could see the castle only dimly through it; the lightning blazed out flash upon flash and pierced the castle and set it on fire, and the flames shone out red and fierce through the cloud, and the people came flying out, shriek-
30   ing, but Satan brushed them back, paying no attention to our begging and crying and imploring; and in the midst of the howling of the wind and vol- leying of the thunder the magazine blew up, the earthquake rent the ground wide, and the castle's wreck and ruin tumbled into the chasm, which swal- lowed it from sight, and closed upon it, with all that innocent life, not one of
35   the five hundred poor creatures escaping. Our hearts were broken; we could not keep from crying.

"Don't cry," Satan said; "they were of no value."

"B.t they are gone to hell!"

"Oh, it is no matter; we can make plenty more."

40   It was of no use to try to move him; evidently he was wholly without feelings and could not understand. He was full of bubbling spirits, and as gay as if this were a wedding instead of a fiendish massacre. And he was bent on making us feel as he did, and of course his magic accomplished his desire. It was no trouble to him; he did whatever he pleased with us. In a little while
45   we were dancing on that grave, and he was playing to us on a strange, sweet instrument which he took out of his pocket; and the music—but there is no music like that, unless perhaps in heaven, and that was where he brought it

from, he said. It made one mad, for pleasure; and we could not take our eyes from him, and the looks that went out of our eyes came from our hearts, and their dumb speech was worship. He brought the dance from heaven, too, and the bliss of paradise was in it.

Presently he said he must go away on an errand. But we could not bear the 5 thought of it, and clung to him, and pleaded with him to stay; and that pleased him, and he said so, and said he would not go yet, but would wait a little while and we would sit down and talk a few minutes longer; and he told us Satan was only his real name, and he was to be known by it to us alone, but he had chosen another one to be called by in the presence of others; just 10 a common one, such as people have—Philip Traum.

It sounded so odd and mean for such a being! But it was his decision, and we said nothing; his decision was sufficient.

We had seen wonders this day; and my thoughts began to run on the pleasure it would be to tell them when I got home, but he noticed those 15 thoughts, and said:

"No, all these matters are a secret among us four. I do not mind your trying to tell them, if you like, but I will protect your tongues and nothing of the secret will escape from them."

It was a disappointment, but it couldn't be helped, and it cost us a sigh or 20 two. We talked pleasantly along, and he was always reading our thoughts and responding to them, and it seemed to me that this was the most wonderful of all the things he did, but he interrupted my musings, and said:

"No, it would be wonderful for you, but it is not wonderful for me. I am not limited like you. I am not subject to human conditions. I can measure 25 and understand your human weaknesses, for I have studied them; but I have none of them. My flesh is not real, although it would seem firm to your touch; my clothes are not real; I am a spirit. Father Peter is coming.["] We looked around, but did not see any one. "He is not in sight yet, but you will see him presently." 30

"Do you know him, Satan?"

"No."

"Won't you talk with him when he comes? He is not ignorant and dull, like us, and he would so like to talk with you. Will you?"

"Another time, yes, but not now. I must go on my errand after a little. 35 There he is now; you can see him. Sit still, and don't say anything."

We looked up and saw Father Peter approaching through the chestnuts. We three were sitting together in the grass, and Satan sat in front of us in the path. Father Peter came slowly along with his head down, thinking, and stopped within a couple of yards of us and took off his hat and got out his silk 40 handkerchief, and stood there mopping his face and looking as if he were going to speak to us, but he didn't. Presently he muttered, "I can't think what brought me here; it seems as if I were in my study a minute ago—but I suppose I have been dreaming along for an hour and have come all this stretch without noticing; for I am not myself in these troubled days." Then he went 45 mumbling along to himself and walked straight through Satan, just as if

---

11. **Traum**—German for "Dream."

nothing were there. It made us catch our breath to see it. We had the impulse
to cry out, the way you nearly always do when a startling thing happens, but
something mysteriously restrained us and we remained quiet, only breathing
fast. Then the trees hid Father Peter after a little, and Satan said:

5   "It is as I told you—I am only a spirit."

"Yes, one perceives it now," said Nikolaus, "but we are not spirits. It is plain
he did not see you, but were we invisible, too? He looked at us, but he didn't
seem to see us."

"No, none of us was visible to him, for I wished it so."

10   It seemed almost too good to be true, that we were actually seeing these
romantic and wonderful things, and that it was not a dream. And there he
sat, looking just like anybody—so natural and simple and charming, and
chatting along again the same as ever, and—well, words cannot make you
understand what we felt. It was an ecstasy; and an ecstasy is a thing that will

15   not go into words; it feels like music, and one cannot tell about music so
that another person can get the feeling of it. He was back in the old ages once
more now, and making them live before us. He had seen so much, so much!
It was just a wonder to look at him and try to think how it must seem to have
such experience behind one.

20   But it made you seem sorrowfully trivial, and the creature of a day, and such
a short and paltry day, too. And he didn't say anything to raise up your drooping pride—no, not a word. He always spoke of men in the same old indifferent
way—just as one speaks of bricks and manure-piles and such things; you could
see that they were of no consequence to him, one way or the other. He didn't

25   mean to hurt us, you could see that; just as we don't mean to insult a brick
when we disparage it; a brick's emotions are nothing to us; it never occurs
to us to think whether it has any or not.

Once when he was bunching the most illustrious kings and conquerors and
poets and prophets and pirates and beggars together—just a brick-pile—I was

30   shamed into putting in a word for man, and asked him why he made so
much difference between men and himself. He had to struggle with that a
moment; he didn't seem to understand how I could ask such a strange question. Then he said:

"The difference between man and me? The difference between a mortal

35   and an immortal? between a cloud and a spirit?" He picked up a wood-louse
that was creeping along a piece of bark: "What is the difference between
Cæsar and this?"

I said, "One cannot compare things which by their nature and by the interval between them are not comparable."

40   "You have answered your own question," he said. "I will expand it. Man
is made of dirt—I saw him made. I am not made of dirt. Man is a museum of
diseases, a home of impurities; he comes to-day and is gone to-morrow; he
begins as dirt and departs as stench; I am of the aristocracy of the Imperish-
ables. And man has the *Moral Sense*. You understand? He has the *Moral

45   Sense*. That would seem to be difference enough between us, all by itself."

He stopped there, as if that settled the matter. I was sorry, for at that time
I had but a dim idea of what the Moral Sense was. I merely knew that we

were proud of having it, and when he talked like that about it, it wounded me, and I felt as a girl feels who thinks her dearest finery is being admired and then overhears strangers making fun of it. For a while we were all silent, and I, for one, was depressed. Then Satan began to chat again, and soon he was sparkling along in such a cheerful and vivacious vein that my spirits rose 5 once more. He told some very cunning things that put us in a gale of laughter; and when he was telling about the time that Samson tied the torches to the foxes' tails and set them loose in the Philistines' corn, and Samson sitting on the fence slapping his thighs and laughing, with the tears running down his cheeks, and lost his balance and fell off the fence, the memory of that picture 10 got him to laughing, too, and we did have a most lovely and jolly time. By and by he said:

"I am going on my errand now."

"Don't!" we all said. "Don't go; stay with us. You won't come back."

"Yes, I will; I give you my word."   15

"When? To-night? Say when."

"It won't be long. You will see."

"We like you."

"And I you. And as a proof of it I will show you something fine to see. Usually when I go I merely vanish; but now I will dissolve myself and let 20 you see me do it."

He stood up and it was quickly finished. He thinned away and thinned away until he was a soap-bubble, except that he kept his shape. You could see the bushes through him as clearly as you see things through a soap-bubble, and all over him played and flashed the delicate iridescent colors of the bubble, 25 and along with them was that thing shaped like a window-sash which you always see on the globe of the bubble. You have seen a bubble strike the carpet and lightly bound along two or three times before it bursts. He did that. He sprang—touched the grass—bounded—floated along—touched again— and so on, and presently exploded—puff! and in his place was vacancy.   30

It was a strange and beautiful thing to see. We did not say anything, but sat wondering and dreaming and blinking; and finally Seppi roused up and said, mournfully sighing:

"I suppose none of it has happened."

Nikolaus sighed and said about the same.   35

I was miserable to hear them say it, for it was the same cold fear that was in my own mind. Then we saw poor old Father Peter wandering along back, with his head bent down, searching the ground. When he was pretty close to us he looked up and saw us, and said, "How long have you been here, boys?"

"A little while, Father."   40

"Then it is since I came by, and maybe you can help me. Did you come up by the path?"

"Yes, Father."

"That is good. I came the same way. I have lost my wallet. There wasn't much in it, but a very little is much to me, for it was all I had. I suppose you 45 haven't seen anything of it?"

7 ff. **Samson**—*cf.* Judg. 15:4-8.

"No, Father, but we will help you hunt."

"It is what I was going to ask you. Why, here it is!"

We hadn't noticed it; yet there it lay, right where Satan stood when he began to melt—if he did melt and it wasn't a delusion. Father Peter picked it
5 up and looked very much surprised.

"It is mine," he said, "but not the contents. This is fat; mine was flat; mine was light; this is heavy." He opened it; it was stuffed as full as it could hold with gold coins. He let us gaze our fill; and of course we did gaze, for we had never seen so much money at one time before. All our mouths came open to
10 say "Satan did it!" but nothing came out. There it was, you see—we couldn't tell what Satan didn't want told; he had said so himself.

"Boys, did you do this?"

It made us laugh. And it made him laugh, too, as soon as he thought what a foolish question it was.

15 "Who has been here?"

Our mouths came open to answer, but stood so for a moment, because we couldn't say "Nobody," for it wouldn't be true, and the right word didn't seem to come; then I thought of the right one, and said it:

"Not a human being."

20 "That is so," said the others, and let their mouths go shut.

"It is not so," said Father Peter, and looked at us very severely. "I came by here a while ago, and there was no one here, but that is nothing; some one has been here since. I don't mean to say that the person didn't pass here before you came, and I don't mean to say that you saw him, but some one did pass,
25 that I know. On your honor—you saw no one?"

"Not a human being."

"That is sufficient; I know you are telling me the truth."

He began to count the money on the path, we on our knees eagerly helping to stack it in little piles.

30 "It's eleven hundred ducats odd!" he said. "Oh dear! if it were only mine— and I need it so!" and his voice broke and his lips quivered.

"It is yours, sir!" we all cried out at once, "every heller!"

"No—it isn't mine. Only four ducats are mine; the rest . . . !" He fell to dreaming, poor old soul, and caressing some of the coins in his hands, and
35 forgot where he was, sitting there on his heels with his old gray head bare; it was pitiful to see. "No," he said, waking up, "it isn't mine. I can't account for it. I think some enemy . . . it must be a trap."

Nikolaus said: "Father Peter, with the exception of the astrologer you haven't a real enemy in the village—nor Marget, either. And not even a half-enemy
40 that's rich enough to chance eleven hundred ducats to do you a mean turn. I'll ask you if that's so or not?"

He couldn't get around that argument, and it cheered him up. "But it isn't mine, you see—it isn't mine, in any case."

He said it in a wistful way, like a person that wouldn't be sorry, but glad, if
45 anybody would contradict him.

"It is yours, Father Peter, and we are witness to it. Aren't we, boys?"

---

32. heller—i.e., "every nickel." A heller was a small silver Austrian coin.

"Yes, we are—and we'll stand by it, too."

"Bless your hearts, you do almost persuade me; you do, indeed. If I had only a hundred-odd ducats of it! The house is mortgaged for it, and we've no home for our heads if we don't pay to-morrow. And that four ducats is all we've got in the—"   5

"It's yours, every bit of it, and you've got to take it—we are bail that it's all right. Aren't we, Theodor? Aren't we, Seppi?"

We two said yes, and Nikolaus stuffed the money back into the shabby old wallet and made the owner take it. So he said he would use two hundred of it, for his house was good enough security for that, and would put the rest at   10 interest till the rightful owner came for it; and on our side we must sign a paper showing how he got the money—a paper to show to the villagers as proof that he had not got out of his troubles dishonestly.

CHAPTER IV

It made immense talk next day, when Father Peter paid Solomon Isaacs in   15 gold and left the rest of the money with him at interest. Also, there was a pleasant change; many people called at the house to congratulate him, and a number of cool old friends became kind and friendly again; and to top all, Marget was invited to a party.

And there was no mystery; Father Peter told the whole circumstance just as   20 it happened, and said he could not account for it, only it was the plain hand of Providence, so far as he could see.

One or two shook their heads and said privately it looked more like the hand of Satan; and really that seemed a surprisingly good guess for ignorant people like that. Some came slyly buzzing around and tried to coax us boys   25 to come out and "tell the truth"; and promised they wouldn't ever tell but only wanted to know for their own satisfaction, because the whole thing was so curious. They even wanted to buy the secret, and pay money for it; and if we could have invented something that would answer—but we couldn't; we hadn't the ingenuity, so we had to let the chance go by, and it was a pity.   30

We carried that secret around without any trouble, but the other one, the big one, the splendid one, burned the very vitals of us, it was so hot to get out and we so hot to let it out and astonish people with it. But we had to keep it in; in fact, it kept itself in. Satan said it would, and it did. We went off every day and got to ourselves in the woods so that we could talk about   35 Satan, and really that was the only subject we thought of or cared anything about; and day and night we watched for him and hoped he would come, and we got more and more impatient all the time. We hadn't any interest in the other boys any more, and wouldn't take part in their games and enter-prises. They seemed so tame, after Satan; and their doings so trifling and   40 commonplace after his adventures in antiquity and the constellations, and his miracles and meltings and explosions, and all that.

During the first day we were in a state of anxiety on account of one thing, and we kept going to Father Peter's house on one pretext or another to keep

6. **bail**—security.

track of it. That was the gold coin; we were afraid it would crumble and turn
to dust, like fairy money. If it did— But it didn't. At the end of the day no
complaint had been made about it, so after that we were satisfied that it was
real gold, and dropped the anxiety out of our minds.

5   There was a question which we wanted to ask Father Peter, and finally we
went there the second evening, a little diffidently, after drawing straws, and I
asked it as casually as I could, though it did not sound as casual as I wanted,
because I didn't know how:

"What is the Moral Sense, sir?"

10   He looked down, surprised, over his great spectacles, and said, "Why, it
is the faculty which enables us to distinguish good from evil."

It threw some light, but not a glare, and I was a little disappointed, also to
some degree embarrassed. He was waiting for me to go on, so, in default of
anything else to say, I asked, "Is it valuable?"

15   "Valuable? Heavens! lad, it is the one thing that lifts man above the beasts
that perish and makes him heir to immortality!"

This did not remind me of anything further to say, so I got out, with the
other boys, and we went away with that indefinite sense you have often had
of being filled but not fatted. They wanted me to explain but I was tired.

20   We passed out through the parlor, and there was Marget at the spinet
teaching Marie Lueger. So one of the deserting pupils was back; and an influential one too; the others would follow. Marget jumped up and ran and
thanked us again with tears in her eyes—this was the third time—for saving
her and her uncle from being turned into the street, and we told her again

25   we hadn't done it; but that was her way, she never could be grateful enough
for anything a person did for her; so we let her have her say. And as we
passed through the garden, there was Wilhelm Meidling sitting there waiting, for it was getting toward the edge of the evening, and he would be asking Marget to take a walk along the river with him when she was done

30   with the lesson. He was a young lawyer, and succeeding fairly well and
working his way along, little by little. He was very fond of Marget, and she
of him. He had not deserted along with the others, but had stood his ground
all through. His faithfulness was not lost on Marget and her uncle. He hadn't
so very much talent but he was handsome and good, and these are a kind of

35   talents themselves and help along. He asked us how the lesson was getting
along, and we told him it was about done. And maybe it was so; we didn't
know anything about it, but we judged it would please him, and it did, and
it didn't cost us anything.

CHAPTER V

40   On the fourth day comes the astrologer from his crumbling old tower up
the valley, where he had heard the news, I reckon. He had a private talk with
us, and we told him what we could, for we were mightily in dread of him.
He sat there studying and studying awhile to himself; then he asked:

"How many ducats did you say?"

45   "Eleven hundred and seven, sir."

Then he said, as if he were talking to himself: "It is ver-y singular. Yes . . .

very strange. A curious coincidence." Then he began to ask questions, and went over the whole ground from the beginning, we answering. By and by he said: "Eleven hundred and six ducats. It is a large sum."

"Seven," said Seppi, correcting him.

"Oh, seven, was it? Of course a ducat more or less isn't of consequence, but 5 you said eleven hundred and six before."

It would not have been safe for us to say he was mistaken, but we knew he was. Nikolaus said, "We ask pardon for the mistake, but we meant to say seven."

"Oh, it is no matter, lad; it was merely that I noticed the discrepancy. It is 10 several days, and you cannot be expected to remember precisely. One is apt to be inexact when there is no particular circumstance to impress the count upon the memory."

"But there was one, sir," said Seppi, eagerly.

"What was it, my son?" asked the astrologer, indifferently. 15

"First, we all counted the piles of coin, each in turn, and all made it the same—eleven hundred and six. But I had slipped one out, for fun, when the count began, and now I slipped it back and said, 'I think there is a mistake—there are eleven hundred and seven; let us count again.' We did, and of course I was right. They were astonished; then I told how it came about." 20

The astrologer asked us if this was so, and we said it was.

"That settles it," he said. "I know the thief now. Lads, the money was stolen."

Then he went away, leaving us very much troubled, and wondering what he could mean. In about an hour we found out; for by that time it was all over 25 the village that Father Peter had been arrested for stealing a great sum of money from the astrologer. Everybody's tongue was loose and going. Many said it was not in Father Peter's character and must be a mistake; but the others shook their heads and said misery and want could drive a suffering man to almost anything. About one detail there were no differences; all agreed that 30 Father Peter's account of how the money came into his hands was just about unbelievable—it had such an impossible look. They said it might have come into the astrologer's hands in some such way, but into Father Peter's, never! Our characters began to suffer now. We were Father Peter's only witnesses; how much did he probably pay us to back up his fantastic tale? People talked 35 that kind of talk to us pretty freely and frankly, and were full of scoffings when we begged them to believe really we had told only the truth. Our parents were harder on us than any one else. Our fathers said we were disgracing our families, and they commanded us to purge ourselves of our lie, and there was no limit to their anger when we continued to say we had spoken 40 true. Our mothers cried over us and begged us to give back our bribe and get back our honest names and save our families from shame, and come out and honorably confess. And at last we were so worried and harassed that we tried to tell the whole thing, Satan and all—but no, it wouldn't come out. We were hoping and longing all the time that Satan would come and help us out of 45 our trouble, but there was no sign of him.

Within an hour after the astrologer's talk with us, Father Peter was in

prison and the money sealed up and in the hands of the officers of the law. The money was in a bag, and Solomon Isaacs said he had not touched it since he had counted it; his oath was taken that it was the same money, and that the amount was eleven hundred and seven ducats. Father Peter claimed trial
5 by the ecclesiastical court, but our other priest, Father Adolf, said an ecclesiastical court hadn't jurisdiction over a suspended priest. The bishop upheld him. That settled it; the case would go to trial in the civil court. The court would not sit for some time to come. Wilhelm Meidling would be Father Peter's lawyer and do the best he could, of course, but he told us privately that
10 a weak case on his side and all the power and prejudice on the other made the outlook bad.

So Marget's new happiness died a quick death. No friends came to condole with her, and none were expected; an unsigned note withdrew her invitation to the party. There would be no scholars to take lessons. How could she sup-
15 port herself? She could remain in the house, for the mortgage was paid off, though the government and not poor Solomon Isaacs had the mortgage-money in its grip for the present. Old Ursula, who was cook, chambermaid, housekeeper, laundress, and everything else for Father Peter, and had been Marget's nurse in earlier years, said God would provide. But she said that from habit,
20 for she was a good Christian. She meant to help in the providing, to make sure, if she could find a way.

We boys wanted to go and see Marget and show friendliness for her, but our parents were afraid of offending the community and wouldn't let us. The astrologer was going around inflaming everybody against Father Peter, and
25 saying he was an abandoned thief and had stolen eleven hundred and seven gold ducats from him. He said he knew he was a thief from that fact, for it was exactly the sum he had lost and which Father Peter pretended he had "found."

In the afternoon of the fourth day after the catastrophe old Ursula appeared
30 at our house and asked for some washing to do, and begged my mother to keep this secret, to save Marget's pride, who would stop this project if she found it out, yet Marget had not enough to eat and was growing weak. Ursula was growing weak herself, and showed it; and she ate of the food that was offered her like a starving person, but could not be persuaded to
35 carry any home, for Marget would not eat charity food. She took some clothes down to the stream to wash them, but we saw from the window that handling the bat was too much for her strength; so she was called back and a trifle of money offered her, which she was afraid to take lest Marget should suspect; then she took it, saying she would explain that she found it in the road. To
40 keep it from being a lie and damning her soul, she got me to drop it while she watched; then she went along by there and found it, and exclaimed with surprise and joy, and picked it up and went her way. Like the rest of the village, she could tell every-day lies fast enough and without taking any precautions against fire and brimstone on their account; but this was a new kind
45 of lie, and it had a dangerous look because she hadn't had any practice in it.

37. **bat**—a specially shaped piece of wood used for pounding clothes when they are washed in a stream.

After a week's practice it wouldn't have given her any trouble. It is the way we are made.

I was in trouble, for how would Marget live? Ursula could not find a coin in the road every day—perhaps not even a second one. And I was ashamed, too, for not having been near Marget, and she so in need of friends; but that was my parents' fault, not mine, and I couldn't help it.

I was walking along the path, feeling very downhearted, when a most cheery and tingling freshening-up sensation went rippling through me, and I was too glad for any words, for I knew by that sign that Satan was by. I had noticed it before. Next moment he was alongside of me and I was telling him all my trouble and what had been happening to Marget and her uncle. While we were talking we turned a curve and saw old Ursula resting in the shade of a tree, and she had a lean stray kitten in her lap and was petting it. I asked her where she got it, and she said it came out of the woods and followed her; and she said it probably hadn't any mother or any friends and she was going to take it home and take care of it. Satan said:

"I understand you are very poor. Why do you want to add another mouth to feed? Why don't you give it to some rich person?"

Ursula bridled at this and said: "Perhaps you would like to have it. You must be rich, with your fine clothes and quality airs." Then she sniffed and said: "Give it to the rich—the idea! The rich don't care for anybody but themselves; it's only the poor that have feeling for the poor, and help them. The poor and God. God will provide for this kitten."

"What makes you think so?"

Ursula's eyes snapped with anger. "Because I know it!" she said. "Not a sparrow falls to the ground without His seeing it."

"But it falls, just the same. What good is seeing it fall?"

Old Ursula's jaws worked, but she could not get any word out for the moment, she was so horrified. When she got her tongue she stormed out, "Go about your business, you puppy, or I will take a stick to you!"

I could not speak, I was so scared. I knew that with his notions about the human race Satan would consider it a matter of no consequence to strike her dead, there being "plenty more"; but my tongue stood still, I could give her no warning. But nothing happened; Satan remained tranquil—tranquil and indifferent. I suppose he could not be insulted by Ursula any more than the king could be insulted by a tumble-bug. The old woman jumped to her feet when she made her remark, and did it as briskly as a young girl. It had been many years since she had done the like of that. That was Satan's influence; he was a fresh breeze to the weak and the sick, wherever he came. His presence affected even the lean kitten, and it skipped to the ground and began to chase a leaf. This surprised Ursula, and she stood looking at the creature and nodding her head wonderingly, her anger quite forgotten.

"What's come over it?" she said. "Awhile ago it could hardly walk."

"You have not seen a kitten of that breed before," said Satan.

Ursula was not proposing to be friendly with the mocking stranger, and she gave him an ungentle look and retorted: "Who asked you to come here

26. sparrow—cf. Matt. 10:29.

and pester me, I'd like to know? And what do you know about what I've seen and what I haven't seen?"

"You haven't seen a kitten with the hair-spines on its tongue pointing to the front, have you?"

5 "No—nor you, either."

"Well, examine this one and see."

Ursula was become pretty spry, but the kitten was spryer, and she could not catch it, and had to give it up. Then Satan said:

"Give it a name, and maybe it will come."

10 Ursula tried several names, but the kitten was not interested.

"Call it Agnes. Try that."

The creature answered to the name and came. Ursula examined its tongue. "Upon my word, it's true!" she said. "I have not seen this kind of a cat before. Is it yours?"

15 "No."

"Then how did you know its name so pat?"

"Because all cats of that breed are named Agnes; they will not answer to any other."

Ursula was impressed. "It is the most wonderful thing!" Then a shadow 20 of trouble came into her face, for her superstitions were aroused, and she reluctantly put the creature down, saying: "I suppose I must let it go; I am not afraid—no, not exactly that, though the priest—well, I've heard people—indeed, many people . . . And, besides, it is quite well now and can take care of itself." She sighed, and turned to go, murmuring: "It is such a pretty one, 25 too, and would be such company—and the house is so sad and lonesome these troubled days . . . Miss Marget so mournful and just a shadow, and the old master shut up in jail."

"It seems a pity not to keep it," said Satan.

Ursula turned quickly—just as if she were hoping some one would en-30 courage her.

"Why?" she asked, wistfully.

"Because this breed brings luck."

"Does it? Is it true? Young man, do you know it to be true? How does it bring luck?"

35 "Well, it brings money, anyway."

Ursula looked disappointed. "Money? A cat bring money? The idea! You could never sell it here; people do not buy cats here; one can't even give them away." She turned to go.

"I don't mean sell it. I mean have an income from it. This kind is called 40 the Lucky Cat. Its owner finds four silver groschen in his pocket every morning."

I saw the indignation rising in the old woman's face. She was insulted. This boy was making fun of her. That was her thought. She thrust her hands into her pockets and straightened up to give him a piece of her mind. Her temper 45 was all up, and hot. Her mouth came open and let out three words of a bitter

---

40. groschen—small silver coin. The original text misspells the word a little later, but the error is here corrected.

sentence, . . . then it fell silent, and the anger in her face turned to surprise
or wonder or fear, or something, and she slowly brought out her hands from
her pockets and opened them and held them so. In one was my piece of
money, in the other lay four silver groschen. She gazed a little while, perhaps
to see if the groschen would vanish away; then she said, fervently: 5

"It's true—it's true—and I'm ashamed and beg forgiveness, O dear master
and benefactor!" And she ran to Satan and kissed his hand, over and over
again, according to the Austrian custom.

In her heart she probably believed it was a witch-cat and an agent of the
Devil; but no matter, it was all the more certain to be able to keep its contract   10
and furnish a daily good living for the family, for in matters of finance even
the piousest of our peasants would have more confidence in an arrangement
with the Devil than with an archangel. Ursula started homeward with Agnes
in her arms, and I said I wished I had her privilege of seeing Marget.

Then I caught my breath, for we were there. There in the parlor, and Mar-   15
get standing looking at us, astonished. She was feeble and pale, but I knew
that those conditions would not last in Satan's atmosphere, and it turned out
so. I introduced Satan—that is, Philip Traum—and we sat down and talked.
There was no constraint. We were simple folk, in our village, and when a
stranger was a pleasant person we were soon friends. Marget wondered how   20
we got in without her hearing us. Traum said the door was open, and we
walked in and waited until she should turn around and greet us. This was
not true; no door was open; we entered through the walls or the roof or
down the chimney, or somehow; but no matter, what Satan wished a person
to believe, the person was sure to believe, and so Marget was quite satisfied   25
with that explanation. And then the main part of her mind was on Traum,
anyway; she couldn't keep her eyes off him, he was so beautiful. That gratified me, and made me proud. I hoped he would show off some, but he didn't.
He seemed only interested in being friendly and telling lies. He said he was
an orphan. That made Marget pity him. The water came into her eyes. He   30
said he had never known his mamma; she passed away while he was a young
thing; and said his papa was in shattered health, and had no property to
speak of—in fact, none of any earthly value—but he had an uncle in business
down in the tropics, and he was very well off and had a monopoly, and it was
from this uncle that he drew his support. The very mention of a kind uncle   35
was enough to remind Marget of her own, and her eyes filled again. She
said she hoped their two uncles would meet, some day. It made me shudder.
Philip said he hoped so, too; and that made me shudder again.

"Maybe they will," said Marget. "Does your uncle travel much?"

"Oh yes, he goes all about; he has business everywhere."   40

And so they went on chatting, and poor Marget forgot her sorrow for one
little while, anyway. It was probably the only really bright and cheery hour
she had known lately. I saw she liked Philip, and I knew she would. And
when he told her he was studying for the ministry I could see that she liked
him better than ever. And then, when he promised to get her admitted to the   45
jail so that she could see her uncle, that was the capstone. He said he would
give the guards a little present, and she must always go in the evening after

dark, and say nothing "but just show this paper and pass in, and show it
again when you come out"—and he scribbled some queer marks on the paper
and gave it to her, and she was ever so thankful, and right away was in a fever
for the sun to go down; for in that old, cruel time prisoners were not allowed
5   to see their friends, and sometimes they spent years in the jails without ever
seeing a friendly face. I judged that the marks on the paper were an enchantment, and that the guards would not know what they were doing, nor have
any memory of it afterward; and that was indeed the way of it. Ursula put her
head in at the door now and said:

10   "Supper's ready, miss." Then she saw us and looked frightened, and motioned me to come to her, which I did, and she asked if we had told about the
cat. I said no, and she was relieved and said please don't, for if Miss Marget
knew, she would think it was an unholy cat and would send for a priest and
have its gifts all purified out of it, and then there wouldn't be any more divi-
15   dends. So I said we wouldn't tell, and she was satisfied. Then I was beginning to say good-by to Marget, but Satan interrupted and said, ever so politely
—well, I don't remember just the words, but anyway he as good as invited
himself to supper, and me, too. Of course Marget was miserably embarrassed,
for she had no reason to suppose there would be half enough for a sick bird.
20   Ursula heard him, and she came straight into the room, not a bit pleased. At
first she was astonished to see Marget looking so fresh and rosy, and said so;
then she spoke up in her native tongue, which was Bohemian, and said—as I
learned afterward—"Send him away, Miss Marget; there's not victuals
enough."

25   Before Marget could speak, Satan had the word, and was talking back to
Ursula in her own language—which was a surprise to her, and for her mistress, too. He said, "Didn't I see you down the road awhile ago?"

"Yes, sir."

"Ah, that pleases me; I see you remember me." He stepped to her and
30   whispered: "I told you it is a Lucky Cat. Don't be troubled; it will provide."

That sponged the slate of Ursula's feelings clean of its anxieties, and a deep,
financial joy shone in her eyes. The cat's value was augmenting. It was getting full time for Marget to take some sort of notice of Satan's invitation, and
she did it in the best way, the honest way that was natural to her. She said
35   she had little to offer, but that we were welcome if he would share it with her.

We had supper in the kitchen, and Ursula waited at table. A small fish was
in the frying-pan, crisp and brown and tempting, and one could see that Marget was not expecting such respectable food as this. Ursula brought it, and
Marget divided it between Satan and me, declining to take any of it herself;
40   and was beginning to say she did not care for fish to-day, but she did not finish
the remark. It was because she noticed that another fish had appeared in the
pan. She looked surprised, but did not say anything. She probably meant to
inquire of Ursula about this later. There were other surprises: flesh and game
and wines and fruits—things which had been strangers in that house lately;
45   but Marget made no exclamations, and now even looked unsurprised, which
was Satan's influence, of course. Satan talked right along, and was entertaining, and made the time pass pleasantly and cheerfully; and although he told

a good many lies, it was no harm in him, for he was only an angel and did not know any better. They do not know right from wrong; I knew this, because I remembered what he had said about it. He got on the good side of Ursula. He praised her to Marget, confidentially, but speaking just loud enough for Ursula to hear. He said she was a fine woman, and he hoped some 5 day to bring her and his uncle together. Very soon Ursula was mincing and simpering around in a ridiculous, girly way, and smoothing out her gown and prinking at herself like a foolish old hen, and all the time pretending she was not hearing what Satan was saying. I was ashamed, for it showed us to be what Satan considered us, a silly race and trivial. Satan said his uncle enter- 10 tained a great deal, and to have a clever woman presiding over the festivities would double the attractions of the place.

"But your uncle is a gentleman, isn't he?" asked Marget.

"Yes," said Satan indifferently; "some even call him a Prince, out of compliment, but he is not bigoted; to him personal merit is everything, rank 15 nothing."

My hand was hanging down by my chair; Agnes came along and licked it; by this act a secret was revealed. I started to say, "It is all a mistake; this is just a common, ordinary cat; the hair-needles on her tongue point inward, not outward." But the words did not come, because they couldn't. Satan smiled 20 upon me, and I understood.

When it was dark Marget took food and wine and fruit, in a basket, and hurried away to the jail, and Satan and I walked toward my home. I was thinking to myself that I should like to see what the inside of the jail was like; Satan overheard the thought, and the next moment we were in the jail. 25 We were in the torture-chamber, Satan said. The rack was there, and the other instruments, and there was a smoky lantern or two hanging on the walls and helping to make the place look dim and dreadful. There were people there—and executioners—but as they took no notice of us, it meant that we were invisible. A young man lay bound, and Satan said he was sus- 30 pected of being a heretic, and the executioners were about to inquire into it. They asked the man to confess to the charge, and he said he could not, for it was not true. Then they drove splinter after splinter under his nails, and he shrieked with the pain. Satan was not disturbed, but I could not endure it, and had to be whisked out of there. I was faint and sick, but the fresh air 35 revived me, and we walked toward my home. I said it was a brutal thing.

"No, it was a human thing. You should not insult the brutes by such a misuse of that word; they have not deserved it," and he went on talking like that. "It is like your paltry race—always lying, always claiming virtues which it hasn't got, always denying them to the higher animals, which alone possess 40 them. No brute ever does a cruel thing—that is the monopoly of those with the Moral Sense. When a brute inflicts pain he does it innocently; it is not wrong; for him there is no such thing as wrong. And he does not inflict pain for the pleasure of inflicting it—only man does that. Inspired by that mongrel Moral Sense of his! A sense whose function is to distinguish between right 45 and wrong, with liberty to choose which of them he will do. Now what advantage can he get out of that? He is always choosing, and in nine cases out of ten he prefers the wrong. There shouldn't be any wrong; and without the Moral Sense there couldn't be any. And yet he is such an unreasoning creature that he is not able to perceive that the Moral Sense degrades him to the bottom layer of animated beings and is a shameful possession. Are you feeling better? Let me show you something."

CHAPTER VI

In a moment we were in a French village. We walked through a great factory of some sort, where men and women and little children were toiling in heat and dirt and a fog of dust; and they were clothed in rags, and drooped at their work, for they were worn and half starved, and weak and drowsy. Satan said:

"It is some more Moral Sense. The proprietors are rich, and very holy; but the wage they pay to these poor brothers and sisters of theirs is only enough to keep them from dropping dead with hunger. The work-hours are fourteen per day, winter and summer—from six in the morning till eight at night— little children and all. And they walk to and from the pigsties which they inhabit——four miles each way, through mud and slush, rain, snow, sleet, and storm, daily, year in and year out. They get four hours of sleep. They kennel together, three families in a room, in unimaginable filth and stench; and disease comes, and they die off like flies. Have they committed a crime, these mangy things? No. What have they done, that they are punished so? Nothing at all, except getting themselves born into your foolish race. You have seen how they treat a misdoer there in the jail; now you see how they treat the innocent and the worthy. Is your race logical? Are these ill-smelling innocents better off than that heretic? Indeed, no; his punishment is trivial compared with theirs. They broke him on the wheel and smashed him to rags and pulp after we left, and he is dead now, and free of your precious race; but these poor slaves here—why, they have been dying for years, and some of them will not escape from life for years to come. It is the Moral Sense which teaches the factory proprietors the difference between right and wrong—you perceive the result. They think themselves better than dogs. Ah, you are such an il- logical, unreasoning race! And paltry—oh, unspeakably!"

Then he dropped all seriousness and just overstrained himself making fun of us, and deriding our pride in our warlike deeds, our great heroes, our imperishable fames, our mighty kings, our ancient aristocracies, our venerable history—and laughed and laughed till it was enough to make a person sick to hear him; and finally he sobered a little and said, "But, after all, it is not all ridiculous; there is a sort of pathos about it when one remembers how few are your days, how childish your pomps, and what shadows you are!"

Presently all things vanished suddenly from my sight, and I knew what it meant. The next moment we were walking along in our village; and down toward the river I saw the twinkling lights of the Golden Stag. Then in the dark I heard a joyful cry:

"He's come again!"

It was Seppi Wohlmeyer. He had felt his blood leap and his spirits rise in a

way that could mean only one thing, and he knew Satan was near, although it was too dark to see him. He came to us, and we walked along together, and Seppi poured out his gladness like water. It was as if he were a lover and had found his sweetheart who had been lost. Seppi was a smart and animated boy, and had enthusiasm and expression, and was a contrast to Nikolaus and 5
me. He was full of the last new mystery, now—the disappearance of Hans Oppert, the village loafer. People were beginning to be curious about it, he said. He did not say anxious—curious was the right word, and strong enough. No one had seen Hans for a couple of days.

"Not since he did that brutal thing, you know," he said. 10

"What brutal thing?" It was Satan that asked.

"Well, he is always clubbing his dog, which is a good dog and his only friend, and is faithful, and loves him, and does no one any harm; and two days ago he was at it again, just for nothing—just for pleasure—and the dog was howling and begging, and Theodor and I begged, too, but he threatened 15
us, and struck the dog again with all his might and knocked one of his eyes out, and he said to us, 'There, I hope you are satisfied now; that's what you have got for him by your damned meddling'—and he laughed, the heartless brute." Seppi's voice trembled with pity and anger. I guessed what Satan would say, and he said it. 20

"There is that misused word again—that shabby slander. Brutes do not act like that, but only men."

"Well, it was inhuman, anyway."

"No, it wasn't, Seppi; it was human—quite distinctly human. It is not pleasant to hear you libel the higher animals by attributing to them dispositions 25
which they are free from, and which are found nowhere but in the human heart. None of the higher animals is tainted with the disease called the Moral Sense. Purify your language, Seppi; drop those lying phrases out of it."

He spoke pretty sternly—for him—and I was sorry I hadn't warned Seppi to be more particular about the word he used. I knew how he was feeling. He 30
would not want to offend Satan; he would rather offend all his kin. There was an uncomfortable silence, but relief soon came, for that poor dog came along now, with his eye hanging down, and went straight to Satan, and began to moan and mutter brokenly, and Satan began to answer in the same way, and it was plain that they were talking together in the dog language. We all sat 35
down in the grass, in the moonlight, for the clouds were breaking away now, and Satan took the dog's head in his lap and put the eye back in its place, and the dog was comfortable, and he wagged his tail and licked Satan's hand, and looked thankful and said the same; I knew he was saying it, though I did not understand the words. Then the two talked together a bit, and Satan said: 40

"He says his master was drunk."

"Yes, he was," said we.

"And an hour later he fell over the precipice there beyond the Cliff Pasture."

"We know the place; it is three miles from here."

"And the dog has been often to the village, begging people to go there, but 45
he was only driven away and not listened to."

We remembered it, but hadn't understood what he wanted.

"He only wanted help for the man who had misused him, and he thought only of that, and has had no food nor sought any. He has watched by his master two nights. What do you think of your race? Is heaven reserved for it, and this dog ruled out, as your teachers tell you? Can your race add anything
5 to this dog's stock of morals and magnanimities?" He spoke to the creature, who jumped up, eager and happy, and apparently ready for orders and impatient to execute them. "Get some men; go with the dog—he will show you that carrion; and take a priest along to arrange about insurance, for death is near."

10 With the last word he vanished, to our sorrow and disappointment. We got the men and Father Adolf, and we saw the man die. Nobody cared but the dog; he mourned and grieved, and licked the dead face, and could not be comforted. We buried him where he was, and without a coffin, for he had no money, and no friend but the dog. If we had been an hour earlier the priest
15 would have been in time to send that poor creature to heaven, but now he was gone down into the awful fires, to burn forever. It seemed such a pity that in a world where so many people have difficulty to put in their time, one little hour could not have been spared for this poor creature who needed it so much, and to whom it would have made the difference between eternal joy
20 and eternal pain. It gave an appalling idea of the value of an hour, and I thought I could never waste one again without remorse and terror. Seppi was depressed and grieved, and said it must be so much better to be a dog and not run such awful risks. We took this one home with us and kept him for our own. Seppi had a very good thought as we were walking along, and it
25 cheered us up and made us feel much better. He said the dog had forgiven the man that had wronged him so, and maybe God would accept that absolution.

There was a very dull week, now, for Satan did not come, nothing much was going on, and we boys could not venture to go and see Marget, because
30 the nights were moonlit and our parents might find us out if we tried. But we came across Ursula a couple of times taking a walk in the meadows beyond the river to air the cat, and we learned from her that things were going well. She had natty new clothes on and bore a prosperous look. The four groschen a day were arriving without a break, but were not being spent for food and
35 wine and such things—the cat attended to all that.

Marget was enduring her forsakenness and isolation fairly well, all things considered, and was cheerful, by help of Wilhelm Meidling. She spent an hour or two every night in the jail with her uncle, and had fattened him up with the cat's contributions. But she was curious to know more about Philip
40 Traum, and hoped I would bring him again. Ursula was curious about him herself, and asked a good many questions about his uncle. It made the boys laugh, for I had told them the nonsense Satan had been stuffing her with. She got no satisfaction out of us, our tongues being tied.

Ursula gave us a small item of information: money being plenty now, she
45 had taken on a servant to help about the house and run errands. She tried to tell it in a commonplace, matter-of-course way, but she was so set up by it and so vain of it that her pride in it leaked out pretty plainly. It was beautiful

to see her veiled delight in this grandeur, poor old thing, but when we heard
the name of the servant we wondered if she had been altogether wise; for
although we were young, and often thoughtless, we had fairly good perception on some matters. This boy was Gottfried Narr, a dull, good creature,
with no harm in him and nothing against him personally; still, he was under 5
a cloud, and properly so, for it had not been six months since a social blight
had mildewed the family—his grandmother had been burned as a witch.
When that kind of a malady is in the blood it does not always come out with
just one burning. Just now was not a good time for Ursula and Marget to be
having dealings with a member of such a family, for the witch-terror had 10
risen higher during the past year than it had ever reached in the memory of
the oldest villagers. The mere mention of a witch was almost enough to
frighten us out of our wits. This was natural enough, because of late years
there were more kinds of witches than there used to be; in old times it had
been only old women, but of late years they were of all ages—even children 15
of eight and nine; it was getting so that anybody might turn out to be a
familiar of the Devil—age and sex hadn't anything to do with it. In our little
region we had tried to extirpate the witches, but the more of them we burned
the more of the breed rose up in their places.

   Once, in a school for girls only ten miles away, the teachers found that the 20
back of one of the girls was all red and inflamed, and they were greatly frightened, believing it to be the Devil's marks. The girl was scared, and begged
them not to denounce her, and said it was only fleas; but of course it would
not do to let the matter rest there. All the girls were examined, and eleven out
of the fifty were badly marked, the rest less so. A commission was appointed, 25
but the eleven only cried for their mothers and would not confess. Then they
were shut up, each by herself, in the dark, and put on black bread and water
for ten days and nights; and by that time they were haggard and wild, and
their eyes were dry and they did not cry any more, but only sat and mumbled,
and would not take the food. Then one of them confessed, and said they had 30
often ridden through the air on broomsticks to the witches' Sabbath, and in
a bleak place high up in the mountains had danced and drunk and caroused
with several hundred other witches and the Evil One, and all had conducted
themselves in a scandalous way and had reviled the priests and blasphemed
God. That is what she said—not in narrative form, for she was not able to 35
remember any of the details without having them called to her mind one after
the other; but the commission did that, for they knew just what questions to
ask, they being all written down for the use of witch-commissioners two centuries before. They asked, "Did you do so and so?" and she always said yes,
and looked weary and tired, and took no interest in it. And so when the other 40
ten heard that this one confessed, they confessed, too, and answered yes to
the questions. Then they were burned at the stake all together, which was
just and right; and everybody went from all the countryside to see it. I went,
too; but when I saw that one of them was a bonny, sweet girl I used to play
with, and looked so pitiful there chained to the stake, and her mother crying 45

4. **Narr**—i.e., "Fool." **31. witches' Sabbath**—any midnight meeting of witches and
demons.

over her and devouring her with kisses and clinging around her neck, and
saying, "Oh, my God! oh, my God!" it was too dreadful, and I went away.

　　It was bitter cold weather when Gottfried's grandmother was burned. It
was charged that she had cured bad headaches by kneading the person's head
5　and neck with her fingers——as she said——but really by the Devil's help, as
everybody knew. They were going to examine her, but she stopped them, and
confessed straight off that her power was from the Devil. So they appointed to
burn her next morning, early, in our market-square. The officer who was to
prepare the fire was there first, and prepared it. She was there next—brought
10　by the constables, who left her and went to fetch another witch. Her family
did not come with her. They might be reviled, maybe stoned, if the people
were excited. I came, and gave her an apple. She was squatting at the fire,
warming herself and waiting; and her old lips and hands were blue with the
cold. A stranger came next. He was a traveler, passing through; and he spoke
15　to her gently, and, seeing nobody but me there to hear, said he was sorry for
her. And he asked if what she confessed was true, and she said no. He looked
surprised and still more sorry then, and asked her:

　　"Then why did you confess?"

　　"I am old and very poor," she said, "and I work for my living. There was
20　no way but to confess. If I hadn't they might have set me free. That would
ruin me, for no one would forget that I had been suspected of being a witch,
and so I would get no more work, and wherever I went they would set the
dogs on me. In a little while I would starve. The fire is best; it is soon over.
You have been good to me, you two, and I thank you."

25　She snuggled closer to the fire, and put out her hands to warm them, the
snow-flakes descending soft and still on her old gray head and making it white
and whiter. The crowd was gathering now, and an egg came flying and struck
her in the eye, and broke and ran down her face. There was a laugh at that.

　　I told Satan all about the eleven girls and the old woman, once, but it did
30　not affect him. He only said it was the human race, and what the human race
did was of no consequence. And he said he had seen it made; and it was not
made of clay; it was made of mud—part of it was, anyway. I knew what he
meant by that—the Moral Sense. He saw the thought in my head, and it tickled
him and made him laugh. Then he called a bullock out of a pasture and petted
35　it and talked with it, and said:

　　"There—he wouldn't drive children mad with hunger and fright and loneliness, and then burn them for confessing to things invented for them which
had never happened. And neither would he break the hearts of innocent, poor
old women and make them afraid to trust themselves among their own race;
40　and he would not insult them in their death-agony. For he is not besmirched
with the Moral Sense, but is as the angels are, and knows no wrong, and never
does it."

　　Lovely as he was, Satan could be cruelly offensive when he chose; and he
always chose when the human race was brought to his attention. He always
45　turned up his nose at it, and never had a kind word for it.

　　Well, as I was saying, we boys doubted if it was a good time for Ursula to
be hiring a member of the Narr family. We were right. When the people found

it out they were naturally indignant. And, moreover, since Marget and Ursula hadn't enough to eat themselves, where was the money coming from to feed another mouth? That is what they wanted to know; and in order to find out they stopped avoiding Gottfried and began to seek his society and have sociable conversations with him. He was pleased—not thinking any harm and not see- 5 ing the trap—and so he talked innocently along, and was no discreeter than a cow.

"Money!" he said; "they've got plenty of it. They pay me two groschen a week, besides my keep. And they live on the fat of the land, I can tell you; the prince himself can't beat their table." 10

This astonishing statement was conveyed by the astrologer to Father Adolf on a Sunday morning when he was returning from mass. He was deeply moved, and said:

"This must be looked into."

He said there must be witchcraft at the bottom of it, and told the villagers 15 to resume relations with Marget and Ursula in a private and unostentatious way, and keep both eyes open. They were told to keep their own counsel and not rouse the suspicions of the household. The villagers were at first a bit re- luctant to enter such a dreadful place, but the priest said they would be under his protection while there, and no harm could come to them, particularly if they 20 carried a trifle of holy water along and kept their beads and crosses handy. This satisfied them and made them willing to go; envy and malice made the baser sort even eager to go.

And so poor Marget began to have company again, and was as pleased as a cat. She was like 'most anybody else—just human, and happy in her prosperities 25 and not averse from showing them off a little; and she was humanly grateful to have the warm shoulder turned to her and be smiled upon by her friends and the village again; for of all the hard things to bear, to be cut by your neigh- bors and left in contemptuous solitude is maybe the hardest.

The bars were down, and we could all go there now, and we did—our parents 30 and all—day after day. The cat began to strain herself. She provided the top of everything for those companies, and in abundance—among them many a dish and many a wine which they had not tasted before and which they had not even heard of except at second-hand from the prince's servants. And the tableware was much above ordinary, too. 35

Marget was troubled at times, and pursued Ursula with questions to an un- comfortable degree; but Ursula stood her ground and stuck to it that it was Providence, and said no word about the cat. Marget knew that nothing was impossible to Providence, but she could not help having doubts that this effort was from there, though she was afraid to say so, lest disaster come of it. Witch- 40 craft occurred to her, but she put the thought aside, for this was before Gott- fried joined the household, and she knew Ursula was pious and a bitter hater of witches. By the time Gottfried arrived Providence was established, unshak- ably intrenched, and getting all the gratitude. The cat made no murmur, but went on composedly improving in style and prodigality by experience. 45

In any community, big or little, there is always a fair proportion of people who are not malicious or unkind by nature, and who never do unkind things

except when they are overmastered by fear, or when their self-interest is greatly in danger, or some such matter as that. Eseldorf had its proportion of such people, and ordinarily their good and gentle influence was felt, but these were not ordinary times—on account of the witch-dread—and so we did not seem
5 to have any gentle and compassionate hearts left, to speak of. Every person was frightened at the unaccountable state of things at Marget's house, not doubting that witchcraft was at the bottom of it, and fright frenzied their reason. Naturally there were some who pitied Marget and Ursula for the danger that was gathering about them, but naturally they did not say so; it would not have been
10 safe. So the others had it all their own way, and there was none to advise the ignorant girl and the foolish woman and warn them to modify their doings. We boys wanted to warn them, but we backed down when it came to the pinch, being afraid. We found that we were not manly enough nor brave enough to do a generous action when there was a chance that it could get us
15 into trouble. Neither of us confessed this poor spirit to the others, but did as other people would have done—dropped the subject and talked about something else. And I knew we all felt mean, eating and drinking Marget's fine things along with those companies of spies, and petting her and complimenting her with the rest, and seeing with self-reproach how foolishly happy she was,
20 and never saying a word to put her on her guard. And, indeed, she was happy, and as proud as a princess, and so grateful to have friends again. And all the time these people were watching with all their eyes and reporting all they saw to Father Adolf.

But he couldn't make head or tail of the situation. There must be an en-
25 chanter somewhere on the premises, but who was it? Marget was not seen to do any jugglery, nor was Ursula, nor yet Gottfried; and still the wines and dainties never ran short, and a guest could not call for a thing and not get it. To produce these effects was usual enough with witches and enchanters—that part of it was not new; but to do it without any incantations, or even any rum-
30 blings or earthquakes or lightnings or apparitions—that was new, novel, wholly irregular. There was nothing in the books like this. Enchanted things were always unreal. Gold turned to dirt in an unenchanted atmosphere, food withered away and vanished. But this test failed in the present case. The spies brought samples: Father Adolf prayed over them, exorcised them, but it did
35 no good; they remained sound and real, they yielded to natural decay only, and took the usual time to do it.

Father Adolf was not merely puzzled, he was also exasperated; for these evidences very nearly convinced him—privately—that there was no witchcraft in the matter. It did not wholly convince him, for this could be a new kind
40 of witchcraft. There was a way to find out as to this: if this prodigal abundance of provender was not brought in from the outside, but produced on the premises, there was witchcraft, sure.

CHAPTER VII

Marget announced a party and invited forty people; the date for it was seven
45 days away. This was a fine opportunity. Marget's house stood by itself, and it

could be easily watched. All the week it was watched night and day. Marget's household went out and in as usual, but they carried nothing in their hands, and neither they nor others brought anything to the house. This was ascertained. Evidently rations for forty people were not being fetched. If they were furnished any sustenance it would have to be made on the premises. It was 5 true that Marget went out with a basket every evening, but the spies ascertained that she always brought it back empty.

The guests arrived at noon and filled the place. Father Adolf followed; also, after a little, the astrologer, without invitation. The spies had informed him that neither at the back nor the front had any parcels been brought in. He 10 entered and found the eating and drinking going on finely, and everything progressing in a lively and festive way. He glanced around and perceived that many of the cooked delicacies and all of the native and foreign fruits were of a perishable character, and he also recognized that these were fresh and perfect. No apparitions, no incantations, no thunder. That settled it. This was witch- 15 craft. And not only that, but of a new kind——a kind never dreamed of before. It was a prodigious power, an illustrious power; he resolved to discover its secret. The announcement of it would resound throughout the world, penetrate to the remotest lands, paralyze all the nations with amazement—and carry his name with it, and make him renowned forever. It was a wonderful piece 20 of luck, a splendid piece of luck; the glory of it made him dizzy.

All the house made room for him; Marget politely seated him; Ursula ordered Gottfried to bring a special table for him. Then she decked it and furnished it, and asked for his orders.

"Bring me what you will," he said.   25

The two servants brought supplies from the pantry, together with white wine and red—a bottle of each. The astrologer, who very likely had never seen such delicacies before, poured out a beaker of red wine, drank it off, poured another, then began to eat with a grand appetite.

I was not expecting Satan, for it was more than a week since I had seen or 30 heard of him but now he came in—I knew it by the feel, though people were in the way and I could not see him. I heard him apologizing for intruding; and he was going away, but Marget urged him to stay, and he thanked her and stayed. She brought him along, introducing him to the girls, and to Meidling, and to some of the elders; and there was quite a rustle of whispers: 35 "It's the young stranger we hear so much about and can't get sight of, he is away so much." "Dear, dear, but he is beautiful—what is his name?" "Philip Traum." "Ah, it fits him!" (You see, "Traum" is German for "Dream.") "What does he do?" "Studying for the ministry, they say." "His face is his fortune—he'll be a cardinal some day." "Where is his home?" "Away down 40 somewhere in the tropics, they say—has a rich uncle down there." And so on. He made his way at once; everybody was anxious to know him and talk with him. Everybody noticed how cool and fresh it was all of a sudden, and wondered at it, for they could see that the sun was beating down the same as before, outside, and the sky was clear of clouds, but no one guessed the reason, of 45 course.

The astrologer had drunk his second beaker; he poured out a third. He set the bottle down, and by accident overturned it. He seized it before much was spilled, and held it up to the light, saying, "What a pity—it is royal wine." Then his face lighted with joy or triumph, or something, and he said, "Quick! Bring a bowl."

5   It was brought—a four-quart one. He took up that two-pint bottle and began to pour; went on pouring, the red liquor gurgling and gushing into the white bowl and rising higher and higher up its sides, everybody staring and holding their breath—and presently the bowl was full to the brim.

"Look at the bottle," he said, holding it up, "it is full yet!" I glanced at Satan,
10   and in that moment he vanished. Then Father Adolf rose up, flushed and excited, crossed himself, and began to thunder in his great voice, "This house is bewitched and accursed!" People began to cry and shriek and crowd toward the door. "I summon this detected household to—"

His words were cut off short. His face became red, then purple, but he could
15   not utter another sound. Then I saw Satan, a transparent film, melt into the astrologer's body; then the astrologer put up his hand, and apparently in his own voice said, "Wait—remain where you are." All stopped where they stood. "Bring a funnel!" Ursula brought it, trembling and scared, and he stuck it in the bottle and took up the great bowl and began to pour the wine back, the
20   people gazing and dazed with astonishment, for they knew the bottle was already full before he began. He emptied the whole of the bowl into the bottle, then smiled out over the room, chuckled, and said, indifferently, "It is nothing —anybody can do it! With my powers I can even do much more."

A frightened cry burst out everywhere. "Oh, my God, he is possessed!" and
25   there was a tumultuous rush for the door which swiftly emptied the house of all who did not belong in it except us boys and Meidling. We boys knew the secret, and would have told it if we could, but we couldn't. We were very thankful to Satan for furnishing that good help at the needful time.

Marget was pale, and crying; Meidling looked kind of petrified; Ursula the
30   same; but Gottfried was the worst—he couldn't stand, he was so weak and scared. For he was of a witch family, you know, and it would be bad for him to be suspected. Agnes came loafing in, looking pious and unaware, and wanted to rub up against Ursula and be petted, but Ursula was afraid of her and shrank away from her, but pretending she was not meaning any incivility, for
35   she knew very well it wouldn't answer to have strained relations with that kind of a cat. But we boys took Agnes and petted her, for Satan would not have befriended her if he had not had a good opinion of her, and that was indorsement enough for us. He seemed to trust anything that hadn't the Moral Sense.

40   Outside, the guests, panic-stricken, scattered in every direction and fled in a pitiable state of terror; and such a tumult as they made with their running and sobbing and shrieking and shouting that soon all the village came flocking from their houses to see what had happened, and they thronged the street and shouldered and jostled one another in excitement and fright; and then Father
45   Adolf appeared, and they fell apart in two walls like the cloven Red Sea, and presently down this lane the astrologer came striding and mumbling, and

45. cloven Red Sea—cf. Exod. 14:21 ff.

where he passed the lanes surged back in packed masses, and fell silent with
awe, and their eyes stared and their breasts heaved, and several women fainted;
and when he was gone by the crowd swarmed together and followed him at
a distance, talking excitedly and asking questions and finding out the facts.
Finding out the facts and passing them on to others, with improvements—im- 5
provements which soon enlarged the bowl of wine to a barrel, and made the
one bottle hold it all and yet remain empty to the last.

When the astrologer reached the market-square he went straight to a juggler,
fantastically dressed, who was keeping three brass balls in the air, and took
them from him and faced around upon the approaching crowd and said: "This 10
poor clown is ignorant of his art. Come forward and see an expert perform."

So saying, he tossed the balls up one after another and set them whirling in
a slender bright oval in the air, and added another, then another and another,
and soon—no one seeing whence he got them—adding, adding, adding, the
oval lengthening all the time, his hands moving so swiftly that they were just 15
a web or a blur and not distinguishable as hands; and such as counted said
there were now a hundred balls in the air. The spinning great oval reached up
twenty feet in the air and was a shining and glinting and wonderful sight.
Then he folded his arms and told the balls to go on spinning without his help
—and they did it. After a couple of minutes he said, "There, that will do," and 20
the oval broke and came crashing down, and the balls scattered abroad and
rolled every whither. And wherever one of them came the people fell back in
dread, and no one would touch it. It made him laugh, and he scoffed at the
people and called them cowards and old women. Then he turned and saw
the tight-rope, and said foolish people were daily wasting their money to see 25
a clumsy and ignorant varlet degrade that beautiful art; now they should see
the work of a master. With that he made a spring into the air and lit firm on
his feet on the rope. Then he hopped the whole length of it back and forth
on one foot, with his hands clasped over his eyes; and next he began to throw
somersaults, both backward and forward, and threw twenty-seven. 30

The people murmured, for the astrologer was old, and always before had
been halting of movement and at times even lame, but he was nimble enough
now and went on with his antics in the liveliest manner. Finally he sprang
lightly down and walked away, and passed up the road and around the corner
and disappeared. Then that great, pale, silent, solid crowd drew a deep breath 35
and looked into one another's faces as if they said: "Was it real? Did you see
it, or was it only I—and I was dreaming?" Then they broke into a low murmur of talking, and fell apart in couples, and moved toward their homes, still
talking in that awed way, with faces close together and laying a hand on an
arm and making other such gestures as people make when they have been 40
deeply impressed by something.

We boys followed behind our fathers, and listened, catching all we could
of what they said; and when they sat down in our house and continued their
talk they still had us for company. They were in a sad mood, for it was certain,
they said, that disaster for the village must follow this awful visitation of 45
witches and devils. Then my father remembered that Father Adolf had been
struck dumb at the moment of his denunciation.

"They have not ventured to lay their hands upon an anointed servant of God before," he said; "and how they could have dared it this time I cannot make out, for he wore his crucifix. Isn't it so?"

"Yes," said the others, "we saw it."

5 "It is serious, friends, it is very serious. Always before, we had a protection. It has failed."

The others shook, as with a sort of chill, and muttered those words over— "It has failed." "God has forsaken us."

"It is true," said Seppi Wohlmeyer's father; "there is nowhere to look for 10 help."

"The people will realize this," said Nikolaus' father, the judge, "and despair will take away their courage and their energies. We have indeed fallen upon evil times."

He sighed, and Wohlmeyer said, in a troubled voice, "The report of it all 15 will go about the country, and our village will be shunned as being under the displeasure of God. The Golden Stag will know hard times."

"True, neighbor," said my father, "all of us will suffer—all in repute, many in estate. And, good God!—"

"What is it?"

20 "That can come—to finish us!"

"Name it—um Gottes Willen!"

"The Interdict!"

It smote like a thunderclap, and they were like to swoon with the terror of it. Then the dread of this calamity roused their energies, and they stopped 25 brooding and began to consider ways to avert it. They discussed this, that, and the other way, and talked till the afternoon was far spent, then confessed that at present they could arrive at no decision. So they parted sorrowfully, with oppressed hearts which were filled with bodings.

While they were saying their parting words I slipped out and set my course 30 for Marget's house to see what was happening there. I met many people, but none of them greeted me. It ought to have been surprising, but it was not, for they were so distraught with fear and dread that they were not in their right minds, I think; they were white and haggard, and walked like persons in a dream, their eyes open but seeing nothing, their lips moving but uttering 35 nothing, and worriedly clasping and unclasping their hands without knowing it.

At Marget's it was like a funeral. She and Wilhelm sat together on the sofa, but said nothing, and not even holding hands. Both were steeped in gloom, and Marget's eyes were red from the crying she had been doing. She said:

40 "I have been begging him to go, and come no more, and so save himself alive. I cannot bear to be his murderer. This house is bewitched, and no inmate will escape the fire. But he will not go, and he will be lost with the rest."

Wilhelm said he would not go; if there was danger for her, his place was 45 by her, and there he would remain. Then she began to cry again, and it was

21. **um Gottes Willen**—"For God's sake!" 22. **Interdict**—the formal sentence by ecclesiastical authority barring a person or place from ecclesiastical functions or privileges or both.

all so mournful that I wished I had stayed away. There was a knock, now, and Satan came in, fresh and cheery and beautiful, and brought that winy atmosphere of his and changed the whole thing. He never said a word about what had been happening, nor about the awful fears which were freezing the blood in the hearts of the community, but began to talk and rattle on about 5 all manner of gay and pleasant things: and next about music—an artful stroke which cleared away the remnant of Marget's depression and brought her spirits and her interests broad awake. She had not heard any one talk so well and so knowingly on that subject before, and she was so uplifted by it and so charmed that what she was feeling lit up her face and came out in her words; and 10 Wilhelm noticed it and did not look as pleased as he ought to have done. And next Satan branched off into poetry, and recited some, and did it well, and Marget was charmed again; and again Wilhelm was not as pleased as he ought to have been, and this time Marget noticed it and was remorseful.

I fell asleep to pleasant music that night—the patter of rain upon the panes 15 and the dull growling of distant thunder. Away in the night Satan came and roused me and said: "Come with me. Where shall we go?"

"Anywhere—so it is with you."

Then there was a fierce glare of sunlight, and he said, "This is China."

That was a grand surprise, and made me sort of drunk with vanity and 20 gladness to think I had come so far—so much, much farther than anybody else in our village, including Bartel Sperling, who had such a great opinion of his travels. We buzzed around over that empire for more than half an hour, and saw the whole of it. It was wonderful, the spectacles we saw; and some were beautiful, others too horrible to think. For instance— However, I may go into 25 that by and by, and also why Satan chose China for this excursion instead of another place; it would interrupt my tale to do it now. Finally we stopped flitting and lit.

We sat upon a mountain commanding a vast landscape of mountain-range and gorge and valley and plain and river, with cities and villages slumbering 30 in the sunlight, and a glimpse of blue sea on the farther verge. It was a tranquil and dreamy picture, beautiful to the eye and restful to the spirit. If we could only make a change like that whenever we wanted to, the world would be easier to live in than it is, for change of scene shifts the mind's burdens to the other shoulder and banishes old, shop-worn weariness from mind and body 35 both.

We talked together, and I had the idea of trying to reform Satan and persuade him to lead a better life. I told him about all those things he had been doing, and begged him to be more considerate and stop making people unhappy. I said I knew he did not mean any harm, but that he ought to stop and 40 consider the possible consequences of a thing before launching it in that impulsive and random way of his; then he would not make so much trouble. He was not hurt by this plain speech; he only looked amused and surprised, and said:

"What? I do random things? Indeed, I never do. I stop and consider pos- 45 sible consequences? Where is the need? I know what the consequences are going to be—always."

"Oh, Satan, then how could you do these things?"

"Well, I will tell you, and you must understand if you can. You belong to a singular race. Every man is a suffering-machine and a happiness-machine combined. The two functions work together harmoniously, with a fine and
5 delicate precision, on the give-and-take principle. For every happiness turned out in the one department the other stands ready to modify it with a sorrow or a pain—maybe a dozen. In most cases the man's life is about equally divided between happiness and unhappiness. When this is not the case the unhappiness predominates—always; never the other. Sometimes a man's make and disposi-
10 tion are such that his misery-machine is able to do nearly all the business. Such a man goes through life almost ignorant of what happiness is. Everything he touches, everything he does, brings a misfortune upon him. You have seen such people? To that kind of a person life is not an advantage, is it? It is only a disaster. Sometimes for an hour's happiness a man's machinery makes him
15 pay years of misery. Don't you know that? It happens every now and then. I will give you a case or two presently. Now the people of your village are nothing to me—you know that, don't you?"

I did not like to speak out too flatly, so I said I had suspected it.

"Well, it is true that they are nothing to me. It is not possible that they should
20 be. The difference between them and me is abysmal, immeasurable. They have no intellect."

"No intellect?"

"Nothing that resembles it. At a future time I will examine what man calls his mind and give you the details of that chaos, then you will see and under-
25 stand. Men have nothing in common with me—there is no point of contact; they have foolish little feelings and foolish little vanities and impertinences and ambitions; their foolish little life is but a laugh, a sigh, and extinction; and they have no sense. Only the Moral Sense. I will show you what I mean. Here is a red spider, not so big as a pin's head. Can you imagine an elephant
30 being interested in him—caring whether he is happy or isn't, or whether he is wealthy or poor, or whether his sweetheart returns his love or not, or whether his mother is sick or well, or whether he is looked up to in society or not, or whether his enemies will smite him or his friends desert him, or whether his hopes will suffer blight or his political ambitions fail, or whether he shall
35 die in the bosom of his family or neglected and despised in a foreign land? These things can never be important to the elephant; they are nothing to him; he cannot shrink his sympathies to the microscopic size of them. Man is to me as the red spider is to the elephant. The elephant has nothing against the spider—he cannot get down to that remote level; I have nothing against man.
40 The elephant is indifferent; I am indifferent. The elephant would not take the trouble to do the spider an ill turn; if he took the notion he might do him a good turn, if it came in his way and cost nothing. I have done men good service, but no ill turns.

"The elephant lives a century, the red spider a day; in power, intellect, and
45 dignity the one creature is separated from the other by a distance which is simply astronomical. Yet in these, as in all qualities, man is immeasurably further below me than is the wee spider below the elephant.

"Man's mind clumsily and tediously and laboriously patches little trivialities together and gets a result—such as it is. My mind creates! Do you get the force of that? Creates anything it desires—and in a moment. Creates without material. Creates fluids, solids, colors—anything, everything—out of the airy nothing which is called Thought. A man imagines a silk thread, imagines a machine to make it, imagines a picture, then by weeks of labor embroiders it on canvas with the thread. I think the whole thing, and in a moment it is before you—created.

"I think a poem, music, the record of a game of chess—anything—and it is there. This is the immortal mind—nothing is beyond its reach. Nothing can obstruct my vision; the rocks are transparent to me, and darkness is daylight. I do not need to open a book; I take the whole of its contents into my mind at a single glance, through the cover; and in a million years I could not forget a single word of it, or its place in the volume. Nothing goes on in the skull of man, bird, fish, insect, or other creature which can be hidden from me. I pierce the learned man's brain with a single glance, and the treasures which cost him threescore years to accumulate are mine; he can forget and he does forget, but I retain.

"Now, then, I perceive by your thoughts that you are understanding me fairly well. Let us proceed. Circumstances might so fall out that the elephant could like the spider—supposing he can see it—but he could not love it. His love is for his own kind—for his equals. An angel's love is sublime, adorable, divine, beyond the imagination of man—infinitely beyond it! But it is limited to his own august order. If it fell upon one of your race for only an instant, it would consume its object to ashes. No, we cannot love men, but we can be harmlessly indifferent to them; we can also like them, sometimes. I like you and the boys, I like Father Peter, and for your sakes I am doing all these things for the villagers."

He saw that I was thinking a sarcasm and he explained his position.

"I have wrought well for the villagers, though it does not look like it on the surface. Your race never know good fortune from ill. They are always mistaking the one for the other. It is because they cannot see into the future. What I am doing for the villagers will bear good fruit some day; in some cases to themselves; in others, to unborn generations of men. No one will ever know that I was the cause, but it will be none the less true, for all that. Among you boys you have a game: you stand a row of bricks on end a few inches apart; you push a brick, it knocks its neighbor over, the neighbor knocks over the next brick—and so on till all the row is prostrate. That is human life. A child's first act knocks over the initial brick, and the rest will follow inexorably. If you could see into the future, as I can, you would see everything that was going to happen to that creature; for nothing can change the order of its life after the first event has determined it. That is, nothing will change it, because each act unfailingly begets an act, that act begets another, and so on to the end, and the seer can look forward down the line and see just when each act is to have birth, from cradle to grave."

"Does God order the career?"

"Foreordain it? No. The man's circumstances and environment order it. His

first act determines the second and all that follow after. But suppose, for argument's sake, that the man should skip one of these acts; an apparently trifling
one, for instance; suppose that it had been appointed that on a certain day, at
a certain hour and minute and second and fraction of a second he should go
5   to the well, and he didn't go. That man's career would change utterly, from
that moment; thence to the grave it would be wholly different from the career
which his first act as a child had arranged for him. Indeed, it might be that
if he had gone to the well he would have ended his career on a throne, and
that omitting to do it would set him upon a career that would lead to beggary
10   and a pauper's grave. For instance: if at any time—say in boyhood—Columbus
had skipped the triflingest little link in the chain of acts projected and made
inevitable by his first childish act, it would have changed his whole subsequent life, and he would have become a priest and died obscure in an Italian
village, and America would not have been discovered for two centuries after-
15   ward. I know this. To skip any one of the billion acts in Columbus's chain
would have wholly changed his life. I have examined his billion of possible
careers, and in only one of them occurs the discovery of America. You people
do not suspect that all of your acts are of one size and importance, but it is
true; to snatch at an appointed fly is as big with fate for you as is any other
20   appointed act—"
   "As the conquering of a continent, for instance?"
   "Yes. Now, then, no man ever does drop a link—the thing has never happened! Even when he is trying to make up his mind as to whether he will do
a thing or not, that itself is a link, an act, and has its proper place in his chain;
25   and when he finally decides an act, that also was the thing which he was absolutely certain to do. You see, now, that a man will never drop a link in his
chain. He cannot. If he made up his mind to try, that project would itself be
an unavoidable link—a thought bound to occur to him at that precise moment,
and made certain by the first act of his babyhood."
30   It seemed so dismal!
   "He is a prisoner for life," I said sorrowfully, "and cannot get free."
   "No, of himself he cannot get away from the consequences of his first
childish act. But I can free him."
   I looked up wistfully.
35   "I have changed the careers of a number of your villagers."
   I tried to thank him but found it difficult, and let it drop.
   "I shall make some other changes. You know that little Lisa Brandt?"
   "Oh yes, everybody does. My mother says she is so sweet and so lovely that
she is not like any other child. She says she will be the pride of the village when
40   she grows up; and its idol, too, just as she is now."
   "I shall change her future."
   "Make it better?" I asked.
   "Yes. And I will change the future of Nikolaus."
   I was glad, this time, and said, "I don't need to ask about his case; you will
45   be sure to do generously by him."
   "It is my intention."
   Straight off I was building that great future of Nicky's in my imagination,

and had already made a renowned general of him and hofmeister at the court, when I noticed that Satan was waiting for me to get ready to listen again. I was ashamed of having exposed my cheap imaginings to him and was expecting some sarcasms, but it did not happen. He proceeded with his subject:

"Nicky's appointed life is sixty-two years."   5

"That's grand!" I said.

"Lisa's, thirty-six. But, as I told you, I shall change their lives and those ages. Two minutes and a quarter from now Nikolaus will wake out of his sleep and find the rain blowing in. It was appointed that he should turn over and go to sleep again. But I have appointed that he shall get up and close the window   10 first. That trifle will change his career entirely. He will rise in the morning two minutes later than the chain of his life had appointed him to rise. By consequence, thenceforth nothing will ever happen to him in accordance with the details of the old chain." He took out his watch and sat looking at it a few moments, then said: "Nikolaus has risen to close the window. His life is   15 changed, his new career has begun. There will be consequences."

It made me feel creepy; it was uncanny.

"But for this change certain things would happen twelve days from now. For instance, Nikolaus would save Lisa from drowning. He would arrive on the scene at exactly the right moment—four minutes past ten, the long-ago   20 appointed instant of time—and the water would be shoal, the achievement easy and certain. But he will arrive some seconds too late, now; Lisa will have struggled into deeper water. He will do his best but both will drown."

"Oh, Satan! oh, dear Satan!" I cried, with the tears rising in my eyes, "save them! Don't let it happen. I can't bear to lose Nikolaus, he is my loving play-   25 mate and friend; and think of Lisa's poor mother!"

I clung to him and begged and pleaded, but he was not moved. He made me sit down again, and told me I must hear him out.

"I have changed Nikolaus's life, and this has changed Lisa's. If I had not done this, Nikolaus would save Lisa, then he would catch cold from his drench-   30 ing; one of your race's fantastic and desolating scarlet fevers would follow, with pathetic after-effects; for forty-six years he would lie in his bed a paralytic log, deaf, dumb, blind, and praying night and day for the blessed relief of death. Shall I change his life back?"

"Oh no! Oh, not for the world! In charity and pity leave it as it is."   35

"It is best so. I could not have changed any other link in his life and done him so good a service. He had a billion possible careers, but not one of them was worth living; they were charged full with miseries and disasters. But for my intervention he would do his brave deed twelve days from now—a deed begun and ended in six minutes—and get for all reward those forty-six years   40 of sorrow and suffering I told you of. It is one of the cases I was thinking of awhile ago when I said that sometimes an act which brings the actor an hour's happiness and self-satisfaction is paid for—or punished—by years of suffering."

I wondered what poor little Lisa's early death would save her from. He answered the thought: 45

"From ten years of pain and slow recovery from an accident, and then from

---

1. **hofmeister**—literally, "court-master," a title of honor.

nineteen years' pollution, shame, depravity, crime, ending with death at the hands of the executioner. Twelve days hence she will die; her mother would save her life if she could. Am I not kinder than her mother?"

"Yes—oh, indeed yes; and wiser."

5 "Father Peter's case is coming on presently. He will be acquitted, through unassailable proofs of his innocence."

"Why, Satan, how can that be? Do you really think it?"

"Indeed, I know it. His good name will be restored, and the rest of his life will be happy."

10 "I can believe it. To restore his good name will have that effect."

"His happiness will not proceed from that cause. I shall change his life that day, for his good. He will never know his good name has been restored."

In my mind—and modestly—I asked for particulars but Satan paid no attention to my thought. Next, my mind wandered to the astrologer, and I won-
15 dered where he might be.

"In the moon," said Satan, with a fleeting sound which I believed was a chuckle. "I've got him on the cold side of it, too. He doesn't know where he is, and is not having a pleasant time; still, it is good enough for him, a good place for his star studies. I shall need him presently; then I shall bring him
20 back and possess him again. He has a long and cruel and odious life before him, but I will change that, for I have no feeling against him and am quite willing to do him a kindness. I think I shall get him burned."

He had such strange notions of kindness! But angels are made so, and do not know any better. Their ways are not like our ways; and, besides, human
25 beings are nothing to them; they think they are only freaks. It seems to me odd that he should put the astrologer so far away; he could have dumped him in Germany just as well, where he would be handy.

"Far away?" said Satan. "To me no place is far away; distance does not exist for me. The sun is less than a hundred million miles from here, and the
30 light that is falling upon us has taken eight minutes to come; but I can make that flight, or any other, in a fraction of time so minute that it cannot be measured by a watch. I have but to think the journey, and it is accomplished."

I held out my hand and said, "The light lies upon it; think it into a glass of wine, Satan."

35 He did it. I drank the wine.

"Break the glass," he said.

I broke it.

"There—you see it is real. The villagers thought the brass balls were magic stuff and as perishable as smoke. They were afraid to touch them. You are a
40 curious lot—your race. But come along; I have business. I will put you to bed."

Said and done. Then he was gone; but his voice came back to me through the rain and darkness saying, "Yes, tell Seppi, but no other."

It was the answer to my thought.

CHAPTER VIII

Sleep would not come. It was not because I was proud of my travels and excited about having been around the big world to China, and feeling contemptuous of Bartel Sperling, "the traveler," as he called himself, and looked down upon us others because he had been to Vienna once and was the only Eseldorf boy who had made such a journey and seen the world's wonders. At another time that would have kept me awake, but it did not affect me now. No, my mind was filled with Nikolaus, my thoughts ran upon him only, and the good days we had seen together at romps and frolics in the woods and the fields and the river in the long summer days, and skating and sliding in the winter when our parents thought we were in school. And now he was going out of this young life, and the summers and winters would come and go, and we others would rove and play as before, but his place would be vacant; we should see him no more. To-morrow he would not suspect, but would be as he had always been, and it would shock me to hear him laugh, and see him do lightsome and frivolous things, for to me he would be a corpse, with waxen hands and dull eyes, and I should see the shroud around his face; and next day he would not suspect, nor the next, and all the time his handful of days would be wasting swiftly away and that awful thing coming nearer and nearer, his fate closing steadily around him and no one knowing it but Seppi and me. Twelve days—only twelve days. It was awful to think of. I noticed that in my thoughts I was not calling him by his familiar names, Nick and Nicky, but was speaking of him by his full name, and reverently, as one speaks of the dead. Also, as incident after incident of our comradeship came thronging into my mind out of the past, I noticed that they were mainly cases where I had wronged him or hurt him, and they rebuked me and reproached me, and my heart was wrung with remorse, just as it is when we remember our unkindnesses to friends who have passed beyond the veil, and we wish we could have them back again, if only for a moment, so that we could go on our knees to them and say, "Have pity and forgive."

Once when we were nine years old he went a long errand of nearly two miles for the fruiterer, who gave him a splendid big apple for reward, and he was flying home with it, almost beside himself with astonishment and delight, and I met him, and he let me look at the apple, not thinking of treachery, and I ran off with it, eating it as I ran, he following me and begging; and when he overtook me I offered him the core, which was all that was left; and I laughed. Then he turned away, crying, and said he had meant to give it to his little sister. That smote me, for she was slowly getting well of a sickness, and it would have been a proud moment for him, to see her joy and surprise and have her caresses. But I was ashamed to say I was ashamed, and only said something rude and mean, to pretend I did not care, and he made no reply in words, but there was a wounded look in his face as he turned away toward his home which rose before me many times in after years, in the night, and reproached me and made me ashamed again. It had grown dim in my mind, by and by, then it disappeared; but it was back now, and not dim.

Once at school, when we were eleven, I upset my ink and spoiled four copy-books, and was in danger of severe punishment; but I put it upon him, and he got the whipping.

And only last year I had cheated him in a trade, giving him a large fish-hook which was partly broken through for three small sound ones. The first fish
5   he caught broke the hook, but he did not know I was blamable, and he refused to take back one of the small hooks which my conscience forced me to offer him, but said, "A trade is a trade; the hook was bad, but that was not your fault."

No, I could not sleep. These little, shabby wrongs upbraided me and tortured
10   me, and with a pain much sharper than one feels when the wrongs have been done to the living. Nikolaus was living but no matter; he was to me as one already dead. The wind was still moaning about the eaves, the rain still pattering upon the panes.

In the morning I sought out Seppi and told him. It was down by the river.
15   His lips moved, but he did not say anything, he only looked dazed and stunned, and his face turned very white. He stood like that a few moments, the tears welling into his eyes, then he turned away and I locked my arm in his and we walked along thinking, but not speaking. We crossed the bridge and wandered through the meadows and up among the hills and the woods,
20   and at last the talk came and flowed freely, and it was all about Nikolaus and was a recalling of the life we had lived with him. And every now and then Seppi said, as if to himself:

"Twelve days!—less than twelve."

We said we must be with him all the time; we must have all of him we
25   could; the days were precious now. Yet we did not go to seek him. It would be like meeting the dead, and we were afraid. We did not say it, but that was what we were feeling. And so it gave us a shock when we turned a curve and came upon Nikolaus face to face. He shouted, gaily:

"Hi-hi! What is the matter? Have you seen a ghost?"

30   We couldn't speak, but there was no occasion; he was willing to talk for us all, for he had just seen Satan and was in high spirits about it. Satan had told him about our trip to China, and he had begged Satan to take him on a journey, and Satan had promised. It was to be a far journey, and wonderful and beautiful; and Nikolaus had begged him to take us, too, but he said no,
35   he would take us some day, maybe, but not now. Satan would come for him on the 13th, and Nikolaus was already counting the hours, he was so impatient.

That was the fatal day. We were already counting the hours, too.

We wandered many a mile, always following paths which had been our favorites from the days when we were little, and always we talked about the
40   old times. All the blitheness was with Nikolaus; we others could not shake off our depression. Our tone toward Nikolaus was so strangely gentle and tender and yearning that he noticed it, and was pleased, and we were constantly doing him deferential little offices of courtesy, and saying, "Wait, let me do that for you," and that pleased him, too. I gave him seven fish-hooks—all I had—
45   and made him take them, and Seppi gave him his new knife and a humming-top painted red and yellow—atonements for swindles practised upon him formerly, as I learned later, and probably no longer remembered by Nikolaus

now. These things touched him, and he said he could not have believed that we loved him so; and his pride in it and gratefulness for it cut us to the heart, we were so undeserving of them. When we parted at last, he was radiant, and said he had never had such a happy day.

As we walked along homeward, Seppi said, "We always prized him but never so much as now, when we are going to lose him."

Next day and every day we spent all of our spare time with Nikolaus, and also added to it time which we (and he) stole from work and other duties, and this cost the three of us some sharp scoldings, and some threats of punishment. Every morning two of us woke with a start and a shudder, saying, as the days flew along, "Only ten days left"; "only nine days left"; "only eight"; "only seven." Always it was narrowing. Always Nikolaus was gay and happy, and always puzzled because we were not. He wore his invention to the bone trying to invent ways to cheer us up, but it was only a hollow success; he could see that our jollity had no heart in it, and that the laughs we broke into came up against some obstruction or other and suffered damage and decayed into a sigh. He tried to find out what the matter was, so that he could help us out of our trouble or make it lighter by sharing it with us; so we had to tell many lies to deceive him and appease him.

But the most distressing thing of all was that he was always making plans, and often they went beyond the 13th! Whenever that happened it made us groan in spirit. All his mind was fixed upon finding some way to conquer our depression and cheer us up; and at last, when he had but three days to live he fell upon the right idea and was jubilant over it—a boys-and-girls' frolic and dance in the woods, up there where we first met Satan, and this was to occur on the 14th. It was ghastly, for that was his funeral day. We couldn't venture to protest; it would only have brought a "Why?" which we could not answer. He wanted us to help him invite his guests, and we did it— one can refuse nothing to a dying friend. But it was dreadful, for really we were inviting them to his funeral.

It was an awful eleven days; and yet, with a lifetime stretching back between to-day and then, they are still a grateful memory to me, and beautiful. In effect they were days of companionship with one's sacred dead, and I have known no comradeship that was so close or so precious. We clung to the hours and the minutes, counting them as they wasted away, and parting with them with that pain and bereavement which a miser feels who sees his hoard filched from him coin by coin by robbers and is helpless to prevent it.

When the evening of the last day came we stayed out too long; Seppi and I were in fault for that; we could not bear to part with Nikolaus; so it was very late when we left him at his door. We lingered near awhile, listening; and that happened which we were fearing. His father gave him the promised punishment, and we heard his shrieks. But we listened only a moment, then hurried away, remorseful for this thing which we had caused. And sorry for the father, too; our thought being, "If he only knew—if he only knew!"

In the morning Nikolaus did not meet us at the appointed place, so we went to his home to see what the matter was. His mother said:

"His father is out of all patience with these goings-on, and will not have

any more of it. Half the time when Nick is needed he is not to be found; then it turns out that he has been gadding around with you two. His father gave him a flogging last night. It always grieved me before, and many's the time I have begged him off and saved him, but this time he appealed to me
5 in vain, for I was out of patience myself."

"I wish you had saved him just this one time," I said, my voice trembling a little; "it would ease a pain in your heart to remember it some day."

She was ironing at the time, and her back was partly toward me. She turned about with a startled or wondering look in her face and said, "What do you
10 mean by that?"

I was not prepared, and didn't know anything to say; so it was awkward, for she kept looking at me; but Seppi was alert and spoke up:

"Why, of course it would be pleasant to remember, for the very reason we were out so late was that Nikolaus got to telling how good you are to him,
15 and how he never got whipped when you were by to save him; and he was so full of it, and we were so full of the interest of it, that none of us noticed how late it was getting."

"Did he say that? Did he?" and she put her apron to her eyes.

"You can ask Theodor—he will tell you the same."

20 "It is a dear, good lad, my Nick," she said. "I am sorry I let him get whipped; I will never do it again. To think—all the time I was sitting here last night, fretting and angry at him, he was loving me and praising me! Dear, dear, if we could only know! Then we shouldn't ever go wrong; but we are only poor, dumb beasts groping around and making mistakes. I sha'n't
25 ever think of last night without a pang."

She was like all the rest; it seemed as if nobody could open a mouth, in these wretched days, without saying something that made us shiver. They were "groping around," and did not know what true, sorrowfully true things they were saying by accident.

30 Seppi asked if Nikolaus might go out with us.

"I am sorry," she answered, "but he can't. To punish him further, his father doesn't allow him to go out of the house to-day."

We had a great hope! I saw it in Seppi's eyes. We thought, "If he cannot leave the house, he cannot be drowned." Seppi asked, to make sure:

35 "Must he stay in all day, or only the morning?"

"All day. It's such a pity, too; it's a beautiful day, and he is so unused to being shut up. But he is busy planning his party, and maybe that is company for him. I do hope he isn't too lonesome."

Seppi saw that in her eye which emboldened him to ask if we might go
40 up and help him pass his time.

"And welcome!" she said, right heartily. "Now I call that real friendship, when you might be abroad in the fields and the woods, having a happy time. You are good boys, I'll allow that, though you don't always find satisfactory ways of improving it. Take these cakes—for yourselves—and give him this
45 one, from his mother."

The first thing we noticed when we entered Nikolaus's room was the time —a quarter to 10. Could that be correct? Only such a few minutes to live! I

felt a contraction at my heart. Nikolaus jumped up and gave us a glad welcome. He was in good spirits over his plannings for his party and had not
been lonesome.

"Sit down," he said, "and look at what I've been doing. And I've finished a
kite that you will say is a beauty. It's drying in the kitchen; I'll fetch it."   5

He had been spending his penny savings in fanciful trifles of various kinds,
to go as prizes in the games, and they were marshaled with fine and showy
effect upon the table. He said:

"Examine them at your leisure while I get mother to touch up the kite with
her iron if it isn't dry enough yet."   10

Then he tripped out and went clattering down-stairs, whistling.

We did not look at the things; we couldn't take any interest in anything
but the clock. We sat staring at it in silence, listening to the ticking, and every
time the minute-hand jumped we nodded recognition—one minute fewer to
cover in the race for life or for death. Finally Seppi drew a deep breath and   15
said:

"Two minutes to ten. Seven minutes more and he will pass the death-point.
Theodor, he is going to be saved! He's going to—"

"Hush! I'm on needles. Watch the clock and keep still."

Five minutes more. We were panting with the strain and the excitement.   20
Another three minutes, and there was a footstep on the stair.

"Saved!" And we jumped up and faced the door.

The old mother entered, bringing the kite. "Isn't it a beauty?" she said.
"And, dear me, how he has slaved over it—ever since daylight, I think, and
only finished it awhile before you came." She stood it against the wall and   25
stepped back to take a view of it. "He drew the pictures his own self, and I
think they are very good. The church isn't so very good, I'll have to admit,
but look at the bridge—any one can recognize the bridge in a minute. He
asked me to bring it up. . . . Dear me! it's seven minutes past ten, and I—"

"But where is he?"   30

"He? Oh, he'll be here soon; he's gone out a minute."

"Gone out?"

"Yes. Just as he came down-stairs little Lisa's mother came in and said the
child had wandered off somewhere, and as she was a little uneasy I told
Nikolaus to never mind about his father's orders—go and look her up. . . .   35
Why, how white you two do look! I do believe you are sick. Sit down; I'll
fetch something. That cake has disagreed with you. It is a little heavy, but I
thought—"

She disappeared without finishing her sentence, and we hurried at once to
the back window and looked toward the river. There was a great crowd at   40
the other end of the bridge, and people were flying toward that point from
every direction.

"Oh, it is all over—poor Nikolaus! Why, oh, why did she let him get out of
the house!"

"Come away," said Seppi, half sobbing, "come quick—we can't bear to meet   45
her; in five minutes she will know."

But we were not to escape. She came upon us at the foot of the stairs, with her cordials in her hands, and made us come in and sit down and take the medicine. Then she watched the effect, and it did not satisfy her; so she made us wait longer, and kept upbraiding herself for giving us the unwholesome cake.

5 Presently the thing happened which we were dreading. There was a sound of tramping and scraping outside, and a crowd came solemnly in, with heads uncovered, and laid the two drowned bodies on the bed.

"Oh, my God!" that poor mother cried out, and fell on her knees, and put her arms about her dead boy and began to cover the wet face with kisses.
10 "Oh, it was I that sent him, and I have been his death. If I had obeyed, and kept him in the house, this would not have happened. And I am rightly punished; I was cruel to him last night, and him begging me, his own mother, to be his friend."

And so she went on and on, and all the women cried and pitied her, and
15 tried to comfort her, but she could not forgive herself and could not be comforted, and kept on saying if she had not sent him out he would be alive and well now, and she was the cause of his death.

It shows how foolish people are when they blame themselves for anything they have done. Satan knows, and he said nothing happens that your first act
20 hasn't arranged to happen and made inevitable, and so, of your own motion you can't ever alter the scheme or do a thing that will break a link. Next we heard screams, and Frau Brandt came wildly plowing and plunging through the crowd with her dress in disorder and hair flying loose, and flung herself upon her dead child with moans and kisses and pleadings and endearments;
25 and by and by she rose up almost exhausted with her outpourings of passionate emotion, and clenched her fist and lifted it toward the sky, and her teardrenched face grew hard and resentful, and she said:

"For nearly two weeks I have had dreams and presentiments and warnings that death was going to strike what was most precious to me, and day and
30 night and night and day I have groveled in the dirt before Him praying Him to have pity on my innocent child and save it from harm—and here is His answer!"

Why, He had saved it from harm—but she did not know.

She wiped the tears from her eyes and cheeks, and stood awhile gazing
35 down at the child and caressing its face and its hair with her hand; then she spoke again in that bitter tone, "But in His hard heart is no compassion. I will never pray again."

She gathered her dead child to her bosom and strode away, the crowd falling back to let her pass, and smitten dumb by the awful words they had
40 heard. Ah, that poor woman! It is as Satan said, we do not know good fortune from bad, and are always mistaking the one for the other. Many a time since I have heard people pray to God to spare the life of sick persons, but I have never done it.

Both funerals took place at the same time in our little church next day.
45 Everybody was there, including the party guests. Satan was there, too; which was proper, for it was on account of his efforts that the funerals had happened. Nikolaus had departed this life without absolution, and a collection was taken

up for masses, to get him out of purgatory. Only two-thirds of the required money was gathered, and the parents were going to try to borrow the rest, but Satan furnished it. He told us privately that there was no purgatory, but he had contributed in order that Nikolaus's parents and their friends might be saved from worry and distress. We thought it very good of him, but he said 5 money did not cost him anything.

At the graveyard the body of little Lisa was seized for debt by a carpenter to whom the mother owed fifty groschen for work done the year before. She had never been able to pay this, and was not able now. The carpenter took the corpse home and kept it four days in his cellar, the mother weeping and im- 10 ploring about his house all the time; then he buried it in his brother's cattle-yard, without religious ceremonies. It drove the mother wild with grief and shame, and she forsook her work and went daily about the town, cursing the carpenter and blaspheming the laws of the emperor and the church, and it was pitiful to see. Seppi asked Satan to interfere, but he said the carpenter 15 and the rest were members of the human race and were acting quite neatly for that species of animal. He would interfere if he found a horse acting in such a way, and we must inform him when we came across that kind of horse doing that kind of a human thing, so that he could stop it. We believed this was sarcasm, for of course there wasn't any such horse. 20

But after a few days we found that we could not abide that poor woman's distress, so we begged Satan to examine her several possible careers, and see if he could not change her, to her profit, to a new one. He said the longest of her careers as they now stood gave her forty-two years to live and her short-est one twenty-nine, and that both were charged with grief and hunger and 25 cold and pain. The only improvement he could make would be to enable her to skip a certain three minutes from now, and he asked us if he should do it. This was such a short time to decide in that we went to pieces with nervous excitement, and before we could pull ourselves together and ask for particu-lars he said the time would be up in a few more seconds; so then we gasped 30 out, "Do it!"

"It is done," he said, "she was going around a corner; I have turned her back; it has changed her career."

"Then what will happen, Satan?"

"It is happening now. She is having words with Fischer, the weaver. In his 35 anger Fischer will straightway do what he would not have done but for this accident. He was present when she stood over her child's body and uttered those blasphemies."

"What will he do?"

"He is doing it now—betraying her. In three days she will go to the stake." 40

We could not speak; we were frozen with horror, for if we had not med-dled with her career she would have been spared this awful fate. Satan no-ticed these thoughts, and said:

"What you are thinking is strictly human-like—that is to say, foolish. The woman is advantaged. Die when she might, she would go to heaven. By this 45 prompt death she gets twenty-nine years more of heaven than she is entitled to, and escapes twenty-nine years of misery here."

A moment before we were bitterly making up our minds that we would ask no more favors of Satan for friends of ours, for he did not seem to know any way to do a person a kindness but by killing him; but the whole aspect of the case was changed now, and we were glad of what we had done and full of
5   happiness in the thought of it.

After a little I began to feel troubled about Fischer, and asked, timidly, "Does this episode change Fischer's life-scheme, Satan?"

"Change it? Why, certainly. And radically. If he had not met Frau Brandt awhile ago he would die next year, thirty-four years of age. Now he will live
10   to be ninety, and have a pretty prosperous and comfortable life of it, as human lives go."

We felt a great joy and pride in what we had done for Fischer, and were expecting Satan to sympathize with this feeling; but he showed no sign and this made us uneasy. We waited for him to speak, but he didn't; so, to as-
15   suage our solicitude we had to ask him if there was any defect in Fischer's good luck. Satan considered the question a moment, then said, with some hesitation:

"Well, the fact is, it is a delicate point. Under his several former possible life-careers he was going to heaven."
20   We were aghast. "Oh, Satan! and under this one—"

"There, don't be so distressed. You were sincerely trying to do him a kindness; let that comfort you."

"Oh, dear, dear, that cannot comfort us. You ought to have told us what we were doing, then we wouldn't have acted so."
25   But it made no impression on him. He had never felt a pain or a sorrow, and did not know what they were, in any really informing way. He had no knowledge of them except theoretically—that is to say, intellectually. And of course that is no good. One can never get any but a loose and ignorant notion of such things except by experience. We tried our best to make him
30   comprehend the awful thing that had been done and how we were compromised by it, but he couldn't seem to get hold of it. He said he did not think it important where Fischer went to; in heaven he would not be missed, there were "plenty there." We tried to make him see that he was missing the point entirely, that Fischer, and not other people, was the proper one to decide about
35   the importance of it; but it all went for nothing; he said he did not care for Fischer—there were plenty more Fischers.

The next minute Fischer went by on the other side of the way and it made us sick and faint to see him, remembering the doom that was upon him, and we the cause of it. And how unconscious he was that anything had happened
40   to him! You could see by his elastic step and his alert manner that he was well satisfied with himself for doing that hard turn for poor Frau Brandt. He kept glancing back over his shoulder expectantly. And, sure enough, pretty soon Frau Brandt followed after, in charge of the officers and wearing jingling chains. A mob was in her wake, jeering and shouting, "Blasphemer and
45   heretic!" and some among them were neighbors and friends of her happier days. Some were trying to strike her, and the officers were not taking as much trouble as they might to keep them from it.

"Oh, stop them, Satan!" It was out before we remembered that he could not interrupt them for a moment without changing their whole after-lives. He puffed a little puff toward them with his lips and they began to reel and stagger and grab at the empty air; then they broke apart and fled in every direction, shrieking, as if in intolerable pain. He had crushed a rib of each 5 of them with that little puff. We could not help asking if their life-chart was changed.

"Yes, entirely. Some have gained years, some have lost them. Some few will profit in various ways by the change, but only that few."

We did not ask if we had brought poor Fischer's luck to any of them. We 10 did not wish to know. We fully believed in Satan's desire to do us kindnesses, but we were losing confidence in his judgment. It was at this time that our growing anxiety to have him look over our life-charts and suggest improvements began to fade out and give place to other interests.

For a day or two the whole village was a chattering turmoil over Frau 15 Brandt's case and over the mysterious calamity that had overtaken the mob, and at her trial the place was crowded. She was easily convicted of her blasphemies, for she uttered those terrible words again and said she would not take them back. When warned that she was imperiling her life, she said they could take it in welcome, she did not want it, she would rather live with the 20 professional devils in perdition than with these imitators in the village. They accused her of breaking all those ribs by witchcraft, and asked her if she was not a witch. She answered scornfully:

"No. If I had that power would any of you holy hypocrites be alive five minutes? No; I would strike you all dead. Pronounce your sentence and let 25 me go; I am tired of your society."

So they found her guilty, and she was excommunicated and cut off from the joys of heaven and doomed to the fires of hell; then she was clothed in a coarse robe and delivered to the secular arm, and conducted to the market-place, the bell solemnly tolling the while. We saw her chained to the stake, and saw 30 the first film of blue smoke rise on the still air. Then her hard face softened, and she looked upon the packed crowd in front of her and said, with gentleness:

"We played together once, in long-agone days when we were innocent little creatures. For the sake of that, I forgive you." 35

We went away then and did not see the fires consume her, but we heard the shrieks, although we put our fingers in our ears. When they ceased we knew she was in heaven, notwithstanding the excommunication, and we were glad of her death and not sorry that we had brought it about.

One day, a little while after this, Satan appeared again. We were always 40 watching out for him, for life was never very stagnant when he was by. He came upon us at that place in the woods where we had first met him. Being boys, we wanted to be entertained; we asked him to do a show for us.

"Very well," he said, "would you like to see a history of the progress of the human race?—its development of that product which it calls civilization?" 45

We said we should.

29. **secular arm**—officers of the law. Church officials may not execute a death sentence.

So, with a thought, he turned the place into the Garden of Eden, and we saw Abel praying by his altar; then Cain came walking toward him with his club, and did not seem to see us, and would have stepped on my foot if I had not drawn it in. He spoke to his brother in a language which we did not
5 understand; then he grew violent and threatening, and we knew what was going to happen and turned away our heads for the moment; but we heard the crash of the blows and heard the shrieks and the groans; then there was silence, and we saw Abel lying in his blood and gasping out his life, and Cain standing over him and looking down at him, vengeful and unrepent-
10 ant.

Then the vision vanished, and was followed by a long series of unknown wars, murders, and massacres. Next we had the Flood, and the Ark tossing around in the stormy waters, with lofty mountains in the distance showing veiled and dim through the rain. Satan said:
15 "The progress of your race was not satisfactory. It is to have another chance now."

The scene changed, and we saw Noah overcome with wine.

Next, we had Sodom and Gomorrah, and "the attempt to discover two or three respectable persons there," as Satan described it. Next, Lot and his
20 daughters in the cave.

Next came the Hebraic wars, and we saw the [victors] massacre the survivors and their cattle, and save the young girls alive and distribute them around.

Next we had Jael; and saw her slip into the tent and drive the nail into
25 the temple of her sleeping guest; and we were so close that when the blood gushed out it trickled in a little, red stream to our feet, and we could have stained our hands in it if we had wanted to.

Next we had Egyptian wars, Greek wars, Roman wars, hideous drenchings of the earth with blood; and we saw the treacheries of the Romans toward the
30 Carthaginians, and the sickening spectacle of the massacre of those brave people. Also we saw Cæsar invade Britain—"not that those barbarians had done him any harm, but because he wanted their land, and desired to confer the blessings of civilization upon their widows and orphans," as Satan explained.
35 Next, Christianity was born. Then ages of Europe passed in review before us, and we saw Christianity and Civilization march hand in hand through those ages, "leaving famine and death and desolation in their wake, and other signs of the progress of the human race," as Satan observed.

And always we had wars, and more wars, and still other wars—all over
40 Europe, all over the world. "Sometimes in the private interest of royal families," Satan said, "sometimes to crush a weak nation; but never a war started by the aggressor for any clean purpose—there is no such war in the history of the race."

"Now," said Satan, "you have seen your progress down to the present, and

---

1-20. **Garden of Eden . . . Lot and his daughters**—in general, a summary of Gen. 2:12. **21. Hebraic wars**—*cf.* the Book of Joshua, *et seq.* **21. [victors]**—the original text prints "victims." **24. Jael**—*cf.* Judg. 4:17-22.

you must confess that it is wonderful—in its way. We must now exhibit the future."

He showed us slaughters more terrible in their destruction of life, more devastating in their engines of war, than any we had seen.

"You perceive," he said, "that you have made continual progress. Cain did his murder with a club; the Hebrews did their murders with javelins and swords; the Greeks and Romans added protective armor and the fine arts of military organization and generalship; the Christian has added guns and gunpowder; a few centuries from now he will have so greatly improved the deadly effectiveness of his weapons of slaughter that all men will confess that without Christian civilization war must have remained a poor and trifling thing to the end of time."

Then he began to laugh in the most unfeeling way, and make fun of the human race, although he knew that what he had been saying shamed us and wounded us. No one but an angel could have acted so; but suffering is nothing to them, they do not know what it is, except by hearsay.

More than once Seppi and I had tried in a humble and diffident way to convert him, and as he had remained silent we had taken his silence as a sort of encouragement; necessarily, then, this talk of his was a disappointment to us, for it showed that we had made no deep impression upon him. The thought made us sad, and we knew then how the missionary must feel when he has been cherishing a glad hope and has seen it blighted. We kept our grief to ourselves, knowing that this was not the time to continue our work.

Satan laughed his unkind laugh to a finish; then he said: "It is a remarkable progress. In five or six thousand years five or six high civilizations have risen, flourished, commanded the wonder of the world, then faded out and disappeared; and not one of them except the latest ever invented any sweeping and adequate way to kill people. They all did their best—to kill being the chiefest ambition of the human race and the earliest incident in its history— but only the Christian civilization has scored a triumph to be proud of. Two or three centuries from now it will be recognized that all the competent killers are Christians; then the pagan world will go to school to the Christian—not to acquire his religion, but his guns. The Turk and the Chinaman will buy those to kill missionaries and converts with."

By this time his theater was at work again, and before our eyes nation after nation drifted by, during two or three centuries, a mighty procession, an endless procession, raging, struggling, wallowing through seas of blood, smothered in battle-smoke through which the flags glinted and the red jets from the cannon darted; and always we heard the thunder of the guns and the cries of the dying.

"And what does it amount to?" said Satan, with his evil chuckle. "Nothing at all. You gain nothing; you always come out where you went in. For a million years the race has gone on monotonously propagating itself and monotonously reperforming this dull nonsense—to what end? No wisdom can guess! Who gets a profit out of it? Nobody but a parcel of usurping little monarchs and nobilities who despise you; would feel defiled if you touched them; would shut the door in your face if you proposed to call; whom you slave for, fight

for, die for, and are not ashamed of it but proud; whose existence is a perpetual insult to you and you are afraid to resent it; who are mendicants supported by your alms, yet assume toward you the airs of benefactor toward beggar; who address you in the language of master to slave, and are answered in the lan-
5 guage of slave to master; who are worshiped by you with your mouth, while in your heart—if you have one—you despise yourselves for it. The first man was a hypocrite and a coward, qualities which have not yet failed in his line; it is the foundation upon which all civilizations have been built. Drink to their perpetuation! Drink to their augmentation! Drink to—" Then he saw by our
10 faces how much we were hurt, and he cut his sentence short and stopped chuckling, and his manner changed. He said, gently: "No, we will drink one another's health, and let civilization go. The wine which has flown to our hands out of space by desire is earthly, and good enough for that other toast; but throw away the glasses, we will drink this one in wine which has not
15 visited this world before."

We obeyed, and reached up and received the new cups as they descended. They were shapely and beautiful goblets, but they were not made of any material that we were acquainted with. They seemed to be in motion, they seemed to be alive; and certainly the colors in them were in motion. They were
20 very brilliant and sparkling, and of every tint, and they were never still, but flowed to and fro in rich tides which met and broke and flashed out dainty explosions of enchanting color. I think it was most like opals washing about in waves and flashing out their splendid fires. But there is nothing to compare the wine with. We drank it, and felt a strange and witching ecstasy as of heaven
25 go stealing through us, and Seppi's eyes filled and he said worshipingly:

"We shall be there some day, and then—"

He glanced furtively at Satan, and I think he hoped Satan would say, "Yes, you will be there some day," but Satan seemed to be thinking about something else, and said nothing. This made me feel ghastly, for I knew he had heard;
30 nothing, spoken or unspoken, ever escaped him. Poor Seppi looked distressed, and did not finish his remark. The goblets rose and clove their way into the sky, a triplet of radiant sundogs, and disappeared. Why didn't they stay? It seemed a bad sign, and depressed me. Should I ever see mine again? Would Seppi ever see his?

35   CHAPTER IX

It was wonderful, the mastery Satan had over time and distance. For him they did not exist. He called them human inventions and said they were artificialities. We often went to the most distant parts of the globe with him and stayed weeks and months, and yet were gone only a fraction of a second,
40 as a rule. You could prove it by the clock. One day when our people were in such awful distress because the witch commission were afraid to proceed against the astrologer and Father Peter's household, or against any, indeed, but the poor and the friendless, they lost patience and took to witch-hunting on their own score, and began to chase a born lady who was known to have
45 the habit of curing people by devilish arts, such as bathing them, washing them, and nourishing them instead of bleeding them and purging them

through the ministrations of a barber-surgeon in the proper way. She came
flying down, with the howling and cursing mob after her, and tried to take
refuge in houses, but the doors were shut in her face. They chased her more
than half an hour, we following to see it, and at last she was exhausted and
fell, and they caught her. They dragged her to a tree and threw a rope over   5
the limb, and began to make a noose in it, some holding her, meantime, and
she was crying and begging and her young daughter looking on and weeping,
but afraid to say or do anything.

They hanged the lady, and I threw a stone at her, although in my heart I
was sorry for her; but all were throwing stones and each was watching his   10
neighbor, and if I had not done as the others did it would have been noticed
and spoken of. Satan burst out laughing.

All that were near by turned upon him, astonished and not pleased. It was
an ill time to laugh, for his free and scoffing ways and his supernatural music·
had brought him under suspicion all over the town and turned many privately   15
against him. The big blacksmith called attention to him now, raising his voice
so that all should hear, and said:

"What are you laughing at? Answer! Moreover, please explain to the company why you threw no stone."

"Are you sure I did not throw a stone?"   20

"Yes. You needn't try to get out of it; I had my eye on you."

"And I—I noticed you!" shouted two others.

"Three witnesses," said Satan: "Mueller, the blacksmith; Klein, the butcher's man; Pfeiffer, the weaver's journeyman. Three very ordinary liars. Are
there any more?"   25

"Never mind whether there are others or not, and never mind about what
you consider us—three's enough to settle your matter for you. You'll prove that
you threw a stone or it shall go hard with you."

"That's so!" shouted the crowd, and surged up as closely as they could to
the center of interest.   30

"And first you will answer that other question," cried the blacksmith,
pleased with himself for being mouthpiece to the public and hero of the occasion. "What are you laughing at?"

Satan smiled and answered, pleasantly: "To see three cowards stoning a dying lady when they were so near death themselves."   35

You could see the superstitious crowd shrink and catch their breath, under
the sudden shock. The blacksmith, with a show of bravado, said:

"Pooh! What do you know about it?"

"I? Everything. By profession I am a fortune-teller and I read the hands of
you three—and some others—when you lifted them to stone the woman. One   40
of you will die to-morrow week; another of you will die to-night; the third
has but five minutes to live—and yonder is the clock!"

It made a sensation. The faces of the crowd blanched, and turned mechanically toward the clock. The butcher and the weaver seemed smitten with an
illness, but the blacksmith braced up and said, with spirit: 45

1. **barber-surgeon**—until the eighteenth century the two professions were united; hence,
the red and white on the modern barber's pole.

"It is not long to wait for prediction number one. If it fails, young master, you will not live a whole minute after, I promise you that."

No one said anything; all watched the clock in a deep stillness which was impressive. When four and a half minutes were gone the blacksmith gave a
5 sudden gasp and clapped his hands upon his heart, saying, "Give me breath! Give me room!" and began to sink down. The crowd surged back, no one offering to support him, and he fell lumbering to the ground and was dead. The people stared at him, then at Satan, then at one another; and their lips moved but no words came. Then Satan said:
10 "Three saw that I threw no stone. Perhaps there are others; let them speak."

It struck a kind of panic into them, and, although no one answered him, many began to violently accuse one another, saying, "You said he didn't throw," and getting for reply, "It is a lie, and I will make you eat it!" And so in a moment they were in a raging and noisy turmoil, and beating and
15 banging one another; and in the midst was the only indifferent one—the dead lady hanging from her rope, her troubles forgotten, her spirit at peace.

So we walked away, and I was not at ease, but was saying to myself, "He told them he was laughing at them, but it was a lie—he was laughing at me."

That made him laugh again, and he said, "Yes, I was laughing at you, be-
20 cause, in fear of what others might report about you, you stoned the woman when your heart revolted at the act—but I was laughing at the others, too."

"Why?"

"Because their case was yours."

"How is that?"
25 "Well, there were sixty-eight people there, and sixty-two of them had no more desire to throw a stone than you had."

"Satan!"

"Oh, it's true. I know your race. It is made up of sheep. It is governed by minorities, seldom or never by majorities. It suppresses its feelings and its
30 beliefs and follows the handful that makes the most noise. Sometimes the noisy handful is right, sometimes wrong; but no matter, the crowd follows it. The vast majority of the race, whether savage or civilized, are secretly kind-hearted and shrink from inflicting pain, but in the presence of the aggressive and pitiless minority they don't dare to assert themselves. Think
35 of it! One kind-hearted creature spies upon another, and sees to it that he loyally helps in iniquities which revolt both of them. Speaking as an expert, I know that ninety-nine out of a hundred of your race were strongly against the killing of witches when that foolishness was first agitated by a handful of pious lunatics in the long ago. And I know that even to-day, after ages of
40 transmitted prejudice and silly teaching, only one person in twenty puts any real heart into the harrying of a witch. And yet apparently everybody hates witches and wants them killed. Some day a handful will rise up on the other side and make the most noise—perhaps even a single daring man with a big voice and a determined front will do it—and in a week all the sheep will
45 wheel and follow him, and witch-hunting will come to a sudden end.

"Monarchies, aristocracies, and religions are all based upon that large defect in your race—the individual's distrust of his neighbor, and his desire, for safety's or comfort's sake, to stand well in his neighbor's eye. These institutions will always remain, and always flourish, and always oppress you, affront you, and degrade you, because you will always be and remain slaves of minorities. There was never a country where the majority of the people were in their secret hearts loyal to any of these institutions."

I did not like to hear our race called sheep, and said I did not think they were.

"Still, it is true, lamb," said Satan. "Look at you in war—what mutton you are, and how ridiculous!"

"In war? How?"

"There has never been a just one, never an honorable one—on the part of the instigator of the war. I can see a million years ahead, and this rule will never change in so many as half a dozen instances. The loud little handful—as usual—will shout for the war. The pulpit will—warily and cautiously—object—at first; the great, big, dull bulk of the nation will rub its sleepy eyes and try to make out why there should be a war, and will say, earnestly and indignantly, "It is unjust and dishonorable, and there is no necessity for it." Then the handful will shout louder. A few fair men on the other side will argue and reason against the war with speech and pen, and at first will have a hearing and be applauded; but it will not last long; those others will outshout them, and presently the anti-war audiences will thin out and lose popularity. Before long you will see this curious thing: the speakers stoned from the platform, and free speech strangled by hordes of furious men who in their secret hearts are still at one with those stoned speakers—as earlier—but do not dare to say so. And now the whole nation—pulpit and all—will take up the war-cry, and shout itself hoarse, and mob any honest man who ventures to open his mouth; and presently such mouths will cease to open. Next the statesmen will invent cheap lies, putting the blame upon the nation that is attacked, and every man will be glad of those conscience-soothing falsities, and will diligently study them, and refuse to examine any refutations of them; and thus he will by and by convince himself that the war is just, and will thank God for the better sleep he enjoys after this process of grotesque self-deception."

CHAPTER X

Days and days went by now, and no Satan. It was dull without him. But the astrologer, who had returned from his excursion to the moon, went about the village, braving public opinion, and getting a stone in the middle of his back now and then when some witch-hater got a safe chance to throw it and dodge out of sight. Meantime two influences had been working well for Marget. That Satan, who was quite indifferent to her, had stopped going to her house after a visit or two had hurt her pride, and she had set herself the task of banishing him from her heart. Reports of Wilhelm Meidling's dissipation brought to her from time to time by old Ursula had touched her with remorse, jealousy of Satan being the cause of it; and so now, these two matters working upon her together, she was getting a good profit out of the combination—her interest in Satan was steadily cooling, her interest in Wilhelm as steadily warming. All that was needed to complete her conversion was that Wilhelm should brace up and do something that should cause favorable talk and incline the public toward him again.

The opportunity came now. Marget sent and asked him to defend her uncle
5 in the approaching trial, and he was greatly pleased, and stopped drinking and began his preparations with diligence. With more diligence than hope, in fact, for it was not a promising case. He had many interviews in his office with Seppi and me, and threshed out our testimony pretty thoroughly, thinking to find some valuable grains among the chaff, but the harvest was poor, of
10 course.

If Satan would only come! That was my constant thought. He could invent some way to win the case, for he had said it would be won, so he necessarily knew how it could be done. But the days dragged on, and still he did not come. Of course I did not doubt that it would win, and that Father Peter
15 would be happy for the rest of his life, since Satan had said so; yet I knew I should be much more comfortable if he would come and tell us how to manage it. It was getting high time for Father Peter to have a saving change toward happiness, for by general report he was worn out with his imprisonment and the ignominy that was burdening him, and was like to die of his
20 miseries unless he got relief soon.

At last the trial came on, and the people gathered from all around to witness it; among them many strangers from considerable distances. Yes, everybody was there except the accused. He was too feeble in body for the strain. But Marget was present, and keeping up her hope and her spirit the best she
25 could. The money was present, too. It was emptied on the table, and was handled and caressed and examined by such as were privileged.

The astrologer was put in the witness-box. He had on his best hat and robe for the occasion.

Question. You claim that this money is yours?
30   *Answer.* I do.

Q. How did you come by it?

A. I found the bag in the road when I was returning from a journey.

Q. When?

A. More than two years ago.
35   *Q.* What did you do with it?

A. I brought it home and hid it in a secret place in my observatory, intending to find the owner if I could.

Q. You endeavored to find him?

A. I made diligent inquiry during several months, but nothing came of it.
40   *Q.* And then?

A. I thought it not worth while to look further, and was minded to use the money in finishing the wing of the foundling-asylum connected with the priory and nunnery. So I took it out of its hiding-place and counted it to see if any of it was missing. And then—
45   *Q.* Why do you stop? Proceed.

A. I am sorry to have to say this, but just as I had finished and was restoring the bag to its place, I looked up and there stood Father Peter behind me.

Several murmured. "That looks bad," but others answered, "Ah, but he is such a liar!"

Q. That made you uneasy?

A. No; I thought nothing of it at the time, for Father Peter often came to me unannounced to ask for a little help in his need.   5

Marget blushed crimson at hearing her uncle falsely and impudently charged with begging, especially from one he had always denounced as a fraud, and was going to speak, but remembered herself in time and held her peace.

Q. Proceed.

A. In the end I was afraid to contribute the money to the foundling-asylum,   10
but elected to wait yet another year and continue my inquiries. When I heard of Father Peter's find I was glad, and no suspicion entered my mind; when I came home a day or two later and discovered that my own money was gone I still did not suspect until three circumstances connected with Father Peter's good fortune struck me as being singular coincidences.   15

Q. Pray name them.

A. Father Peter had found his money in a path—I had found mine in a road. Father Peter's find consisted exclusively of gold ducats—mine also. Father Peter found eleven hundred and seven ducats—I exactly the same.

This closed his evidence, and certainly it made a strong impression on the   20
house; one could see that.

Wilhelm Meidling asked him some questions, then called us boys, and we told our tale. It made the people laugh, and we were ashamed. We were feeling pretty badly, anyhow, because Wilhelm was hopeless, and showed it. He was doing as well as he could, poor young fellow, but nothing was in his   25
favor, and such sympathy as there was was now plainly not with his client. It might be difficult for court and people to believe the astrologer's story, considering his character, but it was almost impossible to believe Father Peter's. We were already feeling badly enough, but when the astrologer's lawyer said he believed he would not ask us any questions—for our story was a little deli-   30
cate and it would be cruel for him to put any strain upon it—everybody tittered, and it was almost more than we could bear. Then he made a sarcastic little speech, and got so much fun out of our tale, and it seemed so ridiculous and childish and every way impossible and foolish, that it made everybody laugh till the tears came; and at last Marget could not keep up her courage   35
any longer, but broke down and cried, and I was so sorry for her.

Now I noticed something that braced me up. It was Satan standing along-side of Wilhelm! And there was such a contrast!—Satan looked so confident, had such a spirit in his eyes and face, and Wilhelm looked so depressed and despondent. We two were comfortable now, and judged that he would testify   40
and persuade the bench and the people that black was white and white black, or any other color he wanted it. We glanced around to see what the strangers in the house thought of him, for he was beautiful, you know—stunning, in fact—but no one was noticing him; so we knew by that that he was invisible.

The lawyer was saying his last words; and while he was saying them Satan   45
began to melt into Wilhelm. He melted into him and disappeared; and then there was a change, when his spirit began to look out of Wilhelm's eyes.

That lawyer finished quite seriously, and with dignity. He pointed to the money and said:

"The love of it is the root of all evil. There it lies, the ancient tempter, newly red with the shame of its latest victory—the dishonor of a priest of
5 God and his two poor juvenile helpers in crime. If it could but speak, let us hope that it would be constrained to confess that of all its conquests this was the basest and the most pathetic."

He sat down. Wilhelm rose and said:

"From the testimony of the accuser I gather that he found this money in a
10 road more than two years ago. Correct me, sir, if I misunderstood you."

The astrologer said his understanding of it was correct.

"And the money so found was never out of his hands thenceforth up to a certain definite date—the last day of last year. Correct me, sir, if I am wrong."

The astrologer nodded his head. Wilhelm turned to the bench and said:
15 "If I prove that this money here was not that money, then it is not his?"

"Certainly not; but this is irregular. If you had such a witness it was your duty to give proper notice of it and have him here to—" He broke off and began to consult with the other judges. Meantime that other lawyer got up excited and began to protest against allowing new witnesses to be brought
20 into the case at this late stage.

The judges decided that his contention was just and must be allowed.

"But this is not a new witness," said Wilhelm. "It has already been partly examined. I speak of the coin."

"The coin? What can the coin say?"
25 "It can say it is not the coin that the astrologer once possessed. It can say it was not in existence last December. By its date it can say this."

And it was so! There was the greatest excitement in the court while that lawyer and the judges were reaching for coins and examining them and exclaiming. And everybody was full of admiration of Wilhelm's brightness in
30 happening to think of that neat idea. At last order was called and the court said:

"All of the coins but four are of the date of the present year. The court tenders its sincere sympathy to the accused, and its deep regret that he, an innocent man, through an unfortunate mistake, has suffered the undeserved
35 humiliation of imprisonment and trial. The case is dismissed."

So the money could speak, after all, though that lawyer thought it couldn't. The court rose and almost everybody came forward to shake hands with Marget and congratulate her, and then to shake with Wilhelm and praise him; and Satan had stepped out of Wilhelm and was standing around look-
40 ing on full of interest, and people walking through him every which way, not knowing he was there. And Wilhelm could not explain why he only thought of the date on the coins at the last moment, instead of earlier; he said it just occurred to him all of a sudden, like an inspiration, and he brought it right out without any hesitation, for, although he didn't examine the coins, he
45 seemed, somehow, to know it was true. That was honest of him, and like

3. **love of it** . . . —cf. I Tim. 6:10.

him; another would have pretended he had thought of it earlier, and was keeping it back for a surprise.

He had dulled down a little now; not much, but still you could notice that he hadn't that luminous look in his eyes that he had while Satan was in him. He nearly got it back, though, for a moment when Marget came and praised him and thanked him and couldn't keep him from seeing how proud she was of him. The astrologer went off dissatisfied and cursing, and Solomon Isaacs gathered up the money and carried it away. It was Father Peter's for good and all, now.

Satan was gone. I judged that he had spirited himself away to the jail to tell the prisoner the news; and in this I was right. Marget and the rest of us hurried thither at our best speed, in a great state of rejoicing.

Well, what Satan had done was this: he had appeared before that poor prisoner, exclaiming, "The trial is over, and you stand forever disgraced as a thief—by verdict of the court!"

The shock unseated the old man's reason. When we arrived, ten minutes later, he was parading pompously up and down and delivering commands to this and that and the other constable or jailer, and calling them Grand Chamberlain, and Prince This and Prince That, and Admiral of the Fleet, Field Marshal in Command, and all such fustian, and was as happy as a bird. He thought he was Emperor!

Marget flung herself on his breast and cried, and indeed everybody was moved almost to heartbreak. He recognized Marget, but could not understand why she should cry. He patted her on the shoulder and said:

"Don't do it, dear; remember, there are witnesses, and it is not becoming in the Crown Princess. Tell me your trouble—it shall be mended; there is nothing the Emperor cannot do." Then he looked around and saw old Ursula with her apron to her eyes. He was puzzled at that, and said, "And what is the matter with you?"

Through her sobs she got out words explaining that she was distressed to see him—"so." He reflected over that a moment, then muttered, as if to himself, "A singular old thing, the Dowager Duchess—means well, but is always snuffling and never able to tell what it is about. It is because she doesn't know." His eyes fell on Wilhelm. "Prince of India," he said, "I divine that it is you that the Crown Princess is concerned about. Her tears shall be dried; I will no longer stand between you; she shall share your throne; and between you you shall inherit mine. There, little lady, have I done well? You can smile now—isn't it so?"

He petted Marget and kissed her, and was so contented with himself and with everybody that he could not do enough for us all, but began to give away kingdoms and such things right and left, and the least that any of us got was a principality. And so at last, being persuaded to go home, he marched in imposing state; and when the crowds along the way saw how it gratified him to be hurrahed at, they humored him to the top of his desire, and he responded with condescending bows and gracious smiles and often stretched out a hand and said, "Bless you, my people!"

As pitiful a sight as ever I saw. And Marget, and old Ursula crying all the way.

On my road home I came upon Satan, and reproached him with deceiving me with that lie. He was not embarrassed, but said, quite simply and com-
5 posedly:

"Ah, you mistake; it was the truth. I said he would be happy the rest of his days, and he will, for he will always think he is the Emperor, and his pride in it and his joy in it will endure to the end. He is now, and will remain, the one utterly happy person in this empire."

10   "But the method of it, Satan, the method! Couldn't you have done it without depriving him of his reason?"

It was difficult to irritate Satan, but that accomplished it.

"What an ass you are!" he said. "Are you so unobservant as not to have found out that sanity and happiness are an impossible combination? No sane
15 man can be happy, for to him life is real, and he sees what a fearful thing it is. Only the mad can be happy, and not many of those. The few that imagine themselves kings or gods are happy, the rest are no happier than the sane. Of course, no man is entirely in his right mind at any time, but I have been referring to the extreme cases. I have taken from this man that trumpery
20 thing which the race regards as a Mind; I have replaced his tin life with a silver-gilt fiction; you see the result—and you criticize! I said I would make him permanently happy, and I have done it. I have made him happy by the only means possible to his race—and you are not satisfied!" He heaved a discouraged sigh, and said, "It seems to me that this race is hard to
25 please."

There it was, you see. He didn't seem to know any way to do a person a favor except by killing him or making a lunatic out of him. I apologized, as well as I could; but privately I did not think much of his processes—at that time.

30   Satan was accustomed to say that our race lived a life of continuous and un-interrupted self-deception. It duped itself from cradle to grave with shams and delusions which it mistook for realities, and this made its entire life a sham. Of the score of fine qualities which it imagined it had and was vain of, it really possessed hardly one. It regarded itself as gold, and was only brass. One
35 day when he was in this vein he mentioned a detail—the sense of humor. I cheered up then, and took issue. I said we possessed it.

"There spoke the race!" he said, "always ready to claim what it hasn't got and mistake its ounce of brass filings for a ton of gold-dust. You have a mongrel perception of humor, nothing more; a multitude of you possess that. This
40 multitude see the comic side of a thousand low-grade and trivial things—broad incongruities, mainly; grotesqueries, absurdities, evokers of the horse-laugh. The ten thousand high-grade comicalities which exist in the world are sealed from their dull vision. Will a day come when the race will detect the funniness of these juvenilities and laugh at them—and by laughing at them
45 destroy them? For your race, in its poverty, has unquestionably one really

21. silver-gilt—silver-foil varnished with yellow lacquer.

effective weapon—laughter. Power, money, persuasion, supplication, persecution—these can lift at a colossal humbug—push it a little—weaken it a little,
century by century; but only laughter can blow it to rags and atoms at a blast.
Against the assault of laughter nothing can stand. You are always fussing and
fighting with your other weapons. Do you ever use that one? No, you leave   5
it lying rusting. As a race, do you ever use it at all? No, you lack sense and
the courage."

We were traveling at the time and stopped at a little city in India and
looked on while a juggler did his tricks before a group of natives. They were
wonderful, but I knew Satan could beat that game, and I begged him to show   10
off a little, and he said he would. He changed himself into a native in turban
and breech-cloth, and very considerately conferred on me a temporary knowledge of the language.

The juggler exhibited a seed, covered it with earth in a small flower-pot,
then put a rag over the pot; after a minute the rag began to rise; in ten min-   15
utes it had risen a foot; then the rag was removed and a little tree was exposed, with leaves upon it and ripe fruit. We ate the fruit, and it was good.
But Satan said:

"Why do you cover the pot? Can't you grow the tree in the sunlight?"

"No," said the juggler, "no one can do that."   20

"You are only an apprentice; you don't know your trade. Give me the seed.
I will show you." He took the seed and said, "What shall I raise from it?"

"It is a cherry seed; of course you will raise a cherry."

"Oh no; that is a trifle; any novice can do that. Shall I raise an orange-tree
from it?"   25

"Oh yes!" and the juggler laughed.

"And shall I make it bear other fruits as well as oranges?"

"If God wills!" and they all laughed.

Satan put the seed in the ground, put a handful of dust on it, and said,
"Rise!"   30

A tiny stem shot up and began to grow, and grew so fast that in five minutes it was a great tree, and we were sitting in the shade of it. There was a
murmur of wonder, then all looked up and saw a strange and pretty sight,
for the branches were heavy with fruits of many kinds and colors—oranges,
grapes, bananas, peaches, cherries, apricots, and so on. Baskets were brought   35
and the unlading of the tree began; and the people crowded around Satan
and kissed his hand, and praised him, calling him the prince of jugglers. The
news went about the town, and everybody came running to see the wonder—
and they remembered to bring baskets, too. But the tree was equal to the occasion; it put out new fruits as fast as any were removed; baskets were filled   40
by the score and by the hundred, but always the supply remained undiminished. At last a foreigner in white linen and sun-helmet arrived and exclaimed,
angrily:

"Away from here! Clear out, you dogs; the tree is on my lands and is my
property."   45

The natives put down their baskets and made humble obeisance. Satan made humble obeisance, too, with his fingers to his forehead, in the native way, and said:

"Please let them have their pleasure for an hour, sir—only that, and no longer. Afterward you may forbid them, and you will still have more fruit than you and the state together can consume in a year."

This made the foreigner very angry, and he cried out, "Who are you, you vagabond, to tell your betters what they may do and what they mayn't!" and he struck Satan with his cane and followed this error with a kick.

The fruits rotted on the branches, and the leaves withered and fell. The foreigner gazed at the bare limbs with the look of one who is surprised, and not gratified. Satan said:

"Take good care of the tree, for its health and yours are bound together. It will never bear again, but if you tend it well it will live long. Water its roots once in each hour every night—and do it yourself; it must not be done by proxy, and to do it in daylight will not answer. If you fail only once in any night, the tree will die, and you likewise. Do not go home to your own country any more—you would not reach there; make no business or pleasure engagements which require you to go outside your gate at night—you cannot afford the risk; do not rent or sell this place—it would be injudicious."

The foreigner was proud and wouldn't beg but I thought he looked as if he would like to. While he stood gazing at Satan we vanished away and landed in Ceylon.

I was sorry for that man; sorry Satan hadn't been his customary self and killed him or made him a lunatic. It would have been a mercy. Satan overheard the thought, and said:

"I would have done it but for his wife, who has not offended me. She is coming to him presently from their native land, Portugal. She is well, but has not long to live and has been yearning to see him and persuade him to go back with her next year. She will die without knowing he can't leave that place."

"He won't tell her?"

"He? He will not trust that secret with any one; he will reflect that it could be revealed in sleep, in the hearing of some Portuguese guest's servant some time or other."

"Did none of those natives understand what you said to him?"

"None of them understood, but he will always be afraid that some of them did. That fear will be torture to him, for he has been a harsh master to them. In his dreams he will imagine them chopping his tree down. That will make his days uncomfortable—I have already arranged for his nights."

It grieved me, though not sharply, to see him take such a malicious satisfaction in his plans for this foreigner.

"Does he believe what you told him, Satan?"

"He thought he didn't, but our vanishing helped. The tree, where there had been no tree before—that helped. The insane and uncanny variety of fruits —the sudden withering—all these things are helps. Let him think as he may, reason as he may, one thing is certain, he will water the tree. But between

30. place?—The question mark is in the original text.

this and night he will begin his changed career with a very natural precaution—for him."

"What is that?"

"He will fetch a priest to cast out the tree's devil. You are such a humorous race—and don't suspect it."   5

"Will he tell the priest?"

"No. He will say a juggler from Bombay created it, and that he wants the
juggler's devil driven out of it, so that it will thrive and be fruitful again.
The priest's incantations will fail; then the Portuguese will give up that
scheme and get his watering-pot ready."   10

"But the priest will burn the tree. I know it; he will not allow it to remain."

"Yes, and anywhere in Europe he would burn the man, too. But in India
the people are civilized, and these things will not happen. The man will drive
the priest away and take care of the tree."

I reflected a little, then said, "Satan, you have given him a hard life, I   15
think."

"Comparatively. It must not be mistaken for a holiday."

We flitted from place to place around the world as we had done before,
Satan showing me a hundred wonders, most of them reflecting in some way
the weakness and triviality of our race. He did this now every few days—not 20
out of malice—I am sure of that—it only seemed to amuse and interest him,
just as a naturalist might be amused and interested by a collection of ants.

CHAPTER XI

For as much as a year Satan continued these visits, but at last he came less
often, and then for a long time he did not come at all. This always made me   25
lonely and melancholy. I felt that he was losing interest in our tiny world and
might at any time abandon his visits entirely. When one day he finally came
to me I was overjoyed, but only for a little while. He had come to say good-by,
he told me, and for the last time. He had investigations and undertakings in
other corners of the universe, he said, that would keep him busy for a longer 30
period than I could wait for his return.

"And you are going away, and will not come back any more?"

"Yes," he said. "We have comraded long together, and it has been pleasant
—pleasant for both; but I must go now, and we shall not see each other any
more."   35

"In this life, Satan, but in another? We shall meet in another, surely?"

Then, all tranquilly and soberly, he made the strange answer, *"There is no
other."*

A subtle influence blew upon my spirit from his, bringing with it a vague,
dim, but blessed and hopeful feeling that the incredible words might be true— 40
even *must* be true.

"Have you never suspected this, Theodor?"

"No. How could I? But if it can only be true—"

"It is true."

A gust of thankfulness rose in my breast, but a doubt checked it before it   45

could issue in words, and I said, "But—but—we have seen that future life—
seen it in its actuality, and so—"

"It was a vision—it had no existence."

I could hardly breathe for the great hope that was struggling in me. "A
5   vision?—a vi—"

"Life itself is only a vision, a dream."

It was electrical. By God! I had had that very thought a thousand times in
my musings!

"Nothing exists; all is a dream. God—man—the world—the sun, the moon,
10 the wilderness of stars—a dream, all a dream; they have no existence. *Nothing exists save empty space—and you!"*

"I!"

"And you are not you—you have no body, no blood, no bones, you are but
a *thought.* I myself have no existence; I am but a dream—your dream, crea-
15 ture of your imagination. In a moment you will have realized this, then you
will banish me from your visions and I shall dissolve into the nothingness out
of which you made me. . . .

"I am perishing already—I am failing—I am passing away. In a little while
you will be alone in shoreless space, to wander its limitless solitudes without
20 friend or comrade forever—for you will remain a *thought,* the only existent
thought, and by your nature inextinguishable, indestructible. But I, your poor
servant, have revealed you to yourself and set you free. Dream other dreams,
and better!

"Strange! that you should not have suspected years ago—centuries, ages,
25 eons, ago!—for you have existed, companionless, through all the eternities.
Strange, indeed, that you should not have suspected that your universe and
its contents were only dreams, visions, fiction! Strange, because they are so
frankly and hysterically insane—like all dreams: a God who could make good
children as easily as bad, yet preferred to make bad ones; who could have
30 made every one of them happy, yet never made a single happy one; who
made them prize their bitter life, yet stingily cut it short; who gave his angels
eternal happiness unearned, yet required his other children to earn it; who
gave his angels painless lives, yet cursed his other children with biting miseries and maladies of mind and body; who mouths justice and invented hell—
35 mouths mercy and invented hell—mouths Golden Rules, and forgiveness multiplied by seventy times seven, and invented hell; who mouths morals to other
people and has none himself; who frowns upon crimes, yet commits them all;
who created man without invitation, then tries to shuffle the responsibility
for man's acts upon man, instead of honorably placing it where it belongs,
40 upon himself; and finally, with altogether divine obtuseness, invites this poor,
abused slave to worship him! . . .

"You perceive, *now,* that these things are all impossible except in a dream.
You perceive that they are pure and puerile insanities, the silly creations of
an imagination that is not conscious of its freaks—in a word, that they are
45 a dream, and you the maker of it. The dream-marks are all present; you
should have recognized them earlier.

36. seventy times seven—*cf.* Matt. 18:22.

"It is true, that which I have revealed to you; there is no God, no universe, no human race, no earthly life, no heaven, no hell. It is all a dream—a grotesque and foolish dream. Nothing exists but you. And you are but a *thought* —a vagrant thought, a useless thought, a homeless thought, wandering forlorn among the empty eternities!"   5

He vanished and left me appalled, for I knew, and realized, that all he had said was true.

WILLIAM DEAN HOWELLS

1837-1920

I. THE YOUNG PRINTER AND TRAVELER (1837–1866)

1837 Born at Martin's Ferry, Ohio, March 1, the second son of William Cooper Howells and Mary Dean Howells. His father was a country printer and druggist of bookish inclination.

1845 Began typesetting at nine and was reading Goldsmith, Irving, Cervantes, and others.

1849 Removed to Dayton, Ohio, and a year later to a log cabin on Little Miami River.

1851–1859 Newspaper experience as compositor on the *Ohio State Journal* (Columbus), reporter for the Cincinnati *Gazette,* and editor of the *Ohio State Journal.*

1860 Contributed poems to the *Atlantic Monthly.* Published with J. J. Piatt *Poems of Two Friends.* First trip to Boston, where he met Lowell and other New England Brahmins. Published campaign life of Lincoln.

1861–1865 Consul in Venice, Italy.

1862 Married Elinor Mead of Vermont, whom he had met in Columbus.

1865 Editorial assistant on the *Nation.*

II. THE BOSTON PERIOD (1866–1885)

1866 Published *Venetian Life,* and became assistant editor of the *Atlantic Monthly* under James T. Fields.

1867 Published *Italian Journeys,* his second travel-book.

1871–1881 Editor of the *Atlantic Monthly,* to which he brought such diversified contributors as Henry James and Mark Twain.

1872 Published *Their Wedding Journey,* his first book of fiction, based on travel.

1873 *Poems* and *A Chance Acquaintance* published.

1875 *A Foregone Conclusion* published.

1876 *The Parlor Car* published, first of a dozen farces like *The Mouse Trap* (1889).

1879 Published *The Lady of the Aroostook,* a novel of social conflicts and contrasts.

1880 Published *The Undiscovered Country,* unsympathetic treatment of spiritualism.

1881 Published *Doctor Breen's Practice* and *A Modern Instance,* containing Howells's best-drawn heroine. For the next four years Howells was abroad.

1884 Published *The Rise of Silas Lapham,* his best-known work.

III. PERIOD OF SOCIAL INTEREST (1885–1900)

1885 Moved to New York and began service on the staff of *Harper's Magazine,* conducting "The Editor's Study," 1886-91, in which he battled for realism. Social interest promoted by reading Tolstoy.

1886 Published *Indian Summer,* which Howells thought his best work.

1888 Published *April Hopes* and *Annie Kilburn.*

1890 Published *A Hazard of New Fortunes,* which incorporates his social criticism and has a large variety of distinctly drawn characters. *A Boy's Town* published.

1891 Published *Criticism and Fiction,* manual of realism, drawn from "The Editor's Study."

1892–1893 Published *The Quality of Mercy* and *The World of Chance,* further studies of social injustice.

1894 Published *A Traveler from Altruria,* utopian romance, influenced by William Morris.

1897 Published *The Landlord at Lion's Head.*

IV. THE DEAN OF AMERICAN LETTERS (1900–1920)

1900–1920 "Easy Chair" essayist in *Harper's Magazine.*

1900 Published *Literary Friends and Acquaintances.*

1902 Published *The Kentons.*

1907 Published *Through the Eye of the Needle,* sequel to *A Traveler from Altruria.*

1910 Published *My Mark Twain,* his tribute to an intimate friendship.

1915 Became a member of the National Institute of Arts and Letters.

1916 Published *The Leatherwood God* in which he returned to a mid-Western background.

1920 Died May 11.

BIOGRAPHIES: Consult the autobiographic books, *A Boy's Town* (1890); *My Year in a Log-Cabin* (1893); *Impressions and Experiences,* 1896; *Literary Friends and Acquaintances,* 1900; and *Years of My Youth* (1916)—all Harper. Alexander Harvey, *William Dean Howells,* Huebsch, 1917 (socialistic); D. G. Cooke, *William Dean Howells: A Critical Study,* Dutton, 1922; O. W. Firkins, *William Dean Howells: A Study,* Harvard University Press, 1924; *Life in Letters of William Dean Howells,* ed. by Mildred Howells, Doubleday, Doran, 1928, 2 vols. See also *Mark Twain's Letters,* Harper, 1917, 2 vols.; *Letters of Henry James,* Scribner, 1920, 2 vols. For articles and essays interpreting Howells, see the bibliography in the *Literary History of the United States,* listed below.

BIBLIOGRAPHY AND EDITIONS: For bibliography consult William M. Gibson and George Arms, *A Bibliography of William Dean Howells,* New York Public Library, 1948; *Literary History of the United States,* Vol. III, pp. 571-76.

No complete collected edition of Howells's writings exists; Harper and Houghton Mifflin publish uniform editions of the more important works. *The Rise of Silas Lapham* is available in various reprints. *Selected Writings,* ed. with an introduction by Henry S. Commager, Random House, 1950, is workmanlike.

Howells was the most conspicuous American figure in the advance of realism during the last quarter of the nineteenth century. In season and out he decried the mawkish sentimentalism that had prevailed in fiction for decades, and led the way in substituting therefor a more honest, if less sensational, transcript of manners. Reticent as his realism seems today, it fought the initial battles for such candor as we now possess.

But Howells's achievements do not stop there. He could tell a story; and he was the first of the moderns to manage the art of dialogue. He understood, as few others have understood, how to present the conflict between different grades of sophistication. In his works events follow one another with the delays and indirections attending such matters in actual life. If he does not picture heart-rending decisions, such are not often exacted in life. The higher ironics of existence he describes as well as did his beloved Jane Austen.

As he grew older his sense of social justice deepened, his vision looking, as he said, "toward the happiness of the whole human family." His criticism of American life for the discrepancy between its democratic profession and its undemocratic practice demonstrated beyond cavil the effectiveness of the novel as a socializing instrument.

CRITICISM AND FICTION

This book, published in 1891, contains Howells's view of the art of fiction, his opposition to the romantic fiction then current, and his advocacy of realism, democracy, decency, in American novels. The selection opens with a passage from the *Philosophical Inquiry into the Origin of Our Ideas of the Sublime and Beautiful* (1756) by Edmund Burke (1729-1797), author also of *Conciliation with the American Colonies* (1775).

II

. . . "As FOR those called critics," the author says, "they have generally sought the rule of the arts in the wrong place; they have sought among poems, pictures, engravings, statues, and buildings; but art can never give the rules that
5   make an art. This is, I believe, the reason why artists in general, and poets principally, have been confined in so narrow a circle; they have been rather imitators of one another than of nature. Critics follow them, and therefore can do little as guides. I can judge but poorly of anything while I measure it by no other standard than itself. The true standard of the arts is in every man's
10 power; and an easy observation of the most common, sometimes of the meanest things, in nature will give the truest lights, where the greatest sagacity and industry that slights such observation must leave us in the dark, or, what is worse, amuse and mislead us by false lights."

If this should happen to be true—and it certainly commends itself to accept-
15 ance—it might portend an immediate danger to the vested interests of criticism, only that it was written a hundred years ago; and we shall probably have the "sagacity and industry that slights the observation" of nature long enough yet to allow most critics the time to learn some more useful trade than criticism as they pursue it. Nevertheless, I am in hopes that the communistic era in taste
20 foreshadowed by Burke is approaching, and that it will occur within the lives of men now overawed by the foolish old superstition that literature and art are anything but the expression of life, and are to be judged by any other test

than that of their fidelity to it. The time is coming, I hope, when each new author, each new artist, will be considered, not in his proportion to any other author or artist, but in his relation to the human nature, known to us all, which it is his privilege, his high duty, to interpret. "The true standard of the artist is in every man's power" already, as Burke says; Michelangelo's "light of the 5 piazza," the glance of the common eye, is and always was the best light on a statue; Goethe's "boys and blackbirds" have in all ages been the real connoisseurs of berries; but hitherto the mass of common men have been afraid to apply their own simplicity, naturalness, and honesty to the appreciation of the beautiful. They have always cast about for the instruction of some one who professed 10 to know better, and who browbeat wholesome common-sense into the self-distrust that ends in sophistication. They have fallen generally to the worst of this bad species, and have been "amused and misled" (how pretty that quaint old use of amuse is!) "by the false lights" of critical vanity and self-righteousness. They have been taught to compare what they see and what they read, not 15 with the things that they have observed and known, but with the things that some other artist or writer has done. Especially if they have themselves the artistic impulse in any direction they are taught to form themselves, not upon life, but upon the masters who became masters only by forming themselves upon life. The seeds of death are planted in them, and they can produce only the 20 still-born, the academic. They are not told to take their work into the public square and see if it seems true to the chance passer, but to test it by the work of the very men who refused and decried any other test of their own work. The young writer who attempts to report the phrase and carriage of every-day life, who tries to tell just how he has heard men talk and seen them look, is made 25 to feel guilty of something low and unworthy by the stupid people who would like to have him show how Shakespeare's men talked and looked, or Scott's, or Thackeray's, or Balzac's, or Hawthorne's, or Dickens's; he is instructed to idealize his personages, that is, to take the life-likeness out of them, and put the book-likeness into them. He is approached in the spirit of the wretched pedantry 30 into which learning, much or little, always decays when it withdraws itself and stands apart from experience in an attitude of imagined superiority, and which would say with the same confidence to the scientists: "I see that you are looking at a grasshopper there which you have found in the grass, and I suppose you intend to describe it. Now don't waste your time and sin against culture in that 35 way. I've got a grasshopper here, which has been evolved at considerable pains and expense out of the grasshopper in general; in fact, it's a type. It's made up of wire and card-board, very prettily painted in a conventional tint, and it's perfectly indestructible. It isn't very much like a real grasshopper, but it's a great deal nicer, and it's served to represent the notion of a grasshopper ever since 40 man emerged from barbarism. You may say that it's artificial. Well, it is artificial; but then it's ideal too; and what you want to do is to cultivate the ideal. You'll find the books full of my kind of grasshopper, and scarcely a trace of yours in any of them. The thing that you are proposing to do is commonplace;

5. **Michelangelo**—Michelangelo Buonarroti (1475-1564), Florentine sculptor, painter, poet. 7. **Goethe**—Johann Wolfgang von Goethe (1749-1832), German poet and critic. 14. **amuse**—that is, in the sense of beguile

but if you say that it isn't commonplace, for the very reason that it hasn't been done before, you'll have to admit that it's photographic."

As I said, I hope the time is coming when not only the artist, but the common, average man, who always "has the standard of the arts in his power,"
5 will have also the courage to apply it, and will reject the ideal grasshopper wherever he finds it, in science, in literature, in art, because it is not "simple, natural, and honest," because it is not like a real grasshopper. But I will own that I think the time is yet far off, and that the people who have been brought up on the ideal grasshopper, the heroic grasshopper, the impassioned grass-
10 hopper, the self-devoted, adventureful, good old romantic card-board grasshopper, must die out before the simple, honest, and natural grasshopper can have a fair field. I am in no haste to compass the end of these good people, whom I find in the mean time very amusing. It is delightful to meet one of them, either in print or out of it—some sweet elderly lady or excellent gentleman
15 whose youth was pastured on the literature of thirty or forty years ago—and to witness the confidence with which they preach their favorite authors as all the law and the prophets. They have commonly read little or nothing since, or, if they have, they have judged it by a standard taken from these authors, and never dreamed of judging it by nature; they are destitute of the documents
20 in the case of the later writers; they suppose that Balzac was the beginning of realism, and that Zola is its wicked end; they are quite ignorant, but they are ready to talk you down, if you differ from them, with an assumption of knowledge sufficient for any occasion. The horror, the resentment, with which they receive any question of their literary saints is genuine; you descend at once very
25 far in the moral and social scale, and anything short of offensive personality is too good for you; it is expressed to you that you are one to be avoided, and put down even a little lower than you have naturally fallen.

These worthy persons are not to blame; it is part of their intellectual mission to represent the petrifaction of taste, and to preserve an image of a smaller and
30 cruder and emptier world than we now live in, a world which was feeling its way towards the simple, the natural, the honest, but was a good deal "amused and misled" by lights now no longer mistakable for heavenly luminaries. They belong to a time, just passing away, when certain authors were considered authorities in certain kinds, when they must be accepted entire and not ques-
35 tioned in any particular. Now we are beginning to see and to say that no author is an authority except in those moments when he held his ear close to Nature's lips and caught her very accent. These moments are not continuous with any authors in the past, and they are rare with all. Therefore I am not afraid to say now that the greatest classics are sometimes not at all great, and
40 that we can profit by them only when we hold them, like our meanest contemporaries, to a strict accounting, and verify their work by the standard of the arts which we all have in our power, the simple, the natural, and the honest.

Those good people, those curious and interesting if somewhat musty back-

---

20-21. Balzac . . . Zola—Honoré de Balzac (1799-1850), whose serried novels, known as the *Comédie humaine,* preceded the Rougon-Macquart series of Emile Zola (1840-1902) as an orderly panoramic picture of French society.

numbers, must always have a hero, an idol of some sort, and it is droll to find
Balzac, who suffered from their sort such bitter scorn and hate for his realism
while he was alive, now become a fetich in his turn, to be shaken in the faces
of those who will not blindly worship him. But it is no new thing in the history
of literature: (whatever is established is sacred with those who do not think.) 5
At the beginning of the century, when romance was making the same fight
against effete classicism which realism is making to-day against effete romanticism, the Italian poet Monti declared that "the romantic was the cold grave
of the Beautiful," just as the realistic is now supposed to be. The romantic of
that day and the real of this are in certain degree the same. Romanticism then 10
sought, as realism seeks now, to widen the bounds of sympathy, to level every
barrier against æsthetic freedom, to escape from the paralysis of tradition. It
exhausted itself in this impulse; and it remained for realism to assert that
fidelity to experience and probability of motive are essential conditions of a
great imaginative literature. It is not a new theory, but it has never before 15
universally characterized literary endeavor. When realism becomes false to itself,
when it heaps up facts merely, and maps life instead of picturing it, realism will
perish too. Every true realist instinctively knows this, and it is perhaps the reason
why he is careful of every fact, and feels himself bound to express or to indicate
its meaning at the risk of over-moralizing. In life he finds nothing insignificant; 20
all tells for destiny and character; nothing that God has made is contemptible.
He cannot look upon human life and declare this thing or that thing unworthy
of notice, any more than the scientist can declare a fact of the material world
beneath the dignity of his inquiry. He feels in every nerve the equality of things
and the unity of men; his soul is exalted, not by vain shows and shadows and 25
ideals, but by realities, in which alone the truth lives. In criticism it is his business to break the images of false gods and misshapen heroes, to take away the
poor silly toys that many grown people would still like to play with. He cannot
keep terms with Jack the Giant-killer or Puss in Boots, under any name or in
any place, even when they reappear as the convict Vautrec, or the Marquis de 30
Montrivaut, or the Sworn Thirteen Noblemen. He must say to himself that
Balzac, when he imagined these monsters, was not Balzac, he was Dumas;
he was not realistic, he was romantic.

XV

Which brings us again, after this long way about, to the divine Jane and her 35
novels, and that troublesome question about them. She was great and they
were beautiful, because she and they were honest, and dealt with nature nearly a
hundred years ago as realism deals with it to-day. Realism is nothing more and
nothing less than the truthful treatment of material, and Jane Austen was the

8. **Monti**—Vincenzo Monti (1754-1828), Italian poet, author of a Dantesque epic, *Bassvilliana,*
a "classical" tragedy, *Aristodemo,* and other works. **30-31. Vautrec . . . Noblemen**—characters in Balzac's *Comédie humaine.* **32. Dumas**—Alexandre Dumas the elder (1802-1870), author
of *The Three Musketeers* and *The Count of Monte Cristo.* **35. Which brings**—Howells had
asked in Section XIII, "How . . . could people who had once known the simple verity, the refined
perfection of Miss Austen, enjoy anything less refined and less perfect?" By way of answer he cited
passages from the Spanish novelist Valdés.

first and the last of the English novelists to treat material with entire truthfulness. Because she did this, she remains the most artistic of the English novelists, and alone worthy to be matched with the great Scandinavian and Slavic and Latin artists. It is not a question of intellect, or not wholly that. The English
5 have mind enough; but they have not taste enough; or, rather, their taste has been perverted by their false criticism, which is based upon personal preference, and not upon principle; which instructs a man to think that what he likes is good, instead of teaching him first to distinguish what is good before he likes it. The art of fiction, as Jane Austen knew it, declined from her through Scott,
10 and Bulwer, and Dickens, and Charlotte Brontë, and Thackeray, and even George Eliot, because the mania of romanticism had seized upon all Europe, and these great writers could not escape the taint of their time; but it has shown few signs of recovery in England, because English criticism, in the presence of the Continental masterpieces, has continued provincial and special
15 and personal, and has expressed a love and a hate which had to do with the quality of the artist rather than the character of his work. It was inevitable that in their time the English romanticists should treat, as Señor Valdés says, "the barbarous customs of the Middle Ages, softening and disfiguring them, as Walter Scott and his kind did"; that they should "devote themselves to falsify-
20 ing nature, refining and subtilizing sentiment, and modifying psychology after their own fancy," like Bulwer and Dickens, as well as like Rousseau and Madame de Staël, not to mention Balzac, the worst of all that sort at his worst. This was the natural course of the disease; but it really seems as if it were their criticism that was to blame for the rest: not, indeed, for the performance of this
25 writer or that, for criticism can never affect the actual doing of a thing; but for the esteem in which this writer or that is held through the perpetuation of false ideals. The only observer of English middle-class life since Jane Austen worthy to be named with her was not George Eliot, who was first ethical and then artistic, who transcended her in everything but the form and method most
30 essential to art, and there fell hopelessly below her. It was Anthony Trollope who was most like her in simple honesty and instinctive truth, as unphilosophized as the light of common day; but he was so warped from a wholesome ideal as to wish at times to be like the caricaturist Thackeray, and to stand about in his scene, talking it over with his hands in his pockets, interrupting the action,
35 and spoiling the illusion in which alone the truth of art resides. Mainly, his instinct was too much for his ideal, and with a low view of life in its civic relations and a thoroughly bourgeois soul, he yet produced works whose beauty is surpassed only by the effect of a more poetic writer in the novels of Thomas Hardy. Yet if a vote of English criticism even at this late day, when all conti-
40 nental Europe has the light of æsthetic truth, could be taken, the majority against these artists would be overwhelmingly in favor of a writer who had so little artistic sensibility, that he never hesitated on any occasion, great or small,

17. **Valdés**—Armando Palacio Valdés (1853-1938), Spanish realistic novelist. *Cf.* Howells, *My Literary Passions*. 22. **Madame de Staël**—the Baronne de Staël-Holstein (1766-1817), French novelist. 30. **Trollope**—Anthony Trollope (1815-1882), English novelist of Barsetshire stories. 39. **Hardy**—Thomas Hardy (1840-1928), English novelist and poet of Wessex, who published *Tess of the D'Urbervilles* the year in which *Criticism and Fiction* appeared.

to make a foray among his characters, and catch them up to show them to the reader and tell him how beautiful or ugly they were; and cry out over their amazing properties.

Doubtless the ideal of those poor islanders will be finally changed. If the truth could become a fad it would be accepted by all their "smart people," but truth is something rather too large for that; and we must await the gradual advance of civilization among them. Then they will see that their criticism has misled them; and that it is to this false guide they owe, not precisely the decline of fiction among them, but its continued debasement as an art.

XVI

"How few materials," says Emerson, "are yet used by our arts! The mass of creatures and of qualities are still hid and expectant," and to break new ground is still one of the uncommonest and most heroic of the virtues. The artists are not alone to blame for the timidity that keeps them in the old furrows of the worn-out fields; most of those whom they live to please, or live by pleasing, prefer to have them remain there; it wants rare virtue to appreciate what is new, as well as to invent it; and the "easy things to understand" are the conventional things. This is why the ordinary English novel, with its hackneyed plot, scenes, and figures, is more comfortable to the ordinary American than an American novel, which deals, at its worst, with comparatively new interests and motives. To adjust one's self to the enjoyment of these costs an intellectual effort, and an intellectual effort is what no ordinary person likes to make. It is only the extraordinary person who can say, with Emerson: "I ask not for the great, the remote, the romantic. . . . I embrace the common; I sit at the feet of the familiar and the low. . . . Man is surprised to find that things near are not less beautiful and wondrous than things remote. . . . The perception of the worth of the vulgar is fruitful in discoveries. . . . The foolish man wonders at the unusual, but the wise man at the usual. . . . To-day always looks mean to the thoughtless; but to-day is a king in disguise. . . . Banks and tariffs, the newspaper and caucus, Methodism and Unitarianism, are flat and dull to dull people, but rest on the same foundations of wonder as the town of Troy and the temple of Delphos."

Perhaps we ought not to deny their town of Troy and their temple of Delphos to the dull people; but if we ought, and if we did, they would still insist upon having them. An English novel, full of titles and rank, is apparently essential to the happiness of such people; their weak and childish imagination is at home in its familiar environment; they know what they are reading; the fact that it is hash many times warmed over reassures them; whereas a story of our own life, honestly studied and faithfully represented, troubles them with varied misgiving. They are not sure that it is literature; they do not feel that it is good society; its characters, so like their own, strike them as commonplace; they say they do not wish to know such people.

11. **Emerson**—The passages in this paragraph are from "The American Scholar" and "The Poet."

Everything in England is appreciable to the literary sense, while the sense of the literary worth of things in America is still faint and weak with most people, with the vast majority who "ask for the great, the remote, the romantic," who cannot "embrace the common," cannot "sit at the feet of the familiar and the
5 low," in the good company of Emerson. We are all, or nearly all, struggling to be distinguished from the mass, and to be set apart in select circles and upper classes like the fine people we have read about. We are really a mixture of the plebeian ingredients of the whole world; but that is not bad; our vulgarity consists in trying to ignore "the worth of 'the vulgar," in believing that the
10 superfine is better.

XXI

It used to be one of the disadvantages of the practice of romance in America, which Hawthorne more or less whimsically lamented, that there were so few shadows and inequalities in our broad level of prosperity; and it is one of the
15 reflections suggested by Dostoïevsky's novel, *The Crime and the Punishment,* that whoever struck a note so profoundly tragic in American fiction would do a false and mistaken thing—as false and as mistaken in its way as dealing in American fiction with certain nudities which the Latin peoples seem to find edifying. Whatever their deserts, very few American novelists have been led out
20 to be shot, or finally exiled to the rigors of a winter at Duluth; and in a land where journeyman carpenters and plumbers strike for four dollars a day the sum of hunger and cold is comparatively small, and the wrong from class to class has been almost inappreciable, though all this is changing for the worse. Our novelists, therefore, concern themselves with the more smiling aspects of
25 life, which are the more American, and seek the universal in the individual rather than the social interests. It is worth while, even at the risk of being called commonplace, to be true to our well-to-do actualities; the very passions themselves seem to be softened and modified by conditions which formerly at least could not be said to wrong any one, to cramp endeavor, or to cross lawful desire.
30 Sin and suffering and shame there must always be in the world, I suppose, but I believe that in this new world of ours it is still mainly from one to another one, and oftener still from one to one's self. We have death, too, in America, and a great deal of disagreeable and painful disease, which the multiplicity of our patent medicines does not seem to cure; but this is tragedy that
35 comes in the very nature of things, and is not peculiarly American, as the large, cheerful average of health and success and happy life is. It will not do to boast, but it is well to be true to the facts, and to see that, apart from these purely mortal troubles, the race here has enjoyed conditions in which most of the ills that have darkened its annals might be averted by honest work and unselfish
40 behavior.

Fine artists we have among us, and right-minded as far as they go; and we must not forget this at evil moments when it seems as if all the women had taken to writing hysterical improprieties, and some of the men were trying to be

---

13. **Hawthorne**—in the Preface to *The Marble Faun.* 15. **Dostoïevsky's**—Feodor Mikhailovich Dostoevsky (1821-1881), Russian novelist, whose *Crime and Punishment* was published in 1866.

at least as hysterical in despair of being as improper. If we kept to the complexion of a certain school—which sadly needs a school-master—we might very
well be despondent; but after all, that school is not representative of our conditions or our intentions. Other traits are much more characteristic of our life
and our fiction. In most American novels, vivid and graphic as the best of   5
them are, the people are segregated if not sequestered, and the scene is sparsely
populated. The effect may be in instinctive response to the vacancy of our social
life, and I shall not make haste to blame it. There are few places, few occasions
among us, in which a novelist can get a large number of polite people together,
or at least keep them together. Unless he carries a snap-camera his picture of   10
them has no probability; they affect one like the figures perfunctorily associated
in such deadly old engravings as that of "Washington Irving and his Friends."
Perhaps it is for this reason that we excel in small pieces with three or four
figures, or in studies of rustic communities, where there is propinquity if not
society. Our grasp of more urbane life is feeble; most attempts to assemble it in   15
our pictures are failures, possibly because it is too transitory, too intangible in
its nature with us, to be truthfully represented as really existent.

I am not sure that the Americans have not brought the short story nearer
perfection in the all-round sense than almost any other people, and for reasons
very simple and near at hand. It might be argued from the national hurry and   20
impatience that it was a literary form peculiarly adapted to the American
temperament, but I suspect that its extraordinary development among us is
owing much more to more tangible facts. The success of American magazines,
which is nothing less than prodigious, is only commensurate with their excellence. Their sort of success is not only from the courage to decide which ought   25
to please, but from the knowledge of what does please; and it is probable that,
aside from the pictures, it is the short stories which please the readers of our
best magazines. The serial novels they must have, of course; but rather more of
course they must have short stories, and by operation of the law of supply and
demand, the short stories, abundant in quantity and excellent in quality, are   30
forthcoming because they are wanted. By another operation of the same law,
which political economists have more recently taken account of, the demand follows the supply, and short stories are sought for because there is a proven ability
to furnish them, and people read them willingly because they are usually very
good. The art of writing them is now so disciplined and diffused with us that   35
there is no lack either for the magazines or for the newspaper "syndicates"
which deal in them almost to the exclusion of the serials.

An interesting fact in regard to the different varieties of the short story among
us is that the sketches and studies by the women seem faithfuller and more
realistic than those of the men, in proportion to their number. Their tendency   40
is more distinctly in that direction, and there is a solidity, an honest observation,
in the work of such women, which often leaves little to be desired. I should,

---

10. **snap-camera**—kodak; *cf.* snapshot. 12. **"Washington Irving and his Friends"**—
Howells refers to a famous drawing by F. O. C. Darley (1822-1888), engraved by Thomas Oldham
Barlow (1824-1889), London, 1864, and widely popular in America. A reproduction can be seen
in *The Colophon,* Part 20. **42. women**—In the first edition Howells here named Mrs. Cooke, Miss
Murfree, Miss Wilkins (Mrs. Freeman), and Miss Jewett.

upon the whole, be disposed to rank American short stories only below those of such Russian writers as I have read, and I should praise rather than blame their free use of our different local parlances, or "dialects," as people call them. I like this because I hope that our inherited English may be constantly freshened and
5 revived from the native sources which our literary decentralization will help to keep open, and I will own that as I turn over novels coming from Philadelphia, from New Mexico, from Boston, from Tennessee, from rural New England, from New York, every local flavor of diction gives me courage and pleasure. Alphonse Daudet, in a conversation with H. H. Boyesen said, speaking of
10 Tourguenief, "What a luxury it must be to have a great big untrodden barbaric language to wade into! We poor fellows who work in the language of an old civilization, we may sit and chisel our little verbal felicities, only to find in the end that it is a borrowed jewel we are polishing. The crown-jewels of our French tongue have passed through the hands of so many generations of
15 monarchs that it seems like presumption on the part of any late-born pretender to attempt to wear them."

This grief is, of course, a little whimsical, yet it has a certain measure of reason in it, and the same regret has been more seriously expressed by the Italian poet Aleardi:

20   "Muse of an aged people, in the eve
            Of fading civilization, I was born.
            . . . . . . Oh, fortunate,
            My sisters, who in the heroic dawn
            Of races sung! To them did destiny give
25   The virgin fire and chaste ingenuousness
            Of their land's speech; and, reverenced, their hands
            Ran over potent strings."

It will never do to allow that we are at such a desperate pass in English, but something of this divine despair we may feel too in thinking of "the spacious
30 times of great Elizabeth," when the poets were trying the stops of the young language, and thrilling with the surprises of their own music. We may comfort ourselves, however, unless we prefer a luxury of grief by remembering that no language is ever old on the lips of those who speak it, no matter how decrepit it drops from the pen. We have only to leave our studies, editorial and other,
35 and go into the shops and fields to find the "spacious times" again; and from the beginning Realism, before she had put on her capital letter, had divined this near-at-hand truth along with the rest. Lowell, almost the greatest and finest realist who ever wrought in verse, showed us that Elizabeth was still Queen where he heard Yankee farmers talk. One need not invite slang into the
40 company of its betters, though perhaps slang has been dropping its "s" and becoming language ever since the world began, and is certainly sometimes delight-

9. Daudet—Alphonse Daudet (1840-1897), French novelist. 9. Boyesen—H. H. Boyesen (1848-1895), Norwegian-American scholar and realistic novelist. 10. Tourguenief—Ivan Turgenev (1818-1883), Russian novelist. 19. Aleardi—Aleardo Aleardi (1812-1878), Italian poet and patriot. The passage in verse appears in Howells' Modern Italian Poets (1887). 29-30. "the spacious . . . Elizabeth"—from the second stanza of Tennyson's "A Dream of Fair Women"; divine despair is also from Tennyson, the second lyric of Bk. IV of The Princess. 37. Lowell —The reference here is to Lowell's use of dialect in The Biglow Papers and his defence thereof.

ful and forcible beyond the reach of the dictionary. I would not have any one go about for new words, but if one of them came aptly, not to reject its help. For our novelists to try to write Americanly, from any motive, would be a dismal error, but being born Americans, I would have them use "Americanisms" whenever these serve their turn; and when their characters speak, I should 5 like to hear them speak true American, with all the varying Tennesseean, Philadelphian, Bostonian, and New York accents. If we bother ourselves to write what the critics imagine to be "English," we shall be priggish and artificial, and still more so if we make our Americans talk "English." There is also this serious disadvantage about "English," that if we wrote the best "English" in the world, 10 probably the English themselves would not know it, or, if they did, certainly would not own it. It has always been supposed by grammarians and purists that a language can be kept as they find it; but languages, while they live, are perpetually changing. God apparently meant them for the common people; and the common people will use them freely as they use other gifts of God. On their 15 lips our continental English will differ more and more from the insular English, and I believe that this is not deplorable, but desirable.

In fine, I would have our American novelists be as American as they unconsciously can. Matthew Arnold complained that he found no "distinction" in our life, and I would gladly persuade all artists intending greatness in any 20 kind among us that the recognition of the fact pointed out by Mr. Arnold ought to be a source of inspiration to them, and not discouragement. We have been now some hundred years building up a state on the affirmation of the essential equality of men in their rights and duties, and whether we have been right or been wrong the gods have taken us at our word, and have responded to us with 25 a civilization in which there is no "distinction" perceptible to the eye that loves and values it. Such beauty and such grandeur as we have is common beauty, common grandeur, or the beauty and grandeur in which the quality of solidarity so prevails that neither distinguishes itself to the disadvantage of anything else. It seems to me that these conditions invite the artist to the study 30 and the appreciation of the common, and to the portrayal in every art of those finer and higher aspects which unite rather than sever humanity, if he would thrive in our new order of things. The talent that is robust enough to front the every-day world and catch the charm of its work-worn, care-worn, brave, kindly face, need not fear the encounter, though it seems terrible to the sort nurtured in 35 the superstition of the romantic, the bizarre, the heroic, the distinguished, as the things alone worthy of painting or carving or writing. The arts must become democratic, and then we shall have the expression of America in art; and the reproach which Arnold was half right in making us shall have no justice in it any longer; we shall be "distinguished." 40

XXIII

One of the great newspapers the other day invited the prominent American authors to speak their minds upon a point in the theory and practice of fiction

19. Matthew Arnold—(1822-1888); *Discourses in America* (1885).

which had already vexed some of them. It was the question of how much or how little the American novel ought to deal with certain facts of life which are not usually talked of before young people, and especially young ladies. Of course the question was not decided, and I forget just how far the balance
5 inclined in favor of a larger freedom in the matter. But it certainly inclined that way; one or two writers of the sex which is somehow supposed to have purity in its keeping (as if purity were a thing that did not practically concern the other sex, preoccupied with serious affairs) gave it a rather vigorous tilt to that side. In view of this fact it would not be the part of prudence to make
10 an effort to dress the balance; and indeed I do not know that I was going to make any such effort. But there are some things to say, around and about the subject, which I should like to have some one else say, and which I may myself possibly be safe in suggesting.

One of the first of these is the fact, generally lost sight of by those who censure
15 the Anglo-Saxon novel for its prudishness, that it is really not such a prude after all; and that if it is sometimes apparently anxious to avoid those experiences of life not spoken of before young people, this may be an appearance only. Sometimes a novel which has this shuffling air, this effect of truckling to propriety, might defend itself, if it could speak for itself, by saying that such experiences
20 happened not to come within its scheme, and that, so far from maiming or mutilating itself in ignoring them, it was all the more faithfully representative of the tone of modern life in dealing with love that was chaste, and with passion so honest that it could be openly spoken of before the tenderest society bud at dinner. It might say that the guilty intrigue, the betrayal, the extreme flirtation
25 even, was the exceptional thing in life, and unless the scheme of the story necessarily involved it, that it would be bad art to lug it in, and as bad taste as to introduce such topics in a mixed company. It could say very justly that the novel in our civilization now always addresses a mixed company, and that the vast majority of the company are ladies, and that very many, if not most, of
30 these ladies are young girls. If the novel were written for men and for married women alone, as in continental Europe, it might be altogether different. But the simple fact is that it is not written for them alone among us, and it is a question of writing, under cover of our universal acceptance, things for young girls to read which you would be put out-of-doors for saying to them, or of frankly
35 giving notice of your intention, and so cutting yourself off from the pleasure— and it is a very high and sweet one—of appealing to these vivid, responsive intelligences, which are none the less brilliant and admirable because they are innocent.

One day a novelist who liked, after the manner of other men, to repine at
40 his hard fate, complained to his friend, a critic, that he was tired of the restriction he had put upon himself in this regard; for it is a mistake, as can be readly shown, to suppose that others impose it. "See how free those French fellows are!" he rebelled. "Shall we always be shut up to our tradition of decency?"

"Do you think it's much worse than being shut up to their tradition of in-
45 decency?" said his friend.

Then that novelist began to reflect, and he remembered how sick the invariable motive of the French novel made him. He perceived finally that, convention for convention, ours was not only more tolerable, but on the whole was truer to life, not only to its complexion, but also to its texture. No one will pretend that there is not vicious love beneath the surface of our society; if he did, the fetid explosions of the divorce trials would refute him; but if he pretended that it was in any just sense characteristic of our society, he could be still more easily refuted. Yet it exists, and it is unquestionably the material of tragedy, the stuff from which intense effects are wrought. The question, after owning this fact, is whether these intense effects are not rather cheap effects. I incline to think they are, and I will try to say why I think so, if I may do so without offence. The material itself, the mere mention of it, has an instant fascination; it arrests, it detains, till the last word is said, and while there is anything to be hinted. This is what makes a love intrigue of some sort all but essential to the popularity of any fiction. Without such an intrigue the intellectual equipment of the author must be of the highest, and then he will succeed only with the highest class of readers. But any author who will deal with a guilty love intrigue holds all readers in his hand, the highest with the lowest, as long as he hints the slightest hope of the smallest potential naughtiness. He need not at all be a great author; he may be a very shabby wretch, if he has but the courage or the trick of that sort of thing. The critics will call him "virile" and "passionate"; decent people will be ashamed to have been limned by him; but the low average will only ask another chance of flocking into his net. If he happens to be an able writer, his really fine and costly work will be unheeded, and the lure to the appetite will be chiefly remembered. There may be other qualities which make reputations for other men, but in his case they will count for nothing. He pays this penalty for his success in that kind; and every one pays some such penalty who deals with some such material.

But I do not mean to imply that his case covers the whole ground. So far as it goes, though, it ought to stop the mouths of those who complain that fiction is enslaved to propriety among us. It appears that of a certain kind of impropriety it is free to give us all it will, and more. But this is not what serious men and women writing fiction mean when they rebel against the limitations of their art in our civilization. They have no desire to deal with nakedness, as painters and sculptors freely do in the worship of beauty; or with certain facts of life, as the stage does, in the service of sensation. But they ask why, when the conventions of the plastic and histrionic arts liberate their followers to the portrayal of almost any phase of the physical or of the emotional nature, an American novelist may not write a story on the lines of *Anna Karénina* or *Madame Bovary*. They wish to touch one of the most serious and sorrowful problems of life in the spirit of Tolstoy and Flaubert, and they ask why they may not. At one time, they remind us, the Anglo-Saxon novelist did deal with such problems—De Foe in his spirit, Richardson in his, Goldsmith in his. At what moment did our fiction lose this privilege? In what fatal hour did the Young Girl arise and seal the lips of Fiction, with a touch of her finger, to some of the most vital interests of life?

Whether I wished to oppose them in their aspiration for greater freedom, or

37. **Anna Karénina**—realistic Russian novel by Leo Tolstoy, published 1875-78. 38. **Madame Bovary**—naturalistic French novel by Gustave Flaubert, published 1857.

whether I wished to encourage them, I should begin to answer them by saying that the Young Girl has never done anything of the kind. The manners of the novel have been improving with those of its readers; that is all. Gentlemen no longer swear or fall drunk under the table, or abduct young ladies and shut
5 them up in lonely country-houses, or so habitually set about the ruin of their neighbors' wives, as they once did. Generally, people now call a spade an agricultural implement; they have not grown decent without having also grown a little squeamish, but they have grown comparatively decent; there is no doubt about that. They require of a novelist whom they respect unquestionable proof
10 of his seriousness, if he proposes to deal with certain phases of life; they require a sort of scientific decorum. He can no longer expect to be received on the ground of entertainment only; he assumes a higher function, something like that of a physician or a priest, and they expect him to be bound by laws as sacred as those of such professions; they hold him solemnly pledged not to
15 betray them or abuse their confidence. If he will accept the conditions, they give him their confidence, and he may then treat to his greater honor, and not at all to his disadvantage, of such experiences, such relations of men and women as George Eliot treats in *Adam Bede,* in *Daniel Deronda,* in *Romola,* in almost all her books; such as Hawthorne treats in *The Scarlet Letter;* such as Dickens
20 treats in *David Copperfield;* such as Thackeray treats in *Pendennis,* and glances at in every one of his fictions; such as most of the masters of English fiction have at some time treated more or less openly. It is quite false or quite mistaken to suppose that our novels have left untouched these most important realities of life. They have only not made them their stock in trade; they have kept a
25 true perspective in regard to them; they have relegated them in their pictures of life to the space and place they occupy in life itself, as we know it in England and America. They have kept a correct proportion, knowing perfectly well that unless the novel is to be a map, with everything scrupulously laid down in it, a faithful record of life in far the greater extent could be made to the exclusion of
30 guilty love and all its circumstances and consequences.

I justify them in this view not only because I hate what is cheap and meretricious, and hold in peculiar loathing the cant of the critics who require "passion" as something in itself admirable and desirable in a novel, but because I prize fidelity in the historian of feeling and character. Most of these
35 critics who demand "passion" would seem to have no conception of any passion but one. Yet there are several other passions: the passion of grief, the passion of avarice, the passion of pity, the passion of ambition, the passion of hate, the passion of envy, the passion of devotion, the passion of friendship; and all these have a greater part in the drama of life than the passion of love, and infinitely
40 greater than the passion of guilty love. Wittingly or unwittingly, English fiction and American fiction have recognized this truth, not fully, not in the measure it merits, but in greater degree than most other fiction.

A TRAVELER FROM ALTRURIA

In *A Traveler from Altruria* (1894) Howells questioned the American social order from the standpoint of a representative of an altruistic commonwealth. Howells had voiced his social consciousness in *A Hazard of New Fortunes* (1889), and under the influence of Edward Bellamy, Henry George, and particularly of William Morris he now ventured to extend his criticism in a symposium on the capitalistic order. In the opening pages, the traveling economist Aristides Homos arrives at the railway station, where he is embarrassed by the system of "tipping" for services.

I

. . . THE FAME of my friend's behavior at the station must have spread through the whole place; and everybody wished to know who he was. I answered simply he was a traveller from Altruria; and in some cases I went farther and explained that the Altrurians were peculiar.   5

In much less time than it seemed my friend found me; and then I had a little compensation for my suffering in his behalf. I could see that, whatever people said of him, they felt the same mysterious liking at sight of him that I had felt. He had made a little change in his dress, and I perceived that the women thought him not only good-looking, but well-dressed. They followed 10 him with their eyes as we went into the dining room, and I was rather proud of being with him, as if I somehow shared the credit of his clothes and good looks. The Altrurian himself seemed most struck with the head waiter, who showed us to our places, and while we were waiting for our supper I found a chance to explain that he was a divinity student from one of the fresh-water 15 colleges, and was serving here during his summer vacation. This seemed to interest my friend so much that I went on to tell him that many of the waitresses, whom he saw standing there subject to the order of the guests, were country school mistresses in the winter.

"Ah, that is as it should be," he said; "that is the kind of thing I expected to 20 meet with in America."

"Yes," I responded, in my flattered national vanity, "if America means anything at all it means the honor of work and the recognition of personal worth everywhere. I hope you are going to make a long stay with us. We like to have travellers visit us who can interpret the spirit of our institutions as well as 25 read their letter. As a rule, Europeans never quite get our point of view. Now a great many of these waitresses are ladies, in the true sense of the word; self-respectful, intelligent, refined, and fit to grace—"

I was interrupted by the noise my friend made in suddenly pushing back his chair and getting to his feet. "What's the matter?" I asked. "You're not ill, I 30 hope?"

But he did not hear me. He had run half down the dining hall toward the slender young girl who was bringing us our supper. I had ordered rather generously, for my friend had owned to a good appetite, and I was hungry myself with waiting for him, so that the tray the girl carried was piled up with 35

heavy dishes. To my dismay I saw, rather than heard at that distance, the Altrurian enter into a polite controversy with her, and then, as if overcoming all her scruples by sheer strength of will, possess himself of the tray and make off with it toward our table. The poor child followed him, blushing to her hair;
5 the head waiter stood looking helplessly on; the guests, who at that late hour were fortunately few, were simply aghast at the scandal; the Altrurian alone seemed to think his conduct the most natural thing in the world. He put the tray on the side table near us, and in spite of our waitress's protests insisted upon arranging the little bird-bath dishes before our plates. Then at last he
10 sat down, and the girl, flushed and tremulous, left the room, as I could not help suspecting, to have a good cry in the kitchen: She did not come back, and the head waiter, who was perhaps afraid to send another in her place, looked after our few wants himself. He kept a sharp eye on my friend, as if he were not quite sure he was safe, but the Altrurian resumed the conversation with all that
15 lightness of spirits which I noticed in him after he helped the porter with the baggage. I did not think it the moment to take him to task for what he had just done; I was not even sure that it was the part of a host to do so at all, and between the one doubt and the other I left the burden of the talk to him.

"What a charming young creature!" he began. "I never saw anything prettier
20 than the way she had of refusing my help, absolutely without coquetry or affectation of any kind. She is, as you said, a perfect lady, and she graces her work, as I am sure she would grace any exigency of life. She quite realizes my ideal of an American girl, and I see now what the spirit of your country must be from such an expression of it." I wished to tell him that while a country
25 school teacher who waits at table in a summer hotel is very much to be respected in her sphere, she is not regarded with that high honor which some other women command among us; but I did not find this very easy, after what I had said of our esteem for labor; and while I was thinking how I could hedge, my friend went on. "I liked England greatly, and I liked the English,
30 but I could not like the theory of their civilization, or the aristocratic structure of their society. It seemed to me iniquitous, for we believe that inequality and iniquity are the same in the last analysis."

At this I found myself able to say: "Yes, there is something terrible, something shocking, in the frank brutality with which Englishmen affirm the essential
35 inequality of men. The affirmation of the essential equality of men was the first point of departure with us, when we separated from them."

"I know," said the Altrurian. "How grandly it is expressed in your glorious Declaration."

"Ah, you have read our Declaration of Independence then?"
40 "Every Altrurian has read that," answered my friend.

"Well," I went on smoothly, and I hoped to render what I was going to say the means of enlightening him without offense concerning the little mistake he had just made with the waitress; "of course we don't take that in its closest literality."
45 "I don't understand you," he said.

"Why, you know it was rather the political than the social traditions of England that we broke with, in the revolution."

"How is that?" he returned. "Didn't you break with monarchy and nobility, and ranks and classes?"

"Yes, we broke with all those things."

"But I found them a part of the social as well as the political structure in England. You have no kings or nobles here. Have you any ranks or classes?"   5

"Well, not exactly in the English sense. Our ranks and classes, such as we have, are what I may call voluntary."

"Oh, I understand. I suppose that from time to time certain ones among you feel the need of serving, and ask leave of the commonwealth to subordinate themselves to the rest of the state, and perform all the lowlier offices in it. Such   10
persons must be held in peculiar honor. Is it something like that?"

"Well, no, I can't say it's quite like that. In fact, I think I'd better let you trust to your own observation of our life."

"But I'm sure," said the Altrurian, with a simplicity so fine that it was a long time before I could believe it quite real, "that I shall approach it so much more   15
intelligently with a little instruction from you. You say that your social divisions are voluntary. But do I understand that those who serve among you do not wish to do so?"

"Well, I don't suppose they would serve if they could help it," I replied.

"Surely," said the Altrurian with a look of horror, "you don't mean that   20
they are slaves."

"Oh, no! Oh, no!" I said; "the War put an end to that. We are all free, now, black and white."

"But if they do not wish to serve, and are not held in peculiar honor for serving—"   25

"I see that my word 'voluntary' has misled you," I put in. "It isn't the word exactly. The divisions among us are rather a process of natural selection. You will see, as you get better acquainted with the workings of our institutions, that there are no arbitrary distinctions here, but the fitness of the work for the man and the man for the work determines the social rank that each one holds."   30

"Ah, that is fine!" cried the Altrurian with a glow of enthusiasm. "Then I suppose that these intelligent young people who teach school in the winter and serve at table in the summer are in a sort of provisional state, waiting for the process of natural selection to determine whether they shall finally be teachers or waiters."   35

"Yes, it might be stated in some such terms," I assented, though I was not altogether easy in my mind. It seemed to me that I was not quite candid with this most candid spirit. I added, "You know we are a sort of fatalists here in America. We are great believers in the doctrine that it will all come out right in the end."   40

"Ah, I don't wonder at that," said the Altrurian, "if the process of natural selection works so perfectly among you as you say. But I am afraid I don't understand this matter of your domestic service yet. I believe you said that all honest work is honored in America. Then no social slight attaches to service, I suppose?"   45

27. natural selection—The Darwin-Spencer philosophy of natural selection enjoyed a wide vogue during the eighties, particularly as interpreted by John Fiske.

"Well, I can't say that, exactly. The fact is, a certain social slight does attach to service, and that is one reason why I don't quite like to have students wait at tables. It won't be pleasant for them to remember it in after life, and it won't be pleasant for their children to remember it."

5 "Then the slight would descend?"

"I think it would. One wouldn't like to think one's father or mother had been at service."

The Altrurian said nothing for a moment. Then he remarked, "So it seems that while all honest work is honored among you, there are some kinds of

10 honest work that are not honored so much as others."

"Yes."

"Why?"

"Because some occupations are more degrading than others."

"But why?" he persisted, as I thought a little unreasonably.

15 "Really," I said, "I think I must leave you to imagine."

"I am afraid I can't," he said sadly. "Then, if domestic service is degrading in your eyes, and people are not willingly servants among you, may I ask why any are servants?"

"It is a question of bread and butter. They are obliged to be."

20 "That is, they are forced to do work that is hateful and disgraceful to them because they cannot live without?"

"Excuse me," I said, not at all liking this sort of pursuit, and feeling it fair to turn even upon a guest who kept it up. "Isn't it so with you in Altruria?"

25 "It was so once," he admitted, "but not now. In fact, it is like a waking dream to find oneself in the presence of conditions here that we outlived so long ago."

There was an unconscious superiority in this speech that nettled me, and stung me to retort: "We do not expect to outlive them. We regard them as

30 final, and as indestructibly based in human nature itself."

"Ah," said the Altrurian with a delicate and caressing courtesy, "have I said something offensive?"

"Not at all," I hastened to answer. "It is not surprising that you do not get our point of view exactly. You will, by and by, and then, I think, you will

35 see that it is the true one. We have found that the logic of our convictions could not be applied to the problem of domestic service. It is everywhere a very curious and perplexing problem. The simple old solution of the problem was to own your servants; but we found that this was not consistent with the spirit of our free institutions. As soon as it was abandoned the anomaly began. We

40 had outlived the primitive period when the housekeeper worked with her domestics and they were her help, and were called so; and we had begun to have servants to do all the household work, and to call them so. This state of things never seemed right to some of our purest and best people. They fancied, as you seem to have done, that to compel people through their necessities to do

45 your hateful drudgery, and to wound and shame them with a name which every American instinctively resents, was neither republican nor Christian. Some of our thinkers tried to mend matters by making their domestics a part

of their families; and in the life of Emerson you'll find an amusing account of his attempt to have his servant eat at the same table with himself and his wife. It wouldn't work. He and his wife could stand it, but the servant couldn't."

I paused, for this was where the laugh ought to have come in. The Altrurian did not laugh, he merely asked: "Why?"   5

"Well, because the servant knew, if they didn't, that they were a whole world apart in their traditions, and were no more fit to associate than New Englanders and New Zealanders. In the mere matter of education—"

"But I thought you said that these young girls who wait at table here were teachers."   10

"Oh, I beg your pardon; I ought to have explained. By this time it had become impossible, as it now is, to get American girls to take service except on some such unusual terms as we have in a summer hotel; and the domestics were already ignorant foreigners, fit for nothing else. In such a place as this it isn't so bad. It is more as if the girls worked in a shop or a factory. They 15
command their own time, in a measure; their hours are tolerably fixed, and they have each other's society. In a private family they would be subject to order at all times, and they would have no social life. They would be in the family, but not of it. American girls understand this, and so they won't go out to service in the usual way. Even in a summer hotel the relation has its odious 20
aspects. The system of giving fees seems to me degrading to those who have to take them. To offer a student or a teacher a dollar for personal service—it isn't right, or I can't make it so. In fact, the whole thing is rather anomalous with us. The best that you can say of it is that it works, and we don't know what else to do."   25

"But I don't see yet," said the Altrurian, "just why domestic service is degrading in a country where all kinds of work are honored."

"Well, my dear fellow, I have done my best to explain. As I intimated before, we distinguish; and in the different kinds of labor we distinguish against domestic service. I dare say it is partly because of the loss of independence 30
which it involves. People naturally despise a dependent."

"Why?" asked the Altrurian, with that innocence of his which I was beginning to find rather trying.

"Why?" I retorted. "Because it implies weakness."

"And is weakness considered despicable among you?" he pursued.   35

"In every community it is despised practically, if not theoretically," I tried to explain. "The great thing that America has done is to offer the race an opportunity: the opportunity for any man to rise above the rest, and to take the highest place, if he is able." I had always been proud of this fact, and I thought I had put it very well, but the Altrurian did not seem much im- 40
pressed by it.

He said: "I do not see how it differs from any country of the past in that. But perhaps you mean that to rise carries with it an obligation to those below. 'If any is first among you, let him be your servant.' Is it something like that?"

"Well, it is not quite like that," I answered, remembering how very little 45

1. Emerson—See page 446 of Cabot's *Memoir of Ralph Waldo Emerson* (1887). 44. 'If any is first . . .' —*Cf.* Mark 9:35.

our self-made men as a class had done for others. "Everyone is expected to
look out for himself here. I fancy that there would be very little rising if men
were expected to rise for the sake of others, in America. How is it with you
in Altruria?" I demanded, hoping to get out of a certain discomfort I felt, in
5 that way. "Do your risen men generally devote themselves to the good of the
community after they get to the top?"

"There is no rising among us," he said, with what seemed a perception of
the harsh spirit of my question; and he paused a moment before he asked in
his turn, "How do men rise among you?"

10 "That would be rather a long story," I replied. "But putting it in the rough,
I should say that they rose by their talents, their shrewdness, their ability to seize
an advantage and turn it to their own account."

"And is that considered noble?"

"It is considered smart. It is considered at the worst far better than a dead
15 level of equality. Are all men equal in Altruria? Are they all alike gifted or
beautiful, or short or tall?"

"No, they are only equal in duties and in rights. But, as you said just now,
that is a very long story. Are they equal in nothing here?"

"They are equal in opportunities."

20 "Ah!" breathed the Altrurian, "I am glad to hear that."

I began to feel a little uneasy, and I was not quite sure that this last assertion of mine would hold water. Everybody but ourselves had now left the
dining room, and I saw the head waiter eying us impatiently. I pushed back
my chair and said, "I'm sorry to seem to hurry you, but I should like to show
25 you a very pretty sunset effect we have here before it is too dark. When we
get back, I want to introduce you to a few of my friends. Of course, I needn't
tell you that there is a good deal of curiosity about you, especially among the
ladies."

"Yes, I found that the case in England, largely. It was the women who cared
30 most to meet me. I understand that in America society is managed even more
by women than it is in England."

"It's entirely in their hands," I said, with the satisfaction we all feel in the
fact. "We have no other leisure class. The richest men among us are generally
hard workers; devotion to business is the rule; but as soon as a man reaches
35 the point where he can afford to pay for domestic service, his wife and daughters expect to be released from it to the cultivation of their minds and the
enjoyment of social pleasures. It's quite right. That is what makes them so
delightful to foreigners. You must have heard their praises chanted in England. The English find our men rather stupid, I believe; but they think our
40 women are charming."

"Yes, I was told that the wives of their nobility were sometimes Americans,"
said the Altrurian. "The English think that you regard such marriages as a
great honor, and that they are very gratifying to your national pride."

"Well, I suppose that is so in a measure," I confessed. "I imagine that it
45 will not be long before the English aristocracy derives as largely from American millionaires as from kings' mistresses. Not," I added virtuously, "that we
approve of aristocracy."

"No, I understand that," said the Altrurian. "I shall hope to get your point
of view in this matter more distinctly by and by. As yet, I'm a little vague
about it."

"I think I can gradually make it clear to you," I returned.

II

We left the hotel, and I began to walk my friend across the meadow toward
the lake. I wished him to see the reflection of the afterglow in its still waters,
with the noble lines of the mountain range that glassed itself there; the effect
is one of the greatest charms of that lovely region, the sojourn of the sweetest
summer in the world, and I am always impatient to show it to strangers.

We climbed the meadow wall and passed through a stretch of woods, to a
path leading down to the shore, and as we loitered along in the tender gloom
of the forest, the music of the hermit-thrushes rang all round us, like crystal
bells, like silver flutes, like the drip of fountains, like the choiring of still-eyed
cherubim. We stopped from time to time and listened, while the shy birds
sang unseen in their covert of shadows; but we did not speak till we emerged
from the trees and suddenly stood upon the naked knoll overlooking the lake.

Then I explained, "The woods used to come down to the shore here, and
we had their mystery and music to the water's edge; but last winter the owner
cut the timber off. It looks rather ragged now." I had to recognize the fact,
for I saw the Altrurian staring about him over the clearing, in a kind of horror. It was a squalid ruin, a graceless desolation, which not even the pitying
twilight could soften. The stumps showed their hideous mutilation everywhere; the brush had been burned, and the fires had scorched and blackened
the lean soil of the hill slope, and blasted it with sterility. A few weak saplings,
withered by the flames, drooped and straggled about; it would be a century
before the forces of nature could repair the waste.

"You say the owner did this," said the Altrurian. "Who is the owner?"

"Well, it does seem too bad," I answered evasively. "There has been a good
deal of feeling about it. The neighbors tried to buy him off before he began
the destruction, for they knew the value of the woods as an attraction to
summer-boarders; the city cottagers, of course, wanted to save them, and together they offered for the land pretty nearly as much as the timber was worth.
But he had got it into his head that the land here by the lake would sell for
building lots if it was cleared, and he could make money on that as well as
on the trees; and so they had to go. Of course, one might say that he was deficient in public spirit, but I don't blame him, altogether."

"No," the Altrurian assented, somewhat to my surprise, I confess.

I resumed, "There was no one else to look after his interests, and it was not
only his right but his duty to get the most he could for himself and his own,
according to his best light. That is what I tell people when they fall foul of
him for his want of public spirit."

"The trouble seems to be, then, in the system that obliges each man to be
the guardian of his own interests. Is that what you blame?"

"No, I consider it a very perfect system. It is based upon individuality, and we believe that individuality is the principle that differences civilized men from savages, from the lower animals, and makes us a nation instead of a tribe or a herd. There isn't one of us, no matter how much he censured this man's 5 want of public spirit, but would resent the slightest interference with his property rights. The woods were his; he had the right to do what he pleased with his own."

"Do I understand you that, in America, a man may do what is wrong with his own?"

10 "He may do anything with his own."

"To the injury of others?"

"Well, not in person or property. But he may hurt them in taste and sentiment as much as he likes. Can't a man do what he pleases with his own in Altruria?"

15 "No, he can only do right with his own."

"And if he tries to do wrong, or what the community thinks is wrong?"

"Then the community takes his own from him." Before I could think of anything to say to this he went on: "But I wish you would explain to me why it was left to this man's neighbors to try and get him to sell his portion of 20 the landscape?"

"Why, bless my soul!" I exclaimed, "who else was there? You wouldn't have expected to take up a collection among the summer-boarders?"

"That wouldn't have been so unreasonable; but I didn't mean that. Was there no provision for such an exigency in your laws? Wasn't the state em- 25 powered to buy him off at the full value of his timber and his land?"

"Certainly not," I replied. "That would be rank paternalism."

It began to get dark, and I suggested that we had better be going back to the hotel. The talk seemed already to have taken us away from all pleasure in the prospect; I said, as we found our way through the rich, balsam-scented 30 twilight of the woods, where one joy-haunted thrush was still singing, "You know that in America the law is careful not to meddle with a man's private affairs, and we don't attempt to legislate personal virtue."

"But marriage," he said, "surely you have the institution of marriage?"

I was really annoyed at this. I returned sarcastically, "Yes, I am glad to say 35 that there we can meet your expectation; we have marriage, not only consecrated by the church, but established and defended by the state. What has that to do with the question?"

"And you consider marriage," he pursued, "the citadel of morality, the fountain of all that is pure and good in your private life, the source of home 40 and the image of heaven?"

"There are some marriages," I said with a touch of our national humor, "that do not quite fill the bill, but that is certainly our ideal of marriage."

"Then why do you say that you have not legislated personal virtue in America?" he asked. "You have laws, I believe, against theft and murder and slan- 45 der and incest and perjury and drunkenness?"

"Why, certainly."

"Then it appears to me that you have legislated honesty, regard for human

life, regard for character, abhorrence of unnatural vice, good faith and sobriety.
I was told on the train coming up, by a gentleman who was shocked at the
sight of a man beating his horse, that you even had laws against cruelty to
animals."

"Yes, and I am happy to say that they are enforced to such a degree that a   5
man cannot kill a cat cruelly without being punished for it." The Altrurian
did not follow up his advantage, and I resolved not to be outdone in mag-
nanimity. "Come, I will own that you have the best of me on those points.
I must say you've trapped me very neatly, too; I can enjoy a thing of that
kind when it's well done, and I frankly knock under. But I had in mind   10
something altogether different when I spoke. I was thinking of those idealists
who want to bind us hand and foot, and render us the slaves of a state where
the most intimate relations of life shall be penetrated by legislation, and the
very hearthstone shall be a tablet of laws."

"Isn't marriage a rather intimate relation of life?" asked the Altrurian. "And   15
I understood that gentleman on the train to say that you had laws against
cruelty to children and societies established to see them enforced. You don't
consider such laws an invasion of the home, do you, or a violation of its im-
munities? I imagine," he went on, "that the difference between your civilization and ours is only one of degree, after all, and that America and Altruria   20
are really one at heart."

I thought his compliment a bit hyperbolical, but I saw that it was honestly
meant, and as we Americans are first of all patriots, and vain for our country
before we are vain for ourselves, I was not proof against the flattery it conveyed to me civically if not personally.   25

We were now drawing near the hotel, and I felt a certain glow of pleasure
in its gay effect, on the pretty knoll where it stood. In its artless and accidental
architecture it was not unlike one of our immense coastwise steamboats. The
twilight had thickened to dusk, and the edifice was brilliantly lighted with electrics, story above story, which streamed into the gloom around like the lights   30
of saloon and stateroom. The corner of wood making into the meadow hid the
station; there was no other building in sight; the hotel seemed riding at anchor
on the swell of a placid sea. I was going to call the Altrurian's attention to
this fanciful resemblance when I remembered that he had not been in our
country long enough to have seen a Fall River boat, and I made toward the   35
house without wasting the comparison upon him. But I treasured it up in my
own mind, intending some day to make a literary use of it.

The guests were sitting in friendly groups about the piazzas or in rows
against the walls, the ladies with their gossip and the gentlemen with their
cigars. The night had fallen cool after a hot day, and they all had the effect of   40
having cast off care with the burden of the week that was past and to be
steeping themselves in the innocent and simple enjoyment of the hour. They
were mostly middle-aged married folk, but some were old enough to have
sons and daughters among the young people who went and came in a long,
wandering promenade of the piazzas, or wove themselves through the waltz   45

35. **Fall River boat**—a line of steamships plying between Boston and New York and calling
in Narragansett Bay.

past the open windows of the great parlor; the music seemed one with the light that streamed far out on the lawn flanking the piazzas. Everyone was well dressed and comfortable and at peace, and I felt that our hotel was in some sort a microcosm of the republic.

5   We involuntarily paused, and I heard the Altrurian murmur, "Charming, charming! This is really delightful!"

"Yes, isn't it?" I returned, with a glow of pride. "Our hotel here is a type of the summer hotel everywhere; it's characteristic in not having anything characteristic about it; and I rather like the notion of the people in it being
10   so much like the people in all the others that you would feel yourself at home wherever you met such a company in such a house. All over the country, north and south, wherever you find a group of hills or a pleasant bit of water or a stretch of coast, you'll find some such refuge as this for our weary toilers. We began to discover some time ago that it would not do to cut open the
15   goose that laid our golden eggs, even if it looked like an eagle, and kept on perching on our banners just as if nothing had happened. We discovered that, if we continued to kill ourselves with hard work, there would be no Americans pretty soon."

The Altrurian laughed. "How delightfully you put it! How quaint! How
20   picturesque! Excuse me, but I can't help expressing my pleasure in it. Our own humor is so very different."

"Ah," I said; "what is your humor like?"

"I could hardly tell you, I'm afraid; I've never been much of a humorist myself."

25   Again a cold doubt of something ironical in the man went through me, but I had no means of verifying it, and so I simply remained silent, waiting for him to prompt me if he wished to know anything further about our national transformation from bees perpetually busy into butterflies occasionally idle. "And when you had made that discovery?" he suggested.

30   "Why, we're nothing if not practical, you know, and as soon as we made that discovery we stopped killing ourselves and invented the summer resort. There are very few of our business or professional men, now, who don't take their four or five weeks' vacation. Their wives go off early in the summer, and if they go to some resort within three or four hours of the city, the men
35   leave town Saturday afternoon and run out, or come up, and spend Sunday with their families. For thirty-eight hours or so, a hotel like this is a nest of happy homes."

"That is admirable," said the Altrurian. "You are truly a practical people. The ladies come early in the summer, you say?"

40   "Yes, sometimes in the beginning of June."

"What do they come for?" asked the Altrurian.

"What for? Why, for rest!" I retorted with some little temper.

"But I thought you told me awhile ago that as soon as a husband could af‑ ford it he relieved his wife and daughters from all household work."

45   "So he does."

"Then what do the ladies wish to rest from?"

"From care. It is not work alone that kills. They are not relieved from house‑

hold care even when they are relieved from household work. There is nothing
so killing as household care. Besides, the sex seems to be born tired. To be
sure, there are some observers of our life who contend that with the advance
of athletics among our ladies, with boating and bathing, and lawn-tennis and
mountain climbing and freedom from care, and these long summers of repose, 5
our women are likely to become as superior to the men physically as they now
are intellectually. It is all right. We should like to see it happen. It would be
part of the national joke?"

"Oh, have you a national joke?" asked the Altrurian. "But, of course! You
have so much humor. I wish you could give me some notion of it."   10

"Well, it is rather damaging to any joke to explain it," I replied, "and your
only hope of getting at ours is to live into it. One feature of it is the confusion
of foreigners at the sight of our men's willingness to subordinate themselves to
our women."

"Oh, I don't find that very bewildering," said the Altrurian. "It seems to me 15
a generous and manly trait of the American character. I'm proud to say that it
is one of the points at which your civilization and our own touch. There can be
no doubt that the influence of women in your public affairs must be of the
greatest advantage to you; it has been so with us."

I turned and stared at him, but he remained insensible to my astonishment, 20
perhaps because it was now too dark for him to see it. "Our women have no
influence in public affairs," I said quietly, after a moment.

"They haven't? Is it possible? But didn't I understand you to imply just
now that your women were better educated than your men?"

"Well, I suppose that, taking all sorts and conditions among us, the women 25
are as a rule better schooled, if not better educated."

"Then, apart from the schooling, they are not more cultivated?"

"In a sense you might say they were. They certainly go in for a lot of things:
art and music, and Browning and the drama, and foreign travel and psychology, and political economy and heaven knows what all. They have more leisure 30
for it; they have all the leisure there is, in fact; our young men have to go
into business. I suppose you may say our women are more cultivated than our
men; yes, I think there's no questioning that. They are the great readers
among us. We poor devils of authors would be badly off if it were not for our
women. In fact, no author could make a reputation among us without them. 35
American literature exists because American women appreciate it and love it."

"But surely your men read books?"

"Some of them; not many, comparatively. You will often hear a complacent
ass of a husband and father say to an author: 'My wife and daughters know
your books, but I can't find time for anything but the papers nowadays. I skim 40
them over at breakfast, or when I'm going in to business on the train.' He
isn't the least ashamed to say that he reads nothing but the newspapers."

"Then you think that it would be better for him to read books?"

"Well, in the presence of four or five thousand journalists with drawn scalping knives I should not like to say so. Besides, modesty forbids."   45

"No, but really," the Altrurian persisted, "you think that the literature of a
book is more carefully pondered than the literature of a daily newspaper?"

"I suppose even the four or five thousand journalists with drawn scalping knives would hardly deny that."

"And it stands to reason, doesn't it, that the habitual reader of carefully pondered literature ought to be more thoughtful than the readers of literature
5 which is not carefully pondered, and which they merely skim over on their way to business?"

"I believe we began by assuming the superior culture of our women, didn't we? You'll hardly find an American that isn't proud of it."

"Then," said the Altrurian, "if your women are generally better schooled
10 than your men, and more cultivated and more thoughtful, and are relieved of household work in such great measure, and even of domestic cares, why have they no part in your public affairs?"

I laughed, for I thought I had my friend at last. "For the best of all possible reasons; they don't want it."

15 "Ah, that's no reason," he returned. "Why don't they want it?"

"Really," I said, out of all patience, "I think I must let you ask the ladies themselves," and I turned and moved again toward the hotel, but the Altrurian gently detained me.

"Excuse me," he began.

20 "No, no," I said:

> 'The feast is set, the guests are met,
> May'st hear the merry din.'

Come in and see the young people dance!"

"Wait," he entreated, "tell me a little more about the old people first. This
25 digression about the ladies has been very interesting, but I thought you were going to speak of the men here. Who are they, or rather, what are they?"

"Why, as I said before, they are all business men and professional men; people who spend their lives in studies and counting rooms and offices, and have come up here for a few weeks or a few days of well-earned repose. They
30 are of all kinds of occupations: they are lawyers and doctors and clergymen and merchants and brokers and bankers. There's hardly any calling you won't find represented among them. As I was thinking just now, our hotel is a sort of microcosm of the American republic."

"I am most fortunate in finding you here, where I can avail myself of your
35 intelligence in making my observations of your life under such advantageous circumstances. It seems to me that with your help I might penetrate the fact of American life, possess myself of the mystery of your national joke, without stirring beyond the piazza of your hospitable hotel," said my friend. I doubted it, but one does not lightly put aside a compliment like that to one's intelli-
40 gence, and I said I should be very happy to be of use to him. He thanked me, and said, "Then, to begin with, I understand that these gentlemen are here because they are all overworked."

"Of course. You can have no conception of how hard our business men and our professional men work. I suppose there is nothing like it anywhere else in
45 the world. But, as I said before, we are beginning to find that we cannot burn

21-22. 'The feast . . . din'—Coleridge's *Rime of the Ancient Mariner*, lines 7-8, slightly disarranged.

the candle at both ends and have it last long. So we put one end out for a little while every summer. Still, there are frightful wrecks of men strewn all along the course of our prosperity, wrecks of mind and body. Our insane asylums are full of madmen who have broken under the tremendous strain, and every country in Europe abounds in our dyspeptics." I was rather proud 5 of this terrible fact; there is no doubt but we Americans are proud of over-working ourselves; heaven knows why.

The Altrurian murmured, "Awful! Shocking!" but I thought some how he had not really followed me very attentively in my celebration of our national violation of the laws of life and its consequences. "I am glad," he went on, 10 "that your business men and professional men are beginning to realize the folly and wickedness of overwork. Shall I find some of your other weary work-ers here, too?"

"What other weary workers?" I asked in turn, for I imagined I had gone over pretty much the whole list. 15

"Why," said the Altrurian, "your mechanics and day laborers, your iron moulders and glass blowers, your miners and farmers, your printers and mill operatives, your trainmen and quarry hands. Or do they prefer to go to resorts of their own?"

III   20

It was not easy to make sure of such innocence as prompted this inquiry of my Altrurian friend. The doubt whether he could really be in earnest was something that I had already felt; and it was destined to beset me, as it did now, again and again. My first thought was that of course he was trying a bit of cheap irony on me, a mixture of the feeble sarcasm and false sentiment 25 that makes us smile when we find it in the philippics of the industrial agi-tators. For a moment I did not know but I had fallen victim to a walking-delegate on his vacation, who was employing his summer leisure in going about the country in the guise of a traveler from Altruria, and foisting himself upon people who would have had nothing to do with him in his real character. 30 But in another moment I perceived that this was impossible. I could not sup-pose that the friend who had introduced him to me would be capable of sec-onding so poor a joke, and besides I could not imagine why a walking-delegate should wish to address his clumsy satire to me particularly. For the present, at least, there was nothing for it but to deal with this inquiry as if it were 35 made in good faith, and in the pursuit of useful information. It struck me as grotesque; but it would not have been decent to treat it as if it were so. I was obliged to regard it seriously, and so I decided to shirk it.

"Well," I said, "that opens up rather a large field, which lies somewhat out-side of the province of my own activities. You know, I am a writer of romantic 40 fiction, and my time is so fully occupied in manipulating the destinies of the good old-fashioned hero and heroine, and trying always to make them end in a happy marriage, that I have hardly had a chance to look much into the lives

27-28. **walking-delegate**—member of a trades-union commissioned to visit other labor or-ganizations for the purpose of securing united action in common interests. **43. happy marriage** —Howells here satirizes the conventional romances to which his fiction was opposed.

of agriculturists or artisans; and to tell you the truth I don't know what they
do with their leisure. I'm pretty certain, though, you won't meet any of them
in this hotel; they couldn't afford it, and I fancy they would find themselves
out of their element among our guests. We respect them thoroughly; every
5 American does; and we know that the prosperity of the country rests with
them; we have a theory that they are politically sovereign, but we see very
little of them, and we don't associate with them. In fact, our cultivated people
have so little interest in them socially that they don't like to meet them, even
in fiction; they prefer refined and polished ladies and gentlemen, whom they
10 can have some sympathy with; and I always go to the upper classes for my
types. It won't do to suppose, though, that we are indifferent to the working-
classes in their place. Their condition is being studied a good deal just now,
and there are several persons here who will be able to satisfy your curiosity on
the points you have made, I think. I will introduce you to them."

15   The Altrurian did not try to detain me this time. He said he should be very
glad indeed to meet my friends, and I led the way toward a little group at the
corner of the piazza. They were men whom I particularly liked, for one reason
or another; they were intelligent and open-minded, and they were thoroughly
American. One was a banker; another was a minister; there was a lawyer, and
20 there was a doctor; there was a professor of political economy in one of our
colleges; and there was a retired manufacturer—I do not know what he used
to manufacture: cotton or iron, or something like that. They all rose politely
as I came up with my Altrurian, and I fancied in them a sensation of expectancy created by the rumor of his eccentric behavior which must have
25 spread through the hotel. But they controlled this if they had it, and I could
see, as the light fell upon his face from a spray of electrics on the nearest
pillar, that sort of liking kindle in theirs which I had felt myself at first sight
of him.

I said, "Gentlemen, I wish to introduce my friend, Mr. Homos," and then
30 I presented them severally to him by name. We all sat down, and I explained:
"Mr. Homos is from Altruria. He is visiting our country for the first time, and
is greatly interested in the working of our institutions. He has been asking
me some rather hard questions about certain phases of our civilization; and
the fact is that I have launched him upon you because I don't feel quite able
35 to cope with him."

They all laughed civilly at this sally of mine, but the professor asked, with
a sarcasm that I thought I hardly merited, "What point in our polity can be
obscured to the author of 'Glove and Gauntlet' and 'Airs and Graces'?"

They all laughed again, not so civilly, I felt, and then the banker asked my
40 friend, "Is it long since you left Altruria?"

"It seems a great while ago," the Altrurian answered, "but it is really only
a few weeks."

"You came by way of England, I suppose?"

"Yes; there is no direct line to America," said the Altrurian.

45   "That seems rather odd," I ventured, with some patriotic grudge.

"Oh, the English have direct lines everywhere," the banker instructed me.

"The tariff has killed our shipbuilding," said the professor. No one took up this firebrand, and the professor added, "Your name is Greek, isn't it, Mr. Homos?"

"Yes; we are of one of the early Hellenic families," said the Altrurian.

"And do you think," asked the lawyer, who, like most lawyers, was a lover of romance, and was well read in legendary lore especially, "that there is any 5 reason for supposing that Altruria is identical with the fabled Atlantis?"

"No, I can't say that I do. We have no traditions of a submergence of the continent, and there are only the usual evidences of a glacial epoch which you find everywhere, to support such a theory. Besides, our civilization is strictly Christian, and dates back to no earlier period than that of the first 10 Christian commune after Christ. It is a matter of history with us that one of these communists, when they were dispersed, brought the gospel to our continent; he was cast away on our eastern coast on his way to Britain."

"Yes, we know that," the minister intervened, "but it is perfectly astonishing that an island so large as Altruria should have been lost to the knowledge of 15 the rest of the world ever since the beginning of our era. You would hardly think that there was a space of the ocean's surface a mile square which had not been traversed by a thousand keels since Columbus sailed westward."

"No, you wouldn't. And I wish," the doctor suggested in his turn, "that Mr. Homos would tell us something about his country, instead of asking us 20 about ours."

"Yes," I coincided, "I'm sure we should all find it a good deal easier. At least I should; but I brought our friend up in the hope that the professor would like nothing better than to train a battery of hard facts upon a defenseless stranger." Since the professor had given me that little stab, I was rather anxious to see 25 how he would handle the desire for information in the Altrurian which I had found so prickly.

This turned the laugh on the professor, and he pretended to be as curious about Altruria as the rest, and said he would rather hear of it. But the Altrurian said: "I hope you will excuse me. Sometime I shall be glad to talk of Altruria 30 as long as you like; or if you will come to us, I shall be still happier to show you many things that I couldn't make you understand at a distance. But I am in America to learn, not to teach, and I hope you will have patience with my ignorance. I begin to be afraid that it is so great as to seem a little incredible. I have fancied in my friend here," he went on, with a smile toward me, "a 35 suspicion that I was not entirely single in some of the inquiries I have made, but that I had some ulterior motive, some wish to censure or satirize."

"Oh, not at all!" I protested, for it was not polite to admit a conjecture so accurate. "We are so well satisfied with our condition that we have nothing but pity for the darkened mind of the foreigner, though we believe in it fully: 40 we are used to the English tourist."

My friends laughed, and the Altrurian continued: "I am very glad to hear it, for I feel myself at a peculiar disadvantage among you. I am not only a foreigner, but I am so alien to you in all the traditions and habitudes that I find it very difficult to get upon common ground with you. Of course I know 45

6. **fabled Atlantis**—mythical continent supposed to have been engulfed by the Atlantic Ocean.
10-11. **first Christian commune**—*Cf.* Acts 4: 34-35.

theoretically what you are, but to realize it practically is another thing. I had read so much about America and understood so little that I could not rest without coming to see for myself. Some of the apparent contradictions were so colossal"—

5   "We have everything on a large scale here," said the banker, breaking off the ash of his cigar with the end of his little finger, "and we rather pride ourselves on the size of our inconsistencies, even. I know something of the state of things in Altruria, and, to be frank with you, I will say that it seems to me preposterous. I should say it was impossible, if it were not an accomplished fact; but

10   I always feel bound to recognize the thing done. You have hitched your wagon to a star and you have made the star go; there is never any trouble with wagons, but stars are not easily broken to harness, and you have managed to get yours well in hand. As I said, I don't believe in you, but I respect you." I thought this charming, myself; perhaps because it stated my own mind

15   about Altruria so exactly and in terms so just and generous.

"Pretty good," said the doctor, in a murmur of satisfaction, at my ear, "for a bloated bond-holder."

"Yes," I whispered back, "I wish I had said it. What an American way of putting it! Emerson would have liked it himself. After all, *he* was our prophet."

20   "He must have thought so from the way we kept stoning him," said the doctor, with a soft laugh.

"Which of our contradictions," asked the banker, in the same tone of gentle bonhomie, "has given you and our friend pause, just now?"

The Altrurian answered after a moment: "I am not sure that it is a contra-

25   diction, for as yet I have not ascertained the facts I was seeking. Our friend was telling me of the great change that had taken place in regard to work, and the increased leisure that your professional people are now allowing themselves; and I was asking him where your workingmen spent their leisure."

He went over the list of those he had specified, and I hung my head in

30   shame and pity; it really had such an effect of mawkish sentimentality. But my friends received it in the best possible way. They did not laugh; they heard him out, and then they quietly deferred to the banker, who made answer for us all:

"Well, I can be almost as brief as the historian of Iceland in his chapter on

35   snakes: those people have no leisure to spend."

"Except when they go out on a strike," said the manufacturer, with a certain grim humor of his own; I never heard anything more dramatic than the account he once gave of the way he broke up a labor-union. "I have seen a good many of them at leisure then."

40   "Yes," the doctor chimed in, "and in my younger days, when I necessarily had a good deal of charity-practice, I used to find them at leisure when they were 'laid off.' It always struck me as such a pretty euphemism. It seemed to minify the harm of the thing so. It seemed to take all the hunger and cold

---

10. **hitched your wagon**—from Emerson's "Civilization" in *Society and Solitude*. 17. **bloated bond-holder**—During the speculation of the seventies and eighties bonds registered inflation. 34. **historian of Iceland**—Chap. LXXII of Neil Horrebain's *Natural History of Norway* (translated 1758) observes laconically that there are no snakes in Iceland.

and sickness out of the fact. To be simply 'laid off' was so different from losing your work and having to face beggary or starvation!"

"Those people," said the professor, "never put anything by. They are wasteful and improvident, almost to a man; and they learn nothing by experience, though they know as well as we do that it is simply a question of demand and supply, and that the day of overproduction is sure to come, when their work must stop unless the men that give them work are willing to lose money."

"And I've seen them lose it, sometimes, rather than shut down," the manufacturer remarked; "lose it hand over hand, to keep the men at work; and then as soon as the tide turned the men would strike for higher wages. You have no idea of the ingratitude of those people." He said this towards the minister, as if he did not wish to be thought hard; and in fact he was a very kindly man.

"Yes," replied the minister, "that is one of the most sinister features of the situation. They seem really to regard their employers as their enemies. I don't know how it will end."

"I know how it would end if I had my way," said the professor. "There wouldn't be any labor-unions, and there wouldn't be any strikes."

"That is all very well," said the lawyer, from that judicial mind which I always liked in him, "as far as the strikes are concerned, but I don't understand that the abolition of the unions would affect the impersonal process of laying-off. The law of demand and supply I respect as much as any one—it's something like the constitution; but all the same I should object extremely to have my income stopped by it every now and then. I'm probably not so wasteful as a workingman generally is; still I haven't laid by enough to make it a matter of indifference to me whether my income went on or not. Perhaps the professor has." The professor did not say, and we all took leave to laugh. The lawyer concluded, "I don't see how those fellows stand it."

"They don't, all of them," said the doctor. "Or their wives and children don't. Some of them die."

"I wonder," the lawyer pursued, "what has become of the good old American fact that there is always work for those who are willing to work? I notice that wherever five thousand men strike in the forenoon, there are five thousand men to take their places in the afternoon—and not men who are turning their hands to something new, but men who are used to doing the very thing the strikers have done."

"That is one of the things that teach the futility of strikes," the professor made haste to interpose, as if he had not quite liked to appear averse to the interests of the workman; no one likes to do that. "If there were anything at all to be hoped from them it would be another matter."

"Yes, but that isn't the point, quite," said the lawyer.

"By the way, what is the point?" I asked, with my humorous lightness.

"Why, I supposed," said the banker, "it was the question how the working-classes amused their elegant leisure. But it seems to be almost anything else."

We all applauded the neat touch, but the Altrurian eagerly entreated: "No, no! never mind that, now. That is a matter of comparatively little interest. I would so much rather know something about the status of the workingman among you."

"Do you mean his political status? It's that of every other citizen."

"I don't mean that. I suppose that in America you have learned, as we have
5 in Altruria, that equal political rights are only means to an end, and as an end have no value or reality. I meant the economic status of the workingman, and his social status."

I do not know why we were so long girding up our loins to meet this simple question. I myself could not have hopefully undertaken to answer it: but
10 the others were each in their way men of affairs, and practically acquainted with the facts, except perhaps the professor; but he had devoted a great deal of thought to them, and ought to have been qualified to make some sort of response. But even he was silent; and I had a vague feeling that they were all somehow reluctant to formulate their knowledge, as if it were uncomfort-
15 able or discreditable. The banker continued to smoke quietly on for a moment; then he suddenly threw his cigar away.

"I like to free my mind of cant," he said, with a short laugh, "when I can afford it, and I propose to cast all sorts of American cant out of it, in answering your question. The economic status of the workingman among us is es-
20 sentially the same as that of the workingman all over the civilized world. You will find plenty of people here, especially about election time, to tell you differently, but they will not be telling you the truth, though a great many of them think they are. In fact, I suppose most Americans honestly believe because we have a republican form of government, and manhood-suffrage, and
25 so on, that our economic conditions are peculiar, and that our workingman has a status higher and better than that of the workingman anywhere else. But he has nothing of the kind. His circumstances are better, and provisionally his wages are higher, but it is only a question of years or decades when his circumstances will be the same and his wages the same as the European working-
30 man's. There is nothing in our conditions to prevent this."

"Yes, I understood from our friend here," said the Altrurian, nodding toward me, "that you had broken only with the political tradition of Europe, in your revolution; and he has explained to me that you do not hold all kinds of labor in equal esteem; but"—

35 "What kind of labor did he say we did hold in esteem?" asked the banker.

"Why, I understood him to say that if America meant anything at all it meant the honor of work, but that you distinguished and did not honor some kinds of work so much as others: for instance, domestic service, or personal attendance of any kind."

40 The banker laughed again. "Oh, he drew the line there, did he? Well, we all have to draw the line somewhere. Our friend is a novelist, and I will tell you in strict confidence that the line he has drawn is imaginary. We don't honor any kind of work any more than any other people. If a fellow gets up, the papers make a great ado over his having been a wood-chopper, or a bobbin-
45 boy, or something of that kind, but I doubt if the fellow himself likes it; he doesn't if he's got any sense. The rest of us feel that it's infra dig., and hope

46. **infra dig.**—*infra dignitatem,* beneath one's dignity.

nobody will find out that we ever worked with our hands for a living. I'll go farther," said the banker, with the effect of whistling prudence down the wind, "and I will challenge any of you to gainsay me from his own experience or observation. How does esteem usually express itself? When we wish to honor a man, what do we do?"

"Ask him to dinner," said the lawyer.

"Exactly. We offer him some sort of social recognition. Well, as soon as a fellow gets up, if he gets up high enough, we offer him some sort of social recognition; in fact, all sorts; but upon condition that he has left off working with his hands for a living. We forgive all you please to his past on account of the present. But there isn't a workingman I venture to say, in any city, or town, or even large village, in the whole length and breadth of the United States who has any social recognition, if he is still working at his trade. I don't mean, merely, that he is excluded from rich and fashionable society, but from the society of the average educated and cultivated people. I'm not saying he is fit for it; but I don't care how intelligent and agreeable he might be—and some of them are astonishingly intelligent, and so agreeable in their tone of mind, and their original way of looking at things, that I like nothing better than to talk with them—all of our invisible fences are up against him."

The minister said: "I wonder if that sort of exclusiveness is quite natural? Children seem to feel no sort of social difference among themselves."

"We can hardly go to children for a type of social order," the professor suggested.

"True," the minister meekly admitted. "But somehow there is a protest in us somewhere against these arbitrary distinctions; something that questions whether they are altogether right. We know that they must be, and always have been, and always will be, and yet—well, I will confess it—I never feel at peace when I face them."

"Oh," said the banker, "if you come to the question of right and wrong, that is another matter. I don't say it's right. I'm not discussing that question; though I'm certainly not proposing to level the fences; I should be the last to take my own down. I say simply that you are no more likely to meet a workingman in American society than you are to meet a colored man. Now you can judge," he ended, turning directly to the Altrurian, "how much we honor labor. And I hope I have indirectly satisfied your curiosity as to the social status of the workingman among us."

We were all silent. Perhaps the others were occupied like myself in trying to recall some instance of a workingman whom they had met in society, and perhaps we said nothing because we all failed.

The Altrurian spoke at last.

"You have been so very full and explicit that I feel as if it were almost unseemly to press any further inquiry; but I should very much like to know how your workingmen bear this social exclusion."

"I'm sure I can't say," returned the banker. "A man does not care much to get into society until he has something to eat, and how to get that is always the first question with the workingman."

"But you wouldn't like it yourself?"

"No, certainly, I shouldn't like it myself. I shouldn't complain of not being

asked to people's houses, and the workingmen don't; you can't do that; but
I should feel it an incalculable loss. We may laugh at the emptiness of society, or pretend to be sick of it, but there is no doubt that society is the flower
of civilization, and to be shut out from it is to be denied the best privilege of
5 a civilized man. There are society-women—we have all met them—whose
graciousness and refinement of presence are something of incomparable value;
it is more than a liberal education to have been admitted to it, but it is as inaccessible to the workingman as—what shall I say? The thing is too gro-
tesquely impossible for any sort of comparison. Merely to conceive of its pos-
10 sibility is something that passes a joke; it is a kind of offence."
        Again we were silent.
        "I don't know," the banker continued, "how the notion of our social equality
originated, but I think it has been fostered mainly by the expectation of foreigners, who argued it from our political equality. As a matter of fact, it never
15 existed, except in our poorest and most primitive communities, in the pioneer
days of the West, and among the gold-hunters of California. It was not dreamt
of in our colonial society, either in Virginia, or Pennsylvania, or New York,
or Massachusetts; and the fathers of the republic, who were mostly slavehold-
ers, were practically as stiff-necked aristocrats as any people of their day. We
20 have not a political aristocracy, that is all; but there is as absolute a division
between the orders of men, and as little love, in this country as in any country
on the globe. The severance of the man who works for his living with his
hands from the man who does not work for his living with his hands is so
complete, and apparently so final, that nobody even imagines anything else,
25 not even in fiction. Or, how is that?" he asked, turning to me. "Do you fellows still put the intelligent, high-spirited, handsome young artisan, who wins
the millionaire's daughter into your books? I used sometimes to find him
there."
        "You might still find him in the fiction of the weekly story-papers; but," I
30 was obliged to own, "he would not go down with my readers. Even in the
story-paper fiction he would leave off working as soon as he married the millionaire's daughter, and go to Europe, or he would stay here and become a
social leader, but he would not receive workingmen in his gilded halls."
        The others rewarded my humor with a smile, but the banker said: "Then
35 I wonder you were not ashamed of filling our friend up with that stuff about
our honoring some kinds of labor. It is true that we don't go about openly
and explicitly despising any kind of honest toil—people don't do that anywhere, now; but we contemn it in terms quite as unmistakable. The workingman acquiesces as completely as anybody else. He does not remain a work-
40 ingman a moment longer than he can help; and after he gets up, if he is
weak enough to be proud of having been one it is because he feels that his
low origin is a proof of his prowess in rising to the top against unusual odds.
I don't suppose there is a man in the whole civilized world—outside of Altruria, of course—who is proud of working at a trade, except the shoemaker
45 Tolstoy, and he is a count, and he does not make very good shoes."

45. Tolstoy—Leo Nikolaiëvich Tolstoy (1828-1910), Russian count, novelist, and social reformer. Howells gave him first place in My Literary Passions.

We all laughed again: those shoes of Count Tolstoy's are always such an infallible joke. The Altrurian, however, was cocked and primed with another question; he instantly exploded it. "But are all the workingmen in America eager to rise above their condition? Is there none willing to remain among the mass because the rest could not rise with him, and from the hope of yet bringing labor to honor?"

The banker answered: "I never heard of any. No, the American ideal is not to change the conditions for all, but for each to rise above the rest if he can."

"Do you think it is really so bad as that?" asked the minister timidly.

The banker answered: "Bad? Do you call that bad? I thought it was very good. But good or bad, I don't think you'll find it deniable, if you look into the facts. There may be workingmen willing to remain so for other workingmen's sake, but I have never met any—perhaps because the workingman never goes into society."

The unfailing question of the Altrurian broke the silence which ensued: "Are there many of your workingmen who are intelligent and agreeable—of the type you mentioned a moment since?"

"Perhaps," said the banker, "I had better refer you to one of our friends here, who has had a great deal more to do with them than I have. He is a manufacturer and he has had to do with all kinds of work-people."

"Yes, for my sins," the manufacturer assented; and he added, "They are often confoundedly intelligent, though I haven't often found them very agreeable, either in their tone of mind or their original way of looking at things."

The banker amiably acknowledged his thrust, and the Altrurian asked, "Ah, they are opposed to your own?"

"Well, we have the same trouble here that you must have heard of in England. As you know now that the conditions are the same here, you won't be surprised at the fact."

"But the conditions," the Altrurian pursued; "do you expect them always to continue the same?"

"Well, I don't know," said the manufacturer. "We can't expect them to change themselves, and I shouldn't know how to change them. It was expected that the rise of the trusts and the syndicates would break the unions, but somehow they haven't. The situation remains the same. The unions are not cutting one another's throats, now, any more than we are. The war is on a larger scale—that's all."

"Then let me see," said the Altrurian, "whether I clearly understand the situation, as regards the workingman in America. He is dependent upon the employer for his chance to earn a living, and he is never sure of this. He may be thrown out of work by his employer's disfavor or disaster, and his willingness to work goes for nothing; there is no public provision of work for him; there is nothing to keep him from want, nor the prospect of anything."

"We are all in the same boat," said the professor.

"But some of us have provisioned ourselves rather better and can generally weather it through till we are picked up," the lawyer put in.

"I am always saying the workingman is improvident," returned the professor.

"There are the charities," the minister suggested.

"But his economical status," the Altrurian pursued, "is in a state of perpetual uncertainty, and to save himself in some measure he has organized, and so has constituted himself a danger to the public peace?"

5 "A very great danger," said the professor.

"I guess we can manage him," the manufacturer remarked.

"And socially he is non-existent?"

The Altrurian turned with this question to the banker, who said, "He is certainly not in society."

10 "Then," said my guest, "if the workingman's wages are provisionally so much better here than in Europe, why should they be discontented? What is the real cause of their discontent?"

I have always been suspicious, in the company of practical men, of an atmosphere of condescension to men of my calling, if nothing worse. I fancy

15 they commonly regard artists of all kinds as a sort of harmless eccentrics, and that literary people they look upon as something droll, as weak and soft, as not quite right. I believed that this particular group, indeed, was rather abler to conceive of me as a rational person than most others, but I knew that if even they had expected me to be as reasonable as themselves they would

20 not have been greatly disappointed if I were not; and it seemed to me that I had put myself wrong with them in imparting to the Altrurian that romantic impression that we hold labor in honor here. I had really thought so, but I could not say so now, and I wished to retrieve myself somehow. I wished to show that I was a practical man, too, and so I made answer: "What is the

25 cause of the workingman's discontent? It is very simple: the walking-delegate."

IV

I suppose I could not have fairly claimed any great originality for my notion that the walking-delegate was the cause of the labor troubles: he is regularly assigned as the reason of a strike in the newspapers, and is reprobated

30 for his evil agency by the editors, who do not fail to read the workingmen many solemn lessons, and fervently warn them against him, as soon as the strike begins to go wrong—as it nearly always does. I understand from them that the walking-delegate is an irresponsible tyrant, who emerges from the mystery that habitually hides him and from time to time orders a strike in

35 mere rancor of spirit and plenitude of power, and then leaves the workingmen and their families to suffer the consequences, while he goes off somewhere and rolls in the lap of luxury, careless of the misery he has created. Between his debauches of vicious idleness and his accesses of baleful activity he is employed in poisoning the mind of the workingman against his real in-

40 terests and real friends. This is perfectly easy, because the American workingman, though singularly shrewd and sensible in other respects, is the victim of an unaccountable obliquity of vision which keeps him from seeing his real interests and real friends—or at least from knowing them when he sees them.

There could be no doubt, I thought, in the mind of any reasonable person

45 that the walking-delegate was the source of the discontent among our pro-

letariat, and I alleged him with a confidence which met the approval of the
professor, apparently, for he nodded, as if to say that I had hit the nail on
the head this time; and the minister seemed to be freshly impressed with a
notion that could not be new to him. The lawyer and the doctor were silent,
as if waiting for the banker to speak again; but he was silent, too. The manu-   5
facturer, to my chagrin, broke into a laugh. "I'm afraid," he said, with a sardonic levity which surprised me, "you'll have to go a good deal deeper than
the walking-delegate. He's a symptom; he isn't the disease. The thing keeps
on and on, and it seems to be always about wages; but it isn't about wages
at the bottom. Some of those fellows know it and some of them don't, but   10
the real discontent is with the whole system, with the nature of things. I had
a curious revelation on that point the last time I tried to deal with my men
as a union. They were always bothering me about this and about that, and
there was no end to the bickering. I yielded point after point, but it didn't
make any difference. It seemed as if the more I gave the more they asked.   15
At last I made up my mind to try to get at the real inwardness of the matter,
and I didn't wait for their committee to come to me—I sent for their leading
man, and said I wanted to have it out with him. He wasn't a bad fellow,
and when I got at him, man to man that way, I found he had sense, and
he had ideas—it's no use pretending those fellows are fools; he had thought   20
about his side of the question, any way. I said: 'Now what does it all mean?
Do you want the earth, or don't you? When is it going to end?' I offered him
something to take, but he said he didn't drink, and we compromised on cigars.
'Now when is it going to end?' said I, and I pressed it home, and wouldn't
let him fight off from the point. 'Do you mean when it is all going to end?'   25
said he. 'Yes,' said I, 'all. I'm sick of it. If there's any way out I'd like to know
it.' 'Well,' said he, 'I'll tell you, if you want to know. It's all going to end
when you get the same amount of money for the same amount of work as
we do.'"   *Communism*

We all laughed uproariously. The thing was deliciously comical; and noth-   30
ing, I thought, attested the Altrurian's want of humor like his failure to appreciate this joke. He did not even smile in asking, "And what did you
say?"

"Well," returned the manufacturer, with cosy enjoyment, "I asked him if
the men would take the concern and run it themselves." We laughed again: 35
this seemed even better than the other joke. "But he said 'No;' they would
not like to do that. And then I asked him just what they would like, if they
could have their own way, and he said they would like to have me run the
business, and all share alike. I asked him what was the sense of that, and
why if I could do something that all of them put together couldn't do I   40
shouldn't be paid more than all of them put together; and he said that if a
man did his best he ought to be paid as much as the best man. I asked him
if that was the principle their union was founded on, and he said 'Yes,' that
the very meaning of their union was the protection of the weak by the strong,
and the equalization of earnings among all who do their best."   45

We waited for the manufacturer to go on, but he made a dramatic pause
at this point, as if to let it sink into our minds; and he did not speak until

the Altrurian prompted him with the question, "And what did you finally do?"

"I saw there was only one way out for me, and I told the fellow I did not think I could do business on that principle. We parted friends but the next
5 Saturday I locked them out, and smashed their union. They came back, most of them—they had to—but I've treated with them ever since 'as individuals.'"

"And they're much better off in your hands than they were in the union," said the professor.

"I don't know about that," said the manufacturer, "but I'm sure I am."
10 We laughed with him, all but the minister, whose mind seemed to have caught upon some other point, and who sat absently by.

"And is it your opinion, from what you know of the workingmen generally, that they all have this twist in their heads?" the professor asked.

"They have, until they begin to rise. Then they get rid of it mighty soon.
15 Let a man save something—enough to get a house of his own, and take a boarder or two, and perhaps have a little money at interest—and he sees the matter in another light."

"Do you think he sees it more clearly?" asked the minister.

"He sees it differently."
20 "What do you think?" the minister pursued, turning to the lawyer. "You are used to dealing with questions of justice"—

"Rather more with questions of law, I'm afraid," the other returned pleasantly, putting his feet together before him and looking down at them, in a way he had. "But still, I have a great interest in questions of justice, and I
25 confess that I find a certain wild equity in this principle, which I see nobody could do business on. It strikes me as idyllic—it's a touch of real poetry in the rough-and-tumble prose of our economic life."

He referred this to me as something I might appreciate in my quality of literary man, and I responded in my quality of practical man, "There's cer-
30 tainly more rhyme than reason in it."

He turned again to the minister:

"I suppose the ideal of the Christian state is the family?"

"I hope so," said the minister, with the gratitude that I have seen people of his cloth show when men of the world conceded premises which the world
35 usually contests; it has seemed to me pathetic.

"And if that is the case, why the logic of the postulate is that the prosperity of the weakest is the sacred charge and highest happiness of all the stronger. But the law has not recognized any such principle, in economics at least, and if the labor unions are based upon it they are outlaw, so far as any hope of
40 enforcing it is concerned; and it is bad for men to feel themselves outlaw. How is it," the lawyer continued, turning to the Altrurian, "in your country? We can see no issue here, if the first principle of organized labor antagonizes the first principle of business."

"But I don't understand precisely yet what the first principle of business is,"
45 returned my guest.

"Ah, that raises another interesting question," said the lawyer. "Of course every business man solves the problem practically according to his tempera-

ment and education, and I suppose that on first thoughts every business man
would answer you accordingly. But perhaps the personal equation is something you wish to eliminate from the definition."

"Yes, of course."

"Still, I would rather not venture upon it first," said the lawyer. "Professor, 5
what should you say was the first principle of business?"

"Buying in the cheapest market and selling in the dearest," the professor
promptly answered.

"We will pass the parson and the doctor and the novelist as witnesses of no
value. They can't possibly have any cognizance of the first principle of busi- 10
ness; their affair is to look after the souls and bodies and fancies of other
people. But what should you say it was?" he asked the banker.

"I should say it was an enlightened conception of one's own interests."

"And you?"

The manufacturer had no hesitation in answering: "The good of Number 15
One first, last, and all the time. There may be a difference of opinion about
the best way to get at it; the long way may be the better, or the short way;
the direct way or the oblique way, or the purely selfish way, or the partly
selfish way; but if you ever lose sight of that end you might as well shut up
shop. That seems to be the first law of nature, as well as the first law of 20
business."

"Ah, we mustn't go to nature for our morality," the minister protested.

"We were not talking of morality," said the manufacturer, "we were talking
of business."

This brought the laugh on the minister, but the lawyer cut it short: "Well, 25
then, I don't really see why the trades-unions are not as business-like as the
syndicates in their dealings with all those outside of themselves. Within themselves they practice an altruism of the highest order, but it is a tribal altruism; it is like that which prompts a Sioux to share his last mouthful with
a starving Sioux, and to take the scalp of a starving Apache. How is it with 30
your trades-unions in Altruria?" he asked my friend.

"We have no trades-unions in Altruria," he began.

"Happy Altruria!" cried the professor.

"We had them formerly," the Altrurian went on, "as you have them now.
They claimed, as I suppose yours do, that they were forced into existence by 35
the necessities of the case; that without union the workingman was unable
to meet the capitalist on anything like equal terms, or to withstand his en-
croachments and oppressions. But to maintain themselves they had to extinguish industrial liberty among the workingmen themselves, and they had to
practice great cruelties against those who refused to join them or who re- 40
belled against them."

"They simply destroy them here," said the professor.

"Well," said the lawyer, from his judicial mind, "the great syndicates have
no scruples in destroying a capitalist who won't come into them, or who tries
to go out. They don't club him or stone him, but they undersell him and freeze 45
him out; they don't break his head, but they bankrupt him. The principle is
the same."

"Don't interrupt Mr. Homos," the banker entreated. "I am very curious to know just how they got rid of labor unions in Altruria."

"We had syndicates, too, and finally we had the reductio ad absurdum—we had a federation of labor unions and a federation of syndicates, that di-
5 vided the nation into two camps. The situation was not only impossible, but it was insupportably ridiculous."

I ventured to say, "It hasn't become quite so much of a joke with us yet."

"Isn't it in a fair way to become so?" asked the doctor; and he turned to the lawyer: "What should you say was the logic of events among us for the
10 last ten or twenty years?"

"There's nothing so capricious as the logic of events. It's like a woman's reasoning—you can't tell what it's aimed at, or where it's going to fetch up; all that you can do is to keep out of the way if possible. We may come to some such condition of things as they have in Altruria, where the faith of the
15 whole nation is pledged to secure every citizen in the pursuit of happiness; or we may revert to some former condition, and the master may again own the man; or we may hitch and joggle along indefinitely, as we are doing now."

"But come, now," said the banker, while he laid a caressing touch on the
20 Altrurian's shoulder, "you don't mean to say honestly that everybody works with his hands in Altruria?"

"Yes, certainly. We are mindful, as a whole people, of the divine law, 'In the sweat of thy brow shalt thou eat bread.'"

"But the capitalists? I'm anxious about Number One, you see."
25 "We have none."

"I forgot, of course. But the lawyers, the doctors, the parsons, the novelists?"

"They all do their share of hand work."

The lawyer said: "That seems to dispose of the question of the working-man in society. But how about your minds? When do you cultivate your
30 minds? When do the ladies of Altruria cultivate their minds, if they have to do their own work, as I suppose they do? Or is it only the men who work, if they happen to be the husbands and fathers of the upper classes?"

The Altrurian seemed to be sensible of the kindly skepticism which persisted in our reception of his statements, after all we had read of Altruria. He
35 smiled indulgently, and said: "You mustn't imagine that work in Altruria is the same as it is here. As we all work, the amount that each one need do is very little, a few hours each day at the most, so that every man and woman has abundant leisure and perfect spirits for the higher pleasures which the education of their whole youth has fitted them to enjoy. If you can under-
40 stand a state of things where the sciences and arts and letters are cultivated for their own sake, and not as a means of livelihood"—

"No," said the lawyer, smiling, "I'm afraid we can't conceive of that. We consider the pinch of poverty the highest incentive that a man can have. If our gifted friend here," he said, indicating me, "were not kept like a toad
45 under the harrow, with his nose on the grindstone and the poorhouse staring him in the face"—

22-23. 'In the sweat . . .' —Cf. Gen. 3: 19.

"For heaven's sake," I cried out, "don't mix your metaphors so, anyway!"

"If it were not for that and all the other hardships that literary men undergo—

'Toil, envy, want, the patron and the jail'—

his novels probably wouldn't be worth reading."   5

"Ah!" said the Altrurian, as if he did not quite follow this joking; and to tell the truth, I never find the personal thing in very good taste. "You will understand, then, how extremely difficult it is for me to imagine a condition of things like yours—although I have it under my very eyes—where the money consideration is the first consideration."   10

"Oh, excuse me!" urged the minister, "I don't think that's quite the case."

"I beg your pardon," said the Altrurian, sweetly; "you can see how easily I go astray."

"Why, I don't know," the banker interposed, "that you are so far out in what you say. If you had said that money was always the first motive, I should   15 have been inclined to dispute you, too; but when you say that money is the first consideration, I think you are quite right. Unless a man secures his financial basis for his work, he can't do his work. It's nonsense to pretend otherwise. So the money consideration is the first consideration. People here have to live by their work, and to live they must have money. Of course, we   20 all recognize a difference in the qualities, as well as in the kinds, of work. The work of the laborer may be roughly defined as the necessity of his life; the work of the business man as the means, and the work of the artist and scientist as the end. We might refine upon these definitions and make them closer, but they will serve for illustration as they are. I don't think there can   25 be any question as to which is the highest kind of work; some truths are self-evident. He is a fortunate man whose work is an end, and every business man sees this, and owns it to himself, at least when he meets some man of an aesthetic or scientific occupation. He knows that this luckier fellow has a joy in his work, which he can never feel in business; that his success in it can never   30 be embittered by the thought that it is the failure of another; that if he does it well, it is pure good; that there cannot be any competition in it—there can be only a noble emulation, as far as the work itself is concerned. He can always look up to his work, for it is something above him; and a business man often has to look down upon his business, for it is often beneath him, unless he is a   35 pretty low fellow."

I listened to all this in surprise; I knew that the banker was a cultivated man, a man of university training, and that he was a reader and a thinker; but he had always kept a certain reserve in his talk, which he now seemed to have thrown aside for the sake of the Altrurian, or because the subject had a   40 charm that lured him out of himself. "Well, now," he continued, "the question is of the money consideration, which is the first consideration with us all: does it, or doesn't it degrade the work, which is the life, of those among us whose work is the highest? I understand that this is the misgiving which troubles you in view of our conditions?"   45

4. 'Toil . . . jail'—from Samuel Johnson, *The Vanity of Human Wishes* (1749).

The Altrurian assented, and I thought it a proof of the banker's innate delicacy that he did not refer the matter, as far as it concerned the aesthetic life and work, to me; I was afraid he was going to do so. But he courteously proposed to keep the question impersonal, and he went on to consider it him-
5 self. "Well, I don't suppose any one can satisfy you fully. But I should say that it put such men under a double strain, and perhaps that is the reason why so many of them break down in a calling that is certainly far less exhausting than business. On one side, the artist is kept to the level of the workingman, of the animal, of the creature whose sole affair is to get something to eat and
10 somewhere to sleep. This is through his necessity. On the other side, he is exalted to the height of beings who have no concern but with the excellence of their. work, which they were born and divinely authorized to do. This is through his purpose. Between the two, I should say that he got mixed, and that his work shows it."

15 None of the others said anything, and since I had not been personally appealed to, I felt the freer to speak. "If you will suppose me to be speaking from observation rather than experience," I began.

"By all means," said the banker, "go on," and the rest made haste in various forms to yield me the word.

20 "I should say that such a man certainly got mixed, but that his work kept itself pure from the money consideration, as it were, in spite of him. A painter, or actor, or even a novelist, is glad to get all he can for his work, and, such is our fallen nature, he does get all he knows how to get; but when he has once fairly passed into his work, he loses himself in it. He does not think whether
25 it will pay or not, whether it will be popular or not, but whether he can make it good or not."

"Well, that is conceivable," said the banker. "But wouldn't he rather do something he would get less for, if he could afford it, than the thing he knows he will get more for? Doesn't the money consideration influence his choice
30 of subject?"

"Oddly enough, I don't believe it does," I answered, after a moment's reflection. "A man makes his choice once for all when he embraces the aesthetic life, or rather it is made for him; no other life seems possible. I know there is a general belief that an artist does the kind of thing he has made go because
35 it pays; but this only shows the prevalence of business ideals. If he did not love to do the thing he does he could not do it well, no matter how richly it paid."

"I am glad to hear it," said the banker, and he added to the Altrurian: "So you see we are not so bad as one would think. We are illogically better, in fact."

40 "Yes," the other assented. "I knew something of your literature as well as your conditions before I left home, and I perceived that by some anomaly, the one was not tainted by the other. It is a miraculous proof of the divine mission of the poet."

"And the popular novelist," the lawyer whispered in my ear, but loud enough
45 for the rest to hear, and they all testified their amusement at my cost.

The Altrurian, with his weak sense of humor, passed the joke. "It shows no signs of corruption from greed, but I can't help thinking that fine as it is, it might have been much finer if the authors who produced it had been absolutely freed to their work, and had never felt the spur of need."

"Are they absolutely freed to it in Altruria?" asked the professor. "I understood you that everybody had to work for his living in Altruria."

"That is a mistake. Nobody works for his living in Altruria; he works for 5 others' living."

"Ah, that is precisely what our workingmen object to doing here!" said the manufacturer. "In that last interview of mine with the walking-delegate he had the impudence to ask me why my men should work for my living as well as their own." 10

"He couldn't imagine that you were giving them the work to do—the very means of life," said the professor.

"Oh, no, that's the last thing those fellows want to think of."

"Perhaps," the Altrurian suggested, "they might not have found it such a hardship to work for your living if their own had been assured, as it is with 15 us. If you will excuse my saying it, we should think it monstrous in Altruria for any man to have another's means of life in his power; and in our condition it is hardly imaginable. Do you really have it in your power to take away a man's opportunity to earn a living?"

The manufacturer laughed uneasily. "It is in my power to take away his life; 20 but I don't habitually shoot my fellow men, and I never dismissed a man yet without good reason."

"Oh, I beg your pardon," said the Altrurian. "I didn't dream of accusing you of such inhumanity. But you see our whole system is so very different that, as I said, it is hard for me to conceive of yours, and I am very curious to under- 25 stand its workings. If you shot your fellowman, as you say, the law would punish you; but if for some reason that you decided to be good you took away his means of living, and he actually starved to death—"

"Then the law would have nothing to do with it," the professor replied for the manufacturer, who did not seem ready to answer. "But that is not the way 30 things fall out. The man would be supported in idleness, probably, till he got another job, by his union, which would take the matter up."

"But I thought that our friend did not employ union labor," returned the Altrurian.

I found all this very uncomfortable, and tried to turn the talk back to a point 35 that I felt curious about. "But in Altruria, if the literary class is not exempt from the rule of manual labor where do they find time and strength to write?"

"Why, you must realize that our manual labor is never engrossing or exhausting. It is no more than is necessary to keep the body in health. I do not see how you remain well here, you people of sedentary occupations." 40

"Oh, we all take some sort of exercise. We walk several hours a day, or we row, or we ride a bicycle, or a horse, or we fence."

"But to us," returned the Altrurian, with a growing frankness, which nothing but the sweetness of his manner would have excused, "exercise for exercise would appear stupid. The barren expenditure of force that began and ended in 45 itself, and produced nothing, we should—if you will excuse my saying so—look upon as childish, if not insane or immoral."

IX

. . . The banker turned to the Altrurian, and then went on:

"As I said the other night, this is a business man's country. We are purely commercial people; money is absolutely to the fore; and business, which is
5 the means of getting the most money, is the American ideal. If you like, you may call it the American fetish; I don't mind calling it so myself. The fact that business is our ideal, or our fetish, will account for the popular faith in business men, who form its priesthood, its hierarchy. I don't know, myself, any other reasons for regarding business men as solider than novelists, or artists, or
10 ministers, not to mention lawyers and doctors. They are supposed to have long heads; but it appears that ninety-five times out of a hundred they haven't. They are supposed to be very reliable; but it is almost invariably a business man, of some sort, who gets out to Canada while the state examiner is balancing his books, and it is usually the longest-headed business men who get plundered
15 by him. No, it is simply because business is our national ideal, that the business man is honored above all other men among us. In the aristocratic countries they forward a public object under the patronage of the nobility and gentry; in a plutocratic country they get the business men to endorse it. I suppose that the average American citizen feels that they wouldn't endorse a thing unless it was
20 safe; and the average American citizen likes to be safe—he is cautious. As a matter of fact, business men are always taking risks, and business is a game of chance, in a certain degree. Have I made myself intelligible?"

"Entirely so," said the Altrurian; and he seemed so thoroughly well satisfied, that he forebore asking any question farther.

25 No one else spoke. The banker lighted a cigar, and resumed at the point where he left off when I ventured to enter upon the defense of his class with him. I must say that he had not convinced me at all. At that moment, I would rather have trusted him, in any serious matter of practical concern, than all the novelists I ever heard of. But I thought I would leave the word to him, without
30 further attempt to reinstate him in his self-esteem. In fact, he seemed to be getting along very well without it; or else he was feeling that mysterious control from the Altrurian which I had already suspected him of using. Voluntarily or involuntarily, the banker proceeded with his contribution to the Altrurian's stock of knowledge concerning our civilization:

35 "I don't believe, however, that the higher education is any more of a failure, as a provision for a business career, than the lower education is for the life of labor. I suppose that the hypercritical observer might say that in a wholly commercial civilization, like ours, the business man really needed nothing beyond the three R's, and the workingman needed no R at all. As a practical affair,
40 there is a good deal to be said in favor of that view. The higher education is part of the social ideal which we have derived from the past, from Europe. It is part of the provision for the life of leisure, the life of the aristocrat, which nobody of our generation leads, except women. Our women really have some use for the education of a gentleman, but our men have none. How will that
45 do for a generalization?" the banker asked of me.

"Oh," I admitted, with a laugh, "it is a good deal like one of my own. I have always been struck with that phase of our civilization."

"Well, then," the banker resumed, "take the lower education. This is part of the civic ideal which, I suppose, I may say we evolved from the depths of our inner consciousness of what an American citizen ought to be. It includes instruction in all the R's, and in several other letters of the alphabet. It is given free by the state, and no one can deny that it is thoroughly socialistic in conception and application."

"Distinctly so," said the professor. "Now that the text-books are furnished by the state, we have only to go a step farther, and provide a good, hot lunch for the children every day, as they do in Paris."

"Well," the banker returned, "I don't know that I should have much to say against that. It seems as reasonable as anything in the system of education which we force upon the working-classes. *They* know, perfectly well, whether we do or not, that the three R's will not make their children better mechanics or laborers, and that, if the fight for a mere living is to go on, from generation to generation, they will have no leisure to apply the little learning they get in the public schools for their personal culture. In the meantime, we deprive the parents of their children's labor, in order that they may be better citizens for their schooling, as we imagine; I don't know whether they are or not. We offer them no sort of compensation for their time, and I think we ought to feel obliged to them for not wanting wages for their children while we are teaching them to be better citizens."

"You know," said the professor, "that has been suggested by some of their leaders."

"No, really? Well, that is *too* good!" The banker threw back his head, and roared, and we all laughed with him. When we had sobered down again, he said: "I suppose that when a working man makes all the use he can of his lower education, he becomes a business man, and then he doesn't need the higher. Professor, you seem to be left out in the cold, by our system, whichever way you take it."

"Oh," said the professor, "the law of supply and demand works both ways; it creates the demand, if the supply comes first; and if we keep on giving the sons of business men the education of a gentleman, we may yet make them feel the need of it. We shall evolve a new sort of business man."

"The sort that can't make money, or wouldn't exactly like to, on some terms?" asked the banker. "Well, perhaps we shall work out our democratic salvation in that way. When you have educated your new business man to the point where he can't consent to get rich at the obvious cost of others, you've got him on the way back to work with his hands. He will sink into the ranks of labor, and give the fellow with the lower education a chance. I've no doubt he'll take it. I don't know but you're right, professor."

The lawyer had not spoken, as yet. Now he said: "Then, it is education, after all, that is to bridge the chasm between the classes and the masses, though it seems destined to go a long way around about it. There was a time, I believe, when we expected religion to do that."

"Well, it may still be doing it, for all I know," said the banker. "What do you say?" he asked, turning to the minister. "You ought to be able to give us some statistics on the subject with that large congregation of yours. You preach to more people than any other pulpit in your city."

The banker named one of the principal cities in the east, and the minister
5   answered, with modest pride: "I am not sure of that; but our society is certainly a very large one."

"Well, and how many of the lower classes are there in it—people who work for their living with their hands?"

The minister stirred uneasily in his chair, and at last he said, with evident
10 unhappiness: "They—I suppose—they have their own churches. I have never thought that such a separation of the classes was right; and I have had some of the very best people—socially and financially—with me in the wish that there might be more brotherliness between the rich and poor among us. But as yet"—

He stopped; the banker pursued: "Do you mean there are *no* working-people
15 in your congregation?"

"I cannot think of any," returned the minister so miserably that the banker forbore to press the point.

The lawyer broke the awkward pause which followed: "I have heard it asserted that there is no country in the world, where the separation of the
20 classes is so absolute as in ours. In fact, I once heard a Russian revolutionist, who had lived in exile all over Europe, say that he had never seen anywhere such a want of kindness or sympathy between rich and poor, as he had observed in America. I doubted whether he was right. But he believed that, if it ever came to the industrial revolution with us, the fight would be more
25 uncompromising than any such fight that the world had ever seen. There was no respect from low to high, he said, and no consideration from high to low, as there were in countries with traditions and old associations."

"Well," said the banker, "there may be something in that. Certainly, so far as the two forces have come into conflict here, there has been no disposition,
30 on either side, to 'make war with the water of roses.' It's astonishing, in fact, to see how ruthless the fellows who have just got up are towards the fellows who are still down. And the best of us have been up only a generation or two— and the fellows who are still down know it."

"And what do you think would be the outcome of such a conflict?" I asked,
35 with my soul divided between fear of it, and the perception of its excellence as material. My fancy vividly sketched the outline of a story which should forecast the struggle and its event, somewhat on the plan of the Battle of Dorking.

"We should beat," said the banker, breaking his cigar-ash off with his little
40 finger; and I instantly cast him with his ironic calm, for the part of a great patrician leader, in my Fall of the Republic. Of course, I disguised him somewhat, and travestied his worldly bonhomie with the bluff sang-froid of the soldier; these things are easily done.

"What makes you think we should beat?" asked the manufacturer, with a
45 certain curiosity.

37-38. **Battle of Dorking**—imaginary account of successful invasion of England, in *Blackwood's Magazine* (1871) by General Sir G. T. Chesney.

"Well, all the good jingo reasons: we have got the materials for beating. Those fellows throw away their strength whenever they begin to fight, and they've been so badly generaled, up to the present time, that they have wanted to fight at the outset of every quarrel. They have been beaten in every quarrel, but still they always want to begin by fighting. That is all right. When they 5 have learned enough to begin by *voting,* then we shall have to look out. But if they keep on fighting, and always putting themselves in the wrong and getting the worst of it, perhaps we can fix the voting so we needn't be any more afraid of that than we are of the fighting. It's astonishing how shortsighted they are. They have no conception of any cure for their grievances, except more 10 wages and fewer hours."

"But," I asked, "do you really think they have any just grievances?"

"Of course not, as a business man," said the banker. "If I were a workingman, I should probably think differently. But we will suppose for the sake of argument, that their day is too long and their pay is too short. How do they go 15 about to better themselves? They strike. Well, a strike is a fight, and in a fight, now-a-days, it is always skill and money that win. The workingmen can't stop till they have put themselves outside of the public sympathy which the newspapers say is so potent in their behalf; I never saw that it did them the least good. They begin by boycotting, and breaking the heads of the men who 20 want to work. They destroy property, and they interfere with business—the two absolutely sacred things in the American religion. Then we call out the militia, and shoot a few of them, and their leaders declare the strike off. It is perfectly simple."

"But will it be quite as simple," I asked, reluctant in behalf of my projected 25 romance, to have the matter so soon disposed of, "will it be quite so simple if their leaders ever persuade the workingmen to leave the militia, as they threaten to do, from time to time?"

"No, not quite so simple," the banker admitted. "Still, the fight would be comparatively simple. In the first place, I doubt—though I won't be certain 30 about it—whether there are a great many workingmen in the militia now. I rather fancy it is made up, for the most part, of clerks and small tradesmen, and book-keepers, and such employees of business as have time and money for it. I may be mistaken."

No one seemed able to say whether he was mistaken or not; and, after wait- 35 ing a moment, he proceeded: "I feel pretty sure that it is so in the city companies and regiments, at any rate, and that if every workingman left them, it would not seriously impair their effectiveness. But when the workingmen have left the militia, what have they done? They have eliminated the only thing that disqualifies it for prompt and unsparing use against strikers. As long as 40 they are in it, we might have our misgivings, but if they were once out of it, we should have none. And what would they gain? They would not be allowed to arm and organize as an inimical force. *That* was settled once for all, in Chicago, in the case of the International Groups. A few squads of policemen

44. **International Groups**—On May 4, 1886, a bomb exploded among the Chicago police engaged in dispersing an anarchists' meeting in Haymarket Square. The outrage was attributed to the influence of foreign labor leaders. Howells's reference was especially pertinent, since the great Pullman strike of 1893-94 was much before the public eye.

would break them up. Why," the banker exclaimed, with his good-humored laugh, "how preposterous they are when you come to look at it! They are in the majority, the immense majority, if you count the farmers, and they prefer to behave as if they were the hopeless minority. They say they want an eight-
5 hour law, and every now and then they strike, and try to fight it. Why don't they *vote* it? They could *make* it the law in six months, by such overwhelming numbers that no one would dare to evade or defy it. They can make any law they want, but they prefer to break such laws as we have. That 'alienates public sympathy,' the newspapers say, but the spectacle of their stupidity and helpless
10 wilfulness is so lamentable that I could almost pity them. If they chose, it would take only a few years to transform our government into the likeness of anything they wanted. But they would rather not have what they want, apparently, if they can only keep themselves from getting it, and they have to work hard to do that!"

15 "I suppose," I said, "that they are misled by the un-American principles and methods of the socialists among them."

"Why, no," returned the banker, "I shouldn't say that. As far as I understand it, the socialists are the only fellows among them who propose to vote their ideas into laws, and nothing can be more American than that. I don't believe
20 the socialists stir up the strikes, at least among our workingmen, though the newspapers convict them of it, generally without trying them. The socialists seem to accept the strikes as the inevitable outcome of the situation, and they make use of them as proofs of the industrial discontent. But, luckily for the status, our labor leaders are not socialists, for your socialist, whatever you may
25 say against him, has generally thought himself into a socialist. He knows that until the workingmen stop fighting, and get down to voting—until they consent to be the majority—there is no hope for them. I am not talking of anarchists, mind you, but of socialists, whose philosophy is more law, not less, and who look forward to an order so just that it can't be disturbed."

30 "And what," the minister faintly said, "do you think will be the outcome of it all?"

"We had that question the other night, didn't we? Our legal friend, here, seemed to feel that we might rub along indefinitely as we are doing, or work out an Altruria of our own; or go back to the patriarchal stage, and own our
35 workingmen. He seemed not to have so much faith in the logic of events as I have. I doubt if it is altogether a woman's logic. *Parole femmine, fatti maschi,* and the logic of events isn't altogether words; it's full of hard knocks, too. But I'm no prophet. I can't forecast the future; I prefer to take it as it comes. There's a little tract of William Morris's though—I forget just what he calls it
40 —that is full of curious and interesting speculation on this point. He thinks that if we keep the road we are now going, the last state of labor will be like its first, and it will be owned."

"Oh, I don't believe that will ever happen in America," I protested.

"Why not?" asked the banker. "Practically, it *is* owned already in a vastly
45 greater measure than we recognize. And where would the great harm be?

36. Parole . . . maschi—Italian for womanly words, manly deeds. 39. tract of William Morris's—*News from Nowhere* (1891).

The new slavery would not be like the old. There needn't be irresponsible whipping and separation of families, and private buying and selling. The proletariat would probably be owned by the state, as it was at one time in Greece; or by large corporations, which would be much more in keeping with the genius of our free institutions: and an enlightened public opinion would 5 cast safeguards about it in the form of law to guard it from abuse. But it would be strictly policed, localized, and controlled. There would probably be less suffering than there is now, when a man may be cowed into submission to any terms through the suffering of his family; when he may be starved out and turned out if he is unruly. You may be sure that nothing of that kind 10 would happen in the new slavery. We have not had nineteen hundred years of Christianity for nothing."

The banker paused, and as the silence continued he broke it with a laugh, which was a prodigious relief to my feelings, and I suppose to the feelings of all. I perceived that he had been joking, and I was confirmed in this when 15 he turned to the Altrurian and laid his hand upon his shoulder. "You see," he said, "I'm a kind of Altrurian myself. What is the reason why we should not found a new Altruria here on the lines I've drawn? Have you never had philosophers—well, call them philanthropists; I don't mind—of my way of thinking among you?"   20

"Oh, yes," said the Altrurian. "At one time, just before we emerged from the competitive conditions, there was much serious question whether capital should not own labor, instead of labor owning capital. That was many hundred years ago."

"I am proud to find myself such an advanced thinker," said the banker. 25 "And how came you to decide that labor should own capital?"

"We voted it," answered the Altrurian.

"Well," said the banker, "our fellows are still fighting it, and getting beaten." . . .

[ENGAGED TO BE MARRIED]

This is Section IV of *A Modern Instance*. Bartley Hubbard, a self-satisfied young journalist in Equity, a small New England town, has just realized that Marcia Gaylord, the village belle, is in love with him. He has come to this reflection after having taken her for a sleigh ride after the church sociable the night before. His reflections take him to the Gaylord home on Sunday morning. This selection illustrates Howells's thorough understanding of human nature, and well represents his narrative gift; the conversation is recorded with the ease and colloquial force of actual talk. The novel appeared serially in the *Century Magazine,* December, 1881, to October, 1882, and was published in book form in 1882.

THE FORENOON sunshine, beating strong upon the thin snow along the 30 edges of the porch floor, tattered them with a little thaw here and there; but it had no effect upon the hard-packed levels of the street, up the middle of which Bartley walked in a silence intensified by the muffled voices of exhortation that came to him out of the churches. It was in the very

heart of sermon-time, and he had the whole street to himself on his way up to Squire Gaylord's house. As he drew near, he saw smoke ascending from the chimney of the lawyer's office,—a little white building that stood apart from the dwelling on the left of the gate, and he knew that the old man was
5 within, reading there, with his hat on and his long legs flung out toward the stove, unshaven and unkempt, in a grim protest against the prevalent Christian superstition. He might be reading Hume or Gibbon, or he might be reading the Bible,—a book in which he was deeply versed, and from which he was furnished with texts for the demolition of its friends, his adversaries. He pro-
10 fessed himself a great admirer of its literature, and, in the heat of controversy, he often found himself a defender of its doctrines when he had occasion to expose the fallacy of latitudinarian interpretations. For liberal Christianity he had nothing but contempt, and refuted it with a scorn which spared none of the worldly tendencies of the church in Equity. The idea that souls were to
15 be saved by church sociables filled him with inappeasable rancor; and he maintained the superiority of the old Puritanic discipline against them with a fervor which nothing but its re-establishment could have abated. It was said that Squire Gaylord's influence had largely helped to keep in place the last of the rigidly orthodox ministers, under whom his liberalizing congregation chafed
20 for years of discontent; but this was probably an exaggeration of the native humor. Mrs. Gaylord had belonged to this church, and had never formally withdrawn from it, and the lawyer always contributed to pay the minister's salary. He also managed a little property for him so well as to make him independent when he was at last asked to resign by his deacons.
25   In another mood, Bartley might have stepped aside to look in on the Squire, before asking at the house door for Marcia. They relished each other's company, as people of contrary opinions and of no opinions are apt to do. Bartley loved to hear the Squire get going, as he said, and the old man felt a fascination in the youngster. Bartley was smart; he took a point as quick as lightning; and
30 the Squire did not mind his making friends with the Mammon of Righteousness, as he called the visible church in Equity. It amused him to see Bartley lending the church the zealous support of the press, with an impartial patronage of the different creeds. There had been times in his own career when the silence of his opinions would have greatly advanced him, but he had not chosen
35 to pay this price for success; he liked his freedom, or he liked the bitter tang of his own tongue too well, and he had remained a leading lawyer in Equity, when he might have ended a judge, or even a Congressman. Of late years, however, since people whom he could have joined in their agnosticism so heartily, up to a certain point, had begun to make such fools of themselves
40 about Darwinism and the brotherhood of all men in the monkey he had grown much more tolerant. He still clung to his old-fashioned deistical opinions; but he thought no worse of a man for holding them; he did not deny that a man might be a Christian, and still be a very good man.

7. **Hume . . . Gibbon**—David Hume (1711-1776), Scotch skeptical philosopher, and Edward Gibbon (1737-1794), English historian with a rational turn of mind. **30-31. Mammon of Righteousness**—humorous travesty of the well-known phrase in Luke 16: 9. **40. Darwinism** —This misconception of the theory of evolution advanced by Charles Darwin (1809-1882) was once common. **41. deistical**—See the discussion of Paine in this volume.

The audacious humor of his position sufficed with a people who liked a joke rather better than anything else; in his old age, his infidelity was something that would hardly have been changed, if possible, by a popular vote. Even his wife, to whom it had once been a heavy cross, borne with secret prayer and tears, had long ceased to gainsay it in any wise. Her family had opposed her yoking with an unbeliever when she married him, but she had some such hopes of converting him as women cherish who give themselves to men confirmed in drunkenness. She learned, as other women do, that she could hardly change her husband in the least of his habits, and that, in this great matter of his unbelief, her love was powerless. It became easier at last for her to add self-sacrifice to self-sacrifice than to vex him with her anxieties about his soul, and to act upon the feeling that, if he must be lost, then she did not care to be saved. He had never interfered with her church-going; he had rather promoted it, for he liked to have women go; but the time came when she no longer cared to go without him; she lapsed from her membership, and it was now many years since she had worshipped with the people of her faith, if, indeed, she were still of any faith. Her life was silenced in every way, and, as often happens with aging wives in country towns, she seldom went out of her own door, and never appeared at the social or public solemnities of the village. Her husband and her daughter composed and bounded her world,—she always talked of them, or of other things as related to them. She had grown an elderly woman without losing the color of her yellow hair; and the bloom of girlhood had been stayed in her cheeks as if by the young habit of blushing, which she had kept. She was still what her neighbors called very pretty-appearing, and she must have been a beautiful girl. The silence of her inward life subdued her manner, till now she seemed always to have come from some place on which a deep hush had newly fallen.

She answered the door when Bartley turned the crank that snapped the gong-bell in its centre; and the young man, who was looking at the street while waiting for some one to come, confronted her with a start. "Oh!" he said, "I thought it was Marcia. Good morning, Mrs. Gaylord. Isn't Marcia at home?"

"She went to church, this morning," replied her mother. "Won't you walk in?"

"Why, yes, I guess I will, thank you," faltered Bartley, in the irresolution of his disappointment. "I hope I sha'n't disturb you."

"Come right into the sitting-room. She won't be gone a great while, now," said Mrs. Gaylord, leading the way to the large square room into which a door at the end of the narrow hall opened. A slumberous heat from a sheet-iron wood-stove pervaded the place, and a clock ticked monotonously on a shelf in the corner. Mrs. Gaylord said, "Won't you take a chair?" and herself sank into the rocker, with a deep feather cushion in the seat, and a thinner feather cushion tied half-way up the back. After the more active duties of her housekeeping were done, she sat every day in this chair with her knitting or sewing, and let the clock tick the long hours of her life away, with no more apparent impatience of them, or sense of their dulness, than the cat on the braided rug at her feet, or the geraniums in the pots at the sunny window. "Are you pretty well to-day?" she asked.

"Well, no, Mrs. Gaylord, I'm not," answered Bartley. "I'm all out of sorts. I haven't felt so dyspeptic for I don't know how long."

Mrs. Gaylord smoothed the silk dress across her lap,—the thin old black silk which she still instinctively put on for Sabbath observance, though it was
5 so long since she had worn it to church. "Mr. Gaylord used to have it when we were first married, though he aint been troubled with it of late years. He seemed to think then it was worse Sundays."

"I don't believe Sunday has much to do with it, in my case. I ate some mince-pie and some toasted cheese last night, and I guess they didn't agree
10 with me very well," said Bartley, who did not spare himself the confession of his sins when seeking sympathy: it was this candor that went so far to convince people of his good-heartedness.

"I don't know as I ever heard that meat-pie was bad," said Mrs. Gaylord, thoughtfully. "Mr. Gaylord used to eat it right along all through his dypepsia,
15 and he never complained of it. And the cheese ought to have made it digest."

"Well, I don't know what it was," replied Bartley, plaintively submitting to be exonerated, "but I feel perfectly used up. Oh, I suppose I shall get over it, or forget all about it, by to-morrow," he added, with strenuous cheerfulness. "It isn't anything worth minding."

20 Mrs. Gaylord seemed to differ with him on this point. "Head ache any?" she asked.

"It did this morning, when I first woke up," Bartley assented.

"I don't believe but what a cup of tea would be the best thing for you," she said, critically.

25 Bartley had instinctively practised a social art which ingratiated him with people at Equity as much as his demands for sympathy endeared him: he gave trouble in little unusual ways. He said, "Oh, I wish you would give me a cup, Mrs. Gaylord."

"Why, yes, indeed! That's just what I was going to," she replied. She went
30 to the kitchen, which lay beyond another room, reappeared with the tea directly, proud of her promptness, but having it on her conscience to explain it. "I 'most always keep the pot on the stove hearth, Sunday morning, so's to have it ready if Mr. Gaylord ever wants a cup. He's a master hand for tea, and always was. There: I guess you better take it without milk. I put some
35 sugar in the saucer, if you want any." She dropped noiselessly upon her feather cushion again, and Bartley, who had risen to receive the tea from her, remained standing while he drank it.

"That does seem to go to the spot," he said, as he sipped it, thoughtfully observant of its effect upon his disagreeable feelings. "I wish I had you to take
40 care of me, Mrs. Gaylord, and keep me from making a fool of myself," he added, when he had drained the cup. "No, no!" he cried, at her offering to take it from him. "I'll set it down. I know it will fret you to have it in here, and I'll carry it out into the kitchen." He did so before she could prevent him, and came back, touching his mustache with his handkerchief. "I declare, Mrs.
45 Gaylord, I should love to live in a kitchen like that."

"I guess you wouldn't if you had to," said Mrs. Gaylord, flattered into a smile. "Marcia, she likes to sit out there, she says, better than anywheres in the house. But I always tell her it's because she was there so much when she was little. I don't see as she seems over-anxious to do anything there *but* sit, I tell her. Not but what she knows how well enough. Mr. Gaylord, too, he's great for being round in the kitchen. If he gets up in the night, when he has his waking spells, he had rather take his lamp out there, if there's a fire left, 5 and read, any time, than what he would in the parlor. Well, we used to sit there together a good deal when we were young, and he got the habit of it. There's everything in habit," she added, thoughtfully. "Marcia, she's got quite in the way, lately, of going to the Methodist church."

"Yes, I've seen her there. You know I board round at the different churches, 10 as the schoolmaster used to at the houses in the old times."

Mrs. Gaylord looked up at the clock, and gave a little nervous laugh. "I don't know what Marcia will say to my letting her company stay in the sitting-room. She's pretty late to-day. But I guess you won't have much longer to wait, now." 15

She spoke with that awe of her daughter and her judgments which is one of the pathetic idiosyncrasies of a certain class of American mothers. They feel themselves to be not so well educated as their daughters, whose fancied knowledge of the world they let outweigh their own experience of life; they are used to deferring to them, and they shrink willingly into household drudges 20 before them, and leave them to order the social affairs of the family. Mrs. Gaylord was not much afraid of Bartley for himself, but as Marcia's company he made her more and more uneasy toward the end of the quarter of an hour in which she tried to entertain him with her simple talk, varying from Mr. Gaylord to Marcia, and from Marcia to Mr. Gaylord again. When she recognized 25 the girl's quick touch in the closing of the front door, and her elastic step approached through the hall, the mother made a little deprecating noise in her throat, and fidgeted in her chair. As soon as Marcia opened the sitting-room door, Mrs. Gaylord modestly rose and went out into the kitchen: the mother who remained in the room when her daughter had company was an oddity 30 almost unknown in Equity.

Marcia's face flashed all into a light of joy at sight of Bartley, who scarcely waited for her mother to be gone before he drew her toward him by the hand she had given. She mechanically yielded; and then, as if the recollection of some new resolution forced itself through her pleasure at sight of him, she 35 freed her hand, and, retreating a step or two, confronted him.

"Why, Marcia," he said, "what's the matter?"

"Nothing," she answered.

It might have amused Bartley, if he had felt quite well, to see the girl so defiant of him, when she was really so much in love with him, but it certainly 40 did not amuse him now: it disappointed him in his expectation of finding her femininely soft and comforting, and he did not know just what to do. He stood staring at her in discomfiture, while she gained in outward composure, though her cheeks were of the Jacqueminot red of the ribbon at her throat.

"What have I done, Marcia?" he faltered. 45

"Oh, you haven't done anything."

"Some one has been talking to you against me."

"No one has said a word to me about you."

"Then why are you so cold—so strange—so—so—different?"

"Different?"

"Yes, from what you were last night," he answered, with an aggrieved air.

5   "Oh, we see some things differently by daylight," she lightly explained. "Won't you sit down?"

"No, thank you," Bartley replied, sadly but unresentfully. "I think I had better be going. I see there is something wrong—"

"I don't see why you say there is anything wrong," she retorted. "What have

10 I done?"

"Oh, you have not *done* anything; I take it back. It is all right. But when I came here this morning—encouraged—hoping—that you had the same feeling as myself, and you seem to forget everything but a ceremonious acquaintanceship—why, it is all right, of course. I have no reason to complain; but I

15 must say that I can't help being surprised." He saw her lips quiver and her bosom heave. "Marcia, do you blame me for feeling hurt at your coldness when I came here to tell you—to tell you I—I love you?" With his nerves all unstrung, and his hunger for sympathy, he really believed that he had come to tell her this. "Yes," he added, bitterly, "I *will* tell you, though it seems to

20 be the last word I shall speak to you. I'll go, now."

"Bartley! You shall *never* go!" she cried, throwing herself in his way. "Do you think I don't care for you, too? You may kiss me,—you may *kill* me now!"

The passionate tears sprang to her eyes, without the sound of sobs or the contortion of weeping, and she did not wait for his embrace. She flung her

25 arms around his neck and held him fast, crying, "I wouldn't let you, for your own sake, darling; and if I had died for it—I thought I should die last night— I was never going to let you kiss me again till you said—till—till—now! Don't you see?" She caught him tighter, and hid her face in his neck, and cried and laughed for joy and shame, while he suffered her caresses with a certain

30 bewilderment. "I want to tell you now—I want to explain," she said, lifting her face and letting him from her as far as her arms, caught around his neck, would reach, and fervidly searching his eyes, lest some ray of what he would think should escape her. "Don't speak a word first! Father saw us at the door last night,—he happened to be coming downstairs, because he couldn't sleep,

35 —just when you— Oh, Bartley, don't!" she implored, at the little smile that made his mustache quiver. "And he asked me whether we were engaged; and when I couldn't tell him we were, I know what he thought. I knew how he despised me, and I determined that, if you didn't tell me that you cared for me— And that's the reason, Bartley, and not—not because I didn't care more

40 for you than I do for the whole world. And—and—you don't mind it, now, do you? It was for your sake, dearest."

Whether Bartley perfectly divined or not all the feeling at which her words hinted, it was delicious to be clung about by such a pretty girl as Marcia Gaylord, to have her now darting her face into his neck-scarf with intolerable con-

45 sciousness, and now boldly confronting him with all-defying fondness while she lightly pushed him and pulled him here and there in the vehemence of her appeal. Perhaps such a man, in those fastnesses of his nature which psychology

has not yet explored, never loses, even in the tenderest transports, the sense of prey as to the girl whose love he has won; but if this is certain, it is also certain that he has transports which are tender, and Bartley now felt his soul melted with affection that was very novel and sweet.

"Why, Marcia!" he said, "what a strange girl you are!" He sunk into his chair again and putting his arms around her waist, drew her upon his knee, like a child.

She held herself apart from him at her arm's length, and said, "Wait! Let me say it before it seems as if we had always been engaged, and everything was as right then as it is now. Did you despise me for letting you kiss me before we were engaged?"

"No," he laughed again. "I liked you for it."

"But if you thought I would let any one else, you wouldn't have liked it?"

This diverted him still more. "I shouldn't have liked that more than half as well."

"No," she said thoughtfully. She dropped her face awhile on his shoulder, and seemed to be struggling with herself. Then she lifted it, and "Did you ever—did you—" she gasped.

"If you want me to say that all the other girls in the world are not worth a hair of your head, I'll say that, Marcia. Now, let's talk business!"

This made her laugh, and "I shall want a little lock of yours," she said, as if they had hitherto been talking of nothing but each other's hair.

"And I shall want all of yours," he answered.

"No. Don't be silly." She critically explored his face. "How funny to have a mole in your eyebrow!" She put her finger on it. "I never saw it before."

"You never looked so closely. There's a scar at the corner of your upper lip that I hadn't noticed."

"Can you see that?" she demanded, radiantly. "Well, you *have* got good eyes! The cat did it when I was a little girl."

The door opened, and Mrs. Gaylord surprised them in the celebration of these discoveries,—or, rather, she surprised herself, for she stood holding the door and helpless to move, though in her heart she had an apologetic impulse to retire, and she even believed that she made some murmurs of excuse for her intrusion. Bartley was equally abashed, but Marcia rose with the coolness of her sex in the intimate emergencies which confound a man. "Oh, mother, it's you! I forgot about you. Come in! Or I'll set the table, if that's what you want." As Mrs. Gaylord continued to look from her to Bartley in her daze, Marcia added, simply, "We're engaged, mother. You may as well know it first as last, and I guess you better know it first."

Her mother appeared not to think it safe to relax her hold upon the door, and Bartley went filially to her rescue—if it was rescue to salute her blushing defencelessness as he did. A confused sense of the extraordinary nature and possible impropriety of the proceeding may have suggested her husband to her mind; or it may have been a feeling that some remark was expected of her, even in the mental destitution to which she was reduced.

"Have you told Mr. Gaylord about it?" she asked, of either, or neither, or both, as they chose to take it.

Bartley left the word to Marcia, who answered, "Well, no, mother. We haven't yet. We've only just found it out ourselves. I guess father can wait till he comes in to dinner. I intend to keep Bartley here to prove it."

"He said," remarked Mrs. Gaylord, whom Bartley had led to her chair and placed on her cushion, "'t he had a headache when he first came in," and she appealed to him for corroboration, while she vainly endeavored to gather force to grapple again with the larger fact that he and Marcia were just engaged to be married.

Marcia stooped down, and pulled her mother up out of her chair with a hug. "Oh, come now, mother! You mustn't let it take your breath away," she said, with patronizing fondness. "I'm not afraid of what father will say. You know what he thinks of Bartley,—or Mr. Hubbard, as I presume you'll want me to call him! Now, mother, you just run up stairs, and put on your best cap, and leave me to set the table and get up the dinner. I guess I can get Bartley to help me. Mother, mother, mother!" she cried, in happiness that was otherwise unutterable, and clasping her mother closer in her strong young arms, she kissed her with a fervor that made her blush again before the young man.

"Marcia, Marcia! You hadn't ought to! It's ridiculous!" she protested. But she suffered herself to be thrust out of the room, grateful for exile, in which she could collect her scattered wits and set herself to realize the fact that had dispersed them. It was decorous, also, for her to leave Marcia alone with Mr. Hubbard, far more so now than when he was merely company; she felt that, and she fumbled over the dressing she was sent about, and once she looked out of her chamber window at the office where Mr. Gaylord sat, and wondered what Mr. Gaylord (she thought of him, and even dreamt of him, as Mr. Gaylord, and had never, in the most familiar moments addressed him otherwise) *would* say! But she left the solution of the problem to him and Marcia; she was used to leaving them to the settlement of their own difficulties.

"Now, Bartley," said Marcia, in the business-like way that women assume in such matters, as soon as the great fact is no longer in doubt, "you must help me to set the table. Put up that leaf and I'll put up this. I'm going to do more for mother than I used to," she said, repentant in her bliss. "It's a shame how much I've left to her." The domestic instinct was already astir in her heart.

Bartley pulled the table-cloth straight from her, and vied with her in the rapidity and exactness with which he arranged the knives and forks at right angles beside the plates. When it came to some heavier dishes, they agreed to carry them turn about; but when it was her turn, he put out his hand to support her elbow: "As I did last night, and saved you from dropping a lamp."

This made her laugh, and she dropped the first dish with a crash. "Poor mother!" she exclaimed. "I know she heard that, and she'll be in agony to know which one it is."

Mrs. Gaylord did indeed hear it, far off in her chamber, and quaked with an anxiety which became intolerable at last.

"Marcia! Marcia!" she quavered, down the stairs, "what *have* you broken?"

Marcia opened the door long enough to call back, "Oh, only the old blue-edged platter, mother!" and then she flew at Bartley, crying, "For shame! For shame!" and pressing her hand over his mouth to stifle his laughter. "She'll hear you, Bartley, and think you're laughing at her." But she laughed herself at his struggles, and ended by taking him by the hand and pulling him out into the kitchen, where neither of them could be heard. She abandoned herself to the ecstasy of her soul, and he thought she had never been so charming as in this wild gayety.

"Why, Marsh! I never saw you carry on so before!"

"You never saw me engaged before! That's the way all girls act—if they get the chance. Don't you like me to be so?" she asked, with quick anxiety.

"Rather!" he replied.

"Oh, Bartley!" she exclaimed, "I feel like a child. I surprise myself as much as I do you; for I thought I had got very old, and I didn't suppose I should ever let myself go in this way. But there is something about this that lets me be as silly as I like. It's somehow as if I were a great deal more alone when I'm with you than when I'm by myself! How does it make you feel?"

"Good!" he answered, and that satisfied her better than if he had entered into those subtleties which she had tried to express: it was more like a man. He had his arm about her again, and she put down her hand on his to press it closer against her heart.

"Of course," she explained, recurring to his surprise at her frolic mood, "I don't expect you to be silly because I am."

"No," he assented; "but how can I help it?"

"Oh, I don't mean for the time being; I mean generally speaking. I mean that I care for you because I know you know a great deal more than I do, and because I respect you. I know that everybody expects you to be something great, and I do, too."

Bartley did not deny the justness of her opinions concerning himself, or the reasonableness of the general expectation, though he probably could not see the relation of these cold abstractions to the pleasure of sitting there with a pretty girl in that way. But he said nothing.

"Do you know," she went on, turning her face prettily around him, but holding it a little way off, to secure attention as impersonal as might be under the circumstances, "what pleased me more than anything else you ever said to me?"

"No," answered Bartley. "Something you got out of me when you were trying to make me tell you the difference between you and the other Equity girls?"

She laughed, in glad defiance of her own consciousness. "Well, I *was* trying to make you compliment me; I'm not going to deny it. But I must say I got my come-uppance: you didn't say a thing I cared for. But you did afterward. Don't you remember?"

"No. When?"

She hesitated a moment. "When you told me that my influence had—had—made you better, you know—"

"Oh!" said Bartley. "That! Well," he added carelessly, "it's every word true. Didn't you believe it?"

"I was just as glad as if I did; and it made me resolve never to do or say a thing that could lower your opinion of me; and then, you know, there at the

door—it all seemed part of our trying to make each other better. But when
father looked at me in that way, and asked me if we were engaged, I went
down into the dust with shame. And it seemed to me that you had just been
laughing at me, and amusing yourself with me, and I was so furious I didn't
5 know what to do. Do you know what I wanted to do? I wanted to run downstairs to father, and tell him what you had said, and ask him if he believed
you had ever liked any other girl." She paused a little, but he did not answer,
and she continued. "But now I'm glad I didn't. And I shall never ask you that,
and I shall not care for anything that you—that's happened before to-day.
10 It's all right. And you *do* think I shall always *try* to make you good and happy,
don't you?"

"I don't think you can make me much happier than I am at present, and
I don't believe anybody could make me feel better," answered Bartley.

She gave a little laugh at his refusal to be serious, and let her head, for
15 fondness, fall upon his shoulder, while he turned round and round a ring he
found on her finger.

"Ah, ha!" he said, after a while. "Who gave you this ring, Miss Gaylord?"

"Father, Christmas before last," she promptly answered, without moving.
"I'm glad you asked," she murmured, in a lower voice, full of pride in the
20 maiden love she could give him. "There's never been any one but you, or the
thought of any one." She suddenly started away.

"Now, let's play we're getting dinner." It was quite time; in the next moment
the coffee boiled up, and if she had not caught the lid off and stirred it down
with her spoon, it would have been spoiled. The steam ascended to the ceiling,
25 and filled the kitchen with the fragrant smell of the berry.

"I'm glad we're going to have coffee," she said. "You'll have to put up with
a cold dinner, except potatoes. But the coffee will make up, and I shall need a
cup to keep me awake. I don't believe I slept last night till nearly morning. Do
you like coffee?"

30 "I'd have given all I ever expect to be worth for a cup of it, last night," he
said. "I was awfully hungry when I got back to the hotel, and I couldn't find
anything but a piece of mince-pie and some old cheese, and I had to be
content with cold milk. I felt as if I had lost all my friends this morning when
I woke up."

35 A sense of remembered grievance trembled in his voice, and made her drop
her head on his arm, in pity and derision of him. "Poor Bartley!" she cried.
"And you came up here for a little petting from me, didn't you? I've noticed
that in you! Well, you didn't get it, did you?"

"Well, not at first," he said.

40 "Yes, you can't complain of any want of petting at last," she returned, delighted at his indirect recognition of the difference. Then the daring, the
archness, and caprice that make coquetry in some women and lurk a divine
possibility in all, came out in her; the sweetness, kept back by the whole
strength of her pride, overflowed that broken barrier now, and she seemed to
45 lavish this revelation of herself upon him with a sort of tender joy in his bewilderment. She was not hurt when he crudely expressed the elusive sense
which has been in other men's minds at such times: they cannot believe that
this fascination is inspired, and not practised.

"Well," he said, "I'm glad you told me that I was the first. I should have thought you'd had a good deal of experience in flirtation."

"You wouldn't have thought so if you hadn't been a great flirt yourself," she answered, audaciously. "Perhaps I have been engaged before!"

Their talk was for the most part frivolous, and their thoughts ephemeral; but again they were, with her at least, suddenly and deeply serious. Till then all things seemed to have been held in arrest, and impressions, ideas, feelings, fears, desires, released themselves simultaneously, and sought expression with a rush that defied coherence. "Oh, why do we try to talk?" she asked, at last. "The more we say, the more we leave unsaid. Let us keep still awhile!" But she could not. "Bartley! When did you first think you cared about me?"

"I don't know," said Bartley, "I guess it must have been the first time I saw you."

"Yes, that is when I first knew that I cared for you. But it seems to me that I must have always cared for you, and that I only found it out when I saw you going by the house that day." She mused a little time before she asked again, "Bartley!"

"Well?"

"Did you ever use to be afraid— Oh, no! Wait! I'll *tell* you first, and then I'll *ask* you. I'm not ashamed of it now, though once I thought I couldn't bear to have any one find it out. I used to be awfully afraid you didn't care for me! I would try to make out, from things you did and said, whether you did or not; but I never could be certain. I believe I used to find the most comfort in discouraging myself. I used to say to myself, 'Why, of course he doesn't! How can he? He's been everywhere, and he's seen so many girls. He corresponds with lots of them. Altogether likely he's engaged to some of the young ladies he's met in Boston; and he just goes with me here for a blind.' And then when you would praise me, sometimes, I would just say, 'Oh, he's complimented plenty of girls. I know he's thinking this instant of the young lady he's engaged to in Boston.' And it would almost kill me; and when you did some little thing to show that you liked me, I would think, 'He doesn't like me! He hates, he despises me. He does, he does, he does!' And I would go on that way, with my teeth shut, and my breath held, I don't know *how* long." Bartley broke out into a broad laugh at this image of desperation, but she added, tenderly, "I hope I never made you suffer in that way?"

"What way?" he asked.

"That's what I wanted you to tell me. Did you ever—did you use to be afraid sometimes that I—that you—did you put off telling me that you cared for me so long because you thought, you dreaded— Oh, I don't see what I can ever do to make it up to you if you did! Were you afraid I didn't care for you?"

"No!" shouted Bartley. She had risen and stood before him in the fervor of her entreaty, and he seized her arms, pinioning them to her side, and holding her helpless, while he laughed, and laughed again. "I knew you were dead in love with me from the first moment."

"Bartley! Bartley Hubbard!" she exclaimed; "let me go,—let me go, this instant! I never heard of such a shameless thing!"

But she really made no effort to escape.

HENRY ADAMS

1838-1918

I. SCION OF A DISTINGUISHED FAMILY (1838–1880)

1838   Henry Brooks Adams born in Boston February 16, son of Charles Francis Adams, grandson of John Quincy Adams and great-grandson of John Adams. Abigail Brooks, his mother, was the daughter of the wealthiest man in Boston.

1858   Graduated from Harvard. Influenced only by Agassiz and Lowell. In November went to Berlin to study law, but drifted to Dresden, and then to Italy.

1860   In Florence and Rome. At Palermo met Garibaldi, the liberator. Returned by way of Paris to Quincy, Massachusetts.

1860–1868   Served as his father's secretary during a memorable session of Congress, and thereafter in London, where his father was American Minister.

1868   Returned to the United States and contributed economic articles to the *North American Review*.

1870–1876   Edited the *North American Review*, and taught medieval history at Harvard University.

1872   June 27, married Marian Hooper of Boston.

1877   Gave up his post at Harvard, and went to Washington, partly to write and partly to enjoy the companionship of John Hay and others. Published *The Life of Albert Gallatin* (1879).

II. DISILLUSIONED WANDERER BETWEEN TWO WORLDS
(1880–1918)

1880   Published *Democracy,* an anonymous novel.

1884   *Esther,* a second novel, published under the pseudonym Frances Snow Compton, a failure.

1885   Tragic death of Mrs. Adams. St. Gaudens's commemorative figure in Rock Creek Cemetery, Washington, D. C., a masterpiece of American art.

1886   Sought solace in travel to Japan and the South Seas with John La Farge.

1889–1891   Published *History of the United States during the Administrations of Jefferson and Madison*. Then traveled in the Caribbean and in Europe. Published *Historical Essays* (1891).

1900   His visit to the Paris exposition convinced him that the dynamo and the Virgin were the two integrating forces in the world.

1904   Privately printed *Mont-Saint-Michel and Chartres,* his masterly interpretation of life in the Middle Ages. Revised, and published in 1913.

1906   *The Education of Henry Adams* privately printed. Given to the public in 1918.

1910   Published *A Letter to American Teachers of History.*

1911   Published *The Life of George Cabot Lodge.*

1918 Died March 28.
1920 Posthumous publication of *The Degradation of the Democratic Dogma.*

BIOGRAPHIES: For biographical information see, besides *The Education* (below), *A Cycle of Adams Letters, 1861-1865,* ed. W. C. Ford, Houghton Mifflin, 1920, 2 vols.; *The Letters of Henry Adams,* ed. W. C. Ford, Houghton Mifflin, 1930-38, 2 vols.; C. F. Adams, Jr., *Charles Francis Adams, 1835-1916; an Autobiography,* Houghton Mifflin, 1916; Dictionary of American Biography, Vol. I (1928); J. T. Adams, *Henry Adams,* Boni, 1933; Dictionary of National Biography, Sup., 1927; *Letters to a Niece . . . with a Niece's Memories* by M. La Farge, Houghton Mifflin, 1920; *Henry Adams and His Friends: A Collection of His Unpublished Letters,* ed. Harold D. Cater, Houghton Mifflin, 1947; Ernest Samuels, *The Young Henry Adams,* Harvard, 1948; *The Letters of Mrs. Henry Adams,* ed. Ward Thoron, Houghton Mifflin, 1936.

EDITIONS: *History of the United States during the Administrations of Jefferson and Madison, 1801-1817,* Scribner, 1889-1891, 9 vols.; *Mont-Saint-Michel and Chartres,* Houghton Mifflin, 1904; *The Degradation of the Democratic Dogma,* Macmillan, 1920; *The Education of Henry Adams,* Houghton Mifflin, 1930 (Riverside Library); Modern Library, New York, 1931; *Esther: A Novel,* introduction by Robert E. Spiller, Scholars' Facsimiles and Reprints, 1938. For other works see *Literary History of the United States,* Vol. III, pp. 373-77.

The importance of Henry Adams, says T. K. Whipple, lies in the fact "that he has recorded the experience of a man endowed with the poetic temper and forced to live in a practical society, that he first and most fully formulated the philosophy implicit in American behavior and that therefore he affords the best of all approaches to an understanding of modern American life and literature." The application of this statement is to be found in three important books. In his *History of the United States* Adams interprets the historical and human significance of the Jefferson-Madison administrations; in *Mont-Saint-Michel and Chartres* this son of the Puritans returns after many negations to the mystical certitudes of the Middle Ages and bows in adoration before the Virgin; and in *The Education of Henry Adams* he retraces more fully his experience of disillusion in an age of industrial development. To his inquiring spirit Chaos appears to be the law of nature; Order, the dream of man. Men are victims, not rulers, of their own discoveries and inventions; but art and religion achieve unity amid multiplicity. Thus this sturdy soul finds in the elusive suggestions of medievalism a quiet which modern wit seems unable to supply. If Adams's synthesis of the cult of the Virgin and the worship of the Dynamo is mystifying at times, and his style is paradoxical, yet his challenges may not easily be set aside, nor in an age of industrial materialism be readily ignored.

AMERICAN CHARACTER

This selection is the concluding chapter of the History of the United States, *Book IX, a work on the administrations of Jefferson and Madison, published in 1891.*

UNTIL 1815 nothing in the future of the American Union was regarded as settled. As late as January, 1815, division into several nationalities was still thought to be possible. Such a destiny, repeating the usual experience of history, was not necessarily more unfortunate than the career of a
5   single nationality wholly American; for if the effects of divided nationality were certain to be unhappy, those of a single society with equal certainty defied experience or sound speculation. One uniform and harmonious system appealed to the imagination as a triumph of human progress, offering prospects of peace and ease, contentment and philanthropy, such as the world had
10 not seen; but it invited dangers, formidable because unusual or altogether unknown. The corruption of such a system might prove to be proportionate with its dimensions, and uniformity might lead to evils as serious as were commonly ascribed to diversity.

The laws of human progress were matter not for dogmatic faith, but for
15 study; and although society instinctively regarded small States, with their clashing interests and incessant wars, as the chief obstacle to improvement, such progress as the world knew had been coupled with those drawbacks. The few examples offered by history of great political societies, relieved from external competition or rivalry, were not commonly thought encouraging. War
20 had been the severest test of political and social character, laying bare whatever was feeble, and calling out whatever was strong; and the effect of removing such a test was an untried problem.

In 1815 for the first time Americans ceased to doubt the path they were about to follow. Not only was the unity of their nation established, but its
25 probable divergence from older societies was also well defined. Already in 1817 the difference between Europe and America was decided. In politics the distinction was more evident than in social, religious, literary, or scientific directions; and the result was singular. For a time the aggressions of England and France forced the United States into a path that seemed to lead toward
30 European methods of government; but the popular resistance, or inertia, was so great that the most popular party leaders failed to overcome it, and no sooner did foreign dangers disappear than the system began to revert to American practices; the national government tried to lay aside its assumed powers. When Madison vetoed the bill for internal improvements he could have had
35 no other motive than that of restoring to the government, as far as possible, its original American character.

The result was not easy to understand in theory or to make efficient in practice; but while the drift of public opinion, and still more of practical ne-

---

34. Madison vetoed—On Mar. 3, 1816, President Madison vetoed a bill which had narrowly passed the House of Representatives, but which gained a larger proportionate support in the Senate, for internal improvements at Federal cost. On Mar. 4 he was succeeded by Monroe.

cessity, drew the government slowly toward the European standard of true political sovereignty, nothing showed that the compromise, which must probably
serve the public purpose, was to be European in form or feeling. As far as
politics supplied a test, the national character had already diverged from any
foreign type. Opinions might differ whether the political movement was pro-   5
gressive or retrograde, but in any case the American, in his political character,
was a new variety of man.

The social movement was also decided. The war gave a severe shock to the
Anglican sympathies of society, and peace seemed to widen the breach between
European and American tastes. Interest in Europe languished after Napoleon's 10
overthrow. France ceased to affect American opinion. England became an object of less alarm. Peace produced in the United States a social and economical
revolution which greatly curtailed the influence of New England, and with it
the social authority of Great Britain. The invention of the steamboat counter-
balanced ocean commerce. The South and West gave to society a character   15
more aggressively American than had been known before. That Europe, within
certain limits, might tend toward American ideas was possible, but that
America should under any circumstances follow the experiences of European
development might thenceforward be reckoned as improbable. American character was formed, if not fixed.   20

The scientific interest of American history centred in national character, and
in the workings of a society destined to become vast, in which individuals
were important chiefly as types. Although this kind of interest was different
from that of European history, it was at least as important to the world.
Should history ever become a true science, it must expect to establish its laws, 25
not from the complicated story of rival European nationalities, but from the
economical evolution of a great democracy. North America was the most
favorable field on the globe for the spread of a society so large, uniform, and
isolated as to answer the purposes of science. There a single homogeneous society could easily attain proportions of three or four hundred million persons, 30
under conditions of undisturbed growth.

In Europe or Asia, except perhaps in China, undisturbed social evolution
had been unknown. Without disturbance, evolution seemed to cease. Wherever disturbance occurred, permanence was impossible. Every people in turn
adapted itself to the law of necessity. Such a system as that of the United   35
States could hardly have existed for half a century in Europe except under the
protection of another power. In the fierce struggle characteristic of European
society, systems were permanent in nothing except in the general law, that,
whatever other character they might possess, they must always be chiefly
military.   40

The want of permanence was not the only or the most confusing obstacle
to the treatment of European history as a science. The intensity of the struggle
gave prominence to the individual, until the hero seemed all, society nothing;
and what was worse for science, the men were far more interesting than the
societies. In the dramatic view of history, the hero deserved more to be studied 45

10-11. **Napoleon's overthrow**—Napoleon Bonaparte (1769-1821), defeated at Waterloo in
1815.

than the community to which he belonged; in truth, he was the society, which existed only to produce him and to perish with him. Against such a view historians were among the last to protest, and protested but faintly when they did so at all. They felt as strongly as their audiences that the highest achieve-
5   ments were alone worth remembering either in history or in art, and that a reiteration of commonplaces was commonplace. With all the advantages of European movement and color, few historians succeeded in enlivening or dig- nifying the lack of motive, intelligence, and morality, the helplessness charac- teristic of many long periods in the face of crushing problems, and the fu-
10   tility of human efforts to escape from difficulties religious, political, and social. In a period extending over four or five thousand years, more or less capable of historical treatment, historians were content to illustrate here and there the most dramatic moments of the most striking communities. The hero was their favorite. War was the chief field of heroic action, and even the history of
15   England was chiefly the story of war.

The history of the United States promised to be free from such disturbances. War counted for little, the hero for less; on the people alone the eye could permanently rest. The steady growth of a vast population without the social distinctions that confused other histories,—without kings, nobles, or armies;
20   without church, traditions, and prejudices,—seemed a subject for the man of science rather than for dramatists or poets. To scientific treatment only one great obstacle existed. Americans, like Europeans, were not disposed to make of their history a mechanical evolution. They felt that they even more than other nations needed the heroic element, because they breathed an atmosphere
25   of peace and industry where heroism could seldom be displayed; and in un- conscious protest against their own social conditions they adorned with imag- inary qualities scores of supposed leaders, whose only merit was their faculty of reflecting a popular trait. Instinctively they clung to ancient history as though conscious that of all misfortunes that could befall the national charac-
30   ter, the greatest would be the loss of the established ideals which alone en- nobled human weakness. Without heroes, the national character of the United States had few charms of imagination even to Americans.

Historians and readers maintained Old-World standards. No historian cared to hasten the coming of an epoch when man should study his own history
35   in the same spirit and by the same methods with which he studied the for- mation of a crystal. Yet history had its scientific as well as its human side, and in American history the scientific interest was greater than the human. Elsewhere the student could study under better conditions the evolution of the individual, but nowhere could he study so well the evolution of a race.
40   The interest of such a subject exceeded that of any other branch of science, for it brought mankind within sight of its own end.

Travellers in Switzerland who stepped across the Rhine where it flowed from its glacier could follow its course among mediaeval towns and feudal ruins, until it became a highway for modern industry, and at last arrived at a
45   permanent equilibrium in the ocean. American history followed the same course. With prehistoric glaciers and mediaeval feudalism the story had little to do; but from the moment it came within sight of the ocean it acquired in-

terest almost painful. A child could find his way in a river-valley, and a hoy could float on the waters of Holland; but science alone could sound the depths of the ocean, measure its currents, foretell its storms, or fix its relations to the system of Nature. In a democratic ocean science could see something ultimate. Man could go no further. The atom might move, but the general equilibrium 5 could not change.

Whether the scientific or the heroic view were taken, in either case the starting-point was the same, and the chief object of interest was to define national character. (Whether the figures of history were treated as heroes or as types, they must be taken to represent the people.) American types were 10 especially worth study if they were to represent the greatest democratic evolution the world could know. Readers might judge for themselves what share the individual possessed in creating or shaping the nation; but whether it was small or great, (the nation could be understood only by studying the individual.) For that reason, in the story of Jefferson and Madison individuals re- 15 tained their old interest as types of character, if not as sources of power.

(In the American character antipathy to war ranked first among political traits.) The majority of Americans regarded war in a peculiar light, the consequence of comparative security. No European nation could have conducted a war, as the people of America conducted the War of 1812. The possibility of 20 doing so without destruction explained the existence of the national trait, and assured its continuance. In politics, the divergence of America from Europe perpetuated itself in the popular instinct for peaceable methods. The Union took shape originally on the general lines that divided the civil from the military elements of the British constitution. The party of Jefferson and Gallatin 25 was founded on dislike of every function of government necessary in a military system. Although Jefferson carried his pacific theories to an extreme, and brought about a military reaction, the reactionary movement was neither universal, violent, nor lasting; and society showed no sign of changing its convictions. With greater strength the country might acquire greater familiarity 30 with warlike methods, but in the same degree was less likely to suffer any general change of habits. Nothing but prolonged intestine contests could convert the population of an entire continent into a race of warriors.

A people whose chief trait was antipathy to war, and to any system organized with military energy, could scarcely develop great results in national ad- 35 ministration; yet the Americans prided themselves chiefly on their political capacity. Even the war did not undeceive them, although the incapacity brought into evidence by the war was undisputed, and was most remarkable among the communities which believed themselves to be most gifted with political sagacity. Virginia and Massachusetts by turns admitted failure in dealing with 40 issues so simple that the newest societies, like Tennessee and Ohio, understood them by instinct. That (incapacity in national politics should appear as a leading trait in American character) was unexpected by Americans, but might naturally result from their conditions. The better test of American character was

---

1. **hoy**—a single-masted small coasting vessel, now obsolete. 25. **Jefferson and Gallatin**—the Democratic party. Albert Gallatin (1761-1849) had been Secretary of the Treasury, 1801-13; Adams had edited his works and written his biography (1879).

not political but social, and was to be found not in the government but in the
people.

The sixteen years of Jefferson's and Madison's rule furnished international
tests of popular intelligence upon which Americans could depend. The ocean
5 was the only open field for competition among nations. Americans enjoyed
there no natural or artificial advantages over Englishmen, Frenchmen, or Spaniards; indeed, all these countries possessed navies, resources, and experience
greater than were to be found in the United States. Yet the Americans developed, in the course of twenty years, a surprising degree of skill in naval af-
10 fairs. The evidence of their success was to be found nowhere so complete
as in the avowals of Englishmen who knew best the history of naval progress.
The American invention of the fast-sailing schooner or clipper was the more
remarkable because, of all American inventions, this alone sprang from direct
competition with Europe. During ten centuries of struggle the nations of
15 Europe had labored to obtain superiority over each other in ship-construction,
yet Americans instantly made improvements which gave them superiority,
and which Europeans were unable immediately to imitate even after seeing
them. Not only were American vessels better in model, faster in sailing, easier
and quicker in handling, and more economical in working than the European,
20 but they were also better equipped. The English complained as a grievance
that the Americans adopted new and unwarranted devices in naval warfare;
that their vessels were heavier and better constructed, and their missiles of unusual shape and improper use. The Americans resorted to expedients that had
not been tried before, and excited a mixture of irritation and respect in the
25 English service, until Yankee smartness became a national misdemeanor.

The English admitted themselves to be slow to change their habits, but the
French were both quick and scientific; yet Americans did on the ocean what
the French, under stronger inducements, failed to do. The French privateer
preyed upon British commerce for twenty years without seriously injuring it;
30 but no sooner did the American privateer sail from French ports, than the
rates of insurance doubled in London, and an outcry for protection arose
among English shippers which the Admiralty could not calm. The British
newspapers were filled with assertions that the American cruiser was the superior of any vessel of its class, and threatened to overthrow England's su-
35 premacy on the ocean.

Another test of relative intelligence was furnished by the battles at sea.
Instantly after the loss of the "Guerriere" the English discovered and complained that American gunnery was superior to their own. They explained
their inferiority by the length of time that had elapsed since their navy had
40 found on the ocean an enemy to fight. Every vestige of hostile fleets had been
swept away, until, after the battle of Trafalgar, British frigates ceased practice
with their guns. Doubtless the British navy had become somewhat careless in
the absence of a dangerous enemy, but Englishmen were themselves aware
that some other cause must have affected their losses. Nothing showed that

---

32. Admiralty—the department of the British Government in charge of naval affairs. **37.
"Guerriere"**—Its defeat by the *Constitution* occurred in the Gulf of St. Lawrence, Aug. 19, 1812.
41. Trafalgar—Nelson defeated the French and Spanish fleets off this Spanish cape, Oct. 21, 1805.

Nelson's line-of-battle ships, frigates, or sloops were as a rule better fought than the "Macedonian" and "Java," the "Avon" and "Reindeer." Sir Howard Douglas, the chief authority on the subject, attempted in vain to explain British reverses by the deterioration of British gunnery. His analysis showed only that American gunnery was extraordinarily good. Of all vessels, the sloop-of- 5 war,—on account of its smallness, its quick motion, and its more accurate armament of thirty-two-pound carronades,—offered the best test of relative gunnery, and Sir Howard Douglas in commenting upon the destruction of the "Peacock" and "Avon" could only say,—

"In these two actions it is clear that the fire of the British vessels was thrown too 10 high, and that the ordnance of their opponents were expressly and carefully aimed at and took effect chiefly in the hull."

The battle of the "Hornet" and "Penguin" as well as those of the "Reindeer" and "Avon," showed that the excellence of American gunnery continued till the close of the war. Whether at point-blank range or at long-distance prac- 15 tice, the Americans used guns as they had never been used at sea before.

None of the reports of former British victories showed that the British fire had been more destructive at any previous time than in 1812, and no report of any commander since the British navy existed showed so much damage inflicted on an opponent in so short a time as was proved to have been inflicted 20 on themselves by the reports of British commanders in the American war. The strongest proof of American superiority was given by the best British officers, like Broke, who strained every nerve to maintain an equality with American gunnery. So instantaneous and energetic was the effort that, according to the British historian of the war, "a British forty-six-gun frigate of 25 1813 was half as effective again as a British forty-six-gun frigate of 1812;" and, as he justly said, "the slaughtered crews and the shattered hulks" of the captured British ships proved that no want of their old fighting qualities accounted for their repeated and almost habitual mortifications.

Unwilling as the English were to admit the superior skill of Americans on 30 the ocean, they did not hesitate to admit it, in certain respects, on land. The American rifle in American hands was affirmed to have no equal in the world. This admission could scarcely be withheld after the lists of killed and wounded which followed almost every battle; but the admission served to check a wider inquiry. In truth, the rifle played but a small part in the war. Winchester's 35 men at the river Raisin may have owed their over-confidence, as the British

2. **"Macedonian . . . Reindeer"**—On Oct. 25, 1812, Stephen Decatur in the *United States* defeated the British frigate *Macedonian* near the Azores; the U. S. *Constitution* defeated the *Java* in December, 1812, off the Brazilian coast; the U. S. *Wasp* defeated the *Avon* the night of Sept. 1, 1814, off the coast of France, having previously captured the *Reindeer* June 28 in the British Channel. 3. **Douglas**—Sir Howard Douglas (1776-1861). His *Naval Gunnery* (1822) first treated naval warfare adequately. 7. **carronades**—ordnance pieces of large caliber and short range. 9. **"Peacock"**—defeated off Demerara River by the U. S. *Hornet* Feb. 24, 1813. 13. **"Penguin"** —a British sloop defeated by the U. S. *Hornet* Mar. 23, 1815. 23. **Broke**—Sir Philip Bowes Vere Broke (1776-1841), in command of the British frigate *Shannon* during her engagement with the U. S. *Chesapeake* off Boston, June 1, 1813. 29. **mortifications**—"[William] James, pp. 525, 528." (Adams's note) The reference is to his *Naval Occurrences* (1817). 35. **Winchester's**— Winchester's men were surprised and most of them massacred on the Raisin River, Michigan, Jan. 22, 1813.

Forty-first owed its losses, to that weapon, and at New Orleans five or six hundred of Coffee's men, who were out of range, were armed with the rifle; but the surprising losses of the British were commonly due to artillery and musketry fire. At New Orleans the artillery was chiefly engaged. The artillery
5 battle of January 1, according to British accounts, amply proved the superiority of American gunnery on that occasion, which was probably the fairest test during the war. The battle of January 8 was also chiefly an artillery battle; the main British column never arrived within fair musket range; Pakenham was killed by a grapeshot, and the main column of his troops
10 halted more than one hundred yards from the parapet.

The best test of British and American military qualities, both for men and weapons, was Scott's battle of Chippawa. Nothing intervened to throw a doubt over the fairness of the trial. Two parallel lines of regular soldiers, practically equal in numbers, armed with similar weapons, moved in close order toward
15 each other, across a wide open plain, without cover or advantage of position, stopping at intervals to load and fire, until one line broke and retired. At the same time two three-gun batteries, the British being the heavier, maintained a steady fire from positions opposite each other. According to the reports, the two infantry lines in the centre never came nearer than eighty yards. Major-
20 General Riall reported that then, owing to severe losses, his troops broke and could not be rallied. Comparison of the official reports showed that the British lost in killed and wounded four hundred and sixty-nine men; the Americans, two hundred and ninety-six. Some doubts always affect the returns of wounded, because the severity of the wound cannot be known; but dead men
25 tell their own tale. Riall reported one hundred and forty-eight killed; Scott reported sixty-one. The severity of the losses showed that the battle was sharply contested, and proved the personal bravery of both armies. Marksmanship decided the result, and the returns proved that the American fire was superior to that of the British in the proportion of more than fifty per cent if estimated
30 by the entire loss, and of two hundred and forty-two to one hundred if estimated by the deaths alone.

The conclusion seemed incredible, but it was supported by the results of the naval battles. The Americans showed superiority amounting in some cases to twice the efficiency of their enemies in the use of weapons. The best French
35 critic of the naval war, Jurien de la Gravière, said: "An enormous superiority in the rapidity and precision of their fire can alone explain the difference in the losses sustained by the combatants." So far from denying this conclusion the British press constantly alleged it, and the British officers complained of it. The discovery caused great surprise, and in both British services much atten-
40 tion was at once directed to improvement in artillery and musketry. Nothing could exceed the frankness with which Englishmen avowed their inferiority. According to Sir Francis Head, "gunnery was in naval warfare in the ex-

2. Coffee's—Colonel John Coffee commanded the Tennessee militia at the Battle of New Orleans. 9. Pakenham—Sir Edward Michael Pakenham (1778-1815), British Commander at New Orleans. 12. Scott's . . . Chippawa—near Fort Erie, July 5, 1814. General Winfield Scott (1786-1866) was opposed by Major General Riall. 35. de la Gravière—Jean Pierre Edmond Jurien de la Gravière (1812-1892), French authority on naval history. The reference is to his Guerres Maritimes, Vol. II, pp. 286, 287. 42. Head—Sir Francis Bond Head (1793-1875), colonial governor and writer.

traordinary state of ignorance we have just described, when our lean children, the American people, taught us, rod in hand, our first lesson in the art." The English textbook on Naval Gunnery, written by Major-General Sir Howard Douglas immediately after the peace, devoted more attention to the short American war than to all the battles of Napoleon, and began by admitting 5 that Great Britain had "entered with too great confidence on war with a marine much more expert than that of any of our European enemies." The admission appeared "objectionable" even to the author; but he did not add, what was equally true, that it applied as well to the land as to the sea service.

No one questioned the bravery of the British forces, or the ease with which 10 they often routed larger bodies of militia; but the losses they inflicted were rarely as great as those they suffered. Even at Bladensburg, where they met little resistance, their loss was several times greater than that of the Americans. At Plattsburg, where the intelligence and quickness of Macdonough and his men alone won the victory, his ships were in effect stationary batteries, and 15 enjoyed the same superiority in gunnery. "The 'Saratoga,' " said his official report, "had fifty-five round-shot in her hull; the 'Confiance,' one hundred and five. The enemy's shot passed principally just over our heads, as there were not twenty whole hammocks in the nettings at the close of the action."

The greater skill of the Americans was not due to special training, for the 20 British service was better trained in gunnery, as in everything else, than the motley armies and fleets that fought at New Orleans and on the Lakes. Critics constantly said that every American had learned from his childhood the use of the rifle, but he certainly had not learned to use the cannon in shooting birds or hunting deer, and he knew less than the Englishman about the handling 25 of artillery and muskets. As if to add unnecessary evidence, the battle of Chrystler's Farm proved only too well that this American efficiency was not confined to citizens of the United States.

Another significant result of the war was the sudden development of scientific engineering in the United States. This branch of the military service 30 owed its efficiency and almost its existence to the military school at West Point, established in 1802. The school was at first much neglected by the government. The number of graduates before the year 1812 was very small; but at the outbreak of the war the corps of engineers was already efficient. Its chief was Colonel Joseph Gardner Swift, of Massachusetts, the first graduate 35 of the academy: Colonel Swift planned the defences of New York harbor. The lieutenant-colonel in 1812 was Walker Keith Armistead, of Virginia,— the third graduate, who planned the defences of Norfolk. Major William McRee, of North Carolina, became chief engineer to General Brown, and constructed the fortifications at Fort Erie, which cost the British General Gor- 40 don Drummond the loss of half his army, besides the mortification of defeat. Captain Eleazer Derby Wood, of New York, constructed Fort Meigs, which

12. **Bladensburg**—village in Maryland at which the British defeated the Americans Aug. 24, 1814, and as a result captured the town of Washington. 14. **Plattsburg**—on Lake Champlain, where in September, 1814, the American fleet under Thomas Macdonough (1783-1825) repulsed the British. 27. **Chrystler's Farm**—On Nov. 11, 1813, the British utterly routed an American force under General Wilkinson at Chrystler's Farm, near Lake Champlain. 39. **Brown**—Jacob Brown (1775-1828), American major general, who fought brilliantly in the Niagara campaign.

enabled Harrison to defeat the attack of Proctor in May, 1813. Captain Joseph Gilbert Totten, of New York, was chief engineer to General Izard at Platts- burg, where he directed the fortifications that stopped the advance of Prevost's great army. None of the works constructed by a graduate of West Point was 5 captured by the enemy; and had an engineer been employed at Washington by Armstrong and Winder, the city would have been easily saved.

Perhaps without exaggeration the West Point Academy might be said to have decided, next to the navy, the result of the war. The works at New Or- leans were simple in character, and as far as they were due to engineering skill 10 were directed by Major Latour, a Frenchman; but the war was already ended when the battle of New Orleans was fought. During the critical campaign of 1814, the West Point engineers doubled the capacity of the little American army for resistance, and introduced a new and scientific character into Ameri- can life.

15 In the application of science the steamboat was the most striking success; but Fulton's invention, however useful, was neither the most original nor the most ingenious of American efforts, nor did it offer the best example of popular characteristics. Perhaps Fulton's torpedo and Stevens's screw-propeller showed more originality than was proved by the "Clermont." The fast-sailing 20 schooner with its pivot-gun—an invention that grew out of the common stock of nautical intelligence—best illustrated the character of the people.

(That the individual should rise to a higher order either of intelligence or morality than had existed in former ages was not to be expected, for the United States offered less field for the development of individuality than had 25 been offered by older and smaller societies.) (The chief function of the American Union was to raise the average standard of popular intelligence and well-being, and at the close of the War of 1812 the superior average intelligence of Ameri- cans was so far admitted that Yankee acuteness, or smartness, became a na- tional reproach; but much doubt remained whether the intelligence belonged 30 to a high order, or proved a high morality.) From the earliest ages, shrewdness was associated with unscrupulousness; and Americans were freely charged with wanting honesty. The charge could neither be proved nor disproved. American morality was such as suited a people so endowed, and was high when compared with the morality of many older societies; but, like American 35 intelligence, it discouraged excess. Probably the political morality shown by the government and by public men during the first sixteen years of the cen- tury offered a fair gauge of social morality. Like the character of the popular inventions, the character of the morals corresponded to the wants of a grow- ing democratic society; but time alone could decide whether it would result 40 in a high or a low national ideal.

Finer analysis showed other signs of divergence from ordinary standards. If Englishmen took pride in one trait more than in another, it was in the steady uniformity of their progress. The innovating and revolutionary quality of

---

6. Armstrong and Winder—John Armstrong (1758-1843), Secretary of War in Madison's cabinet; William Henry Winder (1775-1824), in command at Bladensburg. **16. Fulton's inven- tion**—Robert Fulton (1765-1815) operated the steamboat *Clermont* on the Hudson in 1807. **18. Stevens's**—Robert Livingston Stevens (1787-1856), American inventor.

the French mind irritated them. America showed an un-English rapidity in
movement. In politics, the American people between 1787 and 1817 accepted
greater changes than had been known in England since 1688. In religion,
the Unitarian movement of Boston and Harvard College would never have
been possible in England, where the defection of Oxford or Cambridge, and   5
the best educated society in the United Kingdom, would have shaken Church
and State to their foundations. In literature the American school was chiefly
remarkable for the rapidity with which it matured. The first book of Irving
was a successful burlesque of his own ancestral history; the first poem of
Bryant sang of the earth only as a universal tomb; the first preaching of Chan-   10
ning assumed to overthrow the Trinity; and the first paintings of Allston
aspired to recover the ideal perfection of Raphael and Titian. In all these
directions the American mind showed tendencies that surprised Englishmen
more than they struck Americans. Allston defended himself from the criticism of friends who made complaint of his return to America. He found there,   15
as he maintained, not only a growing taste for art, but "a quicker appreciation"
of artistic effort than in any European land. If the highest intelligence of
American society were to move with such rapidity, the time could not be far
distant when it would pass into regions which England never liked to contemplate.   20
Another intellectual trait, as has been already noticed, was the disposition
to relax severity. Between the theology of Jonathan Edwards and that of William Ellery Channing was an enormous gap, not only in doctrines but also
in methods. Whatever might be thought of the conclusions reached by Edwards and Hopkins, the force of their reasoning commanded respect. Not   25
often had a more strenuous effort than theirs been made to ascertain God's
will, and to follow it without regard to weaknesses of the flesh. The idea that
the nature of God's attributes was to be preached only as subordinate to the
improvement of man, agreed little with the spirit of their religion. The Unitarian and Universalist movements marked the beginning of an epoch when   30
ethical and humanitarian ideas took the place of metaphysics, and even New
England turned from contemplating the omnipotence of the Deity in order
to praise the perfections of his creatures.
The spread of great popular sects like the Universalists and Campbellites,
founded on assumptions such as no orthodox theology could tolerate, showed   35
a growing tendency to relaxation of thought in that direction. The struggle
for existence was already mitigated, and the first effect of the change was
seen in the increasing cheerfulness of religion. Only when men found their
actual world almost a heaven, could they lose overpowering anxiety about the
world to come. Life had taken a softer aspect, and as a consequence God   40

4. **Unitarian**—sect believing God exists in one person, as opposed to Trinitarians. William
Ellery Channing (1780-1842) in his sermon on *Unitarian Christianity* (1819) made the first defini-
tive statement of the new theology. 11. **Allston**—Washington Allston (1779-1843), American
painter and poet. 25. **Hopkins**—Dr. Samuel Hopkins (1721-1803), Calvinistic minister, pupil of
Jonathan Edwards. He believed the inability of the unregenerate was owing to moral and not to
natural causes. 30. **Universalist**—Universalists believe that all souls will finally be saved and that
God will triumph universally. 34. **Campbellites**—or Disciples of Christ, a sect founded by
Thomas Campbell (1763-1854) and Alexander Campbell, his son (1788-1866), about 1809.

was no longer terrible. Even the wicked became less mischievous in an atmosphere where virtue was easier than vice. Punishments seemed mild in a society where every offender could cast off his past, and create a new career. For the first time in history, great bodies of men turned away from their old
5   religion, giving no better reason than that it required them to believe in a cruel Deity, and rejected necessary conclusions of theology because they were inconsistent with human self-esteem.

The same optimism marked the political movement. Society was weary of strife, and settled gladly into a political system which left every disputed point
10 undetermined. The public seemed obstinate only in believing that all was for the best, as far as the United States were concerned, in the affairs of mankind. The contrast was great between this temper of mind and that in which the Constitution had been framed; but it was no greater than the contrast in the religious opinions of the two periods, while the same reaction against severity
15 marked the new literature. The rapid accumulation of wealth and increase in physical comfort told the same story from the standpoint of economy. On every side society showed that ease was for a time to take the place of severity, and enjoyment was to have its full share in the future national existence.

The traits of intelligence, rapidity, and mildness seemed fixed in the national
20 character as early as 1817, and were likely to become more marked as time should pass. A vast amount of conservatism still lingered among the people; but the future spirit of society could hardly fail to be intelligent, rapid in movement, and mild in method. Only in the distant future could serious change occur, and even then no return to European characteristics seemed
25 likely. The American continent was happier in its conditions and easier in its resources than the regions of Europe and Asia, where Nature revelled in diversity and conflict. If at any time American character should change, it might as probably become sluggish as revert to the violence and extravagances of Old-World development. The inertia of several hundred million people,
30 all formed in a similar social mould, was as likely to stifle energy as to stimulate evolution.

With the establishment of these conclusions, a new episode in American history began in 1815. New subjects demanded new treatment, no longer dramatic but steadily tending to becoming scientific. The traits of American
35 character were fixed; the rate of physical and economical growth was established; and history, certain that at a given distance of time the Union would contain so many millions of people, with wealth valued at so many millions of dollars, became thenceforward chiefly concerned to know what kind of people these millions were to be. They were intelligent, but what paths would
40 their intelligence select? They were quick, but what solution of insoluble problems would quickness hurry? They were scientific, and what control would their science exercise over their destiny? They were mild, but what corruptions would their relaxations bring? They were peaceful, but by what machinery were their corruptions to be purged? What interests were to vivify
45 a society so vast and uniform? What ideals were to ennoble it? What object, besides physical content, must a democratic continent aspire to attain? For the treatment of such questions history required another century of experience.

THE VIRGIN OF CHARTRES

This selection is Chapter VI in *Mont-Saint-Michel and Chartres,* privately printed in 1904, published in 1914, a remarkably penetrating study of medieval civilization. The Cathedral of Chartres, fifty miles southwest of Paris, was founded in the eleventh century by Bishop Fulbert, and the main part of the present structure was completed in 1240.

W E MUST take ten minutes to accustom our eyes to the light, and we had better use them to seek the reason why we come to Chartres rather than to Rheims or Amiens or Bourges, for the cathedral that fills our ideal. The truth is, there are several reasons; there generally are, for doing the things we like; and after you have studied Chartres to the ground, 5 and got your reasons settled, you will never find an antiquarian to agree with you; the architects will probably listen to you with contempt; and even these excellent priests, whose kindness is great, whose patience is heavenly, and whose good opinion you would so gladly gain, will turn from you with pain, if not with horror. The Gothic is singular in this; one seems easily at home 10 in the Renaissance; one is not too strange in the Byzantine; as for the Roman, it is ourselves; and we could walk blindfolded through every chink and cranny of the Greek mind; all these styles seem modern, when we come close to them; but the Gothic gets away. No two men think alike about it, and no woman agrees with either man. The Church itself never agreed about it, and 15 the architects agree even less than the priests. To most minds it casts too many shadows; it wraps itself in mystery; and when people talk of mystery, they commonly mean fear. To others, the Gothic seems hoary with age and decrepitude, and its shadows mean death. What is curious to watch is the fanatical conviction of the Gothic enthusiast, to whom the twelfth century means 20 exuberant youth, the eternal child of Wordsworth, over whom its immortality broods like the day; it loves so many toys and cares for so few necessities; its youth is so young, its age so old, and its youthful yearning for old thought is so disconcerting, like the mysterious senility of the baby that—

> Deaf and silent, reads the eternal deep,   25
> Haunted forever by the eternal mind.

One need not take it more seriously than one takes the baby itself. Our amusement is to play with it, and to catch its meaning in its smile; and whatever Chartres may be now, when young it was a smile. To the Church, no doubt, its cathedral here has a fixed and administrative meaning, which is the same 30 as that of every other bishop's seat and with which we have nothing whatever to do. To us, it is a child's fancy; a toyhouse to please the Queen of Heaven,—to please her so much that she would be happy in it,—to charm her till she smiled.

The Queen Mother was as majestic as you like; she was absolute; she could 35

25-26. **Deaf . . . mind**—slightly altered from Wordsworth's *Intimations* ode, lines 112-13. 31. **bishop's seat**—*cathedra* in Latin; whence "cathedral."

be stern; she was not above being angry; but she was still a woman, who loved grace, beauty, ornament,—her toilette, robes, jewels;—who considered the arrangements of her palace with attention, and liked both light and colour; who kept a keen eye on her Court, and exacted prompt and willing
5   obedience from king and archbishops as well as from beggars and drunken priests. She protected her friends and punished her enemies. She required space, beyond what was known in the Courts of kings, because she was liable at all times to have ten thousand people begging her for favours—mostly inconsistent with law—and deaf to refusal. She was extremely sensitive to neg-
10 lect, to disagreeable impressions, to want of intelligence in her surroundings. She was the greatest artist, as she was the greatest philosopher and musician and theologist, that ever lived on earth, except her Son, Who, at Chartres, is still an Infant under her guardianship. Her taste was infallible; her sentence eternally final. This church was built for her in this spirit of simple-minded,
15 practical, utilitarian faith,—in this singleness of thought, exactly as a little girl sets up a doll-house for her favourite blonde doll. Unless you can go back to your dolls, you are out of place here. If you can go back to them, and get rid for one small hour of the weight of custom, you shall see Chartres in glory.

The palaces of earthly queens were hovels compared with these palaces of
20 the Queen of Heaven at Chartres, Paris, Laon, Noyon, Rheims, Amiens, Rouen, Bayeux, Coutances,—a list that might be stretched into a volume. The nearest approach we have made to a palace was the Merveille at Mont-Saint-Michel, but no Queen had a palace equal to that. The Merveille was built, or designed, about the year 1200; toward the year 1500 Louis XI built a great
25 castle at Loches in Touraine, and there Queen Anne de Bretagne had apartments which still exist, and which we will visit. At Blois you shall see the residence which served for Catherine de Medicis till her death in 1589. Anne de Bretagne was trebly queen, and Catherine de Medicis took her standard of comfort from the luxury of Florence. At Versailles you can see the apart-
30 ments which the queens of the Bourbon line occupied through their century of magnificence. All put together, and then trebled in importance, could not rival the splendour of any single cathedral dedicated to Queen Mary in the thirteenth century; and of them all, Chartres was built to be peculiarly and exceptionally her delight. . . .

35 (The measure of this devotion, which proves to any religious American mind, beyond possible cavil, its serious and practical reality, is the money it cost.) According to statistics, in the single century between 1170 and 1270, the French built eighty cathedrals and nearly five hundred churches of the cathedral class, which would have cost, according to an estimate made in 1840, more
40 than five thousand millions to replace. Five thousand million francs is a thousand million dollars, and this covered only the great churches of a single century. The same scale of expenditure had been going on since the year 1000,

27. **Catherine**—Catharine de' Medici (1519-1589), daughter of a Florentine banker and wife of Henry II of France. 27. **Anne**—Anne of Brittany (1417-1514). Anne was "trebly queen," first, as daughter of Francis II; second, through marriage to Charles VIII, who aimed to establish authority over her; and third, through marriage to Louis XII, who had just repudiated Joan of France.

and almost every parish in France had rebuilt its church in stone; to this day France is strewn with the ruins of this architecture and yet the still preserved churches of the eleventh and twelfth centuries, among the churches that be-long to the Romanesque and Transition period, are numbered by hundreds until they reach well into the thousands. The share of this capital which was— if one may use a commercial figure—invested in the Virgin cannot be fixed, any more than the total sum given to religious objects between 1000 and 1300; but in a spiritual and artistic sense, it was almost the whole, and expressed an intensity of conviction never again reached by any passion, whether of reli-gion, of loyalty, of patriotism, or of wealth; perhaps never even parallelled by any single economic effort, except in war. Nearly every great church of the twelfth and thirteenth centuries belonged to Mary, until in France one asks for the church of Notre Dame as though it meant cathedral; but, not satis-fied with this, she contracted the habit of requiring in all churches a chapel of her own, called in English the "Lady Chapel," which was apt to be as large as the church but was always meant to be handsomer; and there, be-hind the high altar, in her own private apartment, Mary sat, receiving her in-numerable suppliants, and ready at any moment to step up upon the high altar itself to support the tottering authority of the local saint.

Expenditure like this rests invariably on an economic idea. Just as the French of the nineteenth century invested their surplus capital in a railway system in the belief that they would make money by it in this life, in the thirteenth they trusted their money to the Queen of Heaven because of their belief in her power to repay it with interest in the life to come. The invest-ment was based on the power of Mary as Queen rather than on any orthodox Church conception of the Virgin's legitimate station. Papal Rome never greatly loved Byzantine empresses or French queens. The Virgin of Chartres was never wholly sympathetic to the Roman Curia. To this day the Church writers —like the Abbé Bulteau or M. Rohault de Fleury—are singularly shy of the true Virgin of majesty, whether at Chartres or at Byzantium or wherever she is seen. The fathers Martin and Cahier at Bourges alone felt her true value. Had the Church controlled her, the Virgin would perhaps have remained prostrate at the foot of the Cross. Dragged by a Byzantine Court, backed by popular insistence and impelled by overpowering self-interest, the Church ac-cepted the Virgin throned and crowned, seated by Christ, the Judge throned and crowned; but even this did not wholly satisfy the French of the thirteenth century who seemed bent on absorbing Christ in His Mother, and making the Mother the Church, and Christ the Symbol. . . .

Constantly—one might better say at once, officially, she was addressed in these terms of supreme majesty: "Imperatrix supernorum!" "Coeli Regina!" "Aula regalis!" but the century seemed determined to carry the idea out to its logical conclusion in defiance of dogma. Not only was the Son absorbed in

---

28. **Curia**—collective body of officials of the papal government. 29. **Bulteau . . . Fleury** —Louis Bulteau (1625-1693), French ecclesiastical writer; Georges Rohault de Fleury (1835-1905), architectural authority. 31. **Martin and Cahier**—Arthur-Marie Martin (1801-1856), who, with Charles Cahier (1807-1882), became an authority on the antiquities of the Bourges cathedral. 40-41. **"Imperatrix . . . regalis"**—"Empress of the Celestials! Queen of Heaven! Imperial Court!"

the Mother, or represented as under her guardianship, but the Father fared no better, and the Holy Ghost followed. The poets regarded the Virgin as the "Templum Trinitatis"; "totius Trinitatis nobile Triclinium."—She was the refectory· of the Trinity—the "Triclinium"—because the refectory was the
5 largest room and contained the whole of the members, and was divided in three parts by two rows of columns. She was the "Templum Trinitatis," the Church itself, with its triple aisle. The Trinity was absorbed in her.

This is a delicate subject in the Church, and you must feel it with delicacy, without brutally insisting on its necessary contradictions. All theology and all
10 philosophy are full of contradictions quite as flagrant and far less sympathetic. This particular variety of religious faith is simply human, and has made its appearance in one form or another in nearly all religions; but though the twelfth century carried it to an extreme, and at Chartres you see it in its most charming expression, we have got always to make allowances for what was
15 going on beneath the surface in men's minds, consciously or unconsciously, and for the latent scepticism which lurks behind all faith. The Church itself never quite accepted the full claims of what was called Mariolatry. One may be sure, too, that the bourgeois capitalist and the student of the schools, each from his own point of view, watched the Virgin with anxious interest. The
20 bourgeois had put an enormous share of his capital into what was in fact an economical speculation, not unlike the South Sea Scheme, or the railway system of our own time; except that in one case the energy was devoted to shortening the road to Heaven; in the other, to shortening the road to Paris; but no serious schoolman could have felt entirely convinced that God would enter
25 into a business partnership with man, to establish a sort of joint-stock society for altering the operation of divine and universal laws. The bourgeois cared little for the philosophical doubt if the economical result proved to be good, but he watched this result with his usual practical sagacity, and required an experience of only about three generations (1200-1300) to satisfy himself that
30 relics were not certain in their effects; that the Saints were not always able or willing to help; that Mary herself could not certainly be bought or bribed; that prayer without money seemed to be quite as efficacious as prayer with money; and that neither the road to Heaven nor Heaven itself had been made surer or brought nearer by an investment of capital which amounted
35 to the best part of the wealth of France. Economically speaking, he became satisfied that his enormous money-investment had proved to be an almost total loss, and the reaction on his mind was as violent as the emotion. For three hundred years it prostrated France. The efforts of the bourgeoisie and the peasantry to recover their property, so far as it was recoverable, have lasted to the
40 present day and we had best take care not to get mixed in those passions.

If you are to get the full enjoyment of Chartres, you must, for the time, believe in Mary as Bernard and Adam did, and feel her presence as the archi-

3. **Templum**—The context makes the meaning clear. 17. **Mariolatry**—term of opprobrium for the worship of Mary. 21. **South Sea Scheme**—In 1711 a British company offered to take over the national debt in return for trading-monopolies with South America and the Pacific islands. Soon hundreds of similar companies were formed and the mania of speculation resulted in disaster. 42. **Bernard and Adam**—St. Bernard of Clairvaux (1090-1153); Adam of St. Victor (12th century).

tects did, in every stone they placed, and every touch they chiselled. You must try first to rid your mind of the traditional idea that the Gothic is an intentional expression of religious gloom. The necessity for light was the motive of the Gothic architects. They needed light and always more light, until they sacrificed safety and common sense in trying to get it. They converted 5 their walls into windows, raised their vaults, diminished their piers, until their churches could no longer stand. You will see the limits at Beauvais; at Chartres we have not got so far, but even here, in places where the Virgin wanted it,—as above the high altar,—the architect has taken all the light there was to take. For the same reason, fenestration became the most impor- 10 tant part of the Gothic architect's work, and at Chartres was uncommonly interesting because the architect was obliged to design a new system, which should at the same time satisfy the laws of construction and the taste and imagination of Mary. No doubt the first command of the Queen of Heaven was for light, but the second, at least equally imperative, was for colour. Any 15 earthly queen, even though she were not Byzantine in taste, loved colour; and the truest of queens—the only true Queen of Queens—had richer and finer taste in colour than the queens of fifty earthly kingdoms, as you will see when you come to the immense effort to gratify her in the glass of her windows. Illusion for illusion,—granting for the moment that Mary was an 20 illusion,—the Virgin Mother in this instance repaid to her worshippers a larger return for their money than the capitalist has ever been able to get, at least in this world, from any other illusion of wealth which he has tried to make a source of pleasure and profit.

The next point on which Mary evidently insisted was the arrangement for 25 her private apartments, the apse, as distinguished from her throne-room, the choir; both being quite distinct from the hall, or reception-room of the public, which was the nave with its enlargements in the transepts. This arrangement marks the distinction between churches built as shrines for the deity and churches built as halls of worship for the public. The difference is chiefly in 30 the apse, and the apse of Chartres is the most interesting of all apses from this point of view.

The Virgin required chiefly these three things, or, if you like, these four: space, light, convenience; and colour decoration to unite and harmonize the whole. This concerns the interior; on the exterior she required statuary, and 35 the only complete system of decorative sculpture that existed seems to belong to her churches:—Paris, Rheims, Amiens, and Chartres. Mary required all this magnificence at Chartres for herself alone, not for the public. As far as one can see into the spirit of the builders, Chartres was exclusively intended for the Virgin, as the Temple of Abydos was intended for Osiris. The wants 40 of man, beyond a mere roof-cover, and perhaps space to some degree, enter to no very great extent into the problem of Chartres. Man came to render homage or to ask favours. The Queen received him in her palace, where she alone was at home, and alone gave commands.

The artist's second thought was to exclude from his work everything that 45

10. **fenestration**—arrangement of windows. 40. **Abydos**—magnificent temple in Upper Egypt; Osiris was the Egyptian god of light, health, and agriculture.

could displease Mary; and since Mary differed from living queens only in
infinitely greater majesty and refinement, the artist could admit only what
pleased the actual taste of the great ladies who dictated taste at the Courts of
France and England, which surrounded the little Court of the Counts of
5 Chartres. What they were—these women of the twelfth and thirteenth centuries—we shall have to see or seek in other directions; but Chartres is
perhaps the most magnificent and permanent monument they left of their
taste, and we can begin here with learning certain things which they were
not.

10   In the first place, they were not in the least vague, dreamy, or mystical in
a modern sense;—far from it. They seemed anxious only to throw the mysteries into a blaze of light; not so much physical, perhaps,—since they, like
all women, liked moderate shadow for their toilettes,—but luminous in the
sense of faith. There is nothing about Chartres that you would think mystical,
15 who know your Lohengrin, Siegfried, and Parsifal. If you care to make a
study of the whole literature of the subject, read M. Mâle's "Art Religieux du
XIIIᵉ Siècle en France," and use it for a guide-book. Here you need only note
how symbolic and how simple the sculpture is, on the portals and porches.
Even what seems a grotesque or an abstract idea is no more than the simplest
20 child's personification. On the walls you may have noticed the *Ane qui vielle*,
—the ass playing the lyre; and on all the old churches you can see "bestiaries,"
as they were called, of fabulous animals, symbolic or not; but the symbolism
is as simple as the realism of the oxen at Laon. It gave play to the artist in his
effort for variety of decoration, and it amused the people,—probably the
25 Virgin also was not above being amused;—now and then it seems about to
suggest what you would call an esoteric meaning, that is to say, a meaning
which each one of us can consider private property reserved for our own
amusement, and from which the public is excluded; yet, in truth, in the Virgin's churches the public is never excluded, but invited. The Virgin even had
30 the additional charm to the public that she was popularly supposed to have
no very marked fancy for priests as such; (she was a queen, a woman, and a
mother, functions, all, which priests could not perform) Accordingly, she seems
to have had little taste for mysteries of any sort, and even the symbols that
seem most mysterious were clear to every old peasant-woman in her church.
35 The most pleasing and promising of them all is the woman's figure you saw
on the front of the cathedral in Paris; her eyes bandaged; her head bent down;
her crown falling; without cloak or royal robe; holding in her hand a guidon
or banner with its staff broken in more than one place. On the opposite pier
stands another woman, with royal mantle, erect and commanding. The symbol
40 is so graceful that one is quite eager to know its meaning; but every child in
the Middle Ages would have instantly told you that the woman with the falling crown meant only the Jewish Synagogue, as the one with the royal robe
meant the Church of Christ.
     Another matter for which the female taste seemed not much to care was

15. Lohengrin . . . Parsifal—Wagnerian operas, based on medieval legends. 16. Art
Religieux—Paris, 1902 (new ed.), by Emile Mâle (1862-   ).

theology in the metaphysical sense. Mary troubled herself little about theology except when she retired into the south transept with Pierre de Dreux. Even there one finds little said about the Trinity, always the most metaphysical subtlety of the Church. Indeed, you might find much amusement here in searching the cathedral for any distinct expression at all of the Trinity as a dogma recognized by Mary. One cannot take seriously the idea that the three doors, the three portals, and the three aisles express the Trinity, because, in the first place, there was no rule about it; churches might have what portals and aisles they pleased; both Paris and Bourges have five; the doors themselves are not allotted to the three members of the Trinity, nor are the portals; while other more serious objection is that the side doors and aisles are not of equal importance with the central, but mere adjuncts and dependencies, so that the architect who had misled the ignorant public into accepting so black a heresy would have deserved the stake, and would probably have gone to it. Even this suggestion of trinity is wanting in the transepts, which have only one aisle, and in the choir, which has five, as well as five or seven chapels, and, as far as an ignorant mind can penetrate, no triplets whatever. Occasionally, no doubt, you will discover in some sculpture or window, a symbol of the Trinity, but the discovery itself amounts to an admission of its absence as a controlling idea, for the ordinary worshipper must have been at least as blind as we are, and to him, as to us, it would have seemed a wholly subordinate detail. Even if the Trinity, too, is anywhere expressed, you will hardly find here an attempt to explain its metaphysical meaning—not even a mystic triangle.)

(The church is wholly given up to be the Mother and the Son. The Father seldom appears; the Holy Ghost still more rarely.)At least, this is the impression made on an ordinary visitor who has no motive to be orthodox; and it must have been the same with the thirteenth-century worshipper who came here with his mind absorbed in the perfections of Mary. Chartres represents, not the Trinity, but the identity of the Mother and Son. The Son represents the Trinity, which is thus absorbed in the Mother. The idea is not orthodox, but this is no affair of ours. The Church watches over its own.

The Virgin's wants and tastes, positive and negative, ought now to be clear enough to enable you to feel the artist's sincerity in trying to satisfy them; but first you have still to convince yourselves of the people's sincerity in employing the artists. This point is the easiest of all, for the evidence is express. In the year 1145 when the old flèche was begun,—the year before Saint Bernard preached the second crusade at Vézelay,—Abbot Haimon, of Saint-Pierre-sur-Dives in Normandy, wrote to the monks of Tutbury Abbey in England a famous letter to tell of the great work which the Virgin was doing in France and which began at the Church of Chartres. "Hujus sacrae institutionis ritus apud Carnotensem ecclesiam est inchoatus." From Chartres it had spread through Normandy, where it produced among other things the beautiful spire

---

2. Pierre de Dreux—Pierre Mauclerc, Comte de Dreux, great-grandson of Louis VI, built the south porch at Chartres, as Adams relates in the preceding chapter, and dedicated it to Christ the Son, whom he preferred to Mary. The reference is to this symbolical subordination of Mary. **36. flèche**—spire (literally arrow). **40-41. "Hujus . . . inchoatus"**—The rite of this sacred institution began at the church of Chartres.

which we saw at Saint-Pierre-sur-Dives. "Postremo per totam fere Norman-
niam longe lateque convaluit ac loca per singula Matri misericordiae dicata
praecipue occupavit." The movement affected especially the places devoted to
Mary, but ran through all Normandy, far and wide. Of all Mary's miracles,
5 the best attested, next to the preservation of her church, is the building of it;
not so much because it surprises us as because it surprised even more the
people of the time and the men who were its instruments. Such deep popular
movements are always surprising, and at Chartres the miracle seems to have
occurred three times, coinciding more or less with the dates of the crusades,
10 and taking the organization of a crusade, as Archibishop Hugo of Rouen described it in a letter to Bishop Thierry of Amiens. The most interesting part
of his letter is the evident astonishment of the writer, who might be talking
to us to-day, so modern is he:—

The inhabitants of Chartres have combined to aid in the construction of their
15 church by transporting the materials; our Lord has rewarded their humble zeal by
miracles which have roused the Normans to imitate the piety of their neighbours.
. . . Since then the faithful of our diocese and of other neighbouring regions have
formed associations for the same object; they admit no one into their company
unless he has been to confession, has renounced enmities and revenges, and has
20 reconciled himself with his enemies. That done, they elect a chief, under whose
direction they conduct their waggons in silence and with humility.

The quarries at Berchères-l'Evêque are about five miles from Chartres. The
stone is excessively hard, and was cut in blocks of considerable size, as you
can see for yourselves; blocks which required great effort to transport and lay
25 in place. The work was done with feverish rapidity, as it still shows, but it is
the solidist building of the age, and without a sign of weakness yet. The
Abbot told, with more surprise than pride, of the spirit which was built into
the cathedral with the stone:—

Who has ever seen!—Who has ever heard tell, in times past, that powerful princes
30 of the world, that men brought up in honour and in wealth, that nobles, men and
women, have bent their proud and haughty necks to the harness of carts, and that,
like beasts of burden, they have dragged to the abode of Christ these waggons,
loaded with wines, grains, oil, stone, wood, and all that is necessary for the wants
of life, or for the construction of the church? But while they draw these burdens,
35 there is one thing admirable to observe; it is that often when a thousand persons
and more are attached to the chariots,—so great is the difficulty,—yet they march
in such silence that not a murmur is heard, and truly if one did not see the thing
with one's eyes, one might believe that among such a multitude there was hardly
a person present. When they halt on the road, nothing is heard but the confession
40 of sins, and pure and suppliant prayer to God to obtain pardon. At the voice of
the priests who exhort their hearts to peace, they forget all hatred, discord is thrown
far aside, debts are remitted, the unity of hearts is established. But if any one is so far
advanced in evil as to be unwilling to pardon an offender, or if he rejects the counsel
of the priest who has piously advised him, his offering is instantly thrown from the
45 wagon as impure, and he himself ignominiously and shamefully excluded from the

---

1-3. "Postremo . . . occupavit"—Finally it spread far and wide almost through all Normandy and filled the places one by one especially dedicated to the Mother of Compassion.

society of the holy. There one sees the priests who preside over each chariot exhort
every one to penitence, to confession of faults, to the resolution of better life! There
one sees old people, young people, little children, calling on the Lord with a suppliant
voice, and uttering to Him, from the depth of the heart, sobs and sighs with words
of glory and praise! After the people, warned by the sound of trumpets and the sight   5
of banners, have resumed their road, the march is made with such ease that no
obstacle can retard it. . . . When they have reached the church they arrange the
wagons about it like a spiritual camp, and during the whole night they celebrate
the watch by hymns and canticles. On each waggon they light tapers and lamps; they
place there the infirm and sick, and bring them the precious relics of the Saints for   10
their relief. Afterwards the priests and clerics close the ceremony by processions
which the people follow with devout heart, imploring the clemency of the Lord and
of his Blessed Mother for the recovery of the sick.

Of course, the Virgin was actually and constantly present during all this
labour, and gave her assistance to it, but you would get no light on the archi-   15
tecture from listening to an account of her miracles, nor do they heighten the
effect of popular faith. (Without the conviction of her personal presence, men
would not have been inspired; but, to us, it is rather the inspiration of the
art which proves the Virgin's presence, and we can better see the conviction
of it in the work than in the words.) Every day, as the work went on, the   20
Virgin was present, directing the architects, and it is this direction that we
are going to study, if you have now got a realizing sense of what it meant.
Without this sense, the church is dead. Most persons of a deeply religious
nature would tell you emphatically that nine churches out of ten actually
were dead-born, after the thirteenth century, and that church architecture be-   25
came a pure matter of mechanism and mathematics; but that is a question
for you to decide when you come to it; and the pleasure consists not in seeing
the death, but in feeling the life.

THE DYNAMO AND THE VIRGIN (1900)   *written in 3rd person*

UNTIL the Great Exposition of 1900 closed its doors in November, Adams
haunted it, aching to absorb knowledge, and helpless to find it. He   30
would have liked to know how much of it could be grasped by the
best-informed man in the world. While he was thus meditating chaos, Langley came by, and showed it to him. At Langley's behest, the Exhibition dropped
its superfluous rags and stripped itself to the skin, for Langley knew what to
study, and why, and how; while Adams might as well have stood outside in   35
the night, staring at the Milky Way. Yet Langley said nothing new, and
taught nothing that one might not have learned from Lord Bacon, three hundred years before; but though one should have known the "Advancement of
Science" as well as one knew the "Comedy of Errors," the literary knowledge
counted for nothing until some teacher should show how to apply it. Bacon   40

29. the Great Exposition—at Paris. 32. Langley—Samuel P. Langley (1834-1906), a
physicist friend, who was a pioneer in flight by airplane. 38-39. "Advancement of Science"
—Adams refers to Bacon's *Advancement of Learning* (1603, not 1620), in which he advocated the
reorganization of natural science.

took a vast deal of trouble in teaching King James I and his subjects, American
or other, towards the year 1620, that true science was the development or economy of forces; yet an elderly American in 1900 knew neither the formula nor
the forces; or even so much as to say to himself that his historical business
5   in the Exposition concerned only the economies or developments of force since
1893, when he began the study at Chicago.

Nothing in education is so astonishing as the amount of ignorance it ac-
cumulates in the form of inert facts. Adams had looked at most of the accumulations of art in the storehouses called Art Museums; yet he did not know
10 how to look at the art exhibits of 1900. He had studied Karl Marx and his
doctrines of history with profound attention, yet he could not apply them at
Paris. Langley, with the ease of a great master of experiment, threw out of
the field every exhibit that did not reveal a new application of force, and naturally threw out, to begin with, almost the whole art exhibit. He led his pupil
15 directly to the forces. His chief interest was in new motors to make his air-
ship feasible, and he taught Adams the astonishing complexities of the Daimler motor, and of the automobile, which, since 1893, had become a nightmare
at a hundred kilometres an hour, almost as destructive as the electric tram
which was only ten years older; and threatening to become as terrible as the
20 locomotive steam-engine itself, which was almost exactly Adams's own age.

Then he showed his scholar the great hall of dynamos, and explained how
little he knew about electricity or force of any kind, even of his own special
sun, which spouted heat in inconceivable volume, but which, as far as he
knew, might spout less or more, at any time, for all the certainty he felt in it.
25 To him, the dynamo itself was but an ingenious channel for conveying somewhere the heat latent in a few tons of poor coal hidden in a dirty engine-
house carefully kept out of sight; but to Adams the dynamo became a symbol
of infinity. As he grew accustomed to the great gallery of machines, he began
to feel the forty-foot dynamos as a moral force, much as the early Christians
30 felt the Cross. The planet itself seemed less impressive, in its old-fashioned,
deliberate annual or daily revolution, than this huge wheel, revolving within
arm's-length at some vertiginous speed, and barely murmuring—scarcely humming an audible warning to stand a hair's breadth further for respect of power
—while it would not wake the baby lying close against its frame. Before the
35 end, one began to pray to it; inherited instinct taught the natural expression
of man before silent and infinite force. Among the thousand symbols of ultimate energy, the dynamo was not so human as some, but it was the most
expressive.

Yet the dynamo, next to the steam-engine, was the most familiar of exhibits.
40 For Adams's objects its value lay chiefly in its occult mechanism. Between the
dynamo in the gallery of machines and the engine-house outside, the break
of continuity amounted to abysmal fracture for a historian's objects. No more
relation could he discover between the steam and the electric current than

---

6. Chicago—In Chapter xxii Adams related what impression a former exposition made on
him. 10. Karl Marx—(1818-1883), German socialist, author of *Das Kapital*. 16-17. Daimler
motor—Gottlieb Daimler (1834-1900) greatly improved the gasoline engine in 1884 and became
in a sense the "father of the autombile."

between the Cross and the cathedral. The forces were interchangeable if not reversible, but he could see only an absolute *fiat* in electricity as in faith. Langley could not help him. Indeed, Langley seemed to be worried by the same trouble, for he constantly repeated that the new forces were anarchical, and specially that he was not responsible for the new rays, that were little short of parricidal in their wicked spirit towards science. His own rays, with which he had doubled the solar spectrum, were altogether harmless and beneficent; but Radium denied its God—or, what was to Langley the same thing, denied the truths of his Science. The force was wholly new.

A historian who asked only to learn enough to be as futile as Langley or Kelvin, made rapid progress under this teaching, and mixed himself up in the tangle of ideas until he achieved a sort of Paradise of ignorance vastly consoling to his fatigued senses. He wrapped himself in vibrations and rays which were new, and he would have hugged Marconi and Branly had he met them, as he hugged the dynamo; while he lost his arithmetic in trying to figure out the equation between the discoveries and the economies of force. The economies, like the discoveries, were absolute, super-sensual, occult; incapable of expression in horse-power. What mathematical equivalent could he suggest as the value of a Branly coherer? Frozen air, or the electric furnace, had some scale of measurement, no doubt, if somebody could invent a thermometer adequate to the purpose; but X-rays had played no part whatever in man's consciousness, and the atom itself had figured only as a fiction of thought. In these seven years man had translated himself into a new universe which had no common scale of measurement with the old. He had entered a super-sensual world, in which he could measure nothing except by chance collisions of movements imperceptible to his senses, perhaps even imperceptible to his instruments, but perceptible to each other, and so to some known ray at the end of the scale. Langley seemed prepared for anything, even for an indeterminable number of universes interfused—physics stark mad in metaphysics.

Historians undertake to arrange sequences—called stories, or histories—assuming in silence a relation of cause and effect. These assumptions, hidden in the depths of dusty libraries, have been astounding, but commonly unconscious and childlike; so much so, that if any captious critic were to drag them to light, historians would probably reply, with one voice, that they had never supposed themselves required to know what they were talking about. Adams, for one, had toiled in vain to find out what he meant. He had even published a dozen volumes of American history for no other purpose than to satisfy himself whether, by the severest process of stating, with the least possible comment, such facts as seemed sure, in such order as seemed rigorously consequent, he could fix for a familiar moment a necessary sequence of human movement. The result had satisfied him as little as at Harvard College. Where he saw sequence, other men saw something quite different, and no one saw the same unit of measure. He cared little about his experiments and less about

8. **Radium denied**—It was one of the first "disintegrating" elements discovered. **11. Kelvin** —William Thomson, Lord Kelvin (1824-1907), Scotch physicist, distinguished for attainments in ocean telegraphy and in molecular dynamics. **14. Marconi, Branly**—Guglielmo Marconi (1874-   ), Italian inventor of wireless telegraphy in 1895. Edouard Branly (1844-   ), French physicist, who invented a "coherer," or device for detecting electric waves.

his statesmen, who seemed to him quite as ignorant as himself and, as a rule, no more honest; but he insisted on a relation of sequence, and if he could not reach it by one method, he would try as many methods as science knew. Satisfied that the sequence of men led to nothing and that the sequence of their
5 society could lead no further, while the mere sequence of time was artificial, and the sequence of thought was chaos, he turned at last to the sequence of force; and thus it happened that, after ten years' pursuit, he found himself lying in the Gallery of Machines at the Great Exposition of 1900, his historical neck broken by the sudden irruption of forces totally new.

10 Since no one else showed much concern, an elderly person without other cares had no need to betray alarm. The year 1900 was not the first to upset schoolmasters. Copernicus and Galileo had broken many professorial necks about 1600; Columbus had stood the world on its head towards 1500; but the nearest approach to the revolution of 1900 was that of 310, when Constantine
15 set up the Cross. The rays that Langley disowned, as well as those which he fathered, were occult, super-sensual, irrational; they were a revelation of mysterious energy like that of the Cross; they were what, in terms of mediaeval science, were called immediate modes of the divine substance.

The historian was thus reduced to his last resources. Clearly if he was bound
20 to reduce all these forces to a common value, this common value could have no measure but that of their attraction on his own mind. He must treat them as they had been felt; as convertible, reversible, interchangeable attractions on thought. He made up his mind to venture it; he would risk translating rays into faith. Such a reversible process would vastly amuse a chemist, but the
25 chemist could not deny that he, or some of his fellow physicists, could feel the force of both. When Adams was a boy in Boston, the best chemist in the place had probably never heard of Venus except by way of scandal, or of the Virgin except as idolatry; neither had he heard of dynamos or automobiles or radium; yet his mind was ready to feel the force of it all, though the rays were
30 unborn and the women were dead.

Here opened another totally new education, which promised to be by far the most hazardous of all. The knife-edge along which he must crawl, like Sir Lancelot in the twelfth century, divided two kingdoms of force which had nothing in common but attraction. They were as different as a magnet is from
35 gravitation, supposing one knew what a magnet was, or gravitation, or love. The force of the Virgin was still felt at Lourdes, and seemed to be as potent as X-rays; but in America neither Venus nor Virgin ever had value as force— at most as sentiment. No American had ever been truly afraid of either.

This problem in dynamics gravely perplexed an American historian. The
40 Woman had once been supreme; in France she still seemed potent, not merely as a sentiment, but as a force. Why was she unknown in America? For evidently America was ashamed of her, and she was ashamed of herself, otherwise they would not have strewn fig-leaves so profusely all over her. When

14. **Constantine**—Constantine's conversion to Christianity occurred when the Vision of the Flaming Cross appeared to him at noonday during his march upon Rome. 32. **knife-edge**— Chrétien de Troyes in his *Chevalier du Charatte* records this mode of entering a castle to rescue Guinevere.

she was a true force, she was ignorant of fig-leaves, but the monthly-magazine-made American female had not a feature that would have been recognized by Adam. The trait was notorious, and often humorous, but any one brought up among Puritans knew that sex was sin. In any previous age, sex was strength. Neither art nor beauty was needed. Every one, even among Puritans, knew 5 that neither Diana of the Ephesians nor any of the Oriental goddesses was worshipped for her beauty. She was goddess because of her force; she was the animated dynamo; she was reproduction—the greatest and most mysterious of all energies; all she needed was to be fecund. Singularly enough, not one of Adams's many schools of education had ever drawn his attention to 10 the opening lines of Lucretius, though they were perhaps the finest in all Latin Literature, where the poet invoked Venus exactly as Dante invoked the Virgin:—

"Quae quoniam rerum naturam sola gubernas."

The Venus of Epicurean philosophy survived in the Virgin of the Schools:— 15

"Donna, sei tanto grande, e tanto vali,
Che qual vuol grazia, e a te non ricorre,
Sua disianza vuol volar senz' ali."

All this was to American thought as though it had never existed. The true American knew something of the facts, but nothing of the feelings; he read 20 the letter, but he never felt the law. Before this historical chasm, a mind like that of Adams felt itself helpless; he turned from the Virgin to the Dynamo as though he were a Branly coherer. On one side, at the Louvre and at Chartres, as he knew by the record of work actually done and still before his eyes, was the highest energy ever known to man, the creator of four-fifths of his noblest 25 art, exercising vastly more attraction over the human mind than all the steam-engines and dynamos ever dreamed of; and yet this energy was unknown to the American mind. An American Virgin would never dare command; an American Venus would never dare exist.

The question, which to any plain American of the nineteenth century 30 seemed as remote as it did to Adams, drew him almost violently to study, once it was posed; and on this point Langleys were as useless as though they were Herbert Spencers or dynamos. The idea survived only as art. There one turned as naturally as though the artist were himself a woman. Adams began to ponder, asking himself whether he knew of any American artist who had ever 35 insisted on the power of sex, as every classic had always done; but he could think only of Walt Whitman; Bret Harte, as far as the magazines would let him venture; and one or two painters, for the flesh-tones. All the rest had

6. **Diana of the Ephesians**—*Cf.* Acts 19:24-41. 11. **Lucretius**—Titus Lucretius Carus (95-51? B.C.), Roman Epicurean philosopher. 14. **"Quae . . . gubernas"**—"Since thou then art sole mistress of the nature of things," line 21 of Lucretius, *On the Nature of Things.* 16-18. **"Donna . . . ali"**—

    "So mighty art thou, Lady, and so great
    That he, who grace desireth, and comes not
    To thee for aidance, fain would have desire
    Fly without wings."

Dante, *Divine Comedy:* Paradise, Canto XXXIII, lines 13-16 (Cary translation). 33. **Spencers—**Herbert Spencer (1820-1903), English philosopher, whose writings on organic and social evolution were widely read in America.

used sex for sentiment, never for force; to them, Eve was a tender flower, and Herodias an unfeminine horror. American art, like the American language and American education, was as far as possible sexless. Society regarded this victory over sex as its greatest triumph, and the historian readily admitted
5 it, since the moral issue, for the moment, did not concern one who was studying the relations of unmoral force. He cared nothing for the sex of the dynamo until he could measure its energy.

Vaguely seeking a clue, he wandered through the art exhibit, and, in his stroll, stopped almost every day before St. Gaudens's General Sherman, which
10 had been given the central post of honor. St. Gaudens himself was in Paris, putting on the work his usual interminable last touches, and listening to the usual contradictory suggestions of brother sculptors. Of all the American artists who gave to American art whatever life it breathed in the seventies, St. Gaudens was perhaps the most sympathetic, but certainly the most inar-
15 ticulate. General Grant or Don Cameron had scarcely less instinct of rhetoric than he. All the others—the Hunts, Richardson, John La Farge, Stanford White—were exuberant; only St. Gaudens could never discuss or dilate on an emotion, or suggest artistic arguments for giving to his work the forms that he felt. He never laid down the law, or affected the despot, or became brutal-
20 ized like Whistler by the brutalities of his world. He required no incense; he was no egoist; his simplicity of thought was excessive; he could not imitate, or give any form but his own to the creations of his hand. No one felt more strongly than he the strength of other men, but the idea that they could affect him never stirred an image in his mind.
25 This summer his health was poor and his spirits were low. For such a temper, Adams was not the best companion, since his own gaiety was not *folle;* but he risked going now and then to the studio on Mont Parnasse to draw him out for a stroll in the Bois de Boulogne, or dinner as pleased his moods, and in return St. Gaudens sometimes let Adams go about in his company.
30 Once St. Gaudens took him down to Amiens, with a party of Frenchmen, to see the cathedral. Not until they found themselves actually studying the sculpture of the western portal, did it dawn on Adams's mind that, for his purposes, St. Gaudens on that spot had more interest to him than the cathedral itself. Great men before great monuments express great truths, provided they
35 are not taken too solemnly. Adams never tired of quoting the supreme phrase of his idol Gibbon, before the Gothic cathedrals: "I darted a contemptuous look on the stately monuments of superstition." Even in the footnotes of his

2. Herodias—Herod's wife, responsible for the death of John the Baptist. *Cf.* Matt., Chapter 14. 9. St. Gaudens's—Augustus St. Gaudens (1848-1897), distinguished American sculptor and friend of Adams. The Sherman statue is at the entrance to Central Park, New York. 15. Don Cameron—Senator J. D. Cameron (1833-1918) of Pennsylvania, another friend of Adams. 16-17. Hunts . . . White—Richard Morris Hunt (1828-1895), architect, and William Morris Hunt (1824-1879), painter; Henry H. Richardson (1838-1886), architect; John La Farge (1835-1910), mural painter and sculptor; Stanford White (1853-1906), architect—all Americans who contributed greatly to civic beauty. 20. Whistler—James McNeill Whistler (1834-1903), American artist and etcher, who lived in Europe; noted for his sharp satiric wit. 26. folle—mad (French). 27-28. Parnasse, Boulogne—Parnasse, elevated artist section on the left bank of the Seine; Boulogne, large park in the western part of Paris. 36. Gibbon—Edward Gibbon (1737-1794) English historian, author of *The Decline and Fall of the Roman Empire.*

history, Gibbon had never inserted a bit of humor more human than this, and one would have paid largely for a photograph of the fat little historian, on the background of Notre Dame of Amiens, trying to persuade his readers—perhaps himself—that he was darting a contemptuous look on the stately monument, for which he felt in fact the respect which every man of his vast study   5
and active mind always feels before objects worthy of it; but besides the humor, one felt also the relation. Gibbon ignored the Virgin, because in 1789 religious monuments were out of fashion. In 1900 his remark sounded fresh and simple as the green fields to ears that had heard a hundred years of other remarks, mostly no more fresh and certainly less simple. Without malice, one   10
might find it more instructive than a whole lecture of Ruskin. One sees what one brings, and at that moment Gibbon brought the French Revolution. Ruskin brought reaction against the Revolution. St. Gaudens had passed beyond all. He liked the stately monuments much more than he liked Gibbon or Ruskin; he loved their dignity; their unity; their scale; their lines; their lights   15
and shadows; their decorative sculpture; but he was even less conscious than they of the force that created it all—the Virgin, the Woman—by whose genius "the stately monuments of superstition" were built, through which she was expressed. He would have seen more meaning in Isis with the cow's horns, at Edfoo, who expressed the same thought. The art remained, but the energy   20
was lost even upon the artist.

Yet in mind and person St. Gaudens was a survival of the 1500's; he bore the stamp of the Renaissance, and should have carried an image of the Virgin round his neck, or stuck in his hat, like Louis XI. In mere time he was a lost soul that had strayed by chance into the twentieth century, and forgotten   25
where it came from. He writhed and cursed at his ignorance, much as Adams did at his own, but in the opposite sense. St. Gaudens was a child of Benvenuto Cellini, smothered in an American cradle. Adams was a quintessence of Boston, devoured by curiosity to think like Benvenuto. St. Gaudens's art was starved from birth, and Adams's instinct was blighted from babyhood. Each   30
had but half of a nature, and when they came together before the Virgin of Amiens they ought both to have felt in her the force that made them one; but it was not so. To Adams she became more than ever a channel of force; to St. Gaudens she remained as before a channel of taste.

For a symbol of power, St. Gaudens instinctively preferred the horse, as   35
was plain in his horse and Victory of the Sherman monument. Doubtless Sherman also felt it so. The attitude was so American that, for at least forty years, Adams had never realized that any other could be in sound taste. How many years had he taken to admit a notion of what Michael Angelo and Rubens were driving at? He could not say; but he knew that only since 1895   40
had he begun to feel the Virgin or Venus as force, and not everywhere even so. At Chartres—perhaps at Lourdes—possibly at Cnidos if one could still find there the divinely naked Aphrodite of Praxiteles—but otherwise one must look

19. **Isis**—Egyptian goddess of fertility. Adams and John Hay had seen her statue at Edfu, in Upper Egypt. 24. **Louis XI**—(1423-1483), King of France from 1461 until his death. 42. **Cnidos** —The Aphrodite of Praxiteles was his masterpiece and was placed in the temple at Cnidos in the fourth century B.C.

for force to the goddesses of Indian mythology. The idea died out long ago in
the German and English stock. St. Gaudens at Amiens was hardly less sensitive to the force of the female energy than Matthew Arnold at the Grande
Chartreuse. Neither of them felt goddesses as power—only as reflected emotion,
5 human expression, beauty, purity, taste, scarcely even as sympathy. They felt a
railway train as power; yet they, and all other artists, constantly complained
that the power embodied in a railway train could never be embodied in art.
All the steam in the world could not, like the Virgin, build Chartres.

Yet in mechanics, whatever the mechanicians might think, both energies
10 acted as interchangeable forces on man, (and by action on man all known force
may be measured.) Indeed, few men of science measured force in any other
way. After once admitting that a straight line was the shortest distance between
two points, no serious mathematician cared to deny anything that suited his
convenience, and rejected no symbol, unproved or unproveable, that helped
15 him to accomplish work. The symbol was force, as a compass-needle or a triangle was force, as the mechanist might prove by losing it, and nothing could
be gained by ignoring their value. (Symbol or energy, the Virgin had acted as
the greatest force the Western world ever felt, and had drawn man's activities
to herself more strongly than any other power, natural or supernatural, had
20 ever done; the historian's business was to follow the track of the energy; to
find where it came from and where it went to; its complex source and shifting channels; its values, equivalents, conversions. It could scarcely be more
complex than radium; it could hardly be deflected, diverted, polarized, absorbed more perplexingly than other radiant matter. Adams knew nothing
25 about any of them, but as a mathematical problem of influence on human
progress, though all were occult, all reacted on his mind, and he rather inclined to think the Virgin easiest to handle.)

The pursuit turned out to be long and tortuous, leading at last into the
vast forests of scholastic science. From Zeno to Descartes, hand in hand with
30 Thomas Aquinas, Montaigne, and Pascal, one stumbled as stupidly as though
one were still a German student of 1860. Only with the instinct of despair
could one force one's self into this old thicket of ignorance after having been
repulsed at a score of entrances more promising and more popular. Thus far,
no path had led anywhere, unless perhaps to an exceedingly modest living.
35 Forty-five years of study had proved to be quite futile for the pursuit of power;
one controlled no more force in 1900 than in 1850, although the amount of
force controlled by society had enormously increased. The secret of education
still hid itself somewhere behind ignorance, and one fumbled over it as feebly
as ever. In such labyrinths, the staff is a force almost more necessary than the
40 legs; the pen becomes a sort of blind-man's dog, to keep him from falling into
the gutters. The pen works for itself, and acts like a hand, modelling the
plastic material over and over again to the form that suits it best. The form
is never arbitrary, but is a sort of growth like crystallization, as any artist

4. **Chartreuse**—Arnold was saved by "the Carthusians' world-famed home," as he relates in
"Stanzas from the Grande Chartreuse" (1855). **29-30. Zeno . . . Pascal**—Zeno (342?-270?
B.C.), founder of Greek stoicism; René Descartes (1596-1650), French rationalist; St. Thomas
Aquinas (1225?-1274), Italian Dominican monk and Church Father; Blaise Pascal (1623-1662),
French mathematician and epigrammatist.

knows too well; for often the pencil or pen runs into side-paths and shape-lessness, loses its relations, stops or is bogged. Then it has to return on its trail, and recover, if it can, its line of force. The result of a year's work depends more on what is struck out than on what is left in; on the sequence of the main lines of thought, than on their play or variety. Compelled once more 5 to lean heavily on this support, Adams covered more thousands of pages with figures as formal as though they were algebra, laboriously striking out, altering, burning, experimenting, until the year had expired, the Exposition had long been closed, and winter drawing to its end, before he sailed from Cherbourg, on January 10, 1901, for home. 10

SIDNEY LANIER

1842-1881

I. "SWORDS AND ROSES" (1842-1865)

1842   Born February 3, at Macon, Georgia, the eldest son of Robert Sampson and Mary Jane Anderson Lanier. Irregular education; development as amateur musician; much reading in romantic literature; absorption of chivalric attitude.

1857   Entered sophomore class of Oglethorpe University (Presbyterian) at Midway, near Milledgeville. Influence of Professor James Woodrow, directing young Lanier to liberalism in theology and German ideals in university life.

1860   July 18, graduated from university. Appointed tutor.

1861   June, joined Macon Volunteers. Sent to Virginia.

1862   June-July, participated in the Seven Days' Battle. August 26, transferred with his brother Clifford to the Mounted Signal Service.

1863-1864   Served as mounted scout. During this period Lanier worked at *Tiger-Lilies*.

1864   August, transferred to Wilmington, North Carolina, as signal officer on blockade-runners. Captured in November and imprisoned under miserable conditions at Point Lookout, Maryland. Increasing tendency toward consumption.

1865   February, discharged. Returned to Macon, dangerously ill.

II. STRUGGLE FOR EXISTENCE (1865-1876)

1866   In Montgomery, Alabama, as bookkeeper and clerk.

1867   December 19, married Mary Day. Publication of *Tiger-Lilies*.

1868   Brief career as a teacher. Studied law. Increasingly bad health.

1869   Entered law office in Macon. Increasing output as literary worker. During these years Lanier formed the acquaintance of Paul Hamilton Hayne. Interest in orchestral music in Baltimore.

1872   November, breakdown in health. Visit to San Antonio, Texas.

1873   Return to Baltimore; engagement as flautist in Peabody Orchestra.

1875   Published *Florida*, a guidebook.

1876   Publication of "Corn" in *Lippincott's Magazine* (February), and of "The Symphony" in the same periodical (June). Friendly interest of Charlotte Cushman and Bayard Taylor. Wrote words for Dudley Buck's music, *The Centennial Meditation of Columbia*, which aroused critical controversy.

III. THE MATURING ARTIST (1876-1881)

1876-1877   Residence in Florida in search of health. Published *Poems* (1877).

1878   Removed to Baltimore; lectured on Elizabethan poetry; gave other lectures at the Peabody Institute.

1879   Appointed lecturer in English literature at The Johns Hopkins University.
        Published *The Boy's Froissart* (*The Boy's King Arthur*, 1880; *The Boy's Mabinogion*, 1881; *The Boy's Percy*, 1882).
1880   Published *The Science of English Verse*. During this period Lanier continued to lecture at the Peabody Institute and at the university, notably on Shakespeare. Worked at "The Jacquerie" (unfinished).
1881   January, began lectures on the English novel at the university. In August he removed to the mountainous district of North Carolina (at Lynn), where he died September 7, 1881.
1883   *The English Novel* (from Lanier's lecture notes) published.
1884   *Poems* published (edited by Mrs. Lanier).
1899   *Retrospects and Prospects* published (collected essays).
1902   *Shakespere and His Forerunners* published (lectures).

BIOGRAPHIES: *Letters, 1866-1881*, Scribner, 1899; Edwin Mims, *Sidney Lanier*, Houghton Mifflin, 1905; Aubrey Harrison Starke, *Sidney Lanier: A Biographical and Critical Study*, University of North Carolina Press, 1933; Lincoln Lorenz, *Life of Sidney Lanier*, Coward-McCann, 1935; Richard Webb and E. R. Coulson, *Sidney Lanier, Poet and Prosodist*, Athens, Ga., University of Georgia Press, 1941.

BIBLIOGRAPHY AND WORKS: For bibliography see Starke's life and *Literary History of the United States*, Vol. III, pp. 605-08. Philip Graham, *A Concordance to the Poems of Sidney Lanier*, University of Texas Press, 1939, is useful. *The Centennial Edition*, 10 vols., Johns Hopkins, 1945, is standard. See Henry W. Lanier, ed., *Selections from Sidney Lanier*, Scribners, 1916; Stark Young, ed., *Selected Poems*, Scribners, 1947.

Objective critical judgment of Lanier is difficult to achieve because Southern critics tend to exaggerate his importance, and Northern critics, often unaware of the conditions under which he worked, underestimate his significance. Admiration for his gallant personal struggle becomes involved with critical judgments to the detriment of the latter. Lanier, moreover, shares some of the more glaring defects of romantic and sentimental poetry. But when all deductions are made, he left a small but firmly written body of poetry, musical in sound, lyric (or mainly so) in mood, and at his best tougher in intellectual structure than unfavorable criticism perceives it to be. Most of the comment on Lanier has been on his serious poetry. In addition, however, he wrote a small group of dialect poems expressive of the Southern farmer and the Southern Negro. His prose, which has been curiously neglected, has importance for its descriptive powers and for revealing that Lanier was aware of the economic, political, and cultural problems of his section. His importance historically is that he represents the transition from the romantic modes of older Southern literature to the realism of the present day.

THE SYMPHONY

This poem was first published in *Lippincott's Magazine*, June, 1875; then in revised form in the *Poems* of 1877 (1876); and in its final form in the *Poems* of 1884. In the first version there were many more verse paragraphs than in the text here printed. Although the general movement of the poem is intended to represent various musical instruments of a symphony orchestra, Lanier's method is suggestive only;

he actually includes only the strings (first and second violins, violas, cellos, but not, apparently, the double basses), the flute (his own instrument, and perhaps for that reason given a disproportionate share in the "symphony"), the clarionet, the horn, the oboe (hautboy), the bassoons. The student should note that as a symphony develops certain musical themes, so the poem is centered around the themes of business, love, and humanity. Lanier (wisely) does not try to represent all the movements of a symphony, but he does seek to suggest the ebb and flow of orchestral sound.

> "O Trade! O Trade! would thou wert dead!
> The Time needs heart—'tis tired of head:
> We're all for love," the violins said.
> "Of what avail the rigorous tale
> Of bill for coin and box for bale?   5
> Grant thee, O Trade! thine uttermost hope:
> Level red gold with blue sky-slope,
> And base it deep as devils grope:
> When all's done, what hast thou won
> Of the only sweet that's under the sun?   10
> Ay, canst thou buy a single sigh
> Of true love's least, least ecstasy?"
> Then, with a bridegroom's heart-beats trembling,
> All the mightier strings assembling
> Ranged them on the violins' side   15
> As when the bridegroom leads the bride,
> And, heart in voice, together cried:
> "Yea, what avail the endless tale
> Of gain by cunning and plus by sale?
> Look up the land, look down the land   20
> The poor, the poor, the poor, they stand
> Wedged by the pressing of Trade's hand
> Against an inward-opening door
> That pressure tightens evermore:
> They sigh a monstrous foul-air sigh   25
> For the outside leagues of liberty,
> Where Art, sweet lark, translates the sky
> Into a heavenly melody.
> 'Each day, all day' (these poor folks say),
> 'In the same old year-long, drear-long way,   30
> We weave in the mills and heave in the kilns,
> We sieve mine-meshes under the hills,
> And thieve much gold from the Devil's bank tills,
> To relieve, O God, what manner of ills?—
> The beasts, they hunger, and eat, and die;   35
> And so do we, and the world's a sty;
> Hush, fellow-swine: why nuzzle and cry?
> *Swinehood hath no remedy*
> Say many men, and hasten by,

7. **level**—that is, build it up to the level of the sky slope. 15. **violins'**—In the original form of the poem there was but one violin. 18. **tale**—count. 20. **land**—The original punctuation was a dash after **land**, which makes for clearer sense. 39. **Say many men**—This line originally read "The rich man says, and passes by,".

Clamping the nose and blinking the eye.   40
But who said once, in the lordly tone,
Man shall not live by bread alone
But all that cometh from the Throne?
   Hath God said so?
   But Trade saith *No:*   45
And the kilns and the curt-tongued mills say *Go:*
There's plenty that can, if you can't: we know.
Move out, if you think you're underpaid.
The poor are prolific; we're not afraid;
   Trade is trade.'"   50
Thereat this passionate protesting
Meekly changed, and softened till
It sank to sad requesting
And suggesting sadder still:
"And oh, if men might some time see   55
How piteous-false the poor decree
That trade no more than trade must be!
Does business mean, *Die, you—live, I?*
Then 'Trade is trade' but sings a lie:
'Tis only war grown miserly.   60
If business is battle, name it so:
War-crimes less will shame it so,
And widows less will blame it so.
Alas, for the poor to have some part
In yon sweet living lands of Art,   65
Makes problem not for head, but heart.
Vainly might Plato's brain revolve it:
Plainly the heart of a child could solve it."

And then, as when from words that seem but rude
We pass to silent pain that sits abroad   70
Back in our heart's great dark and solitude,
So sank the strings to gentle throbbing
Of long chords change-marked with sobbing—
Motherly sobbing, not distinctlier heard
Than half wing-openings of the sleeping bird,   75
Some dream of danger to her young hath stirred.
Then stirring and demurring ceased, and lo!
Every least ripple of the string's song-flow
Died to a level with each level bow
And made a great chord tranquil-surfaced so,   80
As a brook beneath his curving bank doth go
To linger in the sacred dark and green
Where many boughs the still pool overlean
And many leaves make shadow with their sheen.
 But presently   85
A velvet flute-note fell down pleasantly
Upon the bosom of that harmony,
And sailed and sailed incessantly,

42-43. Man . . . Throne—*Cf.* Luke 4: 4.

As if a petal from a wild-rose blown
Had fluttered down upon that pool of tone   90
And boatwise dropped o' the convex side
And floated down the glassy tide
And clarified and glorified
The solemn spaces where the shadows bide.
From the warm concave of that fluted note   95
Somewhat, half song, half odor, forth did float,
As if a rose might somehow be a throat:
"When Nature from her far-off glen
Flutes her soft messages to men,
     The flute can say them o'er again;   100
     Yea, Nature, singing sweet and lone,
Breathes through life's strident polyphone
The flute-voice in the world of tone.
     Sweet friends,
     Man's love ascends   105
To finer and diviner ends
Than man's mere thought e'er comprehends:
For I, e'en I,
As here I lie,
A petal on a harmony,   110
Demand of Science whence and why
Man's tender pain, man's inward cry,
When he doth gaze on earth and sky?
I am not overbold:
     I hold   115
Full powers from Nature manifold.
I speak for each no-tonguèd tree
That, spring by spring, doth nobler be,
And dumbly and most wistfully
His mighty prayerful arms outspreads   120
Above men's oft-unheeding heads,
And his big blessing downward sheds.
I speak for all-shaped blooms and leaves,
Lichens on stones and moss on eaves,
Grasses and grains in ranks and sheaves;   125
Broad-fronded ferns and keen-leaved canes,
And briery mazes bounding lanes,
And marsh-plants, thirsty-cupped for rains,
And milky stems and sugary veins;
For every long-armed woman-vine   130
That round a piteous tree doth twine;
For passionate odors, and divine
Pistils, and petals crystalline;
All purities of shady springs,
All shynesses of film-winged things   135
That fly from tree-trunks and bark-rings;

---

101. Yea—The flute song beginning with this line is the only considerable passage in the poem which was not radically revised in style. **102. polyphone**—many-voicedness.

All modesties of mountain-fawns
That leap to covert from wild lawns,
And tremble if the day but dawns;
All sparklings of small beady eyes						140
Of birds, and sidelong glances wise
Wherewith the jay hints tragedies;
All piquancies of prickly burs,
And smoothnesses of downs and furs,
Of eiders and of minevers;							145
All limpid honeys that do lie
At stamen-bases, nor deny
The humming-birds' fine roguery,
Bee-thighs, nor any butterfly;
All gracious curves of slender wings,					150
Bark-mottlings, fibre-spiralings,
Fern-wavings and leaf-flickerings;
Each dial-marked leaf and flower-bell
Wherewith in every lonesome dell
Time to himself his hours doth tell;					155
All tree-sounds, rustlings of pinecones,
Wind-sighings, doves' melodious moans,
And night's unearthly under-tones;
All placid lakes and waveless deeps,
All cool reposing mountain-steeps,					160
Vale-calms and tranquil lotos-sleeps;—
Yea, all fair forms, and sounds, and lights,
And warmths, and mysteries, and mights,
Of Nature's utmost depths and heights,
—These doth my timid tongue present,					165
Their mouthpiece and leal instrument
And servant, all love-eloquent.
I heard, when 'All for love' the violins cried:
So, Nature calls through all her system wide,
Give me thy love, O man, so long denied.					170
Much time is run, and man hath changed his ways,
Since Nature, in the antique fable-days,
Was hid from man's true love by proxy fays,
False fauns and rascal gods that stole her praise.
The nymphs, cold creatures of man's colder brain,				175
Chilled Nature's streams till man's warm heart was fain
Never to lave its love in them again.
Later, a sweet Voice Love thy neighbor said;
Then first the bounds of neighborhood outspread
Beyond all confines of old ethnic dread.					180
Vainly the Jew might wag his covenant head:
'All men are neighbors,' so the sweet Voice said.
So, when man's arms had circled all man's race,
The liberal compass of his warm embrace

---

145. eiders . . . minevers—the eider duck and the stoat. **166. leal**—loyal. **173. proxy**—substitute; in pagan times men worshiped inferior divinities instead of Nature directly. **178. Love thy neighbor**—Cf. Matt. 22: 39.

Stretched bigger yet in the dark bounds of space;   185
With hands a-grope he felt smooth Nature's grace,
Drew her to breast and kissed her sweetheart face:
Yea, man found neighbors in great hills and trees
And streams and clouds and suns and birds and bees,
And throbbed with neighbor-loves in loving these.   190
But oh, the poor! the poor! the poor!
That stand by the inward-opening door
Trade's hand doth tighten ever more,
And sigh their monstrous foul-air sigh
For the outside hills of liberty,   195
Where Nature spreads her wild blue sky
For Art to make into melody!
Thou Trade; thou king of the modern days!
    Change thy ways,
    Change thy ways;   200
Let the sweaty laborers file
    A little while,
    A little while,
Where Art and Nature sing and smile.
Trade! is thy heart all dead, all dead?   205
And hast thou nothing but a head?
I'm all for heart," the flute-voice said,
And into sudden silence fled,
Like as a blush that while 'tis red
Dies to a still, still white instead.   210

    Thereto a thrilling calm succeeds,
Till presently the silence breeds
A little breeze among the reeds
That seems to blow by sea-marsh weeds:
Then from the gentle stir and fret   215
Sings out the melting clarionet,
Like as a lady sings while yet
Her eyes with salty tears are wet.
"O Trade! O Trade!" the Lady said,
"I too will wish thee utterly dead   220
If all thy heart is in thy head.
For O my God! and O my God!
What shameful ways have women trod
At beckoning of Trade's golden rod!
Alas when sighs are traders' lies,   225
And heart's-ease eyes and violet eyes
    Are merchandise!
O purchased lips that kiss with pain!
O cheeks coin-spotted with smirch and stain!
O trafficked hearts that break in twain!   230
—And yet what wonder at my sisters' crime?
So hath Trade withered up Love's sinewy prime,
Men love not women as in olden time.

213. **reeds**—reed instruments of the orchestra.

Ah, not in these cold merchantable days
Deem men their life an opal gray, where plays   235
The one red Sweet of gracious ladies'-praise.
Now, comes a suitor with sharp prying eye—
Says, *Here, you Lady, if you'll sell, I'll buy:*
Come, heart for heart—a trade? What! weeping? why?
Shame on such wooers' dapper mercery!   240
I would my lover kneeling at my feet
In humble manliness should cry, *O sweet!*
I know not if thy heart my heart will greet:
I ask not if thy love my love can meet:
Whate'er thy worshipful soft tongue shall say,   245
I'll kiss thine answer, be it yea or nay:
I do but know I love thee, and I pray
To be thy knight until my dying day.
Woe him that cunning trades in hearts contrives!
Base love good women to base loving drives.   250
If men loved larger, larger were our lives;
And wooed they nobler, won they nobler wives."

There thrust the bold straightforward horn
To battle for that lady lorn,
With heartsome voice of mellow scorn,   255
Like any knight in knighthood's morn.
    "Now comfort thee," said he,
        "Fair Lady.
For God shall right thy grievous wrong,
And man shall sing thee a true-love song,   260
Voiced in act his whole life long,
    Yea, all thy sweet life long,
        Fair Lady.
Where's he that craftily hath said,
The day of chivalry is dead?   265
I'll prove that lie upon his head,
    Or I will die instead,
        Fair Lady.
Is Honor gone into his grave?
Hath Faith become a caitiff knave,   270
And Selfhood turned into a slave
    To work in Mammon's cave,
        Fair Lady?
Will Truth's long blade ne'er gleam again?
Hath Giant Trade in dungeons slain   275
All great contempts of mean-got gain
    And hates of inward stain,
        Fair Lady?
For aye shall name and fame be sold,
And place be hugged for the sake of gold,   280

240. **mercery**—merchandising. 272. **Mammon's cave**—*Cf. The Faerie Queene,* Bk. II,
Canto vii.

And smirch-robed Justice feebly scold
  At Crime all money-bold,
    Fair Lady?
Shall self-wrapt husbands aye forget
Kiss-pardons for the daily fret   285
Wherewith sweet wifely eyes are wet---
  Blind to lips kiss-wise set—
    Fair Lady?
Shall lovers higgle, heart for heart,
Till wooing grows a trading mart   290
Where much for little, and all for part,
  Make love a cheapening art,
    Fair Lady?
Shall woman scorch for a single sin
That her betrayer may revel in,   295
And she be burnt, and he but grin
  When that the flames begin,
    Fair Lady?
Shall ne'er prevail the woman's plea,
We maids would far, far whiter be   300
If that our eyes might sometimes see
  Men maids in purity,
    Fair Lady?
Shall Trade aye salve his conscience-aches
With jibes at Chivalry's old mistakes—   305
The wars that o'erhot knighthood makes
  For Christ's and ladies' sakes,
    Fair Lady?
Now by each knight that e'er hath prayed
To fight like a man and love like a maid,   310
Since Pembroke's life, as Pembroke's blade,
  I' the scabbard, death, was laid,
    Fair Lady,
I dare avouch my faith is bright
That God doth right and God hath might.   315
Nor time hath changed His hair to white,
  Nor His dear love to spite,
    Fair Lady.
I doubt no doubts: I strive, and shrive my clay,
And fight my fight in the patient modern way   320
For true love and for thee—ah me! and pray
  To be thy knight until my dying day,
    Fair Lady."
Made end that knightly horn, and spurred away
Into the thick of the melodious fray.   325

And then the hautboy played and smiled,
And sang like any large-eyed child,

---

292. cheapening—bargaining. **311. Pembroke's**—As none of the Earls of Pembroke seems sufficiently chivalric to fit Lanier's allusion, it is possible from the context that the poet wants to refer to Sir Philip Sidney (1554-1586), whose sister Mary married the second Earl of Pembroke. **326. hautboy**—oboe.

Cool-hearted and all undefiled.
  "Huge Trade!" he said.
"Would thou wouldst lift me on thy head   330
And run where'er my finger led!
Once said a Man—and wise was He—
Never shalt thou the heavens see,
Save as a little child thou be."
Then o'er sea-lashings of commingling tunes   335
The ancient wise bassoons,
   Like weird
   Gray-beard
Old harpers sitting on the high sea-dunes,
Chanted runes: 340
"Bright-waved gain, gray-waved loss,
The sea of all doth lash and toss,
One wave forward and one across:
But now 'twas trough, now 'tis crest,
And worst doth foam and flash to best,   345
   And curst to blest.

Life! Life! thou sea-fugue, writ from east to west,
   Love, Love alone can pore
   On thy dissolving score
   Of harsh half-phrasings,   350
     Blotted ere writ,
   And double erasings
     Of chords most fit.
Yea, Love, sole music-master blest,
May read thy weltering palimpsest.   355
To follow Time's dying melodies through,
And never to lose the old in the new,
And ever to solve the discords true—
   Love alone can do.
And ever Love hears the poor-folks' crying,   360
And ever Love hears the women's sighing,
And ever sweet knighthood's death-defying,
And ever wise childhood's deep implying,
But never a trader's glozing and lying.

And yet shall Love himself be heard,   365
Though long deferred, though long deferred:
O'er the modern waste a dove hath whirred:
Music is Love in search of a word."

333-34. **Never . . . be**—*Cf.* Matt. 19: 14; Mark 10: 15. **355. palimpsest**—a manuscript on which the first writing has been superficially erased so that the parchment could be used again. **367. dove**—*Cf.* Gen. 8: 8-11.

SONG OF THE CHATTAHOOCHEE

According to Mrs. Lanier this poem was first published in *Scott's Magazine* in
1877, but, as Lanier's latest biographer points out, this periodical ceased publication
in 1869, so that the place of first publication of this, the most popular of Lanier's
poems, is unknown.

The Chattahoochee River rises in Habersham County in northeastern Georgia,
flows southwest through the adjoining county of Hall, and, after crossing the state,
eventually forms its western boundary.

> Out of the hills of Habersham,
> 　Down the valleys of Hall,
> I hurry amain to reach the plain,
> Run the rapid and leap the fall,
> Split at the rock and together again,   5
> Accept my bed, or narrow or wide,
> And flee from folly on every side
> With a lover's pain to attain the plain
> 　Far from the hills of Habersham,
> 　Far from the valleys of Hall.   10
>
> All down the hills of Habersham,
> 　All through the valleys of Hall,
> The rushes cried, *Abide, abide,*
> The willful waterweeds held me thrall,
> The laving laurel turned my tide,   15
> The ferns and the fondling grass said, *Stay,*
> The dewberry dipped for to work delay,
> And the little reeds sighed, *Abide, abide,*
> 　*Here in the hills of Habersham,*
> 　*Here in the valleys of Hall.*   20
>
> High o'er the hills of Habersham,
> 　Veiling the valleys of Hall,
> The hickory told me manifold
> Fair tales of shade, the poplar tall
> Wrought me her shadowy self to hold,   25
> The chestnut, the oak, the walnut, the pine,
> Overleaning, with flickering meaning and sign,
> Said, *Pass not, so cold, these manifold*
> 　*Deep shades of the hills of Habersham,*
> 　*These glades in the valleys of Hall.*   30
>
> And oft in the hills of Habersham,
> 　And oft in the valleys of Hall,
> The white quartz shone, and the smooth brook-stone
> Did bar me of passage with friendly brawl,
> And many a luminous jewel lone   35
> —Crystals clear or a-cloud with mist,
> Ruby, garnet, and amethyst—

Made lures with the lights of streaming stone
  In the clefts of the hills of Habersham,
  In the beds of the valleys of Hall.   40

  But oh, not the hills of Habersham,
  And oh, not the valleys of Hall
Avail: I am fain for to water the plain.
Downward the voices of Duty call—
Downward, to toil and be mixed with the main,   45
The dry fields burn, and the mills are to turn,
And a myriad flowers mortally yearn,
And the lordly main from beyond the plain
  Calls o'er the hills of Habersham,
  Calls through the valleys of Hall.   50

THE MARSHES OF GLYNN

  Lanier originally planned six "Hymns of the Marshes," but he did not live to
complete them. "The Marshes of Glynn" is number 4 of the series, and was first
printed in *A Masque of Poets,* a book published in Boston in 1878 under the
editorship of George Parsons Lathrop, the contributions to which were kept anonymous. The book was one of a once celebrated series known as the No Name Series.
No poem of the author's more completely exemplifies the theory of versification set
forth in his *The Science of English Verse.* The marshes in question are near Brunswick, Georgia.

Glooms of the live-oaks, beautiful-braided and woven
With intricate shades of the vines that myriad-cloven
  Clamber the forks of the multiform boughs,—
      Emerald twilights,—
      Virginal shy lights,   5
Wrought of the leaves to allure to the whisper of vows,
When lovers pace timidly down through the green colonnades
Of the dim sweet woods, of the dear dark woods,
  Of the heavenly woods and glades,
That run to the radiant marginal sand-beach within   10
      The wide sea-marshes of Glynn;—

Beautiful glooms, soft dusks in the noon-day fire,—
Wildwood privacies, closets of lone desire,
Chamber from chamber parted with wavering arras of leaves,—
Cells for the passionate pleasure of prayer to the soul that grieves,   15
Pure with a sense of the passing of saints through the wood,
Cool for the dutiful weighing of ill with good;—

O braided dusks of the oak and woven shades of the vine,
While the riotous noon-day sun of the June-day long did shine
Ye held me fast in your heart and I held you fast in mine;   20
But now when the noon is no more, and riot is rest,
And the sun is a-wait at the ponderous gate of the West,

14. **arras**—curtain.

And the slant yellow beam down the wood-aisle doth seem
Like a lane into heaven that leads from a dream,—
Ay, now, when my soul all day hath drunken the soul of the oak,   25
And my heart is at ease from men, and the wearisome sound of the stroke
    Of the scythe of time and the trowel of trade is low,
    And belief overmasters doubt, and I know that I know,
    And my spirit is grown to a lordly great compass within,
That the length and the breadth and the sweep of the marshes of Glynn   30
Will work me no fear like the fear they have wrought me of yore
When length was fatigue, and when breadth was but bitterness sore,
And when terror and shrinking and dreary unnamable pain
Drew over me out of the merciless miles of the plain.—

Oh, now, unafraid, I am fain to face   35
    The vast sweet visage of space.
To the edge of the wood I am drawn, I am drawn,
Where the gray beach glimmering runs, as a belt of the dawn,
    For a mete and a mark
        To the forest-dark:—   40
          So:
Affable live-oak, leaning low,—
Thus—with your favor—soft, with a reverent hand,
(Not lightly touching your person, Lord of the land!)
Bending your beauty aside, with a step I stand   45
On the firm-packed sand,
        Free
By a world of marsh that borders a world of sea.
    Sinuous southward and sinuous northward the shimmering band
    Of the sand-beach fastens the fringe of the marsh to the folds of the land.   50
Inward and outward to northward and southward the beach-lines linger and curl
As a silver-wrought garment that clings to and follows the firm sweet limbs of a girl.
Vanishing, swerving, evermore curving again into sight,
Softly the sand-beach wavers away to a dim gray looping of light.
And what if behind me to westward the wall of the woods stands high?   55
The world lies east: how ample, the marsh and the sea and the sky!
A league and a league of marsh-grass, waist-high, broad in the blade,
Green, and all of a height, and unflecked with a light or a shade,
Stretch leisurely off, in a pleasant plain,
To the terminal blue of the main.   60

Oh, what is abroad in the marsh and the terminal sea?
    Somehow my soul seems suddenly free
From the weighing of fate and the sad discussion of sin,
By the length and the breadth and the sweep of the marshes of Glynn.

Ye marshes, how candid and simple and nothing-withholding and free   65
Ye publish yourselves to the sky and offer yourselves to the sea!
Tolerant plains, that suffer the sea and the rains and the sun,
Ye spread and span like the catholic man who hath mightily won
God out of knowledge and good out of infinite pain
And sight out of blindness and purity out of a stain.   70

39. mete—boundary. **68. catholic**—literally, universal.

As the marsh-hen secretly builds on the watery sod,
Behold I will build me a nest on the greatness of God:
I will fly in the greatness of God as the marsh-hen flies
In the freedom that fills all the space 'twixt the marsh and the skies:
By so many roots as the marsh-grass sends in the sod   75
I will heartily lay me a-hold on the greatness of God:
Oh, like to the greatness of God is the greatness within
The range of the marshes, the liberal marshes of Glynn.

And the sea lends large, as the marsh: lo, out of his plenty the sea
Pours fast: full soon the time of the flood-tide must be: 80
Look how the grace of the sea doth go
About and about through the intricate channels that flow
       Here and there,
             Everywhere,
Till his waters have flooded the uttermost creeks and the low-lying lanes,   85
And the marsh is meshed with a million veins,
That like as with rosy and silvery essences flow
In the rose-and-silver evening glow.
          Farewell, my lord Sun!
The creeks overflow: a thousand rivulets run   90
'Twixt the roots of the sod; the blades of the marsh-grass stir;
Passeth a hurrying sound of wings that westward whirr;
Passeth, and all is still; and the currents cease to run;
And the sea and the marsh are one.

How still the plains of the waters be!   95
The tide is in his ecstasy.
The tide is at his highest height:
         And it is night.
And now from the Vast of the Lord will the waters of sleep
Roll in on the souls of men,   100
But who will reveal to our waking ken
The forms that swim and the shapes that creep
        Under the waters of sleep?
And I would I could know what swimmeth below when the tide comes in
On the length and the breadth of the marvelous marshes of Glynn.   105

A BALLAD OF TREES AND THE MASTER

This poem was originally printed in the *Independent*, December 23, 1880. *Cf.* Matt. 26:36-46.

Into the woods my Master went,
Clean forspent, forspent.
Into the woods my Master came,
Forspent with love and shame.
But the olives they were not blind to Him,
The little gray leaves were kind to Him: 6
The thorn-tree had a mind to Him
When into the woods He came.

Out of the woods my Master went,
And He was well content.   10
Out of the woods my Master came,
Content with death and shame.
When Death and Shame would woo Him
   last,
From under the trees they drew Him last:
'Twas on a tree they slew Him—last   15
When out of the woods He came.

THE NEW SOUTH

Lanier contributed this essay to *Scribner's Monthly Magazine* in October, 1880.
It was posthumously collected into the volume entitled *Retrospects and Prospects*
(1899). As indicated in the second paragraph, the whole essay is divided into
numbered sections. The section numbering has been ignored in this selection, which
puts together paragraphs illustrative of Lanier's interpretation of Southern "small
farming" and Western "wheat mining."

I⊤ WOULD seem that facts may now be arrayed which leave no doubt that
upon the general cycle of American advance the South has described such
an epicycle of individual growth that no profitable discussion of that
region is possible at present which does not clearly define at the outset whether
5 it is to be a discussion of the old South or the new South. Although the movement here called by the latter name is originally neither political, social, moral,
nor aesthetic, yet the term in the present instance connotes all these with surprising completeness. The New South means small farming.

What Southern small farming really signifies, and how it has come to in-
10 volve and determine the whole compass of civilization in that part of the republic, this paper proposes to show, (1) by briefly pointing out its true relation,
in its last or (what one may call, its) poetic outcome, to the "large farming"
now so imminent in the Northwest; (2) by presenting some statistics of the
remarkable increase in the number of Southern small farms from 1860 to 1870,
15 together with some details of the actual cultures and special conditions thereof;
and (3) by contrasting with it a picture of large farming in England three hundred years ago. Indeed, one has only to recall how the connection between marriage and the price of corn is but a crude and partial statement of the intimate
relation between politics, social life, morality, art, on the one hand, and the
20 bread-giver earth on the other; one has only to remember that, particularly here
in America, whatever crop we hope to reap in the future,—whether it be a crop
of poems, of paintings, of symphonies, of constitutional safeguards, of virtuous
behaviors, of religious exaltations,—we have got to bring it out of the ground
with palpable ploughs and with plain farmer's forethought: in order to see that
25 a vital revolution in the farming economy of the South, if it is actually occur-
ring, is necessarily carrying with it all future Southern politics and Southern
social relations and Southern art, and that, therefore, such an agricultural
change is the one substantial fact upon which any really new South can be
predicated.

30 Approached from this direction, the quiet rise of the small farmer in the
Southern States during the last twenty years becomes the notable circumstance
of the period, in comparison with which noisier events signify nothing.

As just now hinted, small farming in the South becomes clear in its remoter
bearings when seen over against the precisely opposite tendency toward large
35 farming in the West. Doubtless recent reports of this tendency have been sometimes exaggerated. In reading them, one has been obliged to remember that
small minds love to bring large news, and, failing a load, will make one. But

certainly enough appears, if only in the single apparently well-authenticated item of the tempting profits realized by some of the great northwestern planters, to authorize the inference that the tendency to cultivate wheat on enormous farms, where the economies possible only to corporation-management can secure the greatest yield with the least expense, is a growing one. 5

And, this being so, the most rapid glance along the peculiar details of the northwestern large farm opens before us a path of thought which quickly passes beyond wheat-raising, and leads among all those other means of life which appertain to this complex creature who cannot live by bread alone. For instance, classify, as a social and moral factor, a farm like the Grandin place, 10 near Fargo, where 4,855 acres are sown in wheat; where five hands do all the work during the six winter months, while as many as two hundred and fifty must be employed in midsummer; where the day's work is nearly thirteen hours; where, out of the numerous structures for farm purposes, but two have any direct relation to man,—one a residence for the superintendent and fore- 15 man, the other a boarding-house for the hands; where no women, children, nor poultry are to be seen; where the economies are such as are wholly out of the power of the small wheat-raisers, insomuch that even the railways can give special rates for grain coming in such convenient large quantities; where the steam machine, the telephone, and the telegraph are brought to the last degree 20 of skilful service; where, finally, the net profits for the current year are $52,239.

It appears plainly enough from these details that, looked upon from the midst of all those associations which cluster about the idea of the farm, large farming is not farming at all. It is mining for wheat.

Or a slight change in the point of view presents it as a manufacturing busi- 25 ness, in which clods are fed to the mill, and grain appears in carloads at Chicago. And perhaps the most exact relations of this large farming to society in general are to be drawn by considering such farmers as corporations, their laborers as mill-operatives for six months in each year and tramps for the other six, their farms as mills where nature mainly turns the wheel, their investment 30 as beyond the reach of strikes or fires, foreign distress their friend, and the world's hunger their steady customer.

It appears further that, while such agricultural communities are so merely in name and are manufacturing communities in fact, they are manufacturing communities only as to the sterner features of that guild,—the order, the ma- 35 chine, the minimum of expense, the maximum of product,—and not as to those pleasanter features, the school-house, the church, the little workingmen's library, the sewing-class, the cookery-class, the line of promotion, the rise of the bright boy and the steady workman,—all the gentler matters which will spring up, even out of the dust-heaps, about any spot where men have the rudest abiding- 40 place. On the large farm is no abiding-place; the laborer must move on; life cannot stand still, to settle and clarify.

It would not seem necessary to disclaim any design to inveigh against the owners of these great factory-farms, if indignation had not been already expressed in such a way as to oblige one to declare that no obligations can be 45

21. $52,239—"According to an anonymous writer in *The Atlantic Monthly,* January, 1880." (Lanier's note) The article in question is entitled "The Bonanza Farms of the West." The Grandin farm is described on pp. 38-39.

cited, as between them and their laborers, which would not equally apply to every manufacturer. If it is wrong to discharge all but ten laborers when only ten are needed, then the mill-owners of Massachusetts must be held bound to run day and night when the market is over-stocked because they ran so when
5 it was booming; and if it is criminal to pay the large-farm hands no more than will hardly support them for thirteen hours' work, every mill-company in the world which pays market rates for work is *particeps*. But, with the coast thus cleared of personality; with the large farm thus classed as a manufacturing company in all its important incidents; and recognizing in the fullest manner
10 that, if wheat can be made most cheaply in this way, it must be so made: a very brief train of thought brings us upon a situation, as between the small farmer on the one hand and the corporation on the other, which reveals them as embodying two tendencies in the republic at this moment whose relations it is the business of statesmanship and of citizenship to understand with the utmost
15 clearness, since we are bound to foster both of them.

For, if we stop our ears to the noisy child's-play of current politics, and remember (1) that in all ages and countries two spirits, or motives, or tendencies exist which are essentially opposed to each other, but both of which are necessary to the state; (2) that the problem of any given period or society is to recog-
20 nize the special forms in which these two tendencies are then and there embodying themselves, and to keep them in such relations that neither shall crush, while each shall healthily check, the other; (3) that these tendencies may be called the spirit of control and the spirit of independence, and that they are so intimately connected with the two undeniable facts which lie at the bottom of
25 moral behavior—namely, the facts of influence from without, on the one hand, and free will on the other—that the questions of morals and of politics coalesce at their roots; (4) that these two tendencies are now most tangibly embodied among us in the corporation and the small farmer—the corporation representing the spirit of control, and the small farmer representing in many curious ways,
30 the spirit of independence; (5) that our republic vitally needs the corporation for the mighty works which only the corporation can do, while it as vitally needs the small farmer for the pure substance of individual and self-reliant manhood which he digs out of the ground, and which, the experience of all peoples would seem to show, must primarily come that way and no other: we are bound to
35 conclude that the practical affair in the United States at the present juncture is to discover how we may cherish at once the corporation and the small farmer into the highest state of competitive activity, less by constitution-straining laws which forbid the corporation to do this and that, or which coddle the small farmer with sop and privilege, than by affording free scope for both to adjust
40 themselves, and by persistently holding sound moral principles to guide the adjustment. . . .

The phrase "small farming," used of the South, crops out in directions curious enough to one unacquainted with the special economies and relations of existence in that part of our country. While large farming in the South means
45 exclusive cotton-growing,—as it means in the West exclusive wheat-growing or exclusive corn-growing,—small farming means *diversified farm-products;* and

---

7. **particeps**—*particeps criminis,* partner in crime.

a special result of the Southern conditions of agriculture has brought about a still more special sense of the word, so that in Georgia, for example, the term "small farmer" brings up to every native mind the idea of a farmer who, besides his cotton crop, raises corn enough to "do" him. But again, the incidents hinging upon this apparently simple matter of making corn enough to do him are so numerous as, in turn, to render *them* the distinctive feature of small farming. Small farming means, in short, meat and bread for which there are no notes in bank; pigs fed with home-made corn, and growing of themselves while the corn and cotton were being tended; yarn spun, stockings knit, butter made and sold (instead of bought); eggs, chickens, peaches, watermelons, the four extra sheep and a little wool, two calves and a beef,—all to sell every year, besides a colt who is now suddenly become, all of himself, a good, serviceable horse; the four oxen, who are as good as gifts made by the grass; and a hundred other items, all representing income from a hundred sources to the small farmer, which equally represent outgo to the large farmer,—items, too, scarcely appearing at all on the expense side of the strictest account-book, because they are either products of odd moments which, if not so applied, would not have been at all applied, or products of natural animal growth, and grass at nothing a ton. All these ideas are inseparably connected with that of the small farmer in the South.

The extent of this diversity of product possible upon a single small farm in Georgia, for instance, and the certain process by which we find these diversified products presently creating demands for the village library, the neighborhood farmers'-club, the amateur Thespian society, the improvement of the public schools, the village orchestra, all manner of betterments and gentilities and openings out into the universe: show significantly, and even picturesquely, in a mass of clippings which I began to make a couple of years ago, from a number of country papers in Georgia, upon the idea that these unconsidered trifles of mere farmers' neighborhood news, with no politics behind them and no argumentative coloring in front of them, would form the best possible picture of actual small-farm life in the South—that is, of the New South. . . .

Nothing seems more sure than that an entirely new direction of cleavage in the structure of Southern polity must come with the wholly different aggregation of particles implied in this development of small farming.

In the identical aims of the small-farmer class, whatever now remains of the color-line must surely disappear out of the Southern political situation. This class, consisting as it already does of black small-farmers and white small-farmers, must necessarily be a body of persons whose privileges, needs, and relations are *not* those which exist as between the black man on the one hand and the white man on the other, but those which exist as between the small farmer on the one hand and whatever affects small farming on the other. For here—as cannot be too often said—the relation of politics to agriculture is that of the turnip-top to the turnip.

The obliteration of the color-line could be reduced to figures if we knew the actual proportion of the new small farms held by negroes. Though, as already remarked, data are here wanting, yet the matter emerges into great distinctness.

... It does not seem possible to doubt ... that there is, in Georgia at least, a strong class of small farmers which powerfully tends to obliterate color from politics, in virtue of its merger of all conflicting elements into the common interest of common agricultural pursuit. ...

5　　It is impossible to end without adverting to a New South which exists in a far more literal sense than that of small farming. How much of this gracious land is yet new to all real cultivation, how much of it lies groaning for the muscle of men, and how doubly mournful is this newness, in view of the fair and fruitful conditions which here hold perpetual session, and press perpetual
10　invitation upon all men to come and have plenty! Surely, along that ample stretch of generous soil, where the Appalachian ruggednesses calm themselves into pleasant hills before dying quite away into the sea-board levels, a man can find such temperance of heaven and earth—enough of struggle with nature to draw out manhood, with enough of bounty to sanction the struggle—that a
15　more exquisite co-adaptation of all blessed circumstances for man's life need not be sought. It is with a part of that region that this writer is most familiar, and one cannot but remember that, as one stands at a certain spot thereof and looks off up and across the Ocmulgee River, the whole prospect seems distinctly to yearn for men. Everywhere the huge and gentle slopes kneel and pray for
20　vineyards, for cornfields, for cottages, for spires to rise up from beyond the oak-groves. It is a land where there is never a day of summer nor of winter when a man cannot do a full day's work in the open field; all the products meet there, as at nature's own agricultural fair; rice grows alongside of wheat, corn alongside of sugar-cane, cotton alongside of clover, apples alongside of peaches, so
25　that a small farm may often miniature the whole United States in growth; the little valleys everywhere run with living waters, asking grasses and cattle and quiet grist-mills; all manner of timbers for economic uses and trees for finer arts cover the earth; in short, here is such a neighborly congregation of climates, soils, minerals, and vegetables, that within the compass of many a hundred-acre
30　farm a man may find wherewithal to build his house of stone, of brick, of oak, or of pine, to furnish it in woods that would delight the most curious eye, and to supply his family with all the necessaries, most of the comforts, and many of the luxuries, of the whole world. It is the country of homes.

　　And, as said, it is because these blissful ranges are still clamorous for human
35　friendship; it is because many of them are actually virgin to plough, pillar, axe, or mill-wheel, while others have known only the insulting and mean cultivation of the earlier immigrants who scratched the surface for cotton a year or two, then carelessly abandoned all to sedge and sassafras, and sauntered on toward Texas: it is thus that these lands are, with sadder significance than that
40　of small farming, also a New South.

18. Ocmulgee River—river in northern Georgia, flowing into the Altamaha.

WILLIAM JAMES

1842-1910

I. APPRENTICE TO LIFE (1842–1872)

1842 Born January 11, at the Astor House, New York City, the eldest son of Henry James, Sr., and Mary Walsh James.

1845–1855 Irregular schooling and "experimental" childhood in Europe, Albany, New York, and New York City, owing to the father's "philosophical" ideas.

1855 June, family sailed for Europe. Five years of wandering. Awakening interest in painting and in biological science.

1860 Return to Newport, Rhode Island. Study under William M. Hunt, the painter.

1861–1864 Student, Lawrence Scientific School, Harvard College. Influence of Charles W. Eliot in chemistry and of Jeffries Wyman in physiology. Friendship with Chauncey Wright, the young positivist.

1865 April, member of the Thayer zoölogical expedition to the Amazon River. Association with Agassiz.

1866 March, resumed medical studies in Boston.

1867 April, trip to Europe partly for health, partly to continue study of science and art in Germany and France. Returned November, 1868. During these years James began reviewing books of technical science for various periodicals and newspapers.

1869 June, took medical degree at Harvard. Beginning of period of depression and uncertainty.

1870 James's "crisis"; that is, delivery from melancholy. Influence of Charles Renouvier's *Traité de psychologie rationelle* in giving James a belief in man's moral freedom.

II. THE PSYCHOLOGIST (1872–1890)

1872 Autumn, appointed instructor in physiology at Harvard; beginning of ten years' teaching of physiology and related subjects.

1873 First "original" magazine article, "The Mood of Science and the Mood of Faith," in the *Nation*.

1875 Offered first course in the relations between physiology and psychology. Influence of German science (Helmholtz, Wundt).

1876 Instituted first psychological laboratory. Published article in the *Nation* pleading for freedom in the teaching of philosophy.

1877 James's courses transferred to department of philosophy.

1878 July 10, married Alice Howe Gibbens. In "Remarks on Spencer's Definition of Mind as Correspondence" (*Journal of Speculative Philosophy*) made first statement of theory developed in his psychology and philosophy. Began work on *The Principles of Psychology* (1890), the chapters of which were often published in preliminary form from 1879 to 1890.

1880–1882   Trips abroad; contact with leading European psychologists, and with influential English philosophical empiricists like Shadworth Hodgson.

1882–1895   Beginning and development of interest in the Society for Psychical Research laid foundation for *Varieties of Religious Experience* (1902).

1884   Article, "What Is an Emotion?" (*Mind*), first statement by James of James-Lange theory of the emotions.

1890   Published *Principles of Psychology*, 2 vols., first great American contribution to the subject. (*Briefer Course,* 1892.)

III. THE PHILOSOPHER (1890–1910)

1890–1897   Transitional years, in which James's interest shifted from psychology to philosophy.

1894–1898   Growing interest in national affairs. Expression of anti-imperialism.

1894   December, delivered presidential address at the meeting of the American Psychological Association, "The Knowing of Things Together," which marks James's drift to philosophical point of view of Henri Bergson.

1896   Delivered address "The Will to Believe" at Yale and Brown universities. Lecture tour made James acquainted with the Middle West.

1897   Delivered the Ingersoll Lectures at Harvard, *Human Immortality* (published 1898). *The Will to Believe and Other Essays* published.

1898   Lecture tour to California. A lecture at the University of California, "Philosophical Conceptions and Practical Results," was the first formal announcement of pragmatism.

1899   Published *Talks to Teachers on Psychology: and to Students on Some of Life's Ideals.*

1899–1901   Illness; trip to Europe for recovery. Delivered the Gifford Lectures at Edinburgh University (first course, 1901; second course, 1902). These became *Varieties of Religious Experience,* published 1902.

1902–1907   Active as a teacher at Harvard, a lecturer, and a writer of philosophical articles.

1906   Second trip to University of California, where he delivered lectures which became *Some Problems of Philosophy* (1911). President of the American Philosophical Association.

1907   Published *Pragmatism,* lectures delivered at the Lowell Institute in 1906 and at Columbia University in 1907. Met last Harvard class January 22.

1909   Published *A Pluralistic Universe,* lectures delivered at Manchester College, Oxford University, 1908–09. Published *The Meaning of Truth: A Sequel to 'Pragmatism.'*

1910   Published "The Moral Equivalent of War" in *McClure's Magazine* (and elsewhere). Died August 26 at Chocorua, New Hampshire.

1911   *Some Problems of Philosophy* and *Memories and Studies* published.

1912   *Essays in Radical Empiricism* published.

1920   *Collected Essays and Reviews* published.

BIOGRAPHIES: The standard life is Ralph B. Perry, *The Thought and Character of William James,* Little, Brown, 1935, 2 vols. See also Henry James, *A Small Boy and Others,* 1913; and *Notes of a Son and Brother,* 1914; and C. H. Grattan, *The Three Jameses,* Longmans, 1932.

BIBLIOGRAPHY: There is no collected edition of William James. For bibliography consult *Literary History of the United States,* Vol. III, pp. 590-93 and R. B. Perry, *An Annotated Bibliography of the Writings of William James,* Longmans, 1920.

The long curve of American philosophical writing begins with Jonathan Edwards, who denied the freedom of the will, and, in a sense, concludes with William James, who affirmed the freedom of belief. There are other American philosophers as important as James—Josiah Royce, his great contemporary, was perhaps a profounder thinker and certainly a more subtle metaphysician; but in the opinion of foreign critics of American thought, William James is the American philosopher par excellence. He taught that the test of truth is its practical workability; and this has been twisted into the American doctrine that whatever is practicably workable must be true. James really does not say this, though at times he comes close to saying it; but his own doctrine, expressed in the two essays here reprinted, is (like Franklin's) a presentation of truth in informal, and even colloquial, terms and intended, unlike much philosophical writing, to be "understanded of the people." The informality of James's attitude helps to explain the wide influence of pragmatism on popular, no less than on philosophical, thought; and if, as James believed, philosophies are best approached from the point of view of the times which produced them and of the temperament of the philosopher, pragmatism amply expresses the temper of American life in the closing decade of the nineteenth century and in the Theodore Roosevelt era. But the student should not believe that this is the whole doctrine of James. One must not forget his interest in psychical and mystical experience—an interest which links him with Edwards, with Emerson, with Whitman, and with a characteristic strain in the national religious life.

THE WILL TO BELIEVE

In February, 1897, William James published *The Will to Believe and Other Essays in Popular Philosophy* (Longmans), dedicated to C. S. Peirce, "my old friend," to whose "philosophic comradeship" James owed "more incitement and help" than he could repay. The preface is dated at Harvard, 1896; and there are ten essays, "The Will to Believe" being the first. A footnote says that it is an address given to the Philosophical Clubs of Yale and Brown universities, and published in the *New World,* June, 1896. The *New World* was a philosophic quarterly edited by a group of professors; James's essay appears in Vol. V, pp. 327-47; and there are important textual variants.

I N THE recently published Life by Leslie Stephen of his brother, Fitz-James, there is an account of a school to which the latter went when he was a boy. The teacher, a certain Mr. Guest, used to converse with his pupils in this wise: "Gurney, what is the difference between justification and sanctification?—Stephen, prove the omnipotence of God!" etc. In the midst of our 5

1. **Leslie Stephen**—Sir Leslie Stephen (1832-1904), English philosopher and man of letters, famous as an agnostic. The life of his brother, Fitz-James Stephen (1829-1894), an English jurist and writer on public affairs, appeared in 1895. The passage quoted by James appears on p. 73 (2d ed.). 4. **justification**—the theological doctrine which represents the basis of the reconciliation of God and sinners. 4. **sanctification**—the doctrine that the Holy Spirit by grace delivers men from sin and redeems them in Christ.

Harvard freethinking and indifference we are prone to imagine that here at your good old orthodox College conversation continues to be somewhat upon this order; and to show you that we at Harvard have not lost all interest in these vital subjects, I have brought with me to-night something like a sermon
5 on justification by faith to read to you,—I mean an essay in justification *of* faith, a defense of our right to adopt a believing attitude in religious matters, in spite of the fact that our merely logical intellect may not have been coerced. 'The Will to Believe,' accordingly, is the title of my paper.

I have long defended to my own students the lawfulness of voluntarily
10 adopted faith; but as soon as they have got well imbued with the logical spirit, they have as a rule refused to admit my contention to be lawful philosophically, even though in point of fact they were personally all the time chock-full of some faith or other themselves. I am all the while, however, so profoundly convinced that my own position is correct, that your invitation has
15 seemed to me a good occasion to make my statements more clear. Perhaps your minds will be more open than those with which I have hitherto had to deal. I will be as little technical as I can, though I must begin by setting up some technical distinctions that will help us in the end.

I

20 Let us give the name of *hypothesis* to anything that may be proposed to our belief; and just as the electricians speak of live and dead wires, let us speak of any hypothesis as either *live* or *dead*. A live hypothesis is one which appeals as a real possibility to him to whom it is proposed. If I ask you to believe in the Mahdi, the notion makes no electric connection with your nature,—it re-
25 fuses to scintillate with any credibility at all. As an hypothesis it is completely dead. To an Arab, however (even if he be not one of the Mahdi's followers), the hypothesis is among the mind's possibilities: it is alive. This shows that deadness and liveness in an hypothesis are not intrinsic properties, but relations to the individual thinker. They are measured by his willingness to act.
30 The maximum of liveness in an hypothesis means willingness to act irrevocably. Practically, that means belief; but there is some believing tendency wherever there is willingness to act at all.

Next, let us call the decision between two hypotheses an *option*. Options may be of several kinds. They may be—1, *living* or *dead;* 2, *forced* or *avoid-*
35 *able;* 3, *momentous* or *trivial;* and for our purposes we may call an option a *genuine* option when it is of the forced, living, and momentous kind.

1. A living option is one in which both hypotheses are live ones. If I say to you: "Be a theosophist or be a Mohammedan," it is probably a dead option, because for you neither hypothesis is likely to be alive. But if I say: "Be an ag-
40 nostic or be a Christian," it is otherwise: trained as you are, each hypothesis makes some appeal, however small, to your belief.

24. **Mahdi**—In general, a mahdi is a Moslem equivalent for a Messiah. James's reference is probably to Mohammed Ahmed, who in the eighties of the last century was proclaimed "Mahdi," overcame Egyptian troops sent to subdue him, and defeated and killed the English General Gordon at Khartum in 1885. 38. **theosophist**—In general, theosophy is a form of mysticism which teaches that superior spirits may have direct intercourse with God through superior illumination. 39. **agnostic**—An agnostic is one who denies the possibility of knowing anything real about God.

2. Next, if I say to you: "Choose between going out with your umbrella or without it," I do not offer you a genuine option, for it is not forced. You can easily avoid it by not going out at all. Similarly, if I say, "Either love me or hate me," "Either call my theory true or call it false," your option is avoidable. You may remain indifferent to me, neither loving nor hating, and you may decline to offer any judgment as to my theory. But if I say, "Either accept this truth or go without it," I put on you a forced option, for there is no standing place outside of the alternative. Every dilemma based on a complete logical disjunction, with no possibility of not choosing, is an option of this forced kind.

3. Finally, if I were Dr. Nansen and proposed to you to join my North Pole expedition, your option would be momentous; for this would probably be your only similar opportunity, and your choice now would either exclude you from the North Pole sort of immortality altogether or put at least the chance of it into your hands. He who refuses to embrace a unique opportunity loses the prize as surely as if he tried and failed. *Per contra,* the option is trivial when the opportunity is not unique, when the stake is insignificant, or when the decision is reversible if it later prove unwise. Such trivial options abound in the scientific life. A chemist finds an hypothesis live enough to spend a year in its verification: he believes in it to that extent. But if his experiments prove inconclusive either way, he is quit for his loss of time, no vital harm being done.

It will facilitate our discussion if we keep all these distinctions well in mind.

II

The next matter to consider is the actual psychology of human opinion. When we look at certain facts, it seems as if our passional and volitional nature lay at the root of all our convictions. When we look at others, it seems as if they could do nothing when the intellect had once said its say. Let us take the latter facts up first.

Does it not seem preposterous on the very face of it to talk of our opinions being modifiable at will? Can our will either help or hinder our intellect in its perceptions of truth? Can we, by just willing it, believe that Abraham Lincoln's existence is a myth, and that the portraits of him in *McClure's Magazine* are all of some one else? Can we, by any effort of our will, or by any strength of wish that it were true, believe ourselves well and about when we are roaring with rheumatism in bed, or feel certain that the sum of the two one-dollar bills in our pocket must be a hundred dollars? We can *say* any of these things, but we are absolutely impotent to believe them; and of just such things is the whole fabric of the truths that we do believe in made up,—matters of fact, immediate or remote, as Hume said, and relations between ideas, which are either there or not there for us if we see them so, and which if not there cannot be put there by any action of our own.

10. **Nansen**—Fridtjof Nansen (1861-1930), famous Polar explorer. James has especially in mind his expedition of 1893-97, on which Nansen wrote an article in *McClure's Magazine,* February, 1898. 15. **Per contra**—Contrariwise. 32-33. **McClure's Magazine**—James's reference is to an article by Ida M. Tarbell in this magazine, February, 1898, "Some Great Portraits of Lincoln," which is profusely illustrated.

In Pascal's Thoughts there is a celebrated passage known in literature as Pascal's wager. In it he tries to force us into Christianity by reasoning as if our concern with truth resembled our concern with the stakes in a game of chance. Translated freely his words are these: You must either believe or not
5 believe that God is—which will you do? Your human reason cannot say. A game is going on between you and the nature of things which at the day of judgment will bring out either heads or tails. Weigh what your gains and your losses would be if you should stake all you have on heads, or God's existence: if you win in such case, you gain eternal beatitude: if you lose, you
10 lose nothing at all. If there were an infinity of chances, and only one for God in this wager, still you ought to stake your all on God; for though you surely risk a finite loss by this procedure, any finite loss is reasonable, even a certain one is reasonable, if there is but the possibility of infinite gain. Go, then, and take holy water, and have masses said; belief will come and stupefy your
15 scruples,—*Cela vous fera croire et vous abêtira.* Why should you not? At bottom, what have you to lose?

You probably feel that when religious faith expresses itself thus, in the language of the gaming-table, it is put to its last trumps. Surely Pascal's own personal belief in masses and holy water had far other springs; and this celebrated
20 page of his is but an argument for others, a last desperate snatch at a weapon against the hardness of the unbelieving heart. We feel that a faith in masses and holy water adopted wilfully after such a mechanical calculation would lack the inner soul of faith's reality; and if we were ourselves in the place of the Deity, we should probably take particular pleasure in cutting off believers
25 of this pattern from their infinite reward. It is evident that unless there be some pre-existing tendency to believe in masses and holy water, the option offered to the will by Pascal is not a living option. Certainly no Turk ever took to masses and holy water on its account; and even to us Protestants these means of salvation seem such foregone impossibilities that Pascal's logic, in-
30 voked for them specifically, leaves us unmoved. As well might the Mahdi write to us, saying, "I am the Expected One whom God has created in his effulgence. You shall be infinitely happy if you confess me; otherwise you shall be cut off from the light of the sun. Weigh, then, your infinite gain if I am genuine against your finite sacrifice if I am not!" His logic would be that
35 of Pascal; but he would vainly use it on us, for the hypothesis he offers us is dead. No tendency to act on it exists in us to any degree.

The talk of believing by our volition seems, then, from one point of view, simply silly. From another point of view it is worse than silly; it is vile. When one turns to the magnificent edifice of the physical sciences, and sees how it
40 was reared; what thousands of disinterested moral lives of men lie buried in its mere foundations; what patience and postponement, what choking down of preference, what submission to the icy laws of outer fact are wrought into its very stones and mortar; how absolutely impersonal it stands in its vast

---

1. **Pascal's Thoughts**—The reference is to the *Pensées* of Blaise Pascal (see note on p. 1384). James's reference is to par. 233, Sec. III of the *Pensées*, ed. L. Brunschvigg, Paris, 1907. The text paraphrases the passage. **15. Cela . . . abêtira**—"That will make you believe and stupefy your self." Part of a sentence from the *Pensées*, p. 441 of the edition cited.

augustness,—then how besotted and contemptible seems every little sentimen-
talist who comes blowing his voluntary smoke-wreaths, and pretending to
decide things from out of his private dream! Can we wonder if those bred in
the rugged and manly school of science should feel like spewing such sub-
jectivism out of their mouths? The whole system of loyalties which grow up   5
in the schools of science go dead against its toleration; so that it is only natural
that those who have caught the scientific fever should pass over to the opposite
extreme, and write sometimes as if the incorruptibly truthful intellect ought
positively to prefer bitterness and unacceptableness to the heart in its cup.

> It fortifies my soul to know   10
> That, though I perish, Truth is so—

sings Clough, while Huxley exclaims: "My only consolation lies in the reflection that, however bad our posterity may become, so far as they hold by the
plain rule of not pretending to believe what they have no reason to believe,
because it may be to their advantage so to pretend [the word 'pretend' is   15
surely here redundant], they will not have reached the lowest depth of immorality." And that delicious *enfant terrible* Clifford writes: "Belief is dese-
crated when given to unproved and unquestioned statements for the solace
and private pleasure of the believer. . . . Whoso would deserve well of his
fellows in this matter will guard the purity of his belief with a very fanati-   20
cism of jealous care, lest at any time it should rest on an unworthy object,
and catch a stain which can never be wiped away. . . . If [a] belief has been
accepted on insufficient evidence [even though the belief be true, as Clifford
on the same page explains] the pleasure is a stolen one. . . . It is sinful because it is stolen in defiance of our duty to mankind. That duty is to guard   25
ourselves from such beliefs as from a pestilence which may shortly master our
own body and then spread to the rest of the town. . . . It is wrong always,
everywhere, and for every one, to believe anything upon insufficient evidence."

III

All this strikes one as healthy, even when expressed, as by Clifford, with   30
somewhat too much of robustious pathos in the voice. Free-will and simple
wishing do seem, in the matter of our credences, to be only fifth wheels to
the coach. Yet if any one should thereupon assume that intellectual insight is
what remains after wish and will and sentimental preference have taken wing,
or that pure reason is what then settles our opinions, he would fly quite as   35
directly in the teeth of the facts.

It is only our already dead hypotheses that our willing nature is unable to
bring to life again. But what has made them dead for us is for the most part
a previous action of our willing nature of an antagonistic kind. When I say
willing nature,' I do not mean only such deliberate volitions as may have   40

10-11. It . . . so—The verse is the opening lines of a short poem, "With Whom Is No Varia-
bleness, Neither Shadow of Turning" from *Ambervalia* (1843) by Arthur Hugh Clough (1819-
1861). 12. Huxley—Thomas Henry Huxley (1825-1895), English biologist and influential essayist.
17. enfant terrible—"bad boy." 17. Clifford—William Kingdon Clifford (1845-1879), English mathematician and philosopher, who held that consciousness is constructed out of "mind-stuff."

set up habits of belief that we cannot now escape from,—I mean all such factors of belief as fear and hope, prejudice and passion, imitation and partisanship, the circumpressure of our caste and set. As a matter of fact we find ourselves believing, we hardly know how or why. Mr. Balfour gives the name of
5 'authority' to all those influences, born of the intellectual climate, that make hypotheses possible or impossible for us, alive or dead. Here in this room, we all of us believe in molecules and the conservation of energy, in democracy and necessary progress, in Protestant Christianity and the duty of fighting for 'the doctrine of the immortal Monroe,' all for no reasons worthy of the name. We
10 see into these matters with no more inner clearness, and probably with much less, than any disbeliever in them might possess. His unconventionality would probably have some grounds to show for its conclusions; but for us, not insight, but the *prestige* of the opinions, is what makes the spark shoot from them and light up our sleeping magazines of faith. Our reason is quite satis-
15 fied, in nine hundred and ninety-nine cases out of every thousand of us, if it can find a few arguments that will do to recite in case our credulity is criticised by some one else. Our faith is faith in some one else's faith, and in the greatest matters this is most the case. Our belief in truth itself, for instance, that there is a truth, and that our minds and it are made for each other,—
20 what is it but a passionate affirmation of desire, in which our social system backs us up? We want to have a truth; we want to believe that our experiments and studies and discussions must put us in a continually better and better position towards it; and on this line we agree to fight out our thinking lives. But if a pyrrhonistic sceptic asks us *how we know* all this, can our
25 logic find a reply? No! certainly it cannot. It is just one volition against another,—we willing to go in for life upon a trust or assumption which he, for his part, does not care to make.

As a rule we disbelieve all facts and theories for which we have no use. Clifford's cosmic emotions find no use for Christian feelings. Huxley belabors
30 the bishops because there is no use for sacerdotalism in his scheme of life. Newman, on the contrary, goes over to Romanism, and finds all sorts of reasons good for staying there, because a priestly system is for him an organic need and delight. Why do so few 'scientists' even look at the evidence for telepathy, so called? Because they think, as a leading biologist, now dead, once said to
35 me, that even if such a thing were true, scientists ought to band together to keep it suppressed and concealed. It would undo the uniformity of Nature and all sorts of other things without which scientists cannot carry on their pursuits. But if this very man had been shown something which as a scientist

---

3. circumpressure—circular pressure. **4. Balfour**—Arthur James Balfour (1848-1930), English statesman and skeptical philosopher. **9. doctrine . . . Monroe**—The doctrine promulgated by President James Monroe in 1823 that European interference in affairs of the New World would be considered "a manifestation of an unfriendly disposition toward the United States." **24. pyrrhonistic**—Pyrrho, a Greek skeptic (about 300 B.C.), taught that it was impossible to attain certain knowledge. **27. make**—"Compare the admirable page 310 in S. H. Hodgson's *Time and Space, London, 1865.*" (James's note) **30. sacerdotalism**—emphasis upon the interests of the priesthood as opposed to those of the laity. **30. Newman**—John Henry Newman (1801-1890), converted from the Anglican faith to the Roman Catholic Church in 1845. Newman's conversion resulted from his search for "authority." **33. telepathy**—the influencing of one mind by another without the use of the ordinary channels of sensation.

he might *do* with telepathy, he might not only have examined the evidence, but even have found it good enough. This very law which the logicians would impose upon us—if I may give the name of logicians to those who would rule out our willing nature here—is based on nothing but their own natural wish to exclude all elements for which they, in their professional quality of logicians, 5 can find no use.

Evidently, then, our non-intellectual nature does influence our convictions. There are passional tendencies and volitions which run before and others which come after belief, and it is only the latter that are too late for the fair; and they are not too late when the previous passional work has been already in 10 their own direction. Pascal's argument, instead of being powerless, then seems a regular clincher, and is the last stroke needed to make our faith in masses and holy water complete. The state of things is evidently far from simple; and pure insight and logic, whatever they might do ideally, are not the only things that really do produce our creeds. 15

IV

Our next duty, having recognized this mixed-up state of affairs, is to ask whether it be simply reprehensible and pathological, or whether, on the contrary, we must treat it as a normal element in making up our minds. The thesis I defend is, briefly stated, this: *Our passional nature not only lawfully* 20 *may, but must, decide an option between propositions, whenever it is a genuine option that cannot by its nature be decided on intellectual grounds; for to say, under such circumstances, "Do not decide, but leave the question open," is itself a passional decision,—just like deciding yes or no,—and is attended with the same risk of losing the truth.* The thesis thus abstractly expressed will, I 25 trust, soon become quite clear. But I must first indulge in a bit more of preliminary work.

V

It will be observed that for the purposes of this discussion we are on 'dogmatic' ground,—ground, I mean, which leaves systematic philosophical 30 scepticism altogether out of account. The postulate that there is truth, and that it is the destiny of our minds to attain it, we are deliberately resolving to make, though the sceptic will not make it. We part company with him, therefore, absolutely, at this point. But the faith that truth exists, and that our minds can find it, may be held in two ways. We may talk of the 35 *empiricist* way and of the *absolutist* way of believing in truth. The absolutists in this matter say that we not only can attain to knowing truth, but we can *know when* we have attained to knowing it; while the empiricists think that although we may attain it, we cannot infallibly know when. To *know* is one thing, and to know for certain *that* we know is another. One may hold to 40 the first being possible without the second; hence the empiricists and the absolutists, although neither of them is a sceptic in the usual philosophic sense of the term, show very different degrees of dogmatism in their lives.

If we look at the history of opinions, we see that the empiricist tendency has largely prevailed in science, while in philosophy the absolutist tendency 45

has had everything its own way. The characteristic sort of happiness, indeed, which philosophies yield has mainly consisted in the conviction felt by each successive school or system that by it bottom-certitude had been attained. "Other philosophies are collections of opinions, mostly false; *my* philosophy gives
5 standing ground forever,"—who does not recognize in this the key-note of every system worthy of the name? A system, to be a system at all, must come as a *closed* system, reversible in this or that detail, perchance, but in its essential features never!

Scholastic orthodoxy, to which one must always go when one wishes to find
10 perfectly clear statement, has beautifully elaborated this absolutist conviction in a doctrine which it calls that of 'objective evidence.' If, for example, I am unable to doubt that I now exist before you, that two is less than three, or that if all men are mortal, then I am mortal too, it is because these things illumine my intellect irresistibly. The final ground of this objective evidence possessed
15 by certain propositions is the *adaequatio intellectûs nostri cum rê.* The certitude it brings involves an *aptitudinem ad extorquendum certum assensum* on the part of the truth envisaged, and on the side of the subject a *quietem in cognitione,* when once the object is mentally received, that leaves no possibility of doubt behind; and in the whole transaction nothing operates but the *entitas*
20 *ipsa* of the object and the *entitas ipsa* of the mind. We slouchy modern thinkers dislike to talk in Latin,—indeed, we dislike to talk in set terms at all; but at bottom our own state of mind is very much like this whenever we uncritically abandon ourselves: You believe in objective evidence, and I do. Of some things we feel that we are certain: we know, and we know that we do know. There
25 is something that gives a click inside of us, a bell that strikes twelve, when the hands of our mental clock have swept the dial and meet over the meridian hour. The greatest empiricists among us are only empiricists on reflection: when left to their instincts, they dogmatize like infallible popes. When the Cliffords tell us how sinful it is to be Christians on such 'insufficient evidence,'
30 insufficiency is really the last thing they have in mind. For them the evidence is absolutely sufficient, only it makes the other way. They believe so completely in an anti-christian order of the universe that there is no living option: Christianity is a dead hypothesis from the start.

VI

35 But now, since we are all such absolutists by instinct, what in our quality of students of philosophy ought we to do about the fact? Shall we espouse and indorse it? Or shall we treat it as a weakness of our nature from which we must free ourselves, if we can?

I sincerely believe that the latter course is the only one we can follow
40 as reflective men. Objective evidence and certitude are doubtless very fine

9. Scholastic orthodoxy—See note on pragmatism, p. 1390. **15. adaequatio . . . rê**—equal correspondence of our mind with the thing perceived. **16. aptitudinem . . . assensum**—capacity to compel sure assent. **17-18. quietem in cognitione**—surety in knowledge. **19-20. entitas ipsa**—the entity itself. **28. infallible popes**—reference to the Catholic doctrine of papal infallibility, or the doctrine that official pronouncement by the Pope is divinely guarded from error, a theory made part of Roman Catholic dogma in 1870.

ideals to play with, but where on this moonlit and dream-visited planet are they found? I am, therefore, myself a complete empiricist so far as my theory of human knowledge goes. I live, to be sure, by the practical faith that we must go on experiencing and thinking over our experience, for only thus can our opinions grow more true; but to hold any one of them—I abso- 5
lutely do not care which—as if it never could be reinterpretable or corrigible, I believe to be a tremendously mistaken attitude, and I think that the whole history of philosophy will bear me out. There is but one indefectibly certain truth, and that is the truth that pyrrhonistic scepticism itself leaves standing, —the truth that the present phenomenon of consciousness exists. That, how- 10
ever, is the bare starting point of knowledge, the mere admission of a stuff to be philosophized about. The various philosophies are but so many attempts at expressing what this stuff really is. And if we repair to our libraries what disagreement do we discover! Where is a certainly true answer found? Apart from abstract propositions of comparison (such as two and two are the same 15
as four), propositions which tell us nothing by themselves about concrete reality, we find no proposition ever regarded by any one as evidently certain that has not either been called a falsehood, or at least had its truth sincerely questioned by some one else. The transcending of the axioms of geometry, not in play but in earnest, by certain of our contemporaries (as Zöllner and Charles 20
H. Hinton), and the rejection of the whole Aristotelian logic by the Hegelians, are striking instances in point.

No concrete test of what is really true has ever been agreed upon. Some make the criterion external to the moment of perception, putting it either in revelation, the *consensus gentium,* the instincts of the heart, or the systematized 25
experience of the race. Others make the perceptive moment its own test,— Descartes, for instance, with his clear and distinct ideas guaranteed by the veracity of God; Reid with his 'common-sense;' and Kant with his forms of synthetic judgment *a priori.* The inconceivability of the opposite; the capacity to be verified by sense; the possession of complete organic unity or self-relation, 30
realized when a thing is its own other,—are standards which, in turn, have been used. The much lauded objective evidence is never triumphantly there; it is a mere aspiration or *Grenzbegriff,* marking the infinitely remote ideal of our thinking life. To claim that certain truths now possess it, is simply to say that when you think them true and they *are* true, then their evidence is 35
objective, otherwise it is not. But practically one's conviction that the evi-dence one goes by is of the real objective brand, is only one more subjective

20. Zöllner—Johann Karl Zöllner (1834-1882), German astronomer and physicist. 21. Hin-ton—Charles H. Hinton (1853-1907), British writer on mathematical and psychical subjects. 21. Aristotelian logic—the system of formal syllogistic logic of Aristotle (384-322 B.C.). 21. Hegelians—followers of Georg Wilhelm Friedrich Hegel (1770-1831), the most abstruse and difficult of German metaphysicians in the nineteenth century. 25. consensus gentium— agreement of all, prevalent opinion. 27. Descartes—René Descartes (1569-1650), French phi-losopher, who in his *Discourse on Method* (1637) sought to find grounds for certitude in belief. 28. Reid—Thomas Reid (1710-1796), Scotch philosopher of the "common sense" school, which sought to ground its theory on the ordinary view of mind, matter, and intuitive ideas. 28. Kant —Immanuel Kant (1724-1804), whose *Critique of Pure Reason* (1781) marks the beginning of nineteenth-century metaphysics. James's reference to "synthetic judgment *a priori*" is to Kant's de-fense of the possibility of making with certainty predictive judgments based on general laws. 33. Grenzbegriff—literally, boundary-idea.

opinion added to the lot. For what a contradictory array of opinions have objective evidence and absolute certitude been claimed! The world is rational through and through,—its existence is an ultimate brute fact; there is a personal God,—a personal God is inconceivable; there is an extra-mental physical
5 world immediately known,—the mind can only know its own ideas; a moral imperative exists,—obligation is only the resultant of desires; a permament spiritual principle is in every one,—there are only shifting states of mind; there is an endless chain of causes,—there is an absolute first cause; an eternal necessity,—a freedom; a purpose,—no purpose; a primal One,—a primal Many;
10 a universal continuity,—an essential discontinuity in things; an infinity,—no infinity. There is this,—there is that; there is indeed nothing which some one has not thought absolutely true, while his neighbor deemed it absolutely false; and not an absolutist among them seems ever to have considered that the trouble may all the time be essential, and that the intellect, even with truth
15 directly in its grasp, may have no infallible signal for knowing whether it be truth or no. When, indeed, one remembers that the most striking practical application to life of the doctrine of objective certitude has been the conscientious labors of the Holy Office of the Inquisition, one feels less tempted than ever to lend the doctrine a respectful ear.
20 But please observe, now, that when as empiricists we give up the doctrine of objective certitude, we do not thereby give up the quest or hope of truth itself. We still pin our faith on its existence, and still believe that we gain an ever better position towards it by systematically continuing to roll up experiences and think. Our great difference from the scholastic lies in the way we
25 face. The strength of his system lies in the principles, the origin, the *terminus a quo* of his thought; for us the strength is in the outcome, the upshot, the *terminus ad quem*. Not where it comes from, but what it leads to is to decide. It matters not to an empiricist from what quarter an hypothesis may come to him: he may have acquired it by fair means or by foul; passion may have
30 whispered or accident suggested it; but if the total drift of thinking continues to confirm it, that is what he means by its being true.

VII

One more point, small but important, and our preliminaries are done. There are two ways of looking at our duty in the matter of opinion,—ways entirely
35 different, and yet ways about whose difference the theory of knowledge seems hitherto to have shown very little concern. *We must know the truth; and we must avoid error,*—these are our first and great commandments as would-be knowers; but they are not two ways of stating an identical commandment, they are two separable laws. Although it may indeed happen that when we be-
40 lieve the truth *A,* we escape as an incidental consequence from believing the falsehood *B,* it hardly ever happens that by merely disbelieving *B* we necessarily believe *A.* We may in escaping *B* fall into believing other falsehoods,

---

18. Holy . . . Inquisition—tribunal of the Roman Catholic Church for suppressing heresy.
25-26. terminus a quo—limit from which, starting-point. 27. terminus ad quem—limit to which, ending-point.

C or *D,* just as bad as *B;* or we may escape *B* by not believing anything at all, not even *A.*

Believe truth! Shun error!—these, we see, are two materially different laws; and by choosing between them we may end, coloring differently our whole intellectual life. We may regard the chase for truth as paramount, and the avoidance of error as secondary; or we may, on the other hand, treat the avoidance of error as more imperative, and let truth take its chance. Clifford, in the instructive passage which I have quoted, exhorts us to the latter course. Believe nothing, he tells us; keep your mind in suspense forever, rather than by closing it on insufficient evidence incur the awful risk of believing lies. You, on the other hand, may think that the risk of being in error is a very small matter when compared with the blessings of real knowledge, and be ready to be duped many times in your investigation rather than postpone indefinitely the chance of guessing true. I myself find it impossible to go with Clifford. We must remember that these feelings of our duty about either truth or error are in any case only expressions of our passional life. Biologically considered, our minds are as ready to grind out falsehood as veracity, and he who says, "Better go without belief forever than believe a lie!" merely shows his own preponderant private horror of becoming a dupe. He may be critical of many of his desires and fears, but this fear he slavishly obeys. He cannot imagine any one questioning its binding force. For my own part, I have also a horror of being duped; but I can believe that worse things than being duped may happen to a man in this world: so Clifford's exhortation has to my ears a thoroughly fantastic sound. It is like a general informing his soldiers that it is better to keep out of battle forever than to risk a single wound. Not so are victories either over enemies or over nature gained. Our errors are surely not such awfully solemn things. In a world where we are so certain to incur them in spite of all our caution, a certain lightness of heart seems healthier than this excessive nervousness on their behalf. At any rate, it seems the fittest thing for the empiricist philosopher.

VIII

And now, after all this introduction, let us go straight at our question. I have said, and now repeat it, that not only as a matter of fact do we find our passional nature influencing us in our opinions, but that there are some options between opinions in which this influence must be regarded both as an inevitable and as a lawful determinant of our choice.

I fear here that some of you my hearers will begin to scent danger, and lend an inhospitable ear. Two first steps of passion you have indeed had to admit as necessary,—we must think so as to avoid dupery, and we must think so as to gain truth; but the surest path to those ideal consummations, you will probably consider, is from now onwards to take no further passional step.

Well, of course, I agree as far as the facts will allow. Wherever the option between losing truth and gaining it is not momentous, we can throw the chance of *gaining truth* away, and at any rate save ourselves from any chance of *believing falsehood,* by not making up our minds at all till objective evi-

dence has come. In scientific questions, this is almost always the case; and even in human affairs in general, the need of acting is seldom so urgent that a false belief to act on is better than no belief at all. Law courts, indeed, have to decide on the best evidence attainable for the moment, because a judge's
5 duty is to make law as well as to ascertain it, and (as a learned judge once said to me) few cases are worth spending much time over: the great thing is to have them decided on *any* acceptable principle, and got out of the way. But in our dealings with objective nature we obviously are recorders, not makers, of the truth; and decisions for the mere sake of deciding promptly and
10 getting on to the next business would be wholly out of place. Throughout the breadth of physical nature facts are what they are quite independently of us, and seldom is there any such hurry about them that the risks of being duped by believing a premature theory need be faced. The questions here are always trivial options, the hypotheses are hardly living (at any rate not
15 living for us spectators), the choice between believing truth or falsehood is seldom forced. The attitude of sceptical balance is therefore the absolutely wise one if we would escape mistakes. What difference, indeed, does it make to most of us whether we have or have not a theory of the Röntgen rays, whether we believe or not in mind-stuff, or have a conviction about the causality of
20 conscious states? It makes no difference. Such options are not forced on us. On every account it is better not to make them, but still keep weighing reasons *pro et contra* with an indifferent hand.

I speak, of course, here of the purely judging mind. For purposes of discovery such indifference is to be less highly recommended, and science would
25 be far less advanced than she is if the passionate desires of individuals to get their own faiths confirmed had been kept out of the game. See, for example, the sagacity which Spencer and Weismann now display. On the other hand, if you want an absolute duffer in an investigation, you must, after all, take the man who has no interest whatever in its results: he is the warranted in-
30 capable, the positive fool. The most useful investigator, because the most sensitive observer, is always he whose eager interest in one side of the question is balanced by an equally keen nervousness lest he become deceived. Science has organized this nervousness into a regular *technique,* her so-called method of verification; and she has fallen so deeply in love with the method that one
35 may even say she has ceased to care for truth by itself at all. It is only truth as technically verified that interests her. The truth of truths might come in merely affirmative form, and she would decline to touch it. Such truth as that, she might repeat with Clifford, would be stolen in defiance of her duty to mankind. Human passions, however, are stronger than technical rules. "Le
40 cœur a ses raisons," as Pascal says, "que la raison ne connaît pas;" and how-

---

18. Röntgen rays—Wilhelm Konrad Röntgen (1845-1923), German physicist, discoverer of X-rays in 1895. **22. pro et contra**—for and against. **27. Spencer**—Herbert Spencer (1820-1903), English philosopher who tried to apply an evolutionary hypothesis to all phases of existence. **27. Weismann**—August Weismann (1834-1914), German zoölogist, who differed from Darwin and Lamarck in his theory of inheritance. Spencer answered his view in *A Rejoinder to Professor Weismann* and *Weismannism Once More.* **32. deceived**—"Compare Wilfrid Ward's Essay, 'The Wish to Believe,' in his *Witnesses to the Unseen,* Macmillan & Co., 1893." (James's note) **39-40. Le cœur . . . pas**—a famous sentence in Pascal's *Pensées:* "The heart has its reasons which reason does not know." (*Pensées,* ed. cit., Sec. IV, par. 277.)

ever indifferent to all but the bare rules of the game the umpire, the abstract intellect, may be, the concrete players who furnish him the materials to judge of are usually, each one of them, in love with some pet 'live hypothesis' of his own. Let us agree, however, that wherever there is no forced option, the dispassionately judicial intellect with no pet hypothesis, saving us, as it does, from dupery at any rate, ought to be our ideal.

The question next arises: Are there not somewhere forced options in our speculative questions, and can we (as men who may be interested at least as much in positively gaining truth as in merely escaping dupery) always wait with impunity till the coercive evidence shall have arrived? It seems *a priori* improbable that the truth should be so nicely adjusted to our needs and powers as that. In the great boarding-house of nature, the cakes and the butter and the syrup seldom come out so even and leave the plates so clean. Indeed, we should view them with scientific suspicion if they did.

IX

Moral questions immediately present themselves as questions whose solution cannot wait for sensible proof. A moral question is a question not of what sensibly exists, but of what is good, or would be good if it did exist. Science can tell us what exists; but to compare the *worths,* both of what exists and what does not exist, we must consult not science, but what Pascal calls our heart. Science herself consults her heart when she lays it down that the infinite ascertainment of fact and correction of false belief are the supreme goods for man. Challenge the statement, and science can only repeat it oracularly, or else prove it by showing that such ascertainment and correction bring man all sorts of other goods which man's heart in turn declares. The question of having moral beliefs at all or not having them is decided by our will. Are our moral preferences true or false, or are they only odd biological phenomena, making things good or bad for *us,* but in themselves indifferent? How can your pure intellect decide? If your heart does not *want* a world of moral reality, your head will assuredly never make you believe in one. Mephistophelian scepticism, indeed, will satisfy the head's play-instincts much better than any rigorous idealism can. Some men (even at the student age) are so naturally cool-hearted that the moralistic hypothesis never has for them any pungent life, and in their supercilious presence the hot young moralist always feels strangely ill at ease. The appearance of knowingness is on their side, of *naïveté* and gullibility on his. Yet, in the inarticulate heart of him, he clings to it that he is not a dupe, and that there is a realm in which (as Emerson says) all their wit and intellectual superiority is no better than the cunning of a fox. Moral scepticism can no more be refuted or proved by logic than intellectual scepticism can. When we stick to it that there *is* truth (be it of either kind), we do so with our whole nature, and resolve to stand or fall by the results. The sceptic with his whole nature adopts the doubting attitude; but which of us is the wiser, Omniscience only knows.

30-31. **Mephistophelian scepticism**—In Goethe's *Faust,* Mephistopheles says he is the spirit who forever denies. (*Faust,* Pt. I, line 1338) 37. **Emerson**—*Natural History of the Intellect,* p. 29 (Riverside edition).

Turn now from these wide questions of good to a certain class of questions of fact, questions concerning personal relations, states of mind between one man and another. *Do you like me or not?*—for example. Whether you do or not depends, in countless instances, on whether I meet you half-way, am willing
5 to assume that you must like me, and show you trust and expectation. The previous faith on my part in your liking's existence is in such cases what makes your liking come. But if I stand aloof, and refuse to budge an inch until I have objective evidence, until you shall have done something apt, as the absolutists say, *ad extorquendum assensum meum,* ten to one your liking
10 never comes. How many women's hearts are vanquished by the mere sanguine insistence of some man that they *must* love him! he will not consent to the hypothesis that they cannot. The desire for a certain kind of truth here brings about that special truth's existence; and so it is in innumerable cases of other sorts. Who gains promotions, boons, appointments, but the man in whose life
15 they are seen to play the part of live hypotheses, who discounts them, sacrifices other things for their sake before they have come, and takes risks for them in advance? His faith acts on the powers above him as a claim, and creates its own verification.

A social organism of any sort whatever, large or small, is what it is because
20 each member proceeds to his own duty with a trust that the other members will simultaneously do theirs. Wherever a desired result is achieved by the co-operation of many independent persons, its existence as a fact is a pure consequence of the precursive faith in one another of those immediately concerned. A government, an army, a commercial system, a ship, a college, an athletic
25 team, all exist on this condition, without which not only is nothing achieved, but nothing is even attempted. A whole train of passengers (individually brave enough) will be looted by a few highwaymen, simply because the latter can count on one another, while each passenger fears that if he makes a move of resistance, he will be shot before any one else backs him up. If we be-
30 lieved that the whole car-full would rise at once with us, we should each severally rise, and train-robbing would never even be attempted. There are, then, cases where a fact cannot come at all unless a preliminary faith exists in its coming. *And where faith in a fact can help create the fact,* that would be an insane logic which should say that faith running ahead of scientific evi-
35 dence is the 'lowest kind of immorality' into which a thinking being can fall. Yet such is the logic by which our scientific absolutists pretend to regulate our lives!

X

In truths dependent on our personal action, then, faith based on desire is
40 certainly a lawful and possibly an indispensable thing.

But now, it will be said, these are all childish human cases, and have nothing to do with great cosmical matters, like the question of religious faith. Let us then pass on to that. Religions differ so much in their accidents that in discussing the religious question we must make it very generic and broad. What
45 then do we now mean by the religious hypothesis? Science says things are;

9. ad . . . meum—for compelling my approval (assent).

morality says some things are better than other things; and religion says essentially two things.

First, she says that the best things are the most eternal things, the overlapping things, the things in the universe that throw the last stone, so to speak, and say the final word. "Perfection is eternal,"—this phrase of Charles Secrétan 5 seems a good way of putting this first affirmation of religion, an affirmation which obviously cannot yet be verified scientifically at all.

The second affirmation of religion is that we are better off even now if we believe her first affirmation to be true.

Now, let us consider what the logical elements of this situation are *in case* 10 *the religious hypothesis in both its branches be really true.* (Of course, we must admit that possibility at the outset. If we are to discuss the question at all, it must involve a living option. If for any of you religion be an hypothesis that cannot, by any living possibility be true, then you need go no farther. I speak to the 'saving remnant' alone.) So proceeding, we see, first, that re- 15 ligion offers itself as a *momentous* option. We are supposed to gain, even now, by our belief, and to lose by our non-belief, a certain vital good. Secondly, re-ligion is a *forced* option, so far as that good goes. We cannot escape the issue by remaining sceptical and waiting for more light, because, although we do avoid error in that way *if religion be untrue,* we lose the good, *if it be true,* 20 just as certainly as if we positively chose to disbelieve. It is as if a man should hesitate indefinitely to ask a certain woman to marry him because he was not perfectly sure that she would prove an angel after he brought her home. Would he not cut himself off from that particular angel-possibility as decisively as if he went and married some one else? Scepticism, then, is not avoidance of 25 option; it is option of a certain particular kind of risk. *Better risk loss of truth than chance of error,*—that is your faith-vetoer's exact position. He is actively playing his stake as much as the believer is; he is backing the field against the religious hypothesis, just as the believer is backing the religious hypothesis against the field. To preach scepticism to us as a duty until 'sufficient evidence' 30 for religion be found, is tantamount therefore to telling us, when in presence of the religious hypothesis, that to yield to our fear of its being error is wiser and better than to yield to our hope that it may be true. It is not intellect against all passions, then; it is only intellect with one passion laying down its law. And by what, forsooth, is the supreme wisdom of this passion warranted? 35 Dupery for dupery, what proof is there that dupery through hope is so much worse than dupery through fear? I, for one, can see no proof; and I simply refuse obedience to the scientist's command to imitate his kind of option, in a case where my own stake is important enough to give me the right to choose my own form of risk. If religion be true and the evidence for it be still 40 insufficient, I do not wish, by putting your extinguisher upon my nature (which feels to me as if it had after all some business in this matter), to forfeit my sole chance in life of getting upon the winning side,—that chance depending, of course, on my willingness to run the risk of acting as if my passional need of taking the world religiously might be prophetic and right. 45

5. **Charles Secrétan**—(1815-1895) Swiss philosopher, who attempted to construct a philo-sophical rational religion.

All this is on the supposition that it really may be prophetic and right, and that, even to us who are discussing the matter, religion is a live hypothesis which may be true. Now, to most of us religion comes in a still further way that makes a veto on our active faith even more illogical. The more perfect
5 and more eternal aspect of the universe is represented in our religions as having personal form. The universe is no longer a mere *It* to us, but a *Thou,* if we are religious; and any relation that may be possible from person to person might be possible here. For instance, although in one sense we are passive portions of the universe, in another we show a curious autonomy, as
10 if we were small active centres on our own account. We feel, too, as if the appeal of religion to us were made to our own active good-will, as if evidence might be forever withheld from us unless we met the hypothesis half-way. To take a trivial illustration: just as a man who in a company of gentlemen made no advances, asked a warrant for every concession, and believed no
15 one's word without proof, would cut himself off by such churlishness from all the social rewards that a more trusting spirit would earn,—so here, one who should shut himself up in snarling logicality and try to make the gods extort his recognition willy-nilly, or not get it at all, might cut himself off forever from his only opportunity of making the gods' acquaintance. This feeling, forced
20 on us we know not whence, that by obstinately believing that there are gods (although not to do so would be so easy both for our logic and our life) we are doing the universe the deepest service we can, seems part of the living essence of the religious hypothesis. If the hypothesis *were* true in all its parts, including this one, then pure intellectualism, with its veto on our making
25 willing advances, would be an absurdity; and some participation of our sympathetic nature would be logically required. I, therefore, for one, cannot see my way to accepting the agnostic rules for truth-seeking, or wilfully agree to keep my willing nature out of the game. I cannot do so for this plain reason, that *a rule of thinking which would absolutely prevent me from*
30 *acknowledging certain kinds of truth if those kinds of truth were really there, would be an irrational rule.* That for me is the long and short of the formal logic of the situation, no matter what the kinds of truth might materially be.

I confess I do not see how this logic can be escaped. But sad experience
35 makes me fear that some of you may still shrink from radically saying with me, *in abstracto,* that we have the right to believe at our own risk any hypothesis that is live enough to tempt our will. I suspect, however, that if this is so, it is because you have got away from the abstract logical point of view altogether, and are thinking (perhaps without realizing it) of some
40 particular religious hypothesis which for you is dead. The freedom to 'believe what we will' you apply to the case of some patent superstition; and the faith you think of is the faith defined by the schoolboy when he said, "Faith is when you believe something that you know ain't true." I can only repeat that this is misapprehension. *In concreto,* the freedom to believe can only cover

36. in abstracto—abstractly. 44. In concreto—Concretely.

living options which the intellect of the individual cannot by itself resolve; and living options never seem absurdities to him who has them to consider. When I look at the religious question as it really puts itself to concrete men, and when I think of all the possibilities which both practically and theoretically it involves, then this command that we shall put a stopper on our heart, in- stincts, and courage, and *wait*—acting of course meanwhile more or less as if religion were *not* true—till doomsday, or till such time as our intellect and senses working together may have raked in evidence enough,—this command, I say, seems to me the queerest idol ever manufactured in the philosophic cave. Were we scholastic absolutists, there might be more excuse. If we had an in- fallible intellect with its objective certitudes, we might feel ourselves disloyal to such a perfect organ of knowledge in not trusting to it exclusively, in not waiting for its releasing word. But if we are empiricists, if we believe that no bell in us tolls to let us know for certain when truth is in our grasp, then it seems a piece of idle fantasticality to preach so solemnly our duty of waiting for the bell. Indeed we *may* wait if we will,—I hope you do not think that I am denying that,—but if we do so, we do so at our peril as much as if we believed. In either case we *act,* taking our life in our hands. No one of us ought to issue vetoes to the other, nor should we bandy words of abuse. We ought, on the contrary, delicately and profoundly to respect one another's mental free- dom: then only shall we bring about the intellectual republic; then only shall we have that spirit of inner tolerance without which all our outer tolerance is soulless, and which is empiricism's glory; then only shall we live and let live, in speculative as well as in practical things.

I began by a reference to Fitz-James Stephen; let me end by a quotation from him. "What do you think of yourself? What do you think of the world? . . . These are questions with which all must deal as it seems good to them. They are riddles of the Sphinx, and in some way or other we must deal with them. . . . In all important transactions of life we have to take a leap in the dark. . . . If we decide to leave the riddles unanswered, that is a choice; if we waver in our answer, that, too, is a choice: but whatever choice we make, we make it at our peril. If a man chooses to turn his back altogether on God and the future, no one can prevent him; no one can show beyond reasonable doubt that he is mistaken. If a man thinks otherwise and acts as he thinks, I do not see that any one can prove that *he* is mistaken. Each must act as he thinks best; and if he is wrong, so much the worse for him. We stand on a mountain pass in the midst of whirling snow and blinding mist, through which we get glimpses now and then of paths which may be deceptive. If we stand still, we shall be frozen to death. If we take the wrong road, we shall be dashed to

---

7. **true**—"Since belief is measured by action, he who forbids us to believe religion to be true, necessarily also forbids us to act as we should if we did believe it to be true. The whole defence of religious faith hinges upon action. If the action required or inspired by the religious hypothesis is in no way different from that dictated by the naturalistic hypothesis, then religious faith is a pure superfluity, better pruned away, and controversy about its legitimacy is a piece of idle trifling, un- worthy of serious minds. I myself believe, of course, that the religious hypothesis gives to the world an expression which specifically determines our reactions, and makes them in a large part unlike what they might be on a purely naturalistic scheme of belief." (James's note) 9. **cave**— The "Idol of the Cave" is that fallacy in which reason is unconsciously overruled by individual preference. The reference is to Bacon's *Novum Organon,* "*Aphorisms,*" Bk. I, xxxix and xlii.

pieces. We do not certainly know whether there is any right one. What must we do? 'Be strong and of a good courage.' Act for the best, hope for the best, and take what comes. . . . If death ends all, we cannot meet death better."

WHAT PRAGMATISM MEANS

This selection is from the second chapter or lecture of *Pragmatism: A New Name for Some Old Ways of Thinking. Popular Lectures on Philosophy,* first printed in June, 1907. As indicated elsewhere, these were originally lectures delivered at the Lowell Institute and at Columbia University. The first is "The Present Dilemma in Philosophy"; the present selection is the second; and the rest are in order: "Some Metaphysical Problems Pragmatically Considered"; "The One and the Many"; "Pragmatism and Common Sense"; "Pragmatism's Conception of Truth"; "Pragmatism and Humanism"; "Pragmatism and Religion." In the preface James refers his readers, among other authors, to John Dewey's *Studies in Logical Theory* and to subsidiary articles by Dewey; and to F. C. S. Schiller's *Studies in Humanism.*

5 SOME years ago, being with a camping party in the mountains, I returned from a solitary ramble to find every one engaged in a ferocious metaphysical dispute. The *corpus* of the dispute was a squirrel—a live squirrel supposed to be clinging to one side of a tree-trunk; while over against the tree's opposite side a human being was imagined to stand. This human witness tries
10 to get sight of the squirrel by moving rapidly round the tree, but no matter how fast he goes, the squirrel moves as fast in the opposite direction, and always keeps the tree between himself and the man, so that never a glimpse of him is caught. The resultant metaphysical problem now is this: *Does the man go round the squirrel or not?* He goes round the tree, sure enough, and
15 the squirrel is on the tree; but does he go round the squirrel? In the unlimited leisure of the wilderness, discussion had been worn threadbare. Every one had taken sides, and was obstinate; and the numbers on both sides were even. Each side, when I appeared therefore appealed to me to make it a majority. Mindful of the scholastic adage that whenever you meet a contra-
20 diction you must make a distinction, I immediately sought and found one, as follows: "Which party is right," I said, "depends on what you *practically mean* by 'going round' the squirrel. If you mean passing from the north of him to the east, then to the south, then to the west, and then to the north of him again, obviously the man does go round him, for he occupies these suc-
25 cessive positions. But if on the contrary you mean being first in front of him, then on the right of him, then behind him, then on his left, and finally in front again, it is quite as obvious that the man fails to go round him, for by the compensating movements the squirrel makes, he keeps his belly turned towards the man all the time, and his back turned away. Make the dis-
30 tinction, and there is no occasion for any farther dispute. You are both right

---

4. **better**—"Liberty, Equality, Fraternity, p. 353, 2d. edition. London, 1874." (James's note)
7. **corpus**—body or substance. 19. **scholastic**—referring to the system of philosophy based on the authority of the Church Fathers which seeks to settle problems of thought through formal logic.

and both wrong according as you conceive the verb 'to go round' in one practical fashion or the other."

Although one or two of the hotter disputants called my speech a shuffling evasion, saying they wanted no quibbling or scholastic hairsplitting, but meant just plain honest English 'round,' the majority seemed to think that the dis- 5 tinction had assuaged the dispute.

I tell this trivial anecdote because it is a peculiarly simple example of what I wish now to speak of as *the pragmatic method*. The pragmatic method is primarily a method of settling metaphysical disputes that otherwise might be interminable. Is the world one or many?—fated or free?—material or spiritual? 10 —here are notions either of which may or may not hold good of the world; and disputes over such notions are unending. The pragmatic method in such cases is to try to interpret each notion by tracing its respective practical conse- quences. What difference would it practically make to any one if this notion rather than that notion were true? If no practical difference whatever can be 15 traced, then the alternatives mean practically the same thing, and all dispute is idle. Whenever a dispute is serious, we ought to be able to show some prac- tical difference that must follow from one side or the other's being right.

A glance at the history of the idea will show you still better what pragmatism means. The term is derived from the same Greek word πράγμα, meaning action, 20 from which our words 'practice' and 'practical' come. It was first introduced into philosophy by Mr. Charles Peirce in 1878. In an article entitled 'How to Make Our Ideas Clear,' in the 'Popular Science Monthly' for January of that year Mr. Peirce, after pointing out that our beliefs are really rules for action, said that, to develop a thought's meaning, we need only determine what con- 25 duct it is fitted to produce: that conduct is for us its sole significance. And the tangible fact at the root of all our thought-distinctions, however subtle, is that there is no one of them so fine as to consist in anything but a possible difference of practice. To attain perfect clearness in our thoughts of an object, then, we need only consider what conceivable effects of a practical kind the 30 object may involve—what sensations we are to expect from it, and what re- actions we must prepare. Our conceptions of these effects, whether immediate or remote, is then for us the whole of our conception of the object, so far as that conception has positive significance at all.

This is the principle of Peirce, the principle of pragmatism. It lay entirely 35 unnoticed by any one for twenty years, until I, in an address before Professor Howison's philosophical union at the University of California, brought it for- ward again and made a special application of it to religion. By that date (1898) the times seemed ripe for its reception. The word 'pragmatism' spread, and at present it fairly spots the pages of the philosophic journals. On all 40

22. Peirce—Charles S. Peirce (1839-1914), an influential American logician and psychologist, already referred to as James's friend. Peirce later denied that he meant by pragmatism what James here says he meant. See F. C. S. Schiller's article in the *Personalist*, Vol. VIII, pp. 81-93, on James's relation to Peirce. **24. year**—"Translated in the *Revue philosophique* for January, 1879 (vol. vii)." (James's note) Peirce's original paper, "Illustrations of the Logic of Science," which James refers to by its subtitle, is in the *Popular Science Monthly*, Vol. XII, pp. 286-302. **37. Howison**— George Holmes Howison (1834-1916), Mills professor of philosophy at the University of California when James lectured there. The University of California is at Berkeley.

hands we find the 'pragmatic movement' spoken of, sometimes with respect, sometimes with contumely, seldom with clear understanding. It is evident that the term applies itself conveniently to a number of tendencies that hitherto have lacked a collective name, and that it has 'come to stay.'

5   To take in the importance of Peirce's principle, one must get accustomed to applying it to concrete cases. I found a few years ago that Ostwald, the illustrious Leipzig chemist, had been making perfectly distinct use of the principle of pragmatism in his lectures on the philosophy of science, though he had not called it by that name.

10   "All realities influence our practice," he wrote me, "and that influence is their meaning for us. I am accustomed to put questions to my classes in this way: In what respects would the world be different if this alternative or that were true? If I can find nothing that would become different, then the alternative has no sense."

15   That is, the rival views mean practically the same thing, and meaning, other than practical, there is for us none. Ostwald in a published lecture gives this example of what he means. Chemists have long wrangled over the inner constitution of certain bodies called 'tautomerous.' Their properties seemed equally consistent with the notion that an instable hydrogen atom oscillates

20   inside of them, or that they are instable mixtures of two bodies. Controversy raged, but never was decided. "It would never have begun," says Ostwald, "if the combatants had asked themselves what particular experimental fact could have been made different by one or the other view being correct. For it would then have appeared that no difference of fact could possibly ensue; and

25   the quarrel was as unreal as if, theorizing in primitive times about the raising of dough by yeast, one party should have invoked a 'brownie,' while another insisted on an 'elf' as the true cause of the phenomenon."

It is astonishing to see how many philosophical disputes collapse into insignificance the moment you subject them to this simple test of tracing a concrete

30   consequence. There can *be* no difference anywhere that doesn't *make* a difference elsewhere—no difference in abstract truth that doesn't express itself in a difference in concrete fact and in conduct consequent upon that fact, imposed on somebody, somehow, somewhere, and somewhen. The whole function of philosophy ought to be to find out what definite difference it will

35   make to you and me at definite instants of our life, if this world-formula or that world-formula be the true one.

There is absolutely nothing new in the pragmatic method. Socrates was an adept at it. Aristotle used it methodically. Locke, Berkeley, and Hume made

6. **Ostwald**—Wilhelm Ostwald (1853-1932), physical chemist. In 1905 he spent a semester at Harvard. **27. phenomenon**—"'Theorie und Praxis,' *Zeitsch. des Oesterreichischen Ingenieur u. Architecten-Vereines,* 1905, Nr. 4 u. 6. I find a still more radical pragmatism than Ostwald's in an address by Professor W. S. Franklin: 'I think that the sickliest notion of physics, even if a student gets it, is that it is "the science of masses, molecules, and the ether." And I think that the healthiest notion, even if a student does not wholly get it, is that physics is the science of the ways of taking hold of bodies and pushing them!' (*Science,* January 2, 1903.)" (James's note) Professor Franklin was the vice president of the American Association for the Advancement of Science; he delivered an address on "Popular Science" to that association Dec. 29, 1902, from which James quotes the concluding sentences (*Science,* N.S., Vol. XVII, pp. 8-15). **38. Locke, Berkeley, and Hume** —John Locke (1632-1704), George Berkeley (1685-1753), David Hume (1711-1776), the three

momentous contributions to truth by its means. Shadworth Hodgson keeps insisting that realities are only what they are 'known as.' But these forerunners of pragmatism used it in fragments: they were preluders only. Not until in our time has it generalized itself, become conscious of a universal mission, pretended to a conquering destiny. I believe in that destiny, and I hope I may 5 end by inspiring you with my belief.

Pragmatism represents a perfectly familiar attitude in philosophy, the empiricist attitude, but it represents it, as it seems to me, both in a more radical and in a less objectionable form than it has ever yet assumed. A pragmatist turns his back resolutely and once for all upon a lot of inveterate habits dear to 10 professional philosophers. He turns away from abstraction and insufficiency, from verbal solutions, from bad *a priori* reasons, from fixed principles, closed systems, and pretended absolutes and origins. He turns towards concreteness and adequacy, towards facts, towards action and towards power. That means the empiricist temper regnant and the rationalist temper sincerely given up. 15 It means the open air and possibilities of nature, as against dogma, artificiality, and the pretence of finality in truth.

At the same time it does not stand for any special results. It is a method only. But the general triumph of that method would mean an enormous change in what I called in my last lecture the 'temperament' of philosophy. 20 Teachers of the ultra-rationalistic type would be frozen out, much as the courtier type is frozen out in republics, as the ultramontane type of priest is frozen out in protestant lands. Science and metaphysics would come much nearer together, would in fact work absolutely hand in hand.

Metaphysics has usually followed a very primitive kind of quest. You know 25 how men have always hankered after unlawful magic, and you know what a great part in magic *words* have always played. If you have his name, or the formula of incantation that binds him, you can control the spirit, genie, afrite, or whatever the power may be. Solomon knew the names of all the spirits, and having their names, he held them subject to his will. So the universe 30 has always appeared to the natural mind as a kind of enigma, of which the key must be sought in the shape of some illuminating or power-bringing word or name. That word names the universe's *principle,* and to possess it is after a fashion to possess the universe itself. 'God,' 'Matter,' 'Reason,' 'the Absolute,' 'Energy,' are so many solving names. You can rest when you have them. You 35 are at the end of your metaphysical quest.

greatest English philosophers of the "classical" period. The general result of their speculations was to question the existence of innate ideas and to insist upon positive proof in metaphysical speculation in place of formal logical proof.

    1. **Shadworth Hodgson**—(1832-1913) metaphysician, whom James met in England. He profoundly influenced James, but later rejected the Jamesian version of pragmatism. **8. empiricist** —referring to the view that experience alone is the source of knowledge. **12. a priori**—that is, reasoning from causes to effects without observation from experience. **15. rationalist**—Here rationalist refers to the theory that reason rather than sensation is the basis of certainty in knowledge. **20. last lecture**—the first lecture in the series, in which James makes the point that one seeks in philosophy temperamental satisfaction, and that philosophical systems reflect the temperaments of their creators. **22. ultramontane**—In Roman Catholic polity the ultramontanist is one who refers everything to papal authority. **29. Solomon**—The source of James's reference is obscure, but there is an ancient rabbinical tradition to the effect that Solomon commanded spirits by knowing their names.

But if you follow the pragmatic method, you cannot look on any such word as closing your quest. You must bring out of each word its practical cash-value, set it at work within the stream of your experience. It appears less as a solution, then, than as a program for more work, and more particularly as an
5   indication of the ways in which existing realities may be *changed*.

Theories thus become instruments, not answers to enigmas, in which we can rest. We don't lie back upon them, we move forward, and, on occasion, make nature over again by their aid. Pragmatism unstiffens all our theories, limbers them up and sets each one at work. Being nothing essentially new, it harmo-
10 nizes with many ancient philosophic tendencies. It agrees with nominalism for instance, in always appealing to particulars; with utilitarianism in emphasizing practical aspects; with positivism in its disdain for verbal solutions, useless questions and metaphysical abstractions.

All these, you see, are *anti-intellectualist* tendencies. Against rationalism as
15 a pretension and a method pragmatism is fully armed and militant. But, at the outset, at least, it stands for no particular results. It has no dogmas, and no doctrines save its method. As the young Italian pragmatist Papini has well said, it lies in the midst of our theories, like a corridor in a hotel. Innumerable chambers open out of it. In one you may find a man writing an atheistic
20 volume; in the next some one on his knees praying for faith and strength; in a third a chemist investigating a body's properties. In a fourth a system of idealistic metaphysics is being excogitated; in a fifth the impossibility of meta-physics is being shown. But they all own the corridor, and all must pass through it if they want a practicable way of getting into or out of their re-
25 spective rooms.

No particular results then, so far, but only an attitude of orientation, is what the pragmatic method means. The *attitude of looking away from first things, principles, 'categories,' supposed necessities; and of looking towards last things, fruits, consequences, facts.*
30 So much for the pragmatic method! You may say that I have been praising it rather than explaining it to you, but I shall presently explain it abundantly enough by showing how it works on some familiar problems. Meanwhile the word pragmatism has come to be used in a still wider sense, as meaning also a certain *theory of truth*. I mean to give a whole lecture to the statement of
35 that theory, after first paving the way, so I can be very brief now. But brevity is hard to follow, so I ask for your redoubled attention for a quarter of an hour. If much remains obscure, I hope to make it clearer in the later lectures.

One of the most successfully cultivated branches of philosophy in our time is what is called inductive logic, the study of the conditions under which our
40 sciences have evolved. Writers on this subject have begun to show a singular unanimity as to what the laws of nature and elements of fact mean, when formulated by mathematicians, physicists and chemists. When the first mathe-

---

10. nominalism—the philosophical theory which regards ideas as pure names without corre-sponding realities. 11. utilitarianism—the doctrine that makes utility the test of conduct and the greatest happiness of the greatest number the final test of utility. 12. positivism—the system of thought commonly associated with Auguste Comte which emphasizes facts and observable phe-nomena and is not concerned with ultimate origins. 17. Papini—Giovanni Papini (1881-), an Italian philosopher and writer, considered by James the leader of Italian pragmatism.

matical, logical, and natural uniformities, the first *laws,* were discovered, men
were so carried away by the clearness, beauty and simplification that resulted,
that they believed themselves to have deciphered authentically the eternal
thoughts of the Almighty. His mind also thundered and reverberated in
syllogisms. He also thought in conic sections, squares and roots and ratios, 5
and geometrized like Euclid. He made Kepler's laws for the planets to follow;
he made velocity increase proportionally to the time in falling bodies; he made
the law of the sines for light to obey when refracted; he established the classes,
orders, families and genera of plants and animals, and fixed the distances between them. He thought the archetypes of all things, and devised their varia- 10
tions; and when we rediscover any one of these his wondrous institutions, we
seize his mind in its very literal intention.

But as the sciences have developed farther, the notion has gained ground
that most, perhaps all, of our laws are only approximations. The laws themselves, moreover, have grown so numerous that there is no counting them; 15
and so many rival formulations are proposed in all the branches of science
that investigators have become accustomed to the notion that no theory is
absolutely a transcript of reality, but that any one of them may from some
point of view be useful. Their great use is to summarize old facts and to lead
to new ones. They are only a man-made language, a conceptual short-hand, 20
as some one calls them, in which we write our reports of nature; and languages,
as is well known, tolerate much choice of expression and many dialects.

Thus human arbitrariness has driven divine necessity from scientific logic.
If I mention the names of Sigwart, Mach, Ostwald, Pearson, Milhaud, Poincaré,
Duhem, Ruyssen, those of you who are students will easily identify the tendency 25
I speak of, and will think of additional names.

Riding now on the front of this wave of scientifiic logic Messrs. Schiller and
Dewey appear with their pragmatistic account of what truth everywhere
signifies. Everywhere, these teachers say, 'truth' in our ideas and beliefs means
the same thing that it means in science. It means, they say, nothing but this, 30
*that ideas (which themselves are but parts of our experience) become true
just in so far as they help us to get into satisfactory relation with other parts*

6. **Euclid**—Alexandrian mathematician (about 300 B.C.). In the seventeenth century especially
there were attempts to make all thought as clear ·and logical as the propositions of Euclid. 6. **Kepler**—Johann Kepler (1571-1630), German astronomer, who first formulated the laws of planetary
motion. 8. **sines**—For a brief statement of the law of the sines with reference to the refraction of
light see the Encyclopaedia Britannica, 11th ed., Vol. XVI, p. 617. 10. **archetypes**—ideal patterns.
24-25. **Sigwart . . . Ruyssen**—Christoph von Sigwart (1830-1894), a German philosopher
whose *Logic* (1873-1878) seeks to find the basis of judgment in psychological realism; Ernst Mach
(1838-1916), Austrian physicist and psychologist, whom James met in Prague in 1882; Karl
Pearson (1857-1936), an English scientist, important in the history of eugenics, and Galton professor
at the University of London; Gaston Milhaud (1858-1918), a French philosopher and historian of
science, one of the "semi-pragmatists"; Wilhelm Ostwald (see note on p. 1392); Jules-Henri Poincaré (1854-1912), French mathematician and physicist, a pragmatist in scientific theory, and the
greatest mathematical genius of his time; Pierre-Maurice Duhem (1861-1916), French mathematician and physicist, who emphasized the historical development of scientific theory; and Theodore
Ruyssen (1868-   ), who inclines to pragmatism in his theory of judgment. 27-28. **Schiller and
Dewey**—F. C. S. Schiller (1864-1937), the leading English exponent of pragmatism, associated
with Oxford University; John Dewey (1859-   ), American philosopher and psychologist, now at
Columbia University, whose theories have profoundly influenced American educational practice.

of our experience, to summarize them and get about them by conceptual short-cuts instead of following the interminable succession of particular phenomena. Any idea upon which we can ride, so to speak; any idea that will carry us prosperously from any one part of our experience to any other part, linking things satisfactorily, working securely, simplifying, saving labor; is true for just so much, true in so far forth, true *instrumentally.* This is the 'instrumental' view of truth taught so successfully at Chicago, the view that truth in our ideas means their power to 'work,' promulgated so brilliantly at Oxford.

Messrs. Dewey, Schiller and their allies, in reaching this general conception of all truth, have only followed the example of geologists, biologists and philologists. In the establishment of these other sciences, the successful stroke was always to take some simple process actually observable in operation—as denudation by weather, say, or variation from parental type, or change of dialect by incorporation of new words and pronunciations—and then to generalize it, making it apply to all times, and produce great results by summating its effects through the ages.

The observable process which Schiller and Dewey particularly singled out for generalization is the familiar one by which any individual settles into *new opinions.* The process here is always the same. The individual has a stock of old opinions already, but he meets a new experience that puts them to a strain. Somebody contradicts them; or in a reflective moment he discovers that they contradict each other; or he hears of facts with which they are incompatible; or desires arise in him which they cease to satisfy. The result is an inward trouble to which his mind till then had been a stranger, and from which he seeks to escape by modifying his previous mass of opinions. He saves as much of it as he can, for in this matter of belief we are all extreme conservatives. So he tries to change first this opinion, and then that (for they resist change very variously), until at last some new idea comes up which he can graft upon the ancient stock with a minimum of disturbance of the latter, some idea that mediates between the stock and the new experience and runs them into one another most felicitously and expediently.

This new idea is then adopted as the true one. It preserves the older stock of truths with a minimum of modification, stretching them just enough to make them admit the novelty, but conceiving that in ways as familiar as the case leaves possible. An *outrée* explanation, violating all our preconceptions, would never pass for a true account of a novelty. We should scratch round industriously till we found something less excentric. The most violent revolutions in an individual's beliefs leave most of his old order standing. Time and space, cause and effect, nature and history, and one's own biography remain untouched. New truth is always a go-between, a smoother-over of transitions. It marries old opinion to new fact so as ever to show a minimum of jolt, a maximum of continuity. We hold a theory true just in proportion to its success in solving this 'problem of maxima and minima.' But success in solving this

---

7-9. Chicago . . . Oxford—When James wrote this lecture, Dewey was at the University of Chicago. Schiller was, of course, at Oxford. **36. outrée**—unusual, fantastic. **44. 'problem of maxima and minima'**—mathematical concepts, on which see Florian Cajori, *A History of Mathematics,* 2d ed., Macmillan, 1919, Index under this phrase.

problem is eminently a matter of approximation. We say this theory solves it on the whole more satisfactorily than that theory; but that means more satisfactorily to ourselves, and individuals will emphasize their points of satisfaction differently. To a certain degree, therefore, everything here is plastic.

The point I now urge you to observe particularly is the part played by the older truths. Failure to take account of it is the source of much of the unjust criticism levelled against pragmatism. Their influence is absolutely controlling. Loyalty to them is the first principle—in most cases it is the only principle; for by far the most usual way of handling phenomena so novel that they would make for a serious rearrangement of our preconception is to ignore them altogether, or to abuse those who bear witness for them.

You doubtless wish examples of this process of truth's growth, and the only trouble is their superabundance. The simplest case of new truth is of course the mere numerical addition of new kinds of facts, or of new single facts of old kinds, to our experience—an addition that involves no alteration in the old beliefs. Day follows day, and its contents are simply added. The new contents themselves are not true, they simply *come* and *are*. Truth is *what we say about* them, and when we say that they have come, truth is satisfied by the plain additive formula.

But often the day's contents oblige a rearrangement. If I should now utter piercing shrieks and act like a maniac on this platform, it would make many of you revise your ideas as to the probable worth of my philosophy. 'Radium' came the other day as part of the day's content, and seemed for a moment to contradict our ideas of the whole order of nature, that order having come to be identified with what is called the conservation of energy. The mere sight of radium paying heat away indefinitely out of its own pocket seemed to violate that conservation. What to think? If the radiations from it were nothing but an escape of unsuspected 'potential' energy, pre-existent inside of the atoms, the principle of conservation would be saved. The discovery of 'helium' as the radiation's outcome, opened a way to this belief. So Ramsay's view is generally held to be true, because, although it extends our old ideas of energy, it causes a minimum of alteration in their nature.

I need not multiply instances. A new opinion counts as 'true' just in proportion as it gratifies the individual's desire to assimilate the novel in his experience to his beliefs in stock. It must both lean on old truth and grasp new fact; and its success (as I said a moment ago) in doing this, is a matter for the individual's appreciation. When old truth grows, then, by new truth's addition, it is for subjective reasons. We are in the process and obey the reasons. That new idea is truest which performs most felicitously its function of satisfying our double urgency. It makes itself true, gets itself classed as true, by the way it works; grafting itself then upon the ancient body of truth, which thus grows much as a tree grows by the activity of a new layer of cambium.

Now Dewey and Schiller proceed to generalize this observation and to apply

22. 'Radium'—Radium was discovered by Professor and Madame Pierre Curie and M. G. Bémont in Paris in 1898. 29. 'helium'—a rare gaseous element. 30. Ramsay—Sir William Ramsay (1852-1916), British chemist, discoverer of argon (1894) and helium (1895). The theory referred to is the transmutation theory. 42. cambium—substance directly under the bark of a tree where the annual growth of wood and bark takes place.

it to the most ancient parts of truth. They also once were plastic. They also were called true for human reasons. They also mediated between still earlier truths and what in those days were novel observations. Purely objective truth, truth in whose establishment the function of giving human satisfaction in
5 marrying previous parts of experience with newer parts played no rôle whatever, is nowhere to be found. The reason why we call things true is the reason why they *are* true, for 'to be true' *means* only to perform this marriage-function.

The trail of the human serpent is thus over everything. Truth independent;
10 truth that we *find* merely; truth no longer malleable to human need; truth incorrigible, in a word; such truth exists indeed superabundantly—or is supposed to exist by rationalistically minded thinkers; but then it means only the dead heart of the living tree, and its being there means only that truth also has its paleontology, and its 'prescription,' and may grow stiff with years
15 of veteran service and petrified in men's regard by sheer antiquity. But how plastic even the oldest truths nevertheless really are has been vividly shown in our day by the transformation of logical and mathematical ideas, a transformation which seems even to be invading physics. The ancient formulas are reinterpreted as special expressions of much wider principles, principles that our
20 ancestors never got a glimpse of in their present shape and formulation.

Mr. Schiller still gives to all this view of truth the name of 'Humanism,' but, for this doctrine too, the name of pragmatism seems fairly to be in the ascendant, so I will treat it under the name of pragmatism in these lectures.

Such then would be the scope of pragmatism—first, a method; and second,
25 a genetic theory of what is meant by truth. And these two things must be our future topics.

What I have said of the theory of truth will, I am sure, have appeared obscure and unsatisfactory to most of you by reason of its brevity. I shall make amends for that hereafter. In a lecture on 'common sense' I shall try to show
30 what I mean by truths grown petrified by antiquity. In another lecture I shall expatiate on the idea that our thoughts become true in proportion as they successfully exert their go-between function. In a third I shall show how hard it is to discriminate subjective from objective factors in Truth's development. You may not follow me wholly in these lectures; and if you do, you may not
35 wholly agree with me. But you will, I know, regard me at least as serious, and treat my effort with respectful consideration.

You will probably be surprised to learn, then, that Messrs. Schiller's and Dewey's theories have suffered a hailstorm of contempt and ridicule. All rationalism has risen against them. In influential quarters Mr. Schiller, in
40 particular, has been treated like an impudent schoolboy who deserves a spanking. I should not mention this, but for the fact that it throws so much side-

---

9. trail . . . serpent—*Cf.* line 207 of "Paradise and the Peri" in *Lalla Rookh* by Thomas Moore: "But the trail of the Serpent is over them all!" 14. paleontology—the science which deals with the study of fossil remains. 14. 'prescription'—claim founded on long use. 21. Humanism—Here Humanism refers to any system of thought concerned with human, as distinguished from divine, interests. 29. 'common sense'—James here refers to Lecture V, "Pragmatism and Common Sense," in the volume *Pragmatism*. 30. another lecture—Lecture VI, "Pragmatism's Conception of Truth." 32. third—Lecture VII, "Pragmatism and Humanism."

light upon that rationalistic temper to which I have opposed the temper of pragmatism. Pragmatism is uncomfortable away from facts. Rationalism is comfortable only in the presence of abstractions. This pragmatist talk about truths in the plural, about their utility and satisfactoriness, about the success with which they 'work,' etc., suggests to the typical intellectualist mind a sort 5 of coarse lame second-rate makeshift article of truth. Such truths are not real truth. Such tests are merely subjective. As against this, objective truth must be something non-utilitarian, haughty, refined, remote, august, exalted. It must be an absolute correspondence of our thoughts with an equally absolute reality. It must be what we *ought* to think unconditionally. The conditioned 10 ways in which we *do* think are so much irrelevance and matter for psychology. Down with psychology, up with logic, in all this question!

See the exquisite contrast of the types of mind! The pragmatist clings to facts and concreteness, observes truth at its work in particular cases, and generalizes. Truth, for him, becomes a class-name for all sorts of definite 15 working-values in experience. For the rationalist it remains a pure abstraction, to the bare name of which we must defer. When the pragmatist undertakes to show in detail just *why* we must defer, the rationalist is unable to recognize the concretes from which his own abstraction is taken. He accuses us of *denying* truth; whereas we have only sought to trace exactly why people follow it. 20 Your typical ultra-abstractionist fairly shudders at concreteness: other things equal, he positively prefers the pale and spectral. If the two universes were offered, he would always choose the skinny outline rather than the rich thicket of reality. It is so much purer, clearer, nobler.

I hope that as these lectures go on, the concreteness and closeness to facts of 25 the pragmatism which they advocate may be what approves itself to you as its most satisfactory peculiarity. It only follows here the example of the sister-sciences, interpreting the unobserved by the observed. It brings old and new harmoniously together. It converts the absolutely empty notion of a static relation of 'correspondence' (what that may mean we must ask later) between 30 our minds and reality, into that of a rich and active commerce (that any one may follow in detail and understand) between particular thoughts of ours, and the great universe of other experiences in which they play their parts and have their uses.

But enough of this at present? The justification of what I say must be post- 35 poned. I wish now to add a word in further explanation of the claim I made at our last meeting, that pragmatism may be a happy harmonizer of empiricist ways of thinking with the more religious demands of human beings.

Men who are strongly of the fact-loving temperament, you may remember me to have said, are liable to be kept at a distance by the small sympathy with 40 facts which that philosophy from the present-day fashion of idealism offers them. It is far too intellectualistic. Old-fashioned theism was bad enough, with its notion of God as an exalted monarch, made up of a lot of unintelligible

41. idealism—any philosophy holding that the universe is an embodiment of the mind, that reality is ultimately mental. 42. theism—Theism is the belief in a God elevated above the world in his nature, who may yet be present in the world.

or preposterous 'attributes'; but, so long as it held strongly by the argument from design, it kept some touch with concrete realities. Since, however, darwinism has once for all displaced design from the minds of the 'scientific,' theism has lost that foothold; and some kind of an immanent or pantheistic
5 deity working *in* things rather than above them is, if any, the kind recommended to our contemporary imagination. Aspirants to a philosophic religion turn, as a rule, more hopefully nowadays towards idealistic pantheism than towards the older dualistic theism, in spite of the fact that the latter still counts able defenders.

10   But, as I said in my first lecture, the brand of pantheism offered is hard for them to assimilate if they are lovers of facts, or empirically minded. It is the absolutistic brand, spurning the dust and reared upon pure logic. It keeps no connexion whatever with concreteness. Affirming the Absolute Mind, which is its substitute for God, to be the rational presupposition of all particulars
15 of fact, whatever they may be, it remains supremely indifferent to what the particular facts in our world actually are. Be they what they may, the Absolute will father them. Like the sick lion in Esop's fable, all footprints lead into his den, but *nulla vestigia retrorsum.* You cannot redescend into the world of particulars by the Absolute's aid, or deduce any necessary consequences of de-
20 tail important for your life from your idea of his nature. He gives you indeed the assurance that all is well with *Him,* and for his eternal way of thinking; but thereupon he leaves you to be finitely saved by your own temporal devices.

Far be it from me to deny the majesty of this conception, or its capacity to yield religious comfort to a most respectable class of minds. But from the
25 human point of view, no one can pretend that it doesn't suffer from the faults of remoteness and abstractness. It is eminently a product of what I have ventured to call the rationalistic temper. It disdains empiricism's needs. It substitutes a pallid outline for the real world's richness. It is dapper, it is noble in the bad sense, in the sense in which to be noble is to be inapt for humble
30 service. In this real world of sweat and dirt, it seems to me that when a view of things is 'noble,' that ought to count as a presumption against its truth, and as a philosophic disqualification. The prince of darkness may be a gentle man, as we are told he is, but whatever the God of earth and heaven is, he can surely be no gentleman. His menial services are needed in the dust of our
35 human trials, even more than his dignity is needed in the empyrean.

Now pragmatism, devoted though she be to facts, has no such materialistic bias as ordinary empiricism labors under. Moreover, she has no objection what-

1-2. **argument from design**—the argument that as a watch implies a watchmaker, so the evidences of design in the universe imply a deity. The argument, though ancient, is usually associated with William Paley (1743-1805). 2. **darwinism**—the theory of the evolution of species through natural selection, adaptation to environment, and so on, associated with Charles Darwin (1809-1882). 4. **immanent**—indwelling. 4. **pantheistic**—Pantheism is the belief that God and the universe are one. 8. **dualistic**—Philosophical systems are said to be dualistic when they assume the reality of both mind and matter. 12. **absolutistic**—Philosophical absolutism considers that all reality is the ultimate fact of existence. As indicated a few lines below, this ultimate fact may be "Absolute Mind." 17. **Esop**—Aesop, putative author of the famous collection of Greek fables. The story is of the lion who feigned sickness and devoured his visitors. 18. **nulla vestigia retrorsum** —no footprints back. (Horace, *Epistles,* I, i, line 74) 32-33. **prince . . . gentleman**—*Cf. King Lear,* Act III, scene iv, line 148. 35. **empyrean**—heaven. 36. **materialistic**—Materialism in philosophy is the doctrine that there is no reality save matter.

ever to the realizing of abstractions, so long as you get about among particulars with their aid and they actually carry you somewhere. Interested in no conclusions but those which our minds and our experiences work out together, she has no *a priori* prejudices against theology. *If theological ideas prove to have a value for concrete life, they will be true, for pragmatism, in the sense* 5 *of being good for so much. For how much more they are true, will depend entirely on their relations to the other truths that also have to be acknowledged.*

What I said just now about the Absolute, of transcendental idealism, is a case in point. First, I called it majestic and said it yielded religious comfort to a class of minds, and then I accused it of remoteness and sterility. But so far as 10 it affords such comfort, it surely is not sterile; it has that amount of value; it performs a concrete function. As a good pragmatist, I myself ought to call the Absolute true 'in so far forth,' then; and I unhesitatingly now do so.

But what does *true in so far forth* mean in this case? To answer, we need only apply the pragmatic method. What do believers in the Absolute mean by 15 saying that their belief affords them comfort? They mean that since, in the Absolute finite evil is 'overruled' already, we may, therefore, whenever we wish, treat the temporal as if it were potentially the eternal, be sure that we can trust its outcome, and, without sin, dismiss our fear and drop the worry of our finite responsibility. In short, they mean that we have a right ever and 20 anon to take a moral holiday, to let the world wag in its own way, feeling that its issues are in better hands than ours and are none of our business.

The universe is a system of which the individual members may relax their anxieties occasionally, in which the don't-care mood is also right for men, and moral holidays in order,—that, if I mistake not, is part, at least, of what 25 the Absolute is 'known-as,' that is the great difference in our particular experiences which his being true makes, for us, that is his cash-value when he is pragmatically interpreted. Farther than that the ordinary lay-reader in philosophy who thinks favorably of absolute idealism does not venture to sharpen his conceptions. He can use the Absolute for so much, and so much is very 30 precious. He is pained at hearing you speak incredulously of the Absolute, therefore, and disregards your criticisms because they deal with aspects of the conception that he fails to follow.

If the Absolute means this, and means no more than this, who can possibly deny the truth of it? To deny it would be to insist that men should never 35 relax, and that holidays are never in order.

I am well aware how odd it must seem to some of you to hear me say that an idea is 'true' so long as to believe it is profitable to our lives. That it is *good,* for as much as it profits, you will gladly admit. If what we do by its aid is good, you will allow the idea itself to be good in so far forth, for we are 40 the better for possessing it. But is it not a strange misuse of the word 'truth,' you will say, to call ideas also 'true' for this reason?

To answer this difficulty fully is impossible at this stage of my account. You touch here upon the very central point of Messrs. Schiller's, Dewey's and my

8. transcendental idealism—the theory associated with Kant that time, space, relation, and so forth are purely parts of the mental structure of the observer, and not derived from sensory experience.

own doctrine of truth, which I can not discuss with detail until my sixth lecture. Let me now say only this, that truth is *one species of good,* and not, as is usually supposed, a category distinct from good, and co-ordinate with it. *The true is the name of whatever proves itself to be good in the way of belief,*
5 *and good, too, for definite, assignable reasons.* Surely you must admit this, that if there were *no* good for life in true ideas, or if the knowledge of them were positively disadvantageous and false ideas the only useful ones, then the current notion that truth is divine and precious, and its pursuit a duty, could never have grown up or become a dogma. In a world like that, our duty would
10 be to *shun* truth, rather. But in this world, just as certain foods are not only agreeable to our taste, but good for our teeth, our stomach, and our tissues; so certain ideas are not only agreeable to think about, or agreeable as supporting other ideas that we are fond of, but they are also helpful in life's practical struggles. If there be any life that it is really better we should lead, and if
15 there be any idea which, if believed in, would help us to lead that life, then it would be really *better for us* to believe in that idea, *unless, indeed, belief in it incidentally clashed with other greater vital benefits.*

'What would be better for us to believe'! This sounds very like a definition of truth. It comes very near to saying 'what we *ought* to believe': and in *that*
20 definition none of you would find any oddity. Ought we ever not to believe what it is *better for us* to believe? And can we then keep the notion of what is better for us, and what is true for us, permanently apart?

Pragmatism says no, and I fully agree with her. Probably you also agree, so far as the abstract statement goes, but with a suspicion that if we practically
25 did believe everything that made for good in our own personal lives, we should be found indulging all kinds of fancies about this world's affairs, and all kinds of sentimental superstitions about a world hereafter. Your suspicion here is undoubtedly well founded, and it is evident that something happens when you pass from the abstract to the concrete that complicates the situation.
30 I said just now that what is better for us to believe is true *unless the belief incidentally clashes with some other vital benefit.* Now in real life what vital benefits is any particular belief of ours most liable to clash with? What indeed except the vital benefits yielded by *other beliefs* when these prove incompatible with the first ones? In other words, the greatest enemy of any one
35 of our truths may be the rest of our truths. Truths have once for all this desperate instinct of self-preservation and of desire to extinguish whatever contradicts them. My belief in the Absolute, based on the good it does me, must run the gauntlet of all my other beliefs. Grant that it may be true in giving me a moral holiday. Nevertheless, as I conceive it,—and let me speak now con-
40 fidentially, as it were, and merely in my own private person,—it clashes with other truths of mine whose benefits I hate to give up on its account. It happens to be associated with a kind of logic of which I am the enemy, I find that it entangles me in metaphysical paradoxes that are inacceptable, etc., etc. But as I have enough trouble in life already without adding the trouble of carrying
45 these intellectual inconsistencies, I personally just give up the Absolute. I just

---

1-2. **sixth lecture**—"Pragmatism's Conception of Truth." 3. **category**—class.

take my moral holidays; or else as a professional philosopher, I try to justify them by some other principle.

If I could restrict my notion of the Absolute to its bare holiday-giving value, it wouldn't clash with my other truths. But we can not easily thus restrict our hypotheses. They carry supernumerary features, and these it is that clash 5 so. My disbelief in the Absolute means then disbelief in those other supernumerary features, for I fully believe in the legitimacy of taking moral holidays.

You see by this what I meant when I called pragmatism a mediator and reconciler and said, borrowing the word from Papini, that she 'unstiffens' 10 our theories. She has in fact no prejudices whatever, no obstructive dogmas, no rigid canons of what shall count as proof. She is completely genial. She will entertain any hypothesis, she will consider any evidence. It follows that in the religious field she is at a great advantage both over positivistic empiricism, with its anti-theological bias, and over religious rationalism, with its ex- 15 clusive interest in the remote, the noble, the simple, and the abstract in the way of conception.

In short, she widens the field of search for God. Rationalism sticks to logic and the empyrean. Empiricism sticks to the external senses. Pragmatism is willing to take anything, to follow either logic or the senses and to count 20 the humblest and most personal experiences. She will count mystical experiences if they have practical consequences. She will take a God who lives in the very dirt of private fact—if that should seem a likely place to find him.

Her only test of probable truth is what works best in the way of leading us, what fits every part of life best and combines with the collectivity of experi- 25 ence's demands, nothing being omitted. If theological ideas should do this, if the notion of God, in particular, should prove to do it, how could pragmatism possibly deny God's existence? She could see no meaning in treating as 'not true' a notion that was pragmatically so successful. What other kind of truth could there be, for her, than all this agreement with concrete reality? 30

In my last lecture I shall return again to the relations of pragmatism with religion. But you see already how democratic she is. Her manners are as various and flexible, her resources as rich and endless, and her conclusions as friendly as those of mother nature.

31. last lecture—"Pragmatism and Religion."

HENRY JAMES

1843-1916

I. A PASSIONATE PILGRIM (1843–1875)

1843   Born April 15, in New York City, son of the well-to-do philosopher-clergy-man Henry James, Sr., and younger brother of William James, the psychol-ogist.

1855–1860   Cosmopolitan education in Geneva, Paris, Bonn, and Newport.

1862–1863   Attended the Harvard Law School.

1864–1868   Residence in Boston and Cambridge; began writing reviews for the *North American Review* and the *Nation,* and short stories for the *Atlantic Monthly* and the *Galaxy.*

1869–1875   Wanderjahre; the visit to Italy in 1869 had a marked influence upon his career; the one in 1872 confirmed it. In the interim he was in Cambridge with Howells, or at Newport.

1870   Death of his cousin Mary Temple, who served as model for the leading character in *The Portrait of a Lady* and *The Wings of the Dove.*

1871   Publication of *A Passionate Pilgrim,* a response to the call of Europe.

II. THE MIDDLE YEARS (1875–1896)

1875   Publication of *Roderick Hudson* in the *Atlantic Monthly,* his first work of importance.

1876   After a brief stay in Paris, where he met Turgenev and Flaubert, he settled in London, but made excursions to Paris and to Italy.

1877   Published *The American,* which had appeared serially in the *Atlantic,* presenting a compatriot against a Parisian setting.

1878   Published *French Poets and Novelists,* containing James's best reviews.

1879   Published *Daisy Miller, An International Episode,* and *Hawthorne.*

1880   Published *Washington Square.*

1881   Published *The Portrait of a Lady,* his best-drawn American woman against a foreign background.

1886   He concentrated interest on British and Continental subjects, as in *The Princess Casamassima.*

1888   Published *Partial Portraits* (essays), followed in 1893 by *Essays in London and Elsewhere.*

1890–1895   Period of unsuccessful plays and of short stories. *The Tragic Muse* (1890), more extended, sets an artistic career against family interference.

III. PERIOD OF THE INVOLVED MANNER (1896–1916)

1896   James moved from London to Lamb House at Rye, southeast coast of England.

1897–1901   Published novels and short stories of remarkable craftsmanship like *What Maisie Knew* (1897), *The Spoils of Poynton* (1897), *The Turn of the Screw* (1898), *The Awkward Age* (1899), and *The Sacred Fount* (1901).

1902–1904   Period of matured art of indirect manner in *The Wings of the Dove* (published in 1902), *The Ambassadors* (1903), and *The Golden Bowl* (1904).

1913–1914   Published reminiscences: *A Small Boy and Others; Notes of a Son and Brother.*

1915   Became a naturalized British subject. Awarded the Order of Merit by King George in 1916.

1916   Died February 28 in apartments at Chelsea, London.

1917   Publication of two unfinished novels, *The Sense of the Past* and *The Ivory Tower,* and the fragment of autobiography and criticism, *The Middle Years.*

BIOGRAPHIES: See three autobiographical volumes: *A Small Boy and Others,* Scribner, 1913; *Notes of a Son and Brother,* Scribner, 1914; and *The Middle Years,* Scribner, 1917; *Letters of Henry James,* ed. by Percy Lubbock, Scribner, 1920, 2 vols.; Van Wyck Brooks, *The Pilgrimage of Henry James,* Dutton, 1925; C. H. Grattan, *The Three Jameses,* Longmans, 1932; Léon Edel, *Henry James: Les Années Dramatiques,* Paris, 1931; F. O. Matthiessen and K. B. Murdock, edd., *The Notebooks of Henry James,* Oxford, 1947.

CRITICISM: E. L. Cary, *The Novels of Henry James,* Putnam, 1905; Rebecca West, *Writers of the Day,* Holt, 1916; S. P. Sherman, *On Contemporary Literature,* Holt, 1917; J. W. Beach, *The Method of Henry James,* Yale University Press, 1918; Morris Roberts, *Henry James's Criticism,* Harvard University Press, 1929; C. P. Kelley, *The Early Development of Henry James,* University of Illinois Press, 1930; F. O. Matthiessen, *Henry James, the Major Phase,* Oxford, 1944, and *The James Family,* Knopf, 1947.

BIBLIOGRAPHY AND EDITIONS: Le Roy Phillips, *A Bibliography of the Writings of Henry James,* Coward-McCann, 1930; *Literary History of the United States,* Vol. III, pp. 584-90. The New York edition of *James's Novels and Tales,* Scribner, 1907-17, 26 vols., has author's introductions discussing his aims and methods. R. P. Blackmur, *The Art of the Novel: Critical Prefaces* [of Henry James], Scribners, 1934. Many novels are available in individual reprints. See also Philip Rahv, ed., *The Great Short Novels of Henry James,* Dial Press, 1944; Clifton Fadiman, ed., *The Short Novels of Henry James,* Random House, 1945; F. O. Matthiessen, *The American Novels and Stories of Henry James,* Knopf, 1947.

In the work of Henry James, the American, having conquered the frontier, turned to the Old World, "the great distributing heart of our traditional life," in his quest for the beauty which eluded him in the thin culture of the New World. Earlier, the American had looked upon Europe through the eyes of Mark Twain. But now he wandered with Henry Adams, Whistler, and others between two worlds, that of the genteel tradition, become obsolescent, and that of the new culture in the throes of being born. As he reflects on his lack of traditions, this American finds in the contemplation of contrasting national cultures a new integration.

In creating the "international novel"—international in the sense of contrasting backgrounds, not of conflicting loyalties—James selected from a multitude of details just those that give the impression he wants to convey. Because there are no clearly outlined sins, no violent passions, in his stories, readers may feel they are deficient in vitality. But for James morality lies partially in esthetic truth, which issues not infrequently in a gentle irony that evokes out of the frustrations of life a note of supreme loveliness. He has bequeathed to American fiction a fine artistic conscience.

DAISY MILLER: A STUDY

This story first appeared in the *Cornhill Magazine,* June-July, 1878. A pirated edition appeared in Boston in 1879. The story was converted into a comedy and privately printed in 1882, and again in the *Atlantic Monthly,* April-June, 1883. In his preface to Vol. XVIII of the New York edition of his Works, James says that the conception of *Daisy Miller* grew out of the casual remark of a Europeanized American group who were censorious of the American girl abroad. Howells reports, in the *Century* for November, 1882, that "tears bedewed our continent in behalf of the 'average American girl' supposed to be satirized in Daisy Miller, and prevented the perception of the fact that, so far as the average American girl was studied at all in Daisy Miller, her indestructible innocence, her invulnerable new-worldliness, had never been so delicately appreciated. . . . Many of his people are humorously imagined, or rather humorously *seen,* like Daisy Miller's mother, but these do not give a dominant color; the business in hand is commonly serious, and the droll people are subordinated." The story as it appears here is taken from the 1892 edition.

PART I

AT THE little town of Vevey, in Switzerland, there is a particularly comfortable hotel. There are, indeed, many hotels; for the entertainment of tourists is the business of the place, which, as many travellers will
5   remember, is seated upon the edge of a remarkably blue lake—a lake that it behooves every tourist to visit. The shore of the lake presents an unbroken array of establishments of this order, of every category, from the "grand hotel" of the newest fashion, with a chalk-white front, a hundred balconies, and a dozen flags flying from its roof, to the little Swiss *pension* of an elder day,
10 with its name inscribed in German-looking lettering upon a pink or yellow wall, and an awkward summer-house in the angle of the garden. One of the hotels at Vevey, however, is famous, even classical, being distinguished from many of its upstart neighbors by an air both of luxury and of maturity. In this region, in the month of June, American travellers are extremely numer-
15 ous; it may be said, indeed, that Vevey assumes at this period some of the characteristics of an American watering-place. There are sights and sounds which evoke a vision, an echo, of Newport and Saratoga. There is a flitting hither and thither of "stylish" young girls, a rustling of muslin flounces, a rattle of dance-music in the morning hours, a sound of high-pitched voices at
20 all times. You receive an impression of these things at the excellent inn of the "Trois Couronnes," and are transported in fancy to the Ocean House or to Congress Hall. But at the "Trois Couronnes," it must be added, there are

2. **Vevey**—a resort at the northeast end of Lake Geneva.

other features that are much at variance with these suggestions: neat German waiters, who look like secretaries of legation; Russian princesses sitting in the garden; little Polish boys walking about, held by the hand, with their governors; a view of the sunny crest of the Dent du Midi and the picturesque towers of the Castle of Chillon. 5

I hardly know whether it was the analogies or the differences that were uppermost in the mind of a young American, who, two or three years ago, sat in the garden of the "Trois Couronnes," looking about him, rather idly, at some of the graceful objects I have mentioned. It was a beautiful summer morning, and in whatever fashion the young American looked at things, they must 10 have seemed to him charming. He had come from Geneva the day before, by the little steamer, to see his aunt, who was staying at the hotel—Geneva having been for a long time his place of residence. But his aunt had a headache— his aunt had almost always a headache—and now she was shut up in her room, smelling camphor, so that he was at liberty to wander about. He was some 15 seven-and-twenty years of age; when his friends spoke of him, they usually said that he was at Geneva, "studying." When his enemies spoke of him, they said—but, after all, he had no enemies; he was an extremely amiable fellow, and universally liked. What I should say is, simply, that when certain persons spoke of him they affirmed that the reason of his spending so much 20 time at Geneva was that he was extremely devoted to a lady who lived there— a foreign lady—a person older than himself. Very few Americans—indeed I think none—had ever seen this lady, about whom there were some singular stories. But Winterbourne had an old attachment for the little metropolis of Calvinism; he had been put to school there as a boy, and he had afterwards 25 gone to college there—circumstances which had led to his forming a great many youthful friendships. Many of these he had kept, and they were a source of great satisfaction to him.

After knocking at his aunt's door and learning that she was indisposed, he had taken a walk about the town, and then he had come in to his breakfast. 30 He had now finished his breakfast; but he was drinking a small cup of coffee, which had been served to him on a little table in the garden by one of the waiters who looked like an *attaché*. At last he finished his coffee and lit a cigarette. Presently a small boy came walking along the path—an urchin of nine or ten. The child, who was diminutive for his years, had an aged ex- 35 pression of countenance, a pale complexion, and sharp little features. He was dressed in knickerbockers, with red stockings, which displayed his poor little spindleshanks; he also wore a brilliant red cravat. He carried in his hand a long alpenstock, the sharp point of which he thrust into everything that he approached—the flower-beds, the garden-benches, the trains of the ladies' 40 dresses. In front of Winterbourne he paused, looking at him with a pair of bright, penetrating little eyes.

"Will you give me a lump of sugar?" he asked, in a sharp, hard little voice— a voice immature, and yet, somehow, not young.

Winterbourne glanced at the small table near him, on which his coffee- 45 service rested, and saw that several morsels of sugar remained. "Yes, you may take one," he answered; "but I don't think sugar is good for little boys."

This little boy stepped forward and carefully selected three of the coveted fragments, two of which he buried in the pocket of his knickerbockers, depositing the other as promptly in another place. He poked his alpenstock, lance-fashion, into Winterbourne's bench, and tried to crack the lump of sugar with his teeth.

"Oh, blazes; it's har-r-d!" he exclaimed, pronouncing the adjective in a peculiar manner.

Winterbourne had immediately perceived that he might have the honour of claiming him as a fellow-countryman. "Take care you don't hurt your teeth," he said, paternally.

"I haven't got any teeth to hurt. They have all come out. I have only got seven teeth. My mother counted them last night, and one came out right afterwards. She said she'd slap me if any more came out. I can't help it. It's this old Europe. It's the climate that makes them come out. In America they didn't come out. It's these hotels."

Winterbourne was much amused. "If you eat three lumps of sugar, your mother will certainly slap you," he said.

"She's got to give me some candy, then," rejoined his young interlocutor. "I can't get any candy here—any American candy. American candy's the best candy."

"And are American little boys the best little boys?" asked Winterbourne.

"I don't know. I'm an American boy," said the child.

"I see you are one of the best!" laughed Winterbourne.

"Are you an American man?" pursued this vivacious infant. And then, on Winterbourne's affirmative reply—"American men are the best," he declared.

His companion thanked him for the compliment; and the child, who had now got astride of his alpenstock, stood looking about him, while he attacked a second lump of sugar. Winterbourne wondered if he himself had been like this in his infancy, for he had been brought to Europe at about this age.

"Here comes my sister!" cried the child, in a moment. "She's an American girl."

Winterbourne looked along the path and saw a beautiful young lady advancing. "American girls are the best girls," he said, cheerfully, to his young companion.

"My sister ain't the best!" the child declared. "She's always blowing at me."

"I imagine that is your fault, not hers," said Winterbourne. The young lady meanwhile had drawn near. She was dressed in white muslin, with a hundred frills and flounces, and knots of pale-colored ribbon. She was bare-headed; but she balanced in her hand a large parasol, with a deep border of embroidery; and she was strikingly, admirably pretty. "How pretty they are!" thought Winterbourne, straightening himself in his seat, as if he were prepared to rise.

The young lady paused in front of his bench, near the parapet of the garden, which overlooked the lake. The little boy had now converted his alpenstock into a vaulting-pole, by the aid of which he was springing about in the gravel, and kicking it up not a little.

"Randolph," said the young lady, "what *are* you doing?"

"I'm going up the Alps," replied Randolph. "This is the way!" And he gave another little jump, scattering the pebbles about Winterbourne's ears.

"That's the way they come down," said Winterbourne.

"He's an American man!" cried Randolph, in his little hard voice.

The young lady gave no heed to this announcement, but looked straight at her brother. "Well, I guess you had better be quiet," she simply observed.

It seemed to Winterbourne that he had been in a manner presented. He got up and stepped slowly towards the young girl, throwing away his cigarette. "This little boy and I have made acquaintance," he said, with great civility. In Geneva, as he had been perfectly aware, a young man was not at 10 liberty to speak to a young unmarried lady except under certain rarely-occurring conditions; but here at Vevey, what conditions could be better than these? —a pretty American girl coming and standing in front of you in a garden. This pretty American girl, however, on hearing Winterbourne's observation, simply glanced at him; she then turned her head and looked over the parapet, 15 at the lake and the opposite mountains. He wondered whether he had gone too far; but he decided that he must advance farther, rather than retreat. While he was thinking of something else to say, the young lady turned to the little boy again.

"I should like to know where you got that pole," she said. 20

"I bought it!" responded Randolph.

"You don't mean to say you're going to take it to Italy."

"Yes, I am going to take it to Italy!" the child declared.

The young girl glanced over the front of her dress, and smoothed out a knot or two of ribbon. Then she rested her eyes upon the prospect again. 25 "Well, I guess you had better leave it somewhere," she said, after a moment.

"Are you going to Italy?" Winterbourne inquired, in a tone of great respect.

The young lady glanced at him again. "Yes, sir," she replied. And she said nothing more.

"Are you—a—going over the Simplon?" Winterbourne pursued, a little em- 30 barrassed.

"I don't know," she said. "I suppose it's some mountain. Randolph, what mountain are we going over?"

"Going where?" the child demanded.

"To Italy," Winterbourne explained. 35

"I don't know," said Randolph. "I don't want to go to Italy. I want to go to America."

"Oh, Italy is a beautiful place!" rejoined the young man.

"Can you get candy there?" Randolph loudly inquired.

"I hope not," said his sister. "I guess you have had enough candy, and 40 mother thinks so too."

"I haven't had any for ever so long—for a hundred weeks!" cried the boy, still jumping about.

The young lady inspected her flounces and smoothed her ribbons again; and Winterbourne presently risked an observation upon the beauty of the 45

30. **Simplon**—the Simplon Pass, one of the two routes through the Alps into Italy.

view. He was ceasing to be embarrassed, for he had begun to perceive that
she was not in the least embarrassed herself. There had not been the slightest
alteration in her charming complexion; she was evidently neither offended
nor fluttered. If she looked another way when he spoke to her, and seemed not
5 particularly to hear him, this was simply her habit, her manner. Yet, as he
talked a little more, and pointed out some of the objects of interest in the view,
with which she appeared quite unacquainted, she gradually gave him more
of the benefit of her glance; and then he saw that this glance was perfectly
direct and unshrinking. It was not, however, what would have been called
10 an immodest glance, for the young girl's eyes were singularly honest and fresh.
They were wonderfully pretty eyes; and, indeed, Winterbourne had not seen
for a long time anything prettier than his fair countrywoman's various features—her complexion, her nose, her ears, her teeth. He had a great relish for
feminine beauty; he was addicted to observing and analyzing it; and as re-
15 gards this young lady's face he made several observations. It was not at all
insipid, but it was not exactly expressive; and though it was eminently delicate Winterbourne mentally accused it—very forgivingly—of a want of finish.
He thought it very possible that Master Randolph's sister was a coquette; he
was sure she had a spirit of her own; but in her bright, sweet, superficial
20 little visage there was no mockery, no irony. Before long it became obvious
that she was much disposed towards conversation. She told him that they
were going to Rome for the winter—she and her mother and Randolph. She
asked him if he was a "real American"; she shouldn't have taken him for
one; he seemed more like a German—this was said after a little hesitation,
25 especially when he spoke. Winterbourne, laughing, answered that he had met
Germans who spoke like Americans; but that he had not, so far as he remembered, met an American who spoke like a German. Then he asked her if she
should not be more comfortable in sitting upon the bench which he had just
quitted. She answered that she liked standing up and walking about; but she
30 presently sat down. She told him she was from New York State—"if you
know where that is." Winterbourne learned more about her by catching hold
of her small, slippery brother and making him stand a few minutes by his
side.

"Tell me your name, my boy," he said.
35 "Randolph C. Miller," said the boy, sharply. "And I'll tell you her name;"
and he levelled his alpenstock at his sister.

"You had better wait till you are asked!" said this young lady, calmly.

"I should like very much to know your name," said Winterbourne.

"Her name is Daisy Miller!" cried the child. "But that isn't her real name;
40 that isn't her name on her cards."

"It's a pity you haven't got one of my cards!" said Miss Miller.

"Her real name is Annie P. Miller," the boy went on.

"Ask him *his* name," said his sister, indicating Winterbourne.

But on this point Randolph seemed perfectly indifferent; he continued to
45 supply information in regard to his own family. "My father's name is Ezra B.
Miller," he announced. "My father ain't in Europe; my father's in a better
place than Europe."

Winterbourne imagined for a moment that this was the manner in which the child had been taught to intimate that Mr. Miller had been removed to the sphere of celestial rewards. But Randolph immediately added, "My father's in Schenectady. He's got a big business. My father's rich, you bet."

"Well!" ejaculated Miss Miller, lowering her parasol and looking at the embroidered border. Winterbourne presently released the child, who departed, dragging his alpenstock along the path. "He doesn't like Europe," said the young girl. "He wants to go back."

"To Schenectady, you mean?"

"Yes; he wants to go right home. He hasn't got any boys here. There is one boy here, but he always goes round with a teacher; they won't let him play."

"And your brother hasn't any teacher?" Winterbourne inquired.

"Mother thought of getting him one to travel round with us. There was a lady told her of a very good teacher; an American lady—perhaps you know her—Mrs. Sanders. I think she came from Boston. She told her of this teacher, and we thought of getting him to travel round with us. But Randolph said he didn't want a teacher travelling round with us. He said he wouldn't have lessons when he was in the cars. And we *are* in the cars about half the time. There was an English lady we met in the cars—I think her name was Miss Featherstone; perhaps you know her. She wanted to know why I didn't give Randolph lessons—give him 'instructions,' she called it. I guess he could give me more instruction than I could give him. He's very smart."

"Yes," said Winterbourne; "he seems very smart."

"Mother's going to get a teacher for him as soon as we get to Italy. Can you get good teachers in Italy?"

"Very good, I should think," said Winterbourne.

"Or else she's going to find some school. He ought to learn some more. He's only nine. He's going to college." And in this way Miss Miller continued to converse upon the affairs of her family, and upon other topics. She sat there with her extremely pretty hands, ornamented with very brilliant rings, folded in her lap, and with her pretty eyes now resting upon those of Winterbourne, now wandering over the garden, the people who passed by, and the beautiful view. She talked to Winterbourne as if she had known him a long time. He found it very pleasant. It was many years since he had heard a young girl talk so much. It might have been said of this unknown young lady, who had come and sat down beside him upon a bench, that she chattered. She was very quiet; she sat in a charming tranquil attitude, but her lips and her eyes were constantly moving. She had a soft, slender, agreeable voice, and her tone was decidedly sociable. She gave Winterbourne a history of her movements and intentions, and those of her mother and brother, in Europe, and enumerated, in particular, the various hotels at which they had stopped. "That English lady, in the cars," she said—"Miss Featherstone—asked me if we didn't all live in hotels in America. I told her I had never been in so many hotels in my life as since I came to Europe. I have never seen so many—it's nothing but hotels." But Miss Miller did not make this remark with a querulous accent; she appeared to be in the best humor with

everything. She declared that the hotels were very good, when once you got used to their ways, and that Europe was perfectly sweet. She was not disappointed—not a bit. Perhaps it was because she had heard so much about it before. She had ever so many intimate friends that had been there ever
5 so many times. And then she had had ever so many dresses and things from Paris. Whenever she put on a Paris dress she felt as if she were in Europe.

"It was a kind of a wishing-cap," said Winterbourne.

"Yes," said Miss Miller, without examining this analogy; "it always made me wish I was here. But I needn't have done that for dresses. I am sure they
10 send all the pretty ones to America; you see the most frightful things here. The only thing I don't like," she proceeded, "is the society. There isn't any society; or, if there is, I don't know where it keeps itself. Do you? I suppose there is some society somewhere, but I haven't seen anything of it. I'm very fond of society, and I have always had a great deal of it. I don't mean only
15 in Schenectady, but in New York. I used to go to New York every winter. In New York I had lots of society. Last winter I had seventeen dinners given me; and three of them were by gentlemen," added Daisy Miller. "I have more friends in New York than in Schenectady—more gentlemen friends; and more young lady friends too," she resumed in a moment. She paused again for an
20 instant; she was looking at Winterbourne with all her prettiness in her lively eyes and in her light, slightly monotonous smile. "I have always had," she said, "a great deal of gentlemen's society."

Poor Winterbourne was amused, perplexed, and decidedly charmed. He had never yet heard a young girl express herself in just this fashion; never, at
25 least, save in cases where to say such things seemed a kind of demonstrative evidence of a certain laxity of deportment. And yet was he to accuse Miss Daisy Miller of actual or potential *inconduite,* as they said at Geneva? He felt that he had lived at Geneva so long that he had lost a good deal; he had become dishabituated to the American tone. Never, indeed, since he had grown
30 old enough to appreciate things, had he encountered a young American girl of so pronounced a type as this. Certainly she was very charming, but how deucedly sociable! Was she simply a pretty girl from New York State—were they all like that, the pretty girls who had a good deal of gentlemen's society? Or was she also a designing, an audacious, an unscrupulous young person?
35 Winterbourne had lost his instinct in this matter, and his reason could not help him. Miss Daisy Miller looked extremely innocent. Some people had told him that, after all, American girls were exceedingly innocent; and others had told him that, after all, they were not. He was inclined to think Miss Daisy Miller was a flirt—a pretty American flirt. He had never, as yet, had any
40 relations with young ladies of this category. He had known, here in Europe, two or three women—persons older than Miss Daisy Miller, and provided, for respectability's sake, with husbands—who were great coquettes—dangerous, terrible women, with whom one's relations were liable to take a serious turn. But this young girl was not a coquette in that sense; she was very unso-
45 phisticated; she was only a pretty American flirt. Winterbourne was almost

27. inconduite—misconduct.

grateful for having found the formula that applied to Miss Daisy Miller. He leaned back in his seat; he remarked to himself that she had the most charming nose he had ever seen; he wondered what were the regular conditions and limitations of one's intercourse with a pretty American flirt. It presently became apparent that he was on the way to learn.   5

"Have you been to that old castle?" asked the young girl, pointing with her parasol to the far-gleaming walls of the Château de Chillon.

"Yes, formerly, more than once," said Winterbourne. "You too, I suppose, have seen it?"

"No; we haven't been there. I want to go there dreadfully. Of course I   10 mean to go there. I wouldn't go away from here without having seen that old castle."

"It's a very pretty excursion," said Winterbourne, "and very easy to make. You can drive, you know, or you can go by the little steamer."

"You can go in the cars," said Miss Miller.   15

"Yes; you can go in the cars," Winterbourne assented.

"Our courier says they take you right up to the castle," the young girl continued. "We were going last week; but my mother gave out. She suffers dreadfully from dyspepsia. She said she couldn't go. Randolph wouldn't go either; he says he doesn't think much of old castles. But I guess we'll go this   20 week, if we can get Randolph."

"Your brother is not interested in ancient monuments?" Winterbourne inquired, smiling.

"He says he don't care much about old castles. He's only nine. He wants to stay at the hotel. Mother's afraid to leave him alone, and the courier won't   25 stay with him; so we haven't been to many places. But it will be too bad if we don't go up there." And Miss Miller pointed again at the Château de Chillon.

"I should think it might be arranged," said Winterbourne. "Couldn't you get some one to stay—for the afternoon—with Randolph?"   30

Miss Miller looked at him a moment; and then, very placidly, "I wish *you* would stay with him!" she said.

Winterbourne hesitated a moment. "I should much rather go to Chillon with you."

"With me?" asked the young girl, with the same placidity.   35

She didn't rise, blushing, as a young girl at Geneva would have done; and yet Winterbourne, conscious that he had been very bold, thought it possible she was offended. "With your mother," he answered, very respectfully.

But it seemed that both his audacity and his respect were lost upon Miss Daisy Miller. "I guess my mother won't go after all," she said. "She don't   40 like to ride round in the afternoon. But did you really mean what you said just now; that you would like to go up there?"

"Most earnestly," Winterbourne declared.

"Then we may arrange it. If mother will stay with Randolph, I guess Eugenio will."   45

7. **Château de Chillon**—the scene of Byron's romantic poem "The Prisoner of Chillon."

"Eugenio?" the young man inquired.

"Eugenio's our courier. He doesn't like to stay with Randolph; he's the most fastidious man I ever saw. But he's a splendid courier. I guess he'll stay at home with Randolph if mother does, and then we can go to the castle."

5 Winterbourne reflected for an instant as lucidly as possible—"we" could only mean Miss Daisy Miller and himself. This programme seemed almost too agreeable for credence; he felt as if he ought to kiss the young lady's hand. Possibly he would have done so—and quite spoiled the project; but at this moment another person—presumably Eugenio—appeared. A tall, handsome

10 man, with superb whiskers, wearing a velvet morning-coat and a brilliant watch-chain, approached Miss Miller, looking sharply at her companion. "Oh, Eugenio!" said Miss Miller, with the friendliest accent.

Eugenio had looked at Winterbourne from head to foot; he now bowed gravely to the young lady. "I have the honour to inform mademoiselle that

15 luncheon is upon the table."

Miss Miller slowly rose. "See here, Eugenio," she said. "I'm going to that old castle, anyway."

"To the Château de Chillon, mademoiselle?" the courier inquired. "Mademoiselle has made arrangements?" he added, in a tone which struck Winter-

20 bourne as very impertinent.

Eugenio's tone apparently threw, even to Miss Miller's own apprehension, a slightly ironical light upon the young girl's situation. She turned to Winterbourne, blushing a little—a very little. "You won't back out?" she said.

"I shall not be happy till we go!" he protested.

25 "And you are staying in this hotel?" she went on. "And you are really an American?"

The courier stood looking at Winterbourne, offensively. The young man, at least, thought his manner of looking an offence to Miss Miller; it conveyed an imputation that she "picked up" acquaintances. "I shall have the honour

30 of presenting to you a person who will tell you all about me," he said, smiling, and referring to his aunt.

"Oh, well, we'll go some day," said Miss Miller. And she gave him a smile and turned away. She put up her parasol and walked back to the inn beside Eugenio. Winterbourne stood looking after her; and as she moved away,

35 drawing her muslin furbelows over the gravel, said to himself that she had the *tournure* of a princess.

He had, however, engaged to do more than proved feasible, in promising to present his aunt, Mrs. Costello, to Miss Daisy Miller. As soon as the former lady had got better of her headache he waited upon her in her apartment;

40 and, after the proper inquiries in regard to her health, he asked her if she had observed, in the hotel, an American family—a mamma, a daughter, and a little boy.

"And a courier?" said Mrs. Costello. "Oh, yes, I have observed them. Seen them—heard them—and kept out of their way." Mrs. Costello was a widow

45 with a fortune; a person of much distinction, who frequently intimated that,

36. tournure—figure

if she were not so dreadfully liable to sick-headaches, she would probably have left a deeper impress upon her time. She had a long pale face, a high nose, and a great deal of very striking white hair, which she wore in large puffs and *rouleaux* over the top of her head. She had two sons married in New York, and another who was now in Europe. This young man was amus- 5 ing himself at Hombourg, and, though he was on his travels, was rarely perceived to visit any particular city at the moment selected by his mother for her own appearance there. Her nephew, who had come up to Vevey expressly to see her, was therefore more attentive than those who, as she said, were nearer to her. He had imbibed at Geneva the idea that one must always be 10 attentive to one's aunt. Mrs. Costello had not seen him for many years, and she was greatly pleased with him, manifesting her approbation by initiating him into many of the secrets of that social sway which, as she gave him to understand, she exerted in the American capital. She admitted that she was very exclusive; but, if he were acquainted with New York, he would see that 15 one had to be. And her picture of the minutely hierarchical constitution of the society of that city, which she presented to him in many different lights, was, to Winterbourne's imagination, almost oppressively striking.

He immediately perceived, from her tone, that Miss Daisy Miller's place in the social scale was low. "I am afraid you don't approve of them," he said.   20

"They are very common," Mrs. Costello declared. "They are the sort of Americans that one does one's duty by not—not accepting."

"Ah, you don't accept them?" said the young man.

"I can't, my dear Frederick. I would if I could, but I can't."

"The young girl is very pretty," said Winterbourne, in a moment.   25

"Of course she's pretty. But she is very common."

"I see what you mean, of course," said Winterbourne, after another pause.

"She has that charming look that they all have," his aunt resumed. "I can't think where they pick it up; and she dresses in perfection—no, you don't know how well she dresses. I can't think where they get their taste."   30

"But, my dear aunt, she is not, after all, a Comanche savage."

"She is a young lady," said Mrs. Costello, "who has an intimacy with her mamma's courier."

"An intimacy with the courier?" the young man demanded.

"Oh, the mother is just as bad! They treat the courier like a familiar friend 35 —like a gentleman. I shouldn't wonder if he dines with them. Very likely they have never seen a man with such good manners, such fine clothes, so like a gentleman. He probably corresponds to the young lady's idea of a count. He sits with them in the garden, in the evening. I think he smokes."

Winterbourne listened with interest to these disclosures; they helped him 40 to make up his mind about Miss Daisy. Evidently she was rather wild.

"Well," he said, "I am not a courier, and yet she was very charming to me."

"You had better have said at first," said Mrs. Costello with dignity, "that you had made her acquaintance."

"We simply met in the garden, and we talked a bit."   45

6. **Hombourg**—a health resort in southwestern Prussia.

"*Tout bonnement!* And pray what did you say?"

"I said I should take the liberty of introducing her to my admirable aunt."

"I am much obliged to you."

"It was to guarantee my respectability," said Winterbourne.

5 "And pray who is to guarantee hers?"

"Ah, you are cruel!" said the young man. "She's a very nice young girl."

"You don't say that as if you believed it," Mrs. Costello observed.

"She is completely uncultivated," Winterbourne went on. "But she is wonderfully pretty, and, in short, she is very nice. To prove that I believe it, I am

10 going to take her to the Château de Chillon."

"You two are going off there together? I should say it proved just the contrary. How long had you known her, may I ask, when this interesting project was formed? You haven't been twenty-four hours in the house."

"I had known her half an hour!" said Winterbourne, smiling.

15 "Dear me!" cried Mrs. Costello. "What a dreadful girl!"

Her nephew was silent for some moments. "You really think, then," he began, earnestly, and with a desire for trustworthy information—"you really think that—" But he paused again.

"Think what, sir?" said his aunt.

20 "That she is the sort of young lady who expects a man—sooner or later—to carry her off?"

"I haven't the least idea what such young ladies expect a man to do. But I really think that you had better not meddle with little American girls that are uncultivated, as you call them. You have lived too long out of the coun-

25 try. You will be sure to make some great mistake. You are too innocent."

"My dear aunt, I am not so innocent," said Winterbourne, smiling and curling his moustache.

"You are too guilty, then!"

Winterbourne continued to curl his moustache, meditatively. "You won't let

30 the poor girl know you, then?" he asked at last.

"Is it literally true that she is going to the Château de Chillon with you?"

"I think that she fully intends it."

"Then, my dear Frederick," said Mrs. Costello, "I must decline the honour of her acquaintance. I am an old woman, but I am not too old—thank Heaven

35 —to be shocked!"

"But don't they all do these things—the young girls in America?" Winterbourne inquired.

Mrs. Costello stared a moment. "I should like to see my granddaughters do them!" she declared, grimly.

40 This seemed to throw some light upon the matter, for Winterbourne remembered to have heard that his pretty cousins in New York were "tremendous flirts." If, therefore, Miss Daisy Miller exceeded the liberal margin allowed to these young ladies, it was probable that anything might be expected of her. Winterbourne was impatient to see her again, and he was vexed with

45 himself that, by instinct, he should not appreciate her justly.

---

1. **Tout bonnement!**—About equivalent to "Good enough," used with light irony.

Though he was impatient to see her, he hardly knew what he should say to her about his aunt's refusal to become acquainted with her; but he discovered, promptly enough, that with Miss Daisy Miller there was no great need of walking on tiptoe. He found her that evening in the garden, wandering about in the warm starlight, like an indolent sylph, and swinging to and fro the largest fan he had ever beheld. It was ten o'clock. He had dined with his aunt, had been sitting with her since dinner, and had just taken leave of her till the morrow. Miss Daisy Miller seemed very glad to see him; she declared it was the longest evening she had ever passed.

"Have you been all alone?" he asked.

"I have been walking round with mother. But mother gets tired walking round," she answered.

"Has she gone to bed?"

"No; she doesn't like to go to bed," said the young girl. "She doesn't sleep— not three hours. She says she doesn't know how she lives. She's dreadfully nervous. I guess she sleeps more than she thinks. She's gone somewhere after Randolph; she wants to try to get him to go to bed. He doesn't like to go to bed."

"Let us hope she will persuade him," observed Winterbourne.

"She will talk to him all she can; but he doesn't like her to talk to him," said Miss Daisy, opening her fan. "She's going to try to get Eugenio to talk to him. But he isn't afraid of Eugenio. Eugenio's a splendid courier, but he can't make much impression on Randolph! I don't believe he'll go to bed before eleven." It appeared that Randolph's vigil was in fact triumphantly prolonged, for Winterbourne strolled about with the young girl for some time without meeting her mother. "I have been looking round for that lady you want to introduce me to," his companion resumed. "She's your aunt." Then, on Winterbourne's admitting the fact, and expressing some curiosity as to how she had learned it, she said she had heard all about Mrs. Costello from the chambermaid. She was very quiet, and very *comme il faut;* she wore white puffs; she spoke to no one, and she never dined at the *table d'hôte.* Every two days she had a headache. "I think that's a lovely description, headache and all!" said Miss Daisy, chattering along in her thin, gay voice. "I want to know her ever so much. I know just what *your* aunt would be; I know I should like her. She would be very exclusive. I like a lady to be exclusive; I'm dying to be exclusive myself. Well, we *are* exclusive, mother and I. We don't speak to every one—or they don't speak to us. I suppose it's about the same thing. Anyway, I shall be ever so glad to know your aunt."

Winterbourne was embarrassed. "She would be most happy," he said; "but I am afraid those headaches will interfere."

The young girl looked at him through the dusk. "But I suppose she doesn't have a headache every day," she said, sympathetically.

Winterbourne was silent a moment. "She tells me she does," he answered at last—not knowing what to say.

Miss Daisy Miller stopped, and stood looking at him. Her prettiness was

---

30. comme il faut—decorous. **31. table d'hôte**—that is, in the hotel dining-room.

still visible in the darkness; she was opening and closing her enormous fan.
"She doesn't want to know me!" she said, suddenly. "Why don't you say so?
You needn't be afraid. I'm not afraid!" And she gave a little laugh.

Winterbourne fancied there was a tremor in her voice; he was touched,
5 shocked, mortified by it. "My dear young lady," he protested, "she knows no
one. It's her wretched health."

The young girl walked on a few steps, laughing still. "You needn't be
afraid," she repeated. "Why should she want to know me?" Then she paused
again; she was close to the parapet of the garden, and in front of her was
10 the starlit lake. There was a vague sheen upon its surface, and in the distance
were dimly-seen mountain forms. Daisy Miller looked out upon the mysterious prospect, and then she gave another little laugh. "Gracious! she *is* exclusive!" she said. Winterbourne wondered whether she was seriously
wounded, and for a moment almost wished that her sense of injury might
15 be such as to make it becoming in him to attempt to reassure and comfort
her. He had a pleasant sense that she would be very approachable for con-
solatory purposes. He felt then, for the instant, quite ready to sacrifice his
aunt, conversationally; to admit that she was a proud, rude woman, and to declare that they needn't mind her. But before he had time to commit himself
20 to this perilous mixture of gallantry and impiety, the young lady, resuming
her walk, gave an exclamation in quite another tone. "Well; here's mother!
I guess she hasn't got Randolph to go to bed." The figure of a lady appeared,
at a distance, very indistinct in the darkness, and advancing with a slow and
wavering movement. Suddenly it seemed to pause.

25 "Are you sure it is your mother? Can you distinguish her in this thick
dusk?" Winterbourne asked.

"Well!" cried Miss Daisy Miller, with a laugh, "I guess I know my own
mother. And when she has got on my shawl, too! She is always wearing my
things."

30 The lady in question, ceasing to advance, hovered vaguely about the spot
at which she had checked her steps.

"I am afraid your mother doesn't see you," said Winterbourne. "Or perhaps," he added—thinking, with Miss Miller, the joke permissible—"perhaps
she feels guilty about your shawl."

35 "Oh, it's a fearful old thing!" the young girl replied, serenely. "I told her
she could wear it. She won't come here, because she sees you."

"Ah, then," said Winterbourne, "I had better leave you."

"Oh, no; come on!" urged Miss Daisy Miller.

"I'm afraid your mother doesn't approve of my walking with you."

40 Miss Miller gave him a serious glance. "It isn't for me; it's for you—that
is, it's for *her*. Well, I don't know who it's for! But mother doesn't like any
of my gentlemen friends. She's right down timid. She always makes a fuss
if I introduce a gentleman. But I *do* introduce them—almost always. If I
didn't introduce my gentlemen friends to mother," the young girl added, in
45 her little soft, flat monotone, "I shouldn't think I was natural."

"To introduce me," said Winterbourne, "you must know my name." And
he proceeded to pronounce it.

"Oh, dear, I can't say all that!" said his companion, with a laugh. But by this time they had come up to Mrs. Miller, who, as they drew near, walked to the parapet of the garden and leaned upon it, looking intently at the lake, and turning her back to them. "Mother!" said the young girl, in a tone of decision. Upon this the elder lady turned round. "Mr. Winterbourne," said 5 Miss Daisy Miller, introducing the young man very frankly and prettily. "Common" she was, as Mrs. Costello had pronounced her; yet it was a wonder to Winterbourne that, with her commonness, she had a singularly delicate grace.

Her mother was a small, spare, light person, with a wandering eye, a very 10 exiguous nose, and a large forehead, decorated with a certain amount of thin, much-frizzled hair. Like her daughter, Mrs. Miller was dressed with extreme elegance; she had enormous diamonds in her ears. So far as Winterbourne could observe, she gave him no greeting—she certainly was not looking at him. Daisy was near her, pulling her shawl straight. "What are you 15 doing, poking round here?" this young lady inquired; but by no means with that harshness of accent which her choice of words may imply.

"I don't know," said her mother, turning towards the lake again.

"I shouldn't think you'd want that shawl!" Daisy exclaimed.

"Well—I do!" her mother answered, with a little laugh. 20

"Did you get Randolph to go to bed?" asked the young girl.

"No; I couldn't induce him," said Mrs. Miller, very gently. "He wants to talk to the waiter. He likes to talk to that waiter."

"I was telling Mr. Winterbourne," the young girl went on; and to the young man's ear her tone might have indicated that she had been uttering 25 his name all her life.

"Oh, yes!" said Winterbourne; "I have the pleasure of knowing your son."

Randolph's mamma was silent; she turned her attention to the lake. But at last she spoke. "Well, I don't see how he lives!"

"Anyhow, it isn't so bad as it was at Dover," said Daisy Miller. 30

"And what occurred at Dover?" Winterbourne asked.

"He wouldn't go to bed at all. I guess he sat up all night—in the public parlour. He wasn't in bed at twelve o'clock; I know that."

"It was half-past twelve," declared Mrs. Miller, with mild emphasis.

"Does he sleep much during the day?" Winterbourne demanded. 35

"I guess he doesn't sleep much," Daisy rejoined.

"I wish he would!" said her mother. "It seems as if he couldn't."

"I think he's real tiresome," Daisy pursued.

Then, for some moments, there was silence. "Well, Daisy Miller," said the elder lady, presently, "I shouldn't think you'd want to talk against your own 40 brother!"

"Well, he *is* tiresome, mother," said Daisy, quite without the asperity of a retort.

"He's only nine," urged Mrs. Miller.

"Well, he wouldn't go to that castle," said the young girl. "I'm going there 45 with Mr. Winterbourne."

To this announcement, very placidly made, Daisy's mamma offered no re-

sponse. Winterbourne took for granted that she deeply disapproved of the
projected excursion; but he said to himself that she was a simple, easily-man-
aged person, and that a few deferential protestations would take the edge
from her displeasure. "Yes," he began; "your daughter has kindly allowed
5 me the honour of being her guide."

Mrs. Miller's wandering eyes attached themselves, with a sort of appealing
air, to Daisy, who, however, strolled a few steps farther, gently humming to
herself. "I presume you will go in the cars," said her mother.

"Yes; or in the boat," said Winterbourne.

10 "Well, of course, I don't know," Mrs. Miller rejoined. "I have never been
to that castle."

"It is a pity you shouldn't go," said Winterbourne, beginning to feel reassured as to her opposition. And yet he was quite prepared to find that, as
a matter of course, she meant to accompany her daughter.

15 "We've been thinking ever so much about going," she pursued; "but it
seems as if we couldn't. Of course Daisy—she wants to go round. But there's
a lady here—I don't know her name—she says she shouldn't think we'd want
to go to see castles *here;* she should think we'd want to wait till we got to
Italy. It seems as if there would be so many there," continued Mrs. Miller,
20 with an air of increasing confidence. "Of course, we only want to see the
principal ones. We visited several in England," she presently added.

"Ah, yes! in England there are beautiful castles," said Winterbourne. "But
Chillon, here, is very well worth seeing."

"Well, if Daisy feels up to it—," said Mrs. Miller, in a tone impregnated
25 with a sense of the magnitude of the enterprise. "It seems as if there was
nothing she wouldn't undertake."

"Oh, I think she'll enjoy it!" Winterbourne declared. And he desired more
and more to make it a certainty that he was to have the privilege of a *tête-à-
tête* with the young lady, who was still strolling along in front of them, softly
30 vocalizing. "You are not disposed, madam," he inquired, "to undertake it
yourself?"

Daisy's mother looked at him, an instant, askance, and then walked forward in silence. Then—"I guess she had better go alone," she said, simply.
Winterbourne observed to himself that this was a very different type of ma-
35 ternity from that of the vigilant matrons who massed themselves in the fore-
front of social intercourse in the dark old city at the other end of the lake.
But his meditations were interrupted by hearing his name very distinctly
pronounced by Mrs. Miller's unprotected daughter.

"Mr. Winterbourne!" murmured Daisy.

40 "Mademoiselle!" said the young man.

"Don't you want to take me out in a boat?"

"At present?" he asked.

"Of course!" said Daisy.

"Well, Annie Miller!" exclaimed her mother.

45 "I beg you, madam, to let her go," said Winterbourne, ardently; for he had
never yet enjoyed the sensation of guiding through the summer starlight a
skiff freighted with a fresh and beautiful young girl.

"I shouldn't think she'd want to," said her mother. "I should think she'd rather go indoors."

"I'm sure Mr. Winterbourne wants to take me," Daisy declared. "He's so awfully devoted!"

"I will row you over to Chillon, in the starlight."   5

"I don't believe it!" said Daisy.

"Well!" ejaculated the elder lady again.

"You haven't spoken to me for half an hour," her daughter went on.

"I have been having some very pleasant conversation with your mother," said Winterbourne.   10

"Well, I want you to take me out in a boat!" Daisy repeated. They had all stopped, and she had turned round and was looking at Winterbourne. Her face wore a charming smile, her pretty eyes were gleaming, she was swinging her great fan about. No; it's impossible to be prettier than that, thought Winterbourne.   15

"There are half a dozen boats moored at that landing-place," he said, pointing to certain steps which descended from the garden to the lake. "If you will do me the honour to accept my arm, we will go and select one of them."

Daisy stood there smiling; she threw back her head and gave a little, light laugh. "I like a gentleman to be formal!" she declared.   20

"I assure you it's a formal offer."

"I was bound I would make you say something," Daisy went on.

"You see it's not very difficult," said Winterbourne. "But I am afraid you are chaffing me."

"I think not, sir," remarked Mrs. Miller, very gently.   25

"Do, then, let me give you a row," he said to the young girl.

"It's quite lovely, the way you say that!" cried Daisy.

"It will be still more lovely to do it."

"Yes, it would be lovely!" said Daisy. But she made no movement to accompany him; she only stood there laughing.   30

"I should think you had better find out what time it is," interposed her mother.

"It is eleven o'clock, madam," said a voice, with a foreign accent, out of the neighbouring darkness; and Winterbourne, turning, perceived the florid personage who was in attendance upon the two ladies. He had apparently   35
just approached.

"Oh, Eugenio," said Daisy, "I am going out in a boat!"

Eugenio bowed. "At eleven o'clock, mademoiselle?"

"I am going with Mr. Winterbourne. This very minute."

"Do tell her she can't," said Mrs. Miller to the courier.   40

"I think you had better not go out in a boat, mademoiselle," Eugenio declared.

Winterbourne wished to Heaven this pretty girl were not so familiar with her courier; but he said nothing.

"I suppose you don't think it's proper!" Daisy exclaimed. "Eugenio doesn't   45
think anything's proper."

"I am at your service," said Winterbourne.

"Does mademoiselle propose to go alone?" asked Eugenio of Mrs. Miller.

"Oh, no; with this gentleman!" answered Daisy's mamma.

The courier looked for a moment at Winterbourne—the latter thought he was smiling—and then, solemnly, with a bow, "As mademoiselle pleases!" he
5 said.

"Oh, I hoped you would make a fuss!" said Daisy. "I don't care to go now."

"I myself shall make a fuss if you don't go," said Winterbourne.

"That's all I want—a little fuss!" And the young girl began to laugh again.

"Mr. Randolph has gone to bed!" the courier announced, frigidly.

10 "Oh, Daisy; now we can go!" said Mrs. Miller.

Daisy turned away from Winterbourne, looking at him, smiling, and fanning herself. "Good-night," she said; "I hope you are disappointed, or disgusted, or something!"

He looked at her, taking the hand she offered him. "I am puzzled," he
15 answered.

"Well, I hope it won't keep you awake!" she said, very smartly; and, under the escort of the privileged Eugenio, the two ladies passed towards the house.

Winterbourne stood looking after them; he was indeed puzzled. He lingered beside the lake for a quarter of an hour, turning over the mystery of
20 the young girl's sudden familiarities and caprices. But the only very definite conclusion he came to was that he should enjoy deucedly "going off" with her somewhere.

Two days afterwards he went off with her to the Castle of Chillon. He waited for her in the large hall of the hotel, where the couriers, the servants,
25 the foreign tourists were lounging about and staring. It was not the place he should have chosen, but she had appointed it. She came tripping downstairs, buttoning her long gloves, squeezing her folded parasol against her pretty figure, dressed in the perfection of a soberly elegant travelling-costume. Winterbourne was a man of imagination and, as our ancestors used to
30 say, sensibility; as he looked at her dress and, on the great staircase, her little rapid, confiding step, he felt as if there were something romantic going forward. He could have believed he was going to elope with her. He passed out with her among all the idle people that were assembled there; they were all looking at her very hard; she had begun to chatter as soon as she joined
35 him. Winterbourne's preference had been that they should be conveyed to Chillon in a carriage; but she expressed a lively wish to go in the little steamer; she declared that she had a passion for steamboats. There was always such a lovely breeze upon the water, and you saw such lots of people. The sail was not long, but Winterbourne's companion found time to say a great many
40 things. To the young man himself their little excursion was so much of an escapade—an adventure—that, even allowing for her habitual sense of freedom, he had some expectation of seeing her regard it in the same way. But it must be confessed that, in this particular, he was disappointed. Daisy Miller was extremely animated, she was in charming spirits; but she was appar-
45 ently not at all excited; she was not fluttered; she avoided neither his eyes nor those of any one else; she blushed neither when she looked at him nor when she felt that people were looking at her. People continued to look at

her a great deal, and Winterbourne took much satisfaction in his pretty companion's distinguished air. He had been a little afraid that she would talk loud, laugh overmuch, and even, perhaps, desire to move about the boat a good deal. But he quite forgot his fears; he sat smiling, with his eyes upon her face, while, without moving from her place, she delivered herself of a 5 great number of original reflections. It was the most charming garrulity he had ever heard. He had assented to the idea that she was "common"; but was she so, after all, or was he simply getting used to her commonness? Her conversation was chiefly of what metaphysicians term the objective cast; but every now and then it took a subjective turn. 10

"What on *earth* are you so grave about?" she suddenly demanded, fixing her agreeable eyes upon Winterbourne's.

"Am I grave?" he asked. "I had an idea I was grinning from ear to ear."

"You look as if you were taking me to a funeral. If that's a grin, your ears are very near together." 15

"Should you like me to dance a hornpipe on the deck?"

"Pray do, and I'll carry round your hat. It will pay the expenses of our journey."

"I never was better pleased in my life," murmured Winterbourne.

She looked at him a moment, and then burst into a little laugh. "I like to 20 make you say those things! You're a queer mixture!"

In the castle, after they had landed, the subjective element decidedly prevailed. Daisy tripped about the vaulted chambers, rustled her skirts in the corkscrew staircases, flirted back with a pretty little cry and a shudder from the edge of the *oubliettes,* and turned a singularly well-shaped ear to every- 25 thing that Winterbourne told her about the place. But he saw that she cared very little for feudal antiquities, and that the dusky traditions of Chillon made but a slight impression upon her. They had the good fortune to have been able to walk without other companionship than that of the custodian; and Winterbourne arranged with this functionary that they should not be 30 hurried—that they should linger and pause wherever they chose. The custodian interpreted the bargain generously—Winterbourne, on his side, had been generous—and ended by leaving them quite to themselves. Miss Miller's observations were not remarkable for logical consistency; for anything she wanted to say she was sure to find a pretext. She found a great many pretexts 35 in the rugged embrasures of Chillon for asking Winterbourne sudden questions about himself—his family, his previous history, his tastes, his habits, his intentions—and for supplying information upon corresponding points in her own personality. Of her own tastes, habits, and intentions Miss Miller was prepared to give the most definite, and, indeed, the most favourable, 40 account.

"Well, I hope you know enough!" she said to her companion, after he had told her the history of the unhappy Bonnivard. "I never saw a man that knew so much!" The history of Bonnivard had evidently, as they say, gone into one ear and out of the other. But Daisy went on to say that she wished 45

25. oubliettes—medieval dungeons with entrance only through the top. 43. Bonnivard— See Byron's poem "The Prisoner of Chillon."

Winterbourne would travel with them, and "go round" with them; they might know something, in that case. "Don't you want to come and teach Randolph?" she asked. Winterbourne said that nothing could possibly please him so much; but that he had unfortunately other occupations. "Other occu-
5 pations? I don't believe it!" said Miss Daisy. "What do you mean? You are not in business." The young man admitted that he was not in business; but he had engagements which, even within a day or two, would force him to go back to Geneva. "Oh, bother!" she said; "I don't believe it!" and she began to talk about something else. But a few moments later, when he was point-
10 ing out to her the pretty design of an antique fireplace, she broke out irrele-vantly, "You don't mean to say you are going back to Geneva?"
   "It is a melancholy fact that I shall have to return to-morrow."
   "Well, Mr. Winterbourne," said Daisy, "I think you're horrid!"
   "Oh, don't say such dreadful things!" said Winterbourne—"just at the
15 last!"
   "The last!" cried the young girl; "I call it the first. I have half a mind to leave you here and go straight back to the hotel alone." And for the next ten minutes she did nothing but call him horrid. Poor Winterbourne was fairly bewildered; no young lady had as yet done him the honour to be so
20 agitated by the announcement of his movements. His companion, after this, ceased to pay any attention to the curiosities of Chillon or the beauties of the lake; she opened fire upon the mysterious charmer in Geneva, whom she ap-peared to have instantly taken for granted that he was hurrying back to see. How did Miss Daisy Miller know that there was a charmer in Geneva? Win-
25 terbourne, who denied the existence of such a person, was quite unable to discover; and he was divided between amazement at the rapidity of her in-duction and amusement at the frankness of her *persiflage*. She seemed to him, in all this, an extraordinary mixture of innocence and crudity. "Does she never allow you more than three days at a time?" asked Daisy, ironically.
30 "Doesn't she give you a vacation in summer? There is no one so hard worked but they can get leave to go off somewhere at this season. I suppose, if you stay another day, she'll come after you in the boat. Do wait over till Friday, and I will go down to the landing to see her arrive!" Winterbourne began to think he had been wrong to feel disappointed in the temper in which
35 the young lady had embarked. If he had missed the personal accent, the per-sonal accent was now making its appearance. It sounded very distinctly, at last, in her telling him she would stop "teasing" him if he would promise her solemnly to come down to Rome in the winter.
   "That's not a difficult promise to make," said Winterbourne. "My aunt has
40 taken an apartment in Rome for the winter, and has already asked me to come and see her."
   "I don't want you to come for your aunt," said Daisy; "I want you to come for me." And this was the only allusion that the young man was ever to hear her make to his invidious kinswoman. He declared that, at any rate,
45 he would certainly come. After this Daisy stopped teasing. Winterbourne took a carriage, and they drove back to Vevey in the dusk; the young girl was very quiet.

In the evening Winterbourne mentioned to Mrs. Costello that he had spent the afternoon at Chillon with Miss Daisy Miller.

"The Americans—of the courier?" asked this lady.

"Ah, happily," said Winterbourne, "the courier stayed at home."

"She went with you all alone?" 5

"All alone."

Mrs. Costello sniffed a little at her smelling-bottle. "And that," she exclaimed, "is the young person whom you wanted me to know!"

PART II

Winterbourne, who had returned to Geneva the day after his excursion to 10
Chillon, went to Rome towards the end of January. His aunt had been established there for several weeks, and he had received a couple of letters from her. "Those people you were so devoted to last summer at Vevey have turned up here, courier and all," she wrote. "They seem to have made several acquaintances, but the courier continues to be the most *intime*. The young 15
lady, however, is also very intimate with some third-rate Italians, with whom she rackets about in a way that makes much talk. Bring me that pretty novel of Cherbuliez's—'*Paule Méré*'—and don't come later than the 23rd."

In the natural course of events, Winterbourne, on arriving in Rome, would presently have ascertained Mrs. Miller's address at the American banker's, and 20
have gone to pay his compliments to Miss Daisy. "After what happened at Vevey I think I may certainly call upon them," he said to Mrs. Costello.

"If, after what happens—at Vevey and everywhere—you desire to keep up the acquaintance, you are very welcome. Of course a man may know every one. Men are welcome to the privilege!" 25

"Pray what is it that happens—here, for instance?" Winterbourne demanded.

"The girl goes about alone with her foreigners. As to what happens further, you must apply elsewhere for information. She has picked up half-a-dozen of the regular Roman fortune-hunters, and she takes them about to people's 30
houses. When she comes to a party she brings with her a gentleman with a good deal of manner and a wonderful moustache."

"And where is the mother?"

"I haven't the least idea. They are very dreadful people."

Winterbourne meditated a moment. "They are very ignorant—very inno- 35
cent only. Depend upon it they are not bad."

"They are hopelessly vulgar," said Mrs. Costello. "Whether or no being hopelessly vulgar is being 'bad' is a question for the metaphysicians. They are bad enough to dislike, at any rate; and for this short life that is quite enough." 40

The news that Daisy Miller was surrounded by half-a-dozen wonderful moustaches checked Winterbourne's impulse to go straightway to see her. He had perhaps not definitely flattered himself that he had made an ineffaceable

9. **Part II**—Later editions have the caption, Rome. 18. **Cherbuliez**—Victor Cherbuliez (1829-1899), novelist of Swiss origin, technically skillful, but unconvincing.

impression upon her heart, but he was annoyed at hearing of a state of affairs
so little in harmony with an image that had lately flitted in and out of his own
meditations; the image of a very pretty girl looking out of an old Roman
window and asking herself urgently when Mr. Winterbourne would arrive.
5   If, however, he determined to wait a little before reminding Miss Miller of
his claims to her consideration, he went very soon to call upon two or three
other friends. One of these friends was an American lady who had spent
several winters at Geneva, where she had placed her children at school. She
was a very accomplished woman, and she lived in the Via Gregoriana. Winter-
10 bourne found her in a little crimson drawing-room, on a third floor; the room
was filled with southern sunshine. He had not been there ten minutes when
the servant came in, announcing "Madame Mila!" This announcement was
presently followed by the entrance of little Randolph Miller, who stopped in
the middle of the room and stood staring at Winterbourne. An instant later
15 his pretty sister crossed the threshold; and then, after a considerable interval,
Mrs. Miller slowly advanced.

"I know you!" said Randolph.

"I'm sure you know a great many things," exclaimed Winterbourne, taking
him by the hand. "How is your education coming on?"
20 Daisy was exchanging greetings very prettily with her hostess; but when
she heard Winterbourne's voice she quickly turned her head. "Well, I declare!"
she said.

"I told you I should come, you know," Winterbourne rejoined, smiling.

"Well—I didn't believe it," said Miss Daisy.
25 "I am much obliged to you," laughed the young man.

"You might have come to see me!" said Daisy.

"I arrived only yesterday."

"I don't believe that!" the young girl declared.

Winterbourne turned with a protesting smile to her mother; but this lady
30 evaded his glance, and, seating herself, fixed her eyes upon her son. "We've
got a bigger place than this," said Randolph. "It's all gold on the walls."

Mrs. Miller turned uneasily in her chair. "I told you if I were going to bring
you, you would say something!" she murmured.

"I told *you!*" Randolph exclaimed. "I tell *you,* sir!" he added, jocosely, giv-
35 ing Winterbourne a thump on the knee. "It *is* bigger, too!"

Daisy had entered upon a lively conversation with her hostess; and Winterbourne judged it becoming to address a few words to her mother. "I hope
you have been well since we parted at Vevey," he said.

Mrs. Miller now certainly looked at him—at his chin. "Not very well, sir,"
40 she answered.

"She's got the dyspepsia," said Randolph. "I've got it, too. Father's got it.
I've got it most!"

This announcement, instead of embarrassing Mrs. Miller, seemed to relieve
her. "I suffer from the liver," she said. "I think it's this climate; it's less bracing
45 than Schenectady, especially in the winter season. I don't know whether you
know we reside at Schenectady. I was saying to Daisy that I certainly hadn't
found any one like Dr. Davis, and I didn't believe I should. Oh, at Schenectady
he stands first; they think everything of him. He has so much to do, and yet

there was nothing he wouldn't do for me. He said he never saw anything like my dyspepsia, but he was bound to cure it. I'm sure there was nothing he wouldn't try. He was just going to try something new when we came off. Mr. Miller wanted Daisy to see Europe for herself. But I wrote to Mr. Miller that it seems as if I couldn't get on without Dr. Davis. At Schenectady 5 he stands at the very top; and there's a great deal of sickness there, too. It affects my sleep."

Winterbourne had a good deal of pathological gossip with Dr. Davis's patient, during which Daisy chattered unremittingly to her own companion. The young man asked Mrs. Miller how she was pleased with Rome. "Well, 10 I must say I am disappointed," she answered. "We had heard so much about it; I suppose we had heard too much. But we couldn't help that. We had been led to expect something different."

"Ah, wait a little, and you will become very fond of it," said Winterbourne.

"I hate it worse and worse every day!" cried Randolph. 15

"You are like the infant Hannibal," said Winterbourne.

"No, I ain't!" Randolph declared, at a venture.

"You are not much like an infant," said his mother. "But we have seen places," she resumed, "that I should put a long way before Rome." And in reply to Winterbourne's interrogation, "There's Zürich," she concluded; "I 20 think Zürich is lovely; and we hadn't heard half so much about it."

"The best place we've seen is the City of Richmond!" said Randolph.

"He means the ship," his mother explained. "We crossed in that ship. Randolph had a good time on the *City of Richmond.*"

"It's the best place I've seen," the child repeated. "Only it was turned the 25 wrong way."

"Well, we've got to turn the right way some time," said Mrs. Miller, with a little laugh. Winterbourne expressed the hope that her daughter at least found some gratification in Rome, and she declared that Daisy was quite carried away. "It's on account of the society—the society's splendid. She goes 30 round everywhere; she has made a great number of acquaintances. Of course she goes round more than I do. I must say they have been very sociable; they have taken her right in. And then she knows a great many gentlemen. Oh, she thinks there's nothing like Rome. Of course, it's a great deal pleasanter for a young lady if she knows plenty of gentlemen." 35

By this time Daisy had turned her attention again to Winterbourne. "I've been telling Mrs. Walker how mean you were!" the young girl announced.

"And what is the evidence you have offered?" asked Winterbourne, rather annoyed at Miss Miller's want of appreciation of the zeal of an admirer who on his way down to Rome had stopped neither at Bologna nor at Florence, 40 simply because of a certain sentimental impatience. He remembered that a cynical compatriot had once told him that American women—the pretty ones, and this gave a largeness to the axiom—were at once the most exacting in the world and the least endowed with a sense of indebtedness.

"Why, you were awfully mean at Vevey," said Daisy. "You wouldn't do 45 anything. You wouldn't stay there when I asked you."

16. **infant Hannibal**—dedicated by his father to undying hatred of Rome.

"My dearest young lady," cried Winterbourne, with eloquence, "have I come all the way to Rome to encounter your reproaches?"

"Just hear him say that!" said Daisy to her hostess, giving a twist to a bow on this lady's dress. "Did you ever hear anything so quaint?"

5   "So quaint, my dear?" murmured Mrs. Walker, in a tone of a partisan of Winterbourne.

"Well, I don't know," said Daisy, fingering Mrs. Walker's ribbons. "Mrs. Walker, I want to tell you something."

"Mother-r," interposed Randolph, with his rough ends to his words, "I tell
10   you you've got to go. Eugenio'll raise—something!"

"I'm not afraid of Eugenio," said Daisy, with a toss of her head. "Look here, Mrs. Walker," she went on, "you know I'm coming to your party."

"I am delighted to hear it."

"I've got a lovely dress!"

15   "I am very sure of that."

"But I want to ask a favour—permission to bring a friend."

"I shall be happy to see any of your friends," said Mrs. Walker, turning with a smile to Mrs. Miller.

"Oh, they are not my friends," answered Daisy's mamma, smiling shyly,
20   in her own fashion. "I never spoke to them."

"It's an intimate friend of mine—Mr. Giovanelli," said Daisy, without a tremor in her clear little voice, or a shadow on her brilliant little face.

Mrs. Walker was silent a moment; she gave a rapid glance at Winterbourne. "I shall be glad to see Mr. Giovanelli," she then said.

25   "He's an Italian," Daisy pursued, with the prettiest serenity. "He's a great friend of mine—he's the handsomest man in the world—except Mr. Winter-bourne! He knows plenty of Italians, but he wants to know some Americans. He thinks ever so much of Americans. He's tremendously clever. He's per-fectly lovely!"

30   It was settled that this brilliant personage should be brought to Mrs. Walker's party, and then Mrs. Miller prepared to take her leave. "I guess we'll go back to the hotel," she said.

"You may go back to the hotel, mother, but I'm going to take a walk," said Daisy.

35   "She's going to walk with Mr. Giovanelli," Randolph proclaimed.

"I am going to the Pincio," said Daisy, smiling.

"Alone, my dear—at this hour?" Mrs. Walker asked. The afternoon was drawing to a close—it was the hour for the throng of carriages and of con-templative pedestrians. "I don't think it's safe, my dear," said Mrs. Walker.

40   "Neither do I," subjoined Mrs. Miller. "You'll get the fever, as sure as you live. Remember what Dr. Davis told you!"

"Give her some medicine before she goes," said Randolph.

The company had risen to its feet; Daisy, still showing her pretty teeth, bent over and kissed her hostess. "Mrs. Walker, you are too perfect," she said.

45   "I'm not going alone; I am going to meet a friend."

36. **Pincio**—Monte Pincio, one of the hills of Rome.

"Your friend won't keep you from getting the fever," Mrs. Miller observed.
"Is it Mr. Giovanelli?" asked the hostess.

Winterbourne was watching the young girl; at this question his attention quickened. She stood there smiling and smoothing her bonnet ribbons; she glanced at Winterbourne. Then, while she glanced and smiled, she answered, 5 without a shade of hesitation, "Mr. Giovanelli—the beautiful Giovanelli."

"My dear young friend," said Mrs. Walker, taking her hand, pleadingly, "don't walk off to the Pincio at this hour to meet a beautiful Italian."

"Well, he speaks English," said Mrs. Miller.

"Gracious me!" Daisy exclaimed, "I don't want to do anything improper. 10 There's an easy way to settle it." She continued to glance at Winterbourne. "The Pincio is only a hundred yards distant, and if Mr. Winterbourne were as polite as he pretends, he would offer to walk with me!"

Winterbourne's politeness hastened to affirm itself, and the young girl gave him gracious leave to accompany her. They passed down stairs before her 15 mother, and at the door Winterbourne perceived Mrs. Miller's carriage drawn up, with the ornamental courier whose acquaintance he had made at Vevey seated within. "Good-bye, Eugenio!" cried Daisy, "I'm going to take a walk." The distance from the Via Gregoriana to the beautiful garden at the other end of the Pincian Hill is, in fact, rapidly traversed. As the day was splendid, how- 20 ever, and the concourse of vehicles, walkers, and loungers numerous, the young Americans found their progress much delayed. This fact was highly agreeable to Winterbourne, in spite of his consciousness of his singular situation. The slow-moving, idly-gazing Roman crowd bestowed much attention upon the extremely pretty young foreign lady who was passing through it upon his arm; 25 and he wondered what on earth had been in Daisy's mind when she proposed to expose herself, unattended, to its appreciation. His own mission, to her sense, apparently, was to consign her to the hands of Mr. Giovanelli; but Winterbourne, at once annoyed and gratified, resolved that he would do no such thing. 30

"Why haven't you been to see me?" asked Daisy. "You can't get out of that."

"I have had the honour of telling you that I have only just stepped out of the train."

"You must have stayed in the train a good while after it stopped!" cried the young girl, with her little laugh. "I suppose you were asleep. You have had 35 time to go to see Mrs. Walker."

"I knew Mrs. Walker—" Winterbourne began to explain.

"I know where you knew her. You knew her at Geneva. She told me so. Well, you knew me at Vevey. That's just as good. So you ought to have come." She asked him no other question than this; she began to prattle about 40 her own affairs. "We've got splendid rooms at the hotel; Eugenio says they're the best rooms in Rome. We are going to stay all winter, if we don't die of the fever; and I guess we'll stay then. It's a great deal nicer than I thought; I thought it would be fearfully quiet; I was sure it would be awfully poky. I was sure we should be going round all the time with one of those dreadful 45 old men that explain about the pictures and things. But we only had about a week of that, and now I'm enjoying myself. I know ever so many people,

and they are all so charming. The society's extremely select. There are all kinds
—English, and Germans, and Italians. I think I like the English best. I like
their style of conversation. But there are some lovely Americans. I never saw
anything so hospitable. There's something or other every day. There's not
5 much dancing; but I must say I never thought dancing was everything. I was
always fond of conversation. I guess I shall have plenty at Mrs. Walker's—
her rooms are so small." When they had passed the gate of the Pincian Gardens, Miss Miller began to wonder where Mr. Giovanelli might be. "We had
better go straight to that place in front," she said, "where you look at the view."
10   "I certainly shall not help you to find him," Winterbourne declared.
    "Then I shall find him without you," said Miss Daisy.
    "You certainly won't leave me!" cried Winterbourne.
    She burst into her little laugh. "Are you afraid you'll get lost—or run over?
But there's Giovanelli, leaning against that tree. He's staring at the women in
15 the carriages; did you ever see anything so cool?"
    Winterbourne perceived at some distance a little man standing with folded
arms, nursing his cane. He had a handsome face, an artfully poised hat, a
glass in one eye, and a nosegay in his buttonhole. Winterbourne looked at him
a moment, and then said, "Do you mean to speak to that man?"
20   "Do I mean to speak to him? Why, you don't suppose I mean to communicate by signs?"
    "Pray understand, then," said Winterbourne, "that I intend to remain with
you."
    Daisy stopped and looked at him, without a sign of troubled consciousness
25 in her face; with nothing but the presence of her charming eyes and her happy
dimples. "Well, she's a cool one!" thought the young man.
    "I don't like the way you say that," said Daisy. "It's too imperious."
    "I beg your pardon if I say it wrong. The main point is to give you an idea
of my meaning."
30   The young girl looked at him more gravely, but with eyes that were prettier
than ever. "I have never allowed a gentleman to dictate to me, or to interfere
with anything I do."
    "I think you have made a mistake," said Winterbourne. "You should some-
times listen to a gentleman—the right one."
35   Daisy began to laugh again. "I do nothing but listen to gentlemen!" she
exclaimed. "Tell me if Mr. Giovanelli is the right one."
    The gentleman with the nosegay in his bosom had now perceived our two
friends, and was approaching the young girl with obsequious rapidity. He
bowed to Winterbourne as well as to the latter's companion; he had a brilliant
40 smile, an intelligent eye; Winterbourne thought him not a bad-looking fellow.
But he nevertheless said to Daisy, "No, he's not the right one."
    Daisy evidently had a natural talent for performing introductions; she
mentioned the name of each of her companions to the other. She strolled
along with one of them on each side of her; Mr. Giovanelli, who spoke English
45 very cleverly—Winterbourne afterwards learned that he had practised the
idiom upon a great many American heiresses—addressed to her a great deal
of very polite nonsense; he was extremely urbane, and the young American,

who said nothing, reflected upon that profundity of Italian cleverness which
enables people to appear more gracious in proportion as they are more acutely
disappointed. Giovanelli, of course, had counted upon something more intimate; he had not bargained for a party of three. But he kept his temper in a
manner which suggested far-stretching intentions. Winterbourne flattered him- 5
self that he had taken his measure. "He is not a gentleman," said the young
American; "he is only a clever imitation of one. He is a music-master, or a
penny-a-liner, or a third-rate artist. Damn his good looks!" Mr. Giovanelli had
certainly a very pretty face; but Winterbourne felt a superior indignation at
his own lovely fellow-country woman's not knowing the difference between 10
a spurious gentleman and a real one. Giovanelli chattered and jested, and made
himself wonderfully agreeable. It was true that, if he was an imitation, the
imitation was brilliant. "Nevertheless," Winterbourne said to himself, "a nice
girl ought to know!" And then he came back to the question whether this was,
in fact, a nice girl. Would a nice girl—even allowing for her being a little 15
American flirt—make a rendezvous with a presumably low-lived foreigner?
The rendezvous in this case, indeed, had been in broad daylight, and in the
most crowded corner of Rome; but was it not impossible to regard the choice
of these circumstances as a proof of extreme cynicism? Singular though it may
seem, Winterbourne was vexed that the young girl, in joining her *amoroso,* 20
should not appear more impatient of his own company, and he was vexed
because of his inclination. It was impossible to regard her as a perfectly well-
conducted young lady; she was wanting in a certain indispensable delicacy.
It would therefore simplify matters greatly to be able to treat her as the object
of one of those sentiments which are called by romancers "lawless passions." 25
That she should seem to wish to get rid of him would help him to think more
lightly of her, and to be able to think more lightly of her would make her
much less perplexing. But Daisy, on this occasion, continued to present herself
as an inscrutable combination of audacity and innocence.

She had been walking some quarter of an hour, attended by her two cava- 30
liers, and responding in a tone of very childish gaiety, as it seemed to Winterbourne, to the pretty speeches of Mr. Giovanelli, when a carriage that had
detached itself from the revolving train drew up beside the path. At the same
moment Winterbourne perceived that his friend Mrs. Walker—the lady whose
house he had lately left—was seated in the vehicle, and was beckoning to him. 35
Leaving Miss Miller's side, he hastened to obey her summons. Mrs. Walker
was flushed; she wore an excited air. "It is really too dreadful," she said.
"That girl must not do this sort of thing. She must not walk here with you
two men. Fifty people have noticed her."

Winterbourne raised his eyebrows. "I think it's a pity to make too much 40
fuss about it."

"It's a pity to let the girl ruin herself!"

"She is very innocent," said Winterbourne.

"She's very crazy!" cried Mrs. Walker. "Did you ever see anything so
imbecile as her mother? After you had all left me, just now, I could not sit 45

20. amoroso—lover.

still for thinking of it. It seemed too pitiful not even to attempt to save her.
I ordered the carriage and put on my bonnet, and came here as quickly as
possible. Thank Heaven I have found you!"

"What do you propose to do with us?" asked Winterbourne, smiling.

5   "To ask her to get in, to drive her about here for half-an-hour, so that the
world may see that she is not running absolutely wild, and then to take her
safely home."

"I don't think it's a very happy thought," said Winterbourne; "but you can
try."

10   Mrs. Walker tried. The young man went in pursuit of Miss Miller, who had
simply nodded and smiled at his interlocutor in the carriage, and had gone
her way with her companion. Daisy, on learning that Mrs. Walker wished to
speak to her, retraced her steps with a perfect good grace and with Mr.
Giovanelli at her side. She declared that she was delighted to have a chance to
15 present this gentleman to Mrs. Walker. She immediately achieved the introduction, and declared that she had never in her life seen anything so lovely as
Mrs. Walker's carriage-rug.

"I am glad you admire it," said this lady, smiling sweetly. "Will you get in
and let me put it over you?"

20   "Oh no, thank you," said Daisy. "I shall admire it much more as I see you
driving round with it."

"Do get in and drive with me!" said Mrs. Walker.

"That would be charming, but it's so enchanting just as I am!" and Daisy
gave a brilliant glance at the gentlemen on either side of her.

25   "It may be enchanting, dear child, but it is not the custom here," urged
Mrs. Walker, leaning forward in her victoria, with her hands devoutly clasped.

"Well, it ought to be, then!" said Daisy. "If I didn't walk I should expire."

"You should walk with your mother, dear," cried the lady from Geneva,
losing patience.

30   "With my mother, dear!" exclaimed the young girl. Winterbourne saw that
she scented interference. "My mother never walked ten steps in her life. And
then, you know," she added, with a laugh, "I am more than five years old."

"You are old enough to be more reasonable. You are old enough, dear Miss
Miller, to be talked about."

35   Daisy looked at Mrs. Walker, smiling intensely. "Talked about? What do
you mean?"

"Come into my carriage, and I will tell you."

Daisy turned her quickened glance again from one of the gentlemen beside
her to the other. Mr. Giovanelli was bowing to and fro, rubbing down his
40 gloves and laughing very agreeably; Winterbourne thought it a most unpleasant scene. "I don't think I want to know what you mean," said Daisy,
presently. "I don't think I should like it."

Winterbourne wished that Mrs. Walker would tuck in her carriage-rug and
drive away; but this lady did not enjoy being defied, as she afterwards told
45 him. "Should you prefer being thought a very reckless girl?" she demanded.

"Gracious!" exclaimed Daisy. She looked again at Mr. Giovanelli, then she
turned to Winterbourne. There was a little pink flush in her cheek; she was

tremendously pretty. "Does Mr. Winterbourne think," she asked slowly, smiling, throwing back her head and glancing at him from head to foot, "that —to save my reputation—I ought to get into the carriage?"

Winterbourne coloured; for an instant he hesitated greatly. It seemed so strange to hear her speak that way of her "reputation." But he himself, in fact, must speak in accordance with gallantry. The finest gallantry here was simply to tell her the truth; and the truth for Winterbourne—as the few indications I have been able to give have made him known to the reader— was that Daisy Miller should take Mrs. Walker's advice. He looked at her exquisite prettiness; and then said, very gently, "I think you should get into the carriage."

Daisy gave a violent laugh. "I never heard anything so stiff! If this is improper, Mrs. Walker," she pursued, "then I am all improper, and you must give me up. Good-bye; I hope you'll have a lovely ride!" and, with Mr. Giovanelli, who made a triumphantly obsequious salute, she turned away.

Mrs. Walker sat looking after her, and there were tears in Mrs. Walker's eyes. "Get in here, sir," she said to Winterbourne, indicating the place beside her. The young man answered that he felt bound to accompany Miss Miller; whereupon Mrs. Walker declared that if he refused her this favour she would never speak to him again. She was evidently in earnest. Winterbourne overtook Daisy and her companion, and, offering the young girl his hand, told her that Mrs. Walker had made an imperious claim upon his society. He expected that in answer she would say something rather free, something to commit herself still further to that "recklessness" from which Mrs. Walker had so charitably endeavoured to dissuade her. But she only shook his hand, hardly looking at him; while Mr. Giovanelli bade him farewell with a too emphatic flourish of the hat.

Winterbourne was not in the best possible humour as he took his seat in Mrs. Walker's victoria. "That was not clever of you," he said, candidly, while the vehicle mingled again with the throng of carriages.

"In such a case," his companion answered, "I don't wish to be clever; I wish to be *earnest!*"

"Well, your earnestness has only offended her and put her off."

"It has happened very well," said Mrs. Walker. "If she is so perfectly determined to compromise herself, the sooner one knows it the better; one can act accordingly."

"I suspect she meant no harm," Winterbourne rejoined.

"So I thought a month ago. But she has been going too far."

"What has she been doing?"

"Everything that is not done here. Flirting with any man she could pick up; sitting in corners with mysterious Italians; dancing all the evening with the same partners; receiving visits at eleven o'clock at night. Her mother goes away when visitors come."

"But her brother," said Winterbourne, laughing, "sits up till midnight."

"He must be edified by what he sees. I'm told that at their hotel every one is talking about her, and that a smile goes round among all the servants when a gentleman comes and asks for Miss Miller."

"The servants be hanged!" said Winterbourne, angrily. "The poor girl's only fault," he presently added, "is that she is very uncultivated."

"She is naturally indelicate," Mrs. Walker declared. "Take that example this morning. How long had you known her at Vevey?"

5   "A couple of days."

"Fancy, then, her making it a personal matter that you should have left the place!"

Winterbourne was silent for some moments; then he said, "I suspect, Mrs. Walker, that you and I have lived too long at Geneva!" And he added a re-
10   quest that she should inform him with what particular design she had made him enter her carriage.

"I wished to beg you to cease your relations with Miss Miller—not to flirt with her—to give her no further opportunity to expose herself—to let her alone, in short."

15   "I'm afraid I can't do that," said Winterbourne. "I like her extremely."

"All the more reason that you shouldn't help her to make a scandal."

"There shall be nothing scandalous in my attentions to her."

"There certainly will be in the way she takes them. But I have said what I had on my conscience," Mrs. Walker pursued. "If you wish to rejoin the
20   young lady I will put you down. Here, by-the-way, you have a chance."

The carriage was traversing that part of the Pincian Garden that overhangs the wall of Rome and overlooks the beautiful Villa Borghese. It is bordered by a large parapet, near which there are several seats. One of the seats, at a distance, was occupied by a gentleman and a lady, towards whom Mrs. Walker
25   gave a toss of her head. At the same moment these persons rose and walked towards the parapet. Winterbourne had asked the coachman to stop; he now descended from the carriage. His companion looked at him a moment in silence; then, while he raised his hat, she drove majestically away. Winterbourne stood there: he had turned his eyes towards Daisy and her cavalier.
30   They evidently saw no one; they were too deeply occupied with each other. When they reached the low garden-wall they stood a moment looking off at the great flat-topped pine-clusters of the Villa Borghese; then Giovanelli seated himself familiarly upon the broad ledge of the wall. The western sun in the opposite sky sent out a brilliant shaft through a couple of cloud-bars,
35   whereupon Daisy's companion took her parasol out of her hands and opened it. She came a little nearer, and he held the parasol over her; then, still holding it, he let it rest upon her shoulder, so that both of their heads were hidden from Winterbourne. This young man lingered a moment, then he began to walk. But he walked—not towards the couple with the parasol—towards the
40   residence of his aunt, Mrs. Costello.

He flattered himself on the following day that there was no smiling among the servants when he, at least, asked for Mrs. Miller at her hotel. This lady and her daughter, however, were not at home; and on the next day after, repeating his visit, Winterbourne again had the misfortune not to find them.
45   Mrs. Walker's party took place on the evening of the third day, and, in spite of the frigidity of his last interview with the hostess, Winterbourne was among the guests. Mrs. Walker was one of those American ladies who, while

residing abroad, make a point, in their own phrase, of studying European society; and she had on this occasion collected several specimens of her diversely-born fellow-mortals to serve, as it were, as text-books. When Winterbourne arrived, Daisy Miller was not there, but in a few moments he saw her mother come in alone, very shyly and ruefully. Mrs. Miller's hair above her   5 exposed-looking temples was more frizzled than ever. As she approached Mrs. Walker, Winterbourne also drew near.

"You see I've come all alone," said poor Mrs. Miller. "I'm so frightened I don't know what to do. It's the first time I've ever been to a party alone, especially in this country. I wanted to bring Randolph, or Eugenio, or some   10 one, but Daisy just pushed me off by myself. I ain't used to going round alone."

"And does not your daughter intend to favour us with her society?" demanded Mrs. Walker, impressively.

"Well, Daisy's all dressed," said Mrs. Miller, with that accent of the dis-   15 passionate, if not of the philosophic, historian with which she always recorded the current incidents of her daughter's career. "She got dressed on purpose before dinner. But she's got a friend of hers there; that gentleman—the Italian —that she wanted to bring. They've got going at the piano; it seems as if they couldn't leave off. Mr. Giovanelli sings splendidly. But I guess they'll come   20 before very long," concluded Mrs. Miller, hopefully.

"I'm sorry she should come—in that way," said Mrs. Walker.

"Well, I told her that there was no use in her getting dressed before dinner if she was going to wait three hours," responded Daisy's mamma. "I didn't see the use of her putting on such a dress as that to sit round with Mr. Giovanelli."   21

"This is most horrible!" said Mrs. Walker, turning away and addressing herself to Winterbourne. *"Elle s'affiche.* It's her revenge for my having ventured to remonstrate with her. When she comes I shall not speak to her."

Daisy came after eleven o'clock; but she was not, on such an occasion, a young lady to wait to be spoken to. She rustled forward in radiant loveliness,   30 smiling and chattering, carrying a large bouquet, and attended by Mr. Giovanelli. Every one stopped talking, and turned and looked at her. She came straight to Mrs. Walker. "I'm afraid you thought I never was coming, so I sent mother off to tell you. I wanted to make Mr. Giovanelli practise some things before he came; you know he sings beautifully, and I want you to ask   35 him to sing. This is Mr. Giovanelli; you know I introduced him to you; he's got the most lovely voice, and he knows the most charming set of songs. I made him go over them this evening on purpose; we had the greatest time at the hotel." Of all this Daisy delivered herself with the sweetest, brightest audibleness, looking now at her hostess and now round the room, while she   40 gave a series of little pats round her shoulders to the edges of her dress. "Is there any one I know?" she asked.

"I think every one knows you!" said Mrs. Walker, pregnantly, and she gave a very cursory greeting to Mr. Giovanelli. This gentleman bore himself gallantly. He smiled and bowed, and showed his white teeth; he curled his   45

---

27. Elle s'affiche—She's making a show of herself.

moustaches and rolled his eyes, and performed all the proper functions of a handsome Italian at an evening party. He sang very prettily half-a-dozen songs, though Mrs. Walker afterwards declared that she had been quite unable to find out who asked him. It was apparently not Daisy who had given him
5 his orders. Daisy sat at a distance from the piano; and though she had publicly, as it were, professed a high admiration for his singing, talked, not inaudibly, while it was going on.

"It's a pity these rooms are so small; we can't dance," she said to Winterbourne, as if she had seen him five minutes before.
10 "I am not sorry we can't dance," Winterbourne answered; "I don't dance."

"Of course you don't dance; you're too stiff," said Miss Daisy. "I hope you enjoyed your drive with Mrs. Walker!"

"No, I didn't enjoy it; I preferred walking with you."

"We paired off; that was much better," said Daisy. "But did you ever hear
15 anything so cool as Mrs. Walker's wanting me to get into her carriage and drop poor Mr. Giovanelli, and under the pretext that it was proper? People have different ideas! It would have been most unkind; he had been talking about that walk for ten days."

"He should not have talked about it at all," said Winterbourne; "he would
20 never have proposed to a young lady of this country to walk about the streets with him."

"About the streets?" cried Daisy, with her pretty stare. "Where, then, would he have proposed to her to walk? The Pincio is not the streets, either; and I, thank goodness, am not a young lady of this country. The young ladies of
25 this country have a dreadfully poky time of it, so far as I can learn; I don't see why I should change my habits for *them*."

"I am afraid your habits are those of a flirt," said Winterbourne, gravely.

"Of course they are," she cried, giving him her little smiling stare again. "I'm a fearful, frightful flirt! Did you ever hear of a nice girl that was not?
30 But I suppose you will tell me now that I am not a nice girl."

"You're a very nice girl; but I wish you would flirt with me, and me only," said Winterbourne.

"Ah! thank you—thank you very much; you are the last man I should think of flirting with. As I have had the pleasure of informing you, you are too
35 stiff."

"You say that too often," said Winterbourne.

Daisy gave a delighted laugh. "If I could have the sweet hope of making you angry, I should say it again."

"Don't do that; when I am angry I'm stiffer than ever. But if you won't
40 flirt with me, do cease, at least, to flirt with your friend at the piano; they don't understand that sort of thing here."

"I thought they understood nothing else!" exclaimed Daisy.

"Not in young unmarried women."

"It seems to me much more proper in young unmarried women than in old
45 married ones," Daisy declared.

"Well," said Winterbourne, "when you deal with natives you must go by the custom of the place. Flirting is a purely American custom; it doesn't exist here. So when you show yourself in public with Mr. Giovanelli, and without your mother—"

"Gracious! poor mother!" interposed Daisy.

"Though you may be flirting, Mr. Giovanelli is not; he means something else."

"He isn't preaching, at any rate," said Daisy with vivacity. "And if you want very much to know, we are neither of us flirting; we are too good friends for that; we are very intimate friends."

"Ah!" rejoined Winterbourne, "if you are in love with each other it is another affair."

She had allowed him up to this point to talk so frankly that he had no expectation of shocking her by this ejaculation; but she immediately got up, blushing visibly, and leaving him to exclaim mentally that little American flirts were the queerest creatures in the world. "Mr. Giovanelli, at least," she said, giving her interlocutor a single glance, "never says such very disagreeable things to me."

Winterbourne was bewildered; he stood staring. Mr. Giovanelli had finished singing; he left the piano and came over to Daisy. "Won't you come into the other room and have some tea?" he asked, bending before her with his ornamental smile.

Daisy turned to Winterbourne, beginning to smile again. He was still more perplexed, for this inconsequent smile made nothing clear, though it seemed to prove, indeed, that she had a sweetness and softness that reverted instinctively to the pardon of offences. "It has never occurred to Mr. Winterbourne to offer me any tea," she said, with her little tormenting manner.

"I have offered you advice," Winterbourne rejoined.

"I prefer weak tea!" cried Daisy, and she went off with the brilliant Giovanelli. She sat with him in the adjoining room, in the embrasure of the window, for the rest of the evening. There was an interesting performance at the piano, but neither of these young people gave heed to it. When Daisy came to take leave of Mrs. Walker, this lady conscientiously repaired the weakness of which she had been guilty at the moment of the young girl's arrival. She turned her back straight upon Miss Miller and left her to depart with what grace she might. Winterbourne was standing near the door; he saw it all. Daisy turned very pale and looked at her mother, but Mrs. Miller was humbly unconscious of any violation of the usual social forms. She appeared, indeed, to have felt an incongruous impulse to draw attention to her own striking observance of them. "Good-night, Mrs. Walker," she said; "we've had a beautiful evening. You see, if I let Daisy come to parties without me, I don't want her to go away without me." Daisy turned away, looking with a pale, grave face at the circle near the door; Winterbourne saw that, for the first moment, she was too much shocked and puzzled even for indignation. He on his side was greatly touched.

"That was very cruel," he said to Mrs. Walker.

"She never enters my drawing-room again!" replied his hostess.

Since Winterbourne was not to meet her in Mrs. Walker's drawing-room, he went as often as possible to Mrs. Miller's hotel. The ladies were rarely at

home; but when he found them the devoted Giovanelli was always present. Very often the brilliant little Roman was in the drawing-room with Daisy alone, Mrs. Miller being apparently constantly of the opinion that discretion is the better part of surveillance. Winterbourne noted, at first with surprise, that
5 Daisy on these occasions was never embarrassed or annoyed by his own entrance; but he very presently began to feel that she had no more surprises for him; the unexpected in her behaviour was the only thing to expect. She showed no displeasure at her *tête-à-tête* with Giovanelli being interrupted; she could chatter as freshly and freely with two gentlemen as with one; there was
10 always, in her conversation, the same odd mixture of audacity and puerility. Winterbourne remarked to himself that if she was seriously interested in Giovanelli, it was very singular that she should not take more trouble to preserve the sanctity of their interviews; and he liked her the more for her innocent-looking indifference and her apparently inexhaustible good humour. He
15 could hardly have said why, but she seemed to him a girl who would never be jealous. At the risk of exciting a somewhat derisive smile on the reader's part, I may affirm that with regard to the women who had hitherto interested him, it very often seemed to Winterbourne among the possibilities that, given certain contingencies, he should be afraid—literally afraid—of these ladies;
20 he had a pleasant sense that he should never be afraid of Daisy Miller. It must be added that this sentiment was not altogether flattering to Daisy; it was part of his conviction, or rather of his apprehension, that she would prove a very light young person.

But she was evidently very much interested in Giovanelli. She looked at him
25 whenever he spoke; she was perpetually telling him to do this and to do that; she was constantly "chaffing" and abusing him. She appeared completely to have forgotten that Winterbourne had said anything to displease her at Mrs. Walker's little party. One Sunday afternoon, having gone to St. Peter's with his aunt, Winterbourne perceived Daisy strolling about the great church in
30 company with the inevitable Giovanelli. Presently he pointed out the young girl and her cavalier to Mrs. Costello. This lady looked at them a moment through her eyeglass, and then she said,

"That's what makes you so pensive in these days, eh?"

"I had not the least idea I was pensive," said the young man.
35 "You are very much pre-occupied; you are thinking of something."

"And what is it," he asked, "that you accuse me of thinking of?"

"Of that young lady's—Miss Baker's, Miss Chandler's—what's her name?— Miss Miller's intrigue with that little barber's block."

"Do you call it an intrigue," Winterbourne asked—"an affair that goes on
40 with such peculiar publicity?"

"That's their folly," said Mrs. Costello, "it's not their merit."

"No," rejoined Winterbourne, with something of that pensiveness to which his aunt had alluded. "I don't believe that there is anything to be called an intrigue."
45 "I have heard a dozen people speak of it; they say she is quite carried away by him."

"They are certainly very intimate," said Winterbourne.

Mrs. Costello inspected the young couple again with her optical instrument. "He is very handsome. One easily sees how it is. She thinks him the most elegant man in the world, the finest gentleman. She has never seen anything like him; he is better even than the courier. It was the courier, probably, who introduced him; and if he succeeds in marrying the young lady, the courier 5 will come in for a magnificent commission."

"I don't believe she thinks of marrying him," said Winterbourne, "and I don't believe he hopes to marry her."

"You may be very sure she thinks of nothing. She goes on from day to day, from hour to hour, as they did in the Golden Age. I can imagine nothing 10 more vulgar. And at the same time," added Mrs. Costello, "depend upon it that she may tell you any moment that she is 'engaged.'"

"I think that is more than Giovanelli expects," said Winterbourne.

"Who is Giovanelli?"

"The little Italian. I have asked questions about him and learned something. 15 He is apparently a perfectly respectable little man. I believe he is, in a small way, a *cavaliere avvocato*. But he doesn't move in what are called the first circles. I think it is really not absolutely impossible that the courier introduced him. He is evidently immensely charmed with Miss Miller. If she thinks him the finest gentleman in the world, he, on his side, has never found himself in 20 personal contact with such splendour, such opulence, such expensiveness, as this young lady's. And then she must seem to him wonderfully pretty and interesting. I rather doubt that he dreams of marrying her. That must appear to him too impossible a piece of luck. He has nothing but his handsome face to offer, and there is a substantial Mr. Miller in that mysterious land of dollars. 25 Giovanelli knows that he hasn't a title to offer. If he were only a count or a *marchese!* He must wonder at his luck, at the way they have taken him up."

"He accounts for it by his handsome face, and thinks Miss Miller a young lady *qui se passe ses fantaisies!*" said Mrs. Costello.

"It is very true," Winterbourne pursued, "that Daisy and her mamma have 30 not yet risen to that stage of—what shall I call it?—of culture, at which the idea of catching a count or a *marchese* begins. I believe that they are intellectually incapable of that conception."

"Ah! but the *avvocato* can't believe it," said Mrs. Costello.

Of the observation excited by Daisy's "intrigue," Winterbourne gathered 35 that day at St. Peter's sufficient evidence. A dozen of the American colonists in Rome came to talk with Mrs. Costello, who sat on a little portable stool at the base of one of the great pilasters. The vesper service was going forward in splendid chants and organ-tones in the adjacent choir, and meanwhile, between Mrs. Costello and her friends, there was a great deal said about poor little 40 Miss Miller's going really "too far." Winterbourne was not pleased with what he heard; but when, coming out upon the great steps of the church, he saw Daisy, who had emerged before him, get into an open cab with her accomplice and roll away through the cynical streets of Rome, he could not deny to himself that she was going very far indeed. He felt very sorry for her—not exactly 45

17. **cavaliere avvocato**—that is, he is a lawyer. 29. **qui . . . fantaisies**—who is satisfying her caprices.

that he believed that she had completely lost her head, but because it was painful to hear so much that was pretty, and undefended, and natural, assigned to
a vulgar place among the categories of disorder. He made an attempt after this
to give a hint to Mrs. Miller. He met one day in the Corso a friend—a tourist
5 like himself, who had just come out of the Doria Palace, where he had been
walking through the beautiful gallery. His friend talked for a moment about
the superb portrait of Innocent X., by Velasquez, which hangs in one of the
cabinets of the palace, and then said, "And in the same cabinet, by-the-way, I
had the pleasure of contemplating a picture of a different kind—that pretty
10 American girl whom you pointed out to me last week." In answer to Winterbourne's inquiries, his friend narrated that the pretty American girl—prettier
than ever—was seated with a companion in the secluded nook in which the
great papal portrait was enshrined.

"Who was her companion?" asked Winterbourne.

15 "A little Italian with a bouquet in his button-hole. The girl is delightfully
pretty; but I thought I understood from you the other day that she was a
young lady *du meilleur monde*."

"So she is!" answered Winterbourne; and having assured himself that his
informant had seen Daisy and her companion but five minutes before, he
20 jumped into a cab and went to call on Mrs. Miller. She was at home; but she
apologized to him for receiving him in Daisy's absence.

"She's gone out somewhere with Mr. Giovanelli," said Mrs. Miller. "She's
always going round with Mr. Giovanelli."

"I have noticed that they are very intimate," Winterbourne observed.

25 "Oh, it seems as if they couldn't live without each other!" said Mrs. Miller.
"Well, he's a real gentleman, anyhow. I keep telling Daisy she's engaged!"

"And what does Daisy say?"

"Oh, she says she isn't engaged. But she might as well be!" this impartial
parent resumed. "She goes on as if she was. But I've made Mr. Giovanelli
30 promise to tell me, if *she* doesn't. I should want to write to Mr. Miller about
it—shouldn't you?"

Winterbourne replied that he certainly should; and the state of mind of
Daisy's mamma struck him as so unprecedented in the annals of parental
vigilance that he gave up as utterly irrelevant the attempt to place her upon her
35 guard.

After this Daisy was never at home, and Winterbourne ceased to meet her
at the houses of their common acquaintances because, as he perceived, these
shrewd people had quite made up their minds that she was going too far.
They ceased to invite her, and they intimated that they desired to express to
40 observant Europeans the great truth that, though Miss Daisy Miller was a
young American lady, her behaviour was not representative—was regarded by
her compatriots as abnormal. Winterbourne wondered how she felt about all
the cold shoulders that were turned towards her, and sometimes it annoyed
him to suspect that she did not feel at all. He said to himself that she was too
45 light and childish, too uncultivated and unreasoning, too provincial, to have

---

4. **Corso**—principal street of Rome. 7. **Velasquez**—Diego Rodriguez da Silva y Velásquez
(1599-1660), celebrated Spanish painter. 17. **du meilleur monde**—of the best society.

reflected upon her ostracism, or even to have perceived it. Then at other moments he believed that she carried about in her elegant and irresponsible little organism a defiant, passionate, perfectly observant consciousness of the impression she produced. He asked himself whether Daisy's defiance came from the consciousness of innocence, or from her being, essentially, a young 5 person of the reckless class. It must be admitted that holding one's self to a belief in Daisy's "innocence" came to seem to Winterbourne more and more a matter of fine-spun gallantry. As I have already had occasion to relate, he was angry at finding himself reduced to chopping logic about this young lady; he was vexed at his want of instinctive certitude as to how far her eccentricities 10 were generic, national, and how far they were personal. From either view of them he had somehow missed her, and now it was too late. She was "carried away" by Mr. Giovanelli.

A few days after his brief interview with her mother, he encountered her in that beautiful abode of flowering desolation known as the Palace of the 15 Caesars. The early Roman spring had filled the air with bloom and perfume, and the rugged surface of the Palatine was muffled with tender verdure. Daisy was strolling along the top of one of those great mounds of ruin that are embanked with mossy marble and paved with monumental inscriptions. It seemed to him that Rome had never been so lovely as just then. He stood 20 looking off at the enchanting harmony of line and colour that remotely encircles the city, inhaling the softly humid odours, and feeling the freshness of the year and the antiquity of the place reaffirm themselves in mysterious interfusion. It seemed to him, also, that Daisy had never looked so pretty; but this had been an observation of his whenever he met her. Giovanelli was 25 at her side, and Giovanelli, too, wore an aspect of even unwonted brilliancy.

"Well," said Daisy, "I should think you would be lonesome!"

"Lonesome?" asked Winterbourne.

"You are always going round by yourself. Can't you get any one to walk with you?" 30

"I am not so fortunate," said Winterbourne, "as your companion."

Giovanelli, from the first, had treated Winterbourne with distinguished politeness; he listened with a deferential air to his remarks; he laughed, punctiliously, at his pleasantries; he seemed disposed to testify to his belief that Winterbourne was a superior young man. He carried himself in no degree 35 like a jealous wooer; he had obviously a great deal of tact; he had no objection to your expecting a little humility of him. It even seemed to Winterbourne at times that Giovanelli would find a certain mental relief in being able to have a private understanding with him—to say to him, as an intelligent man, that, bless you, *he* knew how extraordinary was this young lady, and didn't flatter 40 himself with delusive—or, at least, *too* delusive—hopes of matrimony and dollars. On this occasion he strolled away from his companion to pluck a sprig of almond-blossom, which he carefully arranged in his button-hole.

"I know why you say that," said Daisy, watching Giovanelli. "Because you think I go round too much with *him*." And she nodded at her attendant. 45

15-16. **Palace of the Caesars**—near the Colosseum. 17. **Palatine**—one of the Seven Hills of Rome.

"Every one thinks so—if you care to know," said Winterbourne.

"Of course I care to know!" Daisy exclaimed, seriously. "But I don't believe it. They are only pretending to be shocked. They don't really care a straw what I do. Besides, I don't go round so much."

5   "I think you will find they do care. They will show it—disagreeably."

Daisy looked at him a moment. "How—disagreeably?"

"Haven't you noticed anything?" Winterbourne asked.

"I have noticed you. But I noticed you were as stiff as an umbrella the first time I saw you."

10   "You will find I am not so stiff as several others," said Winterbourne, smiling.

"How shall I find it?"

"By going to see the others."

"What will they do to me?"

"They will give you the cold shoulder. Do you know what that means?"

15   Daisy was looking at him intently; she began to colour.

"Do you mean as Mrs. Walker did the other night?"

"Exactly!" said Winterbourne.

She looked away at Giovanelli, who was decorating himself with his almond-blossom. Then, looking back at Winterbourne, "I shouldn't think you

20   would let people be so unkind!" she said.

"How can I help it?" he asked.

"I should think you would say something."

"I did say something;" and he paused a moment. "I say that your mother tells me that she believes you are engaged."

25   "Well, she does," said Daisy very simply.

Winterbourne began to laugh. "And does Randolph believe it?" he asked.

"I guess Randolph doesn't believe anything," said Daisy. Randolph's scepticism excited Winterbourne to further hilarity, and he observed that Giovanelli was coming back to them. Daisy, observing it too, addressed herself again to

30   her countryman. "Since you have mentioned it," she said, "I *am* engaged."

. . . Winterbourne looked at her; he had stopped laughing. "You don't believe it!" she added.

He was silent a moment; and then, "Yes, I believe it," he said.

"Oh, no, you don't!" she answered. "Well, then—I am not!"

35   The young girl and her cicerone were on their way to the gate of the enclosure, so that Winterbourne, who had but lately entered, presently took leave of them. A week afterwards he went to dine at a beautiful villa on the Caelian Hill, and, on arriving, dismissed his hired vehicle. The evening was charming, and he promised himself the satisfaction of walking home beneath

40   the Arch of Constantine and past the vaguely-lighted monuments of the Forum. There was a waning moon in the sky, and her radiance was not brilliant, but she was veiled in a thin cloud-curtain which seemed to diffuse and equalize it. When, on his return from the villa (it was eleven o'clock),

---

38. Caelian Hill—southeast of the Forum. **40. Arch of Constantine**—built A.D. 328 to mark the triumphal entry of Constantine into Rome after he had wrested control of the Empire from competing candidates. **41. Forum**—Forum Romanum, a place of public assembly in Rome between the Palatine and Capitoline hills.

Winterbourne approached the dusky circle of the Colosseum, it occurred to him, as a lover of the picturesque, that the interior, in the pale moonshine, would be well worth a glance. He turned aside and walked to one of the empty arches, near which, as he observed, an open carriage—one of the little Roman street-cabs—was stationed. Then he passed in, among the cavernous shadows 5 of the great structure, and emerged upon the clear and silent arena. The place had never seemed to him more impressive. One-half of the gigantic circus was in deep shade; the other was sleeping in the luminous dusk. As he stood there he began to murmur Byron's famous lines, out of "Manfred"; but before he had finished his quotation he remembered that if nocturnal meditations in the 10 Colosseum are recommended by the poets, they are deprecated by the doctors. The historic atmosphere was there, certainly; but the historic atmosphere, scientifically considered, was no better than a villa[i]nous miasma. Winterbourne walked to the middle of the arena, to take a more general glance, intending thereafter to make a hasty retreat. The great cross in the centre was 15 covered with shadow; it was only as he drew near it that he made it out distinctly. Then he saw that two persons were stationed upon the low steps which formed its base. One of these was a woman, seated; her companion was standing in front of her.

Presently the sound of the woman's voice came to him distinctly in the warm 20 night-air. "Well, he looks at us as one of the old lions or tigers may have looked at the Christian martyrs!" These were the words he heard, in the familiar accent of Miss Daisy Miller.

"Let us hope he is not very hungry," responded the ingenious Giovanelli. "He will have to take me first; you will serve for dessert!" 25

Winterbourne stopped, with a sort of horror; and, it must be added, with a sort of relief. It was as if a sudden illumination had been flashed upon the ambiguity of Daisy's behaviour, and the riddle had become easy to read. She was a young lady whom a gentleman need no longer be at pains to respect. He stood there looking at her—looking at her companion, and not reflecting 30 that though he saw them vaguely, he himself must have been more brightly visible. He felt angry with himself that he had bothered so much about the right way of regarding Miss Daisy Miller. Then, as he was going to advance again, he checked himself; not from the fear that he was doing her injustice, but from the sense of the danger of appearing unbecomingly exhilarated by 35 this sudden revulsion from cautious criticism. He turned away towards the entrance of the place; but, as he did so, he heard Daisy speak again.

"Why, it was Mr. Winterbourne! He saw me—and he cuts me!"

What a clever little reprobate she was, and how smartly she played at injured innocence! But he wouldn't cut her. Winterbourne came forward 40 again, and went towards the great cross. Daisy had got up; Giovanelli lifted his hat. Winterbourne had now begun to think simply of the craziness, from a sanitary point of view, of a delicate young girl lounging away the evening in this nest of malaria. What if she *were* a clever little reprobate? that was no

1. **Colosseum**—the Flavian amphitheatre in Rome, built by Vespasian and Titus in A.D. 75-80. It seated 87,000 spectators. The Arch of Constantine and the Colosseum are at the east end of the Forum. 9. **"Manfred"**—*Cf*. Act III, Scene iv, lines 270 ff.

reason for her dying of the *perniciosa.* "How long have you been here?" he asked, almost brutally.

Daisy, lovely in the flattering moonlight, looked at him a moment. Then— "All the evening," she answered, gently. . . . "I never saw anything so pretty."

5   "I am afraid," said Winterbourne, "that you will not think Roman fever very pretty. This is the way people catch it. I wonder," he added, turning to Giovanelli, "that you, a native Roman, should countenance such a terrible indiscretion."

"Ah," said the handsome native, "for myself I am not afraid."

10   "Neither am I—for you! I am speaking for this young lady."

Giovanelli lifted his well-shaped eyebrows and showed his brilliant teeth. But he took Winterbourne's rebuke with docility. "I told the signorina it was a grave indiscretion; but when was the signorina ever prudent?"

"I never was sick, and I don't mean to be!" the signorina declared. "I don't
15   look like much, but I'm healthy! I was bound to see the Colosseum by moonlight; I shouldn't have wanted to go home without that; and we have had the most beautiful time, haven't we, Mr. Giovanelli? If there has been any danger, Eugenio can give me some pills. He has got some splendid pills."

"I should advise you," said Winterbourne, "to drive home as fast as possible
20   and take one!"

"What you say is very wise," Giovanelli rejoined. "I will go and make sure the carriage is at hand." And he went forward rapidly.

Daisy followed with Winterbourne. He kept looking at her; she seemed not in the least embarrassed. Winterbourne said nothing; Daisy chattered about the
25   beauty of the place. "Well, I *have* seen the Colosseum by moonlight!" she exclaimed. "That's one good thing." Then, noticing Winterbourne's silence, she asked him why he didn't speak. He made no answer; he only began to laugh. They passed under one of the dark archways; Giovanelli was in front with the carriage. Here Daisy stopped a moment, looking at the young Ameri-
30   can. "*Did* you believe I was engaged the other day?" she asked.

"It doesn't matter what I believed the other day," said Winterbourne, still laughing.

"Well, what do you believe now?"

"I believe that it makes very little difference whether you are engaged or
35   not!"

He felt the young girl's pretty eyes fixed upon him through the thick gloom of the archway; she was apparently going to answer. But Giovanelli hurried her forward. "Quick! quick!" he said; "if we get in by midnight we are quite safe."

40   Daisy took her seat in the carriage, and the fortunate Italian placed himself beside her. "Don't forget Eugenio's pills!" said Winterbourne, as he lifted his hat.

"I don't care," said Daisy, in a little strange tone, "whether I have Roman fever or not!" Upon this the cab-driver cracked his whip, and they rolled
45   away over the desultory patches of the antique pavement.

    1. perniciosa—Italian for malaria.

Winterbourne—to do him justice, as it were—mentioned to no one that he
had encountered Miss Miller, at midnight, in the Colosseum with a gentleman;
but, nevertheless, a couple of days later, the fact of her having been there
under these circumstances was known to every member of the little American
circle, and commented accordingly. Winterbourne reflected that they had of   5
course known it at the hotel, and that, after Daisy's return, there had been an
exchange of remarks between the porter and the cab-driver. But the young
man was conscious, at the same moment, that it had ceased to be a matter of
serious regret to him that the little American flirt should be "talked about"
by low-minded menials. These people, a day or two later, had serious informa- 10
tion to give: the little American flirt was alarmingly ill. Winterbourne, when
the rumour came to him, immediately went to the hotel for more news. He
found that two or three charitable friends had preceded him, and that they
were being entertained in Mrs. Miller's salon by Randolph.

"It's going round at night," said Randolph—"that's what made her sick.   15
She's always going round at night. I shouldn't think she'd want to—it's so
plaguy dark. You can't see anything here at night, except when there's a moon!
In America there's always a moon!" Mrs. Miller was invisible; she was now,
at least, giving her daughter the advantage of her society. It was evident that
Daisy was dangerously ill.   20

Winterbourne went often to ask for news of her, and once he saw Mrs.
Miller, who, though deeply alarmed, was—rather to his surprise—perfectly
composed, and, as it appeared, a most efficient and judicious nurse. She talked
a good deal about Dr. Davis, but Winterbourne paid her the compliment of
saying to himself that she was not, after all, such a monstrous goose. "Daisy   25
spoke of you the other day," she said to him. "Half the time she doesn't know
what she's saying, but that time I think she did. She gave me a message; she
told me to tell you—she told me to tell you that she never was engaged to that
handsome Italian. I am sure I am very glad; Mr. Giovanelli hasn't been near
us since she was taken ill. I thought he was so much of a gentleman; but I   30
don't call that very polite! A lady told me that he was afraid I was angry with
him for taking Daisy round at night. Well, so I am; but I suppose he knows
I'm a lady. I would scorn to scold him. Anyway, she says she's not engaged.
I don't know why she wanted you to know; but she said to me three times,
'Mind you tell Mr. Winterbourne.' And then she told me to ask if you remem- 35
bered the time you went to that castle in Switzerland. But I said I wouldn't
give any such messages as that. Only, if she is not engaged, I'm sure I'm
glad to know it."

But, as Winterbourne had said, it mattered very little. A week after this
the poor girl died; it had been a terrible case of the fever. Daisy's grave was   40
in the little Protestant cemetery, in an angle of the wall of imperial Rome,
beneath the cypresses and the thick spring-flowers. Winterbourne stood there
beside it, with a number of other mourners—a number larger than the scandal excited by the young lady's career would have led you to expect. Near
him stood Giovanelli, who came nearer still before Winterbourne turned away. 45
Giovanelli was very pale; on this occasion he had no flower in his button-

hole; he seemed to wish to say something. At last he said, "She was the most beautiful young lady I ever saw, and the most amiable." And then he added in a moment, "and she was the most innocent."

5 Winterbourne looked at him, and presently repeated his words, "And the most innocent?"

"The most innocent!"

Winterbourne felt sore and angry. "Why the devil," he asked, "did you take her to that fatal place?"

10 Mr. Giovanelli's urbanity was apparently imperturbable. He looked on the ground a moment, and then he said, "For myself, I had no fear; and she wanted to go."

"That was no reason!" Winterbourne declared.

The subtle Roman again dropped his eyes. "If she had lived, I should have got nothing. She would never have married me, I am sure."

15 "She would never have married you?"

"For a moment I hoped so. But no, I am sure."

Winterbourne listened to him; he stood staring at the raw protuberance among the April daisies. When he turned away again, Mr. Giovanelli with his light, slow step, had retired.

20 Winterbourne almost immediately left Rome; but the following summer he again met his aunt, Mrs. Costello, at Vevey. Mrs. Costello was fond of Vevey. In the interval Winterbourne had often thought of Daisy Miller and her mystifying manners. One day he spoke of her to his aunt—said it was on his conscience that he had done her injustice.

25 "I am sure I don't know," said Mrs. Costello. "How did your injustice affect her?"

"She sent me a message before her death which I didn't understand at the time. But I have understood it since. She would have appreciated one's esteem."

30 "Is that a modest way," asked Mrs. Costello, "of saying that she would have reciprocated one's affection?"

Winterbourne offered no answer to this question; but he presently said, "You were right in that remark that you made last summer. I was booked to make a mistake. I have lived too long in foreign parts."

35 Nevertheless, he went back to live at Geneva, whence there continue to come the most contradictory accounts of his motives of sojourn: a report that he is "studying" hard—an intimation that he is much interested in a very clever foreign lady.

THE ART OF FICTION

Appeared originally in *Longmans' Magazine,* September, 1884; in 1885 it was published with Walter Besant's "The Art of Fiction" in book form, and in 1888 was included in *Partial Portraits.* Robert Louis Stevenson discussed this essay in "A Humble Remonstrance," reprinted in *Memories and Portraits.* The text is that of 1888.

I SHOULD not have affixed so comprehensive a title to these few remarks, necessarily wanting in any completeness upon a subject the full consideration of which would carry us far, did I not seem to discover a pretext for my temerity in the interesting pamphlet lately published under this name by Mr. Walter Besant. Mr. Besant's lecture at the Royal Institution—the orig-   5
inal form of his pamphlet—appears to indicate that many persons are interested in the art of fiction, and are not indifferent to such remarks, as those who practise it may attempt to make about it. I am therefore anxious not to lose the benefit of this favourable association, and to edge in a few words under cover of the attention which Mr. Besant is sure to have excited. There   10
is something very encouraging in his having put into form certain of his ideas on the mystery of story-telling.

It is a proof of life and curiosity—curiosity on the part of the brotherhood of novelists as well as on the part of their readers. Only a short time ago it might have been supposed that the English novel was not what the French   15
call *discutable*. It had no air of having a theory, a conviction, a consciousness of itself behind it—of being the expression of an artistic faith, the result of choice and comparison. I do not say it was necessarily the worse for that: it would take much more courage than I possess to intimate that the form of novel as Dickens and Thackeray (for instance) saw it had any taint of in-   20
completeness. It was, however, *naïf* (if I may help myself out with another French word); and evidently if it be destined to suffer in any way for having lost its *naïveté* it has now an idea of making sure of the corresponding advantages. During the period I have alluded to there was a comfortable good-humoured feeling abroad that a novel is a novel, as a pudding is a pudding,   25
and that our only business with it could be to swallow it. But within a year or two, for some reason or other, there have been signs of returning animation—the era of discussion would appear to have been to a certain extent opened. Art lives upon discussion, upon experiment, upon curiosity, upon variety of attempt, upon the exchange of views and the comparison of stand-   30
points; and there is a presumption that those times when no one has anything particular to say about it, and has no reason to give for practice or preference, though they may be times of honour, are not times of development —are times, possibly, even a little of dulness. The successful application of any art is a delightful spectacle, but the theory too is interesting; and though there   35
is a great deal of the latter without the former I suspect there has never been a genuine success that has not had a latent core of conviction. Discussion, suggestion, formulation, these things are fertilizing when they are frank and sincere. Mr. Besant has set an excellent example in saying what he thinks, for his part, about the way in which fiction should be written, as well as   40
about the way in which it should be published; for his view of the "art," carried on into an appendix, covers that too. Other labourers in the same field will doubtless take up the argument, they will give it the light of their experience, and the effect will surely be to make our interest in the novel a little more what it had for some time threatened to fail to be—a serious, active, in-   45

---

5. **Besant**—Sir Walter Besant (1836-1901), English novelist and critic. The lecture had been delivered at the Royal Institution, Apr. 25, 1884. 16. **discutable**—debatable.

quiring interest, under protection of which this delightful study may, in moments of confidence, venture to say a little more what it thinks of itself.

It must take itself seriously for the public to take it so. The old superstition
about fiction being "wicked" has doubtless died out in England; but the spirit
5 of it lingers in a certain oblique regard directed toward any story which does
not more or less admit that it is only a joke. Even the most jocular novel feels
in some degree the weight of the proscription that was formerly directed
against literary levity: the jocularity does not always succeed in passing for
orthodoxy. It is still expected, though perhaps people are ashamed to say it,
10 that a production which is after all only a "make-believe" (for what else is a
"story"?) shall be in some degree apologetic—shall renounce the pretension
of attempting really to represent life. This, of course, any sensible, wide-awake
story declines to do, for it quickly perceives that the tolerance granted to it
on such a condition is only an attempt to stifle it disguised in the form of
15 generosity. The old evangelical hostility to the novel, which was as explicit
as it was narrow, and which regarded it as little less favourable to our immortal part than a stage-play, was in reality far less insulting. The only reason
for the existence of a novel is that it does attempt to represent life. When it
relinquishes this attempt, the same attempt that we see on the canvas of the
20 painter, it will have arrived at a very strange pass. It is not expected of the
picture that it will make itself humble in order to be forgiven; and the analogy
between the art of the painter and the art of the novelist is, so far as I am
able to see, complete. Their inspiration is the same, their process (allowing
for the different quality of the vehicle) is the same, their success is the same.
25 They may learn from each other, they may explain and sustain each other.
Their cause is the same, and the honour of one is the honour of another.
The Mahometans think a picture an unholy thing, but it is a long time since
any Christian did, and it is therefore the more odd that in the Christian mind
the traces (dissimulated though they may be) of a suspicion of the sister art
30 should linger to this day. The only effectual way to lay it to rest is to em-
phasise the analogy to which I just alluded—to insist on the fact that as the
picture is reality, so the novel is history. That is the only general description
(which does it justice) that we may give of the novel. But history also is allowed to represent life; it is not, any more than painting, expected to apolo-
35 gize. The subject-matter of fiction is stored up likewise in documents and
records, and if it will not give itself away, as they say in California, it must
speak with assurance, with the tone of the historian. Certain accomplished
novelists have a habit of giving themselves away which must often bring tears
to the eyes of people who take their fiction seriously. I was lately struck, in
40 reading over many pages of Anthony Trollope, with his want of discretion in
this particular. In a digression, a parenthesis or an aside, he concedes to the
reader that he and this trusting friend are only "making believe." He admits
that the events he narrates have not really happened, and that he can give
his narrative any turn the reader may like best. Such a betrayal of a sacred
45 office seems to me, I confess, a terrible crime; it is what I mean by the atti

40. Trollope—See note 30, p. 1268.

tude of apology, and it shocks me every whit as much in Trollope as it would
have shocked me in Gibbon or Macaulay. It implies that the novelist is less
occupied in looking for the truth (the truth, of course I mean, that he assumes, the premises that we must grant him, whatever they may be) than
the historian, and in doing so it deprives him at a stroke of all his standing- 5
room. To represent and illustrate the past, the actions of men, is the task of
either writer, and the only difference that I can see is, in proportion as he
succeeds, to the honour of the novelist, consisting as it does in his having
more difficulty in collecting his evidence, which is so far from being purely
literary. It seems to me to give him a great character, the fact that he has at 10
once so much in common with the philosopher and the painter; this double
analogy is a magnificent heritage.

It is of all this evidently that Mr. Besant is full when he insists upon the
fact that fiction is one of the *fine* arts, deserving in its turn of all the honours
and emoluments that have hitherto been reserved for the successful profes- 15
sion of music, poetry, painting, architecture. It is impossible to insist too much
on so important a truth, and the place that Mr. Besant demands for the work
of the novelist may be represented, a trifle less abstractly, by saying that he
demands not only that it shall be reputed artistic, but that it shall be reputed
very artistic indeed. It is excellent that he should have struck this note, for his 20
doing so indicates that there was need of it, that his proposition may be to
many people a novelty. One rubs one's eyes at the thought; but the rest of
Mr. Besant's essay confirms the revelation. I suspect in truth that it would be
possible to confirm it still further, and that one would not be far wrong in
saying that in addition to the people to whom it has never occurred that a 25
novel ought to be artistic, there are a great many others who, if this principle
were urged upon them, would be filled with an indefinable mistrust. They
would find it difficult to explain their repugnance, but it would operate
strongly to put them on their guard. "Art," in our Protestant communities,
where so many things have got so strangely twisted about, is supposed in 30
certain circles to have some vague injurious effect upon those who make it an
important consideration, who let it weigh in the balance. It is assumed to be
opposed in some mysterious manner to morality, to amusement, to instruction. When it is embodied in the work of the painter (the sculptor is another
affair!) you know what it is: it stands there before you, in the honesty of 35
pink and green and a gilt frame; you can see the worst of it at a glance,
and you can be on your guard. But when it is introduced into literature it becomes more insidious—there is danger of its hurting you before you know
it. Literature should be either instructive or amusing, and there is in many
minds an impression that these artistic preoccupations, the search for form, 40
contribute to neither end, interfere indeed with both. They are too frivolous
to be edifying, and too serious to be diverting; and they are moreover priggish
and paradoxical and superfluous. That, I think, represents the manner in
which the latent thought of many people who read novels as an exercise in
skipping would explain itself if it were to become articulate. They would 45
argue, of course, that a novel ought to be "good," but they would interpret
this term in a fashion of their own, which indeed would vary considerably

from one critic to another. One would say that being good means representing virtuous and aspiring characters placed in prominent positions; another
would say that it depends on a "happy ending," on a distribution at the last of
prizes, pensions, husbands, wives, babies, millions, appended paragraphs, and
5 cheerful remarks. Another still would say that it means being full of incident
and movement, so that we shall wish to jump ahead, to see who was the
mysterious stranger, and if the stolen will was ever found, and shall not be
distracted from this pleasure by any tiresome analysis or "description." But
they would all agree that the "artistic" idea would spoil some of their fun.
10 One would hold it accountable for all the description, another would see it
revealed in the absence of sympathy. Its hostility to a happy ending would be
evident, and it might even in some cases render any ending at all impossible.
The "ending" of a novel is, for many persons, like that of a good dinner, a
course of dessert and ices, and the artist in fiction is regarded as a sort of
15 meddlesome doctor who forbids agreeable aftertastes. It is therefore true that
this conception of Mr. Besant's of the novel as a superior form encounters
not only a negative but a positive indifference. It matters little that as a work
of art it should really be as little or as much of its essence to supply happy
endings, sympathetic characters, and an objective tone, as if it were a work
20 of mechanics: the association of ideas, however incongruous, might easily be
too much for it if an eloquent voice were not sometimes raised to call attention to the fact that it is at once as free and as serious a branch of literature
as any other.

Certainly this might sometimes be doubted in presence of the enormous
25 number of works of fiction that appeal to the credulity of our generation,
for it might easily seem that there could be no great character in a com-
modity so quickly and easily produced. It must be admitted that good novels
are much compromised by bad ones, and that the field at large suffers discredit from overcrowding. I think, however, that this injury is only super-
30 ficial, and that the superabundance of written fiction proves nothing against
the principle itself. It has been vulgarised, like all other kinds of literature,
like everything else to-day, and it has proved more than some kinds accessible
to vulgarisation. But there is as much difference as there ever was between
a good novel and a bad one: the bad is swept with all the daubed canvases
35 and spoiled marble into some unvisited limbo, or infinite rubbish-yard beneath
the back-windows of the world, and the good subsists and emits its light and
stimulates our desire for perfection. As I shall take the liberty of making but
a single criticism of Mr. Besant, whose tone is so full of love of his art, I may as
well have done with it at once. He seems to me to mistake, in attempting
40 to say so definitely beforehand, what sort of an affair the good novel will be.
To indicate the danger of such an error as that has been the purpose of these
few pages; to suggest that certain traditions on the subject, applied *a priori,*
have already had much to answer for, and that the good health of an art
which undertakes so immediately to reproduce life must demand that it be
45 perfectly free. It lives upon exercise, and the very meaning of exercise is freedom. The only obligation to which in advance we may hold a novel, without
incurring the accusation of being arbitrary, is that it be interesting. That gen-

eral responsibility rests upon it, but it is the only one I can think of. The
ways in which it is at liberty to accomplish this result (of interesting us)
strike me as innumerable, and such as can only suffer from being marked out
or fenced in by prescription. They are as various as the temperament of man,
and they are successful in proportion as they reveal a particular mind, differ-   5
ent from others. A novel is in its broadest definition a personal, a direct impression of life: that, to begin with, constitutes its value, which is greater or
less according to the intensity of the impression. But there will be no intensity at all, and therefore no value, unless there is freedom to feel and say.
The tracing of a line to be followed, of a tone to be taken, of a form to be   10
filled out, is a limitation of that freedom and a suppression of the very thing
that we are most curious about. The form, it seems to me, is to be appreciated
after the fact: then the author's choice has been made, his standard has been
indicated; then we can follow lines and directions and compare tones and
resemblances. Then in a word we can enjoy one of the most charming of   15
pleasures, we can estimate quality, we can apply the test of execution. The
execution belongs to the author alone; it is what is most personal to him,
and we measure him by that. The advantage, the luxury, as well as the torment and responsibility of the novelist, is that there is no limit to what he
may attempt as an executant—no limit to his possible experiments, efforts,   20
discoveries, successes. Here it is especially that he works, step by step, like
his brother of the brush, of whom we may always say that he has painted his
picture in a manner best known to himself. His manner is his secret, not
necessarily a jealous one. He cannot disclose it as a general thing if he would;
he would be at a loss to teach it to others. I say this with a due recollection   25
of having insisted on the community of method of the artist who paints a
picture and the artist who writes a novel. The painter *is* able to teach the
rudiments of his practice, and it is possible, from the study of good work
(granted the aptitude), both to learn how to paint and to learn how to write.
Yet it remains true, without injury to the *rapprochement,* that the literary   30
artist would be obliged to say to his pupil much more than the other, "Ah,
well, you must do it as you can!" It is a question of degree, a matter of delicacy. If there are exact sciences, there are also exact arts, and the grammar
of painting is so much more definite that it makes the difference.

 I ought to add, however, that if Mr. Besant says at the beginning of his   35
essay that the "laws of fiction may be laid down and taught with as much
precision and exactness as the laws of harmony, perspective, and proportion,"
he mitigates what might appear to be an extravagance by applying his remark to "general" laws, and by expressing most of these rules in a manner with
which it would certainly be unaccommodating to disagree. That the novelist   40
must write from his experience, that his "characters must be real and such as
might be met with in actual life;" that "a young lady brought up in a quiet
country village should avoid descriptions of garrison life," and "a writer
whose friends and personal experiences belong to the lower middle-class
should carefully avoid introducing his characters into society;" that one should   45

30. **rapprochement**—sympathetic approach.

enter one's notes in a common-place book; that one's figures should be clear
in outline; that making them clear by some trick of speech or of carriage is
a bad method, and "describing them at length" is a worse one; that English
Fiction should have a "conscious moral purpose;" that "it is almost impossible
5   to estimate too highly the value of careful workmanship—that is, of style;"
that "the most important point of all is the story," that "the story is everything:"
these are principles with most of which it is surely impossible not to sympathise. That remark about the lower middle-class writer and his knowing his
place is perhaps rather chilling; but for the rest I should find it difficult to
10 dissent from any one of these recommendations. At the same time, I should find
it difficult positively to assent to them, with the exception, perhaps, of the
injunction as to entering one's notes in a common-place book. They scarcely
seem to me to have the quality that Mr. Besant attributes to the rules of the
novelist—the "precision and exactness" of "the laws of harmony, perspective,
15 and proportion." They are suggestive, they are even inspiring, but they are
not exact, though they are doubtless as much so as the case admits of: which
is a proof of that liberty of interpretation for which I just contended. For the
value of these different injunctions—so beautiful and so vague—is wholly in
the meaning one attaches to them. The characters, the situation, which strike
20 one as real will be those that touch and interest one most, but the measure
of reality is very difficult to fix. The reality of Don Quixote or of Mr. Micawber is a very delicate shade; it is a reality so coloured by the author's vision
that, vivid as it may be, one would hesitate to propose it as a model: one
would expose one's self to some very embarrassing questions on the part of a
25 pupil. It goes without saying that you will not write a good novel unless you
possess the sense of reality; but it will be difficult to give you a recipe for
calling that sense into being. Humanity is immense, and reality has a myriad
forms; the most one can affirm is that some of the flowers of fiction have
the odour of it, and others have not; as for telling you in advance how your
30 nosegay should be composed, that is another affair. It is equally excellent and
inconclusive to say that one must write from experience; to our supposititious
aspirant such a declaration might savour of mockery. What kind of experience is intended, and where does it begin and end? Experience is never limited, and it is never complete; it is an immense sensibility, a kind of huge
35 spiderweb of the finest silken threads suspended in the chamber of consciousness, and catching every air-borne particle in its tissue. It is the very atmosphere of the mind; and when the mind is imaginative—much more when it
happens to be that of a man of genius—it takes to itself the faintest hints
of life, it converts the very pulses of the air into revelations. The young lady
40 living in a village has only to be a damsel upon whom nothing is lost to
make it quite unfair (as it seems to me) to declare to her that she shall have
nothing to say about the military. Greater miracles have been seen than that,
imagination assisting, she should speak the truth about some of these gentlemen. I remember an English novelist, a woman of genius, telling me that
45 she was much commended for the impression she had managed to give in

21. **Micawber**—comic character in *David Copperfield*. **Don Quixote** is of course in
Cervantes' novel.

one of her tales of the nature and way of life of the French Protestant youth. She had been asked where she learned so much about this recondite being, she had been congratulated on her peculiar opportunities. These opportunities consisted in her having once, in Paris, as she ascended a staircase, passed an open door where, in the household of a *pasteur,* some of the young Protes- 5 tants were seated at table round a finished meal. The glimpse made a picture; it lasted only a moment, but that moment was experience. She had got her direct personal impression, and she turned out her type. She knew what youth was, and what Protestantism; she also had the advantage of having seen what it was to be French, so that she converted these ideas into a con- 10 crete image and produced a reality. Above all, however, she was blessed with the faculty which when you give it an inch takes an ell, and which for the artist is a much greater source of strength than any accident of residence or of place in the social scale. The power to guess the unseen from the seen, to trace the implication of things, to judge the whole piece by the pattern, the 15 condition of feeling life in general so completely that you are well on your way to knowing any particular corner of it—this cluster of gifts may almost be said to constitute experience, and they occur in country and in town, and in the most differing stages of education. If experience consists of impres- sions, it may be said that impressions *are* experience, just as (have we not 20 seen it?) they are the very air we breathe. Therefore, if I should certainly say to a novice, "Write from experience and experience only," I should feel that this was rather a tantalising monition if I were not careful immediately to add, "Try to be one of the people on whom nothing is lost!"

I am far from intending by this to minimise the importance of exactness— 25 of truth of detail. One can speak best from one's own taste, and I may there- fore venture to say that the air of reality (solidity of specification) seems to me to be the supreme virtue of a novel—the merit on which all its other merits (including that conscious moral purpose of which Mr. Besant speaks) helplessly and submissively depend. If it be not there they are all as nothing, 30 and if these be there, they owe their effect to the success with which the author has produced the illusion of life. The cultivation of this success, the study of this exquisite process, form, to my taste, the beginning and the end of the art of the novelist. They are his inspiration, his despair, his reward, his torment, his delight. It is here in very truth that he competes with life; 35 it is here that he competes with his brother the painter in *his* attempt to ren- der the look of things, the look that conveys their meaning, to catch the colour, the relief, the expression, the surface, the substance of the human spec- tacle. It is in regard to this that Mr. Besant is well inspired when he bids him take notes. He cannot possibly take too many, he cannot possibly take 40 enough. All life solicits him, and to "render" the simplest surface, to produce the most momentary illusion, is a very complicated business. His case would be easier, and the rule would be more exact, if Mr. Besant had been able to tell him what notes to take. But this, I fear, he can never learn in any man- ual; it is the business of his life. He has to take a great many in order to se- 45

5. **pasteur**—pastor.

lect a few, he has to work them up as he can, and even the guides and philosophers who might have most to say to him must leave him alone when it
comes to the application of precepts, as we leave the painter in communion
with his palette. That his characters "must be clear in outline," as Mr. Besant
5 says—he feels that down to his boots; but how he shall make them so is a
secret between his good angel and himself. It would be absurdly simple if
he could be taught that a great deal of "description" would make them so, or
that on the contrary the absence of description and the cultivation of dialogue,
or the absence of dialogue and the multiplication of "incident," would rescue
10 him from his difficulties. Nothing, for instance, is more possible than that
he be of a turn of mind for which this odd, literal opposition of description
and dialogue, incident and description, has little meaning and light. People
often talk of these things as if they had a kind of internecine distinctness, instead of melting into each other at every breath, and being intimately asso-
15 ciated parts of one general effort of expression. I cannot imagine composition
existing in a series of blocks, nor conceive, in any novel worth discussing at
all, of a passage of description that is not in its intention narrative, a passage
of dialogue that is not in its intention descriptive, a touch of truth of any
sort that does not partake of the nature of incident, or an incident that de-
20 rives its interest from any other source than the general and only source of
the success of a work of art—that of being illustrative. A novel is a living
thing, all one and continuous, like any other organism, and in proportion
as it lives will it be found, I think, that in each of the parts there is something of each of the other parts. The critic who over the close texture of a
25 finished work shall pretend to trace a geography of items will mark some
frontiers as artificial, I fear, as any that have been known to history. There is
an old-fashioned distinction between the novel of character and the novel of
incident which must have cost many a smile to the intending fabulist who
was keen about his work. It appears to me as little to the point as the equally
30 celebrated distinction between the novel and the romance—to answer as little
to any reality. There are bad novels and good novels, as there are bad pictures
and good pictures; but that is the only distinction in which I see any meaning, and I can as little imagine speaking of a novel of character as I can imagine speaking of a picture of character. When one says picture one says of
35 character, when one says novel one says of incident, and the terms may be
transposed at will. What is character but the determination of incident?
What is incident but the illustration of character? What is either a picture or
a novel that is *not* of character? What else do we seek in it and find in it? It
is an incident for a woman to stand up with her hand resting on a table
40 and look at you in a certain way; or if it be not an incident I think it will be
hard to say what it is. At the same time it is an expression of character. If
you say you don't see it (character in *that—allons donc!*), this is exactly what
the artist who has reasons of his own for thinking he *does* see it undertakes
to show you. When a young man makes up his mind that he has not faith
45 enough after all to enter the church as he intended, that is an incident, though

42. allons donc!—come, come!

you may not hurry to the end of the chapter to see whether perhaps he doesn't change once more. I do not say that these are extraordinary or startling incidents. I do not pretend to estimate the degree of interest proceeding from them, for this will depend upon the skill of the painter. It sounds almost puerile to say that some incidents are intrinsically much more important than 5 others, and I need not take this precaution after having professed my sympathy for the major ones in remarking that the only classification of the novel that I can understand is into that which has life and that which has it not.

The novel and the romance, the novel of incident and that of character—these clumsy separations appear to me to have been made by critics and read- 10 ers for their own convenience, and to help them out of some of their occasional predicaments, but to have little reality or interest for the producer, from whose point of view it is of course that we are attempting to consider the art of fiction. The case is the same with another shadowy category which Mr. Besant apparently is disposed to set up—that of the "modern English 15 novel;" unless indeed it be that in this matter he has fallen into an accidental confusion of standpoints. It is not quite clear whether he intends the remarks in which he alludes to it to be didactic or historical. It is as difficult to suppose a person intending to write a modern English as to suppose him writing an ancient English novel: that is a label which begs the question. One writes 20 the novel, one paints the picture, of one's language and of one's time, and calling it modern English will not, alas! make the difficult task any easier. No more, unfortunately, will calling this or that work of one's fellow-artist a romance—unless it be, of course, simply for the pleasantness of the thing, as for instance when Hawthorne gave this heading to his story of *Blithedale*. 25 The French, who have brought the theory of fiction to remarkable completeness, have but one name for the novel, and have not attempted smaller things in it, that I can see, for that. I can think of no obligation to which the "romancer" would not be held equally with the novelist; the standard of execution is equally high for each. Of course it is of execution that we are 30 talking—that being the only point of a novel that is open to contention. This is perhaps too often lost sight of, only to produce interminable confusions and cross-purposes. We must grant the artist his subject, his idea, his *donnée*: our criticism is applied only to what he makes of it. Naturally I do not mean that we are bound to like it or find it interesting: in case we do not our 35 course is perfectly simple—to let it alone. We may believe that of a certain idea even the most sincere novelist can make nothing at all, and the event may perfectly justify our belief; but the failure will have been a failure to execute, and it is in the execution that the fatal weakness is recorded. If we pretend to respect the artist at all, we must allow him his freedom of choice, 40 in the face, in particular cases, of innumerable presumptions that the choice will not fructify. Art derives a considerable part of its beneficial exercise from flying in the face of presumptions, and some of the most interesting experiments of which it is capable are hidden in the bosom of common things. Gustave Flaubert has written a story about the devotion of a servant-girl to a 45

9. **novel, romance**—*Cf.* the distinction in Hawthorne's "Preface" to *The House of Seven Gables*. 33. **donnée**—conception, theme. 45. **Flaubert**—*A Simple Heart*.

parrot, and the production, highly finished as it is, cannot on the whole be called a success. We are perfectly free to find it flat, but I think it might have been interesting; and I, for my part, am extremely glad he should have written it; it is a contribution to our knowledge of what can be done—or what
5 cannot. Ivan Turgénieff has written a tale about a deaf and dumb serf and a lap-dog, and the thing is touching, loving, a little masterpiece. He struck the note of life where Gustave Flaubert missed it—he flew in the face of a presumption and achieved a victory.

Nothing, of course, will ever take the place of the good old fashion of
10 "liking" a work of art or not liking it: the most improved criticism will not abolish that primitive, that ultimate test. I mention this to guard myself from the accusation of intimating that the idea, the subject, of a novel or a picture, does not matter. It matters, to my sense, in the highest degree, and if I might put up a prayer it would be that artists should select none but the richest.
15 Some, as I have already hastened to admit, are much more remunerative than others, and it would be a world happily arranged in which persons intending to treat them should be exempt from confusions and mistakes. This fortunate condition will arrive only, I fear, on the same day that critics become purged from error. Meanwhile, I repeat, we do not judge the artist with fairness un-
20 less we say to him, "Oh, I grant you your starting-point, because if I did not I should seem to prescribe to you, and heaven forbid I should take that responsibility. If I pretend to tell you what you must not take, you will call upon me to tell you then what you must take; in which case I shall be prettily caught. Moreover, it isn't till I have accepted your data that I can begin
25 to measure you. I have the standard, the pitch; I have no right to tamper with your flute and then criticise your music. Of course I may not care for your idea at all; I may think it silly, or stale, or unclean; in which case I wash my hands of you altogether. I may content myself with believing that you will not have succeeded in being interesting, but I shall, of course, not
30 attempt to demonstrate it, and you will be as indifferent to me as I am to you. I needn't remind you that there are all sorts of tastes: who can know it better? Some people, for excellent reasons, don't like to read about carpenters; others, for reasons even better, don't like to read about courtesans. Many object to Americans. Others (I believe they are mainly editors and publishers)
35 won't look at Italians. Some readers don't like quiet subjects; others don't like bustling ones. Some enjoy a complete illusion, others the consciousness of large concessions. They choose their novels accordingly, and if they don't care about your idea they won't, a fortiori, care about your treatment."

So that it comes back very quickly, as I have said, to the liking: in spite
40 of M. Zola, who reasons less powerfully than he represents, and who will not reconcile himself to this absoluteness of taste, thinking that there are certain things that people ought to like, and that they can be made to like. I am quite at a loss to imagine anything (at any rate in this matter of fiction) that people ought to like or to dislike. Selection will be sure to take care of itself,
45 for it has a constant motive behind it. That motive is simply experience. As

5. Turgénieff—See note 10, p. 1272. 38. a fortiori—by the stronger reason; all the more. 40. Zola—The reference is to Zola's Le roman expérimental (1880).

people feel life, so they will feel the art that is most closely related to it. This closeness of relation is what we should never forget in talking of the effort of the novel. Many people speak of it as a factitious, artificial form, a product of ingenuity, the business of which it is to alter and arrange the things that sur- round us, to translate them into conventional, traditional moulds. This, how- 5 ever, is a view of the matter which carries us but a very short way, condemns the art to an eternal repetition of a few familiar *clichés,* cuts short its develop- ment, and leads us straight up to a dead wall. Catching the very note and trick, the strange irregular rhythm of life, that is the attempt whose strenuous force keeps Fiction upon her feet. In proportion as in what she offers us we 10 see life *without* rearrangement do we feel that we are touching the truth; in proportion as we see it *with* rearrangement do we feel that we are being put off with a substitute, a compromise and convention. It is not uncommon to hear an extraordinary assurance of remark in regard to this matter of rearranging, which is often spoken of as if it were the last word of art. Mr. Besant seems 15 to me in danger of falling into the great error with his rather unguarded talk about "selection." Art is essentially selection, but it is a selection whose main care is to be typical, to be inclusive. For many people art means rose-coloured window-panes, and selection means picking a bouquet for Mrs. Grundy. They will tell you glibly that artistic considerations have nothing to do with the 20 disagreeable, with the ugly; they will rattle off shallow commonplaces about the province of art and the limits of art till you are moved to some wonder in return as to the province and the limits of ignorance. It appears to me that no one can ever have made a seriously artistic attempt without becoming conscious of an immense increase—a kind of revelation—of freedom. One per- 25 ceives in that case—by the light of a heavenly ray—that the province of art is all life, all feeling, all observation, all vision. As Mr. Besant so justly inti- mates, it is all experience. That is a sufficient answer to those who maintain that it must not touch the sad things of life, who stick into its divine un- conscious bosom little prohibitory inscriptions on the end of sticks, such as 30 we see in public gardens—"It is forbidden to walk on the grass; it is forbidden to touch the flowers; it is not allowed to introduce dogs or to remain after dark; it is requested to keep to the right." The young aspirant in the line of fiction whom we continue to imagine will do nothing without taste, for in that case his freedom would be of little use to him; but the first advantage 35 of his taste will be to reveal to him the absurdity of the little sticks and tick- ets. If he have taste, I must add, of course, he will have ingenuity, and my dis- respectful reference to that quality just now was not meant to imply that it is useless in fiction. But it is only a secondary aid; the first is a capacity for receiving straight impressions. 40

 Mr. Besant has some remarks on the question of "the story" which I shall not attempt to criticise, though they seem to me to contain a singular ambiguity, because I do not think I understand them. I cannot see what is meant by talking as if there were a part of a novel which is the story and part of it which for mystical reasons is not—unless indeed the distinction be made in 45

---

7. clichés—hackneyed terms. **19. selection . . . for Mrs. Grundy**—a squeamish, artificial selection. Mrs. Grundy, a character in Thomas Morton's comedy *Speed the Plough* (1798), has become the stock symbol of prudery.

a sense in which it is difficult to suppose that any one should attempt to convey anything. "The story," if it represents anything, represents the subject, the idea, the *donnée* of the novel; and there is surely no "school"—Mr. Besant speaks of a school—which urges that a novel should be all treatment and no
5   subject. There must assuredly be something to treat; every school is intimately conscious of that. This sense of the story being the idea, the starting-point, of the novel, is the only one that I see in which it can be spoken of as something different from its organic whole; and since in proportion as the work is successful the idea permeates and penetrates it, informs and animates it,
10 so that every word and every punctuation-point contribute directly to the expression, in that proportion do we lose our sense of the story being a blade which may be drawn more or less out of its sheath. The story and the novel, the idea and the form, are the needle and thread, and I never heard of a guild of tailors who recommended the use of the thread without the needle, or the
15 needle without the thread. Mr. Besant is not the only critic who may be observed to have spoken as if there were certain things in life which constitute stories, and certain others which do not. I find the same odd implication in an entertaining article in the *Pall Mall Gazette,* devoted, as it happens, to Mr. Besant's lecture. "The story is the thing!" says this graceful writer, as if
20 with a tone of opposition to some other idea. I should think it was, as every painter who, as the time for "sending in" his picture looms in the distance, finds himself still in quest of a subject—as every belated artist not fixed about his theme will heartily agree. There are some subjects which speak to us and others which do not, but he would be a clever man who should undertake to
25 give a rule—an index expurgatorius—by which the story and the no-story should be known apart. It is impossible (to me at least) to imagine any such rule which shall not be altogether arbitrary. The writer in the *Pall Mall* opposes the delightful (as I suppose) novel of *Margot la Balafrée* to certain tales in which "Bostonian nymphs" appear to have "rejected English dukes for psy-
30 chological reasons." I am not acquainted with the romance just designated, and can scarcely forgive the *Pall Mall* critic for not mentioning the name of the author, but the title appears to refer to a lady who may have received a scar in some heroic adventure. I am inconsolable at not being acquainted with this episode, but am utterly at a loss to see why it is a story when the
35 rejection (or acceptance) of a duke is not, and why a reason, psychological or other, is not a subject when a cicatrix is. They are all particles of the multitudinous life with which the novel deals, and surely no dogma which pretends to make it lawful to touch the one and unlawful to touch the other will stand for a moment on its feet. It is the special picture that must stand
40 or fall, according as it seems to possess truth or to lack it. Mr. Besant does not, to my sense, light up the subject by intimating that a story must, under penalty of not being a story, consist of "adventures." Why of adventures more

---

18. **Pall Mall Gazette**—A newspaper of the day not to be confused with the *Pall Mall Maga-zine*. 25. **index expurgatorius**—a list of books from which passages must be eliminated before they may be read. 28. **Balafrée**—James's reference is to *Margot la Balafrée,* a novel by Fortuné Du Boisgobey (1821-1891), published in 1884. 36. **cicatrix**—scar or seam; la Balafrée means the woman with a scar.

than of green spectacles? He mentions a category of impossible things, and among them he places "fiction without adventure." Why without adventure, more than without matrimony, or celibacy, or parturition, or cholera, or hydropathy, or Jansenism? This seems to me to bring the novel back to the hapless little *rôle* of being an artificial, ingenious thing—bring it down from its large, free character of an immense and exquisite correspondence with life. And what *is* adventure when it comes to that, and by what sign is the listening pupil to recognize it? It is an adventure—an immense one—for me to write this little article; and for a Bostonian nymph to reject an English duke is an adventure only less stirring, I should say, than for an English duke to be rejected by a Bostonian nymph. I see dramas within dramas in that, and innumerable points of view. A psychological reason is, to my imagination, an object adorably pictorial; to catch the tint of its complexion—I feel as if that idea might inspire one to Titianesque efforts. There are few things more exciting to me, in short, than a psychological reason, and yet, I protest, the novel seems to me the most magnificent form of art. I have just been reading, at the same time, the delightful story of *Treasure Island,* by Mr. Robert Louis Stevenson and, in a manner less consecutive, the last tale from M. Edmond de Goncourt, which is entitled *Chérie.* One of these works treats of murders, mysteries, islands of dreadful renown, hairbreadth escapes, miraculous coincidences, and buried doubloons. The other treats of a little French girl who lived in a fine house in Paris, and died of wounded sensibility because no one would marry her. I call *Treasure Island* delightful, because it appears to me to have succeeded wonderfully in what it attempts; and I venture to bestow no epithet upon *Chérie,* which strikes me as having failed deplorably in what it attempts—that is, in tracing the development of the moral consciousness of a child. But one of these productions strikes me as exactly as much of a novel as the other, and as having a "story" quite as much. The moral consciousness of a child is as much a part of life as the islands of the Spanish Main, and the one sort of geography seems to me to have those "surprises" of which Mr. Besant speaks quite as much as the other. For myself (since it comes back in the last resort, as I say, to the preference of the individual), the picture of the child's experience has the advantage that I can at successive steps (an immense luxury, near to the "sensual pleasure" of which Mr. Besant's critic in the *Pall Mall* speaks) say Yes or No, as it may be, to what the artist puts before me. I have been a child in fact, but I have been on a quest for a buried treasure only in supposition, and it is a simple accident that with M. de Goncourt I should have for the most part to say No. With George Eliot, when she painted that country with a far other intelligence, I always said Yes.

The most interesting part of Mr. Besant's lecture is unfortunately the briefest passage—his very cursory allusion to the "conscious moral purpose" of the

---

1. **green spectacles**—The reference is to the episode of Moses and the green spectacles in Goldsmith's *The Vicar of Wakefield*. 3-4. **hydropathy**—treatment of disease by the use of water. 4. **Jansenism**—doctrine of irresistible grace and utter natural depravity deduced from St. Augustine's writings by Cornelius Jansen (1585-1638), Catholic bishop of Ypres in Flanders. 14. **Titianesque**—like Titian (Tiziano Vecellio, 1477-1576), distinguished Venetian painter and colorist.

novel. Here again it is not very clear whether he be recording a fact or laying down a principle; it is a great pity that in the latter case he should not
have developed his idea. This branch of the subject is of immense importance,
and Mr. Besant's few words point to considerations of the widest reach, not
5 to be lightly disposed of. He will have treated the art of fiction but superficially who is not prepared to go every inch of the way that these considerations will carry him. It is for this reason that at the beginning of these remarks I was careful to notify the reader that my reflections on so large a
theme have no pretension to be exhaustive. Like Mr. Besant, I have left the
10 question of the morality of the novel till the last, and at the last I find I
have used up my space. It is a question surrounded with difficulties, as witness the very first that meets us, in the form of a definite question, on the
threshold. Vagueness, in such a discussion, is fatal, and what is the meaning
of your morality and your conscious moral purpose? Will you not define
15 your terms and explain how (a novel being a picture) a picture can be either
moral or immoral? You wish to paint a moral picture or carve a moral statue:
will you not tell us how you would set about it? We are discussing the Art
of Fiction; questions of art are questions (in the widest sense) of execution;
questions of morality are quite another affair, and will you not let us see how
20 it is that you find it so easy to mix them up? These things are so clear to
Mr. Besant that he has deduced from them a law which he sees embodied
in English Fiction, and which is "a truly admirable thing and a great cause
for congratulation." It is a great cause for congratulation indeed when such
thorny problems become as smooth as silk. I may add that in so far as Mr.
25 Besant perceives that in point of fact English Fiction has addressed itself pre-
ponderantly to these delicate questions he will appear to many people to have
made a vain discovery. They will have been positively struck, on the contrary,
with the moral timidity of the usual English novelist; with his (or with her)
aversion to face the difficulties with which on every side the treatment of
30 reality bristles. He is apt to be extremely shy (whereas the picture that
Mr. Besant draws is a picture of boldness), and the sign of his work, for the
most part, is a cautious silence on certain subjects. In the English novel (by
which of course I mean the American as well), more than in any other, there
is a traditional difference between that which people know and that which
35 they agree to admit that they know, that which they see and that which they
speak of, that which they feel to be a part of life and that which they allow
to enter into literature. There is the great difference, in short, between what
they talk of in conversation and what they talk of in print. The essence of
moral energy is to survey the whole field, and I should directly reverse Mr.
40 Besant's remark and say not that the English novel has a purpose, but that
it has a diffidence. To what degree a purpose in a work of art is a source of
corruption I shall not attempt to inquire; the one that seems to me least dangerous is the purpose of making a perfect work. As for our novel, I may say
lastly on this score that as we find it in England to-day it strikes me as ad-
45 dressed in a large degree to "young people," and that this in itself constitutes
a presumption that it will be rather shy. There are certain things which it is
generally agreed not to discuss, not even to mention, before young people.
That is very well, but the absence of discussion is not a symptom of the moral

passion. The purpose of the English novel—"a truly admirable thing, and a great cause for congratulation"—strikes me therefore as rather negative.

There is one point at which the moral sense and the artistic sense lie very near together; that is in the light of the very obvious truth that the deepest quality of a work of art will always be the quality of the mind of the pro- 5 ducer. In proportion as that intelligence is fine will the novel, the picture, the statue partake of the substance of beauty and truth. To be constituted of such elements is, to my vision, to have purpose enough. No good novel will ever proceed from a superficial mind; that seems to me an axiom which, for the artist in fiction, will cover all needful moral ground: if the youthful aspirant 10 take it to heart it will illuminate for him many of the mysteries of "purpose." There are many other useful things that might be said to him, but I have come to the end of my article, and can only touch them as I pass. The critic in the *Pall Mall Gazette,* whom I have already quoted, draws attention to the danger, in speaking of the art of fiction, of generalising. The danger that 15 he has in mind is rather, I imagine, that of particularising, for there are some comprehensive remarks which, in addition to those embodied in Mr. Besant's suggestive lecture, might without fear of misleading him be addressed to the ingenuous student. I should remind him first of the magnificence of the form that is open to him, which offers to sight so few restrictions and such in- 20 numerable opportunities. The other arts, in comparison, appear confined and hampered; the various conditions under which they are exercised are so rigid and definite. But the only condition that I can think of attaching to the composition of the novel is, as I have already said, that it be sincere. This freedom is a splendid privilege, and the first lesson of the young novelist is 25 to learn to be worthy of it. "Enjoy it as it deserves," I should say to him; "take possession of it, explore it to its utmost extent, publish it, rejoice in it. All life belongs to you, and do not listen either to those who would shut you up into corners of it and tell you that it is only here and there that art inhabits, or to those who would persuade you that this heavenly messenger wings her 30 way outside of life altogether, breathing a superfine air, and turning away her head from the truth of things. There is no impression of life, no manner of seeing it and feeling it, to which the plan of the novelist may not offer a place; you have only to remember that talents so dissimilar as those of Alexandre Dumas and Jane Austen, Charles Dickens and Gustave Flaubert have 35 worked in this field with equal glory. Do not think too much about optimism and pessimism; try and catch the colour of life itself. In France to-day we see a prodigious effort (that of Emile Zola, to whose solid and serious work no explorer of the capacity of the novel can allude without respect), we see an extraordinary effort, vitiated by a spirit of pessimism on a narrow basis. M. 40 Zola is magnificent, but he strikes an English reader as ignorant; he has an air of working in the dark; if he had as much light as energy, his results would be of the highest value. As for the aberrations of a shallow optimism, the ground (of English fiction especially) is strewn with their brittle particles as with broken glass. If you must indulge in conclusions, let them have the 45 taste of a wide knowledge. Remember that your first duty is to be as complete as possible—to make as perfect a work. Be generous and delicate and pursue the prize."

EDWIN ARLINGTON ROBINSON

1869-1935

I. OBSCURITY (1869–1916)

1869   Born in Head-of-Tide, Maine, December 22, son of Edward and Mary E. Robinson, a descendant of Anne Bradstreet. The family soon moved to Gardiner, Maine, the "Tilbury Town" of his poems.

1880   Wrote verse from the age of eleven; often lonely.

1891–1893   Attended Harvard College, but withdrew when the death of his father necessitated earning a living. Struggling for a philosophy.

1896   After his mother's death went to New York, a taciturn hermit. At one time a subway inspector. Published *The Torrent* and *The Night Before*. These poems, privately printed, showed the influence of Hardy's poetry.

1897   *The Children of the Night,* included some poems previously printed as well as new ones.

1898–1899   Working in Cambridge, he received encouragement from Josephine Preston Peabody.

1902   *Captain Craig* (rev. ed., 1915) attracted the attention of President Theodore Roosevelt, who, by appointing him clerk in the New York Custom House, rescued him from poverty.

1905–1909   Clerk in the New York Custom House and self-effacing bohemian. Friendship with Ridgely Torrence, D. G. Mason, E. C. Stedman.

1910   *The Town down the River.* He now devoted himself to poetry.

1911   Joined the MacDowell Colony of artists and writers at Peterborough, New Hampshire.

1914–1915   Experimented in playwriting: *Van Zorn* and *The Porcupine.* Interested, with Josephine Preston Peabody, Percy Mackaye, William Vaughn Moody, and others, in reviving poetic drama.

II. FAME (1916–1928)

1916   *The Man against the Sky* brought him recognition.

1917   Interest in Arthurian legends: *Merlin.*

1920   *Lancelot. The Three Taverns.*

1921   *Avon's Harvest. Collected Poems;* won the Pulitzer Prize for Poetry in 1922.

1923   *Roman Bartholow.* Spent several months in England with John Drinkwater, J. C. Squire, and others.

1924   *The Man Who Died Twice.* Received the Pulitzer Prize for Poetry in 1925.

1925   *Dionysus in Doubt.* Received the Litt.D. degree from Bowdoin College.

1927   *Tristram* published by the Literary Guild; awarded the Pulitzer Prize for Poetry in 1928.

1928   *Sonnets, 1889-1927. Fortunatus.*

III. STUDIES IN MODERN LIFE (1929–1935)

1929 *Modred, a Fragment. Cavender's House. The Prodigal Son.*
1930 *The Glory of the Nightingales.*
1931 *Matthias at the Door.*
1932 *Nicodemus.*
1933 *Talifer.*
1934 *Amaranth.*
1935 *King Jasper,* an involved allegory. Death, April 6, in New York.
1940 *Selected Letters.*

BIOGRAPHIES AND CRITICISM: Amy Lowell, *Tendencies in Modern American Poetry,* Houghton Mifflin, 1917; L. Morris, *The Poetry of Edwin Arlington Robinson,* Doran, 1923; Mark Van Doren, *Edwin Arlington Robinson,* Literary Guild, 1927; L. M. Beebe, *Edwin Arlington Robinson and the Arthurian Legend,* Dunster House, 1927; H. R. Fairclough, "The Classics of Our Twentieth Century Poets," *Stanford University Publications in Language and Literature,* Vol. II (1927), pp. 1-50; J. C. Squire, *Contemporary American Authors,* Holt, 1928, pp. 121-48; E. E. Pipkin, "The Arthur of Edwin Arlington Robinson," *English Journal,* March, 1930; C. Cestre, *An Introduction to Edwin Arlington Robinson,* Macmillan, 1930; David Brown, "Some Rejected Poems of Edwin Arlington Robinson," *American Literature,* Vol. VII (1936), pp. 394-414; M. D. Zabel, *Literary Opinion in America,* Harper, 1937, pp. 397-406; R. W. Brown, *Next Door to a Poet,* Appleton-Century, 1937; H. Hagedorn, *Edwin Arlington Robinson,* Macmillan, 1938; R. P. T. Coffin, *New Poetry of New England: Frost and Robinson,* Johns Hopkins Press, 1938; Floyd Stovall, "The Optimism behind Robinson's Tragedies," *American Literature,* Vol. X (1938), pp. 1-24; E. Kaplan, *Philosophy in the Poetry of Edwin Arlington Robinson,* Columbia University Press, 1940; Yvor Winters, *Edwin Arlington Robinson,* New Directions, 1946.

BIBLIOGRAPHIES AND EDITIONS: C. B. Hogan, *A Bibliography of Edwin Arlington Robinson,* Yale University Press, 1936; L. Lippincott, *A Bibliography of the Writings and Criticisms of Edwin Arlington Robinson,* Faxon, 1937; *Literary History of the United States,* Vol. III, pp. 705-08.

Editions of Robinson's *Collected Poems* were published by Macmillan in 1921, in 1924, in 1927, in 1929, and in 1937; this house also published *Selected Letters,* compiled by R. Torrence, 1940. See also Denham Sutcliffe, ed., *Untriangulated Stars: Letters to Harry De Forest Smith, 1890-1905,* Harvard, 1947.

Robinson began writing in the nineties, when the movement to reform and control romantic lawlessness in poetic expression was at its height, and when, as instruments of that control, the French forms of verse (recently imported by way of London), the sonnet, and other patterns of poetry requiring the utmost technical finish were in vogue. Robinson was a patient, and even an enthusiastic, scholar in this school of the Muses. At the same time, the impact upon sensitive American writers of evolutionary and materialistic philosophies from Europe was very great, inducing an alternation of despair and hope about human destiny and of alternate attraction and repulsion face to face with human nature. The old nineteenth-century values were no longer satisfactory, and no sufficient substitute was to be immediately found unless one accepted the pragmatism of William James.

Robinson cannot be understood unless this paradoxical fusion of superb technical control and troubled doubt is understood. He wrote with austere vigor poems of character and fate that were alternately studies of human frustration and studies of inner spiritual triumph; and these he couched in precise verse forms. Eventually he developed a blank verse of his own that is one of the wonders of American poetry, a blank verse which, though it approximates the rhythm of human speech, as in *Tristram,* has the metrical perfection he learned from sonnet and ballade. In the meantime the intellectual severity of this discipline fused with an astringent quality of mind, a dry and sagacious wit, so that whether Robinson's subject be the legendary Tristram or the contemporary Cliff Klingenhagen or Mr. Flood, he finds mankind forever the same. Disillusioned about man's grandeur, Robinson is yet filled with tender sympathy for man's fate; his ironic detachment does not affect his insight. Therefore his delineation of man's struggle against an unkind fate is heartening; and his awareness of the changeless values by which we live, amid constant change, gives his poetry a quiet philosophic dignity and a beauty that place him high among recent poets.

LUKE HAVERGAL

This poem and the nine immediately following were published in *The Children of the Night,* 1897. The bitterness of Luke's search lies in his vain hope of a perfect solution.

Go to the western gate, Luke Havergal,
There where the vines cling crimson on the
   wall,
And in the twilight wait for what will come.
The leaves will whisper there for her, and
   some,
Like flying words, will strike you as they
   fall;   5
But go, and if you listen she will call.
Go to the western gate, Luke Havergal—
Luke Havergal.

No, there is not a dawn in eastern skies
To rift the fiery night that's in your eyes;
But there, where western glooms are gath-
   ering,   11
The dark will end the dark, if anything:
God slays Himself with every leaf that flies,
And hell is more than half of paradise.
No, there is not a dawn in eastern skies— 15
In eastern skies.

Out of a grave I come to tell you this,
Out of a grave I come to quench the kiss
That flames upon your forehead with a glow
That blinds you to the way that you must
   go.   20
Yes, there is yet one way to where she is,
Bitter, but one that faith may never miss.
Out of a grave I come to tell you this—
To tell you this.

There is the western gate, Luke Haver-
   gal,   25
There are the crimson leaves upon the wall.
Go, for the winds are tearing them away,—
Nor think to riddle the dead words they say,
Nor any more to feel them as they fall;
But go, and if you trust her she will call. 30
There is the western gate, Luke Havergal—
Luke Havergal.

THE HOUSE ON THE HILL

They are all gone away,
   The House is shut and still,
There is nothing more to say.

Through broken walls and gray
   The winds blow bleak and shrill: 5
They are all gone away.

Nor is there one to-day
   To speak them good or ill:
There is nothing more to say.

Why is it then we stray   10
  Around that sunken sill?
They are all gone away,

And our poor fancy-play
  For them is wasted skill:
There is nothing more to say.   15

There is ruin and decay
  In the House on the Hill:
They are all gone away,
There is nothing more to say.

RICHARD CORY

Whenever Richard Cory went down town,
We people on the pavement looked at him:
He was a gentleman from sole to crown,
Clean favored, and imperially slim.

And he was always quietly arrayed,   5
And he was always human when he talked;
But still he fluttered pulses when he said,
'Good-morning," and he glittered when he
  walked.

And he was rich—yes, richer than a king—
And admirably schooled in every grace: 10
In fine, we thought that he was everything
To make us wish that we were in his place.

So on we worked, and waited for the light,
And went without the meat, and cursed the
  bread;
And Richard Cory, one calm summer night,
Went home and put a bullet through his
  head.   16

CALVARY

Friendless and faint, with martyred steps
  and slow,
Faint for the flesh, but for the spirit free,
Stung by the mob that came to see the show,
The Master toiled along to Calvary;
We gibed him, as he went, with houndish
  glee,   5
Till his dimmed eyes for us did overflow;

We cursed his vengeless hands thrice wretch-
  edly,—
And this was nineteen hundred years ago.

But after nineteen hundred years the shame
Still clings, and we have not made good the
  loss   10
That outraged faith has entered in his name.
Ah, when shall come love's courage to be
  strong!
Tell me, O Lord—tell me, O Lord, how
  long
Are we to keep Christ writhing on the cross!

ZOLA*

Because he puts the compromising chart
Of hell before your eyes, you are afraid;
Because he counts the price that you have
  paid
For innocence, and counts it from the start,
You loathe him. But he sees the human
  heart   5
Of God meanwhile, and in His hand was
  weighed
Your squeamish and emasculate crusade
Against the grim dominion of his art.

Never until we conquer the uncouth
Connivings of our shamed indifference   10
(We call it Christian faith) are we to scan
The racked and shrieking hideousness of
  Truth
To find, in hate's polluted self-defence
Throbbing, the pulse, the divine heart of
  man.

CLIFF KLINGENHAGEN

Cliff Klingenhagen had me in to dine
With him one day; and after soup and meat,
And all the other things that were to eat,
Cliff took two glasses and filled one with
  wine
And one with wormwood. Then, without a
  sign   5
For me to choose at all, he took the draught

* **Zola**—Emile Zola (1840-1902), novelist and leader of the naturalists in France.

Of bitterness himself, and lightly quaffed
It off, and said the other one was mine.

And when I asked him what the deuce he
   meant
By doing that, he only looked at me   10
And smiled, and said it was a way of his.
And though I know the fellow, I have spent
Long time a-wondering when I shall be
As happy as Cliff Klingenhagen is.

SONNET

Oh for a poet—for a beacon bright
To rift this changeless glimmer of dead gray;
To spirit back the Muses, long astray,
And flush Parnassus with a newer light;
To put these little sonnet-men to flight   5
Who fashion, in a shrewd mechanic way,
Songs without souls, that flicker for a day,
To vanish in irrevocable night.

What does it mean, this barren age of ours?
Here are the men, the women, and the
   flowers,   10
The seasons, and the sunset, as before.
What does it mean? Shall there not one
   arise
To wrench one banner from the western
   skies,
And mark it with his name forevermore?

GEORGE CRABBE

George Crabbe (1754-1832), English poet,
author of *The Village* and other poems, was
among the first to treat life realistically instead of sentimentally.

Give him the darkest inch your shelf allows,
Hide him in lonely garrets, if you will,—
But his hard, human pulse is throbbing still
With the sure strength that fearless truth
   endows.
In spite of all fine science disavows,   5
Of his plain excellence and stubborn skill
There yet remains what fashion cannot kill,

Though years have thinned the laurel from
   his brows.

Whether or not we read him, we can feel
From time to time the vigor of his name   10
Against us like the finger for the shame
And emptiness of what our souls reveal
In books that are as altars where we kneel
To consecrate the flicker, not the flame.

CREDO

Composed about 1894; published in *The
Torrent* and *The Night Before,* 1896; then
included in *The Children of the Night,*
1897.

I cannot find my way: there is no star
In all the shrouded heavens anywhere:
And there is not a whisper in the air
Of any living voice but one so far
That I can hear it only as a bar
Of lost, imperial music, played when fair
And angel fingers wove, and unaware,
Dead leaves to garlands where no roses are.

No, there is not a glimmer, nor a call,
For one that welcomes, welcomes when he
   fears,   10
The black and awful chaos of the night; *
For through it all—above, beyond it all—
I know the far-sent message of the years,
I feel the coming glory of the Light.

MINIVER CHEEVY

Published in *Scribner's Magazine,* March,
1907, and in *The Town down the River,*
1910.

Miniver Cheevy, child of scorn,
   Grew lean while he assailed the seasons;
He wept that he was ever born,
   And he had reasons.

Miniver loved the days of old   5
   When swords were bright and steeds were
     prancing;

* **night**—life of the senses, contrasted with "Light" (line 14), or the intuition of the spirit.

The vision of a warrior bold
Would set him dancing.

Miniver sighed for what was not,
  And dreamed, and rested from his labors;
He dreamed of Thebes and Camelot,   11
  And Priam's neighbors.

Miniver mourned the ripe renown
  That made so many a name so fragrant;
He mourned Romance, now on the town,
  And Art, a vagrant.   16

Miniver loved the Medici,
  Albeit he had never seen one;
He would have sinned incessantly
  Could he have been one.   20

Miniver cursed the commonplace
  And eyed a khaki suit with loathing;
He missed the medieval grace
  Of iron clothing.

Miniver scorned the gold he sought,   25
  But sore annoyed was he without it;
Miniver thought, and thought, and thought,
  And thought about it.

Miniver Cheevy, born too late,
  Scratched his head and kept on thinking;
Miniver coughed, and called it fate, 31
  And kept on drinking.

BEN JONSON ENTERTAINS A MAN FROM STRATFORD

Published in *Drama*, November, 1915; reprinted during the Shakespeare Tercen-
enary in *The Man against the Sky*, 1916.
The classicist Ben Jonson, in talking to an
Alderman who has known Shakespeare
"from his origin," is bewildered over the
romantic genius who seems indifferent to
all but retirement to a large house in his native town. The portrait drawn in this dramatic monologue is revealing not only of
Shakespeare but of Robinson.

You are a friend, then, as I make it out,
Of our man Shakespeare, who alone of us
Will put an ass's head in Fairyland
As he would add a shilling to more shillings,
All most harmonious,—and out of his   5
Miraculous inviolable increase
Fills Ilion, Rome, or any town you like
Of olden time with timeless Englishmen;
And I must wonder what you think of
  him—
All you down there where your small Avon
  flows   10
By Stratford, and where you're an Alder-
  man.
Some, for a guess, would have him riding
  back
To be a farrier there, or say a dyer;
Or maybe one of your adept surveyors;
Or like enough the wizard of all tanners. 15
Not you—no fear of that; for I discern
In you a kindling of the flame that saves—
The nimble element, the true phlogiston;
I see it, and was told of it, moreover,
By our discriminate friend himself, no other.
Had you been one of the sad average,   21
As he would have it,—meaning, as I take it,
The sinew and the solvent of our Island,
You'd not be buying beer for this Terpan-
  der's
Approved and estimated friend Ben Jonson;
He'd never foist it as a part of his   26
Contingent entertainment of a townsman
While he goes off rehearsing, as he must,
If he shall ever be the Duke of Stratford.
And my words are no shadow on your
  town—   30
Far from it; for one town's as like another
As all are unlike London. Oh, he knows
  it,—
And there's the Stratford in him; he denies
  it,

---

11. Thebes—Greek city celebrated in the Peloponnesian and other wars. **11. Camelot**—
capital city of Arthurian legend. **12. Priam's**—king of Troy when it was besieged by the
Greeks, twelfth century B.C. **17. Medici**—Florentine banker family, rather unprincipled, but
patrons of art and learning during the Renaissance. **3. ass's head**—In *A Midsummer Night's
Dream* and elsewhere Shakespeare intermingled comedy and tragedy contrary to the classical rules.
13. farrier—blacksmith. **18. phlogiston**—heat. **24. Terpander's**—famous Lesbian musician
of the seventh century B.C., called "the father of Greek music."

And there's the Shakespeare in him. So,
   God help him!   34
I tell him he needs Greek; but neither God
Nor Greek will help him. Nothing will help
   that man.
You see the fates have given him so much,
He must have all or perish,—or look out
Of London, where he sees too many lords.
They're part of half what ails him: I sup-
   pose   40
There's nothing fouler down among the
   demons
Than what it is he feels when he remembers
The dust and sweat and ointment of his
   calling
With his lords looking on and laughing at
   him.
King as he is, he can't be king *de facto,*   45
And that's as well, because he wouldn't like
   it;
He'd frame a lower rating of men then
Than he has now; and after that would
   come
An abdication or an apoplexy.
He can't be king, not even king of Strat-
   ford,—   50
Though half the world, if not the whole of
   it,
May crown him with a crown that fits no
   king
Save Lord Apollo's homesick emissary:
Not there on Avon, or on any stream
Where Naiads and their white arms are no
   more,   55
Shall he find home again. It's all too bad.
But there's a comfort, for he'll have that
   House—
The best you ever saw; and he'll be there
Anon, as you're an Alderman. Good God!
He makes me lie awake. o'nights and
   laugh.   60

And you have known him from his origin,
You tell me; and a most uncommon urchin
He must have been to the few seeing ones—
A trifle terrifying, I dare say,
Discovering a world with his man's eyes,   65

Quite as another lad might see some finches,
If he looked hard and had an eye for nature.
But this one had his eyes and their fore-
   telling,
And he had you to fare with, and what else?
He must have had a father and a mother—
In fact I've heard him say so—and a dog,   71
As a boy should, I venture; and the dog,
Most likely, was the only man who knew
   him.
A dog, for all I know, is what he needs
As much as anything right here today,   75
To counsel him about his disillusions,
Old aches, and parturitions of what's com-
   ing,—
A dog of orders, an emeritus,
To wag his tail at him when he comes
   home,   79
And then to put his paws up on his knees
And say, "For God's sake, what's it all
   about?"

I don't know whether he needs a dog or
   not—
Or what he needs. I tell him he needs
   Greek;
I'll talk of rules and Aristotle with him,
And if his tongue's at home he'll say to that,
"I have your word that Aristotle knows,   86
And you mine that I don't know Aristotle."
He's all at odds with all the unities,
And what's yet worse, it doesn't seem to
   matter;
He treads along through Time's old wilder-
   ness   90
As if the tramp of all the centuries
Had left no roads—and there are none, for
   him;
He doesn't see them, even with those eyes,—
And that's a pity, or I say it is.   94
Accordingly we have him as we have him—
Going his way, the way that he goes best,
A pleasant animal with no great noise
Or nonsense anywhere to set him off—
Save only divers and inclement devils
Have made of late his heart their dwelling
   place.   100

---

45. de facto—in reality. **53. Lord Apollo's . . . emissary**—a poet or musician. **55. Naiads**—nymphs associated with streams. **66. finches**—seed-eating birds. **84. Aristotle**— Aristotle's *Poetics* formulated the rules of Greek literary art, including the three unities. **90. treads along**—that is, Shakespeare has his own rules.

A flame half ready to fly out sometimes
At some annoyance may be fanned up in him,
But soon it falls, and when it falls goes out;
He knows how little room there is in there
For crude and futile animosities, 105
And how much for the joy of being whole,
And how much for long sorrow and old pain.
On our side there are some who may be given
To grow old wondering what he thinks of us
And some above us, who are, in his eyes,
Above himself,—and that's quite right and English. 111
Yet here we smile, or disappoint the gods
Who made it so: the gods have always eyes
To see men scratch; and they see one down here
Who itches, manor-bitten to the bone, 115
Albeit he knows himself—yes, yes, he knows—
The lord of more than England and of more
Than all the seas of England in all time
Shall ever wash. D'ye wonder that I laugh?
He sees me, and he doesn't seem to care;
And why the devil should he? I can't tell you. 121

I'll meet him out alone of a bright Sunday,
Trim, rather spruce, and quite the gentleman.
"What ho, my lord!" say I. He doesn't hear me; 124
Wherefore I have to pause and look at him.
He's not enormous, but one looks at him.
A little on the round if you insist,
For now, God save the mark, he's growing old;
He's five and forty, and to hear him talk
These days you'd call him eighty; then you'd add 130
More years to that. He's old enough to be
The father of a world, and so he is.
"Ben, you're a scholar, what's the time of day?"

Says he; and there shines out of him again
An aged light that has no age or station—
The mystery that's his—a mischievous 136
Half-mad serenity that laughs at fame
For being won so easy, and at friends
Who laugh at him for what he wants the most,
And for his dukedom down in Warwickshire;— 140
By which you see we're all a little jealous. . . .
Poor Greene! I fear the color of his name
Was even as that of his ascending soul;
And he was one where there are many others, 144
Some scrivening to the end against their fate,
Their puppets all in ink and all to die there:
And some with hands that once would shade an eye
That scanned Euripides and Aeschylus
Will reach by this time for a pot-house mop
To slush their first and last of royalties. 150
Poor devils! and they all play to his hand;
For so it was in Athens and old Rome.
But that's not here or there; I've wandered off.
Greene does it, or I'm careful. Where's that boy?

Yes, he'll go back to Stratford. And we'll miss him? 155
Dear sir, there'll be no London here without him.
We'll all be riding, one of these fine days,
Down there to see him—and his wife won't like us;
And then we'll think of what he never said
Of women—which, if taken all in all 160
With what he did say, would buy many horses.
Though nowadays he's not so much for women:
"So few of them," he says, "are worth the guessing."
But there's a worm at work when he says that, 164
And while he says it one feels in the air
A deal of circumambient hocus-pocus.

115. manor-bitten—Shakespeare is eager to have a manor house in Stratford, Warwickshire. 142. Greene—Robert Greene (1560?-1592), Elizabethan playwright. 148. Euripides . . . Aeschylus—Greek writers of tragedy, whose Elizabethan disciples now follow Shakespeare.

They've had him dancing till his toes were
   tender,
And he can feel 'em now, come chilly rains.
There's no long cry for going into it,   169
However, and we don't know much about
   it.
The Fitton thing was worst of all, I fancy;
And you in Stratford, like most here in
   London,
Have more now in the *Sonnets* than you
   paid for;
He's put one there with all her poison on,
To make a singing fiction of a shadow   175
That's in his life a fact, and always will be.
But she's no care of ours, though Time, I
   fear,
Will have a more reverberant ado
About her than about another one
Who seems to have decoyed him, married
   him,   180
And sent him scuttling on his way to Lon-
   don,—
With much already learned, and more to
   learn,
And more to follow. Lord! how I see him
   now,
Pretending, maybe trying, to be like us.
Whatever he may have meant, we never had
   him;   185
He failed us, or escaped, or what you will,—
And there was that about him (God knows
   what,—
We'd flayed another had he tried it on us)
That made as many of us as had wits
More fond of all his easy distances   190
Than one another's noise and clap-your-
   shoulder.
But think you not, my friend, he'd never
   talk!
Talk? He was eldritch at it; and we lis-
   tened—
Thereby acquiring much we knew before
About ourselves, and hitherto had held   195
Irrelevant, or not prime to the purpose.
And there were some, of course, and there
   be now,
Disordered and reduced amazedly

To resignation by the mystic seal
Of young finality the gods had laid   200
On everything that made him a young
   demon;
And one or two shot looks at him already
As he had been their executioner;
And once or twice he was, not knowing it,—
Or knowing, being sorry for poor clay   205
And saying nothing. . . . Yet, for all his
   engines,
You'll meet a thousand of an afternoon
Who strut and sun themselves and see
   around 'em
A world made out of more that has a reason
Than his, I swear, that he sees here today;
Though he may scarcely give a Fool an exit
But we mark how he sees in everything   212
A law that, given we flout it once too often,
Brings fire and iron down on our naked
   heads.
To me it looks as if the power that made
   him,
For fear of giving all things to one creature,
Left out the first,—faith, innocence, illusion,
Whatever 'tis that keeps us out o' Bedlam,—
And thereby, for his too consuming vision,
Empowered him out of nature; though to
   see him,   220
You'd never guess what's going on inside
   him.
He'll break out some day like a keg of ale
With too much independent frenzy in it;
And all for cellaring what he knows won't
   keep,
And what he'd best forget—but that he
   can't.   225
You'll have it, and have more than I'm
   foretelling;
And there'll be such a roaring at the Globe
As never stunned the bleeding gladiators.
He'll have to change the color of its hair
A bit, for now he calls it Cleopatra.   230
Black hair would never do for Cleopatra.

But you and I are not yet two old women,
And you're a man of office. What he does
Is more to you than how it is he does it,—

173-74. Sonnets . . . one—The *Sonnets* are supposed to have autobiographical information, including reference to a certain "dark lady." **193. eldritch**—weird, uncanny. **206. engines**
—contrivances. **218. Bedlam**—Bethlehem Hospital for the insane, London. **224. cellaring**—
Shakespeare's fertile, effervescent brain.

And that's what the Lord God has never
   told him.   235
They work together, and the Devil helps
   'em;
They do it of a morning, or if not,
They do it of a night; in which event
He's peevish of a morning. He seems old;
He's not the proper stomach or the sleep—
And they're two sovran agents to conserve
   him   241
Against the fiery art that has no mercy
But what's in that prodigious grand new
   House.
I gather something happening in his boy-
   hood   244
Fulfilled him with a boy's determination
To make all Stratford 'ware of him. Well,
   well,
I hope at last he'll have his joy of it,
And all his pigs and sheep and bellowing
   beeves,
And frogs and owls and unicorns, moreover,
Be less than hell to his attendant ears.   250
Oh, past a doubt we'll all go down to see
   him.

He may be wise. With London two days off,
Down there some wind of heaven may yet
   revive him;
But there's no quickening breath from any-
   where
Shall make of him again the poised young
   faun   255
From Warwickshire, who'd made, it seems,
   already
A legend of himself before I came
To blink before the last of his first lightning.
Whatever there be, there'll be no more of
   that;
The coming on of his old monster Time
Has made him a still man; and he has
   dreams   261
Were fair to think on once, and all found
   hollow.
He knows how much of what men paint
   themselves
Would blister in the light of what they are;
He sees how much of what was great now
   shares   265
An eminence transformed and ordinary;

He knows too much of what the world has
   hushed
In others, to be loud now for himself;
He knows now at what height low enemies
May reach his heart, and high friends let
   him fall;   270
But what not even such as he may know
Bedevils him the worst: his lark may sing
At heaven's gate how he will, and for as
   long
As joy may listen, but *he* sees no gate,   274
Save one whereat the spent clay waits a little
Before the churchyard as it, and the worm.
Not long ago, late in an afternoon,
I came on him unseen down Lambeth way,
And on my life I was afear'd of him:
He gloomed and mumbled like a soul from
   Tophet,   280
His hands behind him and his head bent
   solemn.
"What is it now," said I,—"another
   woman?"
That made him sorry for me, and he smiled.
"No, Ben," he mused; "it's Nothing. It's
   all Nothing.
We come, we go; and when we're done,
   we're done.   285
Spiders and flies—we're mostly one or
   t'other—
We come, we go; and when we're done,
   we're done."
"By God, you sing that song as if you knew
   it!"
Said I, by way of cheering him; "what ails
   ye?"
"I think I must have come down here to
   think,"   290
Says he to that, and pulls his little beard;
"Your fly will serve as well as anybody,
And what's his hour? He flies, and flies, and
   flies,
And in his fly's mind has a brave appear-
   ance;   294
And then your spider gets him in her net,
And eats him out, and hangs him up to dry.
That's Nature, the kind mother of us all.
And then your slattern housemaid swings
   her broom,
And where's your spider? And that's Na-
   ture, also.

---

272. lark—*Cf. Cymbeline,* Act II, sc. iii, line 21. **280. Tophet**—hell.

It's Nature, and it's Nothing. It's all
  Nothing.   300
It's all a world where bugs and emperors
Go singularly back to the same dust,
Each in his time; and the old, ordered stars
That sang together, Ben, will sing the same
Old stave tomorrow."

           When he talks like that,
There's nothing for a human man to do 306
But lead him to some grateful nook like this
Where we be now, and there to make him
  drink.
He'll drink, for love of me, and then be sick;
A sad sign always in a man of parts,   310
And always very ominous. The great
Should be as large in liquor as in love,—
And our great friend is not so large in either:
One disaffects him, and the other fails him;
Whatso he drinks that has an antic in it,
He's wondering what's to pay in his in-
  sides;   316
And while his eyes are on the Cyprian
He's fribbling all the time with that damned
  House.
We laugh here at his thrift, but after all
It may be thrift that saves him from the
  devil;   320
God gave it, anyhow,—and we'll suppose
He knew the compound of his handiwork.
Today the clouds are with him, but anon
He'll out of 'em enough to shake the tree
Of life itself and bring down fruit unheard-
  of,—   325
And, throwing in the bruised and whole
  together,
Prepare a wine to make us drunk with
  wonder;
And if he live, there'll be a sunset spell
Thrown over him as over a glassed lake 329
That yesterday was all a black wild water.

God send he live to give us, if no more,
What now's a-rampage in him, and exhibit,
With a decent half-allegiance to the ages
An earnest of at least a casual eye   334
Turned once on what he owes to Gutenberg,
And to the fealty of more centuries

Than are as yet a picture in our vision.
"There's time enough,—I'll do it when I'm
  old,
And we're immortal men," he says to that;
And then he says to me, "Ben, what's 'im-
  mortal'?   340
Think you by any force of ordination
It may be nothing of a sort more noisy
Than a small oblivion of component ashes
That of a dream-addicted world was once
A moving atomy much like your friend
  here?"   345
Nothing will help that man. To make him
  laugh,
I said then he was a mad mountebank,—
And by the Lord I nearer made him cry.
I could have eat an eft then, on my knees,
Tail, claws, and all of him; for I had stung
The king of men, who had no sting for
  me,   351
And I had hurt him in his memories;
And I say now, as I shall say again,
I love the man this side idolatry.

He'll do it when he's old, he says. I wonder.
He may not be so ancient as all that.   356
For such as he, the thing that is to do
Will do itself,—but there's a reckoning;
The sessions that are now too much his own,
The roiling inward of a stilled outside,   360
The churning out of all those blood-fed lines,
The nights of many schemes and little sleep,
The full brain hammered hot with too much
  thinking,
The vexed heart over-worn with too much
  aching,—   364
This weary jangling of conjoined affairs
Made out of elements that have no end,
And all confused at once, I understand,
Is not what makes a man to live forever.
O no, not now! He'll not be going now:
There'll be time yet for God knows what
  explosions   370
Before he goes. He'll stay awhile. Just wait:
Just wait a year or two for Cleopatra,
For she's to be a balsam and a comfort;
And that's not all a jape of mine now, either.
For granted once the old way of Apollo 375

---

317. Cyprian—wine from Cyprus. 335. Gutenberg—that is, the art of printing. 349.
eft—a small lizard. 354. idolatry—Cf. Jonson's Discoveries (de Shakespeare nostrat), 1641. See
also his "To the Memory of My Beloved Master Shakespeare."

Sings in a man, he may then, if he's able,
Strike unafraid whatever strings he will
Upon the last and wildest of new lyres;
Nor out of his new magic, though it hymn
The shrieks of dungeoned hell, shall he
  create   380
A madness or a gloom to shut quite out
A cleaving daylight, and a last great calm
Triumphant over shipwreck and all storms.
He might have given Aristotle creeps,
But surely would have given him his *kathar-
sis*.   385

He'll not be going yet. There's too much yet
Unsung within the man. But when he goes,
I'd stake ye coin o' the realm his only care
For a phantom world he sounded and found
  wanting
Will be a portion here, a portion there,   390
Of this or that thing or some other thing
That has a patent and intrinsical
Equivalence in those egregious shillings.
And yet he knows, God help him! Tell me,
  now,
If ever there was anything let loose   395
On earth by gods or devils heretofore
Like this mad, careful, proud, indifferent
  Shakespeare!
Where was it, if it ever was? By heaven,
'Twas never yet in Rhodes or Pergamon—
In Thebes or Nineveh, a thing like this! 400
No thing like this was ever out of England;
And that he knows. I wonder if he cares.
Perhaps he does. . . . O Lord, that House
  in Stratford!

FLAMMONDE

Published in the *Outlook*, January 6, 1915,
and in *The Man against the Sky*, 1916.

The man Flammonde, from God knows
  where,
With firm address and foreign air,
With news of nations in his talk

And something royal in his walk,
With glint of iron in his eyes,   5
But never doubt, nor yet surprise,
Appeared, and stayed, and held his head
As one by kings accredited.

Erect, with his alert repose
About him, and about his clothes,   10
He pictured all tradition hears
Of what we owe to fifty years.
His cleansing heritage of taste
Paraded neither want nor waste;
And what he needed for his fee   15
To live, he borrowed graciously.
He never told us what he was,
Or what mischance, or other cause,
Had banished him from better days
To play the Prince of Castaways.   20
Meanwhile he played surpassing well
A part, for most, unplayable;
In fine, one pauses, half afraid
To say for certain that he played.

For that, one may as well forego   25
Conviction as to yes or no;
Nor can I say just how intense
Would then have been the difference
To several, who, having striven
In vain to get what he was given,   30
Would see the stranger taken on
By friends not easy to be won.

Moreover, many a malcontent
He soothed and found munificent;
His courtesy beguiled and foiled   35
Suspicion that his years were soiled;
His mien distinguished any crowd,
His credit strengthened when he bowed;
And women, young and old, were fond
Of looking at the man Flammonde.   40

There was a woman in our town
On whom the fashion was to frown;
But while our talk renewed the tinge
Of a long-faded scarlet fringe,
The man Flammonde saw none of that,   45
And what he saw we wondered at—

385. katharsis—Aristotle suggested that true tragedy produced a purgation of the emotions in the spectator. **399-400. Rhodes . . . Nineveh**—At Rhodes was the gigantic statue of Apollo; Pergamon was the citadel of Troy in Homer's *Iliad;* Thebes was the ancient capital of Upper Egypt; Nineveh was the capital of Assyria. **12. fifty years**—Flammonde was a fifty-year-old regal castaway who "borrowed graciously" and who helped the poor.

That none of us, in her distress,
Could hide or find our littleness.

There was a boy that all agreed
Had shut within him the rare seed   50
Of learning. We could understand,
But none of us could lift a hand.
The man Flammonde appraised the youth,
And told a few of us the truth;
And thereby, for a little gold,   55
A flowered future was unrolled.

There were two citizens who fought
For years and years, and over nought;
They made life awkward for their friends,
And shortened their own dividends.   60
The man Flammonde said what was wrong
Should be made right; nor was it long
Before they were again in line,
And had each other in to dine.

And these I mention are but four   65
Of many out of many more.
So much for them. But what of him—
So firm in every look and limb?
What small satanic sort of kink
Was in his brain? What broken link   70
Withheld him from the destinies
That came so near to being his?

What was he, when we came to sift
His meaning, and to note the drift
Of incommunicable ways   75
That make us ponder while we praise?
Why was it that his charm revealed
Somehow the surface of a shield?
What was it that we never caught?
What was he, and what was he not?   80

How much it was of him we met
We cannot ever know; nor yet
Shall all he gave us quite atone
For what was his, and his alone;
Nor need we now, since he knew best,   85
Nourish an ethical unrest:
Rarely at once will nature give
The power to be Flammonde and live.

We cannot know how much we learn
From those who never will return,   90
Until a flash of unforeseen

Remembrance falls on what has been.
We've each a darkening hill to climb;
And this is why, from time to time
In Tilbury Town, we look beyond   95
Horizons for the man Flammonde.

MR. FLOOD'S PARTY

Published in the *Nation*, November 24,
1920, and in the *Collected Poems,* 1921.

Old Eben Flood, climbing alone one night
Over the hill between the town below
And the forsaken upland hermitage
That held as much as he should ever know
On earth again of home, paused warily.   5
The road was his with not a native near;
And Eben, having leisure, said aloud,
For no man else in Tilbury Town to hear:

"Well, Mr. Flood, we have the harvest moon
Again, and we may not have many more;
The bird is on the wing, the poet says,   10
And you and I have said it here before.
Drink to the bird." He raised up to the light
The jug that he had gone so far to fill,
And answered huskily: "Well, Mr. Flood,
Since you propose it, I believe I will."   16
Alone, as if enduring to the end
A valiant armor of scarred hopes outworn,
He stood there in the middle of the road
Like Roland's ghost winding a silent horn
Below him, in the town among the trees,   21
Where friends of other days had honored
   him,
A phantom salutation of the dead
Rang thinly till old Eben's eyes were dim.

Then, as a mother lays her sleeping child
Down tenderly, fearing it may awake,   26
He set the jug down slowly at his feet
With trembling care, knowing that most
   things break
And only when assured that on firm earth
It stood, as the uncertain lives of men   30
Assuredly did not, he paced away,
And with his hand extended paused again:

95. Tilbury Town—Gardiner, Maine, but applicable anywhere. 11. poet—Omar Khay-
yám, *The Rubáiyát,* Fitzgerald translation, stanza 7. 20. Roland's ghost—*Cf.* the end of
Browning's "Childe Roland to the Dark Tower Came."

"Well, Mr. Flood, we have not met like this
In a long time; and many a change has
  come
To both of us, I fear, since last it was   35
We had a drop together. Welcome home!"
Convivially returning with himself,
Again he raised the jug up to the light;
And with an acquiescent quaver said:
"Well, Mr. Flood, if you insist, I might.   40

"Only a very little, Mr. Flood—
For auld lang syne. No more, sir; that will
  do."
So, for the time, apparently it did,
And Eben evidently thought so too;
For soon amid the silver loneliness   45

Of night he lifted up his voice and sang,
Secure, with only two moons listening,
Until the whole harmonious landscape
  rang—

"For auld lang syne." The weary throat
  gave out,
The last word wavered; and the song was
  done.   50
He raised again the jug regretfully
And shook his head, and was again alone.
There was not much that was ahead of him,
And there was nothing in the town below—
Where strangers would have shut the many
  doors   55
That many friends had opened long ago.

From TRISTRAM

Published in 1927. The Arthurian story of Tristram and the two Isolts as Robinson retells it begins on the eve of the marriage of Tristram's uncle Mark, King of Cornwall, to young Isolt of Ireland. Tristram had brought Isolt from Ireland to Cornwall, but realized too late that she loved him rather than the senile King. Sulking, he is deaf to all appeals to participate in the festivities, when Isolt herself appears.

          At last Isolt
Released herself enough to look at him.
With a world burning for him in her eyes,
And two worlds crumbling for him in her
  words:
"What have I done to you, Tristram!" she
  said;   5
"What have you done to me! What have we
  done
To Fate, that she should hate us and destroy
  us,
Waiting for us to speak. What have we done
So false or foul as to be burned alive   9
And then be buried alive—as we shall be—
As I shall be!"

          He gazed upon a face
Where all there was of beauty and of love
That was alive for him, and not for him,
Was his while it was there. "I shall have
  burned
And buried us both," he said. "Your pride
would not   15

Have healed my blindness then, even had
  you prayed
For God to let you speak. When a man sues
The fairest of all women for her love,
He does not cleave the skull first of her kins-
  man   19
To mark himself a man. That was my way;
And it was not the wisest—if your eyes
Had any truth in them for a long time.
Your pride would not have let me tell them
  more—
Had you prayed God, I say."

                    "I did do that,
Tristram, but he was then too far from
  heaven   25
To hear so little a thing as I was, praying
For you on earth. You had not seen my
  eyes
Before you fought with Morhaus; and for
  that,
There was your side and ours. All history
  sings

19. **kinsman**—In combat with Isolt's kinsman Morhaus, Tristram had been wounded, and during his recovery had been cared for by Isolt. Later Tristram came back as "Mark's ambassador."

Of two sides, and will do so till all men   30
Are quiet; and then there will be no men
    left,
Or women alive to hear them. It was long
Before I learned so little as that; and you
It was who taught me while I nursed and
    healed
Your wound, only to see you go away."   35

"And once having seen me go away from
    you,
You saw me coming back to you again,
Cheerful and healed, as Mark's ambassador.
Would God foresee such folly alive as that
In any thing he had made, and still make
    more?   40
If so, his ways are darker than divines
Have drawn them for our best bewilder-
    ments.
Be it so or not, my share in this is clear.
I have prepared a way for us to take,
Because a king was not so much a devil   45
When I was young as not to be a friend,
An uncle, and an easy counsellor.
Later, when love was yet no more for me
Than a gay folly glancing everywhere   49
For triumph easier sometimes than defeat,
Having made sure that I was blind enough,
He sealed me with an oath to make you his
Before I had my eyes, or my heart woke
From pleasure in a dream of other faces   54
That now are nothing else than silly skulls
Covered with skin and hair. The right was
    his
To make of me a shining knight at arms,
By fortune may be not the least adept
And emulous. But God! for seizing you,
And having you here tonight, and all his
    life   60
Having you here, by the blind means of me,
I could tear all the cords out of his neck
To make a rope, and hang the rest of him.
Isolt, forgive me! This is only sound   64
That I am making with a tongue gone mad
That you should be so near me as to hear
    me
Saying how far away you are to go
When you go back to him, driven by—me!

A fool may die with no great noise or loss;
And whether a fool should always live or
    not . . ."   70

Isolt, almost as with a frightened leap
Muffled his mouth with hers in a long kiss,
Blending in their catastrophe two fires
That made one fire. When she could look at
    him
Again, her tears, unwilling still to flow,   75
Made of her eyes two shining lakes of pain
With moonlight living in them; and she
    said
"There is no time for you to tell me this;
And you are younger than time says you are
Or you would not be losing it, saying over
All that I know too well, or for my sake   81
Giving yourself these names that are worth
    nothing.
It was our curse that you were not to see
Until you saw too late. No scourge of names
That you may lay for me upon yourself   85
Will have more consequence for me, or you,
Than beating with a leaf would have or
    horses;
So give yourself no more of them tonight.
The King says you are coming back with
    me.
How can you come? And how can you not
    come!   90
It will be cruel enough for me without you
But with you there alive in the same walls
I shall be hardly worthy of life tonight
If I stay there alive—although I shall,
For this may not be all. This thing has come
For us, and you are not to see the end   96
Through any such fog of honor and self
    hate
As you may seek to throw around yourself
For being yourself. Had you been someone
    else,
You might have been one like your cousin
    Andred,   100
Who looks at me as if he were a snake
That has heard something. Had you been
    someone else,
You might have been like Modred, or like
    Mark.

---

100. **Andred**—Mark's spy, whom Tristram discovers eavesdropping and wounds in a fight.
Andred bides his time and gets revenge later in the story. 103. **Modred**—King Arthur's treacherous nephew.

God—you like Mark! You might have been
 a slave.   104
We cannot say what either of us had been
Had we been something else. All we can say
Is that this thing has come to us tonight.
You can do nothing more unless you kill
 him.
And that would be the end of you and me.
Time on our side, this may not be the
 end."   110

"I might have been a slave, by you unseen,"
He answered, "and you still Isolt of Ireland,
To me unknown. That would have been for
 you
The better way. But that was not the
 way."   114

"No it was not," she said, trying to smile;
And weary then for trying, held him closer.
"But I can feel the hands of time on me,
And they will soon be tearing me away.
Tristram, say to me once before I go, 119
What you believe and what you see for us
Before you. Are you sure that a word given
Is always worth more than a world for-
 saken?
Who knows there may not be a lonely place
In heaven for souls that are ashamed and
 sorry
For fearing hell?"

    "It is not hell tonight, 125
Isolt," he said, "or any beyond the grave,
That I fear most for you or for myself.
Fate has adjusted and made sure of that
Where we are now—though we see not the
 end,
And time be on our side. Praise God for
 time,   130
And for such hope of what may come of it
As time like this may grant. I could be
 strong,
But to be over-strong now at this hour
Would only be destruction. The King's ways
Are not those of one man against another,
And you must live, and I must live—for
 you.   136
If there were not an army of guards below
 us

To bring you back to fruitless ignominy,
There would soon be an end of this offense
To God and the long insult of this mar-
 riage.   140
But to be twice a fool is not the least
Insane of ways to cure a first affliction.
God!—is it so—that you are going back
To be up there with him—with Mark—to-
 night?   144
Before you came, I had been staring down
On those eternal rocks and the white foam
Around them; and I thought how sound
 and long
A sleep would soon begin for us down there
If we were there together—before you
 came.   149
That was a fancy, born of circumstance,
And I was only visioning some such thing
As that. The moon may have been part of it.
I think there was a demon born with me
And in the malediction of my name, 154
And that his work is to make others suffer—
Which is the worst of burdens for a man
Whose death tonight were nothing, could
 the death
Of one be the best end of this for two."

"If that was to be said," Isolt replied, 159
"It will at least not have to be said over.
For since the death of one would only give
The other a twofold weight of wretchedness
To bear, why do you pour these frozen
 words
On one who cannot be so confident
As you that we may not be nearer life, 165
Even here tonight, than we are near to
 death?
I must know more than you have told me
 yet
Before I see, so clearly as you see it,
The sword that must for ever be between
 us.   169
Something in you was always in my father:
A darkness always was around my father,
Since my first eyes remembered him. He
 saw
Nothing, but he would see the shadow of it
Before he saw the color or shape it had,
Or where the sun was. Tristram, fair things
 yet   175

154. **malediction**—sorrow, doom, as the name Tristram suggests.

Will have a shadow black as night before
  them,
And soon will have a shadow black as night
Behind them. And all this may be a shadow,
Sometime, that we may live to see behind
  us—   179
Wishing that we had not been all so sure
Tonight that it was always to be night."

"Your father may have fancied where the
  sun was
When first he saw the shadow of King Mark
Coming with mine before me. You are brave
Tonight, my love. A bravery like yours
  now   185
Would be the summons for a mightier love
Than mine, if there were room for such a
  love
Among things hidden in the hearts of men.
Isolt! Isolt! . . ."

                    Out of her struggling eyes
There were tears flowing, and withheld in
  his,   190
Tears were a veil of pity and desperation
Through which he saw the dim face of Isolt
Before him like a phantom in a mist—
Till to be sure that she was not a phantom,
He clutched and held her fast against his
  heart,   195
And through the cloak she wore felt the
  warm life
Within her trembling to the life in him,
And to the sorrow and the passion there
That would be always there. "Isolt! Isolt!"
Was all the language there was left in
  him   200
And she was all that was left anywhere—
She that would soon be so much worse than
  gone
That if he must have seen her lying still,
Dead where she was, he could have said
  that fate
Was merciful at least to one of them.   205
He would have worn through life a living
  crown
Of death, for memory more to be desired
Than any furtive and forsworn desire,
Or shattered oath of his to serve a King,
His mother's brother, without wilful stain,

Was like to be with all else it might be. 211
So Tristram, in so far as there was reason
Left in him, would have reasoned—when
  Isolt
Drew his face down to hers with all her
  strength,
Or so it seemed, and kissed his eyes and
  cheeks   215
And mouth until there was no reason left
In life but love—love that was not to be,
Save as a wrenching and a separation
Past reason or reprieve. If she forgot
For long enough to smile at him through
  tears,   220
He may have read it as a sign that God
Was watching her and all might yet be well;
And if he knew that all might not be well,
Some God might still be watching over her,
With no more power than theirs now against
  Rome,   225
Or the pernicious valor of sure ruin,
Or against fate, that like an unseen ogre
Made hungry sport of these two there alone
Above the moaning wash of Cornish water,
Cold upon Cornish rocks.

[Fate having intervened between these
unhappy lovers, Tristram returns indifferent to a youthful love in Brittany. In time
she, "Isolt of the white hands," and he are
wed. But he yearns still for Isolt of Ireland,
and while King Mark is in captivity the
two find a brief fulfillment of love at Joyous Gard. But Mark soon is free again and
takes Isolt back to Cornwall with him. Tristram comes there for their last talk together.]

                  "I would to God
That we might fly together away from
  here,   231
Like two birds over the sea," she murmured
  then,
And her words sang to him. "The sea was
  never
So still as it is now, and the wind never
So dead. It is like dying, and not like
  death.   235
No, do not say things now. This is not you,
Tristram. There was a mercy in fate for you

---

225. **Rome**—the Church of Rome.

That later will be clear, when you see bet-
ter
That you need see today. Only remember
That all there was of me was always
yours.   240
There was no more of me. Was it enough?
Tell me, was it enough? You said it was,
And I have still to ask. Women have ears
That will hold love as deserts will hold rain,
But you have told Isolt it was enough, 245
And she knows all there is. When first we
met
In darkness, and were groping there to-
gether,
Not seeing ourselves—and there was all that
time—
She was all yours. But time has died since
then,
Time and the world, and she is always
yours.   250
Pray God she be no burden. You that are
still
To fly, pray God for that."

                          He raised his eyes
And found hers waiting for them. "Time
is not life—
For me," he said. "But your life was for
you.
It was not mine to take away from you."
He went on wanderingly, and his words
ached   256
Like slaves feeling a lash: "It was not mine.
I should have let you go away from there.
I should have made you go, or should have
gone   259
Myself, leaving you there to tell yourself
It was your fear for me that frightened me,
And made me go."

                    "If you should hear my ghost
Laughing at you sometime, you will know
why,
Tristram," she said. And over her calm eyes
A smile of pity passed like a small cloud
Over two pools of violet in warm white, 266
Pallid with change and pain. "It was your
life,
For mine was nothing alone. It was not
time,
For you or me, when we were there to-
gether.

It was too much like always to be time. 270
If you said anything, love, you said it only
Because you are afraid to see me die—
Which is so little, now. There was no more;
And when I knew that I was here again,
I knew there was no more. . . . It was
enough,   275
And it was all there was."

                    Once more she drew him
Closer, and held him; and once more his
head
Was lying upon her with her arms around it
As they would hold a child. She felt the
strength
Of a man shaking in his helplessness,   280
And would not see it. Lying with eyes closed
And all her senses tired with pain and love,
And pity for love that was to die, she saw
him
More as a thunder-stricken tower of life
Brought down by fire, than as a stricken
man   285
Brought down by fate, and always to wear
scars
That in his eyes and voice were changelessly
Revealed and hidden. There was another
voice,
Telling of when there should be left for
him
No place among the living any longer;   290
And there was peace and wisdom, saying to
her,
It will be best then, when it is all done.
But her own peace and wisdom frightened
her,
And she would see him only as he had been
Before. That was the best for her to see;
And it was best that each should see the
other   296
Unseen, and as they were before the world
Was done with them, and for a little while,
In silence, to forget and to remember.
They did not see the ocean or the sky,   300
Or the one ship that moved, if it was mov-
ing,
Or the still leaves on trees. They did not see
The stairs where they had stood once in the
moonlight,
Before the moon went out and Tristram
went
From her to darkness, into time and rain,

Leaving her there with Mark and the cold
    sound   306
Of waves that foamed all night. They did
    not see
The silent shore below, or the black rocks,
Or the black shadow of fate that came un-
    felt,
Or, following it, like evil dressed as man,
A shape that crept and crawled along to
    Tristram,   311
And leapt upon him with a shining knife
That ceased to shine. After one cry to God,
And her last cry, she could hear Tristram,
    saying,
"If it was Andred—give him thanks—for
    me. . . .   315
It was not Mark. . . . Isolt!"

                  She heard no more.
There was no more for either of them to
    hear,
Or tell. It was all done. So there they lay,
And her white arms around his head still
    held him,
Closer than life. They did not hear the
    sound   320
Of Andred laughing, and they did not hear
The cry of Brangwaine, who had seen too
    late,
Andred ascending stealthily alone,
Like death, and with death shining in his
    hand,   324
And in his eyes. They did not hear the steps
Of Mark, who followed, or of Gouvernail,
Who followed Mark.

                They were all silent there
While Mark, nearer the couch and watching
    it,
And all that there was on it, and half on it,
Was unaware of Andred at his knees,   330
Until he seized them and stared up at him
With unclean gleaming eyes. "Tell me, my
    lord
And master," he crooned, with fawning con-
    fidence,
"Tell me—and say if I have not done well!
See him—and say if I'm a lizard now!   335
See him, my master! Have I not done well?"

Mark, for a time withheld in angry wonder
At what he saw, and with accusing sorrow

For what he felt, said nothing and did noth-
    ing,
Till at the sight of Andred's upturned face
He reached and seized him, saying no word
    at all,   341
And like a still machine with hands began
Slowly to strangle him. Then, with a curse,
He flung him half alive upon the floor,
Where now, for the first time, a knife was
    lying,   345
All wet with Tristram's blood. He stared
    at it,
Almost as if his hands had left it there;
And having seen all he would of it, he flung
    it
Over the parapet and into the sea;   349
And where it fell, the faint sound of a splash
Far down was the one sound the sea had
    made
That afternoon. Only the ship had moved—
And was a smaller ship, farther away.
He watched it for a long time, silently,
And then stood watching Tristram and
    Isolt,   355
Who made no sound. "I do not know," he
    said,
And gazed away again from everything.

"No sea was ever so still as this before,"
Gouvernail said, at last; and while he spoke
His eyes were on the two that were to-
    gether   360
Where they were lying as silent as the sea.
"They will not ask me why it is not strange
Of me to say so little."

                "No," Mark answered,
"Nothing was ever so still as this be-
    fore. . . .
She said it was like something after life,
And it was not like death. She may have
    meant   366
To say to me it was like this; and this
Is peace."
        .   .   .   .   .

        And peace, that lay so heavy and dark
That night on Cornwall, lay as dark that
    night   370
On Brittany, where Isolt of the white hands
Sat watching, as Mark had watched, a silent
    sea
That was all stars and darkness. She was
    looking

With her gray eyes again, in her old way,
Into the north, and for she knew not
what 375
Tonight. She was not looking for a ship,
And there was no ship coming. Yet there
she sat,
And long into the night she sat there, look-
ing
Away into the darkness to the north,
Where there was only darkness, and more
stars. 380
No ship was coming that night to Brittany
From Cornwall. There was time enough for
ships;
And when one came at last, with Gouver-
nail,
Alone, she had seen in him the end of wait-
ing, 384
Before her father's eyes and his bowed head
Confirmed her sight and sense.

           King Howel paused,
Like one who shifts a grievous weight he
carries,
Hoping always in vain to make it lighter,
And after gazing at the large gray eyes
In the wan face before him, would have
spoken, 390
But no speech came. Dimly from where he
was,
Through mist that filled his eyes, he pic-
tured her
More as a white and lovely thing to kill
With words than as a woman who was
waiting 394
For truth already told. "Isolt—my child!"
He faltered, and because he was her father,
His anguish for the blow that he was giving
Felt the blow first for her.

           "You are so kind
To me, my father," she said softly to him,
"That you will hold behind you now the
knife 400
You bring with you, first having let me see
it.
You are too kind. I said then to Gawaine
That he would not come back. Tristram is
dead.
So—tell me all there is. I shall not die.
I have died too many times already for
that.

I shall not ever die. Where was he,
father?" 406
Her face was whiter and her large gray eyes
Glimmered with tears that waited.

                 He told her then
A tale, by Gouvernail and himself twice-
tempered,
Of Tristram on his way to Brittany, 410
Having seen that other Isolt, by Mark's re-
prieve,
Only once more before she was to die.
It was an insane sort of kinsman, Andred,
Not Mark, who slew him in a jealous hate;
All which was nebulously true enough 415
To serve, her father trusted, willing to leave
The rest of it unheard, whatever it was,
For time to bury and melt. With Tristram
dead,
This child of his, with her gray eyes that
saw
So much, seeing so far, might one day see
A reason to live without him—which, to
him, 421
Her father, was not so hard as to conceive
A reason for man's once having and leaving
her.
That night the King prayed heaven to make
her see, 424
And in the morning found his child asleep—
After a night of tears and stifled words,
They told him. She had made almost no
sound
That whole night; and for many a day to
follow
She made almost no sound.

               One afternoon
Her father found her by the sea, alone, 430
Where the cold waves that rolled along the
sand
Were saying to her unceasingly, "Tristram—
Tristram." She heard them and was un-
aware
That they had uttered once another name
For Tristram's ears. She did not know of
that, 435
More than a woman or man today may
know
What women or men may hear when some-
one says
Familiar things forgotten, and did not see

Her father until she turned, hearing him
   speak: 439

"Two years ago it was that he came here
To make you his unhappy wife, my child,
Telling you then, and in a thousand ways,
Without the need of language, that his love
Was far from here. His willingness and my
   wish   444
Were more to save you then, so I believed,
Than to deceive you. You were not de-
   ceived;
And you are as far now from all deception,
Or living need of it. You are not going
On always with a ghost for company,
Until you die. If you do so, my way,   450
Which cannot be a long way now, may still
Be more than yours. If Tristram were alive,
You would be Tristram's queen, and the
   world's eyes
And mind would be content, seeing it so.
But he is dead, and you have dreamed too
   long,   455
Partly because your dream was partly true—
Which was the worst of all, but yet a dream.
Now it is time for those large solemn eyes
Of yours to open slowly, and to see
Before them, not behind. Tristram is dead,
And you are a king's daughter, fairer than
   fame   461
Has told—which are two seeds for you to
   plant
In your wise little head as in a garden,
Letting me see what grows. We pay for
   dreams
In waking out of them, and we forget 465
As much as needs forgetting. I'm not a king
With you; I am a father and a man—
A man not over wise or over foolish,
Who has not long to live, and has one child
To be his life when he is gone from here.
You will be Queen some day, if you will
   live,   471
My child, and all you are will shine for me.
You are my life, and I must live in you.
Kings that are marked with nothing else
   than honor
Are not remembered long."

                      "I shall be Queen
Of Here or There, may be—sometime," she
   said;   476

"And as for dreaming, you might hesitate
In shaking me too soon out of my sleep
In which I'm walking. Am I doing so ill
To dream a little, if dreams will help me
   now?   480
You are not educating me, my father,
When you would seize too soon, for my im-
   provement,
All that I have. You are the dreamer now.
You are not playing today with the same
   child
Whose dream amused you once when you
   supposed   485
That she was learning wisdom at your knees.
Wisdom was never learned at any knees,
Not even a father's, and that father a king.
If I am wiser now than while I waited
For Tristram coming, knowing that he
   would come,   490
I may not wait so long for Tristram going,
For he will never go. I am not one
Who must have everything, yet I must have
My dreams if I must live, for they are mine.
Wisdom is not one word and then another,
Till words are like dry leaves under a tree;
Wisdom is like a dawn that comes up
   slowly   497
Out of an unknown ocean."

                     "And goes down
Sometimes," the king said, "into the same
   ocean.
You live still in the night, and are not ready
For the new dawn. When the dawn comes,
   my child,   501
You will forget. No, you will not forget,
But you will change. There are no mortal
   houses
That are so providently barred and fastened
As to keep change and death from coming
   in.   505
Tristram is dead, and change is at your
   door.
Two years have made you more than two
   years older,
And you must change."

                  "The dawn has come," she said,
"And wisdom will come with it. If it sinks
Away from me, and into night again— 510
Then I shall be alone, and I shall die.
But I shall never be all alone—not now;

And I shall know there was a fate more
  swift
Than yours or mine that hurried him far-
  ther on
Than we are yet. I would have been the
  world   515
And heaven to Tristram, and was nothing
  to him;
And that was why the night came down so
  dark
On me when Tristram died. But there was
  always
Attending him an almost visible doom
That I see now; and while he moved and
  looked   520
As one too mighty and too secure to die,
He was not mingled and equipped to live
Very long. It was not earth in him that
  burned
Itself to death; and she that died for him
Must have been more than earth. If he had
  lived,   525
He would have pitied me and smiled at me,
And he would always have been kind to
  me—
If he had lived; and I should not have
  known,
Not even when in his arms, how far away
He was from me. Now, when I cannot
  sleep,   530
Thinking of him, I shall know where he is."

King Howel shook his head. "Thank God,
  my child,
That I was wise enough never to thwart you
When you were never a child. If that was
  wisdom,
Say on my tomb that I was a wise man."
He laid his hands upon her sun-touched
  hair,   536
Which in Gawaine's appraisal had no color
That was a name, and saying no more to
  her
While he stood looking into her gray eyes,

He smiled, like one with nothing else to do;
And with a backward glance unsatisfied,
He walked away.

                    Isolt of the white hands,
Isolt with her gray eyes and her white face,
Still gazed across the water to the north
But not now for a ship. Were ships to come,
No fleet of them could hold a golden
  cargo   546
That would be worth one agate that was
  hers—
One toy that he had given her long ago,
And long ago forgotten. Yet there she gazed
Across the water, over the white waves,
Upon a castle that she had never seen, 551
And would not see, save as a phantom shape
Against a phantom sky. He had been there,
She thought, but not with her. He had died
  there,
But not for her. He had not thought of
  her,   555
Perhaps, and that was strange. He had been
  all,
And would be always all there was for her,
And he had not come back to her alive,
Not even to go again. It was like that
For women, sometimes, and might be so too
  often   560
For women like her. She hoped there were
  not many
Of them, or many of them to be, not know-
  ing
More about that than about waves and foam,
And white birds everywhere, flying, and
  flying;
Alone, with her white face and her gray
  eyes,   565
She watched them there till even her
  thoughts were white,
And there was nothing alive but white birds
  flying,
Flying, and always flying, and still flying,
And the white sunlight flashing on the sea

STEPHEN CRANE

1871-1900

I. EARLY YEARS (1871–1891)

1871 Born November 1 in Newark, New Jersey, fourteenth and youngest child of Reverend Jonathan Townley and Mary (Peck) Crane.

1879 Family finally settled in Port Jervis, New York, after living in Bloomington, Paterson, and Jersey City—the composite background for Crane's *Whilomville Stories.*

1880 Death of Crane's father.

1880–1882 Family moved to Newark, returned to Port Jervis, settled eventually in Asbury Park, New Jersey, where Stephen's brother Townley ran a news reporting agency.

1882–1888 Schooling in Asbury Park, at Pennington Seminary in New Jersey, and at the Hudson River Institute (a military school) in Claverack, New York.

1890–1891 Spent the fall term at Lafáyette College, the spring term at Syracuse University. Excelled in baseball, sold sketches to the Detroit *Free Press,* spent his summers as news reporter. Wrote *Maggie* "in two days before Christmas" (1891) but could not find a publisher.

II. BRIEF SUCCESS (1892–1900)

1892 Free-lance reporter in New York City. Sold sketches to the New York *Tribune,* lived in poverty, learned to know the Bowery.

1893 Borrowed money to print 700 copies of *Maggie: A Girl of the Streets.* Story appeared in yellow paper wrappers under pseudonym of "Johnston Smith," remained unsold.

1894 *The Red Badge of Courage: An Episode of the American Civil War* appeared in the Philadelphia *Press,* December 3-8, a war novel by a man who had never been to war.

1895 *The Red Badge of Courage* published by D. Appleton and Company. An instantaneous success. *The Black Riders and Other Lines* (poems) also published.

1896 *Maggie* republished in book form, with Crane's name on the title page. Also this year: *A Souvenir and a Medley: Seven Poems and a Sketch; George's Mother* (novel); *The Little Regiment and Other Episodes of the American Civil War.* On way to Cuba as foreign correspondent, Crane was aboard the *Commodore* when it sank. Survived after several days at sea in an open boat.

1897 *The Third Violet,* a minor novel, appeared. Crane reported Greco-Turkish War for the New York *Journal* and the Westminster *Gazette.* In Athens, married Cora Taylor, an American woman he had known in Florida. Returned to England with her, living at Oxted, Surrey.

1898 *The Open Boat and Other Tales of Adventure* published. Left in March from New York as correspondent in Spanish-American War. Cited for bravery in Guantánamo, Cuba. Returned to New York in October.

1899 Published *War is Kind* (poems); *Active Service* (novel); *The Monster and Other Stories* (including the famous "The Blue Hotel"). Returned to England and settled finally in Brede Place, Sussex. Host here to numerous literary friends including Joseph Conrad, H. G. Wells, Henry James, James M. Barrie, and Ford Maddox Heuffer (Ford).

1900 *Whilomville Stories; Wounds in the Rain: War Stories.* Died of tuberculosis on June 5 at Badenweiler, Germany, where he had been rushed for treatment. Buried in Elizabeth, New Jersey.

III. POSTHUMOUS PUBLICATIONS

1901 *Great Battles of the World.*
1902 *Last Words* (sketches and stories).
1903 *The O'Ruddy: A Romance* (finished by Robert Barr).
1936 *A Battle in Greece.*
1949 *The Sullivan County Sketches of Stephen Crane,* ed. by Melvin Schoberlin.

BIOGRAPHY AND CRITICISM: The chief source of biographical information is Thomas Beer's *Stephen Crane: A Study in American Letters,* Knopf, 1923. See also Thomas Beer, "Mrs. Stephen Crane," *American Mercury,* March, 1934, pp. 289-95 and Helen R. Crane, "My Uncle: Stephen Crane," *American Mercury,* January, 1934, pp. 24-29. John Berryman's *Stephen Crane,* Sloane, 1950, is a new and valuable study.

Other shorter articles on Crane are Hamlin Garland, "Stephen Crane as I Knew Him," *Yale Review,* April, 1914, pp. 494-506; Harriet Monroe, "Stephen Crane," *Poetry,* June, 1919, pp. 148-52; Edward Garnett, *Friday Nights,* Knopf, 1922, pp. 201-17; Carl Van Doren, "Stephen Crane," *American Mercury,* January, 1924, pp. 11-14; Floyd Dell, "Stephen Crane and the Genius Myth," *Nation,* December 10, 1924, pp. 637-38; Joseph Conrad, *Last Essays,* Doubleday, 1926, pp. 135-73, 175-83; Matthew Josephson, *Portrait of the Artist as American,* Harcourt, Brace, 1930, pp. 232-64; Don C. Seitz, "Stephen Crane: War Correspondent," *Bookman,* February, 1933, pp. 137-40; Alfred Kazin, *On Native Grounds,* Reynal and Hitchcock, 1942, pp. 67-72; and William L. Werner, "Stephen Crane and *The Red Badge of Courage,*" *New York Times Book Review,* September 30, 1945, p. 4.

For additional articles and studies see *Literary History of the United States,* Vol. III, pp. 458-61, and John Berryman, "A Bibliographical Note," in his *Stephen Crane,* Sloane, 1950, pp. 326-31.

EDITIONS: *The Works of Stephen Crane,* ed. by Wilson Follett, 12 vols., Knopf, 1925-27 and *The Collected Poems of Stephen Crane,* ed., by Wilson Follett, Knopf, 1930, are standard, but not completely adequate and are now out of print. Useful single volumes are *The Red Badge of Courage* (several editions, including the inexpensive Modern Library) and *Twenty Stories of Stephen Crane,* ed. with an introduction by Carl Van Doren, Knopf, 1940 (including *Maggie, The Monster,* and "The Blue Hotel").

BIBLIOGRAPHY: There are three useful check lists: Vincent Starrett, *Stephen Crane: A Bibliography,* Centaur Book Shop, 1923; Benjamin J. R. Stolper, *Stephen Crane: A List of His Writings and Articles About Him,* Newark Public Library, 1930; and Ames W. Williams and Vincent Starrett, *Stephen Crane: A Bibliography,* Valentine Press, 1948.

When Stephen Crane wrote in a letter of 1896 that "my creed was identical with one of Howells and Garland," he was acknowledging more than a literary debt to his predecessors in realistic fiction. The publication of *Maggie* had won him William Dean Howells' valuable friendship and admiration. When Crane could afford to pay for the typing of only half of *The Red Badge of Courage,* Hamlin Garland read that half, liked it, paid for the rest of the typing, and urged that it be syndicated. Crane was an eager disciple of the realism of Howells and the "creed of veritism" which Garland advocated in *Main-Travelled Roads.* He believed strongly that the very best reporting achieved the level of art and that personal experience, even though it be brutal and inartistic by nature, could be utilized with powerful effect (as in *Maggie*) by the literary artist. He belongs with the early American naturalists or pseudo-naturalists who continued where Garland turned aside: Frank Norris (*McTeague, The Octopus, The Pit*), Jack London (*The People of the Abyss, The Game*), Theodore Dreiser (*Sister Carrie, Jennie Gerhardt*), and other lesser writers. They shouldered the responsibility of depicting life in the light of the new deterministic sociology, which conceived of man as controlled by his instincts and emotions or by his social environment, without free will, without need for moral judgment, especially from the novelist. In this sense, Crane leads directly to Sherwood Anderson, Dos Passos, Farrell, and the later work of Dreiser.

But ironically Crane's best novel, the work which gained him an international reputation at the age of twenty-six, was written before he ever had opportunity to observe his material at first hand. Whereas "The Open Boat" retells what Crane himself experienced in a lifeboat at sea and "The Blue Hotel" began with his seeing a Nebraska hotel that was painted an ugly blue, the sources of *The Red Badge of Courage* include only tales he heard veterans tell of the American Civil War, Matthew Brady's remarkable photographs, and such books as *Battles and Leaders of the Civil War.* To these Crane brought his tremendous imagination, his incisive style and keen perception, his determination to write of nothing but what could have happened to this most unheroic hero in an unheroic fragment of a great war. *The Red Badge* could only be the product of a man who, as Howells said, had sprung into life fully armed. If it is true that Crane wrote it in ten days, it is believable that the novel poured from his pen with the intensity of an infantry engagement and all the concomitant emotions. Its supreme understatement, its grim honesty and avoidance of heroics in spite of its tensions, endeared it to the decade of the 1920's, especially to Ernest Hemingway who, with Thomas Beer, became Crane's champion (among many other critics) during the years between the two World Wars. Now that Crane's stories have been re-issued and new light shed on his fantastic life, we can begin to enlarge our portrait of this American phenomenon.

THE RED BADGE OF COURAGE

After being serialized in condensed form in the Philadelphia *Press* (December 3-8, 1894) and immediately being printed in a number of other newspapers, *The Red Badge of Courage* was issued in book form in October, 1895, by D. Appleton and Company. Shortly thereafter (1896), it was issued by William Heinemann in London.

Inasmuch as Crane seems to have paid little attention to later editions of the book, the present text is that of the original American edition.

CHAPTER I

THE cold passed reluctantly from the earth, and the retiring fogs revealed an army stretched out on the hills, resting. As the landscape changed from brown to green, the army awakened, and began to tremble with eagerness at the noise of rumors. It cast its eyes upon the roads, which were growing from long troughs of liquid mud to proper thorough-fares. A river, amber-tinted in the shadow of its banks, purled at the army's feet; and at night, when the stream had become of a sorrowful blackness, one could see across it the red, eyelike gleam of hostile camp-fires set in the low brows of distant hills.

Once a certain tall soldier developed virtues and went resolutely to wash a shirt. He came flying back from a brook waving his garment bannerlike. He was swelled with a tale he had heard from a reliable friend, who had heard it from a truthful cavalryman, who had heard it from his trustworthy brother, one of the orderlies at division headquarters. He adopted the important air of a herald in red and gold.

"We're goin' t' move t' morrah—sure," he said pompously to a group in the company street. "We're goin' 'way up the river, cut across, an' come around in behint 'em."

To his attentive audience he drew a loud and elaborate plan of a very brilliant campaign. When he had finished, the blue-clothed men scattered into small arguing groups between the rows of squat brown huts. A negro teamster who had been dancing upon a cracker box with the hilarious encouragement of twoscore soldiers was deserted. He sat mournfully down. Smoke drifted lazily from a multitude of quaint chimneys.

"It's a lie! that's all it is—a thunderin' lie!" said another private loudly. His smooth face was flushed, and his hands were thrust sulkily into his trousers' pockets. He took the matter as an affront to him. "I don't believe the derned old army's ever going to move. We're set. I've got ready to move eight times in the last two weeks, and we ain't moved yet."

The tall soldier felt called upon to defend the truth of a rumor he himself had introduced. He and the loud one came near to fighting over it.

A corporal began to swear before the assemblage. He had just put a costly board floor in his house, he said. During the early spring he had refrained from adding extensively to the comfort of his environment because he had felt that the army might start on the march at any moment. Of late, however, he had been impressed that they were in a sort of eternal camp.

Many of the men engaged in a spirited debate. One outlined in a peculiarly lucid manner all the plans of the commanding general. He was opposed by men who advocated that there were other plans of campaign. They clamored at each other, numbers making futile bids for the popular attention. Meanwhile, the soldier who had fetched the rumor bustled about with much importance. He was continually assailed by questions.

"What's up, Jim?"

"Th' army's goin' t' move."

"Ah, what yeh talkin' about? How yeh know it is?"

"Well, yeh kin b'lieve me er not, jest as yeh like. I don't care a hang."

5   There was much food for thought in the manner in which he replied. He came near to convincing them by disdaining to produce proofs. They grew much excited over it.

There was a youthful private who listened with eager ears to the words of the tall soldier and to the varied comments of his comrades. After receiving
10 a fill of discussions concerning marches and attacks, he went to his hut and crawled through an intricate hole that served it as a door. He wished to be alone with some new thoughts that had lately come to him.

He lay down on a wide bank that stretched across the end of the room. In the other end, cracker boxes were made to serve as furniture. They were
15 grouped about the fireplace. A picture from an illustrated weekly was upon the log walls, and three rifles were paralleled on pegs. Equipments hung on handy projections, and some tin dishes lay upon a small pile of firewood. A folded tent was serving as a roof. The sunlight, without, beating upon it, made it glow a light yellow shade. A small window shot an oblique square
20 of whiter light upon the cluttered floor. The smoke from the fire at times neglected the clay chimney and wreathed into the room, and this flimsy chimney of clay and sticks made endless threats to set ablaze the whole establishment.

The youth was in a little trance of astonishment. So they were at last going
25 to fight. On the morrow, perhaps, there would be a battle, and he would be in it. For a time he was obliged to labor to make himself believe. He could not accept with assurance an omen that he was about to mingle in one of those great affairs of the earth.

He had, of course, dreamed of battles all his life—of vague and bloody con-
30 flicts that had thrilled him with their sweep and fire. In visions he had seen himself in many struggles. He had imagined peoples secure in the shadow of his eagle-eyed prowess. But awake he had regarded battles as crimson blotches on the pages of the past. He had put them as things of the bygone with his thought-images of heavy crowns and high castles. There was a por-
35 tion of the world's history which he had regarded as the time of wars, but it, he thought, had been long gone over the horizon and had disappeared forever.

From his home his youthful eyes had looked upon the war in his own country with distrust. It must be some sort of a play affair. He had long
40 despaired of witnessing a Greeklike struggle. Such would be no more, he had said. Men were better, or more timid. Secular and religious education had effaced the throat-grappling instinct, or else firm finance held in check the passions.

He had burned several times to enlist. Tales of great movements shook
45 the land. They might not be distinctly Homeric, but there seemed to be much glory in them. He had read of marches, sieges, conflicts, and he had

13. **bank**—so spelled in the original text. Probably the author intended *bunk*.

longed to see it all. His busy mind had drawn for him large pictures extravagant in color, lurid with breathless deeds.)

But his mother had discouraged him. She had affected to look with some contempt upon the quality of his war ardor and patriotism. She could calmly seat herself and with no apparent difficulty give him many hundreds of reasons why he was of vastly more importance on the farm than on the field of battle. She had had certain ways of expression that told him that her statements on the subject came from a deep conviction. Moreover, on her side, was his belief that her ethical motive in the argument was impregnable.

At last, however, he had made firm rebellion against this yellow light thrown upon the color of his ambitions. The newspapers, the gossip of the village, his own picturings, had aroused him to an uncheckable degree. They were in truth fighting finely down there. Almost every day the newspapers printed accounts of a decisive victory.

One night, as he lay in bed, the winds had carried to him the clangoring of the church bell as some enthusiast jerked the rope frantically to tell the twisted news of a great battle. This voice of the people rejoicing in the night had made him shiver in a prolonged ecstasy of excitement. Later, he had gone down to his mother's room and had spoken thus: "Ma, I'm going to enlist."

"Henry, don't you be a fool," his mother had replied. She had then covered her face with the quilt. There was an end to the matter for that night.

Nevertheless, the next morning he had gone to a town that was near his mother's farm and had enlisted in a company that was forming there. When he had returned home his mother was milking the brindle cow. Four others stood waiting. "Ma, I've enlisted," he had said to her diffidently. There was a short silence. "The Lord's will be done, Henry," she had finally replied, and had then continued to milk the brindle cow.

When he had stood in the doorway with his soldier's clothes on his back, and with the light of excitement and expectancy in his eyes almost defeating the glow of regret for the home bonds, he had seen two tears leaving their trails on his mother's scarred cheeks.

Still, she had disappointed him by saying nothing whatever about returning with his shield or on it. He had privately primed himself for a beautiful scene. He had prepared certain sentences which he thought could be used with touching effect. But her words destroyed his plans. She had doggedly peeled potatoes and addressed him as follows: "You watch out, Henry, an' take good care of yerself in this here fighting business—you watch out, an' take good care of yerself. Don't go a-thinkin' you can lick the hull rebel army at the start, because yeh can't. Yer jest one little feller amongst a hull lot of others, and yeh've got to keep quiet an' do what they tell yeh. I know how you are, Henry.

"I've knet yeh eight pair of socks, Henry, and I've put in all yer best shirts, because I want my boy to be jest as warm and comf'able as anybody in the army. Whenever they get holes in 'em, I want yeh to send 'em right-away back to me, so's I kin dern 'em.

"An' allus be careful an' choose yer comp'ny. There's lots of bad men in

the army, Henry. The army makes 'em wild, and they like nothing better than the job of leading off a young feller like you, as ain't never been away from home much and has allus had a mother, an' a-learning 'em to drink and swear. Keep clear of them folks, Henry. I don't want yeh to ever do
5   anything, Henry, that yeh would be 'shamed to let me know about. Jest think as if I was a-watchin' yeh. If yeh keep that in yer mind allus, I guess yeh'll come out about right.

"Yeh must allus remember yer father, too, child, an' remember he never drunk a drop of licker in his life, and seldom swore a cross oath.

10   "I don't know what else to tell yeh, Henry, excepting that yeh must never do no shirking, child, on my account. If so be a time comes when yeh have to be kilt or do a mean thing, why, Henry, don't think of anything 'cept what's right, because there's many a woman has to bear up 'ginst sech things these times, and the Lord'll take keer of us all.

15   "Don't forgit about the socks and the shirts, child; and I've put a cup of blackberry jam with yer bundle, because I know yeh like it above all things. Good-by, Henry. Watch out, and be a good boy."

He had, of course, been impatient under the ordeal of this speech. It had not been quite what he expected, and he had borne it with an air of irrita-
20   tion. He departed feeling vague relief.

Still, when he had looked back from the gate, he had seen his mother kneeling among the potato parings. Her brown face, upraised, was stained with tears, and her spare form was quivering. He bowed his head and went on, feeling suddenly ashamed of his purposes.

25   From his home he had gone to the seminary to bid adieu to many school-mates. They had thronged about him with wonder and admiration. He had felt the gulf now between them and had swelled with calm pride. He and some of his fellows who had donned blue were quite overwhelmed with privileges for all of one afternoon, and it had been a very delicious thing.
30   They had strutted.

A certain light-haired girl had made vivacious fun at his martial spirit, but there was another and darker girl whom he had gazed at steadfastly, and he thought she grew demure and sad at sight of his blue and brass. As he had walked down the path between the rows of oaks, he had turned his head
35   and detected her at a window watching his departure. As he perceived her, she had immediately begun to stare up through the high tree branches at the sky. He had seen a good deal of flurry and haste in her movement as she changed her attitude. He often thought of it.

On the way to Washington his spirit had soared. The regiment was fed
40   and caressed at station after station until the youth had believed that he must be a hero. There was a lavish expenditure of bread and cold meats, coffee, and pickles and cheese. As he basked in the smiles of the girls and was patted and complimented by the old men, he had felt growing within him the strength to do mighty deeds of arms.

45   After complicated journeyings with many pauses, there had come months of monotonous life in a camp. He had had the belief that real war was a

    25. seminary—local school, not a theological institution.

series of death struggles with small time in between for sleep and meals; but since his regiment had come to the field the army had done little but sit still and try to keep warm.)

(He was brought then gradually back to his old ideas. Greeklike struggles would be no more. Men were better, or more timid. Secular and religious 5 education had effaced the throat-grappling instinct, or else firm finance held in check the passions.)

He had grown to regard himself merely as a part of a vast blue demonstration. His province was to look out, as far as he could, for his personal comfort. For recreation he could twiddle his thumbs and speculate on the 10 thoughts which must agitate the minds of the generals. Also, he was drilled and drilled and reviewed, and drilled and drilled and reviewed.

The only foes he had seen were some pickets along the river bank. They were a sun-tanned, philosophical lot, who sometimes shot reflectively at the blue pickets. When reproached for this afterward, they usually expressed 15 sorrow, and swore by their gods that the guns had exploded without their permission. The youth, on guard duty one night, conversed across the stream with one of them. He was a slightly ragged man, who spat skillfully between his shoes and possessed a great fund of bland and infantile assurance. The youth liked him personally. 20

"Yank," the other had informed him, "yer a right dum good feller." This sentiment, floating to him upon the still air, had made him temporarily regret war.

Various veterans had told him tales. Some talked of gray, bewhiskered hordes who were advancing with relentless curses and chewing tobacco with 25 unspeakable valor; tremendous bodies of fierce soldiery who were sweeping along like the Huns. Others spoke of tattered and eternally hungry men who fired despondent powders. "They'll charge through hell's fire an' brimstone t' git a holt on a haversack, an' sech stomachs ain't a-lastin' long," he was told. From the stories, the youth imagined the red, live bones sticking 30 out through slits in the faded uniforms.

Still, he could not put a whole faith in veterans' tales, for recruits were their prey. They talked much of smoke, fire, and blood, but he could not tell how much might be lies. They persistently yelled, "Fresh fish!" at him, and were in no wise to be trusted. 35

However, he perceived now that it did not greatly matter what kind of soldiers he was going to fight, so long as they fought, which fact no one disputed. There was a more serious problem. He lay in his bunk pondering upon it. He tried to mathematically prove to himself that he would not run from a battle. 40

Previously he had never felt obliged to wrestle too seriously with this question. In his life he had taken certain things for granted, never challenging his belief in ultimate success, and bothering little about means and roads. But here he was confronted with a thing of moment. It had suddenly ap-

27. **Huns**—a tribe of barbarians from Asia who were the terror of Europe in the fifth century A.D. 29. **haversack**—a bag of canvas, worn over a strap on the shoulder, in which the soldier carried his provisions.

peared to him that perhaps in a battle he might run. He was forced to admit
that as far as war was concerned he knew nothing of himself.

A sufficient time before he would have allowed the problem to kick its
heels at the outer portals of his mind, but now he felt compelled to give
5 serious attention to it.

A little panic-fear grew in his mind. As his imagination went forward to
a fight, he saw hideous possibilities. He contemplated the lurking menaces
of the future, and failed in an effort to see himself standing stoutly in the
midst of them. He recalled his visions of broken-bladed glory, but in the
10 shadow of the impending tumult he suspected them to be impossible pictures.

He sprang from the bunk and began to pace nervously to and fro. "Good
Lord, what's th' matter with me?" he said aloud.

He felt that in this crisis his laws of life were useless. Whatever he had
learned of himself was here of no avail. He was an unknown quantity. He
15 saw that he would again be obliged to experiment as he had in early youth.
He must accumulate information of himself, and meanwhile he resolved to
remain close upon his guard lest those qualities of which he knew nothing
should everlastingly disgrace him. "Good Lord!" he repeated in dismay.

After a time the tall soldier slid dexterously through the hole. The loud
20 private followed. They were wrangling.

"That's all right," said the tall soldier as he entered. He waved his hand
expressively. "You can believe me or not, jest as you like. All you got to do
is to sit down and wait as quiet as you can. Then pretty soon you'll find out
I was right."

25 His comrade grunted stubbornly. For a moment he seemed to be searching for a formidable reply. Finally he said: "Well, you don't know everything
in the world, do you?"

"Didn't say I knew everything in the world," retorted the other sharply.
He began to stow various articles snugly into his knapsack.

30 The youth, pausing in his nervous walk, looked down at the busy figure.
"Going to be a battle, sure, is there, Jim?" he asked.

"Of course there is," replied the tall soldier. "Of course there is. You jest
wait 'til to-morrow, and you'll see one of the biggest battles ever was. You
jest wait."

35 "Thunder!" said the youth.

"Oh, you'll see fighting this time, my boy, what'll be regular out-and-out
fighting," added the tall soldier, with the air of a man who is about to exhibit
a battle for the benefit of his friends.

"Huh!" said the loud one from a corner.

40 "Well," remarked the youth, "like as not this story'll turn out jest like
them others did."

"Not much it won't," replied the tall soldier, exasperated. "Not much it
won't. Didn't the cavalry all start this morning?" He glared about him. No
one denied his statement. "The cavalry started this morning," he continued.
45 "They say there ain't hardly any cavalry left in camp. They're going to
Richmond, or some place, while we fight all the Johnnies. It's some dodge

46. Johnnies—Johnny Rebs, i.e., Confederate soldiers.

like that. The regiment's got orders, too. A feller what seen 'em go to headquarters told me a little while ago. And they're raising blazes all over camp
—anybody can see that."

"Shucks!" said the loud one.

The youth remained silent for a time. At last he spoke to the tall soldier. 5
"Jim!"

"What?"

"How do you think the reg'ment 'll do?"

"Oh, they'll fight all right, I guess, after they once get into it," said the
other with cold judgment. He made a fine use of the third person. "There's 10
been heaps of fun poked at 'em because they're new, of course, and all that;
but they'll fight all right, I guess."

"Think any of the boys 'll run?" persisted the youth.

"Oh, there may be a few of 'em run, but there's them kind in every regiment, 'specially when they first goes under fire," said the other in a tolerant 15
way. "Of course it might happen that the hull kit-and-boodle might start
and run, if some big fighting came first-off, and then again they might stay
and fight like fun. But you can't bet on nothing. Of course they ain't never
been under fire yet, and it ain't likely they'll lick the hull rebel army all-to-
oncet the first time; but I think they'll fight better than some, if worse than 20
others. That's the way I figger. They call the reg'ment 'Fresh fish' and
everything; but the boys come of good stock, and most of 'em 'll fight like
sin after they oncet git shootin'," he added, with a mighty emphasis on the
last four words.

"Oh, you think you know—" began the loud soldier with scorn.   25

The other turned savagely upon him. They had a rapid altercation, in
which they fastened upon each other various strange epithets.

The youth at last interrupted them. "Did you ever think you might run
yourself, Jim?" he asked. On concluding the sentence he laughed as if he
had meant to aim a joke. The loud soldier also giggled.   30

The tall private waved his hand. "Well," said he profoundly, "I've thought
it might get too hot for Jim Conklin in some of them scrimmages, and if a
whole lot of boys started and run, why, I s'pose I'd start and run. And if
I once started to run, I'd run like the devil, and no mistake. But if everybody
was a-standing and a-fighting, why, I'd stand and fight. Be jiminey, I would. 35
I'll bet on it."

"Huh!" said the loud one.

The youth of this tale felt gratitude for these words of his comrade. He
had feared that all of the untried men possessed a great and correct confidence. He now was in a measure reassured.   40

CHAPTER II

The next morning the youth discovered that his tall comrade had been
the fast-flying messenger of a mistake. There was much scoffing at the latter
by those who had yesterday been firm adherents of his views, and there was
even a little sneering by men who had never believed the rumor. The tall 45

one fought with a man from Chatfield Corners and beat him severely.

The youth felt, however, that his problem was in no wise lifted from him. There was, on the contrary, an irritating prolongation. The tale had created in him a great concern for himself. Now, with the newborn question in his
5 mind, he was compelled to sink back into his old place as part of a blue demonstration.

For days he made ceaseless calculations, but they were all wondrously unsatisfactory. He found that he could establish nothing. He finally concluded that the only way to prove himself was to go into the blaze, and then
10 figuratively to watch his legs to discover their merits and faults. He reluctantly admitted that he could not sit still and with a mental slate and pencil derive an answer. To gain it, he must have blaze, blood, and danger, even as a chemist requires this, that, and the other. So he fretted for an opportunity.

Meanwhile he continually tried to measure himself by his comrades. The
15 tall soldier, for one, gave him some assurance. This man's serene unconcern dealt him a measure of confidence, for he had known him since childhood, and from his intimate knowledge he did not see how he could be capable of anything that was beyond him, the youth. Still, he thought that his comrade might be mistaken about himself. Or, on the other hand, he might be
20 a man heretofore doomed to peace and obscurity, but, in reality, made to shine in war.

The youth would have liked to have discovered another who suspected himself. A sympathetic comparison of mental notes would have been a joy to him.

25 He occasionally tried to fathom a comrade with seductive sentences. He looked about to find men in the proper mood. All attempts failed to bring forth any statement which looked in any way like a confession to those doubts which he privately acknowledged in himself. He was afraid to make an open declaration of his concern, because he dreaded to place some un-
30 scrupulous confidant upon the high plane of the unconfessed from which elevation he could be derided.

In regard to his companions his mind wavered between two opinions, according to his mood. Sometimes he inclined to believing them all heroes. In fact, he usually admitted in secret the superior development of the
35 higher qualities in others. He could conceive of men going very insignificantly about the world bearing a load of courage unseen, and, although he had known many of his comrades through boyhood, he began to fear that his judgment of them had been blind. Then, in other moments, he flouted these theories, and assured himself that his fellows were all privately wondering
40 and quaking.

His emotions made him feel strange in the presence of men who talked excitedly of a prospective battle as of a drama they were about to witness, with nothing but eagerness and curiosity apparent in their faces. It was often that he suspected them to be liars.

45 He did not pass such thoughts without severe condemnation of himself. He dinned reproaches at times. He was convicted by himself of many shameful crimes against the gods of traditions.

In his great anxiety his heart was continually clamoring at what he considered the intolerable slowness of the generals. They seemed content to perch tranquilly on the river bank, and leave him bowed down by the weight of a great problem. He wanted it settled forthwith. He could not long bear such a load, he said. Sometimes his anger at the commanders reached an acute stage, and he grumbled about the camp like a veteran.

One morning, however, he found himself in the ranks of his prepared regiment. The men were whispering speculations and recounting the old rumors. In the gloom before the break of the day their uniforms glowed a deep purple hue. From across the river the red eyes were still peering. In the eastern sky there was a yellow patch like a rug laid for the feet of the coming sun; and against it, black and patternlike, loomed the gigantic figure of the colonel on a gigantic horse.

From off in the darkness came the trampling of feet. The youth could occasionally see dark shadows that moved like monsters. The regiment stood at rest for what seemed a long time. The youth grew impatient. It was unendurable the way these affairs were managed. He wondered how long they were to be kept waiting.

As he looked all about him and pondered upon the mystic gloom, he began to believe that at any moment the ominous distance might be aflare, and the rolling crashes of an engagement come to his ears. Staring once at the red eyes across the river, he conceived them to be growing larger, as the orbs of a row of dragons advancing. He turned toward the colonel and saw him lift his gigantic arm and calmly stroke his mustache.

At last he heard from along the road at the foot of the hill the clatter of a horse's galloping hoofs. It must be the coming of orders. He bent forward, scarce breathing. The exciting clickety-click, as it grew louder and louder, seemed to be beating upon his soul. Presently a horseman with jangling equipment drew rein before the colonel of the regiment. The two held a short, sharp-worded conversation. The men in the foremost ranks craned their necks.

As the horseman wheeled his animal and galloped away he turned to shout over his shoulder, "Don't forget that box of cigars!" The colonel mumbled in reply. The youth wondered what a box of cigars had to do with war.

A moment later the regiment went swinging off into the darkness. It was now like one of those moving monsters wending with many feet. The air was heavy, and cold with dew. A mass of wet grass, marched upon, rustled like silk.

There was an occasional flash and glimmer of steel from the backs of all these huge crawling reptiles. From the road came creakings and grumblings as some surly guns were dragged away.

The men stumbled along still muttering speculations. There was a subdued debate. Once a man fell down, and as he reached for his rifle a comrade, unseeing, trod upon his hand. He of the injured fingers swore bitterly and aloud. A low, low, tittering laugh went among his fellows.

Presently they passed into a roadway and marched forward with easy strides. A dark regiment moved before them, and from behind also came the tinkle of equipments on the bodies of marching men.

The rushing yellow of the developing day went on behind their backs. When the sunrays at last struck full and mellowingly upon the earth, the 5 youth saw that the landscape was streaked with two long, thin, black columns which disappeared on the brow of a hill in front and rearward vanished in a wood. They were like two serpents crawling from the cavern of the night.

The river was not in view. The tall soldier burst into praises of what he thought to be his powers of perception.

10 Some of the tall one's companions cried with emphasis that they, too, had evolved the same thing, and they congratulated themselves upon it. But there were others who said that the tall one's plan was not the true one at all. They persisted with other theories. There was a vigorous discussion.

15 The youth took no part in them. As he walked along in careless line he was engaged with his own eternal debate. He could not hinder himself from dwelling upon it. He was despondent and sullen, and threw shifting glances about him. He looked ahead, often expecting to hear from the advance the rattle of firing.

20 But the long serpents crawled slowly from hill to hill without bluster of smoke. A dun-colored cloud of dust floated away to the right. The sky overhead was of a fairy blue.

The youth studied the faces of his companions, ever on the watch to detect kindred emotions. He suffered disappointment. Some ardor of the air 25 which was causing the veteran commands to move with glee—almost with song—had infected the new regiment. The men began to speak of victory as of a thing they knew. Also, the tall soldier received his vindication. They were certainly going to come around in behind the enemy. They expressed commiseration for that part of the army which had been left upon the river 30 bank, felicitating themselves upon being a part of a blasting host.

The youth, considering himself as separated from the others, was saddened by the blithe and merry speeches that went from rank to rank. The company wags all made their best endeavors. The regiment tramped to the tune of laughter.

35 The blatant soldier often convulsed whole files by his biting sarcasms aimed at the tall one.

And it was not long before all the men seemed to forget their mission. Whole brigades grinned in unison, and regiments laughed.

A rather fat soldier attempted to pilfer a horse from a dooryard. He planned 40 to load his knapsack upon it. He was escaping with his prize when a young girl rushed from the house and grabbed the animal's mane. There followed a wrangle. The young girl, with pink cheeks and shining eyes, stood like a dauntless statue.

The observant regiment, standing at rest in the roadway, whooped at once, 45 and entered whole-souled upon the side of the maiden. The men became so engrossed in this affair that they entirely ceased to remember their own large war. They jeered the piratical private, and called attention to various defects in his personal appearance; and they were wildly enthusiastic in support of the young girl. ·

To her, from some distance, came bold advice. "Hit him with a stick."

There were crows and catcalls showered upon him when he retreated without the horse. The regiment rejoiced at his downfall. Loud and vociferous congratulations were showered upon the maiden, who stood panting and regarding the troops with defiance.

At nightfall the column broke into regimental pieces, and the fragments went into the fields to camp. Tents sprang up like strange plants. Camp fires, like red, peculiar blossoms, dotted the night.

The youth kept from intercourse with his companions as much as circumstances would allow him. In the evening he wandered a few paces into the gloom. From this little distance the many fires, with the black forms of men passing to and fro before the crimson rays, made weird and satanic effects.

He lay down in the grass. The blades pressed tenderly against his cheek. The moon had been lighted and was hung in a treetop. The liquid stillness of the night enveloping him made him feel vast pity for himself. There was a caress in the soft winds; and the whole mood of the darkness, he thought, was one of sympathy for himself in his distress.

He wished, without reserve, that he was at home again making the endless rounds from the house to the barn, from the barn to the fields, from the fields to the barn, from the barn to the house. He remembered he had often cursed the brindle cow and her mates, and had sometimes flung milking stools. But, from his present point of view, there was a halo of happiness about each of their heads, and he would have sacrificed all the brass buttons on the continent to have been enabled to return to them. He told himself that he was not formed for a soldier. And he mused seriously upon the radical differences between himself and those men who were dodging implike around the fires.

As he mused thus he heard the rustle of grass, and, upon turning his head, discovered the loud soldier. He called out, "Oh, Wilson!"

The latter approached and looked down. "Why, hello, Henry; is it you? What you doing here?"

"Oh, thinking," said the youth.

The other sat down and carefully lighted his pipe. "You're getting blue, my boy. You're looking thundering peeked. What the dickens is wrong with you?"

"Oh, nothing," said the youth.

The loud soldier launched then into the subject of the anticipated fight. "Oh, we've got 'em now!" As he spoke his boyish face was wreathed in a gleeful smile, and his voice had an exultant ring. "We've got 'em now. At last, by the eternal thunders, we'll lick 'em good!"

"If the truth was known," he added, more soberly, "*they've* licked *us* about every clip up to now; but this time—this time—we'll lick 'em good!"

"I thought you was objecting to this march a little while ago," said the youth coldly.

"Oh, it wasn't that," explained the other. "I don't mind marching, if there's going to be fighting at the end of it. What I hate is this getting moved here and moved there, with no good coming of it, as far as I can see, excepting sore feet and damned short rations."

"Well, Jim Conklin says we'll get a plenty of fighting this time."

5   "He's right for once, I guess, though I can't see how it come. This time we're in for a big battle, and we've got the best end of it, certain sure. Gee rod! how we will thump 'em!"

He arose and began to pace to and fro excitedly. The thrill of his enthusiasm made him walk with an elastic step. He was sprightly, vigorous, fiery
10 in his belief in success. He looked into the future with clear, proud eye, and he swore with the air of an old soldier.

The youth watched him for a moment in silence. When he finally spoke his voice was as bitter as dregs. "Oh, you're going to do great things, I s'pose!"

15   The loud soldier blew a thoughtful cloud of smoke from his pipe. "Oh, I don't know," he remarked with dignity; "I don't know. I s'pose I'll do as well as the rest. I'm going to try like thunder." He evidently complimented himself upon the modesty of this statement.

"How do you know you won't run when the time comes?" asked the youth.
20   "Run?" said the loud one; "run?—of course not!" He laughed.

"Well," continued the youth, "lots of good-a-'nough men have thought they was going to do great things before the fight, but when the time come they skedaddled."

"Oh, that's all true, I s'pose," replied the other; "but I'm not going to ske-
25   daddle. The man that bets on my running will lose his money, that's all." He nodded confidently.

"Oh, shucks!" said the youth. "You ain't the bravest man in the world, are you?"

"No, I ain't," exclaimed the loud soldier indignantly; "and I didn't say
30   I was the bravest man in the world, neither. I said I was going to do my share of fighting—that's what I said. And I am, too. Who are you, anyhow? You talk as if you thought you was Napoleon Bonaparte." He glared at the youth for a moment, and then strode away.

The youth called in a savage voice after his comrade: "Well, you needn't
35   git mad about it!" But the other continued on his way and made no reply.

He felt alone in space when his injured comrade had disappeared. His failure to discover any mite of resemblance in their view points made him more miserable than before. No one seemed to be wrestling with such a
40   terrific personal problem. He was a mental outcast.

He went slowly to his tent and stretched himself on a blanket by the side of the snoring tall soldier. In the darkness he saw visions of a thousand-tongued fear that would babble at his back and cause him to flee, while others were going coolly about their country's business. He admitted that
45   he would not be able to cope with this monster. He felt that every nerve in his body would be an ear to hear the voices, while other men would remain stolid and deaf.

And as he sweated with the pain of these thoughts, he could hear low, serene sentences. "I'll bid five." "Make it six." "Seven." "Seven goes."

He stared at the red, shivering reflection of a fire on the white wall of his tent until, exhausted and ill from the monotony of his suffering, he fell asleep.

CHAPTER III

When another night came the columns, changed to purple streaks, filed across two pontoon bridges. A glaring fire wine-tinted the waters of the river. Its rays, shining upon the moving masses of troops, brought forth here and there sudden gleams of silver or gold. Upon the other shore a dark and mysterious range of hills was curved against the sky. The insect voices of the night sang solemnly.

After this crossing the youth assured himself that at any moment they might be suddenly and fearfully assaulted from the caves of the lowering woods. He kept his eyes watchfully upon the darkness.

But his regiment went unmolested to a camping place, and its soldiers slept the brave sleep of wearied men. In the morning they were routed out with early energy, and hustled along a narrow road that led deep into the forest.

It was during this rapid march that the regiment lost many of the marks of a new command.

The men had begun to count the miles upon their fingers, and they grew tired. "Sore feet an' damned short rations, that's all," said the loud soldier. There was perspiration and grumblings. After a time they began to shed their knapsacks. Some tossed them unconcernedly down; others hid them carefully, asserting their plans to return for them at some convenient time. Men extricated themselves from thick shirts. Presently few carried anything but their necessary clothing, blankets, haversacks, canteens, and arms and ammunition. "You can now eat and shoot," said the tall soldier to the youth. "That's all you want to do."

There was sudden change from the ponderous infantry of theory to the light and speedy infantry of practice. The regiment, relieved of a burden, received a new impetus. But there was much loss of valuable knapsacks, and, on the whole, very good shirts.

But the regiment was not yet veteranlike in appearance. Veteran regiments in the army were likely to be very small aggregations of men. Once, when the command had first come to the field, some perambulating veterans, noting the length of their column, had accosted them thus: "Hey, fellers, what brigade is that?" And when the men had replied that they formed a regiment and not a brigade, the older soldiers had laughed, and said, "O Gawd!"

Also, there was too great a similarity in the hats. The hats of a regiment should properly represent the history of headgear for a period of years. And, moreover, there were no letters of faded gold speaking from the colors. They were new and beautiful, and the color bearer habitually oiled the pole.

Presently the army again sat down to think. The odor of the peaceful

7. **pontoon bridges**—bridge supported by flat-bottomed boats. **22. was**—as printed in the original text.

pines was in the men's nostrils. The sound of monotonous axe blows rang through the forest, and the insects, nodding upon their perches, crooned like old women. The youth returned to his theory of a blue demonstration.

One gray dawn, however, he was kicked in the leg by the tall soldier, and
5 then, before he was entirely awake, he found himself running down a wood road in the midst of men who were panting from the first effects of speed. His canteen banged rhythmically upon his thigh, and his haversack bobbed softly. His musket bounced a trifle from his shoulder at each stride and made his cap feel uncertain upon his head.

10 He could hear the men whisper jerky sentences: "Say—what's all this— about?" "What th' thunder—we—skedaddlin' this way fer?" "Billie—keep off m' feet. Yeh run—like a cow." And the loud soldier's shrill voice could be heard: "What th' devil they in sich a hurry for?"

The youth thought the damp fog of early morning moved from the rush
15 of a great body of troops. From the distance came a sudden spatter of firing.

He was bewildered. As he ran with his comrades he strenuously tried to think, but all he knew was that if he fell down those coming behind would tread upon him. All his faculties seemed to be needed to guide him over and past obstructions. He felt carried along by a mob.

20 The sun spread disclosing rays, and, one by one, regiments burst into view like armed men just born of the earth. The youth perceived that the time had come. He was about to be measured. For a moment he felt in the face of his great trial like a babe, and the flesh over his heart seemed very thin. He seized time to look about him calculatingly.

25 But he instantly saw that it would be impossible for him to escape from the regiment. It inclosed him. And there were iron laws of tradition and law on four sides. He was in a moving box.

As he perceived this fact it occurred to him that he had never wished to come to the war. He had not enlisted of his free will. He had been dragged
30 by the merciless government. And now they were taking him out to be slaughtered.

The regiment slid down a bank and wallowed across a little stream. The mournful current moved slowly on, and from the water, shaded black, some white bubble eyes looked at the men.

35 As they climbed the hill on the farther side artillery began to boom. Here the youth forgot many things as he felt a sudden impulse of curiosity. He scrambled up the bank with a speed that could not be exceeded by a bloodthirsty man.

He expected a battle scene.

40 There were some little fields girted and squeezed by a forest. Spread over the grass and in among the tree trunks, he could see knots and waving lines of skirmishers who were running hither and thither and firing at the landscape. A dark battle line lay upon a sunstruck clearing that gleamed orange color. A flag fluttered.

45 Other regiments floundered up the bank. The brigade was formed in line of battle, and after a pause started slowly through the woods in the rear

7. **canteen**—a small tin or container for water or any other liquid.

of the receding skirmishers, who were continually melting into the scene to appear again farther on. They were always busy as bees, deeply absorbed in their little combats.

The youth tried to observe everything. He did not use care to avoid trees and branches, and his forgotten feet were constantly knocking against stones 5 or getting entangled in briers. He was aware that these battalions with their commotions were woven red and startling into the gentle fabric of softened greens and browns. It looked to be a wrong place for a battle field.

The skirmishers in advance fascinated him. Their shots into thickets and at distant and prominent trees spoke to him of tragedies—hidden, mysterious, 10 solemn.

Once the line encountered the body of a dead soldier. He lay upon his back staring at the sky. He was dressed in an awkward suit of yellowish brown. The youth could see that the soles of his shoes had been worn to the thinness of writing paper, and from a great rent in one the dead foot pro- 15 jected piteously. And it was as if fate had betrayed the soldier. In death it exposed to his enemies that poverty which in life he had perhaps concealed from his friends.

The ranks opened covertly to avoid the corpse. The invulnerable dead man forced a way for himself. The youth looked keenly at the ashen face. 20 The wind raised the tawny beard. It moved as if a hand were stroking it. He vaguely desired to walk around and around the body and stare; the impulse of the living to try to read in dead eyes the answer to the Question.

During the march the ardor which the youth had acquired when out of view of the field rapidly faded to nothing. His curiosity was quite easily 25 satisfied. If an intense scene had caught him with its wild swing as he came to the top of the bank, he might have gone roaring on. This advance upon Nature was too calm. He had opportunity to reflect. He had time in which to wonder about himself and to attempt to probe his sensations.

Absurd ideas took hold upon him. He thought that he did not relish the 30 landscape. It threatened him. A coldness swept over his back, and it is true that his trousers felt to him that they were no fit for his legs at all.

A house standing placidly in distant fields had to him an ominous look. The shadows of the woods were formidable. He was certain that in this vista there lurked fierce-eyed hosts. The swift thought came to him that the gen- 35 erals did not know what they were about. It was all a trap. Suddenly those close forests would bristle with rifle barrels. Ironlike brigades would appear in the rear. They were all going to be sacrificed. The generals were stupids. The enemy would presently swallow the whole command. He glared about him, expecting to see the stealthy approach of his death. 40

He thought that he must break from the ranks and harangue his comrades. They must not all be killed like pigs; and he was sure it would come to pass unless they were informed of these dangers. The generals were idiots to send them marching into a regular pen. There was but one pair of eyes in the corps. He would step forth and make a speech. Shrill and passionate 45 words came to his lips.

The line, broken into moving fragments by the ground, went calmly on through fields and woods. The youth looked at the men nearest him, and saw, for the most part, expressions of deep interest, as if they were investigating something that had fascinated them. One or two stepped with over-valiant airs as if they were already plunged into war. Others walked as 5 upon thin ice. The greater part of the untested men appeared quiet and absorbed. They were going to look at war, the red animal—war, the blood-swollen god. And they were deeply engrossed in this march.

As he looked the youth gripped his outcry at his throat. He saw that even if the men were tottering with fear they would laugh at his warning. They 10 would jeer him, and, if practicable, pelt him with missiles. Admitting that he might be wrong, a frenzied declamation of the kind would turn him into a worm.

He assumed, then, the demeanor of one who knows that he is doomed alone to unwritten responsibilities. He lagged, with tragic glances at the sky. 15 He was surprised presently by the young lieutenant of his company, who began heartily to beat him with a sword, calling out in a loud and insolent voice: "Come, young man, get up into ranks there. No skulking 'll do here." He mended his pace with suitable haste. And he hated the lieutenant, who had no appreciation of fine minds. He was a mere brute.

20 After a time the brigade was halted in the cathedral light of a forest. The busy skirmishers were still popping. Through the aisles of the wood could be seen the floating smoke from their rifles. Sometimes it went up in little balls, white and compact.

During this halt many men in the regiment began erecting tiny hills in 25 front of them. They used stones, sticks, earth, and anything they thought might turn a bullet. Some built comparatively large ones, while others seemed content with little ones.

This procedure caused a discussion among the men. Some wished to fight like duelists, believing it to be correct to stand erect and be, from their feet 30 to their foreheads, a mark. They said they scorned the devices of the cautious. But the others scoffed in reply, and pointed to the veterans on the flanks who were digging at the ground like terriers. In a short time there was quite a barricade along the regimental fronts. Directly, however, they were ordered to withdraw from that place.

35 This astounded the youth. He forgot his stewing over the advance movement. "Well, then, what did they march us out here for?" he demanded of the tall soldier. The latter with calm faith began a heavy explanation, although he had been compelled to leave a little protection of stones and dirt to which he had devoted much care and skill.

40 When the regiment was aligned in another position each man's regard for his safety caused another line of small intrenchments. They ate their noon meal behind a third one. They were moved from this one also. They were marched from place to place with apparent aimlessness.

The youth had been taught that a man became another thing in a battle. 45 He saw his salvation in such a change. Hence this waiting was an ordeal to him. He was in a fever of impatience. He considered that there was denoted a lack of purpose on the part of the generals. He began to complain to the tall soldier. "I can't stand this much longer," he cried. "I don't see what good it does to make us wear out our legs for nothin'." He wished to return to camp, knowing that this affair was a blue demonstration; or else to go into a battle and discover that he had been a fool in his doubts, and was, in truth, a man of traditional courage. The strain of present circum- 5 stances he felt to be intolerable.

The philosophical tall soldier measured a sandwich of cracker and pork and swallowed it in a nonchalant manner. "Oh, I suppose we must go re- connoitering around the country jest to keep 'em from getting too close, or to develop 'em, or something." 10

"Huh!" said the loud soldier.

"Well," cried the youth, still fidgeting, "I'd rather do anything 'most than go tramping 'round the country all day doing no good to nobody and jest tiring ourselves out."

"So would I," said the loud soldier. "It ain't right. I tell you if anybody 15 with any sense was a-runnin' this army it—"

"Oh, shut up!" roared the tall private. "You little fool. You little damn' cuss. You ain't had that there coat and them pants on for six months, and yet you talk as if—"

"Well, I wanta do some fighting anyway," interrupted the other. "I didn't 20 come here to walk. I could 'ave walked to home—'round an 'round the barn, if I jest wanted to walk."

The tall one, red-faced, swallowed another sandwich as if taking poison in despair.

But gradually, as he chewed, his face became again quiet and contented. 25 He could not rage in fierce argument in the presence of such sandwiches. During his meals he always wore an air of blissful contemplation of the food he had swallowed. His spirit seemed then to be communing with the viands.

He accepted new environment and circumstance with great coolness, eating 30 from his haversack at every opportunity. On the march he went along with the stride of a hunter, objecting to neither gait nor distance. And he had not raised his voice when he had been ordered away from three little protective piles of earth and stone, each of which had been an engineering feat worthy of being made sacred to the name of his grandmother. 35

In the afternoon the regiment went out over the same ground it had taken in the morning. The landscape then ceased to threaten the youth. He had been close to it and become familiar with it.

When, however, they began to pass into a new region, his old fears of stupidity and incompetence reassailed him, but this time he doggedly let 40 them babble. He was occupied with his problem, and in his desperation he concluded that the stupidity did not greatly matter.

Once he thought he had concluded that it would be better to get killed directly and end his troubles. Regarding death thus out of the corner of his eye, he conceived it to be nothing but rest, and he was filled with a mo- 45 mentary astonishment that he should have made an extraordinary commotion

7. cracker—hard-tack.

over the mere matter of getting killed. He would die; he would go to some place where he would be understood. It was useless to expect appreciation of his profound and fine senses from such men as the lieutenant. He must look to the grave for comprehension.

5   The skirmish fire increased to a long clattering sound. With it was mingled far-away cheering. A battery spoke.

Directly the youth would see the skirmishers running. They were pursued by the sound of musketry fire. After a time the hot, dangerous flashes of the rifles were visible. Smoke clouds went slowly and insolently across the fields 10 like observant phantoms. The din became crescendo, like the roar of an on-coming train.

A brigade ahead of them and on the right went into action with a rending roar. It was as if it had exploded. And thereafter it lay stretched in the distance behind a long gray wall, that one was obliged to look twice at to 15 make sure that it was smoke.

The youth, forgetting his neat plan of getting killed, gazed spell bound. His eyes grew wide and busy with the action of the scene. His mouth was a little ways open.

Of a sudden he felt a heavy and sad hand laid upon his shoulder. Awaken-20 ing from his trance of observation he turned and beheld the loud soldier.

"It's my first and last battle, old boy," said the latter, with intense gloom. He was quite pale and his girlish lip was trembling.

"Eh?" murmured the youth in great astonishment.

"It's my first and last battle, old boy," continued the loud soldier. "Some-25 thing tells me—"

"What?"

"I'm a gone coon this first time and—and I w-want you to take these here things—to—my—folks." He ended in a quavering sob of pity for himself. He handed the youth a little packet done up in a yellow envelope.

30   "Why, what the devil—" began the youth again.

But the other gave him a glance as from the depths of a tomb, and raised his limp hand in a prophetic manner and turned away.

CHAPTER IV

The brigade was halted in the fringe of a grove. The men crouched among 35 the trees and pointed their restless guns out at the fields. They tried to look beyond the smoke.

Out of this haze they could see running men. Some shouted information and gestured as they hurried.

The men of the new regiment watched and listened eagerly, while their 40 tongues ran on in gossip of the battle. They mouthed rumors that had flown like birds out of the unknown.

"They say Perry has been driven in with big loss."

"Yes, Carrott went t' th' hospital. He said he was sick. That smart lieutenant is commanding 'G' Company. Th' boys say they won't be under Car-45 rott no more if they all have t' desert. They allus knew he was a—"

"Hannises' batt'ry is took."

"It ain't either. I saw Hannises' batt'ry off on th' left not more'n fifteen minutes ago."

"Well—"

"Th' general, he ses he is goin' t' take th' hull cammand of th' 304th 5 when we go inteh action, an' then he ses we'll do sech fightin' as never another one reg'ment done."

"They say we're catchin' it over on th' left. They say th' enemy driv' our line inteh a devil of a swamp an' took Hannises' batt'ry."

"No sech thing. Hannises' batt'ry was 'long here 'bout a minute ago." 10

"That young Hasbrouck, he makes a good off'cer. He ain't afraid 'a nothin'."

"I met one of th' 148th Maine boys an' he ses his brigade fit th' hull rebel army fer four hours over on th' turnpike road an' killed about five thousand of 'em. He ses one more sech fight as that an' th' war 'll be over."

"Bill wasn't scared either. No, sir! It wasn't that. Bill ain't a-gittin' scared 15 easy. He was jest mad, that's what he was. When that feller trod on his hand, he up an' sed that he was willin' t' give his hand t' his country, but he be dumbed if he was goin' t' have every dumb bushwacker in th' kentry walkin' 'round on it. Se he went t' th' hospital disregardless of th' fight. Three fingers was crunched. Th' dern doctor wanted t' amputate 'm, an' Bill, he raised a 20 heluva row, I hear. He's a funny feller."

The din in front swelled to a tremendous chorus. The youth and his fellows were frozen to silence. They could see a flag that tossed in the smoke angrily. Near it were the blurred and agitated forms of troops. There came a turbulent stream of men across the fields. A battery changing position at a frantic 25 gallop scattered the stragglers right and left.

A shell screaming like a storm banshee went over the huddled heads of the reserves. It landed in the grove, and exploding redly flung the brown earth. There was a little shower of pine needles.

Bullets began to whistle among the branches and nip at the trees. Twigs 30 and leaves came sailing down. It was as if a thousand axes, wee and invisible, were being wielded. Many of the men were constantly dodging and ducking their heads.

The lieutenant of the youth's company was shot in the hand. He began to swear so wondrously that a nervous laugh went along the regimental line. 35 The officer's profanity sounded conventional. It relieved the tightened senses of the new men. It was as if he had hit his fingers with a tack hammer at home.

He held the wounded member carefully away from his side so that the blood would not drip upon his trousers. 40

The captain of the company, tucking his sword under his arm, produced a handkerchief and began to bind with it the lieutenant's wound. And they disputed as to how the binding should be done.

The battle flag in the distance jerked about madly. It seemed to be struggling to free itself from an agony. The billowing smoke was filled with hori- 45 zontal flashes.

18. **bushwacker**—irregular (i.e., unenlisted) combatant.

Men running swiftly emerged from it. They grew in numbers until it was seen that the whole command was fleeing. The flag suddenly sank down as if dying. Its motion as it fell was a gesture of despair.

Wild yells came from behind the walls of smoke. A sketch in gray and red
5 dissolved into a moblike body of men who galloped like wild horses.

The veteran regiments on the right and left of the 304th immediately began to jeer. With the passionate song of the bullets and the banshee shrieks of shells were mingled loud catcalls and bits of facetious advice concerning places of safety.

10 But the new regiment was breathless with horror. "Gawd! Saunders's got crushed!" whispered the man at the youth's elbow. They shrank back and crouched as if compelled to await a flood.

The youth shot a swift glance along the blue ranks of the regiment. The profiles were motionless, carven; and afterward he remembered that the color
15 sergeant was standing with his legs apart, as if he expected to be pushed to the ground.

The following throng went whirling around the flank. Here and there were officers carried along on the stream like exasperated chips. They were striking about them with their swords and with their left fists, punching every head
20 they could reach. They cursed like highwaymen.

A mounted officer displayed the furious anger of a spoiled child. He raged with his head, his arms, and his legs.

Another, the commander of the brigade, was galloping about bawling. His hat was gone and his clothes were awry. He resembled a man who has come
25 from bed to go to a fire. The hoofs of his horse often threatened the heads of the running men, but they scampered with singular fortune. In this rush they were apparently all deaf and blind. They heeded not the largest and longest of the oaths that were thrown at them from all directions.

Frequently over this tumult could be heard the grim jokes of the critical
30 veterans; but the retreating men apparently were not even conscious of the presence of an audience.

The battle reflection that shone for an instant in the faces on the mad current made the youth feel that forceful hands from heaven would not have been able to have held him in place if he could have got intelligent control of
35 his legs.

There was an appalling imprint upon these faces. The struggle in the smoke had pictured an exaggeration of itself on the bleached cheeks and in the eyes wild with one desire.

The sight of this stampede exerted a floodlike force that seemed able to
40 drag sticks and stones and men from the ground. They of the reserves had to hold on. They grew pale and firm, and red and quaking.

The youth achieved one little thought in the midst of this chaos. The composite monster which had caused the other troops to flee had not then appeared. He resolved to get a view of it, and then, he thought he might very
45 likely run better than the best of them.

CHAPTER V

There were moments of waiting. The youth thought of the village street
at home before the arrival of the circus parade on a day in the spring. He
remembered how he had stood, a small, thrillful boy, prepared to follow the
dingy lady upon the white horse, or the band in its faded chariot. He saw the
yellow road, the lines of expectant people, and the sober houses. He particularly remembered an old fellow who used to sit upon a cracker box in front
of the store and feign to despise such exhibitions. A thousand details of color
and form surged in his mind. The old fellow upon the cracker box appeared
in middle prominence.

Some one cried, "Here they come!"

There was rustling and muttering among the men. They displayed a feverish desire to have every possible cartridge ready to their hands. The boxes
were pulled around into various positions, and adjusted with great care. It
was as if seven hundred new bonnets were being tried on.

The tall soldier, having prepared his rifle, produced a red handkerchief of
some kind. He was engaged in knitting it about his throat with exquisite
attention to its position, when the cry was repeated up and down the line in
a muffled roar of sound.

"Here they come! Here they come!" Gun locks clicked.

Across the smoke-infested fields came a brown swarm of running men who
were giving shrill yells. They came on, stooping and swinging their rifles at
all angles. A flag, tilted forward, sped near the front.

As he caught sight of them the youth was momentarily startled by a
thought that perhaps his gun was not loaded. He stood trying to rally his
faltering intellect so that he might recollect the moment when he had loaded,
but he could not.

A hatless general pulled his dripping horse to a stand near the colonel of
the 304th. He shook his fist in the other's face. "You've got to hold 'em back!"
he shouted, savagely; "you've got to hold 'em back!"

In his agitation the colonel began to stammer. "A-all r-right, General, all
right, by Gawd! We-we'll do our—we-we'll d-d-do—do our best, General."
The general made a passionate gesture and galloped away. The colonel, perchance to relieve his feelings, began to scold like a wet parrot. The youth,
turning swiftly to make sure that the rear was unmolested, saw the commander regarding his men in a highly resentful manner, as if he regretted
above everything his association with them.

The man at the youth's elbow was mumbling, as if to himself: "Oh, we're
in for it now! oh, we're in for it now!"

The captain of the company had been pacing excitedly to and fro in the
rear. He coaxed in schoolmistress fashion, as to a congregation of boys with
primers. His talk was an endless repetition. "Reserve your fire, boys—don't
shoot till I tell you—save your fire—wait till they get close up—don't be
damned fools—"

Perspiration streamed down the youth's face, which was soiled like that of a weeping urchin. He frequently, with a nervous movement, wiped his eyes with his coat sleeve. His mouth was still a little ways open.

He got the one glance at the foe-swarming field in front of him, and instantly ceased to debate the question of his piece being loaded. Before he was
5 ready to begin—before he had announced to himself that he was about to fight—he threw the obedient, well-balanced rifle into position and fired a first wild shot. Directly he was working at his weapon like an automatic affair.

He suddenly lost concern for himself, and forgot to look at a menacing fate. He became not a man but a member. He felt that something of which he
10 was a part—a regiment, an army, a cause, or a country—was in a crisis. He was welded into a common personality which was dominated by a single desire. For some moments he could not flee no more than a little finger can commit a revolution from a hand.

If he had thought the regiment was about to be annihilated perhaps he
15 could have amputated himself from it. But its noise gave him assurance. The regiment was like a firework that, once ignited, proceeds superior to circumstances until its blazing vitality fades. It wheezed and banged with a mighty power. He pictured the ground before it as strewn with the discomfited.

There was a consciousness always of the presence of his comrades about
20 him. He felt the subtle battle brotherhood more potent even than the cause for which they were fighting. It was a mysterious fraternity born of the smoke and danger of death.

He was at a task. He was like a carpenter who has made many boxes, making still another box, only there was furious haste in his movements. He, in
25 his thought, was careering off in other places, even as the carpenter who as he works whistles and thinks of his friend or his enemy, his home or a saloon. And these jolted dreams were never perfect to him afterward, but remained a mass of blurred shapes.

Presently he began to feel the effects of the war atmosphere—a blistering
30 sweat, a sensation that his eyeballs were about to crack like hot stones. A burning roar filled his ears.

Following this came a red rage. He developed the acute exasperation of a pestered animal, a well-meaning cow worried by dogs. He had a mad feeling against his rifle, which could only be used against one life at a time. He
35 wished to rush forward and strangle with his fingers. He craved a power that would enable him to make a world-sweeping gesture and brush all back. His impotency appeared to him, and made his rage into that of a driven beast.

Buried in the smoke of many rifles his anger was directed not so much
40 against men whom he knew were rushing toward him as against the swirling battle phantoms which were choking him, stuffing their smoke robes down his parched throat. He fought frantically for respite for his senses, for air, as a babe being smothered attacks the deadly blankets.

There was a blare of heated rage mingled with a certain expression of in-
45 tentness on all faces. Many of the men were making low-toned noises with their mouths, and these subdued cheers, snarls, imprecations, prayers, made a wild, barbaric song that went as an undercurrent of sound, strange and chant-

like with the resounding chords of the war march. The man at the youth's elbow was babbling. In it there was something soft and tender like the monologue of a babe. The tall soldier was swearing in a loud voice. From his lips came a black procession of curious oaths. Of a sudden another broke out in a querulous way like a man who has mislaid his hat. "Well, why don't they 5 support us? Why don't they send supports? Do they think—"

The youth in his battle sleep heard this as one who dozes hears.

There was a singular absence of heroic poses. The men bending and surging in their haste and rage were in every impossible attitude. The steel ramrods clanked and clanged with incessant din as the men pounded them furi- 10 ously into the hot rifle barrels. The flaps of the cartridge boxes were all unfastened, and bobbed idiotically with each movement. The rifles, once loaded, were jerked to the shoulder and fired without apparent aim into the smoke or at one of the blurred and shifting forms which upon the field before the regiment had been growing larger and larger like puppets under a magician's 15 hand.

The officers, at their intervals, rearward, neglected to stand in picturesque attitudes. They were bobbing to and fro roaring directions and encouragements. The dimensions of their howls were extraordinary. They expended their lungs with prodigal wills. And often they nearly stood upon their heads 20 in their anxiety to observe the enemy on the other side of the tumbling smoke.

The lieutenant of the youth's company had encountered a soldier who had fled screaming at the first volley of his comrades. Behind the lines these two were acting a little isolated scene. The man was blubbering and staring with sheeplike eyes at the lieutenant, who had seized him by the collar and was 25 pommeling him. He drove him back into the ranks with many blows. The soldier went mechanically, dully, with his animal-like eyes upon the officer. Perhaps there was to him a divinity expressed in the voice of the other—stern, hard, with no reflection of fear in it. He tried to reload his gun, but his shaking hands prevented. The lieutenant was obliged to assist him. 30

The men dropped here and there like bundles. The captain of the youth's company had been killed in an early part of the action. His body lay stretched out in the position of a tired man resting, but upon his face there was an astonished and sorrowful look, as if he thought some friend had done him an ill turn. The babbling man was grazed by a shot that made the blood stream 35 widely down his face. He clapped both hands to his head. "Oh!" he said, and ran. Another grunted suddenly as if he had been struck by a club in the stomach. He sat down and gazed ruefully. In his eyes there was mute, indefinite reproach. Farther up the line a man, standing behind a tree, had had his knee joint splintered by a ball. Immediately he had dropped his rifle and 40 gripped the tree with both arms. And there he remained, clinging desperately and crying for assistance that he might withdraw his hold upon the tree.

At last an exultant yell went along the quivering line. The firing dwindled

---

9-10. ramrods—Although Crane uses the terms "musket" and "rifle" interchangeably, it is evident that the "304th," like actual regiments sent to the front in the early years of the Civil War, was armed with muskets only, which required that the cartridge be tamped down into the barrel by a ramrod.

from an uproar to a last vindictive popping. As the smoke slowly eddied away, the youth saw that the charge had been repulsed. The enemy were scattered into reluctant groups. He saw a man climb to the top of the fence, straddle the rail, and fire a parting shot. The waves had receded, leaving bits
5   of dark *débris* upon the ground.

Some in the regiment began to whoop frenziedly. Many were silent. Apparently they were trying to contemplate themselves.

After the fever had left his veins, the youth thought that at last he was going to suffocate. He became aware of the foul atmosphere in which he
10 had been struggling. He was grimy and dripping like a laborer in a foundry. He grasped his canteen and took a long swallow of the warmed water.

A sentence with variations went up and down the line. "Well, we've helt 'em back. We've helt 'em back; derned if we haven't." The men said it blissfully, leering at each other with dirty smiles.

15 The youth turned to look behind him and off to the right and off to the left. He experienced the joy of a man who at last finds leisure in which to look about him.

Under foot there were a few ghastly forms motionless. They lay twisted in fantastic contortions. Arms were bent and heads were turned in incredible
20 ways. It seemed that the dead men must have fallen from some great height to get into such positions. They looked to be dumped out upon the ground from the sky.

From a position in the rear of the grove a battery was throwing shells over it. The flash of the guns startled the youth at first. He thought they were
25 aimed directly at him. Through the trees he watched the black figures of the gunners as they worked swiftly and intently. Their labor seemed a complicated thing. He wondered how they could remember its formula in the midst of confusion.

The guns squatted in a row like savage chiefs. They argued with abrupt
30 violence. It was a grim pow-wow. Their busy servants ran hither and thither.

A small procession of wounded men were going drearily toward the rear. It was a flow of blood from the torn body of the brigade.

To the right and to the left were the dark lines of other troops. Far in front he thought he could see lighter masses protruding in points from the forest.
35 They were suggestive of unnumbered thousands.

Once he saw a tiny battery go dashing along the line of the horizon. The tiny riders were beating the tiny horses.

From a sloping hill came the sound of cheerings and clashes. Smoke welled slowly through the leaves.

40 Batteries were speaking with thunderous oratorical effort. Here and there were flags, the red in the stripes dominating. They splashed bits of warm color upon the dark lines of troops.

The youth felt the old thrill at the sight of the emblem. They were like beautiful birds strangely undaunted in a storm.

45 As he listened to the din from the hillside, to a deep pulsating thunder that came from afar to the left, and to the lesser clamors which came from many directions, it occurred to him that they were fighting, too, over there, and

over there, and over there. Heretofore he had supposed that all the battle was directly under his nose.

As he gazed around him the youth felt a flash of astonishment at the blue, pure sky and the sun gleamings on the trees and fields. It was surprising that Nature had gone tranquilly on with her golden process in the midst of so much devilment.

CHAPTER VI

The youth awakened slowly. He came gradually back to a position from which he could regard himself. For moments he had been scrutinizing his person in a dazed way as if he had never before seen himself. Then he picked up his cap from the ground. He wriggled in his jacket to make a more comfortable fit, and kneeling relaced his shoe. He thoughtfully mopped his reeking features.

(So it was all over at last! The supreme trial had been passed. The red, formidable difficulties of war had been vanquished.

He went into an ecstasy of self-satisfaction. He had the most delightful sensations of his life. Standing as if apart from himself, he viewed that last scene. He perceived that the man who had fought thus was magnificent.

He felt that he was a fine fellow. He saw himself even with those ideals which he had considered as far beyond him. He smiled in deep gratification.)

Upon his fellows he beamed tenderness and good will. "Gee! ain't it hot, hey?" he said affably to a man who was polishing his streaming face with his coat sleeves.

"You bet!" said the other, grinning sociably. "I never seen sech dumb hotness." He sprawled out luxuriously on the ground. "Gee, yes! An' I hope we don't have no more fightin' till a week from Monday."

There were some handshakings and deep speeches with men whose features were familiar, but with whom the youth now felt the bonds of tied hearts. He helped a cursing comrade to bind up a wound of the shin.

But, of a sudden, cries of amazement broke out along the ranks of the new regiment. "Here they come ag'in! Here they come ag'in!" The man who had sprawled upon the ground started up and said, "Gosh!"

The youth turned quick eyes upon the field. He discerned forms begin to swell in masses out of a distant wood. He again saw the tilted flag speeding forward.

The shells, which had ceased to trouble the regiment for a time, came swirling again, and exploded in the grass or among the leaves of the trees. They looked to be strange war flowers bursting into fierce bloom.

The men groaned. The luster faded from their eyes. Their smudged countenances now expressed a profound dejection. They moved their stiffened bodies slowly, and watched in sullen mood the frantic approach of the enemy. The slaves toiling in the temple of this god began to feel rebellion at his harsh tasks.

They fretted and complained each to each. "Oh, say, this is too much of a good thing! Why can't somebody send us supports?"

"We ain't never goin' to stand this second banging. I didn't come here to fight the hull damn' rebel army."

There was one who raised a doleful cry. "I wish Bill Smithers had trod on my hand, insteader me treddin' on his'n." The sore joints of the regiment
5 creaked as it painfully floundered into position to repulse.

The youth stared. Surely, he thought, this impossible thing was not about to happen. He waited as if he expected the enemy to suddenly stop, apologize, and retire bowing. It was all a mistake.

But the firing began somewhere on the regimental line and ripped along in
10 both directions. The level sheeets of flame developed great clouds of smoke that tumbled and tossed in the mild wind near the ground for a moment, and then rolled through the ranks as through a gate. The clouds were tinged an earthlike yellow in the sunrays and in the shadow were a sorry blue. The flag was sometimes eaten and lost in this mass of vapor, but more often it
15 projected, sun-touched, resplendent.

Into the youth's eyes there came a look that one can see in the orbs of a jaded horse. His neck was quivering with nervous weakness and the muscles of his arms felt numb and bloodless. His hands, too, seemed large and awkward as if he was wearing invisible mittens. And there was a great uncer-
20 tainty about his knee joints.

The words that comrades had uttered previous to the firing began to recur to him. "Oh, say, this is too much of a good thing! What do they take us for—why don't they send supports? I didn't come here to fight the hull damned rebel army."
25 He began to exaggerate the endurance, the skill, and the valor of those who were coming. Himself reeling from exhaustion, he was astonished beyond measure at such persistency. They must be machines of steel. It was very gloomy struggling against such affairs, wound up perhaps to fight until sundown.
30 He slowly lifted his rifle and catching a glimpse of the thickspread field he blazed at a cantering cluster. He stopped then and began to peer as best he could through the smoke. He caught changing views of the ground covered with men who were all running like pursued imps, and yelling.

To the youth it was an onslaught of redoubtable dragons. He became like
35 the man who lost his legs at the approach of the red and green monster. He waited in a sort of a horrified, listening attitude. He seemed to shut his eyes and wait to be gobbled.

A man near him who up to this time had been working feverishly at his rifle suddenly stopped and ran with howls. A lad whose face had borne an
40 expression of exalted courage, the majesty of he who dares give his life, was, at an instant, smitten abject. He blanched like one who has come to the edge of a cliff at midnight and is suddenly made aware. There was a revelation. He, too, threw down his gun and fled. There was no shame in his face. He ran like a rabbit.
45 Others began to scamper away through the smoke. The youth turned his head, shaken from his trance by this movement as if the regiment was leaving him behind. He saw the few fleeting forms.

He yelled then with fright and swung about. For a moment, in the great clamor, he was like a proverbial chicken. He lost the direction of safety. Destruction threatened him from all points.

Directly he began to speed toward the rear in great leaps. His rifle and cap were gone. His unbuttoned coat bulged in the wind. The flap of his cartridge box bobbed wildly, and his canteen, by its slender cord, swung out behind. On his face was all the horror of those things which he imagined.

The lieutenant sprang forward bawling. The youth saw his features wrathfully red, and saw him make a dab with his sword. His one thought of the incident was that the lieutenant was a peculiar creature to feel interested in such matters upon this occasion.

He ran like a blind man. Two or three times he fell down. Once he knocked his shoulder so heavily against a tree that he went headlong.

Since he had turned his back upon the fight his fears had been wondrously magnified. Death about to thrust him between the shoulder blades was far more dreadful than death about to smite him between the eyes. When he thought of it later, he conceived the impression that it is better to view the appalling than to be merely within hearing. The noises of the battle were like stones; he believed himself liable to be crushed.

As he ran on he mingled with others. He dimly saw men on his right and on his left, and he heard footsteps behind him. He thought that all the regiment was fleeing, pursued by these ominous crashes.

In his flight the sound of these following footsteps gave him his one meager relief. He felt vaguely that death must make a first choice of the men who were nearest; the initial morsels for the dragons would be then those who were following him. So he displayed the zeal of an insane sprinter in his purpose to keep them in the rear. There was a race.

As he, leading, went across a little field, he found himself in a region of shells. They hurtled over his head with long wild screams. As he listened he imagined them to have rows of cruel teeth that grinned at him. Once one lit before him and the livid lightning of the explosion effectually barred the way in his chosen direction. He groveled on the ground and then springing up went careering off through some bushes.

He experienced a thrill of amazement when he came within view of a battery in action. The men there seemed to be in conventional moods, altogether unaware of the impending annihilation. The battery was disputing with a distant antagonist and the gunners were wrapped in admiration of their shooting. They were continually bending in coaxing postures over the guns. They seemed to be patting them on the back and encouraging them with words. The guns, stolid and undaunted, spoke with dogged valor.

The precise gunners were coolly enthusiastic. They lifted their eyes every chance to the smoke-wreathed hillock from whence the hostile battery addressed them. The youth pitied them as he ran. Methodical idiots! Machine-like fools! The refined joy of planting shells in the midst of the other battery's formation would appear a little thing when the infantry came swooping out of the woods.

The face of a youthful rider, who was jerking his frantic horse with an abandon of temper he might display in a placid barnyard, was impressed deeply upon his mind. He knew that he looked upon a man who would presently be dead.

Too, he felt a pity for the guns, standing, six good comrades, in a bold row.

5   He saw a brigade going to the relief of its pestered fellows. He scrambled upon a wee hill and watched it sweeping finely, keeping formation in difficult places. The blue of the line was crusted with steel color, and the brilliant flags projected. Officers were shouting.

This sight also filled him with wonder. The brigade was hurrying briskly
10 to be gulped into the infernal mouths of the war god. What manner of men were they, anyhow? Ah, it was some wondrous breed! Or else they didn't comprehend—the fools.

A furious order caused commotion in the artillery. An officer on a bounding horse made maniacal motions with his arms. The teams went swinging up
15 from the rear, the guns were whirled about, and the battery scampered away. The cannon with their noses poked slantingly at the ground grunted and grumbled like stout men, brave but with objections to hurry.

The youth went on, moderating his pace since he had left the place of noises.

20 Later he came upon a general of division seated upon a horse that pricked its ears in an interested way at the battle. There was a great gleaming of yellow and patent leather about the saddle and bridle. The quiet man astride looked mouse-colored upon such a splendid charger.

A jingling staff was galloping hither and thither. Sometimes the general
25 was surrounded by horsemen and at other times he was quite alone. He looked to be much harassed. He had the appearance of a business man whose market is swinging up and down.

The youth went slinking around this spot. He went as near as he dared trying to overhear words. Perhaps the general, unable to comprehend chaos,
30 might call upon him for information. And he could tell him. He knew all concerning it. Of a surety the force was in a fix, and any fool could see that if they did not retreat while they had opportunity—why—

He felt that he would like to thrash the general, or at least approach and tell him in plain words exactly what he thought him to be. It was criminal to
35 stay calmly in one spot and make no effort to stay destruction. He loitered in a fever of eagerness for the division commander to apply to him.

As he warily moved about, he heard the general call out irritably: "Tompkins, go over an' see Taylor, an' tell him not t' be in such an all-fired hurry; tell him t' halt his brigade in th' edge of th' woods; tell him t' detach a
40 reg'ment—say I think th' center 'll break if we don't help it out some; tell him t' hurry up."

A slim youth on a fine chestnut horse caught these swift words from the mouth of his superior. He made his horse bound into a gallop almost from a walk in his haste to go upon his mission. There was a cloud of dust.

45 A moment later the youth saw the general bounce excitedly in his saddle.

"Yes, by heavens, they have!" The officer leaned forward. His face was aflame with excitement. "Yes, by heavens, they've held 'im! They've held 'im!"

He began to blithely roar at his staff: "We'll wallop 'im now. We'll wallop 'im now. We've got 'em sure." He turned suddenly upon an aid: "Here—you —Jones—quick—ride after Tompkins—see Taylor—tell him t' go in—everlastingly—like blazes—anything."

As another officer sped his horse after the first messenger, the general   5 beamed upon the earth like a sun. In his eyes was a desire to chant a pæan. He kept repeating, "They've held 'em, by heavens!"

His excitement made his horse plunge, and he merrily kicked and swore at it. He held a little carnival of joy on horseback.

CHAPTER VII   10

The youth cringed as if discovered in a crime. By heavens, they had won after all! The imbecile line had remained and become victors. He could hear cheering.

He lifted himself upon his toes and looked in the direction of the fight. A yellow fog lay wallowing on the treetops. From beneath it came the clatter   15 of musketry. Hoarse cries told of an advance.

He turned away amazed and angry. He felt that he had been wronged.

He had fled, he told himself, because annihilation approached. He had done a good part in saving himself, who was a little piece of the army. He had considered the time, he said, to be one in which it was the duty of every little   20 piece to rescue itself if possible. Later the officers could fit the little pieces together again, and make a battle front. If none of the little pieces were wise enough to save themselves from the flurry of death at such a time, why, then, where would be the army? It was all plain that he had proceeded according to very correct and commendable rules. His actions had been sagacious things.   25 They had been full of strategy. They were the work of a master's legs.

Thoughts of his comrades came to him. The brittle blue line had withstood the blows and won. He grew bitter over it. It seemed that the blind ignorance and stupidity of those little pieces had betrayed him. He had been overturned and crushed by their lack of sense in holding the position, when intelligent   30 deliberation would have convinced them that it was impossible. He, the enlightened man who looks afar in the dark, had fled because of his superior perceptions and knowledge. He felt a great anger against his comrades. He knew it could be proved that they had been fools.

He wondered what they would remark when later he appeared in camp.   35 His mind heard howls of derision. Their destiny would not enable them to understand his sharper point of view.

He began to pity himself acutely. He was ill used. He was trodden beneath the feet of an iron injustice. He had proceeded with wisdom and from the most righteous motives under heaven's blue only to be frustrated by hateful   40 circumstances.

A dull, animal-like rebellion against his fellows, war in the abstract, and fate grew within him. He shambled along with bowed head, his brain in a tumult of agony and despair. When he looked loweringly up, quivering at

12. **imbecile**—powerless.

each sound, his eyes had the expression of those of a criminal who thinks his guilt and his punishment great, and knows that he can find no words.

He went from the fields into a thick woods, as if resolved to bury himself. He wished to get out of hearing of the crackling shots which were to him 5 like voices.

The ground was cluttered with vines and bushes, and the trees grew close and spread out like bouquets. He was obliged to force his way with much noise. The creepers, catching against his legs, cried out harshly as their sprays were torn from the barks of trees. The swishing saplings tried to make known 10 his presence to the world. He could not conciliate the forest. As he made his way, it was always calling out protestations. When he separated embraces of trees and vines the disturbed foliages waved their arms and turned their face leaves toward him. He dreaded lest these noisy motions and cries should bring men to look at him. So he went far, seeking dark and intricate places.

15 After a time the sound of musketry grew faint and the cannon boomed in the distance. The sun, suddenly apparent, blazed among the trees. The insects were making rhythmical noises. They seemed to be grinding their teeth in unison. A woodpecker stuck his impudent head around the side of a tree. A bird flew on lighthearted wing.

20 Off was the rumble of death. It seemed now that Nature had no ears.

This landscape gave him assurance. A fair field holding life. It was the religion of peace. It would die if its timid eyes were compelled to see blood. He conceived Nature to be a woman with a deep aversion to tragedy.

He threw a pine cone at a jovial squirrel, and he ran with chattering fear. 25 High in a treetop he stopped, and, poking his head cautiously from behind a branch, looked down with an air of trepidation.

The youth felt triumphant at this exhibition. There was the law, he said. Nature had given him a sign. The squirrel, immediately upon recognizing danger, had taken to his legs without ado. He did not stand stolidly baring 30 his furry belly to the missile, and die with an upward glance at the sympathetic heavens. On the contrary, he had fled as fast as his legs could carry him; and he was but an ordinary squirrel, too—doubtless no philosopher of his race. The youth wended, feeling that Nature was of his mind. She re-enforced his argument with proofs that lived where the sun shone.

35 Once he found himself almost into a swamp. He was obliged to walk upon bog tufts and watch his feet to keep from the oily mire. Pausing at one time to look about him he saw, out at some black water, a small animal pounce in and emerge directly with a gleaming fish.

The youth went again into the deep thickets. The brushed branches made 40 a noise that drowned the sounds of cannon. He walked on, going from obscurity into promises of a greater obscurity.

At length he reached a place where the high, arching boughs made a chapel. He softly pushed the green doors aside and entered. Pine needles were a gentle brown carpet. There was a religious half light.

45 Near the threshold he stopped, horror-stricken at the sight of a thing.

He was being looked at by a dead man who was seated with his back against a columnlike tree. The corpse was dressed in a uniform that once had been blue, but was now faded to a melancholy shade of green. The eyes, staring at the youth, had changed to the dull hue to be seen on the side of a dead fish. The mouth was open. Its red had changed to an appalling yellow. Over the gray skin of the face ran little ants. One was trundling some sort of a bundle along the upper lip.

The youth gave a shriek as he confronted the thing. He was for moments turned to stone before it. He remained staring into the liquid-looking eyes. The dead man and the living man exchanged a long look. Then the youth cautiously put one hand behind him and brought it against a tree. Leaning upon this he retreated, step by step, with his face still toward the thing. He feared that if he turned his back the body might spring up and stealthily pursue him.

The branches, pushing against him, threatened to throw him over upon it. His unguided feet, too, caught aggravatingly in brambles; and with it all he received a subtle suggestion to touch the corpse. As he thought of his hand upon it he shuddered profoundly.

At last he burst the bonds which had fastened him to the spot and fled, unheeding the underbrush. He was pursued by a sight of the black ants swarming greedily upon the gray face and venturing horribly near to the eyes.

After a time he paused, and, breathless and panting, listened. He imagined some strange voice would come from the dead throat and squawk after him in horrible menaces.

The trees about the portals of the chapel moved soughingly in a soft wind. A sad silence was upon the little guarding edifice.

CHAPTER VIII

The trees began softly to sing a hymn of twilight. The sun sank until slanted bronze rays struck the forest. There was a lull in the noises of insects as if they had bowed their beaks and were making a devotional pause. There was silence save for the chanted chorus of the trees.

Then, upon this stillness, there suddenly broke a tremendous clangor of sounds. A crimson roar came from the distance.

The youth stopped. He was transfixed by this terrific medley of all noises. It was as if worlds were being rended. There was the ripping sound of musketry and the breaking crash of the artillery.

His mind flew in all directions. He conceived the two armies to be at each other panther fashion. He listened for a time. Then he began to run in the direction of the battle. He saw that it was an ironical thing for him to be running thus toward that which he had been at such pains to avoid. But he said, in substance, to himself that if the earth and the moon were about to clash, many persons would doubtless plan to get upon the roofs to witness the collision.

As he ran, he became aware that the forest had stopped its music, as if at last becoming capable of hearing the foreign sounds. The trees hushed and stood motionless. Everything seemed to be listening to the crackle and clatter and ear-shaking thunder. The chorus pealed over the still earth.

It suddenly occurred to the youth that the fight in which he had been was, after all, but perfunctory popping. In the hearing of this present din he was doubtful if he had seen real battle scenes. This uproar explained a celestial battle; it was tumbling hordes a-struggle in the air.

5   Reflecting, he saw a sort of a humor in the point of view of himself and his fellows during the late encounter. They had taken themselves and the enemy very seriously and had imagined that they were deciding the war. Individuals must have supposed that they were cutting the letters of their names deep into everlasting tablets of brass, or enshrining their reputations forever in the
10 hearts of their countrymen, while, as to fact, the affair would appear in printed reports under a meek and immaterial title. But he saw that it was good, else, he said, in battle every one would surely run save forlorn hopes and their ilk.

He went rapidly on. He wished to come to the edge of the forest that he might peer out.

15 As he hastened, there passed through his mind pictures of stupendous conflicts. His accumulated thought upon such subjects was used to form scenes. The noise was as the voice of an eloquent being, describing.

Sometimes the brambles formed chains and tried to hold him back. Trees, confronting him, stretched out their arms and forbade him to pass. After its
20 previous hostility this new resistance of the forest filled him with a fine bitterness. It seemed that Nature could not be quite ready to kill him.

But he obstinately took roundabout ways, and presently he was where he could see long gray walls of vapor where lay battle lines. The voices of cannon shook him. The musketry sounded in long irregular surges that played
25 havoc with his ears. He stood regardant for a moment. His eyes had an awestruck expression. He gawked in the direction of the fight.

Presently he proceeded again on his forward way. The battle was like the grinding of an immense and terrible machine to him. Its complexities and powers, its grim processes, fascinated him. He must go close and see it pro-
30 duce corpses.

He came to a fence and clambered over it. On the far side, the ground was littered with clothes and guns. A newspaper, folded up, lay in the dirt. A dead soldier was stretched with his face hidden in his arm. Farther off there was a group of four or five corpses keeping mournful company. A hot sun
35 had blazed upon the spot.

In this place the youth felt that he was an invader. This forgotten part of the battle ground was owned by the dead men, and he hurried, in the vague apprehension that one of the swollen forms would rise and tell him to begone.

He came finally to a road from which he could see in the distance dark and
40 agitated bodies of troops, smoke-fringed. In the lane was a blood-stained crowd streaming to the rear. The wounded men were cursing, groaning, and wailing. In the air, always, was a mighty swell of sound that it seemed could sway the earth. With the courageous words of the artillery and the spiteful sentences of the musketry mingled red cheers. And from this region of noises
45 came the steady current of the maimed.

One of the wounded men had a shoeful of blood. He hopped like a schoolboy in a game. He was laughing hysterically.

One was swearing that he had been shot in the arm through the commanding general's mismanagement of the army. One was marching with an air
imitative of some sublime drum major. Upon his features was an unholy
mixture of merriment and agony. As he marched he sang a bit of doggerel in
a high and quavering voice: 5

> "Sing a song 'a vic'try,
> A pocketful 'a bullets,
> Five an' twenty dead men
> Baked in a—pie."

Parts of the procession limped and staggered to this tune.   10

Another had the gray seal of death already upon his face. His lips were
curled in hard lines and his teeth were clinched. His hands were bloody from
where he had pressed them upon his wound. He seemed to be awaiting the
moment when he should pitch headlong. He stalked like the specter of a
soldier, his eyes burning with the power of a stare into the unknown.   15

There were some who proceeded sullenly, full of anger at their wounds,
and ready to turn upon anything as an obscure cause.

An officer was carried along by two privates. He was peevish. "Don't joggle
so, Johnson, yeh fool," he cried. "Think m' leg is made of iron? If yeh can't
carry me decent, put me down an' let some one else do it."   20

He bellowed at the tottering crowd who blocked the quick march of his
bearers. "Say, make way there, can't yeh? Make way, dickens take it all."

They sulkily parted and went to the roadsides. As he was carried past they
made pert remarks to him. When he raged in reply and threatened them, they
told him to be damned.   25

The shoulder of one of the tramping bearers knocked heavily against the
spectral soldier who was staring into the unknown.

The youth joined this crowd and marched along with it. The torn bodies
expressed the awful machinery in which the men had been entangled.

Orderlies and couriers occasionally broke through the throng in the road-   30
way, scattering wounded men right and left, galloping on followed by howls.
The melancholy march was continually disturbed by the messengers, and
sometimes by bustling batteries that came swinging and thumping down upon
them, the officers shouting orders to clear the way.

There was a tattered man, fouled with dust, blood and powder stain from   35
hair to shoes, who trudged quietly at the youth's side. He was listening with
eagerness and much humility to the lurid descriptions of a bearded sergeant.
His lean features wore an expression of awe and admiration. He was like a
listener in a country store to wondrous tales told among the sugar barrels.
He eyed the story-teller with unspeakable wonder. His mouth was agape in   40
yokel fashion.

The sergeant, taking note of this, gave pause to his elaborate history while
he administered a sardonic comment. "Be keerful, honey, you'll be a-ketchin'
flies," he said.

The tattered man shrank back abashed.   45

After a time he began to sidle near to the youth, and in a different way try to make him a friend. His voice was gentle as a girl's voice and his eyes were pleading. The youth saw with surprise that the soldier had two wounds, one in the head, bound with a blood-soaked rag, and the other in the arm, making that member dangle like a broken bough.

5 After they had walked together for some time the tattered man mustered sufficient courage to speak. "Was pretty good fight, wa'n't it?" he timidly said. The youth, deep in thought, glanced up at the bloody and grim figure with its lamblike eyes. "What?"

"Was pretty good fight, wa'n't it?"

10 "Yes," said the youth shortly. He quickened his pace.

But the other hobbled industriously after him. There was an air of apology in his manner, but he evidently thought that he needed only to talk for a time, and the youth would perceive that he was a good fellow.

"Was pretty good fight, wa'n't it?" he began in a small voice, and then
15 he achieved the fortitude to continue. "Dern me if I ever see fellers fight so. Laws, how they did fight! I knowed th' boys 'd like when they onct got square at it. Th' boys ain't had no fair chanct up t' now, but this time they showed what they was. I knowed it 'd turn out this way. Yeh can't lick them boys. No, sir! They're fighters, they be."

20 He breathed a deep breath of humble admiration. He had looked at the youth for encouragement several times. He received none, but gradually he seemed to get absorbed in his subject.

"I was talkin' 'cross pickets with a boy from Georgie, onct, an' that boy, he ses, 'Your fellers 'll all run like hell when they onct hearn a gun,' he ses.
25 'Mebbe they will,' I ses, 'but I don't b'lieve none of it,' I ses; 'an' b'jiminey,' I ses back t' 'um, 'mebbe your fellers 'll all run like hell when they onct hearn a gun,' I ses. He larfed. Well, they didn't run t'-day, did they, hey? No, sir! They fit, an' fit, an' fit."

His homely face was suffused with a light of love for the army which was
30 to him all things beautiful and powerful.

After a time he turned to the youth, "Where yeh hit, ol' boy?" he asked in a brotherly tone.

The youth felt instant panic at this question, although at first its full import was not borne in upon him.

35 "What?" he asked.

"Where yeh hit?" repeated the tattered man.

"Why," began the youth, "I—I—that is—why—I—"

He turned away suddenly and slid through the crowd. His brow was heavily flushed, and his fingers were picking nervously at one of his buttons. He
40 bent his head and fastened his eyes studiously upon the button as if it were a little problem.

The tattered man looked after him in astonishment.

CHAPTER IX

The youth fell back in the procession until the tattered soldier was not in
45 sight. Then he started to walk on with the others.

But he was amid wounds. The mob of men was bleeding. Because of the tattered soldier's question he now felt that his shame could be viewed. He was continually casting sidelong glances to see if the men were contemplating the letters of guilt he felt burned into his brow.

At times he regarded the wounded soldiers in an envious way. He conceived persons with torn bodies to be peculiarly happy. He wished that he, too, had a wound, a red badge of courage.

The spectral soldier was at his side like a stalking reproach. The man's eyes were still fixed in a stare into the unknown. His gray, appalling face had attracted attention in the crowd, and men, slowing to his dreary pace, were walking with him. They were discussing his plight, questioning him and giving him advice. In a dogged way he repelled them, signing to them to go on and leave him alone. The shadows of his face were deepening and his tight lips seemed holding in check the moan of great despair. There could be seen a certain stiffness in the movements of his body, as if he were taking infinite care not to arouse the passion of his wounds. As he went on, he seemed always looking for a place, like one who goes to choose a grave.

Something in the gesture of the man as he waved the bloody and pitying soldiers away made the youth start as if bitten. He yelled in horror. Tottering forward he laid a quivering hand upon the man's arm. As the latter slowly turned his waxlike features toward him, the youth screamed:

"Gawd! Jim Conklin!"

The tall soldier made a little commonplace smile. "Hello, Henry," he said.

The youth swayed on his legs and glared strangely. He stuttered and stammered. "Oh, Jim—oh, Jim—oh, Jim—"

The tall soldier held out his gory hand. There was a curious red and black combination of new blood and old blood upon it. "Where yeh been, Henry?" he asked. He continued in a monotonous voice, "I thought mebbe yeh got keeled over. There's been thunder t' pay t'-day. I was worryin' about it a good deal."

The youth still lamented. "Oh, Jim—oh, Jim—oh, Jim—"

"Yeh know," said the tall soldier, "I was out there." He made a careful gesture. "An', Lord, what a circus! An', b'jiminey, I got shot—I got shot. Yes, b'jiminey, I got shot." He reiterated this fact in a bewildered way, as if he did not know how it came about.

The youth put forth anxious arms to assist him, but the tall soldier went firmly on as if propelled. Since the youth's arrival as a guardian for his friend, the other wounded men had ceased to display much interest. They occupied themselves again in dragging their own tragedies toward the rear.

Suddenly, as the two friends marched on, the tall soldier seemed to be overcome by a terror. His face turned to a semblance of gray paste. He clutched the youth's arm and looked all about him, as if dreading to be overheard. Then he began to speak in a shaking whisper:

"I tell yeh what I'm 'fraid of, Henry—I'll tell yeh what I'm 'fraid of. I'm 'fraid I'll fall down—an' then yeh know—them damned artillery wagons—they like as not 'll run over me. That's what I'm 'fraid of—"

The youth cried out to him hysterically: "I'll take care of yeh, Jim! I'll take care of yeh! I swear t' Gawd I will!"

"Sure—will yeh, Henry?" the tall soldier beseeched.

"Yes—yes—I tell yeh—I'll take care of yeh, Jim!" protested the youth. He
5 could not speak accurately because of the gulpings in his throat.

But the tall soldier continued to beg in a lowly way. He now hung babelike to the youth's arm. His eyes rolled in the wildness of his terror. "I was allus a good friend t' yeh, wa'n't I, Henry? I've allus been a pretty good feller, ain't I? An' it ain't much t' ask, is it? Jest t' pull me along outer th' road? I'd do it
10 fer you, wouldn't I, Henry?"

He paused in piteous anxiety to await his friend's reply.

The youth had reached an anguish where the sobs scorched him. He strove to express his loyalty, but he could only make fantastic gestures.

However, the tall soldier seemed suddenly to forget all those fears. He be-
15 came again the grim, stalking specter of a soldier. He went stonily forward. The youth wished his friend to lean upon him, but the other always shook his head and strangely protested. "No—no—no—leave me be—leave me be—"

His look was fixed again upon the unknown. He moved with mysterious purpose, and all of the youth's offers he brushed aside. "No—no—leave me
20 be—leave me be—"

The youth had to follow.

Presently the latter heard a voice talking softly near his shoulders. Turning he saw that it belonged to the tattered soldier. "Ye'd better take 'im outa th' road, pardner. There's a batt'ry comin' helitywhoop down th' road an' he'll
25 git runned over. He's a goner anyhow in about five minutes—yeh kin see that. Ye'd better take 'im outa th' road. Where th' blazes does he git his stren'th from?"

"Lord knows!" cried the youth. He was shaking his hands helplessly.

He ran forward presently and grasped the tall soldier by the arm. "Jim!
30 Jim!" he coaxed, "come with me."

The tall soldier weakly tried to wrench himself free. "Huh," he said vacantly. He stared at the youth for a moment. At last he spoke as if dimly comprehending. "Oh! Inteh th' fields? Oh!"

He started blindly through the grass.

35 The youth turned once to look at the lashing riders and jouncing guns of the battery. He was startled from this view by a shrill outcry from the tattered man.

"Gawd! He's runnin'!"

Turning his head swiftly, the youth saw his friend running in a staggering
40 and stumbling way toward a little clump of bushes. His heart seemed to wrench itself almost free from his body at this sight. He made a noise of pain. He and the tattered man began a pursuit. There was a singular race.

When he overtook the tall soldier he began to plead with all the words he could find. "Jim—Jim—what are you doing—what makes you do this way
45 —you'll hurt yerself."

The same purpose was in the tall soldier's face. He protested in a dulled way, keeping his eyes fastened on the mystic place of his intentions. "No—no —don't tech me—leave me be—leave me be—"

The youth, aghast and filled with wonder at the tall soldier, began quaveringly to question him. "Where yeh goin', Jim? What you thinking about? Where you going? Tell me, won't you, Jim?"

The tall soldier faced about as upon relentless pursuers. In his eyes there was a great appeal. "Leave me be, can't yeh? Leave me be fer a minnit."

The youth recoiled. "Why, Jim," he said, in a dazed way, "what's the matter with you?"

The tall soldier turned and, lurching dangerously, went on. The youth and the tattered soldier followed, sneaking as if whipped, feeling unable to face the stricken man if he should again confront them. They began to have thoughts of a solemn ceremony. There was something ritelike in these movements of the doomed soldier. And there was a resemblance in him to a devotee of a mad religion, blood-sucking, muscle-wrenching, bone-crushing. They were awed and afraid. They hung back lest he have at command a dreadful weapon.

At last, they saw him stop and stand motionless. Hastening up, they perceived that his face wore an expression telling that he had at last found the place for which he had struggled. His spare figure was erect; his bloody hands were quietly at his side. He was waiting with patience for something that he had come to meet. He was at the rendezvous. They paused and stood, expectant.

There was a silence.

Finally, the chest of the doomed soldier began to heave with a strained motion. It increased in violence until it was as if an animal was within and was kicking and tumbling furiously to be free.

This spectacle of gradual strangulation made the youth writhe, and once as his friend rolled his eyes, he saw something in them that made him sink wailing to the ground. He raised his voice in a last supreme call.

"Jim—Jim—Jim—"

The tall soldier opened his lips and spoke. He made a gesture. "Leave me be—don't tech me—leave me be—"

There was another silence while he waited.

Suddenly, his form stiffened and straightened. Then it was shaken by a prolonged ague. He stared into space. To the two watchers there was a curious and profound dignity in the firm lines of his awful face.

He was invaded by a creeping strangeness that slowly enveloped him. For a moment the tremor of his legs caused him to dance a sort of hideous hornpipe. His arms beat wildly about his head in expression of implike enthusiasm.

His tall figure stretched itself to its full height. There was a slight rending sound. Then it began to swing forward, slow and straight, in the manner of a falling tree. A swift muscular contortion made the left shoulder strike the ground first.

The body seemed to bounce a little way from the earth. "God!" said the tattered soldier.

The youth had watched, spellbound, this ceremony at the place of meeting. His face had been twisted into an expression of every agony he had imagined for his friend.

He now sprang to his feet and, going closer, gazed upon the pastelike
5 face. The mouth was opened and the teeth showed in a laugh.

As the flap of the blue jacket fell away from the body, he could see that the side looked as if it had been chewed by wolves.

The youth turned, with sudden, livid rage, toward the battlefield. He shook his fist. He seemed about to deliver a philippic.

10 "Hell—"

The red sun was pasted in the sky like a wafer.)

CHAPTER X

The tattered man stood musing.

"Well, he was reg'lar jim-dandy fer nerve, wa'n't he," said he finally in a
15 little awestruck voice. "A reg'lar jim-dandy." He thoughtfully poked one of the docile hands with his foot. "I wonner where he got 'is stren'th from? I never seen a man do like that before. It was a funny thing. Well, he was a reg'lar jim-dandy."

The youth desired to screech out his grief. He was stabbed, but his tongue
20 lay dead in the tomb of his mouth. He threw himself again upon the ground and began to brood.

The tattered man stood musing.

"Look-a-here, pardner," he said, after a time. He regarded the corpse as he spoke. "He's up an' gone, ain' 'e, an' we might as well begin t' look out fer
25 ol' number one. This here thing is all over. He's up an' gone, ain't 'e? An' he's all right here. Nobody won't bother 'im. An' I must say I ain't enjoying any great health m'self these days."

The youth, awakened by the tattered soldier's tone, looked quickly up. He saw that he was swinging uncertainly on his legs and that his face had turned
30 to a shade of blue.

"Good Lord!" he cried, "you ain't goin' t'—not you, too."

The tattered man waved his hand. "Nary die," he said. "All I want is some pea soup an' a good bed. Some pea soup," he repeated dreamfully.

The youth arose from the ground. "I wonder where he came from. I left
35 him over there." He pointed. "And now I find 'im here. And he was coming from over there, too." He indicated a new direction. They both turned toward the body as if to ask of it a question.

"Well," at length spoke the tattered man, "there ain't no use in our stayin' here an' tryin' t' ask him anything."

40 The youth nodded an assent wearily. They both turned to gaze for a moment at the corpse.

The youth murmured something.

"Well, he was a jim-dandy, wa'n't 'e?" said the tattered man as if in response.

9. **philippic**—a discourse or speech of bitter denunciation.

They turned their backs upon it and started away. For a time they stole softly, treading with their toes. It remained laughing there in the grass.

"I'm commencin' t' feel pretty bad," said the tattered man, suddenly breaking one of his little silences. "I'm commencin' t' feel pretty damn' bad."

The youth groaned. "O Lord!" He wondered if he was to be the tortured witness of another grim encounter.

But his companion waved his hand reassuringly. "Oh, I'm not goin' t' die yit! There too much dependin' on me fer me t' die yit. No, sir! Nary die! I *can't!* Ye'd oughta see th' swad a' chil'ren I've got, an' all like that."

The youth glancing at his companion could see by the shadow of a smile that he was making some kind of fun.

As they plodded on the tattered soldier continued to talk. "Besides, if I died, I wouldn't die th' way that feller did. That was th' funniest thing. I'd jest flop down, I would. I never seen a feller die th' way that feller did.

"Yeh know Tom Jamison, he lives next door t' me up home. He's a nice feller, he is, an' we was allus good friends. Smart, too. Smart as a steel trap. Well, when we was a-fightin' this atternoon, all-of-a-sudden he begin t' rip up an' cuss an' beller at me. 'Yer shot, yeh blamed infernal!'—he swear horrible—he ses t' me. I put up m' hand t' m' head an' when I looked at m' fingers, I seen, sure 'nough, I was shot. I give a holler an' begin t' run, but b'fore I could git away another one hit me in th' arm an' whirl' me clean 'round. I got skeared when they was all a-shootin' b'hind me an' I run t' beat all, but I cotch it pretty bad. I've an idee I'd a' been fightin' yit, if t'was n't fer Tom Jamison."

Then he made a calm announcement: "There's two of 'em—little ones—but they're beginnin' t' have fun with me now. I don't b'lieve I kin walk much furder."

They went slowly on in silence. "Yeh look pretty peek-ed yerself," said the tattered man at last. "I bet yeh 've got a worser one than yeh think. Ye'd better take keer of yer hurt. It don't do t' let sech things go. It might be inside mostly, an' them plays thunder. Where is it located?" But he continued his harangue without waiting for a reply. "I see' a feller git hit plum in th' head when my reg'ment was a-standin' at ease onct. An' everybody yelled out to 'im: Hurt, John? Are yeh hurt much? 'No,' ses he. He looked kinder surprised, an' he went on tellin' 'em how he felt. He sed he didn't feel nothin'. But, by dad, th' first thing that feller knowed he was dead. Yes, he was dead—stone dead. So, yeh wanta watch out. Yeh might have some queer kind 'a hurt yerself. Yeh can't never tell. Where is your'n located?"

The youth had been wriggling since the introduction of this topic. He now gave a cry of exasperation and made a furious motion with his hand. "Oh, don't bother me!" he said. He was enraged against the tattered man, and could have strangled him. His companions seemed ever to play intolerable parts. They were ever upraising the ghost of shame on the stick of their curiosity. He turned toward the tattered man as one at bay. "Now, don't bother me," he repeated with desperate menace.

"Well, Lord knows I don't wanta bother anybody," said the other. There was a little accent of despair in his voice as he replied, "Lord knows I've gota 'nough m' own t' tend to."

The youth, who had been holding a bitter debate with himself and casting glances of hatred and contempt at the tattered man, here spoke in a hard
5   voice. "Good-by," he said.

The tattered man looked at him in gaping amazement. "Why—why, pardner, where yeh goin'?" he asked unsteadily. The youth looking at him, could see that he, too, like that other one, was beginning to act dumb and animal-like. His thoughts seemed to be floundering about in his head. "Now—now—
10 look—a—here, you Tom Jamison—now—I won't have this—this here won't do. Where—where yeh goin'?"

The youth pointed vaguely. "Over there," he replied.

"Well, now look—a—here—now," said the tattered man, rambling on in idiot fashion. His head was hanging forward and his words were slurred.
15 "This thing won't do, now, Tom Jamison. It won't do. I know yeh, yeh pig-headed devil. Yeh wanta go trompin' off with a bad hurt. It ain't right—now —Tom Jamison—it ain't. Yeh wanta leave me take keer of yeh, Tom Jamison. It ain't—right—it ain't—fer yeh t' go—trompin' off—with a bad hurt—it ain't —ain't—ain't right—it ain't."
20 In reply the youth climbed a fence and started away. He could hear the tattered man bleating plaintively.

Once he faced about angrily. "What?"

"Look—a—here, now, Tom Jamison—now—it ain't—"

The youth went on. Turning at a distance he saw the tattered man wander-
25 ing about helplessly in the field.

He now thought that he wished he was dead. He believed that he envied those men whose bodies lay strewn over the grass of the fields and on the fallen leaves of the forest.

The simple questions of the tattered man had been knife thrusts to him.
30 They asserted a society that probes pitilessly at secrets until all is apparent. His late companion's chance persistency made him feel that he could not keep his crime concealed in his bosom. It was sure to be brought plain by one of those arrows which cloud the air and are constantly pricking, discovering, proclaiming those things which are willed to be forever hidden. He admitted
35 that he could not defend himself against this agency. It was not within the power of vigilance.

CHAPTER XI

He became aware that the furnace roar of the battle was growing louder. Great brown clouds had floated to the still heights of air before him. The
40 noise, too, was approaching. The woods filtered men and the fields became dotted.

As he rounded a hillock, he perceived that the roadway was now a crying mass of wagons, teams, and men. From the heaving tangle issued exhortations, commands, imprecations. Fear was sweeping it all along. The cracking whips
45 bit and horses plunged and tugged. The white-topped wagons strained and stumbled in their exertions like fat sheep.

The youth felt comforted in a measure by this sight. They were all retreating. Perhaps, then, he was not so bad after all. He seated himself and watched the terror-stricken wagons. They fled like soft, ungainly animals. All the roarers and lashers served to help him to magnify the dangers and horrors of the engagement that he might try to prove to himself that the thing with which men could charge him was in truth a symmetrical act. There was an amount of pleasure to him in watching the wild march of this vindication.

Presently the calm head of a forward-going column of infantry appeared in the road. It came swiftly on. Avoiding the obstructions gave it the sinuous movement of a serpent. The men at the head butted mules with their musket stocks. They prodded teamsters indifferent to all howls. The men forced their way through parts of the dense mass by strength. The blunt head of the column pushed. The raving teamsters swore many strange oaths.

The commands to make way had the ring of a great importance in them. The men were going forward to the heart of the din. They were to confront the eager rush of the enemy. They felt the pride of their onward movement when the remainder of the army seemed trying to dribble down this road. They tumbled teams about with a fine feeling that it was no matter so long as their column got to the front in time. This importance made their faces grave and stern. And the backs of the officers were very rigid.

As the youth looked at them the black weight of his woe returned to him. He felt that he was regarding a procession of chosen beings. The separation was as great to him as if they had marched with weapons of flame and banners of sunlight. He could never be like them. He could have wept in his longings.

He searched about in his mind for an adequate malediction for the indefinite cause, the thing upon which men turn the words of final blame. It—whatever it was—was responsible for him, he said. There lay the fault.

The haste of the column to reach the battle seemed to the forlorn young man to be something much finer than stout fighting. Heroes, he thought, could find excuses in that long seething lane. They could retire with perfect self-respect and make excuses to the stars.

He wondered what those men had eaten that they could be in such haste to force their way to grim chances of death. As he watched his envy grew until he thought that he wished to change lives with one of them. He would have liked to have used a tremendous force, he said, throw off himself and become a better. Swift pictures of himself, apart, yet in himself, came to him—a blue desperate figure leading lurid charges with one knee forward and a broken blade high—a blue, determined figure standing before a crimson and steel assault, getting calmly killed on a high place before the eyes of all. He thought of the magnificent pathos of his dead body.

These thoughts uplifted him. He felt the quiver of war desire. In his ears, he heard the ring of victory. He knew the frenzy of a rapid successful charge. The music of the trampling feet, the sharp voices, the clanking arms of the column near him made him soar on the red wings of war. For a few moments he was sublime.

He thought that he was about to start for the front. Indeed, he saw a picture of himself, dust-stained, haggard, panting, flying to the front at the proper moment to seize and throttle the dark, leering witch of calamity.

Then the difficulties of the thing began to drag at him. He hesitated, balancing awkwardly on one foot.

5   He had no rifle; he could not fight with his hands, said he resentfully to his plan. Well, rifles could be had for the picking. They were extraordinarily profuse.

Also, he continued, it would be a miracle if he found his regiment. Well, he could fight with any regiment.

10   He started forward slowly. He stepped as if he expected to tread upon some explosive thing. Doubts and he were struggling.

He would truly be a worm if any of his comrades should see him returning thus, the marks of his flight upon him. There was a reply that the intent fighters did not care for what happened rearward saving that no hostile bay-

15 onets appeared there. In the battle-blur his face would in a way be hidden, like the face of a cowled man.

But then he said that his tireless fate would bring forth, when the strife lulled for a moment, a man to ask of him an explanation. In imagination he felt the scrutiny of his companions as he painfully labored through some lies.

20   Eventually, his courage expended itself upon these objections. The debates drained him of his fire.

He was not cast down by this defeat of his plan, for, upon studying the affair carefully, he could not but admit that the objections were very formidable.

25   Furthermore, various ailments had begun to cry out. In their presence he could not persist in flying high with the wings of war; they rendered it almost impossible for him to see himself in a heroic light. He tumbled headlong.

He discovered that he had a scorching thirst. His face was so dry and grimy

30 that he thought he could feel his skin crackle. Each bone of his body had an ache in it, and seemingly threatened to break with each movement. His feet were like two sores. Also, his body was calling for food. It was more powerful than a direct hunger. There was a dull, weight like feeling in his stomach, and, when he tried to walk, his head swayed and he tottered. He could not

35 see with distinctness. Small patches of green mist floated before his vision.

While he had been tossed by many emotions, he had not been aware of ailments. Now they beset him and made clamor. As he was at last compelled to pay attention to them, his capacity for self-hate was multiplied. In despair, he declared that he was not like those others. He now conceded it to be im-

40 possible that he should ever become a hero. He was a craven loon. Those pictures of glory were piteous things. He groaned from his heart and went staggering off.

A certain mothlike quality within him kept him in the vicinity of the battle. He had a great desire to see, and to get news. He wished to know

45 who was winning.

He told himself that, despite his unprecedented suffering, he had never lost his greed for a victory, yet, he said, in a half-apologetic manner to his conscience, he could not but know that a defeat for the army this time might mean many favorable things for him. The blows of the enemy would splinter regiments into fragments. Thus, many men of courage, he considered, would be obliged to desert the colors and scurry like chickens. He would appear as one of them. They would be sullen brothers in distress, and he could then 5 easily believe he had not run any farther or faster than they. And if he himself could believe in his virtuous perfection, he conceived that there would be small trouble in convincing all others.

He said, as if in excuse for this hope, that previously the army had encountered great defeats and in a few months had shaken off all blood and 10 tradition of them, emerging as bright and valiant as a new one; thrusting out of sight the memory of disaster, and appearing with the valor and confidence of unconquered legions. The shrilling voices of the people at home would pipe dismally for a time, but various generals were usually compelled to listen to these ditties. He of course felt no compunctions for proposing a 15 general as a sacrifice. He could not tell who the chosen for the barbs might be, so he could center no direct sympathy upon him. The people were afar and he did not conceive public opinion to be accurate at long range. It was quite probable they would hit the wrong man who, after he had recovered from his amazement would perhaps spend the rest of his days in writing 20 replies to the songs of his alleged failure. It would be very unfortunate, no doubt, but in this case a general was of no consequence to the youth.

In a defeat there would be a roundabout vindication of himself. He thought it would prove, in a manner, that he had fled early because of his superior powers of perception. A serious prophet upon predicting a flood should be 25 the first man to climb a tree. This would demonstrate that he was indeed a seer.

A moral vindication was regarded by the youth as a very important thing. Without salve, he could not, he thought, wear the sore badge of his dishonor through life. With his heart continually assuring him that he was despicable, 30 he could not exist without making it, through his actions, apparent to all men.

If the army had gone gloriously on he would be lost. If the din meant that now his army's flags were tilted forward he was a condemned wretch. He would be compelled to doom himself to isolation. If the men were advanc- 35 ing, their indifferent feet were trampling upon his chances for a successful life.

As these thoughts went rapidly through his mind, he turned upon them and tried to thrust them away. He denounced himself as a villain. He said that he was the most unutterably selfish man in existence. His mind pictured 40 the soldiers who would place their defiant bodies before the spear of the yelling battle fiend, and as he saw their dripping corpses on an imagined field, he said that he was their murderer.

Again he thought that he wished he was dead. He believed that he envied a corpse. Thinking of the slain, he achieved a great contempt for some of 45 them, as if they were guilty for thus becoming lifeless. They might have been killed by lucky chances, he said, before they had had opportunities to flee or before they had been really tested. Yet they would receive laurels from tradition. He cried out bitterly that their crowns were stolen and their robes of glorious memories were shams. However, he still said that it was a great pity he was not as they.

5   A defeat of the army had suggested itself to him as a means of escape from the consequences of his fall. He considered, now, however, that it was useless to think of such a possibility. His education had been that success for that mighty blue machine was certain; that it would make victories as a contrivance turns out buttons. He presently discarded all his speculations in
10 the other direction. He returned to the creed of soldiers.

When he perceived again that it was not possible for the army to be defeated, he tried to bethink him of a fine tale which he could take back to his regiment, and with it turn the expected shafts of derision.

But, as he mortally feared these shafts, it became impossible for him to
15 invent a tale he felt he could trust. He experimented with many schemes, but threw them aside one by one as flimsy. He was quick to see vulnerable places in them all.

Furthermore, he was much afraid that some arrow of scorn might lay him mentally low before he could raise his protecting tale.

20 He imagined the whole regiment saying: "Where's Henry Fleming? He run, didn't 'e? Oh, my!" He recalled various persons who would be quite sure to leave him no peace about it. They would doubtless question him with sneers, and laugh at his stammering hesitation. In the next engagement they would try to keep watch of him to discover when he would run.

25 Wherever he went in camp, he would encounter insolent and lingeringly cruel stares. As he imagined himself passing near a crowd of comrades, he could hear some one say, "There he goes!"

Then, as if the heads were moved by one muscle, all the faces were turned toward him with wide, derisive grins. He seemed to hear some one make a
30 humorous remark in a low tone. At it the others all crowed and cackled. He was a slang phrase.

CHAPTER XII

The column that had butted stoutly at the obstacles in the roadway was barely out of the youth's sight before he saw dark waves of men come sweep-
35 ing out of the woods and down through the fields. He knew at once that the steel fibers had been washed from their hearts. They were bursting from their coats and their equipments as from entanglements. They charged down upon him like terrified buffaloes.

Behind them blue smoke curled and clouded above the treetops, and through
40 the thickets he could sometimes see a distant pink glare. The voices of the cannon were clamoring in interminable chorus.

The youth was horrorstricken. He stared in agony and amazement. He forgot that he was engaged in combating the universe. He threw aside his mental pamphlets on the philosophy of the retreated and rules for the guid-
45 ance of the damned.

The fight was lost. The dragons were coming with invincible strides. The army, helpless in the matted thickets and blinded by the overhanging night, was going to be swallowed. War, the red animal, war, the blood-swollen god, would have bloated fill.

Within him something bade to cry out. He had the impulse to make a rallying speech, to sing a battle hymn, but he could only get his tongue to 5 call into the air: "Why—why—what—what's th' matter?"

Soon he was in the midst of them. They were leaping and scampering all about him. Their blanched faces shone in the dusk. They seemed, for the most part, to be very burly men. The youth turned from one to another of them as they galloped along. His incoherent questions were lost. They were 10 heedless of his appeals. They did not seem to see him.

They sometimes gabbled insanely. One huge man was asking of the sky: "Say, where de plank road? Where de plank road!" It was as if he had lost a child. He wept in his pain and dismay.

Presently, men were running hither and thither in all ways. The artillery 15 booming, forward, rearward, and on the flanks made jumble of ideas of direction. Landmarks had vanished into the gathered gloom. The youth began to imagine that he had got into the center of the tremendous quarrel, and he could perceive no way out of it. From the mouths of the fleeing men came a thousand wild questions, but no one made answers. 20

The youth, after rushing about and throwing interrogations at the heedless bands of retreating infantry, finally clutched a man by the arm. They swung around face to face.

"Why—why—" stammered the youth struggling with his balking tongue.

The man screamed: "Let go me! Let go me!" His face was livid and his 25 eyes were rolling uncontrolled. He was heaving and panting. He still grasped his rifle, perhaps having forgotten to release his hold upon it. He tugged frantically, and the youth being compelled to lean forward was dragged several paces.

"Let go me! Let go me!" 30

"Why—why—" stuttered the youth.

"Well, then!" bawled the man in a lurid rage. He adroitly and fiercely swung his rifle. It crushed upon the youth's head. The man ran on.

The youth's fingers had turned to paste upon the other's arm. The energy was smitten from his muscles. He saw the flaming wings of lightning flash 35 before his vision. There was a deafening rumble of thunder within his head.

Suddenly his legs seemed to die. He sank writhing to the ground. He tried to arise. In his efforts against the numbing pain he was like a man wrestling with a creature of the air.

There was a sinister struggle. 40

Sometimes he would achieve a position half erect, battle with the air for a moment, and then fall again, grabbing at the grass. His face was of a clammy pallor. Deep groans were wrenched from him.

At last, with a twisting movement, he got upon his hands and knees, and 45 from thence, like a babe trying to walk, to his feet. Pressing his hands to his temples he went lurching over the grass.

He fought an intense battle with his body. His dulled senses wished him to swoon and he opposed them stubbornly, his mind portraying unknown dangers and mutilations if he should fall upon the field. He went tall soldier fashion. He imagined secluded spots where he could fall and be unmolested.
5 To search for one he strove against the tide of his pain.

Once he put his hand to the top of his head and timidly touched the wound. The scratching pain of the contact made him draw a long breath through his clinched teeth. His fingers were dabbled with blood. He regarded them with a fixed stare.

10 Around him he could hear the grumble of jolted cannon as the scurrying horses were lashed toward the front. Once, a young officer on a besplashed charger nearly ran him down. He turned and watched the mass of guns, men, and horses sweeping in a wide curve toward a gap in a fence. The officer was making excited motions with a gauntleted hand. The guns followed the teams
15 with an air of unwillingness, of being dragged by the heels.

Some officers of the scattered infantry were cursing and railing like fishwives. Their scolding voices could be heard above the din. Into the unspeakable jumble in the roadway rode a squadron of cavalry. The faded yellow of their facings shone bravely. There was a mighty altercation.

20 The artillery were assembling as if for a conference.

The blue haze of evening was upon the field. The lines of forest were long purple shadows. One cloud lay along the western sky partly smothering the red.

As the youth left the scene behind him, he heard the guns suddenly roar
25 out. He imagined them shaking in black rage. They belched and howled like brass devils guarding a gate. The soft air was filled with the tremendous remonstrance. With it came the shattering peal of opposing infantry. Turning to look behind him, he could see sheets of orange light illumine the shadowy distance. There were subtle and sudden lightnings in the far air. At times
30 he thought he could see heaving masses of men.

He hurried on in the dusk. The day had faded until he could barely distinguish place for his feet. The purple darkness was filled with men who lectured and jabbered. Sometimes he could see them gesticulating against the blue and somber sky. There seemed to be a great ruck of men and munitions
35 spread about in the forest and in the fields.

The little narrow roadway now lay lifeless. There were overturned wagons like sun-dried bowlders. The bed of the former torrent was choked with the bodies of horses and splintered parts of war machines.

It had come to pass that his wound pained him but little. He was afraid to
40 move rapidly, however, for a dread of disturbing it. He held his head very still and took many precautions against stumbling. He was filled with anxiety, and his face was pinched and drawn in anticipation of the pain of any sudden mistake of his feet in the gloom.

His thoughts, as he walked, fixed intently upon his hurt. There was a cool,
45 liquid feeling about it and he imagined blood moving slowly down under his

19. **facings**—that with which a military garment is "faced"; especially the cuffs and collar of a military coat when these parts are of a color differing from that of the rest of the coat.

hair. His head seemed swollen to a size that made him think his neck to be inadequate.

The new silence of his wound made much worriment. The little blistering voices of pain that had called out from his scalp were, he thought, definite in their expression of danger. By them he believed that he could measure his plight. But when they remained ominously silent he became frightened and imagined terrible fingers that clutched into his brain.

Amid it he began to reflect upon various incidents and conditions of the past. He bethought him of certain meals his mother had cooked at home, in which those dishes of which he was particularly fond had occupied prominent positions. He saw the spread table. The pine walls of the kitchen were glowing in the warm light from the stove. Too, he remembered how he and his companions used to go from the schoolhouse to the bank of a shaded pool. He saw his clothes in disorderly array upon the grass of the bank. He felt the swash of the fragrant water upon his body. The leaves of the overhanging maple rustled with melody in the wind of youthful summer.

He was overcome presently by a dragging weariness. His head hung forward and his shoulders were stooped as if he were bearing a great bundle. His feet shuffled along the ground.

He held continuous arguments as to whether he should lie down and sleep at some near spot, or force himself on until he reached a certain haven. He often tried to dismiss the question, but his body persisted in rebellion and his senses nagged at him like pampered babies.

At last he heard a cheery voice near his shoulder: "Yeh seem t' be in a pretty bad way, boy?"

The youth did not look up, but he assented with thick tongue. "Uh!"

The owner of the cheery voice took him firmly by the arm. "Well," he said, with a round laugh, "I'm goin' your way. Th' hull gang is goin' your way. An' I guess I kin give yeh a lift." They began to walk like a drunken man and his friend.

As they went along, the man questioned the youth and assisted him with the replies like one manipulating the mind of a child. Sometimes he interjected anecdotes. "What reg'ment do yeh b'long teh? Eh? What's that? Th' 304th N' York? Why, what corps is that in? Oh, it is? Why, I thought they wasn't engaged t'-day—they're 'way over in th' center. Oh, they was, eh? Well, pretty nearly everybody got their share 'a fightin' t'-day. By dad, I give myself up fer dead any number 'a times. There was shootin' here an' shootin' there, an' hollerin' here an' hollerin' there, in th' damn' darkness, until I couldn't tell t' save m' soul which side I was on. Sometimes I thought I was sure 'nough from Ohier, an' other times I could a' swore I was from th' bitter end of Florida. It was th' most mixed up dern thing I ever see. An' these here hull woods is a reg'lar mess. It'll be a miracle if we find our reg'ments t'-night. Pretty soon, though, we'll meet a-plenty of guards an' provost-guards, an' one thing an' another. Ho! there they go with an off'cer, I guess. Look at his hand a-draggin'. He's got all th' war he wants, I bet. He won't be talkin' so big about his reputation an' all when they go t' sawin' off his leg. Poor feller! My brother's got whiskers jest like that. How did yeh git 'way over

here, anyhow? Your reg'ment is a long way from here, ain't it? Well, I
guess we can find it. Yeh know there was a boy killed in my comp'ny t'-day
that I thought th' world an' all of. Jack was a nice feller. By ginger, it hurt
like thunder t' see ol' Jack jest git knocked flat. We was a-standin' purty
5 peaceable fer a spell, 'though there was men runnin' ev'ry way all 'round us,
an' while we was a-standin' like that, 'long come a big fat feller. He began
t' peck at Jack's elbow, an' he ses: 'Say, where 's th' road t' th' river?' An'
Jack, he never paid no attention, an' th' feller kept on a-peckin' at his elbow
an' sayin': 'Say, where's th' road t' th' river?' Jack was a-lookin' ahead all th'
10 time tryin' t' see th' Johnnies comin' through th' woods, an' he never paid
no attention t' this big fat feller fer a long time, but at last he turned 'round
an' he ses: 'Ah, go t' hell an' find th' road t' th' river!' An' jest then a shot
slapped him bang on th' side th' head. He was a sergeant, too. Them was
his last words. Thunder, I wish we was sure 'a findin' our reg'ments t'-night.
15 It's goin' t' be long huntin'. But I guess we kin do it."

In the search which followed, the man of the cheery voice seemed to the
youth to possess a wand of a magic kind. He threaded the mazes of the
tangled forest with a strange fortune. In encounters with guards and patrols
he displayed the keenness of a detective and the valor of a gamin. Obstacles
20 fell before him and became of assistance. The youth, with his chin still on
his breast, stood woodenly by while his companion beat ways and means out
of sullen things.

The forest seemed a vast hive of men buzzing about in frantic circles, but
the cheery man conducted the youth without mistakes, until at last he began
25 to chuckle with glee and self-satisfaction. "Ah, there yeh are! See that fire?"

The youth nodded stupidly.

"Well, there's where your reg'ment is. An' now, good-by, ol' boy, good luck
t' yeh."

A warm and strong hand clasped the youth's languid fingers for an in-
30 stant, and then he heard a cheerful and audacious whistling as the man strode
away. As he who had so befriended him was thus passing out of his life, it
suddenly occurred to the youth that he had not once seen his face.

CHAPTER XIII

The youth went slowly toward the fire indicated by his departed friend.
35 As he reeled, he bethought him of the welcome his comrades would give
him. He had a conviction that he would soon feel in his sore heart the barbed
missiles of ridicule. He had no strength to invent a tale; he would be a soft
target.

He made vague plans to go off into the deeper darkness and hide, but
40 they were all destroyed by the voices of exhaustion and pain from his body.
His ailments, clamoring, forced him to seek the place of food and rest, at
whatever cost.

He swung unsteadily toward the fire. He could see the forms of men throwing black shadows in the red light, and as he went nearer it became known
45 to him in some way that the ground was strewn with sleeping men.

Of a sudden he confronted a black and monstrous figure. A rifle barrel caught some glinting beams. "Halt! halt!" He was dismayed for a moment, but he presently thought that he recognized the nervous voice. As he stood tottering before the rifle barrel, he called out: "Why, hello, Wilson, you— you here?" 5

The rifle was lowered to a position of caution and the loud soldier came slowly forward. He peered into the youth's face. "That you, Henry?"

"Yes it's—it's me."

"Well, well, ol' boy," said the other, "by ginger, I'm glad t' see yeh! I give yeh up fer a goner. I thought yeh was dead sure enough." There was husky 10 emotion in his voice.

The youth found that now he could barely stand upon his feet. There was a sudden sinking of his forces. He thought he must hasten to produce his tale to protect him from the missiles already at the lips of his redoubtable comrades. So, staggering before the loud soldier, he began: "Yes, yes. I've— 15 I've had an awful time. I've been all over. Way over on th' right. Ter'ble fightin' over there. I had an awful time. I got separated from th' reg'ment. Over on th' right, I got shot. In th' head. I never see sech fightin'. Awful time. I don't see how I could a' got separated from th' reg'ment. I got shot, too." 20

His friend had stepped forward quickly. "What? Got shot? Why didn't yeh say so first? Poor ol' boy, we must—hol' on a minnit; what am I doin'. I'll call Simpson."

Another figure at that moment loomed in the gloom. They could see that it was the corporal. "Who yeh talkin' to, Wilson?" he demanded. His voice 25 was anger-toned. "Who yeh talkin' to? Yeh th' derndest sentinel—why— hello, Henry, you here? Why, I thought you was dead four hours ago! Great Jerusalem, they keep turnin' up every ten minutes or so! We thought we'd lost forty-two men by straight count, but if they keep on a-comin' this way, we'll git th' comp'ny all back by mornin' yit. Where was yeh?" 30

"Over on th' right. I got separated"—began the youth with considerable glibness.

But his friend had interrupted hastily. "Yes, an' he got shot in th' head an' he's in a fix, an' we must see t' him right away." He rested his rifle in the hollow of his left arm and his right around the youth's shoulder. 35

"Gee, it must hurt like thunder!" he said.

The youth leaned heavily upon his friend. "Yes, it hurts—hurts a good deal," he replied. There was a faltering in his voice.

"Oh," said the corporal. He linked his arm in the youth's and drew him forward. "Come on, Henry. I'll take keer 'a yeh." 40

As they went on together the loud private called out after them: "Put 'im t' sleep in my blanket, Simpson. An'—hol' on a minnit—here's my canteen. It's full 'a coffee. Look at his head by th' fire an' see how it looks. Maybe it's a pretty bad un. When I git relieved in a couple 'a minnits, I'll be over an' see t' him." 45

The youth's senses were so deadened that his friend's voice sounded from afar and he could scarcely feel the pressure of the corporal's arm. He submitted passively to the latter's directing strength. His head was in the old manner hanging forward upon his breast. His knees wobbled.

The corporal led him into the glare of the fire. "Now, Henry," he said, "let's have look at yer ol' head."

5 The youth sat down obediently and the corporal, laying aside his rifle, began to fumble in the bushy hair of his comrade. He was obliged to turn the other's head so that the full flush of the fire light would beam upon it. He puckered his mouth with a critical air. He drew back his lips and whistled through his teeth when his fingers came in contact with the splashed blood
10 and the rare wound.

"Ah, here we are!" he said. He awkwardly made further investigations. "Jest as I thought," he added, presently. "Yeh've been grazed by a ball. It's raised a queer lump jest as if some feller had lammed yeh on th' head with a club. It stopped a-bleedin' long time ago. Th' most about it is that in th'
15 mornin' yeh'll feel that a number ten hat wouldn't fit yeh. An' your head 'll be all het up an' feel as dry as burnt pork. An' yeh may git a lot 'a other sicknesses, too, by mornin'. Yeh can't never tell. Still, I don't much think so. It's jest a damn' good belt on th' head, an' nothin' more. Now, you jest sit here an' don't move, while I go rout out th' relief. Then I'll send Wilson t'
20 take keer 'a yeh."

The corporal went away. The youth remained on the ground like a parcel. He stared with a vacant look into the fire.

After a time he aroused, for some part, and the things about him began to take form. He saw that the ground in the deep shadows was cluttered
25 with men, sprawling in every conceivable posture. Glancing narrowly into the more distant darkness, he caught occasional glimpses of visages that loomed pallid and ghostly, lit with a phosphorescent glow. These faces expressed in their lines the deep stupor of the tired soldiers. They made them appear like men drunk with wine. This bit of forest might have appeared to
30 an ethereal wanderer as a scene of the result of some frightful debauch.

On the other side of the fire the youth observed an officer asleep, seated bolt upright, with his back against a tree. There was something perilous in his position. Badgered by dreams, perhaps, he swayed with little bounces and starts, like an old, toddy-stricken grandfather in a chimney corner. Dust and
35 stains were upon his face. His lower jaw hung down as if lacking strength to assume its normal position. He was the picture of an exhausted soldier after a feast of war.

He had evidently gone to sleep with his sword in his arms. These two had slumbered in an embrace, but the weapon had been allowed in time to
40 fall unheeded to the ground. The brass-mounted hilt lay in contact with some parts of the fire.

Within the gleam of rose and orange light from the burning sticks were other soldiers, snoring and heaving, or lying deathlike in slumber. A few pairs of legs were stuck forth, rigid and straight. The shoes displayed the
45 mud or dust of marches and bits of rounded trousers, protruding from the blankets, showed rents and tears from hurried pitchings through the dense brambles.

The fire crackled musically. From it swelled light smoke. Overhead the foliage moved softly. The leaves, with their faces turned toward the blaze, were colored shifting hues of silver, often edged with red. Far off to the right, through a window in the forest, could be seen a handful of stars lying, like glittering pebbles, on the black level of the night.   5

Occasionally, in this low-arched hall, a soldier would arouse and turn his body to a new position, the experience of his sleep having taught him of uneven and objectionable places upon the ground under him. Or, perhaps, he would lift himself to a sitting posture, blink at the fire for an unintelligent moment, throw a swift glance at his prostrate companion, and then cuddle   10 down again with a grunt of sleepy content.

The youth sat in a forlorn heap until his friend the loud young soldier came, swinging two canteens by their light strings. "Well, now, Henry, ol' boy," said the latter, "we'll have yeh fixed up in jest about a minnit."

He had the bustling ways of an amateur nurse. He fussed around the fire   15 and stirred the sticks to brilliant exertions. He made his patient drink largely from the canteen that contained the coffee. It was to the youth a delicious draught. He tilted his head afar back and held the canteen long to his lips. The cool mixture went caressingly down his blistered throat. Having finished, he sighed with comfortable delight.   20

The loud young soldier watched his comrade with an air of satisfaction. He later produced an extensive handkerchief from his pocket. He folded it into a manner of bandage and soused water from the other canteen upon the middle of it. This crude arrangement he bound over the youth's head, tying the ends in a queer knot at the back of the neck.   25

"There," he said, moving off and surveying his deed, "yeh look like th' devil, but I bet yeh feel better."

The youth contemplated his friend with grateful eyes. Upon his aching and swelling head the cold cloth was like a tender woman's hand.

"Yeh don't holler ner say nothin'," remarked his friend approvingly. "I   30 know I'm a blacksmith at takin' keer 'a sick folks, an' yeh never squeaked. Yer a good un, Henry. Most 'a men would a' been in th' hospital long ago. A shot in th' head ain't foolin' business."

The youth made no reply, but began to fumble with the buttons of his jacket.   35

"Well, come, now," continued his friend, "come on. I must put yeh t' bed an' see that yeh git a good night's rest."

The other got carefully erect, and the loud young soldier led him among the sleeping forms lying in groups and rows. Presently he stooped and picked up his blankets. He spread the rubber one upon the ground and placed the   40 woolen one about the youth's shoulders.

"There now," he said, "lie down an' git some sleep."

The youth, with his manner of doglike obedience, got carefully down like a crone stooping. He stretched out with a murmur of relief and comfort. The ground felt like the softest couch.   45

But of a sudden he ejaculated: "Hol' on a minnit! Where you goin' t' sleep?"

His friend waved his hand impatiently. "Right down there by yeh."

"Well, but hol' on a minnit," continued the youth. "What yeh goin' t' sleep in? I've got your—"

The loud young soldier snarled: "Shet up an' go on t' sleep. Don't be
5 makin' a damn' fool 'a yerself," he said severely.

After the reproof the youth said no more. An exquisite drowsiness had spread through him. The warm comfort of the blanket enveloped him and made a gentle languor. His head fell forward on his crooked arm and his weighted lids went slowly down over his eyes. Hearing a splatter of mus-
10 ketry from the distance, he wondered indifferently if those men sometimes slept. He gave a long sigh, snuggled down into his blanket, and in a moment was like his comrades.

CHAPTER XIV

When the youth awoke it seemed to him that he had been asleep for a thou-
15 sand years, and he felt sure that he opened his eyes upon an unexpected world. Gray mists were slowly shifting before the first efforts of the sun-rays. An impending splendor could be seen in the eastern sky. An icy dew had chilled his face, and immediately upon arousing he curled farther down into his blankets. He stared for a while at the leaves overhead, moving in a heraldic wind of the
20 day.

The distance was splintering and blaring with the noise of fighting. There was in the sound an expression of a deadly persistency, as if it had not begun and was not to cease.

About him were the rows and groups of men that he had dimly seen the
25 previous night. They were getting a last draught of sleep before the awakening. The gaunt, careworn features and dusty figures were made plain by this quaint light at the dawning, but it dressed the skin of the men in corpselike hues and made the tangled limbs appear pulseless and dead. The youth started up with a little cry when his eyes first swept over this motionless mass of men,
30 thick-spread upon the ground, pallid, and in strange postures. His disordered mind interpreted the hall of the forest as a charnel place. He believed for an instant that he was in the house of the dead, and he did not dare to move lest these corpses start up, squalling and squawking. In a second, however, he achieved his proper mind. He swore a complicated oath at himself. He saw
35 that this somber picture was not a fact of the present, but a mere prophecy.

He heard then the noise of a fire crackling briskly in the cold air, and, turning his head, he saw his friend pottering busily about a small blaze. A few other figures moved in the fog, and he heard the hard cracking of axe blows.

Suddenly there was a hollow rumble of drums. A distant bugle sang faintly.
40 Similar sounds, varying in strength, came from near and far over the forest. The bugles called to each other like brazen gamecocks. The near thunder of the regimental drums rolled.

The body of men in the woods rustled. There was a general uplifting of heads. A murmuring of voices broke upon the air. In it there was much bass
45 of grumbling oaths. Strange gods were addressed in condemnation of the

early hours necessary to correct war. An officer's peremptory tenor rang out and quickened the stiffened movement of the men. The tangled limbs unraveled. The corpse-hued faces were hidden behind fists that twisted slowly in the eye sockets.

The youth sat up and gave vent to an enormous yawn. "Thunder!" he re- 5
marked petulantly. He rubbed his eyes, and then putting up his hand felt carefully of the bandage over his wound. His friend, perceiving him to be awake, came from the fire. "Well, Henry, ol' man, how do yeh feel this mornin'?" he demanded.

The youth yawned again. Then he puckered his mouth to a little pucker. 10
His head, in truth, felt precisely like a melon, and there was an unpleasant sensation at his stomach.

"Oh, Lord, I feel pretty bad," he said.

"Thunder!" exclaimed the other. "I hoped ye'd feel all right this mornin'. Let's see th' bandage—I guess it's slipped." He began to tinker at the wound 15
in rather a clumsy way until the youth exploded.

"Gosh-dern it!" he said in sharp irritation; "you're the hangdest man I ever saw! You wear muffs on your hands. Why in good thunderation can't you be more easy? I'd rather you'd stand off an' throw guns at it. Now, go slow, an' don't act as if you was nailing down carpet." 20

He glared with insolent command at his friend, but the latter answered soothingly. "Well, well, come now, an' git some grub," he said. "Then, maybe, yeh'll feel better."

At the fireside the loud young soldier watched over his comrade's wants with tenderness and care. He was very busy marshaling the little black vagabonds of 25
tin cups and pouring into them the streaming, iron colored mixture from a small and sooty tin pail. He had some fresh meat, which he roasted hurriedly upon a stick. He sat down then and contemplated the youth's appetite with glee.

The youth took note of a remarkable change in his comrade since those days 30
of camp life upon the river bank. He seemed no more to be continually regarding the proportions of his personal prowess. He was not furious at small words that pricked his conceits. He was no more a loud young soldier. There was about him now a fine reliance. He showed a quiet belief in his purposes and his abilities. And this inward confidence evidently enabled him to be indifferent 35
to little words of other men aimed at him.

The youth reflected. He had been used to regarding his comrade as a blatant child with an audacity grown from his inexperience, thoughtless, headstrong, jealous, and filled with a tinsel courage. A swaggering babe accustomed to strut in his own dooryard. The youth wondered where had been born these 40
new eyes; when his comrade had made the great discovery that there were many men who would refuse to be subjected by him. Apparently, the other had now climbed a peak of wisdom from which he could perceive himself as a very wee thing. And the youth saw that ever after it would be easier to live in his friend's neighborhood. 45

His comrade balanced his ebony coffee-cup on his knee. "Well, Henry," he said, "what d'yeh think th' chances are? D'yeh think we'll wallop 'em?"

The youth considered for a moment. "Day-b'fore-yesterday," he finally replied, with boldness, "you would 'a' bet you'd lick the hull kit-an'-boodle all by yourself."

His friend looked a trifle amazed. "Would I?" he asked. He pondered. "Well,
5 perhaps I would," he decided at last. He stared humbly at the fire.

The youth was quite disconcerted at this surprising reception of his remarks. "Oh, no, you wouldn't either," he said, hastily trying to retrace.

But the other made a deprecating gesture. "Oh, yeh needn't mind, Henry," he said. "I believe I was a pretty big fool in those days." He spoke as after a
10 lapse of years.

There was a little pause.

"All th' officers say we've got th' rebs in a pretty tight box," said the friend, clearing his throat in a commonplace way. "They all seem t' think we've got 'em jest where we want 'em."
15 "I don't know about that," the youth replied. "What I seen over on th' right makes me think it was th' other way about. From where I was, it looked as if we was gettin' a good poundin' yestirday."

"D'yeh think so?" inquired the friend. "I thought we handled 'em pretty rough yestirday."
20 "Not a bit," said 'the youth. "Why, lord, man, you didn't see nothing of the fight. Why!" Then a sudden thought came to him. "Oh! Jim Conklin's dead."

His friend started. "What? Is he? Jim Conklin?"

The youth spoke slowly. "Yes. He's dead. Shot in th' side."
25 "Yeh don't say so. Jim Conklin . . . poor cuss!"

All about them were other small fires surrounded by men with their little black utensils. From one of these near came sudden sharp voices in a row. It appeared that two light-footed soldiers had been teasing a huge, bearded man, causing him to spill coffee upon his blue knees. The man had gone into a rage
30 and had sworn comprehensively. Stung by his language, his tormentors had immediately bristled at him with a great show of resenting unjust oaths. Possibly there was going to be a fight.

The friend arose and went over to them, making pacific motions with his arms. "Oh, here, now, boys, what's th' use?" he said. "We'll be at th' rebs in
35 less'n an hour. What's th' good fightin' 'mong ourselves?"

One of the light-footed soldiers turned upon him red-faced and violent. "Yeh needn't come around here with yer preachin'. I s'pose yeh don't approve 'a fightin' since Charley Morgan licked yeh; but I don't see what business this here is 'a yours or anybody else."
40 "Well, it ain't," said the friend mildly. "Still I hate t' see—"

That was a tangled argument.

"Well, he—," said the two, indicating their opponent with accusative forefingers.

The huge soldier was quite purple with rage. He pointed at the two soldiers
45 with his great hand, extended clawlike. "Well, they—"

But during this argumentative time the desire to deal blows seemed to pass, although they said much to each other. Finally the friend returned to his old seat. In a short while the three antagonists could be seen together in an amiable bunch.

"Jimmie Rogers ses I'll have t' fight him after th' battle t'-day," announced the friend as he again seated himself. "He ses he don't allow no interferin' in his business. I hate t' see th' boys fightin' 'mong themselves."

The youth laughed. "Yer changed a good bit. Yeh ain't at all like yeh was. I remember when you an' that Irish feller—" He stopped and laughed again.

"No, I didn't use t' be that way," said his friend thoughtfully. "That's true 'nough."

"Well, I didn't mean—" began the youth.

The friend made another deprecatory gesture. "Oh, yeh needn't mind, Henry."

There was another little pause.

"Th' reg'ment lost over half th' men yestirday," remarked the friend eventually. "I thought a course they was all dead, but, laws, they kep' a-comin' back last night until it seems, after all, we didn't lose but a few. They'd been scattered all over, wanderin' around in th' woods, fightin' with other reg'ments, an' everything. Jest like you done."

"So?" said the youth.

CHAPTER XV

The regiment was standing at order arms at the side of a lane, waiting for the command to march, when suddenly the youth remembered the little packet enwrapped in a faded yellow envelope which the loud young soldier with lugubrious words had intrusted to him. It made him start. He uttered an exclamation and turned toward his comrade.

"Wilson!"

"What?"

His friend, at his side in the ranks, was thoughtfully staring down the road. From some cause his expression was at that moment very meek. The youth, regarding him with sidelong glances, felt impelled to change his purpose. "Oh, nothing," he said.

His friend turned his head in some surprise, "Why, what was yeh goin' t' say?"

"Oh, nothing," repeated the youth.

He resolved not to deal the little blow. It was sufficient that the fact made him glad. It was not necessary to knock his friend on the head with the misguided packet.

He had been possessed of much fear of his friend, for he saw how easily questionings could make holes in his feelings. Lately, he had assured himself that the altered comrade would not tantalize him with a persistent curiosity, but he felt certain that during the first period of leisure his friend would ask him to relate his adventures of the previous day.

He now rejoiced in the possession of a small weapon with which he could prostrate his comrade at the first signs of a cross-examination. He was master. It would now be he who could laugh and shoot the shafts of derision.

The friend had, in a weak hour, spoken with sobs of his own death. He had delivered a melancholy oration previous to his funeral, and had doubtless in the packet of letters, presented various keepsakes to relatives. But he had not died, and thus he had delivered himself into the hands of the youth.

5 The latter felt immensely superior to his friend, but he inclined to condescension. He adopted toward him an air of patronizing good humor.

His self-pride was now entirely restored. In the shade of its flourishing growth he stood with braced and self-confident legs, and since nothing could now be discovered he did not shrink from an encounter with the eyes of judges, and allowed no thoughts of his own to keep him from an attitude of manfulness.
10 (He had performed his mistakes in the dark, so he was still a man.)

Indeed, when he remembered his fortunes of yesterday, and looked at them from a distance he began to see something fine there. He had license to be pompous and veteranlike.

His panting agonies of the past he put out of his sight.

15 In the present, he declared to himself that it was only the doomed and the damned who roared with sincerity at circumstance. Few but they ever did it. A man with a full stomach and the respect of his fellows had no business to scold about anything that he might think to be wrong in the ways of the universe, or even with the ways of society. Let the unfortunates rail; the others
20 may play marbles.

He did not give a great deal of thought to these battles that lay directly before him. It was not essential that he should plan his ways in regard to them. He had been taught that many obligations of a life were easily avoided. The lessons of yesterday had been that retribution was a laggard and blind. With
25 these facts before him he did not deem it necessary that he should become feverish over the possibilities of the ensuing twenty-four hours. He could leave much to chance. Besides, a faith in himself had secretly blossomed. There was a little flower of confidence growing within him. He was now a man of experience. He had been out among the dragons, he said, and he assured himself
30 that they were not so hideous as he had imagined them. Also, they were inaccurate; they did not sting with precision. A stout heart often defied, and defying, escaped.

And, furthermore, how could they kill him who was the chosen of gods and doomed to greatness?

35 He remembered how some of the men had run from the battle. As he recalled their terror-struck faces he felt a scorn for them. They had surely been more fleet and more wild than was absolutely necessary. They were weak mortals. As for himself, he had fled with discretion and dignity.

He was aroused from this reverie by his friend, who, having hitched about
40 nervously and blinked at the trees for a time, suddenly coughed in an introductory way, and spoke.

"Fleming!"

"What?"

The friend put his hand up to his mouth and coughed again. He fidgeted in
45 his jacket.

"Well," he gulped, at last, "I guess yeh might as well give me back them letters." Dark, prickling blood had flushed into his cheeks and brow.

"All right, Wilson," said the youth. He loosened two buttons of his coat, thrust in his hand, and brought forth the packet. As he extended it to his friend the latter's face was turned from him.

He had been slow in the act of producing the packet because during it he had been trying to invent a remarkable comment upon the affair. He could conjure nothing of sufficient point. He was compelled to allow his friend to escape unmolested with his packet. And for this he took unto himself considerable credit. It was a generous thing.

His friend at his side seemed suffering great shame. As he contemplated him, the youth felt his heart grow more strong and stout. He had never been compelled to blush in such manner for his acts; he was an individual of extraordinary virtues.

He reflected, with condescending pity: "Too bad! Too bad! The poor devil, it makes him feel tough!"

After this incident, and as he reviewed the battle pictures he had seen, he felt quite competent to return home and make the hearts of the people glow with stories of war. He could see himself in a room of warm tints telling tales to listeners. He could exhibit laurels. They were insignificant; still, in a district where laurels were infrequent, they might shine.

He saw his gaping audience picturing him as the central figure in blazing scenes. And he imagined the consternation and the ejaculations of his mother and the young lady at the seminary as they drank his recitals. Their vague feminine formula for beloved ones doing brave deeds on the field of battle without risk of life would be destroyed.

CHAPTER XVI

A sputtering of musketry was always to be heard. Later, the cannon had entered the dispute. In the fog-filled air their voices made a thudding sound. The reverberations were continued. This part of the world led a strange, battleful existence.

The youth's regiment was marched to relieve a command that had lain long in some damp trenches. The men took positions behind a curving line of rifle pits that had been turned up, like a large furrow, along the line of woods. Before them was a level stretch, peopled with short, deformed stumps. From the woods beyond came the dull popping of the skirmishers and pickets, firing in the fog. From the right came the noise of a terrific fracas.

The men cuddled behind the small embankment and sat in easy attitudes awaiting their turn. Many had their backs to the firing. The youth's friend lay down, buried his face in his arms, and almost instantly, it seemed, he was in a deep sleep.

The youth leaned his breast against the brown dirt and peered over at the woods and up and down the line. Curtains of trees interfered with his ways of vision. He could see the low line of trenches but for a short distance. A few idle flags were perched on the dirt hills. Behind them were rows of dark bodies with a few heads sticking curiously over the top.

Always the noise of skirmishers came from the woods on the front and left, and the din on the right had grown to frightful proportions. The guns were roaring without an instant's pause for breath. It seemed that the cannon had come from all parts and were engaged in a stupendous wrangle. It became impossible to make a sentence heard.

5 　　The youth wished to launch a joke—a quotation from newspapers. He desired to say, "All quiet on the Rappahannock," but the guns refused to permit even a comment upon their uproar. He never successfully concluded the sentence. But at last the guns stopped, and among the men in the rifle pits rumors again flew, like birds, but they were now for the most part black creatures who
10 flapped their wings drearily near to the ground and refused to rise on any wings of hope. The men's faces grew doleful from the interpreting of omens. Tales of hesitation and uncertainty on the part of those high in place and responsibility came to their ears. Stories of disaster were borne into their minds with many proofs. This din of musketry on the right, growing like a released
15 genie of sound, expressed and emphasized the army's plight.

　　The men were disheartened and began to mutter. They made gestures expressive of the sentence: "Ah, what more can we do?" And it could always be seen that they were bewildered by the alleged news and could not fully comprehend a defeat.

20 　　Before the gray mists had been totally obliterated by the sunrays, the regiment was marching in a spread column that was retiring carefully through the woods. The disordered, hurrying lines of the enemy could sometimes be seen down through the groves and little fields. They were yelling, shrill and exultant.

25 　　At this sight the youth forgot many personal matters and became greatly enraged. He exploded in loud sentences. "B'jiminey, we're generaled by a lot 'a lunkheads."

　　"More than one feller has said that t'-day," observed a man.

　　His friend, recently aroused, was still very drowsy. He looked behind him
30 until his mind took in the meaning of the movement. Then he sighed. "Oh, well, I s'pose we got licked," he remarked sadly.

　　The youth had a thought that it would not be handsome for him to freely condemn other men. He made an attempt to restrain himself, but the words upon his tongue were too bitter. He presently began a long and intricate de-
35 nunciation of the commander of the forces.

　　"Mebbe, it wa'n't all his fault—not all together. He did th' best he knowed. It's our luck t' git licked often," said his friend in a weary tone. He was trudging along with stooped shoulders and shifting eyes like a man who has been caned and kicked.

40 　　"Well, don't we fight like the devil? Don't we do all that men can?" demanded the youth loudly.

　　He was secretly dumbfounded at this sentiment when it came from his lips. For a moment his face lost its valor and he looked guiltily about him. But no one questioned his right to deal in such words, and presently he recovered his
45 air of courage. He went on to repeat a statement he had heard going from

　　6. All quiet on the Rappahannock—satiric reference to the common newspaper phrase during the Civil War, "All quiet along the Potomac."

group to group at the camp that morning. "The brigadier said he never saw a new reg'ment fight the way we fought yestirday, didn't he? And we didn't do better than many another reg'ment, did we? Well, then, you can't say it's th' army's fault, can you?"

In his reply, the friend's voice was stern. " 'A course not," he said. "No man   5
dare say we don't fight like th' devil. No man will ever dare say it. Th' boys fight like hell-roosters. But still—still, we don't have no luck."

"Well, then, if we fight like the devil an' don't ever whip, it must be the general's fault," said the youth grandly and decisively. "And I don't see any sense in fighting and fighting and fighting, yet always losing through some   10
derned old lunkhead of a general."

A sarcastic man who was tramping at the youth's side, then spoke lazily. "Mebbe yeh think yeh fit th' hull battle yestirday, Fleming," he remarked.

The speech pierced the youth. Inwardly he was reduced to an abject pulp by these chance words. His legs quaked privately. He cast a frightened glance   15
at the sarcastic man.

"Why, no," he hastened to say in a conciliating voice, "I don't think I fought the whole battle yesterday."

But the other seemed innocent of any deeper meaning. Apparently, he had no information. It was merely his habit. "Oh!" he replied in the same tone of   20
calm derision.

The youth, nevertheless, felt a threat. His mind shrank from going near to the danger, and thereafter he was silent. The significance of the sarcastic man's words took from him all loud moods that would make him appear prominent. He became suddenly a modest person.   25

There was low-toned talk among the troops. The officers were impatient and snappy, their countenances clouded with the tales of misfortune. The troops, sifting through the forest, were sullen. In the youth's company once a man's laugh rang out. A dozen soldiers turned their faces quickly toward him and frowned with vague displeasure.   30

The noise of firing dogged their footsteps. Sometimes, it seemed to be driven a little way, but it always returned again with increased insolence. The men muttered and cursed, throwing black looks in its direction.

In a clear space the troops were at last halted. Regiments and brigades, broken and detached through their encounters with thickets, grew together again and   35
lines were faced toward the pursuing bark of the enemy's infantry.

This noise, following like the yellings of eager, metallic hounds, increased to a loud and joyous burst, and then, as the sun went serenely up the sky, throwing illuminating rays into the gloomy thickets, it broke forth into prolonged pealings. The woods began to crackle as if afire.   40

"Whoop-a-dadee," said a man, "here we are! Everybody fightin'. Blood an' destruction."

"I was willin' t' bet they'd attack as soon as th' sun got fairly up," savagely asserted the lieutenant who commanded the youth's company. He jerked without mercy at his little mustache. He strode to and fro with dark dignity in   45
the rear of his men, who were lying down behind whatever protection they had collected.

A battery had trundled into position in the rear and was thoughtfully shelling the distance. The regiment, unmolested as yet, awaited the moment when the gray shadows of the woods before them should be slashed by the lines of flame. There was much growling and swearing.

5   "Good Gawd," the youth grumbled, "we're always being chased around like rats! It makes me sick. Nobody seems to know where we go or why we go. We just get fired around from pillar to post and get licked here and get licked there, and nobody knows what it's done for. It makes a man feel like a damn' kitten in a bag. Now, I'd like to know what the eternal thunders we was
10 marched into these woods for anyhow, unless it was to give the rebs a regular pot shot at us. We came in here and got our legs all tangled up in these cussed briers, and then we begin to fight and the rebs had an easy time of it. Don't tell me it's just luck! I know better. It's this derned old—"

The friend seemed jaded, but he interrupted his comrade with a voice of
15 calm confidence. "It'll turn out all right in th' end," he said.

"Oh, the devil it will! You always talk like a dog-hanged parson. Don't tell me! I know—"

At this time there was an interposition by the savage-minded lieutenant, who was obliged to vent some of his inward dissatisfaction upon his men. "You boys
20 shut right up! There no need 'a your wastin' your breath in long-winded arguments about this an' that an' th' other. You've been jawin' like a lot 'a old hens. All you've got t' do is to fight, an' you'll get plenty 'a that t' do in about ten minutes. Less talkin' an' more fightin' is what's best for you boys. I never saw sech gabbling jackasses."

25 He paused, ready to pounce upon any man who might have the temerity to reply. No words being said, he resumed his dignified pacing.

"There's too much chin music an' too little fightin' in this war, anyhow," he said to them, turning his head for a final remark.

The day had grown more white, until the sun shed his full radiance upon
30 the thronged forest. A sort of a gust of battle came sweeping toward that part of the line where lay the youth's regiment. The front shifted a trifle to meet it squarely. There was a wait. In this part of the field there passed slowly the intense moments that precede the tempest.

A single rifle flashed in a thicket before the regiment. In an instant it was
35 joined by many others. There was a mighty song of clashes and crashes that went sweeping through the woods. The guns in the rear, aroused and enraged by shells that had been thrown burlike at them, suddenly involved themselves in a hideous altercation with another band of guns. The battle roar settled to a rolling thunder, which was a single, long explosion.

40 In the regiment there was a peculiar kind of hesitation denoted in the attitudes of the men. They were worn, exhausted, having slept but little and labored much. They rolled their eyes toward the advancing battle as they stood awaiting the shock. Some shrank and flinched. They stood as men tied to stakes.

---

37. **burlike**—so spelled in the original text.

CHAPTER XVII

This advance of the enemy had seemed to the youth like a ruthless hunting. He began to fume with rage and exasperation. He beat his foot upon the ground, and scowled with hate at the swirling smoke that was approaching like a phantom flood. There was a maddening quality in this seeming reso- 5 lution of the foe to give him no rest, to give him no time to sit down and think. Yesterday he had fought and had fled rapidly. There had been many adventures. For to-day he felt that he had earned opportunities for contemplative repose. He could have enjoyed portraying to uninitiated listeners various scenes at which he had been a witness or ably discussing the processes 10 of war with other proved men. Too it was important that he should have time for physical recuperation. He was sore and stiff from his experiences. He had received his fill of all exertions, and he wished to rest.

But those other men seemed never to grow weary; they were fighting with their old speed. He had a wild hate for the relentless foe. Yesterday, when he 15 had imagined the universe to be against him, he had hated it, little gods and big gods; to-day he hated the army of the foe with the same great hatred. He was not going to be badgered of his life, like a kitten chased by boys, he said. It was not well to drive men into final corners; at those moments they could all develop teeth and claws. 20

He leaned and spoke into his friend's ear. He menaced the woods with a gesture. "If they keep on chasing us, by Gawd, they'd better watch out. Can't stand *too* much."

The friend twisted his head and made a calm reply. "If they keep on a-chasin' us they'll drive us all inteh th' river." 25

The youth cried out savagely at this statement. He crouched behind a little tree, with his eyes burning hatefully and his teeth set in a curlike snarl. The awkward bandage was still about his head, and upon it, over his wound, there was a spot of dry blood. His hair was wondrously tousled, and some straggling, moving locks hung over the cloth of the bandage down toward his 30 forehead. His jacket and shirt were open at the throat, and exposed his young bronzed neck. There could be seen spasmodic gulpings at his throat.

His fingers twined nervously about his rifle. He wished that it was an engine of annihilating power. He felt that he and his companions were being taunted and derided from sincere convictions that they were poor and puny. 35 His knowledge of his inability to take vengeance for it made his rage into a dark and stormy specter, that possessed him and made him dream of abominable cruelties. The tormentors were flies sucking insolently at his blood, and he thought that he would have given his life for a revenge of seeing their faces in pitiful plights. 40

The winds of battle had swept all about the regiment, until the one rifle, instantly followed by others, flashed in its front. A moment later the regiment roared forth its sudden and valiant retort. A dense wall of smoke settled slowly down. It was furiously slit and slashed by the knifelike fire from the rifles. 45

To the youth the fighters resembled animals tossed for a death struggle into a dark pit. There was a sensation that he and his fellows, at bay, were pushing back, always pushing fierce onslaughts of creatures who were slippery. Their beams of crimson seemed to get no purchase upon the bodies of
5 their foes; the latter seemed to evade them with ease, and come through, between, around, and about with unopposed skill.

When, in a dream, it occurred to the youth that his rifle was an impotent stick, he lost sense of everything but his hate, his desire to smash into pulp the glittering smile of victory which he could feel upon the faces of his
10 enemies.

The blue smoke-swallowed line curled and writhed like a snake stepped upon. It swung its ends to and fro in an agony of fear and rage.

The youth was not conscious that he was erect upon his feet. He did not know the direction of the ground. Indeed, once he even lost the habit of bal-
15 ance and fell heavily. He was up again immediately. One thought went through the chaos of his brain at the time. He wondered if he had fallen because he had been shot. But the suspicion flew away at once. He did not think more of it.

He had taken up a first position behind the little tree, with a direct de-
20 termination to hold it against the world. He had not deemed it possible that his army could that day succeed, and from this he felt the ability to fight harder. But the throng had surged in all ways, until he lost directions and locations, save that he knew where lay the enemy.

The flames bit him, and the hot smoke broiled his skin. His rifle barrel
25 grew so hot that ordinarily he could not have borne it upon his palms; but he kept on stuffing cartridges into it, and pounding them with his clanking, bending ramrod. If he aimed at some changing form through the smoke, he pulled his trigger with a fierce grunt, as if he were dealing a blow of the fist with all his strength.

30 When the enemy seemed falling back before him and his fellows, he went instantly forward, like a dog who, seeing his foes lagging, turns and insists upon being pursued. And when he was compelled to retire again, he did it slowly, sullenly, taking steps of wrathful despair.

Once he, in his intent hate, was almost alone, and was firing, when all those
35 near him had ceased. He was so engrossed in his occupation that he was not aware of a lull.

He was recalled by a hoarse laugh and a sentence that came to his ears in a voice of contempt and amazement. "Yeh infernal fool, don't yeh know enough t' quit when there ain't anything t' shoot at? Good Gawd!"

40 He turned then and, pausing with his rifle thrown half into position, looked at the blue line of his comrades. During this moment of leisure they seemed all to be engaged in staring with astonishment at him. They had become spectators. Turning to the front again he saw, under the lifted smoke, a deserted ground.

45 He looked bewildered for a moment. Then there appeared upon the glazed vacancy of his eyes a diamond point of intelligence. "Oh," he said, comprehending.

He returned to his comrades and threw himself upon the ground. He sprawled like a man who had been thrashed. His flesh seemed strangely on fire, and the sounds of the battle continued in his ears. He groped blindly for his canteen.

The lieutenant was crowing. He seemed drunk with fighting. He called out 5 to the youth: "By heavens, if I had ten thousand wild cats like you I could tear th' stomach outa this war in less'n a week!" He puffed out his chest with large dignity as he said it.

Some of the men muttered and looked at the youth in awe-struck ways. It was plain that as he had gone on loading and firing and cursing without 10 the proper intermission, they had found time to regard him. And they now looked upon him as a war devil.

The friend came staggering to him. There was some fright and dismay in his voice. "Are yeh all right, Fleming? Do yeh feel all right? There ain't nothin' th' matter with yeh, Henry, is there?" 15

"No," said the youth with difficulty. His throat seemed full of knobs and burs.

These incidents made the youth ponder. It was revealed to him that he had been a barbarian, a beast. He had fought like a pagan who defends his religion. Regarding it, he saw that it was fine, wild, and, in some ways, easy. 20 He had been a tremendous figure, no doubt. By this struggle he had overcome obstacles which he had admitted to be mountains. They had fallen like paper peaks, and he was now what he called a hero. And he had not been aware of the process. He had slept and, awakening, found himself a knight.

He lay and basked in the occasional stares of his comrades. Their faces 25 were varied in degrees of blackness from the burned powder. Some were utterly smudged. They were reeking with perspiration, and their breaths came hard and wheezing. And from these soiled expanses they peered at him.

"Hot work! Hot work!" cried the lieutenant deliriously. He walked up and down, restless and eager. Sometimes his voice could be heard in a wild, in- 30 comprehensible laugh.

When he had a particularly profound thought upon the science of war he always unconsciously addressed himself to the youth.

There was some grim rejoicing by the men. "By thunder, I bet this army'll never see another new reg'ment like us!" 35

"You bet!

> "A dog, a woman, an' a walnut tree,
> Th' more yeh beat 'em, th' better they be!"

That's like us."

"Lost a piler men, they did. If an' ol' woman swep' up th' woods she'd 40 git a dustpanful."

"Yes, an' if she'll come around ag'in in 'bout an' hour she'll git a pile more."

The forest still bore its burden of clamor. From off under the trees came the rolling clatter of the musketry. Each distant thicket seemed a strange porcupine with quills of flame. A cloud of dark smoke, as from smoldering 45 ruins, went up toward the sun now bright and gay in the blue, enameled sky.

CHAPTER XVIII

The ragged line had respite for some minutes, but during its pause the struggle in the forest became magnified until the trees seemed to quiver from the firing and the ground to shake from the rushing of the men. The voices
5 of the cannon were mingled in a long and interminable row. It seemed difficult to live in such an atmosphere. The chests of the men strained for a bit of freshness, and their throats craved water.

There was one shot through the body, who raised a cry of bitter lamentation when came this lull. Perhaps he had been calling out during the fight-
10 ing also, but at that time no one had heard him. But now the men turned at the woeful complaints of him upon the ground.

"Who is it? Who is it?"

"It's Jimmie Rogers. Jimmie Rogers."

When their eyes first encountered him there was a sudden halt, as if they
15 feared to go near. He was thrashing about in the grass, twisting his shuddering body into many strange postures. He was screaming loudly. This instant's hesitation seemed to fill him with a tremendous, fantastic contempt, and he damned them in shrieked sentences.

The youth's friend had a geographical illusion concerning a stream, and he
20 obtained permission to go for some water. Immediately canteens were showered upon him. "Fill mine, will yeh?" "Bring me some, too." "And me, too." He departed, laden. The youth went with his friend, feeling a desire to throw his heated body onto the stream and, soaking there, drink quarts.

They made a hurried search for the supposed stream, but did not find it.
25 "No water here," said the youth. They turned without delay and began to retrace their steps.

From their position as they again faced toward the place of the fighting, they could of course comprehend a greater amount of the battle than when their visions had been blurred by the hurling smoke of the line. They could
30 see dark stretches winding along the land, and on one cleared space there was a row of guns making gray clouds, which were filled with large flashes of orange-colored flame. Over some foliage they could see the roof of a house. One window, glowing a deep murder red, shone squarely through the leaves. From the edifice a tall leaning tower of smoke went far into the sky.

35 Looking over their own troops, they saw mixed masses slowly getting into regular form. The sunlight made twinkling points of the bright steel. To the rear there was a glimpse of a distant roadway as it curved over a slope. It was crowded with retreating infantry. From all the interwoven forest arose the smoke and bluster of the battle. The air was always occupied by a blaring.

40 Near where they stood shells were flip-flapping and hooting. Occasional bullets buzzed in the air and spanged into tree trunks. Wounded men and other stragglers were slinking through the woods.

Looking down an aisle of the grove, the youth and his companion saw a jangling general and his staff almost ride upon a wounded man, who was
45 crawling on his hands and knees. The general reined strongly at his charger's

opened and foamy mouth and guided it with dexterous horsemanship past the man. The latter scrambled in wild and torturing haste. His strength evidently failed him as he reached a place of safety. One of his arms suddenly weakened, and he fell, sliding over upon his back. He lay stretched out, breathing gently.

A moment later the small, creaking cavalcade was directly in front of the two soldiers. Another officer, riding with the skillful abandon of a cowboy, galloped his horse to a position directly before the general. The two unnoticed foot soldiers made a little show of going on, but they lingered near in the desire to overhear the conversation. Perhaps, they thought, some great inner historical things would be said.

The general, whom the boys knew as the commander of their division, looked at the other officer and spoke coolly, as if he were criticising his clothes. "Th' enemy's formin' over there for another charge," he said. "It'll be directed against Whiterside, an' I fear they'll break through there unless we work like thunder t' stop them."

The other swore at his restive horse, and then cleared his throat. He made a gesture toward his cap. "It'll be hell t' pay stoppin' them," he said shortly.

"I presume so," remarked the general. Then he began to talk rapidly and in a lower tone. He frequently illustrated his words with a pointing finger. The two infantrymen could hear nothing until finally he asked: "What troops can you spare?"

The officer who rode like a cowboy reflected for an instant. "Well," he said, "I had to order in th' 12th to help th' 76th, an' I haven't really got any. But there's th' 304th. They fight like a lot 'a mule drivers. I can spare them best of any."

The youth and his friend exchanged glances of astonishment.

The general spoke sharply. "Get 'em ready, then. I'll watch developments from here, an' send you word when t' start them. It'll happen in five minutes."

As the other officer tossed his fingers toward his cap and wheeling his horse, started away, the general called out to him in a sober voice: "I don't believe many of your mule drivers will get back."

The other shouted something in reply. He smiled.

With scared faces, the youth and his companion hurried back to the line. These happenings had occupied an incredibly short time, yet the youth felt that in them he had been made aged. New eyes were given to him. And the most startling thing was to learn suddenly that he was very insignificant. The officer spoke of the regiment as if he referred to a broom. Some part of the woods needed sweeping, perhaps, and he merely indicated a broom in a tone properly indifferent to its fate. It was war, no doubt, but it appeared strange.

As the two boys approached the line, the lieutenant perceived them and swelled with wrath. "Fleming—Wilson—how long does it take yeh to git water, anyhow—where yeh been to."

But his oration ceased as he saw their eyes, which were large with great tales. "We're goin' t' charge—we're goin' t' charge!" cried the youth's friend, hastening with his news.

"Charge?" said the lieutenant. "Charge? Well, b'Gawd! Now; this is real fightin'." Over his soiled countenance there went a boastful smile. "Charge? Well, b'Gawd!"

A little group of soldiers surrounded the two youths. "Are we, sure 'nough? Well, I'll be derned! Charge? What fer? What at? Wilson, you're lyin'."

5 "I hope to die," said the youth, pitching his tones to the key of angry remonstrance. "Sure as shooting, I tell you."

And his friend spoke in re-enforcement. "Not by a blame sight, he ain't lyin'. We heard 'em talkin'."

They caught sight of two mounted figures a short distance from them. 10 One was the colonel of the regiment and the other was the officer who had received orders from the commander of the division. They were gesticulating at each other. The soldier, pointing at them, interpreted the scene.

One man had a final objection: "How could yeh hear 'em talkin'?" But the men, for a large part, nodded, admitting that previously the two friends 15 had spoken truth.

They settled back into reposeful attitudes with airs of having accepted the matter. And they mused upon it, with a hundred varieties of expression. It was an engrossing thing to think about. Many tightened their belts carefully and hitched at their trousers.

20 A moment later the officers began to bustle among the men, pushing them into a more compact mass and into a better alignment. They chased those that straggled and fumed at a few men who seemed to show by their attitudes that they had decided to remain at that spot. They were like critical shepherds struggling with sheep.

25 Presently, the regiment seemed to draw itself up and heave a deep breath. None of the men's faces were mirrors of large thoughts. The soldiers were bended and stooped like sprinters before a signal. Many pairs of glinting eyes peered from the grimy faces toward the curtains of the deeper woods. They seemed to be engaged in deep calculations of time and distance.

30 They were surrounded by the noises of the monstrous altercation between the two armies. The world was fully interested in other matters. Apparently, the regiment had its small affair to itself.

The youth, turning, shot a quick, inquiring glance at his friend. The latter returned to him the same manner of look. They were the only ones who 35 possessed an inner knowledge. "Mule drivers—hell t' pay—don't believe many will get back." It was an ironical secret. Still, they saw no hesitation in each other's faces, and they nodded a mute and unprotesting assent when a shaggy man near them said in a meek voice: "We'll git swallowed."

CHAPTER XIX

40 The youth stared at the land in front of him. Its foliages now seemed to veil powers and horrors. He was unaware of the machinery of orders that started the charge, although from the corners of his eyes he saw an officer, who looked like a boy a-horseback, come galloping, waving his hat. Suddenly he felt a straining and heaving among the men. The line fell slowly 45 forward like a toppling wall, and, with a convulsive gasp that was intended

for a cheer, the regiment began its journey. The youth was pushed and jostled for a moment before he understood the movement at all, but directly he lunged ahead and began to run.

He fixed his eye upon a distant and prominent clump of trees where he had concluded the enemy were to be met, and he ran toward it as toward 5 a goal. He had believed throughout that it was a mere question of getting over an unpleasant matter as quickly as possible, and he ran desperately, as if pursued for a murder. His face was drawn hard and tight with the stress of his endeavor. His eyes were fixed in a lurid glare. And with his soiled and disordered dress, his red and inflamed features surmounted by the dingy rag 10 with its spot of blood, his wildly swinging rifle and banging accouterments, he looked to be an insane soldier.

As the regiment swung from its position out into a cleared space the woods and thickets before it awakened. Yellow flames leaped toward it from many directions. The forest made a tremendous objection. 15

The line lurched straight for a moment. Then the right wing sprung forward; it in turn was surpassed by the left. Afterward the center careered to the front until the regiment was a wedge-shaped mass, but an instant later the opposition of the bushes, trees, and uneven places on the ground split the command and scattered it into detached clusters. 20

The youth, light-footed, was unconsciously in advance. His eyes still kept note of the clump of trees. From all places near it the clannish yell of the enemy could be heard. The little flames of rifles leaped from it. The song of the bullets was in the air and shells snarled among the tree-tops. One tumbled directly into the middle of a hurrying group and exploded in crimson fury. 25 There was an instant's spectacle of a man, almost over it, throwing up his hands to shield his eyes.

Other men, punched by bullets, fell in grotesque agonies. The regiment left a coherent trail of bodies.

They had passed into a clearer atmosphere. There was an effect like a 30 revelation in the new appearance of the landscape. Some men working madly at a battery were plain to them, and the opposing infantry's lines were defined by the gray walls and fringes of smoke.

It seemed to the youth that he saw everything. Each blade of the green grass was bold and clear. He thought that he was aware of every change in 35 the thin, transparent vapor that floated idly in sheets. The brown or gray trunks of the trees showed each roughness of their surfaces. And the men of the regiment, with their starting eyes and sweating faces, running madly, or falling, as if thrown headlong, [in]to queer, heaped-up corpses—all were comprehended. His mind took a mechanical but firm impression, so that after- 40 ward everything was pictured and explained to him, save why he himself was there.

But there was a frenzy made from this furious rush. The men, pitching forward insanely, had burst into cheerings, moblike and barbaric, but tuned in strange keys that can arouse the dullard and the stoic. It made a mad enthu- 45 siasm that, it seemed, would be incapable of checking itself before granite

11. **accouterments**—so spelled in the original text.

and brass. There was the delirium that encounters despair and death, and is heedless and blind to the odds. It is a temporary but sublime absence of self-ishness. And because it was of this order was the reason, perhaps, why the youth wondered, afterward, what reasons he could have had for being there.

5   Presently the straining pace ate up the energies of the men. As if by agreement, the leaders began to slacken their speed. The volleys directed against them had had a seeming windlike effect. The regiment snorted and blew. Among some stolid trees it began to falter and hesitate. The men, staring intently, began to wait for some of the distant walls of smoke to move and
10 disclose to them the scene. Since much of their strength and their breath had vanished, they returned to caution. They were become men again.

The youth had a vague belief that he had run miles, and he thought, in a way, that he was now in some new and unknown land.

The moment the regiment ceased its advance the protesting splutter of
15 musketry became a steadied roar. Long and accurate fringes of smoke spread out. From the top of a small hill came level belchings of yellow flame that caused an inhuman whistling in the air.

The men, halted, had opportunity to see some of their comrades dropping with moans and shrieks. A few lay under foot, still or wailing. And now for
20 an instant the men stood, their rifles slack in their hands, and watched the regiment dwindle. They appeared dazed and stupid. This spectacle seemed to paralyze them, overcome them with a fatal fascination. They stared woodenly at the sights, and, lowering their eyes, looked from face to face. It was a strange pause, and a strange silence.

25   Then, above the sounds of the outside commotion, arose the roar of the lieutenant. He strode suddenly forth, his infantile features black with rage.

"Come on, yeh fools!" he bellowed. "Come on! Yeh can't stay here. Yeh must come on." He said more, but much of it could not be understood.

He started rapidly forward, with his head turned toward the men. "Come
30 on," he was shouting. The men stared with blank and yokel-like eyes at him. He was obliged to halt and retrace his steps. He stood then with his back to the enemy and delivered gigantic curses into the faces of the men. His body vibrated from the weight and force of his imprecations. And he could string oaths with the facility of a maiden who strings beads.

35   The friend of the youth aroused. Lurching suddenly forward and dropping to his knees, he fired an angry shot at the persistent woods. This action awakened the men. They huddled no more like sheep. They seemed suddenly to bethink them of their weapons, and at once commenced firing. Belabored by their officers, they began to move forward. The regiment, involved like a cart
40 involved in mud and muddle, started unevenly with many jolts and jerks. The men stopped now every few paces to fire and load, and in this manner moved slowly on from trees to trees.

The flaming opposition in their front grew with their advance until it seemed that all forward ways were barred by the thin leaping tongues, and off
45 to the right an ominous demonstration could sometimes be dimly discerned. The smoke lately generated was in confusing clouds that made it difficult for the regiment to proceed with intelligence. As he passed through each curling mass the youth wondered what would confront him on the farther side.

The command went painfully forward until an open space interposed between them and the lurid lines. Here, crouching and cowering behind some trees, the men clung with desperation, as if threatened by a wave. They looked wild-eyed, and as if amazed at this furious disturbance they had stirred. In the storm there was an ironical expression of their importance. The faces of the men, too, showed a lack of a certain feeling of responsibility for being there. It was as if they had been driven. It was the dominant animal failing to remember in the supreme moments the forceful causes of various superficial qualities. The whole affair seemed incomprehensible to many of them.

As they halted thus the lieutenant again began to bellow profanely. Regardless of the vindictive threats of the bullets, he went about coaxing, berating, and bedamning. His lips, that were habitually in a soft and childlike curve, were now writhed into unholy contortions. He swore by all possible deities.

Once he grabbed the youth by the arm. "Come on, yeh lunkhead!" he roared. "Come on! We'll all git killed if we stay here. We've on'y got t' go across that lot. An' then"—the remainder of his idea disappeared in a blue haze of curses.

The youth stretched forth his arm. "Cross there?" His mouth was puckered in doubt and awe.

"Certainly. Jest 'cross th' lot! We can't stay here," screamed the lieutenant. He poked his face close to the youth and waved his bandaged hand. "Come on!" Presently he grappled with him as if for a wrestling bout. It was as if he planned to drag the youth by the ear on to the assault.

The private felt a sudden unspeakable indignation against his officer. He wrenched fiercely and shook him off.

"Come on yerself, then," he yelled. There was a bitter challenge in his voice.

They galloped together down the regimental front. The friend scrambled after them. In front of the colors the three men began to bawl: "Come on! come on!" They danced and gyrated like tortured savages.

The flag, obedient to these appeals, bended its glittering form and swept toward them. The men wavered in indecision for a moment, and then with a long, wailful cry the dilapidated regiment surged forward and began its new journey.

Over the field went the scurrying mass. It was a handful of men splattered into the faces of the enemy. Toward it instantly sprang the yellow tongues. A vast quantity of blue smoke hung before them. A mighty banging made ears valueless.

The youth ran like a madman to reach the woods before a bullet could discover him. He ducked his head low, like a football player. In his haste his eyes almost closed, and the scene was a wild blur. Pulsating saliva stood at the corners of his mouth.

Within him, as he hurled himself forward, was born a love, a despairing fondness for this flag which was near him. It was a creation of beauty and invulnerability. It was a goddess, radiant, that bended its form with an imperious gesture to him. It was a woman, red and white, hating and loving, that called him with the voice of his hopes. Because no harm could come to it he endowed it with power. He kept near, as if it could be a saver of lives, and an imploring cry went from his mind.

In the mad scramble he was aware that the color sergeant flinched suddenly, as if struck by a bludgeon. He faltered, and then became motionless, save for his quivering knees.

He made a spring and a clutch at the pole. At the same instant his friend grabbed it from the other side. They jerked at it, stout and furious, but the
5 color sergeant was dead, and the corpse would not relinquish its trust. For a moment there was a grim encounter. The dead man, swinging with bended back, seemed to be obstinately tugging, in ludicrous and awful ways, for the possession of the flag.

It was past in an instant of time. They wrenched the flag furiously from the
10 dead man, and, as they turned again, the corpse swayed forward with bowed head. One arm swung high, and the curved hand fell with heavy protest on the friend's unheeding shoulder.

CHAPTER XX

When the two youths turned with the flag they saw that much of the regi-
15 ment had crumbled away, and the dejected remnant was coming back. The men, having hurled themselves in projectile fashion, had presently expended their forces. They slowly retreated, with their faces still toward the spluttering woods, and their hot rifles still replying to the din. Several officers were giving orders, their voices keyed to screams.
20 "Where in hell yeh goin'?" the lieutenant was asking in a sarcastic howl. And a red-bearded officer, whose voice of triple brass could plainly be heard, was commanding: "Shoot into 'em! Shoot into 'em, Gawd damn their souls!" There was a *melée* of screeches, in which the men were ordered to do conflicting and impossible things.
25 The youth and his friend had a small scuffle over the flag. "Give it t' me!" "No, let me keep it!" Each felt satisfied with the other's possession of it, but each felt bound to declare, by an offer to carry the emblem, his willingness to further risk himself. The youth roughly pushed his friend away.

The regiment fell back to the stolid trees. There it halted for a moment to
30 blaze at some dark forms that had begun to steal upon its track. Presently it resumed its march again, curving among the tree trunks. By the time the depleted regiment had again reached the first open space they were receiving a fast and merciless fire. There seemed to be mobs all about them.

The greater part of the men, discouraged, their spirits worn by the turmoil,
35 acted as if stunned. They accepted the pelting of the bullets with bowed and weary heads. It was of no purpose to strive against walls. It was of no use to batter themselves against granite. And from this consciousness that they had attempted to conquer an unconquerable thing there seemed to arise a feeling that they had been betrayed. They glowered with bent brows, but dangerously,
40 upon some of the officers, more particularly upon the red-bearded one with the voice of triple brass.

However, the rear of the regiment was fringed with men, who continued to shoot irritably at the advancing foes. They seemed resolved to make every trouble. The youthful lieutenant was perhaps the last man in the disordered
45 mass. His forgotten back was toward the enemy. He had been shot in the arm. It hung straight and rigid. Occasionally he would cease to remember

it, and be about to emphasize an oath with a sweeping gesture. The multiplied pain caused him to swear with incredible power.

The youth went along with slipping, uncertain feet. He kept watchful eyes rearward. A scowl of mortification and rage was upon his face. He had thought of a fine revenge upon the officer who had referred to him and his fellows as mule drivers. But he saw that it could not come to pass. His dreams had collapsed when the mule drivers, dwindling rapidly, had wavered and hesitated on the little clearing, and then had recoiled. And now the retreat of the mule drivers was a march of shame to him.

A dagger-pointed gaze from without his blackened face was held toward the enemy, but his greater hatred was riveted upon the man, who, not knowing him, had called him a mule driver.

When he knew that he and his comrades had failed to do anything in successful ways that might bring the little pangs of a kind of remorse upon the officer, the youth allowed the rage of the baffled to possess him. This cold officer upon a monument, who dropped epithets unconcernedly down, would be finer as a dead man, he thought. So grievous did he think it that he could never possess the secret right to taunt truly in answer.

He had pictured red letters of curious revenge. "We *are* mule drivers, are we?" And now he was compelled to throw them away.

He presently wrapped his heart in the cloak of his pride and kept the flag erect. He harangued his fellows, pushing against their chests with his free hand. To those he knew well he made frantic appeals, beseeching them by name. Between him and the lieutenant, scolding and near to losing his mind with rage, there was felt a subtle fellowship and equality. They supported each other in all manner of hoarse, howling protests.

But the regiment was a machine run down. The two men babbled at a forceless thing. The soldiers who had heart to go slowly were continually shaken in their resolves by a knowledge that comrades were slipping with speed back to the lines. It was difficult to think of reputation when others were thinking of skins. Wounded men were left crying on this black journey.

The smoke fringes and flames blustered always. The youth, peering once through a sudden rift in a cloud, saw a brown mass of troops, interwoven and magnified until they appeared to be thousands. A fierce-hued flag flashed before his vision.

Immediately, as if the uplifting of the smoke had been prearranged, the discovered troops burst into a rasping yell, and a hundred flames jetted toward the retreating band. A rolling gray cloud again interposed as the regiment doggedly replied. The youth had to depend again upon his misused ears, which were trembling and buzzing from the *melée* of musketry and yells.

The way seemed eternal. In the clouded haze men became panicstricken with the thought that the regiment had lost its path, and was proceeding in a perilous direction. Once the men who headed the wild procession turned and came pushing back against their comrades, screaming that they were being fired upon from points which they had considered to be toward their own lines. At this cry a hysterical fear and dismay beset the troops. A soldier, who heretofore had been ambitious to make the regiment into a wise little band

that would proceed calmly amid the huge-appearing difficulties, suddenly sank down and buried his face in his arms with an air of bowing to a doom. From another a shrill lamentation rang out filled with profane illusions to a general. Men ran hither and thither, seeking with their eyes roads of es-
5 cape. With serene regularity, as if controlled by a schedule, bullets buffed into [the] men.

The youth walked stolidly into the midst of the mob, and with his flag in his hands took a stand as if he expected an attempt to push him to the ground. He unconsciously assumed the attitude of the color bearer in the fight of the
10 preceding day. He passed over his brow a hand that trembled. His breath did not come freely. He was choking during this small wait for the crisis.

His friend came to him. "Well, Henry, I guess this is good-by—John."

"Oh, shut up, you damned fool!" replied the youth, and he would not look at the other.
15 The officers labored like politicians to beat the mass into a proper circle to face the menaces. The ground was uneven and torn. The men curled into depressions and fitted themselves snugly behind whatever would frustrate a bullet.

The youth noted with vague surprise that the lieutenant was standing
20 mutely with his legs far apart and his sword held in the manner of a cane. The youth wondered what had happened to his vocal organs that he no more cursed.

There was something curious in this little intent pause of the lieutenant. He was like a babe which, having wept its fill, raises its eyes and fixes upon
25 a distant toy. He was engrossed in this contemplation, and the soft under lip quivered from self-whispered words.

Some lazy and ignorant smoke curled slowly. The men, hiding from the bullets, waited anxiously for it to lift and disclose the plight of the regiment.

The silent ranks were suddenly thrilled by the eager voice of the youthful
30 lieutenant bawling out: "Here they come! Right on to us, b'Gawd!" His further words were lost in a roar of wicked thunder from the men's rifles.

The youth's eyes had instantly turned in the direction indicated by the awakened and agitated lieutenant, and he had seen the haze of treachery disclosing a body of soldiers of the enemy. They were so near that he could see
35 their features. There was a recognition as he looked at the types of faces. Also he perceived with dim amazement that their uniforms were rather gay in effect, being light gray, accented with a brilliant-hued facing. Too, the clothes seemed new.

These troops had apparently been going forward with caution, their rifles
40 held in readiness, when the youthful lieutenant had discovered them and their movement had been interrupted by the volley from the blue regiment. From the moment's glimpse, it was derived that they had been unaware of the proximity of their dark-suited foes or had mistaken the direction. Almost instantly they were shut utterly from the youth's sight by the smoke from the
45 energetic rifles of his companions. He strained his vision to learn the accomplishment of the volley, but the smoke hung before him.

The two bodies of troops exchanged blows in the manner of a pair of

3. illusions—as printed in the original text. The author apparently meant *allusions.*

boxers. The fast angry firings went back and forth. The men in blue were intent with the despair of their circumstances and they seized upon the revenge to be had at close range. Their thunder swelled loud and valiant. Their curving front bristled with flashes and the place resounded with the clangor of their ramrods. The youth ducked and dodged for a time and achieved a few 5 unsatisfactory views of the enemy. There appeared to be many of them and they were replying swiftly. They seemed moving toward the blue regiment, step by step. He seated himself gloomily on the ground with his flag between his knees.

As he noted the vicious, wolflike temper of his comrades he had a sweet 10 thought that if the enemy was about to swallow the regimental broom as a large prisoner, it could at least have the consolation of going down with bristles forward.

But the blows of the antagonist began to grow more weak. Fewer bullets ripped the air, and finally, when the men slackened to learn of the fight, they 15 could see only dark, floating smoke. The regiment lay still and gazed. Presently some chance whim came to the pestering blur, and it began to coil heavily away. The men saw a ground vacant of fighters. It would have been an empty stage if it were not for a few corpses that lay thrown and twisted into fantastic shapes upon the sward. 20

At sight of this tableau, many of the men in blue sprang from behind their covers and made an ungainly dance of joy. Their eyes burned and a hoarse cheer of elation broke from their dry lips.

It had begun to seem to them that events were trying to prove that they were impotent. These little battles had evidently endeavored to demonstrate 25 that the men could not fight well. When on the verge of submission to these opinions, the small duel had showed them that the proportions were not impossible, and by it they had revenged themselves upon their misgivings and upon the foe.

The impetus of enthusiasm was theirs again. They gazed about them with 30 looks of uplifted pride, feeling new trust in the grim, always confident weapons in their hands. And they were men.

CHAPTER XXI

Presently they knew that no fighting threatened them. All ways seemed once more opened to them. The dusty blue lines of their friends were dis- 35 closed a short distance away. In the distance there were many colossal noises, but in all this part of the field there was a sudden stillness.

They perceived that they were free. The depleted band drew a long breath of relief and gathered itself into a bunch to complete its trip.

In this last length of journey the men began to show strange emotions. 40 They hurried with nervous fear. Some who had been dark and unfaltering in the grimmest moments now could not conceal an anxiety that made them frantic. It was perhaps that they dreaded to be killed in insignificant ways after the times for proper military deaths had passed. Or, perhaps, they thought it would be too ironical to get killed at the portals of safety. With backward 45 looks of perturbation, they hastened.

As they approached their own lines there was some sarcasm exhibited on the part of a gaunt and bronzed regiment that lay resting in the shade of trees. Questions were wafted to them.

"Where th' hell yeh been?"

5 "What yeh comin' back fer?"

"Why didn't yeh stay there?"

"Was it warm out there, sonny?"

"Goin' home now, boys?"

One shouted in taunting mimicry: "Oh, mother, come quick an' look at th'
10 sojers!"

There was no reply from the bruised and battered regiment, save that one man made broadcast challenges to fist fights and the red-bearded officer walked rather near and glared in great swashbuckler style at a tall captain in the other regiment. But the lieutenant suppressed the man who wished to fist
15 fight, and the tall captain, flushing at the little fanfare of the red-bearded one, was obliged to look intently at some trees.

The youth's tender flesh was deeply stung by these remarks. From under his creased brows he glowered with hate at the mockers. He meditated upon a few revenges. Still, many in the regiment hung their heads in criminal fash-
20 ion, so that it came to pass that the men trudged with sudden heaviness, as if they bore upon their bended shoulders the coffin of their honor. And the youthful lieutenant, recollecting himself, began to mutter softly in black curses.

They turned when they arrived at their old position to regard the ground over which they had charged.

25 The youth in this contemplation was smitten with a large astonishment. He discovered that the distances, as compared with the brilliant measurings of his mind, were trivial and ridiculous. The stolid trees, where much had taken place, seemed incredibly near. The time, too, now that he reflected, he saw to have been short. He wondered at the number of emotions and events
30 that had been crowded into such little spaces. Elfin thoughts must have ex- aggerated and enlarged everything, he said.

It seemed, then, that there was bitter justice in the speeches of the gaunt and bronzed veterans. He veiled a glance of disdain at his fellows who strewed the ground, choking with dust, red from perspiration, misty-eyed, disheveled.
35 They were gulping at their canteens, fierce to wring every mite of water from them, and they polished at their swollen and watery features with coat sleeves and bunches of grass.

However, to the youth there was a considerable joy in musing upon his performances during the charge. He had had very little time previously in
40 which to appreciate himself, so that there was now much satisfaction in quietly thinking of his actions. He recalled bits of color that in the flurry had stamped themselves unawares upon his engaged senses.

As the regiment lay heaving from its hot exertions the officer who had named them as mule drivers came galloping along the line. He had lost his
45 cap. His tousled hair streamed wildly, and his face was dark with vexation and wrath. His temper was displayed with more clearness by the way in which he managed his horse. He jerked and wrenched savagely at his bridle, stop- ping the hard-breathing animal with a furious pull near the colonel of the

regiment. He immediately exploded in reproaches which came unbidden to the ears of the men. They were suddenly alert, being always curious about black words between officers.

"Oh, thunder, MacChesnay, what an awful bull you made of this thing!" began the officer. He attempted low tones, but his indignation caused certain 5 of the men to learn the sense of his words. "What an awful mess you made! Good Lord, man, you stopped about a hundred feet this side of a very pretty success! If your men had gone a hundred feet farther you would have made a great charge, but as it is—what a lot of mud diggers you've got any- way!" 10

The men, listening with bated breath, now turned their curious eyes upon the colonel. They had a ragamuffin interest in this affair.

The colonel was seen to straighten his form and put one hand forth in oratorical fashion. He wore an injured air; it was as if a deacon had been ac- cused of stealing. The men were wiggling in an ecstasy of excitement. 15

But of a sudden the colonel's manner changed from that of a deacon to that of a Frenchman. He shrugged his shoulders. "Oh, well, general, we went as far as we could," he said calmly.

"As far as you could? Did you, b'Gawd?" snorted the other. "Well, that wasn't very far, was it?" he added, with a glance of cold contempt into the 20 other's eyes. "Not very far, I think. You were intended to make a diversion in favor of Whiterside. How well you succeeded your own ears can now tell you." He wheeled his horse and rode stiffly away.

The colonel, bidden to hear the jarring noises of an engagement in the woods to the left, broke out in vague damnations. 25

The lieutenant, who had listened with an air of impotent rage to the inter- view, spoke suddenly in firm and undaunted tones. "I don't care what a man is—whether he is a general or what—if he says th' boys didn't put up a good fight out there he's a damned fool."

"Lieutenant," began the colonel, severely, "this is my own affair, and I'll 30 trouble you—"

The lieutenant made an obedient gesture. "All right, colonel, all right," he said. He sat down with an air of being content with himself.

The news that the regiment had been reproached went along the line. For a time the men were bewildered by it. "Good thunder!" they ejaculated, star- 35 ing at the vanishing form of the general. They conceived it to be a huge mistake.

Presently, however, they began to believe that in truth their efforts had been called light. The youth could see this conviction weigh upon the entire regiment until the men were like cuffed and cursed animals, but withal re- 40 bellious.

The friend, with a grievance in his eye, went to the youth. "I wonder what he does want," he said. "He must think we went out there an' played marbles! I never see sech a man!"

The youth developed a tranquil philosophy for these moments of irritation. 45 "Oh, well," he rejoined, "he probably didn't see nothing of it at all and got mad as blazes, and concluded we were a lot of sheep, just because we didn't do what he wanted done. It's a pity old Grandpa Henderson got killed yestirday—he'd have known that we did our best and fought good. It's just our awful luck, that's what."

"I should say so," replied the friend. He seemed to be deeply wounded at an injustice. "I should say we did have awful luck! There's no fun in fightin'
5 fer people when everything yeh do—no matter what—ain't done right. I have a notion t' stay behind next time an' let 'em take their ol' charge an' go t' th' devil with it."

The youth spoke soothingly to his comrade. "Well, we both did good. I'd like to see the fool what'd say we both didn't do as good as we could!"
10 "Of course we did," declared the friend stoutly. "An' I'd break th' feller's neck if he was as big as a church. But we're all right, anyhow, for I heard one feller say that we two fit th' best in th' reg'ment, an' they had a great argument 'bout it. Another feller, 'a course, he had t' up an' say it was a lie—he seen all what was goin' on an' he never seen us from th' beginnin' t' th' end. An'
15 a lot more struck in an' ses it wasn't a lie—we did fight like thunder, an' they give us quite a send-off. But this is what I can't stand—these everlastin' ol' soldiers, titterin' an' laughin', an' then that general, he's crazy."

The youth exclaimed with sudden exasperation: "He's a lunkhead! He makes me mad. I wish he'd come along next time. We'd show 'im
20 what—"

He ceased because several men had come hurrying up. Their faces expressed a bringing of great news.

"O Flem, yeh jest oughta heard!" cried one, eagerly.

"Heard what?" said the youth.
25 "Yeh jest oughta heard!" repeated the other, and he arranged himself to tell his tidings. The others made an excited circle. "Well, sir, th' colonel met your lieutenant right by us—it was damnedest thing I ever heard—an' he ses: 'Ahem! ahem!' he ses. 'Mr. Hasbrouck!' he ses, 'by th' way, who was that lad what carried th' flag?' he ses. There, Flemin', what d' yeh think 'a that?
30 'Who was th' lad what carried th' flag?' he ses, an' th' lieutenant, he speaks up right away: 'That's Flemin', an' he's a jimhickey,' he ses, right away. What? I say he did. 'A jimhickey,' he ses—those 'r his words. He did, too. I say he did. If you kin tell this story better than I kin, go ahead an' tell it. Well, then, keep yer mouth shet. Th' lieutenant, he ses: 'He's a jimhickey,' an' th'
35 colonel, he ses: 'Ahem! ahem! he is, indeed, a very good man t' have, ahem! He kep' th' flag 'way t' th' front. I saw 'im. He's a good un,' ses th' colonel. 'You bet,' ses th' lieutenant, 'he an' a feller named Wilson was at th' head 'a th' charge, an' howlin' like Indians all th' time,' he ses. 'Head a' th' charge all th' time,' he ses. 'A feller named Wilson,' he ses. There, Wilson, m'boy,
40 put that in a letter an' send it hum t' yer mother, hay? 'A feller named Wilson,' he ses. An' th' colonel, he ses: 'Were they, indeed? Ahem! ahem! My sakes!' he ses. 'At th' head a' th' reg'ment?' he ses. 'They were,' ses th' lieutenant. 'My sakes!' ses th' colonel. He ses: 'Well, well, well,' he ses, 'those two babies?' 'They were,' ses th' lieutenant. 'Well, well,' ses th' colonel, 'they de-
45 serve t' be major-generals,' he ses. 'They deserve t' be major-generals.'"

The youth and his friend had said: "Huh!" "Yer lyin', Thompson." "Oh, go t' blazes!" "He never sed it." "Oh, what a lie!" "Huh!" But despite these youthful scoffings and embarrassments, they knew that their faces were deeply flushing from thrills of pleasure. They exchanged a secret glance of joy and congratulation.

They speedily forgot many things. The past held no pictures of error and disappointment. They were very happy, and their hearts swelled with grateful affection for the colonel and the youthful lieutenant.   5

CHAPTER XXII

When the woods again began to pour forth the dark-hued masses of the enemy the youth felt serene self-confidence. He smiled briefly when he saw men dodge and duck at the long screechings of shells that were thrown in giant handfuls over them. He stood, erect and tranquil, watching the attack   10
begin against a part of the line that made a blue curve along the side of an adjacent hill. His vision being unmolested by smoke from the rifles of his companions, he had opportunities to see parts of the hard fight. It was a relief to perceive at last from whence came some of these noises which had been roared into his ears.   15

Off a short way he saw two regiments fighting a little separate battle with two other regiments. It was in a cleared space, wearing a set-apart look. They were blazing as if upon a wager, giving and taking tremendous blows. The firings were incredibly fierce and rapid. These intent regiments apparently were oblivious of all larger purposes of war, and were slugging each other   20
as if at a matched game.

In another direction he saw a magnificent brigade going with the evident intention of driving the enemy from a wood. They passed in out of sight and presently there was a most awe-inspiring racket in the wood. The noise was unspeakable. Having stirred this prodigious uproar, and, apparently, finding   25
it too prodigious, the brigade, after a little time, came marching airily out again with its fine formation in nowise disturbed. There were no traces of speed in its movements. The brigade was jaunty and seemed to point a proud thumb at the yelling wood.

On a slope to the left there was a long row of guns, gruff and maddened,   30
denouncing the enemy, who, down through the woods, were forming for another attack in the pitiless monotony of conflicts. The round red discharges from the guns made a crimson flare and a high, thick smoke. Occasional glimpses could be caught of groups of the toiling artillerymen. In the rear of this row of guns stood a house, calm and white, amid bursting shells. A con-   35
gregation of horses, tied to a long railing, were tugging frenziedly at their bridles. Men were running hither and thither.

The detached battle between the four regiments lasted for some time. There chanced to be no interference, and they settled their dispute by themselves. They struck savagely and powerfully at each other for a period of minutes,   40
and then the lighter-hued regiments faltered and drew back, leaving the dark-blue lines shouting. The youth could see the two flags shaking with laughter amid the smoke remnants.

Presently there was a stillness, pregnant with meaning. The blue lines shifted and changed a trifle and stared expectantly at the silent woods and fields be-   45
fore them. The hush was solemn and churchlike, save for a distant battery

that, evidently unable to remain quiet, sent a faint rolling thunder over the
ground. It irritated, like the noises of unimpressed boys. The men imagined
that it would prevent their perched ears from hearing the first words of the
new battle.

5   Of a sudden the guns on the slope roared out a message of warning. A
spluttering sound had begun in the woods. It swelled with amazing speed to
a profound clamor that involved the earth in noises. The splitting crashes
swept along the lines until an interminable roar was developed. To those in
the midst of it it became a din fitted to the universe. It was the whirring and
10   thumping of gigantic machinery, complications among the smaller stars. The
youth's ears were filled up. They were incapable of hearing more.

On an incline over which a road wound he saw wild and desperate rushes
of men perpetually backward and forward in riotous surges. These parts of
the opposing armies were two long waves that pitched upon each other madly
15   at dictated points. To and fro they swelled. Sometimes, one side by its yells
and cheers would proclaim decisive blows, but a moment later the other side
would be all yells and cheers. Once the youth saw a spray of light forms go
in houndlike leaps toward the waving blue lines. There was much howling,
and presently it went away with a vast mouthful of prisoners. Again, he saw
20   a blue wave dash with such thunderous force against a gray obstruction that
it seemed to clear the earth of it and leave nothing but trampled sod. And always in their swift and deadly rushes to and fro the men screamed and
yelled like maniacs.

Particular pieces of fence or secure positions behind collections of trees were
25   wrangled over, as gold thrones or pearl bedsteads. There were desperate
lunges at these chosen spots seemingly every instant, and most of them were
bandied like light toys between the contending forces. The youth could not
tell from the battle flags flying like crimson foam in many directions which
color of cloth was winning.

30   His emaciated regiment bustled forth with undiminished fierceness when
its time came. When assaulted again by bullets, the men burst out in a barbaric cry of rage and pain. They bent their heads in aims of intent hatred behind the projected hammers of their guns. Their ramrods clanged loud with
fury as their eager arms pounded the cartridges into the rifle barrels. The front
35   of the regiment was a smoke-wall penetrated by the flashing points of yellow
and red.

Wallowing in the fight, they were in an astonishingly short time resmudged.
They surpassed in stain and dirt all their previous appearances. Moving to and
fro with strained exertion, jabbering the while, they were, with their swaying
40   bodies, black faces, and glowing eyes, like strange and ugly friends jigging
heavily in the smoke.

The lieutenant, returning from a tour after a bandage, produced from a
hidden receptacle of his mind new and portentous oaths suited to the emergency. Strings of expletives he swung lashlike over the backs of his men, and
45   it was evident that his previous efforts had in nowise impaired his resources.

The youth, still the bearer of the colors, did not feel his idleness. He was
deeply absorbed as a spectator. The crash and swing of the great drama made

40. friends—so printed in the original text. The author probably meant *fiends*.

him lean forward, intent-eyed, his face working in small contortions. Sometimes he prattled, words coming unconsciously from him in grotesque exclamations. He did not know that he breathed; that the flag hung silently over him, so absorbed was he.

A formidable line of the enemy came within dangerous range. They could 5
be seen plainly—tall, gaunt men with excited faces running with long strides toward a wandering fence.

At sight of this danger the men suddenly ceased their cursing monotone. There was an instant of strained silence before they threw up their rifles and fired a plumping volley at the foes. There had been no order given; the men, 10
upon recognizing the menace, had immediately let drive their flock of bullets without waiting for word of command.

But the enemy were quick to gain the protection of the wandering line of fence. They slid down behind it with remarkable celerity, and from this position they began briskly to slice up the blue men. 15

These latter braced their energies for a great struggle. Often, white clinched teeth shone from the dusky faces. Many heads surged to and fro, floating upon a pale sea of smoke. Those behind the fence frequently shouted and yelped in taunts and gibelike cries, but the regiment maintained a stressed silence. Perhaps, at this new assault the men recalled the fact that they had been named 20
mud diggers, and it made their situation thrice bitter. They were breathlessly intent upon keeping the ground and thrusting away the rejoicing body of the enemy. They fought swiftly and with a despairing savageness denoted in their expressions.

The youth had resolved not to budge whatever should happen. Some arrows 25
of scorn that had buried themselves in his heart had generated strange and unspeakable hatred. It was clear to him that his final and absolute revenge was to be achieved by his dead body lying, torn and gluttering, upon the field. This was to be a poignant retaliation upon the officer who had said "mule drivers," and later "mud diggers," for in all the wild graspings of his 30
mind for a unit responsible for his sufferings and commotions he always seized upon the man who had dubbed him wrongly. And it was his idea, vaguely formulated, that his corpse would be for those eyes a great and salt reproach.

The regiment bled extravagantly. Grunting bundles of blue began to drop. 35
The orderly sergeant of the youth's company was shot through the cheeks. Its supports being injured, his jaw hung afar down, disclosing in the wide cavern of his mouth a pulsing mass of blood and teeth. And with all he made attempts to cry out. In his endeavor there was a dreadful earnestness, as if he conceived that one great shriek would make him well. 40

The youth saw him presently go rearward. His strength seemed in nowise impaired. He ran swiftly, casting wild glances for succor.

Others fell down about the feet of their companions. Some of the wounded crawled out and away, but many lay still, their bodies twisted into impossible shapes. 45

The youth looked once for his friend. He saw a vehement young man,

28. **gluttering**—so printed in the original text. The author probably meant *guttering* or *glittering*.

powder-smeared and frowzled, whom he knew to be him. The lieutenant, also, was unscathed in his position at the rear. He had continued to curse, but it was now with the air of a man who was using his last box of oaths.

For the fire of the regiment had begun to wane and drip. The robust voice, that had come strangely from the thin ranks, was growing rapidly weak.

CHAPTER XXIII

The colonel came running along back of the line. There were other officers following him. "We must charge'm!" they shouted. "We must charge'm!" they cried with resentful voices, as if anticipating a rebellion against this plan by the men.

The youth, upon hearing the shouts, began to study the distance between him and the enemy. He made vague calculations. He saw that to be firm soldiers they must go forward. It would be death to stay in the present place, and with all the circumstances to go backward would exalt too many others. Their hope was to push the galling foes away from the fence.

He expected that his companions, weary and stiffened, would have to be driven to this assault, but as he turned toward them he perceived with a certain surprise that they were giving quick and unqualified expressions of assent. There was an ominous, clanging overture to the charge when the shafts of the bayonets rattled upon the rifle barrels. At the yelled words of command the soldiers sprang forward in eager leaps. There was new and unexpected force in the movement of the regiment. A knowledge of its faded and jaded condition made the charge appear like a paroxysm, a display of the strength that comes before a final feebleness. The men scampered in insane fever of haste, racing as if to achieve a sudden success before an exhilarating fluid should leave them. It was a blind and despairing rush by the collection of men in dusty and tattered blue, over a green sward and under a sapphire sky, toward a fence, dimly outlined in smoke, from behind which spluttered the fierce rifles of enemies.

The youth kept the bright colors to the front. He was waving his free arm in furious circles, the while shrieking mad calls and appeals, urging on those that did not need to be urged, for it seemed that the mob of blue men hurling themselves on the dangerous group of rifles were again grown suddenly wild with an enthusiasm of unselfishness. From the many firings starting toward them, it looked as if they would merely succeed in making a great sprinkling of corpses on the grass between their former position and the fence. But they were in a state of frenzy, perhaps because of forgotten vanities, and it made an exhibition of sublime recklessness. There was no obvious questioning, nor figurings, nor diagrams. There was, apparently, no considered loopholes. It appeared that the swift wings of their desires would have shattered against the iron gates of the impossible.

He himself felt the daring spirit of a savage religion mad. He was capable of profound sacrifices, a tremendous death. He had no time for dissections,

---

1. **frowzled**—appears in the original text. 1. **him**—appears in the original text. 42. **He . . . mad**—The sentence appears here as it appears in the original text. The author probably meant "the daring spirit of a savage [who was] religion-mad."

but he knew that he thought of the bullets only as things that could prevent him from reaching the place of his endeavor. There were subtle flashings of joy within him that thus should be his mind.

He strained all his strength. His eyesight was shaken and dazzled by the tension of thought and muscle. He did not see anything excepting the mist of 5 smoke gashed by the little knives of fire, but he knew that in it lay the aged fence of a vanished farmer protecting the snuggled bodies of the gray men.

As he ran a thought of the shock of contact gleamed in his mind. He expected a great concussion when the two bodies of troops crashed together. This became a part of his wild battle madness. He could feel the onward 10 swing of the regiment about him and he conceived of a thunderous, crushing blow that would prostrate the resistance and spread consternation and amazement for miles. The flying regiment was going to have a catapultian effect. This dream made him run faster among his comrades, who were giving vent to hoarse and frantic cheers. 15

But presently he could see that many of the men in gray did not intend to abide the blow. The smoke, rolling, disclosed men who ran, their faces still turned. These grew to a crowd, who retired stubbornly. Individuals wheeled frequently to send a bullet at the blue wave.

But at one part of the line there was a grim and obdurate group that made 20 no movement. They were settled firmly down behind posts and rails. A flag, ruffled and fierce, waved over them and their rifles dinned fiercely.

The blue whirl of men got very near, until it seemed that in truth there would be a close and frightful scuffle. There was an expressed disdain in the opposition of the little group, that changed the meaning of the cheers of the 25 men in blue. They became yells of wrath, directed, personal. The cries of the two parties were now in sound an interchange of scathing insults.

They in blue showed their teeth; their eyes shone all white. They launched themselves as at the throats of those who stood resisting. The space between dwindled to an insignificant distance. 30

The youth had centered the gaze of his soul upon that other flag. Its possession would be high pride. It would express bloody minglings, near blows. He had a gigantic hatred for those who made great difficulties and complications. They caused it to be as a craved treasure of mythology, hung amid tasks and contrivances of danger. 35

He plunged like a mad horse at it. He was resolved it should not escape if wild blows and darings of blows could seize it. His own emblem, quivering and aflare, was winging toward the other. It seemed there would shortly be an encounter of strange beaks and claws, as of eagles.

The swirling body of blue men came to a sudden halt at close and disastrous 40 range and roared a swift volley. The group in gray was split and broken by this fire, but its riddled body still fought. The men in blue yelled again and rushed in upon it.

The youth, in his leapings, saw, as through a mist, a picture of four or five men stretched upon the ground or writhing upon their knees with bowed 45 heads as if they had been stricken by bolts from the sky. Tottering among

13. **catapultian**—A military machine used in particular by the Romans to hurl darts and stones against the enemy was called a catapult.

them was the rival color bearer, whom the youth saw had been bitten vitally by the bullets of the last formidable volley. He perceived this man fighting a last struggle, the struggle of one whose legs are grasped by demons. It was a ghastly battle. Over his face was the bleach of death, but set upon it was the
5   dark and hard lines of desperate purpose. With this terrible grin of resolution he hugged his precious flag to him and was stumbling and staggering in his design to go the way that led to safety for it.

But his wounds always made it seem that his feet were retarded, held, and he fought a grim fight, as with invisible ghouls fastened greedily upon his
10   limbs. Those in advance of the scampering blue men, howling cheers, leaped at the fence. The despair of the lost was in his eyes as he glanced back at them.

The youth's friend went over the obstruction in a tumbling heap and sprang at the flag as a panther at prey. He pulled at it and, wrenching it free, swung
15   up its red brilliancy with a mad cry of exultation even as the color bearer, gasping, lurched over in a final throe and, stiffening convulsively, turned his dead face to the ground. There was much blood upon the grass blades.

At the place of success there began more wild clamorings of cheers. The men gesticulated and bellowed in an ecstasy. When they spoke it was as if
20   they considered their listener to be a mile away. What hats and caps were left to them they often slung high in the air.

At one part of the line four men had been swooped upon, and they now sat as prisoners. Some blue men were about them in an eager and curious circle. The soldiers had trapped strange birds, and there was an examination.
25   A flurry of fast questions was in the air.

One of the prisoners was nursing a superficial wound in the foot. He cuddled it, baby-wise, but he looked up from it often to curse with an astonishing utter abandon straight at the noses of his captors. He consigned them to red regions; he called upon the pestilential wrath of strange gods. And with
30   it all he was singularly free from recognition of the finer points of the conduct of prisoners of war. It was as if a clumsy clod had trod upon his toe and he conceived it to be his privilege, his duty, to use deep, resentful oaths.

Another, who was a boy in years, took his plight with great calmness and apparent good nature. He conversed with the men in blue, studying their
35   faces with his bright and keen eyes. They spoke of battles and conditions. There was an acute interest in all their faces during this exchange of view points. It seemed a great satisfaction to hear voices from where all had been darkness and speculation.

The third captive sat with a morose countenance. He preserved a stoical and
40   cold attitude. To all advances he made one reply without variation, "Ah, go t' hell!"

The last of the four was always silent and, for the most part, kept his face turned in unmolested directions. From the views the youth received he seemed to be in a state of absolute dejection. Shame was upon him, and with it pro-
45   found regret that he was, perhaps, no more to be counted in the ranks of his fellows. The youth could detect no expression that would allow him to be-

---

1. **whom**—appears in the original text. 4. **was**—appears in the original text.

lieve that the other was giving a thought to his narrowed future, the pictured dungeons, perhaps, and starvations and brutalities, liable to the imagination. All to be seen was shame for captivity and regret for the right to antagonize.

After the men had celebrated sufficiently they settled down behind the old rail fence, on the opposite side to the one from which their foes had been 5 driven. A few shot perfunctorily at distant marks.

There was some long grass. The youth nestled in it and rested, making a convenient rail support the flag. His friend, jubilant and glorified, holding his treasure with vanity, came to him there. They sat side by side and congratulated each other. 10

CHAPTER XXIV

The roarings that had stretched in a long line of sound across the face of the forest began to grow intermittent and weaker. The stentorian speeches of the artillery continued in some distant encounter, but the crashes of the musketry had almost ceased. The youth and his friend of a sudden looked up, 15 feeling a deadened form of distress at the waning of these noises, which had become a part of life. They could see changes going on among the troops. There were marchings this way and that way. A battery wheeled leisurely. On the crest of a small hill was the thick gleam of many departing muskets.

The youth arose. "Well, what now, I wonder?" he said. By his tone he 20 seemed to be preparing to resent some new monstrosity in the way of dins and smashes. He shaded his eyes with his grimy hand and gazed over the field.

His friend also arose and stared. "I bet we're goin' t' git along out of this an' back over th' river," said he. 25

"Well, I swan!" said the youth.

They waited, watching. Within a little while the regiment received orders to retrace its way. The men got up grunting from the grass, regretting the soft repose. They jerked their stiffened legs, and stretched their arms over their heads. One man swore as he rubbed his eyes. They all groaned "O Lord!" 30 They had as many objections to this change as they would have had to a proposal for a new battle.

They trampled slowly back over the field across which they had run in a mad scamper.

The regiment marched until it had joined its fellows. The reformed brigade, 35 in column, aimed through a wood at the road. Directly they were in a mass of dust-covered troops, and were trudging along in a way parallel to the enemy's lines as these had been defined by the previous turmoil.

They passed within view of a stolid white house, and saw in front of it groups of their comrades lying in wait behind a neat breastwork. A row of 40 guns were booming at a distant enemy. Shells thrown in reply were raising clouds of dust and splinters. Horsemen dashed along the line of intrenchments.

At this point of its march the division curved away from the field and went winding off in the direction of the river. When the significance of this move- 45 ment had impressed itself upon the youth he turned his head and looked over his shoulder toward the trampled and *débris*-strewed ground. He breathed a breath of new satisfaction. He finally nudged his friend. "Well, it's all over," he said to him.

His friend gazed backward. "B'Gawd, it is," he assented. They mused.

5   For a time the youth was obliged to reflect in a puzzled and uncertain way. His mind was undergoing a subtle change. It took moments for it to cast off its battleful ways and resume its accustomed course of thought. Gradually his brain emerged from the clogged clouds, and at last he was enabled to more closely comprehend himself and circumstance.

10 He understood then that the existence of shot and counter-shot was in the past. He had dwelt in a land of strange, squalling upheavals and had come forth. He had been where there was red of blood and black of passion, and he was escaped. His first thoughts were given to rejoicings at this fact.

Later he began to study his deeds, his failures, and his achievements. Thus,
15 fresh from scenes where many of his usual machines of reflection had been idle, from where he had proceeded sheeplike, he struggled to marshal all his acts.

At last they marched before him clearly. From this present view point he was enabled to look upon them in spectator fashion and to criticize them with
20 some correctness, for his new condition had already defeated certain sympathies.

Regarding his procession of memory he felt gleeful and unregretting, for in it his public deeds were paraded in great and shining prominence. Those performances which had been witnessed by his fellows marched now in wide
25 purple and gold, having various deflections. They went gayly with music. It was pleasure to watch these things. He spent delightful minutes viewing the gilded images of memory.

He saw that he was good. He recalled with a thrill of joy the respectful comments of his fellows upon his conduct.

30 Nevertheless, the ghost of his flight from the first engagement appeared to him and danced. There were small shoutings in his brain about these matters. For a moment he blushed, and the light of his soul flickered with shame.

A specter of reproach came to him. There loomed the dogging memory of the tattered soldier—he who, gored by bullets and faint for blood, had fretted
35 concerning an imagined wound in another; he who had loaned his last of strength and intellect for the tall soldier; he who, blind with weariness and pain, had been deserted in the field.

For an instant a wretched chill of sweat was upon him at the thought that he might be detected in the thing. As he stood persistently before his vision,
40 he gave vent to a cry of sharp irritation and agony.

His friend turned. "What's the matter, Henry?" he demanded. The youth's reply was an outburst of crimson oaths.

As he marched along the little branch-hung roadway among his prattling companions this vision of cruelty brooded over him. It clung near him always
45 and darkened his view of these deeds in purple and gold. Whichever way his thoughts turned they were followed by the somber phantom of the desertion in the fields. He looked stealthily at his companions, feeling sure that they

must discern in his face evidences of this pursuit. But they were plodding in
ragged array, discussing with quick tongues the accomplishments of the late
battle.

"Oh, if a man should come up an' ask me, I'd say we got a dum good
lickin'."

"Lickin'—in yer eye! We ain't licked, sonny. We're going down here aways,
swing aroun', an' come in behint 'em."

"Oh, hush, with your comin' in behint 'em. I've seen all 'a that I wanta.
Don't tell me about comin' in behint—"

"Bill Smithers, he ses he'd rather been in ten hundred battles than been in
that heluva hospital. He ses they got shootin' in th' night-time, an' shells
dropped plum among 'em in th' hospital. He ses sech hollerin' he never see."

"Hasbrouck? He's th' best off'cer in this here reg'ment. He's a whale."

"Didn't I tell yeh we'd come aroun' in behint 'em? Didn't I tell yeh so?
We—"

"Oh, shet yer mouth!"

For a time this pursuing recollection of the tattered man took all elation
from the youth's veins. He saw his vivid error, and he was afraid that it
would stand before him all his life. He took no share in the chatter of his
comrades, nor did he look at them or know them, save when he felt sudden
suspicion that they were seeing his thoughts and scrutinizing each detail of the
scene with the tattered soldier.

Yet gradually he mustered force to put the sin at a distance. And at last
his eyes seemed to open to some new ways. He found that he could look back
upon the brass and bombast of his earlier gospels and see them truly. He was
gleeful when he discovered that he now despised them.

With this conviction came a store of assurance. He felt a quiet manhood,
nonassertive but of sturdy and strong blood. He knew that he would no more
quail before his guides wherever they should point. He had been to touch
the great death, and found that, after all, it was but the great death. He was a
man.

So it came to pass that as he trudged from the place of blood and wrath
his soul changed. He came from hot plowshares to prospects of clover tranquilly, and it was as if hot plowshares were not. Scars faded as flowers.

It rained. The procession of weary soldiers became a bedraggled train, despondent and muttering, marching with churning effort in a trough of liquid
brown mud under a low, wretched sky. Yet the youth smiled, for he saw
that the world was a world for him, though many discovered it to be made
of oaths and walking sticks. He had rid himself of the red sickness of battle.
The sultry nightmare was in the past. He had been an animal blistered and
sweating in the heat and pain of war. He turned now with a lover's thirst to
images of tranquil skies, fresh meadows, cool brooks—an existence of soft and
eternal peace.

Over the river a golden ray of sun came through the hosts of leaden rain
clouds.

ELLEN GLASGOW

1874-1945

I. REBEL AGAINST THE ROMANTIC TRADITION (1874–1925)

1874   Born April 22 in Richmond, Virginia, the ninth child of Francis Thomas and Anne Jane (Gholson) Glasgow. The father was the manager of the Tredegar Iron Works, which had supplied cannon to the Confederate Army.

1882–1892   Sent to school, which she acutely disliked. This dislike, and delicate health, led to withdrawal and to education at home by private tutors. She read widely in the English classics, philosophy, and history. Under the instruction of Dr. George Frederick Holmes of the University of Virginia (which did not admit women), she passed examination in political economy. Also influenced by *The Origin of Species* and by writers stemming from it.

1892   After destroying a first novel, she began writing *The Descendant,* but laid it aside under the shock of her mother's death.

1897   Published (anonymously) *The Descendant,* a story of the disinherited. Much of the scene is laid in New York City. This is also true of *Phases of an Inferior Planet* (1898).

1900   *The Voice of the People,* the "first work of genuine realism to appear in Southern fiction," revealing the effects of social recovery after the Civil War.

1902   *The Freeman and Other Poems;* also *The Battle Ground,* a novel of the Civil War, the first of a series presenting the social history of Virginia.

1904   *The Deliverance,* a novel of the "tobacco country."

1906   *The Wheel of Life.*

1908   *The Ancient Law.*

1909   *The Romance of a Plain Man,* a companion piece to *The Voice of the People.*

1911   *The Miller of Old Church,* a novel of the "countryfolk" paralleling *The Deliverance.*

1913   *Virginia,* "a candid portrait of a lady."

1916   *Life and Gabriella,* the story of a woman who breaks with the Victorian (and Virginian) tradition of the lady. Her only novel written outside Virginia.

1919   *The Builders.*

1922   *One Man in His Time.*

1923   *The Shadowy Third and Other Stories,* a volume of psychic or supernatural narratives which stands outside the Virginia series.

1925   *Barren Ground,* a novel of "good people" as contrasted with the aristocratic estate of "good families." Widely praised.

II. HISTORIAN OF THE CONTEMPORARY SOUTH AND ITS MANNERS (1926–1945)

1926   *The Romantic Comedians,* first of the Queenborough trilogy of tragicomedies of urban happiness-hunters between the two World Wars.

1929   *They Stooped to Folly,* second in the series.

1929–1933   Issuance of the Old Dominion Edition of her novels in 8 volumes.

1930   Received an honorary Litt.D. from the University of North Carolina.

1932   *The Sheltered Life,* third of the trilogy.

1935   *Vein of Iron,* last of her novels of the country, covering the depression years, and most nearly akin to *Barren Ground.*

1938   Issuance of the Virginia Edition of her novels in 12 volumes. For this she wrote a succession of prefaces later collected and published separately as *A Certain Measure,* 1943. Honorary degrees from the University of Richmond and Duke University. In 1939 an honorary degree from the College of William and Mary.

1940   Awarded the Quinquennial Howells Medal by the American Academy of Arts and Letters for "eminence in creative literature."

1941   *In This Our Life,* an analysis of the modern temper as revealed in a single community in the crucial year 1938-39. Awarded the Saturday Review of Literature plaque for outstanding service to American letters.

1942   Awarded the Pulitzer Prize in Fiction for *In This Our Life.*

1945   Died November 21 in Richmond, Virginia.

BIOGRAPHIES: There is no formal biography. Consult, however, *A Certain Measure,* Harcourt, Brace, 1943, and "What I Believe," *Nation,* April 12, 1935, by this author; and Louise M. Field, *Ellen Glasgow: Novelist of the Old and New South,* Doubleday, Doran, 1923; Douglas S. Freeman, "Ellen Glasgow: Idealist," *Saturday Review of Literature,* August 31, 1935; Dorothea L. Mann, *Ellen Glasgow* (with critical essays by James Branch Cabell, Joseph Collins, and Carl Van Vechten), Doubleday, Doran, 1927; Isaac F. Marcosson, "The Personal Ellen Glasgow," *Bookman,* August, 1909; and the sketch in Fred B. Millett, *Contemporary American Authors,* Harcourt, Brace, 1940.

BIBLIOGRAPHY AND EDITIONS: Consult the bibliography in the appendix of *A Certain Measure,* and also that in Millett. The two "collected" editions are not "complete." These are the Old Dominion Edition, 8 vols., Doubleday, Doran, 1929-33, the texts of the novels therein included being revised and each furnished with a new preface; and the Virginia Edition, 12 vols., Doubleday, Doran, 1938, with new prefaces.

CRITICISM: Fr. Brie, *Ellen Glasgow,* Freiburg i. Br., 1931; J. Donald Adams, "The Virginia Edition of the Works of Ellen Glasgow," *New York Times Book Review,* December 18, 1938; Herschel Brickell, "Miss Glasgow and Mr. Marquand," *Virginia Quarterly Review,* Summer, 1941; James Branch Cabell, "Two Sides of the Shield," *New York Herald Tribune Books,* April 20, 1930; Henry S. Canby, "Ellen Glasgow: Ironic Tragedian," *Saturday Review of Literature,* September 10, 1938; Emily Clark, *Innocence Abroad,* Knopf, 1931; Sara Haardt, "Ellen Glasgow and the South," *Bookman,* April, 1929; H. M. Jones, "Product of the Tragic Muse," *Saturday Review of Literature,* March 29, 1941; "The Virginia Edition of the Works of Ellen Glasgow," *New York Herald Tribune Books,* July 24, 1938; Alfred

Kazin, *On Native Grounds,* Reynal and Hitchcock, 1942; H. L. Mencken, "A Southern Skeptic," *American Mercury,* August, 1933; Edwin Mims, "The Social Philosophy of Ellen Glasgow," *Social Forces,* March, 1926; Isabel Patterson, "Rue with a Difference," *New York Herald Tribune Books,* August 4, 1929; Robert Van Gelder, "An Interview with Ellen Glasgow," *New York Times Book Review,* October 8, 1942; James S. Wilson, "Ellen Glasgow; Ironic Idealist," *Virginia Quarterly Review,* 1939, and "Ellen Glasgow," *ibid.,* Spring, 1941; Stark Young, "Prefaces to Distinction," *New Republic,* June 7, 1933.

Ellen Glasgow is the only American novelist to complete a vast fictional project comparable to that of Balzac or Zola; that is, to give through a series of novels an orderly interpretation of the changing social mores of a great social unit. Her unit has been the commonwealth of Virginia, both the countryside and the city life of Richmond (the Queenborough of her later books). The arrangement of novels included in the Virginia Edition marks the completion of this extraordinary survey. But besides being a "secretary to society," Miss Glasgow belongs to a tradition of fiction-writing older than naturalism and represents a group of writers of whom Willa Cather and Dorothy Canfield Fisher are other examples. This tradition she enunciates and defends in the prefaces cumulated in *A Certain Measure.* For her the novel is an instrument of culture, not merely a bit of laboratory science or a document in propaganda. Possessed of wisdom and wit, mistress of a pure and flexible prose, adapting herself to experimentation in style but not of the "advanced guard," Miss Glasgow brings distinction into an art perpetually under commercial temptations to become undistinguished; and in an age of naturalism she has insisted that men are objects of human evaluation, not mere biological units in a world of physical determinism.

THE DEEP PAST

The following excerpt is Part II of *The Sheltered Life,* first of the "novels of the city" in the social history of Virginia. As the preface indicates, the title, implying no particular age or place, intends rather to suggest the "effort of one human being to stand between another and life." As the theme develops, it reveals as well the tragic futility of standing blindly between oneself and life, but, falling mainly within the year 1917, the beginning (for this country) of the First World War and of the accompanying cultural changes, the novel fits perfectly into Miss Glasgow's over-all plan of portraying this society in transition.

Part I of the novel ("The Age of Make-Believe") opens in 1910, when Jenny Blair Archbald, aged nine, begins to be aware of herself and her world, a world made especially resplendent by the somewhat faded glamour of Queenborough's most romantic pair, Eva and George Birdsong—especially George. In Part II, seven years later, the point of view shifts to Jenny Blair's grandfather, old General Archbald, now eighty-three, to whom Eva, gallant and beautiful, stands as the last of her queenly kind. About to undergo a serious operation, she summons him to her bedside at the hospital, and it is on the way to see her that he pauses to rest in the park while his troubled mind, "oppressed by the burden of remembrance," reviews his own past, its frustrations, and its painful lessons in wisdom. Miss Glasgow, always successful with her older characters, is especially sympathetic with the aged

General, into whose "lonely spirit," she confesses, she has put much of her own "ultimate feeling about life." The text is that of the edition of 1934.

"Yes, it is true," said old General Archbald, for he had passed his eighty-third birthday, and had found that phrases, like events, often repeat themselves, "you can't mend things by thinking."
Though thought may have created life in the beginning, though the whole visible world may hang suspended in an invisible web of mind, one could not 5 by taking heed mend the smallest break, not the tiniest loosened thread in the pattern. All the thinking in the world, he mused, with a sense of unreality as vague as smoke, could not help Eva Birdsong. For months he had suspected that something was wrong. Not more than ten days ago, he had seen her stop suddenly in the midst of a sentence, while a shiver ran through her 10 body, the smile twisted and died on her lips, and she looked at him with the eyes of a woman in torture. Then she had seemed, by sheer strength of will, to drive the spasm away, to keep the returning pain at a distance. "What is it, Eva?" he had asked, and she had answered with a laugh of protest, "Oh, nothing." That was all, "Oh, nothing." Yet he had not been satisfied; he had felt 15 uneasy and agitated; he had known in his heart that something was wrong with her. And now he had just heard that they had taken her to the hospital.
"They have given her morphine," Mrs. Archbald was saying, "and George telephoned me that she will be operated on in the morning. If you'll go up late this afternoon, she thinks she will be able to talk to you. There is some- 20 thing she has on her mind." Arrested by the pain in his eyes, she added, "I sometimes think, Father, that Eva is more to you than anyone in the world."
With his hands clasped on the ebony crook of his walking-stick, he stood on the front porch and blinked up at his daughter-in-law, while William (an old dog now, but carrying his years well) waited for him to go out into the 25 April sunshine in Jefferson Park.
"Is there danger?" he asked, without answering her question. For it was true that Eva was more than a daughter, and nothing is so hard to speak aloud as the truth.
"There is, of course, always danger. For a year she has been really ill; but 30 you know how long it took us to make her submit even to an examination."
"Yes, I know." The brooding eyes beneath the sardonic eyebrows did not waver.
"It does seem exaggerated to carry modesty to the point of endangering one's life. But with Eva, I think, it was less her own shrinking than the feel- 35 ing that George might—well, might— Oh, I don't know, of course, but she told me once he had a horror of what he called maimed women."
"Any man worth his salt would think first of her health."
"That is exactly what George said to me an hour ago. But women, especially romantic women like Eva," she added sagaciously, "make the mistake 40 of measuring a man's love by his theories. She told me about it the day she was seized with that dreadful pain and I telephoned for Doctor Bridges." She broke off abruptly, with the feeling probably, the General reminded himself, that she was giving away some solemn league and covenant of woman.

If only she would tell him more! While the thought crossed his mind, he flinched and raised his eyes to the clement sky. If only she would tell him nothing! After all, there was wisdom in an era that smothered truth in words. For truth, in spite of the stern probings of science, is an ugly and a terrible
5   thing.

"If women could begin to realize," he said, "how little what a man thinks has to do with what he feels."

"Had I ever doubted that, the way George has risen to this crisis would have convinced me. He seems to feel the pain more than Eva does. For three
10   nights he has sat up with her, and he refused to go to bed even after he fell asleep in his chair. The night nurse made him lie down on a couch last night; but he looks dreadfully haggard this morning, and his nerves are on edge. No man," she concluded emphatically, "could have shown a greater devotion."

"I can well believe that."
15   "Then why—? Why—?"

"Those other things, my dear, have nothing to do with his marriage."

Mrs. Archbald looked puzzled. "But that is just what I mean. There have been so many things in his life that have had nothing to do with his marriage."
20   The General sighed with the usual male helplessness before the embarrassing logic of the feminine mind. "Well, George has the kindest heart in the world. But even the kindest heart in the world sometimes fails to get the better of nature. All that side of his life has no more to do with his devotion to Eva than if—than if it were malaria from the bite of a mosquito. That's
25   what women, especially women like Eva, are never able to understand."

"No wonder. It seems so illogical."

"Men aren't logical creatures, my dear. Nor, for that matter, is life logical." Then he asked, "Have you seen Isabella today?"

"Yes, she stopped as she was taking little Erminia to the dentist. There's
30   something wrong with her teeth. It's such a pity, for she is a beautiful child."

"All three of them are beautiful children. Nature seems to be on the side of Isabella. Well, so am I, if only because she let our family skeleton out of the closet. The only way to be rid of a skeleton is to drag it into the light and clothe it in flesh and blood."
35   Mrs. Archbald looked puzzled. "I don't understand, Father."

"I didn't mean you to, my dear, but Isabella would. She is like every other Archbald, only more so, and though she is happily unaware of it, the more so has been her salvation."

Seven years before, three days after the renewal of her engagement to
40   Thomas Lunsford, Isabella had taken the morning train to Washington, and had returned the next afternoon as the wife of Joseph Crocker. "Life is too short," she had explained, with the dash of coarseness that embarrassed her sister and her sister-in-law, "not to have the right man for your first husband at least. As for what people say—well, if talk could kill, I should have been
45   dead long ago." Etta had been prostrated; but Mrs. Archbald had been too busy readjusting the Crockers' station in life to give way to prejudice. When so few standards remained unimpaired, the distinction between plain people

and quiet people was almost obliterated by the first important step from the Baptist Communion to the Episcopal Church. And everything, of course, was made easier because Joseph had so little religion. . . .

"You look tired, Father," Mrs. Archbald remarked, when she had studied him for a moment. "Hadn't you better lie down?"

"No, I like to feel the sun on me, and so does William. We'll sit in the park awhile and then walk up to the hospital."

"Jenny Blair will go with you. She can wait downstairs while you are in Eva's room. The child is so distressed. She has always adored Eva."

"Everyone adores her."

"Well, try not to worry. Something tells me that she will come through. Doctor Bridges feels very hopeful."

"He would naturally—but maimed for life—" his voice trembled.

"We must try not to think of that. If only she comes through it well." Then after a moment's thought, she added cheerfully, "It isn't as if she were a younger woman and still hoped to have children. She is forty-two, and has been married almost twenty years. One would never suspect that to look at her."

After she finished, he lingered a moment, hoping and fearing that she might, if only by accident, become more explicit. Was she shielding Eva's modesty from him, an old man, who would have loved her had she been stripped bare not only of modesty but of every cardinal virtue? Or was such evasion merely an incurable habit of mind? Would George tell him the truth? Or was it conceivable that George did not know?

"Will Jenny Blair come in time?" he asked, pricked by sudden fear. "I should not like to be late."

"Why, you've at least two hours, Father, and if Jenny Blair isn't back in time, I'll go with you myself."

"But I don't need anybody. I am able to go alone." No man needed protection less; but because he had lived a solitary male among women, he could never escape it, and because these women depended upon him, he had remained at their mercy. It was impossible to wound the feelings of women who owed him the bread they ate and the roof over their heads, and so long as he did not hurt their feelings, they would be stronger than he was. Always, from his earliest childhood, he mused, with a curious resentment against life, he had been the victim of pity. Of his own pity, not another's. Of that double-edged nerve of sympathy, like the aching nerve in a tooth, which throbbed alive at the sight of injustice or cruelty. One woman after another had enslaved his sympathy more than his passion, and never had she seemed to be the woman his passion demanded.

Well, it is over, he thought, and knew that it would never be over. Again this secret hostility swept through his nerves, surprising him by its vehemence. Was it possible that he was beginning to break in mind before the infirmities of the flesh had attacked a single physical organ? Only yesterday, Bridges had told him that a man of sixty might be proud of his arteries. Only yesterday! And today he was annoyed by this queer tingling in his limbs, by this hollow drumming which advanced along his nerves and then receded into the distance. "Let us sit down a bit, William," he murmured, walking very erect, with a proper pride in his straight back and thighs and his well-set-up figure for a man of his years. "I suppose this bad news about Eva has disturbed me. I'd rather lose my right arm than have anything happen to her."

5   Dropping down on a green bench in the park, beneath a disfigured tulip tree, which was putting out into bud, he tried to imagine her ill, suffering, and waiting calmly for that dreaded hour under the knife. But no, she chose, as always capriciously, her own hour and mood to return to him. Never had he seen her cast aside her armour of gaiety. Never, among all the women he
10 had known, had she asked him for sympathy. Never once had she tried to take care of him. For all her loveliness, she was, he found himself thinking aloud to William, curled up on the grass by the bench, a strong soul in affliction. A strong soul, still undefeated by life, she came to him now. She came to him out of the pale green distance, out of the flying clouds, out of the
15 April bloom of the sky. Even today, he mused proudly, there wasn't a girl in Queenborough who was worthy to step into her shoes. Not one of them. Not Jenny Blair, a vivid little thing, but lacking in queenliness.

    Resting there, with his tired old hands clasped on the crook of his stick, he told himself that Eva Birdsong in her prime, before misfortune had sapped
20 her ardent vitality, would have put to shame all the professional beauties of Paris or London. Why, he had seen Mrs. Langtry, and had considered her deficient in presence. "Eva would have had all London at her feet," he meditated, without jealousy, since his devotion, at eighty-three, was of the mind alone. Or was this deception? Did one go down into the grave with the senses
25 still alive in the sterile flesh? Well, no matter. The thread had snapped, and the question had floated out of his thoughts. Airy and fragile as mist, he watched it blown away into the April world, into that windy vastness which contained the end of all loving and all living.

    At least she had had, he pondered, sitting beside a triangular flower-bed,
30 beneath the pale buds on the tulip tree, what she believed that she wanted. True, her life might have been easier if they hadn't been poor. Yet being poor, which kept her from parties where she once shone so brilliantly, had saved her also from brooding, from that fatal introspection which is the curse of women and poets. She had not had time to fall out of love. She had not had
35 time to discover that George was unworthy.

    Or was it conceivable, as Cora suspected, that Eva knew the truth, and was merely preserving appearances? No, he could not believe this, he mused, poking the end of his stick into a tuft of young dandelions. Yet, while he rejected Cora's suspicion, he admitted that life would be more agreeable if
40 women could realize that man is not a monogamous animal, and that even a man in love does not necessarily wish to love all the time. Certainly, there would be less unhappiness abroad in the world if good women could either accept or reject the moral nature of man. Over and over, he had seen the faithful lover lose to the rake in an affair of the heart. Over and over, he had
45 seen a miracle of love that failed to make a conversion. Yet he knew, having

---

21. **Mrs. Langtry**—Lily Langtry (1852-1929), known as "The Jersey Lily," British actress painted by Millais, said to have been the most beautiful woman of her day.

much experience to build on, that even loose-living men are not all of one
quality. It was not a simple question of merit. The diversity went deeper,
far down through the nature of man into nature itself. George had lived according to life; his very faults were the too lavish defects of generosity. He
was generous with himself always, and with his money whenever he was   5
affluent. Not without a pang, the General remembered that long ago, when he
was caught on the verge of financial ruin, George alone among his sympathetic friends had offered him help. The year before George had inherited
his father's modest estate, and he would have sacrificed this fortune to save
a friend from disaster. Later on, to be sure, he had speculated unwisely and   10
lost his inheritance—but it was not of this that the General was thinking
while he poked at the dandelions.

He saw George, with his thick wind-blown hair, his smiling eyes, his look
of virile hardness, of inexhaustible energy. Well-favoured enough if you
judged by appearances, and did women, or men either for that matter, ever   15
judge by anything else? But it was more than George's fine features, ruddy
skin, and friendly grey eyes that made one reluctant to blame him. Yes, there
was something more, some full-bodied virtue, some compensating humanity.
"But I am human too," thought old General Archbald, "and what good has
it done me?" . . .   20

As a child, at Stillwater, they had called him a milksop, because he saw
visions in the night and wanted to be a poet. The sight of blood sickened
him; yet his grandfather assured him, with truth, that hunting had given
greater pleasure to a greater number of human beings than all the poetry
since Homer. Pity, said the men who had none, is a woman's virtue; but he   25
had known better than this. A poet's virtue, it may be. He was not sure. So
much virtue passed into a poet when he was dead; when his immortal part
was bound in English calf and put into a library. Little girls, however, were
not pitiful. Little girls were as savage as boys, only weaker. They had never
failed to torment him. They had laughed when he was made sick; they had   30
mocked at his visions; they had stolen his poems and used them for curl-
papers. Strange, the images that were dragged up like bits of shell, in a net
of the memory! All his life curl-papers had remained, for him, the untidy
symbol of an aversion. No, little girls were not gentle. And even his tender-
hearted mother, who nursed her servants in illness, and had never used the   35
word "slave" except in the historical sense—even his mother was incapable
of the pity that becomes a torment to the nerves. She accepted meekly, as an
act of God's inscrutable wisdom, all the ancient wrongs and savage punishments of civilization. . . .

Again General Archbald sighed and prodded the dandelions. Again the   40
thread snapped and a flock of unrelated images darted into his mind. . . .

"Where did the boy get his tomfool ideas?" his robust grandfather inquired
sternly. "Was he born lacking?"

"Not lacking, Father," his mother protested, "but different. Some very nice
people," she added, with an encouraging glance at her peculiar child, "are   45
born different. He may even turn out to be a poet."

"Do you think," his father asked in a troubled tone, "that we had better

try changing his tutor? Is it possible that Mr. Davis has infected him with
newfangled ideas?"

His mother shook her head in perplexity, for it distressed her that one of
her sons should be deficient in manliness. "But the other boys are all manly.
5   Even if Mr. Davis has talked of abolition, after giving us his word that he
would treat the—the institution with respect, I have never heard that New
Englanders disliked bloodshed. I thought, indeed, it was exactly the opposite.
Don't you remember I opposed your engaging Mr. Davis because I had always heard the Puritans were a hard and cruel people? Perhaps," she con-
10 fessed bravely, "he may inherit his eccentric notions from me. Though I try
to be broad-minded, I can't help having a sentiment against cock-fights."

"Pooh! Pooh!" his grandfather blustered, for he belonged to the Georgian
school of a gentleman. "Would you deprive the lower classes of their favourite
sport? As for this young nincompoop, I'll take him deer-hunting tomorrow.
15 If he is too much of a mollycoddle to kill his buck, we'll try to scare up a
fawn for him."

A famous hunter in his prime, the old gentleman still pursued with hounds
any animal that was able to flee. Fortunately, game was plentiful and game
laws unknown in the fields and forests of Stillwater. For nothing escaped his
20 knife or his gun, not the mole in the earth, not the lark in the air. He could
no more look at a wild creature without lusting to kill than he could look
at a pretty girl without lusting to kiss. Well, it was a pity he had not lived
to enjoy the war; for the killing nerve, as his grandson had once said of him,
was the only nerve in his body. Yet he had fallen in love with a woman be-
25 cause of her fragile appearance; and when she had gone into a decline after
the birth of her fifth child, and had lost her reason for a number of years, he
had remained still devoted to her. Against the advice of his family and his
physician, he had refused to send her away, and had kept her, behind barred
windows, in the west wing of the house. To be sure, when she died, he had
30 married again within seven months; but only his first wife, though he had
buried two others, had given him children, and through her the strain of
melancholy had passed into the Archbald blood. . . .

From his father, with filial patience, "For my part, I try not to kill a doe
or a fawn."

35 "Fiddlesticks, sir! You talk like an abolitionist. Didn't the Lord provide
negroes for our servants and animals for our sport? Haven't you been told
this from the pulpit? I hope, sir, I shan't live to see the day when every sort
of sport is no longer welcome at Stillwater." Even the field hands in the quarters, General Archbald remembered, had their "coon or possum dawgs," and
40 went rabbit chasing on holidays when there were no cock-fights. High or
low, good or bad, manners at Stillwater were a perpetual celebration of being
alive. No other way of living had ever seemed to him so deeply rooted in the
spirit of place, in an established feeling for life. Not for happiness alone, not
for life at its best only, but for the whole fresh or salty range of experience.

---

6. institution—Slavery was sometimes euphemistically referred to as "the peculiar institution." **12-13. Georgian school**—"Country gentlemen" under George III and George IV were
supposed to be especially addicted to manly sports, especially hunting.

There was, too, a quality, apart from physical zest, that he had found nowhere else in the world, a mellow flavour he had never forgotten.

Naturally, as a child, he did not hunt or shoot with his grandfather; but several weeks later, on a brilliant November morning, he watched a buck at bay pulled down by the hounds in a rocky stream. He could not remember how it had happened. By accident, probably, when he was out with his tutor. At first, watching the death, he had felt nothing. Then, in a spasm, the retch of physical nausea. For the eyes of the hunted had looked into his at the end; and that look was to return to him again and again, as a childish fear of the dark returns to the grown man when his nerves are unstrung. In how many faces of men, women, children, and animals, all over the world, had he seen that look of the hunted reflected? A look of bewilderment, of doubt, of agony, of wondering despair; but most of all a look that is seeking some God who might, but does not, show mercy. All over the world! North, South, East, West. On the heights, in the desert.

With blood on his hands and a savage joy inflaming his face, his grandfather strode over to smear stains on a milksop. "If you don't like the taste of blood better than milk, you'll have to be blooded. Hold still, sir, I say, and be blooded." Then, as the blood touched him, the boy retched with sickness, and vomited over the anointing hand and the outstretched arm. "Damn you, sir!" the old gentleman bellowed, while he wiped away the mess with his silk handkerchief. "Go back to the nursery where you belong!"

Still retching, furious and humiliated because he had been born a milksop, the boy rode home with his tutor. "I don't love people!" he sobbed passionately. "I don't love people!" Was it fair to blame him because he had been born different? Was anybody to blame for the way God had let him be born?

How close that day seemed to him now, that day and others at Stillwater. The more distant a scene, the clearer it appeared in his vision. Things near at hand he could barely remember. Even yesterday was smothered in fog. But when he looked far back in the past, at the end of seventy years or more, the fog lifted, and persons and objects started out in the sunken glow on the horizon. Instead of diminishing with time, events in the deep past grew larger, and the faces of persons long dead became more vivid and lifelike than life itself. "It is old age," he thought wearily. "It is a sign of old age to lack proper control." Or was the cause deeper still? he mused, while the shadow of a bird flitted over the grass and was gone. Was this second self of his mind, as variable as wind, as nebulous as mist, merely the forgotten consciousness of the poet who might have been? Sitting here in the spring sunshine, was he living again, was he thinking again, with that long buried part of his nature? For his very words, he realized, were the words of that second self, of the self he had always been in dreams and never been in reality. Again the bird flitted by. He did not know. He could not tell. No matter how hard he tried, it was impossible to keep his thoughts from rambling back into the past. It was impossible to trace a connection between the past and present. Was he growing, in his old age, like poor Rodney, who had surrendered to shadows? Better let the past disappear, and hold firmly to the bare structure of living.

For an instant his look wandered from the trees in the park to the few carriages and many motor cars in Washington Street. Yes, the world was changing rapidly, and he wondered what was waiting ahead. He could remember when Queenborough had the charm of a village; but now, wherever
5 he looked, he found ugliness. Beauty, like every other variation from type, was treated more or less as a pathological symptom. Did Americans, especially Southerners, prefer ugliness? Did ugliness conform, he pondered fancifully, to some automatic esthetic spring in the dynamo? But even if the scientific method destroyed beauty, there would be no more great wars, only
10 little wars that no one remembered, said John Welch. What, indeed, would be left to fight about when people thought alike everywhere, and exact knowledge had spread in a vast cemetery for ideals all over the world?

So John Welch, being very advanced in opinion, would argue for hours; but when argument was ended, old General Archbald could not see that
15 human nature was different from what it had been in his youth. To be sure, idealism, like patriotism, appeared to diminish with every material peace between conflicts; but he was near enough to the Spanish War, and indeed to the Civil War, to realize that the last battle has never been fought and the last empty word has never been spoken. Not that it mattered. All he knew
20 now was that he was too old to bother about life. He was too old to bother about cruelty, which he had seen all over the world, in every system invented by man; which he had seen in a velvet mask, in rags, and naked except for its own skin. Yes, he was too old to suffer over the evils that could not be cured. Only, whenever he listened to John Welch assailing the present order,
25 he was reminded of his own revolt against slavery in the eighteen fifties. The reformers of that age had believed that all the world needed was to have negro slavery abolished. Yet negro slavery was gone, and where it had been, John said, another system had ushered in the old evils with a clean, or at least a freshly wiped face. What the world needed now, cried the modern reform-
30 ers, like John Welch, was the new realism of science. For one confirmed habit had not changed with the ages. Mankind was still calling human nature a system and trying vainly to put something else in its place.

But a world made, or even made over, by science was only a stark and colourless spectacle to old David Archbald. A thin-lipped world of facts with-
35 out faith, of bones without flesh. Better the red waistcoats and the soulful vapouring of early Romanticism. Better even the excessive sensibility of mid-Victorian esthetics. Since he belonged to the past, if he belonged anywhere, his mental processes, it seemed, were obliged to be disorderly. When he said, "I am more than myself," when he said, "Life is more than living," when he
40 blundered about "the nature of reality," he was still, or so John Welch declared, harping on a discredited idealism. "Transcendental!" John would snap when he meant "Nonsense!"

Glancing from the street to the sky, while the thread broke again, General Archbald reflected that it was easy to be an idealist in this pleasant spring of

17. **Spanish War**—Spanish-American War, 1898. **35. red waistcoats**—Young Théophile Gautier made his red waistcoat the symbol of the romantic school of literature in Paris in the 1830's.

the year 1914, and to look with hope, if not with confidence, to the future.
It was true that the familiar signs of uneasiness were abroad in the world.
There was trouble not only in China and Mexico, where one naturally ex-
pected trouble to be, but among a part at least of the population of Europe.
Power everywhere was growing more arrogant, and unrest more unrestful. 5
Socialism was springing up and taking root in soil that appeared sterile. In
Great Britain, Ulster and the suffragettes were disturbing a peace that turned
in its broken sleep and dreamed of civil war. Nearer home, pirates had de-
serted the seas and embarked afresh as captains of industry.

But in the realm of ideas, where hope reigned, the prospect was brighter. 10
There the crust of civilization, so thin and brittle over the world outside, was
beginning to thicken. Religion and science, those hoary antagonists, were
reconciled and clasped in a fraternal embrace. Together, in spite of nationalism, in spite even of nature, they would build, or invent, the New Jerusalem
for mankind. In that favoured province, smooth, smiling, well-travelled, 15
there would be neither sin nor disease, and without wars all the ancient
wrongs would be righted. Nobody, not even the old sunning themselves on
green benches, would be allowed to ramble in mind.

Well, perhaps. . . . No harm could come, he supposed, of a sanguine outlook. Only—only, did not that outlook approach a little too close to a formula? 20
Were material ends all the world needed to build on? Was passion, even in
the old, a simple problem of lowering your blood pressure and abandoning
salt? Could a man discard his thinking self as lightly as he discarded the doctrine of an ultimate truth? When John said, "A green bench is only a green
bench," was he wiser than old David Archbald, who replied, "A green bench 25
is not the green bench I touch"? True, men no longer wrangled in public
halls over the nature of reality. But he could not see that exact knowledge
and precision of language had improved the quality of mankind. Well, the
wonder in every age, he supposed, was not that most men were savage, but
that a few men were civilized. Only a few in every age, and these few were 30
the clowns in the parade. . . .

Suddenly, while he meditated, it seemed to him that the shape of the external world, this world of brick and asphalt, of men and women and machines moving, broke apart and dissolved from blown dust into thought. Until
this moment he had remembered with the skin of his mind, not with the 35
arteries; but now, when the concrete world disappeared, he plunged downward through a dim vista of time, where scattered scenes from the past flickered and died and flickered again. At eighty-three, the past was always like
this. Never the whole of it. Fragments, and then more fragments. No single
part, not even an episode, complete as it had happened. 40

In each hour, when he had lived it, life had seemed important to him; but

3. **China . . . Mexico**—The Chinese Revolution of Dr. Sun Yat-sen began in 1912 with
the overthrow of the Manchu dynasty. A succession of violent events involving American policy
convulsed the Republic of Mexico from 1913 to 1917. **7. Ulster . . . suffragettes**—Rather
than accept Home Rule for Ireland in 1914, the Northern Counties (Ulster) organized an army
and even set up a provisional government to oppose the measure by violence. During the same
period embattled advocates of woman suffrage staged a series of violent episodes in and around
the Houses of Parliament in London.

now he saw that it was composed of things that were all little things in themselves, of mere fractions of time, of activities so insignificant that they had
passed away with the moment in which they had quivered and vanished.
How could anyone, he asked, resting there alone at the end, find a meaning,
5 a pattern? Yet, though his mind rambled now, he had walked in beaten
tracks in his maturity. His soul, it is true, had been a rebel; but he had given
lip-homage, like other men all over the world, to creeds that were husks. Like
other men all over the world, he had sacrificed to gods as fragile as the bloom
of light on the tulip tree. And what was time itself but the bloom, the sheath
10 enfolding experience? Within time, and within time alone, there was life—
the gleam, the quiver, the heart-beat, the immeasurable joy and anguish of
being. . . .

The trail plunged straight and deep into the November forest. There was
the tang of woodsmoke far off in a clearing. Frost was spun over the ground.
15 The trees were brilliant with the yellow of hickory, the scarlet of sweet gum,
the wine-red of oaks.

Why was he here? How had he come? Was he awake or asleep? Ah, he
knew the place now. A forest trail at Stillwater. But they had left Stillwater
fifty years ago. Well, no matter. No matter that he was a boy and an old
20 man together, or that the boy wanted to be a poet. It was all the same life.
A solitary fragment, but the same fragment of time. Time was stranger than
memory. Stranger than his roaming again through this old forest, with his
snack and a thin volume of Byron tucked away in his pocket. Here was the
place he had stopped to eat his snack, while his pointer puppies, Pat and Tom,
25 started game in the underbrush.

Then, as he stood with his head up and his eyes on the westering sun
through the trees, he knew that he was watched. He knew that there were
eyes somewhere among the leaves, and that these eyes, the eyes of the hunted,
were watching him. It was the look in the eyes of the dying buck, but now it
30 was everywhere. In the trees, in the sky, in the leaf-strewn pool, in the underbrush, in the very rocks by the trail. All these things reflected and magnified
to his quivering nerves the look of the hunted. Because of the fear in his
nerves, he cried out, expecting no answer. But before his call ended, there
was a stir in the woods; the leaves scattered; and through the thick branches,
35 he met the eyes of a runaway slave. Ragged, starved, shuddering, a slave
crouched on the forest mould, and stared at the bread and meat in the boy's
hand. When the food was given to him, he gulped it down and sat watching.
Haggard with terror and pain, a dirty rag wrapping his swollen jaw, his
clothes as tattered as the shirt of a scarecrow, he had been driven by hunger
40 and cold up from the swamps. His breath came with a wheezing sound, and
his flesh shed the sour smell of a wild animal. (A sour smell and a filthy rag
after nearly seventy years!)

For weeks—for months, even, he may have lain hidden; but the deep
swamps were far away, and he was the first fugitive slave to come within
45 the boundaries of Stillwater. Beyond speech, beyond prayer, nothing remained
in his eyes but bewilderment. "Nobody will hurt you," the boy said, emptying

his pockets of the cornbread he had brought for the puppies. "Nobody will hurt you," he repeated, as if the creature were deaf or inarticulate. While he gave the promise, a wave of courage, of daring, of high adventure, rushed over him. For the second time in his young life he was defying the established order, he was in conflict with the moral notions of men. Is it true, he asked 5 himself now, that man's pity and man's morality are for ever in conflict? Is it true that pity is by nature an outlaw? Well, he liked to think that he had not hesitated; no, not for an instant.

Again that day he had returned to the hidden place in the forest. He had brought clothes taken from the old garments in his father's and his grand- 10 father's closets, food that he had found put away in the pantry, and a little wine that had been left over in the glasses at lunch. From his own bed he had stolen a blanket, and from his grandfather's "body servant" he had borrowed, as if in jest, the "ticket" that permitted Abram Jonas to visit his wife in another county. "When it is over, they will have to know," the boy thought, 15 as he trudged back into the forest with the help he had come to fetch. "When it is over."

And then what had happened? His memory faded, died down to ashes, and shot up more brightly. Two mornings later, he had set out in an old buggy, with a decently clothed servant on the seat at his side. Miles away, 20 screened from the turnpike, he had put a knapsack of food and the money he was saving to buy a colt into the hands of the runaway. "Your name is Abram Jonas. This is a paper that says so. You belong to Gideon Archbald, and you are going to visit your wife in Spottsylvania. Do you remember that? What is your name? Say it once more." "Abram Jonas, marster." "You'd bet- 25 ter repeat it as you go along. I am Abram Jonas. Here is the paper that says so." "I'se Abram Jonas, marster. Dis heah is de paper." The fugitive looked up at him, first with the fear of the hunted, then with a dawning intelligence. "Thanky, marster," and turning, he had limped away from the turnpike into a forest trail. What had become of him? Had he escaped? Was he caught? 30 Did he drop down like an animal and die of the shuddering misery of life?

After all these years General Archbald was still curious. But no word had come. Only silence. Only silence, and the feeling that he had taken his stand against the forces men about him called civilization. He had defied not only the moral notions of his age and his place, but the law and the Constitution 35 and the highest court in the land. The truth came out at last when the real Abram Jonas asked for the return of his "ticket"; and, as a measure of disci- pline, David's father sent his youngest son abroad to be educated. He was six- teen then; and years afterwards, when he left Oxford, he had lived in Paris and London. Ironically, he had begun to think of himself as a stranger in his 40 world and his age. Yet when the war came, he was drawn back to his own. He was drawn back to fight for old loyalties. After the war he had endured poverty and self-denial and, worst of all, darned clothes for a number of years. Then, while he was still burdened by defeat, he had compromised Erminia and proposed to her the next morning. Well, the past was woven of contradic- 45 tions. For eighty-three years he had lived two lives, and between these two different lives, which corresponded only in time, he could trace no connection. What he had wanted, he had never had; what he had wished to do, he had never done. . . .

5   A fog clouded his mind, and he heard a voice like his own remark testily, "Rambling is a sign of age, but I can't keep hold of the present." He couldn't keep hold of yesterday, of last month, of last year, of the faces he knew best, of the features even of his wife, which had grown vague since her death. Now, at the end, all faces of women, even the faces of women he had slept with, looked alike to him. All faces of women, except, perhaps—he wasn't sure
10 —the face of Eva Birdsong. "No, I can't remember," he repeated, while this suppressed irritation clotted his thoughts. "I'm too old to remember that any- thing, especially any woman, made a difference in life."

    Then, softly, while he was thinking this, the fog in his mind dispersed, and the crowd of women's faces melted to air, and reassembled in a solitary
15 face he had not forgotten. Fifty years—nearer sixty years now—since he had lost her. What was the use, he pondered resentfully, in dragging back that old memory, that old passion? Why couldn't the dead stay dead when one had put them away? Half a century of dust! Yet she came to him, unspoiled by time, out of the drifting haze of the present. Was it because he had loved
20 her alone? Or did she shine there, lost, solitary, unforgotten, merely because she was farther away than the others? Not that it mattered. The cause was unimportant beside the vast significance of that remembrance.

    But why, after all, had he loved her? Even when he had fallen in love with her that April in England, he could not point to a single perfection and say,
25 "I love her because she is beautiful, or brilliant, or gifted." There was noth- ing unusual about her, his friends had remarked wonderingly. Dozens of women he knew in London were handsomer, or wittier, or more conspicu- ously good. Small, shy, pale, she was utterly lacking in the presence so much admired by English society in the eighteen fifties.
30   When he first met her, she was married to the wrong man, and was the mother of two delicate children. Had he fallen in love with a veiled emptiness, a shadow without substance? Yet her blue eyes, as soft as hyacinths, had prom- ised joy that was infinite. Or had he loved her because he had seen in her face the old fear and bewilderment of the hunted? Had her memory endured
35 because it was rooted not in desire but in pity? Happier loves, lighter women, he had forgotten. No matter what people say, he thought moodily, it takes more than going to bed with a woman to fix her face in one's mind. For this woman alone he had loved and lost without wholly possessing. Yet she was there when he turned back, clear, soft, vivid, with some secret in her look
40 that thrilled, beckoned, and for ever eluded him. Her eyes were still eloquent with light; the promised joy was still infinite; the merest glimmer of a smile had outlasted the monuments of experience.

    Yet like everything else in his life, important or unimportant, his passion seemed, when it occurred, to come at the wrong moment. He had intended
45 to leave London; his ticket to Paris was in his pocket; his bags were packed. Then a tooth had begun to ache—a tooth he had lost only last year—and he had decided to stay over a day or two and consult an English dentist who

had once treated him for an abscess. Not an act of God, he told himself (unless a twinge of pain were an act of God), but a toothache had decided his destiny. Had the pain come a day later, just one sunrise and one sunset afterwards, he might have escaped. But falling as it did in that infinitesimal pin point of time, his fate had been imprisoned in a single luminous drop of experience.

Looking back, he had often wondered why there had been no suspicion of danger, no visible or invisible warning that he was approaching the crossroads. Even the voice of his old friend was not ruffled when she met him on his way to the dentist and asked him to dinner. Someone had dropped out at the last moment. Tony Bracken (he had not forgotten that it was Tony Bracken) had been summoned to the deathbed of his great-uncle, and since Tony was the heir, he was obliged, naturally, to go when he was summoned. So, in spite of an occasional twinge, young David had braced himself with whiskey, applied laudanum to his tooth, and set out on an adventure beside which all the other occasions of his life were as flat as balloons that are pricked.

Even then, if she had not stood alone in that particular spot, between a lamp and a window, he might never have noticed her. "I wonder who she is," he thought, observing her loneliness; and then, as she raised her lowered lashes and he met her gaze, "She looks frightened." Was he called or driven when he went straight to her through the crowded room? Was it pity or the compulsion of sex that awakened while he watched her hesitate, bite her lip with a nervous tremor, and try in vain to think of something to say? "What can have frightened her?" he thought, as his hand closed over hers. Her eyes held him, and he asked, "Are you alone?" She shook her head. "No, my husband is with me." Her husband! Well, most women had husbands, especially most women one met at dinner in London. It was too late after that first look to think of a husband. It was too late to think even of children. In the end her marriage had won, as dead sounds inevitably win over living voices; but while he stood there and looked into her upturned face, that sulky, well-set-up sportsman and his two vague children had no part in the moment. Nothing mattered to him but the swift, tumultuous, utterly blissful sense of recognition —of now, here, this is my hour. Not the indefinite perhaps, tomorrow, some day in the future. The world, so colourless an instant before, had become alive to the touch. People and objects, sights, sounds, scents even, were vibrating with light.

And now, after sixty years, he could see that moment as clearly and coldly as if it were embedded in crystal. What is memory, a voice asked on the surface of thought, that it should outlast emotion? For he remembered, but he could feel nothing. Nothing of the old rapture, the wildness, the illusion of love's immortality. He still mused with remorseful sympathy of Erminia, whom he had never loved, whose death had brought him release; but the burning ecstasy of desire had left only emptiness. Only emptiness, and the gradual chill of decay. Why had it happened? What was the meaning of it all? he demanded, caught within the twisting vision of age. Why had passion strong enough to ruin his life forsaken him while he lived? Why had it left

only two diminished shapes, performing conventional gestures in a medium that was not time—that was not eternity? Did they still exist, those diminished shapes, in a timeless reality? Were they blown off from time into some transparent substance superior to duration? Did he survive there and here
5   also? Which was the real David Archbald, the lover in memory, or the old man warming his inelastic arteries in the April sunshine? Or were they both merely spirals of cosmic dust, used and discarded in some experimental design? . . .

For an hour, a single hour, of her love he would have given his life when
10 he was young. Her death had left a jagged rent in the universe. Yet if she returned to him now, he knew that it would mean only an effort—only the embarrassment that comes to persons who have loved and separated when they were young, and then meet again, unexpectedly, after they have grown old apart. Strangely enough, if any woman were to return from the dead, he
15 preferred that she should be Erminia. Were the dead like that to the old? Were the intenser desires obliterated by the duller sensations? Joy, longing, disappointment, personalities that impinged upon one another, and then, separating, left only a faint outline of dust. Life was not worth the trouble, he thought. Life was not worth the pang of being, if only that faint outline re-
20 mained. For the passion of his youth had ended as swiftly as it had begun, and at first he had not even suspected that the vehement craving was love. Helpless, bewildered, he had struggled blindly in the grasp of a power he could not resist and could not understand. All he knew was that her presence brought the world into beauty, that his whole being was a palpitating
25 ache for her when she was absent. Inarticulate, passive, without the compelling ardour of sex, she had exercised that ruthless tyranny over desire. Or was it true, as he had sometimes imagined, that he himself was a rare, or perhaps a solitary, variation from sex? Were his deeper instincts awakened only by pity? As the generations went on, would there be others and still others of
30 his breed born into an aging world? Was he more civilized than the average race of males, or simply more white-livered, as his virile grandfather believed? Well, he was too old, he repeated stubbornly, and life was too long over, to bother about what couldn't be helped. All he asked now was to sit in the April sunshine and wait for death with William beside him.
35 But was it really long over? What if it were true that some fragment of his lost ecstasy still survived there, burning with its own radiance, beyond that dim vista of time? What if it were true that such bliss, such agony, such unavailing passion, could never end? All that spring and a part of the summer they had met secretly and joyously; and their secret joy had overflowed into
40 the visible world. The landscape in which they moved borrowed the intense, quivering brightness of a place seen beneath the first or the last sunbeams. Spring was as fair as it looks to a man about to be hanged. Never again were the fields so starry with flowers, the green so luminous on the trees, the blue of the April sky so unearthly.
45 Years afterwards (sometimes as a young man in a strange bed, or again in the long fidelity to a wife he had never desired) a flitting dream of that English spring would flood his heart with an extraordinary delight. For a mo-

ment, no longer, since he invariably awoke while the joy flickered and died. Always, except in dreams, the past had escaped him. The anguish alone had stayed by him in the beginning, closer than the flesh to his bones or the nerves to his brain. And even in sleep, his bliss, when it returned, was only the tremor of light before a dawn that never approached. 5

Would it have been different if she had lived? For she had not lived, and he could never know what his life might have been without that ugly twist in the centre. They had planned to go away together, he devoured by love and longing, she fearful, passive, yielding mutely to that implacable power. In July, they would go to Venice and begin life over in Italy. The tickets were 10 bought; her few boxes were at the station; the compartment was reserved; and then the merest accident had detained them. In the middle of that last night, while she was destroying her letters, one of the children had awakened with a sore throat. The nurse had come for her; she had sat till dawn beside the crib in the nursery; and when morning came she had lost the courage for 15 flight. Fear, the old fear of life, of the unknown, had triumphed over them both.

For an eternity, it seemed to him, he walked the station platform. The guard shut the doors fast; the train drew out slowly. Still he watched with an intolerable ache of desolation while the engine was sliding over the straight 20 track to the gradual curve in the distance. Then, turning away, he wandered, distraught with misery, out into the street. Why? why? why? he demanded of a heaven that seemed as unstable as water. Overhead, low, flying clouds scudded like foam driven by wind. In the country, he walked for hours through rain vague as suspense, soft, fine, slow as mist falling. Afterwards, 25 she wrote that the struggle was over; she could not give up her children—and in the early autumn he heard from a stranger that she had drowned herself in a lake. Lost, vanished, destroyed by the fear for which he had loved her in the beginning!

When he knew that she was dead, he went alone into the country, to the 30 secret places where they had met and loved in the spring. In his memory, these places shone out suddenly, one after another, as scattered lights come out in a landscape at dusk. The woods, the fields, the stream where cowslips bloomed, the grey bench with its blurred marking, the flowers, the bright grass. Now it was spring, but in this flickering scene, he walked there in 35 autumn. Everything returned to him; the falling leaves, the trail of autumn scents in the air, everything but the vital warmth in his agony. Yet he knew, while this light flashed out and moved on again, through the encompassing darkness, that the form, if not the essence, of his passion had lain hidden somewhere beneath the surface of life. 40

In his anguish, he had flung himself beyond time, beyond space, beyond the boundaries of ultimate pain. A panic stillness was in the air; the whole external world, the blue sky, the half-bared trees, the slow fall of the leaves, the grass sprinkled with bloom,—all this was as hollow as a bubble blown from a pipe. Nothing remained alive, nothing but his despair in a universe 45 that was dead to the touch. Again and again, he had cried her name in this panic stillness. He had cried her name; but she was gone; she could never

return. Not though he waited for ever in the place she had left, could she
return to him. In the end, she had escaped the terror of life. She had escaped
his love and his pity. She had escaped into hollowness. But while the light
shone in that vacant place, every twig on the trees, every blade of grass stood
5   out illuminated.

Then this also had passed. Anguish, he discovered, was scarcely less brief
than joy. The light went out and moved on again. Days, weeks, months, years
passed, and a thick deposit of time hardened into a crust of despair over his
wound. "I do not wish to forget," he said, and in forming the thought had
10 already begun to forget and to recover. Yet, though he enjoyed life again, he
never lost entirely the feeling that he was crippled in spirit, that there was a
twisted root, an ugly scar, at the source of his being. The poet had died in
him, and with the poet had died the old living torment of pity. When he
sailed home to fight with his people, he found that the hunted buck, the
15 driven slave, the killing of men in battle, left him more annoyed than distressed. Nothing, not even death, not even dying, seemed important; yet it
was amazing to discover how much pleasure could come after one had ceased
to expect happiness. Little things began to matter supremely. A smile, a kiss,
a drink, a chance encounter in love or war. Appetite, he told himself, with
20 gay cynicism, had taken the place of desire; and it was well that it should
be so. There was much to be said in favour of living if only one were careful
not to probe deeply, not to touch life on the nerve. If only one were careful,
too, not to shatter the hardened crust of despair.

Even so, there were moments, there were hours when he was visited by
25 the old sensation of something missing, as if he were part of a circle that
was bent and distorted and broken in pieces. Life, as well as himself, seemed
to be crippled, to have lost irrevocably a part of the whole. Still, in the solitude of the night, he would awake from his dream of a bliss that hovered
near but never approached, and think, with a start of surprise, "If I awoke and
30 found her beside me, would all the broken pieces come together again? Should
I find that life was simple and right and natural and whole once more?" Then
the dream, the surprise, the pang of expectancy, would fade and mingle and
dissolve into emptiness. Like a man hopelessly ill who realizes that his malady is incurable, he would distract his mind with those blessed little things of
35 life that bear thinking about. Well, he was used to it now, he would repeat
again and again; he was used to the ache, the blankness, even to the stab of
delight which pierced him in sleep. He had accepted the sense of something
missing as a man accepts bodily disfigurement. After the first years of his
loss, he was prepared, he felt, for all the malicious pranks grief can play on
40 the memory. He was prepared even for those mocking resemblances that
beckoned him in the street, for those arrowy glimpses of her in the faces of
strange women, for that sudden wonder, poignant as a flame, "What if the
past were a delusion! What if she were within reach of my arms!" No, it had
been many years, thirty, almost forty years, since life had so mocked him.

45 He had fought through the war. Strange, how insignificant, how futile, any
war appeared to him now! He could never, not even when he took an active
part in one, understand the fascination war exercised over the human mind.

Then, when it was over, he had let life have its way with him. Though the poet in him was lost, he became in later years a prosperous attorney, and a member in good standing, so long as one did not inquire too closely, of the Episcopal Church. . . .

Sitting there in the pale sunshine, so carefully brushed and dressed by his 5 man Robert, he told himself that, in spite of the ugly twist in the centre, he had had a fair life. Nothing that he wanted, but everything that was good for him. Few men at eighty-three were able to look back upon so firm and rich a past, upon so smooth and variegated a surface. A surface! Yes, that, he realized now, was the flaw in the structure. Except for that one defeated pas- 10 sion in his youth, he had lived entirely upon the shifting surface of facts. He had been a good citizen, a successful lawyer, a faithful husband, an indulgent father; he had been, indeed, everything but himself. Always he had fallen into the right pattern; but the centre of the pattern was missing. Once again, the old heartbreaking question returned. Why and what is human personal- 15 ity? An immortal essence? A light that is never blown out? Or a breath, a murmur, the rhythm of molecular changes, scarcely more than the roving whisper of wind in the tree-tops? A multitude of women people the earth: fair women, dark women; tall women, short women; kind women, cruel women; warm women, cold 20 women; tender women, sullen women—a multitude of women, and only one among them all had been able to appease the deep unrest in his nature. Only one unit of being, one cluster of living cells, one vital ray from the sun's warmth, only one ripple in the endless cycle of time or eternity, could restore the splintered roots of his life, could bring back to him the sense of fulfilment, 25 completeness, perfection. A single personality out of the immense profusion, the infinite numbers! A reality that eluded analysis! And yet he had been happy as men use the word happiness. Rarely, since his youth, had he remem- bered that something was missing, that he had lost irrevocably a part from the whole, lost that sense of fulfilment not only in himself but in what men 30 call Divine goodness. Irrevocably—but suppose, after all, the loss were not ir- revocable! Suddenly, without warning, a wave of joy rose from the unconscious depths. Suppose that somewhere beyond, in some central radiance of being, he should find again that ecstasy he had lost without ever possessing. For one heart-beat, 35 while the wave broke and the dazzling spray flooded his thoughts, he told himself that he was immortal, that here on this green bench in the sun, he had found the confirmation of love, faith, truth, right, Divine goodness. Then, as swiftly as it had broken, the wave of joy spent itself. The glow, the surprise, the startled wonder, faded into the apathetic weariness of the end. He was 40 only an old man warming his withered flesh in the April sunshine. "My life is nearly over," he thought, "but who knows what life is in the end?" A cloud passed overhead; the changeable blue of the sky darkened and paled; a sudden wind rocked the buds on the tulip tree; and in the street, where life hurried by, a pillar of dust wavered into the air, held together an 45 instant, and then sank down and whirled in broken eddies over the pavement.

ONE WAY TO WRITE NOVELS

This essay originally appeared in the *Saturday Review of Literature,* December 8, 1934, entitled "One Way to Write Novels," the title used here. The text differs in the magazine version from that of the final version in the Virginia Edition, where it serves as the Preface to *The Sheltered Life.* This second version was reprinted in *A Certain Measure,* Harcourt, Brace, 1943, from which the present text is taken. In the division of the novels indicated in the Virginia Edition, *The Sheltered Life* is the first of the "Novels of the City"; and in *A Certain Measure* the prefaces from this group of novels are preceded by this epigraph:

What was time itself but the bloom, the sheath enfolding experience? Within time, and within time alone, there was life—the gleam, the quiver, the heartbeat, the immeasurable joy and anguish of being. . . .

Nothing, except the weather report or a general maxim of conduct, is so unsafe to rely upon as a theory of fiction. Every great novel has broken many conventions. The greatest of all novels defies every formula; and only Mr. Percy Lubbock believed that *War and Peace* would
5 be greater if it were another, and an entirely different, book. By this I do not mean to question Mr. Lubbock's critical insight. *The Craft of Fiction* is the best work in its limited field, and it may be studied to advantage by any novelist. In the first chapters there is a masterly analysis of *War and Peace.* Yet, after reading this with appreciation, I still think that Tolstoy was the best
10 judge of what his book was about and how long it should be.

This brings us, in the beginning, to the most sensitive, and, therefore, the most controversial, point in the criticism of prose fiction. It is the habit of overworked or frugal critics to speak as if economy were a virtue, and not a necessity. Yet there are faithful readers who feel with me that a good novel
15 cannot be too long or a bad novel too short. Our company is small but picked with care, and we would die upon the literary barricade defending the noble proportions of *War and Peace,* of *The Brothers Karamazov,* of *Clarissa Harlowe* in eight volumes, of *Tom Jones,* of *David Copperfield,* of *The Chronicles of Barsetshire,* of *A la Recherche du Temps Perdu,* of *Le Vicomte de*
20 *Bragelonne.* Tennyson was with us when he said he had no criticism to make of *Clarissa,* except that it might have been longer.

The true novel (I am not concerned with the run-of-the-mill variety) is, like pure poetry, an act of birth, not a device or an invention. It awaits its own time and has its own way to be born, and it cannot, by scientific meth-
25 ods, be pushed into the world from behind. After it is born, a separate individual, an organic structure, it obeys its own vital impulses. The heart quickens; the blood circulates; the pulses beat; the whole body moves in response to some inward rhythm; and in time the expanding vitality attains its full stature. But until the breath of life enters a novel, it is as spiritless as inani-
30 mate matter.

4. **Lubbock**—*Cf.* his *The Craft of Fiction,* Scribner, 1921, Chap. III. **17-20. War . . . Bragelonne**—These examples of lengthy fiction are, in order, by Tolstoi, Dostoevski, Richardson, Fielding, Dickens, Trollope, Proust, and Dumas.

Having said this much, I may confess that spinning theories of fiction is my favourite amusement. This is, I think, a good habit to cultivate. The exercise encourages readiness and agility while it keeps both head and hand in practice. Besides, if it did nothing else, it would still protect one from the radio and the moving picture and other sleepless, if less sinister, enemies to 5 the lost mood of contemplation. This alone would justify every precept that was ever evolved. Although a work of fiction may be written without a formula or a method, I doubt if the true novel has ever been created without the long brooding season.

I have read, I believe, with as much interest as if it were a novel itself, every 10 treatise on the art of fiction that appeared to me to be promising. That variable branch of letters shares with philosophy the favourite shelf in my library. I know all that such sources of learning as Sir Leslie Stephen, Sir Walter Raleigh, Mr. Percy Lubbock, Sir Arthur Quiller-Couch, Mr. E. M. Forster, and others less eminent, but often more earnest, were able to teach me, or I 15 was able to acquire. Indeed, I know more than they could teach me, for I know also how very little their knowledge can help one in the actual writing of novels. If I were giving advice to a beginner (but there are no beginners nowadays, there is only the inspired amateur or the infant pathologist), I should say, probably, something like this: "Learn the technique of writing, 20 and having learned it thoroughly, try to forget it. Study the principles of construction, the value of continuity, the arrangement of masses, the consistent point of view, the revealing episode, the careful handling of detail, and the fatal pitfalls of dialogue. Then, having mastered, if possible, every rule of thumb, dismiss it into the labyrinth of the memory. Leave it there to make 25 its own signals and flash its own warnings." The sensitive feeling, "this is not right" or "something ought to be different" will prove that these signals are working. Or, perhaps, this inner voice may be only the sounder instinct of the born novelist.

The truth is that I began being a novelist, as naturally as I began talking 30 or walking, so early that I cannot remember when the impulse first seized me. Far back in my childhood, before I had learned the letters of the alphabet, a character named Little Willie wandered into the country of my mind, just as every other major character in my novels has strolled across my mental horizon when I was not expecting him, when I was not even thinking of the novel 35 in which he would finally take his place. From what or where he had sprung, why he was named Little Willie, or why I should have selected a hero instead of a heroine—all this is still as much of a mystery to me as it was in my childhood. But there he was, and there he remained, alive and active, threading his own adventures, from the time I was three until I was seven or eight, and 40 discovered Hans Andersen and *Grimms' Fairy Tales*. Every night, as I was

13-14. Stephen . . . Forster—These works are, presumably, Sir Leslie Stephen, *Studies of a Biographer*, 4 vols., Putnam, 1898-1903 (or else *Hours in a Library*, 4 vols., 1907); Sir Walter Alexander Raleigh, *The English Novel*, Scribner, 1894; Percy Lubbock, *The Craft of Fiction;* Sir Arthur Quiller-Couch, *Charles Dickens and Other Victorians*, Putnam, 1925; E. M. Forster, *Aspects of the Novel*, Harcourt, Brace, 1927. **41. Andersen**—Hans Christian Andersen (1805-1875), Danish writer, whose "The Little Tin Soldier" is characteristic. **Grimm**—The latest edition of the *Fairy Tales* of the brothers Grimm is that based on the translation of Margaret Hunt, revised by James Stern, and illustrated in color, Pantheon Books, 1944.

undressed and put to bed by my coloured Mammy, the romance of Little
Willie would begin again exactly where it had broken off the evening before.
In winter, I was undressed in the firelight on the hearth-rug; but in summer,
we moved over to an open window, which looked out on the sunset, and
5 presently on the first stars in the long green twilight. For years Little Willie
lasted, never growing older, always pursuing his own narrative and weaving
his situations out of his own personality. I can still see him, small, wiry, with
lank brown hair like a thatch, and eyes that seemed to say, "I know a secret!
I know a secret!" Hans Andersen and the brothers Grimm were his familiar
10 companions. He returned once, though somewhat sadly, after I had read all
the Waverley Novels; but when I was twelve years old and entered the world
of Dickens, he vanished forever.

In those earliest formative years Little Willie outlined, however vaguely, a
general pattern of work. He showed me that a novelist must write, not by
15 taking thought alone, but with every cell of his being, that nothing can occur
to him that may not sooner or later find its way into his craft. Whatever happened to me or to Mammy Lizzie happened also, strangely transfigured, to
Little Willie. I learned, too, and never forgot, that ideas would not come to
me if I went out to hunt for them. They would fly when I pursued; but if I
20 stopped and sank down into a watchful reverie, they would flock back again
like friendly pigeons. All I had to do before the novel had formed was to
leave the creative faculty (or subconscious mind) free to work its own way
without urging and without effort. After Dorinda in *Barren Ground* first appeared to me, I pushed her back into some glimmering obscurity, where she
25 remained, buried but alive, for a decade, when she emerged from the yeasty
medium with hard round limbs and the bloom of health in her cheeks. Thus
I have never wanted for subjects; but on several occasions when, because of
illness or from external compulsion, I have tried to invent, rather than subconsciously create, a theme or a character, invariably the effort has resulted
30 in failure. These are the anaemic offspring of the brain, not children of my
complete being; and a brood whom I would wish, were it possible, to dis-
inherit.

It is not easy to tell how much of this dependence upon intuition may be
attributed to the lack of harmony between my inner life and my early environ-
35 ment. A thoughtful and imaginative child, haunted by that strange sense of
exile which visits the subjective mind when it is unhappily placed (and always,
apparently, it is unhappily placed or it would not be subjective), I grew up in
a charming society, where ideas were accepted as naturally as the universe or
the weather, and cards for the old, dancing for the young, and conversation
40 flavoured with personalities for the middle-aged, were the only arts practised.
Several members of my family, it is true, possessed brilliant minds, and were
widely and deeply read; but all despised what they called "local talent"; and
my early work was written in secret to escape ridicule, alert, pointed, and not
the less destructive because it was playful. There is more truth than wit in the
45 gibe that every Southern novelist must first make his reputation in the North.
Perhaps this is why so many Southern novelists write of the South as if it
were a fabulous country. When a bound copy of my first book reached me,

I hid it under my pillow while a cousin, who had run in for breakfast, prattled beside my bed of the young men who had quarrelled over the privilege of taking her to the Easter German, as the Cotillion was called. Had I entered the world by way of Oxford, or even by way of Bloomsbury, I might now be able to speak or write of my books without a feeling of outraged reserve. And 5 yet, in the very act of writing these words, my literary conscience, a nuisance to any writer, inquires if ideas were really free at Oxford, or even in Bloomsbury, at the end of the century, and if all the enfranchised spirits who nowadays babble of prohibited subjects are either wiser or better than the happy hypocrites of the 'nineties. 10

From this dubious prelude it might be inferred that I consider the craft of fiction merely another form of mental inertia. On the contrary, I agree with those writers who have found actual writing to be the hardest work in the world. What I am concerned with at the moment, however, is the beginning of a novel alone, not the endless drudgery that wrung from Stevenson the 15 complaint, "The practice of letters is miserably harassing to the mind; and after an hour or two's work, all the more human portion of an author is extinct; he will bully, backbite, and speak daggers." For being a true novelist, even if one's work is not worth the price of a cherry to public or publisher, takes all that one has to give and still something more. Yet the matter is not 20 one of choice, but of fatality. As with the enjoyment of music, or a love for El Greco, or a pleasure in gardening, or the taste for pomegranates, or a liking for Santayana's prose, the bent of nature is either there or it is not there.

For my own part, the only method I have deliberately cultivated has been 25 a system of constant renewal. If novels should be, as Sir Leslie Stephen has said, "transfigured experience," then I have endeavoured, whenever it was possible, to deepen experience and to heighten what I prefer to call illumination, to increase my understanding of that truth of life which has not ever become completely reconciled with the truth of fiction. I do not mean by this 30 that life should necessarily be eventful or filled with variable activities. Profound emotion does not inevitably bear "the pageant of a bleeding heart." Several of the most thrilling lives in all literature were lived amid the unconquerable desolation of the Yorkshire moors. Yet it is doubtful if either the exposed heart of Byron or the brazen trumpet of D. H. Lawrence contained such burn- 35 ing realities as were hidden beneath the quiet fortitude of Emily Brontë.

Because of some natural inability to observe and record instead of create, I have never used an actual scene until the impression it left had sifted down

4. **Bloomsbury**—Bloomsbury Square in London, once a center of literary life. 9-10. **happy hypocrites**—Max Beerbohm, most brilliant of the essayists in the 1890's, published *The Happy Hypocrite.* 15. **Stevenson**—Robert Louis Stevenson (1850-1894), Scottish novelist and poet. 22. **El Greco**—El Greco (Domenico Theotocopuli; d. 1614), a taste for whose paintings has had great vogue in twentieth-century America as part of the theory of distortion in art. 23. **Santayana's**—George Santayana (1863-   ), American philosopher, whose prose moves in a somewhat rarefied atmosphere. 32. **pageant . . . heart**—This phrase describing Byron, from Matthew Arnold's poem, "Stanzas from the Grande Chartreuse," is commonly used to characterize "romantic" literature of self-confession. 34. **Yorkshire moors**—home of the Brontës. 35. **Lawrence**—David Herbert Lawrence (1885-1930), English novelist, whose confessional novels are in a general sense Byronic. 36. **Emily Brontë**—(1818-1848), author of *Wuthering Heights.*

into imagined surroundings. A theme becomes real to me only after it is
clothed in living values; but these values must be drawn directly from the
imagination and indirectly, if at all, from experience. Invariably the characters
appear first, and slowly and gradually build up their own world, and spin
5   the situation and atmosphere out of themselves. Strangely enough, the horizon
of this real or visionary world is limited by the impressions or recollections
of my early childhood. If I were to walk out into the country and pick a scene
for a book, it would remain as flat and lifeless as cardboard; but the places I
loved or hated between the ages of three and thirteen compose an inexhaust-
10 ible landscape of memory. Occasionally, it is true, I have returned to a scene
to verify details, though for freshness and force I have trusted implicitly to
the vision within. And just as my scene is built up from fragments of the
past, whether that past existed in fact or in a dream, so the human figures,
though not one of them has been copied from my acquaintances, will startle
15 me by displaying a familiar trait or gesture, and I will recognize with a shock
some special blending of characteristics.

Frequently these impressions had been buried so long and so deep that I
had entirely forgotten them until they floated upward to the surface of
thought. Yet they were not dead but living, and recovered warmth and anima-
20 tion after the creative faculty had revived them. In the same way, half-obliter-
ated images, events, or episodes, observed in moments of intense experience,
will flash back into a scene or a figure; and this is equally true of the most
trivial detail my memory has registered. For example, in one of the tragic
hours of my youth, I looked out of a window and saw two sparrows quarrel-
25 ling in the rain on a roof. Twenty years or more afterwards, a character in
one of my novels looks out of a window, in a moment of heartbreak, and
sees two sparrows quarrelling in the rain. And immediately, light streamed
back, as if it were cast by the rays of a lantern, into the unlit recesses of memory, and I felt the old grief in my heart, and saw the rain fall on the roof
30 and the two sparrows quarrelling there.

Because everything one has seen or heard or thought or felt leaves a deposit
that never filters entirely through the essence of mind, I believe a novelist
should be perpetually engaged in this effort to refresh and replenish his source.
I am confident, moreover, that nothing I have learned either from life or
35 from literature has been wasted. Whatever I have thought or felt deeply has
stayed with me, if only in fragments or in a distillation of memory. But the
untiring critic within has winnowed, reassorted, and disposed the material I
needed.

Not until the unconscious worker has withdrawn from the task, or taken
40 a brief holiday, and the characters have woven their own background and
circumstances, does the actual drudgery of moulding the mass-substance begin.
Even now, after the groundwork is completed and the subject assembled, I
still give time and thought (brooding is the more accurate term) to the construction. I try to avoid hastening the process, and to leave the invisible agent
45 free to flash directions or warnings. The book must have a form. This is essential. It may be shaped like a mill-stone or an hour-glass or an Indian toma-
hawk or a lace fan—but a shape it must have. Usually a novel assumes its own

figure when it enters the world, and the underlying idea moulds the plastic material to its own structure. More deliberately, the point of view is considered and selected, though this may, and often does, proceed naturally from the unities of time and place, or from one completely dominant figure. In *Barren Ground,* a long novel, I felt from the moment Dorinda entered the book that here could be but one point of view. From the first page to the last, no scene or episode or human figure appears outside her field of vision or imagination.

In *The Sheltered Life,* where I knew intuitively that the angle of vision must create the form, I employed two points of view alone, though they were separated by the whole range of experience. Age and youth look on the same scene, the same persons, the same events and occasions, the same tragedy in the end. Between these conflicting points of view the story flows on, as a stream flows in a narrow valley. Nothing happens that is not seen, on one side, through the steady gaze of the old man, seeing life as it is, and, on the other side, by the troubled eyes of the young girl, seeing life as she would wish it to be. Purposely, I have tried here to interpret reality through the dissimilar mediums of thought and emotion. I have been careful to allow no other aspects to impinge on the contrasting visions which create between them the organic whole of the book. This convention, which appears uncertain, when one thinks of it, becomes natural, and even involuntary, when the work grows, develops, pushes out with its own energy, and finds its own tempo.

Patiently, but without success, I have tried to trace the roots of *The Sheltered Life.* The background is that of my girlhood, and the rudiments of the theme must have lain buried somewhere in my consciousness. But I can recall no definite beginning or voluntary act of creation. One moment there was a mental landscape without figures; the next moment, as if they had been summoned by the stroke of a bell, all the characters trooped in together, with every contour, every feature, every attitude, every gesture and expression, complete. In their origin, I exerted no control over them. They were too real for dismemberment; but I could, and I did, select or eliminate whatever in their appearances or behavior seemed to conflict with the general scheme of the book. It was my part to see that the unities were recognized and obeyed.

It is only logical to infer that when a group of imaginary beings assembles, there must be a motive, or at least an adequate reason, for the particular gathering. I knew, or thought I knew, that no visitor had ever entered my mind without a definite cause. These people were there, I felt, according to a design, for a planned attack upon life, and to push them out of the way would spur them to more vehement activity. It was best to ignore them, and this, as nearly as possible, was the course I pursued. Sooner or later, they would let me know why they had come, and what I was expected to do. For me, they were already alive, though I could not as yet distinguish the intricate ties that bound this isolated group into a detached segment of life. So this state of affairs continued for several years. Another novel, *They Stooped to Folly,* engaged my attention, while some distant range of my imagination was still occupied by the Birdsongs and the Archbalds.

Then, at last, *They Stooped to Folly* was finished, was over. Presently it

was published; and in company with all my other books that had gone out into the world, it became a homeless wanderer and a stranger. It had ceased to belong to me. I might almost say that it had ceased even to interest me. The place where it had been, the place it had filled to overflowing for nearly
5   three years, was now empty. Were there no other inhabitants? What had become of those troublesome intruders I had once banished to some vague Siberia of the mind?

It was at this crucial instant that the Birdsongs and the Archbalds, under their own names, and wearing their own outward semblances, escaped from
10   remote exile. While I waited, in that unhappy brooding season, which cannot be forced, which cannot be hurried, the vacant scene was flooded with light and animation, and the emerging figures began to breathe, move, speak, and round out their own destinies. I knew instantly, as soon as they returned, what the integral drama would be and why it had occurred. The theme was im-
15   plicit in the inevitable title. Beyond this, I saw a shallow and aimless society of happiness-hunters, who lived in a perpetual flight from reality, and grasped at any effort-saving illusion of passion or pleasure. Against this background of futility was projected the contrasting character of General Archbald, a lover of wisdom, a humane and civilized soul, oppressed by the burden of tragic
20   remembrance. The stream of events would pass before him, for he would re- main permanently at the centre of vision, while, opposing him on the farther side, he would meet the wide, blank, unreflective gaze of inexperience.

In a sudden wholeness of perception, one of those complex apprehensions which come so seldom, yet possess a miraculous power of conviction, I saw
25   the meaning, not only of these special figures, but of their essential place in this theme of age and youth, of the past and the present. They had been drawn together by some sympathetic attraction, or by some deeper sense of recognition in my own consciousness. My task was the simple one of extract- ing from the situation every thread of significance, every quiver of vitality,
30   every glimmer of understanding. The contours were moulded. I could see the articulation of the parts, as well as the shape of the structure. I could see, too, the fragile surface of a style that I must strive, however unsuccessfully, to make delicate yet unbreakable. I could feel the peculiar density of light and shadow. I could breathe in that strange symbolic smell which was woven and
35   interwoven through the gradually thickening atmosphere of the scene.

As at least one critic has recognized, the old man, left behind by the years, is the central character of the book; and into his lonely spirit I have put much of my ultimate feeling about life. He represents the tragedy, wherever it ap- pears, of the civilized man in a world that is not civilized. And even the title,
40   which I have called inevitable, implies no special age or place. What it im- plies, to me, is the effort of one human being to stand between another and life. In a larger sense, as this critic perceives, the same tragedy was being re- peated in spheres far wider than Queenborough. The First World War was beginning and men were killing each other from the highest possible ideals.
45   This is the final scope of the book's theme. The old man, his point of view,

43. **Queenborough**—fictional equivalent of Richmond, Virginia, in Miss Glasgow's novels. **First World War**—beginning in 1914.

his thwarted strong body, saw the age pass by him. Not in the South especially; it was throughout the world that ideas, forms, were changing, the familiar order going, the beliefs and certainties. The shelter for men's lives, of religion, convention, social prejudice, was at the crumbling point, just as was the case with the little human figures in the story. . . .   5

While I am at work on a book I remain, or try to remain, in a state of immersion. The first draft of a novel, if it is long, will take two years, and still another year is required for the final writing. All this time the imaginary setting becomes the native country of my mind, and the characters are seldom out of my thoughts. I live with them day and night; they are more real to   10
me than acquaintances in the flesh. In our nursery copy of *Gulliver's Travels* there was a picture which seems, when I recall it now, to illustrate my predicament in the final draft of a novel. Gulliver lies bound in threads, while the Lilliputians swarm over him and hamper his struggles. So words swarm over me and hamper my efforts to seize the right one among them, to find   15
the right rhythm, the right tone, the right accent. But, here again, intuition, or perhaps only a flare of organized memory, will come to my aid. Often, when I have searched for hours for some special word or phrase, and given up in despair, I have awakened with a start in the night, because the hunted word or phrase had darted into my mind while I was asleep.   20

Nevertheless, it is the act of scrupulous revision (the endless pruning and trimming for the sake of a valid and flexible prose style) that provides the writer's best solace even while it makes drudgery. Every literary craftsman who respects his work has, I dare say, this same feeling, and remains restless and wandering in mind until, in the beginning, he has entered the right cli-   25
mate and, at the end, has tracked down the right word. Although my characters may develop traits or actions I had not anticipated, though scenes may shift and alter in perspective, and new episodes may spring out on the way, still the end shines always as the solitary fixed star above the flux of creation. I have never written the first word of the first sentence until I knew what   30
the last word of the last sentence would be. Sometimes I may rewrite the beginning many times, as I did in *They Stooped to Folly,* and sometimes (though this has actually occurred but once) a shorter book like *The Romantic Comedians,* completely realized before pen was put to paper, may ripple out, of itself, with its own energy. Yet in the difficult first chapter   35
of *They Stooped to Folly,* I could still look ahead, over a procession of characters that had slipped from my control, to the subdued scene at the end, while the concluding paragraph of *The Romantic Comedians* echoed the keynote of the book, and reflected the ironic mood.

The final words to be said of any activity will always be, I suppose, was it   40
worth what it cost? Well, the writing of fiction is worth, I imagine, exactly what digging a ditch or charting the heavens may be worth to the worker, which is not a penny more or less than the release of mind that it brings. Although I may not speak as an authority, at least I can speak from long perseverance. I became a novelist before I was old enough to resist, and I remained   45

11. **Gulliver's Travels**—For this episode see Gulliver's first voyage—that to Lilliput.

a novelist because no other enterprise in life has afforded me the same interest, or provided me with equal contentment. It is true that I have written
only for the biased judgment within; but this inner critic has held up an
unattainable standard, and has infused a moderate zest of adventure into what
5 may appear, on the surface, to be merely another humdrum way of earning a
livelihood. Still, to a beginner who is young and cherishes an ambition to be
celebrated, I should recommend the short cut (or royal road) through the
radio and Hollywood; and certainly more than one creative writer, in search
of swift economic security, would do well to buy a new broom and to set out
10 for the next crossing. But, incredible as it may appear in this practical decade,
there are novelists so wanting in a sense of proper values that they place artistic integrity above the voice on the air, the flash on the screen, and the dividends in the bank. There are others who possess an unreasoning faith in their
own work; and there are yet others endowed with a comic spirit so robust,
15 or so lively, that it can find diversion anywhere, even in our national exaltation of the inferior. To this happy company of neglected novelists, the ironic
art of fiction will reveal its own special delights, and may even, as the years
pass, yield its own sufficient, if imponderable, rewards.

In looking back through a long vista, I can see that what I have called the
20 method of constant renewal may be reduced to three ruling principles. Obedience to this self-imposed discipline has enabled me to write novels for nearly
forty years, and yet to feel that the substance from which I draw material and
energy is as fresh today as it was in my first youthful failure. As time moves
on, I still see life in beginnings, moods in conflict, and change as the only
25 permanent law. But the value of these qualities (which may be self-deluding,
and are derived, in fact, more from temperament than from technique) has
been mellowed by long saturation with experience—by that essence of reality
which one distils from life only after it has been lived.

Among the many strange superstitions of the age of science revels the cheer-
30 ful belief that immaturity alone is enough. Pompous illiteracy, escaped from
some Freudian cage, is in the saddle, and the voice of the amateur is the voice
of authority. When we turn to the field of prose fiction, we find that it is
filled with literary sky-rockets sputtering out in the fog. But the trouble with
sky-rockets has always been that they do not stay up in the air. One has only
35 to glance back over the post-war years to discover that the roads of the jazz
age are matted thick with fireworks which went off too soon. To the poet,
it is true, especially if he can arrange with destiny to die young, the glow of
adolescence may impart an unfading magic. But the novel (which must be
conceived with a subdued rapture, or with none at all, or even with the un-
40 poetic virtues of industry and patience) requires more substantial ingredients
than a little ignorance of life and a great yearning to tell everything one has
never known. When I remember Defoe, the father of us all, I am persuaded

---

31. **Freudian cage**—The theories of Sigmund Freud (1856-1939), Austrian psychiatrist,
which include the doctrine that the mind consciously or otherwise "cages" or suppresses dark and
unlovely motives, thoughts, and emotions, have had a profound influence on American fiction.
35-36. **jazz age**—the 1920's. 42. **Defoe**—Daniel Defoe (1661-1731) is "the father of us all" in
the sense that he was perhaps the first professional writer of fiction in English literature.

that the novelist who has harvested well the years, and laid by a rich store of experience, will find his latter period the ripening time of his career.

Transposed into an impersonal method, the three rules of which I have spoken may be so arranged:

1. Always wait between books for the springs to fill up and flow over.　　　5

2. Always preserve, within a wild sanctuary, an inaccessible valley of reveries.

3. Always, and as far as it is possible, endeavour to touch life on every side; but keep the central vision of the mind, the inmost light, untouched and untouchable.　　　10

In my modest way, these rules have helped me, not only to pursue the one calling for which I was designed alike by character and inclination, but even to enjoy the prolonged study of a world that, as the sardonic insight of Henry Adams perceived, no "sensitive and timid natures could regard without a shudder."　　　15

ROBERT FROST

1874-

I. "A BOY'S WILL" (1874–1915)

1874 Born in San Francisco, March 26, son of William P. Frost, Jr., and Isabelle Moodie Frost, New Englanders, and christened Robert Lee Frost.

1885 After father's death, taken to Lawrence, Massachusetts, farm.

1890 Published first poem "La Noche Triste" in Lawrence High School *Bulletin*. Became a bobbin boy in a cotton mill; also made shoes.

1892 Attended Dartmouth College a short time, but gave it up to edit a country newspaper, to teach school, and to farm.

1895 Married Elinor White, December 28, rival valedictorian in high school and his basic inspiration until her death in 1938.

1897–1899 Attended Harvard College, without taking a degree. His poetry declined by leading magazines, 1890-1910.

1900–1909 Farmed near Derry, New Hampshire, reared four children, taught English at Pinkerton Academy, 1906-1911, and psychology at State Normal School.

1912–1915 Sold farm and moved to England, where he enjoyed friendship of Lascelles Abercrombie, Wilfred Gibson, and Rupert Brooke.

1913 *A Boy's Will,* published in England.

1914 *North of Boston,* which established his reputation.

1915 Returned to the United States and settled on a farm near Franconia, New Hampshire.

II. "MOUNTAIN INTERVAL" (1916–1933)

1916 Published *Mountain Interval.* Read Phi Beta Kappa poem "The Axe-Helve" at Harvard University. Member of Amherst College faculty, 1916-1920.

1920 Co-founder of The Bread Loaf School of English, Middlebury, Vermont.

1921–1923 Poet in Residence at the University of Michigan. Published *Selected Poems,* 1923; revised, 1928.

1923–1925 Professor of English, Amherst College; also in 1936-1938. *New Hampshire* (1923) won the Pulitzer Prize in 1924.

1926–1927 Visiting Professor at Wesleyan, Amherst, Michigan, Dartmouth.

1928 Published *West-Running Brook.* Revisited England.

1929 *A Way Out,* a prose play.

1930 *Collected Poems* published; awarded Pulitzer Prize, 1931. Elected a member of American Academy of Arts and Letters.

1933 Associate Fellow at Yale University.

III. "A FURTHER RANGE" (1933–   )

1936 *A Further Range;* awarded Pulitzer Prize, 1937. Appointed Charles Eliot
      Norton Professor of Poetry for 1936, Harvard University.
1938 Holder of Ralph Waldo Emerson Fellowship, Harvard University. Death of
      Mrs. Frost.
1939 A new edition of *Collected Poems.*
1942 *A Witness Tree;* won Pulitzer Prize, 1943.
1943 Fellow in Humanities, Dartmouth College.
1945 *A Masque of Reason.*
1947 *Steeple Bush* and *A Masque of Mercy.*
1949 *Complete Poems of Robert Frost.*

BIOGRAPHIES AND CRITICISM: Amy Lowell, *Tendencies in Modern American Poetry,*
    Houghton Mifflin, 1917; P. H. Boynton, *Some Contemporary Americans,*
    University of Chicago Press, 1924; G. B. Munson, *Robert Frost,* Holt, 1927;
    John Freeman in J. C. Squires' *Contemporary American Authors,* Holt,
    1928; Sidney Cox, *Robert Frost, Original "Ordinary Man,"* Holt, 1929;
    C. Ford, *The Less Traveled Road, A Study of Robert Frost,* Harvard Uni-
    versity Press, 1935; Mark Van Doren, "The Permanence of Robert Frost,"
    American Scholar, March, 1936; R. S. Newdick, "The Early Verse of Robert
    Frost and Some of His Revisions," *American Literature,* May, 1935, and
    "Robert Frost and the Sound of Sense," *American Literature,* November,
    1937; Richard Thornton, ed., *Recognition of Robert Frost,* Holt, 1937; R. P. T.
    Coffin, *New Poetry of New England: Frost and Robinson,* Johns Hopkins
    University Press, 1938; H. H. Waggoner, "The Humanistic Idealism of
    Robert Frost," *American Literature,* November, 1941; L. R. Thompson, *Fire
    and Ice,* Holt, 1942; Malcolm Cowley, "Frost: A Dissenting Opinion," *New
    Republic,* September 11, September 18, 1944.
BIBLIOGRAPHY AND EDITIONS: W. B. Clymer and C. R. Green, *Robert Frost,* the
    chief bibliography, was published by the Jones Library, Amherst, 1937. See
    also Louis and Esther Mertins, *The Intervals of Robert Frost, A Critical Bib-
    liography,* University of California, 1947. *Collected Poems* (Holt), pub-
    lished in 1930, was reissued with additions in 1939 and 1949. *Selected Poems,*
    Holt, 1923, 1934, 1936 (London).

Frost, like Robinson, has little concern for institutional life, or for reform, or
even for wild nature; instead, his poetry is close to daily living, to the comedies and
tragedies and the philosophy of hard-handed folk. He has the power of integrating
his work with the country as few poets have been able to do; he is as indigenous
to New England as its granitic countryside, its woodpiles and dusty blueberries, as
apple picking and mending wall. His lines are said rather than sung; they have the
accents of the cranky humor and stern gravity of folk speech. They have wisdom,
too, the power of revelation that is time's last gift to the mature mind.

Much as Frost loves the soil and his neighbors, he writes for the sophisticated
as well as for the many who naïvely enjoy the conversational tone of his verse. He
takes a tentative, critical attitude toward experience, and though he may sympathize with the conventions, is never deceived by them. He likes to entertain an idea.
He will take a young colt, a mower, a mountain, and make it a symbol of something deeper than itself. He has described poetry as "words that have become
deeds." His is not a whimsical mind at play but a searching mind in meditation.

There is a wistful trying to make something of things that gives his poetry a touch of irony. For him "a poem begins with a lump in the throat; a homesickness or a lovesickness. It is a reaching-out toward expression; an effort to find fulfilment" that ends "in a clarification of life . . . a momentary stay against confusion." Life as he accepts it and dramatizes it is often tragic, though not without a frugal, gallant hope. He is, in his own words, "a pursuitist, not an escapist."

THE TUFT OF FLOWERS

Written in 1904; first published in *A Boy's Will*, 1913. *Cf.* Wordsworth's "the meanest flower that blows" . . .

I went to turn the grass once after one
Who mowed it in the dew before the sun.

The dew was gone that made his blade so keen
Before I came to view the levelled scene.

I looked for him behind an isle of trees;   5
I listened for his whetstone on the breeze.

But he had gone his way, the grass all mown,
And I must be, as he had been,—alone,

'As all must be,' I said within my heart,
'Whether they work together or apart.'   10

But as I said it, swift there passed me by
On noiseless wing a bewildered butterfly,

Seeking with memories grown dim o'er night
Some resting flower of yesterday's delight.

And once I marked his flight go round and round,   15
As where some flower lay withering on the ground.

And then he flew as far as eye could see,
And then on tremulous wing came back to me.

I thought of questions that have no reply,
And would have turned to toss the grass to dry;   20

But he turned first, and led my eye to look
At a tall tuft of flowers beside a brook,

A leaping tongue of bloom the scythe had spared
Beside a reedy brook the scythe had bared.

I left my place to know them by their name,   25
Finding them butterfly weed when I came.

The mower in the dew had loved them thus,
By leaving them to flourish, not for us,

Nor yet to draw one thought of ours to him,
But from sheer morning gladness at the brim.   30

The butterfly and I had lit upon,
Nevertheless, a message from the dawn,

That made me hear the wakening birds around,
And hear his long scythe whispering to the ground,

And feel a spirit kindred to my own;   35
So that henceforth I worked no more alone;

But glad with him, I worked as with his aid,
And weary, sought at noon with him the shade;

And dreaming, as it were, held brotherly speech
With one whose thought I had not hoped to reach.   40

'Men work together,' I told him from the heart,
'Whether they work together or apart.'

MENDING WALL

Written in 1913 and published in *North of Boston,* 1914. Based on the custom of New England farmers to replace stones dislodged from fences by winter's "ground-swell" or by hunters. The neighbor is unimaginative and conventional.

Something there is that doesn't love a wall,
That sends the frozen-ground-swell under it,
And spills the upper boulders in the sun;
And makes gaps even two can pass abreast.
The work of hunters is another thing: 5
I have come after them and made repair
Where they have left not one stone on a stone,
But they would have the rabbit out of hiding,
To please the yelping dogs. The gaps I mean,
No one has seen them made or heard them made,   10
But at spring mending-time we find them there.
I let my neighbour know beyond the hill;
And on a day we meet to walk the line
And set the wall between us once again.
We keep the wall between us as we go.   15
To each the boulders that have fallen to each.
And some are loaves and some so nearly balls
We have to use a spell to make them balance:
'Stay where you are until our backs are turned!'
We wear our fingers rough with handling them.   20

Oh, just another kind of out-door game,
One on a side. It comes to little more:
There where it is we do not need the wall:
He is all pine and I am apple orchard.
My apple trees will never get across   25
And eat the cones under his pines, I tell him.
He only says, 'Good fences make good neighbours.'
Spring is the mischief in me, and I wonder
If I could put a notion in his head:
'*Why* do they make good neighbours? Isn't it   30
Where there are cows? But here there are no cows.
Before I built a wall I'd ask to know
What I was walling in or walling out,
And to whom I was like to give offence.
Something there is that doesn't love a wall,   35
That wants it down.' I could say 'Elves' to him,
But it's not elves exactly, and I'd rather
He said it for himself. I see him there
Bringing a stone grasped firmly by the top
In each hand, like an old-stone savage armed.   40
He moves in darkness as it seems to me,
Not of woods only and the shade of trees.
He will not go behind his father's saying,
And he likes having thought of it so well
He says again, 'Good fences make good neighbours.'   45

THE FEAR

Printed in *Poetry and Drama*, December, 1913, and collected in *North of Boston*,
1914. An eloping couple fears a figure met in the road at night.

A lantern light from deeper in the barn
Shone on a man and woman in the door
And threw their lurching shadows on a house
Near by, all dark in every glossy window.
A horse's hoof pawed once the hollow floor,   5
And the back of the gig they stood beside
Moved in a little. The man grasped a wheel,
The woman spoke out sharply, 'Whoa, stand still!
I saw it just as plain as a white plate,'
She said, 'as the light on the dashboard ran   10
Along the bushes at the roadside—a man's face.
You *must* have seen it too.'

                          'I didn't see it.

Are you sure—'

          'Yes, I'm sure!'

                    '—it was a face?'

'Joel, I'll have to look. I can't go in,
I can't, and leave a thing like that unsettled.   15
Doors locked and curtains drawn will make no difference.
I always have felt strange when we came home
To the dark house after so long an absence,
And the key rattled loudly into place
Seemed to warn someone to be getting out   20
At one door as we entered at another.
What if I'm right, and someone all the time—
Don't hold my arm!'

                'I say it's someone passing.'

'You speak as if this were a travelled road.
You forget where we are. What is beyond   25
That he'd be going to or coming from
At such an hour of night, and on foot too?
What was he standing still for in the bushes?'

'It's not so very late—it's only dark.
There's more in it than you're inclined to say.   30
Did he look like—?'
              'He looked like anyone.
I'll never rest tonight unless I know.
Give me the lantern.'

            'You don't want the lantern.'

She pushed past him and got it for herself.

'You're not to come,' she said. 'This is my business.   35
If the time's come to face it, I'm the one
To put it the right way. He'd never dare—
Listen! He kicked a stone. Hear that, hear that!
He's coming towards us. Joel, go in—please.
Hark!—I don't hear him now. But please go in.'   40

'In the first place you can't make me believe it's—'

'It is—or someone else he's sent to watch.
And now's the time to have it out with him
While we know definitely where he is.
Let him get off and he'll be everywhere   45
Around us, looking out of trees and bushes
Till I sha' n't dare to set a foot outdoors.
And I can't stand it. Joel, let me go!'

'But it's nonsense to think he'd care enough.'

'You mean you couldn't understand his caring.   50
Oh, but you see he hadn't had enough—
Joel, I won't—I won't—I promise you.
We mustn't say hard things. You mustn't either.'

'I'll be the one, if anybody goes!
But you give him the advantage with this light.   55
What couldn't he do to us standing here!
And if to see was what he wanted, why
He has seen all there was to see and gone.'

He appeared to forget to keep his hold,
But advanced with her as she crossed the grass.   60

'What do you want?' she cried to all the dark.
She stretched up tall to overlook the light
That hung in both hands hot against her skirt.

'There's no one; so you're wrong,' he said.

        'There is.—
What do you want?' she cried, and then herself   65
Was startled when an answer really came.

'Nothing.' It came from well along the road.

She reached a hand to Joel for support:
The smell of scorching woollen made her faint.

'What are you doing round this house at night?'   70

'Nothing.' A pause: there seemed no more to say.

And then the voice again: 'You seem afraid.
I saw by the way you whipped up the horse.
I'll just come forward in the lantern light
And let you see.'

    'Yes, do.—Joel, go back!'   75

She stood her ground against the noisy steps
That came on, but her body rocked a little.

'You see,' the voice said.

      'Oh.' She looked and looked.

'You don't see—I've a child here by the hand.
A robber wouldn't have his family with him.'   80

'What's a child doing at this time of night—?'

'Out walking. Every child should have the memory
Of at least one long-after-bedtime walk.
What, son?'

'Then I should think you'd try to find   85
Somewhere to walk—'

'The highway, as it happens—
We're stopping for the fortnight down at Dean's.'

'But if that's all—Joel—you realize—
You won't think anything. You understand?
You understand that we have to be careful.   90
This is a very, very lonely place.
Joel!' She spoke as if she couldn't turn.
The swinging lantern lengthened to the ground,
It touched, it struck, it clattered and went out.

THE ROAD NOT TAKEN

Printed in the *Atlantic Monthly,* August, 1915, and collected in *Mountain Interval,* 1916.

Two roads diverged in a yellow wood,
And sorry I could not travel both
And be one traveler, long I stood
And looked down one as far as I could
To where it bent in the undergrowth;   5

Then took the other, as just as fair,
And having perhaps the better claim,
Because it was grassy and wanted wear;
Though as for that the passing there
Had worn them really about the same,   10

And both that morning equally lay
In leaves no step had trodden black.
Oh, I kept the first for another day!
Yet knowing how way leads on to way,
I doubted if I should ever come back.   15

I shall be telling this with a sigh
Somewhere ages and ages hence:
Two roads diverged in a wood, and I—
I took the one less traveled by,
And that has made all the difference.   20

AN OLD MAN'S WINTER NIGHT

Published in *Mountain Interval,* 1916.

All out of doors looked darkly in at him
Through the thin frost, almost in separate stars,
That gathers on the pane in empty rooms.
What kept his eyes from giving back the gaze
Was the lamp tilted near them in his hand.   5

What kept him from remembering the need
That brought him to that creaking room was age.
He stood with barrels round him—at a loss.
And having scared the cellar under him
In clomping there, he scared it once again   10
In clomping off;—and scared the outer night,
Which has its sounds, familiar, like the roar
Of trees and crack of branches, common things,
But nothing so like beating on a box.
A light he was to no one but himself   15
Where now he sat, concerned with he knew what,
A quiet light, and then not even that.
He consigned to the moon, such as she was,
So late-arising, to the broken moon
As better than the sun in any case   20
For such a charge, his snow upon the roof,
His icicles along the wall to keep;
And slept. The log that shifted with a jolt
Once in the stove, disturbed him and he shifted,
And eased his heavy breathing, but still slept.   25
One aged man—one man—can't fill a house,
A farm, a countryside, or if he can,
It's thus he does it of a winter night.

'OUT, OUT—'

Printed in *McClure's Magazine,* July 16, 1916, and collected in *Mountain Interval,* 1916.

The buzz-saw snarled and rattled in the yard
And made dust and dropped stove-length sticks of wood,
Sweet-scented stuff when the breeze drew across it.
And from there those that lifted eyes could count
Five mountain ranges one behind the other   5
Under the sunset far into Vermont.
And the saw snarled and rattled, snarled and rattled,
As it ran light, or had to bear a load.
And nothing happened: day was all but done.
Call it a day, I wish they might have said   10
To please the boy by giving him the half hour
That a boy counts so much when saved from work.
His sister stood beside them in her apron
To tell them 'Supper.' At the word, the saw,
As if to prove saws knew what supper meant,   15
Leaped out at the boy's hand, or seemed to leap—
He must have given the hand. However it was,
Neither refused the meeting. But the hand!
The boy's first outcry was a rueful laugh,
As he swung toward them holding up the hand   20
Half in appeal, but half as if to keep

The life from spilling. Then the boy saw all—
Since he was old enough to know, big boy
Doing a man's work, though a child at heart—
He saw all spoiled. 'Don't let him cut my hand off—   25
The doctor, when he comes. Don't let him, sister!'
So. But the hand was gone already.
The doctor put him in the dark of ether.
He lay and puffed his lips out with his breath.
And then—the watcher at his pulse took fright.   30
No one believed. They listened at his heart.
Little—less—nothing!—and that ended it.
No more to build on there. And they, since they
Were not the one dead, turned to their affairs.

SNOW

Printed in *Poetry,* November, 1916, and collected in *Mountain Interval,* 1916.

The three stood listening to a fresh access
Of wind that caught against the house a moment,
Gulped snow, and then blew free again—the Coles
Dressed, but dishevelled from some hours of sleep,
Meserve belittled in the great skin coat he wore.   5

Meserve was first to speak. He pointed backward
Over his shoulder with his pipe-stem, saying,
'You can just see it glancing off the roof
Making a great scroll upward toward the sky,
Long enough for recording all our names on.—   10
I think I'll just call up my wife and tell her
I'm here—so far—and starting on again.
I'll call her softly so that if she's wise
And gone to sleep, she needn't wake to answer.'
Three times he barely stirred the bell, then listened.   15
'Why, Lett, still up? Lett, I'm at Cole's. I'm late.
I called you up to say Good-night from here
Before I went to say Good-morning there.—
I thought I would.—I know, but, Lett—I know—
I could, but what's the sense? The rest won't be   20
So bad.—Give me an hour for it.—Ho, ho,
Three hours to here! But that was all up hill;
The rest is down.—Why no, no, not a wallow:
They kept their heads and took their time to it
Like darlings, both of them. They're in the barn.—   25
My dear, I'm coming just the same. I didn't
Call you to ask you to invite me home.—'
He lingered for some word she wouldn't say,
Said it at last himself, 'Good-night,' and then
Getting no answer, closed the telephone.   30
The three stood in the lamplight round the table

With lowered eyes a moment till he said,
'I'll just see how the horses are.'

                              'Yes, do,'
Both the Coles said together. Mrs. Cole
Added: 'You can judge better after seeing.—   35
I want you here with me, Fred. Leave him here,
Brother Meserve. You know to find your way
Out through the shed.'

                         'I guess I know my way,
I guess I know where I can find my name
Carved in the shed to tell me who I am   40
If it don't tell me where I am. I used
To play—'

           'You tend your horses and come back.
Fred Cole, you're going to let him!'

                              'Well, aren't you?
How can you help yourself?'

                              'I called him Brother.

Why did I call him that?'

                              'It's right enough.   45
That's all you ever heard him called round here.
He seems to have lost off his Christian name.'

'Christian enough I should call that myself.
He took no notice, did he? Well, at least
I didn't use it out of love of him,   50
The dear knows. I detest the thought of him
With his ten children under ten years old.
I hate his wretched little Racker Sect,
All's ever I heard of it, which isn't much.
But that's not saying— Look, Fred Cole, it's twelve,   55
Isn't it, now? He's been here half an hour.
He says he left the village store at nine.
Three hours to do four miles—a mile an hour
Or not much better. Why, it doesn't seem
As if a man could move that slow and move.   60
Try to think what he did with all that time.
And three miles more to go!'

                              'Don't let him go.
Stick to him, Helen. Make him answer you.
That sort of man talks straight on all his life
From the last thing he said himself, stone deaf   65

53. **Racker Sect**—an idealistic group of which Meserve is the dictatorial pastor.

To anything anyone else may say.
I should have thought, though, you could make him hear you.'

'What is he doing out a night like this?
Why can't he stay at home?'

                          'He had to preach.'

'It's no night to be out.'

                    'He may be small,   70
He may be good, but one thing's sure, he's tough.'

'And strong of stale tobacco.'

                          'He'll pull through.'

'You only say so. Not another house
Or shelter to put into from this place
To theirs. I'm going to call his wife again.'   75

'Wait and he may. Let's see what he will do.
Let's see if he will think of her again.
But then I doubt he's thinking of himself.
He doesn't look on it as anything.'

'He shan't go—there!'

                    'It *is* a night, my dear.'   80

'One thing: he didn't drag God into it.'

'He don't consider it a case for God.'

'You think so, do you? You don't know the kind.
He's getting up a miracle this minute.
Privately—to himself, right now, he's thinking   85
He'll make a case of it if he succeeds,
But keep still if he fails.'

                    'Keep still all over.
He'll be dead—dead and buried.'

                          'Such a trouble!
Not but I've every reason not to care
What happens to him if it only takes   90
Some of the sanctimonious conceit
Out of one of those pious scalawags.'

'Nonsense to that! You want to see him safe.'

'You like the runt.'

         'Don't you a little?'

                                   'Well,
I don't like what he's doing, which is what   95
You like, and like him for.'

                        'Oh, yes you do.
You like your fun as well as anyone;
Only you women have to put these airs on
To impress men. You've got us so ashamed
Of being men we can't look at a good fight   100
Between two boys and not feel bound to stop it.
Let the man freeze an ear or two, I say.—
He's here. I leave him all to you. Go in
And save his life.—All right, come in, Meserve.
Sit down, sit down. How did you find the horses?'   105

'Fine, fine.'

             'And ready for some more? My wife here
Says it won't do. You've got to give it up.'

'Won't you to please me? Please! If I say please?
Mr. Meserve, I'll leave it to *your* wife.
What *did* your wife say on the telephone?'   110

Meserve seemed to heed nothing but the lamp
Or something not far from it on the table.
By straightening out and lifting a forefinger,
He pointed with his hand from where it lay
Like a white crumpled spider on his knee: 115
'That leaf there in your open book! It moved
Just then, I thought. It's stood erect like that,
There on the table, ever since I came,
Trying to turn itself backward or forward,
I've had my eye on it to make out which;   120
If forward, then it's with a friend's impatience—
You see I know—to get you on to things
It wants to see how you will take, if backward
It's from regret for something you have passed
And failed to see the good of. Never mind,   125
Things must expect to come in front of us
A many times—I don't say just how many—
That varies with the things—before we see them.
One of the lies would make it out that nothing
Ever presents itself before us twice.   130
Where would we be at last if that were so?
Our very life depends on everything's
Recurring till we answer from within.

The thousandth time may prove the charm.—That leaf!
It can't turn either way. It needs the wind's help.   135
But the wind didn't move it if it moved.
It moved itself. The wind's at naught in here.
It couldn't stir so sensitively poised
A thing as that. It couldn't reach the lamp
To get a puff of black smoke from the flame,   140
Or blow a rumple in the collie's coat.
You make a little foursquare block of air,
Quiet and light and warm, in spite of all
The illimitable dark and cold and storm,
And by so doing give these three, lamp, dog,   145
And book-leaf, that keep near you, their repose;
Though for all anyone can tell, repose
May be the thing you haven't, yet you give it.
So false it is that what we haven't we can't give;
So false, that what we always say is true.   150
I'll have to turn the leaf if no one else will.
It won't lie down. Then let it stand. Who cares?'

'I shouldn't want to hurry you, Meserve,
But if you're going— Say you'll stay, you know.
But let me raise this curtain on a scene,   155
And show you how it's piling up against you.
You see the snow-white through the white of frost?
Ask Helen how far up the sash it's climbed
Since last we read the gage.'

                               'It looks as if
Some pallid thing had squashed its features flat   160
And its eyes shut with overeagerness
To see what people found so interesting
In one another, and had gone to sleep
Of its own stupid lack of understanding,
Or broken its white neck of mushroom stuff   165
Short off, and died against the window-pane.'

'Brother Meserve, take care, you'll scare yourself
More than you will us with such nightmare talk.
It's you it matters to, because it's you
Who have to go out into it alone.'   170

'Let him talk, Helen, and perhaps he'll stay.'

'Before you drop the curtain—I'm reminded:
You recollect the boy who came out here
To breathe the air one winter—had a room
Down at the Averys'? Well, one sunny morning   175
After a downy storm, he passed our place

159. gage—barometer.

And found me banking up the house with snow.
And I was burrowing in deep for warmth,
Piling it well above the window-sills.
The snow against the window caught his eye.   180
"Hey, that's a pretty thought"—those were his words.
"So you can think it's six feet deep outside,
While you sit warm and read up balanced rations.
You can't get too much winter in the winter."
Those were his words. And he went home and all   185
But banked the daylight out of Avery's windows.
Now you and I would go to no such length.
At the same time you can't deny it makes
It not a mite worse, sitting here, we three,
Playing our fancy, to have the snowline run   190
So high across the pane outside. There where
There is a sort of tunnel in the frost
More like a tunnel than a hole—way down
At the far end of it you see a stir
And quiver like the frayed edge of the drift   195
Blown in the wind. I *like* that—I like *that*.
Well, now I leave you, people.'

                        'Come, Meserve,
We thought you were deciding not to go—
The ways you found to say the praise of comfort
And being where you are. You want to stay.'   200

'I'll own it's cold for such a fall of snow.
This house is frozen brittle, all except
This room you sit in. If you think the wind
Sounds further off, it's not because it's dying;
You're further under in the snow—that's all—   205
And feel it less. Hear the soft bombs of dust
It bursts against us at the chimney mouth,
And at the eaves. I like it from inside
More than I shall out in it. But the horses
Are rested and it's time to say good-night,   210
And let you get to bed again. Good-night,
Sorry I had to break in on your sleep.'

'Lucky for you you did. Lucky for you
You had us for a half-way station
To stop at. If you were the kind of man   215
Paid heed to women, you'd take my advice
And for your family's sake stay where you are.
But what good is my saying it over and over?
You've done more than you had a right to think
You could do—*now*. You know the risk you take   220
In going on.'

                'Our snow-storms as a rule
Aren't looked on as man-killers, and although

I'd rather be the beast that sleeps the sleep
Under it all, his door sealed up and lost,
Than the man fighting it to keep above it,   225
Yet think of the small birds at roost and not
In nests. Shall I be counted less than they are?
Their bulk in water would be frozen rock
In no time out tonight. And yet tomorrow
They will come budding boughs from tree to tree   230
Flirting their wings and saying Chickadee,
As if not knowing what you meant by the word storm.'

'But why when no one wants you to go on?
Your wife—she doesn't want you to. We don't,
And you yourself don't want to. Who else is there?'   235

'Save us from being cornered by a woman.
Well, there's'— She told Fred afterward that in
The pause right there, she thought the dreaded word
Was coming, 'God.' But no, he only said
'Well, there's—the storm. That says I must go on.   240
That wants me as a war might if it came.
Ask any man.'

                    He threw her that as something
To last her till he got outside the door.
He had Cole with him to the barn to see him off.
When Cole returned he found his wife still standing   245
Beside the table near the open book,
Not reading it.

                    'Well, what kind of a man
Do you call that?' she said.

                    'He had the gift
Of words, or is it tongues, I ought to say?'

'Was ever such a man for seeing likeness?'   250

'Or disregarding people's civil questions—
What? We've found out in one hour more about him
Than we had seeing him pass by in the road
A thousand times. If that's the way he preaches!
You didn't think you'd keep him after all.   255
Oh, I'm not blaming you. He didn't leave you
Much say in the matter, and I'm just as glad
We're not in for a night of him. No sleep
If he had stayed. The least thing set him going.
It's quiet as an empty church without him.'   260

'But how much better off are we as it is?
We'll have to sit here till we know he's safe.'

'Yes, I suppose you'll want to, but I shouldn't.
He knows what he can do, or he wouldn't try.
Get into bed I say, and get some rest.   265
He won't come back, and if he telephones,
It won't be for an hour or two.'

                                 'Well then.
We can't be any help by sitting here
And living his fight through with him, I suppose.'

Cole had been telephoning in the dark.   270
Mrs. Cole's voice came from an inner room:
'Did she call you or you call her?'

                               'She me.
You'd better dress: you won't go back to bed.
We must have been asleep: it's three and after.'

'Had she been ringing long? I'll get my wrapper.   275
I want to speak to her.'

                        'All she said was,
He hadn't come and had he really started.'

'She knew he had, poor thing, two hours ago.'

'He had the shovel. He'll have made a fight.'

'Why did I ever let him leave this house!'   280

'Don't begin that. You did the best you could
To keep him—though perhaps you didn't quite
Conceal a wish to see him show the spunk
To disobey you. Much his wife'll thank you.'

'Fred, after all I said! You shan't make out   285
That it was any way but what it was.
Did she let on by any word she said
She didn't thank me?'

                      'When I told her "Gone,"
"Well then," she said, and "Well then"—like a threat.
And then her voice came scraping slow: "Oh, you,   290
Why did you let him go?"'

                      'Asked why we let him?
You let me there. I'll ask her why she let him.
She didn't dare to speak when he was here.
Their number's—twenty-one? The thing won't work.
Someone's receiver's down. The handle stumbles.   295
The stubborn thing, the way it jars your arm!
It's theirs. She's dropped it from her hand and gone.'

'Try speaking. Say "Hello!"'

                    'Hello. Hello.'

'What do you hear?'

                    'I hear an empty room—
You know—it sounds that way. And yes, I hear—   300
I think I hear a clock—and windows rattling.
No step though. If she's there she's sitting down.'

'Shout, she may hear you.'

                    'Shouting is no good.'

'Keep speaking then.'

                    'Hello. Hello. Hello.
You don't suppose—? She wouldn't go out doors?'   305

'I'm half afraid that's just what she might do.'

'And leave the children?'

                    'Wait and call again.
You can't hear whether she has left the door
Wide open and the wind's blown out the lamp
And the fire's died and the room's dark and cold?'   310

'One of two things, either she's gone to bed
Or gone out doors.'

                    'In which case both are lost.
Do you know what she's like? Have you ever met her?
It's strange she doesn't want to speak to us.'

                    'Fred, see if you can hear what I hear. Come.'   315

'A clock maybe.'

                    'Don't you hear something else?'

'Not talking.'

          'No.'

                    'Why, yes, I hear—what is it?'

'What do you say it is?'

                    'A baby's crying!
Frantic it sounds, though muffled and far off.
Its mother wouldn't let it cry like that,   320
Not if she's there.'

'What do you make of it?'

'There's only one thing possible to make,
That is, assuming—that she has gone out.
Of course she hasn't though.' They both sat down
Helpless. 'There's nothing we can do till morning.'   325

'Fred, I shan't let you think of going out.'

'Hold on.' The double bell began to chirp.
They started up. Fred took the telephone.
'Hello, Meserve. You're there, then!—And your wife?
Good! Why I asked—she didn't seem to answer.   330
He says she went to let him in the barn.—
We're glad. Oh, say no more about it, man.
Drop in and see us when you're passing.'

                                        'Well,
She has him then, though what she wants him for
I *don't* see.'

                    'Possibly not for herself.   335
Maybe she only wants him for the children.'

'The whole to-do seems to have been for nothing.
What spoiled our night was to him just his fun.
What did he come in for?—To talk and visit?
Thought he'd just call to tell us it was snowing.   340
If he thinks he is going to make our house
A half-way coffee house 'twixt town and nowhere—'

'I thought you'd feel you'd been too much concerned.'

'You think you haven't been concerned yourself.'

'If you mean he was inconsiderate   345
To rout us out to think for him at midnight
And then take our advice no more than nothing,
Why, I agree with you. But let's forgive him.
We've had a share in one night of his life.
What'll you bet he ever calls again?'   350

NEW HAMPSHIRE

Title poem of *New Hampshire,* 1923. In this poem Frost raises New Hampshire idiom and thought to the dignity of a literary language. Metaphorically, New Hampshire is a symbol of introversion motivated by the sense of property.

I met a lady from the South who said
(You won't believe she said it, but she said it):
'None of my family ever worked, or had

A thing to sell.' I don't suppose the work
Much matters. You may work for all of me.   5
I've seen the time I've had to work myself.
The having anything to sell is what
Is the disgrace in man or state or nation.

I met a traveller from Arkansas
Who boasted of his state as beautiful   10
For diamonds and apples. 'Diamonds
And apples in commercial quantities?'
I asked him, on my guard. 'Oh yes,' he answered,
Off his. The time was evening in the Pullman.
'I see the porter's made your bed,' I told him.   15

I met a Californian who would
Talk California—a state so blessed,
He said, in climate, none had ever died there
A natural death, and Vigilance Committees
Had had to organize to stock the graveyards   20
And vindicate the state's humanity.
'Just the way Steffanson runs on,' I murmured,
'About the British Arctic. That's what comes
Of being in the market with a climate.'

I met a poet from another state,   25
A zealot full of fluid inspiration,
Who in the name of fluid inspiration,
But in the best style of bad salesmanship,
Angrily tried to make me write a protest
(In verse I think) against the Volstead Act.   30
He didn't even offer me a drink
Until I asked for one to steady *him*.
This is called having an idea to sell.

It never could have happened in New Hampshire.

The only person really soiled with trade   35
I ever stumbled on in old New Hampshire
Was someone who had just come back ashamed
From selling things in California.
He'd built a noble mansard roof with balls
On turrets like Constantinople, deep   40
In woods some ten miles from a railroad station,
As if to put forever out of mind
The hope of being, as we say, received.
I found him standing at the close of day
Inside the threshold of his open barn,   45
Like a lone actor on a gloomy stage—
And recognized him through the iron grey

22. Steffanson—Vilhjalmur Stefansson (1879-   ), Canadian explorer of Arctic regions.
30. Volstead Act—an act passed to enforce the Eighteenth Amendment to the Constitution,
adopted in 1919, which prohibited the manufacture and sale of intoxicating liquors.

In which his face was muffled to the eyes
As an old boyhood friend, and once indeed
A drover with me on the road to Brighton.   50
His farm was 'grounds,' and not a farm at all;
His house among the local sheds and shanties
Rose like a factor's at a trading station.
And he was rich, and I was still a rascal.
I couldn't keep from asking impolitely,   55
Where had he been and what had he been doing?
How did he get so? (Rich was understood.)
In dealing in 'old rags' in San Francisco.
Oh it was terrible as well could be.
We both of us turned over in our graves.   60
Just specimens is all New Hampshire has,
One each of everything as in a show-case
Which naturally she doesn't care to sell.

She had one President (pronounce him Purse,
And make the most of it for better or worse.   65
He's your one chance to score against the state).
She had one Daniel Webster. He was all
The Daniel Webster ever was or shall be.
She had the Dartmouth needed to produce him.

I call her old. She has one family   70
Whose claim is good to being settled here
Before the era of colonization,
And before that of exploration even.
John Smith remarked them as he coasted by
Dangling their legs and fishing off a wharf   75
At the Isles of Shoals, and satisfied himself
They weren't Red Indians, but veritable
Pre-primitives of the white race, dawn people,
Like those who furnished Adam's sons with wives;
However uninnocent they may have been   80
In being there so early in our history.
They'd been there then a hundred years or more.
Pity he didn't ask what they were up to
At that date with a wharf already built,
And take their name. They've since told me their name—   85
Today an honored one in Nottingham.
As for what they were up to more than fishing—
Suppose they weren't behaving Puritanly,
The hour had not yet struck for being good,
Mankind had not yet gone on the Sabbatical.   90
It became an explorer of the deep
Not to explore too deep in others' business.

---

53. **factor's**—manager, agent. 64. **Purse**—Franklin Pierce (1804-1869), fourteenth President of the United States. 67. **Webster**—Daniel Webster (1782-1852), statesman who won fame in the Dartmouth College case in 1819 when the Supreme Court declared its charter inviolable. 76. **Isles of Shoals**—off the coast at Portsmouth, New Hampshire. 90. **Sabbatical**—here, devoting each seventh day to worship.

Did you but know of him, New Hampshire has
One real reformer who would change the world
So it would be accepted by two classes,   95
Artists the minute they set up as artists,
Before, that is, they are themselves accepted,
And boys the minute they get out of college.
I can't help thinking those are tests to go by.

And she has one I don't know what to call him,   100
Who comes from Philadelphia every year
With a great flock of chickens of rare breeds
He wants to give the educational
Advantages of growing almost wild
Under the watchful eye of hawk and eagle—   105
Dorkings because they're spoken of by Chaucer,
Sussex because they're spoken of by Herrick.

She has a touch of gold. New Hampshire gold—
You may have heard of it. I had a farm
Offered me not long since up Berlin way   110
With a mine on it that was worked for gold;
But not gold in commercial quantities.
Just enough gold to make the engagement rings
And marriage rings of those who owned the farm.
What gold more innocent could one have asked for?   115
One of my children ranging after rocks
Lately brought home from Andover or Canaan
A specimen of beryl with a trace
Of radium. I know with radium
The trace would have to be the merest trace   120
To be below the threshold of commercial;
But trust New Hampshire not to have enough
Of radium or anything to sell.

A specimen of everything, I said.
She has one witch—old style. She lives in Colebrook. 125
(The only other witch I ever met
Was lately at a cut-glass dinner in Boston.
There were four candles and four people present.
The witch was young, and beautiful (new style),
And open-minded. She was free to question   130
Her gift for reading letters locked in boxes.
Why was it so much greater when the boxes
Were metal than it was when they were wooden?
It made the world seem so mysterious.
The S'ciety for Psychical Research   135
Was cognizant. Her husband was worth millions.
I think he owned some shares in Harvard College.)

---

106. **Dorkings**—not in the Chaucer Concordance. Evidently a facetious reference to Chantecleer in *Nun's Priest's Tale.* 107. **Herrick**—Robert Herrick (1591-1674), one of England's most famous lyric poets. 125. **witch**—*Cf.* Frost's poem "The Witch of Coös." . . .

New Hampshire *used* to have at Salem
A company we called the White Corpuscles,
Whose duty was at any hour of night   140
To rush in sheets and fools' caps where they smelled
A thing the least bit doubtfully perscented
And give someone the Skipper Ireson's Ride.

One each of everything. as in a show-case.
More than enough land for a specimen   145
You'll say she has, but there there enters in
Something else to protect her from herself.
There quality makes up for quantity.
Not even New Hampshire farms are much for sale.
The farm I made my home on in the mountains   150
I had to take by force rather than buy.
I caught the owner outdoors by himself
Raking up after winter, and I said,
'I'm going to put you off this farm: I want it.'
'Where are you going to put me? In the road?'   155
'I'm going to put you on the farm next to it.'
'Why won't the farm next to it do for you?'
'I like this better.' It was really better.

Apples? New Hampshire has them, but unsprayed,
With no suspicion in stem-end or blossom-end   160
Of vitriol or arsenate of lead,
And so not good for anything but cider.
Her unpruned grapes are flung like lariats
Far up the birches out of reach of man.

A state producing precious metals, stones,   165
And—writing; none of these except perhaps
The precious literature in quantity
Or quality to worry the producer
About disposing of it. Do you know,
Considering the market, there are more   170
Poems produced than any other thing?
No wonder poets sometimes have to *seem*
So much more business-like than business men.
Their wares are so much harder to get rid of.

She's one of the two best states in the Union.   175
Vermont's the other. And the two have been
Yoke-fellows in the sap-yoke from of old
In many Marches. And they lie like wedges,
Thick end to thin end and thin end to thick end,
And are a figure of the way the strong   180
Of mind and strong of arm should fit together,
One thick where one is thin and vice versa.
New Hampshire raises the Connecticut

143. **Skipper Ireson's Ride**—See p. 662 for Whittier's poem on the subject. 161. **vitriol . . . arsenate of lead**—poisons sprayed on fruit trees to destroy insects.

In a trout hatchery near Canada,
But soon divides the river with Vermont.   185
Both are delightful states for their absurdly
Small towns—Lost Nation, Bungey, Muddy Boo,
Poplin, Still Corners (so called not because
The place is silent all day long, nor yet
Because it boasts a whisky still—because   190
It set out once to be a city and still
Is only corners, cross-roads in a wood).
And I remember one whose name appeared
Between the pictures on a movie screen
Election night once in Franconia,   195
When everything had gone Republican
And Democrats were sore in need of comfort:
Easton goes Democratic, Wilson 4
Hughes 2. And everybody to the saddest
Laughed the loud laugh, the big laugh at the little.   200
New York (five million) laughs at Manchester,
Manchester (sixty or seventy thousand) laughs
At Littleton (four thousand), Littleton
Laughs at Franconia (seven hundred), and
Franconia laughs, I fear,—did laugh that night—   205
At Easton. What has Easton left to laugh at,
And like the actress exclaim, 'Oh my God' at?
There's Bungey; and for Bungey there are towns,
Whole townships named but without population.

Anything I can say about New Hampshire   210
Will serve almost as well about Vermont,
Excepting that they differ in their mountains.
The Vermont mountains stretch extended straight;
New Hampshire mountains curl up in a coil.

I had been coming to New Hampshire mountains.   215
And here I am and what am I to say?
Here first my theme becomes embarrassing.
Emerson said, 'The God who made New Hampshire
Taunted the lofty land with little men.'
Another Massachusetts poet said,   220
'I go no more to summer in New Hampshire.
I've given up my summer place in Dublin.'
But when I asked to know what ailed New Hampshire,
She said she couldn't stand the people in it,
The little men (it's Massachusetts speaking).   225
And when I asked to know what ailed the people,
She said, 'Go read your own books and find out.'
I may as well confess myself the author
Of several books against the world in general.
To take them as against a special state   230
Or even nation's to restrict my meaning.

218. Emerson—in his "Ode to W. H. Channing," lines 23-26. **220. Another . . . poet**—
Amy Lowell.

I'm what is called a sensibilist,
Or otherwise an environmentalist.
I refuse to adapt myself a mite
To any change from hot to cold, from wet   235
To dry, from poor to rich, or back again.
I make a virtue of my suffering
From nearly everything that goes on round me.
In other words, I know wherever I am,
Being the creature of literature I am,   240
I shall not lack for pain to keep me awake.
Kit Marlowe taught me how to say my prayers:
'Why, this is Hell, nor am I out of it.'
Samoa, Russia, Ireland I complain of,
No less than England, France and Italy.   245
Because I wrote my novels in New Hampshire
Is no proof that I aimed them at New Hampshire.

When I left Massachusetts years ago
Between two days, the reason why I sought
New Hampshire, not Connecticut,   250
Rhode Island, New York, or Vermont was this:
Where I was living then, New Hampshire offered
The nearest boundary to escape across.
I hadn't an illusion in my hand-bag
About the people being better there   255
Than those I left behind. I thought they weren't.
I thought they couldn't be. And yet they were.
I'd sure had no such friends in Massachusetts
As Hall of Windham, Gay of Atkinson,
Bartlett of Raymond (now of Colorado),   260
Harris of Derry, and Lynch of Bethlehem.

The glorious bards of Massachusetts seem
To want to make New Hampshire people over.
They taunt the lofty land with little men.
I don't know what to say about the people.   265
For art's sake one could almost wish them worse
Rather than better. How are we to write
The Russian novel in America
As long as life goes so unterribly?
There is the pinch from which our only outcry   270
In literature to date is heard to come.
We get what little misery we can
Out of not having cause for misery.
It makes the guild of novel writers sick
To be expected to be Dostoievskis   275
On nothing worse than too much luck and comfort.

242. Marlowe—*Cf. Doctor Faustus*, Act V, line 125. **246. novels**—For "novels" read "poems." Frost has written no novels. **259-61. Hall . . . Lynch**—actual friends of Frost. **275. Dostoievskis**—Feodor M. Dostoievsky (1821-1881), Russian naturalistic novelist, author of *Crime and Punishment.*

This is not sorrow, though; it's just the vapors,
And recognized as such in Russia itself
Under the new regime, and so forbidden.
If well it is with Russia, then feel free   280
To say so or be stood against the wall
And shot. It's Pollyanna now or death.
This, then, is the new freedom we hear tell of;
And very sensible. No state can build
A literature that shall at once be sound   285
And sad on a foundation of well-being.

To show the level of intelligence
Among us: it was just a Warren farmer
Whose horse had pulled him short up in the road
By me, a stranger. This is what he said,   290
From nothing but embarrassment and want
Of anything more sociable to say:
'You hear those hound-dogs sing on Moosilauke?
Well they remind me of the hue and cry
We've heard against the Mid-Victorians   295
And never rightly understood till Bryan
Retired from politics and joined the chorus.
The matter with the Mid-Victorians
Seems to have been a man named John L. Darwin.'
'Go 'long,' I said to him, he to his horse.   300

I knew a man who failing as a farmer
Burned down his farmhouse for the fire insurance,
And spent the proceeds on a telescope
To satisfy a life-long curiosity
About our place among the infinities.   305
And how was that for other-worldliness?

If I must choose which I would elevate—
The people or the already lofty mountains,
I'd elevate the already lofty mountains.
The only fault I find with old New Hampshire   310
Is that her mountains aren't quite high enough.
I was not always so; I've come to be so.
How, to my sorrow, how have I attained
A height from which to look down critical
On mountains? What has given me assurance   315
To say what height becomes New Hampshire mountains,
Or any mountains? Can it be some strength
I feel as of an earthquake in my back
To heave them higher to the morning star?
Can it be foreign travel in the Alps?   320

277. vapors—hypochondria. **282. Pollyanna**—insipid character in Eleanor Porter's popular
sentimental novel *Pollyanna, the Glad Book*, 1913. **296. Bryan**—William Jennings Bryan (1860-
1925), American statesman, who in the year of his death defended the Tennessee anti-evolution
act in the Scopes trial. Frost purposely mistakes Charles Darwin's given name three lines later.

Or having seen and credited a moment
The solid moulding of vast peaks of cloud
Behind the pitiful reality
Of Lincoln, Lafayette and Liberty?
Or some such sense as says how high shall jet   325
The fountain in proportion to the basin?
No, none of these has raised me to my throne
Of intellectual dissatisfaction,
But the sad accident of having seen
Our actual mountains given in a map   330
Of early times as twice the height they are—
Ten thousand feet instead of only five—
Which shows how sad an accident may be.
Five thousand is no longer high enough.
Whereas I never had a good idea   335
About improving people in the world,
Here I am over-fertile in suggestion,
And cannot rest from planning day or night
How high I'd thrust the peaks in summer snow
To tap the upper sky and draw a flow   340
Of frosty night air on the vale below
Down from the stars to freeze the dew as starry.

The more the sensibilist I am
The more I seem to want my mountains wild;
The way the wiry gang-boss liked the log-jam.   345
After he'd picked the lock and got it started,
He dodged a log that lifted like an arm
Against the sky to break his back for him,
Then came in dancing, skipping, with his life
Across the roar and chaos, and the words   350
We saw him say along the zigzag journey
Were doubtless as the words we heard him say
On coming nearer: 'Wasn't she an *i*-deal
Son-of-a-bitch? You bet she was an *i*-deal.'

For all her mountains fall a little short,   355
Her people not quite short enough for Art,
She's still New Hampshire, a most restful state.

Lately in converse with a New York alec
About the new school of the pseudo-phallic,
I found myself in a close corner where   360
I had to make an almost funny choice.
'Choose you which you will be—a prude, or puke,
Mewling and puking in the public arms.'
'Me for the hills where I don't have to choose.'
'But if you had to choose, which would you be?'   365
I wouldn't be a prude afraid of nature.

324. **Lincoln . . . Liberty**—peaks, though not the highest, in New Hampshire. **359.**
pseudo-phallic—Frost satirizes the emphasis by twentieth-century writers on sex. **363.**
mewling—Cf. *As You Like It*, Act II, sc. vii, line 144.

I know a man who took a double axe
And went alone against a grove of trees;
But his heart failing him, he dropped the axe
And ran for shelter quoting Matthew Arnold: 370
'Nature is cruel, man is sick of blood;
There's been enough shed without shedding mine.
Remember Birnam Wood! The wood's in flux!'
He had a special terror of the flux
That showed itself in dendrophobia. 375
The only decent tree had been to mill
And educated into boards, he said.
He knew too well for any earthly use
The line where man leaves off and nature starts,
And never over-stepped it save in dreams. 380
He stood on the safe side of the line talking;
Which is sheer Matthew Arnoldism,
The cult of one who owned himself 'a foiled,
Circuitous wanderer,' and 'took dejectedly
His seat upon the intellectual throne.' 385
Agreed in frowning on these improvised
Altars the woods are full of nowadays,
Again as in the days when Ahaz sinned
By worship under green trees in the open.
Scarcely a mile but that I come on one, 390
A black-cheeked stone and stick of rain-washed charcoal.
Even to say the groves were God's first temples
Comes too near to Ahaz' sin for safety.
Nothing not built with hands of course is sacred.
But here is not a question of what's sacred; 395
Rather of what to face or run away from.
I'd hate to be a runaway from nature.
And neither would I choose to be a puke
Who cares not what he does in company,
And, when he can't do anything, falls back 400
On words, and tries his worst to make words speak
Louder than actions, and sometimes achieves it.
It seems a narrow choice the age insists on.
How about being a good Greek, for instance?
That course, they tell me, isn't offered this year. 405
'Come, but this isn't choosing—puke or prude?'
Well, if I have to choose one or the other,
I choose to be a plain New Hampshire farmer
With an income in cash of say a thousand
(From say a publisher in New York City). 410
It's restful to arrive at a decision,

370. Matthew Arnold—*Cf.* "In Harmony with Nature," line 7. **373. Birnam Wood**—*Cf. Macbeth,* Act IV, sc. i, line 93. **375. dendrophobia**—fear of trees. **383-85. "a foiled . . . throne"**—*Cf.* "The Scholar Gipsy," lines 183-84. **388. Ahaz**—King of Judah (742-727 B.C.), who paid homage to the Assyrian King Tiglath Pileser, a policy of appeasement which resulted in the destruction of the kingdom of Israel. **392. God's first temples**—*Cf.* Bryant's "A Forest Hymn," p. 338. **404. good Greek**—referring to the Greek worship of nature, or possibly to the balanced, well-poised ideal of Greek life.

And restful just to think about New Hampshire.
At present I am living in Vermont.

FIRE AND ICE

Composed in 1919, published in *Harper's Magazine,* December, 1920, and in
New Hampshire, 1923.

Some say the world will end in fire,
Some say in ice.
From what I've tasted of desire
I hold with those who favor fire.
But if it had to perish twice,   5
I think I know enough of hate
To say that for destruction ice
Is also great
And would suffice.

NOTHING GOLD CAN STAY

This and the next poem were published in the *Yale Review,* October, 1914, and
in *New Hampshire,* 1923.

Nature's first green is gold,
Her hardest hue to hold.
Her early leaf's a flower;
But only so an hour.
Then leaf subsides to leaf.   5
So Eden sank to grief,
So dawn goes down to day.
Nothing gold can stay.

TO EARTHWARD

Love at the lips was touch
As sweet as I could bear;
And once that seemed too much;
I lived on air

That crossed me from sweet things,   5
The flow of—was it musk
From hidden grapevine springs
Down hill at dusk?

I had the swirl and ache
From sprays of honeysuckle   10
That when they're gathered shake
Dew on the knuckle.

I craved strong sweets, but those
Seemed strong when I was young;
The petal of the rose   15
It was that stung.

Now no joy but lacks salt
That is not dashed with pain
And weariness and fault;
I crave the stain   20

Of tears, the aftermark
Of almost too much love,
The sweet of bitter bark
And burning clove.

When stiff and sore and scarred   25
I take away my hand
From leaning on it hard
In grass and sand,

The hurt is not enough:
I long for weight and strength   30
To feel the earth as rough
To all my length.

TWO LOOK AT TWO

Published in *New Hampshire*, 1923.

Love and forgetting might have carried them
A little further up the mountain side
With night so near, but not much further up.
They must have halted soon in any case
With thoughts of the path back, how rough it was   5
With rock and washout, and unsafe in darkness;
When they were halted by a tumbled wall
With barbed-wire binding. They stood facing this,
Spending what onward impulse they still had
In one last look the way they must not go,   10
On up the failing path, where, if a stone
Or earthslide moved at night, it moved itself;
No footstep moved it. 'This is all,' they sighed,
'Good-night to woods.' But not so; there was more.
A doe from round a spruce stood looking at them   15
Across the wall, as near the wall as they.
She saw them in their field, they her in hers.
The difficulty of seeing what stood still,
Like some up-ended boulder split in two,
Was in her clouded eyes: they saw no fear there.   20
She seemed to think that two thus they were safe.
Then, as if they were something that, though strange,
She could not trouble her mind with too long,

She sighed and passed unscared along the wall.
'This, then, is all. What more is there to ask?'   25
But no, not yet. A snort to bid them wait.
A buck from round the spruce stood looking at them
Across the wall as near the wall as they.
This was an antlered buck of lusty nostril,
Not the same doe come back into her place.   30
He viewed them quizzically with jerks of head,
As if to ask, 'Why don't you make some motion?
Or give some sign of life? Because you can't.
I doubt if you're as living as you look.'
Thus till he had them almost feeling dared   35
To stretch a proffering hand—and a spell-breaking.
Then he too passed unscared along the wall.
Two had seen two, whichever side you spoke from.
'This *must* be all.' It was all. Still they stood,
A great wave from it going over them,   40
As if the earth in one unlooked-for favor
Had made them certain earth returned their love.

SPRING POOLS

Published in the *Dearborn Independent,* April 23, 1927, and in *West-Running Brook,* 1928.

These pools that, though in forests, still reflect
The total sky almost without defect,
And like the flowers beside them, chill and shiver,
Will like the flowers beside them soon be gone,
And yet not out by any brook or river,   5
But up by roots to bring dark foliage on.

The trees that have it in their pent-up buds
To darken nature and be summer woods—
Let them think twice before they use their powers
To blot out and drink up and sweep away   10
These flowery waters and these watery flowers
From snow that melted only yesterday.

ONCE BY THE PACIFIC

Published in the *New Republic,* December 29, 1926, and in *West-Running Brook,* 1928.

The shattered water made a misty din.
Great waves looked over others coming in,
And thought of doing something to the shore
That water never did to land before.

The clouds were low and hairy in the skies,   5
Like locks blown forward in the gleam of eyes.
You could not tell, and yet it looked as if
The shore was lucky in being backed by cliff,
The cliff in being backed by continent;
It looked as if a night of dark intent   10
Was coming, and not only a night, an age.
Someone had better be prepared for rage.
There would be more than ocean-water broken
Before God's last *Put out the Light* was spoken.

TREE AT MY WINDOW

Published in the *Yale Review,* July, 1927, and in *West-Running Brook,* 1928.

Tree at my window, window tree,
My sash is lowered when night comes on;
But let there never be curtain drawn
Between you and me.

Vague dream-head lifted out of the ground,   5
And thing next most diffuse to cloud,
Not all your light tongues talking aloud
Could be profound.

But tree, I have seen you taken and tossed,
And if you have seen me when I slept,   10
You have seen me when I was taken and swept
And all but lost.

That day she put our heads together,
Fate had her imagination about her,
Your head so much concerned with outer,   15
Mine with inner, weather.

A SOLDIER

Published in *West-Running Brook,* 1928.

He is that fallen lance that lies as hurled,
That lies unlifted now, come dew, come rust,
But still lies pointed as it plowed the dust.
If we who sight along it round the world,
See nothing worthy to have been its mark,   5
It is because like men we look too near,
Forgetting that as fitted to the sphere,
Our missiles always make too short an arc.

They fall, they rip the grass, they intersect
The curve of earth, and striking, break their own;   10
They make us cringe for metal-point on stone.
But this we know, the obstacle that checked
And tripped the body, shot the spirit on
Further than target ever showed or shone.

TWO TRAMPS IN MUD TIME

Published in the *Saturday Review of Literature,* October 6, 1934, and in *A Further Range,* 1936.

Out of the mud two strangers came
And caught me splitting wood in the yard.
And one of them put me off my aim
By hailing cheerily 'Hit them hard!'
I knew pretty well why he dropped behind   5
And let the other go on a way.
I knew pretty well what he had in mind:
He wanted to take my job for pay.

Good blocks of beech it was I split,
As large around as the chopping block;   10
And every piece I squarely hit
Fell splinterless as a cloven rock.
The blows that a life of self-control
Spares to strike for the common good
That day, giving a loose to my soul,   15
I spent on the unimportant wood.

The sun was warm but the wind was chill.
You know how it is with an April day
When the sun is out and the wind is still,
You're one month on in the middle of May.   20
But if you so much as dare to speak,
A cloud comes over the sunlit arch,
A wind comes off a frozen peak,
And you're two months back in the middle of March.

A bluebird comes tenderly up to alight   25
And fronts the wind to unruffle a plume,
His song so pitched as not to excite
A single flower as yet to bloom.
It is snowing a flake: and he half knew
Winter was only playing possum.   30
Except in color he isn't blue,
But he wouldn't advise a thing to blossom.

The water for which we may have to look
In summertime with a witching-wand,

34. **witching-wand**—a forked stick supposed to indicate underground water.

In every wheelrut's now a brook,   35
In every print of a hoof a pond.
Be glad of water, but don't forget
The lurking frost in the earth beneath
That will steal forth after the sun is set
And show on the water its crystal teeth.   40

The time when most I loved my task
These two must make me love it more
By coming with what they came to ask.
You'd think I never had felt before
The weight of an ax-head poised aloft,   45
The grip on earth of outspread feet,
The life of muscles rocking soft
And smooth and moist in vernal heat.

Out of the woods two hulking tramps
(From sleeping God knows where last night,   50
But not long since in the lumber camps).
They thought all chopping was theirs of right.
Men of the woods and lumberjacks,
They judged me by their appropriate tool.
Except as a fellow handled an ax,   55
They had no way of knowing a fool.

Nothing on either side was said.
They knew they had but to stay their stay
And all their logic would fill my head:
As that I had no right to play   60
With what was another man's work for gain.
My right might be love but theirs was need.
And where the two exist in twain
Theirs was the better right-agreed.

But yield who will to their separation,   65
My object in living is to unite
My avocation and my vocation
As my two eyes make one in sight.
Only where love and need are one,
And the work is play for mortal stakes,   70
Is the deed ever really done
For Heaven and the future's sakes.

DESERT PLACES

Published in the *American Mercury,* April, 1934, and in *A Further Range,* 1936.

Snow falling and night falling fast oh fast
In a field I looked into going past,
And the ground almost covered smooth in snow,
But a few weeds and stubble showing last.

The woods around it have it—it is theirs.   5
All animals are smothered in their lairs.
I am too absent-spirited to count;
The loneliness includes me unawares.

And lonely as it is that loneliness
Will be more lonely ere it will be less—   10
A blanker whiteness of benighted snow
With no expression, nothing to express.

They cannot scare me with their empty spaces
Between stars—on stars where no human race is.
.I have it in me so much nearer home   15
To scare myself with my own desert places.

NEITHER OUT FAR NOR IN DEEP

Published in the *Yale Review,* March, 1932, and in *A Further Range,* 1936.

The people along the sand
All turn and look one way.
They turn their back on the land.
They look at the sea all day.

As long as it takes to pass   5
A ship keeps raising its hull;
The wetter ground like glass
Reflects a standing gull.

The land may vary more;
But wherever the truth may be—   10
The water comes ashore,
And the people look at the sea.

They cannot look out far.
They cannot look in deep.
But when was that ever a bar   15
To any watch they keep?

BUILD SOIL—A POLITICAL PASTORAL

Published in *A Further Range,* 1936.

Why Tityrus! But you've forgotten me.
I'm Meliboeus the potato man,
The one you had the talk with, you remember,
Here on this very campus years ago.
Hard times have struck me and I'm on the move.   5

1. **Tityrus**—shepherd in Virgil's First Eclogue, sometimes referring to Virgil himself. 2. **Meli-boeus**—the second shepherd in the same poem.

I've had to give my interval farm up
For interest, and I've bought a mountain farm
For nothing down, all-out-doors of a place,
All woods and pasture only fit for sheep.
But sheep is what I'm going into next.   10
I'm done forever with potato crops
At thirty cents a bushel. Give me sheep.
I know wool's down to seven cents a pound.
But I don't calculate to sell my wool.
I didn't my potatoes. I consumed them.   15
I'll dress up in sheep's clothing and eat sheep.
The Muse takes care of you. You live by writing
Your poems on a farm and call that farming.
Oh I don't blame you. I say take life easy.
I should myself, only I don't know how.   20
But have some pity on us who have to work.
Why don't you use your talents as a writer
To advertise our farms to city buyers,
Or else write something to improve food prices.
Get in a poem toward the next election.   25

Oh Meliboeus, I have half a mind
To take a writing hand in politics.
Before now poetry has taken notice
Of wars, and what are wars but politics
Transformed from chronic to acute and bloody?   30

I may be wrong, but Tityrus to me
The times seem revolutionary bad.

The question is whether they've reached a depth
Of desperation that would warrant poetry's
Leaving love's alternations, joy and grief,   35
The weather's alternations, summer and winter,
Our age-long theme, for the uncertainty
Of judging who is a contemporary liar—
Who in particular, when all alike
Get called as much in clashes of ambition.   40
Life may be tragically bad, and I
Make bold to sing it so, but do I dare
Name names and tell you who by name is wicked?
Whittier's luck with Skipper Ireson awes me.
Many men's luck with Greatest Washington   45
(Who sat for Stuart's portrait, but who sat
Equally for the nation's Constitution).
I prefer to sing safely in the realm
Of types, composite and imagined people:
To affirm there is such a thing as evil   50
Personified, but ask to be excused
From saying on a jury 'Here's the guilty.'

44. Whittier's luck—*Cf.* note, p. 1624, line 143. The poem is on p. 662 above. **46. Stuart's portrait**—Gilbert Stuart (1755-1828) painted the best-known portrait of Washington.

I doubt if you're convinced the times are bad.
I keep my eye on Congress, Meliboeus.
They're in the best position of us all   55
To know if anything is very wrong.
I mean they could be trusted to give the alarm
If earth were thought about to change its axis,
Or a star coming to dilate the sun.
As long as lightly all their live-long sessions,   60
Like a yard full of school boys out at recess
Before their plays and games were organized,
They yelling mix tag, hide-and-seek, hop-scotch,
And leap frog in each other's way,—all's well.
Let newspapers profess to fear the worst!   65
Nothing's portentous, I am reassured.

Is socialism needed, do you think?

We have it now. For socialism is
An element in any government.
There's no such thing as socialism pure—   70
Except as an abstraction of the mind.
There's only democratic socialism
Monarchic socialism—oligarchic,
The last being what they seem to have in Russia.
You often get it most in monarchy,   75
Least in democracy. In practice, pure,
I don't know what it would be. No one knows.
I have no doubt like all the loves when
Philosophized together into one—
One sickness of the body and the soul.   80

Thank God our practice holds the loves apart
Beyond embarrassing self-consciousness
Where natural friends are met, where dogs are kept,
Where women pray with priests. There is no love.
There's only love of men and women, love   85
Of children, love of friends, of men, of God,
Divine love, human love, parental love,
Roughly discriminated for the rough.

Poetry, itself once more, is back in love.

Pardon the analogy, my Meliboeus,   90
For sweeping me away. Let's see, where was I?

But don't you think more should be socialized
Than is?

                    What should you mean by socialized?

Made good for everyone—things like inventions—
Made so we all should get the good of them—   95
All, not just great exploiting businesses.

We sometimes only get the bad of them.
In your sense of the word ambition has
Been socialized—the first propensity
To be attempted. Greed may well come next.   100
But the worst one of all to leave uncurbed,
Unsocialized, is ingenuity:
Which for no sordid self-aggrandizement,
For nothing but its own blind satisfaction
(In this it is as much like hate as love)   105
Works in the dark as much against as for us.
Even while we talk some chemist at Columbia
Is stealthily contriving wool from jute
That when let loose upon the grazing world
Will put ten thousand farmers out of sheep.   110
Everyone asks for freedom for himself,
The man free love, the business man free trade,
The writer and talker free speech and free press.
Political ambition has been taught,
By being punished back, it is not free: 115
It must at some point gracefully refrain.
Greed has been taught a little abnegation
And shall be more before we're done with it.
It is just fool enough to think itself
Self-taught. But our brute snarling and lashing taught it.   120
None shall be as ambitious as he can.
None should be as ingenious as he could,
Not if I had my say. Bounds should be set
To ingenuity for being so cruel
In bringing change unheralded on the unready.   125

I elect you to put the curb on it.

Were I dictator, I'll tell you what I'd do.

What should you do?

                    I'd let things take their course
And then I'd claim the credit for the outcome.

You'd make a sort of safety-first dictator.   130

Don't let the things I say against myself
Betray you into taking sides against me,
Or it might get you into trouble with me.
I'm not afraid to prophesy the future,
And be judged by the outcome, Meliboeus.   135
Listen and I will take my dearest risk.
We're always too much out or too much in.
At present from a cosmical dilation
We're so much out that the odds are against
Our ever getting inside in again.   140
But inside in is where we've got to get.

My friends all know I'm interpersonal.
But long before I'm interpersonal
Away 'way down inside I'm personal.
Just so before we're international   145
We're national and act as nationals.
The colors are kept unmixed on the palette,
Or better on dish plates all around the room,
So the effect when they are mixed on canvas
May seem almost exclusively designed.   150
Some minds are so confounded intermental
They remind me of pictures on a palette.
'Look at what happened. Surely some God pinxit.
Come look at my significant mud pie.'
It's hard to tell which is the worse abhorrence   155
Whether it's persons pied or nations pied.
Don't let me seem to say the exchange, the encounter,
May not be the important thing at last.
It well may be. We meet—I don't say when—
But must bring to the meeting the maturest,   160
The longest-saved-up, raciest, localest
We have strength of reserve in us to bring.

Tityrus, sometimes I'm perplexed myself
To find the good of commerce. Why should I
Have to sell you my apples and buy yours?   165
It can't be just to give the robber a chance
To catch them and take toll of them in transit.
Too mean a thought to get much comfort out of.
I figure that like any bandying
Of words or toys, it ministers to health.   170
It very likely quickens and refines us.

To market 'tis our destiny to go.
But much as in the end we bring for sale there
There is still more we never bring or should bring;
More that should be kept back—the soil for instance   175
In my opinion,—though we both know poets
Who fall all over each other to bring soil
And even subsoil and hardpan to market.
To sell the hay off, let alone the soil,
Is an unpardonable sin in farming.   180
The moral is, make a late start to market.
Let me preach to you, will you Meliboeus?

Preach on. I thought you were already preaching.
But preach and see if I can tell the difference.

Needless to say to you, my argument   185
Is not to lure the city to the country.
Let those possess the land and only those,

---

153. **pinxit**—He painted it; sometimes put at the bottom of a painting with the artist's initials.
156. **pied**—variously mottled. 178. **hardpan**—a layer of detritus under soft soil.

Who love it with a love so strong and stupid
That they may be abused and taken advantage of
And made fun of by business, law and art;   190
They still hang on. That so much of the earth's
Unoccupied need not make us uneasy.
We don't pretend to complete occupancy.
The world's one globe, human society
Another softer globe that slightly flattened   195
Rests on the world, and clinging slowly rolls.
We have our own round shape to keep unbroken.
The world's size has no more to do with us
Than has the universe's. We are balls,
We are round from the same source of roundness.   200
We are both round because the mind is round,
Because all reasoning is in a circle.
At least that's why the universe is round.

If what you're preaching is a line of conduct,
Just what am I supposed to do about it?   205
Reason in circles?

                    No, refuse to be
Seduced back to the land by any claim
The land may seem to have on man to use it.
Let none assume to till the land but farmers.
I only speak to you as one of them.   210
You shall go to your run-out mountain farm,
Poor cast-away of commerce, and so live
That none shall ever see you come to market—
Not for a long long time. Plant, breed, produce,
But what will you raise or grow, why feed it out,   215
Eat it or plow it under where it stands
To build the soil. For what is more accursed
Than an impoverished soil pale and metallic?
What cries more to our kind for sympathy?
I'll make a compact with you, Meliboeus,   220
To match you deed for deed and plan for plan.
Friends crowd around me with their five year plans
That Soviet Russia has made fashionable.
You come to me and I'll unfold to you
A five year plan I call so, not because   225
It takes ten years or so to carry out,
Rather because it took five years at least
To think it out. Come close, let us conspire—
In self-restraint, if in restraint of trade.
You will go to your run-out mountain farm   230
And do what I command you. I take care
To command only what you meant to do
Anyway. That is my style of dictator.
Build soil. Turn the farm in upon itself
Until it can contain itself no more,   235

But sweating-full, drips wine and oil a little.
I will go to my run-out social mind
And be as unsocial with it as I can.
The thought I have, and my first impulse is
To take to market—I will turn it under.   240
The thought from that thought—I will turn it under.
And so on to the limit of my nature.
We are too much out, and if we won't draw in
We shall be driven in. I was brought up
A state-rights free-trade Democrat. What's that?   245
An inconsistency. The state shall be
Laws to itself, it seems, and yet have no
Control of what it sells or what it buys.
Suppose someone comes near me who in rate
Of speech and thinking is so much my better   250
I am imposed on, silenced and discouraged.
Do I submit to being supplied by him
As the more economical producer,
More wonderful, more beautiful producer?
No I unostentatiously move off   255
Far enough for my thought-flow to resume.
Thought product and food product are to me
Nothing compared to the producing of them.
I sent you once a song with the refrain:

    Let me be the one   260
    To do what is done—

My share at least lest I be empty-idle.
Keep off each other and keep each other off.
You see the beauty of my proposal is
It needn't wait on general revolution.   265
I bid you to a one-man revolution—
The only revolution that is coming.
We're too unseparate out among each other—
With goods to sell and notions to impart.
A youngster comes to me with half a quatrain   270
To ask me if I think it worth the pains
Of working out the rest, the other half.
I am brought guaranteed young prattle poems
Made publicly in school, above suspicion
Of plagiarism and help of cheating parents.   275
We congregate embracing from distrust
As much as love, and too close in to strike
And be so very striking. Steal away
The song says. Steal away and stay away.
Don't join too many gangs. Join few if any.   280
Join the United States and join the family—
But not much in between unless a college.
Is it a bargain, Shepherd Meliboeus?

260-61. Let . . . done—*Cf.* "Assertive" in the section "Ten Mills" found in *A Further
Range.* **278. Steal away**—well-known Negro spiritual.

Probably but you're far too fast and strong
For my mind to keep working in your presence.   285
I can tell better after I get home,
Better a month from now when cutting posts
Or mending fence it all comes back to me
What I was thinking when you interrupted
My life-train logic. I agree with you   290
We're too unseparate. And going home
From company means coming to our senses.

COME IN

Published in the *Atlantic Monthly,* Feb-
uary, 1941, and in *A Witness Tree,* 1942.

As I came to the edge of the woods,
Thrush music—hark!
Now if it was dusk outside,
Inside it was dark.

Too dark in the woods for a bird   5
By sleight of wing
To better its perch for the night,
Though it still could sing.

The last of the light of the sun
That had died in the west   10
Still lived for one song more
In a thrush's breast.

Far in the pillared dark
Thrush music went—
Almost like a call to come in   15
To the dark and lament.

But no, I was out for stars:
I would not come in.
I meant not even if asked,
And I hadn't been.   20

THE GIFT OUTRIGHT

Read before the Phi Beta Kappa Society at William and Mary College, December
5, 1941, and published in *A Witness Tree,* 1942.

The land was ours before we were the land's.
She was our land more than a hundred years
Before we were her people. She was ours
In Massachusetts, in Virginia,
But we were England's, still colonials,   5
Possessing what we still were unpossessed by,
Possessed by what we now no more possessed.
Something we were withholding made us weak
Until we found it was ourselves
We were withholding from our land of living,   10
And forthwith found salvation in surrender.
Such as we were we gave ourselves outright
(The deed of gift was many deeds of war)
To the land vaguely realizing westward,
But still unstoried, artless, unenhanced,   15
Such as she was, such as she would become.

CARL SANDBURG

1878 -

I. LABORER AND SOLDIER (1878–1902)

1878   Born January 6, the son of August and Clara (Anderson) Sandburg, at Galesburg, Illinois, the family being Swedish immigrants.

1891–1898   Left school to work as a casual laborer. Traveled in Kansas, Nebraska, and Colorado.

1898   Returned to Galesburg as a housepainter. Enlisted in the Sixth Illinois Infantry as a volunteer in the Spanish-American War, the enlistment terminating in eight months.

1898–1902   Worked his way through Lombard College, Galesburg, where he began literary work, won prizes in declamation, and was captain of the basketball team.

II. POLITICIAN, JOURNALIST, AND POET (1902–1933)

1902–1910   Traveled over the country, settling in Milwaukee as an organizer for the Wisconsin Socialist Democratic party.

1904   Published *In Reckless Ecstasy,* a pamphlet of twenty-two pages.

1908   Married (June 15) Lillian Steichen, sister of a well-known photographer, whose biography Sandburg published in 1929.

1910–1912   Secretary to the mayor of Milwaukee.

1913   Removed to Chicago, where he began his career as a journalist and editor.

1914   Publication of "Chicago" and other poems in *Poetry: A Magazine of Verse.* Awarded the Helen Haire Levinson Prize.

1916   *Chicago Poems.*

1918   *Cornhuskers.* After a period as Stockholm correspondent for Newspaper Enterprise Associates, joined the staff of the *Chicago Daily News* as editorial writer.

1919   *The Chicago Race Riots* (pamphlet). Shared with others (and again in 1921) the Poetry Society of America Prize.

1920   *Smoke and Steel.* Began tours as a lecturer and folk-song singer and collector.

1922   *Slabs of the Sunburnt West* and *Rootabaga Stories,* the latter a book for children.

1923   *Rootabaga Pigeons.*

1926   *Abraham Lincoln: The Prairie Years,* 2 vols., the first section of his gigantic life of Lincoln.

1927   Edited *The American Songbag,* folk songs collected on his lecture tours.

1928   Phi Beta Kappa poet at Harvard. Published *Good Morning, America.*

1930   Published *Potato Face* and *Early Moon* (for children).

1932   *Mary Lincoln: Wife and Widow* (with Paul Angle); reprinted in 1944.

1933   Retired from the *News* to his home at Harbert, Michigan, to work on his biography of Lincoln.

III. BIOGRAPHER AND DEMOCRAT (1933–   )

1934   Lecturer at the University of Hawaii.
1936   *The People, Yes.*
1939   *Abraham Lincoln: The War Years,* 4 vols., awarded the Pulitzer Prize in 1940.
1940   Elected a member of the American Academy of Arts and Letters; awarded a Litt.D. by Harvard University, one among many honorary degrees.
1942   *Storm over the Land.*
1943   *Home Front Memo.*
1944   Co-author (with Frederick H. Meserve) of *The Photographs of Abraham Lincoln.*
1949   *The Lincoln Collector.*
1950   *Complete Poems: Carl Sandburg;* and *Carl Sandburg's New American Songbag.*

BIOGRAPHY: There is no formal biography. However, Karl Detzer, *Carl Sandburg: A Study in Personality and Background,* Harcourt, Brace, 1941, is useful; so is the sketch in *Current Biography, 1940,* pp. 708-11.

STUDIES: There are innumerable reviews and "notices." It is hard to choose among much that is ephemeral, but the following critiques seem to have importance: Newton Arvin, "Carl Sandburg," *New Republic,* September 9, 1936, pp. 119-21; Babette Deutsch, "Poetry for the People," *English Journal,* April, 1937, pp. 265-74; Harry Hansen, *Midwest Portraits,* Harcourt, Brace, 1923; Howard Mumford Jones, "Backgrounds of Sorrow," *Virginia Quarterly Review,* January, 1927, pp. 111-23; Amy Lowell, *Tendencies in Modern American Poetry,* Houghton Mifflin, 1917; Harriet Monroe, "Carl Sandburg," *Poetry,* September, 1924, pp. 320-26 (see also *Poets & Their Art,* rev. ed., Macmillan, 1932); T. K. Whipple, *Spokesmen,* New York, 1928; Morton D. Zabel, "Sandburg's Testament," *Poetry,* October, 1936, pp. 33-45 (see also *Literary Opinion in America,* Harper, 1937). The introduction by Rebecca West to *Selected Poems of Carl Sandburg,* Harcourt, Brace, 1926, has value.

Reviews of Sandburg's two works on Lincoln are important. For *The Prairie Years* see, among others, C. M. Morrison, *Literary Review,* February 13, 1926; R. E. Roberts, *New Statesman,* June 5, 1926, Literary Supplement, pp. iii-iv; L. E. Robinson, *Yale Review,* October, 1926, pp. 184-85; Stuart P. Sherman, *New York Herald Tribune Books,* February 7, 1926 (reprinted in *The Main Stream,* Scribner, 1927); Mark Van Doren, *Nation,* February 10, 1926, pp. 122-149; and Leonard Woolf, *Nation and Athenaeum,* May 1, 1926, p. 130.

For *The War Years* see *The Lincoln of Carl Sandburg* (a collection of reviews by Charles A. Beard, Robert E. Sherwood, Lloyd Lewis, and others), Harcourt, Brace, 1940; Allan Nevins, *Saturday Review of Literature,* December 2, 1939, p. 3. Consult the professional historical journals for other reviews.

BIBLIOGRAPHY AND EDITIONS: For bibliography to 1936 see William P. Schenk, "Carl Sandburg—A Bibliography," *Bulletin of Bibliography,* September-December, 1936, pp. 4-7; and to 1940, Fred B. Millett, *Contemporary American Au-*

thors, Harcourt, Brace, 1940, pp. 557-61. The best selection of the poems is that of Rebecca West, listed above.

In a good many ways Carl Sandburg is the spiritual legatee of Whitman. This inheritance goes beyond the "free-verse" techniques of both poets. In fact, Sandburg's versification, though it abjures rhyme and regular meter as Whitman's does, differs importantly from that of the elder poet, whose catalogue methods, Biblical parallels, and triplicate constructions are not characteristic of the younger man. But like Whitman, Sandburg has a mystic's belief in the brotherhood of man, upon which alone a democratic state can be founded; like Whitman he employs the gusty American lingo for poetical purposes because it seems to him to express the American character; like Whitman he has participated in a critical war; like Whitman he has devoted himself to the memory of Abraham Lincoln; and like Whitman he feels that a new culture is emerging on the American continent.

But Sandburg is no mere replica. He touches life and literature on more sides. His great service in preserving American popular verse and song, his active work in arousing the nation against the menace of fascism, and above all the prodigious patience and skill of his biographical work are activities not paralleled in his predecessor. He is also a writer for children, which Whitman was not. It would be idle to attempt to divide between the two writers an award for a firmer philosophic grasp upon American values, but, confronting an immensely more complicated America than Whitman did, Sandburg has accomplished a fusion of values of immense complexity into a confession of faith—*The People, Yes!*

FISH CRIER

First published in *Chicago Poems,* 1916.

> I know a Jew fish crier down on Maxwell Street with a
>   voice like a north wind blowing over corn stubble
>   in January.
> He dangles herring before prospective customers evinc-
>   ing a joy identical with that of Pavlowa dancing.   5
> His face is that of a man terribly glad to be selling fish,
>   terribly glad that God made fish, and customers to
>   whom he may call his wares from a pushcart.

LOST

First published in *Poetry: A Magazine of Verse,* March, 1914, then collected into *Chicago Poems,* 1916.

> Desolate and lone
> All night long on the lake

1. **Maxwell Street**—in the Jewish section of Chicago, on the near West Side. 5. **Pavlowa** —Anna Pavlova (1885-1931), Russian-trained ballet dancer whose tours of the United States were a triumphant success. 2. **the lake**—Lake Michigan.

Where fog trails and mist creeps,
The whistle of a boat
Calls and cries unendingly,   5
Like some lost child
In tears and trouble
Hunting the harbor's breast
And the harbor's eyes.

COOL TOMBS

First published in the *Craftsman*, July, 1916, then collected into *Cornhuskers*, 1918.

When Abraham Lincoln was shoveled into the tombs,
he forgot the copperheads and the assassin . . .
in the dust, in the cool tombs.

And Ulysses Grant lost all thought of con men and Wall
Street, cash and collateral turned ashes . . . in the   5
dust, in the cool tombs.

Pocahontas' body, lovely as a poplar, sweet as a red haw
in November or a pawpaw in May, did she wonder?
does she remember? . . . in the dust, in the cool
tombs?   10

Take any streetful of people buying clothes and groceries, cheering a hero or throwing confetti and blowing
tin horns . . . tell me if the lovers are losers . . .
tell me if any get more than the lovers . . . in the
dust . . . in the cool tombs.   15

SMOKE AND STEEL

First published in *Poetry: A Magazine of Verse*, February, 1920. In that year it became the title poem of *Smoke and Steel*.

Smoke of the fields in spring is one,
Smoke of the leaves in autumn another.
Smoke of a steel-mill roof or a battleship funnel,
They all go up in a line with a smokestack,
Or they twist . . . in the slow twist . . . of the wind.   5

2. **copperheads**—in the 1860's, Northern sympathizers with the Confederate cause. **assassin**—John Wilkes Booth (1839-1865). **4-5. Ulysses Grant . . . Wall Street**—After retiring from the Presidency in 1877, General U. S. Grant (1822-1885) lost his private fortune because of the collapse of a private banking house. During his Presidency he was accused of winking at an unholy alliance between the United States Treasury and the stock exchange in Wall Street. **7. Pocahontas**—Pocahontas (c. 1595-1617), daughter of Powhatan, the savior of Captain John Smith at Jamestown, died in England.

If the north wind comes they run to the south.
If the west wind comes they run to the east.
    By this sign
    all smokes
    know each other.   10
Smoke of the fields in spring and leaves in autumn,
Smoke of the finished steel, chilled and blue,
By the oath of work they swear: "I know you."

Hunted and hissed from the center
Deep down long ago when God made us over,   15
Deep down are the cinders we came from—
You and I and our heads of smoke.

   .   .   .   .

Some of the smokes God dropped on the job
Cross on the sky and count our years
And sing in the secrets of our numbers;   20
Sing their dawns and sing their evenings,
Sing an old log-fire song:
    You may put the damper up,
    You may put the damper down,
    The smoke goes up the chimney just the same.   25

Smoke of a city sunset skyline,
Smoke of a country dusk horizon—
    They cross on the sky and count our years.

   .   .   .   .

Smoke of a brick-red dust
    Winds on a spiral   30
    Out of the stacks
For a hidden and glimpsing moon.
This, said the bar-iron shed to the blooming mill,
This is the slang of coal and steel.
The day-gang hands it to the night-gang,   35
The night-gang hands it back.

Stammer at the slang of this—
Let us understand half of it.
    In the rolling mills and sheet mills,
    In the harr and boom of the blast fires,   40
    The smoke changes its shadow
    And men change their shadow;
    A nigger, a wop, a bohunk changes.

    A bar of steel—it is only
Smoke at the heart of it, smoke and the blood of a man.   45
A runner of fire ran in it, ran out, ran somewhere else,

33. bar-iron shed . . . blooming mill—structure in which bars of iron are stored; establishment for making malleable iron directly from ore. **40. harr**—snarl. **43. wop . . . bohunk**—The heavy labor in steel mills has been performed by immigrants (or the children of immigrants) from the south and center of Europe.

And left—smoke and the blood of a man
And the finished steel, chilled and blue.

So fire runs in, runs out, runs somewhere else again,
And the bar of steel is a gun, a wheel, a nail, a shovel,   50
A rudder under the sea, a steering-gear in the sky;
And always dark in the heart and through it,
   Smoke and the blood of a man.
Pittsburg, Youngstown, Gary—they make their steel with men.

In the blood of men and the ink of chimneys   55
The smoke nights write their oaths:
Smoke into steel and blood into steel;
Homestead, Braddock, Birmingham, they make their steel with men.
Smoke and blood is the mix of steel.

  The birdmen drone   60
  in the blue; it is steel
  a motor sings and zooms.

  · · · · · · ·

Steel barb-wire around The Works.
Steel guns in the holsters of the guards at the gates of The Works.
Steel ore-boats bring the loads clawed from the earth by steel, lifted and lugged
 by arms of steel, sung on its way by the clanking clam-shells.   65
The runners now, the handlers now, are steel; they dig and clutch and haul; they
 hoist their automatic knuckles from job to job; they are steel making steel.
Fire and dust and air fight in the furnaces; the pour is timed, the billets wriggle;
 the clinkers are dumped:
Liners on the sea, skyscrapers on the land; diving steel in the sea, climbing steel
 in the sky.

  · · · · · · ·

Finders in the dark, you Steve with a dinner bucket, you Steve clumping in the
 dusk on the sidewalks with an evening paper for the woman and kids, you
 Steve with your head wondering where we all end up—
Finders in the dark, Steve: I hook my arm in cinder sleeves; we go down the
 street together; it is all the same to us; you Steve and the rest of us end on
 the same stars; we all wear a hat in hell together, in hell or heaven.   70

  Smoke nights now, Steve.
  Smoke, smoke, lost in the sieves of yesterday;
  Dumped again to the scoops and hooks to-day.
  Smoke like the clocks and whistles, always.
    Smoke nights now.   75
    To-morrow something else.

  · · · · · · ·

54. Pittsburg, Youngstown, Gary—Pittsburgh, Pennsylvania, Youngstown, Ohio, and Gary, Indiana, considered as representative "steel towns." **58. Homestead, Braddock, Birmingham**—Homestead, Pennsylvania; Braddock, Pennsylvania; Birmingham, Alabama. **65. clamshells**—that is, clam-shell dredges. **66. runners**—that is, the distributors, the messengers. Their work is now done by steel mechanisms. **they**—refers to "handlers." **67. pour**—A single filling of the molds is called a pour. **billets wriggle**—The surface of liquid steel in a mold seems to shimmer and wriggle because of the intense heat. **69. Steve**—slang term for a Slav workman in an American steel mill.

Luck moons come and go;
Five men swim in a pot of red steel.
Their bones are kneaded into the bread of steel:
Their bones are knocked into coils and anvils   80
And the sucking plungers of sea-fighting turbines.
Look for them in the woven frame of a wireless station.

So ghosts hide in steel like heavy-armed men in mirrors.
Peepers, skulkers—they shadow-dance in laughing tombs.
They are always there and they never answer.   85

One of them said: "I like my job, the company is good to me, America is a won-
    derful country."
One: "Jesus, my bones ache; the company is a liar; this is a free country, like hell."
One: "I got a girl, a peach; we save up and go on a farm and raise pigs and be
    the boss ourselves."
And the others were roughneck singers a long ways from home.
Look for them back of a steel vault door.   90

      They laugh at the cost.
      They lift the birdmen into the blue.
      It is steel a motor sings and zooms.

In the subway plugs and drums,
In the slow hydraulic drills, in gumbo or gravel,   95
Under dynamo shafts in the webs of armature spiders,
They shadow-dance and laugh at the cost.

   .   .   .   .   .   .

The ovens light a red dome.
Spools of fire wind and wind.
Quadrangles of crimson sputter.   100
The lashes of dying maroon let down.
Fire and wind wash out the slag.
Forever the slag gets washed in fire and wind.

The anthem learned by the steel is:
      Do this or go hungry.   105
Look for our rust on a plow.
Listen to us in a threshing-engine razz.
Look at our job in the running wagon wheat.

   .   .   .   .

Fire and wind wash at the slag.
Box-cars, clocks, steam-shovels, churns, pistons, boilers, scissors—   110
Oh, the sleeping slag from the mountains, the slag-heavy pig-iron will go down
    many roads.
Men will stab and shoot with it, and make butter and tunnel rivers, and mow hay
    in swaths, and slit hogs and skin beeves, and steer airplanes across North
    America, Europe, Asia, round the world.

Hacked from a hard rock country, broken and baked in mills and smelters, the
    rusty dust waits

    95. gumbo—thick mud.

Till the clean hard weave of its atoms cripples and blunts the drills chewing a hole in it.
The steel of its plinths and flanges is reckoned, O God, in one-millionth of an inch.　　　　115

．　　　．　　　．　　　．　　　．　　　．

Once when I saw the curves of fire, the rough scarf women dancing,
Dancing out of the flues and smokestacks—flying hair of fire, flying feet upside down;
Buckets and baskets of fire exploding and chortling, fire running wild out of the steady and fastened ovens;
Sparks cracking a harr-harr-huff from a solar-plexus of rock-ribs of the earth taking a laugh for themselves;
Ears and noses of fire, gibbering gorilla arms of fire, gold mud-pies, gold bird-wings, red jackets riding purple mules, scarlet autocrats tumbling from the humps of camels, assassinated czars straddling vermilion balloons;　　120
I saw then the fires flash one by one: good-by: then smoke, smoke;
And in the screens the great sisters of night and cool stars, sitting women arranging their hair,
Waiting in the sky, waiting with slow easy eyes, waiting and half-murmuring:
　　"Since you know all
　　　and I know nothing,
　　　tell me what I dreamed last night."　　　125

．　　　．　　　．　　　．　　　．　　　．

Pearl cobwebs in the windy rain,
in only a flicker of wind,
are caught and lost and never known again.

A pool of moonshine comes and waits,　　　130
but never waits long: the wind picks up
loose gold like this and is gone.

A bar of steel sleeps and looks slant-eyed
on the pearl cobwebs, the pools of moonshine;
sleeps slant-eyed a million years,　　　135
sleeps with a coat of rust, a vest of moths,
a shirt of gathering sod and loam.

The wind never bothers . . . a bar of steel.
The wind picks only . . . pearl cobwebs . . . pools of moonshine.

THE SINS OF KALAMAZOO

First published in *Smoke and Steel*, 1920. Kalamazoo, in southern Michigan, is here taken as a symbol of small Midwestern cities.

The sins of Kalamazoo are neither scarlet nor crimson.
The sins of Kalamazoo are a convict gray, a dishwater drab.
And the people who sin the sins of Kalamazoo are neither scarlet nor crimson.

115. plinths—a slab, block, or stone which supports a column, or a thin, projecting course of a wall; flanges—projecting rims.

They run to drabs and grays—and some of them sing
    they shall be washed whiter than snow—and   5
    some: We should worry.

Yes, Kalamazoo is a spot on the map
And the passenger trains stop there
And the factory smokestacks smoke
And the grocery stores are open Saturday nights   10
And the streets are free for citizens who vote
And inhabitants counted in the census.
Saturday night is the big night.
    Listen with your ears on a Saturday night in Kalamazoo
    And say to yourself: I hear America, I hear, *what* do I hear?   15

Main street there runs through the middle of the town
And there is a dirty postoffice
And a dirty city hall
And a dirty railroad station
And the United States flag cries, cries the Stars and   20
    Stripes to the four winds on Lincoln's birthday
    and the Fourth of July.

Kalamazoo kisses a hand to something far off.
Kalamazoo calls to a long horizon, to a shivering silver angel, to a creeping mystic
    what-is-it.
"We're here because we're here," is the song of Kalamazoo.   25
"We don't know where we're going but we're on our way," are the words.
There are hound dogs of bronze on the public square, hound dogs looking far be-
    yond the public square.

Sweethearts there in Kalamazoo
Go to the general delivery window of the postoffice
And speak their names and ask for letters   30
And ask again, "Are you sure there is nothing for me?
I wish you'd look again—there must be a letter for me."

And sweethearts go to the city hall
And tell their names and say, "We want a license."
And they go to an installment house and buy a bed on time and a clock,   35
And the children grow up asking each other, "What can we do to kill time?"
They grow up and go to the railroad station and buy tickets for Texas, Pennsyl-
    vania, Alaska.
"Kalamazoo is all right," they say. "But I want to see the world."
And when they have looked the world over they come back saying it is all like
    Kalamazoo.

The trains come in from the east and hoot for the crossings,   40
And buzz away to the peach country and Chicago to the west;
Or they come from the west and shoot on to the Battle Creek breakfast bazaars
And the speedbug heavens of Detroit.

    5. washed whiter than snow—*Cf.* Isaiah 1:18. **6. We should worry**—popular slang
expression in 1920. **41. peach country**—western Michigan. **42. Battle . . . bazaars**—Battle
Creek, Michigan, is a center for the manufacture of prepared breakfast foods. **43. speedbug
heavens**—Detroit as the center of the automotive industry.

"I hear America, I hear, *what* do I hear?"
Said a loafer lagging along on the sidewalks of Kalamazoo,   45
Lagging along and asking questions, reading signs.

Oh yes, there is a town named Kalamazoo,
A spot on the map where the trains hesitate.
I saw the sign of a five and ten cent store there
And the Standard Oil Company and the International Harvester   50
And a graveyard and a ball grounds
And a short order counter where a man can get a stack of wheats
And a pool hall where a rounder leered confidential like and said:
"Lookin' for a quiet game?"

The loafer lagged along and asked,   55
"Do you make guitars here?
Do you make boxes the singing wood winds ask to sleep in?
Do you rig up strings the singing wood winds sift over and sing low?"
The answer: "We manufacture musical instruments here."

Here I saw churches with steeples like hatpins,   60
Undertaking rooms with sample coffins in the show window
And signs everywhere satisfaction is guaranteed,
Shooting galleries where men kill imitation pigeons,
And there were doctors for the sick,
And lawyers for people waiting in jail,   65
And a dog catcher and a superintendent of streets,
And telephones, water-works, trolley cars,
And newspapers with a splatter of telegrams from
        sister cities of Kalamazoo the round world over.

And the loafer lagging along said: 70
Kalamazoo, you ain't in a class by yourself;
I seen you before in a lot of places.
If you are nuts America is nuts.
        And lagging along he said bitterly:
        Before I came to Kalamazoo I was silent.   75
        Now I am gabby, God help me, I am gabby.

Kalamazoo, both of us will do a fadeaway.
I will be carried out feet first
And time and the rain will chew you to dust
And the winds blow you away.   80
And an old, old mother will lay a green moss cover on my bones
And a green moss cover on the stones of your postoffice and city hall.

        Best of all
I have loved your kiddies playing run-sheep-run
And cutting their initials on the ball ground fence.   85
They knew every time I fooled them who was fooled and how.

        Best of all
I have loved the red gold smoke of your sunsets;

I have loved a moon with a ring around it
Floating over your public square;   90
I have loved the white dawn frost of early winter silver
And purple over your railroad tracks and lumber yards.

   The wishing heart of you I loved, Kalamazoo.
   I sang bye-lo, bye-lo to your dreams.
I sang bye-lo to your hopes and songs.   95
I wished to God there were hound dogs of bronze on your public square,
Hound dogs with bronze paws looking to a long
  horizon with a shivering silver angel,
  a creeping mystic what-is-it.

BROKEN-FACE GARGOYLES

From *Smoke and Steel,* 1920, in which it forms the title poem of the third section. First published in the *Dial,* March, 1920.

All I can give you is broken-face gargoyles.
It is too early to sing and dance at funerals,
Though I can whisper to you I am looking for an undertaker humming a lullaby
  and throwing his feet in a swift and mystic buck-and-wing, now you see it and
  now you don't.

Fish to swim a pool in your garden flashing a speckled silver,
A basket of wine-saps filling your room with flame-dark for your eyes and the tang
  of valley orchards for your nose,   5
Such a beautiful pail of fish, such a beautiful peck of apples, I cannot bring you
  now.
It is too early and I am not footloose yet.

I shall come in the night when I come with a hammer and saw.
I shall come near your window, where you look out when your eyes open in the
  morning,
And there I shall slam together bird-houses and bird-baths for wing-loose wrens and
  hummers to live in, birds with yellow wing tips to blur and buzz soft all
  summer,   10
So I shall make little fool homes with doors, always open doors for all and each to
  run away when they want to.
I shall come just like that even though now it is early and I am not yet footloose,
Even though I am still looking for an undertaker with a raw, wind-bitten face and
  a dance in his feet.
I make a date with you (put it down) for six o'clock in the evening a thousand
  years from now.

All I can give you now is broken-face gargoyles.   15
All I can give you now is a double gorilla head with two fish mouths and four
  eagle eyes hooked on a street wall, spouting water and looking two ways to

  3. buck-and-wing—an American dance. **5. wine-saps**—a variety of apple. **10. hummers**
—hummingbirds.

the ends of the street for the new people, the young strangers, coming, coming, always coming.

It is early.
I shall yet be footloose.

FOUR PRELUDES ON PLAYTHINGS OF THE WIND

"The past is a bucket of ashes."

After publication in the *New Republic*, July 21, 1920, this became the title poem of the fourth section of *Smoke and Steel*, 1920.

I

The woman named To-morrow
sits with a hairpin in her teeth
and takes her time
and does her hair the way she wants it
and fastens at last the last braid and coil   5
and puts the hairpin where it belongs
and turns and drawls: Well, what of it?
My grandmother, Yesterday, is gone.
What of it? Let the dead be dead.

II

The doors were cedar   10
and the panels strips of gold
and the girls were golden girls
and the panels read and the girls chanted:
    We are the greatest city,
      the greatest nation: 15
      nothing like us ever was.
The doors are twisted on broken hinges.
Sheets of rain swish through on the wind
    where the golden girls ran and the panels read:
    We are the greatest city,   20
    the greatest nation,
    nothing like us ever was.

III

It has happened before.
Strong men put up a city and got
    a nation together,   25
And paid singers to sing and women
    to warble: We are the greatest city,
      the greatest nation,
      nothing like us ever was.

10. **cedar**—In a vague way this description of lost magnificence is based on Solomon's building of the Temple. *Cf.* I Kings, Chapters 6-7.

And while the singers sang   30
and the strong men listened
and paid the singers well
and felt good about it all,
    there were rats and lizards who listened
    . . . and the only listeners left now   35
    . . . are . . . the rats . . . and the lizards.

And there are black crows
crying, "Caw, caw,"
bringing mud and sticks
building a nest   40
over the words carved
on the doors where the panels were cedar
and the strips on the panels were gold
and the golden girls came singing:
    We are the greatest city,   45
    the greatest nation:
    nothing like us ever was.

The only singers now are crows crying, "Caw, caw,"
And the sheets of rain whine in the wind and doorways.
And the only listeners now are . . . the rats . . . and the lizards.   50

IV

    The feet of the rats
    scribble on the door sills;
    the hieroglyphs of the rat footprints
    chatter the pedigrees of the rats
    and babble of the blood   55
    and gabble of the breed
    of the grandfathers and the great-grandfathers
    of the rats.

    And the wind shifts
    and the dust on the door sill shifts   60
    and even the writing of the rat footprints
    tells us nothing, nothing at all
    about the greatest city, the greatest nation
    where the strong men listened
    and the women warbled: Nothing like us ever was.   65

KILLERS

Although Sandburg published a poem with this title in *Poetry* for October, 1915, the present poem seems to have been first printed in the fourth section of *Smoke and Steel*, 1920.

I am put high over all others in the city today.
I am the killer who kills for those who wish a killing today.

Here is a strong young man who killed.
There was a driving wind of city dust and horse dung blowing and he stood at an
    intersection of five sewers and there pumped the bullets of an automatic pistol
    into another man, a fellow citizen.
Therefore, the prosecuting attorneys, fellow citizens, and a jury of his peers, also
    fellow citizens, listened to the testimony of other fellow citizens, policemen,
    doctors, and after a verdict of guilty, the judge, a fellow citizen, said: I sen-
    tence you to be hanged by the neck till you are dead.   5

So there is a killer to be killed and I am the killer of the killer for today.
I don't know why it beats in my head in the lines I read once in an old school
    reader: I'm to be queen of the May, mother, I'm to be queen of the May.
Anyhow it comes back in language just like that today.

I am the high honorable killer today.
There are five million people in the state, five million killers for whom I kill   10
I am the killer who kills today for five million killers who wish a killing.

WIND SONG

From the section of *Smoke and Steel,* 1920, called "Mist Forms."

Long ago I learned how to sleep,
In an old apple orchard where the wind swept by
    counting its money and throwing it away,
In a wind-gaunt orchard where the limbs forked out
    and listened or never listened at all,   5
In a passel of trees where the branches trapped the
    wind into whistling, "Who, who are you?"
I slept with my head in an elbow on a summer after-
    noon and there I took a sleep lesson.
There I went away saying: I know why they sleep,   10
    I know how they trap the tricky winds.
Long ago I learned how to listen to the singing wind
    and how to forget and how to hear the deep whine,
Slapping and lapsing under the day blue and the night stars:
    Who, who are you?   15

        Who can ever forget
        listening to the wind go by
        counting its money
        and throwing it away?

   7. I'm to be . . . May—The refrain of Tennyson's poem "The May Queen." **6. passel**—
folk pronunciation of "parcel," meaning here an indefinite number, a collection.

BABY VAMPS

From the "Circles of Doors" section of *Smoke and Steel*, 1920.

Baby vamps, is it harder work than it used to be?
Are the new soda parlors worse than the old time saloons?
  Baby vamps, do you have jobs in the day time
        or is this all you do?
        do you come out only at night?   5
In the winter at the skating rinks, in the summer at the
        roller coaster parks,
Wherever figure eights are carved, by skates in winter, by roller coasters in summer,
Wherever the whirligigs are going and chicken spanish and hot dog are sold,
There you come, giggling baby vamp, there you come with your blue baby eyes,
    saying: 10
        Take me along.

AND SO TO-DAY

On November 11, 1921, the body of an unknown soldier, which had been lying in state under the rotunda of the National Capitol, was taken in solemn procession from there to its final resting place in the Arlington National Cemetery. The pallbearers were generals of the Army and the Marine Corps, and admirals of the Navy, and in the procession were Woodrow Wilson, President during the First World War, Warren Gamaliel Harding (the "peace commander" mentioned in the poem), and General Pershing, who marched with President Harding immediately behind the caisson. After an address by the President and other ceremonies, the body was taken into the sarcophagus, there to remain forever. In 1931 the present cenotaph was erected, replacing the earlier, temporary tomb. On it is the inscription: "Here rests in honored glory an American soldier known but to God."

The burial procession was primarily a military affair. Consultation of any good map of Washington will make clear the path of the procession, which is also the path of the procession of skeletons in Sandburg's imagined parade.

This poem first appeared in *Slabs of the Sunburnt West*, 1922.

And so to-day—they lay him away—
the boy nobody knows the name of—
the buck private—the unknown soldier—
the doughboy who dug under and died
when they told him to—that's him.   5

Down Pennsylvania Avenue to-day the riders go,
men and boys riding horses, roses in their teeth,
stems of roses, rose leaf stalks, rose dark leaves—
the line of the green ends in a red rose flash.

2. **soda parlors . . . saloons**—When this poem was written, prohibition was just coming into effect as a result of adopting the Eighteenth Amendment. The irony of the poem is that this "noble experiment" was supposed to elevate public morals.

Skeleton men and boys riding skeleton horses,   10
the rib bones shine, the rib bones curve,
shine with savage, elegant curves—
a jawbone runs with a long white slant,
a skull dome runs with a long white arch,
bone triangles click and rattle,   15
elbows, ankles, white line slants—
shining in the sun, past the White House,
past the Treasury Building, Army and Navy Buildings,
on to the mystic white Capitol Dome—
so they go down Pennsylvania Avenue to-day,   20
skeleton men and boys riding skeleton horses,
stems of roses in their teeth,
rose dark leaves at their white jaw slants—
and a hoarse laugh question nickers and whinnies,
moans with a whistle out of horse head teeth: 25
why? who? where?

       ("The big fish—eat the little fish—
       the little fish—eat the shrimps—
       and the shrimps—eat mud."—
       said a cadaverous man—with a black umbrella—   30
       spotted with white polka dots—with a missing
       ear—with a missing foot and arms—
       with a missing sheath of muscles
       singing to the silver sashes of the sun.)

And so to-day—they lay him away—   35
the boy nobody knows the name of—
the buck private—the unknown soldier—
the doughboy who dug under and died
when they told him to—that's him.

If he picked himself and said, "I am ready to die,"   40
if he gave his name and said, "My country, take me,"
then the baskets of roses to-day are for the Boy,
the flowers, the songs, the steamboat whistles,
the proclamations of the honorable orators,
they are all for the Boy—that's him.   45
If the government of the Republic picked him saying,
"You are wanted, your country takes you"—
if the Republic put a stethoscope to his heart
and looked at his teeth and tested his eyes and said,
"You are a citizen of the Republic and a sound animal   50
in all parts and functions—the Republic takes you"—
then to-day the baskets of flowers are all for the Republic,
the roses, the songs, the steamboat whistles,
the proclamations of the honorable orators—
they are all for the Republic.   55

   46. picked him—that is, if he was drafted.

And so to-day—they lay him away—
and an understanding goes—his long sleep shall be
under arms and arches near the Capitol Dome—
there is an authorization—he shall have tomb companions—
the martyred presidents of the Republic—   60
the buck private—the unknown soldier—that's him.

The man who was war commander of the armies of the Republic
rides down Pennsylvania Avenue—
The man who is peace commander of the armies of the Republic
rides down Pennsylvania Avenue—   65
for the sake of the Boy, for the sake of the Republic.

    (And the hoofs of the skeleton horses
    all drum soft on the asphalt footing—
    so soft is the drumming, so soft the roll call
    of the grinning sergeants calling the roll call—   70
    so soft is it all—a camera man murmurs, "Moonshine.")

Look—who salutes the coffin—
lays a wreath of remembrance
on the box where a buck private
sleeps a clean dry sleep at last—   75
look—it is the highest ranking general
of the officers of the armies of the Republic.

    (Among pigeon corners of the Congressional Library—they file documents
        quietly, casually, all in a day's work—this human document, the buck
        private nobody knows the name of—they file away in granite and steel—
        with music and roses, salutes, proclamations of the honorable orators.)

Across the country, between two ocean shore lines,
where cities cling to rail and water routes,   80
there people and horses stop in their foot tracks,
cars and wagons stop in their wheel tracks—
faces at street crossings shine with a silence
of eggs laid in a row on a pantry shelf—
among the ways and paths of the flow of the Republic   85
faces come to a standstill, sixty clockticks count—
in the name of the Boy, in the name of the Republic.

    (A million faces a thousand miles from Pennsylvania Avenue stay frozen
        with a look, a clocktick, a moment—skeleton riders on skeleton horses
        —the nickering high horse laugh, the whinny and the howl up Penn-
        sylvania Avenue: who? why? where?)

60. martyred presidents—The catafalque on which the body of the Unknown Soldier lay in state also served for the bodies of Presidents Lincoln, Garfield, and McKinley, each of whom had been assassinated. **62. war commander**—Woodrow Wilson. **64. peace commander**—Warren Gamaliel Harding. **76. highest ranking general**—John J. Pershing, General of the Armies of the United States. **78. pigeon corners**—pigeonhole corners. **81. stop in their foot tracks**—A national "moment of silence" was observed on the day in question.

(So people far from the asphalt footing of Pennsylvania Avenue look, wonder, mumble—the riding white-jaw phantoms ride hi-eeee, hi-eeee, hi-yi,
hi-yi, hi-eeee—the proclamations of the honorable orators mix with the
top-sergeants whistling the roll call.)

If when the clockticks counted sixty,   90
when the heartbeats of the Republic
came to a stop for a minute,
if the Boy had happened to sit up,
happening to sit up as Lazarus sat up, in the story,
then the first shivering language to drip off his mouth   95
might have come as, "Thank God," or "Am I dreaming?"
or "What the hell" or "When do we eat?"
or "Kill 'em, kill 'em, the . . ."
or "Was that . . . a rat . . . ran over my face?"
or "For Christ's sake, gimme water, gimme water,"   100
or "Blub blub, bloo bloo . . . . . ."
or any bubbles of shell shock gibberish
from the gashes of No Man's Land.

Maybe some buddy knows,
some sister, mother, sweetheart,   105
maybe some girl who sat with him once
when a two-horn silver moon
slid on the peak of a house-roof gable,
and promises lived in the air of the night,
when the air was filled with promises,   110
when any little slip-shoe lovey
could pick a promise out of the air.

        "Feed it to 'em,
            they lap it up,
            bull . . . bull . . . bull,"   115
Said a movie news reel camera man,
Said a Washington newspaper correspondent,
Said a baggage handler lugging a trunk,
Said a two-a-day vaudeville juggler,
Said a hanky-pank selling jumping-jacks.   120
"Hokum—they lap it up," said the bunch.

And a tall scar-face ball player,
Played out as a ball player,
Made a speech of his own for the hero boy,
Sent an earful of his own to the dead buck private: 125
        "It's all safe now, buddy,
            Safe when you say yes,
            Safe for the yes-men."

94. **Lazarus**—*Cf.* John, Chapter 11. 103. **No Man's Land**—space between the trenches of
the contending armies in the First World War. 119. **two-a-day vaudeville juggler**—that is,
he gave an afternoon and an evening performance daily. 120. **hanky-pank**—street pedlar.

He was a tall scar-face battler
With his face in a newspaper   130
Reading want ads, reading jokes,
Reading love, murder, politics,
Jumping from jokes back to the want ads,
Reading the want ads first and last,
The letters of the word JOB, "J-O-B,"   135
Burnt like a shot of bootleg booze
In the bones of his head—
In the wish of his scar-face eyes.

The honorable orators,
Always the honorable orators,   140
Buttoning the buttons on their prinz alberts,
Pronouncing the syllables "sac-ri-fice,"
Juggling those bitter salt-soaked syllables—
Do they ever gag with hot ashes in their mouths?
Do their tongues ever shrivel with a pain of fire   145
Across those simple syllables "sac-ri-fice"?

(There was one orator people far off saw.
He had on a gunnysack shirt over his bones,
And he lifted an elbow socket over his head,
And he lifted a skinny signal finger.   150
And he had nothing to say, nothing easy—
He mentioned ten million men, mentioned them as having gone west, mentioned
     them as shoving up the daisies.
We could write it all on a postage stamp, what he said.
He said it and quit and faded away,
A gunnysack shirt on his bones.)   155

        Stars of the night sky,
        did you see that phantom fadeout,
        did you see those phantom riders,
        skeleton riders on skeleton horses,
        stems of roses in their teeth,   160
        rose leaves red on white-jaw slants,
        grinning along on Pennsylvania Avenue,
        the top-sergeants calling roll calls—
        did their horses bicker a horse laugh?
        did the ghosts of the boney battalions   165
        move out and on, up the Potomac, over on the Ohio,
        and out to the Mississippi, the Missouri, the Red River,
        and down to the Rio Grande, and on to the Yazoo,
        over to the Chattahoochee and up to the Rappahannock?
        did you see 'em, stars of the night sky?   170

        And so to-day—they lay him away—
        the boy nobody knows the name of—

136. bootleg booze—The prohibition amendment was then in force. 141. prinz alberts
—properly Prince Albert, a cutaway coat worn on formal occasions. 142. "sac-ri-fice"—the
theme of President Harding's oration. 152. gone west—died. 157. fadeout—as in a movie.

they lay him away in granite and steel—
with music and roses—under a flag—
under a sky of promises.   175

SEA SLANT

First published in the *New Republic*, February 22, 1922, this poem was collected into *Slabs of the Sunburnt West*, 1922.

On up the sea slant,
On up the horizon,
This ship limps.

The bone of her nose fog-gray,
The heart of her sea-strong,   5
She came a long way,
She goes a long way.

On up the horizon,
On up the sea-slant,
She limps sea-strong, fog-gray.   10

She is a green-lit night gray.
She comes and goes in sea fog.
Up the horizon slant she limps.

SKETCH OF A POET

From the "Valley Mist" section of *Good Morning, America*, 1928. With this
whimsical definition of a poet the student should compare the thirty-eight "definitions" of poetry which open that volume.

He wastes time walking and telling the air, "I am superior
even to the wind."

On several proud days he has addressed the wide circumambient atmosphere, "I am the wind myself."

He has poet's license 4-11-44; he got it even before writing   5
of those "silver bugs that come on the sky without warning
every evening."

He stops for the buzzing of bumblebees on bright Tuesdays
in any summer month; he performs with a pencil all alone
among dun cat-tails, amid climbing juniper bushes, nota-   10
tions rivaling the foot tracks of anxious spiders; he finds
mice homes under beach logs in the sand and pursues inquiries on how mice have one room for bed-room, dining-
room, sitting-room and how they have no front porch where
they sit publicly and watch passers-by.   15

He asks himself, "Who else is the emperor of such elegant
english? Who else has slipped so often on perilous banana
peels and yet lived to put praise of banana peels on sonorous pages?"

One minute he accuses God of having started the world on
a shoestring; the next minute he executes a simple twist of   20
the wrist and a slight motion of the hand and insinuates
these bones shall rise again.

Yet he wastes time walking and telling the air, "I am superior to the wind," or on proud days, "I am the wind myself."

SELECTIONS FROM *THE PEOPLE, YES*

The People, Yes, a book of almost three hundred pages, is Sandburg's confession
of faith in the long-run strength and sagacity of the plain people. It is a volume in
107 sections, mingling prose and poetry, short sections and long sections, heaping
up popular phrases, folk wisdom, anecdotes, conversations, and myths. The theme
is that the people can be momentarily tricked and betrayed, but as the opening of
the last section states, "The people will live on." In bulk it is Sandburg's most impressive book except for the enormous biography of Lincoln; in scope and insight
it is probably his richest and most characteristic "poetical" work. Incidentally, it is
one in which he departs most widely from conventional notions of the technique
of poetry and of the dignity of poetry.

38

Have you seen men handed refusals
    till they began to laugh
       at the notion of ever landing a job again—
Muttering with the laugh,
    "It's driving me nuts and the family too,"   5
Mumbling of hoodoos and jinx,
    fear of defeat creeping in their vitals—
Have you never seen this?
    or do you kid yourself
    with the fond soothing syrup of four words   10
    "Some folks won't work"??
Of course some folks won't work—
    they are sick or wornout or lazy
    or misled with the big idea
the idle poor should imitate the idle rich.   15

Have you seen women and kids
    step out and hustle for the family
    some in night life on the streets
    some fighting other women and kids
    for the leavings of fruit and vegetable markets   20
    or searching alleys and garbage dumps for scraps?

Have you seen them with savings gone
    furniture and keepsakes pawned
    and the pawntickets blown away in cold winds?
    by one letdown and another ending   25
    in what you might call slums—
To be named perhaps in case reports
    and tabulated and classified
    among those who have crossed over
    from the employables into the *un*employables?   30

What is the saga of the employables?
    what are the breaks they get?
What are the dramas of personal fate
    spilled over from industrial transitions?
    what punishments handed bottom people   35
    who have wronged no man's house
    or things or person?

    Stocks are property, yes.
    Bonds are property, yes.
Machines, land, buildings, are property, yes.   40
    A job is property,
    no, nix, nah nah.

The rights of property are guarded
    by ten thousand laws and fortresses.
The right of a man to live by his work—   45
        what is this right?
        and why does it clamor?
        and who can hush it
        so it will stay hushed?
        and why does it speak   56
        and though put down speak again
        with strengths out of the earth?

45

    They have yarns
Of a skyscraper so tall they had to put hinges
On the two top stories so to let the moon go by
Of one corn crop in Missouri when the roots
Went so deep and drew off so much water   5
The Mississippi riverbed that year was dry,
Of pancakes so thin they had only one side,
Of "a fog so thick we shingled the barn and six feet out on the fog,"
Of Pecos Pete straddling a cyclone in Texas and riding it to the west coast where "it
    rained out under him,"
Of the man who drove a swarm of bees across the Rocky Mountains and the
    Desert "and didn't lose a bee,"   10

9. Pecos Pete—also known as Pecos Bill, Southwestern folk hero whose figure is the center
of numerous tall stories.

Of a mountain railroad curve where the engineer in his cab can touch the caboose
    and spit in the conductor's eye,
Of the boy who climbed a cornstalk growing so fast he would have starved to
    death if they hadn't shot biscuits up to him,
Of the old man's whiskers: "When the wind was with him his whiskers arrived a
    day before he did,"
Of the hen laying a square egg and cackling, "Ouch!" and of hens laying eggs
    with the dates printed on them,
Of the ship captain's shadow: it froze to the deck one cold winter night,   15
Of mutineers on that same ship put to chipping rust with rubber hammers,
Of the sheep counter who was fast and accurate: "I just count their feet and divide
    by four,"
Of the man so tall he must climb a ladder to shave himself,
Of the runt so teeny-weeny it takes two men and a boy to see him,
Of mosquitoes: one can kill a dog, two of them a man,   20
Of a cyclone that sucked cookstoves out of the kitchen, up the chimney flue, and
    on to the next town,
Of the same cyclone picking up wagon-tracks in Nebraska and dropping them
    over in the Dakotas,
Of the hook-and-eye snake unlocking itself into forty pieces, each piece two inches
    long, then in nine seconds flat snapping itself together again,
Of the watch swallowed by the cow—when they butchered her a year later the
    watch was running and had the correct time,
Of horned snakes, hoop snakes that roll themselves where they want to go, and
    rattlesnakes carrying bells instead of rattles on their tails,   25
Of the herd of cattle in California getting lost in a giant redwood tree that had
    hollowed out,
Of the man who killed a snake by putting its tail in its mouth so it swallowed
    itself,
Of railroad trains whizzing along so fast they reach the station before the whistle,
Of pigs so thin the farmer had to tie knots in their tails to keep them from crawl-
    ing through the cracks in their pens,
Of Paul Bunyan's big blue ox, Babe, measuring between the eyes forty-two ax-
    handles and a plug of Star tobacco exactly,   30
Of John Henry's hammer and the curve of its swing and his singing of it as "a
    rainbow round my shoulder."

                    "Do tell!"
                    "I want to know!"
                    "You don't say so!"
                    "For the land's sake!"   35
                    "Gosh all fish-hooks!"
                    "Tell me some more.
                    I don't believe a word you say
                    but I love to listen
                    to your sweet harmonica   40
                    to your chin-music.
                    Your fish stories hang together

30. **Paul Bunyan**—giant mythical hero of the lumber camps, whose big blue ox, Babe, is part of the dramatis personae of Bunyan legends. 31. **John Henry**—Negro folk hero, a steel driver who died in a heroic attempt to surpass a steam drill.

when they're just a pack of lies:
you ought to have a leather medal:
you ought to have a statue   45
carved of butter: you deserve
a large bouquet of turnips."

"Yessir," the traveler drawled,
"Away out there in the petrified forest
everything goes on the same as usual.   50
The petrified birds sit in their petrified nests
and hatch their petrified young from petrified eggs."

A high pressure salesman jumped off the Brooklyn Bridge and was saved by a policeman. But it didn't take him long to sell the idea to the policeman. So together they jumped off the bridge.

One of the oil men in heaven started a rumor of a gusher down in hell. All the other oil men left in a hurry for hell. As he gets to thinking about the rumor he had started he says to himself there might be something in it after all. So he leaves for hell in a hurry.

"The number 42 will win this raffle, that's my number." And when he won they asked whether he guessed the number or had a system. He said he had a system, "I took up the old family album and there on page 7 was my grandfather and grandmother both on page 7. I said to myself this is easy for 7 times 7 is the number that will win and 7 times 7 is 42."   55

Once a shipwrecked sailor caught hold of a stateroom door and floated for hours till friendly hands from out of the darkness threw him a rope. And he called across the night, "What country is this?" and hearing voices answer, "New Jersey," he took a fresh hold on the floating stateroom door and called back half-wearily, "I guess I'll float a little farther."

An Ohio man bundled up the tin roof of a summer kitchen and sent it to a motor car maker with a complaint of his car not giving service. In three weeks a new car arrived for him and a letter: "We regret delay in shipment but your car was received in a very bad order."
A Dakota cousin of this Ohio man sent six years of tin can accumulations to the same works, asking them to overhaul his car. Two weeks later came a rebuilt car, five old tin cans, and a letter: "We are also forwarding you five parts not necessary in our new model."
Thus fantasies heard at filling stations in the midwest. Another relates to a Missouri mule who took aim with his heels at an automobile rattling by. The car turned a somersault, lit next a fence, ran right along through a cornfield till it came to a gate, moved onto the road and went on its way as though nothing had happened. The mule heehawed with desolation, "What's the use?"
Another tells of a farmer and his family stalled on a railroad crossing, how they jumped out in time to see a limited express knock it into flinders, the farmer calling, "Well, I always did say that car was no shucks in a real pinch."   60

When the Masonic Temple in Chicago was the tallest building in the United States west of New York, two men who would cheat the eyes out of you if you gave 'em a chance, took an Iowa farmer to the top of the building and asked him, "How is this for high?" They told him that for $25 they would go down in the basement and turn the building around on its turn-table for him while he stood on the roof and saw how this seventh wonder of the world worked. He handed them $25. They went. He waited. They never came back.

This is told in Chicago as a folk tale, the same as the legend of Mrs. O'Leary's cow kicking over the barn lamp that started the Chicago fire, when the Georgia visitor, Robert Toombs, telegraphed an Atlanta crony, "Chicago is on fire, the whole city burning down, God be praised!"

Nor is the prize sleeper Rip Van Winkle and his scolding wife forgotten, nor the headless horseman scooting through Sleepy Hollow

Nor the sunken treasure-ships in coves and harbors, the hideouts of gold and silver sought by Coronado, nor the Flying Dutchman rounding the Cape doomed to nevermore pound his ear nor ever again take a snooze for himself

Nor the sailor's caretaker Mother Carey seeing to it that every seafaring man in the afterworld has a seabird to bring him news of ships and women, an alba-tross for the admiral, a gull for the deckhand   65

Nor the sailor with a sweetheart in every port of the world, nor the ships that set out with flying colors and all the promises you could ask, the ships never heard of again,

Nor Jim Liverpool, the riverman who could jump across any river and back with-out touching land he was that quick on his feet,

Nor Mike Fink along the Ohio and the Mississippi, half wild horse and half cock-eyed alligator, the rest of him snags and snapping turtle. "I can out-run, out-jump, out-shoot, out-brag, out-drink, and out-fight, rough and tumble, no holts barred, any man on both sides of the river from Pittsburgh to New Orleans and back again to St. Louis. My trigger finger itches and I want to go redhot. War, famine and bloodshed puts flesh on my bones, and hardship's my daily bread."

Nor the man so lean he threw no shadow: six rattlesnakes struck at him at one time and every one missed him.

87

The people learn, unlearn, learn,
a builder, a wrecker, a builder again,
a juggler of shifting puppets.
   In so few eyeblinks
   In transition lightning streaks,   5
the people protect midgets into giants,
the people shrink titans into dwarfs.

62. Mrs. O'Leary's cow—The great Chicago fire of 1871 was started, according to legend, through the upsetting of a kerosene lantern by a cow belonging to Mrs. O'Leary. **Robert Toombs**—Robert Toombs (1810-1885) of Georgia, Secretary of State in the Confederate govern-ment. **63. Rip Van Winkle**—hero of Washington Irving's famous tale. **headless horse-man . . . Sleepy Hollow**—*Cf.* pp. 236 ff., above. **64. Coronado**—Francisco Vásquez de Cor-onado (c. 1500-1554), Spanish explorer who in 1540-42 led an expedition into our Southwest to locate the fabulous and wealthy Seven Cities of Cibola. **Flying Dutchman**—mythical hero who, as a result of a rash curse, is forever doomed to fail to make port in his ghost ship; subject of Wagner's opera. **65. Mother Carey**—Stormy petrels are known as "Mother Carey's chickens" because they are supposed to look after the souls of sailors. Mother Carey is derived from *"mater cara."* **67. Jim Liverpool**—sometimes a minor character in the Paul Bunyan saga and sometimes an independent folk hero. **68. Mike Fink**—Mississippi-Missouri River folk hero.

Faiths blow on the winds
and become shibboleths
and deep growths   10
with men ready to die
for a living word on the tongue,
for a light alive in the bones,
for dreams fluttering in the wrists.

For liberty and authority they die   15
though one is fire and the other water
and the balances of freedom and discipline
are a moving target with changing decoys.

Revolt and terror pay a price.
Order andd law have a cost.   20
What is this double use of fire and water?
Where are the rulers who know this riddle?
On the fingers of one hand you can number them.
How often has a governor of the people first
    learned to govern himself?   25

The free man willing to pay and struggle and die
    for the freedom for himself and others
Knowing how far to subject himself to discipline
    and obedience for the sake of an ordered so-
    ciety free from tyrants, exploiters and   30
    legalized frauds—
This free man is a rare bird and when you meet
    him take a good look at him and try
    to figure him out because
Some day when the United States of the Earth   35
    gets going and runs smooth and pretty there
    will be more of him than we have now.

103

The wind in the corn leaves among the naked stalks
and the assurances of the October cornhuskers
throwing the yellow and gold ears into wagons
and the weatherworn boards of the oblong corncribs
and the heavy boots of winter roaring   5
    around the barn doors
and the cows drowsing in peace at the feed-boxes—
while sheet steel is riveted into ships and bridges
and the hangar night shift meets the air mail
and the steam shovels scoop gravel by the ton   10
and the interstate trucks parade on the hard roads
and the bread line silhouettes stand in a drizzle
and in Iowa the state fair prize hog crunches corn
and on the truck farms this year's scarecrows
lose the clothes they wore this summer   15
and stand next year in a change of rags—
these are chapters interwoven of the people.

When a slow dim light moves
on the face of vast waters
and in its slow dim changing   20
baffles keen old captains
the reading of the light
in its shifting resolves
is the same as trying to read
the hosts of circumstance   25
deepening the paths of action
with a decree for the people:
    "Tomorrow you do this because
    you can do nothing else."

    What is it now   30
in the hosts of circumstance
where plainspoken men multiply,
what is it now the people are saying
near enough to the ribs of life
and the flowing face of vast waters   35
so they will go on saying it
in deepening paths of action
running toward a slow dim decree:
    "You do this because
    you can do nothing else"?   40

105

Always the storm of propaganda blows.
Buy a paper. Read a book. Start the radio.
Listen in the railroad car, in the bus,
Go to church, to a movie, to a saloon.
And always the breezes of personal opinion   5
are blowing mixed with the doctrines
of propaganda or the chatter of selling spiels.
Believe this, believe that. Buy these, buy them.
Love one-two-three, hate four-five-six.
Remember 7-8-9, forget 10-11-12.   10
Go now, don't wait, go now at once and buy
Dada Salts Incorporated, Crazy Horse Crystals,
for whatever ails you and if nothing ails you
it is good for that and we are telling you
for your own good. Whatever you are told,   15
you are told it is for your own good and not
for the special interest of those telling you.
Planned economy is forethought and care.
Planned economy is regimentation and tyranny.
What do you know about planned economy   20
and how did this argument get statred and why?
Let the argument go on.

The storm of propaganda blows always.
In every air of today the germs float and hover.

The shock and contact of ideas goes on.   25
Planned economy will arrive, stand up,
and stay a long time—or planned economy will
take a beating and be smothered.
> The people have the say-so
> Let the argument go on.   30
> Let the people listen.
Tomorrow the people say Yes or No by one question:
> "What else can be done?"
In the drive of faiths on the wind today the people know:
"We have come far and we are going farther yet."   35

Who was the quiet silver-toned agitator who
said he loved every stone of the streets of
Boston, who was a believer in sidewalks, and
had it, "The talk of the sidewalk today is
the law of the land tomorrow"?   40

"The people," said a farmer's wife in a Minnesota country store
    while her husband was buying a new post-hole digger,
"The people," she went on, "will stick around a long time.
"The people run the works, only they don't know it yet—you wait and see."

   .   Who knows the answers, the cold inviolable truth?   45
And when have the paid and professional liars done else than
    bring wrath and fire, wreck and doom?
And how few they are who search and hesitate and say:
"I stand in this whirlpool and tell you I don't know and if I did
    know I would tell you and all I am doing now is to guess   50
    and I give you my guess for what it is worth as one man's guess.
"Yet I have worked out this guess for myself as nobody's yes-man
    and when it happens I no longer own the priceless little piece
    of territory under my own hat, so far gone that I can't even
    do my own guessing for myself,   55
"Then I will know I am one of the unburied dead, one of the
    moving walking stalking talking unburied dead."

107

The people will live on.
The learning and blundering people will live on.
> They will be tricked and sold and again sold
And go back to the nourishing earth for rootholds,
> The people so peculiar in renewal and comeback,   5
> You can't laugh off their capacity to take it.
The mammoth rests between his cyclonic dramas.

The people so often sleepy, weary, enigmatic,
is a vast huddle with many units saying:
> "I earn my living.   10
> I make enough to get by
> and it takes all my time.

If I had more time
I could do more for myself
and maybe for others.   15
I could read and study
and talk things over
and find out about things.
It takes time.
I wish I had the time."   20

The people is a tragic and comic two-face:
hero and hoodlum: phantom and gorilla twisting to moan with a gargoyle mouth: "They
buy me and sell me . . . it's a game . . .
some time I'll break loose . . ."   25

            Once having marched
        Over the margins of animal necessity,
        Over the grim line of sheer subsistence
            Then man came
        To the deeper rituals of his bones,   30
        To the lights lighter than any bones,
        To the time for thinking things over,
        To the dance, the song, the story,
        Or the hours given over to dreaming,
            Once having so marched.   35

Between the finite limitations of the five senses
and the endless yearnings of man for the beyond
the people hold to the humdrum bidding of work and food
while reaching out when it comes their way
for lights beyond the prison of the five senses,   40
for keepsakes lasting beyond any hunger or death.
        This reaching is alive.
The panderers and liars have violated and smutted it.
        Yet this reaching is alive yet
        for lights and keepsakes.   45

            The people know the salt of the sea
            and the strength of the winds
            lashing the corners of the earth.
            The people take the earth
            as a tomb of rest and a cradle of hope.   50
            Who else speaks for the Family of Man?
            They are in tune and step
            with constellations of universal law.
            The people is a polychrome,
            a spectrum and a prism   55
            held in a moving monolith,
            a console organ of changing themes,
            a clavilux of color poems

58. clavilux—the so-called color organ, a machine for throwing lights on walls or screens
and constantly modifying the colors and patterns thus created.

wherein the sea offers fog
and the fog moves off in rain   60
and the labrador sunset shortens
to a nocturne of clear stars
serene over the shot spray
of northern lights.

The steel mill sky is alive.   65
The fire breaks white and zigzag
Shot on a gun-metal gloaming.
Man is a long time coming.
Man will yet win.
Brother may yet line up with brother: 70

This old anvil laughs at many broken hammers.
There are men who can't be bought.
The fireborn are at home in fire.
The stars make no noise.
You can't hinder the wind from blowing.   75
Time is a great teacher.
Who can live without hope?

In the darkness with a great bundle of grief
the people march.
In the night, and overhead a shovel of stars for   80
keeps, the people march:
                              "Where to? what next?"

HENRY LOUIS MENCKEN

1880-

I. NEWSPAPER MAN IN BALTIMORE (1880–1914)

1880 September 12, born in Baltimore, the eldest son of August and Anna (Abhau) Mencken, of mixed German and Irish ancestry. The family long distinguished for learning.

1892 After education at F. Knapp's Institute, a private school, entered Baltimore Polytechnic Institute, graduating at sixteen (though he had no interest in engineering). Worked until the death of his father in the paternal tobacco business.

1899–1906 On staff of the *Baltimore Morning Herald* (reporter, 1899-1903; city editor, 1903-1905; editor, 1905-1906) until the collapse of the paper.

1903 *Ventures into Verse.*

1905 *George Bernard Shaw: His Plays,* said to be the first book about Shaw published in this country.

1906–1941 On staff of one or the other of the Baltimore "Sunpapers" as editorial writer in varying capacities, beginning as Sunday editor.

1908 *The Philosophy of Friedrich Nietzsche.* Became literary critic for *The Smart Set.*

1909 First meeting with George Jean Nathan.

1910 Established a department of his own in the *Baltimore Sun,* "The Free Lance," in which he exercised complete editorial freedom (to 1916). Controversy carried on in this column did much to strengthen the right of freedom of expression in newspapers. Published *Men versus the Man: A Correspondence . . .* a statement of Mencken's conservative position vis-à-vis Socialism.

1912 *The Artist: A Drama without Words* (republished 1917 as *The Artist: A Satire in One Act* (1920). This, with *Heliogabalus: A Buffoonery* (with George Jean Nathan), is Mencken's principal contribution to the American theater.

II. CRITIC OF AMERICAN CULTURE (1914–   )

1914 *Europe after 8:15* (with Nathan and Willard Huntington Wright). Became (with Nathan) editor of *The Smart Set* (to 1923).

1916 *A Little Book in C Major,* also *A Book of Burlesques.*

1916–1918 American newspaper correspondent in Germany (previous European trips in 1908 and 1910).

1917 Beginning of long association with Alfred A. Knopf. Published *A Book of Prefaces;* also (under a pseudonym, with Nathan) *Pistols for Two,* and other pamphlets.

1918 *Damn! A Book of Calumny; In Defense of Women.*

1919   *The American Language* (second ed., 1921; third ed., 1923; fourth ed., 1936; fifth ed., 1948). *Prejudices: First Series* (*Second Series*, 1920; *Third Series*, 1922; *Fourth Series*, 1924; *Fifth Series*, 1926; *Sixth Series*, 1927; *Selected Prejudices*, 1926; *Second Series* of *Selected Prejudices*, 1927). After *A Book of Prefaces*, these constitute the heart of Mencken's critical writing.

1920   *The American Credo: A Contribution toward the Interpretation of the National Mind* (with Nathan).

1923–1933   Editor of the *American Mercury* (with Nathan to 1924).

1924–1932   Contributing editor of the *Nation*.

1930   Married Sara Powell Haardt, August 27. (She died in 1935.) Published *Treatise on the Gods*.

1934   *Treatise on Right and Wrong*.

1940   His autobiographical *Happy Days, 1880-1892*, followed by *Newspaper Days, 1899-1906* (1941) and *Heathen Days, 1890-1936* (1943).

1942   Edited and published *A New Dictionary of Quotations*.

1949   *A Mencken Chrestomathy*.

BIBLIOGRAPHIES: Besides that in Millett (below), see that by F. C. Henderson in Burton Rascoe, ed., *H. L. Mencken* (*Fanfare—The American Critic—Bibliography*), Knopf, 1920; Carroll Frey, *A Bibliography of the Writings of H. L. Mencken*, Centaur Book Shop, Philadelphia, 1924; *Literary History of the United States*, Vol. III, pp. 654-56. In addition to the titles in the biographical outline above, the student should consult Millett for the enormous number of miscellaneous publications, works edited and translated, and fugitive material.

BIOGRAPHIES: Consult, of course, the autobiographical books listed above. But much of Mencken is autobiographical. See also Ernest A. Boyd, *H. L. Mencken*, McBride, 1925; Isaac Goldberg, *The Man Mencken: A Biographical and Critical Survey*, Simon and Schuster, 1925; Walter Lippmann, *H. L. Mencken*, Knopf, 1926; the essays by Burton Rascoe and Vincent O'Sullivan in *H. L. Mencken* (*Fanfare . . .*) listed above; Edgar Kemler, *The Irreverent Mr. Mencken*, Atlantic Press, 1950.

CRITICAL COMMENT: There is an enormous critical and controversial literature, listed and codified in Fred B. Millett, *Contemporary American Authors*, Harcourt, Brace, 1940, pp. 484-96, which should be consulted. For later interpretations see Oscar Cargill, *Intellectual America: Ideas on the March*, Macmillan, 1941, especially Chaps. II and V; and Alfred Kazin, *On Native Grounds*, Reynal and Hitchcock, 1942, *passim*.

A glance at the outline of Mencken's life will show that before and after the twenties he was concerned with philosophy; during the twenties he was a notable literary and social critic. This aspect of his career begins before 1917, but that year saw the appearance of *A Book of Prefaces*, with its classic attack upon the genteel tradition in letters (here reprinted). The twenties open, so to speak, with *Prejudices*, the first of a series of collected essays of literary and social comment; and also with *The American Language*, which in the same decade underwent a series of revisions. And the mid-twenties saw the creation of the *American Mercury*. These were the means by which the extraordinary vogue of the Sage of Hollins Street was exercised.

Politically and economically conservative, Mencken appeared in literary circles as an iconoclast. He battled uproariously against the fading relics of American Victorianism and against what he considered the stifling quality of academic literary theory. An amateur of science, he accepted the scientific postulates of Huxley and therefore of literary naturalism and, in a general sense, of a samurai class of intellectuals. On the one hand, he seemed to be educating a simpler America into the "sophistication" of Europe; on the other hand, his inimitable style was an expression of American nationalism. But his buffoonery was on the surface; underneath the flippancy was a solid substructure of learning different in kind but like in capacity to that of the professors Mencken attacked. The rising literary generation therefore found in him the coryphaeus of the "revolt from the village"; and Mencken became one of the principal proponents of the theory that Dreiser, Conrad, and Huneker were superior to Howells, James, and Lowell.

PURITANISM AS A LITERARY FORCE

This essay first appeared as the terminal chapter of *A Book of Prefaces*, 1917, one of the most characteristic and influential of the author's volumes. Previous chapters discuss Joseph Conrad, Theodore Dreiser, and James G. Huneker, all of whom Mencken regards as important forces in breaking down the restricted outlook of American "Puritanism." Aside from the range and drive of the essay, it is important as illustrating the determined attack upon nineteenth-century literary and moral standards, which helped to create the intellectual climate of the 1920's. Mencken, of course, makes no pretense of confining "Puritanism" to its proper theological meaning. The text is from the 1917 edition, often reprinted.

C ALVINISM," says Dr. Leon Kellner, in his excellent little history of American literature, "is the natural theology of the disinherited; it never flourished, therefore, anywhere as it did in the barren hills of Scot-
5 land and in the wilds of North America." The learned doctor is here speaking of theology in what may be called its narrow technical sense—that is, as a theory of God. Under Calvinism, in the New World as well as in the Old, it became no more than a luxuriant demonology; even God himself was transformed into a superior sort of devil, ever wary and wholly merciless. That
10 primitive demonology still survives in the barbaric doctrines of the Methodists and Baptists, particularly in the South; but it has been ameliorated, even there, by a growing sense of the divine grace, and so the old God of Plymouth Rock, as practically conceived, is now scarcely worse than the average jail warden or Italian padrone. On the ethical side, however, Calvinism is dying a much
15 harder death, and we are still a long way from the enlightenment. Save where Continental influences have measurably corrupted the Puritan idea—*e.g.,* in such cities as New York, San Francisco and New Orleans,—the prevailing American view of the world and its mysteries is still a moral one, and no other human concern gets half the attention that is endlessly lavished upon
20 the problem of conduct, particularly of the other fellow. It needed no official announcement to define the function and office of the republic as that of an international expert in morals, and the mentor and exemplar of the more back-

---

3. literature—American Literature, tr. by Julia Franklin; New York, Doubleday, Page & Co., 1915. (Author's note) The quotation is on p. 40. **14. padrone**—labor contractor who holds unskilled workers in virtual slavery.

ward nations. Within, as well as without, the eternal rapping of knuckles and proclaiming of new austerities goes on. The American, save in moments of conscious and swiftly lamented deviltry, casts up all ponderable values, including even the values of beauty, in terms of right and wrong. He is beyond all things else, a judge and a policeman; he believes firmly that there is a 5 mysterious power in law; he supports and embellishes its operation with a fanatical vigilance.

Naturally enough, this moral obsession has given a strong colour to American literature. In truth, it has coloured it so brilliantly that American literature is set off sharply from all other literatures. In none other will you find so 10 wholesale and ecstatic a sacrifice of aesthetic ideas, of all the fine gusto of passion and beauty, to notions of what is meet, proper and nice. From the books of grisly sermons that were the first American contribution to letters down to that amazing literature of "inspiration" which now flowers so prodigiously, with two literary ex-Presidents among its chief virtuosi, one observes no relax- 15 ation of the moral pressure. In the history of every other literature there have been periods of what might be called moral innocence—periods in which a naif *joie de vivre* has broken through all concepts of duty and responsibility, and the wonder and glory of the universe have been hymned with unashamed zest. The age of Shakespeare comes to mind at once: the violence of the Puri- 20 tan reaction offers a measure of the pendulum's wild swing. But in America no such general rising of the blood has ever been seen. The literature of the nation, even the literature of the enlightened minority, has been under harsh Puritan restraints from the beginning, and despite a few stealthy efforts at revolt—usually quite without artistic value or even common honesty, as in the 25 case of the cheap fiction magazines and that of smutty plays on Broadway, and always very short-lived—it shows not the slightest sign of emancipating itself today. The American, try as he will, can never imagine any work of the imagination as wholly devoid of moral content. It must either tend toward the promotion of virtue, or be suspect and abominable. 30

If any doubt of this is in your mind, turn to the critical articles in the newspapers and literary weeklies; you will encounter enough proofs in a month's explorations to convince you forever. A novel or a play is judged among us, not by its dignity of conception, its artistic honesty, its perfection of workmanship, but almost entirely by its orthodoxy of doctrine, its platitudinousness, its 35 usefulness as a moral tract. A digest of the reviews of such a book as David Graham Phillips' "Susan Lenox" or of such a play as Ibsen's "Hedda Gabler" would make astounding reading for a Continental European. Not only the childish incompetents who write for the daily press, but also most of our critics of experience and reputation, seem quite unable to estimate a piece of 40 writing as a piece of writing, a work of art as a work of art; they almost in-

15. **two literary ex-Presidents**—In 1917 these would presumably be Theodore Roosevelt (1858-1919) and William Howard Taft (1857-1930), who published *Ethics in Service* in 1915. 18. **joie de vivre**—gaiety. 37. **"Susan Lenox"**—In 1917 David Graham Phillips (1867-1911) published a "naturalistic novel," *Susan Lenox: Her Fall and Rise,* revolving around the problem of self-supporting women. The heroine for a brief interval takes to prostitution. **"Hedda Gabler"**—This great play by Henrik Ibsen (1828-1906), which dates from 1890, has for its central figure a woman of "egotistic ferocity."

evitably drag in irrelevant gabble as to whether this or that personage in it is respectable, or this or that situation in accordance with the national notions of what is edifying and nice. Fully nine-tenths of the reviews of Dreiser's "The Titan," without question the best American novel of its year, were devoted
5 chiefly to indignant denunciations of the morals of Frank Cowperwood, its central character. That the man was superbly imagined and magnificently depicted, that he stood out from the book in all the flashing vigour of life, that his creation was an artistic achievement of a very high and difficult order —these facts seem to have made no impression upon the reviewers whatever.
10 They were Puritans writing for Puritans, and all they could see in Cowperwood was an anti-Puritan, and in his creator another. It will remain for Europeans, I daresay, to discover the true stature of "The Titan," as it remained for Europeans to discover the true stature of "Sister Carrie."

Just how deeply this corrective knife has cut you may find plainly displayed
15 in Dr. Kellner's little book. He sees the throttling influence of an ever alert and bellicose Puritanism, not only in our grand literature, but also in our petit literature, our minor poetry, even in our humour. The Puritan's utter lack of aesthetic sense, his distrust of all romantic emotion, his unmatchable intolerance of opposition, his unbreakable belief in his own bleak and narrow
20 views, his savage cruelty of attack, his lust for relentless and barbarous persecution—these things have put an almost unbearable burden upon the exchange of ideas in the United States, and particularly upon that form of it which involves playing with them for the mere game's sake. On the one hand, the writer who would deal seriously and honestly with the larger problems of
25 life, particularly in the rigidly-partitioned ethical field, is restrained by laws that would have kept a Balzac or a Zola in prison from year's end to year's end; and on the other hand the writer who would proceed against the reigning superstitions by mockery has been silenced by taboos that are quite as stringent, and by an indifference that is even worse. For all our professed de-
30 light in and capacity for jocosity, we have produced so far but one genuine wit—Ambrose Bierce—and, save to a small circle, he remains unknown today. Our great humourists, including even Mark Twain, have had to take protective colouration, whether willingly or unwillingly, from the prevailing ethical foliage, and so one finds them levelling their darts, not at the stupidities
35 of the Puritan majority, but at the evidences of lessening stupidity in the anti-Puritan minority. In other words, they have done battle, not against, but *for* Philistinism—and Philistinism is no more than another name for Puritanism. Both wage a ceaseless warfare upon beauty in its every form, from painting

---

12. **"The Titan"**—This novel, by Theodore Dreiser (1871-1945), published in 1914, has for its central character Frank Cowperwood, an amoral self-made financier. 13. **"Sister Carrie"**— a novel by Dreiser published in 1900, suppressed on moral grounds, and later republished. Its merits were hailed by Arnold Bennett, H. G. Wells, and Hugh Walpole in England before they were widely recognized in the United States. 26. **Balzac**—Honoré de Balzac (1799-1850), whose collected novels, *La Comédie humaine,* are a pitiless exposé of Napoleonic and post-Napoleonic France. **Zola**—Emile Zola (1840-1902), whose linked novels, known as the Rougon-Macquart series, are a similar exposé of the France of Napoleon III. 31. **Bierce**—Ambrose Gwinett Bierce (1842-1914?), most of whose writings represent the comment of a cynic upon human life and American society. 37. **Philistinism**—Matthew Arnold's famous term for the character and habits of the uninspiring middle class.

to religious ritual, and from the drama to the dance—the first because it holds beauty to be a mean and stupid thing, and the second because it holds beauty to be distracting and corrupting.

Mark Twain, without question, was a great artist; there was in him something of that prodigality of imagination, that aloof engrossment in the human comedy, that penetrating cynicism, which one associates with the great artists of the Renaissance. But his nationality hung around his neck like a millstone; he could never throw off his native Philistinism. One ploughs through "The Innocents Abroad" and through parts of "A Tramp Abroad" with incredulous amazement. Is such coarse and ignorant clowning to be accepted as humour, as great humour, as the best humour that the most humorous of peoples has produced? Is it really the mark of a smart fellow to lift a peasant's cackle over "Lohengrin"? Is Titian's chromo of Moses in the bullrushes seriously to be regarded as the noblest picture in Europe? Is there nothing in Latin Christianity, after all, save petty grafting, monastic scandals and the worship of the knuckles and shin-bones of dubious saints? May not a civilized man, disbelieving in it, still find himself profoundly moved by its dazzling history, the lingering remnants of its old magnificence, the charm of its gorgeous and melancholy loveliness? In the presence of all beauty of man's creation—in brief, of what we roughly call art, whatever its form—the voice of Mark Twain was the voice of the Philistine. A literary artist of very high rank himself, with instinctive gifts that lifted him, in "Huckleberry Finn" to kinship with Cervantes and Aristophanes, he was yet so far the victim of his nationality that he seems to have had no capacity for distinguishing between the good and the bad in the work of other men of his own craft. The literary criticism that one occasionally finds in his writings is chiefly trivial and ignorant; his private inclination appears to have been toward such romantic sentimentality as entrances school-boys; the thing that interested him in Shakespeare was not the man's colossal genius, but the absurd theory that Bacon wrote his plays. Had he been born in France (the country of his chief abomination!) instead of in a Puritan village of the American hinterland, I venture that he would have conquered the world. But try as he would, being what he was, he could not get rid of the Puritan smugness and cocksureness, the Puritan distrust of new ideas, the Puritan incapacity for seeing beauty as a thing in itself, and the full peer of the true and the good.

It is, indeed, precisely in the works of such men as Mark Twain that one finds the best proofs of the Puritan influence in American letters, for it is there that it is least expected and hence most significant. Our native critics, unanimously Puritans themselves, are anaesthetic to the flavour, but to Dr. Kellner, with his half-European, half-Oriental culture, it is always distinctly perceptible. He senses it, not only in the harsh Calvinistic fables of Hawthorne and the pious gurglings of Longfellow, but also in the poetry of Bryant, the tea-party

13. "Lohengrin"—opera by Richard Wagner (1813-1883), completed in 1848. For Mark Twain's comment on Wagner see Chap. v of *A Tramp Abroad*. **Titian's . . . bullrushes** —For typical comment by Mark Twain on Italian art see Chaps. xvii-xxvi of *Innocents Abroad*. **23. Cervantes**—Miguel de Cervantes Saavedra (1547-1616), here cited as the author of *Don Quixote*. **Aristophanes**—Greek comic dramatist (c. 448-385 B.C.). **29. Bacon**—See Mark Twain, *Is Shakespeare Dead?* **40. half-European, half-Oriental culture**—Dr. Kellner was born in Galicia and trained as a Hebrew scholar.

niceness of Howells, the "maiden-like reserve" of James Lane Allen, and even in the work of Joel Chandler Harris. What! A Southern Puritan? Well, why not? What could be more erroneous than the common assumption that Puritanism is exclusively a Northern, a New England, madness? The truth is that
5   it is as thoroughly national as the kindred belief in the devil, and runs almost unobstructed from Portland to Portland and from the Lakes to the Gulf. It is in the South, indeed, and not in the North, that it takes on its most bellicose and extravagant forms. Between the upper tier of New England and the Potomac river there was not a single prohibition state—but thereafter, alas,
10 they came in huge blocks! And behind that infinitely prosperous Puritanism there is a long and unbroken tradition. Berkeley, the last of the Cavaliers, was kicked out of power in Virginia so long ago as 1650. Lord Baltimore, the Proprietor of Maryland, was brought to terms by the Puritans of the Severn in 1657. The Scotch Covenanter, the most uncompromising and unenlightened
15 of all Puritans, flourished in the Carolinas from the start, and in 1698, or thereabout, he was reinforced from New England. In 1757 a band of Puritans invaded what is now Georgia—and Georgia has been a Puritan barbarism ever since. Even while the early (and half-mythical) Cavaliers were still in nominal control of all these Southern plantations, they clung to the sea-coast.
20 The population that moved down the chain of the Appalachians during the latter part of the eighteenth century, and then swept over them into the Mississippi valley, was composed almost entirely of Puritans—chiefly intransigeants from New England (where Unitarianism was getting on its legs), kirk-crazy Scotch, and that plupious and beauty-hating folk, the Scotch-Irish.
25 "In the South today," said John Fiske a generation ago, "there is more Puritanism surviving than in New England." In that whole region, an area three times as large as France or Germany, there is not a single orchestra capable of playing Beethoven's C minor symphony, or a single painting worth looking at, or a single public building or monument of any genuine distinction,

        1. James Lane Allen—James Lane Allen (1849-1925), whose *The Choir Invisible* (1897) is representative. **2. Joel Chandler Harris**—Joel Chandler Harris (1848-1908), creator of Uncle Remus, whose other writings, however, lack depth. **6. Portland to Portland**—that is, from Portland, Maine, to Portland, Oregon. **9. prohibition state**—In August, 1917, national legislation forbade the use of food products for making distilled beverages. In December Congress adopted the Eighteenth Amendment, which was part of the constitution in January, 1919. Mencken vigorously opposes prohibition as an invasion of personal liberty. **11. Berkeley**—Sir William Berkeley (1606-1677), colonial governor of Virginia, deposed as chief magistrate by a British fleet under Parliament. However, he returned to the governor's chair at the Restoration in 1660. **12. Lord Baltimore**—In November, 1657, articles of agreement terminating civil war in Maryland were signed in London between the second Lord Baltimore and representatives of "Bennett and other people in Maryland, now or late in opposition to his Lordship's government." It is not clear that the Puritans won a victory. See Bernard C. Steiner, *Maryland under the Commonwealth,* Johns Hopkins Press, 1911. **14. Scotch Covenanter**—one of the more fanatical Presbyterians of the seventeenth century, who refused to recognize either Cromwell's settlement of the ecclesiastical problems of Great Britain or that of Charles II. Many such fled to America and settled in the Shenandoah Valley and in the Piedmont and Appalachian regions of North and South Carolina. **15-16. 1698, or thereabout**—In 1691 Massachusetts became a royal colony, to the dissatisfaction of those in favor of a theocratic government. **16-17. 1757 . . . Georgia**—In 1756-57 numbers of Scotch-Irish Presbyterians began to take up land along the Ogeechee River in Georgia. **24. kirk-crazy**—In Scotland the national church is the "kirk." **plupious**—excessively pious. **25. John Fiske**—John Fiske (1842-1901), Harvard philosopher and colonial historian. **28. C minor symphony**—The famous "Fifth Symphony," here cited as an example of familiar music.

or a single factory devoted to the making of beautiful things, or a single poet, novelist, historian, musician, painter or sculptor whose reputation extends beyond his own country. Between the Mason and Dixon line and the mouth of the Mississippi there is but one opera-house, and that one was built by a Frenchman, and is now, I believe, closed. The only domestic art this huge and opulent empire knows is in the hands of Mexican greasers; its only native music it owes to the despised Negro; its only genuine poet was permitted to die up an alley like a stray dog.

2

In studying the anatomy and physiology of American Puritanism, and its effects upon the national literature, one quickly discerns two main streams of influence. On the one hand, there is the influence of the original Puritans— whether of New England or of the South—, who came to the New World with a ready-made philosophy of the utmost clarity, positiveness and inclusiveness of scope, and who attained to such a position of political and intellectual leadership that they were able to force it almost unchanged upon the whole population, and to endow it with such vitality that it successfully resisted alien opposition later on. And on the other hand, one sees a complex of social and economic conditions which worked in countless irresistible ways against the rise of that dionysian spirit, that joyful acquiescence in life, that philosophy of the *Ja-sager,* which offers to Puritanism, today as in times past, its chief and perhaps only effective antagonism. In other words, the American of the days since the Revolution has had Puritanism diligently pressed upon him from without, and at the same time he has led, in the main, a life that has engendered a chronic hospitality to it, or at all events to its salient principles, within.

Dr. Kellner accurately describes the process whereby the esthetic spirit, and its concomitant spirit of joy, were squeezed out of the original New Englanders, so that no trace of it showed in their literature, or even in their lives, for a century and a half after the first settlements. "Absorption in God," he says, "seems incompatible with the presentation (*i.e.,* esthetically) of mankind. The God of the Puritans was in this respect a jealous God who brooked no sort of creative rivalry. The inspired moments of the loftiest souls were filled with the thought of God and His designs; spiritual life was wholly dominated by solicitude regarding salvation, the hereafter, grace; how could such petty concerns as personal experience of a lyric nature, the transports or the pangs of love, find utterance? What did a lyric occurrence like the first call of the cuckoo, elsewhere so welcome, or the first sight of the snowdrop, signify compared with the last Sunday's sermon and the new interpretation of the old riddle of evil in the world? And apart from the fact that everything of a personal nature must have appeared so trivial, all the sources of secular lyric

3. **Mason and Dixon line**—the boundary between Pennsylvania and Maryland (and hence, by imaginary extension, between the North and the South) laid out by two English astronomers, Charles Mason and Jeremiah Dixon, between 1763 and 1767. 4. **opera-house**—the French opera house in New Orleans, built in 1859, destroyed by fire in 1919. 7. **genuine poet**—Poe. 21. **Ja-sager**—Yes-sayer. 30 ff. **"Absorption . . ."**—Kellner, *op. cit.,* pp. 7-9.

poetry were offensive and impious to Puritan theology. . . . One thing is an established fact: up to the close of the eighteenth century America had no belletristic literature."

5   This Puritan bedevilment by the idea of personal sin, this reign of the God-crazy, gave way in later years, as we shall see, to other and somewhat milder forms of pious enthusiasm. At the time of the Revolution, indeed, the importation of French political ideas was accompanied by an importation of French theological ideas, and such men as Franklin and Jefferson dallied with what, in those days at least, was regarded as downright atheism. Even in New Eng-10 land this influence made itself felt; there was a gradual letting down of Calvinism to the softness of Unitarianism, and that change was presently to flower in the vague temporizing of Transcendentalism. But as Puritanism, in the strict sense, declined in virulence and took deceptive new forms, there was a compensating growth of its brother, Philistinism, and by the first quarter of 15 the nineteenth century, the distrust of beauty, and of the joy that is its object, was as firmly established throughout the land as it had ever been in New England. The original Puritans had at least been men of a certain education, and even of a certain austere culture. They were inordinately hostile to beauty in all its forms, but one somehow suspects that much of their hostility was due 20 to a sense of their weakness before it, a realization of its disarming psychical pull. But the American of the new republic was of a different kidney. He was not so much hostile to beauty as devoid of any consciousness of it; he stood as unmoved before its phenomena as a savage before a table of logarithms. What he had set up on this continent, in brief, was a commonwealth of peasants 25 and small traders, a paradise of the third-rate, and its national philosophy, almost wholly unchecked by the more sophisticated and civilized ideas of an aristocracy, was precisely the philosophy that one finds among peasants and small traders at all times and everywhere. The difference between the United States and any other nation did not lie in any essential difference between 30 American peasants and other peasants, but simply in the fact that here, alone, the voice of the peasant was the single voice of the nation—that here, alone, the only way to eminence and public influence was the way of acquiescence in the opinions and prejudices of the untutored and Philistine mob. Jackson was the *Stammvater* of the new statesmen and philosophers; he carried the 35 mob's distrust of good taste even into the field of conduct; he was the first to put the rewards of conformity above the dictates of common decency; he founded a whole hierarchy of Philistine messiahs, the roaring of which still belabours the ear.

   Once established, this culture of the intellectually disinherited tended to de-40 fend and perpetuate itself. On the one hand, there was no appearance of a challenge from within, for the exigent problems of existence in a country that was yet but half settled and organized left its people with no energy for questioning what at least satisfied their gross needs, and so met the pragmatic test. And on the other hand, there was no critical pressure from without, for

---

   7-8. French theological ideas—that is, deism and materialism. **33. Jackson**—Andrew Jackson (1767-1845), whose election to the Presidency in 1828 marks the beginning of the "Jacksonian" or popular revolution in American political history. **34. Stammvater**—begetter.

the English culture which alone reached over the sea was itself entering upon its Victorian decline, and the influence of the native aristocracy—the degenerating *Junkers* of the great estates and the boorish magnates of the city *bourgeoisie*—was quite without any cultural direction at all. The chief concern of the American people, even above the bread-and-butter question, was politics. They were incessantly hag-ridden by political difficulties, both internal and external, of an inordinate complexity, and these occupied all the leisure they could steal from the sordid work of everyday. More, their new and troubled political ideas tended to absorb all the rancorous certainty of their fading religious ideas, so that devotion to a theory or a candidate became translated into devotion to a revelation, and the game of politics turned itself into a holy war. The custom of connecting purely political doctrines with pietistic concepts of an inflammable nature, then firmly set up by skilful persuaders of the mob, has never quite died out in the United States. There has not been a presidential contest since Jackson's day without its Armageddons, its marching of Christian soldiers, its crosses of gold, its crowns of thorns. The most successful American politicians, beginning with the anti-slavery agitators, have been those most adept at twisting the ancient gauds and shibboleths of Puritanism to partisan uses. Every campaign that we have seen for eighty years has been, on each side, a pursuit of bugaboos, a denunciation of heresies, a snouting up of immoralities.

But it was during the long contest against slavery, beginning with the appearance of William Lloyd Garrison's *Liberator* in 1831 and ending at Appomattox, that this gigantic supernaturalization of politics reached its most astounding heights. In those days, indeed, politics and religion coalesced in a manner not seen in the world since the Middle Ages, and the combined pull of the two was so powerful that none could quite resist it. All men of any ability and ambition turned to political activity for self-expression. It engaged the press to the exclusion of everything else; it conquered the pulpit; it even laid its hand upon industry and trade. Drawing the best imaginative talent into its service—Jefferson and Lincoln may well stand as examples—it left the cultivation of belles lettres, and of all the other arts no less, to women and admittedly second-rate men. And when, breaking through this taboo, some chance first-rate man gave himself over to purely esthetic expression, his reward was not only neglect, but even a sort of ignominy, as if such enterprises were not fitting for males with hair on their chests. I need not point to Poe and Whitman, both disdained as dreamers and wasters, and both proceeded against with the utmost rigours of outraged Philistinism.

3. **Junkers**—Prussian term for landholding aristocracy, humorously applied to Southern plantation owners. 4. **bourgeoisie**—middle class. 15. **Armageddons**—When Theodore Roosevelt ran for President on the Progressive party ticket in 1913, the slogan was "We stand at Armageddon and we battle for the Lord." *Cf.* Rev. 16: 16. 16. **Christian soldiers**—that is, "Onward, Christian soldiers," the well-known hymn. **crosses of gold . . . thorns**—The concluding phrases of William Jennings Bryan's famous speech at the Democratic National Convention of 1896 are: "You shall not press down upon the brow of labor this crown of thorns; you shall not crucify mankind upon a cross of gold." This speech won him the presidential nomination. 18. **gauds**—gewgaws. **shibboleths**—test words. *Cf.* Judges 12: 4-6. 23. **Liberator**—The most outspoken of the antislavery journals. 23-24. **Appomattox**—Lee's surrender at Appomattox Court House, Virginia, April 9, 1865, is the conventional date for the end of the American Civil War.

In brief, the literature of that whole period, as Algernon Tassin shows in "The Magazine in America," was almost completely disassociated from life as men were then living it. Save one counts in such crude politico-puritan tracts as "Uncle Tom's Cabin," it is difficult to find a single contemporaneous work
5 that interprets the culture of the time, or even accurately represents it. Later on, it found historians and anatomists, and in one work, at least, to wit, "Huckleberry Finn," it was studied and projected with the highest art, but no such impulse to make imaginative use of it showed itself contemporaneously, and there was not even the crude sentimentalization of here and now that
10 one finds in the popular novels of today. Fenimore Cooper filled his romances, not with the people about him, but with the Indians beyond the skyline, and made them half-fabulous to boot. Irving told fairy tales about the forgotten Knickerbockers; Hawthorne turned backward to the Puritans of Plymouth Rock; Longfellow to the Acadians and the prehistoric Indians;
15 Emerson took flight from earth altogether; even Poe sought refuge in a land of fantasy. It was only the frank second-raters—*e.g.,* Whittier and Lowell— who ventured to turn to the life around them, and the banality of the result is a sufficient indication of the crudeness of the current taste, and the mean position assigned to the art of letters. This was pre-eminently the era of the
20 moral tale, the Sunday-school book. Literature was conceived, not as a thing in itself, but merely as a hand-maiden to politics or religion. The great celebrity of Emerson in New England was not the celebrity of a literary artist, but that of a theologian and metaphysician; he was esteemed in much the same way that Jonathan Edwards had been esteemed. Even down to our own
25 time, indeed, his vague and empty philosophizing has been put above his undeniable capacity for graceful utterance, and it remained for Dr. Kellner to consider him purely as a literary artist, and to give him due praise for his skill.

The Civil War brought that era of sterility to an end. As I shall show later
30 on, the shock of it completely reorganized the American scheme of things, and even made certain important changes in the national Puritanism, or, at all events, in its machinery. Whitman, whose career straddled, so to speak, the four years of the war, was the leader—and for a long while, the only trooper—of a double revolt. On the one hand he offered a courageous chal-
35 lenge to the intolerable prudishness and dirty-mindedness of Puritanism, and on the other hand he boldly sought the themes and even the modes of expression of his poetry in the arduous, contentious and highly melodramatic life that lay all about him. Whitman, however, was clearly before his time. His countrymen could see him only as immoralist; save for a pitiful few of them, they
40 were dead to any understanding of his stature as artist, and even unaware that such a category of men existed. He was put down as an invader of the public decencies, a disturber of the public peace; even his eloquent war poems, surely the best of all his work, were insufficient to get him a hearing; the sentimental rubbish of "The Blue and the Gray" and the ecstatic supernatural-

---

2. **"The Magazine in America"**—"New York, Dodd, Mead & Co., 1916." (Author's note)
44. **"The Blue and the Gray"**—poem by Francis Miles Finch (1827-1907), first published in the *Atlantic Monthly* in September, 1867, the sentiment of which helped to create a feeling for Memorial Day and to obliterate sectional bitterness between North and South.

ism of "The Battle Hymn of the Republic" were far more to the public taste. Where Whitman failed, indeed, all subsequent explorers of the same field have failed with him, and the great war has left no more mark upon American letters than if it had never been fought. Nothing remotely approaching the bulk and beam of Tolstoi's "War and Peace," or, to descend to a smaller scale, Zola's "The Attack on the Mill," has come out of it. Its appeal to the national imagination was undoubtedly of the most profound character; it coloured politics for fifty years, and is today a dominating influence in the thought of whole sections of the American people. But in all that stirring up there was no upheaval of artistic consciousness, for the plain reason that there was no artistic consciousness there to heave up, and all we have in the way of Civil War literature is a few conventional melodramas, a few half-forgotten short stories by Ambrose Bierce and Stephen Crane, and a half dozen idiotic popular songs in the manner of Randall's "Maryland, My Maryland."

In the seventies and eighties, with the appearance of such men as Henry James, William Dean Howells, Mark Twain and Bret Harte, a better day seemed to be dawning. Here, after a full century of infantile romanticizing, were four writers who at least deserved respectful consideration as literary artists, and what is more, three of them turned from the conventionalized themes of the past to the teeming and colourful life that lay under their noses. But this promise of better things was soon found to be no more than a promise. Mark Twain, after "The Gilded Age," slipped back into romanticism tempered by Philistinism, and was presently in the era before the Civil War, and finally in the Middle Ages, and even beyond. Harte, a brilliant technician, had displayed his whole stock when he had displayed his technique: his stories were not even superficially true to the life they presumed to depict; one searched them in vain for an interpretation of it; they were simply idle tales. As for Howells and James, both quickly showed that timorousness and reticence which are the distinguishing marks of the Puritan, even in his most intellectual incarnations. The American scene that they depicted with such meticulous care was chiefly peopled with marionettes. They shrunk, characteristically, from those larger, harsher clashes of will and purpose which one finds in all truly first-rate literature. In particular, they shrunk from any interpretation of life which grounded itself upon an acknowledgment of its inexorable and inexplicable tragedy. In the vast combat of instincts and aspirations about them they saw only a feeble jousting of comedians, unserious and insignificant. Of the great questions that have agitated the minds of men in Howells' time one gets no more than a faint and far-away echo in his novels.

1. "The Battle Hymn of the Republic"—by Julia Ward Howe (1819-1910), first published in the *Atlantic Monthly* in 1862. 5. "War and Peace"—the great historical novel of the Russian resistance to Napoleon, published in 1864-66 by Count Leo N. Tolstoi (1828-1910). 6. "The Attack on the Mill"—This short story first appeared in book form in *Les Soirées de Médan*, Paris, 1880. 13. stories by Ambrose Bierce and Stephen Crane—that is, *Tales of Soldiers and Civilians* by Bierce (1891); and *The Red Badge of Courage* (1895) and *The Little Regiment and Other Episodes of the Civil War* (1896) by Stephen Crane (1871-1900). However, *The Red Badge of Courage* "sold amazingly, and Crane rose to sudden fame." 14. "Maryland, My Maryland"—James Ryder Randall (1839-1908), upon hearing of the attack on the Sixth Massachusetts in Baltimore, being in New Orleans, published this famous song in the *New Orleans Delta* April 26, 1861. It became one of the battle songs of the Confederacy.

His investigations, one may say, are carried on *in vacuo;* his discoveries are not expressed in terms of passion, but in terms of giggles.

In the followers of Howells and James one finds little save an empty imitation of their emptiness, a somewhat puerile parodying of their highly artful but essentially personal technique. To wade through the books of such characteristic American fictioneers as Frances Hodgson Burnett, Mary E. Wilkins Freeman, F. Hopkinson Smith, Alice Brown, James Lane Allen, Winston Churchill, Ellen Glasgow, Gertrude Atherton and Sarah Orne Jewett is to undergo an experience that is almost terrible. The flow of words is completely purged of ideas; in place of them one finds no more than a romantic restatement of all the old platitudes and formulae. To call such an emission of graceful poppycock a literature, of course, is to mouth an absurdity, and yet, if the college professors who write treatises on letters are to be believed, it is the best we have to show. Turn, for example, to "A History of American Literature Since 1870," by Prof. Fred Lewis Pattee, one of the latest and undoubtedly one of the least unintelligent of these books. In it the gifted pedagogue gives extended notice to no less than six of the nine writers I have mentioned, and upon all of them his verdicts are flattering. He bestows high praises, direct and indirect, upon Mrs. Freeman's "grim and austere" manner, her "repression," her entire lack of poetical illumination. He compares Miss Jewett to both Howells and Hawthorne, not to mention Mrs. Gaskell—and Addison! He grows enthusiastic over a hollow piece of fine writing by Miss Brown. And he forgets altogether to mention Dreiser, or Sinclair, or Medill Patterson, or Harry Leon Wilson, or George Ade! . . .

So much for the best. The worst is beyond description. France has her Brieux and her Henry Bordeaux; Germany has her Mühlbach, her stars of the *Gartenlaube;* England contributes Caine, Corelli, Oppenheim and com-

6-9. Frances Hodgson Burnett . . . Sarah Orne Jewett—Frances Eliza Hodgson Burnett (1849-1924), now best remembered for *Little Lord Fauntleroy* (1886); **Mary E. Wilkins Freeman** (1852-1930), best known for short stories of New England life, such as *A Humble Romance* (1887); **F. Hopkinson Smith** (1838-1915), creator of *Colonel Carter of Cartersville* (1891); **Alice Brown** (1857-1948), whose *Country Neighbors* (1910) is typical; **James Lane Allen** (see above); **Winston Churchill** (1871-1947), whose *The Inside of the Cup* (1913) is a novel of religious life; **Ellen Glasgow** (1874-1945), whose works since 1917 scarcely justify Mencken's condemnation; **Gertrude Atherton** (1857-1948), author of *Senator North* (1900) and other novels of American manners; **Sarah Orne Jewett** (1849-1909), fictionist of Maine, whose first success was *Deephaven* (1877). **24. Sinclair**—Upton Sinclair (1878-   ), Socialist poet, propagandist, and novelist. **Patterson**—Joseph Medill Patterson (1879-1946), author of *Little Brother of the Rich* (1908). **24. Wilson**—Harry Leon Wilson (1867-1939), author of *Ruggles of Red Gap* (1915). **24. Ade**—George Ade (1866-1944), author of *Fables in Slang* (1900). **26. Brieux**—Eugène Brieux (1858-1932), whose *Les avariés,* translated as *Damaged Goods,* had great vogue after 1911 as an earnest drama of moral reform. He was introduced to American readers by George Bernard Shaw. **Bordeaux**—Henri Bordeaux (1870-   ), voluminous French novelist, critic, historian, and propagandist, whose *The Awakening* had considerable vogue in the United States in 1914-15. **Mühlbach**—Louisa Mühlbach, whose real name was Klara Müller Mundt (1814-1873), German author of innumerable sentimental historical novels. **27. Gartenlaube**—A sentimental family magazine long published in Germany. **Caine**—Sir Thomas Henry Hall Caine (1853-1931), better known as Hall Caine, noted for his novels of Manx life, such as *The Deemster* (1887). **Corelli**—Marie Corelli (1855-1924), who became famous in 1886 with *The Romance of Two Worlds*. **Oppenheim** —E. Phillips Oppenheim (1866-1944), voluminous author of mystery stories and "international" romances.

pany. But it is in our country alone that banality in letters takes on the proportions of a national movement; it is only here that a work of the imagination is habitually judged by its sheer emptiness of ideas, its fundamental platitudinousness, its correspondence with the imbecility of mob thinking; it is only here that "glad" books run up sales of hundreds of thousands. Richard 5 Harding Davis, with his ideals of a floorwalker; Gene Stratton-Porter, with her snuffling sentimentality; Robert W. Chambers, with his "society" romances for shop-girls; Irvin Cobb, with his laboured, *Ayers' Almanac* jocosity; the authors of the *Saturday Evening Post* school, with their heroic drummers and stockbrokers, their ecstatic celebration of the stupid, the sordid, the ignoble 10 —these, after all, are our typical *literati*. The Puritan fear of ideas is the master of them all. Some of them, in truth, most of them, have undeniable talent; in a more favourable environment not a few of them might be doing sound work. But they see how small the ring is, and they make their tricks small to fit it. Not many of them ever venture a leg outside. The lash of the 15 ringmaster is swift, and it stings damnably. . . .

I say not many; I surely do not mean none at all. As a matter of fact, there have been intermittent rebellions against the prevailing pecksniffery and sentimentality ever since the days of Irving and Hawthorne. Poe led one of them —as critic more than as creative artist. His scathing attacks upon the Gerald 20 Stanley Lees, the Hamilton Wright Mabies and the George E. Woodberrys of his time keep a liveliness and appositeness that the years have not staled; his criticism deserves to be better remembered. Poe sensed the Philistine pull of a Puritan civilization as none had before him, and combated it with his whole artillery of rhetoric. Another rebel, of course, was Whitman; how he 25 came to grief is too well known to need recalling. What is less familiar is the fact that both the *Atlantic Monthly* and the *Century* (first called *Scribner's*) were set up by men in revolt against the reign of mush, as *Putnam's* and the *Dial* had been before them. The salutatory of the *Dial,* dated 1840, stated the case against the national mugginess clearly. The aim of the magazine, it said, 30 was to oppose "that rigour of our conventions of religion and education which is turning us to stone" and to give expression to "new views and the dreams of youth." Alas, for these brave *révoltés! Putnam's* succumbed to the circumambient rigours and duly turned to stone, and is now no more. The *Atlantic,* once so heretical, has become as respectable as the New York *Evening Post.* 35 As for the *Dial,* it was until lately the very pope of orthodoxy and jealously guarded the college professors who read it from the pollution of ideas. Only

---

6. Davis—Richard Harding Davis (1864-1916), newspaper correspondent and fictionist, whose *Ransom's Folly* (1902) is representative. **Stratton-Porter**—Gene Stratton Porter (Mrs. Charles Darwin Porter) (1868-1924), author of *Freckles* (1904) and other sentimental books. **7. Chambers**—Robert William Chambers (1865-1933), whose *The Common Law* (1912) is representative. **8. Cobb**—Irvin Shrewsbury Cobb (1876-1945), author of *Old Judge Priest* (1915). **Ayers' Almanac**—a "family almanac" founded in 1852 and published in various languages by Dr. J. C. Ayer & Company of Lowell, Massachusetts, a patent-medicine concern. **21. Lees**—Rev. Gerald Stanley Lee (1862-1944), author of *Crowds* (1913) and other books. **Mabies**—Hamilton Wright Mabie (1845-1916), teacher, critic, and editor of the *Outlook* (1893-1916). **Woodberrys**—George Edward Woodberry (1855-1930), poet and critic of an idealizing tendency. **27-29. Atlantic Monthly . . . Dial**—On these magazines consult Frank Luther Mott, *A History of American Magazines, 1850-1865,* Appleton, 1938. **33. révoltés**—rebels.

the *Century* has kept the faith unbrokenly. It is, indeed, the one first-class
American magazine that has always welcomed newcomers, and that maintains
an intelligent contact with the literature that is in being, and that consistently
tries to make the best terms possible with the dominant Philistinism. It cannot
5 go the whole way without running into danger; let it be said to the credit
of its editors that they have more than once braved that danger.

The tale might be lengthened. Mark Twain, in his day, felt the stirrings of
revolt, and not all his Philistinism was sufficient to hold him altogether in
check. If you want to find out about the struggle that went on within him,
10 read the biography by Albert Bigelow Paine, or, better still, "The Mysterious
Stranger" and "What is Man?" Alive, he had his position to consider; dead,
he now speaks out. In the preface to "What is Man?" dated 1905, there is a
curious confession of his incapacity for defying the taboos which surrounded
him. The studies for the book, he says, were begun "twenty-five or twenty-
15 seven years ago"—the period of "A Tramp Abroad" and "The Prince and the
Pauper." It was actually written "seven years ago"—that is, just after "Following the Equator" and "Personal Recollections of Joan of Arc." And why did
it lie so long in manuscript, and finally go out stealthily, under a private imprint? Simply because, as Mark frankly confesses, he "dreaded (*and could
20 not bear*) the disapproval of the people around" him. He knew how hard his
fight for recognition had been; he knew what direful penalties outraged orthodoxy could inflict; he had in him the somewhat pathetic discretion of a respectable family man. But, dead, he is safely beyond reprisal, and so, after a
prudent interval, the faithful Paine begins printing books in which, writing
25 knowingly behind six feet of earth, he could set down his true ideas without
fear. Some day, perhaps, we shall have his microbe story, and maybe even his
picture of the court of Elizabeth.

A sneer in Prof. Pattee's history, before mentioned, recalls the fact that
Hamlin Garland was also a rebel in his day and bawled for the Truth with a
30 capital T. That was in 1893. Two years later the guardians of the national
rectitude fell afoul of "Rose of Dutchers' Coolly" and Garland began to think
it over; today he devotes himself to the safer enterprise of chasing spooks; his
name is conspicuously absent from the Dreiser Protest. Nine years before his
brief offending John Hay had set off a discreet bomb in "The Bread-Winners"
35 —anonymously because "my standing would be seriously compromised" by an
avowal. Six years later Frank Norris shook up the Phelpses and Mores of the
time with "McTeague." Since then there have been assaults timorous and as-

1. Century—This magazine ceased publication in 1930. 18-19. imprint—The first edition
for public sale did not appear until June, 1917, and in it the preface was suppressed. (Author's
note) 29. Garland—Hamlin Garland (1860-1940), pioneer realist, who took up spiritualism in
later life. 33. Dreiser Protest—After the publication of Dreiser's *The Genius* the book was
attacked as immoral; groups of British and American authors issued statements denouncing this
form of censorship. See Mencken's essay on Dreiser in *A Book of Prefaces,* 5th ed., Garden City
Publishing Company, 1927, pp. 67-148. 34. John Hay—John Hay (1838-1905) diplomat and
biographer, published *The Breadwinners* anonymously in 1884. 36. Frank Norris—Frank
Norris (1870-1902) published *McTeague,* sometimes called the first American naturalistic novel,
in 1899. Phelpses . . . Mores—William Lyon Phelps (1865-1944), popular Yale professor
of literature; Paul Elmer More (1864-1937), leader of the neo-humanists, opposed to Mencken.

saults head-long—by Bierce, by Dreiser, by Phillips, by Fuller—by Mary Mac-
Lanes and by Upton Sinclairs—by ploughboy poets from the Middle West
and by jitney geniuses in Greenwich Village—assaults gradually tapering off
to a mere sophomoric brashness and deviltry. And all of them like snow-ball-
ings of Verdun. All of them petered out and ineffectual. The normal, the   5
typical American book of today is as fully a remouthing of old husks as the
normal book of Griswold's day. The whole atmosphere of our literature, in
William James' phrase, is "mawkish and dishwatery." Books are still judged
among us, not by their form and organization as works of art, their accuracy
and vividness as representations of life, their validity and perspicacity as inter- 10
pretations of it, but by their conformity to the national prejudices, their accordance with set standards of niceness and propriety. The thing irrevocably demanded is a "sane" book; the ideal is a "clean," an "inspiring," a "glad" book.

3

All this may be called the Puritan impulse from within. It is, indeed, but a   15
single manifestation of one of the deepest prejudices of a religious and half-
cultured people—the prejudice against beauty as a form of debauchery and
corruption—the distrust of all ideas that do not fit readily into certain accepted
axioms—the belief in the eternal validity of moral concepts—in brief, the whole
mental sluggishness of the lower orders of men. But in addition to this in-   20
ternal resistance, there has been laid upon American letters the heavy hand
of a Puritan authority from without, and no examination of the history and
present condition of our literature could be of any value which did not take
it constantly into account, and work out the means of its influence and operation. That authority, as I shall show, transcends both in power and in alert-   25
ness the natural reactions of the national mind, and is incomparably more
potent in combating ideas. It is supported by a body of law that is unmatched
in any other country of Christendom, and it is exercised with a fanatical harshness and vigilance that make escape from its operations well nigh impossible.
Some of its effects, both direct and indirect, I shall describe later, but before   30
doing so it may be well to trace its genesis and development.

At bottom, of course, it rests upon the inherent Puritanism of the people;
it could not survive a year if they were opposed to the principle visible in it.
That deep-seated and uncorrupted Puritanism, that conviction of the per-
vasiveness of sin, of the supreme importance of moral correctness, of the need   35
of savage and inquisitorial laws, has been a dominating force in American
life since the very beginning. There has never been any question before the
nation, whether political or economic, religious or military, diplomatic or sociological, which did not resolve itself, soon or late, into a purely moral question. Nor has there ever been any surcease of the spiritual eagerness which lay   40

1. **Fuller**—Henry Blake Fuller (1857-1929), Chicago realistic novelist, whose *The Cliff-
Dwellers* (1893) is representative. **1-2. Mary MacLanes**—The reference is to an autobiographical volume, *I, Mary MacLane*, published in 1917 (1881-1929). **3. Greenwich Village**—When
this essay was published, this part of New York City was first becoming known as the home of
self-conscious bohemianism. **5. Verdun**—The heroic defense of the fortress-city of Verdun by the
French against incessant German attacks in 1916 was one of the turning points of the First World
War. **7. Griswold**—Rufus Wilmot Griswold (1815-1857), anthologist and hack writer.

at the bottom of the original Puritan's moral obsession: the American has
been, from the very start, a man genuinely interested in the eternal mysteries,
and fearful of missing their correct solution. The frank theocracy of the New
England colonies had scarcely succumbed to the libertarianism of a godless
5 Crown before there came the Great Awakening of 1734, with its orgies of
homiletics and its restoration of talmudism to the first place among polite
sciences. The Revolution, of course, brought a set-back: the colonists faced so
urgent a need of unity in politics that they declared a sort of *Treuga Dei* in
religion, and that truce, armed though it was, left its imprint upon the First
10 Amendment to the Constitution. But immediately the young Republic emerged
from the stresses of adolescence, a missionary army took to the field again, and
before long the Asbury revival was paling that of Whitefield, Wesley and
Jonathan Edwards, not only in its hortatory violence but also in the length of
its lists of slain.

15   Thereafter, down to the outbreak of the Civil War, the country was rocked
again and again by furious attacks upon the devil. On the one hand, this great
campaign took a purely theological form, with a hundred new and fantastic
creeds as its fruits; on the other hand, it crystallized into the hysterical temperance movement of the 30's and 40's, which penetrated to the very floor of
20 Congress and put "dry" laws upon the statute-books of ten States; and on the
third hand, as it were, it established a prudery in speech and thought from
which we are yet but half delivered. Such ancient and innocent words as
"bitch" and "bastard" disappeared from the American language; Bartlett tells
us, indeed, in his "Dictionary of Americanisms," that even "bull" was softened
25 to "male cow." This was the Golden Age of euphemism, as it was of euphu-
ism; the worst inventions of the English mid-Victorians were adopted and
improved. The word "woman" became a term of opprobrium, verging close
upon downright libel; legs became the inimitable "limbs"; the stomach began
to run from the "bosom" to the pelvic arch; pantaloons faded into "unmen-
30 tionables"; the newspapers spun their parts of speech into such gossamer webs
as "a statutory offence," "a house of questionable repute" and "an interesting
condition." And meanwhile the Good Templars and Sons of Temperance
swarmed in the land like a plague of celestial locusts. There was not a hamlet
without its uniformed phalanx, its affecting exhibit of reformed drunkards.
35 The Kentucky Legislature succumbed to a travelling recruiting officer, and
two-thirds of the members signed the pledge. The National House of Representatives took recess after recess to hear eminent excoriators of the Rum
Demon, and more than a dozen of its members forsook their duties to carry
the new gospel to the bucolic heathen—the vanguard, one may note in pass-
40 ing, of the innumerable Chautauquan caravan of later years.

4-5. **godless Crown**—The reference is to Massachusetts' becoming a royal colony in
1684. 6. **talmudism**—here humorously misused in the sense of book worship. 8. **Treuga
Dei**—Truce of God. 9-10. **First Amendment**—This guarantees religious liberty. 12. **Asbury**
—Rev. Francis Asbury (1745-1816), first bishop of the Methodist Church in America. 12-13.
Whitefield, Wesley . . . Edwards—Rev. George Whitefield (1714-1770), who launched
a series of revival meetings in eighteenth-century colonial America; Rev. John Wesley (1702-
1791), English founder of the Methodist Church, who visited Georgia as a missionary (1735-38);
Jonathan Edwards, see pp. 39 ff. of this volume. 24. **"Dictionary of Americanisms"**—Second edition; Boston, Little, Brown & Co., 1859, xxvi. (Author's note)

Beneath all this bubbling on the surface, of course, ran the deep and swift undercurrent of anti-slavery feeling—a tide of passion which historians now attempt to account for on economic grounds, but which showed no trace of economic origin while it lasted. Its true quality was moral, devout, ecstatic; it culminated, to change the figure, in a supreme discharge of moral electricity, almost fatal to the nation. The crack of that great spark emptied the jar; the American people forgot all about their pledges and pruderies during the four years of Civil War. The Good Templars, indeed, were never heard of again, and with them into memory went many other singular virtuosi of virtue—for example, the Millerites. But almost before the last smoke of battle cleared away, a renaissance of Puritan ardour began, and by the middle of the 70's it was in full flower. Its high points and flashing lighthouses halt the backward-looking eye; the Moody and Sankey uproar, the triumphal entry of the Salvation Army, the recrudescence of the temperance agitation and its culmination in prohibition, the rise of the Young Men's Christian Association and of the Sunday-school, the almost miraculous growth of the Christian Endeavour movement, the beginnings of the vice crusade, the renewed injection of moral conceptions and rages into party politics (the "crime" of 1873!), the furious preaching of baroque Utopias, the invention of muckraking, the mad, glad war of extermination upon the Mormons, the hysteria over the Breckenridge-Pollard case and other like causes, the enormous multiplication of moral and religious associations, the spread of zoöphilia, the attack upon Mammon, the dawn of the uplift, and last but far from least, comstockery.

In comstockery, if I do not err, the new Puritanism gave a sign of its formal departure from the old, and moral endeavour suffered a general overhauling and tightening of the screws. The difference between the two forms is very well represented by the difference between the program of the half-forgotten Good Templars and the program set forth in the Webb Law of 1913, or by that between the somewhat diffident prudery of the 40's and the astoundingly ferocious and uncompromising vice-crusading of today. In brief, a difference between the *r*enunciation and *d*enunciation, asceticism and Mohammedanism, the hair

10. **Millerites**—Followers of the Rev. William Miller (1782-1849), who in 1836 published a book to demonstrate that the second coming of Christ must occur in 1843. 13. **Moody and Sankey uproar**—Rev. Dwight Lyman Moody (1837-1899), with the singer Ira David Sankey (1840-1908), conducted a remarkable series of revival meetings in Great Britain, the United States, and Canada during the last quarter of the nineteenth century, making use of "crowd psychology." 14. **Salvation Army**—This religious organization officially began work in the United States in March, 1880. 15. **Young . . . Association**—The Y.M.C.A. was founded in England in 1844, and soon after spread to the United States. 16. **Sunday-school**—Founded in Gloucester, England, in 1780; by 1824 Sunday schools had so increased in the United States as to lead to the organization of the American Sunday School Union. **Christian Endeavour** —founded in 1881 in Portland, Maine. 18. **"crime" of 1873!**—The cant phrase for the bill demonetizing silver in that year. 20. **Mormons**—From their founding in 1830 almost to the end of the nineteenth century Mormons (members of the Church of Jesus Christ of Latter-Day Saints) have been subjected to mob violence. 20-21. **Breckenridge-Pollard case**—See P. Pollard, *Their Day in Court*. 22. **zoöphilia**—literally, the love of animals; the reference is to the antivivisection crusade. **Mammon**—emblem of materialistic wealth. 23. **comstockery**—Anthony Comstock (1844-1915) was the chief figure associated with the Society for the Suppression of Vice, devoting a good deal of time to the moral censorship of art. The term "comstockery" was coined by George Bernard Shaw. 28. **Webb Law**—In 1913 the California Legislature passed legislation forbidding aliens incapable of citizenship to own agricultural land in that state. The law was intended to prevent Japanese from buying land.

shirt and the flaming sword. The distinguishing mark of the elder Puritanism, at least after it had attained to the stature of a national philosophy, was its appeal to the individual conscience, its exclusive concern with the elect, its strong flavour of self-accusing. Even the rage against slavery was, in large measure,
5 an emotion of the mourners' bench. The thing that worried the more ecstatic Abolitionists was their sneaking sense of responsibility, the fear that they themselves were flouting the fire by letting slavery go on. The thirst to punish the concrete slave-owner, as an end in itself, did not appear until opposition had added exasperation to fervour. In most of the earlier harangues against his
10 practice, indeed, you will find a perfect willingness to grant that slave-owner's good faith, and even to compensate him for his property. But the new Puritanism—or, perhaps more accurately, considering the shades of prefixes, the neo-Puritanism—is a frank harking back to the primitive spirit. The original Puritan of the bleak New England coast was not content to flay his own way-
15 ward carcass: full satisfaction did not sit upon him until he had jailed a Quaker. That is to say, the sinner who excited his highest zeal and passion was not so much himself as his neighbour; to borrow a term from psychopathology, he was less the masochist than the sadist. And it is that very peculiarity which sets off his descendant of today from the ameliorated Puritan
20 of the era between the Revolution and the Civil War. The new Puritanism is not ascetic, but militant. Its aim is not to lift up saints but to knock down sinners. Its supreme manifestation is the vice crusade, an armed pursuit of helpless outcasts by the whole military and naval forces of the Republic. Its supreme hero is Comstock Himself, with his pious boast that the sinners
25 he jailed during his astounding career, if gathered into one penitential party, would have filled a train of sixty-one coaches, allowing sixty to the coach.

So much for the general trend and tenor of the movement. At the bottom of it, it is plain, there lies that insistent presentation of the idea of sin, that
30 enchantment by concepts of carnality, which has engaged a certain type of man, to the exclusion of all other notions, since the dawn of history. The remote ancestors of our Puritan-Philistines of today are to be met with in the Old Testament and the New, and their nearer grandfathers clamoured against the snares of the flesh in all the councils of the Early Church. Not only West-
35 ern Christianity has had to reckon with them: they have brothers today among the Mohammedan Sufi and in obscure Buddhist sects, and they were the chief preachers of the Russian Raskol, or Reformation. "The Ironsides of Cromwell and the Puritans of New England," says Heard, in his book on the Russian church, "bear a strong resemblance to the Old Believers." But here, in the
40 main, we have asceticism more than Puritanism, as it is now visible; here the sinner combated is chiefly the one within. How are we to account for the wholesale transvaluation of values that came after the Civil War, the transfer of ire from the Old Adam to the happy rascal across the street, the sinister rise of a new Inquisition in the midst of a growing luxury that even the Puri-

36. Sufi—an ascetic mystic. 37. Raskol—dissenter from the Russian Orthodox Church. 38. Heard—Albert F. Heard, *The Russian Church and Russian Dissent*, Harper, 1887. 43. Old Adam—unregenerate mankind.

tans themselves succumbed to? The answer is to be sought, it seems to me, in the direction of the Golden Calf—in the direction of the fat fields of our Midlands, the full nets of our lakes and coasts, the factory smoke of our cities —even in the direction of Wall Street, that devil's chasm. In brief, Puritanism has become bellicose and tyrannical by becoming rich. The will to power has 5 been aroused to a high flame by an increase in the available draught and fuel, as militarism is engendered and nourished by the presence of men and materials. Wealth, discovering its power, has reached out its long arms to grab the distant and innumerable sinner; it has gone down into its deep pockets to pay for his costly pursuit and flaying; it has created the Puritan *entre-* 10 *preneur,* the daring and imaginative organizer of Puritanism, the baron of moral endeavour, the invincible prophet of new austerities. And, by the same token, it has issued its letters of marque to the Puritan mercenary, the professional hound of heaven, the moral *Junker,* the Comstock, and out of his skill at his trade there has arisen the whole machinery, so complicated and so ef- 15 fective, of the new Holy Office.

Poverty is a soft pedal upon all branches of human activity, not excepting the spiritual, and even the original Puritans, for all their fire, felt its throttling caress. I think it is Bill Nye who has humorously pictured their arduous life: how they had to dig clams all winter that they would have strength enough 20 to plant corn, and how they had to hoe corn all summer that they would have strength enough to dig clams. That low ebb of fortune worked against the full satisfaction of their zeal in two distinct ways. On the one hand, it kept them but ill-prepared for the cost of offensive enterprise: even their occasional missionarying raids upon the Indians took too much productive energy from 25 their business with the corn and the clams. And on the other hand, it kept a certain restraining humility in their hearts, so that for every Quaker they hanged, they let a dozen go. Poverty, of course, is no discredit, but at all events, it is a subtle criticism. The man oppressed by material wants is not in the best of moods for the more ambitious forms of moral adventure. He 30 not only lacks the means; he is also deficient in the self-assurance, the sense of superiority, the secure and lofty point of departure. If he is haunted by notions of the sinfulness of his neighbours, he is apt to see some of its worst manifestations within himself, and that disquieting discovery will tend to take his thoughts from the other fellow. It is by no arbitrary fiat, indeed, that the 35 brothers of all the expiatory orders are vowed to poverty. History teaches us that wealth, whenever it has come to them by chance, has put an end to their soul-searching. The Puritans of the elder generations, with few exceptions, were poor. Nearly all Americans, down to the Civil War, were poor. And being poor, they subscribed to a *Sklavenmoral.* That is to say, they were spirit- 40 ually humble. Their eyes were fixed, not upon the abyss below them, but upon the long and rocky road ahead of them. Their moral passion spent most of its force in self-accusing, self-denial and self-scourging. They began by

---

2. **Golden Calf**—*Cf.* Exod. 32: 1-13. **10-11. entrepreneur**—literally, undertaker; in technical economic theory, one who launches new enterprises. **14. hound of heaven**—See Francis Thompson's poem by this name. **16. Holy Office**—the Inquisition. **19. Nye**—See *Bill Nye's History of the United States* by Edgar Wilson Nye (1850-1896), Lippincott, 1894, pp. 49 f. **40. Sklavenmoral**—morale of the dispossessed.

howling their sins from the mourners' bench; they came to their end, many of
them, in the supreme immolation of battle.

But out of the War came prosperity, and out of prosperity came a new morality, to wit, the *Herrenmoral*. Many great fortunes were made in the War
5 itself; an uncountable number got started during the two decades following.
What is more, this material prosperity was generally dispersed through all
classes: it affected the common workman and the remote farmer quite as much
as the actual merchant and manufacturer. Its first effect, as we all know, was
a universal cockiness, a rise in pretensions, a comforting feeling that the Re-
10 public was a success, and with it, its every citizen. This change made itself
quickly obvious, and even odious, in all the secular relations of life. The American became a sort of braggart playboy of the western world, enormously sure
of himself and ludicrously contemptuous of all other men. And on the ghostly
side there appeared the same accession of confidence, the same sure assump-
15 tion of authority, though at first less self-evidently and offensively. The religion of the American thus began to lose its inward direction; it became less
and less a scheme of personal salvation and more and more a scheme of pious
derring-do. The revivals of the 70's had all the bounce and fervour of those of
half a century before, but the mourners' bench began to lose its standing as
20 their symbol, and in its place appeared the collection basket. Instead of accusing himself, the convert volunteered to track down and bring in the other
fellow. His enthusiasm was not for repentance, but for what he began to call
service. In brief, the national sense of energy and fitness gradually superim-
posed itself upon the national Puritanism, and from that marriage sprung a
25 keen *Wille zur Macht,* a lusty will to power. The American Puritan, by now,
was not content with the rescue of his own soul; he felt an irresistible impulse
to hand salvation on, to disperse and multiply it, to ram it down reluctant
throats, to make it free, universal and compulsory. He had the men, he had
the guns and he had the money too. All that was needed was organization.
30 The rescue of the unsaved could be converted into a wholesale business, un-
sentimentally and economically conducted, and with all the usual aids to efficiency, from skilful sales management to seductive advertising, and from rigorous accounting to the diligent shutting off of competition.

Out of that new will to power came many enterprises more or less futile
35 and harmless, with the "institutional" church at their head. Piety was cunningly disguised as basketball, billiards and squash; the sinner was lured to
grace with Turkish baths, lectures on foreign travel, and free instructions in
stenography, rhetoric and double-entry book-keeping. Religion lost all its old
contemplative and esoteric character, and became a frankly worldly enterprise,
40 a thing of balance-sheets and ponderable profits, heavily capitalized and
astutely manned. There was no longer any room for the spiritual type of

4. **Herrenmoral**—morale of the master class. 12. **playboy . . . world**—title of a famous play by John Millington Synge (1871-1909), Irish dramatist, first produced in 1907. 13.
ghostly—spiritual. 25. **Wille zur Macht**—will to power. This, like *Sklavenmoral* and
Herrenmoral above, Mencken takes over from Friedrich Nietzsche (1844-1900), who occasioned
Mencken's second book. **power**—*Cf.* The Puritan, by Owen Hatteras, *The Smart Set*, July,
1916; and The Puritan's Will to Power, by Randolph S. Bourne, *The Seven Arts*, April, 1917.
(Author's note) Owen Hatteras is a pseudonym for Mencken. **28-29. He had . . . too**—from
the chorus of a popular song.

leader, with his white choker and his interminable fourthlies. He was displaced by a brisk gentleman in a "business suit" who looked, talked and thought like a seller of Mexican mine stock. Scheme after scheme for the swift evangelization of the nation was launched, some of them of truly astonishing sweep and daring. They kept pace, step by step, with the mushroom growth of enterprise in the commercial field. The Y.M.C.A. swelled to the proportions of a Standard Oil Company, a United States Steel Corporation. Its huge buildings began to rise in every city; it developed a swarm of specialists in new and fantastic moral and social sciences; it enlisted the same gargantuan talent which managed the railroads, the big banks and the larger national industries. And beside it rose the Young People's Society of Christian Endeavour, the Sunday-school associations and a score of other such grandiose organizations, each with its seductive baits for recruits and money. Even the enterprises that had come down from an elder and less expansive day were pumped up and put on a Wall Street basis: the American Bible Society, for example, began to give away Bibles by the million instead of by the thousand, and the venerable Tract Society took on the feverish ardour of a daily newspaper, even of a yellow journal. Down into our own day this trustification of pious endeavour has gone on. The Men and Religion Forward Movement proposed to convert the whole country by 12 o'clock noon of such and such a day; the Order of Gideons plans to make every traveller read the Bible (American Revised Version!) whether he will or not; in a score of cities there are committees of opulent devotees who take half-pages in the newspapers, and advertise the Decalogue and the Beatitudes as if they were commodities of trade.

Thus the national energy which created the Beef Trust and the Oil Trust achieved equal marvels in the field of religious organization and by exactly the same methods. One needs be no psychologist to perceive in all this a good deal less actual religious zeal than mere lust for staggering accomplishment, for empty bigness, for the unprecedented and the prodigious. Many of these great religious enterprises, indeed, soon lost all save the faintest flavour of devotion—for example, the Y.M.C.A., which is now no more than a sort of national club system, with its doors open to anyone not palpably felonious. (I have drunk cocktails in Y.M.C.A. lamaseries, and helped fallen lamas to bed.) But while the war upon godlessness thus degenerated into a secular sport in one direction, it maintained all its pristine quality, and even took on a new ferocity in another direction. Here it was that the lamp of American Puritanism kept on burning; here, it was, indeed, that the lamp became converted

15. **Bible Society**—founded in 1816 "to encourage a wider circulation of the Holy Scriptures, without note or comment." It circulates (in English) only the King James and the English and American Revised Versions of the Bible. 17. **Tract Society**—The American Tract Society was founded in New York City in 1825. It absorbed various older societies. 19. **Men . . . Movement**—In 1912 Fred B. Smith, international secretary of the Y.M.C.A., founded the Men and Religion Forward Movement in sixty North American cities, to gain strength for the "Y." 21. **Gideons**—organized in 1899 at Janesville, Wisconsin, to place a copy of the Bible in every hotel bedroom. 21-22. **Revised Version**—Dissatisfied with the Revised Version of the Bible produced by British scholars, American scholars published their own version in 1901. Mencken's point is that the point of view of the Gideons is narrow. 23-24. **Decalogue**—*Cf.* Exod. 20: 3-17. 24. **Beatitudes**—*Cf.* Matt. 5: 3-12. 33. **lamaseries**—humorous misuse of the Tibetan word for "monastery." A lama is a Tibetan Buddhist priest.

into a huge bonfire, or rather a blast-furnace, with flames mounting to the
very heavens, and sinners stacked like cordwood at the hand of an eager black
gang. In brief, the new will to power, working in the true Puritan as in the
mere religious sportsman, stimulated him to a campaign of repression and
5 punishment perhaps unequalled in the history of the world, and developed
an art of militant morality as complex in technique and as rich in professors as
the elder art of iniquity.

If we take the passage of the Comstock Postal Act, on March 3, 1873, as a
starting point, the legislative stakes of this new Puritan movement sweep up-
10 ward in a grand curve to the passage of the Mann and Webb Acts, in 1910
and 1913, the first of which ratifies the Seventh Commandment with a salvo
of artillery, and the second of which put the overwhelming power of the Federal Government behind the enforcement of the prohibition laws in the so-
called "dry" States. The mind at once recalls the salient campaigns of this
15 war of a generation: first the attack upon "vicious" literature, begun by Comstock and the New York Society for the Suppression of Vice, but quickly extending to every city in the land; then the long fight upon the open gambling
house, culminating in its practical disappearance; then the recrudescence of
prohibition, abandoned at the outbreak of the Civil War, and the attempt to
20 enforce it in a rapidly growing list of States; then the successful onslaught
upon the Louisiana lottery, and upon its swarm of rivals and successors; then
the gradual stamping-out of horse-racing, until finally but two or three States
permitted it, and the consequent attack upon the poolroom; then the rise of a
theatre-censorship in most of the large cities, and of a moving picture censor-
25 ship following it; then the revival of Sabbatarianism, with the Lord's Day
Alliance, a Canadian invention, in the van; then the gradual tightening of the
laws against sexual irregularity, with the unenforceable New York Adultery
Act as a typical product; and lastly, the general ploughing up and emotional
discussion of sexual matters, with compulsory instruction in "sex hygiene" as
30 its mildest manifestation and the mediaeval fury of the vice crusade as its worst.
Differing widely in their targets, these various Puritan enterprises had one
character in common: they were all efforts to combat immorality with the
weapons designed for crime. In each of them there was a visible effort to erect
the individual's offence against himself into an offence against society. Be-
35 neath all of them there was the dubious principle—the very determining principle, indeed, of Puritanism—that it is competent for the community to limit
and condition the private acts of its members, and with it the inevitable corol-
lary that there are some members of the community who have a special talent
for such legislation, and that their arbitrary fiats are, and of a right ought to
40 be, binding upon all.

10. **Mann**—The so-called Mann Act forbids the transportation of women across state lines for
immoral purposes. Its enforcement has sometimes led to individual persecution. 11. **Seventh
Commandment**—against adultery. 21. **lottery**—The fight to abolish the Louisiana State Lottery Company in that state extended from 1868 to 1893. 25. **Sabbatarianism**—belief in an excessively strict observance of Sunday. 27-28. **New York . . . Act**—In New York state divorce is granted only when adultery can be proved.

4

This is the essential fact of the new Puritanism; its recognition of the moral expert, the professional sinhound, the virtuoso of virtue. Under the original Puritan theocracy, as in Scotland, for example, the chase and punishment of sinners was a purely ecclesiastical function, and during the slow disintegration of the theocracy the only change introduced was the extension of that function to lay helpers, and finally to the whole body of laymen. This change, however, did not materially corrupt the ecclesiastical quality of the enterprise: the leader in the so-called militant field still remained the same man who led in the spiritual field. But with the capitalization of Puritan effort there came a radical overhauling of method. The secular arm, as it were, conquered as it helped. That is to say, the special business of forcing sinners to be good was taken away from the preachers and put into the hands of laymen trained in its technique and mystery, and there it remains. The new Puritanism has created an army of gladiators who are not only distinct from the hierarchy, but who, in many instances, actually command and intimidate the hierarchy. This is conspicuously evident in the case of the Anti-Saloon League, an enormously effective fighting organization, with a large staff of highly accomplished experts in its service. These experts do not wait for ecclesiastical support, nor even ask for it; they force it. The clergyman who presumes to protest against their war upon the saloon, even upon the quite virtuous ground that it is not effective enough, runs a risk of condign and merciless punishment. So plainly is this understood, indeed, that in more than one State the clergy of the Puritan denominations openly take orders from these specialists in excoriation, and court their favour without shame. Here a single moral enterprise, heavily capitalized and carefully officered, has engulfed the entire Puritan movement, and a part has become more than the whole.

In a dozen other directions this tendency to transform a religious business into a purely secular business, with lay backers and lay officers, is plainly visible. The increasing wealth of Puritanism has not only augmented its scope and its daring, but it has also had the effect of attracting clever men, of no particular spiritual enthusiasm, to its service. Moral endeavour, in brief, has become a recognized trade, or rather a profession, and there have appeared men who pretend to a special and enormous knowledge of it, and who show enough truth in their pretension to gain the unlimited support of Puritan capitalists. The vice crusade, to mention one example, has produced a large crop of such self-constituted experts, and some of them are in such demand that they are overwhelmed with engagements. The majority of these men have wholly lost the flavour of sacerdotalism. They are not pastors, but detectives, statisticians and mob orators, and not infrequently their secularity becomes distressingly evident. Their aim, as they say, is to do things. Assuming that "moral sentiment" is behind them, they override all criticism and opposition without argument, and proceed to the business of dispersing prostitutes,

27. whole—An instructive account of the organization and methods of the Anti-Saloon League, a thoroughly typical Puritan engine, is to be found in Alcohol and Society, by John Koren; New York, Henry Holt & Co., 1916. (Author's note)

of browbeating and terrorizing weak officials, and of forcing legislation of their own invention through City Councils and State Legislatures. Their very cocksureness is their chief source of strength. They combat objection with such violence and with such a devastating cynicism that it quickly fades away.
5 The more astute politicians, in the face of so ruthless a fire, commonly profess conversion and join the colours, just as their brethren went over to prohibition in the "dry" States, and the newspapers seldom hold out much longer. The result is that the "investigation" of the social evil becomes an orgy, and that the ensuing "report" of the inevitable "vice commission" is made up of
10 two parts sensational fiction and three parts platitude. Of all the vice commissions that have sat of late in the United States, not one has done its work without the aid of these singularly confident experts, and not one has contributed an original and sagacious idea, nor even an idea of ordinary common sense, to the solution of the problem.
15 I need not go on piling up examples of this new form of Puritan activity, with its definite departure from a religious foundation and its elaborate development as an everyday business. The impulse behind it I have called a *Wille zur Macht,* a will to power. In terms more homely, it was described by John Fiske as "the disposition to domineer," and in his usual unerring way, he saw
20 its dependence on the gratuitous assumption of infallibility. But even stronger than the Puritan's belief in his own inspiration is his yearning to make some one jump. In other words, he has an ineradicable liking for cruelty in him: he is a sportsman even before he is a moralist, and very often his blood-lust leads him into lamentable excesses. The various vice crusades afford innumer-
25 able cases in point. In one city, if the press dispatches are to be believed, the proscribed women of the Tenderloin were pursued with such ferocity that seven of them were driven to suicide. And in another city, after a campaign of repression so unfortunate in its effects that there were actually protests against it by clergymen elsewhere, a distinguished (and very friendly) con-
30 noisseur of such affairs referred to it ingenuously as more fun "than a fleet of aeroplanes." Such disorderly combats with evil, of course, produce no permanent good. It is a commonplace, indeed, that a city is usually in worse condition after it has been "cleaned up" than it was before, and I need not point to New York, Los Angeles and Des Moines for the evidence as to the social
35 evil, and to any large city, East, West, North, South, for the evidence as to the saloon. But the Puritans who finance such enterprises get their thrills, not out of any possible obliteration of vice, but out of the galloping pursuit of the vicious. The new Puritan gives no more serious thought to the rights and feelings of his quarry than the gunner gives to the rights and feelings of his birds.
40 From the beginning of the prohibition campaign, for example, the principle of compensation has been violently opposed, despite its obvious justice, and a complaisant judiciary has ratified the Puritan position. In England and on the Continent that principle is safeguarded by the fundamental laws, and during the early days of the anti-slavery agitation in this country it was accepted as
45 incontrovertible, but if any American statesman were to propose today that it

26. **Tenderloin**—red-light district.

be applied to the license-holder whose lawful franchise has been taken away from him arbitrarily, or to the brewer or distiller whose costly plant has been rendered useless and valueless, he would see the days of his statesmanship brought to a quick and violent close.

But does all this argue a total lack of justice in the American character, or even a lack of common decency? I doubt that it would be well to go so far in accusation. What it does argue is a tendency to put moral considerations above all other considerations, and to define morality in the narrow Puritan sense. The American, in other words, thinks that the sinner has no rights that any-one is bound to respect, and he is prone to mistake an unsupported charge of sinning, provided it be made violently enough, for actual proof and confession. What is more, he takes an intense joy in the mere chase: he has the true Puri-tan taste for an *auto da fé* in him. "I am ag'inst capital punishment," said Mr. Dooley, "but we won't get rid av it so long as the people enjie it so much." But though he is thus an eager spectator, and may even be lured into taking part in the pursuit, the average American is not disposed to initiate it, nor to pay for it. The larger Puritan enterprises of today are not popular in the sense of originating in the bleachers, but only in the sense of being applauded from the bleachers. The burdens of the fray, both of toil and of expense, are always upon a relatively small number of men. In a State rocked and racked by a war upon the saloon, it was recently shown, for example, that but five per cent of the members of the Puritan denominations contributed to the war-chest. And yet the Anti-Saloon League of that State was so sure of support from below that it presumed to stand as the spokesman of the whole Christian community, and even ventured to launch excommunications upon contuma-cious Christians, both lay and clerical, who objected to its methods. Moreover, the great majority of the persons included in the contributing five per cent gave no more than a few cents a year. The whole support of the League de-volved upon a dozen men, all of them rich and all of them Puritans of purest ray serene. These men supported a costly organization for their private enter-tainment and stimulation. It was their means of recreation, their sporting club. They were willing to spend a lot of money to procure good sport for them-selves—*i.e.,* to procure the best crusading talent available—and they were so successful in that endeavour that they enchanted the populace too, and so shook the State.

Naturally enough, this organization of Puritanism upon a business and sporting basis has had a tendency to attract and create a type of "expert" cru-sader whose determination to give his employers a good show is uncontami-nated by any consideration for the public welfare. The result has been a steady increase of scandals, a constant collapse of moral organizations, a fre-quent unveiling of whited sepulchres. Various observers have sought to direct the public attention to this significant corruption of the new Puritanism. The New York *Sun,* for example, in the course of a protest against the appoint-ment of a vice commission for New York, has denounced the paid agents of

13. auto da fé—literally, act of faith; term used for the execution of heretics under the In-quisition in Spain. 14. Dooley—the comic creation of Finley Peter Dunne (1867-1936), whose comments on public affairs first appeared in book form in *Mr. Dooley in Peace and War* (1898).

private reform organizations as "notoriously corrupt, undependable and dishonest," and the Rev. Dr. W. S. Rainsford, supporting the charge, has borne testimony out of his own wide experience to their lawlessness, their absurd pretensions to special knowledge, their habit of manufacturing evidence, and
5 their devious methods of shutting off criticism. But so far, at all events, no organized war upon them has been undertaken, and they seem to flourish more luxuriantly year after year. The individual whose common rights are invaded by such persons has little chance of getting justice, and less of getting redress. When he attempts to defend himself he finds that he is opposed,
10 not only by a financial power that is ample for all purposes of the combat and that does not shrink at intimidating juries, prosecuting officers and judges, but also by a shrewdness which shapes the laws to its own uses, and takes full advantage of the miserable cowardice of legislatures. The moral gladiators, in brief, know the game. They come before a legislature with a bill ostensibly
15 designed to cure some great and admitted evil, they procure its enactment by scarcely veiled insinuations that all who stand against it must be apologists for the evil itself, and then they proceed to extend its aims by bold inferences, and to dragoon the courts into ratifying those inferences, and to employ it as a means of persecution, terrorism and blackmail. The history of the Mann
20 Act offers a shining example of this purpose. It was carried through Congress, over the veto of President Taft, who discerned its extravagance, on the plea that it was needed to put down the traffic in prostitutes; it is enforced today against men who are no more engaged in the traffic in prostitutes than you or I. Naturally enough, the effect of this extension of its purposes, against
25 which its author has publicly protested, has been to make it a truly deadly weapon in the hands of professional Puritans and of denouncers of delinquency even less honest. "Blackmailers of both sexes have arisen," says Mr. Justice McKenna, "using the terrors of the construction now sanctioned by the [Supreme] Court as a help—indeed, the means—for their brigandage. The re-
30 sult is grave and should give us pause."

But that is as far as objection has yet gone; the majority of the learned jurist's colleagues swallowed both the statute and its consequences. There is, indeed, no sign as yet of any organized war upon the alliance between the blackmailing Puritan and the pseudo-Puritan blackmailer. It must wait until a sense
35 of reason and justice shows itself in the American people, strong enough to overcome their prejudice in favour of the moralist on the one hand, and their delight in barbarous pursuits and punishments on the other. I see but faint promise of that change today.

5

40 I have gone into the anatomy and physiology of militant Puritanism because, so far as I know, the inquiry has not been attempted before, and because a somewhat detailed acquaintance with the forces behind so grotesque a manifestation as comstockery, the particular business of the present essay,

---

2. **Rainsford**—Rev. William Stephen Rainsford (1850-1933), Protestant Episcopal clergyman who turned St. George's Church in Stuyvesant Square, New York City, facing collapse in 1883, into a noted center of social service. **30. pause**—U. S. Rep., vol. 242, no. 7, p. 502. (Author's note) **32. consequences**—The majority opinion, written by Mr. Justice Day, is given in U. S. Rep., vol. 242, no. 7, pp. 482-496. (Author's note)

is necessary to an understanding of its workings, and of its prosperity, and of its influence upon the arts. Save one turn to England or to the British colonies, it is impossible to find a parallel for the astounding absolutism of Comstock and his imitators in any civilized country. No other nation has laws which oppress the arts so ignorantly and so abominably as ours do, nor has any 5 other nation handed over the enforcement of the statutes which exist to agencies so openly pledged to reduce all aesthetic expression to the service of a stupid and unworkable scheme of rectitude. I have before me as I write a pamphlet in explanation of his aims and principles, prepared by Comstock himself and presented to me by his successor. Its very title is a sufficient state- 10 ment of the Puritan position: "MORALS, Not Art or Literature." The capitals are in the original. And within, as a sort of general text, the idea is amplified: "It is a question of peace, good order and morals, and not art, literature or science." Here we have a statement of principle that, at all events, is at least quite frank. There is not the slightest effort to beg the question; there is no 15 hypocritical pretension to a desire to purify or safeguard the arts; they are dismissed at once as trivial and degrading. And jury after jury has acquiesced in this; it was old Anthony's boast, in his last days, that his percentage of convictions, in 40 years, had run to 98.5.

Comstockery is thus grounded firmly upon that profound national suspi- 20 cion of the arts, that truculent and almost unanimous Philistinism, which I have described. It would be absurd to dismiss it as an excrescence, and untypical of the American mind. But it is typical, too, in the manner in which it has gone beyond that mere partiality to the accumulation of a definite power, and made that power irresponsible and almost irresistible. It was Comstock 25 himself, in fact, who invented the process whereby his followers in other fields of moral endeavour have forced laws into the statute books upon the pretence of putting down John Doe, an acknowledged malefactor, and then turned them savagely upon Richard Roe, a peaceable, well-meaning and hitherto law-abiding man. And it was Comstock who first capitalized moral 30 endeavour like baseball or the soap business, and made himself the first of its kept professors, and erected about himself a rampart of legal and financial immunity which rid him of all fear of mistakes and their consequences, and so enabled him to pursue his jehad with all the advantages in his favour. He was, in brief, more than the greatest Puritan gladiator of his time; he was the 35 Copernicus of a quite new art and science, and he devised a technique and handed down a professional ethic that no rival has been able to better.

The whole story is naïvely told in "Anthony Comstock, Fighter," a work

11. "Morals . . . Literature"—New York (1914). (Author's note) 19. 98.5—I quote from page 157 of Anthony Comstock, Fighter, the official biography. On page 299 the number of his prosecutions is given as 3,646, with 2,682 convictions, which works out to but 73 per cent. He is credited with having destroyed 50 tons of books, 28,425 pounds of stereotype plates, 16,900 photographic negatives, and 3,984,063 photographs—enough to fill "sixteen freight cars, fifteen loaded with ten tons each, and the other nearly full." (Author's note) 28-29. Doe . . . Roe—two legal fictions, used when the real names of persons cannot be known. 34. jehad— fanatical crusade. 36. Copernicus—Nicolaus Copernicus (1473-1543), the Polish astronomer, whose De revolutionibus orbium celestium (1543) established the modern theory that the planets revolve around the sun. 38. "Anthony Comstock, Fighter"—By Charles Gallaudet Trumbull; New York, Fleming H. Revell Co. (1913). (Author's note) See also Heywood Broun and Margaret Leech, Anthony Comstock, Roundsman of the Lord; Albert & Charles Boni, 1927, which is more critical.

which passed under the approving eye of the old war horse himself and is
full of his characteristic pecksniffery. His beginnings, it appears, were very
modest. When he arrived in New York from the Connecticut hinterland, he
was a penniless and uneducated clodhopper, just out of the Union army, and
5 his first job was that of a porter in a wholesale dry-goods house. But he had in
him several qualities of the traditional Yankee which almost always insure
success, and it was not long before he began to make his way. One of these
qualities was a talent for bold and ingratiating address; another was a vast
appetite for thrusting himself into affairs, a yearning to run things—what the
10 Puritan calls public spirit. The two constituted his fortune. The second brought
him into intimate relations with the newly-organized Young Men's Christian
Association, and led him to the discovery of a form of moral endeavour that
was at once novel and fascinating—the unearthing and denunciation of "immoral" literature. The first, once he had attracted attention thereby, got him
15 the favourable notice, and finally the unlimited support, of the late Morris K.
Jesup, one of the earliest and perhaps the greatest of the moral *entrepreneurs*
that I have described. Jesup was very rich, and very eager to bring the whole
nation up to grace by *force majeure*. He was the banker of at least a dozen
grandiose programs of purification in the seventies and eighties. In Comstock
20 he found precisely the sort of field agent that he was looking for, and the
two presently constituted the most formidable team of professional reformers
that the country had ever seen.

The story of the passage of the Act of Congress of March 3, 1873, under
cover of which the Comstock Society still carries on its campaigns of snouting
25 and suppression, is a classical tale of Puritan impudence and chicanery. Comstock, with Jesup and other rich men backing him financially and politically,
managed the business. First, a number of spectacular raids were made on the
publishers of such pornographic books as "The Memoirs of Fanny Hill" and
"Only a Boy." Then the newspapers were filled with inflammatory matter
30 about the wide dispersal of such stuff, and its demoralizing effects upon the
youth of the republic. Then a committee of self-advertising clergymen and
"Christian millionaires" was organized to launch a definite "movement." And
then a direct attack was made upon Congress, and, to the tune of fiery moral
indignation, the bill prepared by Comstock himself was forced through both
35 houses. All opposition, if only the opposition of inquiry, was overborne in
the usual manner. That is to say, every Congressman who presumed to ask

2. pecksniffery—from Mr. Pecksniff, one of the chief characters (a hypocrite) in Dickens's
Martin Chuzzlewit.—An example: "All the evil men in New York cannot harm a hair of my
head, were it not the will of God. If it be His will, what right have I or anyone to say aught?
I am only a speck, a mite, before God, yet not a hair of my head can be harmed unless it be
His will. Oh, to live, to feel, to be—Thy will be done!" (pp. 84-5). Again: "I prayed that, if my
bill might not pass, I might go back to New York submissive to God's will, feeling that it was
for the best. I asked for forgiveness and asked that my bill might pass, if possible; but over and
above all, that the will of God be done" (p. 6). Nevertheless, Comstock neglected no chance
to apply his backstairs pressure to the members of both Houses. (Author's note) **16. Jesup**—
Morris Ketchum Jesup (1830-1908), capitalist and philanthropist. Mencken's picture is scarcely
just. **18. force majeure**—pressure. **23. 1873**—Now, with amendments, sections 211, 212 and
245 of the United States Criminal Code. (Author's note) **26. politically**—*Vide* Anthony Comstock, Fighter, pp. 81, 85, 94. (Author's note)

what it was all about, or to point out obvious defects in the bill, was disposed of by the insinuation, or even the direct charge, that he was a covert defender of obscene books, and, by inference, of the carnal recreations described in them. We have grown familiar of late with this process: it was displayed at full length in the passage of the Mann Act, and again when the Webb Act   5
and the Prohibition Amendment were before Congress. In 1873 its effectiveness was helped out by its novelty, and so the Comstock bill was rushed through both houses in the closing days of a busy session, and President Grant accommodatingly signed it.

Once it was upon the books, Comstock made further use of the prevailing   10
uproar to have himself appointed a special agent of the Postoffice Department to enforce it, and with characteristic cunning refused to take any salary. Had his job carried a salary, it would have excited the acquisitiveness of other virtuosi; as it was, he was secure. As for the necessary sinews of war, he knew well that he could get them from Jesup. Within a few weeks, indeed, the latter   15
had perfected a special organization for the enforcement of the new statute, and it still flourishes as the New York Society for the Suppression of Vice; or, as it is better known, the Comstock Society. The new Federal Act, dealing only with the mails, left certain loopholes; they were plugged up by fastening drastic amendments upon the New York Code of Criminal Procedure—   20
amendments forced through the legislature precisely as the Federal Act had been forced through Congress. With these laws in his hands Comstock was ready for his career. It was his part of the arrangement to supply the thrills of the chase; it was Jesup's part to find the money. The partnership kept up until the death of Jesup, in 1908, and after that Comstock readily found new   25
backers. Even his own death, in 1915, did not materially alter a scheme of things which offered such admirable opportunities for the exercise of the Puritan love of spectacular and relentless pursuit, the Puritan delusion of moral grandeur and infallibility, the Puritan will to power.

Ostensibly, as I have said, the new laws were designed to put down the   30
traffic in frankly pornographic books and pictures—a traffic which, of course, found no defenders—but Comstock had so drawn them that their actual sweep was vastly wider, and once he was firmly in the saddle his enterprises scarcely knew limits. Having disposed of "The Confessions of Maria Monk" and "Night Life in Paris," he turned to Rabelais and the Decameron, and having   35
driven these ancients under the book-counters, he pounced upon Zola, Balzac and Daudet, and having disposed of these too, he began a *pogrom* which, in other hands, eventually brought down such astounding victims as Thomas Hardy's "Jude the Obscure" and Harold Frederic's "The Damnation of Theron Ware." All through the eighties and nineties this ecstatic campaign   40
continued, always increasing in violence and effectiveness. Comstock became a national celebrity; his doings were as copiously reported by the newspapers

22. Congress—Now sections 1141, 1142 and 1143 of the Penal Laws of New York. (Author's note) **35-40. Rabelais . . . Ware**—The literary figures alluded to are familiar enough, with the possible exception of **Harold Frederic** (1856-1898), whose *The Damnation of Theron Ware* (1896) has a shallow Methodist minister for its central figure. **37. pogrom**—persecution.

as those of P. T. Barnum or John L. Sullivan. Imitators sprang up in all the larger cities: there was hardly a public library in the land that did not begin feverishly expurgating its shelves; the publication of fiction, and particularly of foreign fiction, took on the character of an extra hazardous enterprise. Not,

5 of course, that the reign of terror was not challenged, and Comstock himself denounced. So early as 1876 a national organization demanding a reasonable amendment of the postal laws got on its legs; in the late eighties "Citizen" George Francis Train defied the whirlwind by printing the Old Testament as a serial; many indignant victims, acquitted by some chance in the courts,

10 brought suit against Comstock for damages. Moreover, an occasional judge, standing out boldly against the usual intimidation, denounced him from the bench; one of them, Judge Jenkins, accused him specifically of "fraud and lying" and other "dishonest practices." But the spirit of American Puritanism was on his side. His very extravagances at once stimulated and satisfied the

15 national yearning for a hot chase, a good show—and in the complaints of his victims, that the art of letters was being degraded, that the country was made ridiculous, the newspaper-reading populace could see no more than an affectation. The reform organization of 1876 lasted but five years; and then disbanded without having accomplished anything; Train was put on trial for

20 "debauching the young" with an "obscene" serial; juries refused to bring in punitive verdicts against the master showman.

In carrying on this way of extermination upon all ideas that violated their private notions of virtue and decorum, Comstock and his followers were very greatly aided by the vagueness of the law. It prohibited the use of the mails

25 for transporting all matter of an "obscene, lewd, lascivious . . . or filthy" character, but conveniently failed to define these adjectives. As a result, of course, it was possible to bring an accusation against practically *any* publication that aroused the comstockian blood-lust, however innocently, and to subject the persons responsible for it to costly, embarrassing and often dangerous

30 persecution. No man, said Dr. Johnson, would care to go on trial for his life once a week, even if possessed of absolute proofs of his innocence. By the same token, no man wants to be arraigned in a criminal court, and displayed in the sensational newspapers, as a purveyor of indecency, however strong his assurance of innocence. Comstock made use of this fact in an adroit and

35 characteristically unconscionable manner. He held the menace of prosecution

---

1. **Barnum**—Phineas Taylor Barnum (1810-1891), "the great American showman," who declared the public liked to be cheated. **Sullivan**—John Lawrence Sullivan (1858-1918), who, after defeating Paddy Ryan in 1882 and thus winning the American heavyweight championship, was defeated by James Corbett in 1892. **8. Train**—George Francis Train (1829-1904), Boston-born merchant who, in the course of a spectacular career, came to the defense of Victoria Woodhull in the Tilton-Beecher divorce case, and actually printed the Bible in his paper, *The Train Line,* to test the obscenity statute. For this he was arrested and confined in the Ludlow Street Jail in New York for months, refusing to avail himself of bail. **12-13. Jenkins . . . practices**—U. S. *vs.* Casper, reported in the *Twentieth Century,* Feb. 11, 1892. (Author's note) **20. serial**—The trial court dodged the issue by directing the jury to find the prisoner not guilty on the ground of insanity. The necessary implication, of course, was that the publication complained of was actually obscene. In 1895, one Wise, of Clay Center, Kansas, sent a quotation from the Bible through the mails, and was found guilty of mailing obscene matter. See The Free Press Anthology, compiled by Theodore Schroeder, New York, Truth Seeker Pub. Co., 1909, p. 258. (Author's note) **30. Johnson**—*Cf.* Boswell's *Life of Johnson* under date of April 3, 1776.

over all who presumed to dispute his tyranny, and when he could not prevail
by a mere threat, he did not hesitate to begin proceedings, and to carry them
forward with the aid of florid proclamations to the newspapers and ill concealed intimidations of judges and juries.

The last-named business succeeded as it always does in this country, where   5
the judiciary is quite as sensitive to the suspicion of sinfulness as the legislative arm. A glance at the decisions handed down during the forty years of
Comstock's chief activity shows a truly amazing willingness to accommodate
him in his pious enterprises. On the one hand, there was gradually built up a
court-made definition of obscenity which eventually embraced almost every   10
conceivable violation of Puritan prudery, and on the other hand the victim's
means of defence were steadily restricted and conditioned, until in the end he
had scarcely any at all. This is the state of the law today. It is held in the
leading cases that anything is obscene which may excite "impure thoughts"
in "the minds . . . of persons that are susceptible to impure thoughts," or   15
which "tends to deprave the minds" of any who, because they are "young and
inexperienced," are "open to such influences"—in brief, that anything is obscene that is not fit to be handed to a child just learning to read, or that may
imaginably stimulate the lubricity of the most foul-minded. It is held further
that words that are perfectly innocent in themselves—"words, abstractly con-   20
sidered, [that] may be free from vulgarism"—may yet be assumed, by a
friendly jury, to be likely to "arouse a libidinous passion . . . in the mind of
a modest woman." (I quote exactly! The court failed to define "modest
woman.") Yet further, it is held that any book is obscene "which is unbecoming, immodest. . . ." Obviously, this last decision throws open the door to   25
endless imbecilities, for its definition merely begs the question, and so makes
a reasonable solution ten times harder. It is in such mazes that the Comstocks
safely lurk. Almost any printed allusion to sex may be argued against as unbecoming in a moral republic, and once it is unbecoming it is also obscene.

In meeting such attacks the defendant must do his fighting without weap-   30
ons. He cannot allege in his defence that the offending work was put forth
for a legitimate, necessary and decent purpose; he cannot allege that a passage
complained of is from a standard work, itself in general circulation; he cannot offer evidence that the person to whom a book or picture was sold or exhibited was not actually depraved by it, or likely to be depraved by it; he can-   35
not rest his defence on its lack of such effect upon the jurymen themselves;
he cannot plead that the alleged obscenity, in point of fact, is couched in decent and unobjectionable language; he cannot plead that the same or a similar

14. thoughts—U. S. vs. Bennett, 16 Blatchford, 368-9 (1877). (Author's note) 17. influences—Idem, 362; People vs. Muller, 96 N. Y., 411; U. S. vs. Clark, 38 Fed. Rep. 734.
(Author's note) 23. modest woman—U. S. vs. Moore, 129 Fed., 160-1 (1904). (Author's note)
25. immodest—U. S. vs. Heywood, judge's charge, Boston, 1877. Quoted in U. S. vs. Bennett,
16 Blatchford. (Author's note) 32. purpose—U. S. vs. Slenker, 32 Fed. Rep., 693; People vs.
Muller, 96 N. Y. 408-414; Anti-Vice Motion Picture Co. vs. Bell, reported in the New York Law
Journal, Sept. 22, 1916; Sociological Research Film Corporation vs. the City of New York, 83
Misc. 815; Steele vs. Bannon, 7 L.R.C. L. Series, 267; U. S. vs. Means, 42 Fed. Rep. 605, etc.
(Author's note) 33. circulation—U. S. vs. Cheseman, 19 Fed. Rep., 597 (1884). (Author's
note) 35. by it—People vs. Muller, 96 N. Y., 413. (Author's note) 36. themselves—U. S. vs.
Bennett, 16 Blatchford, 368-9. (Author's note) 38. language—U. S. vs. Smith, 45 Fed. Rep.
478. (Author's note)

work has gone unchallenged elsewhere; he cannot argue that the circulation of works of the same class has set up a presumption of toleration, and a tacit limitation of the definition of obscenity. The general character of a book is not a defence of a particular passage, however unimportant; if there is the
5   slightest descent to what is "unbecoming," the whole may be ruthlessly condemned. Nor is it an admissible defence to argue that the book was not generally circulated, and that the copy in evidence was obtained by an *agent provocateur,* and by false representations. Finally, all the decisions deny the defendant the right to introduce any testimony, whether expert or otherwise,
10 that a book is of artistic value and not pornographic, and that its effect upon normal persons is not pernicious. Upon this point the jury is the sole judge, and it cannot be helped to its decision by taking other opinions, or by hearing evidence as to what is the general opinion.
   Occasionally, as I have said, a judge has revolted against this intolerable
15 state of the court- and Comstock-made law, and directed a jury to disregard these astounding decisions. In a recent New York case Judge Samuel Seabury actually ruled that "it is no part of the duty of courts to exercise a censorship over literary productions." But in general the judiciary has been curiously complaisant, and more than once a Puritan on the bench has delighted the
20 Comstocks by prosecuting their case for them. With such decisions in their hands and such aid from the other side of the bar, it is no wonder that they enter upon their campaigns with impudence and assurance. All the odds are in their favour from the start. They have statutes deliberately designed to make the defence onerous; they are familiar by long experience with all the
25 tricks and surprises of the game; they are sheltered behind organizations, incorporated without capital and liberally chartered by trembling legislatures, which make reprisals impossible in case of failure; above all, they have perfected the business of playing upon the cowardice and vanity of judges and prosecuting officers. The newspapers, with very few exceptions, give them
30 ready aid. Theoretically, perhaps, many newspaper editors are opposed to comstockery, and sometimes they denounce it with great eloquence, but when a good show is offered they are always in favour of the showman—and the

---

1. **elsewhere**—U. S. *vs.* Bennett, 16 Blatchford, 360-1; People *vs.* Berry, 1 N. Y., Crim. R., 32. (Author's note) 3. **obscenity**—People *vs.* Muller, 32 Hun., 212-215. (Author's note) 5-6. **condemned**—U. S. *vs.* Bennett, 16 Blatchford, 361. (Author's note) 7-8. **agent provocateur** —one hired to provoke deliberately a violation of law. 8. **representations**—U. S. *vs.* Moore, 16 Fed. Rep., 39; U. S. *vs.* Wright, 38 Fed. Rep., 106; U. S. *vs.* Dorsey, 40 Fed. Rep., 752; U. S. *vs.* Baker, 155 Mass., 287; U. S. *vs.* Grimm, 15 Supreme Court Rep., 472. (Author's note) 16. **decisions**—Various cases in point are cited in the Brief on Behalf of Plaintiff in Dreiser *vs.* John Lane Co., App. Div. 1st Dept. N. Y., 1917. I cite a few: People *vs.* Eastman, 188 N. Y., 478; U. S. *vs.* Swearingen, 161 U. S., 446; People *vs.* Tylkoff, 212 N. Y., 197; In the matter of Worthington Co., 62 St. Rep. 116-7; St. Hubert Guild *vs.* Quinn, 64 Misc., 336-341. But nearly all such decisions are in New York cases. In the Federal courts the Comstocks usually have their way. (Author's note) 18. **productions**—St. Hubert Guild *vs.* Quinn, 64 Misc., 339. (Author's note) 20. **case for them**—For example, Judge Chas. L. Benedict, sitting in U. S. *vs.* Bennett, *op. cit.* This is a leading case, and the Comstocks make much of it. Nevertheless, a contemporary newspaper denounces Judge Benedict for his "intense bigotry" and alleges that "the only evidence which he permitted to be given was on the side of the prosecution." (Port Jervis, N. Y. *Evening Gazette,* March 22, 1879.) Moreover, a juror in the case, Alfred A. Valentine, thought it necessary to inform the newspapers that he voted guilty only in obedience to judicial instructions. (Author's note) 32. **showman**—*Vide* Newspaper Morals, by H. L. Mencken, the *Atlantic Monthly,* March, 1914. (Author's note)

Comstocks are showmen of undoubted skill. They know how to make a victim jump and writhe in the ring; they have a talent for finding victims who are prominent enough to arrest attention; they shrewdly capitalize the fact that the pursuer appears more heroic than the prey, and the further fact that the newspaper reader is impatient of artistic pretensions and glad to see an 5 artist made ridiculous. And behind them there is always the steady pressure of Puritan prejudice—the Puritan feeling that "immorality" is the blackest of crimes, and that its practitioner has no rights. It was by making use of these elements that Comstock achieved his prodigies, and it is by making use of them that his heirs and assigns keep up the sport today. Their livelihood de- 10 pends upon the money they can raise among the righteous, and the amount they can raise depends upon the quality of the entertainment they offer. Hence their adept search for shining marks. Hence, for example, the spectacular raid upon the Art Students' League, on August 2, 1906. Hence the artful turning to their own use of the vogue of such sensational dramatists as Eugène Brieux 15 and George Bernard Shaw, and of such isolated plays as "Trilby" and "Sapho." Hence the barring from the mails of the inflammatory report of the Chicago Vice Commission—a strange, strange case of dog eating dog.

But here we have humour. There is, however, no humour in the case of a serious author who sees his work damaged and perhaps ruined by a malicious 20 and unintelligent attack, and himself held up to public obloquy as one with the vendors of pamphlets of flagellation and filthy "marriage guides." He finds opposing him a flat denial of his decent purpose as an artist, and a stupid and ill-natured logic that baffles sober answer. He finds on his side only the half-hearted support of a publisher whose interest in a single book is 25 limited to his profits from it, and who desires above all things to evade a nuisance and an expense. Not a few publishers, knowing the constant possibility of sudden and arbitrary attack, insert a clause in their contracts whereby an author must secure them against damage from any "immoral" matter in his book. They read and approve the manuscript, they print the book and 30 sell it—but if it is unlucky enough to attract the comstockian lightning, the author has the whole burden to bear, and if they seek safety and economy

16. "Trilby" . . . "Sapho"—Paul M. Potter dramatized *Trilby,* George Du Maurier's celebrated novel, for the Boston Museum Stock Company, where it was first produced in 1895. The play aroused moral controversy. In 1900 Clyde Fitch adapted Daudet's novel *Sapho* as a play for Olga Nethersole. The production was stopped on moral grounds, although Réjane and Bernhardt had produced French versions. 24. answer—As a fair specimen of the sort of reasoning that prevails among the consecrated brethren I offer the following extract from an argument against birth control delivered by the present active head of the New York Society for the Suppression of Vice before the Women's City Club of New York, Nov. 17, 1916: "Natural and inevitable conditions, over which we can have no control, will assert themselves wherever population becomes too dense. This has been exemplified time after time in the history of the world where over-population has been corrected by manifestations of nature or by war, flood or pestilence. . . . Belgium may have been regarded as an over-populated country. Is it a coincidence that, during the past two years, the territory of Belgium has been devastated and its population scattered throughout the other countries of the world?" (Author's note) 32. bear—For example, the printed contract of the John Lane Co., publisher of Dreiser's The "Genius," contains this provision: "The author hereby guarantees . . . that the work . . . contains nothing of a scandalous, an immoral or a libelous nature." The contract for the publication of The "Genius" was signed on July 30, 1914. The manuscript had been carefully read by representatives of the publisher, and presumably passed as not scandalous or immoral, inasmuch as the publication of a scandalous or immoral book would have exposed the publisher to prosecution. About 8,000 copies were sold under this

by yielding, as often happens, he must consent to the mutilation or even the
suppression of his work. The result is that a writer in such a situation, is
practically beaten before he can offer a defence. The professional book-baiters
have laws to their liking, and courts pliant to their exactions; they fill the
newspapers with inflammatory charges before the accused gets his day in
court; they have the aid of prosecuting officers who fear the political damage
of their enmity, and of the enmity of their wealthy and influential backers;
above all, they have the command of far more money than any author
can hope to muster. Finally, they derive an advantage from two of the most
widespread of human weaknesses, the first being envy and the second being
fear. When an author is attacked, a good many of his rivals see only a personal benefit in his difficulties, and not a menace to the whole order, and a
good many others are afraid to go to his aid because of the danger of bringing down the moralists' rage upon themselves. Both of these weaknesses revealed themselves very amusingly in the Dreiser case, and I hope to detail
their operations at some length later on, when I describe that *cause célèbre* in
a separate work.

Now add to the unfairness and malignancy of the attack its no less disconcerting arbitrariness and fortuitousness, and the path of the American author
is seen to be strewn with formidable entanglements indeed. With the law
what it is, he is quite unable to decide *a priori* what is permitted by the national delicacy and what is not, nor can he get any light from the recorded
campaigns of the moralists. They seem to strike blindly, unintelligently, without any coherent theory or plan. "Trilby" is assaulted by the united comstockery of a dozen cities, and "The Yoke" somehow escapes. "Hagar Revelly" is
made the subject of a double prosecution in the State and Federal courts, and
"Love's Pilgrimage" and "One Man" go unmolested. The publisher of
Przybyszewski's "Homo Sapiens" is forced to withdraw it; the publisher of
Artzibashef's "Sanine" follows it with "The Breaking Point." The serious
work of a Forel is brought into court as pornography, and the books of
Havelock Ellis are barred from the mails; the innumerable volumes on "sex
hygiene" by tawdry clergymen and smutty old maids are circulated by the
million and without challenge. Frank Harris is deprived of a publisher for his

contract. Two years later, in July, 1916, the Society for the Suppression of Vice threatened to
begin a prosecution unless the book was withdrawn. It was withdrawn forthwith, and Dreiser
was compelled to enter suit for a performance of the contract. The withdrawal, it will be noticed, was not in obedience to a court order, but followed a mere comstockian threat. Yet Dreiser
was at once deprived of his royalties, and forced into expensive litigation. Had it not been that
eminent counsel volunteered for his defence, his personal means would have been insufficient to
have got him even a day in court. (Author's note) **16. cause célèbre**—case much talked about.
21. a priori—without examination. **25. "The Yoke"**—a novel by this title, published in 1908.
The author is "Hubert Wales" (William Piggott, 1872-1943). **"Hagar Revelly"**—by Daniel Carson Goodman (1883-   ), published in 1913. **27. "Love's Pilgrimage"**—by Upton
Sinclair (1878-   ), 1911. **"One Man"**—a novel by Robert Steele, 1915. **28. "Homo
Sapiens"**—by Stanislaw Przybyszewski (1868-1927), 1909. **29. "The Breaking Point"**—by
Mikhail Petrovich Artsybashev (1878-1927), translated in 1915. *Sanine* was translated in 1914.
30. Forel—Auguste Forel (1848-1931), French psychologist and biologist, whose *The Sexual
Question* (translated in 1908) aroused controversy. **31. Ellis**—Henry Havelock Ellis (1859-1944)
author of *Studies in the Psychology of Sex,* one of the classics of irrational psychology, first published in 7 vols., 1897-1928, later in 4 vols. by Random House. **33. Harris**—Frank Harris (1855-
1931). His book on Oscar Wilde was first printed in 1916. Since then it has been republished.

"Oscar Wilde: His Life and Confession" by threats of immediate prosecution; the newspapers meanwhile dedicate thousands of columns to the filthy amusements of Harry Thaw. George Moore's "Memoirs of My Dead Life" are bowdlerized, James Lane Allen's "A Summer in Arcady" is barred from libraries, and a book by D. H. Lawrence is forbidden publication altogether; 5 at the same time half a dozen cheap magazines devoted to sensational sex stories attain to hundreds of thousands of circulation. A serious book by David Graham Phillips, published serially in a popular monthly, is raided the moment it appears between covers; a trashy piece of nastiness by Elinor Glyn goes unmolested. Worse, books are sold for months and even years without 10 protest, and then suddenly attacked; Dreiser's "The 'Genius,'" Kreymborg's "Edna" and Forel's "The Sexual Question" are examples. Still worse, what is held to be unobjectionable in one State is forbidden in another as *contra bonos mores*. Altogether, there is madness, and no method in it. The livelihoods and good names of hard-striving and decent men are at the mercy of the 15 whims of a horde of fanatics and mountebanks, and they have no way of securing themselves against attack, and no redress for their loss when it comes.

6

So beset, it is no wonder that the typical American maker of books becomes a timorous and ineffective fellow, whose work tends inevitably toward a feeble 20 superficiality. Sucking in the Puritan spirit with the very air he breathes, and perhaps burdened inwardly with an inheritance of the actual Puritan stupidity, he is further kept upon the straight path of chemical purity by the very real perils that I have just rehearsed. The result is a literature full of the mawkishness that the late Henry James so often roared against—a literature almost 25 wholly detached from life as men are living it in the world—in George Moore's phrase, a literature still at nurse. It is on the side of sex that the appointed virtuosi of virtue exercise their chief repressions, for it is sex that especially fascinates the lubricious Puritan mind; but the conventual reticence that thus becomes the enforced fashion in one field extends itself to all others. Our fic- 30 tion, in general, is marked by an artificiality as marked as that of Eighteenth Century poetry or the later Georgian drama. The romance in it runs to set forms and stale situations; the revelation, by such a book as "The Titan," that there may be a glamour as entrancing in the way of a conqueror of men as in the way of a youth with a maid, remains isolated and exotic. We have 35

---

3. **Thaw**—The trial of Harry K. Thaw for the murder of Stanford White (1853-1906), whom he accused of adultery with Mrs. Thaw, was notably unsavory. **Moore**—George Moore (1852-1933) first published this book in 1906; it was republished in 1920. 4. **bowdlerize**—to omit parts considered offensive or indelicate, as Thomas Bowdler did in his edition of Shakespeare. "**A Summer in Arcady**"—Macmillan, 1896. 5. **Lawrence**—David Herbert Lawrence (1885-1930), British novelist whose novels and poems show how powerful is sex motivation. *The Rainbow* (1915) was prosecuted by the police, a fact which "seemed for a time to check Lawrence's fertility." 7. **serious book**—*Susan Lenox*, referred to above, p. 1677. 9. **Glyn**—*Three Weeks* by Elinor (Sutherland) Glyn was a popular "smash hit" in 1907. 11-12. **Kreymborg's "Edna"**—On December 13, 1916, Guido Bruno, a New York bookseller, was arrested for selling a copy of *Edna* by Alfred Kreymborg (1883-   ), a short tale which had been in print for two and one-half years. 13-14. **contra bonos mores**—against good customs.—The chief sufferers from this conflict are the authors of moving pictures. What they face at the hands of imbecile State boards of censorship is described at length by Channing Pollock in an article entitled "Swinging the Censor" in the *Bulletin* of the Authors' League of America for March, 1917. (Author's note)

no first-rate political or religious novel; we have no first-rate war story; despite
all our national engrossment in commercial enterprise, we have few second-
rate tales of business. Romance, in American fiction, still means only a somewhat childish amorousness and sentimentality—the love affairs of Paul and
5 Virginia, or the pale adulteries of their elders. And on the side of realism
there is an almost equal vacuity and lack of veracity. The action of all the
novels of the Howells school goes on within four walls of painted canvas;
they begin to shock once they describe an attack of asthma or a steak burning
below stairs; they never penetrate beneath the flow of social concealments and
10 urbanities to the passions that actually move men and women to their acts,
and the great forces that circumscribe and condition personality. So obvious a
piece of reporting as Upton Sinclair's "The Jungle" or Robert Herrick's
"Together" makes a sensation; the appearance of a "Jennie Gerhardt" or a
"Hagar Revelly" brings forth a growl of astonishment and rage.

15   In all this dread of free inquiry, this childish skittishness in both writers and
public, this dearth of courage and even of curiosity, the influence of comstockery is undoubtedly to be detected. It constitutes a sinister and ever-present
menace to all men of ideas; it affrights the publisher and paralyzes the author;
no one on the outside can imagine its burden as a practical concern. I am, in
20 moments borrowed from more palatable business, the editor of an American
magazine, and I thus know at first hand what the burden is. That magazine
is anything but a popular one, in the current sense. It sells at a relatively high
price; it contains no pictures or other baits for the childish; it is frankly addressed to a sophisticated minority. I may thus assume reasonably, I believe,
25 that its readers are not sex-curious and itching adolescents, just as my col-
league of the *Atlantic Monthly* may assume reasonably that his readers are
not Italian immigrants. Nevertheless, as a practical editor, I find that the
Comstocks, near and far, are oftener in my mind's eye than my actual patrons.
The thing I always have to decide about a manuscript offered for publication,
30 before ever I give any thought to its artistic merit and suitability, is the question whether its publication will be permitted—not even whether it is intrinsically good or evil, moral or immoral, but whether some roving Methodist preacher, self-commissioned to keep watch on letters, will read indecency
into it. Not a week passes that I do not decline some sound and honest piece
35 of work for no other reason. I have a long list of such things by American authors, well-devised, well-imagined, well-executed, respectable as human documents and as works of art—but never to be printed in mine or any other
American magazine. It includes four or five short stories of the very first
rank, and the best one-act play yet done, to my knowledge, by an American.
40 All of these pieces would go into type at once on the Continent; no sane man
would think of objecting to them; they are no more obscene, to a normal
adult, than his own bare legs. But they simply cannot be printed in the United
States, with the law what it is and the courts what they are.

4-5. **Paul and Virginia**—sentimental tale of young love by Bernardin de Saint-Pierre (1737-
1814), first published in 1789. 12. **"The Jungle"**—a "naturalistic" novel of life in the old
stockyards district of Chicago (1906). 13. **"Together"**—realistic novel of the psychology of
married life (1908) by Robert Herrick. **"Jennie Gerhardt"**—by Theodore Dreiser (1871-
1945), published in 1911.

I know many other editors. All of them are in the same boat. Some of them try to get around the difficulty by pecksniffery more or less open—for example, by fastening a moral purpose upon works of art, and hawking them as uplifting. Others, facing the intolerable fact, yield to it with resignation. And if they didn't? Well, if one of them didn't, any professional moralist could go 5 before a police magistrate, get a warrant upon a simple affidavit, raid the office of the offending editor, seize all the magazines in sight, and keep them impounded until after the disposition of the case. Editors cannot afford to take this risk. Magazines are perishable goods. Even if, after a trial has been had, they are returned, they are worthless save as waste paper. And what may be 10 done with copies found in the actual office of publication may be done too with copies found on news-stands, and not only in one city, but in two, six, a dozen, a hundred. All the costs and burdens of the contest are on the defendant. Let him be acquitted with honour, and invited to dinner by the judge, he has yet lost his property, and the Comstock hiding behind the war- 15 rant cannot be made to pay. In this concealment, indeed, lurk many sinister things—not forgetting personal enmity and business rivalry. The actual complainant is seldom uncovered; Comstockery, taking on a semi-judicial character, throws its chartered immunity around the whole process. A hypothetical outrage? By no means. It has been perpetrated, in one American city or an- 20 other, upon fully half of the magazines of general circulation published today. Its possibility sticks in the consciousness of every editor and publisher like a recurrent glycosuria.

But though the effects of comstockery are thus abominably insane and irritating, the fact is not to be forgotten that, after all, the thing is no more than 25 an effect itself. The fundamental causes of all the grotesque (and often half-fabulous) phenomena flowing out of it are to be sought in the habits of mind of the American people. They are, as I have shown, besotted by moral concepts, a moral engrossment, a delusion of moral infallibility. In their view of the arts they are still unable to shake off the naïve suspicion of the Fathers. 30 A work of the imagination can justify itself, in their sight, only if it shows a moral purpose, and that purpose must be obvious and unmistakable. Even in their slow progress toward a revolt against the ancestral Philistinism, they cling to this ethical bemusement: a new gallery of pictures is welcomed as "improving," to hear Beethoven "makes one better." Any questioning of the 35 moral ideas that prevail—the principal business, it must be plain, of the novelist, the serious dramatist, the professed inquirer into human motives and acts—is received with the utmost hostility. To attempt such an enterprise is

---

3-4. uplifting—For example, the magazine which printed David Graham Phillips' *Susan Lenox; Her Rise and Fall* as a serial prefaced it with a moral encomium by the Rev. Charles H. Parkhurst. Later, when the novel appeared in book form, the Comstocks began an action to have it suppressed, and forced the publisher to bowdlerize it. (Author's note) **23. glycosuria**—sugar in the urine.—An account of a typical prosecution, arbitrary, unintelligent and disingenuous, is to be found in Sumner and Indecency, by Frank Harris, in *Pearson's Magazine* for June, 1917, p. 556. (Author's note) **30. Fathers**—For further discussions of this point consult Art in America, by Aleister Crowley, *The English Review*, Nov., 1913; Life, Art and America, by Theodore Dreiser, *The Seven Arts*, Feb., 1917; and The American; His Ideas of Beauty, by H. L. Mencken, *The Smart Set*, Sept., 1913. (Author's note)

to disturb the peace—and the disturber of the peace, in the national view, quickly passes over into the downright criminal.

These symptoms, it seems to me, are only partly racial, despite the persistent survival of that third-rate English strain which shows itself so ingenuously
5 in the colonial spirit, the sense of inferiority, the frank craving for praise from home. The race, in truth, grows mongrel, and the protest against that mongrelism only serves to drive in the fact. But a mongrel race is necessarily a race still in the stage of reaching out for culture; it has not yet formulated defensible standards; it must needs rest heavily upon the superstitions that go
10 with inferiority. The Reformation brought Scotland among the civilized nations, but it took Scotland a century and a half to live down the Reformation. Dogmatism, conformity, Philistinism, the fear of rebels, the crusading spirit; these are the marks of an upstart people, uncertain of their rank in the world and even of their direction. A cultured European, reading a typical American
15 critical journal, must needs conceive the United States, says H. G. Wells, as "a vain, garrulous and prosperous female of uncertain age and still more uncertain temper, with unfounded pretensions to intellectuality and an ideal of refinement of the most negative description . . . the Aunt Errant of Christendom." There is always that blushful shyness, that timorous uncertainty, broken
20 by sudden rages, sudden enunciations of impeccable doctrine, sudden runnings amuck. Formalism is the hall-mark of the national culture, and sins against the one are sins against the other. The American is school-mastered out of gusto, out of joy, out of innocence. He can never fathom William Blake's notion that "the lust of the goat is also to the glory of God." He must
25 be correct, or, in his own phrase, he must bust.

Via trita est tutissima. The new generation, urged to curiosity and rebellion by its mounting sap, is rigorously restrained, regimented, policed. The ideal is vacuity, guilelessness, imbecility. "We are looking at this particular book," said Comstock's successor of "The 'Genius,'" "from the standpoint of its
30 harmful effect on female readers of immature mind." To be curious is to be lewd; to know is to yield to fornication. Here we have the mediaeval doctrine still on its legs: a chance word may arouse "a libidinous passion" in the mind of a "modest" woman. Not only youth must be safeguarded, but also the "female," the untrustworthy one, the temptress. "Modest" is a euphemism;
35 it takes laws to keep her "pure." The "locks of chastity" rust in the Cluny Museum; in place of them we have comstockery. . . .

But, as I have said in hymning Huneker, there is yet the munyonic consola-

---

10. **Reformation**—*Vide* The Cambridge History of English Literature, vol. XI, p. 225. (Author's note) 14. **direction**—The point is discussed by H. V. Routh in The Cambridge History of English Literature, vol. XI, p. 290. (Author's note) 18-19. **Christendom**—In Boon; New York, George H. Doran Co., 1915. (Author's note) 24. **Blake**—William Blake (1757-1827), British mystical poet and painter. 26. **Via . . . tutissima**—A dull life is the safest. 29. **successor**—John S. Sumner. 30. **mind**—In a letter to Felix Shay, Nov. 24, 1916. (Author's note) 35-36. **Cluny Museum**—famous medieval museum in France. 37. **Huneker**—James Gibbons Huneker (1860-1921), American impressionist critic of the arts. **munyonic**—coined from the name of "an eminent American wizard of the last century," to wit, James Munyon of Philadelphia. He made a large fortune marketing homeopathic pills in vest pocket size bottles. . . . His trade mark was a portrait of himself, with his right hand held up and his forefinger extended. Underneath was the legend, "There is yet hope!" (Author's note)

tion. Time is a great legalizer, even in the field of morals. We have yet no delivery, but we have at least the beginnings of a revolt, or, at all events, of a protest. We have already reached, in Howells, our Hannah More; in Clemens, our Swift; in Henry James, our Horace Walpole; in Woodberry, Robinson *et al.,* our Cowpers, Southeys and Crabbes; perhaps we might even make a 5 composite and call it our Johnson. We are sweating through our Eighteenth Century, our era of sentiment, our spiritual measles. Maybe a new day is not quite so far off as it seems to be, and with it we may get our Hardy, our Conrad, our Swinburne, our Thoma, our Moore, our Meredith and our Synge.

3-9. **More . . . Synge**—The references not already identified in this list of names are: Hannah **More** (1745-1833), a "serious" writer, whose *Coelebs in Search of a Wife* (1809) is an arch-example of the didactic novel; **Horace Walpole** (1717-1797), appropriate here because his voluminous correspondence, several times edited, is a chronicle of eighteenth-century manners; William **Cowper** (1731-1800), didactic poet of English life; Robert **Southey** (1774-1843), the most "moral" of the English romantic poets; George **Crabbe** (1754-1832), realistic poet of English village life; Joseph **Conrad** (1884-1924), the Polish-English novelist Mencken thinks well of; Algernon Charles **Swinburne** (1837-1900), who, especially in *Poems and Ballads* (1866), flouted Victorian moralism; Ludwig **Thoma** (1868-1921), German novelist of manners. George **Moore** has been mentioned before in the essay; George **Meredith** (1828-1909), novelist of English manners, appropriate here because of the intellectual demands he makes on readers; John Millington **Synge** (1871-1909), perhaps the greatest dramatic genius appearing in the Irish Renaissance.

SINCLAIR LEWIS

1885-1951

I. YOUTH FROM MAIN STREET (1885–1920)

1885 Born in Sauk Center ("Gopher Prairie"), Minnesota, February 7, son of small-town doctor Edwin J. Lewis and Emma Kermott Lewis, of Yankee stock.

1895–1904 Athletic boyhood; inclination to iconoclasm.

1904–1907 Attended Yale University; made two summer voyages to Europe on cattle boats; was editor of a Yale literary magazine; received the A.B. degree with the class of 1908.

1907 Worked for board in Upton Sinclair's Helicon Hall, a New Jersey Socialist colony. Vagabonded through twenty-six states and Mexico.

1907–1915 In the gashouse district of Manhattan, writing verse for household magazines and jokes for *Life* and *Punch*.

1910–1912 Hack writer; magazine editor of *Transatlantic Tales, Volta Review,* and so on. Trip to Panama via steerage, return as stowaway. Reader for F. A. Stokes and for George Doran, publishers.

1914 Married Grace Hegger, April 15; son named after H. G. Wells, born in 1915; divorce, 1925. *Our Mr. Wrenn,* a Wellsian novel of a wandering clerk who goes to England on a cattle boat.

1915 *The Trail of the Hawk,* a realistic novel of marriage, aviation, and journalism, somewhat autobiographic.

1917 *The Job,* a novel of businesswomen in New York, in which Lewis first fully evolved his method of characterization.

1919 *Free Air,* a humorous interlude on a couple's journey to Seattle, serialized in the *Saturday Evening Post. Hobohemia,* a play, produced in New York.

1920 *Main Street,* a novel castigating village complacency and dullness, made him an international figure.

II. SATIRIST OF THE AMERICAN BOURGEOISIE (1922–1930)

1922 *Babbitt,* satiric novel on the "booster" type of businessman.

1925 *Arrowsmith,* a satire on commercialism and cheap publicity in the medical profession; technical information supplied by Paul De Kruif.

1926 Awarded the Pulitzer Prize for Fiction for *Arrowsmith,* but declined it. *Mantrap.*

1927 *Elmer Gantry,* a violent attack on ministerial hypocrisy.

1928 Married Dorothy Thompson, columnist, May 14; one son, Michael, born to this union; divorced, 1942. *The Man Who Knew Coolidge.*

1929   *Dodsworth*, an international novel. Dramatized with Sidney Howard in 1935.
1930   Awarded the Nobel Prize in Literature.

III. "A RESTLESS, DETERMINED, TALL FLAME" (1930–1951)

1933   *Ann Vickers*, a novel depicting a suffragette's interest in prison reform.
1934   *It Can't Happen Here*, a novel on demagoguery. Dramatized with John C. Moffitt (1936) and given in the Federal Theater. Also produced with Lloyd Lewis a pre-Civil War play, *Jayhawker*. *Work of Art*, a novel of a successful hotelman.
1936   Received Litt.D. degree from Yale University.
1938   *The Prodigal Parents*, a novel on modern domestic relations.
1938–1939   Acted in various cities in *Angela Is Twenty-two*.
1940   *Bethel Merriday*, a novel about the career of an actress.
1943   *Gideon Planish*, a withering blast at philanthropists.
1945   *Cass Timberlane*.
1947   *Kingsblood Royal*.
1951   Died in Rome, January 10. *World So Wide*, published posthumously.

BIOGRAPHY AND CRITICISM: Carl Van Doren, *Sinclair Lewis*, Doubleday, Doran, 1933, is the chief work devoted to Lewis. See also "Dilly Tante" (Stanley J. Kunitz), ed., *Living Authors: A Book of Biographies*, H. W. Wilson Company, 1931, and Fred B. Millett, *Contemporary American Authors*, Harcourt, Brace, 1940, pp. 436-41. S. P. Sherman, "The Significance of Sinclair Lewis," in *Points of View*, Scribner, 1924; P. H. Boynton, *More Contemporary Americans*, University of Chicago Press, 1927; M. Waldman in J. C. Squire's *Contemporary American Authors*, Holt, 1928, pp. 71-94; R. Michaud, *The American Novel To-day*, Little, Brown, 1928, pp. 128-53; T. K. Whipple, *Spokesmen*, Appleton, 1928, pp. 208-29; V. L. Parrington, *Main Currents in American Thought*, 3 vols., Harcourt, Brace, 1930, Vol. III, pp. 360-69; H. M. Jones, "Mr. Lewis's America," *Virginia Quarterly Review*, July, 1931, pp. 427-32; L. Mumford, "The America of Sinclair Lewis," *Current History*, January, 1931, pp. 529-33; Sinclair Lewis (with E. A. Karlfeldt), "Why Sinclair Lewis Got the Nobel Prize," Harcourt, Brace, 1931; Bernard De Voto, "Sinclair Lewis," *Saturday Review of Literature*, January 28, 1933, pp. 397-98; W. R. Benét, "The Earlier Lewis," *Saturday Review of Literature*, January 20, 1934, pp. 421-22; H. S. Canby, "Sinclair Lewis's Art of Work," *Saturday Review of Literature*, February 10, 1934, pp. 465-73; H. Hatcher, *Creating the Modern American Novel*, Farrar and Rinehart, 1935, pp. 109-26; G. Hicks, "Sinclair Lewis and the Good Life," *English Journal*, April, 1936, pp. 265-73; T. D. Horton, "The Symbol of an Era," *North American Review*, 1939, pp. 374-93; B. Stolberg, "Sinclair Lewis," *American Mercury*, 1941, pp. 450-60.
BIBLIOGRAPHY: Consult H. Taylor, "Bibliography of the Writings of Sinclair Lewis," in Carl Van Doren, *Sinclair Lewis*, Doubleday, Doran, 1935, pp. 77-187; Merle Johnson, *American First Editions*, R. R. Bowker, 1943; *Literary History of the United States*, Vol. III, pp. 609-11.

After a long discipline in writing magazine fiction, with *Main Street* Sinclair Lewis emerged in the twenties as the popular leader of those novelists whose revolt against the materialism which science and industry seemed to support took the form of protest, attack, and satiric exaggeration. *Main Street*, enormously popular, indicted provincial America for its satisfaction with cheap success, its coarse moral standards, its vulgar taste. Then in *Babbitt* he showed how happy was the ordinary middle-class American in a land that owned every gadget but that failed to own a soul. *Arrowsmith* went deeper: ostensibly the story of a scientist, it really poises the question whether search for lasting truth is not futile in a pragmatic world. In *Elmer Gantry* blame was attached to commercialized religion. In *Dodsworth,* when American values are tested by European standards, the rich industrial magnate recognizes his deficiencies and humbles himself to rebuild his life. Since then, Lewis has turned his mordant satire to themes as disparate as fascism, parenthood, and philanthropical foundations. Caricature is half-truth; and the half-truth of his picture of Americans satisfied the European mind and brought him the Nobel Prize.

But Dr. Kennicott, the central male figure of *Main Street,* possesses professional integrity and courage which sets him apart from his addle-pated, miseducated wife; Babbitt is somehow lovable as Mrs. Babbitt is not; and Fran Dodsworth is every way a cheaper person than her wistful, questing husband. With the exception of Leora Arrowsmith, Lewis celebrates the superiority of the American male in a male civilization. That civilization he essentially loves, as *It Can't Happen Here* exists to show. He is as American as Whitman—and it is interesting to note that the great American writers represented in this book with few exceptions are men—and this "man's country" is something that Lewis scolds because he loves it. His technique is the bold technique of the smoking-car anecdote, the quick jab, the raucous laughter, and the underlined humor of the men he satirizes; not for him the subtle strokes of a Willa Cather or an Ellen Glasgow. In some sense he is therefore the heir of the American tall tale, and in the line of succession to Mark Twain.

BABBITT

The scene of this satire is a flourishing Midwestern city of 361,000 population. Babbitt is a typical self-sufficient, bustling, commonplace businessman of such a metropolis. He accepts its ideals of standardization, respectability, and high-pressure salesmanship, but is restless because he is not creative. He gropes in various directions, most of them unfruitful, for those values which he misses through glib conformity to the Good Fellows whose approval he covets.

CHAPTER I

THE TOWERS of Zenith aspired above the morning mist; austere towers of steel and cement and limestone, sturdy as cliffs and delicate as silver rods. They were neither citadels nor churches, but frankly and beau-
5 tifully office-buildings.

The mist took pity on the fretted structures of earlier generations: the Post Office with its shingle-tortured mansard, the red brick minarets of hulking old houses, factories with stingy and sooted windows, wooden tenements colored like mud. The city was full of such grotesqueries, but the clean towers were
10 thrusting them from the business center, and on the farther hills were shining new houses, homes—they seemed—for laughter and tranquillity.

Over a concrete bridge fled a limousine of long sleek hood and noiseless engine. These people in evening clothes were returning from an all-night re-

hearsal of a Little Theater play, an artistic adventure considerably illuminated
by champagne. Below the bridge curved a railroad, a maze of green and crimson lights. The New York Flyer boomed past, and twenty lines of polished
steel leaped into the glare.

In one of the skyscrapers the wires of the Associated Press were closing   5
down. The telegraph operators wearily raised their celluloid eye-shades after
a night of talking with Paris and Peking. Through the building crawled the
scrubwomen, yawning, their old shoes slapping. The dawn mist spun away.
Cues of men with lunch-boxes clumped toward the immensity of new factories, sheets of glass and hollow tile, glittering shops where five thousand 10
men worked beneath one roof, pouring out the honest wares that would be
sold up the Euphrates and across the veldt. The whistles rolled out in greeting a chorus cheerful as the April dawn; the song of labor in a city built—it
seemed—for giants.

II   15

There was nothing of the giant in the aspect of the man who was beginning
to awaken on the sleeping-porch of a Dutch Colonial house in that residential
district of Zenith known as Floral Heights.

His name was George F. Babbitt. He was forty-six years old now, in April,
1920, and he made nothing in particular, neither butter nor shoes nor poetry, 20
but he was nimble in the calling of selling houses for more than people could
afford to pay.

His large head was pink, his brown hair thin and dry. His face was babyish
in slumber, despite his wrinkles and the red spectacle-dents on the slopes
of his nose. He was not fat but he was exceedingly well fed; his cheeks were 25
pads, and the unroughened hand which lay helpless upon the khaki-colored
blanket was slightly puffy. He seemed prosperous, extremely married and unromantic; and altogether unromantic appeared this sleeping-porch, which
looked on one sizable elm, two respectable grass-plots, a cement driveway,
and a corrugated iron garage. Yet Babbitt was again dreaming of the fairy 30
child, a dream more romantic than scarlet pagodas by a silver sea.

For years the fairy child had come to him. Where others saw but Georgie
Babbitt, she discerned gallant youth. She waited for him, in the darkness beyond mysterious groves. When at last he could slip away from the crowded
house he darted to her. His wife, his clamoring friends, sought to follow, but 35
he escaped, the girl fleet beside him, and they crouched together on a shadowy
hillside. She was so slim, so white, so eager! She cried that he was gay and
valiant, that she would wait for him, that they would sail—

Rumble and bang of the milk-truck.

Babbitt moaned, turned over, struggled back toward his dream. He could 40
see only her face now, beyond misty waters. The furnace-man slammed the
basement door. A dog barked in the next yard. As Babbitt sank blissfully into
a dim warm tide, the paper-carrier went by whistling, and the rolled-up
Advocate thumped the front door. Babbitt roused, his stomach constricted
with alarm. As he relaxed, he was pierced by the familiar and irritating rattle 45
of someone cranking a Ford: snap-ah-ah, snap-ah-ah, snap-ah-ah. Himself a

---

12. **veldt**—level lands of South Africa.

pious motorist, Babbitt cranked with the unseen driver, with him waited
through taut hours for the roar of the starting engine, with him agonized as the
roar ceased and again began the infernal patient snap-ah-ah—a round, flat sound,
a shivering cold-morning sound, a sound infuriating and inescapable. Not till
5 the rising voice of the motor told him that the Ford was moving was he released from the panting tension. He glanced once at his favorite tree, elm
twigs against the gold patina of sky, and fumbled for sleep as for a drug.
He who had been a boy very credulous of life was no longer greatly interested
in the possible and improbable adventures of each new day.

10   He escaped from reality till the alarm-clock rang, at seven-twenty.

III

It was the best of nationally advertised and quantitatively produced alarm-
clocks, with all modern attachments, including cathedral chime, intermittent
alarm, and a phosphorescent dial. Babbitt was proud of being awakened by
15 such a rich device. Socially it was almost as creditable as buying expensive
cord tires.

He sulkily admitted now that there was no more escape, but he lay and
detested the grind of the real-estate business, and disliked his family, and disliked himself for disliking them. The evening before, he had played poker
20 at Vergil Gunch's till midnight, and after such holidays he was irritable before breakfast. It may have been the tremendous home-brewed beer of the
prohibition-era and the cigars to which that beer enticed him; it may have
been resentment of return from this fine, bold man-world to a restricted region of wives and stenographers, and of suggestions not to smoke so much.

25   From the bedroom beside the sleeping-porch, his wife's detestably cheerful
"Time to get up, Georgie boy," and the itchy sound, the brisk and scratchy
sound, of combing hairs out of a stiff brush.

He grunted; he dragged his thick legs, in faded baby-blue pajamas, from
under the khaki blanket; he sat on the edge of the cot, running his fingers
30 through his wild hair, while his plump feet mechanically felt for his slippers.
He looked regretfully at the blanket—forever a suggestion to him of freedom
and heroism. He had bought it for a camping trip which had never come off.
It symbolized gorgeous loafing, gorgeous cursing, virile flannel shirts.

He creaked to his feet, groaning at the waves of pain which passed behind
35 his eyeballs. Though he waited for their scorching recurrence, he looked
blurrily out at the yard. It delighted him, as always; it was the neat yard of
a successful business man of Zenith, that is, it was perfection, and made him
also perfect. He regarded the corrugated iron garage. For the three-hundred-
and-sixty-fifth time in a year he reflected, "No class to that tin shack. Have to
40 build me a frame garage. But by golly it's the only thing on the place that isn't
up-to-date!" While he stared he thought of a community garage for his acreage development, Glen Oriole. He stopped puffing and jiggling. His arms
were akimbo. His petulant, sleep-swollen face was set in harder lines. He suddenly seemed capable, an official, a man to contrive, to direct, to get things
45 done.

On the vigor of his idea he was carried down the hard, clean, unused-looking hall into the bathroom.

Though the house was not large it had, like all houses on Floral Heights, an altogether royal bathroom of porcelain and glazed tile and metal sleek as silver. The towel-rack was a rod of clear glass set in nickel. The tub was long 5 enough for a Prussian Guard, and above the set bowl was a sensational exhibit of tooth-brush holder, shaving-brush holder, soap-dish, sponge-dish, and medicine-cabinet, so glittering and so ingenious that they resembled an electrical instrument-board. But the Babbitt whose god was Modern Appliances was not pleased. The air of the bathroom was thick with the smell of a heathen tooth- 10 paste. "Verona been at it again! 'Stead of sticking to Lilidol, like I've repeatedly asked her, she's gone and gotten some confounded stinkum stuff that makes you sick!"

The bath-mat was wrinkled and the floor was wet. (His daughter Verona eccentrically took baths in the morning, now and then.) He slipped on the 15 mat, and slid against the tub. He said "Damn!" Furiously he snatched up his tube of shaving-cream, furiously he lathered, with a belligerent slapping of the unctuous brush, furiously he raked his plump cheeks with a safety-razor. It pulled. The blade was dull. He said, "Damn—oh—oh—damn it!"

He hunted through the medicine-cabinet for a packet of new razor-blades 20 (reflecting, as invariably, "Be cheaper to buy one of these dinguses and strop your own blades,") and when he discovered the packet, behind the round box of bicarbonate of soda, he thought ill of his wife for putting it there and very well of himself for not saying "Damn." But he did say it, immediately afterward, when with wet and soap-slippery fingers he tried to remove the horrible 25 little envelope and crisp clinging oiled paper from the new blade.

Then there was the problem, oft-pondered, never solved, of what to do with the old blade, which might imperil the fingers of his young. As usual, he tossed it on top of the medicine-cabinet, with a mental note that some day he must remove the fifty or sixty other blades that were also, temporarily, piled 30 up there. He finished his shaving in a growing testiness increased by his spinning headache and by the emptiness in his stomach. When he was done, his round face smooth and streamy and his eyes stinging from soapy water, he reached for a towel. The family towels were wet, wet and clammy and vile, all of them wet, he found, as he blindly snatched them—his own face-towel, 35 his wife's, Verona's, Ted's, Tinka's, and the lone bath-towel with the huge welt of initial. Then George F. Babbitt did a dismaying thing. He wiped his face on the guest-towel! It was a pansy-embroidered trifle which always hung there to indicate that the Babbitts were in the best Floral Heights society. No one had ever used it. No guest had ever dared to. Guests secretively took a 40 corner of the nearest regular towel.

He was raging, "By golly, here they go and use up all the towels, every doggone one of 'em, and they use 'em and get 'em all wet and sopping, and never put out a dry one for me—of course, I'm the goat!—and then I want one and— I'm the only person in the doggone house that's got the slightest 45

6. **Prussian Guard**—Frederick II of Prussia recruited a regiment of guards from men six feet or more in height.

doggone bit of consideration for other people and thoughtfulness and consider there may be others that may want to use the doggone bathroom after me and consider—"

He was pitching the chill abominations into the bath-tub, pleased by the vindictiveness of that desolate flapping sound; and in the midst his wife serenely trotted in, observed serenely, "Why Georgie dear, what are you doing? Are you going to wash out the towels? Why, you needn't wash out the towels. Oh, Georgie, you didn't go and use the guest-towel, did you?"

It is not recorded that he was able to answer.

For the first time in weeks he was sufficiently roused by his wife to look at her.

IV

Myra Babbitt—Mrs. George F. Babbitt—was definitely mature. She had creases from the corners of her mouth to the bottom of her chin, and her plump neck bagged. But the thing that marked her as having passed the line was that she no longer had reticences before her husband, and no longer worried about not having reticences. She was in a petticoat now, and corsets which bulged, and unaware of being seen in bulgy corsets. She had become so dully habituated to married life that in her full matronliness she was as sexless as an anemic nun. She was a good woman, a kind woman, a diligent woman, but no one, save perhaps Tinka her ten-year-old, was at all interested in her or entirely aware that she was alive.

After a rather thorough discussion of all the domestic and social aspects of towels she apologized to Babbitt for his having an alcoholic headache; and he recovered enough to endure the search for a B.V.D. undershirt which had, he pointed out, malevolently been concealed among his clean pajamas.

He was fairly amiable in the conference on the brown suit.

"What do you think, Myra?" He pawed at the clothes hunched on a chair in their bedroom, while she moved about mysteriously adjusting and patting her petticoat and, to his jaundiced eye, never seeming to get on with her dressing. "How about it? Shall I wear the brown suit another day?"

"Well, it looks awfully nice on you."

"I know, but gosh, it needs pressing."

"That's so. Perhaps it does."

"It certainly could stand being pressed, all right."

"Yes, perhaps it wouldn't hurt it to be pressed."

"But gee, the coat doesn't need pressing. No sense in having the whole darn suit pressed, when the coat doesn't need it."

"That's so."

"But the pants certainly need it, all right. Look at them—look at those wrinkles—the pants certainly do need pressing."

"That's so. Oh, Georgie, why couldn't you wear the brown coat with the blue trousers we were wondering what we'd do with them?"

"Good Lord! Did you ever in all my life know me to wear the coat of one suit and the pants of another? What do you think I am? A busted book-keeper?"

"Well, why don't you put on the dark gray suit today, and stop in at the tailor and leave the brown trousers?"

"Well, they certainly need— Now where the devil is that gray suit? Oh, yes, here we are."

He was able to get through the other crises of dressing with comparative resoluteness and calm.

His first adornment was the sleeveless dimity B.V.D. undershirt, in which he resembled a small boy humorlessly wearing a cheesecloth tabard at a civic pageant. He never put on B.V.D.'s without thanking the God of Progress that he didn't wear tight, long, old-fashioned undergarments, like his father-in-law and partner, Henry Thompson. His second embellishment was combing and slicking back his hair. It gave him a tremendous forehead, arching up two inches beyond the former hair-line. But most wonder-working of all was the donning of his spectacles.

There is character in spectacles—the pretentious tortoise-shell, the meek pince-nez of the school teacher, the twisted silver-framed glasses of the old villager. Babbitt's spectacles had huge, circular, frameless lenses of the very best glass; the ear-pieces were thin bars of gold. In them he was the modern business man; one who gave orders to clerks and drove a car and played occasional golf and was scholarly in regard to Salesmanship. His head suddenly appeared not babyish but weighty, and you noted his heavy, blunt nose, his straight mouth and thick, long upper lip, his chin overfleshy but strong; with respect you beheld him put on the rest of his uniform as a Solid Citizen.

The gray suit was well cut, well made, and completely undistinguished. It was a standard suit. White piping on the V of the vest added a flavor of law and learning. His shoes were black laced boots, good boots, honest boots, standard boots, extraordinarily uninteresting boots. The only frivolity was in his purple knitted scarf. With considerable comment on the matter to Mrs. Babbitt (who, acrobatically fastening the back of her blouse to her skirt with a safety-pin, did not hear a word he said), he chose between the purple scarf and a tapestry effect with stringless brown harps among blown palms, and into it he thrust a snake-head pin with opal eyes.

A sensational event was changing from the brown suit to the gray the contents of his pockets. He was earnest about these objects. They were of eternal importance, like baseball or the Republican Party. They included a fountain pen and a silver pencil (always lacking a supply of new leads) which belonged in the righthand upper vest pocket. Without them he would have felt naked. On his watch-chain were a gold penknife, silver cigar-cutter, seven keys (the use of two of which he had forgotten), and incidentally a good watch. Depending from the chain was a large, yellowish elk's-tooth—proclamation of his membership in the Brotherly and Protective Order of Elks. Most significant of all was his loose-leaf pocket note-book, that modern and efficient notebook which contained the addresses of people whom he had forgotten, prudent memoranda of postal money-orders which had reached their destinations months ago, stamps which had lost their mucilage, clippings of verses by T. Cholmondeley Frink and of the newspaper editorials from which Babbitt got his opinions and his polysyllables, notes to be sure and do things which he did not intend to do, and one curious inscription—D.S.S. D.M.Y.P.D.F.

But he had no cigarette-case. No one had ever happened to give him one, so he hadn't the habit, and people who carried cigarette-cases he regarded as effeminate.

5 Last, he stuck in his lapel the Boosters' Club button. With the conciseness of great art the button displayed two words: "Boosters—Pep!" It made Babbitt feel loyal and important. It associated him with Good Fellows, with men who were nice and human, and important in business circles. It was his V.C., his Legion of Honor ribbon, his Phi Beta Kappa key.

10 With the subtleties of dressing ran other complex worries. "I feel kind of punk this morning," he said. "I think I had too much dinner last evening. You oughtn't to serve those heavy banana fritters."

"But you asked me to have some."

"I know, but— I tell you, when a fellow gets past forty he has to look after
15 his digestion. There's a lot of fellows that don't take proper care of themselves. I tell you at forty a man's a fool or his doctor—I mean, his own doctor. Folks don't give enough attention to this matter of dieting. Now I think— Course a man ought to have a good meal after the day's work, but it would be a good thing for both of us if we took lighter lunches."

20 "But Georgie, here at home I always do have a light lunch."

"Mean to imply I make a hog of myself, eating down-town? Yes, sure! You'd have a swell time if you had to eat the truck that new steward hands out to us at the Athletic Club! But I certainly do feel out of sorts, this morning. Funny, got a pain down here on the left side—but no, that wouldn't be
25 appendicitis, would it? Last night, when I was driving over to Verg Gunch's, I felt a pain in my stomach, too. Right here it was—kind of a sharp shooting pain. I— Where'd that dime go to? Why don't you serve more prunes at breakfast? Of course I eat an apple every evening—an apple a day keeps the doctor away—but still, you ought to have more prunes, and not all these fancy
30 doodads."

"The last time I had prunes you didn't eat them."

"Well, I didn't feel like eating 'em, I suppose. Matter of fact, I think I did eat some of 'em. Anyway— I tell you it's mighty important to— I was saying to Verg Gunch, just last evening, most people don't take sufficient care of
35 their diges—"

"Shall we have the Gunches for our dinner, next week?"

"Why sure; you bet."

"Now see here, George: I want you to put on your nice dinner-jacket that evening."

40 "Rats! The rest of 'em won't want to dress."

"Of course they will. You remember when you didn't dress for the Little-fields' supper-party, and all the rest did, and how embarrassed you were."

"Embarrassed, hell! I wasn't embarrassed. Everybody knows I can put on as expensive a Tux. as anybody else, and I should worry if I don't happen to have
45 it on sometimes. All a darn nuisance, anyway. All right for a woman, that

---

8. **V.C.**—Victoria Cross, the highest award for conspicuous bravery in British Army or Navy.
44. **Tux.**—the Tuxedo dinner suit, originated in Tuxedo, New York.

stays around the house all the time, but when a fellow's worked like the dickens all day, he doesn't want to go and hustle his head off getting into the soup-and-fish for a lot of folks that he's seen in just reg'lar ordinary clothes that same day."

"You know you enjoy being seen in one. The other evening you admitted 5 you were glad I'd insisted on your dressing. You said you felt a lot better for it. And oh, Georgie, I do wish you wouldn't say 'Tux.' It's 'dinner-jacket.' "

"Rats, what's the odds?"

"Well, it's what all the nice folks say. Suppose Lucile McKelvey heard you calling it a 'Tux.' " 10

"Well, that's all right now! Lucile McKelvey can't pull anything on me! Her folks are common as mud, even if her husband and her dad are millionaires! I suppose you're trying to rub in *your* exalted social position! Well, let me tell you that your revered paternal ancestor, Henry T., doesn't even call it a 'Tux.'! He calls it a 'bobtail jacket for a ringtail monkey,' and you couldn't 15 get him into one unless you chloroformed him!"

"Now don't be horrid, George."

"Well, I don't want to be horrid, but Lord! you're getting as fussy as Verona. Ever since she got out of college she's been too rambunctious to live with— doesn't know what she wants—well, I know what she wants!—all she wants 20 is to marry a millionaire, and live in Europe, and hold some preacher's hand, and simultaneously at the same time stay right here in Zenith and be some blooming kind of a socialist agitator or boss charity-worker or some damn thing! Lord, and Ted is just as bad! He wants to go to college, and he doesn't want to go to college. Only one of the three that knows her own mind is 25 Tinka. Simply can't understand how I ever came to have a pair of shillyshallying children like Rone and Ted. I may not be any Rockefeller or James J. Shakespeare, but I certainly do know my own mind, and I do keep right on plugging along in the office and— Do you know the latest? Far as I can figure out, Ted's new bee is he'd like to be a movie actor and— And here I've told 30 him a hundred times, if he'll go to college and law-school and make good, I'll set him up in business and— Verona just exactly as bad. Doesn't know what she wants. Well, well, come on! Aren't you ready yet? The girl rang the bell three minutes ago."

v 35

Before he followed his wife, Babbitt stood at the westernmost window of their room. This residential settlement, Floral Heights, was on a rise; and though the center of the city was three miles away—Zenith had between three and four hundred thousand inhabitants now—he could see the top of the Second National Tower, an Indiana limestone building of thirty-five stories. 40

Its shining walls rose against April sky to a simple cornice like a streak of white fire. Integrity was in the tower, and decision. It bore its strength lightly as a tall soldier. As Babbitt stared, the nervousness was soothed from his face, his slack chin lifted in reverence. All he articulated was "That's one lovely sight!" but he was inspired by the rhythm of the city; his love of it renewed. 45

3. **soup-and-fish**—slang for a man's formal evening dress.

He beheld the tower as a temple-spire of the religion of business, a faith passionate, exalted, surpassing common men; and as he clumped down to breakfast he whistled the ballad "Oh, by gee, by gosh, by jingo" as though it were
a hymn melancholy and noble.

₅   CHAPTER II

Relieved of Babbitt's bumbling and the soft grunts with which his wife expressed the sympathy she was too experienced to feel and much too experienced not to show, their bedroom settled instantly into impersonality.

It gave on the sleeping-porch. It served both of them as dressing-room, and
₁₀ on the coldest nights Babbitt luxuriously gave up the duty of being manly
and retreated to the bed inside, to curl his toes in the warmth and laugh at the
January gale.

The room displayed a modest and pleasant color-scheme, after one of the
best standard designs of the decorator who "did the interiors" for most of the
₁₅ speculative-builders' houses in Zenith. The walls were gray, the woodwork
white, the rug a serene blue; and very much like mahogany was the furniture
—the bureau with its great clear mirror, Mrs. Babbitt's dressing-table with
toilet-articles of almost solid silver, the plain twin beds, between them a small
table holding a standard electric bedside lamp, a glass for water, and a standard
₂₀ bedside book with colored illustrations—what particular book it was cannot
be ascertained, since no one had ever opened it. The mattresses were firm but
not hard, triumphant modern mattresses which had cost a great deal of money;
the hot-water radiator was of exactly the proper scientific surface for the cubic
contents of the room. The windows were large and easily opened, with the
₂₅ best catches and cords, and Holland roller-shades guaranteed not to crack. It
was a masterpiece among bedrooms, right out of Cheerful Modern Houses for
Medium Incomes. Only it had nothing to do with the Babbitts, nor with anyone else. If people had ever lived and loved here, read thrillers at midnight
and lain in beautiful indolence on a Sunday morning, there were no signs of
₃₀ it. It had the air of being a very good room in a very good hotel. One expected
the chambermaid to come in and make it ready for people who would stay but
one night, go without looking back, and never think of it again.

Every second house in Floral Heights had a bedroom precisely like this.

The Babbitts' house was five years old. It was all as competent and glossy
₃₅ as this bedroom. It had the best of taste, the best of inexpensive rugs, a simple
and laudable architecture, and the latest conveniences. Throughout, electricity
took the place of candles and slatternly hearth-fires. Along the bedroom base-
board were three plugs for electric lamps, concealed by little brass doors. In
the halls were plugs for the vacuum cleaner, and in the living-room plugs for
₄₀ the piano lamp, for the electric fan. The trim dining-room (with its admirable
oak buffet, its leaded-glass cupboard, its creamy plaster walls, its modest scene
of a salmon expiring upon a pile of oysters) had plugs which supplied the
electric percolator and the electric toaster.

In fact there was but one thing wrong with the Babbitt house: It was not a
₄₅ home.

II

Often of a morning Babbitt came bouncing and jesting in to breakfast. But things were mysteriously awry today. As he pontifically tread the upper hall he looked into Verona's bedroom and protested, "What's the use of giving the family a high-class house when they don't appreciate it and tend to business 5 and get down to brass tacks?"

He marched upon them: Verona, a dumpy brown-haired girl of twenty-two, just out of Bryn Mawr, given to solicitudes about duty and sex and God and the unconquerable bagginess of the gray sports-suit she was now wearing. Ted—Theodore Roosevelt Babbitt—a decorative boy of seventeen. Tinka— 10 Katherine—still a baby at ten, with radiant red hair and a thin skin which hinted of too much candy and too many ice cream sodas. Babbitt did not show his vague irritation as he tramped in. He really disliked being a family tyrant, and his nagging was as meaningless as it was frequent. He shouted at Tinka, "Well, kittiedoolie!" It was the only pet name in his vocabulary, except the 15 "dear" and "hon." with which he recognized his wife, and he flung it at Tinka every morning.

He gulped a cup of coffee in the hope of pacifying his stomach and his soul. His stomach ceased to feel as though it did not belong to him, but Verona began to be conscientious and annoying, and abruptly there returned to Bab- 20 bitt the doubts regarding life and families and business which had clawed at him when his dream-life and the slim fairy girl had fled.

Verona had for six months been filing-clerk at the Gruensberg Leather Company offices, with a prospect of becoming secretary to Mr. Gruensberg and thus, as Babbitt defined it, "getting some good out of your expensive college 25 education till you're ready to marry and settle down."

But now said Verona: "Father! I was talking to a classmate of mine that's working for the Associated Charities—oh, Dad, there's the sweetest little babies that come to the milk-station there!—and I feel as though I ought to be doing something worth while like that." 30

"What do you mean 'worth while'? If you get to be Gruensberg's secretary —and maybe you would, if you kept up your shorthand and didn't go sneaking off to concerts and talk-fests every evening—I guess you'll find thirty-five or forty bones a week worth while!"

"I know, but—oh, I want to—contribute— I wish I were working in a set- 35 tlement-house. I wonder if I could get one of the department-stores to let me put in a welfare-department with a nice rest-room and chintzes and wicker chairs and so on and so forth. Or I could—"

"Now you look here! The first thing you got to understand is that all this uplift and flipflop and settlement-work and recreation is nothing in God's 40 world but the entering wedge for socialism. The sooner a man learns he isn't going to be coddled, and he needn't expect a lot of free grub and, uh, all these free classes and flipflop and doodads for his kids unless he earns 'em, why, the sooner he'll get on the job and produce—produce—produce! That's what the country needs, and not all this fancy stuff that just enfeebles the will-power 45 of the working man and gives his kids a lot of notions above their class. And

you—if you'd tend to business instead of fooling and fussing— All the time!
When I was a young man I made up my mind what I wanted to do, and
stuck to it through thick and thin, and that's why I'm where I am today,
and— Myra! What do you let the girl chop the toast up into these dinky little
5 chunks for? Can't you get your fist onto 'em. Half cold, anyway!"

Ted Babbitt, junior in the great East Side High School, had been making
hiccup-like sounds of interruption. He blurted now, "Say, Rone, you going
to—"

Verona whirled. "Ted! Will you kindly not interrupt us when we're talking
10 about serious matters!"

"Aw punk," said Ted judicially. "Ever since somebody slipped up and let
you out of college, Ammonia, you been pulling these nut conversations about
what-nots and so-on-and-so-forths. Are you going to— I want to use the car
tonight."

15 Babbitt snorted, "Oh, you do! May want it myself!" Verona protested, "Oh,
you do, Mr. Smarty! I'm going to take it myself!" Tinka wailed, "Oh, papa,
you said maybe you'd drive us down to Rosedale!" and Mrs. Babbitt, "Careful, Tinka, your sleeve is in the butter." They glared, and Verona hurled,
"Ted, you're a perfect pig about the car!"

20 "Course you're not! Not a-tall!" Ted could be maddeningly bland. "You
just want to grab it off, right after dinner, and leave it in front of some skirt's
house all evening while you sit and gas about lite'ature and the highbrows
you're going to marry—if they only propose!"

"Well, Dad oughtn't to *ever* let you have it! You and those beastly Jones
25 boys drive like maniacs. The idea of your taking the turn on Chautauqua
Place at forty miles an hour!"

"Aw, where do you get that stuff! You're so darn scared of the car that you
drive up-hill with the emergency brake on!"

"I do not! And you— Always talking about how much you know about
30 motors, and Eunice Littlefield told me you said the battery fed the generator!"

"You—why, my good woman, you don't know a generator from a differen-
tial." Not unreasonably was Ted lofty with her. He was a natural mechanic,
a maker and tinkerer of machines; he lisped in blueprints for the blueprints
came.

35 "That'll do now!" Babbitt flung in mechanically, as he lighted the gloriously
satisfying first cigar of the day and tasted the exhilarating drug of the
Advocate-Times headlines.

Ted negotiated: "Gee, honest, Rone, I don't want to take the old boat, but
I promised couple o' girls in my class I'd drive 'em down to the rehearsal of
40 the school chorus, and, gee, I don't want to, but a gentleman's got to keep
his social engagements."

"Well, upon my word! You and your social engagements! In high school!"

"Oh, ain't we select since we went to that hen college! Let me tell you
there isn't a private school in the state that's got as swell a bunch as we got
45 in Gamma Digamma this year. There's two fellows that their dads are mil-

33. lisped—parody on Pope's "I lisped in numbers, for the numbers came," from "Epistle to
Dr. Arbuthnot," line 128.

lionaires. Say, gee, I ought to have a car of my own, like lots of the fellows."

Babbitt almost rose. "A car of your own! Don't you want a yacht, and a house and lot? That pretty nearly takes the cake! A boy that can't pass his Latin examinations, like any other boy ought to, and he expects me to give him a motor-car, and I suppose a chauffeur, and an aeroplane maybe, as a reward for the hard work he puts in going to the movies with Eunice Littlefield! Well, when you see me giving you—"

Somewhat later, after diplomacies, Ted persuaded Verona to admit that she was merely going to the Armory, that evening, to see the dog and cat show. She was then, Ted planned, to park the car in front of the candy-store across from the Armory and he would pick it up. There were masterly arrangements regarding leaving the key, and having the gasoline tank filled; and passionately, devotees of the Great God Motor, they hymned the patch on the spare inner-tube, and the lost jack-handle.

Their truce dissolving, Ted observed that her friends were "a scream of a bunch—stuck-up gabby four-flushers." His friends, she indicated, were "disgusting imitation sports, and horrid little shrieking ignorant girls." Further: "It's disgusting of you to smoke cigarettes, and so on and so forth, and those clothes you've got on this morning, they're too utterly ridiculous—honestly, simply disgusting."

Ted balanced over to the low beveled mirror in the buffet, regarded his charms, and smirked. His suit, the latest thing in Old Eli Togs, was skintight, with skimpy trousers to the tops of his glaring tan boots, a chorus-man waistline, pattern of an agitated check, and across the back a belt which belted nothing. His scarf was an enormous black silk wad. His flaxen hair was icesmooth, pasted back without parting. When he went to school he would add a cap with a long vizor like a shovel-blade. Proudest of all was his waistcoat, saved for, begged for, plotted for; a real Fancy Vest of fawn with polka dots of a decayed red, the points astoundingly long. On the lower edge of it he wore a high-school button, a class button, and a fraternity pin.

And none of it mattered. He was supple and swift and flushed; his eyes (which he believed to be cynical) were candidly eager. But he was not overgentle. He waved his hand at poor dumpy Verona and drawled: "Yes, I guess we're pretty ridiculous and disgusticulus, and I rather guess our new necktie is some smear!"

Babbitt barked: "It is! And while you're admiring yourself, let me tell you it might add to your manly beauty if you wiped some of that egg off your mouth!"

Verona giggled, momentary victor in the greatest of Great Wars, which is the family war. Ted looked at her hopelessly, then shrieked at Tinka: "For the love o' Pete, quit pouring the whole sugar bowl on your corn flakes!"

When Verona and Ted were gone and Tinka upstairs, Babbitt groaned to his wife: "Nice family, I must say! I don't pretend to be any baa-lamb, and maybe I'm a little cross-grained at breakfast sometimes, but the way they go on jab-jab-jabbering, I simply can't stand it. I swear, I feel like going off some place where I can get a little peace. I do think after a man's spent his lifetime trying to give his kids a chance and a decent education, it's pretty discouraging to hear them all the time scrapping like a bunch of hyenas and never—and never— Curious; here in the paper it says— Never silent for one mom— Seen the morning paper yet?"

"No, dear." In twenty-three years of married life, Mrs. Babbitt had seen the
5 paper before her husband just sixty-seven times.

"Lots of news. Terrible big tornado in the South. Hard luck, all right. But this, say, this is corking! Beginning of the end for those fellows! New York Assembly has passed some bills that ought to completely outlaw the socialists! And there's an elevator-runners' strike in New York and a lot of college
10 boys are taking their places. That's the stuff! And a mass-meeting in Birmingham's demanded that this Mick agitator, this fellow De Valera, be deported. Dead right, by golly! All these agitators paid with German gold anyway. And we got no business interfering with the Irish or any other foreign government. Keep our hands strictly off. And there's another well-authenticated
15 rumor from Russia that Lenin is dead. That's fine. It's beyond me why we don't just step in there and kick those Bolshevik cusses out."

"That's so," said Mrs. Babbitt.

"And it says here a fellow was inaugurated mayor in overalls—a preacher, too! What do you think of that!"
20 "Humph! Well!"

He searched for an attitude, but neither as a Republican, a Presbyterian, an Elk, nor a real-estate broker did he have any doctrine about preacher-mayors laid down for him, so he grunted and went on. She looked sympathetic and did not hear a word. Later she would read the headlines, the society columns,
25 and the department-store advertisements.

"What do you know about this! Charley McKelvey still doing the sassiety stunt as heavy as ever. Here's what that gushy woman reporter says about last night:

Never is Society with the big, big S more flattered than when they are bidden to
30 partake of good cheer at the distinguished and hospitable residence of Mr. and Mrs. Charles L. McKelvey as they were last night. Set in its spacious lawns and landscaping, one of the notable sights crowning Royal Ridge, but merry and homelike despite its mighty stone walls and its vast rooms famed for their decoration, their home was thrown open last night for a dance in honor of Mrs. McKelvey's
35 notable guest, Miss J. Sneeth of Washington. The wide hall is so generous in its proportions that it made a perfect ballroom, its hardwood floor reflecting the charming pageant above its polished surface. Even the delights of dancing paled before the alluring opportunities for tête-à-têtes that invited the soul to loaf in the long library before the baronial fireplace, or in the drawing-room with its deep comfy
40 armchairs, its shaded lamps just made for a sly whisper of pretty nothings all a deux; or even in the billiard room where one could take a cue and show a prowess at still another game than that sponsored by Cupid and Terpsichore.

There was more, a great deal more, in the best urban journalistic style of Miss Elnora Pearl Bates, the popular society editor of the *Advocate-Times*.

11. **De Valera**—Eamon De Valera (1882-   ), Irish revolutionary leader, born in New York and proclaimed President of the Irish Republic in 1919. **15. Lenin**—See note on page 1765.

But Babbitt could not abide it. He grunted. He wrinkled the newspaper. He protested: "Can you beat it! I'm willing to hand a lot of credit to Charley McKelvey. When we were in college together, he was just as hard up as any of us, and he's made a million good bucks out of contracting and hasn't been any dishonester or bought any more city councils than was necessary. And that's a good house of his—though it ain't any 'mighty stone walls' and it ain't worth the ninety thousand it cost him. But when it comes to talking as though Charley McKelvey and all that booze-hoisting set of his are any blooming bunch of of, of Vanderbilts, why, it makes me tired!"

Timidly from Mrs. Babbitt: "I would like to see the inside of their house though. It must be lovely. I've never been inside."

"Well, I have! Lots of—couple of times. To see Chaz about business deals, in the evening. It's not so much. I wouldn't *want* to go there to dinner with that gang of, of highbinders. And I'll bet I make a whole lot more money than some of those tin-horns that spend all they got on dress-suits and haven't got a decent suit of underwear to their name! Hey! What do you think of this!"

Mrs. Babbitt was strangely unmoved by the tidings from the Real Estate and Building column of the *Advocate-Times:*

> Ashtabula Street, 496—J. K. Dawson to Thomas Mullally,
> April 17, 15.7 x 112.2, mtg. $4000 . . . . Nom.

And this morning Babbitt was too disquieted to entertain her with items from Mechanics' Liens, Mortgages Recorded, and Contracts Awarded. He rose. As he looked at her his eyebrows seemed shaggier than usual. Suddenly:

"Yes, maybe— Kind of shame to not keep in touch with folks like the Mc-Kelveys. We might try inviting them to dinner, some evening. Oh, thunder, let's not waste our good time thinking about 'em! Our little bunch has a lot liver times than all those plutes. Just compare a real human like you with these neurotic birds like Lucile McKelvey—all highbrow talk and dressed up like a plush horse! You're a great old girl, hon.!"

He covered his betrayal of softness with a complaining: "Say, don't let Tinka go and eat any more of that poison nut-fudge. For Heaven's sake, try to keep her from ruining her digestion. I tell you, most folks don't appreciate how important it is to have a good digestion and regular habits. Be back 'bout usual time, I guess."

He kissed her—he didn't quite kiss her—he laid unmoving lips against her unflushing cheek. He hurried out to the garage, muttering: "Lord, what a family! And now Myra is going to get pathetic on me because we don't train with this millionaire outfit. Oh, Lord, sometimes I'd like to quit the whole game. And the office worry and detail just as bad. And I act cranky and— I don't mean to, but I get— So darn tired!"

9. **Vanderbilts**—Commodore Cornelius Vanderbilt (1794-1877), a typical capitalist of the Gilded Age, built the family fortune on railway and steamship transportation.

CHAPTER III

To George F. Babbitt, as to most prosperous citizens of Zenith, his motor car was poetry and tragedy, love and heroism. The office was his pirate ship but the car his perilous excursion ashore.

5 Among the tremendous crises of each day none was more dramatic than starting the engine. It was slow on cold mornings; there was the long, anxious whirr of the starter; and sometimes he had to drip ether into the cocks of the cylinders, which was so very interesting that at lunch he would chronicle it drop by drop, and orally calculate how much each drop had cost 10 him.

This morning he was darkly prepared to find something wrong, and he felt belittled when the mixture exploded sweet and strong, and the car didn't even brush the door-jamb, gouged and splintery with many bruisings by fenders, as he backed out of the garage. He was confused. He shouted "Morn-15 ing!" to Sam Doppelbrau with more cordiality than he had intended.

Babbitt's green and white Dutch Colonial house was one of three in that block on Chatham Road. To the left of it was the residence of Mr. Samuel Doppelbrau, secretary of an excellent firm of bathroom-fixture jobbers. His was a comfortable house with no architectural manners whatever; a large 20 wooden box with a squat tower, a broad porch, and glossy paint yellow as a yolk. Babbitt disapproved of Mr. and Mrs. Doppelbrau as "Bohemian." From their house came midnight music and obscene laughter; there were neighborhood rumors of bootlegged whisky and fast motor rides. They furnished Babbitt with many happy evenings of discussion, during which he announced 25 firmly, "I'm not strait-laced, and I don't mind seeing a fellow throw in a drink once in a while, but when it comes to deliberately trying to get away with a lot of hell-raising all the while like the Doppelbraus do, it's too rich for my blood!"

On the other side of Babbitt lived Howard Littlefield, Ph.D., in a strictly 30 modern house whereof the lower part was dark red tapestry brick, with a leaded oriel, the upper part of pale stucco like spattered clay, and the roof red-tiled. Littlefield was the Great Scholar of the neighborhood; the authority on everything in the world except babies, cooking, and motors. He was a Bachelor of Arts of Blodgett College, and a Doctor of Philosophy in economics 35 of Yale. He was the employment-manager and publicity-counsel of the Zenith Street Traction Company. He could, on ten hours' notice, appear before the board of aldermen or the state legislature and prove, absolutely, with figures all in rows and with precedents from Poland and New Zealand, that the streetcar company loved the Public and yearned over its employees; that all its 40 stock was owned by Widows and Orphans; and that whatever it desired to do would benefit property-owners by increasing rental values, and help the poor by lowering rents. All his acquaintances turned to Littlefield when they desired to know the date of the battle of Saragossa, the definition of the word "sabotage," the future of the German mark, the translation of *"hinc illae* 45 *lachrimae,"* or the number of products of coal tar. He awed Babbitt by con-

fessing that he often sat up till midnight reading the figures and footnotes in
Government reports, or skimming (with amusement at the author's mistakes)
the latest volumes of chemistry, archeology, and ichthyology.

But Littlefield's great value was as a spiritual example. Despite his strange
learnings he was as strict a Presbyterian and as firm a Republican as George   5
F. Babbitt. He confirmed the business men in the faith. Where they knew
only by passionate instinct that their system of industry and manners was
perfect, Dr. Howard Littlefield proved it to them, out of history, economics,
and the confessions of reformed radicals.

Babbitt had a good deal of honest pride in being the neighbor of such a   10
savant, and in Ted's intimacy with Eunice Littlefield. At sixteen Eunice was
interested in no statistics save those regarding the ages and salaries of motion-
picture stars, but—as Babbitt definitively put it—"she was her father's
daughter."

The difference between a light man like Sam Doppelbrau and a really fine   15
character like Littlefield was revealed in their appearances. Doppelbrau was
disturbingly young for a man of forty-eight. He wore his derby on the back
of his head, and his red face was wrinkled with meaningless laughter. But
Littlefield was old for a man of forty-two. He was tall, broad, thick; his gold-
rimmed spectacles were engulfed in the folds of his long face; his hair was a   20
tossed mass of greasy blackness; he puffed and rumbled as he talked; his Phi
Beta Kappa key shone against a spotty black vest; he smelled of old pipes;
he was altogether funereal and archidiaconal; and to real-estate brokerage
and the jobbing of bathroom-fixtures he added an aroma of sanctity.

This morning he was in front of his house, inspecting the grass parking   25
between the curb and the broad cement sidewalk. Babbitt stopped his car
and leaned out to shout "Mornin'!" Littlefield lumbered over and stood with
one foot up on the running-board.

"Fine morning," said Babbitt, lighting—illegally early—his second cigar of
the day.   30

"Yes, it's a mighty fine morning," said Littlefield.

"Spring coming along fast now."

"Yes, it's real spring now, all right," said Littlefield.

"Still cold nights, though. Had to have a couple blankets, on the sleeping-
porch last night."   35

"Yes, it wasn't any too warm last night," said Littlefield.

"But I don't anticipate we'll have any more real cold weather now."

"No, but still, there was snow at Tiflis, Montana, yesterday," said the Scholar,
"and you remember the blizzard they had out West three days ago—thirty
inches of snow at Greeley, Colorado—and two years ago we had a snow-   40
squall right here in Zenith on the twenty-fifth of April."

"Is that a fact! Say, old man, what do you think about the Republican candidate? Who'll they nominate for president? Don't you think it's about time
we had a real business administration?"

"In my opinion, what the country needs, first and foremost, is a good, sound,   45

23. **archidiaconal**—in the manner of an archdeacon.

business-like conduct of its affairs. What we need is—a business administration!" said Littlefield.

"I'm glad to hear you say that! I certainly am glad to hear you say that! I didn't know how you'd feel about it, with all your associations with colleges and so on, and I'm glad you feel that way. What the country needs—just at this present juncture—is neither a college president nor a lot of monkeying with foreign affairs, but a good—sound—economical—business—administration, that will give us a chance to have something like a decent turnover."

"Yes. It isn't generally realized that even in China the schoolmen are giving way to more practical men, and of course you can see what that implies."

"Is that a fact! Well, well!" breathed Babbitt, feeling much calmer, and much happier about the way things were going in the world. "Well, it's been nice to stop and parleyvoo a second. Guess I'll have to get down to the office now and sting a few clients. Well, so long, old man. See you tonight. So long."

II

They had labored, these solid citizens. Twenty years before, the hill on which Floral Heights was spread, with its bright roofs and immaculate turf and amazing comfort, had been a wilderness of rank second-growth elms and oaks and maples. Along the precise streets were still a few wooded vacant lots, and the fragment of an old orchard. It was brilliant today; the apple boughs were lit with fresh leaves like torches of green fire. The first white of cherry blossoms flickered down a gully, and robins clamored.

Babbitt sniffed the earth, chuckled at the hysteric robins as he would have chuckled at kittens or at a comic movie. He was, to the eye, the perfect office-going executive—a well-fed man in a correct brown soft hat and frameless spectacles, smoking a large cigar, driving a good motor along a semi-suburban parkway. But in him was some genius of authentic love for his neighborhood, his city, his clan. The winter was over; the time was come for the building, the visible growth, which to him was glory. He lost his dawn depression; he was ruddily cheerful when he stopped on Smith Street to leave the brown trousers, and to have the gasoline-tank filled.

The familiarity of the rite fortified him: the sight of the tall red iron gasoline-pump, the hollow-tile and terra-cotta garage, the window full of the most agreeable accessories—shiny casings, spark-plugs with immaculate porcelain jackets, tire-chains of gold and silver. He was flattered by the friendliness with which Sylvester Moon, dirtiest and most skilled of motor mechanics, came out to serve him. "Mornin', Mr. Babbitt!" said Moon, and Babbitt felt himself a person of importance, one whose name even busy garagemen remembered—not one of these cheap-sports flying around in flivvers. He admired the ingenuity of the automatic dial, clicking off gallon by gallon; admired the smartness of the sign: "A fill in time saves getting stuck—gas today 31 cents"; admired the rhythmic gurgle of the gasoline as it flowed into the tank, and the mechanical regularity with which Moon turned the handle.

"How much we takin' today?" asked Moon, in a manner which combined the independence of the great specialist, the friendliness of a familiar gossip, and respect for a man of weight in the community, like George F. Babbitt.

"Fill 'er up."

"Who you rootin' for for Republican candidate, Mr. Babbitt?"

"It's too early to make any predictions yet. After all, there's still a good month and two weeks—no, three weeks—must be almost three weeks—well, 5 there's more than six weeks in all before the Republican convention, and I feel a fellow ought to keep an open mind and give all the candidates a show— look 'em all over and size 'em up, and then decide carefully."

"That's a fact, Mr. Babbitt."

"But I'll tell you—and my stand on this is just the same as it was four years 10 ago, and eight years ago, and it'll be my stand four years from now—yes, and eight years from now! What I tell everybody, and it can't be too generally understood, is that what we need first, last, and all the time is a good, sound business administration!"

"By golly, that's right!"   15

"How do those front tires look to you?"

"Fine! Fine! Wouldn't be much work for garages if everybody looked after their car the way you do."

"Well, I do try and have some sense about it." Babbitt paid his bill, said adequately, "Oh, keep the change," and drove off in an ecstasy of honest self- 20 appreciation. It was with the manner of a Good Samaritan that he shouted at a respectable-looking man who was waiting for a trolley car, "Have a lift?" As the man climbed in Babbitt condescended, "Going clear down-town? Whenever I see a fellow waiting for a trolley, I always make it a practice to give him a lift—unless, of course, he looks like a bum."   25

"Wish there were more folks that were so generous with their machines," dutifully said the victim of benevolence.

"Oh, no, 'tain't a question of generosity, hardly. Fact, I always feel—I was saying to my son just the other night—it's a fellow's duty to share the good things of this world with his neighbors, and it gets my goat when a fellow 30 gets stuck on himself and goes around tooting his horn merely because he's charitable."

The victim seemed unable to find the right answer. Babbitt boomed on:

"Pretty punk service the Company giving us on these car-lines. Nonsense to only run the Portland Road cars once every seven minutes. Fellow gets mighty 35 cold on a winter morning, waiting on a street corner with the wind nipping at his ankles."

"That's right. The Street Car Company don't care a damn what kind of a deal they give us. Something ought to happen to 'em."

Babbitt was alarmed. "But still, of course it won't do to just keep knocking 40 the Traction Company and not realize the difficulties they're operating under, like these cranks that want municipal ownership. The way these workmen hold up the Company for high wages is simply a crime, and of course the burden falls on you and me that have to pay a seven-cent fare! Fact, there's remarkable service on all their lines—considering."   45

"Well—" uneasily.

"Darn fine morning," Babbitt explained. "Spring coming along fast."

"Yes, it's real spring now."

The victim had no originality, no wit, and Babbitt fell into a great silence and devoted himself to the game of beating trolley cars to the corner: a spurt, a tail-chase, nervous speeding between the huge yellow side of the trolley and
5 the jagged row of parked motors, shooting past just as the trolley stopped—a rare game and valiant.

And all the while he was conscious of the loveliness of Zenith. For weeks together he noticed nothing but clients and the vexing To Rent signs of rival brokers. Today, in mysterious malaise, he raged or rejoiced with equal nervous
10 swiftness, and today the light of spring was so winsome that he lifted his head and saw.

He admired each district along his familiar route to the office: The bungalows and shrubs and winding irregular driveways of Floral Heights. The one-story shops on Smith Street, a glare of plate-glass and new yellow brick;
15 groceries and laundries and drug-stores to supply the more immediate needs of East Side housewives. The market gardens in Dutch Hollow, their shanties patched with corrugated iron and stolen doors. Billboards with crimson goddesses nine feet tall advertising cinema films, pipe tobacco, and talcum powder. The old "mansions" along Ninth Street, S.E., like aged dandies in filthy
20 linen; wooden castles turned into boarding-houses, with muddy walks and rusty hedges, jostled by fast-intruding garages, cheap apartment-houses, and fruit-stands conducted by bland, sleek Athenians. Across the belt of railroad-tracks, factories with high-perched water-tanks and tall stacks—factories producing condensed milk, paper boxes, lighting-fixtures, motor cars. Then the
25 business center, the thickening darting traffic, the crammed trolleys unloading, and high doorways of marble and polished granite.

It was big—and Babbitt respected bigness in anything; in mountains, jewels, muscles, wealth, or words. He was, for a spring-enchanted moment, the lyric and almost unselfish lover of Zenith. He thought of the outlying factory
30 suburbs; of the Chaloosa River with its strangely eroded banks; of the orchard-dappled Tonawanda Hills to the North, and all the fat dairy land and big barns and comfortable herds. As he dropped his passenger he cried, "Gosh, I feel pretty good this morning!"

III

35 Epochal as starting the car was the drama of parking it before he entered his office. As he turned from Oberlin Avenue round the corner into Third Street, N.E., he peered ahead for a space in the line of parked cars. He angrily just missed a space as a rival driver slid into it. Ahead, another car was leaving the curb, and Babbitt slowed up, holding out his hand to the cars press-
40 ing on him from behind, agitatedly motioning an old woman to go ahead, avoiding a truck which bore down on him from one side. With front wheels nicking the wrought-steel bumper of the car in front, he stopped, feverishly cramped his steering-wheel, slid back into the vacant space and, with eighteen inches of room, manoeuvered to bring the car level with the curb. It was a

9. malaise—uneasiness.

virile adventure masterfully executed. With satisfaction he locked a thief-proof steel wedge on the front wheel, and crossed the street to his real-estate office on the ground floor of the Reeves Building.

The Reeves Building was as fireproof as a rock and as efficient as a type-writer; fourteen stories of yellow pressed brick, with clean, upright, unorna- 5
mented lines. It was filled with the offices of lawyers, doctors, agents for ma-chinery, for emery wheels, for wire fencing, for mining-stock. Their gold signs shone on the windows. The entrance was too modern to be flamboyant with pillars; it was quiet, shrewd, neat. Along the Third Street side were a Western Union Telegraph Office, the Blue Delft Candy Shop, Shotwell's Stationery 10
Shop, and the Babbitt-Thompson Realty Company.

Babbitt could have entered his office from the street, as customers did, but it made him feel an insider to go through the corridor of the building and enter by the back door. Thus he was greeted by the villagers.

The little unknown people who inhabited the Reeves Building corridors— 15
elevator-runners, starter, engineers, superintendent, and the doubtful-looking lame man who conducted the news and cigar stand—were in no way city-dwellers. They were rustics, living in a constricted valley, interested only in one another and in The Building. Their Main Street was the entrance hall, with its stone floor, severe marble ceiling, and the inner windows of the shops. 20
The liveliest place on the street was the Reeves Building Barber Shop, but this was also Babbitt's one embarrassment. Himself, he patronized the glittering Pompeian Barber Shop in the Hotel Thornleigh, and every time he passed the Reeves shop—ten times a day, a hundred times—he felt untrue to his own village. 25

Now, as one of the squirearchy, greeted with honorable salutations by the villagers, he marched into his office, and peace and dignity were upon him, and the morning's dissonances all unheard.

They were heard again, immediately.

Stanley Graff, the outside salesman, was talking on the telephone with tragic 30
lack of that firm manner which disciplines clients: "Say, uh, I think I got just the house that would suit you—the Percival House, in Linton. . . . Oh, you've seen it. Well, how'd it strike you? . . . Huh? . . . Oh," irresolutely, "oh, I see."

As Babbitt marched into his private room, a coop with semi-partition of 35
oak and frosted glass, at the back of the office, he reflected how hard it was to find employees who had his own faith that he was going to make sales.

There were nine members of the staff, besides Babbitt and his partner and father-in-law, Henry Thompson, who rarely came to the office. The nine were Stanley Graff, the outside salesman—a youngish man given to cigarettes and 40
the playing of pool; old Mat Penniman, general utility man, collector of rents and salesman of insurance—broken, silent, gray; a mystery, reputed to have been a "crack" real-estate man with a firm of his own in haughty Brooklyn; Chester Kirby Laylock, resident salesman out at the Glen Oriole acreage de-velopment—an enthusiastic person with a silky mustache and much family; 45
Miss Theresa McGoun, the swift and rather pretty stenographer; Miss Wil-

berta Bannigan, the thick, slow, laborious accountant and file-clerk; and four
freelance part-time commission salesmen.

As he looked from his own cage into the main room Babbitt mourned,
"McGoun's a good stenog., smart's a whip, but Stan Graff and all those
5 bums—" The zest of the spring morning was smothered in the stale office air.

Normally he admired the office, with a pleased surprise that he should have
created this sure lovely thing; normally he was stimulated by the clean newness of it and the air of bustle; but today it seemed flat—the tiled floor, like
a bathroom, the ocher-colored metal ceiling, the faded maps on the hard plaster
10 walls, the chairs of varnished pale oak, the desks and filing-cabinets of steel
painted in olive drab. It was a vault, a steel chapel where loafing and laughter
were raw sin.

He hadn't even any satisfaction in the new water-cooler! And it was the
very best of water-coolers, up-to-date, scientific, and right-thinking. It had cost
15 a great deal of money (in itself a virtue). It possessed a non-conducting fiber
ice-container, a porcelain water-jar (guaranteed hygienic), a dripless non-
clogging sanitary faucet, and machine-painted decorations in two tones of gold.
He looked down the relentless stretch of tiled floor at the water-cooler, and
assured himself that no tenant of the Reeves Building had a more expensive
20 one, but he could not recapture the feeling of social superiority it had given
him. He astoundingly grunted, "I'd like to beat it off to the woods right now.
And loaf all day. And go to Gunch's again tonight, and play poker, and cuss
as much as I feel like, and drink a hundred and nine-thousand bottles of
beer."

25 He sighed; he read through his mail; he shouted "Msgoun," which meant
"Miss McGoun"; and began to dictate. . . .

IV

His morning was not sharply marked into divisions. Interwoven with correspondence and advertisement-writing were a thousand nervous details: calls
30 from clerks who were incessantly and hopefully seeking five furnished rooms
and bath at sixty dollars a month; advice to Mat Penniman on getting money
out of tenants who had no money.

Babbitt's virtues as a real-estate broker—as the servant of society in the department of finding homes for families and shops for distributors of food—
35 were steadiness and diligence. He was conventionally honest, he kept his records of buyers and sellers complete, he had experience with leases and titles
and an excellent memory for prices. His shoulders were broad enough, his
voice deep enough, his relish of hearty humor strong enough, to establish him
as one of the ruling caste of Good Fellows. Yet his eventual importance to
40 mankind was perhaps lessened by his large and complacent ignorance of all
architecture save the types of houses turned out by speculative builders; all
landscape gardening save the use of curving roads, grass, and six ordinary
shrubs; and all the commonest axioms of economics. He serenely believed
that the one purpose of the real-estate business was to make money for George
45 F. Babbitt. True, it was a good advertisement at Boosters' Club lunches, and

all the varieties of Annual Banquets to which Good Fellows were invited, to speak sonorously of Unselfish Public Service, the Broker's Obligation to Keep Inviolate the Trust of His Clients, and a thing called Ethics, whose nature was confusing but if you had it you were a High-class Realtor and if you hadn't you were a shyster, a piker, and a fly-by-night. These virtues awakened Confi- 5 dence, and enabled you to handle Bigger Propositions. But they didn't imply that you were to be impractical and refuse to take twice the value of a house if a buyer was such an idiot that he didn't jew you down on the asking-price.

Babbitt spoke well—and often—at these orgies of commercial righteousness about the "realtor's function as a seer of the future development of the com- 10 munity, and as a prophetic engineer clearing the pathway for inevitable changes"—which meant that a real-estate broker could make money by guess-ing which way the town would grow. This guessing he called Vision.

In an address at the Boosters' Club he had admitted, "It is at once the duty and the privilege of the realtor to know everything about his own city and its 15 environs. Where a surgeon is a specialist on every vein and mysterious cell of the human body, and the engineer upon electricity in all its phases, or every bolt of some great bridge majestically arching o'er a mighty flood, the realtor must know his city, inch by inch, and all its faults and virtues."

Though he did know the market-price, inch by inch, of certain districts of 20 Zenith, he did not know whether the police force was too large or too small, or whether it was in alliance with gambling and prostitution. He knew the means of fireproofing buildings and the relation of insurance-rates to fire-proofing, but he did not know how many firemen there were in the city, how they were trained and paid, or how complete their apparatus. He sang elo- 25 quently the advantages of proximity of school-buildings to rentable homes, but he did not know—he did not know that it was worth while to know—whether the city schoolrooms were properly heated, lighted, ventilated, fur-nished; he did not know how the teachers were chosen; and though he chanted "One of the boasts of Zenith is that we pay our teachers adequately," 30 that was because he had read the statement in the *Advocate-Times*. Himself, he could not have given the average salary of teachers in Zenith or anywhere else.

He had heard it said that "conditions" in the County Jail and the Zenith City Prison were not very "scientific"; he had, with indignation at the criti- 35 cism of Zenith, skimmed through a report in which the notorious pessimist Seneca Doane, the radical lawyer, asserted that to throw boys and young girls into a bull-pen crammed with men suffering from syphilis, delirium tremens, and insanity was not the perfect way of educating them. He had controverted the report by growling, "Folks that think a jail ought to be a bloomin' Hotel 40 Thornleigh make me sick. If people don't like a jail, let 'em behave 'emselves and keep out of it. Besides, these reform cranks always exaggerate." That was the beginning and quite completely the end of his investigations into Zenith's charities and corrections; and as to the "vice districts" he brightly expressed it, "Those are things that no decent man monkeys with. Besides, smatter fact, 45 I'll tell you confidentially: it's a protection to our daughters and to decent women to have a district where tough nuts can raise cain. Keeps 'em away from our own homes."

As to industrial conditions, however, Babbitt had thought a great deal, and his opinions may be coördinated as follows:

5   "A good labor union is of value because it keeps out radical unions, which would destroy property. No one ought to be forced to belong to a union, however. All labor agitators who try to force men to join a union should be hanged. In fact, just between ourselves, there oughtn't to be any unions allowed at all; and as it's the best way of fighting the unions, every business man ought to

10 belong to an employers'-association and to the Chamber of Commerce. In union there is strength. So any selfish hog who doesn't join the Chamber of Commerce ought to be forced to." . . .

v

Conrad Lyte was a real-estate speculator. He was a nervous speculator. Be-

15 fore he gambled he consulted bankers, lawyers, architects, contracting builders, and all of their clerks and stenographers who were willing to be cornered and give him advice. He was a bold entrepreneur, and he desired nothing more than complete safety in his investments, freedom from attention to details, and the thirty or forty per cent profit which, according to all authori-

20 ties, a pioneer deserves for his risks and foresight. He was a stubby man with a cap-like mass of short gray curls and clothes which, no matter how well cut, seemed shaggy. Below his eyes were semicircular hollows, as though silver dollars had been pressed against them and had left an imprint.

Particularly and always Lyte consulted Babbitt, and trusted in his slow

25 cautiousness.

Six months ago Babbitt had learned that one Archibald Purdy, a grocer in the indecisive residential district known as Linton, was talking of opening a butcher shop beside his grocery. Looking up the ownership of adjoining parcels of land, Babbitt found that Purdy owned his present shop but did not

30 own the one available lot adjoining. He advised Conrad Lyte to purchase this lot, for eleven thousand dollars, though an appraisal on a basis of rents did not indicate its value as above nine thousand. The rents, declared Babbitt, were too low; and by waiting they could make Purdy come to their price. (This was Vision.) He had to bully Lyte into buying. His first act as agent

35 for Lyte was to increase the rent of the battered store-building on the lot. The tenant said a number of rude things, but he paid.

Now, Purdy seemed ready to buy, and his delay was going to cost him ten thousand extra dollars—the reward paid by the community to Mr. Conrad Lyte for the virtue of employing a broker who had Vision and who under-

40 stood Talking Points, Strategic Values, Key Situations, Underappraisals, and the Psychology of Salesmanship.

Lyte came to the conference exultantly. He was fond of Babbitt, this morning, and called him "old hoss." Purdy, the grocer, a long-nosed man and solemn, seemed to care less for Babbitt and for Vision, but Babbitt met him at the

45 street door of the office and guided him toward the private room with af-

fectionate little cries of "This way, Brother Purdy!" He took from the correspondence-file the entire box of cigars and forced them on his guests. He pushed their chairs two inches forward and three inches back, which gave an hospitable note, then leaned back in his desk-chair and looked plump and jolly. But he spoke to the weakling grocer with firmness.   5

"Well, Brother Purdy, we been having some pretty tempting offers from butchers and a slew of other folks for that lot next to your store, but I persuaded Brother Lyte that we ought to give you a shot at the property first. I said to Lyte, 'It'd be a rotten shame,' I said, 'if somebody went and opened a combination grocery and meat market right next door and ruined Purdy's nice   10 little business.' Especially—" Babbitt leaned forward, and his voice was harsh, "—it would be hard luck if one of these cash-and-carry chain-stores got in there and started cutting prices below cost till they got rid of competition and forced you to the wall!"

Purdy snatched his thin hands from his pockets, pulled up his trousers,   15 thrust his hands back into his pockets, tilted in the heavy oak chair, and tried to look amused, as he struggled:

"Yes, they're bad competition. But I guess you don't realize the Pulling Power that Personality has in a neighborhood business."

The great Babbitt smiled. "That's so. Just as you feel, old man. We thought   20 we'd give you first chance. All right then—"

"Now look here!" Purdy wailed. "I know f'r a fact that a piece of property 'bout same size, right near, sold for less 'n eighty-five hundred, 'twa'n't two years ago, and here you fellows are asking me twenty-four thousand dollars! Why, I'd have to mortgage— I wouldn't mind so much paying twelve thou-   25 sand but— Why good God, Mr. Babbitt, you're asking more 'n twice its value! And threatening to ruin me if I don't take it!"

"Purdy, I don't like your way of talking! I don't like it one little bit! Supposing Lyte and I were stinking enough to want to ruin my fellow human, don't you suppose we know it's to our own selfish interest to have everybody   30 in Zenith prosperous? But all this is beside the point. Tell you what we'll do: We'll come down to twenty-three thousand—five thousand down and the rest on mortgage—and if you want to wreck the old shack and rebuild, I guess I can get Lyte here to loosen up for a building-mortgage on good liberal terms. Heavens, man, we'd be glad to oblige you! We don't like these foreign grocery   35 trusts any better 'n you do! But it isn't reasonable to expect us to sacrifice eleven thousand or more just for neighborliness, is it! How about it, Lyte? You willing to come down?"

By warmly taking Purdy's part, Babbitt persuaded the benevolent Mr. Lyte to reduce his price to twenty-one thousand dollars. At the right moment Bab-   40 bitt snatched from a drawer the agreement he had had Miss McGoun type out a week ago and thrust it into Purdy's hands. He genially shook his fountain pen to make certain that it was flowing, handed it to Purdy, and approvingly watched him sign.

The work of the world was being done. Lyte had made something over   45 nine thousand dollars, Babbitt had made a four-hundred-and-fifty dollar commission, Purdy had, by the sensitive mechanism of modern finance, been provided with a business-building, and soon the happy inhabitants of Linton would have meat lavished upon them at prices only a little higher than those down-town.

It had been a manly battle, but after it Babbitt drooped. This was the only
5 really amusing contest he had been planning. There was nothing ahead save details of leases, appraisals, mortgages.

He muttered, "Makes me sick to think of Lyte carrying off most of the profit when I did all the work, the old skinflint! And— What else have I got to do today? . . . Like to take a good long vacation. Motor trip. Something."
10 He sprang up, rekindled by the thought of lunching with Paul Riesling.

CHAPTER V

Babbitt's preparations for leaving the office to its feeble self during the hour and a half of his lunch-period were somewhat less elaborate than the plans for a general European war.
15 He fretted to Miss McGoun, "What time you going to lunch? Well, make sure Miss Bannigan is in then. Explain to her that if Wiedenfeldt calls up, she's to tell him I'm already having the title traced. And oh, b' the way, remind me tomorrow to have Penniman trace it. Now if anybody comes in looking for a cheap house, remember we got to shove that Bangor Road place
20 off onto somebody. If you need me, I'll be at the Athletic Club. And—uh— And—uh— I'll be back by two."

He dusted the cigar-ashes off his vest. He placed a difficult unanswered letter on the pile of unfinished work, that he might not fail to attend to it that afternoon. (For three noons, now, he had placed the same letter on the un-
25 finished pile.) He scrawled on a sheet of yellow backing-paper the memorandum: "See abt apt h drs," which gave him an agreeable feeling of having already seen about the apartment-house doors.

He discovered that he was smoking another cigar. He threw it away, protesting, "Darn it, I thought you'd quit this darn smoking!" He courageously
30 returned the cigar-box to the correspondence-file, locked it up, hid the key in a more difficult place, and raged, "Ought to take care of myself. And need more exercise—walk to the club, every single noon—just what I'll do—every noon— cut out this motoring all the time."

The resolution made him feel exemplary. Immediately after it he decided
35 that this noon it was too late to walk.

It took but little more time to start his car and edge it into the traffic than it would have taken to walk the three and a half blocks to the club.

II

As he drove he glanced with the fondness of familiarity at the buildings.
40 A stranger suddenly dropped into the business-center of Zenith could not have told whether he was in a city of Oregon or Georgia, Ohio or Maine, Oklahoma or Manitoba. But to Babbitt, every inch was individual and stirring. As always he noted that the California Building across the way was three

stories lower, therefore three stories less beautiful, than his own Reeves Building. As always when he passed the Parthenon Shoe Shine Parlor, a one-story hut which beside the granite and red-brick ponderousness of the old California Building resembled a bath-house under a cliff, he commented, "Gosh, ought to get my shoes shined this afternoon. Keep forgetting it." At the Simplex Office Furniture Shop, the National Cash Register Agency, he yearned for a dictaphone, for a typewriter which would add and multiply, as a poet yearns for quartos or a physician for radium.

At the Nobby Men's Wear Shop he took his left hand off the steering-wheel to touch his scarf, and thought well of himself as one who bought expensive ties "and could pay cash for 'em, too, by golly"; and at the United Cigar Store, with its crimson and gold alertness, he reflected, "Wonder if I need some cigars —idiot—plumb forgot—going t' cut down my fool smoking." He looked at his bank, the Miners' and Drovers' National, and considered how clever and solid he was to bank with so marbled an establishment. His high moment came in the clash of traffic when he was halted at the corner beneath the lofty Second National Tower. His car was banked with four others in a line of steel restless as cavalry, while the cross-town traffic, limousines and enormous moving-vans and insistent motor-cycles, poured by; on the farther corner, pneumatic riveters rang on the sun-plated skeleton of a new building; and out of this tornado flashed the inspiration of a familiar face, and a fellow Booster shouted, "H' are you, George!" Babbitt waved in neighborly affection, and slid on with the traffic as the policeman lifted his hand. He noted how quickly his car picked up. He felt superior and powerful, like a shuttle of polished steel darting in a vast machine.

As always he ignored the next two blocks, decayed blocks not yet reclaimed from the grime and shabbiness of the Zenith of 1885. While he was passing the five-and-ten-cent store, the Dakota Lodging House, Concordia Hall with its lodge-rooms and the offices of fortune-tellers and chiropractors, he thought of how much money he made, and he boasted a little and worried a little and did old familiar sums:

"Four hundred fifty plunks this morning from the Lyte deal. But taxes due. Let's see: I ought to pull out eight thousand net this year, and save fifteen hundred of that—no, not if I put up garage and— Let's see: six hundred and forty clear last month, and twelve times six-forty makes—makes—let see: six times twelve is seventy-two hundred and— Oh rats, anyway, I'll make eight thousand—gee now, that's not so bad; mighty few fellows pulling down eight thousand dollars a year—eight thousand good hard iron dollars—bet there isn't more than five per cent of the people in the whole United States that make more than Uncle George does, by golly! Right up at the top of the heap! But— Way expenses are— Family wasting gasoline, and always dressed like millionaires, and sending that eighty a month to Mother— And all these stenographers and salesmen gouging me for every cent they can get—"

The effect of his scientific budget-planning was that he felt at once triumphantly wealthy and perilously poor, and in the midst of these dissertations he stopped his car, rushed into a small news-and-miscellany shop, and bought the electric cigar-lighter which he had coveted for a week. He dodged his conscience by being jerky and noisy, and by shouting at the clerk, "Guess this will prett' near pay for itself in matches, eh?"

It was a pretty thing, a nickeled cylinder with an almost silvery socket, to be attached to the dashboard of his car. It was not only, as the placard on the counter observed, "a dandy little refinement, lending the last touch of class to a gentleman's auto," but a priceless time-saver. By freeing him from halting the car to light a match, it would in a month or two easily save ten minutes.

As he drove on he glanced at it. "Pretty nice. Always wanted one," he said wistfully. "The one thing a smoker needs, too."

Then he remembered that he had given up smoking.

"Darn it!" he mourned. "Oh well, I suppose I'll hit a cigar once in a while. And— Be a great convenience for other folks. Might make just the difference in getting chummy with some fellow that would put over a sale. And— Certainly looks nice there. Certainly is a mighty clever little jigger. Gives the last touch of refinement and class. I— By golly, I guess I can afford it if I want to! Not going to be the only member of this family that never has a single doggone luxury!"

Thus, laden with treasure, after three and a half blocks of romantic adventure, he drove up to the club.

THOMAS STEARNS ELIOT

1888-

I. THE YOUNG AMERICAN SOPHISTICATE (1888–1914)

1888 Born September 26, St. Louis, the youngest of seven children, the son of Henry Ware and Charlotte Chauncy Stearns Eliot, the parents being of New England stock.

1898–1905 Pupil at Smith Academy, St. Louis.

1905–1906 Pupil at Milton Academy, near Boston.

1906–1910 Studied at Harvard (A.B., 1909; A.M., 1910), where he was influenced by the teaching of Irving Babbitt and George Santayana and later (negatively) by the ideas of Bertrand Russell.

1910–1911 Student in philosophy at the University of Paris.

1911–1914 Student of Sanskrit, Pali, and philosophy in the Harvard Graduate School; 1913-1914, assistant in philosophy; 1914, Sheldon Travelling Fellowship (summer in Germany).

1914–1915 Student in philosophy at Merton College, Oxford University.

II. ENGLAND AND THE WASTE LAND (1915–1927)

1915–1917 Teacher, first at High Wycombe, Buckinghamshire, then at Highgate School, London.

1915 Married Vivien Haigh Haigh-Wood, daughter of a British artist. (Mrs. Eliot died in 1947.)

1917 Published a brochure on Ezra Pound. Published *Prufrock and Other Observations* (poems).

1918–1925 Employed in various capacities in Lloyds Bank.

1920 Published *Poems* and *The Sacred Wood* (essays on poetry and criticism).

1921 To recuperate from overwork, Eliot went to Lausanne, where he worked on the first draft of *The Waste Land,* which was submitted to Pound for criticism.

1922–1939 Edited *The Criterion,* influential literary magazine, in which *The Waste Land* originally appeared in England. It was then published in book form. Won $2,000 Dial Prize.

1924 Published *Homage to John Dryden.*

1925 Joined the board of Faber & Gwyer (now Faber & Faber), publishers. Published *Poems, 1909-1925.*

1926 Clark Lecturer at Trinity College.

1927 Confirmed as a member of the Church of England. Became British subject.

III. PROPAGANDIST OF FAITH, TRADITION, AND CONSERVATISM (1928–   )

1928 *For Lancelot Andrewes,* collection of critical essays.

1930 *Ash-Wednesday,* poem of religious doubt and faith.

1932 *Selected Essays, 1917-1932.*

1932–1933 Charles Eliot Norton Professor of Poetry at Harvard, the lectures being published as *The Use of Poetry and the Use of Criticism,* 1933. Published *Sweeney Agonistes.*

1934 *After Strange Gods. A Primer of Modern Heresy,* lectures delivered on the Page-Barbour Foundation of the University of Virginia. Also published *The Rock* (a pageant) and *Elizabethan Essays.*

1935 *Murder in the Cathedral* (poetic tragedy).

1936 *Essays Ancient and Modern* (includes earlier material) and *Collected Poems, 1909-1935.*

1939 *The Family Reunion* (play); *Old Possum's Book of Practical Cats; The Idea of a Christian Society.*

1942 *The Music of Poetry* (lecture); *The Classics and the Man of Letters* (lecture).

1943 *Four Quartets.* (Three parts of this poem had previously appeared as follows: *Burnt Norton,* 1941; *The Dry Salvages,* 1941; *Little Gidding,* 1942.)

1945 *What is a Classic?* (lecture).

1947 Honorary degrees from Harvard, Yale, and Princeton (previously honorary degrees had been conferred by Columbia, Edinburgh, Cambridge, Bristol, Leeds).

1948 *Notes towards the Definition of Culture.* Awarded Nobel Prize for literature.

1949 *The Cocktail Party* (play), published 1950.

1950 *Poetry and Drama* (lecture).

BIBLIOGRAPHY: Donald Gallup, *A Bibliographical Check-List of the Writings of T. S. Eliot,* Yale, 1947; *Literary History of the United States,* Vol. III, pp. 488-92.

CRITICISM: There is no biography but the material contributed by Eliot to the *Harvard College Class of 1910: Twenty-Fifth Anniversary Report,* Cambridge, 1935, is useful. The best single introduction is F. O. Matthiessen, *The Achievement of T. S. Eliot,* rev. ed., Oxford, 1947. See also George Williamson, *The Talent of T. S. Eliot,* University of Washington, 1929; Edmund Wilson, *Axel's Castle,* Scribner, 1931; H. R. Williamson, *The Poetry of T. S. Eliot,* Hodder, London, 1932; F. R. Leavis, *New Bearings in English Poetry,* Chatto and Windus, London, 1932, pp. 75-132; Theodore Spencer, "The Poetry of T. S. Eliot," *Atlantic Monthly,* January, 1933, pp. 60-68; Allardyce Nicoll, "T. S. Eliot and the Revival of Classicism," *English Journal,* April, 1934, pp. 269-78; R. P. Blackmur, *The Double Agent,* Arrow Editions, 1935; Allen Tate, *Reactionary Essays on Poetry and Ideas,* Scribner, 1936, pp. 210-20; Cleanth Brooks, "The Waste Land: Critique of the Myth," *Modern Poetry and the Tradition,* University of North Carolina Press, 1939; Yvor Winters, *The Anatomy of Nonsense,* New Directions, 1943; Eliseo Vivas, "The Objective Correlative," *American Bookman,* Winter, 1944, pp. 7-18; Clive Sansom, *The Poetry of T. S. Eliot,* Oxford, 1947; Leonard Unger, ed., *T. S. Eliot: A Selected Critique,* Rinehart, 1948; Leonard Unger, ed., *The Art of T. S. Eliot,* Cresset Press, London, 1949. But all discussions of recent and contemporary poetry and most discussions of recent criticism touch on Eliot.

T. S. Eliot abandoned the United States as a place of residence in 1914, at the age of 26, and became a British subject in 1927. He published almost nothing until he had cut his ties with his native Missouri, whereas, in the apposite case of Henry James, another expatriate, James did not settle permanently abroad until his middle thirties, nor did he become a naturalized British subject until he was 72. If James wrote the international novel, the protagonist was commonly an American. But so small is the number of Eliot's poems on American themes and so rare is the discussion of American writers in his prose that, like modernism in architecture, he belongs not so much to the native letters as to the international style. The lack of direct connection with the American theme is emphasized by Eliot's famous pronouncement of 1928 that he was a royalist in politics, a classicist in literature, and an Anglo-Catholic in religion. If he later expressed some distress at the literalness with which these phrases were taken, he has not essentially altered his position.

Eliot's appeal is not to the general audience addressed by Robert Frost in poetry, Sinclair Lewis in fiction, and Henry L. Mencken in prose, but to the metropolitan intellectual and especially to the younger poets of his generation. Though his appeal may be self-limited through the elliptic nature of his poetry and the dogmatic quality of his critical and social dicta, his influence is evident in much of the poetry written in America and England during the 1930's and 1940's. His early poems celebrate the moral imbecility and cultural vacuity of Western man and had their principal audience in the world before Hitler. Prufrock and Gerontion and Sweeney stand for varieties of hollow men who, as Eliot saw them, were being nibbled away by inaction rather than defeated in honest conflict. These poems read strangely now in the light of Dunkirk and Okinawa, the heroism of those who resisted totalitarianism in concentration camp and underground movement, and the great appeals of Eliot's contemporaries, Winston Churchill and Franklin D. Roosevelt, to the traditional heroism and beliefs of the English-speaking world.

Within these cultural and historical limitations, however, the poetry, particularly *The Waste Land,* has had a remarkable influence on English prosody. Eliot has been criticized for an excessive use of recondite bookish allusions for poetical effects and for a compactness of structure which sometimes leads to obscurantism. But along with this bookishness appear great technical mastery of meter and the creation of haunting phrase and lovely music, the poems being commonly organized for "symphonic" effects. They also represent a return upon myth, anthropology, and symbolism, both as an approach to religious belief and as reinvigoration of imaginative energy.

The prose is sometimes as baffling as the poetry. Eliot's formal training in philosophy has not prevented some astonishing lapses in logic, which critics have pointed out, and he is capable of such *obiter dicta* as that Shakespeare's *Pericles* is "that very great play," whereas *Hamlet* is a failure, and these have sometimes embarrassed their author. In general, the prose is a plea for order in society, for Christian orthodoxy in the state (see *The Idea of a Christian Society*) even at a considerable cost in tolerance, and for a special variety of traditionalism in literature. At its best the criticism formulates a theory and psychology of literature, particularly of poetic creation, which has been widely influential and offers an analysis of writers like Dryden and Pascal almost unsurpassed for keenness of insight, sympathy, and imaginative range.

THE LOVE SONG OF J. ALFRED PRUFROCK

This poem first appeared in *Poetry: A Magazine of Verse,* VI: 130-35 in June, 1915, and was then gathered into *Prufrock and Other Observations,* London, 1917, whence it passed into various collections of Eliot's poems. There are some minute differences in spelling and punctuation between earlier states of the poem, and that printed

here, which is based on the *Collected Poems* of 1936. The square brackets of that
edition have been altered to the original parenthesis marks.

> *S'io credesse che mia risposta fosse*
> *A persona che mai tornasse al mondo,*
> *Questa fiamma staria senza piu scosse.*
> *Ma perciocche giammai di questo fondo*
> *Non torno vivo alcun, s'i'odo il vero,*   5
> *Senza tema d'infamia ti rispondo.*

Let us go then, you and I,
When the evening is spread out against the sky
Like a patient etherised upon a table;
Let us go, through certain half-deserted streets,   10
The muttering retreats
Of restless nights in one-night cheap hotels
And sawdust restaurants with oyster-shells:
Streets that follow like a tedious argument
Of insidious intent   15
To lead you to an overwhelming question. . .
Oh, do not ask, "What is it?"
Let us go and make our visit.

In the room the women come and go
Talking of Michelangelo.   20

The yellow fog that rubs its back upon the window-panes,
The yellow smoke that rubs its muzzle on the window-panes
Licked its tongue into the corners of the evening,
Lingered upon the pools that stand in drains,
Let fall upon its back the soot that falls from chimneys,   25
Slipped by the terrace, made a sudden leap,
And seeing that it was a soft October night,
Curled once about the house, and fell asleep.

And indeed there will be time
For the yellow smoke that slides along the street,   30
Rubbing its back upon the window-panes;
There will be time, there will be time
To prepare a face to meet the faces that you meet;
There will be time to murder and create,
And time for all the works and days of hands   35
That lift and drop a question on your plate;

1-6. **"S'io . . . rispondo"**—Dante, "Inferno," Canto XXVII:61-66. This is the reply
made by Guido da Montefeltro to Dante, as Dante passes through the part of Hell devoted to
the punishment by fire of evil counselors. It may be translated: "If I thought that a reply of
mine were being made to someone who might return to earth, this flame would be made without further shaking, but since, if what I hear is true, nobody ever returned alive out of this gulf,
I answer you without fear of infamy." 19-20. **women . . . Michelangelo**—The suggested
background is that of a gathering of women talking art. 24. **drains**—here, about equivalent
to street gutters. 35. **works and days**—title of a poem by Hesiod, Greek poet of the eighth
century, B.C., a collection of maxims on how to live.

Time for you and time for me,
And time yet for a hundred indecisions,
And for a hundred visions and revisions,
Before the taking of a toast and tea.   40

In the room the women come and go
Talking of Michelangelo.

And indeed there will be time
To wonder, "Do I dare?" and, "Do I dare?"
Time to turn back and descend the stair,   45
With a bald spot in the middle of my hair—
(They will say: "How his hair is growing thin!")
My morning coat, my collar mounting firmly to the chin,
My necktie rich and modest, but asserted by a simple pin—
(They will say: "But how his arms and legs are thin!")   50
Do I dare
Disturb the universe?
In a minute there is time
For decisions and revisions which a minute will reverse.

For I have known them all already, known them all—   55
Have known the evenings, mornings, afternoons,
I have measured out my life with coffee spoons;
I know the voices dying with a dying fall
Beneath the music from a farther room.
    So how should I presume?   60

And I have known the eyes already, known them all—
The eyes that fix you in a formulated phrase,
And when I am formulated, sprawling on a pin,
When I am pinned and wriggling on the wall,
Then how should I begin   65
To spit out all the butt-ends of my days and ways?
    And how should I presume?

And I have known the arms already, known them all—
Arms that are braceleted and white and bare
(But in the lamplight, downed with light brown hair!)   70
Is it perfume from a dress
That makes me so digress?
Arms that lie along a table, or wrap about a shawl.
    And should I then presume?
    And how should I begin?   75

            .   .   .   .   .   .

Shall I say, I have gone at dusk through narrow streets
And watched the smoke that rises from the pipes
Of lonely men in shirt-sleeves, leaning out of windows? . . .

I should have been a pair of ragged claws
Scuttling across the floors of silent seas.   80

        .   .   .   .

And the afternoon, the evening, sleeps so peacefully!
Smoothed by long fingers,
Asleep . . . tired . . . or it malingers,
Stretched on the floor, here beside you and me.
Should I, after tea and cakes and ices,   85
Have the strength to force the moment to its crisis?
But though I have wept and fasted, wept and prayed,
Though I have seen my head (grown slightly bald) brought in upon a platter,
I am no prophet—and here's no great matter;
I have seen the moment of my greatness flicker,   90
And I have seen the eternal Footman hold my coat, and snicker,
And in short, I was afraid.

And would it have been worth it, after all,
After the cups, the marmalade, the tea,
Among the porcelain, among some talk of you and me,   95
Would it have been worth while,
To have bitten off the matter with a smile,
To have squeezed the universe into a ball
To roll it toward some overwhelming question,
To say: "I am Lazarus, come from the dead,   100
Come back to tell you all, I shall tell you all"—
If one, settling a pillow by her head,
   Should say: "That is not what I meant at all.
   That is not it, at all."

And would it have been worth it, after all,   105
Would it have been worth while,
After the sunsets and the dooryards and the sprinkled streets,
After the novels, after the teacups, after the skirts that trail along the floor—
And this, and so much more?—
It is impossible to say just what I mean!   110
But as if a magic lantern threw the nerves in patterns on a screen:
Would it have been worth while
If one, settling a pillow or throwing off a shawl,
And turning toward the window, should say:
   "That is not it at all,
   That is not what I meant, at all."   115

          .   .   .   .   .   .

No! I am not Prince Hamlet, nor was meant to be;
Am an attendant lord, one that will do
To swell a progress, start a scene or two,
Advise the prince; no doubt, an easy tool,   120
Deferential, glad to be of use,
Politic, cautious, and meticulous;
Full of high sentence, but a bit obtuse;
At times, indeed, almost ridiculous—
Almost, at times, the Fool.   125

88. head . . . platter—*cf.* Mark 6:22-28. **100. Lazarus**—*cf.* John 11:1-44. **118. attendant lord**—*cf.* the characters of Rosencrantz and Guildenstern in *Hamlet*. **119. progress**
—a state journey made by a royal, ecclesiastical, or noble personage and his attendants. **125. Fool**
—i.e., in Elizabethan drama.

I grow old . . . I grow old . . .
I shall wear the bottoms of my trousers rolled.

Shall I part my hair behind? Do I dare to eat a peach?
I shall wear white flannel trousers, and walk upon the beach.
I have heard the mermaids singing, each to each.   130

I do not think that they will sing to me.

I have seen them riding seaward on the waves
Combing the white hair of the waves blown back
When the wind blows the water white and black.

We have lingered in the chambers of the sea   135
By sea-girls wreathed with seaweed red and brown
Till human voices wake us, and we drown.

SWEENEY AMONG THE NIGHTINGALES

This poem was first printed in the *Little Review*, V:10, for September, 1918.
It was then gathered into *Poems*, London, 1919, then into *Ara Vus* [*Vos*] *Prec*,
London, 1920, and thence into the various collected editions. There are variations
in the text and punctuation in the earlier states of the poem. Up to its inclusion in
Poems, 1919-1925, the Greek epigraph was followed by the sentence: "Why should
I speak of the nightingale? The nightingale sings of adulterous wrong." The present
text is that in *Collected Poems* of 1936.

ὤμοι, πέπληγμαι καιρίαν πληγὴν ἔσω.*

Apeneck Sweeney spreads his knees
Letting his arms hang down to laugh,
The zebra stripes along his jaw
Swelling to maculate giraffe.

The circles of the stormy moon   5
Slide westward toward the River Plate,
Death and the Raven drift above
And Sweeney guards the hornèd gate.

Gloomy Orion and the Dog
Are veiled; and hushed the shrunken seas;   10

*The motto is from Æschylus' *Agamemnon* and means: "Alas, I am struck by a timely blow
within" (line 1343). **6. toward**—reads *to* in earlier version. "The River Plate" is the La Plata,
lying between Uruguay and Argentina and therefore westward. **7. Death and the Raven**—
In Mithraic lore the sacred bull was slain by Mithras after a message had been sent by a Raven
from the Sun, ordering him to do so. The soul of the bull rose to heaven and the raven became
the first or outermost of the planetary spheres. **8. hornèd gate**—According to Greek legend
dreams pass through two gates to reach mankind; those passing through the Gate of Horn are
true dreams. **9. Orion . . . Dog**—the two constellations, Orion and Canis Major. They are
"veiled" either in the sense of having set or of being misted over by early morning. **10. shrunken
seas**—i.e., the tide is out.

The person in the Spanish cape
Tries to sit on Sweeney's knees.

Slips and pulls the table cloth
Overturns a coffee-cup,
Reorganised upon the floor   15
She yawns and draws a stocking up;

The silent man in mocha brown
Sprawls at the window-sill and gapes;
The waiter brings in oranges
Bananas figs and hothouse grapes;   20

The silent vertebrate in brown
Contracts and concentrates, withdraws;
Rachel *née* Rabinovitch
Tears at the grapes with murderous paws;

She and the lady in the cape   25
Are suspect, thought to be in league;
Therefore the man with heavy eyes
Declines the gambit, shows fatigue,

Leaves the room and reappears
Outside the window, leaning in,   30
Branches of wistaria
Circumscribe a golden grin;

The host with someone indistinct
Converses at the door apart,
The nightingales are singing near   35
The Convent of the Sacred Heart,

And sang within the bloody wood
When Agamemnon cried aloud,
And let their liquid siftings fall
To stain the stiff dishonoured shroud.   40

THE WASTE LAND*

Without the author's explanatory notes *The Waste Land* appeared in *The Criterion: A Quarterly Review* (London), I: 50-64, in October, 1922, and in *The Dial* (New York), LXXIII: 473-85 in November, 1922. *The Dial* announced an American

21. in brown—reads "exhalts" in the earliest form of the poem. 28. declines the gambit —In chess, a mode of opening a game in which a piece is sacrificed to secure a position is called a gambit. 35. nightingales—see the headnote to this poem. 36. Convent of the Sacred Heart—There is apparently a concealed association in this line. The Convent of the Sacred Heart in London is near St. Thomas Hospital, and the Nightingale Home for nurses was founded at that hospital by Florence Nightingale. 38. Agamemnon—Upon his return from the Trojan War, Agamemnon was slain by Clytemnestra in his bath, but not in a "bloody wood." * Waste Land—"Not only the title, but the plan and a good deal of the incidental symbolism

edition "presently." The poem appeared as a book in New York in 1922, and in London in 1923. One of the curiosities of the American editions is that, after being correctly printed in an early version, "mountain" in line 339 thereafter appeared as "mount in" for some printings. Eliot's notes were added to the poem in book form. It was gathered into the collected *Poems, 1919-1925*. In this version for the first time appeared the dedication: "For Ezra Pound: *il miglior fabbro*" (i.e., "the better artificer"). The present text is that of the first American edition in book form.

"NAM Sibyllam * quidem Cumis ego ipse
oculis meis vidi in ampulla pendere,
et cum illi pueri dicerent: Σίβυλλα τί
θέλεις; respondebat illa: ἀποθανεῖν θέλω."

I. THE BURIAL † OF THE DEAD

April is the cruellest month, breeding
Lilacs out of the dead land, mixing
Memory and desire, stirring
Dull roots with spring rain.
Winter kept us warm, covering   5
Earth in forgetful snow, feeding
A little life with dried tubers.
Summer surprised us, coming over the Starnbergersee
With a shower of rain; we stopped in the colonnade,
And went on in sunlight, into the Hofgarten,   10
And drank coffee, and talked for an hour.
Bin gar keine Russin, stamm' aus Litauen, echt deutsch.

of the poem were suggested by Miss Jessie L. Weston's book on the Grail legend: *From Ritual to Romance* (Cambridge). Indeed, so deeply am I indebted, Miss Weston's book will elucidate the difficulties of the poem much better than my notes can do; and I recommend it (apart from the great interest of the book itself) to any who think such elucidation of the poem worth the trouble. To another work of anthropology I am indebted in general, one which has influenced our generation profoundly; I mean *The Golden Bough*; I have used especially the two volumes *Adonis, Attis, Osiris*. Anyone who is acquainted with these works will immediately recognise in the poem certain references to vegetation ceremonies" (Eliot). In *From Ritual to Romance* (1920) the waste land appears in the story of the Grail as a sterile country blighted by a curse and ruled by a Fisher King, who is impotent. Release from the spell can come only when a knight visits the castle and asks the meaning of certain symbols at once sexual and religious. In the poem the "waste land" is the impotent twentieth century. From 1890 to 1915 Sir James Frazer (1854-1941) produced at intervals his famous work, *The Golden Bough*, in 12 volumes. The title refers to a branch broken from a sacred tree by Æneas in Virgil's poem, which permits Æneas, though living, to visit the afterworld; and the central problem of Frazer's study, especially in *Adonis, Attis, Osiris*, is to trace the myths and rituals by which the seasonal worship of the fertility god was carried on. This god is buried in the autumn and rises again in the spring. * **Nam Sibyllam**—"For I once saw the Cumaean Sybil, with my own eyes, hanging in a glass bottle, and when the boys said to her, 'Sybil, what do you want?' she answered, 'I want to die.' " (Petronius, *Satyricon*, chap. 48.) The point seems to be that the once powerful Sybil has withered away until she is small enough to go into a bottle. † **Burial**—According to the vegetation myth the god must be buried in order that the resurrection of the deity of fertility may occur in spring, when the poem opens. **1. April**—the month in which Easter usually occurs. **2-7. Lilacs . . . tubers**—reminiscent of life in New England. **8. Starnbergersee**—a lake near Munich in Bavaria, much patronized during the summer by wealthy and fashionable people. The conversation implied in the following lines takes place in the Hofgarten in Munich, a park containing open-air restaurants. **12. Bin . . . deutsch**—"I am no Russian woman, I come from Lithuania, but I am truly German." The point is that the speaker is descended from one of the German families sent to colonize Lithuania, or at least that part of Lithuania which fell to Prussia during the partitions of Poland in the eighteenth century.

And when we were children, staying at the archduke's,
My cousin's, he took me out on a sled,
And I was frightened. He said, Marie,   15
Marie, hold on tight. And down we went.
In the mountains, there you feel free.
I read, much of the night, and go south in the winter.

What are the roots that clutch, what branches grow
Out of this stony rubbish? Son of man,   20
You cannot say, or guess, for you know only
A heap of broken images, where the sun beats,
And the dead tree gives no shelter, the cricket no relief,
And the dry stone no sound of water. Only
There is shadow under this red rock,   25
(Come in under the shadow of this red rock),
And I will show you something different from either
Your shadow at morning striding behind you
Or your shadow at evening rising to meet you;
I will show you fear in a handful of dust.   30

> *Frisch weht der Wind*
> *Der Heimat zu,*
> *Mein Irisch Kind,*
> *Wo weilest du?*

"You gave me hyacinths first a year ago;   35
"They called me the hyacinth girl."
—Yet when we came back, late, from the Hyacinth garden,
Your arms full, and your hair wet, I could not
Speak, and my eyes failed, I was neither
Living nor dead, and I knew nothing,   40
Looking into the heart of light, the silence.
Od' und leer das Meer.

Madame Sosostris, famous clairvoyante,
Had a bad cold, nevertheless
Is known to be the wisest woman in Europe,   45
With a wicked pack of cards. Here, said she,

---

20. Son of man—"Cf. Ezekiel II, i" (Eliot). **23. cricket**—"Cf. Ecclesiastes XII, v" (Eliot). **31-34. Frisch . . . du?**—"V[ide] *Tristan und Isolde,* I, verses 5-8" (Eliot). "The wind of home blows fresh—my Irish child, where do you linger?" From the song by the young sailor which opens Wagner's opera. **42. Od' . . . Meer**—"Id. III, verse 24" (Eliot). "Waste and empty the sea—" a phrase sung by a shepherd at the opening of Act III while the companion of the unconscious Tristan looks for the ship that is to bring Isolde. Printed as "Oed'" in subsequent editions. **43. clairvoyante**—a woman gifted with the ability to see objects not visible to the senses. **45. wisest**—a "wise woman" is a fortune-teller. **46. wicked**—in the slang sense, "terrific." **46. pack of cards**—"I am not familiar with the exact constitution of the Tarot pack of cards, from which I have obviously departed to suit my own convenience. The Hanged Man, a member of the traditional pack, fits my purpose in two ways: because he is associated in my mind with the Hanged God of Frazer, and because I associate him with the hooded figure in the passage of the disciples to Emmaus in Part V. The Phoenician Sailor and Merchant appear later; also the 'crowds of people,' and Death by Water is executed in Part IV. The Man with Three Staves (an authentic member of the Tarot pack) I associate, quite arbitrarily, with the Fisher King himself" (Eliot). Tarot cards, used both for a game and for fortune-telling, are 78 in number, 22 of them being emblematical. The Hanged Man, the Wheel, and the Man with the Three Staves (appropriate to the Fisher King, who has a trident) are actual cards in the pack.

Is your card, the drowned Phoenician Sailor,
(Those are pearls that were his eyes. Look!)
Here is Belladonna, the Lady of the Rocks,
The lady of situations.　　　　　　　　　　　　　　　　　　　50
Here is the man with three staves, and here the Wheel,
And here is the one-eyed merchant, and this card,
Which is blank, is something he carries on his back,
Which I am forbidden to see. I do not find
The Hanged Man. Fear death by water.　　　　　　　　　55
I see crowds of people, walking round in a ring.
Thank you. If you see dear Mrs. Equitone,
Tell her I bring the horoscope myself:
One must be so careful these days.

Unreal City,　　　　　　　　　　　　　　　　　　　　　60
Under the brown fog of a winter dawn,
A crowd flowed over London Bridge, so many,
I had not thought death had undone so many.
Sighs, short and infrequent, were exhaled.
And each man fixed his eyes before his feet.　　　　　　65
Flowed up the hill and down King William Street,
To where Saint Mary Woolnoth kept the hours
With a dead sound on the final stroke of nine.
There I saw one I knew, and stopped him, crying: "Stetson!
"You who were with me in the ships at Mylae!　　　　70
"That corpse you planted last year in your garden,
"Has it begun to sprout? Will it bloom this year?
"Or has the sudden frost disturbed its bed?

48. pearls—"Those are pearls that were his eyes." From Ariel's song in *The Tempest*, Act I,
sc. ii. **49. Belladonna . . . Rocks**—an imagined Tarot card, but there are vague overtones
of an implied reference to Leonardo da Vinci's painting, "Virgin of the Rocks." **60. Unreal
City**—"Cf. Baudelaire:

　　　　　'Fourmillante cité, cité pleine de rêves,
　　　　　'Où le spectre en plein jour raccroche le passant' "　(Eliot).

"Swarming city filled with dreams, where in full daylight a ghost accosts the passerby," the
opening lines of Baudelaire's poem, "Les Sept Veillards." **63. had not thought**—"Cf. *Inferno*
III, 55-57:
　　　　　　　　　　　　'si lunga tratta
　　　　　　　di gente, ch'io non avrei mai creduto
　　　　　　　che morte tanta n'avesse disfatta' "　(Eliot).

"So long a train of people, I never should have believed death had undone so many." Said by
Dante as he sees those this side of Acheron, who were neither for God nor for His enemies. **64.
Sighs . . . exhaled**—"Cf. *Inferno* IV 25-27:
　　　　　　　'Quivi, secondo che per ascoltare,
　　　　　　　non avea pianto, ma' che di sospiri,
　　　　　　　che l'aura eterna facevan tremare' "　(Eliot).

"Here, as one listened, there was no complaining, but only sighs, which made the eternal air
tremble." Dante so describes the life of those in Limbo, who, having lived before Christ and being
virtuous, yet cannot be saved. **65-66. each . . . Street**—reminiscent of another passage in
the *Inferno*, XVIII, 27-33, in which Dante compares the lines of panderers to the throngs passing
in opposite directions over the bridge of Sant' Angelo in Rome during the Jubilee. **67. Mary
Woolnoth**—the church rebuilt in 1716 by Hawksmoore, a pupil of Sir Christopher Wren,
standing at the corner of King William and Lombard Streets in the "City." **68. dead sound**—
"A phenomenon which I have often noticed" (Eliot). **70. Mylae**—The Romans defeated the
Carthaginians in the naval battle of Mylae, 260 B.C., i.e., all wars are the same.

"Oh keep the Dog far hence, that's friend to men,
"Or with his nails he'll dig it up again!
"You! hypocrite lecteur!—mon semblable,—mon frère!"   75

II. A GAME OF CHESS *

The Chair she sat in, like a burnished throne,
Glowed on the marble, where the glass
Held up by standards wrought with fruited vines
From which a golden Cupidon peeped out   80
(Another hid his eyes behind his wing)
Doubled the flames of sevenbranched candelabra
Reflecting light upon the table as
The glitter of her jewels rose to meet it,
From satin cases poured in rich profusion;   85
In vials of ivory and coloured glass
Unstoppered, lurked her strange synthetic perfumes,
Unguent, powdered, or liquid—troubled, confused
And drowned the sense in odours; stirred by the air
That freshened from the window, these ascended   90
In fattening the prolonged candle-flames,
Flung their smoke into the laquearia,
Stirring the pattern on the coffered ceiling.
Huge sea-wood fed with copper
Burned green and orange, framed by the coloured stone,   95
In which sad light a carvèd dolphin swam.
Above the antique mantel was displayed
As though a window gave upon the sylvan scene
The change of Philomel, by the barbarous king
So rudely forced; yet there the nightingale   100
Filled all the desert with inviolable voice
And still she cried, and still the world pursues,
"Jug Jug" to dirty ears.
And other withered stumps of time
Were told upon the walls; staring forms   105
Leaned out, leaning, hushing the room enclosed.
Footsteps shuffled on the stair.
Under the firelight, under the brush, her hair

74-75. **"Oh keep . . . again"**—"Cf. the Dirge in Webster's *White Devil*" (Eliot). This dirge, beginning "But keep the Wolf" is in Act V, sc. iv. **76. "You! . . . frère!"**—"V[ide] Baudelaire, Preface to *Fleurs du Mal*" (Eliot). The phrase means: "hypocritical reader, my likeness, my brother." * **Game of Chess**—*cf.* note to line 138. **77 ff. The Chair**—"Cf. [Shakespeare's] *Antony and Cleopatra*, II, ii. l. 190" (Eliot). And the succeeding lines. **92. laquearia** —"V. *Æneid*, I, 726:

> dependent lychni laquearibus aureis
> incensi, et noctem flammis funalia vincunt" (Eliot).

"There, blazing from the gilded roof, are seen/ Bright lamps, and torches turn the night to day" (E. F. Taylor's translation). **93. coffered**—A coffer is an ornamental panel sunk into a ceiling. **98. sylvan scene**—"V. Milton, *Paradise Lost*, IV, 140" (Eliot). The phrase is the keynote of the description of the Garden of Eden. **99. Philomel**—"V. Ovid, *Metamorphoses*, VI, Philomela" (Eliot). After raping her, King Tereus cut out the tongue of Philomela in order to keep his secret, but Philomela was afterwards changed into a nightingale. **100. nightingale**—"Cf. Part III, l. 204" (Eliot). **103. "Jug Jug"**—vulgar imitation of the nightingale's song.

Spread out in fiery points
Glowed into words, then would be savagely still.   110

"My nerves are bad to-night. Yes, bad. Stay with me.
"Speak to me. Why do you never speak? Speak.
"What are you thinking of? What thinking? What?
"I never know what you are thinking. Think."

I think we are in rats' alley   115
Where the dead men lost their bones.

"What is that noise?"
                        The wind under the door.
"What is that noise now? What is the wind doing?"
                        Nothing again nothing.   120
                                            "Do
"You know nothing? Do you see nothing? Do you remember
"Nothing?"
            I remembeı
Those are pearls that were his eyes.   125
"Are you alive, or not? Is there nothing in your head?"
                                            But

O O O O that Shakespeherian Rag—
It's so elegant
So intelligent   130
"What shall I do now? What shall I do?"
"I shall rush out as I am, and walk the street
"With my hair down, so. What shall we do to-morrow?
"What shall we ever do?"
                        The hot water at ten.   135
And if it rains, a closed car at four.
And we shall play a game of chess,
Pressing lidless eyes and waiting for a knock upon the door.

When Lil's husband got demobbed, I said—
I didn't mince my words, I said to her myself,   140

HURRY UP PLEASE ITS TIME
Now Albert's coming back, make yourself a bit smart.
He'll want to know what you done with that money he gave you
To get yourself some teeth. He did, I was there.
You have them all out, Lil, and get a nice set,   145
He said, I swear, I can't bear to look at you.
And no more can't I, I said, and think of poor Albert,
He's been in the army four years, he wants a good time,

---

115. rats' alley—"Cf. Part III, l. 194" (Eliot). **118. wind . . . door**—"Cf. Webster: 'Is
the wind in that door still?'" (Eliot). **128. Rag**—ragtime. **138. knock upon the door**—
"Cf. the game of chess in Middleton's *Women beware Women*" (Eliot). In Act. II, sc. ii, a
widowed mother is kept occupied playing chess while her daughter-in-law is being more or less
forcibly seduced in another room. Middleton also has a play called *A Game of Chess*. **139. demobbed**—demobilized, i.e., after World War I. **141. Hurry . . . time**—The owner of the
London "pub" where the conversation takes place concerning Lil and Albert is warning his
customers it is closing time.

And if you don't give it him, there's others will, I said.
Oh is there, she said. Something o' that, I said.   150
Then I'll know who to thank, she said, and give me a straight look.
HURRY UP PLEASE ITS TIME
If you don't like it you can get on with it, I said.
Others can pick and choose if you can't.
But if Albert makes off, it won't be for lack of telling.   155
You ought to be ashamed, I said, to look so antique.
(And her only thirty-one.)
I can't help it, she said, pulling a long face,
It's them pills I took, to bring it off, she said.
(She's had five already, and nearly died of young George.)   160
The chemist said it would be alright, but I've never been the same.
You *are* a proper fool, I said.
Well, if Albert won't leave you alone, there it is, I said,
What you get married for if you don't want children?
HURRY UP PLEASE ITS TIME   165
Well, that Sunday Albert was home, they had a hot gammon,
And they asked me in to dinner, to get the beauty of it hot—
HURRY UP PLEASE ITS TIME
HURRY UP PLEASE ITS TIME
Goonight Bill. Goonight Lou. Goonight May. Goonight.   170
Ta ta. Goonight. Goonight.
Good night, ladies, good night, sweet ladies, good night, good night.

III. THE FIRE SERMON *

The river's tent is broken: the last fingers of leaf
Clutch and sink into the wet bank. The wind
Crosses the brown land, unheard. The nymphs are departed.   175
Sweet Thames, run softly, till I end my song.
The river bears no empty bottles, sandwich papers,
Silk handkerchiefs, cardboard boxes, cigarette ends
Or other testimony of summer nights. The nymphs are departed.
And their friends, the loitering heirs of city directors;   180
Departed, have left no addresses.
By the waters of Leman I sat down and wept . . .
Sweet Thames, run softly till I end my song,
Sweet Thames, run softly, for I speak not loud or long.
But at my back in a cold blast I hear   185
The rattle of the bones, and chuckle spread from ear to ear.
A rat crept softly through the vegetation
Dragging its slimy belly on the bank
While I was fishing in the dull canal
On a winter evening round behind the gashouse   190

---

161. chemist—druggist. **161. alright**—so printed in the American edition. **166. gammon**
—the bottom part of a flitch or "side" of bacon. **172. sweet ladies**—*cf. Hamlet,* Act IV, sc. v.
* **The Fire Sermon**—*cf.* note to line 308 below. **176. Sweet . . . song**—"V. Spenser,
Prothalamion" (Eliot). The line is the refrain of the poem by Edmund Spenser. *Cf.* lines 183-84,
also from this poem. **182. By . . . wept**—*cf.* Ps. 137:1. **185. back**—*cf.* note to line 196.
189. fishing—intended to call up associations with the Fisher King image.

Musing upon the king my brother's wreck
And on the king my father's death before him.
White bodies naked on the low damp ground
And bones cast in a little low dry garret,
Rattled by the rat's foot only, year to year.   195
But at my back from time to time I hear
The sound of horns and motors, which shall bring
Sweeney to Mrs. Porter in the spring.
O the moon shone bright on Mrs. Porter
And on her daughter   200
They wash their feet in soda water
Et O ces voix d'enfants, chantant dans la coupole!

Twit twit twit
Jug jug jug jug jug jug
So rudely forc'd.   205
Tereu

Unreal City
Under the brown fog of a winter noon
Mr. Eugenides, the Smyrna merchant
Unshaven, with a pocket full of currants   210
C.i.f. London: documents at sight,
Asked me in demotic French
To luncheon at the Cannon Street Hotel
Followed by a weekend at the Metropole.

At the violet hour, when the eyes and back   215
Turn upward from the desk, when the human engine waits
Like a taxi throbbing waiting,

192. father's death—"Cf. *The Tempest*, I, ii" (Eliot). Ferdinand's first speech includes the lines:

> "Sitting on a bank,
> Weeping again the king my father's wreck,
> This music crept by me upon the waters."

196. at my back—"Cf. Marvell, *To His Coy Mistress*" (Eliot). The passage in Marvell runs: "But at my back I always hear/ Time's wingèd chariot hurrying near" (21-22). **197. sound of horns**—"Cf. Day, *Parliament of Bees*:

> 'When of the sudden, listening, you shall hear,
> 'A noise of horns and hunting, which shall bring
> 'Actaeon to Diana in the spring,
> 'Where all shall see her naked skin . . .'" (Eliot)

John Day (c. 1574-c. 1640) wrote twelve pastoral eclogues called *The Parliament of Bees*. **198. Sweeney**—the type in Eliot's poems of the sordid modern man. **199. O the moon**—"I do not know the origin of the ballad from which these lines are taken: it was reported to me from Sydney, Australia" (Eliot). There is, of course, a popular American song which opens with the line: "Oh the moon shone bright on pretty Redwing." **202. Et . . . coupole!**—"V. Verlaine, *Parsifal*" (Eliot). "And O those voices of children, singing in the dome," i.e., the footwashing in line 199 calls up a more religious image of children singing during the ceremony of footwashing by Parsifal, which precedes the cure of Anfortas and takes away the curse from the waste land. Parsifal has passed his trials and cured the king, and he is ready to see the Grail. Paul Verlaine (1844-1896), after a sordid life, was converted to Roman Catholicism in the 1870's. **206. Tereu**—the nightingale's song, this time in a form suggesting Tereus. Cf. note to line 99. **210. currants**—"The currants were quoted at a price 'carriage and insurance free to London'; and the Bill of Lading etc. were to be handed to the buyer upon payment of the sight draft" (Eliot). Cf. line 211. **212. demotic**—Demotic script was the vulgarized form of Egyptian writing; hence, popular or illiterate is meant.

I Tiresias, though blind, throbbing between two lives,
Old man with wrinkled female breasts, can see
At the violet hour, the evening hour that strives   220
Homeward, and brings the sailor home from sea,
The typist home at teatime, clears her breakfast, lights
Her stove, and lays out food in tins.
Out of the window perilously spread
Her drying combinations touched by the sun's last rays,   225
On the divan are piled (at night her bed)
Stockings, slippers, camisoles, and stays.
I Tiresias, old man with wrinkled dugs
Perceived the scene, and foretold the rest—
I too awaited the expected guest.   230
He, the young man carbuncular, arrives,
A small house agent's clerk, with one bold stare,

218. Tiresias—"Tiresias, although a mere spectator and not indeed a 'character,' is yet the most important personage in the poem, uniting all the rest. Just as the one-eyed merchant, seller of currants, melts into the Phoenician Sailor, and the latter is not wholly distinct from Ferdinand Prince of Naples, so all the women are one woman, and the two sexes meet in Tiresias. What Tiresias *sees,* in fact, is the substance of the poem. The whole passage from Ovid is of great anthropological interest:

> '. . . Cum Iunone iocos et maior vestra profecto est
> Quam, quae contingit maribus,' dixisse, 'voluptas.'
> Illa negat; placuit quae sit sententia docti
> Quaerere Tiresiae: venus huic erat utraque nota.
> Nam duo magnorum viridi coeuntia silva
> Corpora serpentum baculi violaverat ictu
> Deque viro factus, mirabile, femina septem
> Egerat autumnos; octavo rursus eosdem
> Vidit et 'est vestrae si tanta potentia plagae,'
> Dixit 'ut auctoris sortem in contraria mutet,
> Nunc quoque vos feriam!' percussis anguibus isdem
> Forma prior rediit genetivaque venit imago.
> Arbiter hic igitur sumptus de lite iocosa
> Dicta Iovis firmat; gravius Saturnia iusto
> Nec pro materia fertur doluisse suique
> Iudicis aeterna damnavit lumina nocte,
> At pater omnipotens (neque enim licet inrita cuiquam
> Facta dei fecisse deo) pro lumine adempto
> Scire futura dedit poenamque levavit honore." (Eliot)

"(Jupiter, made happy with nectar, put aside his heavy responsibilities in order to abandon himself to frolicking) with Juno, free from every sort of care, and he said to her: Your sex must have a greater pleasure in love than that which men experience. This she denied. Thereupon they agreed to ask the opinion of Tiresias, since he was experienced in the pleasures of both sexes. For with a blow of his staff he once struck two enormous serpents as they were coupling together in the green forest. At once (what a prodigy!) he was transformed into a woman, and kept his new form for seven autumns. In the eighth year, going back, he saw the very same serpents. 'If the blow I gave you was powerful enough to change the sex of your enemy,' he said, 'I am now going to strike you again.' Scarcely had the serpents been struck again when he returned to his former shape and seemed to be born a second time. Chosen to be the umpire of this sportive argument, he affirmed the opinion of Jupiter, but they say the daughter of Saturn thereupon experienced a lively sense of grievance little comporting with the cause which provoked it, and she therefore condemned the eyes of her judge to an eternity of darkness. But the omnipotent father, since no god has the right to annihilate the work of another god, thereupon gave him knowledge of the future in compensation for his blindness, and lightened his suffering by this honor." *Metamorphoses,* III:320-38. **221. Homeward . . . sea**—"This may not appear as exact as Sappho's lines, but I had in mind the 'longshore' or 'dory' fisherman, who returns at nightfall" (Eliot). The 149th fragment of Sappho (b. 600 B.C.?) contains the famous apostrophe to the Evening Star, "star that bringest back all that lightsome Dawn scattered afar."

One of the low on whom assurance sits
As a silk hat on a Bradford millionaire.
The time is now propitious, as he guesses,   235
The meal is ended, she is bored and tired,
Endeavours to engage her in caresses
Which still are unreproved, if undesired.
Flushed and decided, he assaults at once;
Exploring hands encounter no defence;   240
His vanity requires no response,
And makes a welcome of indifference.
(And I Tiresias have foresuffered all
Enacted on this same divan or bed;
I who have sat by Thebes below the wall   245
And walked among the lowest of the dead.)
Bestows one final patronising kiss,
And gropes his way, finding the stairs unlit . . .

She turns and looks a moment in the glass,
Hardly aware of her departed lover;   250
Her brain allows one half-formed thought to pass:
"Well now that's done: and I'm glad it's over."
When lovely woman stoops to folly and
Paces about her room again, alone,
She smoothes her hair with automatic hand,   255
And puts a record on the gramophone.

"This music crept by me upon the waters"
And along the Strand, up Queen Victoria Street.
O City city, I can sometimes hear
Beside a public bar in Lower Thames Street,   260
The pleasant whining of a mandoline
And a clatter and a chatter from within
Where fishmen lounge at noon: where the walls
Of Magnus Martyr hold
Inexplicable splendour of Ionian white and gold.   265

The river sweats
Oil and tar

234. **Bradford millionaire**—Bradford, in the West Riding of Yorkshire, is now a center
of industry and of the wool trade. It became a city in 1897. The implication is that its wealthy
men are vulgarians. **245. Thebes**—In the *Antigone* of Sophocles the blind Teresias is led by a
boy into the presence of the tyrant Creon, and tries in vain to warn him against the doom that
will follow in "slaying o'er the slain." In *Œdipus Tyrannus* he has a similar function. **253.
When lovely . . .**—"V. Goldsmith, the song in *The Vicar of Wakefield*" (Eliot). See
Chapter 24. **257. This music**—"V. *The Tempest,* as above" (Eliot), i.e., note to line 192.
260. Lower Thames Street—i.e., in a part of London frequented by fishermen, as contrasted with the more fashionable and modern Strand. **264. Magnus Martyr**—"The interior
of St. Magnus Martyr is to my mind one of the finest among Wren's interiors. See *The Proposed
Demolition of Nineteen City Churches:* [P. S. King & Son, Ltd.]" (Eliot). **265. Ionian**—here,
loosely equivalent to Athenian. **266. The river sweats**—"The Song of the [three] Thames-
daughters begins here. From line 292 to 306 inclusive they speak in turn. V. *Götterdämmerung,*
III, i: the Rhine-daughters" (Eliot). At the opening of Act III of Wagner's opera the Rhine
maidens sing that the beauty of the Rhine river has gone since the gold of the Nibelungs has
been stolen from them, and ask the hero, Siegfried, to return the treasure to them, threatening
him with destruction if he does not. The meter in which they sing is imitated in this poem, and
the refrain in lines 277-78 is their refrain in the opera.

The barges drift
With the turning tide
Red sails   270
Wide
To leeward, swing on the heavy spar.
The barges wash
Drifting logs
Down Greenwich reach   275
Past the Isle of Dogs.

        Weialala leia
        Wallala leialala

Elizabeth and Leicester
Beating oars   280
The stern was formed
A gilded shell
Red and gold
The brisk swell
Rippled both shores   285
Southwest wind
Carried down stream
The peal of bells
White towers

        Weialala leia   290
        Wallala leialala

"Trams and dusty trees.
Highbury bore me. Richmond and Kew
Undid me. By Richmond I raised my knees
Supine on the floor of a narrow canoe."   295

  "My feet are at Moorgate, and my heart
  Under my feet. After the event

275-76. Greenwich . . . Dogs—at "Greenwich reach" the Thames broadens out; the Isle of Dogs is now the area of wharfs for great ocean-going ships. **279. Elizabeth and Leicester** —"V. Froude, *Elizabeth*, Vol. I, ch. iv, letter of De Quadra to Philip of Spain: 'In the afternoon we were in a barge, watching the games on the river. (The Queen) was alone with Lord Robert and myself on the poop, when they began to talk nonsense, and went so far that Lord Robert at last said, as I was on the spot there was no reason why they should not be married if the queen pleased' " (Eliot). De Quadra was a Catholic bishop and Spanish representative. Leicester was Robert Dudley, Earl of Leicester (1552?-1588), later captain-general of the queen's armies against the Spanish Armada. Note that the description of their barge recalls that of Cleopatra, for which see note to line 77. **293. Highbury**—"Cf. *Purgatorio*, V. 133:

        'Ricorditi di me, che son la Pia;
        Siena mi fe', disfecemi Maremma' " (Eliot).

In the outer part of Purgatory Dante meets the spirits who had delayed repentance and had met death by violence, yet died repentant. One of these was Pia, the wife of Tolomei, who said to Dante: Remember me, who am Pia. Siena made me, Maremma unmade me, i.e., I was born in Siena and put to death in Maremma. In "The Waste Land" a "girl of the people" parodies this passage. Richmond and Kew are park resorts on the Thames. **296. Moorgate**—In 1761 the old Moorgate of London Wall was pulled down. Today the name is preserved in Moorgate Street (near the Bank of England and the Stock Exchange) and in Moorgate Station (on the Underground). Moorfields, a parallel street on the west, preserves the memory of the marshy district outside the old Moorgate, once the resort of archers, washerwomen, and (later) of booksellers.

He wept. He promised 'a new start.'
I made no comment. What should I resent?"

"On Margate Sands.   300
I can connect
Nothing with nothing.
The broken fingernails of dirty hands.
My people humble people who expect
Nothing."   305

                            la la

To Carthage then I came

Burning burning burning burning
O Lord Thou pluckest me out
O Lord Thou pluckest   310

burning

IV. DEATH BY WATER *

Phlebas the Phoenician, a fortnight dead,
Forgot the cry of gulls, and the deep sea swell
And the profit and loss.
                        A current under sea   315
Picked his bones in whispers. As he rose and fell
He passed the stages of his age and youth
Entering the whirlpool.
                        Gentile or Jew
O you who turn the wheel and look to windward,   320
Consider Phlebas, who was once handsome and tall as you.

300. Margate—a seaside town not far from Dover, much frequented by "trippers." **307. To Carthage**—"V. St. Augustine's *Confessions*: 'to Carthage then I came, where a cauldron of unholy loves sang all about mine ears' " (Eliot). The opening phrase of the third book of the *Confessions*. **308. Burning**—"The complete text of the Buddha's Fire Sermon (which corresponds in importance to the Sermon on the Mount) from which these words are taken, will be found translated in the late Henry Clarke Warren's *Buddhism in Translation* (Harvard Oriental Series). Mr. Warren was one of the great pioneers of Buddhist studies in the Occident" (Eliot). Henry Clarke Warren (1854-1899), a wealthy amateur scholar of great distinction, made possible the issuing of the Harvard Oriental Series in 31 volumes, between 1891 and 1932, to which his own *Buddhism in Translation* (1896) was the most influential contribution, since much of it reappeared in the famous Harvard Classics (Five-Foot Shelf) edited by Charles W. Eliot. **309. O Lord**—"From St. Augustine's *Confessions* again. The collection of these two representatives of eastern and western asceticism, as the culmination of this part of the poem, is not an accident" (Eliot). This note is persistently referred to line 312 in editions of the poem. But line 312 has to do with Phlebas the Phoenician, whereas line 309, echoed in line 310, seems to refer to the passage near the end of Book VI of the *Confessions,* wherein Augustine, having suffered the loss of his concubine, praises God for being "continually ready to pluck me out of the mire, and to wash me thoroughly." * **Death by Water**—*cf.* line 55, above. **312. Phlebas**—*cf.* line 47, above. The general tone of this passage is that of the Sepulchral Epigrams in the *Greek Anthology,* many of which concern persons lost at sea.

V. WHAT THE THUNDER * SAID

After the torchlight red on sweaty faces
After the frosty silence in the gardens
After the agony in stony places
The shouting and the crying   325
Prison and palace and reverberation
Of thunder of spring over distant mountains
He who was living is now dead
We who were living are now dying
With a little patience   330

Here is no water but only rock
Rock and no water and the sandy road
The road winding above among the mountains
Which are mountains of rock without water
If there were water we should stop and drink   335
Amongst the rock one cannot stop or think
Sweat is dry and feet are in the sand
If there were only water amongst the rock
Dead mountain mouth of carious teeth that cannot spit
Here one can neither stand nor lie nor sit   340
There is not even silence in the mountains
But dry sterile thunder without rain
There is not even solitude in the mountains
But red sullen faces sneer and snarl
From doors of mudcracked houses   345
                                        If there were water
      And no rock
      If there were rock
      And also water
      And water   350
      A spring
      A pool among the rock
      If there were the sound of water only
      Not the cicada
      And dry grass singing   355
      But sound of water over a rock
      Where the hermit-thrush sings in the pine trees
      Drip drop drip drop drop drop drop
      But there is no water

* **Thunder**—"In the first part of Part V three themes are employed: the journey to Emmaus, the approach to the Chapel Perilous (see Miss Weston's book) and the present decay in eastern Europe" (Eliot). **322. torchlight**—The general picture is that of the arrest of Jesus in the Garden of Gethsemane, the agony, his imprisonment, his trial in the palace of Pilate, and his crucifixion, with the following earthquake (the reverberation of line 326). See, e.g., Mark 28:51 ff. **358. Drip drop**—"This is *Turdus aonalaschkae pallasii*, the hermit-thrush [*cf.* line 357] which I have heard in Quebec County. Chapman says (*Handbook of Birds of Eastern North America*) 'it is most at home in secluded woodland and thickety retreats. . . . Its notes are not remarkable for variety or volume, but in purity and sweetness of tone and exquisite modulation they are unequalled.' Its 'water-dripping song' is justly celebrated" (Eliot).

Who is the third who walks always beside you?   360
When I count, there are only you and I together
But when I look ahead up the white road
There is always another one walking beside you
Gliding wrapt in a brown mantle, hooded
I do not know whether a man or a woman   365
—But who is that on the other side of you?

What is that sound high in the air
Murmur of maternal lamentation
Who are those hooded hordes swarming
Over endless plains, stumbling in cracked earth   370
Ringed by the flat horizon only
What is the city over the mountains
Cracks and reforms and bursts in the violet air
Falling towers
Jerusalem Athens Alexandria   375
Vienna London
Unreal

A woman drew her long black hair out tight
And fiddled whisper music on those strings
And bats with baby faces in the violet light   380
Whistled, and beat their wings
And crawled head downward down a blackened wall
And upside down in air were towers
Tolling reminiscent bells, that kept the hours
And voices singing out of empty cisterns and exhausted wells.   385

In this decayed hole among the mountains
In the faint moonlight, the grass is singing
Over the tumbled graves, about the chapel
There is the empty chapel, only the wind's home.
It has no windows, and the door swings,   390
Dry bones can harm no one.
Only a cock stood on the rooftree

361. **When I count**—"The following lines were stimulated by the account of one of the Antarctic expeditions (I forget which, but I think one of Shackleton's): it was related that the party of explorers, at the extremity of their strength, had the constant delusion that there was *one more member* than could actually be counted" (Eliot). Sir Ernest Henry Shackleton, 1874-1922, made expeditions of major importance into Antarctica in 1908-09, 1914-17, 1921-22. **363. another one**—*cf.* Luke 24:13-31. **367-77. What . . . Unreal**—"Cf. Hermann Hesse, *Blick ins Chaos*: 'Schon ist halb Europa, schon ist zumindest der halbe Osten Europas auf dem Wege zum Chaos, fährt betrunken im heiligem Wahn am Abgrund entlang und singt dazu, singt betrunken und hymnisch wie Dmitri Karamasoff sang. Ueber diese Lieder lacht der Bürger beleidigt, der Heilige und Seher hört sie mit Tränen' " (Eliot). "Half Europe, or at the very least half of eastern Europe, is on the road to chaos, moving drunkenly along with a kind of sanctified insanity into the abyss, and at the same time it sings, sings drunkenly and as if it were singing hymns as Dmitri Karamazov sang [in *The Brothers Karamazov* by Dostoievski]. The insulted citizenry laughs over these songs, the saint and the seer hear them with tears." The book in question was published in 1920. **378. A woman**—This succession of creepy images is apparently occasioned in part by the initiatory mysteries of the visit to the Perilous Chapel in Weston's *From Ritual to Romance*. The chapel is mentioned in line 388. **392. cock**—In folklore the cock is supposed to chase away the powers of evil.

Co co rico co co rico
In a flash of lightning. Then a damp gust
Bringing rain   395
Ganga was sunken, and the limp leaves
Waited for rain, while the black clouds
Gathered far distant, over Himavant.
The jungle crouched, humped in silence.
Then spoke the thunder   400
DA
Datta: what have we given?
My friend, blood shaking my heart
The awful daring of a moment's surrender
Which an age of prudence can never retract   405
By this, and this only, we have existed
Which is not to be found in our obituaries
Or in memories draped by the beneficent spider
Or under seals broken by the lean solicitor
In our empty rooms   410
DA
Dayadhvam: I have heard the key
Turn in the door once and turn once only
We think of the key, each in his prison
Thinking of the key, each confirms a prison   415
Only at nightfall, aethereal rumours
Revive for a moment a broken Coriolanus
DA
Damyata: The boat responded
Gaily, to the hand expert with sail and oar   420
The sea was calm, your heart would have responded
Gaily, when invited, beating obedient
To controlling hands
                      I sat upon the shore
Fishing, with the arid plain behind me   425
Shall I at least set my lands in order?

396. **Ganga**—the river Ganges in India. 398. **Himavant**—Himalayas, the lofty mountains along the border between India and Tibet. 402. **Datta**—" 'Datta, dayadhvam, damyata' (Give, sympathise, control). The fable of the meaning of the Thunder is found in the *Brihadaranyaka-Upanishad*, 5, 1. A translation is found in Deussen's *Sechzig Upanishads des Veda*, p. 489" (Eliot). The Upanishads are a collection of essays on man and the universe dating from the sixth century, B.C., written in Sanskrit, and part of the Vedic writings. Veda ("Knowledge") refers to four sacred books of the Brahmins. 408. **spider**—"Cf. Webster, *The White Devil*, V, vi: '. . . they'll remarry/Ere the worm pierce your winding-sheet, ere the spider/Make a thin curtain for your epitaphs' " (Eliot). 412. **Dayadhvam**—See note to line 402. 412. **key**—"Cf. *Inferno*, XXXIII, 46: 'ed io sentii chiavar l'uscio di sotto/all' orribile torre' " (Eliot). ["And I heard the lower door of the tower being nailed up." Said to Dante by Count Ugolino, in the ninth circle of Hell, who ate his own children.] "Also F. H. Bradley, *Appearance and Reality*, p. 346. 'My external sensations are no less private to myself than are my thoughts or my feelings. In either case my experience falls within my own circle, a circle closed on the outside; and, with all its elements alike, every sphere is opaque to the others which surround it. . . . In brief, regarded as an existence which appears in a soul, the whole world for each is peculiar and private to that soul' " (Eliot). Francis Herbert Bradley (1846-1924), British philosopher, whose *Appearance and Reality* (1893) stirred the world of philosophy as a renewed discussion of the nature of the absolute. 417. **Coriolanus**—*cf.* Shakespeare's tragedy, *Coriolanus*. 419. **Damyata**—*cf.* note to line 402. 425. **Fishing**—"V. Weston: *From Ritual to Romance;* chapter on the Fisher King" (Eliot).

London Bridge is falling down falling down falling down
Poi s'ascose nel foco che gli affina
Quando fiam uti chelidon—O swallow swallow
Le Prince d'Aquitaine à la tour abolie   430
These fragments I have shored against my ruins
Why then Ile fit you. Hieronymo's mad againe.
Datta. Dayadhvam. Damyata.
              Shantih   shantih   shantih

TRADITION AND THE INDIVIDUAL TALENT

This essay first appeared, in two parts, in *The Egoist* (London), September-December, 1919, at a time when Eliot was an assistant editor of the journal. It was collected with other pieces for *The Sacred Wood: Essays on Poetry and Criticism,* London, 1920, and again appeared in *Selected Essays: 1917-1932,* New York, 1932. The text here reprinted is from the latter volume. The essay has been translated into French, German, Spanish, Danish, and Japanese.

In English writing we seldom speak of tradition, though we occasionally apply its name in deploring its absence. We cannot refer to "the tradition" or to "a tradition"; at most, we employ the adjective in saying that the poetry of So-and-so is "traditional" or even "too traditional." Seldom, perhaps, does the word appear except in a phrase of censure. If otherwise, it is vaguely approba- 5 tive, with the implication, as to the work approved, of some pleasing archaeo-logical reconstruction. You can hardly make the word agreeable to English

428. Poi—"V. *Purgatorio,* XXVI, 148.

> 'Ara vos prec per aquella valor
> 'que vos guida al som de l'escalina,
> 'sovegna vos a temps de ma dolor.'
> Poi s'ascose nel foco che gli affina" (Eliot).

In the seventh ledge of the Mountain of Purgatory, devoted to the cleansing of the lustful, Dante meets the Provençal poet, Arnaut Daniel, who says to him in part: " 'I now pray you by that power which guides you to the top of this stairway, remember in proper season my pains.' He then hid himself in the fire which refines them." **429. Quando . . . chelidon.**—"V. *Pervigilium Veneris.* Cf. Philomela in Parts II and III" (Eliot). The quotation means: "When shall I be like a swallow?" The *Pervigilium Veneris,* a Latin poem celebrating love and spring, was written probably in the second century A.D. **430. Le Prince . . . abolie.**—"V. Gerard de Nerval, Sonnet *El Desdichado*" (Eliot). Gérard de Nerval, pen-name of Gérard Labrunie (1808-1855), author of *Les Chimères.* The first poem in this work is "El Desdichado" (The Unhappy One), a series of images implying melancholy. Since the sonnet was suggested by "The Disinherited Knight" in Scott's *Ivanhoe,* the Prince d'Aquitaine is probably Richard Cœur de Lion and the "tour" is the tower in which he was imprisoned. The line means: "The Prince of Aquitaine at the ruined tower." **432. Why . . . againe.**—"V. Kyd's *Spanish Tragedy*" (Eliot). See Act IV, sc. i, line 67 and the subtitle of the play. The words "Why then Ile fit you." (meaning "I will accommodate you in your plans") come at the point in the play when Hieronymo prepares an entertainment to amuse the murderers of his son. **434. Shantih**—"Shantih. Repeated as here, a formal ending to an Upanishad. 'The Peace which passeth understanding' is our equivalent to this word" (Eliot). Cf. Phil. 4:7: "The peace of God, which passeth all understanding."

ears without this comfortable reference to the reassuring science of archaeology.

Certainly the word is not likely to appear in our appreciations of living or dead writers. Every nation, every race, has not only its own creative, but its own
5   critical turn of mind; and is even more oblivious of the shortcomings and limitations of its critical habits than of those of its creative genius. We know, or think we know, from the enormous mass of critical writing that has appeared in the French language the critical method or habit of the French; we only conclude (we are such unconscious people) that the French are "more criti-
10 cal" than we, and sometimes even plume ourselves a little with the fact, as if the French were the less spontaneous. Perhaps they are; but we might remind ourselves that criticism is as inevitable as breathing, and that we should be none the worse for articulating what passes in our minds when we read a book and feel an emotion about it, for criticizing our own minds in their
15 work of criticism. One of the facts that might come to light in this process is our tendency to insist, when we praise a poet, upon those aspects of his work in which he least resembles any one else. In these aspects or parts of his work we pretend to find what is individual, what is the peculiar essence of the man. We dwell with satisfaction upon the poet's difference from his predecessors,
20 especially his immediate predecessors; we endeavour to find something that can be isolated in order to be enjoyed. Whereas if we approach a poet without this prejudice we shall often find that not only the best, but the most individual parts of his work may be those in which the dead poets, his ancestors, assert their immortality most vigorously. And I do not mean the impression-
25 able period of adolescence, but the period of full maturity.

Yet if the only form of tradition, of handing down, consisted in following the ways of the immediate generation before us in a blind or timid adherence to its successes, "tradition" should positively be discouraged. We have seen many such simple currents soon lost in the sand; and novelty is better than
30 repetition. Tradition is a matter of much wider significance. It cannot be inherited, and if you want it you must obtain it by great labour. It involves, in the first place, the historical sense, which we may call nearly indispensable to any one who would continue to be a poet beyond his twenty-fifth year; and the historical sense involves a perception, not only of the pastness of the past,
35 but of its presence; the historical sense compels a man to write not merely with his own generation in his bones, but with a feeling that the whole of the literature of Europe from Homer and within it the whole of the literature of his own country has a simultaneous existence and composes a simultaneous order. This historical sense, which is a sense of the timeless as well as of the
40 temporal and of the timeless and of the temporal together, is what makes a writer traditional. And it is at the same time what makes a writer most acutely conscious of his place in time, of his own contemporaneity.

No poet, no artist of any art, has his complete meaning alone. His significance, his appreciation is the appreciation of his relation to the dead poets and
45 artists. You cannot value him alone; you must set him, for contrast and com-

parison, among the dead. I mean this as a principle of aesthetic, not merely historical, criticism. The necessity that he shall conform, that he shall cohere, is not onesided; what happens when a new work of art is created is something that happens simultaneously to all the works of art which preceded it. The existing monuments form an ideal order among themselves, which is modified by the introduction of the new (the really new) work of art among them. The existing order is complete before the new work arrives; for order to persist after the supervention of novelty, the *whole* existing order must be, if ever so slightly, altered; and so the relations, proportions, values of each work of art toward the whole are readjusted; and this is conformity between the old and the new. Whoever has approved this idea of order, of the form of European, of English literature will not find it preposterous that the past should be altered by the present as much as the present is directed by the past. And the poet who is aware of this will be aware of great difficulties and responsibilities.

In a peculiar sense he will be aware also that he must inevitably be judged by the standards of the past. I say judged, not amputated, by them; not judged to be as good as, or worse or better than, the dead; and certainly not judged by the canons of dead critics. It is a judgment, a comparison, in which two things are measured by each other. To conform merely would be for the new work not really to conform at all; it would not be new, and would therefore not be a work of art. And we do not quite say that the new is more valuable because it fits in; but its fitting in is a test of its value—a test, it is true, which can only be slowly and cautiously applied, for we are none of us infallible judges of conformity. We say: it appears to conform, and is perhaps individual, or it appears individual, and may conform; but we are hardly likely to find that it is one and not the other.

To proceed to a more intelligible exposition of the relation of the poet to the past: he can neither take the past as a lump, an indiscriminate bolus, nor can he form himself wholly on one or two private admirations, nor can he form himself wholly upon one preferred period. The first course is inadmissible, the second is an important experience of youth, and the third is a pleasant and highly desirable supplement. The poet must be very conscious of the main current, which does not at all flow invariably through the most distinguished reputations. He must be quite aware of the obvious fact that art never improves, but that the material of art is never quite the same. He must be aware that the mind of Europe—the mind of his own country—a mind which he learns in time to be much more important than his own private mind—is a mind which changes, and that this change is a development which abandons nothing *en route,* which does not superannuate either Shakespeare, or Homer, or the rock drawing of the Magdalenian draughtsmen. That this develop-

---

29. **bolus**—a large "cure-all" pill. 41. **Magdalenian draughtsmen**—"Magdalenian" is a term referring to the culture of the last part of the Palaeolithic period. In caves in La Madeleine in France prehistoric artists sketched pictures, especially of animals, of surprising beauty on the cave walls.

ment, refinement perhaps, complication certainly, is not, from the point of
view of the artist, any improvement. Perhaps not even an improvement from
the point of view of the psychologist or not to the extent which we imagine;
perhaps only in the end based upon a complication in economics and ma-
5 chinery. But the difference between the present and the past is that the conscious present is an awareness of the past in a way and to an extent which
the past's awareness of itself cannot show.

Some one said: "The dead writers are remote from us because we *know* so
much more than they did." Precisely, and they are that which we know.

10 I am alive to a usual objection to what is clearly part of my programme for
the *métier* of poetry. The objection is that the doctrine requires a ridiculous
amount of erudition (pedantry), a claim which can be rejected by appeal to
the lives of poets in any pantheon. It will even be affirmed that much learning deadens or perverts poetic sensibility. While, however, we persist in be-
15 lieving that a poet ought to know as much as will not encroach upon his necessary receptivity and necessary laziness, it is not desirable to confine knowledge to whatever can be put into a useful shape for examinations, drawing-
rooms, or the still more pretentious modes of publicity. Some can absorb
knowledge, the more tardy must sweat for it. Shakespeare acquired more es-
20 sential history from Plutarch than most men could from the whole British
Museum. What is to be insisted upon is that the poet must develop or procure the consciousness of the past and that he should continue to develop this
consciousness throughout his career.

What happens is a continual surrender of himself as he is at the moment to
25 something which is more valuable. The progress of an artist is a continual
self-sacrifice, a continual extinction of personality.

There remains to define this process of depersonalization and its relation
to the sense of tradition. It is in this depersonalization that art may be said to
approach the condition of science. I, therefore, invite you to consider, as a
30 suggestive analogy, the action which takes place when a bit of finely filiated
platinum is introduced into a chamber containing oxygen and sulphur dioxide.

II

Honest criticism and sensitive appreciation are directed not upon the poet
but upon the poetry. If we attend to the confused cries of the newspaper
35 critics and the *susurrus* of popular repetition that follows, we shall hear the
names of poets in great numbers; if we seek not Blue-book knowledge but
the enjoyment of poetry, and ask for a poem, we shall seldom find it. I have
tried to point out the importance of the relation of the poem to other poems
by other authors, and suggested the conception of poetry as a living whole of
40 all the poetry that has ever been written. The other aspect of this Impersonal
theory of poetry is the relation of the poem to its author. And I hinted, by an

11. **métier**—occupation, business. 35. **susurrus**—whispering. 36. **Blue-book**—official publications of the British government are known as Blue books.

analogy, that the mind of the mature poet differs from that of the immature one not precisely in any valuation of "personality," not being necessarily more interesting, or having "more to say," but rather by being a more finely perfected medium in which special, or very varied, feelings are at liberty to enter into new combinations.   5

The analogy was that of the catalyst. When the two gases previously mentioned are mixed in the presence of a filament of platinum, they form sulphurous acid. This combination takes place only if the platinum is present; nevertheless the newly formed acid contains no trace of platinum and the platinum itself is apparently unaffected; has remained inert, neutral, and unchanged.   10 The mind of the poet is the shred of platinum. It may partly or exclusively operate upon the experience of the man himself; but, the more perfect the artist, the more completely separate in him will be the man who suffers and the mind which creates; the more perfectly will the mind digest and transmute the passions which are its material.   15

The experience, you will notice, the elements which enter the presence of the transforming catalyst, are of two kinds: emotions and feelings. The effect of a work of art upon the person who enjoys it is an experience different in kind from any experience not of art. It may be formed out of one emotion, or may be a combination of several; and various feelings, inhering for the   20 writer in particular words or phrases or images, may be added to compose the final result. Or great poetry may be made without the direct use of any emotion whatever: composed out of feelings solely. Canto XV of the *Inferno* (Brunetto Latini) is a working up of the emotion evident in the situation; but the effect, though single as that of any work of art, is obtained by considerable complexity of detail. The last quatrain gives an image, a feeling attaching to an image, which "came," which did not develop simply out of what precedes, but which was probably in suspension in the poet's mind until the proper combination arrived for it to add itself to. The poet's mind is in fact a receptacle for seizing and storing up numberless feelings, phrases, images,   30 which remain there until all the particles which can unite to form a new compound are present together.

If you compare several representative passages of the greatest poetry you see how great is the variety of types of combination, and also how completely any semi-ethical criterion of "sublimity" misses the mark. For it is not the   35 "greatness," the intensity, of the emotions, the components, but the intensity of the artistic process, the pressure, so to speak, under which the fusion takes place, that counts. The episode of Paolo and Francesca employs a definite emotion, but the intensity of the poetry is something quite different from whatever intensity in the supposed experience it may give the impression of. It is   40

26. last quatrain—lines 121-124 of the Canto, to the effect that he (Brunetto Latini) then turned back like one of those who run across the plain at Verona for the green cloth (prize), and he seemed to be the one who wins and not the one who loses. 38. Paolo and Francesca— In Canto V of the *Inferno* Dante meets the shades of the lovers Paolo and Francesca, whose tragic story so affects him that he swoons.

no more intense, furthermore, than Canto XXVI, the voyage of Ulysses, which
has not the direct dependence upon an emotion. Great variety is possible in
the process of transmutation of emotion: the murder of Agamemnon, or the
agony of Othello, gives an artistic effect apparently closer to a possible original
than the scenes from Dante. In the *Agamemnon,* the artistic emotion approximates to the emotion of an actual spectator; in *Othello* to the emotion of the
protagonist himself. But the difference between art and the event is always
absolute; the combination which is the murder of Agamemnon is probably as
complex as that which is the voyage of Ulysses. In either case there has been a
fusion of elements. The ode of Keats contains a number of feelings which have
nothing particular to do with the nightingale, but which the nightingale,
partly, perhaps, because of its attractive name, and partly because of its reputation, served to bring together.

The point of view which I am struggling to attack is perhaps related to the
metaphysical theory of the substantial unity of the soul: for my meaning is,
that the poet has, not a "personality" to express, but a particular medium,
which is only a medium and not a personality, in which impressions and experiences combine in peculiar and unexpected ways. Impressions and experiences which are important for the man may take no place in the poetry, and
those which become important in the poetry may play quite a negligible part
in the man, the personality.

I will quote a passage which is unfamiliar enough to be regarded with fresh
attention in the light—or darkness—of these observations:

> *And now methinks I could e'en chide myself*
> *For doating on her beauty, though her death*
> *Shall be revenged after no common action.*
> *Does the silkworm expend her yellow labours*
> *For thee? For thee does she undo herself?*
> *Are lordships sold to maintain ladyships*
> *For the poor benefit of a bewildering minute?*
> *Why does yon fellow falsify highways,*
> *And put his life between the judge's lips,*
> *To refine such a thing—keeps horse and men*
> *To beat their valours for her? . . .*

In this passage (as is evident if it is taken in its context) there is a combination of positive and negative emotions: an intensely strong attraction toward
beauty and an equally intense fascination by the ugliness which is contrasted
with it and which destroys it. This balance of contrasted emotion is in the
dramatic situation to which the speech is pertinent, but that situation alone is
inadequate to it. This is, so to speak, the structural emotion, provided by the

1. **Canto XXVI**—of the *Inferno,* in which the supposed voyage of Ulysses reveals a great
deal of medieval geography. **24-34. And now . . . for her?**—Cyril Tourneur, *The Revenger's
Tragedy,* edited by Allardyce Nicoll (London, The Franfrolico Press, 1929), Act III, sc. v,
lines 71-82.

drama. But the whole effect, the dominant tone, is due to the fact that a number of floating feelings, having an affinity to this emotion by no means superficially evident, have combined with it to give us a new art emotion.

It is not in his personal emotions, the emotions provoked by particular events in his life, that the poet is in any way remarkable or interesting. His 5 particular emotions may be simple, or crude, or flat. The emotion in his poetry will be a very complex thing, but not with the complexity of the emotions of people who have very complex or unusual emotions in life. One error, in fact, of eccentricity in poetry is to seek for new human emotions to express; and in this search for novelty in the wrong place it discovers the perverse. The 10 business of the poet is not to find new emotions, but to use the ordinary ones and, in working them up into poetry, to express feelings which are not in actual emotions at all. And emotions which he has never experienced will serve his turn as well as those familiar to him. Consequently, we must believe that "emotion recollected in tranquillity" is an inexact formula. For it is 15 neither emotion, nor recollection, nor, without distortion of meaning, tranquillity. It is a concentration, and a new thing resulting from the concentration, of a very great number of experiences which to the practical and active person would not seem to be experiences at all; it is a concentration which does not happen consciously or of deliberation. These experiences are not 20 "recollected," and they finally unite in an atmosphere which is "tranquil" only in that it is a passive attending upon the event. Of course this is not quite the whole story. There is a great deal, in the writing of poetry, which must be conscious and deliberate. In fact, the bad poet is usually unconscious where he ought to be conscious, and conscious where he ought to be uncon 25 scious. Both errors tend to make him "personal." Poetry is not a turning loose of emotion, but an escape from emotion; it is not the expression of personality, but an escape from personality. But, of course, only those who have personality and emotions know what it means to want to escape from these things. 30

III

ὁ δὲ νοῦς ἴσως Θειότερόν τι καὶ ἀπαθές ἐστιν.

This essay proposes to halt at the frontier of metaphysics or mysticism, and confine itself to such practical conclusions as can be applied by the responsible person interested in poetry. To divert interest from the poet to the poetry is 35 a laudable aim: for it would conduce to a juster estimation of actual poetry, good and bad. There are many people who appreciate the expression of sincere emotion in verse, and there is a smaller number of people who can appreciate technical excellence. But very few know when there is an expression of *significant* emotion, emotion which has its life in the poem and not in the 40

<hr>

16-17. **emotion . . . tranquillity**—a key phrase in Wordsworth's famous preface to the second (1800) edition of *Lyrical Ballads* by Coleridge and Wordsworth. **32.** ὁ δὲ . . . ἐστιν.— "The mind seems to be something diviner and unaffected." See Aristotle, *de Anima*, Chap. IV, 408b29.

history of the poet. The emotion of art is impersonal. And the poet cannot reach this impersonality without surrendering himself wholly to the work to be done. And he is not likely to know what is to be done unless he lives in what is not merely the present, but the present moment of the past, unless he
5 is conscious, not of what is dead, but of what is already living.

ARCHIBALD MAC LEISH

1892 -

I. THE HAMLET OF A. MAC LEISH (1892–1928)

1892 Archibald MacLeish was born in Glencoe, Illinois, May 7, 1892, the son of Andrew and Martha (Hillard) MacLeish.

1911 Entered Yale University after attending public schools and the Hotchkiss School, Lakeville, Connecticut. At Yale he distinguished himself in literature and student activities and was a member of a group including Stephen Vincent Benét and Thornton Wilder.

1915 Graduated from Yale (B.A.), Phi Beta Kappa and class poet. The Yale University Press published both the class poem and a prize poem. MacLeish also published a pamphlet containing a cycle of sonnets, *Songs for a Summer's Day*.

1915–1916 Student in the Harvard Law School (LL.B., 1919).

1916 Married Ada Hitchcock June 21. (Three children were born of this marriage.)

1917 Published *Tower of Ivory*. Enlisted as private in the United States Army and was sent to France, where he was transferred to field artillery and served for twelve months.

1918 Ordered home as a training officer; ended military service as a captain of field artillery; discharged in February, 1919.

1919–1923 Teacher in Harvard Law School; practicing lawyer in Boston.

1923 Removed with his family to Paris; traveled extensively in subsequent years in Southern Europe, the Mediterranean, and the Near East.

1924 *The Happy Marriage.*

1925 *The Pot of Earth,* also *Nobodaddy* (verse plays).

1926 *Streets in the Moon.*

1928 *The Hamlet of A. MacLeish.* Returned to America, living at Stonington, Connecticut.

II. THE REDISCOVERY OF AMERICA (1928–1939)

1929 Trip along Cortés's route from the seacoast to Mexico City, as part of the preparation for *Conquistador*. Won the John Reed Memorial Prize (in the gift of *Poetry: A Magazine of Verse*.)

1929–1930 Beginning of connection with *Fortune* magazine and of research work and travel at home and abroad in the interests of this magazine. Separate articles by him from *Fortune* have been published separately, such as *Housing America* (1932); *Jews in America* (1936); *Background of War* (1937).

1930 *New Found Land.*

1932   *Conquistador,* which won the Pulitzer Prize for Poetry. Awarded an honorary M.A. degree by Tufts College, the first of some twelve honorary degrees.

1933   *Frescoes for Mr. Rockefeller's City,* which aroused controversy; and *Poems, 1929-1933,* a collected edition containing those poems he could reread "without embarrassment."

1934   *Union Pacific: A Ballet.*

1935   *Panic* (verse play).

1936   *Public Speech* (poems).

1937   *The Fall of the City* (verse play for radio). Increasingly alarmed by public indifference to the fight against fascism in Spain, he joined Hemingway and Dos Passos in a campaign of public education.

1938   *The Land of the Free;* also *Air Raid* (verse play for radio). Made curator (and in fact director) of the Nieman Collection of Journalism at Harvard and of the Nieman fellowships in journalism.

III. MAN OF LETTERS AND PUBLIC SERVANT (1939–   )

1939   *America Was Promises.* Appointed Librarian of Congress, a post he held until 1944.

1940   *The Irresponsibles.*

1941   *The American Cause.* Director, United States Office of Facts and Figures, 1941-42, making many influential addresses on war issues. Published *A Time to Speak.*

1942   Rede lecturer at Cambridge University, his lecture being *American Opinion of the War.* Appointed Assistant Director of the Office of War Information, 1942-43. Published *A Time to Act.*

1944   Appointed Assistant Secretary of State, 1944-45.

1945   Chairman American delegation to London Conference which drew up constitution for UNESCO, and later, delegate (to 1947).

1949   Boylston Professor of Rhetoric and Oratory, Harvard University.

There is no biography. For an incomplete bibliography see Frederic G. Melcher, "Check List of Archibald MacLeish," *Publishers' Weekly,* July 15, 1933, p. 180, and Arthur Mizener, *A Catalogue of the First Editions of Archibald MacLeish,* Yale University Library, 1938. See also *Literary History of the United States,* Vol. III, pp. 633-36. For critical comment the list of references in Fred B. Millett, *Contemporary American Authors,* Harcourt, Brace, 1940, p. 473, is useful. Since that work was issued, most of the printed comment on MacLeish has had to do with his official positions. For the controversy over his appointment as Librarian of Congress and the one concerning his nomination as Assistant Secretary of State, consult the *New York Times Index* and the files of *Time* and *News Week.*

Like H. L. Mencken in the twenties, Archibald MacLeish in the thirties has been a powerful force reshaping and altering the direction of literary history in the United States. As a younger man this poet underwent the experiences of the "lost generation" whose emotional sterility he has since repudiated; and no writer has been more obviously a disciple of T. S. Eliot. But though MacLeish admired Eliot, he was not overwhelmed by him; *The Hamlet of A. MacLeish* remains an individual and distinctive confession of spiritual turmoil. Eliot repudiated America;

MacLeish returned to it. He could not rest in the "Hamlet" tradition; and *Conquistador* was an act of faith in the American theme, an outward-facing poem which, though it narrates tragic events, is not, like *The Hamlet,* solipsistic. Mac-Leish's re-examination of American values has conditioned everything he has written since *Conquistador,* and has led him into one of the most astonishing and fruitful transformations in our literary history. He has not merely repudiated the literary values of the twenties, he has experimented with new forms (the radio verse play) and revived the forgotten role of "man of letters," like Franklin and Lowell before him. His essays and addresses have become documents in the history of public opinion. *The Irresponsibles* may in retrospect prove to be one of those crucial utterances (like *The American Scholar*) profoundly altering the course of literature and of literary scholarship in the modern nation. And MacLeish's public offices apparently do not stifle his literary productivity, but rather illustrate how the poet can, as Milton argued he should, serve the state.

YOU, ANDREW MARVELL

This apparently first appeared in *New Found Land* (1930), whence it migrated without change to *Poems, 1924-1933.* The poem begins in Persia, from which country the author returned in 1926. An atlas will make clear the geographical range of the piece. For the emotional and literary background read "To His Coy Mistress" by Andrew Marvell (1621-1678), with its famous passage:

> "But at my back I always hear
> Time's wingèd chariot hurrying near."

A note contributed by the author to the *Oxford Anthology of American Literature* says the impulse to write the poem originated in the following, set down while the poet was in the Mediterranean: "The unforeseen experience—consciousness now of the other side of the earth: the always westward coming on of night—Teheran dark—Pa-i-Tak—the Tigris—the house at Rutba Wells—the Levant shore—Crete—Messina—the Garoupe Light—Saragossa the round domes—ocean."

> And here face down beneath the sun
> And here upon earth's noonward height
> To feel the always coming on
> The always rising of the night
>
> To feel creep up the curving east   5
> The earthy chill of dusk and slow
> Upon those under lands the vast
> And ever climbing shadow grow
>
> And strange at Ecbatan the trees
> Take leaf by leaf the evening strange   10
> The flooding dark about their knees
> The mountains over Persia change
>
> And now at Kermanshah the gate
> Dark empty and the withered grass

And through the twilight now the late   15
Few travelers in the westward pass

And Baghdad darken and the bridge
Across the silent river gone
And through Arabia the edge
Of evening widen and steal on   20

And deepen on Palmyra's street
The wheel rut in the ruined stone
And Lebanon fade out and Crete
High through the clouds and overblown

And over Sicily the air   25
Still flashing with the landward gulls
And loom and slowly disappear
The sails above the shadowy hulls

And Spain go under and the shore
Of Africa the gilded sand   30
And evening vanish and no more
The low pale light across that land

Nor now the long light on the sea

And here face downward in the sun
To feel how swift how secretly   35
The shadow of the night comes on . . .

THE END OF THE WORLD

This first appeared in the *New Republic*, May 20, 1925, where, except for the
first, the lines were printed without initial capitalization and the "Jocko" of the
seventh line reads "Lily." It then formed the concluding poem in *Streets in the
Moon* (1926), where the present text first appears. It was afterward collected into
Poems, 1924-1933.

Quite unexpectedly as Vasserot
The armless ambidextrian was lighting
A match between his great and second toe
And Ralph the lion was engaged in biting
The neck of Madame Sossman while the drum   5
Pointed, and Teeny was about to cough
In waltz-time swinging Jocko by the thumb—
Quite unexpectedly the top blew off:

And there, there overhead, there, there, hung over
Those thousands of white faces, those dazed eyes,   10
There in the starless dark the poise, the hover,
There with vast wings across the canceled skies,
There in the sudden blackness the black pall
Of nothing, nothing, nothing—nothing at all.

ARS POETICA

This first appeared in *Poetry,* June, 1926, where the text differs in punctuation and substance from the final version. It was next collected into *Streets in the Moon* (1926), where it assumed its present form; and was thence transferred to *Poems, 1924-1933.* The student should observe the hidden rhymes and the use of assonance and alliteration in holding the poem together.

> A poem should be palpable and mute
> As a globed fruit
>
> Dumb
> As old medallions to the thumb
>
> Silent as the sleeve-worn stone
> Of casement ledges where the moss has grown—
>
> A poem should be wordless
> As the flight of birds
> .   .   .   .   .   .
>
> A poem should be motionless in time
> As the moon climbs
>
> Leaving, as the moon releases
> Twig by twig the night-entangled trees,
>
> Leaving, as the moon behind the winter leaves,
> Memory by memory the mind—
>
> A poem should be motionless in time
> As the moon climbs
> .   .   .   .   .   °
>
> A poem should be equal to:
> Not true
>
> For all the history of grief
> An empty doorway and a maple leaf
>
> For love
> The leaning grasses and two lights about the sea—
>
> A poem should not mean
> But be.

5

10

15

20

IMMORTAL AUTUMN

This first appeared in the *Yale Review,* Autumn, 1929, where it was printed without punctuation. It was then collected into *New Found Land* (1930) and thence transferred to *Poems, 1924-1933,* the present punctuation being adopted in 1930. Line 5 furnished the epigraph for Van Wyck Brooks's *New England: Indian Summer, 1865-1915,* Dutton, 1940.

I speak this poem now with grave and level voice
In praise of autumn of the far-horn-winding fall
I praise the flower-barren fields the clouds the tall
Unanswering branches where the wind makes sullen noise

I praise the fall it is the human season
                                  now   5
No more the foreign sun does meddle at our earth
Enforce the green and bring the fallow land to birth
Nor winter yet weigh all with silence the pine bough

But now in autumn with the black and outcast crows
Share we the spacious world the whispering year is gone   10
There is more room to live now the once secret dawn
Comes late by daylight and the dark unguarded goes

Between the mutinous brave burning of the leaves
And winter's covering of our hearts with his deep snow
We are alone there are no evening birds we know   15
The naked moon the tame stars circle at our eaves

It is the human season on this sterile air
Do words outcarry breath the sound goes on and on
I hear a dead man's cry from autumn long since gone

I cry to you beyond upon this bitter air   20

IMMORTAL HELIX

This apparently first appeared in *Streets in the Moon* and then in the *Poems, 1924-1933.* A "helix" is a geometrical form like that of a screw thread; that is, any spiral.

> Hereunder Jacob Schmidt who, man and bones,
> Has been his hundred times around the sun
>
> His chronicle is endless—the great curve
> Inscribed in nothing by a point upon
> The spinning surface of a circling sphere.   5
>
> Dead bones roll on.

MOTHER GOOSE'S GARLAND

This was part of *Streets in the Moon;* thence it migrated to *Poems, 1924-1933.*

> Around, around the sun we go:
> The moon goes round the earth.
> We do not die of death:
> We die of vertigo.

FRESCOES FOR MR. ROCKEFELLER'S CITY . . .

This series of poems first appeared in pamphlet form in 1933 and was dedicated to Carl Sandburg. The poems were then collected into *Poems, 1924-1933*.

The decorating of the huge group of buildings in New York City known as Rockefeller Center (originally "Rockefeller City") aroused public interest because Mr. and Mrs. John D. Rockefeller, Jr., were known patrons of advanced modern art. Among the painters and sculptors chosen to contribute to this project were two sculptors, William Zorach and Gwen Lux, and the Mexican revolutionary painter Diego Rivera. The first episode of an unhappy history occurred when, in December, 1932, Samuel L. Rothafel ("Roxy"), then in charge of Radio City Music Hall, banished a nude figure by Zorach, "The Spirit of the Dance," and another by Gwen Lux, "Eve," from the theater lobby. He was quoted as saying: "Mrs. Rockefeller may like them. Mr. Rockefeller may like them. . . . But I don't like them. I think they're ugly. Take them away." Controversy turned upon the perennial problem of the nude in art and upon the right of the "advanced" artist to be protected against philistinism.

But the protest over the sculptures was as nothing compared with the storm over the Rivera mural. A group of three artists (none of them an American citizen, it so happened) had been chosen to decorate the walls of the lobby of the RCA Building. The general theme was "New Frontiers," and the subject assigned Rivera was "Man at the crossroads looking with uncertainty but hope for a new solution." This was a direct invitation for revolutionary treatment, and was apparently so understood. Nevertheless, in May, 1933, the huge mural being still incomplete, Rivera was discharged because he refused to paint out the head of Lenin and substitute some less controversial figure. Protests by leading artists and picketings by excited supporters did not alter this decision. The controversy was darkened by the charge that American artists were being ignored in favor of the foreign-born. In February, 1934, laborers working at night destroyed the unfinished mural, which had meanwhile been concealed from public gaze by a false wall. Inasmuch as these episodes occurred during the depths of the depression, Rivera's discharge was interpreted as "counter-revolutionary" action by the capitalists. Conservatives, on the other hand, hailed the destruction of the mural as both a blow for "American" art and a refusal to countenance "un-American" activities by foreigners.

I

LANDSCAPE AS A NUDE

This poem defiantly pictures the country as a huge nude, and is therefore a protest against the action of Mr. Rothafel.

> She lies on her left side her flank golden:
> Her hair is burned black with the strong sun:
> The scent of her hair is of rain in the dust on her shoulders:
> She has brown breasts and the mouth of no other country:
>
> Ah she is beautiful here in the sun where she lies: 5
> She is not like the soft girls naked in vineyards
> Nor the soft naked girls of the English islands
> Where the rain comes in with the surf on an east wind:

Hers is the west wind and the sunlight: the west
Wind is the long clean wind of the continents—   10
The wind turning with earth: the wind descending
Steadily out of the evening and following on:

The wind here where she lies is west: the trees
Oak ironwood cottonwood hickory: standing in
Great groves they roll on the wind as the sea would: 15
The grasses of Iowa Illinois Indiana

Run with the plunge of the wind as a wave tumbling:

Under her knees there is no green lawn of the Florentines:
Under her dusty knees is the corn stubble:
Her belly is flecked with the flickering light of the corn: 20

She lies on her left side her flank golden:
Her hair is burned black with the strong sun:
The scent of her hair is of dust and of smoke on her shoulders:
She has brown breasts and the mouth of no other country:

2

WILDWEST *

There were none of my blood in this battle:
There were Minneconjous: Sans Arcs: Brules:
Many nations of Sioux: they were few men galloping:

This would have been in the long days in June:
They were galloping well deployed under the plum-trees: 5
They were driving riderless horses: themselves they were few:

Crazy Horse had done it with few numbers:
Crazy Horse was small for a Lakota:
He was riding always alone thinking of something:

He was standing alone by the picket lines by the ropes: 10
He was young then: he was thirty when he died:
Unless there were children to talk he took no notice:

When the soldiers came for him there on the other side
On the Greasy Grass in the villages we were shouting
'Hoka Hey! Crazy Horse will be riding!'   15

They fought in the water: horses and men were drowning:
They rode on the butte: dust settled in sunlight:
Hoka Hey! they lay on the bloody ground:

No one could tell of the dead which man was Custer . . .
That was the end of his luck: by that river: 20
The soldiers beat him at Slim Buttes once:

* Black Elk's memories of Crazy Horse recorded by [John G.] Neihardt. (Author's note.) As a
protest against the genteel tradition that art is merely "nice," MacLeish emphasizes the rude vigor
of Western history. The Indian references will be made clear by consulting the biography of
Crazy Horse (ca. 1849-1877), the great Sioux Indian leader, in the *Dictionary of American Biography*. The Indian names are those of various branches of the Sioux.

They beat him at Willow Creek when the snow lifted:
The last time they beat him was the Tongue:
He had only the meat he had made and of that little:

Do you ask why he should fight? It was his country: 25
My God should he not fight? It was his:
But after the Tongue there were no herds to be hunting:

He cut the knots of the tails and he led them in:
He cried out 'I am Crazy Horse! Do not touch me!'
There were many soldiers between and the gun glinting . . .   30

And a Mister Josiah Perham of Maine had much of the
land Mister Perham was building the Northern Pacific
railroad that is Mister Perham was saying at lunch that

forty say fifty millions of acres in gift and
government grant outright ought to be worth a   35
wide price on the Board at two-fifty and

later a Mister Cooke had relieved Mister Perham and
later a Mister Morgan relieved Mister Cooke:
Mister Morgan converted at prices current:

It was all prices to them: they never looked at it: 40
why should they look at the land: they were Empire Builders:
it was all in the bid and the asked and the ink on their books . . .

When Crazy Horse was there by the Black Hills
His heart would be big with the love he had for that country
And all the game he had seen and the mares he had ridden   45

And how it went out from you wide and clean in the sunlight

3

BURYING GROUND BY THE TIES

Ayee! Ai! This is heavy earth on our shoulders:
There were none of us born to be buried in this earth:
Niggers we were Portuguese Magyars Polacks:

We were born to another look of the sky certainly:
Now we lie here in the river pastures: 5
We lie in the mowings under the thick turf:

31-38. Perham . . . Cooke . . . Morgan—Josiah Perham (1803-1868) pushed through Congress with the aid of Thaddeus Stevens the bill which granted public lands to the Northern Pacific Railroad in order that a northern transcontinental line might be built. He was the first president of the road, but in 1866 he was forced out, and the company was reorganized by John Gregory Smith (1818-1891), who admitted a group of Eastern capitalists, and Smith, who succeeded him as president, was forced in 1872 to resign by pressure from Jay Cooke (1821-1905). The failure of Jay Cooke & Company in 1873 eventually threw the company into the hands of John Pierpont Morgan (1839-1913), who reorganized the Northern Pacific in 1893.

We hear the earth and the all-day rasp of the grasshoppers:
It was we laid the steel on this land from ocean to ocean:
It was we (if you know) put the U. P. through the passes

Bringing her down into Laramie full load   10
Eighteen mile on the granite anticlinal
Forty-three foot to the mile and the grade holding:

It was we did it: hunkies of our kind:
It was we dug the caved-in holes for the cold water:
It was we built the gully spurs and the freight sidings: 15

Who would do it but we and the Irishmen bossing us?
It was all foreign-born men there were in this country:
It was Scotsmen Englishmen Chinese Squareheads Austrians . . .

Ayee! but there's weight to the earth under it:
Not for this did we come out—to be lying here   20
Nameless under the ties in the clay cuts:

There's nothing good in the world but the rich will buy it:
Everything sticks to the grease of a gold note—
Even a continent—even a new sky!

Do not pity us much for the strange grass over us: 25
We laid the steel to the stone stock of these mountains:
The place of our graves is marked by the telegraph poles!

It was not to lie in the bottoms we came out
And the trains going over us here in the dry hollows . . .

4

OIL PAINTING OF THE ARTIST AS THE ARTIST

The satirical suggestion of a head to replace that of Lenin. See the headnote to the whole poem.

The plump Mr. Pl'f is washing his hands of America:
The plump Mr. Pl'f is in ochre with such hair:

America is in blue-black-grey-green-sandcolor:
America is a continent—many lands:

The plump Mr. Pl'f is washing his hands of America: 5
He is pictured at Pau on the *place* and his eyes glaring:

9. U. P.—Union Pacific Railroad, the first great transcontinental line, completed in 1869. 10-11. Laramie . . . anticlinal—Early surveys determined that the route of the Union Pacific should be by way of a pass through the Laramie Mountains. The "grade" into and out of the town of Laramie was in 1868 as represented in the text. Much of the road had to be cut through solid rock of the "anticlinal" or convex bend of a granite stratum. 18. Squareheads— This term of humorous reproach is applied sometimes to Swedes, sometimes to Prussians. 6. Pau —Pau is a summer resort in the French Pyrenees. 6. place—plaza, park or open space in the center of a city.

He thinks of himself as an exile from all this:
As an émigré from his own time into history—

(History being an empty house without owners
A practical man may get in by the privy stones—   10

The dead are excellent hosts: they have no objections—
And once in he can nail the knob on the next one

Living the life of a classic in bad air with
Himself for the Past and his face in the glass for Posterity)

The Cinquecento is nothing at all like Nome   15
Or Natchez or Wounded Knee or the Shenandoah:

Your vulgarity Tennessee: your violence Texas:
The rocks under your fields Ohio Connecticut:

Your clay Missouri your clay: you have driven him out:
You have shadowed his life Appalachians purple mountains: 20

There is much too much of your flowing Mississippi:
He prefers a tidier stream with a terrace for trippers and

Cypresses mentioned in Horace or Henry James:
He prefers a country where everything carries the name of a

Countess or real king or an actual palace or   25
Something in Prose and the stock prices all in Italian:

There is more shade for an artist under a fig
Than under the whole damn range (he finds) of the Big Horns

5

EMPIRE BUILDERS

James J. Hill (1838-1916), who dominated the Northern Pacific—Great Northern—Chicago, Burlington & Quincy railroad system, liked to refer to himself and his contemporaries as "empire builders"; and he so named one of his crack trains.

The Museum Attendant:

This is *The Making of America in Five Panels:*

This is Mister Harriman making America:

15. **Cinquecento**—sixteenth century; that is, the art of the Italian Renaissance. 15. **Nome**—city in Alaska; the poet begins a list of places where life has been rude or violent. 23. **Horace . . . James**—These writers reappear here as representatives of urban culture. 28. **Big Horns**—mountain range in Wyoming. 3. **Harriman**—Edward Henry Harriman (1848-1909), the rival of James J. Hill, who took the Union Pacific out of the hands of receivers and after 1898 dominated that railroad system.

Mister-Harriman-is-buying-the-Union-Pacific-at-Seventy:
The Santa Fe is shining on his hair: 5

This is Commodore Vanderbilt making America:
Mister-Vanderbilt-is-eliminating-the-short-interest-in-Hudson:
Observe the carving on the rocking chair:

This is J. P. Morgan making America:
(The Tennessee Coal is behind to the left of the Steel Company:)   10
Those in mauve are braces he is wearing:

This is Mister Mellon making America:
Mister-Mellon-is-represented-as-a-symbolical-figure-in-aluminum-
Strewing-bank-stocks-on-a-burnished-stair:

This is the Bruce is the Barton making America: 15
Mister-Barton-is-selling-us-Doctor's-Deliciousest-Dentifrice:
This is he in beige with the canary:

You have just beheld the Makers making America:
This is *The Making of America in Five Panels:*
America lies to the west-southwest of the Switch-Tower: 20
There is nothing to see of America but land:

*The Original Document
under the Panel Paint:*
"To Thos. Jefferson Esq. his obd't serv't
M. Lewis: captain: detached: 25
                         Sir:

Having in mind your repeated commands in this matter:
And the worst half of it done and the streams mapped:

4. buying . . . Seventy—refers to the stock "deal" by which Harriman took over the
road from Kuhn, Loeb & Company. **5. Santa Fe**—Control of the Atchison, Topeka & Santa Fe
was one of the weapons by which Harriman sought to force his way into Chicago in competition
with Hill. **6-7. Vanderbilt . . . Hudson**—Cornelius Vanderbilt (1794-1877), creator of the
New York Central Railroad system, in 1862 controlled the New York & Harlem Railroad and
sought to absorb the Hudson River Railroad, a rival line. Daniel Drew and his associates plotted
to sell Vanderbilt "short" on Hudson River stock and force him to retire, but he bought heavily,
sent the price up, and united the two roads in the late sixties as the New York Central & Hudson
River Railroad. **10. Tennessee Coal**—the Tennessee Coal & Iron Company, a powerful company, part of the "steel trust," whose labor policy was disliked by radicals. **12. Mellon**—Andrew
J. Mellon (1855-1937), the dominating genius of the Aluminum Corporation of America. Secretary
of the Treasury under Harding, Coolidge, and Hoover. He was thought by "radicals" to be
responsible for the disastrous financial policies that helped to bring on the depression. He was
also director in various banks and other corporations. **15. Bruce . . . Barton**—Bruce Barton
(1886-   ), former Congressman, advertising man, editor, and writer, whose books were thought
to be too favorable to a "businessman's" America. **25. M. Lewis**—Meriwether Lewis (1774-
1809) of the Lewis and Clark Expedition to the far Northwest and the Pacific (1803-1806). The
following imaginary letter is based upon passages in the *Original Journals of the Lewis and Clark
Expedition,* ed. R. G. Thwaites, 8 vols., Dodd, Mead, 1905, especially upon some of the authentic
letters to Jefferson, which may be read in the Appendix to this work in Vol. VII. See also the
reprint of the original (1814) *History of the Expedition of Captains Lewis and Clark 1804-5-6,*
ed. J. K. Hosmer, 3 vols., McClurg, 1902.

And we here on the back of this beach beholding the
Other ocean—two years gone and the cold   30

Breaking with rain for the third spring since St. Louis:
The crows at the fishbones on the frozen dunes:

The first cranes going over from south north:
And the river down by a mark of the pole since the morning:

And time near to return, and a ship (Spanish)   35
Lying in for the salmon: and fearing chance or the

Drought or the Sioux should deprive you of these discoveries—
Therefore we send by sea in this writing:
                               Above the
Platte there were long plains and a clay country:
Rim of the sky far off: grass under it: 40

Dung for the cook fires by the sulphur licks:
After that there were low hills and the sycamores:

And we poled up by the Great Bend in the skiffs:
The honey bees left us after the Osage River:

The wind was west in the evenings and no dew and the   45
Morning Star larger and whiter than usual—

The winter rattling in the brittle haws:
The second year there was sage and the quail calling:

All that valley is good land by the river:
Three thousand miles and the clay cliffs and   50

Rue and beargrass by the water banks
And many birds and the brant going over and tracks of

Bear elk wolves marten: the buffalo
Numberless so that the cloud of their dust covers them:

The antelope fording the fall creeks: and the mountains and   55
Grazing lands and the meadow lands and the ground

Sweet and open and well-drained:
                          We advise you to
Settle troops at the forks and to issue licenses:

Many men will have living on these lands:
There is wealth in the earth for them all and the wood standing   60

And wild birds on the water where they sleep:
There is stone in the hills for the towns of a great people . . ."

You have just beheld the Makers making America:

They screwed her scrawny and gaunt with their seven-year panics:
 They bought her back on their mortgages old-whore-cheap: 65
They fattened their bonds at her breasts till the thin blood ran from them:

Men have forgotten how full clear and deep
The Yellowstone moved on the gravel and grass grew
When the land lay waiting for her westward people!

6

BACKGROUND WITH REVOLUTIONARIES

And the corn singing Millennium!
Lenin! Millennium! Lennium!

When they're shunting the cars on the Katy a mile off
When they're shunting the cars when they're shunting the cars on the Katy
You can hear the clank of the couplings riding away   5

Also Comrade Devine who writes of America
Most instructively having in 'Seventy-four
Crossed to the Hoboken side on the Barclay Street Ferry

She sits on a settle in the State of North Dakota
O she sits on a settle in the State of North Dakota   10
She can hear the engines whistle over Iowa and Idaho

Also Comrade Edward Remington Ridge
Who has prayed God since the April of 'Seventeen
To replace in his life his lost (M.E.) religion

And The New York Daily Worker *goes a'blowing over Arkansas*   15
The New York Daily Worker *goes a'blowing over Arkansas*
The grasses let it go along the Ozarks over Arkansas

Even Comrade Grenadine Grilt who has tried since
August tenth for something to feel about strongly in
Verses—his personal passions having tired   20

I can tell my land by the jays in the apple-trees
Tell my land by the jays in the apple-trees
I can tell my people by the blue-jays in the apple-trees

Aindt you read in d' books you are all brudders?
D' glassic historic objective broves you are brudders!   25
You and d' Wops and d' Chinks you are all brudders!
Havendt you got it d' same ideology? Havendt you?

2. **Lenin**—Vladimir Ilich Ulyanov, who later took the name Nikolai Lenin (1870-1924), Russian revolutionary leader. **3. Katy**—Missouri, Kansas & Texas Railroad. **8. Hoboken**—New Jersey city across the Hudson River from New York City. **14. M.E.**—Methodist Episcopal. **15. New York Daily Worker**—principal Communist newspaper in the United States.

When it's yesterday in Oregon it's one A M in Maine
And she slides: and the day slides: and it runs: runs over us:
And the bells strike twelve strike twelve strike twelve   30
In Marblehead in Buffalo in Cheyenne in Cherokee
Yesterday runs on the states like a crow's shadow

For Marx has said to us Workers what do you need?
And Stalin has said to us Starvers what do you need?
You need the Dialectical Materialism!   35

She's a tough land under the corn mister:
She has changed the bone in the cheeks of many races:
She has winced the eyes of the soft Slavs with her sun on them:
She has tried the fat from the round rumps of Italians:
Even the voice of the English has gone dry   40
And hard on the tongue and alive in the throat speaking:

She's a tough land under the oak-trees mister:
It may be she can change the word in the book
As she changes the bone of a man's head in his children:
It may be that the earth and the men remain. . . .   45

There is too much sun on the lids of my eyes to be listening

THE IRRESPONSIBLES

First published as a booklet, in 1940.

HISTORY—if honest history continues to be written—will have one question to ask of our generation, people like ourselves. It will be asked of the books we have written, the carbon copies of our correspondence, the photographs of our faces, the minutes of our meetings in the famous rooms   5
before the portraits of our spiritual begetters. The question will be this: Why did the scholars and the writers of our generation in this country, witnesses as they were to the destruction of writing and of scholarship in great areas of Europe and to the exile and the imprisonment and murder of men whose crime was scholarship and writing—witnesses also to the rise in their own   10
country of the same destructive forces with the same impulses, the same motives, the same means—why did the scholars and the writers of our generation in America fail to oppose those forces while they could—while there was still time and still place to oppose them with the arms of scholarship and writing?

It is a question the historians will ask with interest—the gentle, detached,   15
not altogether loving interest with which historians have always questioned the impotent spirits of the dead. Young men working in the paper rubbish of our lives, the old journals, the marginal notations, the printed works, will discover (or so they will think) that the scholars and the writers of our generation in this country had been warned of danger as men were rarely warned   20

33. **Marx**—Karl Marx (1818-1883), author of *Das Kapital.* 34. **Stalin**—Iosif Vissarionovich Dzhugashvili, who later took the name Joseph Stalin (1879-1953), former head of the Soviet Union. "Stalin" means "steel." 35. **Dialectical Materialism**—that form of Marxian theory which argues that economic determinism compels social change.

before. They will discover (or so they will think) that the common inherited culture of the West, by which alone our scholars and our writers lived, had been attacked in other countries with a stated and explicit purpose to destroy. They will discover that that purpose had been realized. They will discover that
5 a similar purpose backed by similar forces, created by similar conditions, was forming here. And it will seem to them strange—ironical and strange—that the great mass of American scholars and American writers made no effort to defend either themselves or the world by which they lived.

They will make of course the necessary reservations. They will note that
10 societies of scholars and associations of writers adopted resolutions declaring their devotion to civilization. They will note that certain young novelists and poets, the most generous and gallant of their time, unable to endure the outrage and injustice, gave up their lives as writers and enlisted in the hopeless armies to fight brutality with force. But of those who truly faced this danger
15 not with their bodies but their minds, of those who fought the enemies of the intellect with the weapons of the intellect, devoting to that warfare all the strength, all the imagination, all the resources of courage and inventiveness, all the watchfulness by day and night, all the last reserves of hope and skill and pain which men must use whose lives and more than lives are put in
20 danger—of those who fought this danger with the weapons by which this danger could be overcome, they will record the names of very few. And they will ask their question. Why did we, scholars and writers in America in this time, we who had been warned of our danger not only by explicit threats but by explicit action, why did we not fight this danger while the weapons we
25 used best—the weapons of ideas and words—could still be used against it?

It is not a question for which we are altogether unprepared. We have been writing out our answer for many years now in action and inaction, in words and in silence—in learned articles in the scientific journals and in controversial aricles in the general magazines, in blank faces after the passionate words,
30 in bored eyes refusing to believe. The answer we have prepared, the answer we have written out for history to find, is the answer Leonardo is said to have given Michelangelo when Michelangelo blamed him for his indifference to the misfortunes of the Florentines. It is the answer of our kind at many other times and places. "Indeed," said Leonardo, "indeed the study of beauty has
35 occupied my whole heart." The study of beauty, the study of history, the study of science, has occupied our whole hearts and the misfortunes of our generation are none of our concern. They are the practical and political concern of practical and political men but the concern of the scholar, the concern of the artist, is with other, purer, more enduring things.
40 This is the answer we have written down for history to find. I doubt whether it will satisfy the ironic men who came to plague us on that waterfront where Teresias was made to drink the blood and answer. I think indeed it will not satisfy them. For it has not satisfied ourselves. We say with great

---

31. **Leonardo**—Leonardo da Vinci (1452-1519), universal genius of the Italian Renaissance. **32. Michelangelo**—Michelangelo Buonarroti (1475-1564), great Florentine sculptor, painter, poet, and architect. **42. Teresias**—In the *Odyssey* (Book XI) Odysseus in the underworld meets the shade of Tiresias the seer by the river Cocytus (the "river of wailing") and gives him the blood of a ram to drink in order that he may have strength to prophesy future events.

firmness and authority, speaking by our words and by our silence, that the
misfortunes of our generation are economic and political misfortunes from
which the scholar can safely hold himself apart. We say this with all the authority of the political scientists of the past to whom the misfortunes of the
people were always political and economic and of no concern to the poet, the   5
pure scholar, the artist intent upon his art. We say it also with the authority
of the political scientists of the present to whom all phenomena of whatever
kind are, by hypothesis, economic and political. But though we say it we do
not believe it. For we have observed these misfortunes. They have been acted
out for us to see. And what we have seen is this: that the misfortunes of our   10
time are not the misfortunes the philosophers, the theorists, the political scientists have described to us. They are not the practical concern of the practical
man and therefore matters of indifference to the scholar. On the contrary, it is
the practical man and the practical man alone—the man whose only care is
for his belly and his roof—who can safely be indifferent to these troubles. The   15
things he lives by are not menaced. And it is precisely the scholar, the poet—
the man whose care is for the structures of the intellect, the houses of the
mind—whose heart is caught. For it is the scholar's goods which are in danger.

It is perhaps because we have seen this and yet refuse to see it—because we
know one thing and yet continue to declare another—that our minds are so   20
confused and our counsels so bewildering. Nothing is more characteristic of
the intellectuals of our generation than their failure to understand what it is
that is happening to their world. And nothing explains that failure as precisely as their unwillingness to see what they have seen and to know what
they do truly know. They have seen the crisis of their time—they have seen it   25
spelled out, played out, fought out as few observers ever before in history saw
the tragedy exposed. They know its ending. And yet they continue to pretend
that they do not know. They continue to speak of the crisis of their time as
though the war in Europe were that crisis—and the war, they say, is no concern of theirs. They continue to speak of the crisis as though the imperialistic   30
maneuvers, the struggles for markets, the propaganda in the newspapers and
the radio, were the crisis—and the maneuvers of imperialism, the propaganda
of the press and the struggles for trade they say are no concern of theirs. And
yet they know—they know very well because they have seen—that these things
are not the crisis but merely its reflections in the mirrors of action. They know   35
that behind the war, behind the diplomatic gestures, behind the black print
on the page and the hysterical voices on the air there is something deeper and
more dangerous—more dangerous to *them*. They know that it is a condition
of men's minds which has produced these things—a condition which existed
and exists not only in Europe but in other parts of the world as well and not   40
least in our own country. And they know that this condition of men's minds
is not a practical, a political, phenomenon of no concern to the scholar and
the man of thought but something very different.

It is not, for example, a matter of purely practical and political interest that
great numbers of men in various parts of the world wish passionately and   45
even violently to give up the long labor of liberty and to surrender their wills

37. **hysterical . . . air**—that is, radio propagandists.

and their bodies and even their minds to the will of a leader, so that they may achieve at least the dignity of order, at least the dignity of obedience. It is not a matter of purely practical and political significance that whole nations of men have gladly and willingly released themselves not only from their rights

5   as individuals but from their responsibilities as individuals so that they are no longer compelled to feel or to respect the individual humanity of others— or to feel or to respect the things that individual humanity has, over many centuries, created. It is not a matter of purely practical and political importance that governments which once, whatever they may have practiced, pro-

10 tested a respect for learning and the arts, should now permit themselves to show not only the power but worse, far worse, the *willingness,* the *purpose,* to enslave both learning and the arts. It is not a matter of purely practical and political importance that societies which once made part of the community of Western culture should now attempt by murder and outrage and exile to

15 root out that culture and to replace it with private and parochial sciences and private and parochial arts so that frontiers are armed, for the first time in the history of the West, not only along the rivers and the mountains and the boundaries of nations, but across the common earth of culture, the free land that was never fenced before.

20   I think no honest man will say that these are matters of practical and po- litical significance alone. I think any man who considers with coolness, and without the preconceptions of the dogmas, the character of the crisis of his time will admit, because he will have no choice but to admit, that this crisis is in essence a cultural crisis—a revolt of certain classes, certain conditions of men

25 against the inherited culture of the West and against all common culture—a revolt by no means limited to those nations alone where it has been successful. Wars we have had before—many wars; murder also: inquisition of scholars: torture of askers: suppression and mutilation of truth. But in the past these things have been done, however hypocritically, in the name of truth, in the

30 name of humanity—even in the name of God. The forms of culture were pre- served—and in the preservation of a civilization as in the preservation of an art the forms are everything. What is new and unexampled in the times we live in is *the repudiation of the forms.* What is new is a cynical brutality which considers moral self-justification unnecessary and therefore—and this is per-

35 haps its worst indecency—dispenses even with the filthy garment of the hypo- crite. To use brutality and force, not in the name of Right nor in the name of God, but in the name of force alone, is to destroy the self-respect and therefore the dignity of the individual life without which the existence of art or learning is inconceivable. To lie, not in the name of truth, but in the

40 name of lies, is to destroy the common basis of communication without which a common culture cannot exist and a work of learning or of art becomes un- intelligible.

The truth is—the plain and simple truth of which we have so many pain- ful evidences—that the disorder of our time, whatever else it may now be or

45 may become, is in its essentials a revolt against the common culture of the West. For against what but the common culture did this disorder continue to struggle in Germany long after it had overthrown the former state? There

was no domestic danger for it to fear. Against what but the Western respect for the dignity of the individual was aimed the long series of outrages against the Jews? The Jews were impotent when they were subjected to the worst abuses. Against what but the Western respect for the common, the nationless, creation of the artist was aimed the destruction of the work of men like Thomas Mann? Thomas Mann had already been repudiated by his people when they accepted the government of his enemies. Against what but the Western belief in the wholeness of Western civilization was aimed the assault upon a church which was no longer a danger to any ruler and the fabrication of a paganism which needed only the blond sopranos on the ends of wires to be Wagner at his worst?

Intellectuals in America and elsewhere—writers, scientists, the men of learning—have attempted to ignore these questions. They have pretended to themselves that the burning of books, the exiling of artists, the invention of mythologies were merely incidents—afterthoughts—decorations: that the true crisis was the crisis of food, the crisis of arms, the crisis created by political forces, by economic collapse,—that they had, and needed to have, no truck with it. They have been wrong. These things are not incidents. They are not after-thoughts. They are the essential nature of the revolution of our age. For with-out this attack upon the habits of the mind, the reliances of the spirit, that revolution could not, by any possibility, have succeeded.

The revolution of our age—the revolution which has finally emerged and declared itself in action—is not the great revolution of the masses of which generous men once dreamed: and which other and less generous men have now so meanly and so bloodily betrayed. The revolution of the masses was a revolution which proposed to set up one faith against another faith, one cul-ture against another culture: a faith in man, a faith in the power of the pat-terns of men's lives, against a faith in institutions and in money; a culture of the people against a culture of the exploiters of the people. The revolution which has finally and successfully emerged in action has no such faith and no such culture.

It is a revolution of negatives, a revolution of the defeated, a revolution of the dispossessed, a revolution of despair. It is a revolution created out of misery by dread of yet more misery, a revolution created out of disorder by terror of disorder. It is a revolution of gangs, a revolution *against*. And the enemy it is against, the enemy it must destroy, is the enemy which, in all times and in all civilizations, has stood against the revolutions of the gangs—the rule of moral law, the rule of spiritual authority, the rule of intellectual truth. To establish the negative revolutions, the revolutions of which the only aim is power, the revolutions which have no means but force, it is necessary first to destroy the authority of the unseen sayings of the mind. It is necessary to de-stroy the things the mind has made. Caliban in the miserable and besotted

5

10

15

20

25

30

35

40

6. **Mann**—Thomas Mann (1875-   ), leading German novelist, whose vigorous protests against the Nazification of his country led to his exile to the United States. **10-11. blond so-pranos . . . wires . . . Wagner**—In those scenes of Wagner's *Ring,* particularly in *Das Rheingold,* supposed to take place in the depths of the Rhine, the "Rhine maidens" or mermaids sing while suspended on piano wires and simulating the action of swimming. **42. Caliban**—the half-human, half-animal "villain" of *The Tempest* of Shakespeare. The following passage refers to Act III, *sc.* ii, lines 144-48.

swamp is the symbol of this revolution. As long as the unseen beauty in the air retains its voices and its seductive music and its stinging whips the revolutions of the gangs are clumsy, blundering, grotesque and foolish. They can bellow and threaten and boast and gesture with their arms but in the end the invisible voices of the air, the invisible power of the ideal will master them. They have one hope of success and only one—the destruction of the whole system of ideas, the whole respect for truth, the whole authority of excellence which places law above force, beauty above cruelty, singleness above numbers.

It is the distinction of our time—perhaps unhappily its most memorable distinction—that it and it alone has provided the formula by which this overthrow could be achieved. Only in our time has the revolution of the gangs discovered a strategy and a leadership brutal enough, cynical enough, cunning enough to destroy the entire authority of the inherited culture and thereafter to seal the doors against the searching and the asking of the scholar's mind, the artist's mind, so that the revolution of force, the revolution of despair could flower and fulfill its possibilities. Only in our time has the revolution of the gangs shown itself openly and admittedly as the thing it is—a revolution of cruelty, cunning and despair against the authority and the discipline of the mind.

It is to this disorder and not to some political and partisan dissension, not to some accidental economic breakdown—practical and political matters for the men of politics and practice—it is to this direct, explicit and intentional attack upon the scholar's world and the scholar's life and the scholar's work that American scholarship has been indifferent. Or if not indifferent, then inactive, merely watchful—fearful, watchful and inactive. And it is there that history will place its questions.

How could we sit back as spectators of a war against ourselves?

Did we suppose the newly discovered techniques of deception, of falsehood as a military force, of strategic fraud, were incapable of reaching us—incapable of crossing sea water? We had seen their methods drive their conquests through the countries of the world more rapidly than Alexander or Napoleon or Tamerlane or any other conqueror or killer.

Or was it something else we thought? Did we believe others would defend us? Did we think the issue was an issue of strategy, an issue of battles? Did we think the British and the French would win their war and so defend us? But we knew very well, because we had seen, that this war was not a war fought in the open on the military front, but a war fought in the back street and the dark stair—a war fought within the city, within the house, within the mind—a war of treason: a war of corruption: a war of lies. And against treason and corruption and lies, battle fleets and grand armies are impotent.

The questions answer themselves and yet provide no answer. For if we did not believe we were safe by sea water, or if we did not believe others would save us, then our failure to act in our own defense becomes a curious thing. What has prevented us from acting? Lack of courage? It is difficult

31-32. **Alexander . . . Tamerlane**—Alexander the Great (356-323 B.C.), the conqueror of Asia; Napoleon I (1769-1821), creator of the First French Empire; and Tamerlane (1336-1405), who overran Asia with much slaughter, are cited here as mere killers.

to indict a generation for lack of courage. Lack of wisdom? There is wisdom
enough in other matters.

I think, speaking only of what I have seen myself and heard—I think it is
neither lack of courage nor lack of wisdom, but a different reason which has
prevented our generation of intellectuals in this country from acting in their   5
own defense. I think it is the organization of the intellectual life of our time.
Specifically, I think it is the division and therefore the destruction of intellectual responsibility. The men of intellectual duty, those who should have
been responsible for action, have divided themselves into two castes, two cults
—the scholars and the writers. Neither accepts responsibility for the common   10
culture or for its defense.

There was a time a century ago, two centuries ago, when men who practiced our professions would have accepted this responsibility without an instant's hesitation. A century ago the professions of the writer and the scholar
were united in the single profession of the man of letters and the man of let-   15
ters was responsible in everything that touched the mind. He was a man of
wholeness of purpose, of singleness of intention—a single intellectual champion, admittedly responsible for the defense of the inherited tradition,
avowedly partisan of its practice. Where those who practice our several professions divide the learned world and the creative world between them in   20
irresponsible and neutral states, the man of letters inhabited both learning and
the world of letters like an empire.

He was a man of learning whose learning was employed not for its own
sake in a kind of academic narcissism but for the sake of decent living in his
time. He was a writer whose writing was used not to mirror an abstract and   25
unrelated present but to illuminate that present by placing it in just relation
to its past. He was therefore and necessarily a man who admitted a responsibility for the survival and vitality of the common and accumulated experience
of the mind, for this experience was to him the air he breathed, the perspective
of his thinking. Learning to him was no plump pigeon carcass to be picked   30
at for his private pleasure and his private fame but a profession practiced for
the common good. Writing was not an ornament, a jewel, but a means to
ends, a weapon, the most powerful of weapons, a weapon to be used. Whatever threatened learning or the ends of learning challenged the man of letters.
Whatever struck at truth or closed off question or defiled an art or violated   35
decency of thinking struck at him. And he struck back with every weapon
masters of the word could find to strike with. Milton defending freedom of
the mind in sentences which outlive every name of those who struck at freedom, Voltaire displaying naked to the grin of history the tyrants who were
great until he made them small, Bartolomé de las Casas gentling cruel priests   40
and brutal captains with the dreadful strokes of truth—Las Casas, Milton and

24. narcissism—In Greek mythology Narcissus fell in love with his own image in a pool and
was drowned. In psychology the term refers to the gratification secured from admiring oneself.
37. Milton—The reference is to *Areopagitica: A Speech of Mr. John Milton for the Liberty of
Unlicenced* [that is, uncensored] *Printing,* 1644. 39. Voltaire—the assumed name of François
Marie Arouet (1694-1778), whose pen was perpetually exercised against tyranny. MacLeish's reference is vague. 40. Bartolomé . . . las Casas—Bartolomé de las Casas (1474?-1566), Bishop
of Chiapa, whose *Very Brief Account of the Ruin of the Indies* (1542) indicts Spanish treatment
of the Indians.

Voltaire were men of letters—men who confessed an obligation to defend the disciplines of thought not in their own but in the general interest.

Had men like these been living in our time—had the intellectuals of our time been whole and loyal—it would, I think, have been impossible for the
5 revolution of the gangs to have succeeded where success has been most dangerous—in the perversion of the judgments of the mind. Murder is not absolved of immorality by committing murder. Murder is absolved of immorality by bringing men to think that murder is not evil. This only the perversion of the mind can bring about. And the perversion of the mind is only possible
10 when those who should be heard in its defense are silent.

They are silent in our time because there are no voices which accept responsibility for speaking. Even the unimaginable indecencies of propaganda—even the corruption of the word itself in Germany and Russia and in Spain and elsewhere—even the open triumph of the lie, produced no answer such as
15 Voltaire in his generation would have given. And for this reason—that the man who could have been Voltaire, who could have been Las Casas, does not live: the man of intellectual *office,* the man of intellectual *calling,* the man who *professes* letters—professes an obligation as a servant of the mind to defend the mind's integrity against every physical power—professes an obliga-
20 tion to defend the labors of the mind and the structures it has created and the means by which it lives, not only privately and safely in his study, not only strictly and securely in the controversies of the learned press, but publicly and at the public risk and danger of his life. He does not exist because the man of letters no longer exists. And the man of letters no longer exists because he
25 has been driven from our world and from our time by the division of his kingdom. The single responsibility, the wholeness of function of the man of letters, has been replaced by the divided function, the mutual antagonism, the isolated irresponsibility of two figures, each free of obligation, each separated from a portion of his duty—the scholar and the writer.

30 Why this substitution has come about—whether because the methods of scientific inquiry, carried over into the humanities, destroyed the loyalties and habits of the mind or for some other reason, I leave to wiser men to say. The point is that there has been a substitution. The country of the man of letters has been divided between his heirs. The country that was once the past and
35 present—the past made useful to the reasons of the present, the present understood against the knowledge of the past—the country that was once the past and present brought together in the mind, is now divided into past on one side, present on the other.

Past is the scholar's country: present is the writer's. The writer sees the
40 present on the faces of the world and leaves the past to rot in its own rubbish. The scholar digs his ivory cellar in the ruins of the past and lets the present sicken as it will. A few exceptions noted here and there—men like Thomas Mann—the gulf between these countries is complete. And the historical novels fashionable at the moment, the vulgarizations of science, the digests of phi-

---

12. propaganda—The verb *propagare* originally meant merely to broaden, to disseminate. In totalitarian theory propaganda refers to the power of manipulating mass psychology to given ends by telling lies of great magnitude. **41. ivory cellar**—satirical inversion of "ivory tower."

losophy only define its depth as a plank across a chasm makes the chasm deeper. That it should be necessary to throw such flimsy flights from one side to the other of the learned world shows how deeply and disastrously the split was made.

That scholarship suffers or that writing suffers by the change is not as- 5 serted. Scholarship may be more scientific: writing may be purer. Indeed there are many who believe, and I among them, that the time we live in has produced more first-rate writers than any but the very greatest ages, and there are scholars of a scholarship as hard, as honest, as devoted as any we have known. But excellence of scholarship and writing are not now in question. 10 What matters now is the defense of culture—the defense truly, and in the most literal terms, of civilization as men have known it for the last two thousand years. And there the substitution for the man of letters of the scholar and the writer, however pure the scholarship, however excellent the writing, is a tragic and immeasurable loss. For neither the modern scholar nor the 15 modern writer admits responsibility for the defense. They assert on the contrary, each in his particular way, an irresponsibility as complete as it is singular.

The irresponsibility of the scholar is the irresponsibility of the scientist upon whose laboratory insulation he has patterned all his work. The scholar has made himself as indifferent to values, as careless of significance, as bored with 20 meanings as the chemist. He is a refugee from consequences, an exile from the responsibilities of moral choice. He has taught himself to say with the physicist—and with some others whom history remembers—"What is truth?" He has taught himself with the biologist to refrain from judgments of better or worse. His words of praise are the laboratory words—objectivity—detach- 25 ment—dispassion. His pride is to be scientific, neuter, skeptical, detached—superior to final judgment or absolute belief. In his capacity as scholar the modern scholar does not occupy the present. In his capacity as scholar he loves the word—but only the word which entails no judgments, involves no decisions, accomplishes no actions. Where the man of letters of other centuries domesti- 30 cated the past within the rustling of the present, making it stand among us like the meaning of a statue among trees, the modern scholar in his capacity as scholar leaves the present and returns across the past where all the men are marble. Where the man of letters of other centuries quarried his learning from the past to build the present the modern scholar quarries his learning 35 from the past to dig the quarries.

It is not for nothing that the modern scholar invented the Ph.D. thesis as his principal contribution to literary form. The Ph.D. thesis is the perfect image of his world. It is work done for the sake of doing work—perfectly conscientious, perfectly laborious, perfectly irresponsible. The modern scholar 40 at his best and worst is both these things—perfectly conscientious, laborious and competent: perfectly irresponsible for the saving of his world. He remembers how in the Civil Wars in England the scholars, devoted only to their proper tasks, founded the Royal Society. He remembers how through other

---

23. some others . . . truth—*Cf.* Luke 18: 38. **44. Royal Society**—Chartered in 1662, the Royal Society grew out of the Philosophical Society, founded in 1645. The English Civil Wars are usually dated 1642-1646 and 1648-1651.

wars and other dangers the scholars kept the lamp of learning lighted. He
does not consider that the scholars then did other things as well as trim the
lamp wicks. He does not consider either that the dangers change and can
be greater. He has his work to do. He has his book to finish. He hopes
5 the war will not destroy the manuscripts he works with. He is the pure, the
perfect type of irresponsibility—the man who acts as though the fire could
not burn him because he has no business with the fire. He knows because he
cannot help but know, reading his papers, talking to his friends—he knows this
fire has consumed the books, the spirit, everything he lives by, flesh itself—in
10 other countries. He knows this but he will not know. It's not his business.
Whose business is it then? He will not answer even that. He has his work
to do. He has his book to finish . . .

The writer's irresponsibility is of a different kind. Where the modern
scholar escapes from the adult judgments of the mind by taking the disinter-
15 ested man of science as his model, the modern writer escapes by imitation of
the artist. He practices his writing as a painter does his painting. He thinks as
artist—which is to say he thinks without responsibility to anything but truth
of feeling. He observes as artist—which is to say that he observes with honesty and truthfulness and without comment. His devotion, as with every hon-
20 est painter, is devotion to the thing observed, the actual thing, the thing without its consequences or its antecedents, naked of judgment, stripped of causes
and effects. The invisible world, the intellectual world, the world of the relation of ideas, the world of judgments, of values, the world in which truth is
good and lies are evil—this world has no existence to the honest artist or to
25 the honest writer who takes the artist for his model. His duty is to strip all
this away—to strip away the moral preference, the intellectual association.

He sees the world as a god sees it—without morality, without care, without
judgment. People look like this. People act like that. He shows them looking,
acting. It is not his business why they look so, why they act so. It is enough
30 that he should "make them happen." This is the whole test, the whole criterion, of the work of the writer-artist—to show things as they "really happen": to write with such skill, such penetration of the physical presence of the
world, that the action seen, the action described, will "really happen" on his
page. If he concerns himself with motive at all he concerns himself with the
35 "real" motive, meaning the discreditable motive which the actor conceals from
himself. His most searching purpose is to find, not the truth of human action,
but the low-down, the discreditable explanation which excuses him from care.
The suggestion that there are things in the world—ideas, conceptions, ways of
thinking—which the writer-artist should defend from attack: the suggestion
40 above all that he was under obligation to defend the inherited culture, would
strike him as ridiculous.

Artists do not save the world. They practice art. They practice it as Goya
practiced it among the cannon in Madrid. And if this war is not Napoleon
in Spain but something even worse than that? They practice art. Or they put

42-44. Goya . . . Spain—Francisco Goya y Lucientes (1746-1828), great Spanish painter,
during Napoleon's invasion of the Spanish Peninsula and the subsequent bloody Peninsular War
found material for his art in the horrors of his time.

the art aside and take a rifle and go out and fight. But not *as artists*. The artist does not fight. The artist's obligations are obligations to his art. His responsibility—his one responsibility—is to his art. He has no other. Not even when his art itself, his chance to practice it, his need to live where it is practiced, may be in danger. The writer-artist will write a bloody story about the expense of blood. He will present the face of agony as it has rarely been presented. But not even then will he take the weapon of his words and carry it to the barricades of intellectual warfare, to the storming of belief, the fortifying of conviction where alone this fighting can be won.

There are examples in history of civilizations made impotent by excess of culture. No one, I think, will say of us that we lost our intellectual liberties on this account. But it may well be said, and said with equally ironic emphasis, that the men of thought, the men of learning in this country were deceived and rendered impotent by the best they knew. To the scholar impartiality, objectivity, detachment were ideal qualities he taught himself laboriously and painfully to acquire. To the writer objectivity and detachment were his writer's pride. Both subjected themselves to inconceivable restraints, endless disciplines to reach these ends. And both succeeded. Both writers and scholars freed themselves of the subjective passions, the emotional preconceptions which color conviction and judgment. Both writers and scholars freed themselves of the personal responsibility associated with personal choice. They emerged free, pure and single into the antiseptic air of objectivity. And by that sublimation of the mind they prepared the mind's disaster.

If it is a consolation to the philosophers of earlier civilization to know that they lost the things they loved because of the purity of their devotion, then perhaps this consolation will be ours as well. I doubt if we will profit by it or receive much praise.

F. SCOTT FITZGERALD

1896-1940

I. THE YEARS OF STRUGGLE (1896–1920)

1896 Born September 24, St. Paul, Minnesota, son of Edward and Mary McQuillan Fitzgerald. Christened Francis Scott Key Fitzgerald, since he was distantly related to the author of "The Star-Spangled Banner." Educated in St. Paul.

1911–1913 Pupil in the Newman School, Hackensack, New Jersey, "in the hopes that he might do more studying."

1913–1917 Student at Princeton. As a freshman he wrote an operetta for the Triangle Club, and with Edmund Wilson wrote other dramatic material. Stories and poems in *The Princeton Tiger* and *The Nassau Literary Magazine*.

1917 Commissioned as infantry lieutenant; aide-de-camp to General J. A. Ryan. Worked on *The Romantic Egoist,* first form of *This Side of Paradise.*

1919–1920 Worked as an advertising writer.

1920 Sold his first story to a magazine, gave up his job, and revised his novel. Published *This Side of Paradise.* Married Zelda Sayre of Montgomery, Alabama.

II. SUCCESS AND FRUSTRATION (1920–1940)

1920 Following success of the novel, he published stories, principally in *The Saturday Evening Post,* collected as *Flappers and Philosophers.* Began wandering life in Europe and the United States.

1922 *The Beautiful and Damned* (novel); *Tales of the Jazz Age* (includes such short stories as "May Day" and "The Diamond as Big as the Ritz").

1923 *The Vegetable* (play).

1925 *The Great Gatsby,* written in Italy and the French Riviera.

1926 *All the Sad Young Men* (short stories).

1928 *John Jackson's Arcady.*

1934 *Tender is the Night* (novel).

1935 *Taps at Reveille* (short stories).

1937–1940 Life in Hollywood, which served as background for *The Last Tycoon* and is the subject of Budd Schulberg's novel, *The Disenchanted* (1950).

1940 Died December 21, in Hollywood.

1941 *The Last Tycoon: An Unfinished Novel.*

1945 *The Crack-Up* (uncollected pieces, notebooks, and unpublished letters, edited by Edmund Wilson).

BIOGRAPHY AND CRITICISM: Arthur Mizener's *The Far Side of Paradise,* Houghton Mifflin, 1951, is the first full-length biography. Delmore Schwartz has another study in preparation. For critical comment see Glenway Wescott and others, "In Memory of Scott Fitzgerald," *New Republic,* Feb. 17, 1941, pp.

213-17, 311-13; Leo and Miriam Gurko, "The Essence of Scott Fitzgerald," *College English,* April, 1944, pp. 372-75; John Berryman, "F. Scott Fitzgerald," *Kenyon Review,* Winter, 1946, pp. 103-112; Maxwell Geismar, *The Last of the Provincials,* Houghton Mifflin, 1947; Alfred Kazin, ed., *F. Scott Fitzgerald: The Man and His Work,* World Publishing Company, 1951. For other references see Fred B. Millett, *Contemporary American Authors,* 3d ed., Harcourt, Brace, 1940.

BIBLIOGRAPHY: See Millett, above, and *Literary History of the United States,* Vol. III, pp. 505-06.

EDITIONS: *The Great Gatsby* is available in the Modern Library, Random House, and in New Directions' New Classic Series. Charles Scribner's Sons has reissued *This Side of Paradise, Tender is the Night,* and in one volume *The Last Tycoon* and *The Great Gatsby.* Malcolm Cowley has selected twenty-eight short stories (including ten never before published in book form) for *The Stories of F. Scott Fitzgerald* (Scribner's, 1951). An excellent collection is the *Portable F. Scott Fitzgerald* (Viking, 1945), selected by Dorothy Parker, with an introduction by John O'Hara.

F. Scott Fitzgerald originally appeared as the voice of youth after World War I, disillusioned by the unwisdom of their elders and seeking in casual sex, casual drink, and casual adventure some escape from spiritual defeatism. "Tales of the Jazz Age," it seemed for a time, might serve as epigraph for all his fiction. Closer reading of *This Side of Paradise* and of the short stories revealed more—it revealed an undercutting of the values of a spending economy, an alert, critical intelligence at work upon the problem of happiness in an industrial economy. Admirable as was (and is) *The Beautiful and Damned* (some critics regard it as Fitzgerald's masterpiece), it was not until *The Great Gatsby* that the mature artist was recognized. Pathetic and ludicrous in his Proustian fixation, Gatsby's attempts to ape society were at once a case study in pathos and a critical parody of the Benjamin Franklin virtues, inasmuch as Gatsby, too, had been diligent in business. *The Last Tycoon* promised even greater things as an analysis of the intellectual and emotional sterility of mere success. It is considered by many as one of the best fictional treatments of that American phenomenon, Hollywood, even though the novel remained unfinished. Fitzgerald is now generally recognized as one of the prose masters of the twentieth century, and his career is regarded as pointing up the problem of the economy of art in contemporary society.

THE RICH BOY

This story was first printed in *Redbook,* January and February, 1926. It appeared again as the opening tale in *All the Sad Young Men,* 1926, the text of which is here followed.

BEGIN with an individual, and before you know it you find that you have created a type; begin with a type, and you find that you have created— nothing. That is because we are all queer fish, queerer behind our faces and voices than we want any one to know or than we know ourselves. When I hear a man proclaiming himself an "average, honest, open fellow," I feel   5 pretty sure that he has some definite and perhaps terrible abnormality which he has agreed to conceal—and his protestation of being average and honest and open is his way of reminding himself of his misprision.

There are no types, no plurals. There is a rich boy, and this is his and not his brothers' story. All my life I have lived among his brothers but this one has been my friend. Besides, if I wrote about his brothers I should have to begin by attacking all the lies that the poor have told about the rich and the
5 rich have told about themselves—such a wild structure they have erected that when we pick up a book about the rich, some instinct prepares us for unreality. Even the intelligent and impassioned reporters of life have made the country of the rich as unreal as fairy-land.

Let me tell you about the very rich. They are different from you and me.
10 They possess and enjoy early, and it does something to them, makes them soft where we are hard, and cynical where we are trustful, in a way that, unless you were born rich, it is very difficult to understand. They think, deep in their hearts, that they are better than we are because we had to discover the compensations and refuges of life for ourselves. Even when they enter deep
15 into our world or sink below us, they still think that they are better than we are. They are different. The only way I can describe young Anson Hunter is to approach him as if he were a foreigner and cling stubbornly to my point of view. If I accept his for a moment I am lost—I have nothing to show but a preposterous movie.

20   II

Anson was the eldest of six children who would some day divide a fortune of fifteen million dollars, and he reached the age of reason—is it seven?—at the beginning of the century when daring young women were already gliding along Fifth Avenue in electric "mobiles." In those days he and his brother
25 had an English governess who spoke the language very clearly and crisply and well, so that the two boys grew to speak as she did—their words and sentences were all crisp and clear and not run together as ours are. They didn't talk exactly like English children but acquired an accent that is peculiar to fashionable people in the city of New York.
30 In the summer the six children were moved from the house on 71st Street to a big estate in northern Connecticut. It was not a fashionable locality—Anson's father wanted to delay as long as possible his children's knowledge of that side of life. He was a man somewhat superior to his class, which composed New York society, and to his period, which was the snobbish and for-
35 malized vulgarity of the Gilded Age, and he wanted his sons to learn habits of concentration and have sound constitutions and grow up into right-living and successful men. He and his wife kept an eye on them as well as they were able until the two older boys went away to school, but in huge establishments this is difficult—it was much simpler in the series of small and medium-sized
40 houses in which my own youth was spent—I was never far out of the reach of my mother's voice, of the sense of her presence, her approval or disapproval.

Anson's first sense of his superiority came to him when he realized the half-grudging American deference that was paid to him in the Connecticut village.
45 The parents of the boys he played with always inquired after his father and

35. **Gilded Age**—title of a novel by Mark Twain and Charles Dudley Warner, 1873.

mother, and were vaguely excited when their own children were asked to the Hunters' house. He accepted this as the natural state of things, and a sort of impatience with all groups of which he was not the center—in money, in position, in authority—remained with him for the rest of his life. He disdained to struggle with other boys for precedence—he expected it to be given him 5 freely, and when it wasn't he withdrew into his family. His family was sufficient, for in the East money is still a somewhat feudal thing, a clan-forming thing. In the snobbish West, money separates families to form "sets."

At eighteen, when he went to New Haven, Anson was tall and thick-set, with a clear complexion and a healthy color from the ordered life he had led 10 in school. His hair was yellow and grew in a funny way on his head, his nose was beaked—these two things kept him from being handsome—but he had a confident charm and a certain brusque style, and the upper-class men who passed him on the street knew without being told that he was a rich boy and had gone to one of the best schools. Nevertheless, his very superiority kept 15 him from being a success in college—the independence was mistaken for egotism, and the refusal to accept Yale standards with the proper awe seemed to belittle all those who had. So, long before he graduated, he began to shift the center of his life to New York.

He was at home in New York—there was his own house with "the kind 20 of servants you can't get any more"—and his own family, of which, because of his good humor and a certain ability to make things go, he was rapidly becoming the centre, and the débutante parties, and the correct manly world of the men's clubs, and the occasional wild spree with the gallant girls whom New Haven only knew from the fifth row. His aspirations were conventional 25 enough—they included even the irreproachable shadow he would some day marry, but they differed from the aspirations of the majority of young men in that there was no mist over them, none of that quality which is variously known as "idealism" or "illusion." Anson accepted without reservation the world of high finance and high extravagance, of divorce and dissipation, of 30 snobbery and of privilege. Most of our lives end as a compromise—it was as a compromise that his life began.

He and I first met in the late summer of 1917 when he was just out of Yale, and, like the rest of us, was swept up into the systematized hysteria of the war. In the blue-green uniform of the naval aviation he came down to Pensa- 35 cola, where the hotel orchestras played "I'm sorry, dear," and we young officers danced with the girls. Every one liked him, and though he ran. with the drinkers and wasn't an especially good pilot, even the instructors treated him with a certain respect. He was always having long talks with them in his confident, logical voice—talks which ended by his getting himself, or, more 40 frequently, another officer, out of some impending trouble. He was convivial, bawdy, robustly avid for pleasure, and we were all surprised when he fell in love with a conservative and rather proper girl.

Her name was Paula Legendre, a dark, serious beauty from somewhere in California. Her family kept a winter residence just outside of town, and in 45 spite of her primness she was enormously popular; there is a large class of men whose egotism can't endure humor in a woman. But Anson wasn't that sort, and I couldn't understand the attraction of her "sincerity"—that was the thing to say about her—for his keen and somewhat sardonic mind.

Nevertheless, they fell in love—and on her terms. He no longer joined the twilight gathering at the De Sota bar, and whenever they were seen together
5 they were engaged in a long, serious dialogue, which must have gone on several weeks. Long afterward he told me that it was not about anything in particular but was composed on both sides of immature and even meaningless statements—the emotional content that gradually came to fill it grew up not out of the words but out of its enormous seriousness. It was a sort of hypnosis.
10 Often it was interrupted, giving way to that emasculated humor we call fun; when they were alone it was resumed again, solemn, low-keyed, and pitched so as to give each other a sense of unity in feeling and thought. They came to resent any interruptions of it, to be unresponsive to facetiousness about life, even to the mild cynicism of their contemporaries. They were only happy
15 when the dialogue was going on, and its seriousness bathed them like the amber glow of an open fire. Toward the end there came an interruption they did not resent—it began to be interrupted by passion.

Oddly enough, Anson was as engrossed in the dialogue as she was and as profoundly affected by it, yet at the same time aware that on his side much
20 was insincere, and on hers much was merely simple. At first, too, he despised her emotional simplicity as well, but with his love her nature deepened and blossomed, and he could despise it no longer. He felt that if he could enter into Paula's warm safe life he would be happy. The long preparation of the dialogue removed any constraint—he taught her some of what he had learned
25 from more adventurous women, and she responded with a rapt holy intensity. One evening after a dance they agreed to marry, and he wrote a long letter about her to his mother. The next day Paula told him that she was rich, that she had a personal fortune of nearly a million dollars.

III

30 It was exactly as if they could say "Neither of us has anything: we shall be poor together"—just as delightful that they should be rich instead. It gave them the same communion of adventure. Yet when Anson got leave in April, and Paula and her mother accompanied him North, she was impressed with the standing of his family in New York and with the scale on which they
35 lived. Alone with Anson for the first time in the rooms where he had played as a boy, she was filled with a comfortable emotion, as though she were pre-eminently safe and taken care of. The pictures of Anson in a skull cap at his first school, of Anson on horseback with the sweetheart of a mysterious for-gotten summer, of Anson in a gay group of ushers and bridesmaids at a wed-
40 ding, made her jealous of his life apart from her in the past, and so com-pletely did his authoritative person seem to sum up and typify these posses-sions of his that she was inspired with the idea of being married immediately and returning to Pensacola as his wife.

But an immediate marriage wasn't discussed—even the engagement was to
45 be secret until after the war. When she realized that only two days of his

leave remained, her dissatisfaction crystallized in the intention of making him as unwilling to wait as she was. They were driving to the country for dinner, and she determined to force the issue that night.

Now a cousin of Paula's was staying with them at the Ritz, a severe, bitter girl who loved Paula but was somewhat jealous of her impressive engage- 5 ment, and as Paula was late in dressing, the cousin, who wasn't going to the party, received Anson in the parlor of the suite.

Anson had met friends at five o'clock and drunk freely and indiscreetly with them for an hour. He left the Yale Club at a proper time, and his moth- er's chauffeur drove him to the Ritz, but his usual capacity was not in evi- 10 dence, and the impact of the steam-heated sitting-room made him suddenly dizzy. He knew it, and he was both amused and sorry.

Paula's cousin was twenty-five, but she was exceptionally naïve, and at first failed to realize what was up. She had never met Anson before, and she was surprised when he mumbled strange information and nearly fell off his chair, 15 but until Paula appeared it didn't occur to her that what she had taken for the odor of a dry-cleaned uniform was really whiskey. But Paula understood as soon as she appeared; her only thought was to get Anson away before her mother saw him, and at the look in her eyes the cousin understood too.

When Paula and Anson descended to the limousine they found two men 20 inside, both asleep; they were the men with whom he had been drinking at the Yale Club, and they were also going to the party. He had entirely for- gotten their presence in the car. On the way to Hempstead they awoke and sang. Some of the songs were rough, and though Paula tried to reconcile her- self to the fact that Anson had few verbal inhibitions, her lips tightened with 25 shame and distaste.

Back at the hotel the cousin, confused and agitated, considered the inci- dent, and then walked into Mrs. Legendre's bedroom, saying: "Isn't he funny?"

"Who is funny?" 30

"Why—Mr. Hunter. He seemed so funny."

Mrs. Legendre looked at her sharply.

"How is he funny?"

"Why, he said he was French. I didn't know he was French."

"That's absurd. You must have misunderstood." She smiled: "It was a 35 joke."

The cousin shook her head stubbornly.

"No. He said he was brought up in France. He said he couldn't speak any English, and that's why he couldn't talk to me. And he couldn't!"

Mrs. Legendre looked away with impatience just as the cousin added 40 thoughtfully, "Perhaps it was because he was so drunk," and walked out of the room.

This curious report was true. Anson, finding his voice thick and uncon- trollable, had taken the unusual refuge of announcing that he spoke no Eng- lish. Years afterward he used to tell that part of the story, and he invariably 45 communicated the uproarious laughter which the memory aroused in him.

23. **Hempstead**—suburb of New York City, on Long Island.

Five times in the next hour Mrs. Legendre tried to get Hempstead on the phone. When she succeeded, there was a ten-minute delay before she heard Paula's voice on the wire.

"Cousin Jo told me Anson was intoxicated."

5   "Oh, no. . . ."

"Oh, yes. Cousin Jo says he was intoxicated. He told her he was French, and fell off his chair and behaved as if he was very intoxicated. I don't want you to come home with him."

"Mother, he's all right! Please don't worry about—"

10   "But I do worry. I think it's dreadful. I want you to promise me not to come home with him."

"I'll take care of it, mother. . . ."

"I don't want you to come home with him."

"All right, mother. Good-by."

15   "Be sure now, Paula. Ask some one to bring you."

Deliberately Paula took the receiver from her ear and hung it up. Her face was flushed with helpless annoyance. Anson was stretched asleep out in a bedroom upstairs, while the dinner-party below was proceeding lamely toward conclusion.

20   The hour's drive had sobered him somewhat—his arrival was merely hilarious—and Paula hoped that the evening was not spoiled, after all, but two imprudent cocktails before dinner completed the disaster. He talked boisterously and somewhat offensively to the party at large for fifteen minutes, and then slid silently under the table; like a man in an old print—but, unlike an

25 old print, it was rather horrible without being at all quaint. None of the young girls present remarked upon the incident—it seemed to merit only silence. His uncle and two other men carried him upstairs, and it was just after this that Paula was called to the phone.

An hour later Anson awoke in a fog of nervous agony, through which he

30 perceived after a moment the figure of his Uncle Robert standing by the door.

". . . I said are you better?"

"What?"

"Do you feel better, old man?"

"Terrible," said Anson.

35   "I'm going to try you on another bromo-seltzer. If you can hold it down, it'll do you good to sleep."

With an effort Anson slid his legs from the bed and stood up.

"I'm all right," he said dully.

"Take it easy."

40   "I thin' if you gave me a glassbrandy I could go downstairs."

"Oh, no—"

"Yes, that's the only thin'. I'm all right now. . . . I suppose I'm in dutch dow' there."

"They know you're a little under the weather," said his uncle deprecatingly.

45 "But don't worry about it. Schuyler didn't even get here. He passed away in the locker-room over at the Links."

45. **passed away**—so runs the text, but "passed out" seems to be demanded.

Indifferent to any opinion, except Paula's, Anson was nevertheless determined to save the débris of the evening, but when after a cold bath he made his appearance most of the party had already left. Paula got up immediately to go home.

In the limousine the old serious dialogue began. She had known that he drank, she admitted, but she had never expected anything like this—it seemed to her that perhaps they were not suited to each other, after all. Their ideas about life were too different, and so forth. When she finished speaking, Anson spoke in turn, very soberly. Then Paula said she'd have to think it over; she wouldn't decide tonight; she was not angry but she was terribly sorry. Nor would she let him come into the hotel with her, but just before she got out of the car she leaned and kissed him unhappily on the cheek.

The next afternoon Anson had a long talk with Mrs. Legendre while Paula sat listening in silence. It was agreed that Paula was to brood over the incident for a proper period and then, if mother and daughter thought it best, they would follow Anson to Pensacola. On his part he apologized with sincerity and dignity—that was all; with every card in her hand Mrs. Legendre was unable to establish any advantage over him. He made no promises, showed no humility, only delivered a few serious comments on life which brought him off with rather a moral superiority at the end. When they came South three weeks later, neither Anson in his satisfaction nor Paula in her relief at the reunion realized that the psychological moment had passed forever.

IV

He dominated and attracted her, and at the same time filled her with anxiety. Confused by his mixture of solidity and self-indulgence, of sentiment and cynicism—incongruities which her gentle mind was unable to resolve—Paula grew to think of him as two alternating personalities. When she saw him alone, or at a formal party, or with his casual inferiors, she felt a tremendous pride in his strong, attractive presence, the paternal, understanding stature of his mind. In other company she became uneasy when what had been a fine imperviousness to mere gentility showed its other face. The other face was gross, humorous, reckless of everything but pleasure. It startled her mind temporarily away from him, even led her into a short covert experiment with an old beau, but it was no use—after four months of Anson's enveloping vitality there was an anæmic pallor in all other men.

In July he was ordered abroad, and their tenderness and desire reached a crescendo. Paula considered a last-minute marriage—decided against it only because there were always cocktails on his breath now, but the parting itself made her physically ill with grief. After his departure she wrote him long letters of regret for the days of love they had missed by waiting. In August Anson's plane slipped down into the North Sea. He was pulled onto a destroyer after a night in the water and sent to hospital with pneumonia; the armistice was signed before he was finally sent home.

Then, with every opportunity given back to them, with no material obstacle to overcome, the secret weavings of their temperaments came between them, drying up their kisses and their tears, making their voices less loud to one another, muffling the intimate chatter of their hearts until the old communication was only possible by letters, from far away. One afternoon a society reporter waited for two hours in the Hunters' house for a confirmation

5 of their engagement. Anson denied it; nevertheless an early issue carried the report as a leading paragraph—they were "constantly seen together at Southampton, Hot Springs, and Tuxedo Park." But the serious dialogue had turned a corner into a long-sustained quarrel, and the affair was almost played out. Anson got drunk flagrantly and missed an engagement with her, whereupon

10 Paula made certain behavioristic demands. His despair was helpless before his pride and his knowledge of himself: the engagement was definitely broken.

"Dearest," said their letters now, "Dearest, Dearest, when I wake up in the middle of the night and realize that after all it was not to be, I feel that I want to die. I can't go on living any more. Perhaps when we meet this sum-

15 mer we may talk things over and decide differently—we were so excited and sad that day, and I don't feel that I can live all my life without you. You speak of other people. Don't you know there are no other people for me, but only you. . . ."

But as Paula drifted here and there around the East she would sometimes

20 mention her gaieties to make him wonder. Anson was too acute to wonder. When he saw a man's name in her letters he felt more sure of her and a little disdainful—he was always superior to such things. But he still hoped that they would some day marry.

Meanwhile he plunged vigorously into all the movement and glitter of post-

25 bellum New York, entering a brokerage house, joining half a dozen clubs, dancing late, and moving in three worlds—his own world, the world of young Yale graduates, and that section of the half-world which rests one end on Broadway. But there was always a thorough and infractible eight hours devoted to his work in Wall Street, where the combination of his influential

30 family connection, his sharp intelligence, and his abundance of sheer physical energy brought him almost immediately forward. He had one of those invaluable minds with partitions in it; sometimes he appeared at his office refreshed by less than an hour's sleep, but such occurrences were rare. So early as 1920 his income in salary and commissions exceeded twelve thousand dollars.

35 As the Yale tradition slipped into the past he became more and more of a popular figure among his classmates in New York, more popular than he had ever been in college. He lived in a great house, and had the means of introducing young men into other great houses. Moreover, his life already seemed secure, while theirs, for the most part, had arrived again at precarious begin-

40 nings. They commenced to turn to him for amusement and escape, and Anson responded readily, taking pleasure in helping people and arranging their affairs.

There were no men in Paula's letters now, but a note of tenderness ran through them that had not been there before. From several sources he heard

45 that she had "a heavy beau," Lowell Thayer, a Bostonian of wealth and posi-

6-7. **Southampton . . . Park**—fashionable resort towns in Long Island, Arkansas, and Orange County, New York, respectively.

tion, and though he was sure she still loved him, it made him uneasy to think that he might lose her, after all. Save for one unsatisfactory day she had not been in New York for almost five months, and as the rumors multiplied he became increasingly anxious to see her. In February he took his vacation and went down to Florida.

Palm Beach sprawled plump and opulent between the sparkling sapphire of Lake Worth, flawed here and there by house-boats at anchor, and the great turquoise bar of the Atlantic Ocean. The huge bulks of the Breakers and the Royal Poinciana rose as twin paunches from the bright level of the sand, and around them clustered the Dancing Glade, Bradley's House of Chance, and a dozen modistes and milliners with goods at triple prices from New York. Upon the trellissed veranda of the Breakers two hundred women stepped right, stepped left, wheeled, and slid in that then celebrated calisthenic known as the double-shuffle, while in half-time to the music two thousand bracelets clicked up and down on two hundred arms.

At the Everglades Club after dark Paula and Lowell Thayer and Anson and a casual fourth played bridge with hot cards. It seemed to Anson that her kind, serious face was wan and tired—she had been around now for four, five, years. He had known her for three.

"Two spades."

"Cigarette? . . . Oh, I beg your pardon. By me."

"By."

"I'll double three spades."

There were a dozen tables of bridge in the room, which was filling up with smoke. Anson's eyes met Paula's, held them persistently even when Thayer's glance fell between them. . . .

"What was bid?" he asked abstractedly.

"Rose of Washington Square"

sang the young people in the corners:

*"I'm withering there
In basement air—"*

The smoke banked like fog, and the opening of a door filled the room with blown swirls of ectoplasm. Little Bright Eyes streaked past the tables seeking Mr. Conan Doyle among the Englishmen who were posing as Englishmen about the lobby.

"You could cut it with a knife."

". . . cut it with a knife."

". . . a knife."

At the end of the rubber Paula suddenly got up and spoke to Anson in a tense, low voice. With scarcely a glance at Lowell Thayer, they walked out the door and descended a long flight of stone steps—in a moment they were walking hand in hand along the moonlit beach.

33. Little Bright Eyes—the medium's "control" in Bayard Veiller's melodrama, *The Thirteenth Chair,* 1922. **34. Conan Doyle**—After the death of his son in World War I, Sir Arthur Conan Doyle (1859-1930), the creator of Sherlock Holmes, became a convinced spiritualist and believer in mediums.

"Darling, darling. . . ." They embraced recklessly, passionately, in a shadow. . . . Then Paula drew back her face to let his lips say what she wanted to hear—she could feel the words forming as they kissed again. . . . Again she broke away, listening, but as he pulled her close once more she
5 realized that he had said nothing—only *Darling! Darling!* in that deep, sad whisper that always made her cry. Humbly, obediently, her emotions yielded to him and the tears streamed down her face, but her heart kept on crying: "Ask me—oh, Anson, dearest, ask me!"

"Paula. . . . *Paula!*"

10 The words wrung her heart like hands, and Anson, feeling her tremble, knew that emotion was enough. He need say no more, commit their destinies to no practical enigma. Why should he, when he might hold her so, biding his own time, for another year—forever? He was considering them both, her more than himself. For a moment, when she said suddenly that she
15 must go back to her hotel, he hesitated, thinking, first, "This is the moment, after all," and then: "No, let it wait—she is mine. . . ."

He had forgotten that Paula too was worn away inside with the strain of three years. Her mood passed forever in the night.

He went back to New York next morning filled with a certain restless dis-
20 satisfaction. Late in April, without warning, he received a telegram from Bar Harbor in which Paula told him that she was engaged to Lowell Thayer, and that they would be married immediately in Boston. What he never really believed could happen had happened at last.

Anson filled himself with whiskey that morning, and going to the office,
25 carried on his work without a break—rather with a fear of what would happen if he stopped. In the evening he went out as usual, saying nothing of what had occurred; he was cordial, humorous, unabstracted. But one thing he could not help—for three days, in any place, in any company, he would suddenly bend his head into his hands and cry like a child.

30   V

In 1922 when Anson went abroad with the junior partner to investigate some London loans, the journey intimated that he was to be taken into the firm. He was twenty-seven now, a little heavy without being definitely stout, and with a manner older than his years. Old people and young people liked
35 him and trusted him, and mothers felt safe when their daughters were in his charge, for he had a way, when he came into a room, of putting himself on a footing with the oldest and most conservative people there. "You and I," he seemed to say, "we're solid. We understand."

He had an instinctive and rather charitable knowledge of the weaknesses
40 of men and women, and, like a priest, it made him the more concerned for the maintenance of outward forms. It was typical of him that every Sunday morning he taught in a fashionable Episcopal Sunday school—even though a cold shower and a quick change into a cutaway coat were all that separated him from the wild night before.

20-21. **Bar Harbor**—well-to-do resort town in Maine.

After his father's death he was the practical head of his family, and, in effect, guided the destinies of the younger children. Through a complication his authority did not extend to his father's estate, which was administrated by his Uncle Robert, who was the horsey member of the family, a good-natured, hard-drinking member of that set which centres about Wheatley Hills.

Uncle Robert and his wife, Edna, had been great friends of Anson's youth, and the former was disappointed when his nephew's superiority failed to take a horsey form. He backed him for a city club which was the most difficult in America to enter—one could only join if one's family had "helped to build up New York" (or, in other words, were rich before 1880)—and when Anson, after his election, neglected it for the Yale Club, Uncle Robert gave him a little talk on the subject. But when on top of that Anson declined to enter Robert Hunter's own conservative and somewhat neglected brokerage house, his manner grew cooler. Like a primary teacher who has taught all he knew, he slipped out of Anson's life.

There were so many friends in Anson's life—scarcely one for whom he had not done some unusual kindness and scarcely one whom he did not occasionally embarrass by his bursts of rough conversation or his habit of getting drunk whenever and however he liked. It annoyed him when any one else blundered in that regard—about his own lapses he was always humorous. Odd things happened to him and he told them with infectious laughter.

I was working in New York that spring, and I used to lunch with him at the Yale Club, which my university was sharing until the completion of our own. I had read of Paula's marriage, and one afternoon, when I asked him about her, something moved him to tell me the story. After that he frequently invited me to family dinners at his house and behaved as though there was a special relation between us, as though with his confidence a little of that consuming memory had passed into me.

I found that despite the trusting mothers, his attitude toward girls was not indiscriminately protective. It was up to the girl—if she showed an inclination toward looseness, she must take care of herself, even with him.

"Life," he would explain sometimes, "has made a cynic of me."

By life he meant Paula. Sometimes, especially when he was drinking, it became a little twisted in his mind, and he thought that she had callously thrown him over.

This "cynicism," or rather his realization that naturally fast girls were not worth sparing, led to his affair with Dolly Karger. It wasn't his only affair in those years, but it came nearest to touching him deeply, and it had a profound effect upon his attitude toward life.

Dolly was the daughter of a notorious "publicist" who had married into society. She herself grew up into the Junior League, came out at the Plaza, and went to the Assembly; and only a few old families like the Hunters could question whether or not she "belonged," for her picture was often in the papers, and she had more enviable attention than many girls who undoubtedly did. She was dark-haired, with carmine lips and a high, lovely color, which she concealed under pinkish-gray powder all through the first

year out, because high color was unfashionable—Victorian-pale was the thing
to be. She wore black, severe suits and stood with her hands in her pockets
leaning a little forward, with a humorous restraint on her face. She danced
exquisitely—better than anything she liked to dance—better than anything ex-
5   cept making love. Since she was ten she had always been in love, and, usually, with some boy who didn't respond to her. Those who did—and there
were many—bored her after a brief encounter, but for her failures she reserved the warmest spot in her heart. When she met them she would always
try once more—sometimes she succeeded, more often she failed.

10   It never occurred to this gypsy of the unattainable that there was a certain
resemblance in those who refused to love her—they shared a hard intuition
that saw through to her weakness, not a weakness of emotion but a weakness
of rudder. Anson perceived this when he first met her, less than a month
after Paula's marriage. He was drinking rather heavily, and he pretended for
15   a week that he was falling in love with her. Then he dropped her abruptly
and forgot—immediately he took up the commanding position in her heart.

Like so many girls of that day Dolly was slackly and indiscreetly wild.
The unconventionality of a slightly older generation had been simply one
facet of a post-war movement to discredit obsolete manners—Dolly's was both
20   older and shabbier, and she saw in Anson the two extremes which the emo-
tionally shiftless woman seeks, an abandon to indulgence alternating with a
protective strength. In his character she felt both the sybarite and the solid
rock, and these two satisfied every need of her nature.

She felt that it was going to be difficult, but she mistook the reason—she
25   thought that Anson and his family expected a more spectacular marriage, but
she guessed immediately that her advantage lay in his tendency to drink.

They met at the large débutante dances, but as her infatuation increased
they managed to be more and more together. Like most mothers, Mrs. Karger
believed that Anson was exceptionally reliable, so she allowed Dolly to go
30   with him to distant country clubs and suburban houses without inquiring
closely into their activities or questioning her explanations when they came in
late. At first these explanations might have been accurate, but Dolly's worldly
ideas of capturing Anson were soon engulfed in the rising sweep of her emotion. Kisses in the back of taxis and motor-cars were no longer enough; they
35   did a curious thing:

They dropped out of their world for a while and made another world just
beneath it where Anson's tippling and Dolly's irregular hours would be less
noticed and commented on. It was composed, this world, of varying elements
—several of Anson's Yale friends and their wives, two or three young brokers
40   and bond salesmen and a handful of unattached men, fresh from college, with
money and a propensity to dissipation. What this world lacked in spaciousness
and scale it made up for by allowing them a liberty that it scarcely permitted
itself. Moreover, it centred around them and permitted Dolly the pleasure of a
faint condescension—a pleasure which Anson, whose whole life was a conde-
45   scension from the certitudes of his childhood, was unable to share.

He was not in love with her, and in the long feverish winter of their affair he frequently told her so. In the spring he was weary—he wanted to re-

new his life at some other source—moreover, he saw that either he must break with her now or accept the responsibility of a definite seduction. Her family's encouraging attitude precipitated his decision—one evening when Mr. Karger knocked discreetly at the library door to announce that he had left a bottle of old brandy in the dining-room, Anson felt that life was hemming him in. That night he wrote her a short letter in which he told her that he was going on his vacation, and that in view of all the circumstances they had better meet no more.

It was June. His family had closed up the house and gone to the country, so he was living temporarily at the Yale Club. I had heard about his affair with Dolly as it developed—accounts salted with humor, for he despised unstable women, and granted them no place in the social edifice in which he believed—and when he told me that night that he was definitely breaking with her I was glad. I had seen Dolly here and there, and each time with a feeling of pity at the hopelessness of her struggle, and of shame at knowing so much about her that I had no right to know. She was what is known as "a pretty little thing," but there was a certain recklessness which rather fascinated me. Her dedication to the goddess of waste would have been less obvious had she been less spirited—she would most certainly throw herself away, but I was glad when I heard that the sacrifice would not be consummated in my sight.

Anson was going to leave the letter of farewell at her house next morning. It was one of the few houses left open in the Fifth Avenue district, and he knew that the Kargers, acting upon erroneous information from Dolly, had foregone a trip abroad to give their daughter her chance. As he stepped out the door of the Yale Club into Madison Avenue the postman passed him, and he followed back inside. The first letter that caught his eye was in Dolly's hand.

He knew what it would be—a lonely and tragic monologue, full of the reproaches he knew, the invoked memories, the "I wonder if's"—all the immemorial intimacies that he had communicated to Paula Legendre in what seemed another age. Thumbing over some bills, he brought it on top again and opened it. To his surprise it was a short, somewhat formal note, which said that Dolly would be unable to go to the country with him for the weekend, because Perry Hull from Chicago had unexpectedly come to town. It added that Anson had brought this on himself: "—if I felt that you loved me as I love you I would go with you at any time, any place, but Perry is *so* nice, and he so much wants me to marry him—"

Anson smiled contemptuously—he had had experience with such decoy epistles. Moreover, he knew how Dolly had labored over this plan, probably sent for the faithful Perry and calculated the time of his arrival—even labored over the note so that it would make him jealous without driving him away. Like most compromises, it had neither force nor vitality but only a timorous despair.

Suddenly he was angry. He sat down in the lobby and read it again. Then he went to the phone, called Dolly and told her in his clear, compelling voice that he had received her note and would call for her at five o'clock as they had previously planned. Scarcely waiting for the pretended uncertainty of her "Perhaps I can see you for an hour," he hung up the receiver and went down to his office. On the way he tore his own letter into bits and dropped it in the street.

5   He was not jealous—she meant nothing to him—but at her pathetic ruse everything stubborn and self-indulgent in him came to the surface. It was a presumption from a mental inferior and it could not be overlooked. If she wanted to know to whom she belonged she would see.

He was on the door-step at quarter past five. Dolly was dressed for the 10 street, and he listened in silence to the paragraph of "I can only see you for an hour," which she had begun on the phone.

"Put on your hat, Dolly," he said, "we'll take a walk."

They strolled up Madison Avenue and over to Fifth while Anson's shirt dampened upon his portly body in the deep heat. He talked little, scolding 15 her, making no love to her, but before they had walked six blocks she was his again, apologizing for the note, offering not to see Perry at all as an atonement, offering anything. She thought that he had come because he was beginning to love her.

"I'm hot," he said when they reached 71st Street. "This is a winter suit. If 20 I stop by the house and change, would you mind waiting for me downstairs? I'll only be a minute."

She was happy; the intimacy of his being hot, of any physical fact about him, thrilled her. When they came to the iron-grated door and Anson took out his key she experienced a sort of delight.

25   Downstairs it was dark, and after he ascended in the lift Dolly raised a curtain and looked out through opaque lace at the houses over the way. She heard the lift machinery stop, and with the notion of teasing him pressed the button that brought it down. Then on what was more than an impulse she got into it and sent it up to what she guessed was his floor.

30   "Anson," she called, laughing a little.

"Just a minute," he answered from his bedroom . . . then after a brief delay: "Now you can come in."

He had changed and was buttoning his vest. "This is my room," he said lightly. "How do you like it?"

35   She caught sight of Paula's picture on the wall and stared at it in fascination, just as Paula had stared at the pictures of Anson's childish sweethearts five years before. She knew something about Paula—sometimes she tortured herself with fragments of the story.

Suddenly she came close to Anson, raising her arms. They embraced. Out-40 side the area window a soft artificial twilight already hovered, though the sun was still bright on a back roof across the way. In half an hour the room would be quite dark. The uncalculated opportunity overwhelmed them, made them both breathless, and they clung more closely. It was eminent, inevitable. Still holding one another, they raised their heads—their eyes fell together 45 upon Paula's picture, staring down at them from the wall.

Suddenly Anson dropped his arms, and sitting down at his desk tried the drawer with a bunch of keys.

"Like a drink?" he asked in a gruff voice.

"No, Anson."

He poured himself half a tumbler of whiskey, swallowed it, and then opened the door into the hall.

"Come on," he said.   5

Dolly hesitated.

"Anson—I'm going to the country with you tonight, after all. You understand that, don't you?"

"Of course," he answered brusquely.

In Dolly's car they rode on to Long Island, closer in their emotions than   10
they had ever been before. They knew what would happen—not with Paula's face to remind them that something was lacking, but when they were alone in the still, hot Long Island night they did not care.

The estate in Port Washington where they were to spend the week-end belonged to a cousin of Anson's who had married a Montana copper operator.   15
An interminable drive began at the lodge and twisted under imported poplar saplings toward a huge, pink, Spanish house. Anson had often visited there before.

After dinner they danced at the Linx Club. About midnight Anson assured himself that his cousins would not leave before two—then he explained that   20
Dolly was tired; he would take her home and return to the dance later. Trembling a little with excitement, they got into a borrowed car together and drove to Port Washington. As they reached the lodge he stopped and spoke to the night-watchman.

"When are you making a round, Carl?"   25

"Right away."

"Then you'll be here till everybody's in?"

"Yes, sir."

"All right. Listen: if any automobile, no matter whose it is, turns in at this gate, I want you to phone the house immediately." He put a five-dollar bill   30
into Carl's hand. "Is that clear?"

"Yes, Mr. Anson." Being of the Old World, he neither winked nor smiled. Yet Dolly sat with her face turned slightly away.

Anson had a key. Once inside he poured a drink for both of them—Dolly left hers untouched—then he ascertained definitely the location of the phone,   35
and found that it was within easy hearing distance of their rooms, both of which were on the first floor.

Five minutes later he knocked at the door of Dolly's room.

"Anson?" He went in, closing the door behind him. She was in bed, leaning up anxiously with elbows on the pillow; sitting beside her he took her in his   40
arms.

"Anson, darling."

He didn't answer.

"Anson. . . . Anson! I love you. . . . Say you love me. Say it now—can't
you say it now? Even if you don't mean it?"   45

He did not listen. Over her head he perceived that the picture of Paula was hanging here upon this wall.

He got up and went close to it. The frame gleamed faintly with thrice-reflected moonlight—within was a blurred shadow of a face that he saw he did not know. Almost sobbing, he turned around and stared with abomination at the little figure on the bed.

5 "This is all foolishness," he said thickly. "I don't know what I was thinking about. I don't love you and you'd better wait for somebody that loves you. I don't love you a bit, can't you understand?"

His voice broke, and he went hurriedly out. Back in the salon he was pouring himself a drink with uneasy fingers, when the front door opened sud-
10 denly, and his cousin came in.

"Why, Anson, I hear Dolly's sick," she began solicitously. "I hear she's sick. . . ."

"It was nothing," he interrupted, raising his voice so that it would carry into Dolly's room. "She was a little tired. She went to bed."

15 For a long time afterward Anson believed that a protective God sometimes interfered in human affairs. But Dolly Karger, lying awake and staring at the ceiling never again believed in anything at all.

VI

When Dolly married during the following autumn, Anson was in London
20 on business. Like Paula's marriage, it was sudden, but it affected him in a different way. At first he felt that it was funny, and had an inclination to laugh when he thought of it. Later it depressed him—it made him feel old.

There was something repetitive about it—why, Paula and Dolly had belonged to different generations. He had a foretaste of the sensation of a man
25 of forty who hears that the daughter of an old flame has married. He wired congratulations and, as was not the case with Paula, they were sincere—he had never really hoped that Paula would be happy.

When he returned to New York, he was made a partner in the firm, and, as his responsibilities increased, he had less time on his hands. The refusal of
30 a life-insurance company to issue him a policy made such an impression on him that he stopped drinking for a year, and claimed that he felt better physically, though I think he missed the convivial recounting of those Celliniesque adventures which, in his early twenties, had played such a part of his life. But he never abandoned the Yale Club. He was a figure there, a personality,
35 and the tendency of his class, who were now seven years out of college, to drift away to more sober haunts was checked by his presence.

His day was never too full nor his mind too weary to give any sort of aid to any one who asked it. What had been done at first through pride and superiority had become a habit and a passion. And there was always some-
40 thing—a younger brother in trouble at New Haven, a quarrel to be patched up between a friend and his wife, a position to be found for this man, an investment for that. But his specialty was the solving of problems for young married people. Young married people fascinated him and their apartments

32. **Celliniesque**—The *Autobiography of Benvenuto Cellini* (1500-1571) is a record of an adventurous and arrogant life.

were almost sacred to him—he knew the story of their love-affair, advised
them where to live and how, and remembered their babies' names. Toward
young wives his attitude was circumspect: he never abused the trust which
their husbands—strangely enough in view of his unconcealed irregularities—
invariably reposed in him.   5

He came to take a vicarious pleasure in happy marriages, and to be inspired
to an almost equally pleasant melancholy by those that went astray. Not a season passed that he did not witness the collapse of an affair that perhaps he
himself had fathered. When Paula was divorced and almost immediately re-
married to another Bostonian, he talked about her to me all one afternoon.   10
He would never love any one as he had loved Paula, but he insisted that he
no longer cared.

"I'll never marry," he came to say; "I've seen too much of it, and I know a
happy marriage is a very rare thing. Besides, I'm too old."

But he did believe in marriage. Like all men who spring from a happy   15
and successful marriage, he believed in it passionately—nothing he had seen
would change his belief, his cynicism dissolved upon it like air. But he did
really believe he was too old. At twenty-eight he began to accept with equanimity the prospect of marrying without romantic love; he resolutely chose a
New York girl of his own class, pretty, intelligent, congenial, above reproach 20
—and set about falling in love with her. The things he had said to Paula
with sincerity, to other girls with grace, he could no longer say at all without
smiling, or with the force necessary to convince.

"When I'm forty," he told his friends, "I'll be ripe. I'll fall for some chorus
girl like the rest."   25

Nevertheless, he persisted in his attempt. His mother wanted to see him
married, and he could now well afford it—he had a seat on the Stock Exchange, and his earned income came to twenty-five thousand a year. The idea
was agreeable: when his friends—he spent most of his time with the set he
and Dolly had evolved—closed themselves in behind domestic doors at night, 30
he no longer rejoiced in his freedom. He even wondered if he should have
married Dolly. Not even Paula had loved him more, and he was learning the
rarity, in a single life, of encountering true emotion.

Just as this mood began to creep over him a disquieting story reached his
ear. His aunt Edna, a woman just this side of forty, was carrying on an open 35
intrigue with a dissolute, hard-drinking young man named Cary Sloane.
Every one knew of it except Anson's Uncle Robert, who for fifteen years had
talked long in clubs and taken his wife for granted.

Anson heard the story again and again with increasing annoyance. Something of his old feeling for his uncle came back to him, a feeling that was   40
more than personal, a reversion toward that family solidarity on which he
had based his pride. His intuition singled out the essential point of the affair,
which was that his uncle shouldn't be hurt. It was his first experiment in
unsolicited meddling, but with his knowledge of Edna's character he felt that
he could handle the matter better than a district judge or his uncle.   45

His uncle was in Hot Springs. Anson traced down the sources of the scandal so that there should be no possibility of mistake and then he called Edna

and asked her to lunch with him at the Plaza next day. Something in his tone must have frightened her, for she was reluctant, but he insisted, putting off the date until she had no excuse for refusing.

5   She met him at the appointed time in the Plaza lobby, a lovely, faded, gray-eyed blonde in a coat of Russian sable. Five great rings, cold with diamonds and emeralds, sparkled on her slender hands. It occurred to Anson that it was his father's intelligence and not his uncle's that had earned the fur and the stones, the rich brilliance that buoyed up her passing beauty.

Though Edna scented his hostility, she was unprepared for the directness of
10   his approach.

"Edna, I'm astonished at the way you've been acting," he said in a strong, frank voice. "At first I couldn't believe it."

"Believe what?" she demanded sharply.

"You needn't pretend with me, Edna. I'm talking about Cary Sloane. Aside
15   from any other consideration, I didn't think you could treat Uncle Robert—"

"Now look here, Anson—" she began angrily, but his peremptory voice broke through hers:

"—and your children in such a way. You've been married eighteen years, and you're old enough to know better."

20   "You can't talk to me like that! You—"

"Yes, I can. Uncle Robert has always been my best friend." He was tremendously moved. He felt a real distress about his uncle, about his three young cousins.

Edna stood up, leaving her crab-flake cocktail untasted.
25   "This is the silliest thing—"

"Very well, if you won't listen to me I'll go to Uncle Robert and tell him the whole story—he's bound to hear it sooner or later. And afterward I'll go to old Moses Sloane."

Edna faltered back into her chair.
30   "Don't talk so loud," she begged him. Her eyes blurred with tears. "You have no idea how your voice carries. You might have chosen a less public place to make all these crazy accusations."

He didn't answer.

"Oh, you never liked me, I know," she went on. "You're just taking ad-
35   vantage of some silly gossip to try and break up the only interesting friendship I've ever had. What did I ever do to make you hate me so?"

Still Anson waited. There would be the appeal to his chivalry, then to his pity, finally to his superior sophistication—when he had shouldered his way through all these there would be admissions, and he could come to grips with
40   her. By being silent, by being impervious, by returning constantly to his main weapon, which was his own true emotion, he bullied her into frantic despair as the luncheon hour slipped away. At two o'clock she took out a mirror and a handkerchief, shined away the marks of her tears and powdered the slight hollows where they had lain. She had agreed to meet him at her own house
45   at five.

When he arrived she was stretched on a *chaise-longue* which was covered with cretonne for the summer, and the tears he had called up at luncheon seemed still to be standing in her eyes. Then he was aware of Cary Sloane's dark anxious presence upon the cold hearth.

"What's this idea of yours?" broke out Sloane immediately. "I understand you invited Edna to lunch and then threatened her on the basis of some cheap scandal."   5

Anson sat down.

"I have no reason to think it's only scandal."

"I hear you're going to take it to Robert Hunter, and to my father."

Anson nodded.

"Either you break it off—or I will," he said.   10

"What God damned business is it of yours, Hunter?"

"Don't lose your temper, Cary," said Edna nervously. "It's only a question of showing him how absurd—"

"For one thing, it's my name that's being handed around," interrupted Anson. "That's all that concerns you, Cary."   15

"Edna isn't a member of your family."

"She most certainly is!" His anger mounted. "Why—she owes this house and the rings on her fingers to my father's brains. When Uncle Robert married her she didn't have a penny."

They all looked at the rings as if they had a significant bearing on the situa-   20
tion. Edna made a gesture to take them from her hand.

"I guess they're not the only rings in the world," said Sloane.

"Oh, this is absurd," cried Edna. "Anson, will you listen to me? I've found out how the silly story started. It was a maid I discharged who went right to the Chilicheffs—all these Russians pump things out of their servants and then   25
put a false meaning on them." She brought down her fist angrily on the table: "And after Tom lent them the limousine for a whole month when we were South last winter—"

"Do you see?" demanded Sloane eagerly. "This maid got hold of the wrong end of the thing. She knew that Edna and I were friends, and she carried it   30
to the Chilicheffs. In Russia they assume that if a man and a woman—"

He enlarged the theme to a disquisition upon social relations in the Caucasus.

"If that's the case it better be explained to Uncle Robert," said Anson dryly, "so that when the rumors do reach him he'll know they're not true."   35

Adopting the method he had followed with Edna at luncheon he let them explain it all away. He knew that they were guilty and that presently they would cross the line from explanation into justification and convict themselves more definitely than he could ever do. By seven they had taken the desperate step of telling him the truth—Robert Hunter's neglect, Edna's empty   40
life, the casual dalliance that had flamed up into passion—but like so many true stories it had the misfortune of being old, and its enfeebled body beat helplessly against the armor of Anson's will. The threat to go to Sloane's father sealed their helplessness, for the latter, a retired cotton broker out of Alabama, was a notorious fundamentalist who controlled his son by a rigid   45
allowance and the promise that at his next vagary the allowance would stop forever.

They dined at a small French restaurant, and the discussion continued—at one time Sloane resorted to physical threats, a little later they were both imploring him to give them time. But Anson was obdurate. He saw that Edna was breaking up, and that her spirit must not be refreshed by any renewal of their passion.

At two o'clock in a small night-club on 53d Street, Edna's nerves suddenly collapsed, and she cried to go home. Sloane had been drinking heavily all evening, and he was faintly maudlin, leaning on the table and weeping a little with his face in his hands. Quickly Anson gave them his terms. Sloane was to leave town for six months, and he must be gone within forty-eight hours. When he returned there was to be no resumption of the affair, but at the end of a year Edna might, if she wished, tell Robert Hunter that she wanted a divorce and go about it in the usual way.

He paused, gaining confidence from their faces for his final word.

"Or there's another thing you can do," he said slowly, "if Edna wants to leave her children, there's nothing I can do to prevent your running off together."

"I want to go home!" cried Edna again. "Oh, haven't you done enough to us for one day?"

Outside it was dark, save for a blurred glow from Sixth Avenue down the street. In that light those two who had been lovers looked for the last time into each other's tragic faces, realizing that between them there was not enough youth and strength to avert their eternal parting. Sloane walked suddenly off down the street and Anson tapped a dozing taxi-driver on the arm.

It was almost four; there was a patient flow of cleaning water along the ghostly pavement of Fifth Avenue, and the shadows of two night women flitted over the dark façade of St. Thomas's church. Then the desolate shrubbery of Central Park where Anson had often played as a child, and the mounting numbers, significant as names, of the marching streets. This was his city, he thought, where his name had flourished through five generations. No change could alter the permanence of its place here, for change itself was the essential substratum by which he and those of his name identified themselves with the spirit of New York. Resourcefulness and a powerful will—for his threats in weaker hands would have been less than nothing—had beaten the gathering dust from his uncle's name, from the name of his family, from even this shivering figure that sat beside him in the car.

Cary Sloane's body was found next morning on the lower shelf of a pillar of Queensboro Bridge. In the darkness and in his excitement he had thought that it was the water flowing black beneath him, but in less than a second it made no possible difference—unless he had planned to think one last thought of Edna, and call out her name as he struggled feebly in the water.

VII

Anson never blamed himself for his part in this affair—the situation which brought it about had not been of his making. But the just suffer with the unjust, and he found that his oldest and somehow his most precious friendship was over. He never knew what distorted story Edna told, but he was welcome in his uncle's house no longer.

Just before Christmas Mrs. Hunter retired to a select Episcopal heaven, and Anson became the responsible head of his family. An unmarried aunt who had lived with them for years ran the house, and attempted with helpless inefficiency to chaperone the younger girls. All the children were less self-reliant than Anson, more conventional both in their virtues and in their shortcomings. Mrs. Hunter's death had postponed the début of one daughter and the wedding of another. Also it had taken something deeply material from all of them, for with her passing the quiet, expensive superiority of the Hunters came to an end.

For one thing, the estate, considerably diminished by two inheritance taxes and soon to be divided among six children, was not a notable fortune any more. Anson saw a tendency in his youngest sisters to speak rather respectfully of families that hadn't "existed" twenty years ago. His own feeling of precedence was not echoed in them—sometimes they were conventionally snobbish, that was all. For another thing, this was the last summer they would spend on the Connecticut estate; the clamor against it was too loud: "Who wants to waste the best months of the year shut up in that dead old town?" Reluctantly he yielded—the house would go into the market in the fall, and next summer they would rent a smaller place in Westchester County. It was a step down from the expensive simplicity of his father's idea, and, while he sympathized with the revolt, it also annoyed him; during his mother's lifetime he had gone up there at least every other week-end—even in the gayest summers.

Yet he himself was part of this change, and his strong instinct for life had turned him in his twenties from the hollow obsequies of that abortive leisure class. He did not see this clearly—he still felt that there was a norm, a standard of society. But there was no norm, it was doubtful if there had ever been a true norm in New York. The few who still paid and fought to enter a particular set succeeded only to find that as a society it scarcely functioned—or, what was more alarming, that the Bohemia from which they fled sat above them at table.

At twenty-nine Anson's chief concern was his own growing loneliness. He was sure now that he would never marry. The number of weddings at which he had officiated as best man or usher was past all counting—there was a drawer at home that bulged with the official neckties of this or that wedding-party, neckties standing for romances that had not endured a year, for couples who had passed completely from his life. Scarfpins, gold pencils, cuff-buttons, presents from a generation of grooms had passed through his jewel-box and been lost—and with every ceremony he was less and less able to imagine himself in the groom's place. Under his hearty good-will toward all those marriages there was despair about his own.

And as he neared thirty he became not a little depressed at the inroads that marriage, especially lately, had made upon his friendships. Groups of people had a disconcerting tendency to dissolve and disappear. The men from his own college—and it was upon them he had expended the most time and affection—were the most elusive of all. Most of them were drawn deep into domesticity, two were dead, one lived abroad, one was in Hollywood writing continuities for pictures that Anson went faithfully to see.

Most of them, however, were permanent commuters with an intricate family life centring around some suburban country club, and it was from these that he felt his estrangement most keenly.

In the early days of their married life they had all needed him; he gave them advice about their slim finances, he exorcised their doubts about the advisability of bringing a baby into two rooms and a bath, especially he stood for the great world outside. But now their financial troubles were in the past and the fearfully expected child had evolved into an absorbing family. They were always glad to see old Anson, but they dressed up for him and tried to impress him with their present importance, and kept their troubles to themselves. They needed him no longer.

A few weeks before his thirtieth birthday the last of his early and intimate friends was married. Anson acted in his usual rôle of best man, gave his usual silver tea-service, and went down to the usual *Homeric* to say good-by. It was a hot Friday afternoon in May, and as he walked from the pier he realized that Saturday closing had begun and he was free until Monday morning.

"Go where?" he asked himself.

The Yale Club, of course; bridge until dinner, then four or five raw cocktails in somebody's room and a pleasant confused evening. He regretted that this afternoon's groom wouldn't be along—they had always been able to cram so much into such nights: they knew how to attach women and how to get rid of them, how much consideration any girl deserved from their intelligent hedonism. A party was an adjusted thing—you took certain girls to certain places and spent just so much on their amusement; you drank a little, not much, more than you ought to drink, and at a certain time in the morning you stood up and said you were going home. You avoided college boys, sponges, future engagements, fights, sentiment, and indiscretions. That was the way it was done. All the rest was dissipation.

In the morning you were never violently sorry—you made no resolutions, but if you had overdone it and your heart was slightly out of order, you went on the wagon for a few days without saying anything about it, and waited until an accumulation of nervous boredom projected you into another party.

The lobby of the Yale Club was unpopulated. In the bar three very young alumni looked up at him, momentarily and without curiosity.

"Hello there, Oscar," he said to the bartender. "Mr. Cahill been around this afternoon?"

"Mr. Cahill's gone to New Haven."

"Oh . . . that so?"

"Gone to the ball game. Lot of men gone up."

Anson looked once again into the lobby, considered for a moment, and then walked out and over to Fifth Avenue. From the broad window of one of his clubs—one that he had scarcely visited in five years—a gray man with watery eyes stared down at him. Anson looked quickly away—that figure sitting in

17. **Homeric**—steamer of the Cunard Line.

vacant resignation, in supercilious solitude, depressed him. He stopped and, retracing his steps, started over 47th Street toward Teak Warden's apartment. Teak and his wife had once been his most familiar friends—it was a household where he and Dolly Karger had been used to go in the days of their affair. But Teak had taken to drink, and his wife had remarked publicly that Anson was a bad influence on him. The remark reached Anson in an exaggerated form—when it was finally cleared up, the delicate spell of intimacy was broken, never to be renewed.

"Is Mr. Warden at home?" he inquired.

"They've gone to the country."

The fact unexpectedly cut at him. They were gone to the country and he hadn't known. Two years before he would have known the date, the hour, come up at the last moment for a final drink, and planned his first visit to them. Now they had gone without a word.

Anson looked at his watch and considered a week-end with his family, but the only train was a local that would jolt through the aggressive heat for three hours. And tomorrow in the country, and Sunday—he was in no mood for porch-bridge with polite undergraduates, and dancing after dinner at a rural road-house, a diminutive of gaiety which his father had estimated too well.

"Oh, no," he said to himself. . . . "No."

He was a dignified, impressive young man, rather stout now, but otherwise unmarked by dissipation. He could have been cast for a pillar of something—at times you were sure it was not society, at others nothing else—for the law, for the church. He stood for a few minutes motionless on the sidewalk in front of a 47th Street apartment-house; for almost the first time in his life he had nothing whatever to do.

Then he began to walk briskly up Fifth Avenue, as if he had just been reminded of an important engagement there. The necessity of dissimulation is one of the few characteristics that we share with dogs, and I think of Anson on that day as some well-bred specimen who had been disappointed at a familiar back door. He was going to see Nick, once a fashionable bartender in demand at all private dances, and now employed in cooling non-alcoholic champagne among the labyrinthine cellars of the Plaza Hotel.

"Nick," he said, "what's happened to everything?"

"Dead," Nick said.

"Make me a whiskey sour." Anson handed a pint bottle over the counter. "Nick, the girls are different; I had a little girl in Brooklyn and she got married last week without letting me know."

"That a fact? Ha-ha-ha," responded Nick diplomatically. "Slipped it over on you."

"Absolutely," said Anson. "And I was out with her the night before."

"Ha-ha-ha," said Nick, "ha-ha-ha!"

"Do you remember the wedding, Nick, in Hot Springs where I had the waiters and the musicians singing 'God save the King'?"

"Now where was that, Mr. Hunter?" Nick concentrated doubtfully. "Seems to me that was—"

"Next time they were back for more, and I began to wonder how much I'd paid them," continued Anson.

"—seems to me that was at Mr. Trenholm's wedding."

"Don't know him," said Anson decisively. He was offended that a strange
5 name should intrude upon his reminiscences; Nick perceived this.

"Naw—aw—" he admitted, "I ought to know that. It was one of *your* crowd —Brakins. . . . Baker—"

"Bicker Baker," said Anson responsively. "They put me in a hearse after it was over and covered me up with flowers and drove me away."

10 "Ha-ha-ha," said Nick. "Ha-ha-ha."

Nick's simulation of the old family servant paled presently and Anson went up-stairs to the lobby. He looked around—his eyes met the glance of an unfamiliar clerk at the desk, then fell upon a flower from the morning's marriage hesitating in the mouth of a brass cuspidor. He went out and walked
15 slowly toward the blood-red sun over Columbus Circle. Suddenly he turned around and, retracing his steps to the Plaza, immured himself in a telephone-booth.

Later he said that he tried to get me three times that afternoon, that he tried every one who might be in New York—men and girls he had not seen for
20 years, an artist's model of his college days whose faded number was still in his address book—Central told him that even the exchange existed no longer. At length his quest roved into the country, and he held brief disappointing conversations with emphatic butlers and maids. So-and-so was out, riding, swimming, playing golf, sailed to Europe last week. Who shall I say phoned?

25 It was intolerable that he should pass the evening alone—the private reckonings which one plans for a moment of leisure lose every charm when the solitude is enforced. There were always women of a sort, but the ones he knew had temporarily vanished, and to pass a New York evening in the hired company of a stranger never occurred to him—he would have consid-
30 ered that that was something shameful and secret, the diversion of a travelling salesman in a strange town.

Anson paid the telephone bill—the girl tried unsuccessfully to joke with him about its size—and for the second time that afternoon started to leave the Plaza and go he knew not where. Near the revolving door the figure of a
35 woman, obviously with child, stood sideways to the light—a sheer beige cape fluttered at her shoulders when the door turned and, each time, she looked impatiently toward it as if she were weary of waiting. At the first sight of her a strong nervous thrill of familiarity went over him, but not until he was within five feet of her did he realize that it was Paula.

40 "Why, Anson Hunter!"

His heart turned over.

"Why, Paula—"

"Why, this is wonderful. I can't believe it, *Anson!*"

She took both his hands, and he saw in the freedom of the gesture that the
45 memory of him had lost poignancy to her. But not to him—he felt that old mood that she evoked in him stealing over his brain, that gentleness with which he had always met her optimism as if afraid to mar its surface.

"We're at Rye for the summer. Pete had to come East on business—you know of course I'm Mrs. Peter Hagerty now—so we brought the children and took a house. You've got to come out and see us."

"Can I?" he asked directly. "When?"

"When you like. Here's Pete." The revolving door functioned, giving up a fine tall man of thirty with a tanned face and a trim mustache. His immaculate fitness made a sharp contrast with Anson's increasing bulk, which was obvious under the faintly tight cutaway coat.

"You oughtn't to be standing," said Hagerty to his wife. "Let's sit down here." He indicated lobby chairs, but Paula hesitated.

"I've got to go right home," she said. "Anson, why don't you—why don't you come out and have dinner with us to-night? We're just getting settled, but if you can stand that—"

Hagerty confirmed the invitation cordially.

"Come out for the night."

Their car waited in front of the hotel, and Paula with a tired gesture sank back against silk cushions in the corner.

"There's so much I want to talk to you about," she said, "it seems hopeless."

"I want to hear about you."

"Well"—she smiled at Hagerty—"that would take a long time too. I have three children—by my first marriage. The oldest is five, then four, then three." She smiled again. "I didn't waste much time having them, did I?"

"Boys?"

"A boy and two girls. Then—oh, a lot of things happened, and I got a divorce in Paris a year ago and married Pete. That's all—except that I'm awfully happy."

In Rye they drove up to a large house near the Beach Club, from which there issued presently three dark, slim children who broke from an English governess and approached them with an esoteric cry. Abstractedly and with difficulty Paula took each one into her arms, a caress which they accepted stiffly, as they had evidently been told not to bump into Mummy. Even against their fresh faces Paula's skin showed scarcely any weariness—for all her physical languor she seemed younger than when he had last seen her at Palm Beach seven years ago.

At dinner she was preoccupied, and afterward, during the homage to the radio, she lay with closed eyes on the sofa, until Anson wondered if his presence at this time were not an intrusion. But at nine o'clock, when Hagerty rose and said pleasantly that he was going to leave them by themselves for a while, she began to talk slowly about herself and the past.

"My first baby," she said—"the one we call Darling, the biggest little girl—I wanted to die when I knew I was going to have her, because Lowell was like a stranger to me. It didn't seem as though she could be my own. I wrote you a letter and tore it up. Oh, you were *so* bad to me, Anson."

It was the dialogue again, rising and falling. Anson felt a sudden quickening of memory.

1. **Rye**—village in Westchester County, New York, on Long Island Sound.

"Weren't you engaged once?" she asked—"a girl named Dolly something?"

"I wasn't ever engaged. I tried to be engaged, but I never loved anybody but you, Paula."

"Oh," she said. Then after a moment: "This baby is the first one I ever
5 really wanted. You see, I'm in love now—at last."

He didn't answer, shocked at the treachery of her remembrance. She must have seen that the "at last" bruised him, for she continued:

"I was infatuated with you, Anson—you could make me do anything you liked. But we wouldn't have been happy. I'm not smart enough for you. I
10 don't like things to be complicated like you do." She paused. "You'll never settle down," she said.

The phrase struck at him from behind—it was an accusation that of all accusations he had never merited.

"I could settle down if women were different," he said. "If I didn't under-
15 stand so much about them, if women didn't spoil you for other women, if they had only a little pride. If I could go to sleep for a while and wake up into a home that was really mine—why, that's what I'm made for, Paula, that's what women have seen in me and liked in me. It's only that I can't get through the preliminaries any more."

20 Hagerty came in a little before eleven; after a whiskey Paula stood up and announced that she was going to bed. She went over and stood by her husband.

"Where did you go, dearest?" she demanded.

"I had a drink with Ed Saunders."

25 "I was worried. I thought maybe you'd run away."

She rested her head against his coat.

"He's sweet, isn't he, Anson?" she demanded.

"Absolutely," said Anson, laughing.

She raised her face to her husband.

30 "Well, I'm ready," she said. She turned to Anson: "Do you want to see our family gymnastic stunt?"

"Yes," he said in an interested voice.

"All right. Here we go!"

Hagerty picked her up easily in his arms.

35 "This is called the family acrobatic stunt," said Paula. "He carries me up-stairs. Isn't it sweet of him?"

"Yes," said Anson.

Hagerty bent his head slightly until his face touched Paula's.

"And I love him," she said. "I've just been telling you, haven't I, Anson?"

40 "Yes," he said.

"He's the dearest thing that ever lived in this world; aren't you, darling?
. . . Well, good night. Here we go. Isn't he strong?"

"Yes," Anson said.

"You'll find a pair of Pete's pajamas laid out for you. Sweet dreams—see
45 you at breakfast."

"Yes," Anson said.

VIII

The older members of the firm insisted that Anson should go abroad for the summer. He had scarcely had a vacation in seven years, they said. He was stale and needed a change. Anson resisted.

"If I go," he declared, "I won't come back any more." 5

"That's absurd, old man. You'll be back in three months with all this depression gone. Fit as ever."

"No." He shook his head stubbornly. "If I stop, I won't go back to work. If I stop, that means I've given up—I'm through."

"We'll take a chance on that. Stay six months if you like—we're not afraid 10 you'll leave us. Why, you'd be miserable if you didn't work."

They arranged his passage for him. They liked Anson—every one liked Anson—and the change that had been coming over him cast a sort of pall over the office. The enthusiasm that had invariably signalled up business, the consideration toward his equals and his inferiors, the lift of his vital presence 15 —within the past four months his intense nervousness had melted down these qualities into the fussy pessimism of a man of forty. On every transaction in which he was involved he acted as a drag and a strain.

"If I go I'll never come back," he said.

Three days before he sailed Paula Legendre Hagerty died in childbirth. I 20 was with him a great deal then, for we were crossing together, but for the first time in our friendship he told me not a word of how he felt, nor did I see the slightest sign of emotion. His chief preoccupation was with the fact that he was thirty years old—he would turn the conversation to the point where he could remind you of it and then fall silent, as if he assumed that 25 the statement would start a chain of thought sufficient to itself. Like his partners, I was amazed at the change in him, and I was glad when the *Paris* moved off into the wet space between the worlds, leaving his principality behind.

"How about a drink?" he suggested. 30

We walked into the bar with that defiant feeling that characterizes the day of departure and ordered four Martinis. After one cocktail a change came over him—he suddenly reached across and slapped my knee with the first joviality I had seen him exhibit for months.

"Did you see that girl in the red tam?" he demanded, "the one with the 35 high color who had the two police dogs down to bid her good-by."

"She's pretty," I agreed.

"I looked her up in the purser's office and found out that she's alone. I'm going down to see the steward in a few minutes. We'll have dinner with her to-night." 40

After a while he left me, and within an hour he was walking up and down the deck with her, talking to her in his strong, clear voice. Her red tam was a bright spot of color against the steel-green sea, and from time to time she looked up with a flashing bob of her head, and smiled with amusement and

interest, and anticipation. At dinner we had champagne, and were very joyous—afterward Anson ran the pool with infectious gusto, and several people
who had seen me with him asked me his name. He and the girl were talking
and laughing together on a lounge in the bar when I went to bed.

5   I saw less of him on the trip than I had hoped. He wanted to arrange a
foursome, but there was no one available, so I saw him only at meals. Sometimes, though, he would have a cocktail in the bar, and he told me about the
girl in the red tam, and his adventures with her, making them all bizarre
and amusing, as he had a way of doing, and I was glad that he was himself
10   again, or at least the self that I knew, and with which I felt at home. I don't
think he was ever happy unless some one was in love with him, responding
to him like filings to a magnet, helping him to explain himself, promising him
something. What it was I do not know. Perhaps they promised that there
would always be women in the world who would spend their brightest, fresh-
15   est, rarest hours to nurse and protect that superiority he cherished in his heart.

THE CRACK-UP

"The Crack-up" was printed serially in *Esquire* in the issues indicated by the dates
at the head of each of the several parts here reprinted; and was then collected by
Edmund Wilson into the posthumous volume of that title, printed in 1945. The text
remained unchanged with the curious exception that the titles of the second and
third parts have been reversed in the book from what they were in magazine form.

February, 1936

O F course all life is a process of breaking down, but the blows that do
the dramatic side of the work—the big sudden blows that come, or
seem to come, from outside—the ones you remember and blame
20   things on and, in moments of weakness, tell your friends about, don't show
their effect all at once. There is another sort of blow that comes from within—
that you don't feel until it's too late to do anything about it, until you realize
with finality that in some regard you will never be as good a man again. The
first sort of breakage seems to happen quick—the second kind happens al-
25   most without your knowing it but is realized suddenly indeed.

Before I go on with this short history, let me make a general observation—
the test of a first-rate intelligence is the ability to hold two opposed ideas in
the mind at the same time, and still retain the ability to function. One should,
for example, be able to see that things are hopeless and yet be determined to
30   make them otherwise. This philosophy fitted on to my early adult life, when
I saw the improbable, the implausible, often the "impossible," come true. Life
was something you dominated if you were any good. Life yielded easily to intelligence and effort, or, to what proportion could be mustered of both. It
seemed a romantic business to be a successful literary man—you were not ever
35   going to be as famous as a movie star but what note you had was probably
longer-lived—you were never going to have the power of a man of strong
political or religious convictions but you were certainly more independent. Of

course within the practice of your trade you were forever unsatisfied—but I, for one, would not have chosen any other.

As the twenties passed, with my own twenties marching a little ahead of them, my two juvenile regrets—at not being big enough (or good enough) to play football in college, and at not getting overseas during the war—resolved themselves into childish waking dreams of imaginary heroism that were good enough to go to sleep on in restless nights. The big problems of life seemed to solve themselves, and if the business of fixing them was difficult, it made one too tired to think of more general problems.

Life, ten years ago, was largely a personal matter. I must hold in balance the sense of the futility of effort and the sense of the necessity to struggle; the conviction of the inevitability of failure and still the determination to "succeed"—and, more than these, the contradiction between the dead hand of the past and the high intentions of the future. If I could do this through the common ills—domestic, professional and personal—then the ego would continue as an arrow shot from nothingness to nothingness with such force that only gravity would bring it to earth at last.

For seventeen years, with a year of deliberate loafing and resting out in the center—things went on like that, with a new chore only a nice prospect for the next day. I was living hard, too, but: "Up to forty-nine it'll be all right," I said. "I can count on that. For a man who's lived as I have, that's all you could ask."

—And then, ten years this side of forty-nine, I suddenly realized that I had prematurely cracked.

II

Now a man can crack in many ways—can crack in the head—in which case the power of decision is taken from you by others! or in the body, when one can but submit to the white hospital world; or in the nerves. William Seabrook in an unsympathetic book tells, with some pride and a movie ending, of how he became a public charge. What led to his alcoholism or was bound up with it, was a collapse of his nervous system. Though the present writer was not so entangled—having at the time not tasted so much as a glass of beer for six months—it was his nervous reflexes that were giving way—too much anger and too many tears.

Moreover, to go back to my thesis that life has a varying offensive, the realization of having cracked was not simultaneous with a blow, but with a reprieve.

Not long before, I had sat in the office of a great doctor and listened to a grave sentence. With what, in retrospect, seems some equanimity, I had gone on about my affairs in the city where I was then living, not caring much, not thinking how much had been left undone, or what would become of this and that responsibility, like people do in books; I was well insured and anyhow I had been only a mediocre caretaker of most of the things left in my hands, even of my talent.

28-29. **William Seabrook**—*Asylum*, by William Buehler Seabrook (1886-1945), appeared in 1935.

But I had a strong sudden instinct that I must be alone. I didn't want to see any people at all. I had seen so many people all my life—I was an average mixer, but more than average in a tendency to identify myself, my ideas, my destiny, with those of all classes that I came in contact with. I was always 5 saving or being saved—in a single morning I would go through the emotions ascribable to Wellington at Waterloo. I lived in a world of inscrutable hostiles and inalienable friends and supporters.

But now I wanted to be absolutely alone and so arranged a certain insulation from ordinary cares.

10 It was not an unhappy time. I went away and there were fewer people. I found I was good-and-tired. I could lie around and was glad to, sleeping or dozing sometimes twenty hours a day and in the intervals trying resolutely not to think—instead I made lists—made lists and tore them up, hundreds of lists: of cavalry leaders and football players and cities, and popular tunes and 15 pitchers, and happy times, and hobbies and houses lived in and how many suits since I left the army and how many pairs of shoes (I didn't count the suit I bought in Sorrento that shrunk, nor the pumps and dress shirt and collar that I carried around for years and never wore, because the pumps got damp and grainy and the shirt and collar got yellow and starch-rotted). And 20 lists of women I'd liked, and of the times I had let myself be snubbed by people who had not been my betters in character or ability.

—And then suddenly, surprisingly, I got better.

—And cracked like an old plate as soon as I heard the news.

That is the real end of this story. What was to be done about it will have 25 to rest in what used to be called the "womb of time." Suffice it to say that after about an hour of solitary pillow-hugging, I began to realize that for two years my life had been a drawing on resources that I did not possess, that I had been mortgaging myself physically and spiritually up to the hilt. What was the small gift of life given back in comparison to that?—when 30 there had once been a pride of direction and a confidence in enduring independence.

I realized that in those two years, in order to preserve something—an inner hush maybe, maybe not—I had weaned myself from all the things I used to love—that every act of life from the morning tooth-brush to the friend at 35 dinner had become an effort. I saw that for a long time I had not liked people and things, but only followed the rickety old pretense of liking. I saw that even my love for those closest to me was become only an attempt to love, that my casual relations—with an editor, a tobacco seller, the child of a friend, were only what I remembered I *should* do, from other days. All in the same 40 month I became bitter about such things as the sound of the radio, the advertisements in the magazines, the screech of tracks, the dead silence of the country—contemptuous at human softness, immediately (if secretively) quarrelsome toward hardness—hating the night when I couldn't sleep and hating the day because it went toward night. I slept on the heart side now because

17. Sorrento—Italian resort town, overlooking the Bay of Naples. **25. "womb of time"** —"hid in the womb of time," from "The Daisy's Eternity," a poem by John Clare (1793-1864), but "womb of time" also appears in Shakespeare.

I knew that the sooner I could tire that out, even a little, the sooner would come that blessed hour of nightmare which, like a catharsis, would enable me to better meet the new day.

There were certain spots, certain faces I could look at. Like most Middle Westerners, I have never had any but the vaguest race prejudices—I always had a secret yen for the lovely Scandinavian blondes who sat on porches in St. Paul but hadn't emerged enough economically to be part of what was then society. They were too nice to be "chickens" and too quickly off the farmlands to seize a place in the sun, but I remember going round blocks to catch a single glimpse of shining hair—the bright shock of a girl I'd never know. This is urban, unpopular talk. It strays afield from the fact that in these latter days I couldn't stand the sight of Celts, English, Politicians, Strangers, Virginians, Negroes (light or dark), Hunting People, or retail clerks, and middlemen in general, all writers (I avoided writers very carefully because they can perpetuate trouble as no one else can)—and all the classes as classes and most of them as members of their class . . .

Trying to cling to something, I liked doctors and girl children up to the age of about thirteen and well-brought-up boy children from about eight years old on. I could have peace and happiness with these few categories of people. I forgot to add that I liked old men—men over seventy, sometimes over sixty if their faces looked seasoned. I liked Katharine Hepburn's face on the screen, no matter what was said about her pretentiousness, and Miriam Hopkins' face, and old friends if I only saw them once a year and could remember their ghosts.

All rather inhuman and undernourished, isn't it? Well, that, children, is the true sign of cracking up.

It is not a pretty picture. Inevitably it was carted here and there within its frame and exposed to various critics. One of them can only be described as a person whose life makes other people's lives seem like death—even this time when she was cast in the usually unappealing role of Job's comforter. In spite of the fact that this story is over, let me append our conversation as a sort of postscript:

"Instead of being so sorry for yourself, listen—" she said. (She always says "Listen," because she thinks while she talks—*really* thinks.) So she said: "Listen. Suppose this wasn't a crack in you—suppose it was a crack in the Grand Canyon."

"The crack's in me," I said heroically.

"Listen! The world only exists in your eyes—your conception of it. You can make it as big or as small as you want to. And you're trying to be a little puny individual. By God, if I ever cracked, I'd try to make the world crack with me. Listen! The world only exists through your apprehension of it, and so it's much better to say that it's not you that's cracked—it's the Grand Canyon."

21. **Katharine Hepburn**—Katharine Hepburn (1909-   ), American stage and screen actress, received the award of the Academy of Motion Picture Arts and Sciences in 1934 for her performance in *Morning Glory*. 22. **Miriam Hopkins**—Miriam Hopkins (1902-   ), motion picture actress. 30. **Job's comforter**—*cf.* Job 16:1.

"Baby et up all her Spinoza?"

"I don't know anything about Spinoza. I know—" She spoke, then, of old woes of her own, that seemed, in the telling, to have been more dolorous than mine, and how she had met them, over-ridden them, beaten them.

5   I felt a certain reaction to what she said, but I am a slow-thinking man, and it occurred to me simultaneously that of all natural forces, vitality is the incommunicable one. In days when juice came into one as an article without duty, one tried to distribute it—but always without success; to further mix metaphors, vitality never "takes." You have it or you haven't it, like health or 10   brown eyes or honor or a baritone voice. I might have asked some of it from her, neatly wrapped and ready for home cooking and digestion, but I could never have got it—not if I'd waited around for a thousand hours with the tin cup of self-pity. I could walk from her door, holding myself very carefully like cracked crockery, and go away into the world of bitterness, where I 15   was making a home with such materials as are found there—and quote to myself after I left her door:

"Ye are the salt of the earth. But if the salt hath lost its savour, wherewith shall it be salted?"

Matthew 5:13.

20   HANDLE WITH CARE

March, 1936

In a previous article this writer told about his realization that what he had before him was not the dish that he had ordered for his forties. In fact— since he and the dish were one, he described himself as a cracked plate, the 25   kind that one wonders whether it is worth preserving. Your editor thought that the article suggested too many aspects without regarding them closely, and probably many readers felt the same way—and there are always those to whom all self-revelation is contemptible, unless it ends with a noble thanks to the gods for the Unconquerable Soul.

30   But I had been thanking the gods too long, and thanking them for nothing. I wanted to put a lament into my record, without even the background of the Euganean Hills to give it color. There weren't any Euganean hills that I could see.

Sometimes, though, the cracked plate has to be retained in the pantry, has 35   to be kept in service as a household necessity. It can never again be warmed on the stove nor shuffled with the other plates in the dishpan; it will not be brought out for company, but it will do to hold crackers late at night or to go into the ice box under left-overs . . .

Hence this sequel—a cracked plate's further history.

40   Now the standard cure for one who is sunk is to consider those in actual destitution or physical suffering—this is an all-weather beatitude for gloom in general and fairly salutory day-time advice for everyone. But at three o'clock

---

1. **"Baby et up all her Spinoza?"**—The phrase "Baby et up all her spinach" became a catchword as a result of the popularity of *Nize Baby* (1926) by Milt Gross. Baruch Spinoza (1632-1677) taught complete trustfulness in the Divine Being. **28-29. thanks . . . Soul**—from "Invictus" by William Ernest Henley (1849-1903). **32. Euganean Hills**—*cf.* "Lines written among the Euganean Hills" by Percy Bysshe Shelley.

in the morning, a forgotten package has the same tragic importance as a death sentence, and the cure doesn't work—and in a real dark night of the soul it is always three o'clock in the morning, day after day. At that hour the tendency is to refuse to face things as long as possible by retiring into an infantile dream—but one is continually startled out of this by various contacts 5 with the world. One meets these occasions as quickly and carelessly as possible and retires once more back into the dream, hoping that things will adjust themselves by some great material or spiritual bonanza. But as the withdrawal persists there is less and less chance of the bonanza—one is not waiting for the fade-out of a single sorrow, but rather being an unwilling witness of an exe- 10 cution, the disintegration of one's own personality . . .

Unless madness or drugs or drink come into it, this phase comes to a dead-end, eventually, and is succeeded by a vacuous quiet. In this you can try to estimate what has been sheared away and what is left. Only when this quiet came to me, did I realize that I had gone through two parallel experiences.   15

The first time was twenty years ago, when I left Princeton in junior year with a complaint diagnosed as malaria. It transpired, through an X-ray taken a dozen years later, that it had been tuberculosis—a mild case, and after a few months of rest I went back to college. But I had lost certain offices, the chief one was the presidency of the Triangle Club, a musical comedy idea, and 20 also I dropped back a class. To me college would never be the same. There were to be no badges of pride, no medals, after all. It seemed on one March afternoon that I had lost every single thing I wanted—and that night was the first time that I hunted down the spectre of womanhood that, for a little while, makes everything else seem unimportant.   25

Years later I realized that my failure as a big shot in college was all right— instead of serving on committees, I took a beating on English poetry; when I got the idea of what it was all about, I set about learning how to write. On Shaw's principle that "If you don't get what you like, you better like what you get," it was a lucky break—at the moment it was a harsh and bitter busi- 30 ness to know that my career as a leader of men was over.

Since that day I have not been able to fire a bad servant, and I am astonished and impressed by people who can. Some old desire for personal dominance was broken and gone. Life around me was a solemn dream, and I lived on the letters I wrote to a girl in another city. A man does not recover from 35 such jolts—he becomes a different person and, eventually, the new person finds new things to care about.

The other episode parallel to my current situation took place after the war, when I had again over-extended my flank. It was one of those tragic loves doomed for lack of money, and one day the girl closed it out on the basis of 40 common sense. During a long summer of despair I wrote a novel instead of letters, so it came out all right, but it came out all right for a different person. The man with the jingle of money in his pocket who married the girl a year later would always cherish an abiding distrust, an animosity, toward the leisure

2-3. **dark night of the soul**—title of an allegorical work by the Spanish mystic, San Juan de la Cruz (1542-1591). **29. Shaw's**—George Bernard Shaw (1856-1950), dramatist, music critic, and Socialist. But the sentence is attributed to a number of others.

class—not the conviction of a revolutionist but the smouldering hatred of a peasant. In the years since then I have never been able to stop wondering where my friends' money came from, nor to stop thinking that at one time a sort of *droit de seigneur* might have been exercised to give one of them my
5 girl.

For sixteen years I lived pretty much as this latter person, distrusting the rich, yet working for money with which to share their mobility and the grace that some of them brought into their lives. During this time I had plenty of the usual horses shot from under me—I remember some of their names—
10 *Punctured Pride, Thwarted Expectation, Faithless, Show-off, Hard Hit, Never Again.* And after awhile I wasn't twenty-five, then not even thirty-five, and nothing was quite as good. But in all these years I don't remember a moment of discouragement. I saw honest men through moods of suicidal gloom —some of them gave up and died; others adjusted themselves and went
15 on to a larger success than mine; but my morale never sank below the level of self-disgust when I had put on some unsightly personal show. Trouble has no necessary connection with discouragement—discouragement has a germ of its own, as different from trouble as arthritis is different from a stiff joint.

20 When a new sky cut off the sun last spring, I didn't at first relate it to what had happened fifteen or twenty years ago. Only gradually did a certain family resemblance come through—an over-extension of the flank, a burning of the candle at both ends; a call upon physical resources that I did not command, like a man over-drawing at his bank. In its impact this blow was more
25 violent than the other two but it was the same in kind—a feeling that I was standing at twilight on a deserted range, with an empty rifle in my hands and the targets down. No problem set—simply a silence with only the sound of my own breathing.

In this silence there was a vast irresponsibility toward every obligation, a
30 deflation of all my values. A passionate belief in order, a disregard of motives or consequences in favor of guess work and prophecy, a feeling that craft and industry would have a place in any world—one by one, these and other convictions were swept away. I saw that the novel, which at my maturity was the strongest and supplest medium for conveying thought and emo-
35 tion from one human being to another, was becoming subordinated to a mechanical and communal art that, whether in the hands of Hollywood merchants or Russian idealists, was capable of reflecting only the tritest thought, the most obvious emotion. It was an art in which words were subordinate to images, where personality was worn down to the inevitable low gear of col-
40 laboration. As long past as 1930, I had a hunch that the talkies would make even the best selling novelist as archaic as silent pictures. People still read, if only Professor Canby's book of the month—curious children nosed at the slime

4. droit de seigneur—also known as the *jus primae noctis,* a custom alleged to exist in the Middle Ages, giving the feudal lord the right to sleep the first night with the bride of any vassal. **36-37. communal . . . Russian idealists**—The reference is to the vogue of the so-called proletarian novels in the 1930's. **42. Canby's**—Henry Seidel Canby (1878-   ), formerly professor of English at Yale University, and one of the governing board of the Book-of-the-Month Club (founded 1926).

of Mr. Tiffany Thayer in the drugstore libraries—but there was a rankling in-
dignity, that to me had become almost an obsession, in seeing the power of
the written word subordinated to another power, a more glittering, a grosser
power . . .

I set that down as an example of what haunted me during the long night—   5
this was something I could neither accept nor struggle against, something
which tended to make my efforts obsolescent, as the chain stores have crippled
the small merchant, an exterior force, unbeatable—

(I have the sense of lecturing now, looking at a watch on the desk before
me and seeing how many more minutes—.)   10

Well, when I had reached this period of silence, I was forced into a measure
that no one ever adopts voluntarily: I was impelled to think. God, was it difficult! The moving about of great secret trunks. In the first exhausted halt, I
wondered whether I had ever thought. After a long time I came to these conclusions, just as I write them here: 15

(1) That I had done very little thinking, save within the problems of my
craft. For twenty years a certain man had been my intellectual conscience.
That was Edmund Wilson.

(2) That another man represented my sense of the "good life," though I saw
him once in a decade, and since then he might have been hung. He is in the   20
fur business in the Northwest and wouldn't like his name set down here. But
in difficult situations I had tried to think what *he* would have thought, how
he would have acted.

(3) That a third contemporary had been an artistic conscience to me—I had
not imitated his infectious style, because my own style, such as it is, was   25
formed before he published anything, but there was an awful pull toward him
when I was on a spot.

(4) That a fourth man had come to dictate my relations with other people
when these relations were successful: how to do, what to say. How to make
people at least momentarily happy (in opposition to Mrs. Post's theories of   30
how to make everyone thoroughly uncomfortable with a sort of systematized
vulgarity). This always confused me and made me want to go out and get
drunk, but this man had seen the game, analyzed it and beaten it, and his
word was good enough for me.

(5) That my political conscience had scarcely existed for ten years save as   35
an element of irony in my stuff. When I became again concerned with the
system I should function under, it was a man much younger than myself who
brought it to me, with a mixture of passion and fresh air.

So there was not an "I" any more—not a basis on which I could organize
my self-respect—save my limitless capacity for toil that it seemed I possessed   40
no more. It was strange to have no self—to be like a little boy left alone in a
big house, who knew that now he could do anything he wanted to do, but
found that there was nothing that he wanted to do—

1. **Tiffany Thayer**—Tiffany Ellsworth Thayer (1902-   ), who writes under a variety of
pen names. Typical titles are *Thirteen Men* (1930) and *Thirteen Women* (1932), books characteristically to be had at rental libraries in American drugstores. **18. Wilson**—Edmund Wilson
(1895-   ), American critic and fictionist and editor of *The Crack-up*. **30. Mrs. Post**—Emily
Price Post (1873?-   ), columnist, whose *Etiquette* (1922) had much vogue.

(The watch is past the hour and I have barely reached my thesis. I have some doubts as to whether this is of general interest, but if anyone wants more, there is plenty left, and your editor will tell me. If you've had enough, say so—but not too loud, because I have the feeling that someone, I'm not
5 sure who, is sound asleep—someone who could have helped me to keep my shop open. It wasn't Lenin, and it wasn't God.)

PASTING IT TOGETHER

April, 1936

I have spoken in these pages of how an exceptionally optimistic young man
10 experienced a crack-up of all values, a crack-up that he scarcely knew of until long after it occurred. I told of the succeeding period of desolation and of the necessity of going on, but without benefit of Henley's familiar heroics, "my head is bloody but unbowed." For a check-up of my spiritual liabilities indicated that I had no particular head to be bowed or unbowed. Once I had had
15 a heart but that was about all I was sure of.

This was at least a starting place out of the morass in which I floundered: "I felt—therefore I was." At one time or another there had been many people who had leaned on me, come to me in difficulties or written me from afar, believed implicitly in my advice and my attitude toward life. The dullest
20 platitude monger or the most unscrupulous Rasputin who can influence the destinies of many people must have some individuality, so the question became one of finding why and where I had changed, where was the leak through which, unknown to myself, my enthusiasm and my vitality had been steadily and prematurely trickling away.

25 One harassed and despairing night I packed a brief case and went off a thousand miles to think it over. I took a dollar room in a drab little town where I knew no one and sunk all the money I had with me in a stock of potted meat, crackers and apples. But don't let me suggest that the change from a rather overstuffed world to a comparative asceticism was any Research
30 Magnificent—I only wanted absolute quiet to think out why I had developed a sad attitude toward sadness, a melancholy attitude toward melancholy and a tragic attitude toward tragedy—*why I had become identified with the objects of my horror or compassion.*

Does this seem a fine distinction? It isn't: identification such as this spells
35 the death of accomplishment. It is something like this that keeps insane people from working. Lenin did not willingly endure the sufferings of his proletariat, nor Washington of his troops, nor Dickens of his London poor. And when Tolstoy tried some such merging of himself with the objects of his attention,

6. **Lenin**—Nikolai Lenin (1870-1924), the leader of the Russian revolution of 1917-18, and now the great hero of Soviet Russia. 12-13. **"my . . . unbowed"**—again, from "Invictus." 17. **"I felt . . . was"**—parody of the famous dictum of Descartes, *Cogito, ergo sum,* "I think, therefore I am." 20. **Rasputin**—Grigori Efimovich Rasputin (1871?-1916), Russian monk and evil genius of the court of the last Russian Czar, assassinated by the nobles. 29-30. **Research Magnificent**—title of a novel by Herbert George Wells (1866-1946), published in 1915. 36. **proletariat**—in Marxian theory, the exploited "hand-to-mouth" workers in the cities. 38. **Tolstoy**—Count Leo Tolstoi (1828-1910), though born to wealth, in his later years abandoned his estates and tried to live as a country peasant.

it was a fake and a failure. I mention these because they are the men best
known to us all.

It was dangerous mist. When Wordsworth decided that "there had passed
away a glory from the earth," he felt no compulsion to pass away with it, and
the Fiery Particle Keats never ceased his struggle against t. b. nor in his last   5
moments relinquished his hope of being among the English poets.

My self-immolation was something sodden-dark. It was very distinctly not
modern—yet I saw it in others, saw it in a dozen men of honor and industry
since the war. (I heard you, but that's too easy—there were Marxians among
these men.) I had stood by while one famous contemporary of mine played   10
with the idea of the Big Out for half a year; I had watched when another,
equally eminent, spent months in an asylum unable to endure any contact
with his fellow men. And of those who had given up and passed on I could
list a score.

This led me to the idea that the ones who had survived had made some   15
sort of clean break. This is a big word and is no parallel to a jail-break when
one is probably headed for a new jail or will be forced back to the old one.
The famous "Escape" or "run away from it all" is an excursion in a trap even
if the trap includes the south seas, which are only for those who want to
paint them or sail them. A clean break is something you cannot come back   20
from; that is irretrievable because it makes the past cease to exist. So, since
I could no longer fulfill the obligations that life had set for me or that I
had set for myself, why not slay the empty shell who had been posturing at
it for four years? I must continue to be a writer because that was my only
way of life, but I would cease any attempts to be a person—to be kind, just   25
or generous. There were plenty of counterfeit coins around that would pass
instead of these and I knew where I could get them at a nickel on the dollar.
In thirty-nine years an observant eye has learned to detect where the milk
is watered and the sugar is sanded, the rhinestone passed for diamond and
the stucco for stone. There was to be no more giving of myself—all giving   30
was to be outlawed henceforth under a new name, and that name was
Waste.

The decision made me rather exuberant, like anything that is both real and
new. As a sort of beginning there was a whole shaft of letters to be tipped into
the waste basket when I went home, letters that wanted something for noth-   35
ing—to read this man's manuscript, market this man's poem, speak free on
the radio, indite notes of introduction, give this interview, help with the plot
of this play, with this domestic situation, perform this act of thoughtfulness
or charity.

The conjuror's hat was empty. To draw things out of it had long been a   40
sort of sleight of hand, and now, to change the metaphor, I was off the dis-
pensing end of the relief roll forever.

The heady villainous feeling continued.

I felt like the beady-eyed men I used to see on the commuting train from

3-4. "there . . . earth"—line 18 of Wordsworth's "Ode on Intimations of Immortality."
5. Fiery . . . Keats—Thinking that John Keats had died of grief because of an unfavorable
review of his poems, Byron wrote in Don Juan, Canto XI:19, " 'Tis strange the mind, that very
fiery particle,/ Should let itself be snuff'd out by an article."

Great Neck fifteen years back—men who didn't care whether the world tumbled into chaos tomorrow if it spared their houses. I was one with them now,
one with the smooth articles who said:

"I'm sorry but business is business." Or:

5 "You ought to have thought of that before you got into this trouble." Or:
"I'm not the person to see about that."

And a smile—ah, I would get me a smile. I'm still working on that smile.
It is to combine the best qualities of a hotel manager, an experienced old social
weasel, a headmaster on visitors' day, a colored elevator man, a pansy pulling
10 a profile, a producer getting stuff at half its market value, a trained nurse
coming on a new job, a body-vender in her first rotogravure, a hopeful extra
swept near the camera, a ballet dancer with an infected toe, and of course the
great beam of loving kindness common to all those from Washington to
Beverly Hills who must exist by virtue of the contorted pan.

15 The voice too—I am working with a teacher on the voice. When I have
perfected it the larynx will show no ring of conviction except the conviction
of the person I am talking to. Since it will be largely called upon for the elici-
tation of the word "Yes," my teacher (a lawyer) and I are concentrating on
that, but in extra hours. I am learning to bring into it that polite acerbity that
20 makes people feel that far from being welcome they are not even tolerated and
are under continual and scathing analysis at every moment. These times will
of course not coincide with the smile. This will be reserved exclusively for
those from whom I have nothing to gain, old worn-out people or young
struggling people. They won't mind—what the hell, they get it most of the
25 time anyhow.

But enough. It is not a matter of levity. If you are young and you should
write asking to see me and learn how to be a sombre literary man writing
pieces upon the state of emotional exhaustion that often overtakes writers in
their prime—if you should be so young and so fatuous as to do this, I would
30 not do so much as acknowledge your letter, unless you were related to someone very rich and important indeed. And if you were dying of starvation outside my window, I would go out quickly and give you the smile and the voice
(if no longer the hand) and stick around till somebody raised a nickel to
phone for the ambulance, that is if I thought there would be any copy in it
35 for me.

I have now at last become a writer only. The man I had persistently tried
to be became such a burden that I have "cut him loose" with as little com-
punction as a Negro lady cuts loose a rival on Saturday night. Let the good
people function as such—let the overworked doctors die in harness, with one
40 week's "vacation" a year that they can devote to straightening out their family affairs, and let the underworked doctors scramble for cases at one dollar a
throw; let the soldiers be killed and enter immediately into the Valhalla of

1. **Great Neck**—fashionable suburb on Long Island. 9. **pansy**—effeminate male. 11. **body-**
vender—female model. 11. **rotogravure**—"picture" supplement common in American Sunday
papers. 14. **Beverly Hills**—suburb of Hollywood inhabited by motion-picture stars; hence,
not merely from the Atlantic to the Pacific Coast, but from politicians, who must please, to actors,
who must also please. 14. **pan**—face. 42. **Valhalla**—In Norse myth the souls of dead warriors
were taken to Valhalla, a hall with 540 gates, from which they may go out and through which
they may re-enter from combat.

their profession. That is their contract with the gods. A writer need have no such ideals unless he makes them for himself, and this one has quit. The old dream of being an entire man in the Goethe-Byron-Shaw tradition, with an opulent American touch, a sort of combination of J. P. Morgan, Topham Beauclerk and St. Francis of Assisi, has been relegated to the junk heap of the shoulder pads worn for one day on the Princeton freshman football field and the overseas cap never worn overseas.

So what? This is what I think now: that the natural state of the sentient adult is a qualified unhappiness. I think also that in an adult the desire to be finer in grain than you are, "a constant striving" (as those people say who gain their bread by saying it) only adds to this unhappiness in the end—that end that comes to our youth and hope. My own happiness in the past often approached such an ecstasy that I could not share it even with the person dearest to me but had to walk it away in quiet streets and lanes with only fragments of it to distil into little lines in books—and I think that my happiness, or talent for self-delusion or what you will, was an exception. It was not the natural thing but the unnatural—unnatural as the Boom; and my recent experience parallels the wave of despair that swept the nation when the Boom was over.

I shall manage to live with the new dispensation, though it has taken some months to be certain of the fact. And just as the laughing stoicism which has enabled the American Negro to endure the intolerable conditions of his existence has cost him his sense of the truth—so in my case there is a price to pay. I do not any longer like the postman, nor the grocer, nor the editor, nor the cousin's husband, and he in turn will come to dislike me, so that life will never be very pleasant again, and the sign *Cave Canem* is hung permanently just above my door. I will try to be a correct animal though, and if you throw me a bone with enough meat on it I may even lick your hand.

4-5. J. P. . . . Assisi—John Pierpont Morgan (1837-1913), American banker, symbol of untold money-power; Topham Beauclerk (1739-1780), friend of Dr. Johnson, a "beau" of that period; St. Francis of Assisi (1181?-1226), founder of the Franciscan Order of "poor friars," type of poverty and love. **17. Boom**—the unexampled false prosperity of the "Twenties," ending in the stock-market collapse of 1929. **25. Cave Canem**—"Beware the Dog," a sign still to be traced in the ruined city of Pompeii.

WILLIAM FAULKNER

1897-

I. YOUTH AND THE TWENTIES (1897–1928)

1897 Born September 25, 1897, at New Albany, Mississippi, the son of Murry C. and Maud (Butler) Falkner (he later changed the spelling to Faulkner). The father was at the time a railroad man, but the family included a great-grand-father, William Falkner, who wrote *The White Rose of Memphis,* a novel.

1918 Removed as a child to Oxford, Mississippi. After desultory schooling, Faulkner joined the Royal Flying Corps, training in Canada.

1919–1921 Attended the University of Mississippi.

1922–1924 Postmaster at the University.

1924–1925 Lived for a time in New Orleans, where he knew Sherwood Anderson and where he contributed poems and criticism to *The Double Dealer.*

1924 *The Marble Faun* (poems, privately printed).

1926 *Soldiers' Pay,* a novel about an aviator who, presumed dead, returns home. During these difficult years, Faulkner worked as a carpenter, house-painter, farmer, and at other odd jobs.

1927 *Mosquitoes,* satirical novel about contemporary writers.

II. THE YEARS OF SUCCESS (1929–   )

1929 *Sartoris,* a novel in which the "saga of Yoknapatawpha County" begins to take shape. *The Sound and the Fury,* a stream-of-consciousness novel in which the lives of the Compson family appear, a key to the social problems of the Sartoris-Compson-Sutpen families. Married Estelle Oldham Franklin, June 20.

1930 *As I Lay Dying* (novel).

1931 *Sanctuary* (originally rejected, then rewritten), a deliberate shocker; *These 13* (short stories); *Idyll in the Desert* (short story).

1932 *Light in August* (novel), central for an understanding of the social problems of Yoknapatawpha County; *Miss Zilphia Gant* (short story); *Salmagundi* and *This Earth* (poems, privately printed).

1933 *A Green Bough* (poems).

1934 *Doctor Martino and Other Stories.*

1935 *Pylon,* a novel concerning air races during Mardi Gras.

1936 *Absalom, Absalom!* (novel), part of the saga, telling the Sutpen story.

1938 *The Unvanquished* (novel), another chronicle of the Sartoris family.

1939 *The Wild Palms* (novel).

1940 *The Hamlet* (novel), which concerns the Snopes family.

1942 *Go Down, Moses, and Other Stories,* including "Was," "The Bear," and "Delta Autumn."

1948 *Intruder in the Dust* (novel).

1949 *Knight's Gambit* (short stories).

1950 *Collected Stories of William Faulkner. Notes on a Horsethief* (short story, printed privately in a limited edition). December 10 in Stockholm, Sweden, awarded the Nobel Prize in literature for 1949.

BIOGRAPHY: There is no biography. Brief facts are available in *Who's Who in America; New York Times Index;* Marshall J. Smith, "Faulkner of Mississippi," *Bookman,* December, 1931, pp. 411-17; Stark Young, "New Year's Craw," *The New Republic,* January 12, 1938, pp. 283-84; and Fred B. Millett, *Contemporary American Authors,* Harcourt, Brace, 1940, pp. 346-48.

BIBLIOGRAPHY: Consult, for the fullest listing up to *Go Down, Moses,* Robert W. Daniel, *A Catalogue of the Writings of William Faulkner,* Yale University Press, 1942. See also Aubrey Starke, "An American Comedy: An Introduction to a Bibliography of William Faulkner," *Colophon,* Pt. 19, 1934, 12 pp., and *Literary History of the United States,* Vol. III, pp. 502-03.

CRITICAL COMMENT: Before 1939 the critical notice of Faulkner's work was chiefly hostile with the exception of brief notes in American fiction surveys, of Evelyn Scott's pamphlet on *The Sound and the Fury* (New York, Jonathan Cape, 1929), and of Wyndham Lewis' study, "William Faulkner, the Moralist with a Corn Cob" in *Men Without Art,* London, 1934, pp. 42-64.

More balanced appraisal begins with George Marion O'Donnell, "Faulkner's Mythology," *Kenyon Review,* Summer, 1939, pp. 285-99; and Warren Beck, "Faulkner and the South," *Antioch Review,* Spring, 1941, pp. 82-94, "Faulkner's Point of View," *College English,* May, 1941, pp. 736-49, and "William Faulkner's Style," *American Prefaces,* Spring, 1941, pp. 195-211. See also Robert Penn Warren, "The Snopes World," *Kenyon Review,* Spring, 1941, pp. 253-57; Malcolm Cowley, "William Faulkner's Human Comedy," *New York Times Book Review,* October 29, 1944, p. 4 and "William Faulkner's Legend of the South," *Saturday Review of Literature,* July, 1945, pp. 343-61; John M. Maclachan, "William Faulkner and the Southern Folk," *Southern Folklore Quarterly,* September, 1945, pp. 153-67; George Snell, "The Fury of William Faulkner," *Western Review,* Autumn, 1946, pp. 29-40; Vincent F. Hopper, "Faulkner's Paradise Lost," *Virginia Quarterly Review,* July, 1947, pp. 405-20; and John Arthos, "Ritual and Humor in the Writing of William Faulkner," *Accent,* 1948, pp. 17-30.

For a more nearly complete bibliography of critical comment on individual novels see John L. Longley, Jr. and Robert Daniel, "Faulkner's Critics: A Selective Bibliography," *Perspective,* Autumn, 1950, pp. 202-08. The best book of selections, with a valuable introduction and editor's notes, is that compiled by Malcolm Cowley, *The Portable Faulkner,* Viking Press, 1946.

In American fiction, the name of William Faulkner has become synonymous with Oxford, Mississippi, where for many years he has lived in a large, century-old house; with the mythical Yoknapatawpha County of his novels; with legends of the decay of the Old South; and, among his fellow novelists especially, with a reputation more envied than understood, more clearly possessing "the elements of simple genius" (as Henry James said of Hawthorne) than the facility and gregariousness of many of his contemporaries. As was Hawthorne, Mr. Faulkner is a solitary worker. When he came out of semi-seclusion to accept the Nobel Prize in Stockholm, he said in his acceptance speech that "the young man or woman writing today has forgotten the problems of the human heart in conflict with itself which alone can make good writing because only that is worth writing about, worth the agony and the sweat."

For more than twenty-five years, Mr. Faulkner has dedicated himself to this task, to creating a world of the imagination such as comes to being once or twice a century in a nation's letters and in this world (Yoknapatawpha County) stating over and over the Southern legend of privilege and its decay, of defeat and reconstruction, in microcosm. He probes these "problems of the human heart" through at least five distinguishable levels of society: the planters and their descendants (the Compson family in *The Sound and the Fury,* the Sutpen clan in *Absalom, Absalom!,* the Sartoris clan in *The Unvanquished* and *Sartoris*—all degenerating from pre-Civil War standards); the townspeople (such as Gavin Stevens, the lawyer in *Intruder in the Dust* and *Knight's Gambit,* or Percy Grimm, the incipient fascist in *Light in August*); the white trash and carpetbaggers (the Bundren family of *As I Lay Dying,* the unwashed Snopes clan of *The Hamlet* who spread over the land like locusts, or the incredibly brutal Popeye of *Sanctuary*); the Negroes (notably the imperturbable Dilsey of *The Sound and the Fury* and the obstinate, shrewd Lucas Beauchamp of *Go Down, Moses* and *Intruder in the Dust*); and finally the Indians (like Ikkemotubbe and Sam Fathers and Boon Hogganbeck in *Go Down, Moses*). Though each novel stands as an entity, one must survey the whole tapestry of this community before one can realize the immensity of its scope and the closeness of its details.

In developing a personal idiom, Faulkner has succumbed to a highly rhetorical style which many critics feel becomes prolix more often than necessary, leading his reader into a literary labyrinth which requires a third and fourth reading for mere comprehension. Still other critics object to the unadulterated violence and brutality of his characters, to his use of insane and morally perverted subjects merely for shock value. A careful study of Mr. Faulkner's intention reveals more than rhetoric and shock technique. His involute style demands an intensity of response which few artists receive; it so involves the reader in its syntax that he becomes a functioning part of the story almost against his will, as it were, and as he discovers for himself the related elements of the action he is re-creating the story anew, on his own level of perception. Though this complexity often challenges patience, it stimulates vibrant reaction. Mr. Faulkner is willing to trade one for the other, just as he is willing to risk censorship of language in order to state his moral indignation in stinging terms. If his people seem crude and unlearned, he would most likely say that the aspects of life as he knows it are in themselves so terrible that only by starting again with simpler people, with naïfs and crazy folk, telling the story as they must have seen it, can he get closer to the truth. He wishes above all to break through the crust of indifference and inhumanity with which mechanized civilization has coated our lives, for only this way leads to recognition of "the problems of the human heart."

THE BEAR

The story which is here reprinted is taken from *Go Down, Moses,* a collection of tales about the McCaslin family, principally about Isaac McCaslin, son of Uncle Buck (Theophilus McCaslin) and grandson of old Carothers McCaslin, progenitor of the clan. Parts of this story first appeared in *Harper's* (December, 1935) under the title "Lion," in which Isaac, however, is not the hero and in which Sam Fathers never appears. Still other parts appeared in the *Saturday Evening Post* (May 9, 1942) in a brief story called "The Bear," which tells of Isaac's relationship to Sam, Old Ben, and a fyce named Nip.

I

THERE was a man and a dog too this time. Two beasts, counting Old Ben, the bear, and two men, counting Boon Hogganbeck, in whom some of the same blood ran which ran in Sam Fathers, even though Boon's was a plebeian strain of it and only Sam and Old Ben and the mongrel Lion were taintless and incorruptible.

He was sixteen. For six years now he had been a man's hunter. For six years now he had heard the best of all talking. It was of the wilderness, the big woods, bigger and older than any recorded document; of white man fatuous enough to believe he had bought any fragment of it, of Indian ruthless enough to pretend that any fragment of it had been his to convey; bigger than Major de Spain and the scrap he pretended to, knowing better; older than old Thomas Sutpen of whom Major de Spain had had it and who knew better; older even than old Ikkemotubbe, the Chickasaw chief, of whom old Sutpen had had it and who knew better in his turn. It was of the men, not white nor black nor red but men, hunters, with the will and hardihood to endure and the humility and skill to survive, and the dogs and the bear and deer juxtaposed and reliefed against it, ordered and compelled by and within the wilderness in the ancient and unremitting contest according to the ancient and immitigable rules which voided all regrets and brooked no quarter;—the best game of all, the best of all breathing and forever the best of all listening, the voices quiet and weighty and deliberate for retrospection and recollection and exactitude among the concrete trophies—the racked guns and the heads and skins—in the libraries of town houses or the offices of plantation houses or (and best of all) in the camps themselves where the intact and still-warm meat yet hung, the men who had slain it sitting before the burning logs on hearths when there were houses and hearths or about the smoky blazing of piled wood in front of stretched tarpaulins when there were not. There was always a bottle present, so that it would seem to him that those fine fierce instants of heart and brain and courage and wiliness and speed were concentrated and distilled into that brown liquor which not women, not boys and children, but only hunters drank, drinking not of the blood they spilled but some condensation of the wild immortal spirit, drinking it moderately, humbly even, not with the pagan's base and baseless hope of acquiring thereby the virtues of cunning and strength and speed but in salute to them. Thus it seemed to him on this December morning not only natural but actually fitting that this should have begun with whisky.

He realized later that it had begun long before that. It had already begun on that day when he first wrote his age in two ciphers and his cousin Mc-Caslin brought him for the first time to the camp, the big woods, to earn for himself from the wilderness the name and state of hunter provided he in his turn were humble and enduring enough. He had already inherited then, without ever having seen it, the big old bear with one trap-ruined foot that in an

5

10

15

20

25

30

35

40

6. **He**—that is, Isaac McCaslin, about whom the whole story is centered. **38-39. his cousin McCaslin**—that is, Carothers McCaslin Edmonds. This man, sixteen years older than Isaac, is sometimes referred to as "Cass" in the story.

area almost a hundred miles square had earned for himself a name, a definite designation like a living man:—the long legend of corn-cribs broken down and rifled, of shoats and grown pigs and even calves carried bodily into the woods and devoured and traps and deadfalls overthrown and dogs mangled and slain
5   and shotgun and even rifle shots delivered at point-blank range yet with no more effect than so many peas blown through a tube by a child—a corridor of wreckage and destruction beginning back before the boy was born, through which sped, not fast but rather with the ruthless and irresistible deliberation of a locomotive, the shaggy tremendous shape. It ran in his knowledge before
10 he ever saw it. It loomed and towered in his dreams before he even saw the unaxed woods where it left its crooked print, shaggy, tremendous, red-eyed, not malevolent but just big, too big for the dogs which tried to bay it, for the horses which tried to ride it down, for the men and the bullets they fired into it; too big for the very country which was its constricting scope. It was as if
15 the boy had already divined what his senses and intellect had not encompassed yet: that doomed wilderness whose edges were being constantly and punily gnawed at by men with plows and axes who feared it because it was wilderness, men myriad and nameless even to one another in the land where the old bear had earned a name, and through which ran not even a mortal beast
20 but an anachronism indomitable and invincible out of an old dead time, a phantom, epitome and apotheosis of the old wild life which the little puny humans swarmed and hacked at in a fury of abhorrence and fear like pygmies about the ankles of a drowsing elephant;—the old bear, solitary, indomitable, and alone; widowered childless and absolved of mortality—old Priam reft of
25 his old wife and outlived all his sons.

Still a child, with three years then two years then one year yet before he too could make one of them, each November he would watch the wagon containing the dogs and the bedding and food and guns and his cousin McCaslin and Tennie's Jim and Sam Fathers too until Sam moved to the camp to live,
30 depart for the Big Bottom, the big woods. To him, they were going not to hunt bear and deer but to keep yearly rendezvous with the bear which they did not even intend to kill. Two weeks later they would return, with no trophy, no skin. He had not expected it. He had not even feared that it might be in the wagon this time with the other skins and heads. He did not even
35 tell himself that in three years or two years or one year more he would be present and that it might even be his gun. He believed that only after he had served his apprenticeship in the woods which would prove him worthy to be a hunter, would he even be permitted to distinguish the crooked print, and that even then for two November weeks he would merely make another minor
40 one, along with his cousin and Major de Spain and General Compson and Walter Ewell and Boon and the dogs which feared to bay it and the shotguns and rifles which failed even to bleed it, in the yearly pageant-rite of the old bear's furious immortality.

His day came at last. In the surrey with his cousin and Major de Spain and

24. **Priam**—King of Troy at the time of the Trojan war, Priam was husband of Hecuba, father of fifty sons and many daughters. 29. **Tennie's Jim**—that is, Jim (a young Negro boy), the son of Tennie Beauchamp. Actually Tennie's Jim and Isaac McCaslin were both grandsons of old Carothers McCaslin, though Jim's mother and grandmother were Negroes.

General Compson he saw the wilderness through a slow drizzle of November rain just above the ice point as it seemed to him later he always saw it or at least always remembered it—the tall and endless wall of dense November woods under the dissolving afternoon and the year's death, sombre, impenetrable (he could not even discern yet how, at what point they could possibly hope to enter it even though he knew that Sam Fathers was waiting there with the wagon), the surrey moving through the skeleton stalks of cotton and corn in the last of open country, the last trace of man's puny gnawing at the immemorial flank, until, dwarfed by that perspective into an almost ridiculous diminishment, the surrey itself seemed to have ceased to move (this too to be completed later, years later, after he had grown to a man and had seen the sea) as a solitary small boat hangs in lonely immobility, merely tossing up and down, in the infinite waste of the ocean while the water and then the apparently impenetrable land which it nears without appreciable progress, swings slowly and opens the widening inlet which is the anchorage. He entered it. Sam was waiting, wrapped in a quilt on the wagon seat behind the patient and steaming mules. He entered his novitiate to the true wilderness with Sam beside him as he had begun his apprenticeship in miniature to manhood after the rabbits and such with Sam beside him, the two of them wrapped in the damp, warm, negro-rank quilt, while the wilderness closed behind his entrance as it had opened momentarily to accept him, opening before his advancement as it closed behind his progress, no fixed path the wagon followed but a channel non-existent ten yards ahead of it and ceasing to exist ten yards after it had passed, the wagon progressing not by its own volition but by attrition of their intact yet fluid circumambience, drowsing, earless, almost lightless.

It seemed to him that at the age of ten he was witnessing his own birth. It was not even strange to him. He had experienced it all before, and not merely in dreams. He saw the camp—a paintless six-room bungalow set on piles above the spring high-water—and he knew already how it was going to look. He helped in the rapid orderly disorder of their establishment in it and even his motions were familiar to him, foreknown. Then for two weeks he ate the coarse, rapid food—the shapeless sour bread, the wild strange meat, venison and bear and turkey and coon which he had never tasted before—which men ate, cooked by men who were hunters first and cooks afterward; he slept in harsh sheetless blankets as hunters slept. Each morning the gray of dawn found him and Sam Fathers on the stand, the crossing, which had been allotted him. It was the poorest one, the most barren. He had expected that; he had not dared yet to hope even to himself that he would even hear the running dogs this first time. But he did hear them. It was on the third morning—a murmur, sourceless, almost indistinguishable, yet he knew what it was although he had never before heard that many dogs running at once, the murmur swelling into separate and distinct voices until he could call the five dogs which his cousin owned from among the others. "Now," Sam said, "slant your gun up a little and draw back the hammers and then stand still."

But it was not for him, not yet. The humility was there; he had learned that. And he could learn the patience. He was only ten, only one week. The instant had passed. It seemed to him that he could actually see the deer, the

buck, smoke-colored, elongated with speed, vanished, the woods, the gray solitude still ringing even when the voices of the dogs had died away; from far
away across the sombre woods and the gray half-liquid morning there came
two shots. "Now let your hammers down," Sam said.

5   He did so. "You knew it too," he said.
"Yes," Sam said. "I want you to learn how to do when you didn't shoot.
It's after the chance for the bear or the deer has done already come and gone
that men and dogs get killed."
"Anyway, it wasn't him," the boy said. "It wasn't even a bear. It was just
10 a deer."
"Yes," Sam said, "it was just a deer."
Then one morning, it was in the second week, he heard the dogs again. This
time before Sam even spoke he readied the too-long, too-heavy, man-size gun
as Sam had taught him, even though this time he knew the dogs and the deer
15 were coming less close than ever, hardly within hearing even. They didn't
sound like any running dogs he had ever heard before even. Then he found
that Sam, who had taught him first of all to cock the gun and take position
where he could see best in all directions and then never to move again, had
himself moved up beside him. "There," he said. "Listen." The boy listened,
20 to no ringing chorus strong and fast on a free scent but, a moiling yapping
an octave too high and with something more than indecision and even abjectness in it which he could not yet recognize, reluctant, not even moving very
fast, taking a long time to pass out of hearing, leaving even then in the air
that echo of thin and almost human hysteria, abject, almost humanly grieving,
25 with this time nothing ahead of it, no sense of a fleeing unseen smoke-colored
shape. He could hear Sam breathing at his shoulder. He saw the arched curve
of the old man's inhaling nostrils.
"It's Old Ben!" he cried, whispering.
Sam didn't move save for the slow gradual turning of his head as the voices
30 faded on and the faint steady rapid arch and collapse of his nostrils. "Hah,"
he said. "Not even running. Walking."
"But up here!" the boy cried. "Way up here!"
"He do it every year," Sam said. "Once. Ash and Boon say he comes up here
to run the other little bears away. Tell them to get to hell out of here and
35 stay out until the hunters are gone. Maybe." The boy no longer heard anything
at all, yet still Sam's head continued to turn gradually and steadily until the
back of it was toward him. Then it turned back and looked down at him—
the same face, grave, familiar, expressionless until it smiled, the same old man's
eyes from which as he watched there faded slowly a quality darkly and fiercely
40 lambent, passionate and proud. "He dont care no more for bears than he does
for dogs or men neither. He come to see who's here, who's new in camp this
year, whether he can shoot or not, can stay or not. Whether we got the dog
yet that can bay and hold him until a man gets there with a gun. Because he's
the head bear. He's the man." It faded, was gone; again they were the eyes as
45 he had known them all his life. "He'll let them follow him to the river. Then
he'll send them home. We might as well go too; see how they look when they
get back to camp."

The dogs were there first, ten of them huddled back under the kitchen, himself and Sam squatting to peer back into the obscurity where they crouched, quiet, the eyes rolling and luminous, vanishing, and no sound, only that effluvium which the boy could not quite place yet, of something more than dog, stronger than dog and not just animal, just beast even. Because there had been nothing in front of the abject and painful yapping except the solitude, the wilderness, so that when the eleventh hound got back about mid-afternoon and he and Tennie's Jim held the passive and still trembling bitch while Sam daubed her tattered ear and raked shoulder with turpentine and axle-grease, it was still no living creature but only the wilderness which, leaning for a moment, had patted lightly once her temerity. "Just like a man," Sam said. "Just like folks. Put off as long as she could having to be brave, knowing all the time that sooner or later she would have to be brave once so she could keep on calling herself a dog, and knowing beforehand what was going to happen when she done it."

He did not know just when Sam left. He only knew that he was gone. For the next three mornings he rose and ate breakfast and Sam was not waiting for him. He went to his stand alone; he found it without help now and stood on it as Sam had taught him. On the third morning he heard the dogs again, running strong and free on a true scent again, and he readied the gun as he had learned to do and heard the hunt sweep past on since he was not ready yet, had not deserved other yet in just one short period of two weeks as compared to all the long life which he had already dedicated to the wilderness with patience and humility; he heard the shot again, one shot, the single clapping report of Walter Ewell's rifle. By now he could not only find his stand and then return to camp without guidance, by using the compass his cousin had given him he reached Walter, waiting beside the buck and the moiling of dogs over the cast entrails before any of the others except Major de Spain and Tennie's Jim on the horses, even before Uncle Ash arrived with the one-eyed wagon-mule which did not mind the smell of blood or even, so they said, of bear.

It was not Uncle Ash on the mule. It was Sam, returned. And Sam was waiting when he finished his dinner and, himself on the one-eyed mule and Sam on the other one of the wagon team, they rode for more than three hours through the rapid shortening sunless afternoon, following no path, no trail even that he could discern, into a section of country he had never seen before. Then he understood why Sam had made him ride the one-eyed mule which would not spook at the smell of blood, of wild animals. The other one, the sound one, stopped short and tried to whirl and bolt even as Sam got down, jerking and wrenching at the rein while Sam held it, coaxing it forward with his voice since he did not dare risk hitching it, drawing it forward while the boy dismounted from the marred one which would stand. Then, standing beside Sam in the thick great gloom of ancient woods and the winter's dying afternoon, he looked quietly down at the rotted log scored and gutted with claw-marks and, in the wet earth beside it, the print of the enormous warped two-toed foot. Now he knew what he had heard in the hounds' voices in the

38. spook—startle or bolt.

woods that morning and what he had smelled when he peered under the
kitchen where they huddled. It was in him too, a little different because they
were brute beasts and he was not, but only a little different—an eagerness, passive; an abjectness, a sense of his own fragility and impotence against the time-
5   less woods, yet without doubt or dread; a flavor like brass in the sudden run
of saliva in his mouth, a hard sharp constriction either in his brain or his
stomach, he could not tell which and it did not matter; he knew only that for
the first time he realized that the bear which had run in his listening and
loomed in his dreams since before he could remember and which therefore
10   must have existed in the listening and the dreams of his cousin and Major de
Spain and even old General Compson before they began to remember in their
turn, was a mortal animal and that they had departed for the camp each
November with no actual intention of slaying it, not because it could not be
slain but because so far they had no actual hope of being able to. "It will be
15   tomorrow," he said.
"You mean we will try tomorrow," Sam said. "We aint got the dog yet."
"We've got eleven," he said. "They ran him Monday."
"And you heard them," Sam said. "Saw them too. We aint got the dog
yet. It wont take but one. But he aint there. Maybe he aint nowhere. The only
20   other way will be for him to run by accident over somebody that had a gun
and knowed how to shoot it."
"That wouldn't be me," the boy said. "It would be Walter or Major or—"
"It might," Sam said. "You watch close tomorrow. Because he's smart. That's
how come he has lived this long. If he gets hemmed up and has got to pick out
25   somebody to run over, he will pick out you."
"How?" he said. "How will he know. . . ." He ceased. "You mean he
already knows me, that I aint never been to the big bottom before, aint had
time to find out yet whether I . . ." He ceased again, staring at Sam; he said
humbly, not even amazed: "It was me he was watching. I dont reckon he did
30   need to come but once."
"You watch tomorrow," Sam said. "I reckon we better start back. It'll be
long after dark now before we get to camp."
The next morning they started three hours earlier than they had ever done.
Even Uncle Ash went, the cook, who called himself by profession a camp cook
35   and who did little else save cook for Major de Spain's hunting and camping
parties, yet who had been marked by the wilderness from simple juxtaposition
to it until he responded as they all did, even the boy who until two weeks ago
had never even seen the wilderness, to a hound's ripped ear and shoulder and
the print of a crooked foot in a patch of wet earth. They rode. It was too far
40   to walk: the boy and Sam and Uncle Ash in the wagon with the dogs, his
cousin and Major de Spain and General Compson and Boon and Walter and
Tennie's Jim riding double on the horses; again the first gray light found
him, as on that first morning two weeks ago, on the stand where Sam had
placed and left him. With the gun which was too big for him, the breech-
45   loader which did not even belong to him but to Major de Spain and which
he had fired only once, at a stump on the first day to learn the recoil and how
to reload it with the paper shells, he stood against a big gum tree beside a

little bayou whose black still water crept without motion out of a cane-brake, across a small clearing and into the cane again, where, invisible, a bird, the big woodpecker called Lord-to-God by negroes, clattered at a dead trunk. It was a stand like any other stand, dissimilar only in incidentals to the one where he had stood each morning for two weeks; a territory new to him yet 5 no less familiar than that other one which after two weeks he had come to believe he knew a little—the same solitude, the same loneliness through which frail and timorous man had merely passed without altering it, leaving no mark nor scar, which looked exactly as it must have looked when the first ancestor of Sam Fathers' Chickasaw predecessors crept into it and looked about him, 10 club or stone axe or bone arrow drawn and ready, different only because, squatting at the edge of the kitchen, he had smelled the dogs huddled and cringing beneath it and saw the raked ear and side of the bitch that, as Sam had said, had to be brave once in order to keep on calling herself a dog, and saw yesterday in the earth beside the gutted log, the print of the living foot. 15 He heard no dogs at all. He never did certainly hear them. He only heard the drumming of the woodpecker stop short off, and knew that the bear was looking at him. He never saw it. He did not know whether it was facing him from the cane or behind him. He did not move, holding the useless gun which he knew now he would never fire at it, now or ever, tasting in his saliva that 20 taint of brass which he had smelled in the huddled dogs when he peered under the kitchen.

Then it was gone. As abruptly as it had stopped, the woodpecker's dry hammering set up again, and after a while he believed he even heard the dogs— a murmur, scarce a sound even, which he had probably been hearing for a 25 time, perhaps a minute or two, before he remarked it, drifting into hearing and then out again, dying away. They came nowhere near him. If it was dogs he heard, he could not have sworn to it; if it was a bear they ran, it was another bear. It was Sam himself who emerged from the cane and crossed the bayou, the injured bitch following at heel as a bird dog is taught to walk. 30 She came and crouched against his leg, trembling. "I didn't see him," he said. "I didn't, Sam."

"I know it," Sam said. "He done the looking. You didn't hear him neither, did you?"

"No," the boy said. "I—" 35

"He's smart," Sam said. "Too smart." Again the boy saw in his eyes that quality of dark and brooding lambence as Sam looked down at the bitch trembling faintly and steadily against the boy's leg. From her raked shoulder a few drops of fresh blood clung like bright berries. "Too big. We aint got the dog yet. But maybe some day." 40

Because there would be a next time, after and after. He was only ten. It seemed to him that he could see them, the two of them, shadowy in the limbo from which time emerged and became time: the old bear absolved of mortality and himself who shared a little of it. Because he recognised now what he had smelled in the huddled dogs and tasted in his own saliva, recognised 45

---

1. **bayou**—a term common to the lower Mississippi basin, meaning an arm or outlet to a river or lake.

fear as a boy, a youth, recognises the existence of love and passion and experience which is his heritage but not yet his patrimony, from entering by chance
the presence or perhaps even merely the bedroom of a woman who has loved
and been loved by many men. *So I will have to see him,* he thought, without
5 dread or even hope. *I will have to look at him.* So it was in June of the next
summer. They were at the camp again, celebrating Major de Spain's and General Compson's birthdays. Although the one had been born in September and
the other in the depth of winter and almost thirty years earlier, each June the
two of them and McCaslin and Boon and Walter Ewell (and the boy too
10 from now on) spent two weeks at the camp, fishing and shooting squirrels and
turkey and running coons and wildcats with the dogs at night. That is, Boon
and the negroes (and the boy too now) fished and shot squirrels and ran the
coons and cats, because the proven hunters, not only Major de Spain and old
General Compson (who spent those two weeks sitting in a rocking chair be-
15 fore a tremendous iron pot of Brunswick stew, stirring and tasting, with Uncle
Ash to quarrel with about how he was making it and Tennie's Jim to pour
whisky into the tin dipper from which he drank it), but even McCaslin and
Walter Ewell who were still young enough, scorned such other than shooting
the wild gobblers with pistols for wagers or to test their marksmanship.
20   That is, his cousin McCaslin and the others thought he was hunting
squirrels. Until the third evening he believed that Sam Fathers thought so
too. Each morning he would leave the camp right after breakfast. He had
his own gun now, a new breech-loader, a Christmas gift; he would own and
shoot it for almost seventy years, through two new pairs of barrels and locks
25 and one new stock, until all that remained of the original gun was the silver-
inlaid trigger-guard with his and McCaslin's engraved names and the date in
1878. He found the tree beside the little bayou where he had stood that morning. Using the compass he ranged from that point; he was teaching himself
to be better than a fair woodsman without even knowing he was doing it.
30 On the third day he even found the gutted log where he had first seen the
print. It was almost completely crumbled now, healing with unbelievable
speed, a passionate and almost visible relinquishment, back into the earth
from which the tree had grown. He ranged the summer woods now, green
with gloom, if anything actually dimmer than they had been in November's
35 gray dissolution, where even at noon the sun fell only in windless dappling
upon the earth which never completely dried and which crawled with snakes—
moccasins and watersnakes and rattlers, themselves the color of the dappled
gloom so that he would not always see them until they moved; returning to
camp later and later and later, first day, second day, passing in the twilight of
40 the third evening the little log pen enclosing the log barn where Sam was
putting up the stock for the night. "You aint looked right yet," Sam said.
He stopped. For a moment he didn't answer. Then he said peacefully, in a
peaceful rushing burst, as when a boy's miniature dam in a little brook gives
way: "All right. Yes. But how? I went to the bayou. I even found that log
45 again. I—"
"I reckon that was all right. Likely he's been watching you. You never saw
his foot?"

"I . . ." the boy said. "I didn't . . . I never thought . . ."

"It's the gun," Sam said. He stood beside the fence, motionless, the old man, son of a negro slave and a Chickasaw chief, in the battered and faded overalls and the frayed five-cent straw hat which had been the badge of the negro's slavery and was now the regalia of his freedom. The camp—the clearing, the house, the barn and its tiny lot with which Major de Spain in his turn had scratched punily and evanescently at the wilderness—faded in the dusk, back into the immemorial darkness of the woods. *The gun,* the boy thought. *The gun.* "You will have to choose," Sam said.

He left the next morning before light, without breakfast, long before Uncle Ash would wake in his quilts on the kitchen floor and start the fire. He had only the compass and a stick for the snakes. He could go almost a mile before he would need to see the compass. He sat on a log, the invisible compass in his hand, while the secret night-sounds which had ceased at his movements, scurried again and then fell still for good and the owls ceased and gave over to the waking day birds and there was light in the gray wet woods and he could see the compass. He went fast yet still quietly, becoming steadily better and better as a woodsman without yet having time to realise it; he jumped a doe and a fawn, walked them out of the bed, close enough to see them—the crash of undergrowth, the white scut, the fawn scudding along behind her, faster than he had known it could have run. He was hunting right, upwind, as Sam had taught him, but that didn't matter now. He had left the gun; by his own will and relinquishment he had accepted not a gambit, not a choice, but a condition in which not only the bear's heretofore inviolable anonymity but all the ancient rules and balances of hunter and hunted had been abrogated. He would not even be afraid, not even in the moment when the fear would take him completely: blood, skin, bowels, bones, memory from the long time before it even became his memory—all save that thin clear quenchless lucidity which alone differed him from this bear and from all the other bears and bucks he would follow during almost seventy years, to which Sam had said: "Be scared. You cant help that. But dont be afraid. Aint nothing in the woods going to hurt you if you dont corner it or it dont smell that you are afraid. A bear or a deer has got to be scared of a coward the same as a brave man has got to be."

By noon he was far beyond the crossing on the little bayou, farther into the new and alien country than he had ever been, travelling now not only by the compass but by the old, heavy, biscuit-thick silver watch which had been his father's. He had left the camp nine hours ago; nine hours from now, dark would already have been an hour old. He stopped, for the first time since he had risen from the log when he could see the compass face at last, and looked about, mopping his sweating face on his sleeve. He had already relinquished, of his will, because of his need, in humility and peace and without regret, yet apparently that had not been enough, the leaving of the gun was not enough. He stood for a moment—a child, alien and lost in the green and soaring gloom of the markless wilderness. Then he relinquished completely to it. It was the watch and the compass. He was still tainted. He removed the linked

---

20. scut—a short tail, especially of a rabbit, hare, or deer.

chain of the one and the looped thong of the other from his overalls and hung them on a bush and leaned the stick beside them and entered it.

5 When he realised he was lost, he did as Sam had coached and drilled him: made a cast to cross his back-track. He had not been going very fast for the last two or three hours, and he had gone even less fast since he left the compass and watch on the bush. So he went slower still now, since the tree could not be very far; in fact, he found it before he really expected to and turned and went to it. But there was no bush beneath it, no compass nor watch, so he did next as Sam had coached and drilled him: made this next circle in the 10 opposite direction and much larger, so that the pattern of the two of them would bisect his track somewhere, but crossing no trace nor mark anywhere of his feet or any feet, and now he was going faster though still not panicked, his heart beating a little more rapidly but strong and steady enough, and this time it was not even the tree because there was a down log beside it which 15 he had never seen before and beyond the log a little swamp, a seepage of moisture somewhere between earth and water, and he did what Sam had coached and drilled him as the next and the last, seeing as he sat down on the log the crooked print, the warped indentation in the wet ground which while he looked at it continued to fill with water until it was level full and the water 20 began to overflow and the sides of the print began to dissolve away. Even as he looked up he saw the next one, and, moving, the one beyond it; moving, not hurrying, running, but merely keeping pace with them as they appeared before him as though they were being shaped out of thin air just one constant pace short of where he would lose them forever and be lost forever himself, 25 tireless, eager, without doubt or dread, panting a little above the strong rapid little hammer of his heart, emerging suddenly into a little glade, and the wilderness coalesced. It rushed, soundless, and solidified—the tree, the bush, the compass and the watch glinting where a ray of sunlight touched them. Then he saw the bear. It did not emerge, appear: it was just there, immobile, 30 fixed in the green and windless noon's hot dappling, not as big as he had dreamed it but as big as he had expected, bigger, dimensionless against the dappled obscurity, looking at him. Then it moved. It crossed the glade without haste, walking for an instant into the sun's full glare and out of it, and stopped again and looked back at him across one shoulder. Then it was gone. 35 It didn't walk into the woods. It faded, sank back into the wilderness without motion as he had watched a fish, a huge old bass, sink back into the dark depths of its pool and vanish without even any movement of its fins.

2

So he should have hated and feared Lion. He was thirteen then. He had 40 killed his buck and Sam Fathers had marked his face with the hot blood, and in the next November he killed a bear. But before that accolade he had become as competent in the woods as many grown men with the same experience. By now he was a better woodsman than most grown men with more. There was no territory within twenty-five miles of the camp that he did not

40. **hot blood**—Sam is here performing a part of the ritual of Indian tribes: the initiation of the young hunter to the hunt by anointing him with the blood of his first kill.

know—bayou, ridge, landmark trees and path; he could have led anyone direct to any spot in it and brought him back. He knew game trails that even Sam Fathers had never seen; in the third fall he found a buck's bedding-place by himself and unbeknown to his cousin he borrowed Walter Ewell's rifle and lay in wait for the buck at dawn and killed it when it walked back to the bed as Sam had told him how the old Chickasaw fathers did.

By now he knew the old bear's footprint better than he did his own, and not only the crooked one. He could see any one of the three sound prints and distinguish it at once from any other, and not only because of its size. There were other bears within that fifty miles which left tracks almost as large, or at least so near that the one would have appeared larger only by juxtaposition. It was more than that. If Sam Fathers had been his mentor and the backyard rabbits and squirrels his kindergarten, then the wilderness the old bear ran was his college and the old male bear itself, so long unwifed and childless as to have become its own ungendered progenitor, was his alma mater.

He could find the crooked print now whenever he wished, ten miles or five miles or sometimes closer than that, to the camp. Twice while on stand during the next three years he heard the dogs strike its trail and once even jump it by chance, the voices high, abject, almost human in their hysteria. Once, still-hunting with Walter Ewell's rifle, he saw it cross a long corridor of down timber where a tornado had passed. It rushed through rather than across the tangle of trunks and branches as a locomotive would, faster than he had ever believed it could have moved, almost as fast as a deer even because the deer would have spent most of that distance in the air; he realised then why it would take a dog not only of abnormal courage but size and speed too ever to bring it to bay. He had a little dog at home, a mongrel, of the sort called fyce by negroes, a ratter, itself not much bigger than a rat and possessing that sort of courage which had long since stopped being bravery and had become foolhardiness. He brought it with him one June and, timing them as if they were meeting an appointment with another human being, himself carrying the fyce with a sack over its head and Sam Fathers with a brace of the hounds on a rope leash, they lay downwind of the trail and actually ambushed the bear. They were so close that it turned at bay although he realised later this might have been from surprise and amazement at the shrill and frantic uproar of the fyce. It turned at bay against the trunk of a big cypress, on its hind feet; it seemed to the boy that it would never stop rising, taller and taller, and even the two hounds seemed to have taken a kind of desperate and despairing courage from the fyce. Then he realised that the fyce was actually not going to stop. He flung the gun down and ran. When he overtook and grasped the shrill, frantically pinwheeling little dog, it seemed to him that he was directly under the bear. He could smell it, strong and hot and rank. Sprawling, he looked up where it loomed and towered over him like a thunderclap. It was quite familiar, until he remembered: this was the way he had used to dream about it.

Then it was gone. He didn't see it go. He knelt, holding the frantic fyce

---

20. still-hunting—that is, hunting for game by stalking or by using cover. **26. fyce**—a variation of the word *feist*, meaning a small dog, like a rat terrier. Also spelled *feice, fice*, or *fist*.

with both hands, hearing the abased wailing of the two hounds drawing further and further away, until Sam came up, carrying the gun. He laid it quietly down beside the boy and stood looking down at him. "You've done seed him twice now, with a gun in your hands," he said. "This time you
5 couldn't have missed him."

The boy rose. He still held the fyce. Even in his arms it continued to yap frantically, surging and straining toward the fading sound of the hounds like a collection of live-wire springs. The boy was panting a little. "Neither could you," he said. "You had the gun. Why didn't you shoot him?"
10 Sam didn't seem to have heard. He put out his hand and touched the little dog in the boy's arms which still yapped and strained even though the two hounds were out of hearing now. "He's done gone," Sam said. "You can slack off and rest now, until next time." He stroked the little dog until it began to grow quiet under his hand. "You's almost the one we wants," he said. "You
15 just aint big enough. We aint got that one yet. He will need to be just a little bigger than smart, and a little braver than either." He withdrew his hand from the fyce's head and stood looking into the woods where the bear and the hounds had vanished. "Somebody is going to, some day."

"I know it," the boy said. "That's why it must be one of us. So it wont be
20 until the last day. When even he dont want it to last any longer."

So he should have hated and feared Lion. It was in the fourth summer, the fourth time he had made one in the celebration of Major de Spain's and General Compson's birthday. In the early spring Major de Spain's mare had foaled a horse colt. One evening when Sam brought the horses and mules up to
25 stable them for the night, the colt was missing and it was all he could do to get the frantic mare into the lot. He had thought at first to let the mare lead him back to where she had become separated from the foal. But she would not do it. She would not even feint toward any particular part of the woods or even in any particular direction. She merely ran, as if she couldn't see, still
30 frantic with terror. She whirled and ran at Sam once, as if to attack him in some ultimate desperation, as if she could not for the moment realise that he was a man and a long-familiar one. He got her into the lot at last. It was too dark by that time to back-track her, to unravel the erratic course she had doubtless pursued.
35 He came to the house and told Major de Spain. It was an animal, of course, a big one, and the colt was dead now, wherever it was. They all knew that. "It's a panther," General Compson said at once. "The same one. That doe and fawn last March." Sam had sent Major de Spain word of it when Boon Hogganbeck came to the camp on a routine visit to see how the stock had win-
40 tered—the doe's throat torn out, and the beast had run down the helpless fawn and killed it too.

"Sam never did say that was a panther," Major de Spain said. Sam said nothing now, standing behind Major de Spain where they sat at supper, inscrutable, as if he were just waiting for them to stop talking so he could go home.
45 He didn't even seem to be looking at anything. "A panther might jump a doe, and he wouldn't have much trouble catching the fawn afterward. But no panther would have jumped that colt with the dam right there with it. It was

Old Ben," Major de Spain said. "I'm disappointed in him. He has broken the rules. I didn't think he would have done that. He has killed mine and Mc-Caslin's dogs, but that was all right. We gambled the dogs against him; we gave each other warning. But now he has come into my house and destroyed my property, out of season too. He broke the rules. It was Old Ben, Sam." Still Sam said nothing, standing there until Major de Spain should stop talking. "We'll back-track her tomorrow and see," Major de Spain said.

Sam departed. He would not live in the camp; he had built himself a little hut something like Joe Baker's, only stouter, tighter, on the bayou a quarter-mile away, and a stout log crib where he stored a little corn for the shoat he raised each year. The next morning he was waiting when they waked. He had already found the colt. They did not even wait for breakfast. It was not far, not five hundred yards from the stable—the three-months' colt lying on its side, its throat torn out and the entrails and one ham partly eaten. It lay not as if it had been dropped but as if it had been struck and hurled, and no cat-mark, no claw-mark where a panther would have gripped it while finding its throat. They read the tracks where the frantic mare had circled and at last rushed in with that same ultimate desperation with which she had whirled on Sam Fathers yesterday evening, and the long tracks of dead and terrified running and those of the beast which had not even rushed at her when she advanced but had merely walked three or four paces toward her until she broke, and General Compson said, "Good God, what a wolf!"

Still Sam said nothing. The boy watched him while the men knelt, measuring the tracks. There was something in Sam's face now. It was neither exultation nor joy nor hope. Later, a man, the boy realised what it had been, and that Sam had known all the time what had made the tracks and what had torn the throat out of the doe in the spring and killed the fawn. It had been foreknowledge in Sam's face that morning. *And he was glad,* he told himself. *He was old. He had no children, no people, none of his blood anywhere above earth that he would ever meet again. And even if he were to, he could not have touched it, spoken to it, because for seventy years now he had had to be a negro. It was almost over now and he was glad.*

They returned to camp and had breakfast and came back with guns and the hounds. Afterward the boy realised that they also should have known then what killed the colt as well as Sam Fathers did. But that was neither the first nor the last time he had seen men rationalise from and even act upon their misconceptions. After Boon, standing astride the colt, had whipped the dogs away from it with his belt, they snuffed at the tracks. One of them, a young dog hound without judgment yet, bayed once, and they ran for a few feet on what seemed to be a trail. Then they stopped, looking back at the men, eager enough, not baffled, merely questioning, as if they were asking "Now what?" Then they rushed back to the colt, where Boon, still astride it, slashed at them with the belt.

"I never knew a trail to get cold that quick," General Compson said.

"Maybe a single wolf big enough to kill a colt with the dam right there beside it dont leave scent," Major de Spain said.

"Maybe it was a hant," Walter Ewell said. He looked at Tennie's Jim. "Hah, Jim?"

Because the hounds would not run it, Major de Spain had Sam hunt out and find the tracks a hundred yards farther on and they put the dogs on it
5 again and again the young one bayed and not one of them realised then that the hound was not baying like a dog striking game but was merely bellowing like a country dog whose yard has been invaded. General Compson spoke to the boy and Boon and Tennie's Jim: to the squirrel hunters. "You boys keep the dogs with you this morning. He's probably hanging around somewhere,
10 waiting to get his breakfast off the colt. You might strike him."

But they did not. The boy remembered how Sam stood watching them as they went into the woods with the leashed hounds—the Indian face in which he had never seen anything until it smiled except that faint arching of the nostrils on that first morning when the hounds had found Old Ben. They
15 took the hounds with them on the next day, though when they reached the place where they hoped to strike a fresh trail, the carcass of the colt was gone. Then on the third morning Sam was waiting again, this time until they had finished breakfast. He said, "Come." He led them to his house, his little hut, to the corn-crib beyond it. He had removed the corn and had made a dead-
20 fall of the door, baiting it with the colt's carcass; peering between the logs, they saw an animal almost the color of a gun or pistol barrel, what little time they had to examine its color or shape. It was not crouched nor even stand-ing. It was in motion, in the air, coming toward them—a heavy body crashing with tremendous force against the door so that the thick door jumped and
25 clattered in its frame, the animal, whatever it was, hurling itself against the door again seemingly before it could have touched the floor and got a new purchase to spring from. "Come away," Sam said, "fore he break his neck." Even when they retreated the heavy and measured crashes continued, the stout door jumping and clattering each time, and still no sound from the
30 beast itself—no snarl, no cry.

"What in hell's name is it?" Major de Spain said.

"It's a dog," Sam said, his nostrils arching and collapsing faintly and stead-ily and that faint, fierce milkiness in his eyes again as on that first morning when the hounds had struck the old bear. "It's the dog."
35 *The* dog?" Major de Spain said.

"That's gonter hold Old Ben."

"Dog the devil," Major de Spain said. "I'd rather have Old Ben himself in my pack than that brute. Shoot him."

"No," Sam said.
40 "You'll never tame him. How do you ever expect to make an animal like that afraid of you?"

"I dont want him tame," Sam said; again the boy watched his nostrils and the fierce milky light in his eyes. "But I almost rather he be tame than scared, of me or any man or any thing. But he wont be neither, of nothing."
45 "Then what are you going to do with it?"

"You can watch," Sam said.

Each morning through the second week they would go to Sam's crib. He

had removed a few shingles from the roof and had put a rope on the colt's
carcass and had drawn it out when the trap fell. Each morning they would
watch him lower a pail of water into the crib while the dog hurled itself tirelessly against the door and dropped back and leaped again. It never made any
sound and there was nothing frenzied in the act but only a cold and grim in-   5
domitable determination. Toward the end of the week it stopped jumping at
the door. Yet it had not weakened appreciably and it was not as if it had
rationalised the fact that the door was not going to give. It was as if for that
time it simply disdained to jump any longer. It was not down. None of them
had ever seen it down. It stood, and they could see it now—part mastiff, some-   10
thing of Airedale and something of a dozen other strains probably, better than
thirty inches at the shoulders and weighing as they guessed almost ninety
pounds, with cold yellow eyes and a tremendous chest and over all that strange
color like a blued gun-barrel.

Then the two weeks were up. They prepared to break camp. The boy   15
begged to remain and his cousin let him. He moved into the little hut with
Sam Fathers. Each morning he watched Sam lower the pail of water into
the crib. By the end of that week the dog was down. It would rise and half
stagger, half crawl to the water and drink and collapse again. One morning it
could not even reach the water, could not raise its forequarters even from the   20
floor. Sam took a short stick and prepared to enter the crib. "Wait," the boy
said. "Let me get the gun—"

"No," Sam said. "He cant move now." Nor could it. It lay on its side while
Sam touched it, its head and the gaunted body, the dog lying motionless, the
yellow eyes open. They were not fierce and there was nothing of petty malev-   25
olence in them, but a cold and almost impersonal malignance like some natural force. It was not even looking at Sam nor at the boy peering at it between the logs.

Sam began to feed it again. The first time he had to raise its head so it
could lap the broth. That night he left a bowl of broth containing lumps of   30
meat where the dog could reach it. The next morning the bowl was empty
and the dog was lying on its belly, its head up, the cold yellow eyes watching
the door as Sam entered, no change whatever in the cold yellow eyes and still
no sound from it even when it sprang, its aim and co-ordination still bad
from weakness so that Sam had time to strike it down with the stick and leap   35
from the crib and slam the door as the dog, still without having had time to
get its feet under it to jump again seemingly, hurled itself against the door as
if the two weeks of starving had never been.

At noon that day someone came whooping through the woods from the
direction of the camp. It was Boon. He came and looked for a while between   40
the logs, at the tremendous dog lying again on its belly, its head up, the yellow
eyes blinking sleepily at nothing: the indomitable and unbroken spirit. "What
we better do," Boon said, "is to let that son of a bitch go and catch Old Ben
and run him on the dog." He turned to the boy his weather-reddened and
beetling face. "Get your traps together. Cass says for you to come on home.   45
You been in here fooling with that horse-eating varmint long enough."

Boon had a borrowed mule at the camp; the buggy was waiting at the edge of the bottom. He was at home that night. He told McCaslin about it. "Sam's going to starve him again until he can go in and touch him. Then he will feed him again. Then he will starve him again, if he has to."

"But why?" McCaslin said. "What for? Even Sam will never tame that
5 brute."

"We dont want him tame. We want him like he is. We just want him to find out at last that the only way he can get out of that crib and stay out of it is to do what Sam or somebody tells him to do. He's the dog that's going to stop Old Ben and hold him. We've already named him. His name is
10 Lion."

Then November came at last. They returned to the camp. With General Compson and Major de Spain and his cousin and Walter and Boon he stood in the yard among the guns and bedding and boxes of food and watched Sam Fathers and Lion come up the lane from the lot—the Indian, the old
15 man in battered overalls and rubber boots and a worn sheepskin coat and a hat which had belonged to the boy's father; the tremendous dog pacing gravely beside him. The hounds rushed out to meet them and stopped, except the young one which still had but little of judgment. It ran up to Lion, fawning. Lion didn't snap at it. He didn't even pause. He struck it rolling
20 and yelping for five or six feet with a blow of one paw as a bear would have done and came on into the yard and stood, blinking sleepily at nothing, looking at no one, while Boon said, "Jesus. Jesus.—Will he let me touch him?"

"You can touch him," Sam said. "He dont care. He dont care about nothing or nobody."

25 The boy watched that too. He watched it for the next two years from that moment when Boon touched Lion's head and then knelt beside him, feeling the bones and muscles, the power. It was as if Lion were a woman—or perhaps Boon was the woman. That was more like it—the big, grave, sleepy-seeming dog which, as Sam Fathers said, cared about no man and no thing;
30 and the violent, insensitive, hard-faced man with his touch of remote Indian blood and the mind almost of a child. He watched Boon take over Lion's feeding from Sam and Uncle Ash both. He would see Boon squatting in the cold rain beside the kitchen while Lion ate. Because Lion neither slept nor ate with the other dogs though none of them knew where he did sleep until in
35 the second November, thinking until then that Lion slept in his kennel beside Sam Fathers' hut, when the boy's cousin McCaslin said something about it to Sam by sheer chance and Sam told him. And that night the boy and Major de Spain and McCaslin with a lamp entered the back room where Boon slept—the little, tight, airless room rank with the smell of Boon's un-
40 washed body and his wet hunting-clothes—where Boon, snoring on his back, choked and waked and Lion raised his head beside him and looked back at them from his cold, slumbrous yellow eyes.

"Damn it, Boon," McCaslin said. "Get that dog out of here. He's got to run Old Ben tomorrow morning. How in hell do you expect him to smell any-
45 thing fainter than a skunk after breathing you all night?"

"The way I smell aint hurt my nose none that I ever noticed," Boon said.

"It wouldn't matter if it had," Major de Spain said. "We're not depending on you to trail a bear. Put him outside. Put him under the house with the other dogs."

Boon began to get up. "He'll kill the first one that happens to yawn or sneeze in his face or touches him."

"I reckon not," Major de Spain said. "None of them are going to risk yawn- 5 ing in his face or touching him either, even asleep. Put him outside. I want his nose right tomorrow. Old Ben fooled him last year. I dont think he will do it again."

Boon put on his shoes without lacing them; in his long soiled underwear, his hair still tousled from sleep, he and Lion went out. The others returned 10 to the front room and the poker game where McCaslin's and Major de Spain's hands waited for them on the table. After a while McCaslin said, "Do you want me to go back and look again?"

"No," Major de Spain said. "I call," he said to Walter Ewell. He spoke to McCaslin again. "If you do, dont tell me. I am beginning to see the first sign 15 of my increasing age: I dont like to know that my orders have been disobeyed, even when I knew when I gave them that they would be.—A small pair," he said to Walter Ewell.

"How small?" Walter said.

"Very small," Major de Spain said.   20

And the boy, lying beneath his piled quilts and blankets waiting for sleep, knew likewise that Lion was already back in Boon's bed, for the rest of that night and the next one and during all the nights of the next November and the next one. He thought then: *I wonder what Sam thinks. He could have Lion with him, even if Boon is a white man. He could ask Major or McCaslin* 25 *either. And more than that. It was Sam's hand that touched Lion first and Lion knows it.* Then he became a man and he knew that too. It had been all right. That was the way it should have been. Sam was the chief, the prince; Boon, the plebeian, was his huntsman. Boon should have nursed the dogs.

On the first morning that Lion led the pack after Old Ben, seven strangers 30 appeared in the camp. They were swampers: gaunt, malaria-ridden men appearing from nowhere, who ran trap-lines for coons or perhaps farmed little patches of cotton and corn along the edge of the bottom, in clothes but little better than Sam Fathers' and nowhere near as good as Tennie's Jim's, with worn shotguns and rifles, already squatting patiently in the cold drizzle in 35 the side yard when day broke. They had a spokesman; afterward Sam Fathers told Major de Spain how all during the past summer and fall they had drifted into the camp singly or in pairs and threes, to look quietly at Lion for a while and then go away: "Mawnin, Major. We heerd you was aimin to put that ere blue dawg on that old two-toed bear this mawnin. We figgered we'd come 40 up and watch, if you dont mind. We wont do no shooting, lessen he runs over us."

"You are welcome," Major de Spain said. "You are welcome to shoot. He's more your bear than ours."

"I reckon that aint no lie. I done fed him enough cawn to have a sheer in 45 him. Not to mention a shoat three years ago."

"I reckon I got a sheer too," another said. "Only it aint in the bear." Major de Spain looked at him. He was chewing tobacco. He spat. "Hit was a heifer calf. Nice un too. Last year. When I finally found her, I reckon she looked about like that colt of yourn looked last June."

"Oh," Major de Spain said. "Be welcome. If you see game in front of my
5 dogs, shoot it."

Nobody shot Old Ben that day. No man saw him. The dogs jumped him within a hundred yards of the glade where the boy had seen him that day in the summer of his eleventh year. The boy was less than a quarter-mile away. He heard the jump but he could distinguish no voice among the dogs
10 that he did not know and therefore would be Lion's, and he thought, believed, that Lion was not among them. Even the fact that they were going much faster than he had ever heard them run behind Old Ben before and that the high thin note of hysteria was missing now from their voices was not enough to disabuse him. He didn't comprehend until that night, when Sam
15 told him that Lion would never cry on a trail. "He gonter growl when he catches Old Ben's throat," Sam said. "But he aint gonter never holler, no more than he ever done when he was jumping at that two-inch door. It's that blue dog in him. What you call it?"

"Airedale," the boy said.

20 Lion was there; the jump was just too close to the river. When Boon returned with Lion about eleven that night, he swore that Lion had stopped Old Ben once but that the hounds would not go in and Old Ben broke away and took to the river and swam for miles down it and he and Lion went down one bank for about ten miles and crossed and came up the other but
25 it had begun to get dark before they struck any trail where Old Ben had come up out of the water, unless he was still in the water when he passed the ford where they crossed. Then he fell to cursing the hounds and ate the supper Uncle Ash had saved for him and went off to bed and after a while the boy opened the door of the little stale room thunderous with snoring and the
30 great grave dog raised its head from Boon's pillow and blinked at him for a moment and lowered its head again.

When the next November came and the last day, the day on which it was now becoming traditional to save for Old Ben, there were more than a dozen strangers waiting. They were not all swampers this time. Some of them were
35 townsmen, from other county seats like Jefferson, who had heard about Lion and Old Ben and had come to watch the great blue dog keep his yearly rendezvous with the old two-toed bear. Some of them didn't even have guns and the hunting-clothes and boots they wore had been on a store shelf yesterday.

40 This time Lion jumped Old Ben more than five miles from the river and bayed and held him and this time the hounds went in, in a sort of desperate emulation. The boy heard them; he was that near. He heard Boon whooping; he heard the two shots when General Compson delivered both barrels, one containing five buckshot, the other a single ball, into the bear from as close
45 as he could force his almost unmanageable horse. He heard the dogs when the bear broke free again. He was running now; panting, stumbling, his lungs bursting, he reached the place where General Compson had fired and where

Old Ben had killed two of the hounds. He saw the blood from General Compson's shots, but he could go no further. He stopped, leaning against a tree for his breathing to ease and his heart to slow, hearing the sound of the dogs as it faded on and died away.

In camp that night—they had as guests five of the still terrified strangers 5 in new hunting coats and boots who had been lost all day until Sam Fathers went out and got them—he heard the rest of it: how Lion had stopped and held the bear again but only the one-eyed mule which did not mind the smell of wild blood would approach and Boon was riding the mule and Boon had never been known to hit anything. He shot at the bear five times with his pump 10 gun, touching nothing, and Old Ben killed another hound and broke free once more and reached the river and was gone. Again Boon and Lion hunted as far down one bank as they dared. Too far; they crossed in the first of dusk and dark overtook them within a mile. And this time Lion found the broken trail, the blood perhaps, in the darkness where Old Ben had come up out of 15 the water, but Boon had him on a rope, luckily, and he got down from the mule and fought Lion hand-to-hand until he got him back to camp. This time Boon didn't even curse. He stood in the door, muddy, spent, his huge gargoyle's face tragic and still amazed. "I missed him," he said. "I was in twenty-five feet of him and I missed him five times." 20

"But we have drawn blood," Major de Spain said. "General Compson drew blood. We have never done that before."

"But I missed him," Boon said. "I missed him five times. With Lion looking right at me."

"Never mind," Major de Spain said. "It was a damned fine race. And we 25 drew blood. Next year we'll let General Compson or Walter ride Katie, and we'll get him."

Then McCaslin said, "Where is Lion, Boon?"

"I left him at Sam's," Boon said. He was already turning away. "I aint fit to sleep with him." 30

So he should have hated and feared Lion. Yet he did not. It seemed to him that there was a fatality in it. It seemed to him that something, he didn't know what, was beginning; had already begun. It was like the last act on a set stage. It was the beginning of the end of something, he didn't know what except that he would not grieve. He would be humble and proud that 35 he had been found worthy to be a part of it too or even just to see it too.

3

It was December. It was the coldest December he had ever remembered. They had been in camp four days over two weeks, waiting for the weather to soften so that Lion and Old Ben could run their yearly race. Then they 40 would break camp and go home. Because of these unforeseen additional days which they had had to pass waiting on the weather, with nothing to do but play poker, the whisky had given out and he and Boon were being sent to Memphis with a suitcase and a note from Major de Spain to Mr Semmes, the

---

10-11. **pump gun**—a repeating shotgun, operated by sliding a hand grip back and forth along the magazine. **31. he**—that is, Isaac.

distiller, to get more. That is, Major de Spain and McCaslin were sending Boon to get the whisky and sending him to see that Boon got back with it or most of it or at least some of it.

Tennie's Jim waked him at three. He dressed rapidly, shivering, not so
5 much from the cold because a fresh fire already boomed and roared on the hearth, but in that dead winter hour when the blood and the heart are slow and sleep is incomplete. He crossed the gap between house and kitchen, the gap of iron earth beneath the brilliant and rigid night where dawn would not begin for three hours yet, tasting, tongue palate and to the very bottom
10 of his lungs the searing dark, and entered the kitchen, the lamp-lit warmth where the stove glowed, fogging the windows, and where Boon already sat at the table at breakfast, hunched over his plate, almost in his plate, his working jaws blue with stubble and his face innocent of water and his coarse, horse-mane hair innocent of comb—the quarter Indian, grandson of a Chicka-
15 saw squaw, who on occasion resented with his hard and furious fists the intimation of one single drop of alien blood and on others, usually after whisky, affirmed with the same fists and the same fury that his father had been the full-blood Chickasaw and even a chief and that even his mother had been only half white. He was four inches over six feet; he had the mind of a
20 child, the heart of a horse, and little hard shoe-button eyes without depth or meanness or generosity or viciousness or gentleness or anything else, in the ugliest face the boy had ever seen. It looked like somebody had found a walnut a little larger than a football and with a machinist's hammer had shaped features into it and then painted it, mostly red; not Indian red but a fine
25 bright ruddy color which whisky might have had something to do with but which was mostly just happy and violent out-of-doors, the wrinkles in it not the residue of the forty years it had survived but from squinting into the sun or into the gloom of cane-brakes where game had run, baked into it by the camp fires before which he had lain trying to sleep on the cold November or
30 December ground while waiting for daylight so he could rise and hunt again, as though time were merely something he walked through as he did through air, aging him no more than air did. He was brave, faithful, improvident and unreliable; he had neither profession job nor trade and owned one vice and one virtue: whisky, and that absolute and unquestioning fidelity to Major de
35 Spain and the boy's cousin McCaslin. "Sometimes I'd call them both virtues," Major de Spain said once. "Or both vices," McCaslin said.

He ate his breakfast, hearing the dogs under the kitchen, wakened by the smell of frying meat or perhaps by the feet overhead. He heard Lion once, short and peremptory, as the best hunter in any camp has only to speak once
40 to all save the fools, and none other of Major de Spain's and McCaslin's dogs were Lion's equal in size and strength and perhaps even in courage, but they were not fools; Old Ben had killed the last fool among them last year.

Tennie's Jim came in as they finished. The wagon was outside. Ash decided he would drive them over to the log-line where they would flag the outbound
45 log-train and let Tennie's Jim wash the dishes. The boy knew why. It would not be the first time he had listened to old Ash badgering Boon.

It was cold. The wagon wheels banged and clattered on the frozen ground;

the sky was fixed and brilliant. He was not shivering, he was shaking, slow and steady and hard, the food he had just eaten still warm and solid inside him while his outside shook slow and steady around it as though his stomach floated loose. "They wont run this morning," he said. "No dog will have any nose today." 5

"Cep Lion," Ash said. "Lion dont need no nose. All he need is a bear." He had wrapped his feet in towsacks and he had a quilt from his pallet bed on the kitchen floor drawn over his head and wrapped around him until in the thin brilliant starlight he looked like nothing at all that the boy had ever seen before. "He run a bear through a thousand-acre ice-house. Catch him too. 10 Them other dogs dont matter because they aint going to keep up with Lion nohow, long as he got a bear in front of him."

"What's wrong with the other dogs?" Boon said. "What the hell do you know about it anyway? This is the first time you've had your tail out of that kitchen since we got here except to chop a little wood." 15

"Aint nothing wrong with them," Ash said. "And long as it's left up to them, aint nothing going to be. I just wish I had knowed all my life how to take care of my health good as them hounds knows."

"Well, they aint going to run this morning," Boon said. His voice was harsh and positive. "Major promised they wouldn't until me and Ike get back." 20

"Weather gonter break today. Gonter soft up. Rain by night." Then Ash laughed, chuckled, somewhere inside the quilt which concealed even his face. "Hum up here, mules!" he said, jerking the reins so that the mules leaped forward and snatched the lurching and banging wagon for several feet before they slowed again into their quick, short-paced, rapid plodding. "Sides, I like 25 to know why Major need to wait on you. It's Lion he aiming to use. I aint never heard tell of you bringing no bear nor no other kind of meat into this camp."

Now Boon's going to curse Ash or maybe even hit him, the boy thought. But Boon never did, never had; the boy knew he never would even though 30 four years ago Boon had shot five times with a borrowed pistol at a negro on the street in Jefferson, with the same result as when he had shot five times at Old Ben last fall. "By God," Boon said, "he aint going to put Lion or no other dog on nothing until I get back tonight. Because he promised me. Whip up them mules and keep them whipped up. Do you want me to freeze to 35 death?"

They reached the log-line and built a fire. After a while the log-train came up out of the woods under the paling east and Boon flagged it. Then in the warm caboose the boy slept again while Boon and the conductor and brakeman talked about Lion and Old Ben as people later would talk about Sullivan 40 and Kilrain and, later still, about Dempsey and Tunney. Dozing, swaying as the springless caboose lurched and clattered, he would hear them still talking,

---

37. log-line—usually a narrow-gauge railroad, used solely for bringing logs out of the woods. **40-41. Sullivan . . . Tunney**—John L. Sullivan (1858-1918), the last of the bare-knuckle boxing champions, defeated Jake Kilrain in 75 rounds, July 8, 1889, in Richburg, Mississippi. Gene Tunney (1898-   ) won the heavyweight championship from Jack Dempsey (1895-   ) on a ten-round decision, September 23, 1926, in Philadelphia. Tunney gave Dempsey a return match in 1927 in Chicago and retained his crown.

about the shoats and calves Old Ben had killed and the cribs he had rifled
and the traps and deadfalls he had wrecked and the lead he probably carried
under his hide—Old Ben, the two-toed bear in a land where bears with trap-
ruined feet had been called Two-Toe or Three-Toe or Cripple-Foot for fifty
5 years, only Old Ben was an extra bear (the head bear, General Compson called
him) and so had earned a name such as a human man could have worn and
not been sorry.

They reached Hoke's at sunup. They emerged from the warm caboose in
their hunting clothes, the muddy boots and stained khaki and Boon's blue
10 unshaven jowls. But that was all right. Hoke's was a sawmill and commissary
and two stores and a loading-chute on a sidetrack from the main line, and all
the men in it wore boots and khaki too. Presently the Memphis train came.
Boon bought three packages of popcorn-and-molasses and a bottle of beer from
the news butch and the boy went to sleep again to the sound of his chew-
15 ing.

But in Memphis it was not all right. It was as if the high buildings and the
hard pavements, the fine carriages and the horse cars and the men in starched
collars and neckties made their boots and khaki look a little rougher and a
little muddier and made Boon's beard look worse and more unshaven and his
20 face look more and more like he should never have brought it out of the
woods at all or at least out of reach of Major de Spain or McCaslin or someone who knew it and could have said, "Dont be afraid. He wont hurt you."
He walked through the station, on the slick floor, his face moving as he
worked the popcorn out of his teeth with his tongue, his legs spraddled and
25 stiff in the hips as if he were walking on buttered glass, and that blue stubble
on his face like the filings from a new gun-barrel. They passed the first saloon.
Even through the closed doors the boy could seem to smell the sawdust and
the reek of old drink. Boon began to cough. He coughed for something less
than a minute. "Damn this cold," he said. "I'd sure like to know where I
30 got it."

"Back there in the station," the boy said.

Boon had started to cough again. He stopped. He looked at the boy.
"What?" he said.

"You never had it when we left camp nor on the train either." Boon looked
35 at him, blinking. Then he stopped blinking. He didn't cough again. He said
quietly:

"Lend me a dollar. Come on. You've got it. If you ever had one, you've
still got it. I dont mean you are tight with your money because you aint. You
just dont never seem to ever think of nothing you want. When I was sixteen
40 a dollar bill melted off of me before I even had time to read the name of the
bank that issued it." He said quietly: "Let me have a dollar, Ike."

"You promised Major. You promised McCaslin. Not till we get back to
camp."

"All right," Boon said in that quiet and patient voice. "What can I do on just
45 one dollar? You aint going to lend me another."

"You're damn right I aint," the boy said, his voice quiet too, cold with rage

14. news butch—newsdealer.

which was not at Boon, remembering: Boon snoring in a hard chair in the kitchen so he could watch the clock and wake him and McCaslin and drive them the seventeen miles in to Jefferson to catch the train to Memphis; the wild, never-bridled Texas paint pony which he had persuaded McCaslin to let him buy and which he and Boon had bought at auction for four dollars and seventy-five cents and fetched home wired between two gentle old mares with pieces of barbed wire and which had never even seen shelled corn before and didn't even know what it was unless the grains were bugs maybe and at last (he was ten and Boon had been ten all his life) Boon said the pony was gentled and with a towsack over its head and four negroes to hold it they backed it into an old two-wheeled cart and hooked up the gear and he and Boon got up and Boon said, "All right, boys. Let him go" and one of the negroes—it was Tennie's Jim—snatched the towsack off and leaped for his life and they lost the first wheel against a post of the open gate only at that moment Boon caught him by the scruff of the neck and flung him into the roadside ditch so he only saw the rest of it in fragments: the other wheel as it slammed through the side gate and crossed the back yard and leaped up onto the gallery and scraps of the cart here and there along the road and Boon vanishing rapidly on his stomach in the leaping and spurting dust and still holding the reins until they broke too and two days later they finally caught the pony seven miles away still wearing the hames and the headstall of the bridle around its neck like a duchess with two necklaces at one time. He gave Boon the dollar.

"All right," Boon said. "Come on in out of the cold."

"I aint cold," he said.

"You can have some lemonade."

"I dont want any lemonade."

The door closed behind him. The sun was well up now. It was a brilliant day, though Ash had said it would rain before night. Already it was warmer; they could run tomorrow. He felt the old lift of the heart, as pristine as ever, as on the first day; he would never lose it, no matter how old in hunting and pursuit: the best, the best of all breathing, the humility and the pride. He must stop thinking about it. Already it seemed to him that he was running, back to the station, to the tracks themselves: the first train going south, he must stop thinking about it. The street was busy. He watched the big Norman draft horses, the Percherons; the trim carriages from which the men in the fine overcoats and the ladies rosy in furs descended and entered the station. (They were still next door to it but one.) Twenty years ago his father had ridden into Memphis as a member of Colonel Sartoris' horse in Forrest's command, up Main street and (the tale told) into the lobby of the Gayoso Hotel where the Yankee officers sat in the leather chairs spitting into the tall bright cuspidors and then out again, scot-free—

The door opened behind him. Boon was wiping his mouth on the back

4. **paint pony**—a pinto, or spotted horse. 18. **gallery**—a piazza, portico, or veranda. 21. **hames**—the two curved pieces lying upon the collar in the harness of an animal, to which the traces are fastened. 21. **headstall**—the part of the bridle or halter which encircles the head. 39. **Forrest**—Nathan Bedford Forrest (1821-1877), lieutenant general and head of a famous Confederate cavalry raiding force.

of his hand. "All right," he said. "Let's go tend to it and get the hell out
of here."

They went and had the suitcase packed. He never knew where or when
Boon got the other bottle. Doubtless Mr Semmes gave it to him. When they
5 reached Hoke's again at sundown, it was empty. They could get a return train
to Hoke's in two hours; they went straight back to the station as Major de
Spain and then McCaslin had told Boon to do and then ordered him to do
and had sent the boy along to see that he did. Boon took the first drink from
his bottle in the wash room. A man in a uniform cap came to tell him he
10 couldn't drink there and looked at Boon's face once and said nothing. The
next time he was pouring into his water glass beneath the edge of a table in
the restaurant when the manager (she was a woman) did tell him he couldn't
drink there and he went back to the washroom. He had been telling the
negro waiter and all the other people in the restaurant who couldn't help
15 but hear him and who had never heard of Lion and didn't want to, about
Lion and Old Ben. Then he happened to think of the zoo. He had found
out that there was another train to Hoke's at three oclock and so they would
spend the time at the zoo and take the three oclock train until he came back
from the washroom for the third time. Then they would take the first train
20 back to camp, get Lion and come back to the zoo where, he said, the bears
were fed on ice cream and lady fingers and he would match Lion against
them all.

So they missed the first train, the one they were supposed to take, but he
got Boon onto the three oclock train and they were all right again, with Boon
25 not even going to the wash-room now but drinking in the aisle and talking
about Lion and the men he buttonholed no more daring to tell Boon he
couldn't drink there than the man in the station had dared.

When they reached Hoke's at sundown, Boon was asleep. The boy waked
him at last and got him and the suitcase off the train and he even persuaded
30 him to eat some supper at the sawmill commissary. So he was all right when
they got in the caboose of the log-train to go back into the woods, with the
sun going down red and the sky already overcast and the ground would not
freeze tonight. It was the boy who slept now, sitting behind the ruby stove
while the springless caboose jumped and clattered and Boon and the brake-
35 man and the conductor talked about Lion and Old Ben because they knew
what Boon was talking about because this was home. "Overcast and already
thawing," Boon said. "Lion will get him tomorrow."

It would have to be Lion, or somebody. It would not be Boon. He had
never hit anything bigger than a squirrel that anybody ever knew, except the
40 negro woman that day when he was shooting at the negro man. He was
a big negro and not ten feet away but Boon shot five times with the pistol
he had borrowed from Major de Spain's negro coachman and the negro he
was shooting at outed with a dollar-and-a-half mail-order pistol and would
have burned Boon down with it only it never went off, it just went snicksnick-
45 snicksnicksnick five times and Boon still blasting away and he broke a plate-

---

25. **wash-room**—Faulkner is inconsistent in the spelling of this word. It appears above as
wash room and *washroom*.

glass window that cost McCaslin forty-five dollars and hit a negro woman who happened to be passing in the leg only Major de Spain paid for that; he and McCaslin cut cards, the plate-glass window against the negro woman's leg. And the first day on stand this year, the first morning in camp, the buck ran right over Boon; he heard Boon's old pump gun go whow. whow. whow. 5 whow. whow. and then his voice: "God damn, here he comes! Head him! Head him!" and when he got there the buck's tracks and the five exploded shells were not twenty paces apart.

There were five guests in camp that night from Jefferson: Mr Bayard Sartoris and his son and General Compson's son and two others. And the next 10 morning he looked out the window, into the gray thin drizzle of daybreak which Ash had predicted, and there they were, standing and squatting beneath the thin rain, almost two dozen of them who had fed Old Ben corn and shoats and even calves for ten years, in their worn hats and hunting coats and overalls which any town negro would have thrown away or burned and only the rub- 15 ber boots strong and sound, and the worn and blueless guns, and some even without guns. While they ate breakfast a dozen more arrived, mounted and on foot: loggers from the camp thirteen miles below and sawmill men from Hoke's and the only gun among them that one which the log-train conductor carried: so that when they went into the woods this morning Major de Spain 20 led a party almost as strong, excepting that some of them were not armed, as some he had led in the last darkening days of '64 and '65. The little yard would not hold them. They overflowed it, into the lane where Major de Spain sat his mare while Ash in his dirty apron thrust the greasy cartridges into his carbine and passed it up to him and the great grave blue dog stood at his stirrup not 25 as a dog stands but as a horse stands, blinking his sleepy topaz eyes at nothing, deaf even to the yelling of the hounds which Boon and Tennie's Jim held on leash.

"We'll put General Compson on Katie this morning," Major de Spain said. "He drew blood last year; if he'd had a mule then that would have stood, he 30 would have—"

"No," General Compson said. "I'm too old to go helling through the woods on a mule or a horse or anything else any more. Besides, I had my chance last year and missed it. I'm going on a stand this morning. I'm going to let that boy ride Katie." 35

"No, wait," McCaslin said. "Ike's got the rest of his life to hunt bears in. Let somebody else—"

"No," General Compson said. "I want Ike to ride Katie. He's already a better woodsman than you or me either and in another ten years he'll be as good as Walter." 40

At first he couldn't believe it, not until Major de Spain spoke to him. Then he was up, on the one-eyed mule which would not spook at wild blood, looking down at the dog motionless at Major de Spain's stirrup, looking in the gray streaming light bigger than a calf, bigger than he knew it actually was—the

9-10. **Mr Bayard Sartoris**—see Faulkner's novels, *Sartoris* (1929) and *The Unvanquished* (1938). 16. **blueless**—After a gun has been used for many years it loses the original blue cast in the steel.

big head, the chest almost as big as his own, the blue hide beneath which the muscles flinched or quivered to no touch since the heart which drove blood to them loved no man and no thing, standing as a horse stands yet different from a horse which infers only weight and speed while Lion inferred not only
5 courage and all else that went to make up the will and desire to pursue and kill, but endurance, the will and desire to endure beyond all imaginable limits of flesh in order to overtake and slay. Then the dog looked at him. It moved its head and looked at him across the trivial uproar of the hounds, out of the yellow eyes as depthless as Boon's, as free as Boon's of meanness or generosity
10 or gentleness or viciousness. They were just cold and sleepy. Then it blinked, and he knew it was not looking at him and never had been, without even bothering to turn its head away.

That morning he heard the first cry. Lion had already vanished while Sam and Tennie's Jim were putting saddles on the mule and horse which had drawn
15 the wagon and he watched the hounds as they crossed and cast, snuffing and whimpering, until they too disappeared. Then he and Major de Spain and Sam and Tennie's Jim rode after them and heard the first cry out of the wet and thawing woods not two hundred yards ahead, high, with that abject, almost human quality he had come to know, and the other hounds joining in until the
20 gloomed woods rang and clamored. They rode then. It seemed to him that he could actually see the big blue dog boring on, silent, and the bear too: the thick, locomotive-like shape which he had seen that day four years ago crossing the blow-down, crashing on ahead of the dogs faster than he had believed it could have moved, drawing away even from the running mules. He heard a shot-
25 gun, once. The woods had opened, they were going fast, the clamor faint and fading on ahead; they passed the man who had fired—a swamper, a pointing arm, a gaunt face, the small black orifice of his yelling studded with rotten teeth.

He heard the changed note in the hounds' uproar and two hundred yards
30 ahead he saw them. The bear had turned. He saw Lion drive in without pausing and saw the bear strike him aside and lunge into the yelling hounds and kill one of them almost in its tracks and whirl and run again. Then they were in a streaming tide of dogs. He heard Major de Spain and Tennie's Jim shouting and the pistol sound of Tennie's Jim's leather thong as he tried to turn
35 them. Then he and Sam Fathers were riding alone. One of the hounds had kept on with Lion though. He recognised its voice. It was the young hound which even a year ago had had no judgment and which, by the lights of the other hounds anyway, still had none. *Maybe that's what courage is,* he thought. "Right," Sam said behind him. "Right. We got to turn him from the river if
40 we can."

Now they were in cane: a brake. He knew the path through it as well as Sam did. They came out of the undergrowth and struck the entrance almost exactly. It would traverse the brake and come out onto a high open ridge above the river. He heard the flat clap of Walter Ewell's rifle, then two more. "No,"
45 Sam said. "I can hear the hound. Go on."

They emerged from the narrow roofless tunnel of snapping and hissing cane,

15. **cast**—searched in all directions for the scent.

still galloping, onto the open ridge below which the thick yellow river, reflectionless in the gray and streaming light, seemed not to move. Now he could hear the hound too. It was not running. The cry was a high frantic yapping and Boon was running along the edge of the bluff, his old gun leaping and jouncing against his back on its sling made of a piece of cotton plow-line. He whirled and ran up to them, wild-faced, and flung himself onto the mule behind the boy. "That damn boat!" he cried. "It's on the other side! He went straight across! Lion was too close to him! That little hound too! Lion was so close I couldn't shoot! Go on!" he cried, beating his heels into the mule's flanks. "Go on!"

They plunged down the bank, slipping and sliding in the thawed earth, crashing through the willows and into the water. He felt no shock, no cold, he on one side of the swimming mule, grasping the pommel with one hand and holding his gun above the water with the other, Boon opposite him. Sam was behind them somewhere, and then the river, the water about them, was full of dogs. They swam faster than the mules; they were scrabbling up the bank before the mules touched bottom. Major de Spain was whooping from the bank they had just left and, looking back, he saw Tennie's Jim and the horse as they went into the water.

Now the woods ahead of them and the rain-heavy air were one uproar. It rang and clamored; it echoed and broke against the bank behind them and reformed and clamored and rang until it seemed to the boy that all the hounds which had ever bayed game in this land were yelling down at him. He got his leg over the mule as it came up out of the water. Boon didn't try to mount again. He grasped one stirrup as they went up the bank and crashed through the undergrowth which fringed the bluff and saw the bear, on its hind feet, its back against a tree while the bellowing hounds swirled around it and once more Lion drove in, leaping clear of the ground.

This time the bear didn't strike him down. It caught the dog in both arms, almost loverlike, and they both went down. He was off the mule now. He drew back both hammers of the gun but he could see nothing but moiling spotted houndbodies until the bear surged up again. Boon was yelling something, he could not tell what; he could see Lion still clinging to the bear's throat and he saw the bear, half erect, strike one of the hounds with one paw and hurl it five or six feet and then, rising and rising as though it would never stop, stand erect again and begin to rake at Lion's belly with its forepaws. Then Boon was running. The boy saw the gleam of the blade in his hand and watched him leap among the hounds, hurdling them, kicking them aside as he ran, and fling himself astride the bear as he had hurled himself onto the mule, his legs locked around the bear's belly, his left arm under the bear's throat where Lion clung, and the glint of the knife as it rose and fell.

It fell just once. For an instant they almost resembled a piece of statuary: the clinging dog, the bear, the man astride its back, working and probing the buried blade. Then they went down, pulled over backward by Boon's weight, Boon underneath. It was the bear's back which reappeared first but at once Boon was astride it again. He had never released the knife and again the boy saw the almost infinitesimal movement of his arm and shoulder as he probed

and sought; then the bear surged erect, raising with it the man and the dog too, and turned and still carrying the man and the dog it took two or three steps toward the woods on its hind feet as a man would have walked and crashed down. It didn't collapse, crumple. It fell all of a piece, as a tree falls, so that all
5 three of them, man dog and bear, seemed to bounce once.

He and Tennie's Jim ran forward. Boon was kneeling at the bear's head. His left ear was shredded, his left coat sleeve was completely gone, his right boot had been ripped from knee to instep; the bright blood thinned in the thin rain down his leg and hand and arm and down the side of his face which
10 was no longer wild but was quite calm. Together they prized Lion's jaws from the bear's throat. "Easy, goddamn it," Boon said. "Cant you see his guts are all out of him?" He began to remove his coat. He spoke to Tennie's Jim in that calm voice: "Bring the boat up. It's about a hundred yards down the bank there. I saw it." Tennie's Jim rose and went away. Then, and he could not re-
15 member if it had been a call or an exclamation from Tennie's Jim or if he had glanced up by chance, he saw Tennie's Jim stooping and saw Sam Fathers lying motionless on his face in the trampled mud.

The mule had not thrown him. He remembered that Sam was down too even before Boon began to run. There was no mark on him whatever and when
20 he and Boon turned him over, his eyes were open and he said something in that tongue which he and Joe Baker had used to speak together. But he couldn't move. Tennie's Jim brought the skiff up; they could hear him shouting to Major de Spain across the river. Boon wrapped Lion in his hunting coat and carried him down to the skiff and they carried Sam down and returned and
25 hitched the bear to the one-eyed mule's saddle-bow with Tennie's Jim's leash-thong and dragged him down to the skiff and got him into it and left Tennie's Jim to swim the horse and the two mules back across. Major de Spain caught the bow of the skiff as Boon jumped out and past him before it touched the bank. He looked at Old Ben and said quietly: "Well." Then he walked into
30 the water and leaned down and touched Sam and Sam looked up at him and said something in that old tongue he and Joe Baker spoke. "You dont know what happened?" Major de Spain said.

"No, sir," the boy said. "It wasn't the mule. It wasn't anything. He was off the mule when Boon ran in on the bear. Then we looked up and he was lying
35 on the ground." Boon was shouting at Tennie's Jim, still in the middle of the river.

"Come on, goddamn it!" he said. "Bring me that mule!"

"What do you want with a mule?" Major de Spain said.

Boon didn't even look at him. "I'm going to Hoke's to get the doctor," he
40 said in that calm voice, his face quite calm beneath the steady thinning of the bright blood.

"You need a doctor yourself," Major de Spain said. "Tennie's Jim—"

"Damn that," Boon said. He turned on Major de Spain. His face was still calm, only his voice was a pitch higher. "Cant you see his goddamn guts are
45 all out of him?"

"Boon!" Major de Spain said. They looked at one another. Boon was a good head taller than Major de Spain; even the boy was taller now than Major de Spain.

"I've got to get the doctor," Boon said. "His goddamn guts—"

"All right," Major de Spain said. Tennie's Jim came up out of the water. The horse and the sound mule had already scented Old Ben; they surged and plunged all the way up to the top of the bluff, dragging Tennie's Jim with them, before he could stop them and tie them and come back. Major de Spain unlooped the leather thong of his compass from his buttonhole and gave it to Tennie's Jim. "Go straight to Hoke's," he said. "Bring Doctor Crawford back with you. Tell him there are two men to be looked at. Take my mare. Can you find the road from here?"

"Yes, sir," Tennie's Jim said.

"All right," Major de Spain said. "Go on." He turned to the boy. "Take the mules and the horse and go back and get the wagon. We'll go on down the river in the boat to Coon bridge. Meet us there. Can you find it again?"

"Yes, sir," the boy said.

"All right. Get started."

He went back to the wagon. He realised then how far they had run. It was already afternoon when he put the mules into the traces and tied the horse's lead-rope to the tail-gate. He reached Coon bridge at dusk. The skiff was already there. Before he could see it and almost before he could see the water he had to leap from the tilting wagon, still holding the reins, and work around to where he could grasp the bit and then the ear of the plunging sound mule and dig his heels and hold it until Boon came up the bank. The rope of the led horse had already snapped and it had already disappeared up the road toward camp. They turned the wagon around and took the mules out and he led the sound mule a hundred yards up the road and tied it. Boon had already brought Lion up to the wagon and Sam was sitting up in the skiff now and when they raised him he tried to walk, up the bank and to the wagon and he tried to climb into the wagon but Boon did not wait; he picked Sam up bodily and set him on the seat. Then they hitched Old Ben to the one-eyed mule's saddle again and dragged him up the bank and set two skid-poles into the open tail-gate and got him into the wagon and he went and got the sound mule and Boon fought it into the traces, striking it across its hard hollow-sounding face until it came into position and stood trembling. Then the rain came down, as though it had held off all day waiting on them.

They returned to camp through it, through the streaming and sightless dark, hearing long before they saw any light the horn and the spaced shots to guide them. When they came to Sam's dark little hut he tried to stand up. He spoke again in the tongue of the old fathers; then he said clearly: "Let me out. Let me out."

"He hasn't got any fire," Major said. "Go on!" he said sharply.

But Sam was struggling now, trying to stand up. "Let me out, master," he said. "Let me go home."

---

20. tail-gate—that is, the tailboard at the back of a wagon or truck. The gate can usually be removed or let down for convenience in loading or unloading.

So he stopped the wagon and Boon got down and lifted Sam out. He did not wait to let Sam try to walk this time. He carried him into the hut and Major de Spain got light on a paper spill from the buried embers on the hearth and lit the lamp and Boon put Sam on his bunk and drew off his boots and Major de 5 Spain covered him and the boy was not there, he was holding the mules, the sound one which was trying again to bolt since when the wagon stopped Old Ben's scent drifted forward again along the streaming blackness of air, but Sam's eyes were probably open again on that profound look which saw further than them or the hut, further than the death of a bear and the dying of a dog. 10 Then they went on, toward the long wailing of the horn and the shots which seemed each to linger intact somewhere in the thick streaming air until the next spaced report joined and blended with it, to the lighted house, the bright streaming windows, the quiet faces as Boon entered, bloody and quite calm, carrying the bundled coat. He laid Lion, blood coat and all, on his stale sheet- 15 less pallet bed which not even Ash, as deft in the house as a woman, could ever make smooth.

The sawmill doctor from Hoke's was already there. Boon would not let the doctor touch him until he had seen to Lion. He wouldn't risk giving Lion chloroform. He put the entrails back and sewed him up without it while Major 20 de Spain held his head and Boon his feet. But he never tried to move. He lay there, the yellow eyes open upon nothing while the quiet men in the new hunt- ing clothes and in the old ones crowded into the little airless room rank with the smell of Boon's body and garments, and watched. Then the doctor cleaned and disinfected Boon's face and arm and leg and bandaged them and, the boy 25 in front with a lantern and the doctor and McCaslin and Major de Spain and General Compson following, they went to Sam Fathers' hut. Tennie's Jim had built up the fire; he squatted before it, dozing. Sam had not moved since Boon had put him in the bunk and Major de Spain had covered him with the blankets, yet he opened his eyes and looked from one to another of the faces 30 and when McCaslin touched his shoulder and said, "Sam. The doctor wants to look at you," he even drew his hands out of the blanket and began to fumble at his shirt buttons until McCaslin said, "Wait. We'll do it." They undressed him. He lay there—the copper-brown, almost hairless body, the old man's body, the old man, the wild man not even one generation from the woods, childless, 35 kinless, peopleless—motionless, his eyes open but no longer looking at any of them, while the doctor examined him and drew the blankets up and put the stethoscope back into his bag and snapped the bag and only the boy knew that Sam too was going to die.

"Exhaustion," the doctor said. "Shock maybe. A man his age swimming 40 rivers in December. He'll be all right. Just make him stay in bed for a day or two. Will there be somebody here with him?"

"There will be somebody here," Major de Spain said.

They went back to the house, to the rank little room where Boon still sat on the pallet bed with Lion's head under his hand while the men, the ones who 45 had hunted behind Lion and the ones who had never seen him before today, came quietly in to look at him and went away. Then it was dawn and they all

3. spill—a slender piece of wood or of twisted paper, for lighting candles, lamps, etc.

went out into the yard to look at Old Ben, with his eyes open too and his lips snarled back from his worn teeth and his mutilated foot and the little hard lumps under his skin which were the old bullets (there were fifty-two of them, buckshot rifle and ball) and the single almost invisible slit under his left shoulder where Boon's blade had finally found his life. Then Ash began to 5 beat on the bottom of the dishpan with a heavy spoon to call them to breakfast and it was the first time he could remember hearing no sound from the dogs under the kitchen while they were eating. It was as if the old bear, even dead there in the yard, was a more potent terror still than they could face without Lion between them.   10

The rain had stopped during the night. By midmorning the thin sun appeared, rapidly burning away mist and cloud, warming the air and the earth; it would be one of those windless Mississippi December days which are a sort of Indian summer's Indian summer. They moved Lion out to the front gallery, into the sun. It was Boon's idea. "Goddamn it," he said, "he never did want to 15 stay in the house until I made him. You know that." He took a crowbar and loosened the floor boards under his pallet bed so it could be raised, mattress and all, without disturbing Lion's position, and they carried him out to the gallery and put him down facing the woods.

Then he and the doctor and McCaslin and Major de Spain went to Sam's hut. 20 This time Sam didn't open his eyes and his breathing was so quiet, so peaceful that they could hardly see that he breathed. The doctor didn't even take out his stethoscope nor even touch him. "He's all right," the doctor said. "He didn't even catch cold. He just quit."

"Quit?" McCaslin said.   25

"Yes. Old people do that sometimes. Then they get a good night's sleep or maybe it's just a drink of whisky, and they change their minds."

They returned to the house. And then they began to arrive—the swamp-dwellers, the gaunt men who ran trap-lines and lived on quinine and coons and river water, the farmers of little corn- and cotton-patches along the bottom's 30 edge whose fields and cribs and pig-pens the old bear had rifled, the loggers from the camp and the sawmill men from Hoke's and the town men from further away than that, whose hounds the old bear had slain and [whose] traps and deadfalls he had wrecked and whose lead he carried. They came up mounted and on foot and in wagons, to enter the yard and look at him and 35 then go on to the front where Lion lay, filling the little yard and overflowing it until there were almost a hundred of them squatting and standing in the warm and drowsing sunlight, talking quietly of hunting, of the game and the dogs which ran it, of hounds and bear and deer and men of yesterday vanished from the earth, while from time to time the great blue dog would open his 40 eyes, not as if he were listening to them but as though to look at the woods for a moment before closing his eyes again, to remember the woods or to see that they were still there. He died at sundown.

Major de Spain broke camp that night. They carried Lion into the woods, or Boon carried him that is, wrapped in a quilt from his bed, just as he had refused 45 to let anyone else touch Lion yesterday until the doctor got there; Boon carry-ing Lion, and the boy and General Compson and Walter and still almost fifty

of them following with lanterns and lighted pine-knots—men from Hoke's and even further, who would have to ride out of the bottom in the dark, and swampers and trappers who would have to walk even, scattering toward the little hidden huts where they lived. And Boon would let nobody else dig the
5   grave either and lay Lion in it and cover him and then General Compson stood at the head of it while the blaze and smoke of the pine-knots streamed away among the winter branches and spoke as he would have spoken over a man. Then they returned to camp. Major de Spain and McCaslin and Ash had rolled and tied all the bedding. The mules were hitched to the wagon and pointed
10   out of the bottom and the wagon was already loaded and the stove in the kitchen was cold and the table was set with scraps of cold food and bread and only the coffee was hot when the boy ran into the kitchen where Major de Spain and McCaslin had already eaten. "What?" he cried. "What? I'm not going."
15   "Yes," McCaslin said, "we're going out tonight. Major wants to get on back home."

"No!" he said. "I'm going to stay."

"You've got to be back in school Monday. You've already missed a week more than I intended. It will take you from now until Monday to catch up.
20   Sam's all right. You heard Doctor Crawford. I'm going to leave Boon and Tennie's Jim both to stay with him until he feels like getting up."

He was panting. The others had come in. He looked rapidly and almost frantically around at the other faces. Boon had a fresh bottle. He upended it and started the cork by striking the bottom of the bottle with the heel of his
25   hand and drew the cork with his teeth and spat it out and drank. "You're damn right you're going back to school," Boon said. "Or I'll burn the tail off of you myself if Cass dont, whether you are sixteen or sixty. Where in hell do you expect to get without education? Where would Cass be? Where in hell would I be if I hadn't never went to school?"
30   He looked at McCaslin again. He could feel his breath coming shorter and shorter and shallower and shallower, as if there were not enough air in the kitchen for that many to breathe. "This is just Thursday. I'll come home Sunday night on one of the horses. I'll come home Sunday, then. I'll make up the time I lost studying Sunday night, McCaslin," he said, without even despair.
35   "No, I tell you," McCaslin said. "Sit down here and eat your supper. We're going out to—"

"Hold up, Cass," General Compson said. The boy did not know General Compson had moved until he put his hand on his shoulder. "What is it, bud?" he said.
40   "I've got to stay," he said. "I've got to."

"All right," General Compson said. "You can stay. If missing an extra week of school is going to throw you so far behind you'll have to sweat to find out what some hired pedagogue put between the covers of a book, you better quit altogether.—And you shut up, Cass," he said, though McCaslin had not spoken.
45   "You've got one foot straddled into a farm and the other foot straddled into a bank; you aint even got a good hand-hold where this boy was already an old

man long before you damned Sartorises and Edmondses invented farms and
banks to keep yourselves from having to find out what this boy was born knowing and fearing too maybe but without being afraid, that could go ten miles on
a compass because he wanted to look at a bear none of us had ever got near
enough to put a bullet in and looked at the bear and came the ten miles back   5
on the compass in the dark; maybe by God that's the why and the wherefore of
farms and banks.—I reckon you still aint going to tell what it is?"

But still he could not. "I've got to stay," he said.

"All right," General Compson said. "There's plenty of grub left. And you'll
come home Sunday, like you promised McCaslin? Not Sunday night: Sun-   10
day."

"Yes, sir," he said.

"All right," General Compson said. "Sit down and eat, boys," he said. "Let's
get started. It's going to be cold before we get home."

They ate. The wagon was already loaded and ready to depart; all they had   15
to do was to get into it. Boon would drive them out to the road, to the farmer's
stable where the surrey had been left. He stood beside the wagon, in silhouette
on the sky, turbaned like a Paythan and taller than any there, the bottle tilted.
Then he flung the bottle from his lips without even lowering it, spinning and
glinting in the faint starlight, empty. "Them that's going," he said, "get in the   20
goddamn wagon. Them that aint, get out of the goddamn way." The others
got in. Boon mounted to the seat beside General Compson and the wagon
moved, on into the obscurity until the boy could no longer see it, even the
moving density of it amid the greater night. But he could still hear it, for a
long while: the slow, deliberate banging of the wooden frame as it lurched   25
from rut to rut. And he could hear Boon even when he could no longer hear
the wagon. He was singing, harsh, tuneless, loud.

That was Thursday. On Saturday morning Tennie's Jim left on McCaslin's
woods-horse which had not been out of the bottom one time now in six years,
and late that afternoon rode through the gate on the spent horse and on to the   30
commissary where McCaslin was rationing the tenants and the wage-hands for
the coming week, and this time McCaslin forestalled any necessity or risk of
having to wait while Major de Spain's surrey was being horsed and harnessed.
He took their own, and with Tennie's Jim already asleep in the back seat he
drove in to Jefferson and waited while Major de Spain changed to boots and   35
put on his overcoat, and they drove the thirty miles in the dark of that night
and at daybreak on Sunday morning they swapped to the waiting mare and
mule and as the sun rose they rode out of the jungle and onto the low ridge
where they had buried Lion: the low mound of unannealed earth where Boon's
spade-marks still showed, and beyond the grave the platform of freshly cut   40
saplings bound between four posts and the blanket-wrapped bundle upon the
platform and Boon and the boy squatting between the platform and the grave
until Boon, the bandage removed, ripped from his head so that the long

---

18. **Paythan**—usually spelled *Paithan;* hence, a resident of this city, located in the northern
sector of the Hyderabad district of India. 39. **unannealed**—i.e., the dirt was still fresh and raw.
Annealed means *glazed.*

scoriations of Old Ben's claws resembled crusted tar in the sunlight, sprang up and threw down upon them with the old gun with which he had never been known to hit anything although McCaslin was already off the mule, kicked both feet free of the irons and vaulted down before the mule had stopped, 5 walking toward Boon.

"Stand back," Boon said. "By God, you wont touch him. Stand back, McCaslin." Still McCaslin came on, fast yet without haste.

"Cass!" Major de Spain said. Then he said, "Boon! You, Boon!" and he was down too and the boy rose too, quickly, and still McCaslin came on not fast 10 but steady and walked up to the grave and reached his hand steadily out, quickly yet still not fast, and took hold the gun by the middle so that he and Boon faced one another across Lion's grave, both holding the gun, Boon's spent indomitable amazed and frantic face almost a head higher than McCaslin's beneath the black scoriations of beast's claws and then Boon's chest began to 15 heave as though there were not enough air in all the woods, in all the wilderness, for all of them, for him and anyone else, even for him alone.

"Turn it loose, Boon," McCaslin said.

"You damn little spindling—" Boon said. "Dont you know I can take it away from you? Dont you know I can tie it around your neck like a damn 20 cravat?"

"Yes," McCaslin said. "Turn it loose, Boon."

"This is the way he wanted it. He told us. He told us exactly how to do it. And by God you aint going to move him. So we did it like he said, and I been sitting here ever since to keep the damn wildcats and varmints away from him 25 and by God—" Then McCaslin had the gun, downslanted while he pumped the slide, the five shells snicking out of it so fast that the last one was almost out before the first one touched the ground and McCaslin dropped the gun behind him without once having taken his eyes from Boon's.

"Did you kill him, Boon?" he said. Then Boon moved. He turned, he moved 30 like he was still drunk and then for a moment blind too, one hand out as he blundered toward the big tree and seemed to stop walking before he reached the tree so that he plunged, fell toward it, flinging up both hands and catching himself against the tree and turning until his back was against it, backing with the tree's trunk his wild spent scoriated face and the tremendous heave and 35 collapse of his chest, McCaslin following, facing him again, never once having moved his eyes from Boon's eyes. "Did you kill him, Boon?"

"No!" Boon said. "No!"

"Tell the truth," McCaslin said. "I would have done it if he had asked me to." Then the boy moved. He was between them, facing McCaslin; the water 40 felt as if it had burst and sprung not from his eyes alone but from his whole face, like sweat.

"Leave him alone!" he cried. "Goddamn it! Leave him alone!"

2-5. threw down . . . toward Boon—as printed in the original text. Faulkner's prose is cloudy here but it is possible he means to say that Boon jumped up, grabbed his gun, and prepared to defend Sam's corpse at exactly the same time that McCaslin kicked his feet free of the stirrups (or irons), jumped off the mule, and walked toward Boon.

[Part 4, by far the longest section of "The Bear," has been omitted by the editors. Although germane to the story, the section is not necessary to an understanding of its intention and power. Mr. Faulkner moves the action ahead in time sequence to Isaac McCaslin's twenty-first birthday when, as inheritor of his grandfather's land, he insists on relinquishing the plantation to atone for old Carothers McCaslin's sins, the sins of privilege and excessive pride. "This whole land," Isaac claims, "the whole South, is cursed, and all of us who derive from it, whom it ever suckled, white and black both, lie under the curse." It is the Negroes, he believes, who will endure because "they are better than we are, stronger than we are, . . . a people who have learned humility through suffering and learned pride through the endurance which survived the suffering." This theme runs through the whole of *Go Down, Moses* and through many of Faulkner's best novels, particularly *The Sound and the Fury* and *Absalom, Absalom!*]

5

He went back to the camp one more time before the lumber company moved in and began to cut the timber. Major de Spain himself never saw it again. But he made them welcome to use the house and hunt the land whenever they liked, and in the winter following the last hunt when Sam   5
Fathers and Lion died, General Compson and Walter Ewell invented a plan to corporate themselves, the old group, into a club and lease the camp and the hunting privileges of the woods—an invention doubtless of the somewhat childish old General but actually worthy of Boon Hogganbeck himself. Even the boy, listening, recognised it for the subterfuge it was: to change the leop-   10
ard's spots when they could not alter the leopard, a baseless and illusory hope to which even McCaslin seemed to subscribe for a while, that once they had persuaded Major de Spain to return to the camp he might revoke himself, which even the boy knew he would not do. And he did not. The boy never knew what occurred when Major de Spain declined. He was not present when   15
the subject was broached and McCaslin never told him. But when June came and the time for the double birthday celebration there was no mention of it and when November came no one spoke of using Major de Spain's house and he never knew whether or not Major de Spain knew they were going on the hunt though without doubt old Ash probably told him: he and McCaslin and   20
General Compson (and that one was the General's last hunt too) and Walter and Boon and Tennie's Jim and old Ash loaded two wagons and drove two days and almost forty miles beyond any country the boy had ever seen before and lived in tents for the two weeks. And the next spring they heard (not from Major de Spain) that he had sold the timber-rights to a Memphis lum-   25
ber company and in June the boy came to town with McCaslin one Saturday and went to Major de Spain's office—the big, airy, book-lined, second-storey room with windows at one end opening upon the shabby hinder purlieus of stores and at the other a door giving onto the railed balcony above the Square, with its curtained alcove where sat a cedar water-bucket and a sugar-bowl   30

10-11. **leopard's spots**—*cf.* Jeremiah 13:23. 17. **double birthday celebration**—that is, the birthday of Major de Spain and General Compson.

and spoon and tumbler and a wicker-covered demijohn of whisky, and the
bamboo-and-paper punkah swinging back and forth above the desk while old
Ash in a tilted chair beside the entrance pulled the cord.

    "Of course," Major de Spain said. "Ash will probably like to get off in the
5 woods himself for a while, where he wont have to eat Daisy's cooking. Complain about it, anyway. Are you going to take anybody with you?"

    "No sir," he said. "I thought that maybe Boon—" For six months now Boon
had been town-marshal at Hoke's; Major de Spain had compounded with the
lumber company—or perhaps compromised was closer, since it was the lum-
10 ber company who had decided that Boon might be better as a town-marshal
than head of a logging gang.

    "Yes," Major de Spain said. "I'll wire him today. He can meet you at Hoke's.
I'll send Ash on by the train and they can take some food in and all you will
have to do will be to mount your horse and ride over."

15   "Yes sir," he said. "Thank you." And he heard his voice again. He didn't
know he was going to say it yet he did know, he had known it all the time:
"Maybe if you . . ." His voice died. It was stopped, he never knew how because Major de Spain did not speak and it was not until his voice ceased that
Major de Spain moved, turned back to the desk and the papers spread on
20 it and even that without moving because he was sitting at the desk with a
paper in his hand when the boy entered, the boy standing there looking down
at the short plumpish gray-haired man in sober fine broadcloth and an immaculate glazed shirt whom he was used to seeing in boots and muddy cor-
duroy, unshaven, sitting the shaggy powerful long-hocked mare with the
25 worn Winchester carbine across the saddlebow and the great blue dog standing motionless as bronze at the stirrup, the two of them in that last year and
to the boy anyway coming to resemble one another somehow as two people
competent for love or for business who have been in love or in business together for a long time sometimes do. Major de Spain did not look up again.
30   "No. I will be too busy. But good luck to you. If you have it, you might
bring me a young squirrel."

    "Yes sir," he said. "I will."

    He rode his mare, the three-year-old filly he had bred and raised and
broken himself. He left home a little after midnight and six hours later,
35 without even having sweated her, he rode into Hoke's, the tiny log-line junc-
tion which he had always thought of as Major de Spain's property too although Major de Spain had merely sold the company (and that many years
ago) the land on which the sidetracks and loading-platforms and the commissary store stood, and looked about in shocked and grieved amazement
40 even though he had had forewarning and had believed himself prepared:
a new planing-mill already half completed which would cover two or three
acres and what looked like miles and miles of stacked steel rails red with the

    1. demijohn—a large small-necked bottle, usually cased in wickerwork. 2. punkah—in the
East Indies, a large swinging screenlike fan hung from the ceiling and kept in motion by a
servant. 25. Winchester carbine—a kind of short, light rifle (or, formerly, musket) especially
used by cavalry. Oliver Fisher Winchester (1810-1880) produced in about 1866 the first breechloading repeating rifle to bear his name.

light bright rust of newness and of piled crossties sharp with creosote, and wire corrals and feeding-troughs for two hundred mules at least and the tents for the men who drove them; so that he arranged for the care and stabling of his mare as rapidly as he could and did not look any more, mounted into the log-train caboose with his gun and climbed into the cupola and looked 5 no more save toward the wall of wilderness ahead within which he would be able to hide himself from it once more anyway.

Then the little locomotive shrieked and began to move: a rapid churning of exhaust, a lethargic deliberate clashing of slack couplings traveling backward along the train, the exhaust changing to the deep slow clapping bites 10 of power as the caboose too began to move and from the cupola he watched the train's head complete the first and only curve in the entire line's length and vanish into the wilderness, dragging its length of train behind it so that it resembled a small dingy harmless snake vanishing into weeds, drawing him with it too until soon it ran once more at its maximum clattering speed 15 between the twin walls of unaxed wilderness as of old. It had been harmless once. Not five years ago Walter Ewell had shot a six-point buck from this same moving caboose, and there was the story of the half-grown bear: the train's first trip in to the cutting thirty miles away, the bear between the rails, its rear end elevated like that of a playing puppy while it dug to see what 20 sort of ants or bugs they might contain or perhaps just to examine the curious symmetrical squared barkless logs which had appeared apparently from nowhere in one endless mathematical line overnight, still digging until the driver on the braked engine not fifty feet away blew the whistle at it, whereupon it broke frantically and took the first tree it came to: an ash sapling not 25 much bigger than a man's thigh and climbed as high as it could and clung there, its head ducked between its arms as a man (a woman perhaps) might have done while the brakeman threw chunks of ballast at it, and when the engine returned three hours later with the first load of outbound logs the bear was halfway down the tree and once more scrambled back up as high 30 as it could and clung again while the train passed and was still there when the engine went in again in the afternoon and still there when it came back out at dusk; and Boon had been in Hoke's with the wagon after a barrel of flour that noon when the train-crew told about it and Boon and Ash, both twenty years younger then, sat under the tree all that night to keep any- 35 body from shooting it and the next morning Major de Spain had the log-train held at Hoke's and just before sundown on the second day, with not only Boon and Ash but Major de Spain and General Compson and Walter and McCaslin, twelve then, watching, it came down the tree after almost thirty-six hours without even water and McCaslin told him how for a minute they 40 thought it was going to stop right there at the barrow-pit where they were standing and drink, how it looked at the water and paused and looked at them and at the water again, but did not, gone, running, as bears run, the two sets of feet, front and back, tracking two separate though parallel courses.

5. cupola—the raised box-like structure on the roof of a caboose, the windows of which give a view on all sides of the moving train.

It had been harmless then. They would hear the passing log-train sometimes from the camp; sometimes, because nobody bothered to listen for it
or not. They would hear it going in, running light and fast, the light clatter
of the trucks, the exhaust of the diminutive locomotive and its shrill peanut-
5 parcher whistle flung for one petty moment and absorbed by the brooding
and inattentive wilderness without even an echo. They would hear it going
out, loaded, not quite so fast now yet giving its frantic and toylike illusion
of crawling speed, not whistling now to conserve steam, flinging its bitten
laboring miniature puffing into the immemorial woodsface with frantic and
10 bootless vainglory, empty and noisy and puerile, carrying to no destination
or purpose sticks which left nowhere any scar or stump as the child's toy
loads and transports and unloads its dead sand and rushes back for more,
tireless and unceasing and rapid yet never quite so fast as the Hand which
plays with it moves the toy burden back to load the toy again. But it was
15 different now. It was the same train, engine cars and caboose, even the same
enginemen brakeman and conductor to whom Boon, drunk then sober then
drunk again then fairly sober once more all in the space of fourteen hours,
had bragged that day two years ago about what they were going to do to
Old Ben tomorrow, running with its same illusion of frantic rapidity be-
20 tween the same twin walls of impenetrable and impervious woods, passing
the old landmarks, the old game crossings over which he had trailed bucks
wounded and not wounded and more than once seen them, anything but
wounded, bot out of the woods and up and across the embankment which
bore the rails and ties then down and into the woods again as the earth-
25 bound supposedly move but crossing as arrows travel, groundless, elongated,
three times its actual length and even paler, different in color, as if there were
a point between immobility and absolute motion where even mass chemically
altered, changing without pain or agony not only in bulk and shape but in
color too, approaching the color of wind, yet this time it was as though the
30 train (and not only the train but himself, not only his vision which had seen
it and his memory which remembered it but his clothes too, as garments
carry back into the clean edgeless blowing of air the lingering effluvium of
a sick-room or of death) had brought with it into the doomed wilderness
even before the actual axe the shadow and portent of the new mill not even
35 finished yet and the rails and ties which were not even laid; and he knew
now what he had known as soon as he saw Hoke's this morning but had not
yet thought into words: why Major de Spain had not come back, and that
after this time he himself, who had had to see it one time other, would return no more.
40   Now they were near. He knew it before the engine-driver whistled to warn
him. Then he saw Ash and the wagon, the reins without doubt wrapped once
more about the brake-lever as within the boy's own memory Major de Spain
had been forbidding him for eight years to do, the train slowing, the slackened couplings jolting and clashing again from car to car, the caboose slowing

---

1. It—the train. 23. bot—as printed in the original text. Faulkner is using either a local word
or, perhaps, the old past tense of the verb *boot*. 32. effluvium—exhalation.

past the wagon as he swung down with his gun, the conductor leaning out
above him to signal the engine, the caboose still slowing, creeping, although
the engine's exhaust was already slatting in mounting tempo against the un-
echoing wilderness, the crashing of drawbars once more traveling backward
along the train, the caboose picking up speed at last. Then it was gone. It had 5
not been. He could no longer hear it. The wilderness soared, musing, inattentive, myriad, eternal, green; older than any mill-shed, longer than any spur-
line. "Mr Boon here yet?" he said.

"He beat me in," Ash said. "Had the wagon loaded and ready for me at
Hoke's yistiddy when I got there and setting on the front steps at camp last 10
night when I got in. He already been in the woods since fo daylight this
morning. Said he gwine up to the Gum Tree and for you to hunt up that
way and meet him." He knew where that was: a single big sweet-gum just
outside the woods, in an old clearing; if you crept up to it very quietly this
time of year and then ran suddenly into the clearing, sometimes you caught 15
as many as a dozen squirrels in it, trapped, since there was no other tree
near they could jump to. So he didn't get into the wagon at all.

"I will," he said.

"I figured you would," Ash said, "I fotch you a box of shells." He passed
the shells down and began to unwrap the lines from the brake-pole. 20

"How many times up to now do you reckon Major has told you not to do
that?" the boy said.

"Do which?" Ash said. Then he said: "And tell Boon Hogganbeck dinner
gonter be on the table in a hour and if yawl want any to come on and eat
it." 25

"In an hour?" he said. "It aint nine oclock yet." He drew out his watch
and extended it face-toward Ash. "Look." Ash didn't even look at the watch.

"That's town time. You aint in town now. You in the woods."

"Look at the sun then."

"Nemmine the sun too," Ash said. "If you and Boon Hogganbeck want 30
any dinner, you better come on in and get it when I tole you. I aim to get
done in that kitchen because I got my wood to chop. And watch your feet.
They're crawling."

"I will," he said.

Then he was in the woods, not alone but solitary; the solitude closed about 35
him, green with summer. They did not change, and, timeless, would not, any
more than would the green of summer and the fire and rain of fall and the
iron cold and sometimes even snow

*the day, the morning when he killed the buck and Sam marked his face
with its hot blood, they returned to camp and he remembered old Ash's blink-* 40
*ing and disgruntled and even outraged disbelief until at last McCaslin had had
to affirm the fact that he had really killed it: and that night Ash sat snarling
and unapproachable behind the stove so that Tennie's Jim had to serve the
supper and waked them with breakfast already on the table the next morning and it was only half-past one oclock and at last out of Major de Spain's* 45
angry cursing and Ash's snarling and sullen rejoinders the fact emerged that

Ash not only wanted to go into the woods and shoot a deer also but he in-
tended to and Major de Spain said, 'By God, if we dont let him we will prob-
ably have to do the cooking from now on:' and Walter Ewell said, 'Or get
up at midnight to eat what Ash cooks:' and since he had already killed his
5   *buck for this hunt and was not to shoot again unless they needed meat, he*
offered his gun to Ash until Major de Spain took command and allotted that
gun to Boon for the day and gave Boon's unpredictable pump gun to Ash,
with two buckshot shells but Ash said, 'I got shells:' and showed them, four:
one buck, one of number three shot for rabbits, two of bird-shot and told
10 *one by one their history and their origin and he remembered not Ash's face*
alone but Major de Spain's and Walter's and General Compson's too. and
Ash's voice: 'Shoot? In course they'll shoot! Genl Cawmpson guv me this
un'—the buckshot—'right outen the same gun he kilt that big buck with
eight years ago. And this un'—it was the rabbit shell: triumphantly—'is
15 *oldern thisyer boy!' And that morning he loaded the gun himself, reversing*
the order: the bird-shot, the rabbit, then the buck so that the buckshot would
feed first into the chamber, and himself without a gun, he and Ash walked
beside Major de Spain's and Tennie's Jim's horses and the dogs (that was
the snow) until they cast and struck, the sweet strong cries ringing away into
20 *the muffled falling air and gone almost immediately, as if the constant and un-*
murmuring flakes had already buried even the unformed echoes beneath their
myriad and weightless falling, Major de Spain and Tennie's Jim gone too,
whooping on into the woods; and then it was all right, he knew as plainly
as if Ash had told him that Ash had now hunted his deer and that even his
25 *tender years had been forgiven for having killed one, and they turned back*
toward home through the falling snow—that is, Ash said, 'Now whut?' and
he said, 'This way'—himself in front because, although they were less than
a mile from camp, he knew that Ash, who had spent two weeks of his life
in the camp each year for the last twenty, had no idea whatever where they
30 *were, until quite soon the manner in which Ash carried Boon's gun was mak-*
ing him a good deal more than just nervous and he made Ash walk in front,
striding on, talking now, an old man's garrulous monologue beginning with
where he was at the moment then of the woods and of camping in the woods
and of eating in camps then of eating then of cooking it and of his wife's
35 *cooking then briefly of his old wife and almost at once and at length of a*
new light-colored woman who nursed next door to Major de Spain's and if she
didn't watch out who she was switching her tail at he would show her how old
was an old man or not if his wife just didn't watch him all the time, the two
of them in a game trail through a dense brake of cane and brier which would
40 *bring them out within a quarter-mile of camp, approaching a big fallen tree-*
trunk lying athwart the path and just as Ash, still talking, was about to step
over it the bear, the yearling, rose suddenly beyond the log, sitting up, its
forearms against its chest and its wrists limply arrested as if it had been sur-
prised in the act of covering its face to pray: and after a certain time Ash's
45 *gun yawed jerkily up and he said, 'You haven't got a shell in the barrel yet.*
Pump it:' but the gun already snicked and he said, 'Pump it. You haven't

got a shell in the barrel yet:' and Ash pumped the action and in a certain
time the gun steadied again and snicked and he said, 'Pump it:' and watched
the buckshot shell jerk, spinning heavily, into the cane. This is the rabbit
shot: he thought and the gun snicked and he thought: The next is bird-shot:
and he didn't have to say Pump it; he cried, 'Dont shoot! Dont shoot!' but 5
that was already too late too, the light dry vicious snick! before he could
speak and the bear turned and dropped to all-fours and then was gone and
there was only the log, the cane, the velvet and constant snow and Ash said,
'Now whut?' and he said, 'This way. Come on:' and began to back away
down the path and Ash said, 'I got to find my shells:' and he said, 'Goddamn 10
it, goddamn it, come on:' but Ash leaned the gun against the log and returned
and stooped and fumbled among the cane roots until he came back and
stooped and found the shells and they rose and at that moment the gun, un-
touched, leaning against the log six feet away and for that while even for-
gotten by both of them, roared, bellowed and flamed, and ceased: and he 15
carried it now, pumped out the last mummified shell and gave that one also
to Ash and, the action still open, himself carried the gun until he stood it in
the corner behind Boon's bed at the camp

—; summer, and fall, and snow, and wet and sap rife spring in their ordered immortal sequence, the deathless and immemorial phases of the mother 20
who had shaped him if any had toward the man he almost was, mother and
father both to the old man born of a Negro slave and a Chickasaw chief who
had been his spirit's father if any had, whom he had revered and harkened
to and loved and lost and grieved: and he would marry someday and they
too would own for their brief while that brief unsubstanced glory which in- 25
herently of itself cannot last and hence why glory: and they would, might,
carry even the remembrance of it into the time when flesh no longer talks
to flesh because memory at least does last: but still the woods would be his
mistress and his wife.

He was not going toward the Gum Tree. Actually he was getting farther 30
from it. Time was and not so long ago either when he would not have been
allowed here without someone with him, and a little later, when he had begun to learn how much he did not know, he would not have dared be here
without someone with him, and later still, beginning to ascertain, even if
only dimly, the limits of what he did not know, he could have attempted and 35
carried it through with a compass, not because of any increased belief in himself but because McCaslin and Major de Spain and Walter and General Compson too had taught him at last to believe the compass regardless of what it
seemed to state. Now he did not even use the compass but merely the sun
and that only subconsciously, yet he could have taken a scaled map and plotted 40
at any time to within a hundred feet of where he actually was; and sure
enough, at almost the exact moment when he expected it, the earth began
to rise faintly, he passed one of the four concrete markers set down by the

---

17. action—the operating mechanism of a breechloading rifle. **22. Negro**—as printed in
the original text. Faulkner is inconsistent in capitalization. **40. plotted**—that is, found his
position on the map by means of the map's co-ordinates (intersecting lines).

lumber company's surveyor to establish the four corners of the plot which
Major de Spain had reserved out of the sale, then he stood on the crest of the
knoll itself, the four corner-markers all visible now, blanched still even beneath the winter's weathering, lifeless and shockingly alien in that place where
5 dissolution itself was a seething turmoil of ejaculation tumescence conception
and birth, and death did not even exist. After two winters' blanketings of
leaves and the flood-waters of two springs, there was no trace of the two
graves any more at all. But those who would have come this far to find them
would not need headstones but would have found them as Sam Fathers him-
10 self had taught him to find such: by bearings on trees: and did, almost the
first thrust of the hunting knife finding (but only to see if it was still there)
the round tin box manufactured for axel-grease and containing now Old Ben's
dried mutilated paw, resting above Lion's bones.

He didn't disturb it. He didn't even look for the other grave where he and
15 McCaslin and Major de Spain and Boon had laid Sam's body, along with
his hunting horn and his knife and his tobacco-pipe, that Sunday morning
two years ago; he didn't have to. He had stepped over it, perhaps on it. But
that was all right. *He probably knew I was in the woods this morning long
before I got here,* he thought, going on to the tree which had supported one
20 end of the platform where Sam lay when McCaslin and Major de Spain found
them—the tree, the other axel-grease tin nailed to the trunk, but weathered,
rusted, alien too yet healed already into the wilderness' concordant generality,
raising no tuneless note, and empty, long since empty of the food and tobacco he had put into it that day, as empty of that as it would presently be
25 of this which he drew from his pocket—the twist of tobacco, the new ban-
danna handkerchief, the small paper sack of the peppermint candy which
Sam had used to love; that gone too, almost before he had turned his back,
not vanished but merely translated into the myriad life which printed the
dark mold of these secret and sunless places with delicate fairy tracks, which,
30 breathing and biding and immobile, watched him from beyond every twig
and leaf until he moved, moving again, walking on; he had not stopped, he
had only paused, quitting the knoll which was no abode of the dead because
there was no death, not Lion and not Sam: not held fast in earth but free in
earth and not in earth but of earth, myriad yet undiffused of every myriad
35 part, leaf and twig and particle, air and sun and rain and dew and night,
acorn oak and leaf and acorn again, dark and dawn and dark and dawn
again in their immutable progression and, being myriad, one: and Old Ben
too, Old Ben too; they would give him his paw back even, certainly they
would give him his paw back: then the long challenge and the long chase,
40 no heart to be driven and outraged, no flesh to be mauled and bled— Even
as he froze himself, he seemed to hear Ash's parting admonition. He could
even hear the voice as he froze, immobile, one foot just taking his weight,
the toe of the other just lifted behind him, not breathing, feeling again and
as always the sharp shocking inrush from when Isaac McCaslin long yet
45 was not, and so it was fear all right but not fright as he looked down at it.

---

12. **axel-grease**—usually spelled *axle,* in modern English.

It had not coiled yet and the buzzer had not sounded either, only one thick rapid contraction, one loop cast sideways as though merely for purchase from which the raised head might start slightly backward, not in fright either, not in threat quite yet, more than six feet of it, the head raised higher than his knee and less than his knee's length away, and old, the once-bright markings 5 of its youth dulled now to a monotone concordant too with the wilderness it crawled and lurked: the old one, the ancient and accursed about the earth, fatal and solitary and he could smell it now: the thin sick smell of rotting cucumbers and something else which had no name, evocative of all knowledge and an old weariness and of pariah-hood and of death. At last it moved. 10 Not the head. The elevation of the head did not change as it began to glide away from him, moving erect yet off the perpendicular as if the head and that elevated third were complete and all: an entity walking on two feet and free of all laws of mass and balance and should have been because even now he could not quite believe that all that shift and flow of shadow behind that 15 walking head could have been one snake: going and then gone; he put the other foot down at last and didn't know it, standing with one hand raised as Sam had stood that afternoon six years ago when Sam led him into the wilderness and showed him and he ceased to be a child, speaking the old tongue which Sam had spoken that day without premeditation either: "Chief," he 20 said: "Grandfather."

He couldn't tell when he first began to hear the sound, because when he became aware of it, it seemed to him that he had been already hearing it for several seconds—a sound as though someone were hammering a gun-barrel against a piece of railroad iron, a sound loud and heavy and not rapid yet with 25 something frenzied about it, as the hammerer were not only a strong man and an earnest one but a little hysterical too. Yet it couldn't be on the log-line because, although the track lay in that direction, it was at least two miles from him and this sound was not three hundred yards away. But even as he thought that, he realised where the sound must be coming from: whoever the man 30 was and whatever he was doing, he was somewhere near the edge of the clearing where the Gum Tree was and where he was to meet Boon. So far, he had been hunting as he advanced, moving slowly and quietly and watching the ground and the trees both. Now he went on, his gun unloaded and the barrel slanted up and back to facilitate its passage through brier and undergrowth, 35 approaching as it grew louder and louder that steady savage somehow queerly hysterical beating of metal on metal, emerging from the woods, into the old clearing, with the solitary gum tree directly before him. At first glance the tree seemed to be alive with frantic squirrels. There appeared to be forty or fifty of them leaping and darting from branch to branch until the whole tree 40 had become one green maelstrom of mad leaves, while from time to time, singly or in twos and threes, squirrels would dart down the trunk then whirl without stopping and rush back up again as though sucked violently back by the vacuum of their fellows' frenzied vortex. Then he saw Boon, sitting, his back against the trunk, his head bent, hammering furiously at something on 45 his lap. What he hammered with was the barrel of his dismembered gun, what he hammered at was the breech of it. The rest of the gun lay scattered about him in a half-dozen pieces while he bent over the piece on his lap his scarlet and streaming walnut face, hammering the disjointed barrel against the gun-breech with the frantic abandon of a madman. He didn't even look up to see who it was. Still hammering, he merely shouted back at the boy in a hoarse strangled voice:

"Get out of here! Dont touch them! Dont touch a one of them! They're mine!"

ERNEST HEMINGWAY

1898-

I. AMERICAN YOUTH (1898–1917)

1898 Born at Oak Park, Illinois, July 21, the second son of Dr. Clarence Edmonds and Grace (Hall) Hemingway; christened Ernest Miller Hemingway.

1898–1913 As a boy he accompanied his father on professional visits and on fishing and hunting trips to Michigan.

1913 Ran away from home, but returned to finish high school, where he excelled in football and boxing.

1917 Graduated from the Oak Park High School, having contributed the class prophecy to the 1917 yearbook.

II. "THE LOST GENERATION" (1917–1936)

1917 Worked as a reporter for the *Kansas City Star*. Volunteered in an American ambulance unit in the First World War. Transferred to the Italian Arditi combat unit; wounded on the Italian front; hospitalized.

1918 Decorated by the Italian Government for valor.

1919 Returned to the United States after the Armistice; married Hadley Richardson, a childhood Michigan friend. Re-entered newspaper work.

1920 After a brief interlude as correspondent covering the Greco-Turkish War, became Paris correspondent for the Hearst syndicate.

1921–1925 Prominent figure in the American colony in Paris, especially the group around Gertrude Stein. Others were F. Scott Fitzgerald and Ezra Pound.

1923 Appearance of his first signed work in *Poetry,* January, 1923. Published *Three Stories & Ten Poems* at Dijon, France.

1924 *In Our Time* (Paris), a collection of stories and sketches, reprinted in New York in 1925.

1926 *The Torrents of Spring,* a burlesque novel (May), and *The Sun Also Rises* (October). Divorced.

1927 *Men without Women.* Married Pauline Pfeiffer, a Paris fashion writer for *Vogue.*

1929 *A Farewell to Arms.*

1932 *Death in the Afternoon,* a book in celebration of bullfighting, which also contains some important statements of literary theory and philosophy.

1933 *Winner Take Nothing.*

1935 *The Green Hills of Africa,* the product of a trip to Africa the previous year.

1936 Raised money to buy ambulances for the Madrid Loyalists in the Spanish War.

1885

III. THE EMBATTLED LIBERTARIAN (1936–   )

1937   In February sailed for Spain for the North American Newspaper Alliance.
Prepared material for a film, *The Spanish Earth*. Returned May 18 to prepare a sound-track. In his first public speech he uttered a scathing indictment
of fascism before the League of American Writers. Returned to Spain August
14. Published *To Have and Have Not*.

1938   January 27 returned to Florida from Spain; thence to New York City to help
direct a play of his composition. During this year he went back and forth
between Europe and the United States in the interests of the fight against
fascism. Published *The Fifth Column and the First Forty-Nine Stories, The
Fifth Column* being his antifascist play about Spain.

1939   Cochairman with William Allan Neilson of the American Committee for
the Protection of the Foreign-Born.

1940   *For Whom the Bell Tolls*. Divorced his second wife and married Martha
Gellhorn, a writer.

1941   Newspaper correspondent in China.

1942   Edited *Men at War*, an anthology of war stories.

1946   Divorced his third wife and married Mary Welsh, a journalist.

1950   *Across the River and Into the Trees*.

BIOGRAPHIES: There is no biography. Consult, however, *Who's Who in America;
New York Times Index;* "All Stories End . . ." in *Time* for October 18,
1937, pp. 79-85; "Dilly Tante" (Stanley J. Kunitz), ed., *Living Authors: A
Book of Biographies,* H. W. Wilson Company, 1931, pp. 175-76; Gertrude
Stein, *The Autobiography of Alice B. Toklas,* Harcourt, Brace, 1933, pp.
261-71; Fred B. Millett, *Contemporary American Authors,* Harcourt, Brace,
1940, pp. 385-88 and references.

BIBLIOGRAPHY: Consult Louis Henry Cohn, *A Bibliography of the Works of Ernest
Hemingway,* Random House, 1931; Merle Johnson, "American First Edi-
tions," *Publishers' Weekly,* February 20, 1932, p. 870; Vrest Orton, "Some
Notes Bibliographical and Otherwise on the Books of Ernest Hemingway,"
Publishers' Weekly, February 15, 1930, pp. 884-86; *Literary History of the
United States,* Vol. III, pp. 559-61.

CRITICAL COMMENT: Joseph Warren Beach, *American Fiction 1920-1940,* Macmillan,
1941, pp. 69-119; Malcolm Cowley, "Hemingway at Midnight," *New Re-
public,* August 14, 1944, pp. 190-95; David Daiches, "Ernest Hemingway,"
College English, May, 1941, pp. 725-36; Clifton Fadiman, "Ernest Heming-
way, an American Byron," *Nation,* January 18, 1933, pp. 63-64; James T.
Farrell, "Ernest Hemingway, Apostle of a 'Lost Generation,' " *New York
Times Book Review,* August 1, 1943, pp. 6, 14; Maxwell Geismar, "No Man
Alone Now," *Virginia Quarterly Review,* Autumn, 1941, pp. 517-34; Edgar
Johnson, "Farewell the Separate Peace," *Sewanee Review,* July-September,
1940, pp. 289-300; Robert Morss Lovett, "Ernest Hemingway," *English
Journal,* October, 1932, pp. 609-17; Herbert J. Muller, *Modern Fiction: A
Study in Values,* Funk & Wagnalls, 1937, pp. 395-403; Edmund Wilson,
"Ernest Hemingway," *Atlantic Monthly,* July, 1939, pp. 36-46; and especially
John K. M. McCaffery, ed., *Ernest Hemingway: The Man and His Work,*
World Publishing Co., 1950, a valuable collection of evaluations by twenty-
one critics. The best book of selections is undoubtedly that edited by Mal-
colm Cowley, *Hemingway,* Viking Press, 1944 (The Viking Portable Library).

The famous phrase of Gertrude Stein, "You are all a lost generation," which is the epigraph of *The Sun Also Rises,* introduces the first phase and the first misunderstanding of Ernest Hemingway. To the war-weary world of the 1920's Hemingway was par excellence the leader of the "hard-boiled" school of disillusioned fictionists. Not merely the themes of aimlessness and frustration, of pointless heroism and pointless death, that occasioned his earlier novels and tales but also the manner of their telling were hailed as the supreme embodiment of a disillusioned view of life. Stripped of all rhetorical adornment, Hemingway's clipped dialogue, which did not express and yet somehow revealed irrational emotionalisms beneath, was felt to be the last word in literary technique. This, it seemed to say, this, stripped of all romantic adornment, is naked reality.

Looking backward, in the light of Hemingway's passionate belief in the righteousness of the Loyalist cause in Spain, more recent criticism revises this judgment. Still acknowledging Hemingway as a great technician, modern criticism finds in him not disillusion but an implied appeal to a higher set of ethical values than that by which most men live; and the sense of frustration in his work is not so much a comment on actual life as a recurrence of that inward psychic fear that haunted the minds of Charles Brockden Brown, Hawthorne, and Poe. The strength of his work is that he digs beneath the accepted metropolitan surfaces of our life into a deeper layer of consciousness that is not so much primitive as primary. In that sense there is a real connection between the uncertainty of the characters in Hemingway and the uncertainty of such a character as George F. Babbitt in Lewis's novel. This uncertainty reflects the uneasiness of the American mind as it moves into novel and uncharted seas in the twentieth century.

MY OLD MAN

"My Old Man" appeared originally in *Three Stories & Ten Poems,* published in 1923 by the Contact Publishing Company and printed in Dijon, France. When E. J. H. O'Brien included it in his *The Best Short Stories of 1923* (Small, Maynard), he offered the first work of Hemingway's to be printed in the United States, although in the dedication of this volume to Hemingway he showed his unfamiliarity with the author by spelling his name "Hemenway." O'Brien also reprinted the story in *The Twenty-Five Finest Short Stories* (Richard R. Smith, 1926). It was included in *In Our Time* (1924). The text below follows that of *The Fifth Column and the First Forty-Nine Stories* (1938).

I GUESS looking at it, now, my old man was cut out for a fat guy, one of those regular little roly fat guys you see around, but he sure never got that way, except a little toward the last, and then it wasn't his fault, he was riding over the jumps only and he could afford to carry plenty of weight then. I remember the way he'd pull on a rubber shirt over a couple of jerseys and a big   5
sweat shirt over that, and get me to run with him in the forenoon in the hot sun. He'd have, maybe, taken a trial trip with one of Razzo's skins early in the morning after just getting in from Torino at four o'clock in the morning and beating it out to the stables in a cab and then with the dew all over everything and the sun just starting to get going, I'd help him pull off   10

3-4. **riding over the jumps**—that is, exercising horses only, not racing. 7. **skins**—horses.

his boots and he'd get into a pair of sneakers and all these sweaters and we'd start out.

"Come on, kid," he'd say, stepping up and down on his toes in front of the jock's dressing room, "let's get moving."

5   Then we'd start off jogging around the infield once, maybe, with him ahead, running nice, and then turn out the gate and along one of those roads with all the trees along both sides of them that run out from San Siro. I'd go ahead of him when we hit the road and I could run pretty stout and I'd look around and he'd be jogging easy just behind me and after a little while I'd look around
10 again and he'd begun to sweat. Sweating heavy and he'd just be dogging it along with his eyes on my back, but when he'd catch me looking at him he'd grin and say, "Sweating plenty?" When my old man grinned, nobody could help but grin too. We'd keep right on running out toward the mountains and then my old man would yell, "Hey, Joe!" and I'd look back and he'd be sit-
15 ting under a tree with a towel he'd had around his waist wrapped around his neck.

I'd come back and sit down beside him and he'd pull a rope out of his pocket and start skipping rope out in the sun with the sweat pouring off his face and him skipping rope out in the white dust with the rope going clop-
20 petty, cloppetty, clop, clop, clop, and the sun hotter, and him working harder up and down a patch of the road. Say, it was a treat to see my old man skip rope, too. He could whirr it fast or lop it slow and fancy. Say, you ought to have seen wops look at us sometimes, when they'd come by, going into town walking along with big white steers hauling the cart. They sure looked as
25 though they thought the old man was nuts. He'd start the rope whirring till they'd stop dead still and watch him, then give the steers a cluck and a poke with the goad and get going again.

When I'd sit watching him working out in the hot sun I sure felt fond of him. He sure was fun and he done his work so hard and he'd finish up with
30 a regular whirring that'd drive the sweat out of his face like water and then sling the rope at the tree and come over and sit down with me and lean back against the tree with the towel and a sweater wrapped around his neck.

"Sure is hell keeping it down, Joe," he'd say and lean back and shut his eyes and breathe long and deep, "it ain't like when you're a kid." Then he'd get
35 up and before he started to cool we'd jog along back to the stables. That's the way it was keeping down to weight. He was worried all the time. Most jocks can just about ride off all they want to. A jock loses about a kilo every time he rides, but my old man was sort of dried out and he couldn't keep down his kilos without all that running.

40   I remember once at San Siro, Regoli, a little wop, that was riding for Buzoni, came out across the paddock going to the bar for something cool; and flicking his boots with his whip, after he'd just weighed in and my old man had just weighed in too, and came out with the saddle under his arm looking red-faced and tired and too big for his silks and he stood there looking at young Regoli
45 standing up to the outdoors bar, cool and kid-looking, and I said; "What's

---

4. jock's—jockey's. **37. kilo**—a weight of a little more than two pounds. **44. silks**—A jockey's shirt is made out of silk.

the matter, Dad?" 'cause I thought maybe Regoli had bumped him or something and he just looked at Regoli and said, "Oh, to hell with it," and went on to the dressing room.

Well, it would have been all right, maybe, if we'd stayed in Milan and ridden at Milan and Torino, 'cause if there ever were any easy courses, it's those   5
two. "Pianola, Joe," my old man said when he dismounted in the winning stall after what the wops thought was a hell of a steeplechase. I asked him once. "This course rides itself. It's the pace you're going at, that makes riding the jumps dangerous, Joe. We ain't going any pace here, and they ain't any really bad jumps either. But it's the pace always—not the jumps—that makes the   10
trouble."

San Siro was the swellest course I'd ever seen but the old man said it was a dog's life. Going back and forth between Mirafiore and San Siro and riding just about every day in the week with a train ride every other night.

I was nuts about the horses, too. There's something about it, when they come   15
out and go up the track to the post. Sort of dancy and tight looking with the jock keeping a tight hold on them and maybe easing off a little and letting them run a little going up. Then once they were at the barrier it got me worse than anything. Especially at San Siro with that big green infield and the mountains way off and the fat wop starter with his big whip and the jocks fiddling   20
them around and then the barrier snapping up and that bell going off and them all getting off in a bunch and then commencing to string out. You know the way a bunch of skins gets off. If you're up in the stand with a pair of glasses all you see is them plunging off and then that bell goes off and it seems like it rings for a thousand years and then they come sweeping round the turn. There   25
wasn't ever anything like it for me.

But my old man said one day, in the dressing room, when he was getting into his street clothes, "None of these things are horses, Joe. They'd kill that bunch of skates for their hides and hoofs up at Paris." That was the day he'd won the Premio Commercio with Lantorna shooting her out of the field the   30
last hundred meters like pulling a cork out of a bottle.

It was right after the Premio Commercio that we pulled out and left Italy. My old man and Holbrook and a fat wop in a straw hat that kept wiping his face with a handkerchief were having an argument at a table in the Galleria. They were all talking French and the two of them was after my old man about   35
something. Finally he didn't say anything any more but just sat there and looked at Holbrook, and the two of them kept after him, first one talking and then the other, and the fat wop always butting in on Holbrook.

"You go out and buy me a *Sportsman,* will you, Joe?" my old man said, and handed me a couple of soldi without looking away from Holbrook.   40

So I went out of the Galleria and walked over to in front of the Scala and bought a paper, and came back and stood a little way away because I didn't want to butt in and my old man was sitting back in his chair looking down at his coffee and fooling with a spoon and Holbrook and the big wop were standing and the big wop was wiping his face and shaking his head. And I came   45

16. **post**—starting post. 30. **Premio Commercio**—Commercial Prize. 40. **soldi**—small Italian coins.

up and my old man acted just as though the two of them weren't standing there and said, "Want an ice, Joe?" Holbrook looked down at my old man and said slow and careful, "You son of a bitch," and he and the fat wop went out through the tables.

5   My old man sat there and sort of smiled at me, but his face was white and he looked sick as hell and I was scared and felt sick inside because I knew something had happened and I didn't see how anybody could call my old man a son of a bitch, and get away with it. My old man opened up the *Sportsman* and studied the handicaps for a while and then he said, "You got to take a 10 lot of things in this world, Joe." And three days later we left Milan for good on the Turin train for Paris, after an auction sale out in front of Turner's stables of everything we couldn't get into a trunk and a suit case.

We got into Paris early in the morning in a long, dirty station the old man told me was the Gare de Lyon. Paris was an awful big town after Milan. Seems 15 like in Milan everybody is going somewhere and all the trams run somewhere and there ain't any sort of a mix-up, but Paris is all balled up and they never do straighten it out. I got to like it, though, part of it, anyway, and say, it's got the best race courses in the world. Seems as though that were the thing that keeps it all going and about the only thing you can figure on is that every 20 day the buses will be going out to whatever track they're running at, going right out through everything to the track. I never really got to know Paris well, because I just came in about once or twice a week with the old man from Maisons and he always sat at the Café de la Paix on the Opera side with the rest of the gang from Maisons and I guess that's one of the busiest parts of the 25 town. But, say, it is funny that a big town like Paris wouldn't have a Galleria, isn't it?

Well, we went out to live at Maisons-Lafitte, where just about everybody lives except the gang at Chantilly, with a Mrs. Meyers that runs a boarding house. Maisons is about the swellest place to live I've ever seen in all my life. 30 The town ain't so much, but there's a lake and a swell forest that we used to go off bumming in all day, a couple of us kids, and my old man made me a sling shot and we got a lot of things with it but the best one was a magpie. Young Dick Atkinson shot a rabbit with it one day and we put it under a tree and were all sitting around and Dick had some cigarettes and all of a sudden 35 the rabbit jumped up and beat it into the brush and we chased it but we couldn't find it. Gee, we had fun at Maisons. Mrs. Meyers used to give me lunch in the morning and I'd be gone all day. I learned to talk French quick. It's an easy language.

As soon as we got to Maisons, my old man wrote to Milan for his license 40 and he was pretty worried till it came. He used to sit around the Café de Paris in Maisons with the gang, there were lots of guys he'd known when he rode up at Paris, before the war, lived at Maisons, and there's a lot of time to sit around because the work around a racing stable, for the jocks, that is, is all cleaned up by nine o'clock in the morning. They take the first bunch of skins 45 out to gallop them at 5.30 in the morning and they work the second lot at

---

15. **trams**—streetcars. 23. **Maisons . . . Café de la Paix**—Consult any large map of Paris.

8 o'clock. That means getting up early all right and going to bed early, too. If a jock's riding for somebody too, he can't go boozing around because the trainer always has an eye on him if he's a kid and if he ain't a kid he's always got an eye on himself. So mostly if a jock ain't working he sits around the Café de Paris with the gang and they can all sit around about two or three   5 hours in front of some drink like a vermouth and seltz and they talk and tell stories and shoot pool and it's sort of like a club or the Galleria in Milan. Only it ain't really like the Galleria because there everybody is going by all the time and there's everybody around at the tables.

Well, my old man got his license all right. They sent it through to him with-   10 out a word and he rode a couple of times. Amiens, up country and that sort of thing, but he didn't seem to get any engagement. Everybody liked him and whenever I'd come in to the Café in the forenoon I'd find somebody drinking with him because my old man wasn't tight like most of these jockeys that have got the first dollar they made riding at the World's Fair in St. Louis in nine-   15 teen ought four. That's what my old man would say when he'd kid George Burns. But it seemed like everybody steered clear of giving my old man any mounts.

We went out to wherever they were running every day with the car from Maisons and that was the most fun of all. I was glad when the horses came   20 back from Deauville and the summer. Even though it meant no more bum- ming in the woods, 'cause then we'd ride to Enghien or Tremblay or St. Cloud and watch them from the trainers' and jockeys' stand. I sure learned about racing from going out with that gang and the fun of it was going every day.   25

I remember once out at St. Cloud. It was a big two hundred thousand franc race with seven entries and Kzar a big favorite. I went around to the paddock to see the horses with my old man and you never saw such horses. This Kzar is a great big yellow horse that looks like just nothing but run. I never saw such a horse. He was being led around the paddocks with his head down and   30 when he went by me I felt all hollow inside he was so beautiful. There never was such a wonderful, lean, running built horse. And he went around the paddock putting his feet just so and quiet and careful and moving easy like he knew just what he had to do and not jerking and standing up on his legs and getting wild eyed like you see these selling platers with a shot of dope in them.   35 The crowd was so thick I couldn't see him again except just his legs going by and some yellow and my old man started out through the crowd and I fol- lowed him over to the jock's dressing room back in the trees and there was a big crowd around there, too, but the man at the door in a derby nodded to my old man and we got in and everybody was sitting around and getting dressed   40 and pulling shirts over their heads and pulling boots on and it all smelled hot and sweaty and linimenty and outside was the crowd looking in.

The old man went over and sat down beside George Gardner that was get- ting into his pants and said, "What's the dope, George?" just in an ordinary

6. **seltz**—seltzer water. **11. Amiens**—city north of Paris. **21. Deauville**—French resort town on the English Channel. **22-23. Enghien . . . St. Cloud**—Parisian suburbs. **35. platers**—horses that compete chiefly in selling races; inferior horses.

tone of voice 'cause there ain't any use him feeling around because George either can tell him or he can't tell him.

"He won't win," George says very low, leaning over and buttoning the bottoms of his pants.

5 "Who will?" my old man says, leaning over close so nobody can hear.

"Kircubbin," George says, "and if he does, save me a couple of tickets."

My old man says something in a regular voice to George and George says, "Don't ever bet on anything I tell you," kidding like, and we beat it out and through all the crowd that was looking in, over to the 100 franc mutuel ma-

10 chine. But I knew something big was up because George is Kzar's jockey. On the way he gets one of the yellow odds-sheets with the starting prices on and Kzar is only paying 5 for 10, Cefisidote is next at 3 to 1 and fifth down the list this Kircubbin at 8 to 1. My old man bets five thousand on Kircubbin to win and puts on a thousand to place and we went around back of the grandstand

15 to go up the stairs and get a place to watch the race.

We were jammed in tight and first a man in a long coat with a gray tall hat and a whip folded up in his hand came out and then one after another the horses, with the jocks up and a stable boy holding the bridle on each side and walking along, followed the old guy. That big yellow horse Kzar came

20 first. He didn't look so big when you first looked at him until you saw the length of his legs and the whole way he's built and the way he moves. Gosh, I never saw such a horse. George Gardner was riding him and they moved along slow, back of the old guy in the gray tall hat that walked along like he was the ring master in a circus. Back of Kzar, moving along smooth and yel-

25 low in the sun, was a good looking black with a nice head with Tommy Archibald riding him; and after the black was a string of five more horses all moving along slow in a procession past the grandstand and the pesage. My old man said the black was Kircubbin and I took a good look at him and he was a nice looking horse, all right, but nothing like Kzar.

30 Everybody cheered Kzar when he went by and he sure was one swell-looking horse. The procession of them went around on the other side past the pelouse and then back up to the near end of the course and the circus master had the stable boys turn them loose one after another so they could gallop by the stands on their way up to the post and let everybody have a good look at

35 them. They weren't at the post hardly any time at all when the gong started and you could see them way off across the infield all in a bunch starting on the first swing like a lot of little toy horses. I was watching them through the glasses and Kzar was running well back, with one of the bays making the pace. They swept down and around and came pounding past and Kzar

40 was way back when they passed us and this Kircubbin horse in front and going smooth. Gee, it's awful when they go by you and then you have to watch them go farther away and get smaller and smaller and then all bunched up on the turns and then come around towards into the stretch and you feel like swearing and goddamming worse and worse. Finally they

9. **mutuel**—a mode of betting. **13. thousand**—francs. A franc was then worth about 5 cents. **27. pesage**—space for spectators outside the grandstand. **32. pelouse**—greensward around the racetrack.

made the last turn and came into the straightaway with this Kircubbin horse
way out in front. Everybody was looking funny and saying "Kzar" in sort of
a sick way and them pounding nearer down the stretch, and then something
came out of the pack right into my glasses like a horse-headed yellow streak
and everybody began to yell "Kzar" as though they were crazy. Kzar came on 5
faster than I'd ever seen anything in my life and pulled up on Kircubbin that
was going fast as any black horse could go with the jock flogging hell out of
him with the gad and they were right dead neck and neck for a second but
Kzar seemed going about twice as fast with those great jumps and that head
out—but it was while they were neck and neck that they passed the winning 10
post and when the numbers went up in the slots the first one was 2 and that
meant Kircubbin had won.

I felt all trembly and funny inside, and then we were all jammed in with
the people going downstairs to stand in front of the board where they'd post
what Kircubbin paid. Honest, watching the race I'd forgot how much my old 15
man had bet on Kircubbin. I'd wanted Kzar to win so damned bad. But now
it was all over it was swell to know we had the winner.

"Wasn't it a swell race, Dad?" I said to him.

He looked at me sort of funny with his derby on the back of his head.
"George Gardner's a swell jockey, all right," he said. "It sure took a great jock 20
to keep that Kzar horse from winning."

Of course I knew it was funny all the time. But my old man saying that
right out like that sure took the kick all out of it for me and I didn't get the
real kick back again ever, even when they posted the numbers up on the board
and the bell rang to pay off and we saw that Kircubbin paid 67.50 for 10. All 25
round people were saying, "Poor Kzar! Poor Kzar!" And I thought, I wish I
were a jockey and could have rode him instead of that son of a bitch. And that
was funny, thinking of George Gardner as a son of a bitch because I'd always
liked him and besides he'd given us the winner, but I guess that's what he is,
all right. 30

My old man had a big lot of money after that race and he took to coming
into Paris oftener. If they raced at Tremblay he'd have them drop him in town
on their way back to Maisons and he and I'd sit out in front of the Café de la
Paix and watch the people go by. It's funny sitting there. There's streams of
people going by and all sorts of guys come up and want to sell you things, and 35
I loved to sit there with my old man. That was when we'd have the most fun.
Guys would come by selling funny rabbits that jumped if you squeezed a bulb
and they'd come up to us and my old man would kid with them. He could
talk French just like English and all those kind of guys knew him 'cause you
can always tell a jockey—and then we always sat at the same table and they 40
got used to seeing us there. There were guys selling matrimonial papers and
girls selling rubber eggs that when you squeezed them a rooster came out of
them and one old wormy-looking guy that went by with post-cards of Paris,
showing them to everybody, and, of course, nobody ever bought any, and then
he would come back and show the under side of the pack and they would all 45
be smutty post-cards and lots of people would dig down and buy them.

8. gad—whip.

Gee, I remember the funny people that used to go by. Girls around supper time looking for somebody to take them out to eat and they'd speak to my old man and he'd make some joke at them in French and they'd pat me on the head and go on. Once there was an American woman sitting with her kid
5 daughter at the next table to us and they were both eating ices and I kept looking at the girl and she was awfully good looking and I smiled at her and she smiled at me but that was all that ever came of it because I looked for her mother and her every day and I made up ways that I was going to speak to her and I wondered if I got to know her if her mother would let me take her
10 out to Auteuil or Tremblay but I never saw either of them again. Anyway, I guess it wouldn't have been any good, anyway, because looking back on it I remember the way I thought out would be best to speak to her was to say, "Pardon me, but perhaps I can give you a winner at Enghien today?" and, after all, maybe she would have thought I was a tout instead of really trying
15 to give her a winner.

We'd sit at the Café de la Paix, my old man and me, and we had a big drag with the waiter because my old man drank whisky and it cost five francs, and that meant a good tip when the saucers were counted up. My old man was drinking more than I'd ever seen him, but he wasn't riding at all now and be-
20 sides he said that whisky kept his weight down. But I noticed he was putting it on, all right, just the same. He'd busted away from his old gang out at Maisons and seemed to like just sitting around on the boulevard with me. But he was dropping money every day at the track. He'd feel sort of doleful after the last race, if he'd lost on the day, until we'd get to our table and he'd have
25 his first whisky and then he'd be fine.

He'd be reading the *Paris-Sport* and he'd look over at me and say, "Where's your girl, Joe?" to kid me on account I had told him about the girl that day at the next table. And I'd get red, but I liked being kidded about her. It gave me a good feeling. "Keep your eye peeled for her, Joe," he'd say, "she'll be
30 back."

He'd ask me questions about things and some of the things I'd say he'd laugh. And then he'd get started talking about things. About riding down in Egypt, or at St. Moritz on the ice before my mother died, and about during the war when they had regular races down in the south of France without any
35 purses, or betting or crowd or anything just to keep the breed up. Regular races with the jocks riding hell out of the horses. Gee, I could listen to my old man talk by the hour, especially when he'd had a couple or so of drinks. He'd tell me about when he was a boy in Kentucky and going coon hunting, and the old days in the States before everything went on the bum there. And he'd
40 say, "Joe, when we've got a decent stake, you're going back there to the States and go to school."

"What've I got to go back there to go to school for when everything's on the bum there?" I'd ask him.

"That's different," he'd say and get the waiter over and pay the pile of

---

18. **saucers**—In French cafés drinks are served on saucers, each saucer representing a certain price. When the customer pays the bill, the saucers are counted up. 33. **St. Moritz**—Swiss resort town.

saucers and we'd get a taxi to the Gare St. Lazare and get on the train out to Maisons.

One day at Auteuil, after a selling steeplechase, my old man bought in the winner for 30,000 francs. He had to bid a little to get him but the stable let the horse go finally and my old man had his permit and his colors in a week. Gee, 5 I felt proud when my old man was an owner. He fixed it up for stable space with Charles Drake and cut out coming in to Paris, and started his running and sweating out again, and him and I were the whole stable gang. Our horse's name was Gilford, he was Irish bred and a nice, sweet jumper. My old man figured that training him and riding him, himself, he was a good investment. 10 I was proud of everything and I thought Gilford was as good a horse as Kzar. He was a good, solid jumper, a bay, with plenty of speed on the flat, if you asked him for it, and he was a nice-looking horse, too.

Gee, I was fond of him. The first time he started with my old man up, he finished third in a 2500 meter hurdle race and when my old man got off him, 15 all sweating and happy in the place stall, and went in to weigh, I felt as proud of him as though it was the first race he'd ever placed in. You see, when a guy ain't been riding for a long time, you can't make yourself really believe that he has ever rode. The whole thing was different now, 'cause down in Milan, even big races never seemed to make any difference to my old man, if he won 20 he wasn't ever excited or anything, and now it was so I couldn't hardly sleep the night before a race and I knew my old man was excited, too, even if he didn't show it. Riding for yourself makes an awful difference.

Second time Gilford and my old man started, was a rainy Sunday at Auteuil, in the Prix du Marat, a 4500 meter steeplechase. As soon as he'd gone out I 25 beat it up in the stand with the new glasses my old man had bought for me to watch them. They started way over at the far end of the course and there was some trouble at the barrier. Something with goggle blinders on was making a great fuss and rearing around and busted the barrier once, but I could see my old man in our black jacket, with a white cross and a black cap, sit- 30 ting up on Gilford, and patting him with his hand. Then they were off in a jump and out of sight behind the trees and the gong going for dear life and the pari-mutuel wickets rattling down. Gosh, I was so excited, I was afraid to look at them, but I fixed the glasses on the place where they would come out back of the trees and then out they came with the old black jacket going third 35 and they all sailing over the jump like birds. Then they went out of sight again and then they came pounding out and down the hill and all going nice and sweet and easy and taking the fence smooth in a bunch, and moving away from us all solid. Looked as though you could walk across on their backs they were all so bunched and going so smooth. Then they bellied over the big 40 double Bullfinch and something came down. I couldn't see who it was, but in a minute the horse was up and galloping free and the field, all bunched still,

---

1. **Gare**—railroad station. 15. **meter**—about a yard. 25. **Prix du Marat**—Marat Prize. 33. **pari-mutuel**—a kind of betting in which the backers of the winning horse divide the total stakes on the other runners. 41. **Bullfinch**—A bullfinch is a quickset hedge with a ditch on one side. It is too high and strong to be cleared, hence the horse must be leaped through it, not over it.

sweeping around the long left turn into the straightaway. They jumped the stone wall and came jammed down the stretch toward the big water-jump right in front of the stands. I saw them coming and hollered at my old man as he went by, and he was leading by about a length and riding way out, and
5 light as a monkey, and they were racing for the water-jump. They took off over the big hedge of the water-jump in a pack and then there was a crash, and two horses pulled sideways out off it, and kept on going, and three others were piled up. I couldn't see my old man anywhere. One horse kneed himself up and the jock had hold of the bridle and mounted and went slamming on
10 after the place money. The other horse was up and away by himself, jerking his head and galloping with the bridle rein hanging and the jock staggered over to one side of the track against the fence. Then Gilford rolled over to one side off my old man and got up and started to run on three legs with his off hoof dangling and there was my old man laying there on the grass flat out
15 with his face up and blood all over the side of his head. I ran down the stand and bumped into a jam of people and got to the rail and a cop grabbed me and held me and two big stretcher-bearers were going out after my old man and around on the other side of the course I saw three horses, strung way out, coming out of the trees and taking the jump.
20 My old man was dead when they brought him in and while a doctor was listening to his heart with a thing plugged in his ears, I heard a shot up the track that meant they'd killed Gilford. I lay down beside my old man, when they carried the stretcher into the hospital room, and hung onto the stretcher and cried and cried, and he looked so white and gone and so awfully dead, and
25 I couldn't help feeling that if my old man was dead maybe they didn't need to have shot Gilford. His hoof might have got well. I don't know. I loved my old man so much.

Then a couple of guys came in and one of them patted me on the back and then went over and looked at my old man and then pulled a sheet off the cot
30 and spread it over him; and the other was telephoning in French for them to send the ambulance to take him out to Maisons. And I couldn't stop crying, crying and choking, sort of, and George Gardner came in and sat down beside me on the floor and put his arm around me and says, "Come on, Joe, old boy. Get up and we'll go out and wait for the ambulance."
35 George and I went out to the gate and I was trying to stop bawling and George wiped off my face with his handkerchief and we were standing back a little ways while the crowd was going out of the gate and a couple of guys stopped near us while we were waiting for the crowd to get through the gate and one of them was counting a bunch of mutuel tickets and he said, "Well,
40 Butler got his, all right."

The other guy said, "I don't give a good goddam if he did, the crook. He had it coming to him on the stuff he's pulled."

"I'll say he had," said the other guy, and tore the bunch of tickets in two.

And George Gardner looked at me to see if I'd heard and I had all right

10. place money—A horse "places" if it comes in second or third; hence, under most systems of betting, the owner will win something. **13-14. off hoof**—the "off" side of a horse is the right side, since one mounts on the left or "near" side.

and he said, "Don't you listen to what those bums said, Joe. Your old man was one swell guy."

But I don't know. Seems like when they get started they don't leave a guy nothing.

THE UNDEFEATED   5

"The Undefeated" was first published in *This Quarter* (Milan) in 1925-26, re-published with slight textual changes in E. J. H. O'Brien's *The Best Short Stories of 1926* (Dodd, Mead), and is included in the collections *Men without Women* (1927); *Present-Day American Stories* (Scribner, 1929); and *The Fifth Column and the First Forty-Nine Stories* (1939), from which this text is taken. Hemingway's *Death in the Afternoon* (1932) is a detailed account of bullfighting.

M ANUEL GARCIA climbed the stairs to Don Miguel Retana's office. He set down his suitcase and knocked on the door. There was no answer. Manuel, standing in the hallway, felt there was someone in the room. He felt it through the door.

"Retana," he said, listening.   10

There was no answer.

He's there, all right, Manuel thought.

"Retana," he said and banged the door.

"Who's there?" said someone in the office.

"Me, Manolo," Manuel said.   15

"What do you want?" asked the voice.

"I want to work," Manuel said.

Something in the door clicked several times and it swung open. Manuel went in, carrying his suitcase.

A little man sat behind a desk at the far side of the room. Over his head was   20
a bull's head, stuffed by a Madrid taxidermist; on the walls were framed photographs and bull-fight posters.

The little man sat looking at Manuel.

"I thought they'd killed you," he said.

Manuel knocked with his knuckles on the desk. The little man sat looking   25
at him across the desk.

"How many corridas you had this year?" Retana asked.

"One," he answered.

"Just that one?" the little man asked.

"That's all."   30

"I read about it in the papers," Retana said. He leaned back in the chair and looked at Manuel.

Manuel looked up at the stuffed bull. He had seen it often before. He felt a certain family interest in it. It had killed his brother, the promising one, about nine years ago. Manuel remembered the day. There was a brass plate   35
on the oak shield the bull's head was mounted on. Manuel could not read it,

27. **corridas**—bullfights.

but he imagined it was in memory of his brother. Well, he had been a good kid.

The plate said: "The Bull 'Mariposa' of the Duke of Veragua, which accepted 9 varas for 7 caballos, and caused the death of Antonio Garcia, Novil-
5 lero, April 27, 1909."

Retana saw him looking at the stuffed bull's head.

"The lot the Duke sent me for Sunday will make a scandal," he said. "They're all bad in the legs. What do they say about them at the Café?"

"I don't know," Manuel said. "I just got in."

10 "Yes," Retana said. "You still have your bag."

He looked at Manuel, leaning back behind the big desk.

"Sit down," he said. "Take off your cap."

Manuel sat down; his cap off, his face was changed. He looked pale, and his coleta pinned forward on his head, so that it would not show under the
15 cap, gave him a strange look.

"You don't look well," Retana said.

"I just got out of the hospital," Manuel said.

"I heard they'd cut your leg off," Retana said.

"No," said Manuel. "It got all right."

20 Retana leaned forward across the desk and pushed a wooden box of cigarettes toward Manuel.

"Have a cigarette," he said.

"Thanks."

Manuel lit it.

25 "Smoke?" he said, offering the match to Retana.

"No," Retana waved his hand, "I never smoke."

Retana watched him smoking.

"Why don't you get a job and go to work?" he said.

"I don't want to work," Manuel said. "I am a bull-fighter."

30 "There aren't any bull-fighters any more," Retana said.

"I'm a bull-fighter," Manuel said.

"Yes, while you're in there," Retana said.

Manuel laughed.

Retana sat, saying nothing and looking at Manuel.

35 "I'll put you in a nocturnal if you want," Retana offered.

"When?" Manuel asked.

"Tomorrow night."

"I don't like to substitute for anybody," Manuel said. That was the way they all got killed. That was the way Salvator got killed. He tapped with his
40 knuckles on the table.

"It's all I've got," Retana said.

"Why don't you put me on next week?" Manuel suggested.

"You wouldn't draw," Retana said. "All they want is Litri and Rubito and La Torre. Those kids are good."

45 "They'd come to see me get it," Manuel said, hopefully.

---

4. **varas**—shafts or pics. **caballos**—horses. 14. **coleta**—bullfighter's pigtail. 35. **nocturnal**—night fight.

"No, they wouldn't. They don't know who you are any more."

"I've got a lot of stuff," Manuel said.

"I'm offering to put you on tomorrow night," Retana said. "You can work with young Hernandez and kill two novillos after the Charlots."

"Whose novillos?" Manuel asked.

"I don't know. Whatever stuff they've got in the corrals. What the veterinaries won't pass in the daytime."

"I don't like to substitute," Manuel said.

"You can take it or leave it," Retana said. He leaned forward over the papers. He was no longer interested. The appeal that Manuel had made to him for a moment when he thought of the old days was gone. He would like to get him to substitute for Larita because he could get him cheaply. He could get others cheaply too. He would like to help him though. Still he had given him the chance. It was up to him.

"How much do I get?" Manuel asked. He was still playing with the idea of refusing. But he knew he could not refuse.

"Two hundred and fifty pesetas," Retana said. He had thought of five hundred, but when he opened his mouth it said two hundred and fifty.

"You pay Villalta seven thousand," Manuel said.

"You're not Villalta," Retana said.

"I know it," Manuel said.

"He draws it, Manolo," Retana said in explanation.

"Sure," said Manuel. He stood up. "Give me three hundred, Retana."

"All right," Retana agreed. He reached in the drawer for a paper.

"Can I have fifty now?" Manuel asked.

"Sure," said Retana. He took a fifty-peseta note out of his pocketbook and laid it, spread out flat, on the table.

Manuel picked it up and put it in his pocket.

"What about a cuadrilla?" he asked.

"There's the boys that always work for me nights," Retana said. "They're all right."

"How about picadors?" Manuel asked.

"They're not much," Retana admitted.

"I've got to have one good pic," Manuel said.

"Get him then," Retana said. "Go and get him."

"Not out of this," Manuel said. "I'm not paying for any cuadrilla out of sixty duros."

Retana said nothing but looked at Manuel across the big desk.

"You know I've got to have one good pic," Manuel said.

Retana said nothing but looked at Manuel from a long way off.

"It isn't right," Manuel said.

Retana was still considering him, leaning back in his chair, considering him from a long way away.

---

4. **novillos**—bulls. **Charlots**—"Charlie Chaplins," comic burlesques by clowns before the fight. 17. **pesetas**—A peseta is a silver coin worth at that time about 20 cents. 29. **cuadrilla**—troupe of bullfighters. 32. **picadors**—men on horseback who "pic" the bulls with lances. 37. **duros**—5-peseta pieces.

"There're the regular pics," he offered.

"I know," Manuel said. "I know your regular pics."

Retana did not smile. Manuel knew it was over.

"All I want is an even break," Manuel said reasoningly. "When I go out
5 there I want to be able to call my shots on the bull. It only takes one good
picador."

He was talking to a man who was no longer listening.

"If you want something extra," Retana said, "go and get it. There will be a
regular cuadrilla out there. Bring as many of your own pics as you want. The
10 charlotada is over by 10.30."

"All right," Manuel said. "If that's the way you feel about it."

"That's the way," Retana said.

"I'll see you tomorrow night," Manuel said.

"I'll be out there," Retana said.

15 Manuel picked up his suitcase and went out.

"Shut the door," Retana called.

Manuel looked back. Retana was sitting forward looking at some papers.
Manuel pulled the door tight until it clicked.

He went down the stairs and out of the door into the hot brightness of the
20 street. It was very hot in the street and the light on the white buildings was
sudden and hard on his eyes. He walked down the shady side of the steep
street toward the Puerta del Sol. The shade felt solid and cool as running water.
The heat came suddenly as he crossed the intersecting streets. Manuel saw no
one he knew in all the people he passed.

25 Just before the Puerta del Sol he turned into a café.

It was quiet in the café. There were a few men sitting at tables against the
wall. At one table four men played cards. Most of the men sat against the wall
smoking, empty coffee-cups and liqueur-glasses before them on the tables. Manuel went through the long room to a small room in back. A man sat at a table
30 in the corner asleep. Manuel sat down at one of the tables.

A waiter came in and stood beside Manuel's table.

"Have you seen Zurito?" Manuel asked him.

"He was in before lunch," the waiter answered. "He won't be back before
five o'clock."

35 "Bring me some coffee and milk and a shot of the ordinary," Manuel said.

The waiter came back into the room carrying a tray with a big coffee-glass
and a liqueur-glass on it. In his left hand he held a bottle of brandy. He
swung these down to the table and a boy who had followed him poured
coffee and milk into the glass from two shiny, spouted pots with long han-
40 dles.

Manuel took off his cap and the waiter noticed his pigtail pinned forward
on his head. He winked at the coffee-boy as he poured out the brandy into
the little glass beside Manuel's coffee. The coffee-boy looked at Manuel's pale
face curiously.

45 "You fighting here?" asked the waiter, corking up the bottle.

10. **charlotada**—the Charlie Chaplin burlesque. 22. **Puerta del Sol**—Gate of the Sun,
famous landmark in Madrid.

"Yes," Manuel said. "Tomorrow."

The waiter stood there, holding the bottle on one hip.

"You in the Charlie Chaplins?" he asked.

The coffee-boy looked away, embarrassed.

"No. In the ordinary."   5

"I thought they were going to have Chaves and Hernandez," the waiter said.

"No. Me and another."

"Who? Chaves or Hernandez?"

"Hernandez, I think."   10

"What's the matter with Chaves?"

"He got hurt."

"Where did you hear that?"

"Retana."

"Hey, Looie," the waiter called to the next room, "Chaves got cogida."   15

Manuel had taken the wrapper off the lumps of sugar and dropped them into his coffee. He stirred it and drank it down, sweet, hot, and warming in his empty stomach. He drank off the brandy.

"Give me another shot of that," he said to the waiter.

The waiter uncorked the bottle and poured the glass full, slopping another   20
drink into the saucer. Another waiter had come up in front of the table. The coffee-boy was gone.

"Is Chaves hurt bad?" the second waiter asked Manuel.

"I don't know," Manuel said, "Retana didn't say."

"A hell of a lot he cares," the tall waiter said. Manuel had not seen him   25
before. He must have just come up.

"If you stand in with Retana in this town, you're a made man," the tall waiter said. "If you aren't in with him, you might just as well go out and shoot yourself."

"You said it," the other waiter who had come in said. "You said it then."   30

"You're right I said it," said the tall waiter. "I know what I'm talking about when I talk about that bird."

"Look what he's done for Villalta," the first waiter said.

"And that ain't all," the tall waiter said. "Look what he's done for Marcial Lalanda. Look what he's done for Nacional."   35

"You said it, kid," agreed the short waiter.

Manuel looked at them, standing talking in front of his table. He had drunk his second brandy. They had forgotten about him. They were not interested in him.

"Look at that bunch of camels," the tall waiter went on. "Did you ever see   40
this Nacional II?"

"I seen him last Sunday, didn't I?" the original waiter said.

"He's a giraffe," the short waiter said.

"What did I tell you?" the tall waiter said. "Those are Retana's boys."

"Say, give me another shot of that," Manuel said. He had poured the brandy   45

15. **cogida**—tossing by the bull.

the waiter had slopped over in the saucer into his glass and drank it while they were talking.

The original waiter poured his glass full mechanically, and the three of them went out of the room talking.

5 In the far corner the man was still asleep, snoring slightly on the intaking breath, his head back against the wall.

Manuel drank his brandy. He felt sleepy himself. It was too hot to go out into the town. Besides there was nothing to do. He wanted to see Zurito. He would go to sleep while he waited. He kicked his suitcase under the table to
10 be sure it was there. Perhaps it would be better to put it back under the seat, against the wall. He leaned down and shoved it under. Then he leaned forward on the table and went to sleep.

When he woke there was someone sitting across the table from him. It was a big man with a heavy brown face like an Indian. He had been sitting there
15 some time. He had waved the waiter away and sat reading the paper and occasionally looking down at Manuel, asleep, his head on the table. He read the paper laboriously, forming the words with his lips as he read. When it tired him he looked at Manuel. He sat heavily in the chair, his black Cordoba hat tipped forward.

20 Manuel sat up and looked at him.

"Hello, Zurito," he said.

"Hello, kid," the big man said.

"I've been asleep." Manuel rubbed his forehead with the back of his fist.

"I thought maybe you were."

25 "How's everything?"

"Good. How is everything with you?"

"Not so good."

They were both silent. Zurito, the picador, looked at Manuel's white face. Manuel looked down at the picador's enormous hands folding the paper to put
30 away in his pocket.

"I got a favor to ask you, Manos," Manuel said.

Manosduros was Zurito's nickname. He never heard it without thinking of his huge hands. He put them forward on the table self-consciously.

"Let's have a drink," he said.

35 "Sure," said Manuel.

The waiter came and went and came again. He went out of the room looking back at the two men at the table.

"What's the matter, Manolo?" Zurito set down his glass.

"Would you pic two bulls for me tomorrow night?" Manuel asked, looking
40 up at Zurito across the table.

"No," said Zurito. "I'm not pic-ing."

Manuel looked down at his glass. He had expected that answer; now he had it. Well, he had it.

"I'm sorry, Manolo, but I'm not pic-ing." Zurito looked at his hands.

45 "That's all right," Manuel said.

32. **Manosduros**—Hard Hands.

"I'm too old," Zurito said.

"I just asked you," Manuel said.

"Is it the nocturnal tomorrow?"

"That's it. I figured if I had just one good pic, I could get away with it."

"How much are you getting?"   5

"Three hundred pesetas."

"I get more than that for pic-ing."

"I know," said Manuel. "I didn't have any right to ask you."

"What do you keep on doing it for?" Zurito asked. "Why don't you cut off your coleta, Manolo?"   10

"I don't know," Manuel said.

"You're pretty near as old as I am," Zurito said.

"I don't know," Manuel said. "I got to do it. If I can fix it so that I get an even break, that's all I want. I got to stick with it, Manos."

"No, you don't."   15

"Yes, I do. I've tried keeping away from it."

"I know how you feel. But it isn't right. You ought to get out and stay out."

"I can't do it. Besides, I've been going good lately."

Zurito looked at his face.

"You've been in the hospital."   20

"But I was going great when I got hurt."

Zurito said nothing. He tipped the cognac out of his saucer into his glass.

"The papers said they never saw a better faena," Manuel said.

Zurito looked at him.

"You know when I get going I'm good," Manuel said.   25

"You're too old," the picador said.

"No," said Manuel. "You're ten years older than I am."

"With me it's different."

"I'm not too old," Manuel said.

They sat silent, Manuel watching the picador's face.   30

"I was going great till I got hurt," Manuel offered.

"You ought to have seen me, Manos," Manuel said, reproachfully.

"I don't want to see you," Zurito said. "It makes me nervous."

"You haven't seen me lately."

"I've seen you plenty."   35

Zurito looked at Manuel, avoiding his eyes.

"You ought to quit it, Manolo."

"I can't," Manuel said. "I'm going good now, I tell you."

Zurito leaned forward, his hands on the table.

"Listen. I'll pic for you and if you don't go big tomorrow night, you'll quit.   40
See? Will you do that?"

"Sure."

Zurito leaned back, relieved.

"You got to quit," he said. "No monkey business. You got to cut the coleta."

"I won't have to quit," Manuel said. "You watch me. I've got the stuff."   45

23. faena—matador's over-all performance in the final third of a bullfight.

Zurito stood up. He felt tired from arguing.

"You got to quit," he said. "I'll cut your coleta myself."

"No, you won't," Manuel said. "You won't have a chance."

Zurito called the waiter.

5   "Come on," said Zurito. "Come on up to the house."

Manuel reached under the seat for his suitcase. He was happy. He knew Zurito would pic for him. He was the best picador living. It was all simple now.

"Come on up to the house and we'll eat," Zurito said.

10   Manuel stood in the patio de caballos waiting for the Charlie Chaplins to be over. Zurito stood beside him. Where they stood it was dark. The high door that led into the bull-ring was shut. Above them they heard a shout, then another shout of laughter. Then there was silence. Manuel liked the smell of the stables about the patio de caballos. It smelt good in the dark. There was another roar from the arena and then applause, prolonged applause, going on and on.

"You ever seen these fellows?" Zurito asked, big and looming beside Manuel in the dark.

"No," Manuel said.

20   "They're pretty funny," Zurito said. He smiled to himself in the dark.

The high, double, tight-fitting door into the bull-ring swung open and Manuel saw the ring in the hard light of the arc-lights, the plaza, dark all the way around, rising high; around the edge of the ring were running and bowing two men dressed like tramps, followed by a third in the uniform of a hotel bell-boy who stooped and picked up the hats and canes thrown down onto the sand and tossed them back up into the darkness.

The electric light went on in the patio.

"I'll climb onto one of those ponies while you collect the kids," Zurito said.

Behind them came the jingle of the mules, coming out to go into the arena and be hitched onto the dead bull.

The members of the cuadrilla, who had been watching the burlesque from the runway between the barrera and the seats, came walking back and stood in a group talking, under the electric light in the patio. A good-looking lad in a silver-and-orange suit came up to Manuel and smiled.

35   "I'm Hernandez," he said and put out his hand.

Manuel shook it.

"They're regular elephants we've got tonight," the boy said cheerfully.

"They're big ones with horns," Manuel agreed.

"You drew the worst lot," the boy said.

40   "That's all right," Manuel said. "The bigger they are, the more meat for the poor."

"Where did you get that one?" Hernandez grinned.

"That's an old one," Manuel said. "You line up your cuadrilla, so I can see what I've got."

10. **patio de caballos**—court where the horses are kept. 32. **barrera**—red wooden fence around the bull ring.

"You've got some good kids," Hernandez said. He was very cheerful. He had been on twice before in nocturnals and was beginning to get a following in Madrid. He was happy the fight would start in a few minutes.

"Where are the pics?" Manuel asked.

"They're back in the corrals fighting about who gets the beautiful horses," 5 Hernandez grinned.

The mules came through the gate in a rush, the whips snapping, bells jangling and the young bull ploughing a furrow of sand.

They formed up for the paseo as soon as the bull had gone through.

Manuel and Hernandez stood in front. The youths of the cuadrillas were 10 behind, their heavy capes furled over their arms. In back, the four picadors, mounted, holding their steel-tipped push-poles erect in the half-dark of the corral.

"It's a wonder Retana wouldn't give us enough light to see the horses by," one picador said.   15

"He knows we'll be happier if we don't get too good a look at these skins," another pic answered.

"This thing I'm on barely keeps me off the ground," the first picador said.

"Well, they're horses."

"Sure, they're horses."   20

They talked, sitting their gaunt horses in the dark.

Zurito said nothing. He had the only steady horse of the lot. He had tried him, wheeling him in the corrals and he responded to the bit and the spurs. He had taken the bandage off his right eye and cut the strings where they had tied his ears tight shut at the base. He was a good, solid horse, solid on his 25 legs. That was all he needed. He intended to ride him all through the corrida. He had already, since he had mounted, sitting in the half-dark in the big, quilted saddle, waiting for the paseo, pic-ed through the whole corrida in his mind. The other picadors went on talking on both sides of him. He did not hear them.   30

The two matadors stood together in front of their three peones, their capes furled over their left arms in the same fashion. Manuel was thinking about the three lads in back of him. They were all three Madrilenos, like Hernandez, boys about nineteen. One of them, a gypsy, serious, aloof, and dark-faced, he liked the look of. He turned.   35

"What's your name, kid?" he asked the gypsy.

"Fuentes," the gypsy said.

"That's a good name," Manuel said.

The gypsy smiled, showing his teeth.

"You take the bull and give him a little run when he comes out," Manuel 40 said.

"All right," the gypsy said. His face was serious. He began to think about just what he would do.

9. **paseo**—bullfighters' entry into the ring and the procession across it. 31. **matadors**—leading bullfighters who finally kill the bull. **peones**—men who fight under direction of a matador, chiefly placing the barbed shafts (banderillas) in the bull. 33. **Madrilenos**—natives of Madrid.

"Here she goes," Manuel said to Hernandez.

"All right. We'll go."

Heads up, swinging with the music, their right arms swinging free, they stepped out, crossing the sanded arena under the arc-lights, the cuadrillas open-
5 ing out behind, the picadors riding after; behind came the bull-ring servants and the jingling mules. The crowd applauded Hernandez as they marched across the arena. Arrogant, swinging, they looked straight ahead as they marched.

They bowed before the president, and the procession broke up into its com-
10 ponent parts. The bull-fighters went over to the barrera and changed their heavy mantles for the light fighting capes. The mules went out. The picadors galloped jerkily around the ring, and two rode out the gate they had come in by. The servants swept the sand smooth.

Manuel drank a glass of water poured for him by one of Retana's deputies,
15 who was acting as his manager and sword-handler. Hernandez came over from speaking with his own manager.

"You got a good hand, kid," Manuel complimented him.

"They like me," Hernandez said happily.

"How did the paseo go?" Manuel asked Retana's man.

20 "Like a wedding," said the handler. "Fine. You came out like Joselito and Belmonte."

Zurito rode by, a bulky equestrian statue. He wheeled his horse and faced him toward the toril on the far side of the ring where the bull would come out. It was strange under the arc-light. He pic-ed in the hot afternoon sun for
25 big money. He didn't like this arc-light business. He wished they would get started.

Manuel went up to him.

"Pic him, Manos," he said. "Cut him down to size for me."

"I'll pic him, kid," Zurito spat on the sand. "I'll make him jump out of the
30 ring."

"Lean on him, Manos," Manuel said.

"I'll lean on him," Zurito said. "What's holding it up?"

"He's coming now," Manuel said.

Zurito sat there, his feet in the box-stirrups, his great legs in the buckskin-
35 covered armor gripping the horse, the reins in his left hand, the long pic held in his right hand, his broad hat well down over his eyes to shade them from the lights, watching the distant door of the toril. His horse's ears quivered. Zurito patted him with his left hand.

The red door of the toril swung back and for a moment Zurito looked into
40 the empty passageway far across the arena. Then the bull came out in a rush, skidding on his four legs as he came out under the lights, then charging in a gallop, moving softly in a fast gallop, silent except as he woofed through wide nostrils as he charged, glad to be free after the dark pen.

In the first row of seats, slightly bored, leaning forward to write on the
45 cement wall in front of his knees, the substitute bull-fight critic of *El Heraldo*

20-21. **Joselito** . . . **Belmonte**—two famous bullfighters. 23. **toril**—bull enclosure.

scribbled: "Campagnero, Negro, 42, came out at 90 miles an hour with plenty of gas—"

Manuel, leaning against the barrera, watching the bull, waved his hand and the gypsy ran out, trailing his cape. The bull, in full gallop, pivoted and charged the cape, his head down, his tail rising. The gypsy moved in a zigzag, 5 and as he passed, the bull caught sight of him and abandoned the cape to charge the man. The gyp sprinted and vaulted the red fence of the barrera as the bull struck it with his horns. He tossed into it twice with his horns, banging into the wood blindly.

The critic of *El Heraldo* lit a cigarette and tossed the match at the bull, then 10 wrote in his note-book, "large and with enough horns to satisfy the cash customers, Campagnero showed a tendency to cut into the terrain of the bull-fighters."

Manuel stepped out on the hard sand as the bull banged into the fence. Out of the corner of his eye he saw Zurito sitting the white horse close to the bar- 15 rera, about a quarter of the way around the ring to the left. Manuel held the cape close in front of him, a fold in each hand, and shouted at the bull. "Huh! Huh!" The bull turned, seemed to brace against the fence as he charged in a scramble, driving into the cape as Manuel side-stepped, pivoted on his heels with the charge of the bull, and swung the cape just ahead of the horns. At 20 the end of the swing he was facing the bull again and held the cape in the same position close in front of his body, and pivoted again as the bull re-charged. Each time, as he swung, the crowd shouted.

Four times he swung with the bull, lifting the cape so it billowed full, and each time bringing the bull around to charge again. Then, at the end of the 25 fifth swing, he held the cape against his hip and pivoted, so the cape swung out like a ballet dancer's skirt and wound the bull around himself like a belt, to step clear, leaving the bull facing Zurito on the white horse, come up and planted firm, the horse facing the bull, its ears forward, its lips nervous, Zurito, his hat over his eyes, leaning forward, the long pole sticking out before and 30 behind in a sharp angle under his right arm, held half-way down, the triangular iron point facing the bull.

El Heraldo's second-string critic, drawing on his cigarette, his eyes on the bull, wrote: "The veteran Manolo designed a series of acceptable veronicas, ending in a very Belmontistic recorte that earned applause from the regulars, 35 and we entered the tercio of the cavalry."

Zurito sat his horse, measuring the distance between the bull and the end of the pic. As he looked, the bull gathered himself together and charged, his eyes on the horse's chest. As he lowered his head to hook, Zurito sunk the point of the pic in the swelling hump of muscle above the bull's shoulder, leaned all 40 his weight on the shaft, and with his left hand pulled the white horse into the air, front hoofs pawing, and swung him to the right as he pushed the bull under and through so the horns passed safely under the horse's belly and the horse came down, quivering, the bull's tail brushing his chest as he charged the cape Hernandez offered him.   45

34. **veronicas**—passes with the cape. 35. **recorte**—a pass with the cape involving quick movements. 36. **tercio**—third part.

Hernandez ran sideways, taking the bull out and away with the cape, toward the other picador. He fixed him with a swing of the cape, squarely facing the horse and rider, and stepped back. As the bull saw the horse he charged. The picador's lance slid along his back, and as the shock of the charge lifted
5   the horse, the picador was already half-way out of the saddle, lifting his right leg clear as he missed with the lance and falling to the left side to keep the horse between him and the bull. The horse, lifted and gored, crashed over with the bull driving into him, the picador gave a shove with his boots against the horse and lay clear, waiting to be lifted and hauled away and put on his feet.
10 Manuel let the bull drive into the fallen horse; he was in no hurry, the picador was safe; besides, it did a picador like that good to worry. He'd stay on longer next time. Lousy pics! He looked across the sand at Zurito a little way out from the barrera, his horse rigid, waiting.

"Huh!" he called to the bull, "Tomar!" holding the cape in both hands so it
15 would catch his eye. The bull detached himself from the horse and charged the cape, and Manuel, running sideways and holding the cape spread wide, stopped, swung on his heels, and brought the bull sharply around facing Zurito.

"Campagnero accepted a pair of varas for the death of one rosinante, with Hernandez and Manolo at the quites," *El Heraldo's* critic wrote. "He pressed
20 on the iron and clearly showed he was no horse-lover. The veteran Zurito resurrected some of his old stuff with the pike-pole, notably the suerte—"

"Olé! Olé!" the man sitting beside him shouted. The shout was lost in the roar of the crowd, and he slapped the critic on the back. The critic looked up to see Zurito, directly below him, leaning far out over his horse, the length
25 of the pic rising in a sharp angle under his armpit, holding the pic almost by the point, bearing down with all his weight, holding the bull off, the bull pushing and driving to get at the horse, and Zurito, far out, on top of him, holding him, holding him, and slowly pivoting the horse against the pressure, so that at last he was clear. Zurito felt the moment when the horse was clear
30 and the bull could come past, and relaxed the absolute steel lock of his resistance, and the triangular steel point of the pic ripped in the bull's hump of shoulder muscle as he tore loose to find Hernandez's cape before his muzzle. He charged blindly into the cape and the boy took him out into the open arena.

Zurito sat patting his horse and looking at the bull charging the cape that
35 Hernandez swung for him out under the bright light while the crowd shouted.

"You see that one?" he said to Manuel.

"It was a wonder," Manuel said.

"I got him that time," Zurito said. "Look at him now."

At the conclusion of a closely turned pass of the cape the bull slid to his
40 knees. He was up at once, but far out across the sand Manuel and Zurito saw the shine of the pumping flow of blood, smooth against the black of the bull's shoulder.

"I got him that time," Zurito said.

"He's a good bull," Manuel said.

---

18. rosinante—old nag; named for Don Quixote's steed. **19. quites**—the turning away or diverting of the bull from anyone endangered by him. **21. suerte**—formal maneuver by fixed rule. **22. Olé!**—Bravo!

"If they gave me another shot at him, I'd kill him," Zurito said.

"They'll change the thirds on us," Manuel said.

"Look at him now," Zurito said.

"I got to go over there," Manuel said, and started on a run for the other side of the ring, where the monos were leading a horse out by the bridle toward the bull, whacking him on the legs with rods and all, in a procession, trying to get him toward the bull, who stood, dropping his head, pawing, unable to make up his mind to charge.

Zurito, sitting his horse, walking him toward the scene, not missing any detail, scowled.

Finally the bull charged, the horse leaders ran for the barrera, the picador hit too far back, and the bull got under the horse, lifted him, threw him onto his back.

Zurito watched. The monos, in their red shirts, running out to drag the picador clear. The picador, now on his feet, swearing and flopping his arms. Manuel and Hernandez standing ready with their capes. And the bull, the great, black bull, with a horse on his back, hooves dangling, the bridle caught in the horns. Black bull with a horse on his back, staggering short-legged, then arching his neck and lifting, thrusting, charging to slide the horse off, horse sliding down. Then the bull into a lunging charge at the cape Manuel spread for him.

The bull was slower now, Manuel felt. He was bleeding badly. There was a sheen of blood all down his flank.

Manuel offered him the cape again. There he came, eyes open, ugly, watching the cape. Manuel stepped to the side and raised his arms, tightening the cape ahead of the bull for the veronica.

Now he was facing the bull. Yes, his head was going down a little. He was carrying it lower. That was Zurito.

Manuel flopped the cape; there he comes; he side-stepped and swung in another veronica. He's shooting awfully accurately, he thought. He's had enough fight, so he's watching now. He's hunting now. Got his eye on me. But I always give him the cape.

He shook the cape at the bull; there he comes; he side-stepped. Awful close that time. I don't want to work that close to him.

The edge of the cape was wet with blood where it had swept along the bull's back as he went by.

All right, here's the last one.

Manuel, facing the bull, having turned with him each charge, offered the cape with his two hands. The bull looked at him. Eyes watching, horns straight forward, the bull looked at him, watching.

"Huh!" Manuel said, "Toro!" and leaning back, swung the cape forward. Here he comes. He side-stepped, swung the cape in back of him, and pivoted, so the bull followed a swirl of cape and then was left with nothing, fixed by the pass, dominated by the cape. Manuel swung the cape under his muzzle with one hand, to show the bull was fixed, and walked away.

There was no applause.

5. **monos**—short for monosabios, bull-ring servants wearing red shirts.

Manuel walked across the sand toward the barrera, while Zurito rode out of the ring. The trumpet had blown to change the act to the planting of the banderillos while Manuel had been working with the bull. He had not consciously noticed it. The monos were spreading canvas over the two dead horses
5   and sprinkling sawdust around them.

Manuel came up to the barrera for a drink of water. Retana's man handed him the heavy porous jug.

Fuentes, the tall gypsy, was standing holding a pair of banderillos, holding them together, slim, red sticks, fish-hook points out. He looked at Manuel.
10 "Go on out there," Manuel said.

The gypsy trotted out. Manuel set down the jug and watched. He wiped his face with his handkerchief.

The critic of *El Heraldo* reached for the bottle of warm champagne that stood between his feet, took a drink, and finished his paragraph.
15 "—the aged Manolo rated no applause for a vulgar series of lances with the cape and we entered the third of the palings."

Alone in the center of the ring the bull stood, still fixed. Fuentes, tall, flat-backed, walking toward him arrogantly, his arms spread out, the two slim, red sticks, one in each hand, held by the fingers, points straight forward.
20 Fuentes walked forward. Back of him and to one side was a peon with a cape. The bull looked at him and was no longer fixed.

His eyes watched Fuentes, now standing still. Now he leaned back, calling to him. Fuentes twitched the two banderillos and the light on the steel points caught the bull's eye.
25 His tail went up and he charged.

He came straight, his eyes on the man. Fuentes stood still, leaning back, the banderillos pointing forward. As the bull lowered his head to hook, Fuentes leaned backward, his arms came together and rose, his two hands touching, the banderillos two descending red lines, and leaning forward drove the points
30 into the bull's shoulder, leaning far in over the bull's horns and pivoting on the two upright sticks, his legs tight together, his body curving to one side to let the bull pass.

"Olé!" from the crowd.

The bull was hooking wildly, jumping like a trout, all four feet off the
35 ground. The red shaft of the banderillos tossed as he jumped.

Manuel, standing at the barrera, noticed that he looked always to the right.

"Tell him to drop the next pair on the right," he said to the kid who started to run out to Fuentes with the new banderillos.

A heavy hand fell on his shoulder. It was Zurito.
40 "How do you feel, kid?" he asked.

Manuel was watching the bull.

Zurito leaned forward on the barrera, leaning the weight of his body on his arms. Manuel turned to him.

"You're going good," Zurito said.
45 Manuel shook his head. He had nothing to do now until the next third. The gypsy was very good with the banderillos. The bull would come to him

3. **banderillos**—fighters who help run with the cape and place the barbs.

in the next third in good shape. He was a good bull. It had all been easy up
to now. The final stuff with the sword was all he worried over. He did not
really worry. He did not even think about it. But standing there he had a
heavy sense of apprehension. He looked out at the bull, planning his faena,
his work with the red cloth that was to reduce the bull, to make him man- 5
ageable.

The gypsy was walking out toward the bull again, walking heel-and-toe, insultingly, like a ballroom dancer, the red shafts of the banderillos twitching
with his walk. The bull watched him, not fixed now, hunting him, but waiting to get close enough so he could be sure of getting him, getting the horns 10
into him.

As Fuentes walked forward the bull charged. Fuentes ran across the quarter
of a circle as the bull charged and, as he passed running backward, stopped,
swung forward, rose on his toes, arm straight out, and sunk the banderillos
straight down into the tight of the big shoulder muscles as the bull missed 15
him.

The crowd were wild about it.

"That kid won't stay in this night stuff long," Retana's man said to Zurito.

"He's good," Zurito said.

"Watch him now." 20

They watched.

Fuentes was standing with his back against the barrera. Two of the cuadrilla
were back of him, with their capes ready to flop over the fence to distract the
bull.

The bull, with his tongue out, his barrel heaving, was watching the gypsy. 25
He thought he had him now. Back against the red planks. Only a short charge
away. The bull watched him.

The gypsy bent back, drew back his arms, the banderillos pointing at the
bull. He called to the bull, stamped one foot. The bull was suspicious. He
wanted the man. No more barbs in the shoulder. 30

Fuentes walked a little closer to the bull. Bent back. Called again. Somebody
in the crowd shouted a warning.

"He's too damn close," Zurito said.

"Watch him," Retana's man said.

Leaning back, inciting the bull with the banderillos, Fuentes jumped, both 35
feet off the ground. As he jumped the bull's tail rose and he charged. Fuentes
came down on his toes, arms straight out, whole body arching forward, and
drove the shafts straight down as he swung his body clear of the right horn.

The bull crashed into the barrera where the flopping capes had attracted his
eye as he lost the man. 40

The gypsy came running along the barrera toward Manuel, taking the applause of the crowd. His vest was ripped where he had not quite cleared the
point of the horn. He was happy about it, showing it to the spectators. He
made the tour of the ring. Zurito saw him go by, smiling, pointing at his vest.
He smiled. 45

Somebody else was planting the last pair of banderillos. Nobody was paying
any attention.

Retana's man tucked a baton inside the red cloth of a muleta, folded the cloth over it, and handed it over the barrera to Manuel. He reached in the leather sword-case, took out a sword, and holding it by its leather scabbard, reached it over the fence to Manuel. Manuel pulled the blade out by the red hilt and the scabbard fell limp.

He looked at Zurito. The big man saw he was sweating.

"Now you get him, kid," Zurito said.

Manuel nodded.

"He's in good shape," Zurito said.

"Just like you want him," Retana's man assured him.

Manuel nodded.

The trumpeter, up under the roof, blew for the final act, and Manuel walked across the arena toward where, up in the dark boxes, the president must be.

In the front row of seats the substitute bull-fight critic of *El Heraldo* took a long drink of the warm champagne. He had decided it was not worth while to write a running story and would write up the corrida back in the office. What the hell was it anyway? Only a nocturnal. If he missed anything he would get it out of the morning papers. He took another drink of the champagne. He had a date at Maxim's at twelve. Who were these bull-fighters anyway? Kids and bums. A bunch of bums. He put his pad of paper in his pocket and looked over toward Manuel, standing very much alone in the ring, gesturing with his hat in a salute toward a box he could not see high up in the dark plaza. Out in the ring the bull stood quiet, looking at nothing.

"I dedicate this bull to you, Mr. President, and to the public of Madrid, the most intelligent and generous of the world," was what Manuel was saying. It was a formula. He said it all. It was a little long for nocturnal use.

He bowed at the dark, straightened, tossed his hat over his shoulder, and, carrying the muleta in his left hand and the sword in his right, walked out toward the bull.

Manuel walked toward the bull. The bull looked at him; his eyes were quick. Manuel noticed the way the banderillos hung down on his left shoulder and the steady sheen of blood from Zurito's pic-ing. He noticed the way the bull's feet were. As he walked forward, holding the muleta in his left hand and the sword in his right, he watched the bull's feet. The bull could not charge without gathering his feet together. Now he stood square on them, dully.

Manuel walked toward him, watching his feet. This was all right. He could do this. He must work to get the bull's head down, so he could go in past the horns and kill him. He did not think about the sword, not about killing the bull. He thought about one thing at a time. The coming things oppressed him, though. Walking forward, watching the bull's feet, he saw successively his eyes, his wet muzzle, and the wide, forward-pointing spread of his horns. The bull had light circles about his eyes. His eyes watched Manuel. He felt he was going to get this little one with the white face.

Standing still now and spreading the red cloth of the muleta with the sword, pricking the point into the cloth so that the sword, now held in his left hand,

1. **muleta**—red flannel flag used by bullfighters.

spread the red flannel like the jib of a boat, Manuel noticed the points of the bull's horns. One of them was splintered from banging against the barrera. The other was sharp as a porcupine quill. Manuel noticed while spreading the muleta that the white base of the horn was stained red. While he noticed these things he did not lose sight of the bull's feet. The bull watched Manuel steadily. 5

He's on the defensive now, Manuel thought. He's reserving himself. I've got to bring him out of that and get his head down. Always get his head down. Zurito had his head down once, but he's come back. He'll bleed when I start him going and that will bring it down.

Holding the muleta, with the sword in his left hand widening it in front 10 of him, he called to the bull.

The bull looked at him.

He leaned back insultingly and shook the wide-spread flannel.

The bull saw the muleta. It was a bright scarlet under the arc-light. The bull's legs tightened. 15

Here he comes. Whoosh! Manuel turned as the bull came and raised the muleta so that it passed over the bull's horns and swept down his broad back from head to tail. The bull had gone clean up in the air with the charge. Manuel had not moved.

At the end of the pass the bull turned like a cat coming around a corner 20 and faced Manuel.

He was on the offensive again. His heaviness was gone. Manuel noted the fresh blood shining down the black shoulder and dripping down the bull's leg. He drew the sword out of the muleta and held it in his right hand. The muleta held low down in his left hand, leaning toward the left, he called to the bull. 25 The bull's legs tightened, his eyes on the muleta. Here he comes, Manuel thought. Yuh!

He swung with the charge, sweeping the muleta ahead of the bull, his feet firm, the sword following the curve, a point of light under the arcs.

The bull recharged as the pase natural finished and Manuel raised the muleta 30 for a pase de pecho. Firmly planted, the bull came by his chest under the raised muleta. Manuel leaned his head back to avoid the clattering banderillo shafts. The hot, black bull body touched his chest as it passed.

Too damn close, Manuel thought. Zurito, leaning on the barrera, spoke rapidly to the gypsy, who trotted out toward Manuel with a cape. Zurito pulled 35 his hat down low and looked out across the arena at Manuel.

Manuel was facing the bull again, the muleta held low and to the left. The bull's head was down as he watched the muleta.

"If it was Belmonte doing that stuff, they'd go crazy," Retana's man said.

Zurito said nothing. He was watching Manuel out in the center of the arena. 40

"Where did the boss dig this fellow up?" Retana's man asked.

"Out of the hospital," Zurito said.

"That's where he's going damn quick," Retana's man said.

Zurito turned on him.

"Knock on that," he said, pointing to the barrera. 45

30. **pase natural**—pass with cape or muleta in the left hand. 31. **pase de pecho**—maneuver by which the bull is made to pass before the matador's chest.

"I was just kidding, man," Retana's man said.

"Knock on the wood."

Retana's man leaned forward and knocked three times on the barrera.

"Watch the faena," Zurito said.

5   Out in the center of the ring, under the lights, Manuel was kneeling, facing the bull, and as he raised the muleta in both hands the bull charged, tail up.

Manuel swung his body clear and, as the bull recharged, brought around the muleta in a half-circle that pulled the bull to his knees.

"Why, that one's a great bull-fighter," Retana's man said.

10   "No, he's not," said Zurito.

Manuel stood up and, the muleta in his left hand, the sword in his right, acknowledged the applause from the dark plaza.

The bull had humped himself up from his knees and stood waiting, his head hung low.

15   Zurito spoke to two of the other lads of the cuadrilla and they ran out to stand back of Manuel with their capes. There were four men back of him now. Hernandez had followed him since he first came out with the muleta. Fuentes stood watching, his cape held against his body, tall, in repose, watching lazy-eyed. Now the two came up. Hernandez motioned them to stand one at each

20 side. Manuel stood alone, facing the bull.

Manuel waved back the men with the capes. Stepping back cautiously, they saw his face was white and sweating.

Didn't they know enough to keep back? Did they want to catch the bull's eye with the capes after he was fixed and ready? He had enough to worry

25 about without that kind of thing.

The bull was standing, his four feet square, looking at the muleta. Manuel furled the muleta in his left hand. The bull's eyes watched it. His body was heavy on his feet. He carried his head low, but not too low.

Manuel lifted the muleta at him. The bull did not move. Only his eyes

30 watched.

He's all lead, Manuel thought. He's all square. He's framed right. He'll take it.

He thought in bull-fight terms. Sometimes he had a thought and the particular piece of slang would not come into his mind and he could not realize

35 the thought. His instincts and his knowledge worked automatically, and his brain worked slowly and in words. He knew all about bulls. He did not have to think about them. He just did the right thing. His eyes noted things and his body performed the necessary measures without thought. If he thought about it, he would be gone.

40   Now, facing the bull, he was conscious of many things at the same time. There were the horns, the one splintered, the other smoothly sharp, the need to profile himself toward the left horn, lance himself short and straight, lower the muleta so the bull would follow it, and, going in over the horns, put the sword all the way into a little spot about as big as a five-peseta piece straight in

45 back of the neck, between the sharp pitch of the bull's shoulders. He must do all this and must then come out from between the horns. He was conscious he must do all this, but his only thought was in words: "Corto y derecho."

"Corto y derecho," he thought, furling the muleta. Short and straight. Corto
y derecho, he drew the sword out of the muleta, profiled on the splintered left
horn, dropped the muleta across his body, so his right hand with the sword on
the level with his eye made the sign of the cross, and, rising on his toes, sighted
along the dipping blade of the sword at the spot high up between the bull's 5
shoulders.

Corto y derecho he launched himself on the bull.

There was a shock, and he felt himself go up in the air. He pushed on the
sword as he went up and over, and it flew out of his hand. He hit the ground
and the bull was on him. Manuel, lying on the ground, kicked at the bull's 10
muzzle with his slippered feet. Kicking, kicking, the bull after him, missing
him in his excitement, bumping him with his head, driving the horns into the
sand. Kicking like a man keeping a ball in the air, Manuel kept the bull from
getting a clean thrust at him.

Manuel felt the wind on his back from the capes flopping at the bull, and 15
then the bull was gone, gone over him in a rush. Dark, as his belly went over.
Not even stepped on.

Manuel stood up and picked up the muleta. Fuentes handed him the sword.
It was bent where it had struck the shoulder-blade. Manuel straightened it
on his knee and ran toward the bull, standing now beside one of the dead 20
horses. As he ran, his jacket flopped where it had been ripped under his arm
pit.

"Get him out of there," Manuel shouted to the gypsy. The bull had smelled
the blood of the dead horse and ripped into the canvas-cover with his horns.
He charged Fuentes's cape, with the canvas hanging from his splintered horn, 25
and the crowd laughed. Out in the ring, he tossed his head to rid himself of
the canvas. Hernandez, running up from behind him, grabbed the end of the
canvas and neatly lifted it off the horn.

The bull followed it in a half-charge and stopped still. He was on the defensive again. Manuel was walking toward him with the sword and muleta. 30
Manuel swung the muleta before him. The bull would not charge.

Manuel profiled toward the bull, sighting along the dipping blade of the
sword. The bull was motionless, seemingly dead on his feet, incapable of another charge.

Manuel rose to his toes, sighting along the steel, and charged. 35

Again there was the shock and he felt himself being borne back in a rush,
to strike hard on the sand. There was no chance of kicking this time. The bull
was on top of him. Manuel lay as though dead, his head on his arms, and the
bull bumped him. Bumped his back, bumped his face in the sand. He felt the
horn go into the sand between his folded arms. The bull hit him in the small 40
of the back. His face drove into the sand. The horn drove through one of his
sleeves and the bull ripped it off. Manuel was tossed clear and the bull followed
the capes.

Manuel got up, found the sword and muleta, tried the point of the sword
with his thumb, and then ran toward the barrera for a new sword. 45

Retana's man handed him the sword over the edge of the barrera.

"Wipe off your face," he said.

Manuel, running again toward the bull, wiped his bloody face with his hand-kerchief. He had not seen Zurito. Where was Zurito?

The cuadrilla had stepped away from the bull and waited with their capes. The bull stood, heavy and dull again after the action.

5 Manuel walked toward him with the muleta. He stopped and shook it. The bull did not respond. He passed it right and left, left and right before the bull's muzzle. The bull's eyes watched it and turned with the swing, but he would not charge. He was waiting for Manuel.

Manuel was worried. There was nothing to do but go in. Corto y derecho.
10 He profiled close to the bull, crossed the muleta in front of his body and charged. As he pushed in the sword, he jerked his body to the left to clear the horn. The bull passed him and the sword shot up in the air, twinkling under the arc-lights, to fall red-hilted on the sand.

Manuel ran over and picked it up. It was bent and he straightened it over
15 his knee.

As he came running toward the bull, fixed again now, he passed Hernandez standing with his cape.

"He's all bone," the boy said encouragingly.

Manuel nodded, wiping his face. He put the bloody handkerchief in his
20 pocket.

There was the bull. He was close to the barrera now. Damn him. Maybe he was all bone. Maybe there was not any place for the sword to go in. The hell there wasn't! He'd show them.

He tried a pass with the muleta and the bull did not move. Manuel chopped
25 the muleta back and forth in front of the bull. Nothing doing.

He furled the muleta, drew the sword out, profiled and drove in on the bull. He felt the sword buckle as he shoved it in, leaning his weight on it, and then it shot high in the air, end-over-ending into the crowd. Manuel had jerked clear as the sword jumped.

30 The first cushions thrown down out of the dark missed him. Then one hit him in the face, his bloody face looking toward the crowd. They were coming down fast. Spotting the sand. Somebody threw an empty champagne-bottle from close range. It hit Manuel on the foot. He stood there watching the dark, where the things were coming from. Then something whished through the air
35 and struck by him. Manuel leaned over and picked it up. It was his sword. He straightened it over his knee and gestured with it to the crowd.

"Thank you," he said. "Thank you."

Oh, the dirty bastards! Dirty bastards! Oh, the lousy, dirty bastards! He kicked into a cushion as he ran.

40 There was the bull. The same as ever. All right, you dirty, lousy bastard!
Manuel passed the muleta in front of the bull's black muzzle.
Nothing doing.

You won't! All right. He stepped close and jammed the sharp peak of the muleta into the bull's damp muzzle.

45 The bull was on him as he jumped back and as he tripped on a cushion he felt the horn go into him, into his side. He grabbed the horn with his two hands and rode backward, holding tight onto the place. The bull

tossed him and he was clear. He lay still. It was all right. The bull was gone.

He got up coughing and feeling broken and gone. The dirty bastards!

"Give me the sword," he shouted. "Give me the stuff."

Fuentes came up with the muleta and the sword.

Hernandez put his arm around him. 5

"Go on to the infirmary, man," he said. "Don't be a damn fool."

"Get away from me," Manuel said. "Get to hell away from me."

He twisted free. Hernandez shrugged his shoulders. Manuel ran toward the bull.

There was the bull standing, heavy, firmly planted. 10

All right, you bastard! Manuel drew the sword out of the muleta, sighted with the same movement, and flung himself onto the bull. He felt the sword go in all the way. Right up to the guard. Four fingers and his thumb into the bull. The blood was hot on his knuckles, and he was on top of the bull.

The bull lurched with him as he lay on, and seemed to sink; then he was 15 standing clear. He looked at the bull going down slowly over on his side, then suddenly four feet in the air.

Then he gestured at the crowd, his hand warm from the bull blood.

All right, you bastards! He wanted to say something, but he started to cough. It was hot and choking. He looked down for the muleta. He must go 20 over and salute the president. President, hell! He was sitting down looking at something. It was the bull. His four feet up. Thick tongue out. Things crawling around on his belly and under his legs. Crawling where the hair was thin. Dead bull. To hell with the bull! To hell with them all! He started to get to his feet and commenced to cough. He sat down again, coughing. Somebody 25 came and pushed him up.

They carried him across the ring to the infirmary, running with him across the sand, standing blocked at the gate as the mules came in, then around under the dark passageway, men grunting as they took him up the stairway, and then laid him down. 30

The doctor and two men in white were waiting for him. They laid him out on the table. They were cutting away his shirt. Manuel felt tired. His whole chest felt scalding inside. He started to cough and they held something to his mouth. Everybody was very busy.

There was an electric light in his eyes. He shut his eyes. 35

He heard someone coming very heavily up the stairs. Then he did not hear it. Then he heard a noise far off. That was the crowd. Well, somebody would have to kill his other bull. They had cut away all his shirt. The doctor smiled at him. There was Retana.

"Hello, Retana!" Manuel said. He could not hear his voice. 40

Retana smiled at him and said something. Manuel could not hear it.

Zurito stood beside the table, bending over where the doctor was working. He was in his picador clothes, without his hat.

Zurito said something to him. Manuel could not hear it.

Zurito was speaking to Retana. One of the men in white smiled and handed 45 Retana a pair of scissors. Retana gave them to Zurito. Zurito said something to Manuel. He could not hear it.

To hell with this operating-table. He'd been on plenty of operating-tables before. He was not going to die. There would be a priest if he was going to die.

Zurito was saying something to him. Holding up the scissors.

5   That was it. They were going to cut off his coleta. They were going to cut off his pigtail.

Manuel sat up on the operating-table. The doctor stepped back, angry. Someone grabbed him and held him.

"You couldn't do a thing like that, Manos," he said.

10   He heard suddenly, clearly, Zurito's voice.

"That's all right," Zurito said. "I won't do it. I was joking."

"I was going good," Manuel said. "I didn't have any luck. That was all."

Manuel lay back. They had put something over his face. It was all familiar. He inhaled deeply. He felt very tired. He was very, very tired. They took the
15 thing away from his face.

"I was going good," Manuel said weakly. "I was going great."

Retana looked at Zurito and started for the door.

"I'll stay here with him," Zurito said.

Retana shrugged his shoulders.

20   Manuel opened his eyes and looked at Zurito.

"Wasn't I going good, Manos?" he asked, for confirmation.

"Sure," said Zurito. "You were going great."

The doctor's assistant put the cone over Manuel's face and he inhaled deeply. Zurito stood awkwardly, watching.

A SELECTED BIBLIOGRAPHY

I. BIBLIOGRAPHY

American Literature; A Journal of Literary History, Criticism, and Bibliography (quarterly), Durham, N. C.

American Quarterly, Philadelphia, Pa.

J. D. Hart, *The Oxford Companion to American Literature,* 2d ed., Oxford University Press, 1948

S. J. Kunitz and H. Haycraft, *American Authors, 1600-1900,* H. W. Wilson, 1938

Literary History of the United States, ed. by Robert E. Spiller, Willard Thorp, Thomas H. Johnson, and Henry Seidel Canby, 3 vols., Macmillan, 1948. (Bibliography in Vol. III)

F. B. Millett, *Contemporary American Authors: A Critical Survey and 219 Bio-bibliographies,* Harcourt, Brace, 1940

L. H. Wright, *American Fiction, 1774-1850: A Contribution toward a Bibliography,* San Marino, Calif., 1948

II. HISTORY (INCLUDING LITERARY HISTORY)

J. T. Adams, *The Epic of America,* Little, Brown, 1933

C. M. Andrews, *The Colonial Period of American History,* Yale University Press, 1934— (Four volumes published)

J. W. Beach, *American Fiction, 1920-1940,* Macmillan, 1941

C. A. and Mary Beard, *The Rise of American Civilization,* 4 vols., Macmillan, 1927-42

Walter Blair, *Horse Sense in American Humor,* University of Chicago Press, 1942

Van Wyck Brooks, *The Flowering of New England, 1815-1865,* Dutton, 1936

————— *New England: Indian Summer, 1865-1915,* Dutton, 1940

————— *The World of Washington Irving,* Dutton, 1944

————— *The Times of Melville and Whitman,* Dutton, 1947

Herbert Brown, *The Sentimental Novel in America, 1789-1860,* Duke University Press, 1940

P. H. Buck, *The Road to Reunion, 1865-1900,* Little, Brown, 1937

William Charvat, *The Origins of American Critical Thought, 1810-1835,* University of Pennsylvania Press, 1936

Chronicles of America series, Yale University Press, 56 vols., 1918-50

H. S. Commager, *The American Mind: An Interpretation of American Thought and Character Since the 1880's,* Yale University Press, 1950

Alexander Cowie, *The Rise of the American Novel,* American Book Company, 1948

Merle Curti, *The Growth of American Thought,* Harper, 1943

Dictionary of American Biography, ed. by Allen Johnson and others, published under the auspices of the American Council of Learned Societies, 21 vols., 1928-44

Dictionary of American History, ed. by J. T. Adams and others, 6 vols., Scribner, 1940

Clement Eaton, *Freedom of Thought in the Old South,* Duke University Press, 1940

R. H. Gabriel, *The Course of American Democratic Thought: An Intellectual History since 1815,* Ronald Press, 1940

Clarence Gohdes, *American Literature in Nineteenth Century England,* Columbia University Press, 1944

Horace Gregory and Marya Zaturenska, *A History of American Poetry: 1900-1940,* Harcourt, Brace, 1946

L. M. Hacker and H. S. Zahler, edd., *The Shaping of the American Tradition,* Columbia University Press, 1947

T. C. Hall, *The Religious Background of American Culture,* Little, Brown, 1930

M. L. Hansen, *The Atlantic Migration, 1607-1860: A History of the Continuing Settlement of the United States,* Harvard University Press, 1940

———— *The Immigrant in American History,* Harvard University Press, 1940

J. D. Hart, *The Popular Book: A History of America's Literary Taste,* Oxford University Press, 1950

I. H. Herron, *The Small Town in American Literature,* Duke University Press, 1939

History of American Life, ed. by A. M. Schlesinger and D. R. Fox, 13 vols., Macmillan, 1927-48

F. J. Hoffman, Charles Allen, and C. F. Ulrich, *The Little Magazine: A History and a Bibliography,* Princeton University Press, 1947

Richard Hofstadter, *Social Darwinism in American Thought, 1860-1915,* University of Pennsylvania Press, 1944

———— *The American Political Tradition and the Men Who Made It,* Knopf, 1948

H. M. Jones, *Ideas in America,* Harvard University Press, 1944

———— *The Theory of American Literature,* Cornell University Press, 1948

G. P. Krapp, *The English Language in America,* 2 vols., Century, 1925

O. W. Larkin, *Art and Life in America,* Rinehart, 1949

Isabel Leighton, ed., *The Aspirin Age, 1919-1941,* Simon and Schuster, 1949

E. E. Leisy, *The American Historical Novel,* University of Oklahoma Press, 1950

Literary History of the United States, ed. by Robert E. Spiller, Willard Thorp, Thomas H. Johnson, and Henry Seidel Canby, 3 vols., Macmillan, 1948

D. C. McMurtie, *A History of Printing in the United States: The Story of the Introduction of the Press . . . in Each State of the Union* (4 vols.?), R. R. Bowker, 1936— (Only Vol. II, covering the Atlantic States, has been published.)

H. L. Mencken, *The American Language,* 4th ed., Knopf, 1936; Supplements I and II, 1945-48

Perry Miller, *The New England Mind: The Seventeenth Century,* Macmillan, 1939

S. E. Morison and H. S. Commager, *The Growth of the American Republic,* 3d ed., 2 vols., Oxford University Press, 1942

F. L. Mott, *A History of American Magazines,* Harvard University Press, 1930. (3 vols. published. Vol. I, covering the period 1741-1850, was originally issued by Appleton.)

K. B. Murdock, *Literature and Theology in Colonial New England,* Harvard University Press, 1949

E. H. O'Neill, *A History of American Biography, 1800-1935,* University of Pennsylvania Press, 1935

V. L. Parrington, *Main Currents in American Thought,* 3 vols., Harcourt, Brace, 1927-30. (Also published in 1 vol.)

F. L. Pattee, *The First Century of American Literature, 1770-1870,* Appleton-Century, 1935

———————— *A History of American Literature since 1870* [to 1900], Century, 1915

———————— *The New American Literature, 1890-1930,* Century, 1930

———————— *The Development of the American Short Story,* Harper, 1923

R. B. Perry, *Puritanism and Democracy,* Vanguard Press, 1944

Albert Post, *Popular Freethought in America, 1825-1850,* Columbia University Press, 1943

A. H. Quinn, *American Fiction: An Historical and Critical Survey,* Appleton-Century, 1936

———————— *A History of the American Drama, from the Beginning to the Civil War,* Crofts, 1923, 2d ed., 1943

———————— *A History of the American Drama, from the Civil War to the Present Day,* 2 vols., Crofts, 1927, rev. ed., 1936

L. N. Richardson, *A History of Early American Magazines, 1741-1789,* Nelson, 1931

Woodbridge Riley, *American Thought from Puritanism to Pragmatism and Beyond,* 2d ed., Holt, 1923

A. K. Rogers, *English and American Philosophy since 1800,* Macmillan, 1922

Romanticism in America, ed. by George Boas, Johns Hopkins Press, 1940

Constance Rourke, *American Humor: A Study of the National Character,* Harcourt, Brace, 1931

———————— *The Roots of American Culture,* Harcourt, Brace, 1942

R. L. Rusk, *The Literature of the Middle Western Frontier,* 2 vols., Columbia University Press, 1925

H. W. Schneider, *The Puritan Mind,* Holt, 1930

———————— *A History of American Philosophy,* Columbia University Press, 1946

Bernard Smith, *Forces in American Criticism,* Harcourt, Brace, 1939

George Snell, *The Shapers of American Fiction, 1798-1947,* Dutton, 1947

R. E. Spiller, *Changing Patterns in American Civilization,* University of Pennsylvania Press, 1949

Wallace Stegner and others, *One Nation,* Houghton Mifflin, 1945

Floyd Stovall, *American Idealism,* University of Oklahoma Press, 1943

W. F. Taylor, *The Economic Novel in America,* University of North Carolina Press, 1942

A. de Tocqueville, *Democracy in America,* ed. by Phillips Bradley, 2 vols., Knopf, 1945

H. G. Townsend, *Philosophical Ideas in the United States,* American Book Company, 1934

M. C. Tyler, *A History of American Literature, 1607-1765,* Cornell University Press, 1949

M C. Tyler, *The Literary History of the American Revolution, 1763-1783*, 2 vols., Putnam, 1897. (Reissued in facsimile, Barnes and Noble, 1940.)

Carl Van Doren, *The American Novel, 1789-1939*, rev. and enl. ed., Macmillan, 1940

W. P. Webb, *The Great Plains*, Ginn, 1931

Dixon Wecter, *The Hero in America: A Chronicle of Hero-Worship*, Scribner, 1941

———— *The Saga of American Society*, Scribner, 1937

M. G. White, *Social Thought in America: The Revolt Against Formalism*, Viking, 1949

Harvey Wish, *Society and Thought in Early America*, Longmans, Green, 1950

L. B. Wright, *The First Gentlemen of Virginia: Intellectual Qualities of the Early Colonial Ruling Class*, Huntington Library, 1940

T. G. Wright, *Literary Culture in Early New England, 1620-1730*, Yale University Press, 1920

III. CRITICISM

R. P. Blackmur, *The Double Agent: Essays in Craft and Elucidation*, Arrow Editions, 1935

———— *The Expense of Greatness*, Arrow Editions, 1940

Ernest Boyd, ed., *Criticism in America*, Harcourt, Brace, 1924

Cleanth Brooks, *Modern Poetry and the Tradition*, University of North Carolina Press, 1939

———— *The Well Wrought Urn*, Reynal and Hitchcock, 1947

W. C. Brownell, *American Prose Masters*, Scribner, 1909.

V. F. Calverton, *The Liberation of American Literature*, Scribner, 1932

H. S. Canby, *Classic Americans*, Harcourt, Brace, 1931

Oscar Cargill, *Intellectual America: Ideas on the March*, Macmillan, 1941

Elizabeth Drew and J. L. Sweeney, *Directions in Modern Poetry*, Norton, 1940

Norman Foerster, *American Criticism*, Houghton Mifflin, 1928

————, ed., *The Reinterpretation of American Literature*, Harcourt, Brace, 1928

Granville Hicks, *The Great Tradition: An Interpretation of American Literature Since the Civil War*, Macmillan, 1933, rev. ed., 1935

Alfred Kazin, *On Native Grounds*, Reynal and Hitchcock, 1942

John Macy, *The Spirit of American Literature*, Doubleday, Page, 1913

F. O. Matthiessen, *American Renaissance: Art and Expression in the Age of Emerson and Whitman*, Oxford University Press, 1941

Lewis Mumford, *The Brown Decade*, Harcourt, Brace, 1931

———— *The Golden Day*, Boni and Liveright, 1926

———— *Sticks and Stones*, Boni and Liveright, 1924

William O'Connor, ed., *Forms of Modern Fiction*, University of Minnesota Press, 1948

J. C. Ransom, *The New Criticism*, New Directions, 1941

J. E. Spingarn, *Creative Criticism and Other Essays*, Harcourt, Brace, 1931

R. W. Stallman, ed., *Critiques and Essays in Criticism*, Ronald Press, 1949

D. A. Stauffer, ed., *The Intent of the Critic,* Princeton University Press, 1941

———————— *The Nature of Poetry,* Norton, 1946

Allen Tate, ed., *The Language of Poetry,* Princeton University Press, 1942

———————— *On the Limits of Poetry: Selected Essays,* Swallow Press—Morrow Company, 1948

Lionel Trilling, *The Liberal Imagination,* Viking, 1950

T. K. Whipple, *Spokesmen,* D. Appleton, 1928

Edmund Wilson, *The Boys in the Backroom: Notes on California Novelists,* Colt Press, 1941

————————, ed., *The Shock of Recognition,* Doubleday, 1943

Yvor Winters, *In Defense of Reason* (including *Maule's Curse, Primitivism and Decadence,* and *The Anatomy*), William Morrow, 1947

IV. COLLECTIONS

E. A. Alderman and others, *A Library of Southern Literature,* 17 vols., New Orleans, The Martin and Hoyt Company, 1908-23

Walter Blair, *Native American Humor, 1800-1900,* American Book Company, 1937

B. A. Botkin, *A Treasury of American Folklore,* Crown, 1944

W. B. Cairns, *Selections from Early American Writers, 1607-1800,* Macmillan, 1909

B. H. Clark and others, *America's Lost Plays,* 20 vols., Princeton University Press, 1940-41

J. T. Flanagan, ed., *America Is West,* University of Minnesota Press, 1945

A. G. Halline, *American Plays,* American Book Company, 1935

A. P. Hudson, *Humor in the Old Deep South,* Macmillan, 1936

J. A. and Alan Lomax, *American Ballads and Folk Songs,* Macmillan, 1934

F. O. Matthiessen, *The Oxford Book of American Verse,* Oxford University Press, 1950

George Mayberry, *A Little Treasury of American Prose,* Scribner, 1949

F. J. Meine, *Tall Tales of the Southwest,* Knopf, 1930

Perry Miller, *The Transcendentalists,* Harvard University Press, 1950

———————— and T. H. Johnson, *The Puritans,* American Book Company, 1938

Louise Pound, *American Ballads and Songs,* Scribner, 1922

A. H. Quinn, *Representative American Plays from 1767 to the Present Day,* 6th ed., Century, 1938

Carl Sandburg, *The American Songbag,* Harcourt, Brace, 1927

E. C. Stedman and E. M. Hutchinson, *Library of American Literature,* 11 vols., Webster, 1888-90

W. P. Trent and B. W. Wells, *Colonial Prose and Poetry,* 3 vols., Crowell, 1901

H. R. Warfel and G. H. Orians, edd., *American Local-Color Stories,* American Book Company, 1941

Oscar Williams, *A Little Treasury of American Poetry,* Scribner, 1948

M. D. Zabel, *Literary Opinion in America,* Harper, 1937

INDEX

FOR VOLUME TWO

xix